Cryptographic and Information Security

Approaches for Images and Videos

Cryptographic and Information Security

Approaches for Images and Videos

Edited by
S. Ramakrishnan

CRC Press
Taylor & Francis Group
Boca Raton London New York

CRC Press is an imprint of the
Taylor & Francis Group, an **informa** business

Revised second edition published by CRC Press 2024

CRC Press
Taylor & Francis Group
6000 Broken Sound Parkway NW, Suite 300
Boca Raton, FL 33487-2742

© 2019 by Taylor & Francis Group, LLC
CRC Press is an imprint of Taylor & Francis Group, an Informa business

---

Library of Congress Cataloging-in-Publication Data

Names: Ramakrishnan, S. (College teacher), editor.
Title: Cryptographic and information security : approaches for images and videos / edited by S. Ramakrishnan.
Description: Boca Raton, Florida : CRC Press, [2019] | Includes bibliographical references and index.
Identifiers: LCCN 2018026578 | ISBN 9781138563841 (hardback : alk. paper) | ISBN 9780429435461 (e-book)
Subjects: LCSH: Computer security. | Multimedia communications--Security measures. | Data encryption (Computer science) | Data protection.
Classification: LCC QA76.9.A25 C843 2019 | DDC 005.8--dc23
LC record available at https://lccn.loc.gov/2018026578

ISBN: 9781032598024 (hbk)
ISBN: 9781032598031 (pbk)
ISBN: 9780429435461 (ebk)

DOI: 10.1201/9780429435461

Contents

SECTION II   WATERMARKING

SECTION III   STEGANOGRAPHY

SECTION IV FORENSICS

SECTION V BIOMETRICS

Acknowledgements

We are directly and indirectly indebted to a number of individuals who assisted in the preparation of this book. In particular, we are grateful to the 53 referees who reviewed chapters and provided valuable suggestions, comments and criticism. Our special thanks and congratulations to the authors of these 31 chapters for successfully submitting their chapter as per the recommendations of the reviewers. The support of Mr. Richard O'Hanley, Publisher—ICT and Security—of CRC Press is really tremendous and greatly appreciated. We are pleased to thank our colleagues for their cooperation in sharing our academic load during this work. We do not find the right words to express our gratitude to our family members for their love, prayers and backing. We sincerely thank our colleague Mrs. A.G. Priyavarshini for her great and tireless support in formatting and handling of the email correspondence. Our sincere thanks are due to the management, secretary, principal in our department and our fellow colleagues for their support that contributed to the successful completion of this book.

We are open to comments and criticisms from the readers in improving the quality of this book during future editions.

S. Ramakrishnan
Dr. Mahalingam College of Engineering and Technology
Pollachi, India

Editor

S. Ramakrishnan received his B.E. degree in Electronics and Communication Engineering in 1998 from the Bharathidasan University, Trichy, and his M.E. degree in Communication Systems in 2000 from the Madurai Kamaraj University, Madurai, India. He received his Ph.D. degree in Information and Communication Engineering from Anna University, Chennai, India, in 2007.

He has 18 years of teaching experience and one year of industry experience. He is a Professor and the Head of the Department of Information Technology, Dr. Mahalingam College of Engineering and Technology, Pollachi, India.

Dr. Ramakrishnan is an Associate Editor of *IEEE Access* and he is a reviewer of 25 international journals including 7 *IEEE Transactions*, 5 Elsevier science journals, 3 *Institute of Engineering and Technology* (*IET*) journals, *ACM (Association for Computing Machinery) Computing Reviews* and Springer and Wiley journals. He is on the editorial board of 7 international journals. He is a Guest Editor of special issues in 3 international journals including Springer's *Telecommunication Systems Journal*. He has published 157 papers in international and national journals, and conference proceedings. S. Ramakrishnan has published the book, *Wireless Sensor Networks* for CRC Press, Boca Raton, FL, and five books on speech processing, pattern recognition and fuzzy logic for InTech Publisher, Croatia, as well as a book on computational techniques for Lambert Academic Publishing, Germany. He has reviewed 3 books for McGraw-Hill International Edition and 15 books for *ACM Computing Reviews*. He was the convenor of the IT board in Anna University of Technology – Coimbatore Board of Studies (BoS) and has guided two Ph.D. scholars and is currently guiding eight scholars. His biography has been included in the Marquis *Whos's Who in the World* 2012 and 2016 editions. His areas of research include digital image processing, information security and soft computing.

Contributors

Adrian Arellano-Delgado
Baja California Autonomous University
(UABC)
Ensenada, Mexico

Syeda Iram Batool Naqvi
Institute of Space Technology
Islamabad, Pakistan

Jignesh S. Bhatt
Indian Institute of Information
Technology Vadodara
Gujarat, India

Ch. Hima Bindu
QIS College of Engineering &
Technology
Ongole, India

Gajanan K. Birajdar
Ramrao Adik Institute of Technology
Maharashtra, India

Komal Borisagar
Atmiya Institute of Technology &
Science
Gujarat, India

Surekha Borra
K.S. Institute of Technology
Bengaluru, India

Chao Chang
Hefei Electronic Engineering Institute
Anhui Province, China

Lokesh Chouhan
National Institute of Technology
Hamirpur, India

César Cruz-Hernández
Scientific Research and Advanced
Studies Center of Ensenada
(CICESE)
Ensenada, Mexico

Mayank Dave
National Institute of Technology
Kurukshetra, Haryana

Robert H. Deng
School of Information System
Singapore Management University
Singapore

Raahat Devender Singh
Panjab University
Chandigarh, India

Nilanjan Dey
Techno India College of Technology
West Bengal, India

Linda Y. Dong
Devery Co. Ltd.
Sydney, Australia

Nishant Doshi
Pandit Deendayal Petroleum
    University (PDPU)
Gujarat, India

Amit Dua
BITS Pilani
Rajasthan, India

Areeba Fatima
Indian Institute of
    Technology-Patna
Bihar, India

Musab Ghadi
University of Bretagne
    Occidentale
Brest, France

SP Ghrera
Jaypee University of Information
    Technology
Himachal Pradesh, India

Inan Guler
Gazi University
Ankara, Turkey

Zahra Hossein-Nejad
Islamic Azad University
Sirjan Branch
Sirjan, Iran

Amit M. Joshi
Malaviya National Institute of
    Technology
Rajasthan, India

Vaibhav B. Joshi
School of Engineering and Applied
    Science
Ahmedabad University
Gujarat, India

Ki-Hyun Jung
Kyungil University
Gyeongbuk, Republic of Korea

Rukiye Karakis
Cumhuriyet University
Sivas, Turkey

G. Jaspher Willsie Kathrine
Karunya University
Coimbatore, India

Majid Khan
Institute of Space Technology
Islamabad, Pakistan

Emir Kremić
Federal Institute of Statistics
Bosnia and Herzegovina, Europe

Pankaj Kumar
Research Scholar
NIT Hamirpur
Hamirpur, India

Amit Kumar Singh
National Institute of Technology
Patna, India

Lamri Laouamer
University of Bretagne Occidentale
Brest, France

Charles Z. Liu
Department of Computing
    Macquarie University
Sydney, Australia

and

Devery Co. Ltd.
Sydney, Australia

Shaohui Liu
Harbin institute of Technology
Harbin, China

Yuliang Lu
Hefei Electronic Engineering Institute
Anhui Province, China

V. T. Manu
Institute for Development and
    Research in Banking Technology
    (IDRBT) and School of Computer
    and Information Sciences (SCIS)
University of Hyderabad
Hyderabad, India

B. M. Mehtre
Institute for Development and
    Research in Banking Technology
Hyderabad, India

Rodrigo Méndez-Ramírez
Scientific Research and Advanced
    Studies Center of Ensenada
    (CICESE)
Ensenada, Mexico

Bhaskar Mondal
Xavier School of Computer Science &
    Engineering
Xavier University
Bhubaneswar, India

Miguel Angel Murillo-Escobar
Scientific Research and Advanced
    Studies Center of Ensenada
    (CICESE
Ensenada, Mexico

Laurent Nana
University of Bretagne Occidentale
Brest, France

Mehdi Nasri
Islamic Azad University
Khomeinishahr Branch
Isfahan, Iran

Naveen Kumar Nishchal
Indian Institute of Technology-Patna
Bihar, India

Padmapriya Praveenkumar
SASTRA University
Thanjavur, India

Anca Pascu
University of Bretagne Occidentale
Brest, France

Mukesh D. Patil
Ramrao Adik Institute
    of Technology
Maharashtra, India

Piyush Raghav
BITS Pilani
Rajasthan, India

Y. Sreenivasa Rao
National Institute of Technology
Warangal, India

Mehul S. Raval
School of Engineering and Applied
Science
Ahmedabad University
Gujarat, India

Amirtharajan Rengarajan
SASTRA University
Thanjavur, India

Raymond P. Shaw
SmartSys Workgroup
Toronto, Ontario, Canada

K. Sitara
Institute for Development and
Research in Banking Technology
(IDRBT) and School of
Computer and Information
Sciences (SCIS)
University of Hyderabad
Hyderabad, India

Ankit Songara
National Institute of Technology
Hamirpur, India

Abdulhamit Subasi
College of Engineering
Effat University
Jeddah, Saudi Arabia

Sandhya Tarar
Gautam Buddha University
Greater Noida, India

Sriti Thakur
Jaypee University of Information
Technology
Himachal Pradesh, India

Rohit Thanki
C. U. Shah University
Wadhwan City, India

Vishwesh A. Vyawahare
Ramrao Adik Institute of
Technology
Maharashtra, India

Song Wan
Hefei Electronic Engineering Institute
Anhui Province, China

Yongjie Wang
Hefei Electronic Engineering Institute
Anhui Province, China

Zhuo Wei
Singapore Research Center
Huawei, Singapore

Swee Won Lo
Singapore University of Social Sciences
Singapore

Yongdong Wu
Institute for Infocomm Research
Astar, Singapore

Xuehu Yan
Hefei Electronic Engineering Institute
Anhui Province, China

Zheng Yan
Xidian University
Xi'an, China

and

Aalto University
Espoo, Finland

Yanjiang Yang
Singapore Research Center
Huawei, Singapore

Reviewer Details

R. Amirtharajan
SASTRA University
Thanjavur, India

Amira S. Ashour
Computers and Information
   Technology College
Taif University
Taif, Saudi Arabia

Kishore Bhamidipati
Manipal Institute of Technology
Manipal, India

Gajanan K. Birajdar
Dr. Babasaheb Ambedkar
   Technological University
Lonere, India

Komal Borisagar
Atmiya Institute of Technology
   and Science
Rajkot, India

Surekha Borra
K.S. Institute of Technology
Bengaluru, India

Yigang Cen
Beijing Jiaotong University
Beijing, China

Ahmet Cihan
Duzce University
Duzce, Turkey

Marisa T. Dery
Audio Video Forensic Analyst
American Board of Recorded
   Evidence
AES, ABRE, NAIS, CARAS
Tamar Forensics
Somerville, Massachusetts

Sellapan Devaraju
Dr. Mahalingam College of
   Engineering and Technology
Pollachi, India

Raahat Devender Singh
Panjab University
Chandigarh, India

Nilanjan Dey
Techno India College of Technology
Kolkata, India

Ravindra N. Duche
Lokmanya Tilak College of
   Engineering
Navi Mumbai, India

Sekar Elango
Bannari Amman Institute of
  Technology
Coimbatore, India

T. Gopalakrishnan
Dr. Mahalingam College of
  Engineering and Technology
Pollachi, India

Ch. Hima Bindu
QIS College of Engineering &
  Technology
Ongole, India

Musab Ghadi
University of Brest
Brittany, France

Madhavi Gudavalli
Department of Information
  Technology
JNTUK
Vizianagaram, India

Jude Hemanth
Karunya University
Coimbatore, India

Divya Jennifer Dsouza
NMAMIT Nitte
Udupi, India

Ki-Hyun Jung
Kyungil University
Gyeongsan, South Korea

G. Jaspher Willsie Kathrine
Karunya University
Coimbatore, India

Hamed Khodadadi
Islamic Azad University
Tehran, Iran

Emir Kremić
Federal Institute of Statistics
Bosnia and Herzegovina, Europe

Ela Kumar
Indira Gandhi Delhi Technical
  University for Women
New Delhi, India

Siva Kumar
Dr. Mahalingam College of
  Engineering and Technology
Pollachi, India

Mohammad Faiz Liew Bin Abdullah
Universiti Tun Hussein Onn
Johor, Malaysia

Charles Z. Liu
Department of Computing
Macquarie University
Sydney, Australia

and

Devery Co. Ltd.
Sydney, Australia

Shaohui Liu
Harbin Institute of Technology
Harbin, China

Rodrigo Méndez-Ramírez
Scientific Research and Advanced
Studies Center of Ensenada
  (CICESE)
Ensenada, Mexico

Bhaskar Mondal
Xavier School of Computer Science &
   Engineering
Xavier University
Bhubaneswar, India

N. S. MurtiSarma
Sreenidhi Institute of Science and
   Technology
Hyderabad, India

Mehdi Nasri
Islamic Azad University
Khomeinishahr Branch
Isfahan, Iran

Naveen Kumar Nishchal
Indian Institute of Technology-Patna
Bihar, India

V. Padmapriya
SASTRA University
Thanjavur, India

Sanjay R. Patil
Maharashtra Institute of Technology
Pune, India

Satya Prasad
KL University
Guntur, India

Om Prakash Sangwan
GJU University
Hisar, India

Shanmuganantham Rajasekar
Anna University
Regional Center
Coimbatore, India

Sourav Samanta
University Institute of Technology
Bardhaman, India

Vijaya Santhi
A.U. College of Engineering (A)
Visakhapatnam, India

Mansi Subhedar
HOC College of Engineering and
   Technology
Khalapur, India

C. N. Sujatha
Sreenidhi Institute of Science and
   Technology
Hyderabad, India

Sandhya Tarar
Gautam Buddha University
Greater Noida, India

Rohit Thanki
C. U. Shah University
Wadhwan City, India

Esteban Tlelo-Cuautle
INAOE
Puebla, Mexico

Rajesh Verma
Regional Forensic Science Laboratory
   (RFSL)
Mandi, India

Song Wan
Hefei Electronic Engineering
   Institute
Anhui Province, China

Shiqi Wang
Department of Computer Science
City University of Hong Kong
Hong Kong, China

Zhuo Wei
Singapore Research Center
Huawei, Teletech Park, Singapore

and

Singapore University of Social
   Sciences
Clementi Road, Singapore

Swee Won Lo
Singapore University of Social Sciences
Singapore

Suneel Yadav
Department of Electronics and
   Communication Engineering
Indian Institute of Information
   Technology
Allahabad, India

Yu Zhou
Chinese Academy of Sciences
Beijing, China

Chapter 1

Introduction

Contents

Securing information is one of the most important concerns for both individuals and organizations. Recently, most of the data is being shared and stored in digital form and it needs careful protection. Over the past two decades academicians, researchers and industry professionals are focusing on information security in the form of text and files. Today, much focus is given to secure information in the form of image and video. Image and video processing books primarily focus on non-cryptographic approaches, whereas books on cryptography and information security primarily focus on text and file security. There is a clear need for a book that comprehensively provides various cryptographic and information security approaches for images and videos. Hence, this book.

1.1 Objectives

Objectives of this book are as follows:

- To provide a comprehensive and up-to-date coverage on various cryptographic and information security approaches for images and videos.
- To encourage both researchers and practitioners to share their experiences and recent studies on image and video security.
- To propose new and innovative solutions for various real-world problems related to image and video security.

DOI: 10.1201/9780429435461-1

■ To present applications and case studies in the areas of image and video encryption, watermarking and steganography.
■ To publish worldwide best practices regarding digital forensics and biometrics.

The diversity, richness and rapid development of the subject make us believe that teamwork alone can yield a good results. We approached CRC Press with our proposal on editing a book on the above said topic during June 2017. CRC Press had accepted our proposal and subsequently we announced the call for book chapters to various academic and industrial experts working in the field world-wide. Consequently, we have collected chapters from the domain experts working in various subfields of cryptography and information security around the globe and have edited the chapters to develop this book.

Forty-eight expert teams have delivered submissions from India, Pakistan, Australia, Malaysia, Canada, Singapore, China, Finland, Chile, Mexico, France, Korea, Turkey, Iran, Bosnia and Herzegovina and Saudi Arabia. The material presented in this book was reviewed by 53 reviewers; we have accepted only 31 out of 48 submissions, based on the recommendations and comments from the reviewers.

This book is written for graduate students, academicians, researchers, scientists and professionals working in computer science and electrical engineering, as well as for developers and practitioners working in information security, image and video processing. The reader is provided with a concise list of references at the end of each chapter.

1.1.1 Organization of the Chapters

These 31 chapters are divided into five parts: Section I: Encryption; Section II: Watermarking; Section III: Steganography; Section IV: Forensics and Section V: Biometrics.

Section I is on image and video encryption. This section has 10 chapters. These chapters cover several topics, namely cryptographic primitives, boolean functions, chaotic maps, scrambling techniques, optical cryptography and various applications. The book begins with an Introduction (Chapter 1). Image scrambling, one of the effective methods for encrypting images, is presented in Chapter 2. This chapter provides mechanisms along with experimental and comparative analysis of various image scrambling techniques, namely matrix scrambling, bit plane scrambling, pixel, row and column swapping. Chaotic maps play a vital role in image cryptography. Chapter 3 discusses various chaotic maps, namely logistics, tent, sine, Bernoulli and Gaussian maps. This chapter contains a case study on biometrics and presents experimental analysis. Substitution box (S-boxes) and boolean functions are indispensable components of cryptosystems and are presented with mathematical analysis in Chapter 4. Relationships between various cryptographic properties such as non-linearity, correlation immunity, avalanche and propagation criterion are also presented in this chapter. One of the widely used cryptosystems, namely optical cryptosystem, is discussed in Chapter 5. This chapter contains some of the applications of phase retrieval in the field of optical security. Iterative phase retrieval techniques have been reviewed in this chapter to provide the groundwork for optical security applications. A lightweight encryption technique called Elliptic Curve Cryptography (ECC) is presented in Chapter 6. Chapter 7 emphasizes the security of scalable video coding. This chapter introduces scalable video coding, its security requirements, applications, partial encryptions and content-based authentication. In Chapter 8, a new encryption technique based on compressive sensing for color imagery is presented along with detailed experimental results and comparisons. Signcryption is a logical combination of encryption and signature, and is used for access control over encrypted data and authenticity of the data sender. A new signcryption algorithm with security analysis is presented in Chapter 9. Chapter 10 discusses the design and experimental implementation of chaotic encryption algorithm applied to a communication protocol to provide confidentiality to multimedia contents, which is reproduced in a smart display. Chapter 11 presents an authenticated secure communication medium to share Electronic Patient Record (EPR) among peers to ensure confidentiality and seclusion along with experimental results.

Section II is on watermarking and has six chapters. Chapter 12 provides a brief survey of various document image watermarking techniques along with its performance analysis. Various tools available for document watermarking are also presented. HEVC (High Efficiency Video Coding)-based real-time watermarking helps to embed the watermark at the time of capturing the video. Chapter 13 presents a video watermarking scheme and its VLSI implementation in HEVC encoders. This chapter also offers experimental results along with comparisons. Various methods for hiding data in compressed images and videos are presented along with illustrations in Chapter 14. Multi-Criteria Decision-Making (MCDM) techniques can be used to solve the imprecision of the image's characteristics in order to achieve image authentication. Chapter 15 provides an overview of the multi-criteria decision making approach, discussing how the texture problem is analyzed using one of the MCDM methods in order to identify highly textured blocks within a host image to hold the watermark with high imperceptibility and robustness. Chapter 16 addresses the role of image fusion for watermarking techniques in the field of medical imaging. Methods for the integration of patient information such as photo, name, gender, age, and so on with Electrocardiogram (ECG) reports, and MRI-CT or MRI-PET by fusion process are also presented in this chapter. Chapter 17 provides an in-depth review of various watermarking techniques applied to tele-health. In addition to various applications of watermarks, possible watermarking attacks are also presented in this chapter.

Section III is on steganography and has five chapters. Chapter 18 presents a steganography algorithm using small S-boxes. Concepts are presented with illustration, statistical analysis and performance analysis. In Chapter 19, an electrocardiogram steganography approach in frequency domain is discussed using fractional Fourier transform. Architecture of ECG steganography for eHealthcare systems is also presented in this chapter along with simulation results. In Chapter 20, a visual secret sharing (VSS) scheme based on the Quick Response (QR) code is presented along with illustrations and experimental analysis. In Chapter 21, reversible data hiding methods using interpolation techniques and edge detection algorithms are described. Performance measurements are also explained including the embedding capacity and visual quality. Chapter 22 describes how steganography can be applied to medical information systems. This chapter also provides the details of Picture Archiving and Communication System (PACS) and Digital Imaging and Communications in Medicine (DICOM), to present medical steganography techniques along with experimental results.

Section IV is on forensics and has five chapters. Chapter 23 provides a detailed account of digital visual media forensics. This chapter discusses source identification, integrity verification, content authentication, tamper detection and hidden data detection and gives an overview of anti-forensics and counter anti-forensics. Chapter 24 surveys tampering detection techniques that can be used for copy-move forgery detection. Chapter 25 describes various network issues and also presents solutions to those issues using blockchain technology. This chapter defines blockchain in detail, its features and importance in networks and its applications in the real world. Chapter 26 surveys various methods available for copy-move forgery detection, and also presents a copy-move forgery detection technique using keypoint elimination methods. Experimental results are also presented in this chapter. In Chapter 27, a survey on anti-forensic methods for impeding passive image and video tampering detection is presented. Methods for countering these anti-forensics are discussed in this chapter.

Section V is on biometrics and has four chapters. Chapter 28 presents various data hiding techniques for securing biometrics, specifically fingerprints. Experimental results are also presented in this chapter. Chapter 29 describes different aspects of security provided by biometrics. It broadly discusses the security techniques such as fingerprint watermarking and fingerprint mosaicking. Chapter 30 discusses an artificial model for facial recognition and its use in mobile security for the Android OS platform. This chapter focuses on information security, access management and personal security in mobile devices. Chapter 31 presents a biometric data-based user authentication scheme to enable a user to login securely to access a Cloud resource. Completeness of the proposed method is tested using Gong Needham and Yahalom (GNY) logic. In addition, experimental results along with performance comparison are provided in this chapter.

MATLAB® is a registered trademark of The MathWorks, Inc. For product information, please contact:

The MathWorks, Inc.
3 Apple Hill Drive
Natick, MA 01760-2098 USA
Tel: 508 647 7000
Fax: 508-647-7001
E-mail: info@mathworks.com
Web: www.mathworks.com

ENCRYPTION

Chapter 2

Cryptographic Image Scrambling Techniques

Bhaskar Mondal

Contents

DOI: 10.1201/9780429435461-3

Image scrambling is the method of rearranging the pixels randomly to make the image visually unreadable and break the correlation between the neighboring pixels. In general, during scrambling the pixel values remains unchanged. In recent past a huge number of image encryption algorithms were being proposed. Most of the image encryption algorithms involve two phases, namely confusion and diffusion. In the confusion phase the pixel positions are permuted using some scrambling technique and in the diffusion phase the pixel values are changed by using some inverse-able function. Image pixels are highly correlated with neighboring pixels and a good scrambling algorithm reduces this correlation near to zero. In this chapter is an in-depth comparative study on different scrambling techniques like matrix transformation, bit plane scrambling, pixel swaping, row and column swapping, row and column swapping with rotation. To determine the quality and efficiency of the scrambling techniques correlation coefficient, entropy, and computation time are considered.

2.1 Introduction

During the past two decades the working habits and social life changed drastically due to the Internet and social media. Every day a huge amount of images are being captured and stored or transmitted over the Internet, which includes personal, organizational, secret and sensitive information. Secure multimedia communication is increasingly becoming important as multimedia data can be easily intercepted by illegal users. Law enforcement agents may find it very difficult to stay afloat above the ill intentions of hackers. Therefore, encrypting those images are highly required [1].

Scrambling is widely used in encryption algorithms [2,3] for adding confusion [4]. Scrambling refers to the permutations of pixel values or permutation of bit values in a bit plane. Transforming a plain image into a meaningless noise and eliminate the high correlation between adjacent pixels are the objective of scrambling. Various image scrambling techniques are used in image and video encryption [5], time synchronization in physical layer, generating randomness in computer generated events etc. The strength and computational overhead of an image encryption algorithm is highly dependent on the scrambling techniques used in the algorithm.

In [6], a matrix based scrambling technique is used, based on Arnold's cat map. Arnold's cat map is a chaotic map named after Vladimir Arnold who proposed the algorithm. The scrambling using Arnold's cat map is also known as Arnold's Transformation. The matrix based scrambling may also be done based on Fibonacci transform [5]. Fibonacci transform [7] has a unique property of uniformity. The pixels that are at equal distance from each other in original image remain at equal distances in the encrypted image as well. The adjacent pixels are also spread as far as possible resulting very low correlation between the adjacent pixels. In [8,9] the authors claimed a comparison of six scrambling methods, But they have kept the scrambling procedure unchanged with six different random matrix generators. Two other permutation measures are presented in [8].

Another image scrambling method based on 2D chaotic mapping [10]. The pseudo-randomness, aperiodicity and being sensitive to change with respect to initial conditions make chaotic maps one of the favorite techniques in scrambling. It is also used in scrambling of large amount of data such as video, audio etc [11].

Key based scrambling for secure image encryption is used in [12–14], based on row and column swapping. Using some random sequences, the rows of the image are swapped. Similarly, the columns are also swapped. Further, circular shifting of the rows and columns are done using the same sequence [15] uses row and column shifting method for permutation of pixels.

Bit-plane scrambling is one of the famous image scrambling techniques. In [16] a quantum image gray-code (GB) with bit-plane scrambling is presented. It is used as one of the basic steps in many encryption algorithm [17]. In [18], a novel chaos-based bit-level permutation scheme is used, in which the image is extended to bit plane binary image and the rows are permuted according to a random sequences. Further, the columns are shifted using the same random sequences. After that, the extended image is divided into 8 blocks of equal size and again permutation is applied on each block using generalized Arnold's Cat Map. The blocks are merged to obtain the cipher image [19,20] using a pixel-level permutation and bit-level permutation for image encryption.

This chapter presents in depth comparative study of some popular cryptographic image scrambling methods like generalized matrix-based scrambling (transformation) [21] using Arnold's transform [6] and Fibonacci transform [7], 2D mapping [10], key based row and column shifting [13,22], gray code with bit plane transformation [23], and key based row and column shifting with bit-level permutation [18]. In this chapter a same pseudo random number generator (PRNG), based on chaotic logistic map, is used for different scrambling techniques to test and compare the cryptographic effect of the scrambling techniques.

For measuring encryption effect of the scrambling techniques correlation coefficient, entropy and computational time are compared in the chapter by simulating and testing on different types of images. Same image, namely the Peeper image, is scrambled using all the scrambling techniques discussed in the chapter for better understanding and comparison of the scrambling techniques.

The rest of the chapter describes different image scrambling techniques and their comparison and performance analysis followed by the chapter summary.

2.2 Scrambling Techniques

This section will present different image scrambling techniques used in image encryption. The techniques are also applied to different types of images to demonstrate their cryptographic effects.

2.2.1 Scrambling by Row and Column Shifting with Circular Rotation

Key based scrambling algorithm is a very effective and simple method of image scrambling and encryption. In this method, the user specifies a key that forms a sequence of two pseudo random numbers $R1$ and $R2$ [12].

In Figure 2.1a representation of scrambling using row and column shifting with circular rotation. In Figure 2.1a an plain image with 16 pixel is presented. In Figure 2.1b the rows of the image are scrambled based on a random number sequence {3,4,2,1}. In Figure 2.1c the columns of the image are scrambled based on a random number sequence {3,1,4,2}. In Figure 2.1c The elements are remains in the same rows or columns, they are only scrambled with in the row or column, which gives lesser security. On the other hand if we apply circular rotation using random sequence {1,2,2,3} on Figure 2.1b after the row shifting we get the result in Figure 2.1d. Then a column shifting in Figure 2.1e using random sequence {4,2,1,3} followed by column wise circular rotation using random sequence {2,3,1,2} which produce the result in Figure 2.1f. All the pixels are scrambled randomly irrespective of rows or columns. Therefore, scrambling using row and column shifting with circular rotation gives a proper scrambling and cryptographic effect.

The scrambling method is shown in Figure 2.2 and given by Algorithm 1.

ALGORITHM 2.1 Row and Column Shifting with Circular Rotation

Input: The original image I.
for $i = 0$ to M **do**
    Cyclic shift the ith row of I to right with step size $R1_i$;
end for
The row scrambled image is denoted as I_1.
for $i = 0$ to N **do**
    Cyclic shift the ith column of I_1 to right with step size $R2_i$;
end for
The column scrambled image is denoted as I'.
Output: The scrambled image I'.

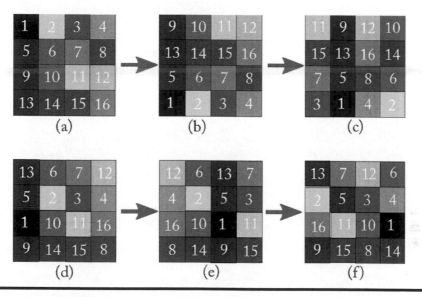

Figure 2.1 Step by step process of scrambling using row and column shifting with circular rotation: (a) plain sub-image with 16 pixels is presented, (b) the rows of the image are scrambled based on a random number sequence {3,4,2,1}, (c) the columns of the image are scrambled based on a random number sequence {3,1,4,2}, (d) shows that the pixels are only scrambled within the row or column, (e) column shifting using random sequence {4,2,1,3}, and (f) column wise circular rotation using random sequence {2,3,1,2}.

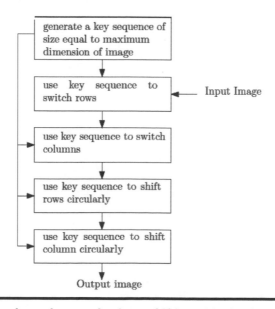

Figure 2.2 Flowchart of row and column shifting with circular rotation.

The row and column shifting with circular rotation is applied on the Peeper image in Figure 2.8a which results in the scrambled image in Figure 2.3b. The plots of the correlation in vertical, horizontal and diagonal direction of the plain Peeper image are presented in Figures 2.17f, 2.12e, 2.12g, respectively, and the plots of the correlation in vertical, horizontal and diagonal direction of the scrambled Peeper image are presented in Figures 2.3d, 2.3f, 2.3h.

The values of the correlation (Corr) in vertical correlation (VC), horizontal correlation (HC) and diagonal correlation (DC) direction of the plain Peeper image are 0.9768, 0.9792, 0.9639 respectively and the entropy is 7.5937. The values of the overall Correlation, vertical VC, HC, and DC direction of the scrambled Peeper image are 0.0217, 0.0252, 0.6936, 0.0345.

2.2.2 Scrambling Based on 2D Mapping

2D mapping is one of the simplest way of scrambling an image I with dimension $(M \times N)$ where M represents the height of the image and N represents the width of the image. The pixel value of any coordinate (i, j) is expressed by $A(i, j)$ where $i = 0, 1, 2, \ldots M - 1$ and $j = 0, 1, 2, \ldots N - 1$. In this method two random matrix are generated $X(i, j)$ and $Y(i, j)$. The elements of the random matrix are acted as new coordinates of the pixels in the scrambled image I'.

ALGORITHM 2.2 Scrambling Using Fibonacci Transformation

Input: $I(i, j)$ the plain image with dimension $(M \times N)$
Generate $X(i, j)$ and $Y(i, j)$.
for each pixel $I(i, j)$ **do**
    $I'(X(i, j), Y(i, j)) = I(i, j)$
end for
Output: $I'(I, J)$, the scrambled image.

The performance of this scheme depends on the PRNG used for generating the random matrix.

The scrambling technique based on 2D mapping is applied on the Peeper image in Figure 2.4a, which results in the scrambled image in Figure 2.4b. The plots of the correlation in vertical, horizontal and diagonal direction of the plain Peeper image are presented in Figures 2.17f, 2.12e, 2.12g, respectively, and the plots of the correlation in vertical, horizontal and diagonal direction of the scrambled Peeper image are presented in Figures 2.4d, 2.4f, and 2.4h.

The values of the overall correlation in vertical, horizontal and diagonal direction of the plain Peeper image are 0.9768, 0.9792, 0.9639, respectively, and the entropy

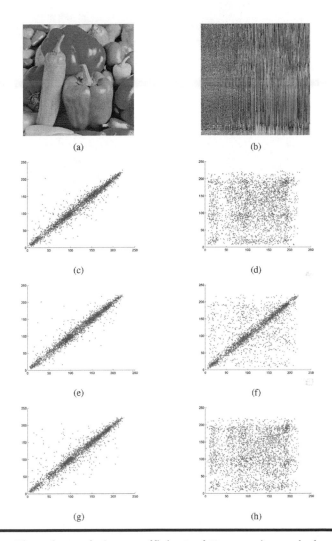

Figure 2.3 **Plot of correlation coefficient of Peppers image before and after scrambling using 2D mapping: (a) Plain Peppers image, (b) scrambled pepper image, (c) correlation in vertical direction of plain image, (d) correlation in vertical direction of scrambled image, (e) correlation in horizontal direction of plain image, (f) correlation in horizontal direction of scrambled image, (g) correlation in diagonal direction of plain image, and (h) correlation in diagonal direction of scrambled image.**

is 7.5937. The values of the overall correlation in vertical, horizontal and diagonal direction of the scrambled Peeper image are 0.0380, 0.0434, 0.0405, 0.0521, respectively, and the entropy is 7.8415. The detailed results are given in Table 2.1.

This method is used to generate a large number of pseudo random number sequences, doubling the size of the plain image.

Table 2.1 Comparative Results of Correlations and Entropy

Test Image	Parameters	Arnold's Transformation	Fibonacci Transformation	Gray Code Bit Plane	2D Mapping	Row and Column Shifting	Row and Column Shifting with Bit Plane Scrambling
Airplane image	Corr	0.0015	0.0117	0.0505	0.0443	0.0954	0.0016
	HC	−0.1114	0.4942	0.3177	−0.0553	0.1691	0.0298
	VC	−0.0733	0.3451	0.3573	−0.0538	0.6425	0.0056
	DC	0.0278	0.3485	0.3008	−0.0550	0.1917	0.0089
	Entropy	6.7025	6.7025	6.7025	0.8236	6.7780	7.9368
Baboon image	Corr	4.5970e-04	0.0097	0.0485	0.0033	0.0569	0.0017
	HC	0.0979	0.3120	0.0485	0.0446	0.0612	0.0481
	VC	0.1232	0.2215	0.0556	0.0722	0.3780	0.0160
	DC	0.1051	0.0296	0.2883	0.0346	0.0087	0.0090
	Entropy	7.2673	7.2673	3.6133	7.2673	7.1782	7.9523

(Continued)

Table 2.1 (*Continued*) Comparative Results of Correlations and Entropy

Test Image	Parameters	Arnold's Transformation	Fibonacci Transformation	Gray Code Bit Plane	2D Mapping	Row and Column Shifting	Row and Column Shifting with Bit Plane Scrambling
Lena image	Corr	2.4868e-05	3.1170e-05	0.0091	0.0423	0.0139	0.0021
	HC	0.0327	0.6513	0.1307	0.0626	0.0646	0.0199
	VC	-0.0875	0.4783	0.1676	0.0660	0.6749	0.0165
	DC	0.1963	0.2036	0.1323	0.0667	0.0680	0.0158
	Entropy	7.4455	7.4455	7.4455	7.691	7.4677	7.9976
Peppers image	Corr	-0.0110	0.0228	0.0022	0.0380	0.0217	0.0011
	HC	0.0979	0.5906	0.1134	-0.0434	0.0252	0.0114
	VC	0.0175	0.3675	0.0556	-0.0405	0.6936	0.0050
	DC	0.1066	0.1561	0.0834	-0.0521	0.0345	0.0398
	Entropy	7.5937	7.5937	7.5937	0.8415	7.6438	7.9966

Note: Correlation between current pixel and horizontal/diagonal/vertical pixel is by choosing 1000 random pixels.

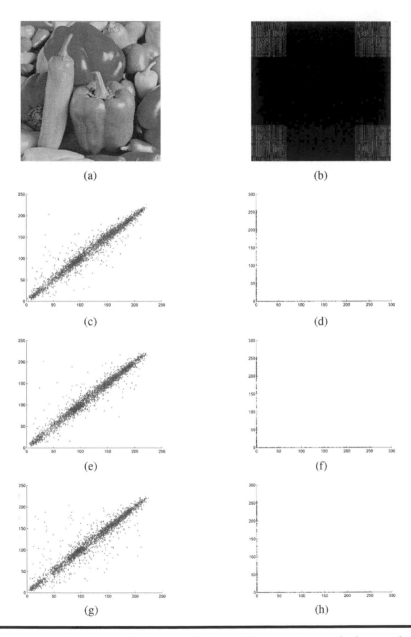

Figure 2.4   Plot of correlation coefficient of Peppers image before and after scrambling using 2D mapping: (a) Plain Peppers image, (b) scrambled pepper image, (c) correlation in vertical direction of plain image, (d) correlation in vertical direction of scrambled image, (e) correlation in horizontal direction of plain image, (f) correlation in horizontal direction of scrambled image, (g) correlation in diagonal direction of plain image, and (h) correlation in diagonal direction of scrambled image.

2.2.3 Bit-level Permutation with Row and Column Shifting

A bit plane of an image is a set of bits corresponding to a given position in each of the binary numbers representing the pixel value of the image. An 8-bit image can be represented by 8-bit planes. The first bit plane contains the set of the most significant bit, and the 8th contains the least significant bit. The bit plane slices of Perrers image are shown in Figure 2.5.

This scheme is based on bit plain permutation based on pseudo random number sequence. The scheme performs the scrambling in two steps, first using a pseudo random sequence and followed by a generalized Arnold transform [18]. The scheme is successful in generating a secure scrambled image with good cryptographic effects. The steps are as follows:

1. Extend the image I of size $M \times N$ to $M \times N \times 8$ bit plane binary image.
2. Generate the pseudo random number sequences S_0 and S_1 of size M and $N \times 8$ respectively.
3. Permute the rows of the binary image using sequence S_0.
4. Permute the columns of binary image using sequence S_1.
5. Now, divide the binary image into 8 blocks of equal size.
6. Permute each block with generalized Arnold cat map (in Equation 2.5) k times.
7. marge the blocks left to right to recover the pixel plane and further generate the cipher image.

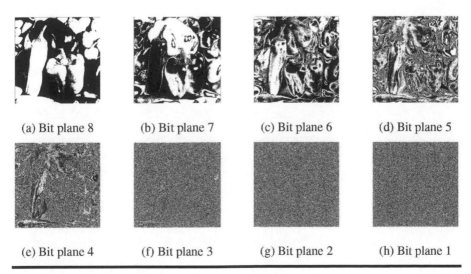

| (a) Bit plane 8 | (b) Bit plane 7 | (c) Bit plane 6 | (d) Bit plane 5 |
| (e) Bit plane 4 | (f) Bit plane 3 | (g) Bit plane 2 | (h) Bit plane 1 |

Figure 2.5   Bit plain slice of the Peppers image.

The scrambling technique based on 2D mapping is applied on the Peeper image in Figure 2.6a which results in the scrambled image in Figure 2.6b. The plots of the correlation in vertical, horizontal and diagonal direction of the plain Peeper image are presented in Figures 2.17f, 2.12e, and 2.17g, respectively, and the plots of the correlation in vertical, horizontal, and diagonal direction of the scrambled Peeper image are presented in Figures 2.6d, 2.6f, and 2.6h.

The values of the overall correlation in vertical correlation, horizontal correlation and diagonal correlation direction of the plain Peeper image are 0.9768, 0.9792, 0.9639 respectively and the entropy is 7.5937. The values of the overall correlation in vertical correlation, horizontal correlation and diagonal correlation direction of the scrambled Peeper image are 0.0011, 0.0114, 0.0050, 0.0398 respectively and the entropy is 7.9966. The detailed results are given in Table 2.1.

2.2.4 Generalized Matrix Based Scrambling (Transformation)

The Equation 2.1 transformation is the general model:

$$\vec{V}_k = A\vec{V}_{k-1} \bmod \vec{N}, k \in Z^+ \tag{2.1}$$

In Equation 2.1, A is a matrix of size $n \times n$. A is known as scrambling parameter matrix. All the elements of A are non-negative integers such that $\det(A) \neq 0$, $\vec{V}_k, \vec{V}_{k-1}, \vec{N}$ are $n \times 1$ vectors and $0 < v_{i,j} \le N_{j-1}$ for $i = k-1, k$ and $j = 1, 2, \ldots, n$ assuming $\vec{V}_{k-1} = (V_{k-1,1} V_{k-1,2} \ldots V_{k-2,n})'$ and $\vec{V}_k = (V_{k,1} V_{k,2} \ldots V_{k,n})'$, $\vec{N} = (N_1 N_2 \ldots N_n)'$ is the module vector in which N_j are positive integers representing the upper limit of the corresponding $v_{ij} = (i, j = 1, 2 \ldots)$. The scrambling times of the image is denoted by a positive integer k. $^+$ denotes the set of +ve integers.

The case with equal module is defined as equi-modulo transformation, i.e., $\vec{N} = (NN \ldots N)'$, then, Equation 2.1 can be transformed into Equation 2.2:

$$\vec{V}_k = A\vec{V}_{k-1} \bmod N, k \in Z^+ \tag{2.2}$$

2.2.4.1 Matrix Based Image Scrambling Using Arnold Transform

Cat map, also known as Arnold transform was proposed by V.I. Arnold in the research of ergodic theory. A process of splicing and clipping which realigns the digital image matrix is called transform. The 2D Arnold transform is an invertible map described by Equation 2.3

$$\begin{pmatrix} x_{n+1} \\ y_{n+1} \end{pmatrix} = \begin{pmatrix} 1 & 1 \\ 1 & 2 \end{pmatrix} \begin{pmatrix} x_n \\ y_n \end{pmatrix} \bmod 1 \tag{2.3}$$

where $(x_n, y_n) \in [0,1) \times [0,1)$

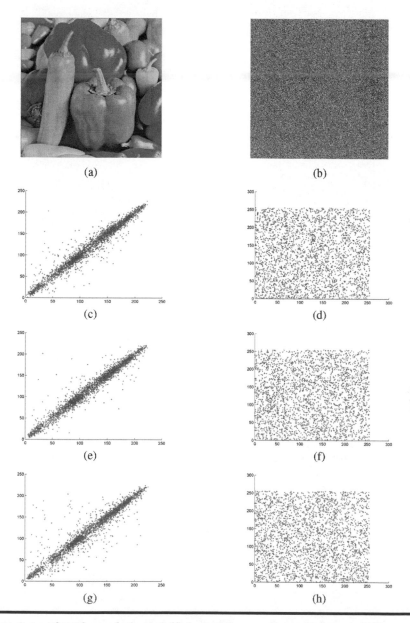

Figure 2.6 Plot of correlation coefficient of Peppers image before and after scrambling using bit-level permutation with row and column shifting: (a) Plain Peppers image, (b) scrambled pepper image, (c) correlation in vertical direction of plain image, (d) correlation in vertical direction of scrambled image, (e) correlation in horizontal direction of plain image, (f) correlation in horizontal direction of scrambled image, (g) correlation in diagonal direction of plain image, and (h) correlation in diagonal direction of scrambled image.

and Arnold transform is given by Equation 2.4

$$\begin{pmatrix} x_{n+1} \\ y_{n+1} \end{pmatrix} = \begin{pmatrix} a_{00} & a_{01} \\ a_{10} & a_{11} \end{pmatrix} \begin{pmatrix} x_n \\ y_n \end{pmatrix} \bmod N \qquad (2.4)$$

where $a_{00} \times a_{11} + a_{01} \times a_{10} = \pm 1$, which makes the scrambling reversible.

It can be applied to scrambled digital images sized $N \times N$ by the discrete form in Equation 2.5:

$$\begin{pmatrix} x_{n+1} \\ y_{n+1} \end{pmatrix} = \begin{pmatrix} 1 & 1 \\ 1 & 2 \end{pmatrix} \begin{pmatrix} x_n \\ y_n \end{pmatrix} \bmod N \qquad (2.5)$$

where $(x_n, y_n) \in [0, N-1] \times [0, N-1]$

is the pixel coordinate of the plain image's; $N \times N$ is the dimension of the in put plain image; (x_{n+1}, y_{n+1}) is the new coordinate for pixel in the resulting image. This method scrambled the pixel positions for a number of times to scramble the image well enough [6].

The digital image can be seen as a two-dimensional matrix. When the size of the image is N, then we have $N \times N$ elements, the subscript x, y stand for the position of pixel, $x, y \in 0, 1, 2 ..., N-1$. Let x, y corresponds to the x, y of Arnold scrambling, for each pair x, y, after all complete Arnold scrambling, become x' and y', which is equivalent to the original image of the point from (x, y) moved to the (x', y'), so realizing the movement of pixels in the image, the image with Arnold scrambling traverse all the points to complete a picture of Arnold scrambling.

Figure 2.7 showing the process of stretching the unit square image in Figure 2.7a by the linear map and the rearrangement of the pieces due to the modulo operation in Figure 2.7b by the arrows.

The cycle of Arnold scrambling is related to the size of the image, but not directly proportional. If size is a 128×128 pixel image of Arnold scrambling cycle

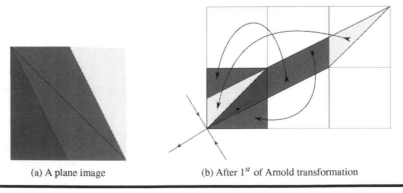

(a) A plane image   (b) After 1st of Arnold transformation

Figure 2.7   1st round of Arnold transformation.

Table 2.2 Two-Dimension Arnold Transform Period with Different Degree N

N	2	3	4	5	6	7	8	9	10	11	12	16	24	25
Period	3	4	3	10	12	8	6	12	30	5	12	12	12	50
N	32	40	48	50	56	60	64	100	120	125	128	256	480	512
Period	24	30	12	150	24	60	48	150	60	250	96	192	120	384

is 96, size 240×240 pixel image of Arnold scrambling for 60 cycles. Dyson and Falk analyze Arnold transform periodicity and the result shows that the period of Arnold transform is $T \leq N^2/2$ with random $N(N > 2)$[2–4]. Table 2.2 shows that matrix degree N is not in direct proportion to the two-dimension period of Arnold transform. Therefore, when we consider the matrix degree of a digital watermark image, we choose less degree for Arnold transform by any possibility, in order to do less computational work.

ALGORITHM 2.3 Scrambling Using Arnold Transform

Input $I(i, j)$ the plain image
for each pixel $I(i, j)$ **do**

$$\begin{pmatrix} I \\ J \end{pmatrix} \leftarrow \begin{pmatrix} 1 & 1 \\ 1 & 2 \end{pmatrix} \begin{pmatrix} I \\ J \end{pmatrix}$$

$\quad I'(I, J) \leftarrow I(i, j)$
end for
Output $I'(i, j)$ the scrambled image

The Arnold transformation is applied on a Peeper image in Figure 2.8a which results in the scrambled image in Figure 2.8b. The plots of the correlation in vertical, horizontal, and diagonal direction of the plain Peeper image are presented in Figures 2.17f, 2.12e, and 2.12g, respectively, and the plots of the correlation in vertical, horizontal and diagonal direction of the scrambled Peeper image are presented in Figures 2.8d, 2.8f, and 2.8h.

The values of the overall correlation in vertical correlation, horizontal correlation and diagonal correlation direction of the plain Peeper image are 0.9768, 0.9792, 0.9639 respectively and the entropy is 7.5937. The values of the overall correlation in vertical correlation, horizontal correlation and diagonal correlation direction of the scrambled Peeper image are 0.0110, 0.0979, 0.0175, 0.1066 respectively and the entropy is 7.9966. The detailed results are given in Table 2.1.

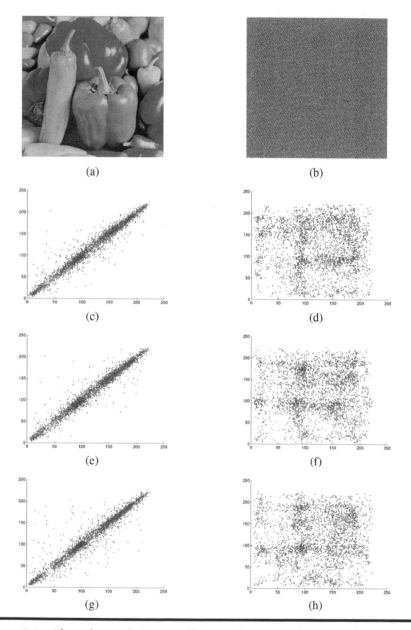

Figure 2.8 Plot of correlation coefficient of Peppers image before and after scrambling using Arnold's transformation: (a) Plain Peppers image, (b) scrambled pepper image, (c) correlation in vertical direction of plain image, (d) correlation in vertical direction of scrambled image, (e) correlation in horizontal direction of plain image, (f) correlation in horizontal direction of scrambled image, (g) correlation in diagonal direction of plain image, and (h) correlation in diagonal direction of scrambled image.

2.2.4.2 Matrix Based Image Scrambling Using Fibonacci Transformation

The numbers 1,1,2,3,5,8,13,21,34,55,89,... known as the Fibonacci numbers have been named by the nineteenth-century French mathematician Edouard Lucas after Leonard Fibonacci of Pisa, one of the best mathematicians of the Middle Ages, who referred to them in his book *Liber Abaci* (1202) in connection with his rabbit problem. The Fibonacci sequence has fascinated both amateurs and professional mathematicians for centuries due to their abundant applications, and their ubiquitous habit of occurring in totally surprising and unrelated places.

Fibonacci transform is the same as Arnold transform, only difference is that the values of $a_{00}, a_{11}, a_{01}, a_{10}$ are four consecutive numbers in the Fibonacci series.

The Fibonacci series is given by Equation 2.6

$$F = \begin{cases} 0 & if \quad n < 1 \\ 1 & if \quad n = 1 \\ F(n-1) + F(n-2) & if \quad n > 1 \end{cases} \tag{2.6}$$

The Fibonacci transformation is represented by Equation 2.7 [7]:

$$\begin{pmatrix} x' \\ y' \end{pmatrix} = \begin{pmatrix} 1 & 1 \\ 1 & 0 \end{pmatrix} \begin{pmatrix} x \\ y \end{pmatrix} \mod N \tag{2.7}$$

where $x, y \in \{0,1,2,3...,N-1\}$

The algorithm 4 presents the scrambling techniques using Fibonacci transformation.

ALGORITHM 2.4 Scrambling Using Fibonacci Transformation

Input: $I(i, j)$ the plain image
for each pixel $I(i, j)$ **do**
$$\begin{pmatrix} I \\ J \end{pmatrix} \leftarrow \begin{pmatrix} 1 & 1 \\ 1 & 0 \end{pmatrix} \begin{pmatrix} i \\ j \end{pmatrix}$$
$I'(I, J) \leftarrow I(i, j)$
end for
Output: $I'(I, J)$, the scrambled image.

The Fibonacci transformation is applied on a Peeper image in Figure 2.9a which results in the scrambled image in Figure 2.9b. The plots of the correlation in vertical, horizontal and diagonal direction of the plain Peeper image are presented in

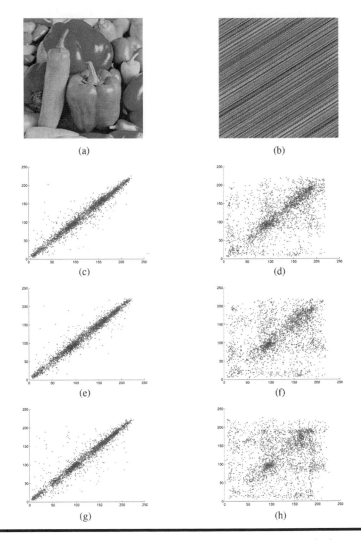

Figure 2.9 **Plot of correlation coefficient of Peppers image before and after scrambling using Fibonacci transformation: (a) Plain Peppers image, (b) scrambled pepper image, (c) correlation in vertical direction of plain image, (d) correlation in vertical direction of scrambled image, (e) correlation in horizontal direction of plain image, (f) correlation in horizontal direction of scrambled image, (g) correlation in diagonal direction of plain image, and (h) correlation in diagonal direction of scrambled image.**

Figures 2.17f, 2.12e, and 2.12g respectively and the plots of the correlation in vertical, horizontal and diagonal direction of the scrambled Peeper image are presented in Figures 2.9d, 2.9f, and 2.9h.

The values of the overall correlation in vertical correlation, horizontal correlation and diagonal correlation direction of the plain Peeper image are 0.9768,

0.9792, 0.9639 respectively and the entropy is 7.5937. The values of the overall correlation in vertical correlation, horizontal correlation and diagonal correlation direction of the scrambled Peeper image are 0.0228, 0.5906, 0.3675, 0.1561 respectively and the entropy is 7.5937. The detailed results are given in Table 2.1.

2.2.5 Gray Code with Bit Plane Scrambling

Novel enhanced quantum representation (NEQR) [24], based on Flexible Representation of Quantum Image (FRQI) is a splendid representation for a quantum image. In [16,23] the authors have presented the gray code with bit plane scrambling in detail. As per the NEQR model, a gray code quantum image can be represented as Equation 2.8

$$
\begin{aligned}
|I\rangle &= \frac{1}{2^n} \sum_{x=0}^{2^n-1} \sum_{y=0}^{2^n-1} |f(X,Y)\rangle |XY\rangle \\
&= \frac{1}{2^n} \sum_{x=0}^{2^n-1} \sum_{y=0}^{2^n-1} \otimes_{i=0}^{q-1} |C_{i=0}^i| |XY\rangle
\end{aligned}
\tag{2.8}
$$

where $|I\rangle$ stands for a image of dimension $2^n \times 2^n$ with 2^q gray range. Then, the gray value of the pixel $f(X,Y)$ is encoded by a binary sequence, described by the Equation 2.9,

$$
\begin{aligned}
f(X,Y) &= C_{XY}^0 C_{XY}^1 \ldots C_{XY}^{q-2} C_{XY}^{q-1}, C_{XY}^k \in [0,1], \\
f(X,Y) &\in [0, 2^q - 1]
\end{aligned}
\tag{2.9}
$$

The Scrambling process: The first operation performed on the image is bit plane slicing. Bit plane information rule states that high bit planes contain most of the information (50.19% information of the pixel is contained in the 8th bit plane) while the lower bit planes contain less information (0.003% information of the pixel is present in the 0th bit plane). According to this rule, the basic Gray Code techniques incur the gray-code transformation in reverse order i.e., 0th bit plane is kept fixed. The basic GB scrambling is denoted by the following Equation 2.10:

$$
\begin{aligned}
|I\rangle &= \frac{1}{2^n} \sum_{x=0}^{2^M-1} \sum_{y=0}^{2^N-1} GB(|f(X,Y)\rangle)|XY\rangle \\
&= \frac{1}{2^n} \sum_{x=0}^{2^M-1} \sum_{y=0}^{2^N-1} |g(X,Y)\rangle|XY\rangle
\end{aligned}
\tag{2.10}
$$

where $n = (M + N)/2$

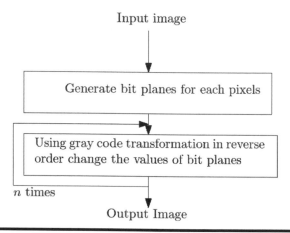

Figure 2.10   Flowchart of gray code scrambling.

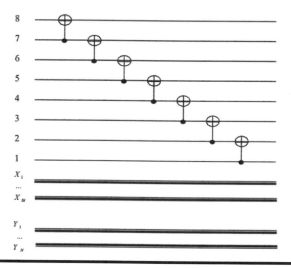

Figure 2.11   The quantum circuit.

The GB in the above equation represents the elementary operations of GB scrambling. In Figure 2.11 a quantum circuit represents the scheme is given below. Numbers 1–8 represent the bit planes. The gates used here is CNOT gates (Controlled NOT gate) (Figures 2.10 and 2.11).

The scrambling technique based on gray code with bit plane scrambling applied on a Peeper image in Figure 2.17d which results in the scrambled image in Figure 2.17e. The plots of the correlation in vertical, horizontal and diagonal direction of the plain Peeper image are presented in Figures 2.17f, 2.12e, and 2.12g respectively and the plots of the correlation in vertical, horizontal and diagonal direction of the scrambled Peeper image are presented in Figures 2.12d, 2.12f, and 2.12h.

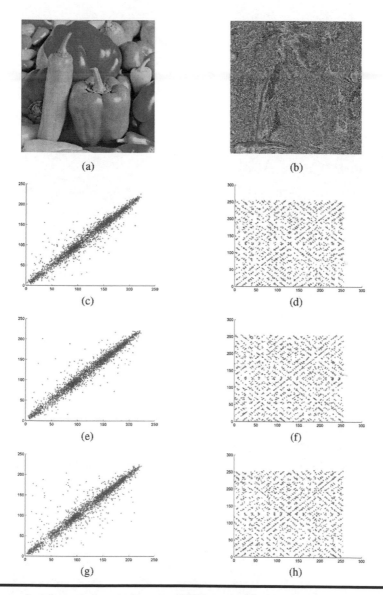

Figure 2.12 Plot of correlation coefficient of Peppers image before and after scrambling using Gray code with bit plane scrambling: (a) Plain Peppers image, (b) scrambled pepper image, (c) correlation in vertical direction of plain image, (d) correlation in vertical direction of scrambled image, (e) correlation in horizontal direction of plain image, (f) correlation in horizontal direction of scrambled image, (g) correlation in diagonal direction of plain image, and (h) correlation in diagonal direction of scrambled image.

The values of the overall correlation in vertical, horizontal, and diagonal direction of the plain Peeper image are 0.9768, 0.9792, 0.9639, respectively, and the entropy is 7.5937. The values of the overall correlation in vertical correlation, horizontal correlation and diagonal correlation direction of the scrambled Peeper image are 0.0022, 0.1134, 0.0556, 0.0834 respectively and the entropy is 7.5937. The detailed results are given in Table 2.1.

2.3 Comparative Analysis

Four images namely Airplane image in Figure 2.13a, Baboon image in Figure 2.13b, and Lena image in Figure 2.13c were used for experiment and to demonstrate comparative results. Those images were scrabbled using all the six methods.

All the results are presented in Table 2.1. In the results it can be noticed that the correlations after scrambling become near to zero, where a good quality scrambling technique reduces the correlation near to zero. The entropy after scrambling remains near to eight where the pixel values are not changed during the scrambling.

The Airplane image in Figure 2.13a is scrambled using circular row and column shifting in Figure 2.14a, scrambled using 2D mapping in Figure 2.14b, scrambled using bit label permutation in Figure 2.14c, scrambled using Arnold transformation in Figure 2.14d, scrambled using Fibonacci transformation in Figure 2.14f, scrambled using gray code in Figure 2.14a.

The Baboon image in Figure 2.13b is scrambled using circular row and column shifting in Figure 2.15a, scrambled using 2D mapping in Figure 2.15b, scrambled using bit label permutation in Figure 2.15c, scrambled using Arnold transformation in Figure 2.15d, scrambled using Fibonacci transformation in Figure 2.15f, scrambled using gray code in Figure 2.15a.

(a) Airplane image (b) Baboon image (c) Lena image

Figure 2.13 Test results using gray code with bit plane scrambling.

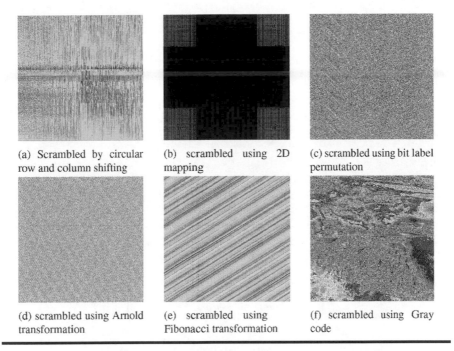

(a) Scrambled by circular row and column shifting

(b) scrambled using 2D mapping

(c) scrambled using bit label permutation

(d) scrambled using Arnold transformation

(e) scrambled using Fibonacci transformation

(f) scrambled using Gray code

Figure 2.14 The Airplane image scrambled using different techniques.

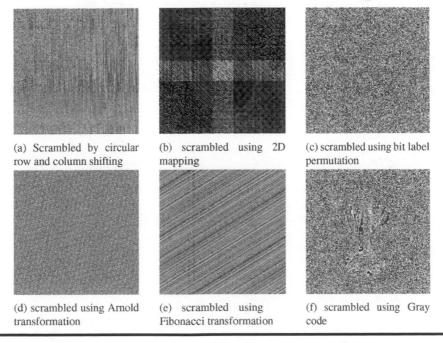

(a) Scrambled by circular row and column shifting

(b) scrambled using 2D mapping

(c) scrambled using bit label permutation

(d) scrambled using Arnold transformation

(e) scrambled using Fibonacci transformation

(f) scrambled using Gray code

Figure 2.15 The Baboon image scrambled using different techniques.

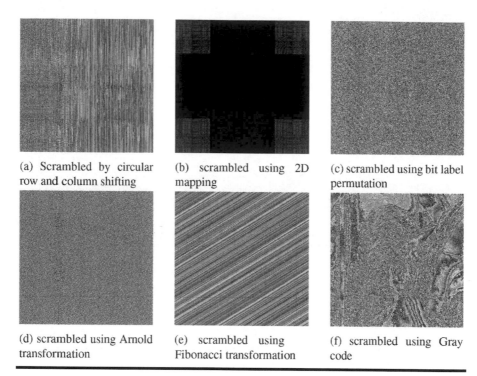

(a) Scrambled by circular row and column shifting

(b) scrambled using 2D mapping

(c) scrambled using bit label permutation

(d) scrambled using Arnold transformation

(e) scrambled using Fibonacci transformation

(f) scrambled using Gray code

Figure 2.16   The Lena image scrambled using different techniques.

The Lena image in Figure 2.13c is scrambled using circular row and column shifting in Figure 2.16a, scrambled using 2D mappiing in Figure 2.16b, scrambled using bit label permutation in Figure 2.16c, scrambled using Arnold transformation in Figure 2.16d, scrambled using Fibonacci transformation in Figure 2.16f, scrambled using gray code in Figure 2.16a.

2.3.1 Entropy Analysis

The information entropy is defined as the degree of uncertainties in the system. The greater the entropy, the more is the randomness in the image, or the image is more uniform [25]. Thus statistical attacks become difficult. Entropy is defined in Equation 2.11 [26].

$$H(m) = \sum_{i=0}^{2^N-1} p(m_i) \times \log_2 \left[\frac{1}{p(m_i)} \right] \tag{2.11}$$

where $p(m_i)$ are the histogram counts returned from the histogram. For an ideal random image, the entropy is calculated to be 8.

Entropy is the measure of randomness and unpredictability in an image. It measures the randomness in the frequency of occurrence of pixels with different intensities present in the image. A small value of entropy demonstrates high statistical correlations and repetition of same values or keys, which is the sweet point for statistical cryptanalysis. In contrast a high value of entropy indicates a less predictable key and high randomness. Therefore, for better is the randomness in the image, the entropy should be closer to 8.

2.3.2 Correlation Coefficient

In any image the adjacent pixels are highly correlated, which gives attacker to apply known plane text attack to break the cipher. Therefore, the encryption system must ensure lowest possible correlation between the adjacent pixels in the cipher image [27].

In this chapter, correlation between vertical, horizontally, and diagonally neighbor pixels and between the same pixels of the original and the encrypted image are analyzed. To calculate, 1000–2000 pairs of two-adjacent pixels were randomly selected in vertical, horizontal, and diagonal direction. It is calculated by the Equation 2.12 [28,29].

$$r = \frac{\text{Cov}(x, y)}{\sigma_x \times \sigma_y} \tag{2.12}$$

$$\text{VAR}(x) = \frac{1}{N} \sum_{i=1}^{N} (x_i - E(x))^2 \tag{2.13}$$

$$\sigma_x = \sqrt{\text{VAR}(x)} \tag{2.14}$$

$$\sigma_y = \sqrt{\text{VAR}(y)} \tag{2.15}$$

$$\text{Cov}(x, y) = \frac{1}{N} \sum_{x=1}^{N} (x_i - E(x))(y_i - E(y)) \tag{2.16}$$

where r is correlation coefficient and Cov is covariance at pixels x and y, where x and y are the gray-scale values of two pixels in the same place in the plaintext and ciphertext images. $\text{VAR}(x)$ is variance at pixel value x in the plaintext image, σ_x is standard deviation, E is the expected value operator and N is the total number of pixels for $N \times N$ matrix. The values were found to be as shown in Table 2.1 (Figure 2.17).

2.3.3 Comparative Computational Complexity

The Comparative numbers of operation are presented in Table 2.3. Where k stands for number of iterations of Arnold-Fibonacci transform-Gray bit plane scrambling.

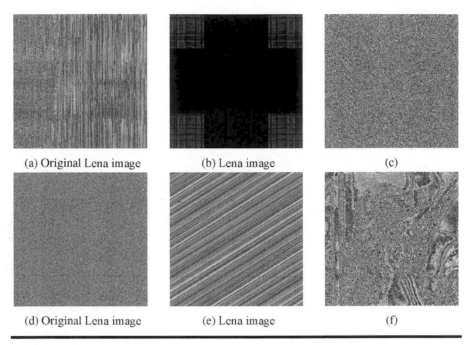

(a) Original Lena image (b) Lena image (c)

(d) Original Lena image (e) Lena image (f)

Figure 2.17 Test results using gray code with bit plane scrambling.

Table 2.3 Comparative Results of Operation

Scheme	Operation
Arnold's transformation	No of mod operations $M \times N \times k$; No of swap operations $M \times N \times k$
Fibonacci transformation	No of mod operations $M \times N \times k$; No of swap operations $M \times N \times k$
Gray code with bit plane transformation	No of xor operations $M \times N$; No of mod operations $M \times N \times 2$; No of copy operations $3 \times M \times N$
2D mapping	No of xor operations $7 \times M \times N \times k$
Row and column shifting	No of swap operations $M \times N + N \times M = 2 \times M \times N$; Worst Case No of shift operations $\max(M, N) \times M + \max(M, N) \times N$
Row and column shifting with bit plane scrambling	No of swap operations $M + N \times 8 + M \times N \times 8 \times k$; No of mod operations $M \times N \times 8 \times k$

2.4 Inverse Scrambling

To restore the image to its pre-scrambled form, one must simply exchange roles of prepared Sudoku puzzles and repeat the scrambling steps with the same iteration numbers. This will successfully restore the image as long as the correct sets of puzzles and iteration numbers are used.

2.5 Conclusion

Scrambling is one of the most important parts of confusion diffusion based image encryption. A huge number of scrambling techniques are available in literature. Therefor choosing the correct scrambling method for an encryption scheme becomes most crucial. The performance of an encryption scheme largely depends on the scrambling technique used. In this chapter a comparative study on different cryptographic scrambling techniques was presented. The study included matrix based, Fibonacci series based, and key based scrambling techniques. Correlation coefficient, entropy and computational time will be compared in the chapter by simulating and testing them on different types of images. There are some other image scrambling techniques readers may go through, namely scrambling based on non-commutative wavelet transform, Queue Transform, Poker Shuffling Transform, Rubiks cubic rotation, scrambling using relative prime numbers, scrambling based on Sudoku puzzle, image scrambling based on 2D cellular automata, etc.

References

1. B. Mondal, T. Mandal, D. A. Khan, and T. Choudhury. A secure image encryption scheme using chaos and wavelet transformations. *Recent Patents on Engineering*, 12(1):5–14, 2018.
2. B. Mondal, N. Sinha, and T. Mandal. A secure image encryption algorithm using lfsr and rc4 key stream generator. In *Proceedings of 3rd International Conference on Advanced Computing, Networking and Informatics*, pp. 227–237. Springer India, New Delhi, India, 2015.
3. B. Mondal and T. Mandal. A nobel chaos based secure image encryption algorithm. *International Journal of Applied Engineering Research*, 11(5):3120–3127, 2016.
4. B. Mondal and S. K. Singh. A highly secure steganography scheme for secure communication. In *Proceedings, International Conference of Computation and Communication Advancement (IC3A)-2013*, Vol. 3, pp. 88–92, January 2013.
5. J. Zou, R. K. Ward, and D. Qi. A new digital image scrambling method based on fibonacci numbers. In *Circuits and Systems, 2004. ISCAS'04. Proceedings of the 2004 International Symposium on*, Vol. 3, pp. III–965–8 Vol. 3, May 2004.
6. N. A. M. Abbas. Image encryption based on independent component analysis and Arnold's cat map. *Egyptian Informatics Journal*, 17(1):139–146, 2016.

7. Y. Zhou, K. Panetta, S. Agaian, and C. L. P. Chen. Image encryption using p-fibonacci transform and decomposition. *Optics Communications*, 285(5):594–608, 2012.
8. S. K. Abd-El-Hafiz, S. H. AbdElHaleem, and A. G. Radwan. Novel permutation measures for image encryption algorithms. *Optics and Lasers in Engineering*, 85:72–83, 2016.
9. B. Mondal and T. Mandal. A multilevel security scheme using chaos based encryption and steganography for secure audio communication. *International Journal of Research in Engineering and Technology*, 2(10):399–403, 2013.
10. W. Yanling. Image scrambling method based on chaotic sequences and mapping. In *Education Technology and Computer Science, 2009. ETCS'09. First International Workshop on*, Vol. 3, pp. 453–457, March 2009.
11. S. M. H. Alwahbani and E. B. M. Bashier. Speech scrambling based on chaotic maps and one time pad. In *Computing, Electrical and Electronics Engineering (ICCEEE), 2013 International Conference on*, pp. 128–133, August 2013.
12. W. Liu, K. Sun, and C. Zhu. A fast image encryption algorithm based on chaotic map. *Optics and Lasers in Engineering*, 84:26–36, 2016.
13. B. Mondal and T. Mandal. A light weight secure image encryption scheme based on chaos dna computing. *Journal of King Saud University-Computer and Information Sciences*, 29(4):499–504, 2017.
14. B. Mondal, T. Mandal, N. Biswas, and P. Kumar. A secure partial encryption scheme based on bit plane manipulation. In *7th International Symposium on Embedded Computing and System Design 2017 (ISED)*, pp. 1–5, 2017.
15. Z. Parvin, H. Seyedarabi, and M. Shamsi. A new secure and sensitive image encryption scheme based on new substitution with chaotic function. *Multimedia Tools and Applications*, 75(17):10631–10648, 2014.
16. J. Chen, Z. Zhu, C. Fu, H. Yu, and L. Zhang. An efficient image encryption scheme using gray code based permutation approach. *Optics and Lasers in Engineering*, 67:191–204, 2015.
17. Y. Zhou, K. Panetta, S. Agaian, and C. L. P. Chen. (n, k, p)-gray code for image systems. *IEEE Transactions on Cybernetics*, 43(2):515–529, 2013.
18. C. Fu, B. Lin, Y. Miao, X. Liu, and J. Chen. A novel chaos-based bit-level permutation scheme for digital image encryption. *Optics Communications*, 284(23):5415–5423, 2011.
19. A. Jolfaei, X. W. Wu, and V. Muthukkumarasamy. On the security of permutation-only image encryption schemes. *IEEE Transactions on Information Forensics and Security*, 11(2):235–246, 2016.
20. Y. Li, C. Wang, and H. Chen. A hyper-chaos-based image encryption algorithm using pixel-level permutation and bit-level permutation. *Optics and Lasers in Engineering*, 90:238–246, 2017.
21. X. Li. A generalized matrix-based scrambling transformation and its properties. In *Young Computer Scientists, 2008. ICYCS 2008. The 9th International Conference for*, pp. 1429–1434, November 2008.
22. P. Premaratne and M. Premaratne. Key-based scrambling for secure image communication. In D.-S. Huang, P. Gupta, X. Zhang, and P. Premaratne, editors, *Emerging Intelligent Computing Technology and Applications*, Vol. 304 of *Communications in Computer and Information Science*, pp. 259–263. Springer, Berlin, Germany, 2012.
23. R.-G. Zhou, Y.-J. Sun, and P. Fan. Quantum image gray-code and bit-plane scrambling. *Quantum Information Processing*, 14(5):1717–1734, 2015.

24. Y. Zhang, K. Lu, Y. Gao, and M. Wang. Neqr: A novel enhanced quantum representation of digital images. *Quantum Information Processing*, 12(8):2833–2860, 2013.
25. Y. Dodis and A. Smith. Entropic security and the encryption of high entropy messages. Cryptology ePrint Archive, Report 2004/219, 2004. http://eprint.iacr.org/2004/219.
26. C. E. Shannon. Communication theory of secrecy systems. *Bell System Technical Journal*, 28:656–715, 1949.
27. T. Siegenthaler. Correlation-immunity of nonlinear combining functions for cryptographic applications (corresp.). *IEEE Transactions on Information Theory*, 30(5):776–780, 1984.
28. H. M. Elkamchouchi and M. A. Makar. Measuring encryption quality for bitmap images encrypted with rijndael and kamkar block ciphers. In *Proceedings of the Twenty-Second National Radio Science Conference, 2005. NRSC 2005*, pp. 277–284, March 2005.
29. M. A. Sutton, J. J. Orteu, and H. Schreier. *Image Correlation for Shape, Motion and Deformation Measurements: Basic Concepts, Theory and Applications*. Springer, New York, 2009.

Chapter 3

Chaos-Based Image Cryptography

Charles Z. Liu, Linda Y. Dong and Raymond P. Shaw

Contents

DOI: 10.1201/9780429435461-4

3.1 Introduction

3.1.1 Background

Information security gains increasing weight in modern information exchanging and system networking, and cryptography serves as an important foundation for guaranteeing the trustworthy data communication. With the access of diverse multimedia content in an information system, data such as image, speech, and video, it brings many new properties to communication as well as challenges in security. Image cryptography is a technique to cipher an original image by encoding its elements (usually pixels) with an algorithm to convert the plaintext information into an encrypted form thats hard to read its meaning. Usually, the ciphered information can be recovered by a corresponding decryption processing to decode the encrypted information back to its original meaning. To build a bridge between encryption and decryption for the plaintext, a key, usually a set of characters, is required as a clue for the algorithm to encode and decode the information correspondingly.

Conventional ciphering strategies, such as Data Encryption Standard (DES), International Data Encryption Algorithm (IDEA), Rivest–Shamir–Adleman (RSA) serve sufficiently for data like words and characters, but are not suitable for information in complex forms like image or voice, thus rendering its weakness on applications. This is especially true for online communication or of data that is complicated and large [4]. Even though conventional methods can be embedded into the encoded part of the system for encrypting the information with transforming the original data like image or voice into a coded form, the efficiency and effectiveness may not be stable. Besides time-consumption, in some cases directly applying traditional methods may cause inferior performance on scrambling. What is more, inappropriate encryption would result in the risk of data loss caused by residual transcoding errors and improper decryption ,thus failing to restore the original data since distortion caused losing partial information.

Furthermore, visual data are different from texts in many aspects, such as high redundancy and correlation, the local structure and broadband power spectrum, and its encoding features. All those differences render the conventional ciphering strategy limitations to image cryptography.

3.1.2 Chaotic Encryption

Chaotic encryption has a potential to sever as a good candidate for image encryption. Chaos refers to a phenomena of pseudo random dynamics generated by deterministic systems. The systems are characterized by sensitive dependence on initial conditions, aperiodic trajectories, bounded trajectories, and mixing orbits. Thanks to its nonlinear and pseudo-random characteristics, schemes involved with cipher-text encryption by chaotic mapping were proposed as early as the 1990s [5,6]. The primary mechanism is using the parameter of the tent map combined with a secret key to generate a chaotic sequence using forwarding iteration of the encryption algorithm, thus obtaining the ciphertext from an initial point which denoted plain text. The deterministic pseudo-random series was generated by chaos dynamic mapping to encrypt the plaintext iteratively. Chaotic mapping has many important properties corresponding to cryptography. Sensitive dependence on initial state and system parameters, similar to random behavior and topological transitivity, are closely related to the demands of encryption such as mixing and diffusion. Therefore, chaotic cryptograph had been seen as a novel direction for the development of practical methodology on cryptograph applications [7].

Chaotic dynamics can be used as a ciphering base to encrypt plaintext information. However, some chaos-based encryptions are not always secure. Ljupco analyzed the risks on weakness and slow cipher of chaotic encryption strategy, and provided an improvement scheme for chaotic encryption methodology with Jakimoski [7–9]. Afterward, many works on improving and applying chaotic cryptosystem stand out to date. Recently, research on improving and extending the chaotic cipher methodology have grabbed the headlines of the linguistics. Kanso and Smaoui studied a random binary generator with chaotic mapping [10]. Behnia et al. generalize the logistic maps to a hierarchy of one parameter families of maps with invariant measure [11]. Sun et al. aiming at the drawbacks of small key space and weak security in one-dimensional chaotic cipher, proposed a spatial chaos method for high degree security image encryption [12]. Ye researches the methods to scramble the encryption of an image with a chaotic map concerning pixel bit [13]. Wang et al. researched a method to accelerate the encryption process by combining the stages of permutation and diffusion to improve the scanning effort [14]. Many of these works focus much on encryption efficiency and scrambling performance concerning correlation distribution analysis by comparing the ciphered result to the plain text.

To improve the hiddenness and scrambling of information, we need to make the encrypted result possess stationary stochastic characteristics similar to white noise so that very little variety in reflecting information appears to provide the cue for cracking. To improve the effectiveness, Belazi et al. investigated whether effectiveness of investigated linear fractional transformation can enhance Substitution-boxes (S-boxes). They introduced permutation-substitution to improve the statistical performance [15]. If only necessary elements of sensitive information in the Lifting Wavelet Transform (LWT) frequency domain will be encrypted, the efficiency of this method can also be improved by partial encryption [16]. Murillo-Escobar et al. drew our attention to the effectiveness pseudo random number generator (PRNG). Based on the logistic map, they proposed a enhanced chaotic map by using *mod* operator to improve random performance [17].

It has been proven that with improved random performance, enhanced chaotic maps can also help to solve the problem of chosen plaintext attacks due to its optimized distribution [18]. The more the cipher-text resembles white noise, the evener statistic characteristics the encryption brings; thus, the more uniform the spatial distribution and frequency distribution are, the better the plaintext information gets hidden.

3.1.3 *Organization of the Chapter*

In this chapter, we will introduce the chaos-based technology for image cryptography, and examples with its applications in biometric protection for security system are given to show its performance. Section 3.1 will give an introduction of the cryptography and discuss the issues and challenges in image cryptography, comparing with the traditional cryptography (e.g., triple DES) methodology. In Section 3.2, several classic the related methods, including triple DES, Bernoulli, and Logistic mapping, are discussed. Section 3.3, focusing on distribution in space domain and uniform diffusion in a frequency domain, we study a compounded chaotic cipher strategy with dynamic Bernoulli mapping for improving the performance of cryptographic text with consideration both of volatility and correlation. Section 3.4 represents an application of a biometric system for privacy and security as an example. Aiming at visual original biometric data, Section 3.5 gives the results of related tests and analysis on key space, sensitivity, correlation and uniform distribution strategy with various biometric data and comparative analysis of their performance. Discussions on effectiveness, implementation and anti-attack are given in Section 3.6 and conclusion is made in Section 3.7.

3.2 Relevant Methods

The chaos-based image encryption methods focus on protecting the original image by scrambling to disguise plain text into noise by chaotic cryptography, which applies the mathematical chaos theory to the cryptography, privately and securely transmitting information with the presence of a form in chaos or randomness.

One dimensional maps can be defined as f that:

$$x(n+1) = f(x(n)) \tag{3.1}$$

where each current state $x(n)$ determines the following state $x(n+1)$, and the iterates of the function f is dynamic orbits. Assume initial value is x_0, the orbit will be chaotic if it leads to aperiodic point.

This section introduces some typical methods for encryption including logistic mapping, tent mapping, sine mapping, Sawtooth-Bernoulli mapping. Gaussian mapping and their aperiodic domain.

3.2.1 Logistic Mapping

Logistic map is polynomial chaotic mapping exhibiting complicated behavior with superb sensitivity to initial conditions [19–21]. The formulation for its state evolution is:

$$x(n+1) = \alpha x(n)\,(1+x(n)) \tag{3.2}$$

where $x(n) \in (0,1)$ is the state of system in time n and α is control parameter for updating, which takes the value ranged within [3.7,4). This map generates a pseudo-random state series by means of the operation of the chaotic discrete-time dynamical system.

3.2.2 Tent Mapping

Tent map [22] is another chaotic mapping. By a real-valued function f_μ in a tent-like shape, it can be formulated with parameter μ as:

$$f_\mu = \mu \min\{x, 1-x\} \tag{3.3}$$

The initial start point x_0 meets $x_0 \in [0,1]$ and yields a sequence x_n as:

$$x(n+1) = f_\mu(x_n) = \begin{cases} \mu x(n) & if \quad x < 1/2 \\ \mu(1-x(n)) & else \end{cases} \tag{3.4}$$

where $\mu > 0$ as a constant and $x(n) \in (0,1)$.

The tent map with parameter $\mu = 2$ is topologically conjugate with the logistic map with parameter $\alpha = 4$, which means the behaviors of the two maps are topologically identical under iteration.

3.2.3 Sine Map

Chaotic series can also be generated by some simple typical nonlinear functions. Sine map [23,24] is a case in point, which is defined as:

$$x(n+1) = \mu \sin(\pi x_n) \tag{3.5}$$

The parameter μ is set as $\mu \in [0,1]$ to make the map unimodal and it has quadratic behavior near maximum, thus showing similar behavior to the logistic map. Its fixed point 0 will be stable when $\mu < 1/\mu$.

3.2.4 Sawtooth-Bernoulli Map

A Sawtooth-Bernoulli mapping [25,26] can be formulated with determined operation as:

$$f(x) = 2x \quad \mathrm{mod}\ 1 \tag{3.6}$$

where $x \in [0,1]$ and $f(x) \in [0,1]$, and x mod 1 is the fractional part of x.

It can be seen that x_{n+1} is the Bernoulli shift of x_n. In the binary number system, coefficient 2 corresponds to the left shift by 1 bit thus taking the fractional part corresponding to a bit truncation. Meanwhile, the Bernoulli process is a discrete-time stochastic process. From any given time, future trials are also a Bernoulli process independent of the past trials. Therefore, the Sawtooth-Bernoulli map can be a candidate for a virtual stochastic independent dynamic generation.

3.2.5 Gaussian Map

A general Gaussian map [27] can be formulated as:

$$x(n+1) = \mu[e^{-(x(n)-a)^2} - c] \tag{3.7}$$

A typical parameters to make this map unimodal in a symmetric and quadratic distribution, which maps $[0,1] \mapsto [0,1]$ with a single maxima at $x = 0.5$, are $a = 0.5$, $c = e^{(-0.25)}$, and

$$\mu_{\max} = \frac{1}{\min([e^{-(x(n)-a)^2} - c])} \tag{3.8}$$

Gaussian map behaviors are similar to the logistic map when it is a unimodal and maxima has quadratic behavior.

3.2.6 Multidimensional Maps

Multidimensional maps can be defined as:

$$x(n+1) = f(x(n)) \tag{3.9}$$

where $x(n)$ represents a vector of current state $[x_1(n), x_2(n), \ldots, x_l(n)]^T$ with l substates, and $\mathbf{f}$ represents an vector operator. iteration vector state $x(n+1) = [x_1(n+1), x_2(n+1), \ldots, x_l(n+1)]^T$. Many types of multidimensional chaotic systems, such as Lorenz systems [28], Rossler systems [29], Lu systems [30], and Chen systems [31], can be extended to hyperchaotic systems (e.g., [32]). The hyperchaotic system can improve the scrambling performance with its enhanced randomness and chaos feature. Due to the pages limitation, this part of the content will not be discussed in this chapter. But, we will introduce in the next section another method to enhance the chaotic randomness with the typical method mentioned above.

3.3 Compounded Chaotic Cryptography

The hyperchaotic map can be used to enhance the chaos dynamics. However, hyperchaotic systems usually are based on the multidimensional chaos map. It implies that more computational resource is needed when computing the vector state iteration. In this section, a compounded chaotic strategy is studied to improve the scrambling performance with virtual stochastic independency dynamic, which makes the process de-coupled in space domain and uniformly stationary in statistic distribution so as to close to the meaningless noise. By introducing stochastic dynamics, the compound chaotic map can also enhance the randomness with less correlation among the adjacent information blocks in the data. To demonstrate the compound strategy, logistic mapping is selected as candidate for compounding and this dynamic maps unit interval onto itself, which can be applied to iteration directly. In order to generate a virtual stochastic independent process, we introduce the Bernoulli model as a coin flipping-like switch strategy and design a dynamic Bernoulli mapping as updating strategy and combine it with Logistic mapping to form a synthetic dynamic system.

In order to enhance the volatility of the pseudo-random series and stationary, we design a compounded strategy by combining Logistic mapping with dynamic Bernoulli and defined as Bernoulli-Logistic Encryption (BLE) (3.10):

$$\begin{cases} x(n+1) = \phi(y(n)) + \psi(y(n)) \\ \\ y(n) = \alpha x(n)\,(1+x(n)) \end{cases} \tag{3.10}$$

For random state evolution, we can design the dynamic Bernoulli updating strategy as follows:

$$x(n+1) = \phi(x(n)) + \psi(x(n)) \tag{3.11}$$

where

$$\begin{cases} \phi(x(n)) = f(x(n))\, \beta(1-x(n)) \\ \psi(x(n)) = (1 - f(x(n)))\, (\beta x(n)) \end{cases} \tag{3.12}$$

$\beta \in (1,2)$ is optional parameter for update control. This updating rule can be seen as a coin flipping-type strategy to generate a series of stochastic sequence. According to the rule, it takes the unit interval [0,1] into itself, which enable the map to be applied in iteration procedure directly. We introduce Bernoulli map to reinforce the random while reducing the correlation for generating series so as to improve the volatility and stationary of the mixture of the cryptograph.

To further de-couple the correlation between the adjacent elements, a space scrambling strategy is introduced as a discrete dynamic system formulated as:

$$x_{i+1,j} + \omega x_{i,j+1} = 1 - ((1+\omega)\mu x_{i,j}) \tag{3.13}$$

where $\omega \in (-1,1)$, $\mu \in (1.55,2)$, which brings the further scrambling dynamic in space domain with chaotic state. Original biometric data I is converted into encrypted form E using results of iteration of BLE chaos map X with optional conditions and parameters dynamics. The encryption is followed with the computation as:

$$E = I \oplus (X \times K \mod T) \tag{3.14}$$

where:
 $\oplus$ is XOR operator
 K is the coefficient matrix
 T is the threshold for data regularization

The cipher structure is symmetric, which the decryption procedure is similar to that of encryption. To obtain the original information it just needs to replace the original plain text by cryptographic result with same BLE map.

3.4 Case Study: Cryptography for Biometrics

3.4.1 Biometrics

Biometrics refers to the science and technology of measuring and analyzing biological data. The past decade witnessed the significant advancement in the capabilities of biometric technologies [33,34]. Topics focusing on methodology and system for biometrics measurement and recognition have received increasing interest with respect to medicine and authentication [35–41].

With the development of information and communication technology (ICT), biometric networks are used more and more frequently for asset management as well. Lots of efforts are made concerning how biometric technology is implemented and applied in services like asset management and authorization through biometric traits like DNA, fingerprints, retinas, irises, and hands, so those biometrics are widely used as IDs to access and as substitutions to passwords. Much weight is given on the biometric implementation and application in service, like asset management and authorization with biometrics [42–46]. By means of biometrics, users no longer have to design and remember different long and complex passwords for diverse safe accessing [47–49]. Instead, they can use their natural body components, which bring users the convenience to access the service without losing the effectiveness of the authentication.

While bringing convenience, biometric data application involves private information that is sensitive for users privacy and safety both of person and asset. Fingerprint, iris, and retina may not be the only physical features of individuals, but also can be used as proof of identity for authentication of ownership to assets. Once breaches, leaks, or hacks happen to such information, it would not only result in the divulging of user's privacy but also threaten the relevant safety of the asset as well. Therefore, on no account should we ignore the significance of the issues on security and privacy of biometric data and its system.

3.4.2 Security of Biometric

Many types of research have been conducted to explore the possible vulnerabilities of the biometric system and feasible measures to guarantee the security. Uludag et al. analyze the challenges involved in biometric applications in authentication systems and limitations of the biometric cryptosystems [50]. Guillen et al. analyzed the vulnerability of fingerprint biometric network system [51]. According to these works, it can be seen that the biometric network is capable of reducing the cost of implementation and making it possible for the mobile and scalable application. In the meanwhile, the works suggest that the system should be designed in parallel with the level of security. Computation complexity and resource consumption for security services should reach the corresponding balance to the level of security that is necessary, rather than simply following the rule of "the higher, the better."

As for the issues on security and privacy, protecting biometric templates is critical for public acceptability. Ignatenko and Willems discuss the security issue of biometric from the secrecy perspective concerning secret-key and privacy leakage [52]. Rathgeb and Uhl discussed biometric template protection technologies involved with cryptosystems and cancelable biometrics [53]. Jain et al. investigated the vulnerabilities of a biometric system and discussed countermeasures to deal with the cruxes [54,55]. It can be seen that the biometric data security falls under three mainly groups:

encryption based protection, biometric cryptosystem, and biometric transform. Each of them has its characteristics: encryption based method is suitable for sophisticated matching so as to preserve the matching accuracy; biometric cryptosystem serves as a good scheme for remote cross-domain authentication; and biometric transform is competent in privacy protection registered in separate multi-terminals. These three techniques can be comprehensively applied as an integrated scheme.

In some especially confidential access control cases, biometric data must be saved as original samples. For example, as for scenarios like intensive care unit, prohibited military zone, prison and restricted vault, the persons while being granted access should also be recognized and logged with his/her biometric data for tracking and inspection purposes. Under this type of scenario, the system must secure the biometric data while preserving privacy so that both the transparency for legitimate users and security against potential attack are maintained.

Aiming at this circumstance, the most direct strategy for this application are encryption based methods that protect the access and recovery by cryptography. Many existing works involved with data access security mainly focus on the protection scheme for remote or local data accessing based on traditional encryption algorithms [55–61]. However, most biometric data in modern practicable application are in visual form [33–36,39,40,42]. Owning to the size of biometric data is greater in than that of texts, direct ciphering these data with traditional cryptosystem is so time-consuming that it is not suitable for quick authentication and cryptic record in the biometric application. It can be seen that conventional encryption cannot be applicable directly to such original biometric data samples, therefore research on a suitable methodology for such biometric raw data is still in need on account of the generality of the method. Issues on encryption based protection for original biometric data still leave much room to study.

3.4.3 Materials

Biometric information is a type of plaintext and chaos-based cryptography that can be used to protect [62–64]. In this section, we take a biometrics encryption as a case to study the feasibility and application of the chaotic image cryptography. Experiments of the encryption method have been given as well.

Three typical biometrics, retina, iris and fingerprint, are selected as test materials A, B,C, where test A is an RGB color map and test B and C are grey-scale maps. The data is stored in an image with the size 256 × 256.

Different from mass media visual data, most biometrics focus on reflecting characteristics, in which the information is expressed as data with strong contrast. Therefore, in order to test the cryptography effect to this type of data, we also use a special image that with intensive black-white contrast saturation as extreme test sample D in 256 × 256 gray level scale map to examine the statistic distribution and scrambling performance of the encryption strategies.

All plain test materials are shown in Figure 3.1.

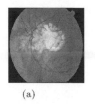 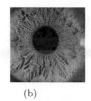 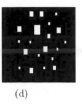

(a)   (b)   (c)   (d)

Figure 3.1 The plain samples for test: (a) Retina for test A, (b) iris for test B, (c) fingerprint for test C, and (d) intensive black-white contrast for test D.

3.4.4 Tests and Results

In this section, several cipher schemes were involved in the test including triple DES (data encryption standard), Logistic mapping, dynamic Bernoulli mapping cipher and compounded BLE mapping. Weight is given both to random scrambling in space domain and stationary in a uniform distribution.

To carry out a performance analysis of different cipher schemes, we take Triple DES (3DES), which is symmetric-key block cipher based on DES algorithm [65–68], as a case of conventional cipher for a comparison study. It increases the key size of DES through applying three times DES to each data block. As an efficient protection against brute-force attacks, 3DES is one of the most widely used cryptosystems. The basic encryption procedure Ξ of 3DES is:

$$C = \Xi(k_1, k_2, k_3, P) = E_{k3}(D_{k2}(E_{k1}(P))) \tag{3.15}$$

where P and C refer to plaintext and ciphertext respectively, and E_{kx}, D_{kx} refer to DES encryption and decryption process with key $kx \in \{k1, k2, k3\}$, respectively. Correspondingly, the basic decryption of 3DES is:

$$P = \Xi^{-1}((k_1, k_2, k_3, C)) = D_{k1}(E_{k2}(D_{k3}(C))) \tag{3.16}$$

The security of 3DES mostly depends on keys $k1, k2, k3$. It is initially equivalent to 168 bit cipher if these three keys are different. 3DES is widely used with left-right key structure, i.e., key $k = (k_l, k_r)$, which amounts to the procedure Ξ and Ξ^{-1} with $k_1 = k_3 = k_l, k_2 = k_r$. In this case, 3DES plays a role as a 112 bit cipher.

The Logistic, dynamic Bernoulli, and the compounded mapping comply with (3.2), (3.11), and (3.10) respectively, where the parameters are set as $K = 10000$, $T = 256$, $\mu = 0.5$, $\omega = 0.4$, $\alpha = 4$, $\beta = 1.732105000$, $x(0) = 0.32105000$.

Meanwhile, 3DES encryption strategy is included as well in the test to present the cipher effect with standard data encryption. Left-right key structure is applied with $k_l = 32105000$ for the first and the third round DES encryption and $k_r = 12345000$ for the second round. We cipher the test materials A-D with 3DES cipher (3DES-C), logistic cipher (LC), dynamic Bernoulli cipher (BC) and Bernoulli-Logistic encryption (BLE) to examine their effectiveness.

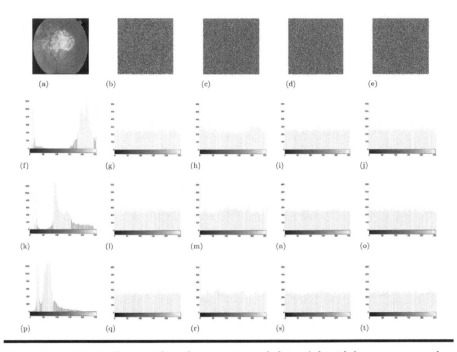

Figure 3.2 Encryption results of test A. From left to right: Plaintext, encryption with 3DES cipher, logistic cipher, Bernoulli cipher, and compounded BLE cipher. The first row shows the space domain information and the other three rows show the corresponding histogram in three channels. In each histogram sub-figures, *X*-axis represents gray level and *Y*-axis represents number of pixels. (a) Plaintext, (b) 3DES-C test Result, (c) LC test result, (d) BC test result, (e) BLE test result, (f) Ch. R plaintext histogram, (g) Ch. R 3DES-C histogram, (h) Ch. R LC histogram, (i) Ch. R BC histogram, (j) Ch. R BLE histogram, (k) Ch. G plaintext histogram, (l) Ch. G 3DES-C histogram, (m) Ch. G LC histogram, (n) Ch. G BC histogram, (o) Ch. G BLE histogram, (p) Ch. B plaintext histogram, (q) Ch. B 3DES-C histogram, (r) Ch. B LC histogram, (s) Ch. B BC histogram, and (t) Ch. B BLE histogram.

In Figure 3.2, the ciphered effect and their corresponding statistics of test A are shown, where sub-figures in the first column show the information in space domain and the other 3 columns present the corresponding histogram in R, G, B channels, respectively. Sub-figures a–e in the first row present the plaintext and its encryption results with 3DES-C, LC, BC, and BLE. Second to fourth rows present the histograms of each result corresponding to the above sub-figure in R, G, B channels, where *X*-axis represents gray level and *Y*-axis represents number of pixels.

Figures 3.3 through 3.5 show the ciphered results of test B–D with strategy 3DES-C, LC, BC, and BLE, respectively, where the first column presents the data in space domain form and second column presents the histogram. The histogram information in Figures 3.3 through 3.5 are all showed in one channel due to the fact that plaintext samples in test B–D are in gray level.

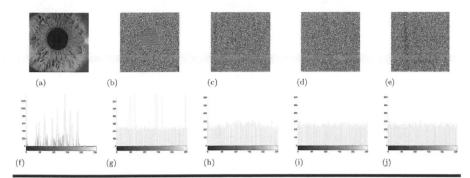

Figure 3.3 Encryption results of test B. From left to right: Plaintext, encryption with 3DES cipher, logistic cipher, Bernoulli cipher, and compounded BLE cipher. The sub-figures in top row shows the space domain information and the bottom row shows the corresponding histogram. In each histogram sub-figure, *X*-axis represents gray level and *Y*-axis represents number of pixels. (a) Plaintext, (b) 3DES-C test Result, (c) LC test result, (d) BC test result, (e) BLE test result, (f) histogram of plaintext, (g) histogram of 3DES-C, (h) histogram of LC, (i) histogram of BC, and (j) histogram of BLE.

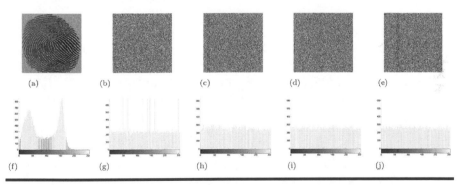

Figure 3.4 Encryption results of test C. From left to right: Plaintext, encryption with 3DES cipher, logistic cipher, Bernoulli cipher, and compounded BLE cipher. The sub-figures in top row shows the space domain information and the bottom row shows the corresponding histogram. In each histogram sub-figures, *X*-axis represents gray level and *Y*-axis represents number of pixels. (a) Plaintext, (b) 3DES-C test Result, (c) LC test Result, (d) BC test Result, (e) BLE test Result, (f) histogram of plaintext, (g) histogram of 3DES-C, (h) histogram of LC, (i) histogram of BC, and (j) histogram of BLE.

It can be seen from the test results that different ciphered images with different methods exhibit various effectiveness. From visual representations of all four schemes, encrypted results of BC and BLE show good performance when randomly scrambled in space domain and fairly uniform in histogram distribution, which is significantly different from that of the plaintext. Comparatively, a result of LC scheme present inferior but acceptable effect as well.

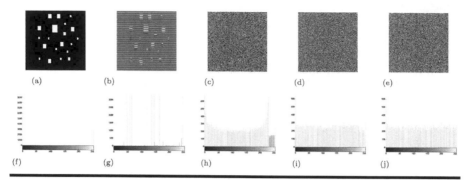

Figure 3.5 Encryption results of test D. From left to right: Plaintext, encryption with 3DES cipher, logistic cipher, Bernoulli cipher, and compounded BLE cipher. The sub-figures in top row shows the space domain information and the bottom row shows the corresponding histogram. In each histogram sub-figures, *X*-axis represents gray level and *Y*-axis represents number of pixels. (a) Plaintext, (b) 3DES-C test Result, (c) LC test Result, (d) BC test Result, (e) BLE test Result, (f) histogram of plaintext, (g) histogram of 3DES-C, (h) histogram of LC, (i) histogram of BC, and (j) histogram of BLE.

Various degrees of information leaking phenomenon take place in space domain when applying the 3DES encryption strategy directly, even with acceptable statistic performance. Visual inspections in Figures 3.2b through 3.5b show that 3DES-C ciphered data still contain some of the original information and the result in test D, shown in Figure 3.5b, can be seen as one failure example of biometric encryption with text-oriented cipher strategy.

One reason for this phenomenon lies in the fact that 3DES uses the DES block cipher that takes little account of the correlation between the pixels in the space domain. Whereas biometric data in the visual form is more space pertinent than text data, thus rendering the interdependency in space domain indispensable. Therefore, it can be safely concluded that attention should be paid not only to statistic diffusion but also to space scrambling when encrypting biometric data. Test results also reveal one fact that biometric data has its characteristic, which is different from text data, and imply that 3DES-C might have risks with encryption failure, especially for those biometric data with distinct characteristics (like test A, B, D).

3.5 Analysis

As for a good cipher scheme with performance against attack, it should be sensitive to the secret keys, and the key space should be large enough to make brute-force attacks infeasible. Next, we will perform the security analysis to show the security of the methods involved in the tests.

3.5.1 Key Space Analysis

As for key parameter, initial value $x(0)$ of LC, gain β of BC, and both $x(0)$ and β of BLE are available for secret keys candidates. Moreover, parameters α, μ, ω can also be used as the secret keys, i.e., there are five candidate parameters for BLE key space.

Key space can be measured by volume H, which is calculated by:

$$H = 10^m p^{-1} \tag{3.17}$$

where m refers to the number of the employed parameter representing the dimensions of key space and p is the precision of parameter representing the unit density of key in the key space. The more dimensions there are, and the lower density there is, the larger the scope of the key space. As an example for BLE, assuming five parameters are used as key, and the precision of each parameter is 10^{-15}, the key space size can reach up to 10^{75}, and the key space can be enlarged further with the improvement of precision. Thus it can be seen that if the precision is long enough, BLE is capable of resisting brute-force attacks.

As for 3DES, it uses three keys to perform three rounds of encryption so as to increase the total key space. The degree of key space is three dimensions less than that of BLE, which is up to 5 parameters as the key dimension. Besides, each dimension of 3DES key space means one round cryptography computation whereas BLE key space can be 5 degrees per round. This implies BLE possesses more free degree with less computation than 3DES. It can be seen that the key space of BLE is flexible and efficient.

3.5.2 Sensitivity Analysis

Several sensitivity tests are performed as well to examine the security performance of diverse schemes. As for 3DES encryption, the sensitivity test focusses on its key parameter. We make a one-bit error in key parameters, changing $k_l = 30215001$ while leaving k_r fixed, to examine its sensitivity. As for Logistic, dynamic Bernoulli and compounded mapping schemes, a subtler change is made in parameter $x(0)$ without modifying the other parameters. We let $x(0) = 0.30215000000000001$ be a key for decryption to test the sensitivity of the cryptography schemes, in which the residual is the unit error with accuracy at the level of 10^{-17}.

Figure 3.6 illustrates the sensitivity of the schemes to the parameters, where sub-figures in the first column shows the plaintext materials, the second shows 3DES sensitivity test result with one bit error key parameters, the third to fifth shows the results of proof test on sensitivity of Logistic, dynamic Bernoulli and compounded BLE strategy with error at level of 10^{-17}.

The proof test shows that a compounded BLE scheme possesses good performance on sensitivity. The compounded method provides larger key space without

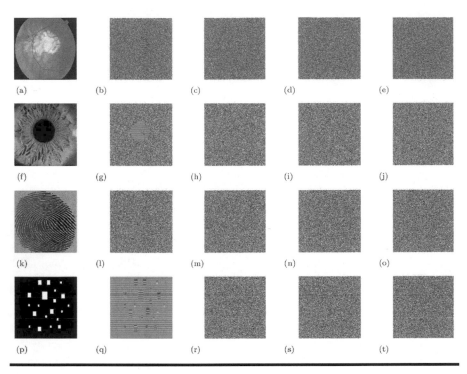

Figure 3.6 Sensitivity test results. From left to right: Plaintext, encryption with 3DES cipher, logistic cipher, Bernoulli cipher, and compounded BLE cipher. From top to bottom: Plaintext A–D sensitivity test corresponding to plaintext A–D. (a) Plaintext A, (b) 3DES-C Sensitivity Test A, (c) LC Sensitivity Test A, (d) BC Sensitivity Test A, (e) BLE Sensitivity Test A, (f) Plaintext B, (g) 3DES-C Sensitivity Test B, (h) LC Sensitivity Test B; (i) BC Sensitivity Test B; (j) BLE Sensitivity Test B, (k) Plaintext C, (l) 3DES-C Sensitivity Test C, (m) LC Sensitivity Test C, (n) BC Sensitivity Test C, (o) BLE Sensitivity Test C, (p) Plaintext D, (q) 3DES-C Sensitivity Test D, (r) LC Sensitivity Test D, (s) BC Sensitivity Test D, and (t) BLE Sensitivity Test D.

lacking sensitivity of security for detection on illegal access. Even if a subtle error happens to the parameters, the mapping will generate a completely different decryption result making the key-trial attack fail to get the correct plain-image. Thus, it can be safely concluded that compounded BLE provides a larger and sensitive key space, which is significant for protection against brute-force attack.

3.5.3 Performance Analysis

To further clarify the performance of the methods involved in this chapter, quantitative analysis has been carried out to assess the effectiveness of 3DES-C, LC, BC, and proposed BLE scheme. In this section, we focus on both performances on space correlation and statistic uniform. Correlation coefficient and volatility are introduced as two criterions to measure the effect of space scrambling and statistic distribution Using correlation analysis and uniform analysis.

3.5.3.1 Correlation Analysis

To test the correlation of the plain and encryption, pairs of pixels horizontally adjacent (HA) $(x, x+1)$, vertically adjacent (VA) $(y, y+1)$, and diagonally adjacent (DA) $(x+1, y+1)$ with their correlation coefficients $R(x, x+1), R(y, y+1), R(x+1, y+1)$ are calculated respectively. The pairs are chosen randomly. The correlation coefficients of each pair are calculated by using the following formulas:

$$R(x, y) = \frac{\text{cov}(x, y)}{\sqrt{D(x)}\sqrt{D(y)}} \tag{3.18}$$

where

$$E(x) = \frac{1}{N} \sum_{i=1}^{N} x_i \tag{3.19}$$

$$D(x) = \frac{1}{N} \sum_{i=1}^{N} (x_i - E(x))^2 \tag{3.20}$$

$$\text{cov}(x, y) = \frac{1}{N} \sum_{i=1}^{N} (x_i - E(x))(y_i - E(y)) \tag{3.21}$$

x and y are grey values of two adjacent pixels in the image. We choose correlation coefficient $R(x, y)$ as criteria to measure the disorder mixture of space domain distribution. The correlation coefficient is the inverse proportion to mixture of the image.

3.5.3.2 Uniform Analysis

In order to assess statistic uniformness of the results, we introduce the criteria volatility to calculate the stationary with the histogram; thus, assessing how fairly uniform the ciphered results are so as to know how much the result approximates the white noise, in which the real information can hide inside. The criteria volatility is defined as:

$$V(h) = \text{cov}(h) - E(h) \tag{3.22}$$

where h is the series vector of histogram value.

This criteria used for uniform analysis reveals how well spread the frequency distribution of the pixel intensity in the image is. The smaller the volatility of a ciphered image is, the more uniform the frequency distribution is and that much closer to well-distributed meaningless noise.

3.5.3.3 Analysis Results

We randomly select 10^6 pairs of two adjacent pixels from the plaintext images and corresponding ciphered results of 3DES-C, LC, BC, and BLE scheme. As to space domain distribution analysis, correlation coefficients of pairs are calculated by using the formulas (3.18) to measure the correlation between horizontally adjacent, vertically adjacent and diagonally adjacent pixels. As to statistic distribution analysis, we measuring the uniform fairness of gray scale histogram by using (3.22) to calculate volatility criteria. This criteria for uniform analysis reveals the extent of well-distribution in frequency domain.

Figures 3.7 through 3.12 show the VA (sub-figures a–e), HA (sub-figures f–j), DA (sub-figures k–o) correlation distributions analysis result aiming at test A–D, where in each HA correlation analysis sub-figure, X-axis represents gray value on location (x, y) and Y-axis represents $(x + 1, y)$; in each VA correlation analysis sub-figure, X-axis represents gray value on location (x, y) and Y-axis represents $(x, y + 1)$; and in each DA correlation analysis sub-figure,

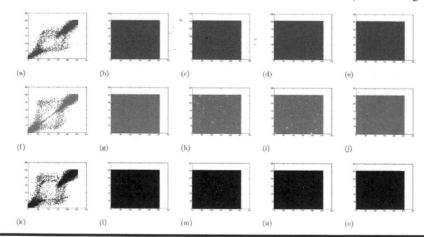

Figure 3.7 **Correlation analysis of test A in channel R. From left to right: Columns for plaintext, encryption with 3DES cipher, logistic cipher, Bernoulli cipher, and BLE cipher. From top to bottom: Rows in order for horizontal analysis (HA), vertical analysis (VA), diagonal analysis (DA). (a) Ch. R Plaintext HA, (b) Ch. R 3DES-C Result HA, (c) Ch. R LC test HA Result, (d) Ch. R BC test HA Result, (e) Ch. R BLE test HA Result, (f) Ch. R Plaintext VA, (g) Ch. R 3DES-C Result VA, (h) Ch. R LC Result VA, (i) Ch. R BC Result VA, (j) Ch. R BLE Result VA, (k) Ch. R Plaintext DA, (l) Ch. R 3DES-C Result DA, (m) Ch. R LC Result DA, (n) Ch. R BC Result HA, and (o) Ch. R BLE Result HA.**

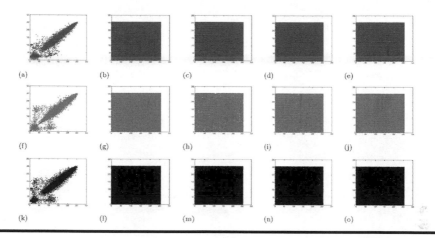

Figure 3.8 Correlation analysis of test A in channel G. From left to right: Columns for plaintext, encryption with 3DES cipher, logistic cipher, Bernoulli cipher, and BLE cipher. From top to bottom: Rows in order for horizontal analysis (HA), vertical analysis (VA), diagonal analysis (DA). (a) Ch. G Plaintext HA, (b) Ch. G 3DES-C Result HA, (c) Ch. G LC test HA Result, (d) Ch. G BC test HA Result, (e) Ch. G BLE test HA Result, (f) Ch. G Plaintext VA, (g) Ch. G 3DES-C Result VA, (h) Ch. G LC Result VA, (i) Ch. G BC Result VA, (j) Ch. G BLE Result VA, (k) Ch. G Plaintext DA, (l) Ch. G 3DES-C Result DA, (m) Ch. G LC Result DA, (n) Ch. G BC Result HA, (o) Ch. G BLE Result HA.

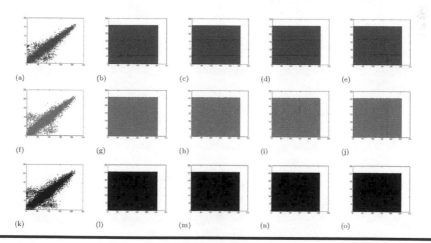

Figure 3.9 Correlation analysis of test A in channel B. From left to right: Columns for plaintext, encryption with 3DES cipher, logistic cipher, Bernoulli cipher, and BLE cipher. From top to bottom: Rows in order for horizontal analysis (HA), vertical analysis (VA), diagonal analysis (DA). (a) Ch. B Plaintext HA, (b) Ch. B 3DES-C Result HA, (c) Ch. B LC test HA Result, (d) Ch. B BC test HA Result, (e) Ch. B BLE test HA Result, (f) Ch. B Plaintext VA, (g) Ch. B 3DES-C Result VA, (h) Ch. B LC Result VA, (i) Ch. B BC Result VA, (j) Ch. B BLE Result VA, (k) Ch. B Plaintext DA, (l) Ch. B 3DES-C Result DA, (m) Ch. B LC Result DA, (n) Ch. B BC Result HA, and (o) Ch. B BLE Result HA.

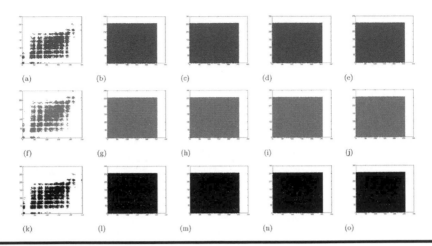

Figure 3.10 Correlation analysis of test B. From left to right: Columns for plaintext, encryption with 3DES cipher, logistic cipher, Bernoulli cipher, and BLE cipher. From top to bottom: Rows in order for horizontal analysis (HA), vertical analysis (VA), diagonal analysis (DA). (a) Plaintext HA, (b) 3DES-C Result HA, (c) LC test HA Result, (d) BC test HA Result, (e) BLE test HA Result, (f) Plaintext VA, (g) 3DES-C Result VA, (h) LC test VA Result, (i) BC test VA Result, (j) BLE test VA Result, (k) Plaintext DA, (l) 3DES-C Result DA, (m) LC test DA Result, (n) BC test DA Result, and (o) BLE test DA Result.

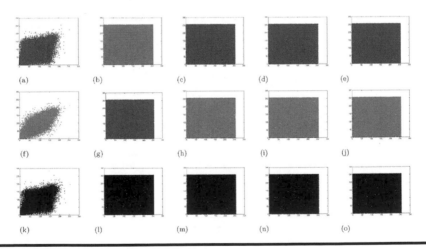

Figure 3.11 Correlation analysis of test C. From left to right: Columns for plaintext, encryption with 3DES cipher, logistic cipher, Bernoulli cipher, and BLE cipher. From top to bottom: Rows in order for horizontal analysis (HA), vertical analysis (VA), diagonal analysis (DA). (a) Plaintext HA, (b) 3DES-C Result HA, (c) LC test HA Result, (d) BC test HA Result, (e) BLE test HA Result, (f) Plaintext VA, (g) 3DES-C Result VA, (h) LC test VA Result, (i) BC test VA Result, (j) BLE test VA Result, (k) Plaintext DA, (l) 3DES-C Result DA, (m) LC test DA Result, (n) BC test DA Result, and (o) BLE test DA Result.

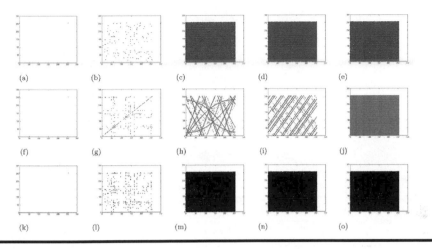

Figure 3.12 Correlation analysis of test D. From left to right: Columns for plaintext, encryption with 3DES cipher, logistic cipher, Bernoulli cipher, and BLE cipher. From top to bottom: Rows in order for horizontal analysis (HA), vertical analysis (VA), diagonal analysis (DA). (a) Plaintext HA, (b) 3DES-C Result HA, (c) LC test HA Result, (d) BC test HA Result, (e) BLE test HA Result, (f) Plaintext VA, (g) 3DES-C Result VA, (h) LC test VA Result, (i) BC test VA Result, (j) BLE test VA Result, (k) Plaintext DA, (l) 3DES-C Result DA, (m) LC test DA Result, (n) BC test DA Result, and (o) BLE test DA Result.

Table 3.1 Space Correlation and Statistic Uniform Analysis on Test Results

Test on	R(x, x+1)	R(y, y+1)	R(x+1,y+1)	Volatility
Test A R Channel				
Plain	0.9875	0.9857	0.9772	17949
3DES Cipher	0.0049	0.0036	−0.0052	488.6745
Logistic Cipher	0.0037	0.0294	−0.0061	822.2118
Bernoulli Cipher	0.0015	0.0263	0.0054	5.4588
Proposed Cipher	0.0160	−0.0086	0.0035	36.0941
Test A G Channel				
Plain	0.9850	0.9809	0.9716	22929
3DES Cipher	−0.0063	−0.0045	0.0086	62.6353
Logistic Cipher	0.0053	−0.0541	−0.0030	484.6980

(Continued)

Table 3.1 (*Continued*)   Space Correlation and Statistic Uniform Analysis on Test Results

Test on	R(x, x+1)	R(y, y+1)	R(x+1,y+1)	Volatility
Bernoulli Cipher	−0.0030	−0.0130	−0.0119	12.1098
Proposed Cipher	−0.0057	0.0028	−0.00004	1.0588
Test A *B Channel*				
Plain	0.9534	0.9458	0.9283	19867
3DES Cipher	0.0017	0.0003	−0.0067	10.3137
Logistic Cipher	−0.0080	−0.0303	−0.0042	451.3569
Bernoulli Cipher	−0.0081	−0.0066	0.0025	26.6353
Proposed Cipher	0.0061	0.00006	−0.00004	11.2941
Test B				
Plain B	0.9225	0.8876	0.8732	241050
3DES Cipher	−0.0160	0.0436	−0.0188	11557
Logistic Cipher	0.0015	−0.0264	−0.0053	526.5020
Bernoulli Cipher	0.0018	−0.0147	−0.0030	14.7922
Proposed Cipher	0.0020	−0.0024	−0.0008	4.3686
Test C				
Plain C	0.7852	0.9183	0.7930	54337
3DES Cipher	0.0066	−0.0051	−0.0005	25.3255
Logistic Cipher	−0.0013	−0.0051	0.0016	180.4392
Bernoulli Cipher	−0.0026	−0.0001	−0.0013	17.0431
Proposed Cipher	0.0055	−0.0008	−0.0006	10.7529
Test D				
Plain D	0.9432	0.9135	0.8629	1511600
3DES Cipher	−0.3189	0.9754	−0.3171	175430
Logistic Cipher	0.0022	0.1191	−0.0105	10829
Bernoulli Cipher	0.0036	0.0284	0.0027	344.3294
Proposed Cipher	0.0294	−0.0022	−0.0017	90.9412

X-axis represents gray value on location (x, y) and *Y*-axis represents $(x + 1, y + 1)$. The corresponding value of correlation coefficient and volatility, calculated by (3.18) and (3.22) respectively, are shown in Table 3.1. It can be seen that correlation distribution of plain text images changed to diffusion distribution after encryption.

In terms of quantity criteria, the magnitude of correlation coefficient corresponding to plain text for test A–D are at 10^{-1} level, and the minimum magnitude of volatility criterions are at 10^5, for each channel (RGB) respectively. The coefficients and volatility of ciphered results are much less. The minimum magnitude of criterions is down to 10^{-5} for correlation coefficient and 10^0 for volatility.

From these results taken together, the effectiveness of BC and BLE is higher than that of the other two, both in view of direct observing flaws appeared in correlation distribution and calculating analysis criterions. Comparatively, the encrypted results with the proposed BLE method exhibit better comprehensive performance than those with BC method to the extent of both diffusion in correlation distribution and uniform in a frequency distribution. Especially in test B–D that data are in gray level form, it can be seen that BLE possesses less volatility than BC even with approximate coefficient distribution.

What is remarkable is an interesting phenomenon that can be seen in Figure 3.12. When dealing with an extreme situation as test D, which possesses data of prominent contrast, 3DES-C fails to mix the correlation into well distribution (see second column in Figure 3.12b, 3.12g, 3.12l), and even though LC and BC scheme give mixture answer to HA (see Figure 3.12c and 3.12d) and DA (see Figure 3.12m and 3.12n) but appears to consist of regularity in VA (see Figure 3.12h and 3.12i). Only results of proposed BLE show a stable performance in HA, VA, and DA (see Figure 3.12e, 3.12j, 3.12o) but also reach the minimum volatility in test D, which is nearly 6.0162×10^{-5} of original data, almost the same with uniform distributed noise.

Form this phenomenon; it can be seen that proposed compounded strategy is a uniform distributed cipher. Especially when facing a data with intensive contrast information, BLE scheme has better adaptiveness and stability for encryption, whether in view of HA, VA, and DA correlation distribution or volatility criteria.

3.6 Discussion

3.6.1 Effectiveness

From the correlation analysis, the correlation distribution of the encrypted result from the proposed BLE method is more fairly uniform with diffusion and mixture than those from 3DES, Logistic chaotic, and single dynamic Bernoulli mapping, which exhibit more leaking flaws in the correlation distribution. Meanwhile, the histogram shows that the result encrypted by proposed strategy is more statically uniform in a frequency distribution, bringing better hiddenness, making it an evener statistic feature, thus more difficult to dig the subtle difference for cracking both the information of cipher system and plain text.

Moreover, according to analysis on key space and sensitivity, BLE possesses larger but sensitive key space compared to 3DES and Logistic map, thus demonstrating the high security of its cryptography. This provides a potential application in online based biometric data network encryption and information transmission.

3.6.2 Implementation

The implementation of proposed compounded strategy is compact and simple, performed by only four elemental operations including plus, multiplication, modulus, and XOR, which are basic operations for common computational hardware, making it feasible for development of compact devices with limited resource while possessing large key space with sensitivity at high accuracy level.

As for authentication, feature extraction for biometric matching is performed after decryption. Readers who are interested in the works involved with bio-feature extraction can refer to [33,34,69–71].

The possible vulnerabilities for intrusion into a biometric system are illegal access including data injection and unclaimed access to the system matching and communication channels. Considering the menaces, implementation with hardware security techniques (e.g., [72]) can stem this type of leak by enclosing the inner access as a hardware encapsulation, thus making the proposed scheme reinforced with physical defense support. With the support of a hardware security technique, enclosing the access part, including decryption and matching, inside the hardware-protected inner module provides a secure boundary access to the biometric system and the user's template upon which administrator wishes to mount against intrusive attack.

3.6.3 Anti-attack

3.6.3.1 Brute Force Attack

In order to perform an efficient brute force attack, a database with a mega quantity of real trial data is needed for searching the target. Under nonpriori condition, the probability of successfully finding the target needed by a brute force attack can be formulated as:

$$P\{A\} = (w \times h \times d \times c)^{-1} \tag{3.23}$$

where A refers to the event of successful target finding in a trial database, w, h, d, c represent width, height, depth (gray level), and channel of the visual biometric data, respectively. This is the natural infimum of probability for blind search. Due to the encryption, the target is protected with scrambling and diffusion, which is typically secret and cannot be utilized or modified without decrypting the data with the correct key. Therefore, an attacker needs to hack the key as well. According to key space analysis, the probability of successful key finding by brute force, as event B, is $P\{B\} = H^{-1}$, where H is key space volume calculated by (3.17). With the proposed BLE protection scheme, its key space possesses up to 5 dimensions, which is larger than 3DES, Logistic, and dynamic Bernoulli updating map. The security strength can be further enhanced by the improvement of parameter precision.

Due to the event A and event B are independent, the probability of successful attack by brute force is:

$$P\{AB\} = P\{A\}P\{B\} = (w \times h \times d \times c \times H)^{-1} \qquad (3.24)$$

Assuming a data with size of $w = h = 256$ in depth $d = 256$ and $c = 1$ channel, and set key with 5 dimensions at precision level of 10^{-15}, the infimum probability of a successful attack is $P_{\text{inf}}\{AB\} \approx 5.9605 \times 10^{-28}$, which can be seen as the probability of a successful attack with once trial. According to this infimum, it needs almost 1.6777×10^{27} times trial at worst.

If an attacker had obtained secret data, brute force is aiming at an attack on key crack trial, then the worst trial for key guess still needs 10^{75} times attempts. Assuming each trial for key cracking trial consumes one nanosecond (10^9 times computation/second), it would take nearly 3.1710×10^{58} years for key trial by brute force attack at worst case. Even if excluding 99% fault trials, it still needs almost billions of years for attempts on the remaining part.

3.6.3.2 Hill Climbing Attack

As an efficient heuristic way of launching attacks, hill climbing strategy is getting more attention and thus widely studied [73–75]. It requires much less resource than the ones needed for a brute force attack, thus making it a popular strategy oriented to biometric breaking. Different from brute- force, this attack generates a series of artificial data, and injecting it into the system and after analyzing the output, modifying such data.

Trying to perform the hill climbing attack on the proposed implementation scheme, an attacker needs a randomly composed database to generate the data most similar to encrypted biometric data and guess the corresponding key to the target. On account of the large key space when the precision is long enough, proposed BLE is capable of resisting brute force attacks. Weak correlated scrambling in space domain and uniform distribution in frequency domain enable BLE robustness against heuristic modification in a search. It makes the heuristic attack hard to synthesize biometric data when requiring thousands of iterations, thus rendering the crack unaffordable and prone to fail [75]. In addition, combining with water-marking based hidden strategy [76], the compounded scheme can further embed anti-counterfeiting information into the host biometric data, providing enhancement security even after decryption.

Taking the implementation of access encapsulation into consideration, enclosing the decryption and matching part of the system with hardware security techniques makes it hard for an attacker to access the scoring system and obtain the result of matching to assess output and generate the modification input for next iteration. Under this condition, the efficiency of hill-climbing attack approximates that of brute force.

3.7 Conclusion

In this chapter, an introduction of chaos-based image encryption is given. We discuss the significance in image encryption and the characteristics of image ciphering. Due to the differences between image data and text based data, the conventional ciphering strategies have limitations to image cryptography, and chaos-based encryption provides another solution with the randomness feature of chaos maps. The typical chaos maps, including tent map, logistic map, sine map, Sawtooth-Bernoulli map, and Gaussian map, are introduced. To improve the scrambling performance for encryption, an encryption scheme with Bernoulli-Logistic map (BLE) is proposed with the consideration of enhancement on mixture and hiddenness of encryption. To demonstrate the performance of the chaotic encryption, the case study of a biometric privacy protection is given with a brief review of the security issues in biometric data application. An analysis of the traditional cipher method and its problems involved with the characteristics of the biometric data application is given, thus highlighting the significance of security issues in a biometric application. In order to examine the effect of the relevant methods, 3DES and Logistic are introduced in tests, comparing them with dynamic Bernoulli updating strategy and proposed BLE scheme. Analysis results are given on experiments involved with keyspace, sensitivity, and performance with criteria correlation coefficients and volatility. Discussing on effectiveness, implementation, and anti-attack, it can be seen that proposed compounded scheme is simple to implement and robust to attack. On account of the performance of both space domain scrambling and statistic diffusion, it proves that the chaotic compound strategy can enhance the encryption performance. It also possesses potential to be competent for the data cryptography tasks in multidimensional systems.

Bibliography

1. B. Schneier. The idea encryption algorithm-the international data encryption algorithm (idea) may be one of the most secure block algorithms available to the public today. Bruce examines its 128-bit-long key. *Dr Dobb's Journal-Software Tools for the Professional Programmer*, 18(13):50–57, 1993.
2. A. Nagar. Biometric template security. PhD thesis, Michigan State University, East Lansing, MI, 2012.

3. A. Kanso and N. Smaoui. Logistic chaotic maps for binary numbers generations. *Chaos, Solitons & Fractals*, 40(5):2557–2568, 2009.
4. C. Rathgeb and A. Uhl. Context-based biometric key generation for iris. *IET Computer Vision*, 5(6):389–397, 2011.
5. M. Pudzs, R. Fuksis, R. Ruskuls, T. Eglitis, A. Kadikis, and M. Greitans. FPGA based palmprint and palm vein biometric system. In *Biometrics Special Interest Group (BIOSIG), 2013 International Conference of the*, pp. 1–4. IEEE, 2013.
6. M. Liu and T. Buma. Biometric mapping of fingertip eccrine glands with optical coherence tomography. *Photonics Technology Letters, IEEE*, 22(22):1677–1679, 2010.
7. L. Kocarev and G. Jakimoski. Logistic map as a block encryption algorithm. *Physics Letters A*, 289(4):199–206, 2001.
8. U. Uludag, S. Pankanti, S. Prabhakar, and A. K. Jain. Biometric cryptosystems: Issues and challenges. *Proceedings of the IEEE*, 92(6):948–960, 2004.
9. A. K. Jain, N. Karthik, and A. Nagar. Biometric template security. *EURASIP Journal on Advances in Signal Processing*, 2008, 2008.
10. C. Rathgeb and A. Uhl. A survey on biometric cryptosystems and cancelable biometrics. *EURASIP Journal on Information Security*, 2011(1):1–25, 2011.
11. S. Behnia, A. Akhshani, H. Mahmodi, and A. Akhavan. A novel algorithm for image encryption based on mixture of chaotic maps. *Chaos, Solitons & Fractals*, 35(2):408–419, 2008.
12. C.-L. Chen, C.-C. Lee, and C.-Y. Hsu. Mobile device integration of a fingerprint biometric remote authentication scheme. *International Journal of Communication Systems*, 25(5):585–597, 2012.
13. G. Chen, Y. Mao, and C. K. Chui. A symmetric image encryption scheme based on 3d chaotic cat maps. *Chaos, Solitons & Fractals*, 21(3):749–761, 2004.
14. R. Kolerman, J. Nissan, and H. Tal. Combined osteotome-induced ridge expansion and guided bone regeneration simultaneous with implant placement: A biometric study. *Clinical Implant Dentistry and Related Research*, 16(5):691–704, 2013.
15. M. Martinez-Diaz, J. Fierrez-Aguilar, F. Alonso-Fernandez, J. Ortega-Garcia, and J. A. Siguenza. Hill-climbing and brute-force attacks on biometric systems: A case study in match-on-card fingerprint verification. In *Carnahan Conferences Security Technology, Proceedings 2006 40th Annual IEEE International*, pp. 151–159. IEEE, 2006.
16. M. Al Ameen, J. Liu, and K. Kwak. Security and privacy issues in wireless sensor networks for healthcare applications. *Journal of Medical Systems*, 36(1):93–101, 2012.
17. S. O. Southern, K. N. Montgomery, C. W. Taylor, B. H. Weigl, B. V. K. Vijaya Kumar, S. Prabhakar, and A. A. Ross. Sensing technologies for global health, military medicine, disaster response, and environmental monitoring; and biometric technology for human identification VIII. In *Proceedings of SPIE*, Vol. 8029, pp. 802901–1, 2011.
18. T. Ignatenko and F. M. J. Willems. Biometric systems: Privacy and secrecy aspects. *Information Forensics and Security, IEEE Transactions on*, 4(4):956–973, 2009.
19. A. Nagar and S. Chaudhury. Biometrics based asymmetric cryptosystem design using modified fuzzy vault scheme. In *Pattern Recognition, 2006. ICPR 2006. 18th International Conference on*, Vol. 4, pp. 537–540. IEEE, 2006.
20. F. Sun, S. Liu, Z. Li, and Z. Lü. A novel image encryption scheme based on spatial chaos map. *Chaos, Solitons & Fractals*, 38(3):631–640, 2008.
21. V. Pasham and S. Trimberger. High-speed des and triple des encryptor/decryptor. *Xilinx Application Notes*, 2001.

22. A. Arakala, S. A. Davis, and K. J. Horadam. Retina features based on vessel graph substructures. In *Biometrics (IJCB), 2011 International Joint Conference on*, pp. 1–6. IEEE, 2011.

23. M. A. Murillo-Escobar, C. Cruz-Hernández, L. Cardoza-Avendaño, and R. Méndez-Ramrez. A novel pseudorandom number generator based on pseudorandomly enhanced logistic map. *Nonlinear Dynamics*, 87(1):407–425, 2017.

24. R. L. Rivest, A. Shamir, and L. Adleman. A method for obtaining digital signatures and public-key cryptosystems. *Communications of the ACM*, 21(2):120–126, 1978.

25. V. Patidar, N. K. Pareek, and K. K. Sud. A new substitution–diffusion based image cipher using chaotic standard and logistic maps. *Communications in Nonlinear Science and Numerical Simulation*, 14(7):3056–3075, 2009.

26. M. K. Khan, L. Xie, and J. Zhang. Chaos and NDFT-based spread spectrum concealing of fingerprint-biometric data into audio signals. *Digital Signal Processing*, 20(1):179–190, 2010.

27. L. Kocarev. Chaos-based cryptography: A brief overview. *Circuits and Systems Magazine, IEEE*, 1(3):6–21, 2001.

28. K. Bae, S. Noh, and J. Kim. Iris feature extraction using independent component analysis. In *Audio-and Video-Based Biometric Person Authentication*, pp. 838–844. Springer, Berlin, Germany, 2003.

29. M. S. Baptista. Cryptography with chaos. *Physics Letters A*, 240(1):50–54, 1998.

30. A. Jain, L. Hong, and S. Pankanti. Biometric identification. *Communications of the ACM*, 43(2):90–98, 2000.

31. M. Barua, M. Shamsul Alam, X. Liang, and X. Shen. Secure and quality of service assurance scheduling scheme for wban with application to ehealth. In *Wireless Communications and Networking Conference (WCNC), 2011 IEEE*, pp. 1102–1106. 2011.

32. A. K. Jain, A. Ross, and S. Prabhakar. An introduction to biometric recognition. *Circuits and Systems for Video Technology, IEEE Transactions on*, 14(1):4–20, 2004.

33. M. E. Smid and D. K. Branstad. Data encryption standard: Past and future. *Proceedings of the IEEE*, 76(5):550–559, 1988.

34. A. K. Awasthi and K. Srivastava. A biometric authentication scheme for telecare medicine information systems with nonce. *Journal of Medical Systems*, 37(5):1–4, 2013.

35. J. Fierrez, J. Ortega-Garcia, A. Esposito, A. Drygajlo, and M. Faundez-Zanuy. Biometric ID Management and Multimodal Communication. In *Joint COST 2101 and 2102 International Conference, BioID_MultiComm 2009, Madrid, Spain, September 16-18, 2009, Proceedings*, Vol. 5707. Springer, Berlin, Germany, 2009.

36. A. H. Kolk, K. N. Montgomery, S. Prabhakar, A. A. Ross, S. O. Southern, C. W. Taylor, and B. V. K. Vijaya Kumar. Sensing technologies for global health, military medicine, disaster response, and environmental monitoring II; and biometric technology for human identification IX. In *Society of Photo-Optical Instrumentation Engineers (SPIE) Conference Series*, Vol. 8371, 2012.

37. S. Krishna and C. Owen. Security chip architecture and implementations for cryptography acceleration, November 29, 2005. US Patent 6,971,006.

38. G. Ye. Image scrambling encryption algorithm of pixel bit based on chaos map. *Pattern Recognition Letters*, 31(5):347–354, 2010.

39. M. S. Tavazoei and M. Haeri. Comparison of different one-dimensional maps as chaotic search pattern in chaos optimization algorithms. *Applied Mathematics and Computation*, 187(2):1076–1085, 2007.

40. A. Vélez. Insecure identities: The approval of a biometric id card in mexico. *Surveillance & Society*, 10(1):42–50, 2012.
41. S. Saleem, S. Ullah, and K. Sup Kwak. Towards security issues and solutions in wireless body area networks. In *Networked Computing (INC), 2010 6th International Conference on*, pp. 1–4. IEEE, 2010.
42. H. Kummert. The PPP triple-DES encryption protocol (3DESE), Internet Engineering Task Force (IETF), RFC 2420 (Proposed Standard), pp. 1–8, 1998.
43. M. M. Yeung and S. Pankanti. Verification watermarks on fingerprint recognition and retrieval. *Journal of Electronic Imaging*, 9(4):468–476, 2000.
44. D. Coppersmith, D. B. Johnson, and S. M. Matyas. A proposed mode for triple-des encryption. *IBM Journal of Research and Development*, 40(2):253–262, 1996.
45. C. Soutar. Biometric system security. White paper, Bioscrypt, http://www.bioscrypt. com, 2002.
46. D. F. Drake and D. B. Williams. Linear, random representations of chaos. *IEEE Transactions on Signal Processing*, 55(4):1379–1389, 2007.
47. G. Qi, G. Chen, S. Du, Z. Chen, and Z. Yuan. Analysis of a new chaotic system. *Physica A: Statistical Mechanics and Its Applications*, 352(2):295–308, 2005.
48. Y. Wang, K.-W. Wong, X. Liao, and G. Chen. A new chaos-based fast image encryption algorithm. *Applied Soft Computing*, 11(1):514–522, 2011.
49. PUB FIPS. 46-3: Data encryption standard (des). *National Institute of Standards and Technology*, 25(10), 1999.
50. D. T. Kaplan and L. Glass. Coarse-grained embeddings of time series: Random walks, gaussian random processes, and deterministic chaos. *Physica D: Nonlinear Phenomena*, 64(4):431–454, 1993.
51. U. Uludag and A. K. Jain. Attacks on biometric systems: A case study in fingerprints. In *Electronic Imaging 2004*, pp. 622–633. International Society for Optics and Photonics, 2004.
52. E. Guillen, L. Alfonso, K. Martinez, and M. Mejia. Vulnerabilities and performance analysis over fingerprint biometric authentication network. In *Proceedings of the World Congress on Engineering and Computer Science*, Vol. 2, 2012.
53. G. Jakimoski and L. Kocarev. Chaos and cryptography: Block encryption ciphers based on chaotic maps. *Circuits and Systems I: Fundamental Theory and Applications, IEEE Transactions on*, 48(2):163–169, 2001.
54. M. A. Murillo-Escobar, C. Cruz-Hernández, F. Abundiz-Pérez, and R. M. López-Gutiérrez. A robust embedded biometric authentication system based on fingerprint and chaotic encryption. *Expert Systems with Applications*, 42(21):8198–8211, 2015.
55. M. Jessa. Designing security for number sequences generated by means of the sawtooth chaotic map. *IEEE Transactions on Circuits and Systems I: Regular Papers*, 53(5):1140–1150, 2006.
56. M. A. Murillo-Escobar, C. Cruz-Hernández, F. Abundiz-Pérez, R. M. López-Gutiérrez, and O. R. Acosta Del Campo. A RGB image encryption algorithm based on total plain image characteristics and chaos. *Signal Processing*, 109:119–131, 2015.
57. L. M. Pecora and T. L. Carroll. Synchronization in chaotic systems. *Physical Review Letters*, 64(8):821, 1990.
58. H. N. Agiza and M. T. Yassen. Synchronization of Rossler and Chen chaotic dynamical systems using active control. *Physics Letters A*, 278(4):191–197, 2001.
59. S. Saleem, S. Ullah, and K. Sup Kwak. A study of ieee 802.15. 4 security framework for wireless body area networks. *Sensors*, 11(2):1383–1395, 2011.

60. R. K. Sande, K. Matre, T. Kiserud, and G. Eide. Op25. 01: The effect of reduced level of ultrasound power on obstetric biometric measurements. *Ultrasound in Obstetrics & Gynecology*, 40(S1):129–129, 2012.

61. H. Li and O. Chutatape. Automated feature extraction in color retinal images by a model based approach. *Biomedical Engineering, IEEE Transactions on*, 51(2):246–254, 2004.

62. M. Agarwal and L. Agarwal. Accessing the bank account without card and password in atm using biometric technology. *Researcher*, 4(3):33–37, 2012.

63. F. Abundiz-Pérez, C. Cruz-Hernández, M. A. Murillo-Escobar, R. M. López-Gutiérrez, and A. Arellano-Delgado. A fingerprint image encryption scheme based on hyperchaotic rössler map. *Mathematical Problems in Engineering*, 2016, 2016.

64. T. Yoshida, H. Mori, and H. Shigematsu. Analytic study of chaos of the tent map: Band structures, power spectra, and critical behaviors. *Journal of Statistical Physics*, 31(2):279–308, 1983.

65. M. Li, W. Lou, and K. Ren. Data security and privacy in wireless body area networks. *Wireless Communications, IEEE*, 17(1):51–58, 2010.

66. A. Belazi, A. A. Abd El-Latif, and S. Belghith. A novel image encryption scheme based on substitution-permutation network and chaos. *Signal Processing*, 128:155–170, 2016.

67. H. Hao, D. K. Kumar, B. Aliahmad, C. Azemin, M. Zulfaezal, and R. Kawasaki. Using color histogram as the trait of retina biometric. In *Biosignals and Biorobotics Conference (BRC), 2013 ISSNIP*, pp. 1–4. IEEE, 2013.

68. X. Yu. Controlling Lorenz chaos. *International Journal of Systems Science*, 27(4): 355–359, 1996.

69. J. H. Park. Adaptive synchronization of hyperchaotic chen system with uncertain parameters. *Chaos, Solitons & Fractals*, 26(3):959–964, 2005.

70. N. K. Pareek, V. Patidar, and K. K. Sud. Image encryption using chaotic logistic map. *Image and Vision Computing*, 24(9):926–934, 2006.

71. A. Bossen, R. Lehmann, and C. Meier. Internal fingerprint identification with optical coherence tomography. *Photonics Technology Letters, IEEE*, 22(7):507–509, 2010.

72. A. Belazi, A. A. Abd El-Latif, A.-V. Diaconu, R. Rhouma, and S. Belghith. Chaos-based partial image encryption scheme based on linear fractional and lifting wavelet transforms. *Optics and Lasers in Engineering*, 88:37–50, 2017.

73. Y. Zhou, L. Bao, and C. L. Philip Chen. A new 1d chaotic system for image encryption. *Signal Processing*, 97:172–182, 2014.

74. T. Habutsu, Y. Nishio, I. Sasase, and S. Mori. A secret key cryptosystem by iterating a chaotic map. In *Advances in Cryptology* UROCRYPT91, pp. 127–140. Springer, Berlin, Germany, 1991.

75. G. Jakimoski and L. Kocarev. Analysis of some recently proposed chaos-based encryption algorithms. *Physics Letters A*, 291(6):381–384, 2001.

76. A. Hariton, M. Creu, L. Nia, and M. Slcianu. Database security on remote patient monitoring system. *International Journal of Telemedicine and Applications*, 9, 2011.

Chapter 4

Fundamental Cryptographic Characteristics of Boolean Functions: A Review

Majid Khan and Syeda Iram Batool Naqvi

Contents

DOI: 10.1201/9780429435461-5

These days, society is immovably encompassed by the circle of the information time, which is arranged by researcher resources and is utilizable inside data being considered outstandingly valuable. Instructive data exists and is utilized as a part of different structures as money related, official (reports), military, and political. The wellbeing of this data in the midst of exchange and sparing, and in routine practice is vital in light of the fact that its bargain may impact the revelation of promoting, money related misfortune, military best insider facts, and even the death toll. Cryptology is a noteworthy way utilized as a part of the review of data security. Three most imperative kinds of security are displayed by cryptology using suitable and sound organized cryptosystems.

These frameworks are known as confidentiality, integrity, and authentication. Confidentiality is offered by ensuring that mystery information is kept individual from informal revelation. Integrity is offered by ensuring the mystery information has not been changed, even circumstantially, amid creation or capacity. Authentication is the system of evaluation that the dispatcher of the information is appropriately perceived and honest to goodness.

The encryption plans are frequently grouped by a few viewpoints, for example, the logic of their key conveyance and the measurement of their input stream. Symmetric encryption designs have a typical mystery key designated to senders and collectors, while asymmetric cryptosystems utilize unique keys for enciphering and deciphering of given information. Symmetric cryptosystems have two principle branches, block or stream ciphers, where the information to the cryptosystem gets the state of either squares or unbroken piece streams, separately. Another sort of encryption conspire is a hash function, which presses data in a process frame for trustworthiness or verification.

Cryptosystems are key imprints for an assailant wanting to trade off the mystery information being monitored by a security calculation. In parade with the three kinds of security necessities referred to over, the typical inspirations of an assailant are to uncover mystery data, to unlawfully and mischievously modify data, and to dishonestly embrace a personality. Besides, an assailant potentially will attempt to take out proof, or even include counterfeit confirmation that an outcome or exchange has occurred.

Trading off a cryptosystem which is mindful to secure the mystery data can either specifically allow these occasions to happen, or eventually debilitate an alternate element of the plan to enable these moves to later make input. Prevailing available cryptanalytic assaults contrary to cryptosystems have adjusted to being unbeaten under these conditions.

The general quality of an encryption calculation is dependent on the quality of the individual parts, for example, the authentication scheme, the secret key management scheme, the data sparing plan, the cryptosystem, the arrangements and techniques, and so on. In like manner, the entire quality of a security framework is dependent on the power of its individual instrument. A blemish in any of the individual procedures may prompt a shattering breakdown in the whole security framework.

Substitution box (S-boxes) and Boolean functions are indispensable components of cryptosystems. These two imperative parts are connected by work amount. That is, an S-box is in general included a few particular yield Boolean functions, however in the event that it is mapped to only a single bit, is indistinguishable to a Boolean function.

Boolean functions are utilized in different parts of block and stream ciphers. Besides, Boolean mappings have additionally displayed some huge properties, which are fundamental to restricting the classic sort of attacks, so these functions are a critical segment in all stream and block ciphers [1].

The S-box is the key segment utilized as a part of numerous block ciphers. It offers a method for substituting different pieces of bits for an absolutely disparate arrangement of yield bits. One thing which is vital is the utilization of secure S-boxes (those which hold astounding encryption properties), keeping in mind the end goal is to make befuddled input and output bits of the S-box. One of the fundamental elements of the substitution box, when utilized as a part of iterative round capacity, is to upgrade the exertion required to investigate any statistical structure in safe information.

S-boxes are competent to give the wellbeing of an encryption algorithm by having incredible encryption properties. Building secure S-boxes to utilize them in various cryptosystems for expanding their security is an ebb and flow issue. This is mostly so on the grounds that the cryptanalytic framework ends up being more refined and, with the changes in computer innovation, that contributes similarly in supporting and against secure correspondence.

The quality of S-boxes has a noteworthy bearing on secure correspondence. Be that as it may, bigger functions typically require extra computational time and exertion, keeping in mind the end goal is to investigate their defects. So to pick up a decent computational multifaceted nature upgrade when attempting to discover vast capacities with astoundingly brilliant measures of appealing encryption properties incorporates an extra piece of many-sided qualities to the examination issue.

4.1 Overview of Boolean Functions Theory

Boolean functions are the main building blocks of most cipher systems. Various aspects of their cryptological characteristics are examined and investigated by many researchers from different fields. The point of this chapter is to display a comprehensive and compact review of the fundamental parts of Boolean functions and S-boxes identified with cryptography. We begin with a few documentations that will be utilized all through the chapter. The initial segment of this section is on Boolean functions. In the first place, we portray distinctive methods for speaking to Boolean functions with regards to cryptography (binary values, truth table, algebraic degree, algebraic immunity and algebraic normal form), together with the essential apparatuses (Walsh and autocorrelation). Identified with the Walsh spectrum, the autocorrelation spectrum, and the structure of truth table and Algebraic normal form, we exhibit the definitions and properties that portray cryptographic Boolean mappings and transformations. Some fundamental developments of Boolean transformations are likewise clarified. Also we will explain in detail about single and multi-valued functions and transformation utilized in the construction of nonlinear component for block and steam ciphers. The common cryptographic properties are also explained along with examples. Moreover, we have explained how a nonlinear component is based on multi-valued Boolean functions (Vectorial Boolean functions) [2].

4.1.1 Boolean Transformation Concepts

We first demonstrate the diverse descriptions and procedures to examine Boolean functions with regards to cryptography. At that point properties and definitions are displayed, together with a smaller strategy to infer the relations and limits on the parameters characterizing the cryptographic properties.

4.1.2 Some Well-Known Characteristics of Boolean Functions

The chief aim of this part is to add some fundamental definitions on Boolean functions. Let $\mathbb{Z}_2^n$ be the vector space of dimension n over the two-element Galois field $\mathbb{Z}_2$. $\mathbb{Z}_2^n$ consist of 2^n vectors written in a binary sequence of length n. The vector space is equipped with the scalar product $< .,. >: \mathbb{Z}_2^n \times \mathbb{Z}_2^n \rightarrow \mathbb{Z}_2$:

$$< \alpha, \beta >= \oplus_{j=1}^{m} \alpha_j . \beta_j, \tag{4.1}$$

where the multiplication $\otimes$ and addition $\oplus$ are over $\mathbb{Z}_2$.

Definition 4.1: *[2] A Boolean function of n variables is a function $g : \mathbb{Z}_2^n \rightarrow \mathbb{Z}_2^n$ (or simply a function on $\mathbb{Z}_2^n$). The $(0,1)$-sequence is defined by $(g(\alpha_0), g(\alpha_1), ..., g(\alpha_{2^n-1}))$, also called the truth table of g, where $\alpha_0 = (0,0,...,0), \alpha_1 = (0,0,...,1),...,\alpha_{2^n-1} = (1,1,...,1)$, ordered by lexicographical order.*

Definition 4.2: *[2] A vector Boolean function is a function that maps a Boolean vector to another Boolean vector:*

$$\zeta : \mathbb{Z}_2^n \rightarrow \mathbb{Z}_2^m. \tag{4.2}$$

This vector Boolean function has n input bits and m output bits. A vector Boolean function can be specified by its definition table: an array containing the output value for each of the 2^n possible input values.

Definition 4.3: *[2] A vector Boolean transformation is a vector Boolean function with the identical number of input bits as output bits which can be expressed as follows:*

$$\zeta : \mathbb{Z}_2^n \to \mathbb{Z}_2^n. \tag{4.3}$$

Definition 4.4: *To each Boolean function $g : \mathbb{Z}_2^n \to \mathbb{Z}_2$, we associate its sign function, or character form, denoted by $\hat{g} : \mathbb{Z}_2^n \to \mathbb{R}^* \subseteq \mathbb{C}^*$, and defined by the following expression (Table 4.1):*

$$\hat{g}(x) = (-1)^{g(x)}. \tag{4.4}$$

Definition 4.5: *The Hamming weight of a Boolean function $g : \mathbb{Z}_2^n \to \mathbb{Z}_2$, is defined as the number of 1's in the binary truth table, or number of -1's in the sign function of g.*

$$\mathbf{wt}(g) = \sum_x g(x) = \frac{1}{2}\left(2^n - \sum_x \hat{g}(x)\right)$$

Definition 4.6: *For two Boolean functions $g, h : \mathbb{Z}_2^n \to \mathbb{Z}_2$, we define the Hamming distance as the number of arguments where g and h differ, that is*

$$d(g,h) = \#\{x \in \mathbb{Z}_2^n \mid g(x) \neq h(x)\} = \mathbf{wt}(g \oplus h). \tag{4.5}$$

Definition 4.7: *The support of a Boolean function g is defined as*

$$\mathbf{supp}(g) = \{x \in \mathbb{Z}_2^n \mid g(x) = 1\}. \tag{4.6}$$

Definition 4.8: *A $(0,1)$-sequence $((1,-1)$-sequence) is called balanced if it contains an equal number of zeros and one (ones and minus ones). A function is balanced if its sequence is balanced that is $\mathbf{wt}(g) = 2^{n-1}$.*

Table 4.1 Truth Table Example for $n = 2$

x_1	x_2	$g(x)$	$\hat{g}(x)$
0	0	0	1
0	1	1	−1
1	0	1	−1
1	1	0	1

Definition 4.9: *The imbalance* **Imb**(g) *of a Boolean function* g *is the number of inputs that maps to* 0 *minus the number of inputs that maps to* 1 *divided by two. The imbalance can have any integer value and ranges from* -2^n *to* 2^n. *We have*

$$\mathbf{Imb}(g) = 1/2(\#\{a \mid g(a) = 0\} - \#\{a \mid g(a) = 1\}) = \left| wt(g) - 2^{n-1} \right| = 2^{n-1} \left| C(f, \mathbf{0}) \right|. \quad (4.7)$$

where $\mathbf{0}$ indicates the constant zero Boolean function.

Definition 4.10: *The autocorrelation function* $\hat{r}_{\hat{g}}(a)$ *with a shift* $a \in \mathbb{Z}_2^n$ *is defined as*

$$\hat{r}_{\hat{g}}(a) = \sum_{x \in \mathbb{Z}_2^n} \hat{g}(x)\hat{g}(x \oplus a). \quad (4.8)$$

Definition 4.11: *Let* g *be a function defined on* $\mathbb{Z}_2^n$. *Let* $a \in \mathbb{Z}_2^n$ *is called a linear structure of* $a \in \mathbb{Z}_2^n$ *if*

$$\hat{r}_{\hat{g}}(a) = 2^n, \quad (4.9)$$

i.e., if $\hat{g}(x)\hat{g}(x \oplus a)$ is constant.

Definition 4.12: *The correlation value between two Boolean functions* g *and* h *is defined by*

$$\begin{aligned} C(g, h) &= 2\Pr(g(x) = h(x)) - 1, \\ &= 2\left[\frac{2^n - d(g, h)}{2^n} \right] - 1, \\ &= \frac{2^{n+1} - 2d(g, h)}{2^n} - 1, \\ &= 1 - \frac{d(g, h)}{2^{n-1}}. \end{aligned} \quad (4.10)$$

Correlation is a rational number in the range $[-1, 1]$. From the definition, we see that the upper bound of 1 is achieved when the Hamming distance between two functions is zero. Similarly, the lower bound -1 is achieved when the Hamming distance between two functions is equal to 2^n. Correlation is an important tool in the analysis of pairs of functions, particularly in relation to the concept of imbalance in a Boolean function.

Example 4.13: *Let f and g be two Boolean functions defined as*

$$f(x, y) = x \oplus y,$$

$$g(x, y) = xy \oplus 1.$$

The truth table of two Boolean function is

x	y	f	g	f ⊕ g
1	1	0	0	0
0	1	1	1	0
1	0	1	1	0
0	0	0	1	1

Hamming weight, support and imbalance of Boolean functions *f* and *g* are given below:

$$wt(f) = d(f, 0),$$
$$wt(f) = 2.$$
$$\sup p(f) = \{x \in GF(2)^n \mid f(x) = 1\},$$
$$\sup p(f) = 2.$$
$$imb(f) = 1/2(\{x \mid f(x) = 0\} - \{x \mid f(x) = 1\}),$$
$$imb(f) = 0.$$

whereas the Hamming distance and correlation between *f* and *g* can be calculated as follows:

$$d(f, g) = \{x \in GF(2)^n \mid g(x) \neq f(x)\},$$
$$d(f, g) = 1.$$
$$d(f, g) = wt(f \oplus g) = 1.$$
$$C(f, g) = 1 - \frac{d(f, g)}{2^{n-1}},$$
$$C(f, g) = 0.5.$$

Definition 4.14: *The number of variables in highest order monomial with zero coefficients is called the algebraic degree.*

Definition 4.15: *The Algebraic Normal Form (ANF) is an n-variables Boolean function which can be written as follows:*

$$g(x) = b_0 \oplus b_0 x_0 \oplus \ldots \oplus b_{01} x_0 x_1 \oplus b_{012\ldots n-1} x_0 x_1 x_2 \ldots x_{n-1}, \tag{4.11}$$

where the coefficients $b \in \mathbb{Z}_2^n$ form the elements of the truth table of the ANF of $g(x)$. Note that each product term in the ANF is calculated by the multiplication of each of the components of that term.

Definition 4.16: *A Boolean function is said to be homogeneous if its algebraic normal form only contains terms of the same degree.*

Definition 4.17: *An n variable Boolean function $g(x)$, which contains all n variables in its ANF is called a nondegenerate function. Conversely, if $g(x)$ does not contain every variable in its ANF representation then the function is degenerate.*

Definition 4.18: *The algebraic degree of a Boolean function $g(x)$, denoted by $deg(g)$, is defined to be the number of variables in the largest product term of the function's ANF having a non-zero coefficient. The algebraic degree of a Boolean function is a good indicator of the function's algebraic complexity. The higher the degree of a function, the greater is its algebraic complexity.*

4.2 Nonlinearity of Boolean Function

Nonlinearity is one of the most important cryptographic properties. As before, we denote with the set of all affine functions and the Hamming distance is the number of arguments where the Boolean functions g and h differ. In addition, Pieprzyk [3] introduced the notion of nonlinearity as follows:

Definition 4.19: *The nonlinearity of a Boolean function g is denoted by N_g and is defined as follows:*

$$N_g = d(g, A_n) = \min_{\alpha \in A_n} d(g, \alpha). \tag{4.12}$$

Example 4.20: *Let $n = 2$, $g(x) = x_1 x_2$ and $a_i \in \mathbb{Z}_2$. Then any affine function can be expressed as*

$$\Lambda_i(x) = a_0 \oplus a_1 x_1 \oplus a_2 x_2.$$

By taking all the combinations of $a_i's$, we can generate all affine functions for $n = 2$ and they are presented in the table. To find the nonlinearity of g, we calculate the distance between g and all affine functions that are presented in Table 4.2. The minimum Hamming distance is nonlinearity of g.

Table 4.2 Distance between *g* and All Affine Functions

g	Λ_1	Λ_2	Λ_3	Λ_4	Λ_5	Λ_6	Λ_7	Λ_8
				Affine Functions				
0	0	0	0	0	1	1	1	1
0	0	1	0	1	1	0	1	0
0	0	0	1	1	1	1	0	0
1	0	1	1	0	1	0	0	1
$d(g, A_i)$	1	1	1	3	3	3	3	1

$$d_{\min} = 1 \Rightarrow N_g = 1.$$

4.3 The Walsh Transform

In this section, we introduce one of the most important tools in cryptography. Namely, the Walsh transforms which is the characteristic 2 case of the discrete Fourier transform. We define the Walsh transform of a Boolean function as follows [2]:

Definition 4.21: *[2] The Walsh transform of a function g on $\mathbb{Z}_2^n$ is a map $\Omega : \mathbb{Z}_2^n \to \mathbb{R}$ defined by*

$$\Omega(g)(u) = \sum_{x \in \mathbb{Z}_2^n} g(x)(-1)^{<u,x>}, \tag{4.13}$$

where $< u, x >$ is the canonical scalar product.

Lemma 4.22: *[2, Lemma 3.2] If $u \in \mathbb{Z}_2^n$, we have*

$$\sum_{x \in \mathbb{Z}_2^n} (-1)^{<u,x>} = \begin{cases} 2^n, & \text{if } u = 0 \\ 0, & \text{else.} \end{cases} \tag{4.14}$$

Theorem 4.23: *[2, Theorem 3.3] The Walsh transform $\Omega : \mathbb{Z}_2^n \to \mathbb{R}$ is bijective and the inversion is given by:*

$$\Omega^{-1} = \Omega / 2^n. \tag{4.15}$$

Definition 4.24: *The Sylvester-Hadamard matrix (or Walsh-Hadamard matrix) of order 2^n, denoted by H_n is generated by the recursive relation*

$$H_n = \begin{bmatrix} H_{n-1} & H_{n-1} \\ H_{n-1} & -H_{n-1} \end{bmatrix} = H_1 \otimes H_{n-1}, \tag{4.16}$$

for $n = 1, 2, \dots$ and $H_0 = (1)$.

Lemma 4.25: *[4] If the Boolean function can be obtained from h by an affine transformation of the input that is $h = g(Av \oplus b)$, with A an invertible matrix and $b \in \mathbb{Z}_2^n$, then the Walsh transform of g and h are related by*

$$\Omega(h)(u) = \pm \Omega(g)(uA^{-1}). \tag{4.17}$$

Corollary 4.26: *[2, Corollary 3.10] In particular $\Omega(\hat{g})(u)$ is always even and we have*

$$-2^n \le \Omega(\hat{g})(u) \le 2^n. \tag{4.18}$$

Definition 4.27: *Let g and h be any Boolean functions on $\mathbb{Z}_2^n$. The Convolution of g and h is defined by*

$$(g * h)(x) = \sum_{y \in \mathbb{Z}_2^n} g(y)h(x \oplus y). \tag{4.19}$$

Corollary 4.28: *(Parseval's equation) For any Boolean function g in n variables, the following equations holds*

$$\sum_{u \in \mathbb{Z}_2^n} \left(\Omega(\hat{g}) \right)(u)^2 = 2^{2n}. \tag{4.20}$$

Lemma 4.29

$$\sum_{u \in \mathbb{Z}_2^n} \Omega(\hat{g})(u)\Omega(\hat{g})(u \oplus v) = \begin{cases} 2^{2n} & \text{if } v = 0, \\ 0 & \text{if } v \ne 0. \end{cases}$$

Theorem 4.30: *A Boolean function on $\mathbb{Z}_2^n$ satisfies*

$$\Omega(\hat{r})(t) = \Omega(\hat{g})^2(t),\tag{4.21}$$

for all $t \in \mathbb{Z}_2^n$.

Definition 4.31 *The spectral radius of a Boolean function $g : \mathbb{Z}_2^n \to \mathbb{Z}_2$ is defined by*

$$R_g = \max\{|\Omega(\hat{g})(u)| : u \in \mathbb{Z}_2^n\}\tag{4.22}$$

This definition provides a measure for linearity. Obviously, the linearity is upper bounded by $2^n \geq R_g$ by. The upper bound is only attainable if g is affine.

Theorem 4.32: *For a Boolean function $g : \mathbb{Z}_2^n \to \mathbb{Z}_2$ the spectral radius is*

$$R_g \geq 2^{\frac{n}{2}},\tag{4.23}$$

and the equality is holds if and only if $\Omega(\hat{g})^2 = 2^n$ is constant.

Theorem 4.33: *The nonlinearity N_g of a Boolean function g is determined by the Walsh transform of $\Omega(\hat{g})(u) = H_{2^n}\hat{g}$, that is,*

$$N_g = 2^{n-1} - \frac{1}{2}\max_{u \in \mathbb{Z}_2^n}|\Omega(\hat{g})(u)|.\tag{4.24}$$

Thus, it is possible to achieve *high nonlinearity if the* maximal Walsh coefficient is of small value.

Example 4.34: *Let us calculate a nonlinearity N_g of Boolean function g: $\mathbb{Z}_2^2 \to \mathbb{Z}_2$ by using above definition (Table 4.3):*

where

$$H_4 = \begin{bmatrix} 1 & 1 & 1 & 1 \\ 1 & -1 & 1 & -1 \\ 1 & 1 & -1 & -1 \\ 1 & -1 & -1 & 1 \end{bmatrix},$$

$$N_g = 2^{2-1} - \frac{1}{2}\max|Walsh\ spectrum| = 2 - \frac{1}{2}(2) = 1.$$

Table 4.3 Polarity and Walsh Spectrum of a Boolean Function *g*

x_1	x_2	g	$\hat{g} = (-1)^{g(x)}$	Walsh Spectrum $= \Omega(\hat{g})(u) = H_4 \cdot \hat{g}$
0	0	0	1	2
0	1	0	1	2
1	0	0	1	2
1	1	1	−1	−2

4.4 Correlation Immune Boolean Functions

Correlation immune functions were introduced by Siegenthaler [5] in order to protect some shift register based on stream ciphers against correlation attacks.

Definition 4.35: *[5] A Boolean function g in n variables is said to be correlation immune of order k, $1 \le k \le n$, if any fixed subset of k variables the probability that, given the value of g(x), the k variables have any fixed set of values, is always 2^{-k}, no matter what the choice of the fixed set of k values is. In other words, g is correlation immune of order k if its values are statistically independent of any subset of input variables.*

We can formulate the definition of correlation immunity to an equivalent information theory condition. If the chosen subset of variables is $(x(i_1), x(i_2), ..., x(i_k))$ then the above definition of correlation immunity of order k is equivalent to the information theory condition that the information obtained about the values of $(x(i_1), x(i_2), ..., x(i_k))$ given is zero. Now we collect some useful equivalent conditions to correlation immunity of order 1 given in [4,6].

Lemma 4.36: *[4] A function g in n variables is correlation immune of order k, $1 \le k \le n$, if and only if all of the Walsh transforms*

$$\Omega(\hat{g})(u) = \sum_{x \in \mathbb{Z}_2^n} (-1)^{g(x) \oplus <u,x>}, \quad 0 \le \mathbf{wt}(u) \le k, \tag{4.25}$$

are equal to zero.

Lemma 4.37: *[?] For Boolean function g the total square correlation of g with the set of all linear functions is equal to one, that is*

$$\sum_{u \in \mathbb{Z}_2^n} c(g; \alpha_u)^2 = 1. \tag{4.26}$$

Definition 4.38: *A Boolean function in variables which is balanced and correlation immune of order* k *is said to be* $k-$ *resilient function.*

Theorem 4.39: *[7] Any Boolean function in n variables is k-resilient if and only if* $\Omega(\hat{g})(u) = 0$, *for all* $u \in \mathbb{Z}_2^n$ *such that* $\mathbf{wt}(u) \leq k$. *Equivalently, g is k-resilient if and only if* $\Omega\left(g\right)(u)$ *for all* $u \in \mathbb{Z}_2^n$ *such that* $0 < \mathbf{wt}(u) \leq k$.

Theorem 4.40: *[2, Theorem 4.7] If g is a Boolean function in n variables, which is correlation immune of order k, then the degree of g is at most n–k. If g is also balanced and k < n–1, then the degree is at most* $n-k-1$.

4.5 Avalanche and Propagation Criterion

The avalanche effect states an appropriate property of cryptography. The avalanche consequence is obvious, when an input is altered to some extent the output changes meaningfully (e.g., half the output bits flip). The idea of avalanche was introduced by Horst Feistel which is based on the concept of Shannon's diffusion. The Strict Avalanche Criterion (SAC for short) was introduced by Webster and Tavares [8]. They write [8] "If a function is to satisfy the strict avalanche criterion, then each of its output bits should change with a probability of one half whenever a single input bit x is complemented to x'." The SAC is a useful property for Boolean functions in cryptographic applications. This means that if a Boolean function is satisfying the SAC, a small change in the input leads to a large change in the output (an avalanche effect). This property is essential in a cryptographic context due to the fact that we cannot infer its input from its output. In addition to SAC we study the Propagation Criterion (PC for short) which was introduced by Preneel et al. [9]. The mathematical expression for avalanche and SAC is defined as follows:

Definition 4.41: *[2] A function* $g : \mathbb{Z}_2^n \rightarrow \mathbb{Z}_2^m$ *has the avalanche effect, if an average of* $1/2$ *of the output bits change whenever a single input bit is complemented i.e.*

$$\frac{1}{2^n} \sum_{u \in \mathbb{Z}_2^n} wt(g(x^i) - g(x)) = \frac{m}{2}, \quad \text{for all } i = 1, 2, ..., n. \qquad (4.27)$$

Definition 4.42: *A function* $g : \mathbb{Z}_2^n \rightarrow \mathbb{Z}_2^m$ *of n input bits into m output bits is said to be complete, if each output bit depends on each input bits, i.e. change whenever a single input bit is complemented, i.e.*

$$\forall \, i = 1, 2, ..., n, \, j = 1, 2, ..., m, \, \exists \, x \in \mathbb{Z}_2^n \text{ with } (g(x^i))_j \neq (g(x))_j. \qquad (4.28)$$

If a cryptographic transformation is complete, then each ciphertext bit must depend on all of the output bits. Thus, if it were possible to find the simplest Boolean expression for each ciphertext bit in terms of the plaintext bits, each of those expressions would have to contain all of the plaintext bits if the function was complete. Alternatively, if there is at least one pair of n-bit plaintext vectors X and X_i that differ only in bit i, $g(X)$ and $g(X_i)$ differ at least in bit j for all $\{(i, j) \mid 1 \le i, j \le n\}$ then the function g must be complete.

Definition 4.43: *A function $g : \mathbb{Z}_2^n \to \mathbb{Z}_2^m$ satisfies the strict avalanche criterion, if each output bit changes with a probability $1/2$ whenever a single input bit is complemented, i.e.*

$$\forall \ i = 1, 2, ..., n, \ j = 1, 2, ..., m, \ Prob(g(x^i))_j \ne Prob(g(x))_j = \frac{1}{2}. \quad (4.29)$$

In the process of building these S-boxes, it was discovered that if an S-box is complete, or even perfect, its inverse function may not be complete. This could become important if these inverse functions are used in the decryption process, for it would be desirable for any changes in the ciphertext to affect all bits in the plaintext in a random fashion, especially if there is not much redundancy in the original plaintext. Complete cryptographic transformations with inverses which are complete are described as being two-way complete, and if the inverse is not complete the transformation is said to be only one-way complete.

Definition 4.44: *The dependence matrix of a function $g : \mathbb{Z}_2^n \to \mathbb{Z}_2^m$ is an $n \times m$ matrix A whose $(i, j)^{th}$ element a_{ij} denotes the number of inputs for which complementing the ith input bit results in a change of the jth output bit,*

$$a_{ij} = \#\{x \in \mathbb{Z}_2^n \mid \mathbf{wt}((g(x^i))_j - (g(x))_j\}, \ \text{for } i = 1, 2, ..., n, \text{ and } j = 1, 2, ..., m. \quad (4.30)$$

Definition 4.45: *The distance matrix of a function $g : \mathbb{Z}_2^n \to \mathbb{Z}_2^m$ is an $n \times (m+1)$ matrix B whose $(i, j)^{th}$ element b_{ij} denotes the number of inputs for which complementing i^{th} input bit results in a change of the jth output bit, i.e.*

$$b_{ij} = \#\{x \in \mathbb{Z}_2^n \mid \}(g(x^i) - g(x)) = j\}, \ \text{for } i = 1, 2, ..., n, \text{ and } j = 1, 2, ..., m. \quad (4.31)$$

Definition 4.46: *For $g : \mathbb{Z}_2^n \to \mathbb{Z}_2$ and $a \in \mathbb{Z}_2^n$, $a \neq 0$, we defined the function by*

$$g_a(x) = g(x) \oplus g(x \oplus a), \qquad (4.32)$$

where g_a is called the directional derivative of g in the direction of a.

Now we are able to express the SAC in connection with the directional derivative.

Lemma 4.47: *[2, Lemma 5.3] A Boolean function $g : \mathbb{Z}_2^n \to \mathbb{Z}_2$ satisfies SAC if and only if the function $g(x) \oplus g(x \oplus a)$ is balanced for every $a \in \mathbb{Z}_2^n$ with $a \neq 0$, Hamming weight 1.*

Definition 4.48: *The autocorrelation (AC) function of a Boolean function in n variables is defined as*

$$r_g(a) = \sum_{i=0}^{2^n-1} g(x_i) g(x_i \oplus a), \qquad (4.33)$$

for all every $a \in \mathbb{Z}_2^n$.

Example 4.49: *Let us study the Boolean function $g(x) = x_3 \oplus x_2 x_1$; then the truth table for g is shown in Table 4.4. The AC coefficient for $a = 001$ are given as follows:*

$$
\begin{aligned}
r_g(000) &= \sum_{i=0}^{2^3-1} g(x_i) \otimes g(x_i \oplus 000), \\
&= g(000)g(000 \oplus 000) + g(001)g(001 \oplus 000) + \dots + g(111)g(111 \oplus 000), \\
&= 0.0 + 0.0 + \dots + 1.1, \\
&= 5.
\end{aligned}
$$

Lemma 4.50: *[2, Lemma 5.5] A Boolean function g in n variables is SAC if and only if the autocorrelation function $r_g(a)$ is equal to 2^{n-1} for all $a \in \mathbb{Z}_2^n$ with the Hamming weight 1.*

Example 4.51: *Now take an example for SAC with $a = 01$, (Table 4.5),*

The given function g doesn't satisfy the SAC, since $g(x).g(x \oplus a)$ is not balance.

Table 4.4   Auto Correlation of a Boolean Function g

X	g	a	$r_g(a)$
$x_3x_2x_1$			
000	0	000	5
001	0	001	4
010	0	010	4
011	1	011	4
100	1	100	2
101	1	101	2
110	1	110	2
111	1	111	2

Table 4.5   Truth Table Example for $n = 2$ with $x = x_1x_2$

x_1	x_2	$g(x)$	$x \oplus a$	$gx \oplus a$	$g(x).g(x \oplus a)$
0	0	0	01	1	0
0	1	1	00	0	0
1	0	1	11	0	0
1	1	0	10	1	0

4.6 The Strict Avalanche Criterion of Higher Order

In this section we study a generalization of the SAC.

Definition 4.52: *A Boolean function g in n variables is said to satisfy the SAC of order k (SAC(k)) if fixing any k in n bits in the input x results in a Boolean function in the remaining n − k variables which satisfy the SAC, where $0 \le k \le n - 2$.*

Lemma 4.53: *Suppose g is a Boolean function in $n > 2$ variables which satisfies the SAC of order $k, 1 \le k \le n - 2$. Then g also satisfies the SAC of order j for any j = 0, 1.*

4.7 The Propagation Criterion

This section generalizes the notion of the strict avalanche criterion to the propagation criterion.

Definition 4.54: *A Boolean function g in n variables is said to satisfy the propagation criterion of degree k (PC(k) for short) if changing any i $(1 \leq i \leq k)$ of the n bits in the x input results in the output of the function being changed for exactly half of the 2^n vectors x.*

Lemma 4.55: *A Boolean function in n variables satisfies PC(1) if and only if all of the given values*

$$r_g(a) = \sum_{x \in \mathbb{Z}_2^n} g(x) \otimes g(x \oplus a), \quad 1 \leq \mathbf{wt}(a) \leq k,$$

of the autocorrelation function are equal to 2^{n-1}.

Lemma 4.56: *A Boolean function g in n variables satisfies PC(k) if and only if all directional derivative $g_a(x) = g(x) \otimes g(x \oplus a), 1 \leq \mathbf{wt}(a) \leq k$, are balanced functions.*

Lemma 4.57: *Let g and h be function on whose (1,-1)-sequences are ξ_g and ξ_h. Then the distance between g and h can be calculated by*

$$d(g,h) = 2^{n-1} - \frac{1}{2}\langle \xi_g, \xi_h \rangle. \tag{4.34}$$

Theorem 4.58: *For any function on $\mathbb{Z}_2^n$ the nonlinearity N_g of g satisfies* $N_g \leq 2^{n-1} - 2^{\frac{n}{2}-1}$.

In case of bent Boolean function the upper bound of nonlinearity is achievable [10].

4.8 S-Box Theory

In this section we now turn our discussions to the area of S-boxes (S-boxes). The basic definitions of S-box theory are provided to support the research work performed in this chapter. Also in this section, a review of relevant cryptographic properties as applied to S-boxes, is provided.

4.8.1 S-Box Definitions and Types

A natural progression from the theory of single output Boolean functions is the extension of that theory to multiple output Boolean functions, collectively referred to as an S-box. The relationship between the input and output bits in terms of dimension and uniqueness gives rise to various types of S-boxes. We list below several necessary S-box definitions, together with a brief description of some S-box types of interest to this research.

An $n \times m$ substitution box (S-box) is a mapping from n input bits to m output bits, $S : \mathbb{Z}_2^n \to \mathbb{Z}_2^m$. The output vector $S(x) = (s_1, s_2, ..., s_m)$ can be decomposed into m component functions $S_i : \mathbb{Z}_2^n \to \mathbb{Z}_2$, $i = 1, 2, ..., m$. There are 2^n inputs and 2^m possible outputs for an $n \times m$ S-box. Often considered as a look-up table, an $n \times m$ S-box, S, is normally symbolized as a matrix of size $2^n \times m$, indexed as $S_{[i]}$ ($0 \le i \le 2^n - 1$) each an m−bit entry. There are, generally speaking, three types of S-boxes: Straight, compressed and expansion S-boxes.

A straight $n \times m$ S-box with $n = m$ (takes in a given number of bits and puts out the same number of bits) may either contain distinct entries where each input is mapped to a distinct output or repeat S-box entries where multiple inputs may be mapped to the same output and all possible outputs are not represented in the S-box. An $n \times m$ S-box which is both injective and surjective is known as a bijective S-box. That is, each input maps to a distinct output entry and all possible outputs are present in the S-box. Bijective S-boxes may only exist when $n = m$ and are also called reversible since there must also exist a mapping from each distinct output entry to its corresponding input. This is the design approached used with the Rijndael cipher.

A compression $n \times m$ S-box $n > m$ with puts out fewer bits than it takes in. A good example of this is the S-box used in data incryption standard (DES). In the case of DES, each S-box takes in 6 bits but only outputs 4 bits. A expansion $n \times m$ S-box with $n < m$ puts out more bits than it takes in. A regular $n \times m$ S-box is one which has each of its possible 2^m output appearing an equal number of times in the S-box. Thus, each of the possible output entries appears a total number of 2^{n-m} times in the S-box. All single output Boolean functions comprising a regular S-box are balanced, as are all linear combinations of these functions. Regular $n \times m$ S-boxes are balanced S-boxes and may only exist when $n \ge m$. An $n \times m$ S-box ($n \ge 2m$ and n is even) is said to be bent if every linear combination of its component Boolean functions is a bent function.

There are issues associated with both compression and expansion S-boxes. The first issue is reversibility, or decryption. Since either type of S-box alters the total number of bits, reversing the process is difficult. The second issue is a loss of information, particularly with compression S-boxes. In the case of DES, prior to the S-box, certain bits are replicated. Thus what is lost in the compression step are duplicate bits and no information is lost. In general working with either compression or expansion S-boxes will introduce significant complexities in your S-box design. Therefore straight S-boxes are far more common.

4.8.2 Cryptographic Properties of S-Boxes

While many of the Boolean function properties discussed in previous sections have conceptual equivalences when applied to S-boxes, there are fundamental differences in the manner by which these properties are derived. As an S-box is comprised of a number of component Boolean functions, it is important to observe that when considering the cryptographic properties of an S-box, it is not sufficient to consider the cryptographic properties of the component Boolean functions individually. Rather, it is also necessary to consider the cryptographic properties of all the linear combinations of the component functions. This is illustrated in the following selection of relevant S-box properties.

An $n \times m$ S-box which is balanced is one whose component Boolean functions and their linear combinations are all balanced. Because of this balance, there does not exist an exploitable bias in that the equally likely number of output bits over all output vector combinations ensures that an attacker is unable to trivially approximate the functions or the output.

The well-known concept of confusion due to Shannon [11,12] is described as a method for ensuring that in a cipher system a complex relationship exists between the ciphertext and the key material. This notion has been extrapolated to mean that a significant reliance on some form of substitution is required as a source of this confusion. The confusion in a cipher system is achieved through the use of nonlinear components. As expected, S-boxes tend to provide the main source of nonlinearity to cryptographic cipher systems. We now define the measure of nonlinearity for an $n \times m$ S-box.

Definition 4.59: *The nonlinearity of an $n \times m$ S-box S, denoted by $N_{S_{n,m}}$ is defined as the minimum nonlinearity of each of its component output Boolean functions and their linear combinations. Let $S = (s_1, s_2, ..., s_m)$ where s_i ($i = 1, ..., m$) are n-variable Boolean functions. Let h_i be the set of linear combinations of s_i ($i = 1, ..., m$) (which includes the functions s_i). Then the nonlinearity of S can be expressed as follows:*

$$N_{S_{n,m}} = \min_h \{N_{S_{n,m}}(h_j)\}(j = 1, ..., 2^m - 1). \tag{4.35}$$

Clearly, as n and m increase, the task of merely computing the nonlinearity value of an $n \times m$ S-box quickly becomes computationally infeasible. The importance of this property for the security of cipher systems becomes evident in the next section when we discuss some of the effective cryptanalytic attacks which exist.

The algebraic degree of an S-box (and similarly a Boolean function) is desired to be as high as possible in order to resist a cryptanalytic attack known as low order approximation [13]. The measure of S-box degree is defined below:

Definition 4.60: *Let* $S = (s_1, s_2, ..., s_m)$ *be an* $n \times m$ *S-box where* s_i $(i = 1, ..., m)$ *are* *n-variable Boolean functions. Let* h_j *be the set of linear combinations of* $s_i (i = 1, ..., m)$ *(which includes the functions* h_i*). Then the algebraic degree of* S*, denoted by* $\deg(S_{n,m})$*, is defined as*

$$\deg(S_{n,m}) = \min_h \{\deg(h_j)\} (j = 1, ..., 2^m - 1). \tag{4.36}$$

A companion concept to confusion, called diffusion, was also proposed by Shannon [12]. Therein it is described as the method by which the data redundancy in a cipher is spread throughout the entire (or large portion of the) data in an effort to reduce the probability of discovering part or all of its statistical structure. Diffusion has long been lined to the avalanche characteristics of a cipher system and, in particular, is achieved by using cipher components which exhibit good avalanche characteristics. In order to measure these characteristics for $n \times m$ S-boxes we require the following definitions:

Definition 4.61: *Let* $S = (s_1, s_2, ..., s_m)$ *be an* $n \times m$ *S-box where* s_i $(i = 1, ..., m)$ *are* *n-variable Boolean functions. Let* h_j *be the set of linear combinations of* s_i $(i = 1, ..., m)$ *(which includes the functions* s_i*), each with autocorrelation function,* $\hat{r}_{h_j}(a)$*. Then the maximum absolute autocorrelation value of* S *is defined as:*

$$\left| AC_{S_{n,m}} \right|_{\max} = \max_h \left| \hat{r}_{h_j}(a) \right|, \tag{4.37}$$

with $a \in \{1, ..., 2^n - 1\}$ and $(j = 1, ..., 2^m - 1)$.

Definition 4.62: *Let* $S = (s_1, s_2, ..., s_m)$ *be an* $n \times m$ *S-box where* s_i $(i = 1, ..., m)$ *and* *n-variable Boolean functions. Let* h_j *be the set of linear combinations of* s_i $(i = 1, ..., m)$ *(which includes the function* s_i*). Then* S *is said to satisfy strict avalanche criterion (SAC) if every* h_j $(j = 1, ..., 2^m - 1)$ *satisfies SAC.*

Definition 4.63: *Let* $S = (s_1, s_2, ..., s_m)$ *be an* $n \times m$ *S-box where* s_i $(i = 1, ..., m)$ *are* *n-variable Boolean functions. Let* h_j *be the set of linear combinations of* s_i $(i = 1, ..., m)$ *(which includes the functions* s_i*). Then* S *is said to satisfy propagation criteria of order* k*,* $PC(k)$*, if every* h_j $(j = 1, ..., 2^m - 1)$ *satisfies* $PC(k)$*.*

The next two definitions outline the way in which, respectively, the correlation immunity and resilience of an S-box are determined.

Definition 4.64: *Let $S = (s_1, s_2, ..., s_m)$ be an $n \times m$ S-box where s_i $(i = 1, ..., m)$ are n-variable Boolean functions. Let h_j be the set of linear combinations of s_i $(i = 1, ..., m)$ (which includes the functions s_i). Then S is a $CI(t)$ S-box if all h_j $(j = 1, ..., 2^m - 1)$ are $CI(t)$ Boolean functions.*

Definition 4.65: *Let $S = (s_1, s_2, ..., s_m)$ be an $n \times m$ S-box where s_i $(i = 1, ..., m)$ are n-variable Boolean functions. Let h_j be the set of linear combinations of s_i $(i = 1, ..., m)$ (which includes the functions s_i). Then S is a t-resilient S-box if all h_j $(j = 1, ..., 2^m - 1)$ are t-resilient Boolean functions.*

4.9 Bit Independent Criterion

Webster and Tavares in 1985, introduced another criterion, called bit independent criterion (BIC) for S-boxes [8]. This property states that the output bits j and k should alter independently, when any single input bit i is reversed, for all i, j and $k \in (1, 2, ..., n)$. This criterion appears to strengthen the effectiveness of the confusion function. To illustrate the bit independent concept, one requires the correlation coefficient between j^{th} and k^{th} components of the output difference string. The bit independence corresponding to the effect of the ith input bit change on the jth and k^{th} bits of is B^{e_i}:

$$BIC(b_j, b_k) = \max_{1 \leq i \leq n} |\operatorname{corr}(b_j^{e_i}, b_k^{e_i})|. \tag{4.38}$$

The BIC parameter for the S-box function $h : \mathbb{Z}_2^n \to \mathbb{Z}_2^n$, is then defined as follows:

$$BIC(h) = \max_{\substack{1 \leq j, k \leq n \\ j \neq k}} BIC(b_j, b_k), \tag{4.39}$$

which shows how close is satisfying the BIC [8],

4.10 Linear and Differential Cryptanalysis of S-Boxes

Linear cryptanalysis was introduced at Eurocrypt conference in 1993 by M. Matsui as a theoretical attack on the DES [14] and later successfully used in the practical cryptanalysis of DES [13]. Linear cryptanalysis works on the principle of finding "high probability occurrences of linear expressions involving plaintext bits, ciphertext bits (actually we shall use bits from the 2nd last round output), and subkey bits" [15]. It is a known plaintext attack in which a large number of plaintext-ciphertext pairs are used to determine the value of key bits [15].

Differential cryptanalysis was first presented at Crypto conference in 1990 by E. Biham and A. Shamir as an attack on DES [16]. Heys [15] describes the main principle: "Differential cryptanalysis exploits the high probability of certain occurrences of plaintext differences and differences into the last round of the cipher." It is a chosen plaintext attack, that means plaintext can be selected and output subsequently calculated in order to derive the key [17]. In this section XOR distribution, linear and differential probability are defined [18,19].

Definition 4.66: *For an vector Boolean function (S-boxes)* $g : \mathbb{Z}_2^n \to \mathbb{Z}_2^n$, *the XOR table has a size of* $2^n \times 2^n$, *with its rows and columns indexed by* $0,1,2,...,2^n - 1$. *Position* (i, j) *in the XOR table contains the number of input vectors:*

$$|\{P \in \mathbb{Z}_2^n : g(P) \oplus g(P \oplus \tau_i) = \tau_j\}|, \tag{4.40}$$

such that $0 \le i, j \le 2^n - 1, \tau_i$ and τ_j are n-bit binary representations of indices i and j. P is the input vector, g corresponds to the cryptographic function of the S-box, and the pair (i, j) is called an input/output XOR pair. Differential cryptanalysis exploits such XOR pairs with large XOR table entries. A cipher can be secured against differential cryptanalysis by selecting S-boxes with low XOR table entries, ideally 0 or 2 (the only exception is the entry $(0,0)$ which has the value of 2^n). The sum of the XOR table entries on each row is equal to 2^n, which is the total number of input vector pairs $(P, P \oplus \tau_i)$ [15].

Definition 4.67: *For a given vector Boolean function* $g : \mathbb{Z}_2^n \to \mathbb{Z}_2^m$ *it is defined the linear approximation table which elements are*

$$LAT_g(a,b) = \#\{x \in \mathbb{Z}_2^n \mid a.x = b.g(x)\} - 2^{n-1}, \tag{4.41}$$

where $a \in \mathbb{Z}_2^n, b \in \mathbb{Z}_2^m \backslash \{0\}$.

Lemma 4.68: *For a given vector Boolean function* $g : \mathbb{Z}_2^n \to \mathbb{Z}_2^m$ *it is defined the linear approximation table which elements are*

$$LAT_g(a,b) = 2^{n-1} - d(a.x,b.g), \tag{4.42}$$

where $a \in \mathbb{Z}_2^n, b \in \mathbb{Z}_2^m \setminus \{0\}$.

Proof. By the definition of LAT, we have

$$
\begin{aligned}
LAT_g(a,b) &= \#\{x \in \mathbb{Z}_2^n \mid a.x = b.g(x)\} - 2^{n-1}, \\
&= 2^n - \#\{x \in \mathbb{Z}_2^n \mid a.x \neq b.g(x)\} - 2^{n-1}, \qquad (4.43) \\
&= 2^{n-1} - d(a.x, b.g).
\end{aligned}
$$

Lemma 4.69: *For a given vector Boolean function $g : \mathbb{Z}_2^n \to \mathbb{Z}_2^m$ one has*

$$
N_g = 2^{n-1} - \max_{a,b} |LAT_g(a,b)|, \qquad (4.44)
$$

where $a \in \mathbb{Z}_2^n, b \in \mathbb{Z}_2^m \setminus \{0\}$.

Definition 4.70: *[20] For any given Δ_x, Δ_y, Γ_x, $\Gamma_y \in \mathbb{Z}_2^n$, the linear and differential approximation probabilities for each vector Boolean function (S-box) are defined as:*

$$
LP^{S_i}(\Gamma_y \to \Gamma_x) = \left(2 \times \frac{\#\{x \in \mathbb{Z}_2^n \mid x\Gamma_x = S_i(x)\Gamma_y\}}{2^n} - 1 \right), \qquad (4.45)
$$

$$
DP^{S_i}(\Delta_x \to \Delta_y) = \left(\frac{\#\{x \in \mathbb{Z}_2^n \mid S_i(x) \oplus S_i(x \oplus \Delta_x) = \Delta_y\}}{2^n} \right), \qquad (4.46)
$$

where $x\Gamma_x$, denotes the parity *(0 or 1)* of the bitwise product of x and Γ_x.

Definition 4.71: *[20] The maximum linear and differential approximation probabilities of vector Boolean function (S-boxes) are defined as:*

$$
p = \max_i \max_{\Gamma_x, \Gamma_y} LP^{S_i}(\Gamma_y \to \Gamma_x), \qquad (4.47)
$$

$$
q = \max_i \max_{\Delta_x, \Delta_y} DP^{S_i}(\Delta_x \to \Delta_y). \qquad (4.48)
$$

4.11 Conclusion

In this chapter, we have defined the relevant supporting theory of both Boolean functions and S-boxes. In particular, we have provided numerous long established definitions and theorems for various aspects of the theory. The necessary cryptographic properties which are used to analyze the strength of single and multiple output functions have also been defined and discussed, as have the inter-relations between pairs of selected properties.

Acknowledgment

The authors of this chapter is highly thankful to Vice Chancellor Brig. (Rtd) Engr. Imran Rahman, Institute of Space Technology, Islamabad, Pakistan, for providing a good atmosphere for research and development.

References

1. M. Khan, T. Shah, H. Mahmood, M. A. Gondal, I. Hussain, A novel technique for constructions of S-Boxes based on chaotic Lorenz systems, *Nonlinear Dyn.*, 70 (2012) 2303–2311.
2. J. Christian, M. Hortmann, and G. Leander, Boolean functions, PhD thesis, University of Bremen, 2012.
3. J. P. Pieprzyk, Non-linearity of exponent permutations, *Lect. Notes. Comput. Sci.*, 434 (1990) 80–92.
4. T. W. Cusick, P. Stanica, *Cryptographic Boolean Functions and Applications*, Elsevier/Academic Press, Amsterdam, the Netherlands, 2009.
5. T. Siegenthaler, Correlation-immunity of nonlinear combining functions for cryptographic applications, *IEEE Trans. Inf. Theory.*, 30(5) (1984) 776–780.
6. S. Chee, S. Lee, D. Lee, S. H. Sung, On the correlation immune functions and their nonlinearity, *Lect. Notes. Comput. Sci.*, 1163 (1996) 232–243.
7. C. Carlet, Boolean functions for cryptography and error correcting codes, chapter of the monography, In *Boolean Models and Methods in Mathematics, Computer Science, and Engineering*, Cambridge University Press, New York, 2010, pp. 257–397.
8. A. F. Webster, S. Tavares, On the design of S-boxes, *Lect. Notes. Comput. Sci.*, 85 (1986) 523–534.
9. B. Preneel, V. Leekwijk, V. Linden, R. Govaerts, J. Vandewalle, Propagation characteristics of boolean functions, *Lect. Notes. Comput. Sci.*, 473 (1991) 161–173.
10. O. S. Rothaus, On bent functions, *J. Combin. Theory Ser. A.*, 20 (1976) 300–305.
11. C. E. Shannon, A mathematical theory of communication, *Bell Labs. Tech. J.*, 27 (1948) 379–423.
12. C. E. Shannon, Communication theory of secrecy systems, *Bell Labs. Tech. J.*, 28 (1949) 656–715.
13. M. Matsui, Linear cryptoanalysis method for DES cipher, *Lect. Notes. Comput. Sci.*, 765 (1994) 386–397.

14. M. Matsui, The first experimental cryptanalysis of the Data Encryption Standard, *Lect. Notes. Comput. Sci.*, 839 (1994) 1–11.
15. H. M. Heys, A tutorial on linear and differential cryptanalysis, technical report CORR 2001–17, Centre for Applied Cryptographic Research, Department of Combinatorics and Optimization, University of Waterloo, Canada, March 2001.
16. E. Biham, A. Shamir, Differential cryptanalysis of DES like cryptosystems, *Lect. Notes. Comput. Sci.*, 537 (1991) 2–21.
17. L. L. Bartosov, Linear and differential cryptanalysis of reduced-round AES, *Tatra Mt. Math. Publ.*, 50(1) (2011) 51–61.
18. M. Khan, T. Shah, A construction of novel chaos base nonlinear component of block cipher, *Nonlinear Dyn.*, 76 (2014) 377–382.
19. M. Khan, T. Shah, H. Mahmood, M. A. Gondal, An efficient method for the construction of block cipher with multi-chaotic systems, *Nonlinear Dyn.*, 71 (2013) 493–504.
20. M. Khan, T. Shah, Construction and applications of chaotic S-boxes in image encryption, *Neural Comput. Appl.*, 27 (2016) 677–685.

Chapter 5

Phase Retrieval in Optical Cryptography

Naveen Kumar Nishchal and Areeba Fatima

Contents

5.1 Introduction

Optical cryptography essentially refers to encoding any information using optical means. The encryption and decryption procedure or either of them is accomplished using the principles of optics. Electromagnetic fields offer various degrees of freedom such as the amplitude, phase, wavelength and state of polarization which can be used as parameters to encrypt information. Moreover, use of optical field for encryption enables faster, parallel processing which is an advantage

DOI: 10.1201/9780429435461-6

over non-optical methods. The first optical encryption technique to be reported was the double random phase encoding (DRPE) [1]. The DRPE involved a simple 4f optical set-up to encrypt an image. The principle being simple and efficient, DRPE saw many variants that aimed at strengthening the security by different means such as using different optical transform instead of the conventional Fourier transform [2,3]. The fractional Fourier transform (FRT) was proposed as a better option to encode plaintexts as it offers a larger key space in the form of fractional order of the system. On similar lines other transforms such as the Fresnel, gyrator, cosine and wavelet transforms were introduced as a platform for encryption [4–11]. Though the DRPE technique offered various advantages, the encrypted information in DRPE was complex and it required a holographic set-up to record the phase of the ciphertext. To overcome this obstacle, other methods such as the diffractive imaging based encryption [12–16] or polarization based encoding [17–19] were introduced, which used intensity information as ciphertexts.

Some of the techniques that generated intensity ciphertexts involved retrieving the lost phase of the plaintexts as they carry the essential information. Apart from this, cryptanalysis also involved retrieving the phase to breach the system [20]. The known plaintext attacks and the specific attacks on different optical cryptosystems were made using phase retrieval techniques [21–25]. Hence, the role of phase retrieval methods finds relevance in the study of optical security schemes.

Phase retrieval refers to the recovery of a function when the amplitude of its Fourier transform is known [26]. Phase recovery problems often arise in microscopy, astronomy, crystallography, and optical imaging to name a few [26]. This is because the phase of the electromagnetic field changes far too rapidly to get recorded, resulting in devices that record only the intensity. One of the ways in which the phase can be recorded is to use holographic set up [3]. But in many cases, this might be cumbersome, adding complexity to the main optical set up. Hence, algorithmic methods were introduced to retrieve the phase from the known Fourier magnitude and other information available about the object or Fourier domain function.

This chapter discusses some of the applications of algorithmic phase retrieval in the field of optical security. Introduction to major iterative phase retrieval techniques has been reviewed in the beginning to provide groundwork for its optical security applications.

5.2 Phase Retrieval Algorithms

In a general problem of phase retrieval, the magnitude of an object's Fourier transform is known, and it is aimed to obtain the object computationally. Alternatively, the intensity information in the object and the Fourier domain is known and it remains to retrieve the phase information from these intensity measurements.

There are various iterative phase retrievals algorithms with different rates of convergence and with different requirement of constraints. In this section, we discuss three major phase retrieval algorithms that have been widely used in optical cryptography.

5.2.1 Gerchberg-Saxton Algorithm (GSA)

The Gerchberg-Saxton algorithm (GSA) is the classical method for retrieving the phase when the amplitude information in the object domain $f(x, y)$ and the Fourier domain (i.e., $G(u, v)$) is given [27]. The algorithm is initiated by assigning a random distribution $\phi_0(u,v)$ lying between the interval $[-\pi, \pi]$ as the phase distribution in the Fourier domain. The subscript 0 in $\phi_0(u,v)$ represents the initial iteration where the iteration number $k = 0$. The basic steps involved in the kth iteration step of the process can be summarized as:

The random phase $\phi_k(u,v)$ is multiplied with the amplitude of the Fourier domain, $G(u,v)$:

$$A_k = G(u,v) \times \phi_k(u,v) \tag{5.1}$$

A_k is then inverse Fourier transformed (IFT) to reach the object domain:

$$F_k' = \mathrm{IFT}(A_k) \tag{5.2}$$

Substitute the amplitude of F_k' with the known amplitude of the object domain i.e. $f(x, y)$. This gives the updated value of the object domain function.

$$F_k = f(x, y) \times \mathrm{phase}\,(F_k') \tag{5.3}$$

F_k is Fourier transformed (FT) and the phase of this Fourier transformed quantity is used to update $\phi_k(u,v)$ to get $\phi_{k+1}(u,v)$. This in turn is multiplied by the Fourier domain amplitude to get A_{k+1}:

$$A_k' = \mathrm{FT}\{F_k\} \tag{5.4}$$

$$\phi_{k+1} = \mathrm{phase}\{A_k'\} \tag{5.5}$$

$$A_{k+1} = G(u,v) \times \phi_{k+1}(u,v) \tag{5.6}$$

The algorithm then proceeds with the above steps forming an iterative loop. The iterations continue till the error between the approximated Fourier amplitude of A_k'

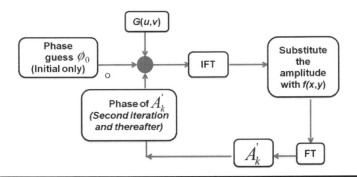

Figure 5.1 Flowchart showing the steps of GSA.

and the actual Fourier domain magnitude $G(u, v)$ reaches a preset threshold value. The entire process is explained in the flowchart shown in Figure 5.1.

The GSA has been used in electron microscopy and other applications involving wavefront sensing [26]. However, the algorithm was modified by Fienup who introduced new set of object constraints to get better convergence [27]. The method came to be known as the error reduction algorithm which is explained in the next section.

5.2.2 Error Reduction Algorithm (ERA)

The ERA aims to obtain the object image given its Fourier domain amplitude and a set of constraints, such as positivity, reality of the pixel values of the image and the support [28–30]. The algorithm mostly follows the GSA except that all those points in the object domain which do not obey the constraints are set to zero before moving on to the next iteration. The initial step comprises assigning a random phase function $\phi_0(u,v)$ in the Fourier domain (same as in GSA). For any kth iteration, the algorithm proceeds in the following manner:

The phase $\phi_k(u,v)$ is multiplied by the Fourier domain amplitude $G(u, v)$ and is inverse Fourier transformed to get the function $F_k'(x, y)$:

$$F_k' = \mathrm{IFT}\left\{G(u,v)\times\phi_k(u,v)\right\} \tag{5.7}$$

The known constraints such as the positivity, reality or the knowledge of support are applied in this domain, to get the new estimate $F_{k+1}(x, y)$. All those pixels which obey the object domain constraints are retained while those pixels which do not conform to these restrictions are set to zero:

$$F_{k+1}(x, y) = \begin{cases} F_k'(x, y) & (x, y) \in \gamma \\ 0, & (x, y) \in \gamma \end{cases} \tag{5.8}$$

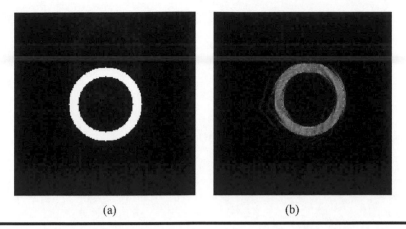

Figure 5.2 **Numerical simulation result for demonstrating ERA (a) input image and (b) recovered image after ERA.**

The updated $F_{k+1}(x, y)$ is Fourier transformed and the amplitude obtained is substituted with the actual value of the Fourier domain amplitude i.e. $G(u, v)$.

As an illustration, Figure 5.2 shows the retrieval of a simple binary image. The constraints used are the support and the positivity in the object domain.

5.2.3 Hybrid Input-Output Algorithm (HIOA)

To further improve the convergence Fienup proposed the hybrid input–output algorithm that would overcome stagnation problems with grey scale objects [28,30]. In this method, the first step remains the same as described in ER algorithm. The constraints application in the second step of ERA described above is modified to a negative feedback process to get the HIOA. The pixels in the image $F_k''(x, y)$ which conform to the constraints, such as positivity, in the object domain are retained. The pixels which do not conform to these constraints are used to modify the previous guess, by means of negative feedback. The application of constraints can be summarized as:

$$F_{k+1}(x, y) = \begin{cases} F_k'(x, y) & (x, y) \in \gamma \\ F_k(x, y) - \beta F_k', & (x, y) \in \gamma \end{cases} \tag{5.9}$$

Here β is a positive parameter selected in the interval (0,1). The above discussed algorithms have been reported to be efficient at solving the phase retrieval problems and have found use in various applications [25,30]. In the next sections, their applications in optical cryptography are discussed.

5.3 Encryption Involving Phase Retrieval Algorithms

Various optical cryptosystems have been proposed in which the decryption or the choice of the random phase masks (RPMs) rely on the method of phase retrieval [31–35]. To exemplify this methodology, two such cryptosystems have been studied.

5.3.1 Diffractive Imaging Based System

An optical encryption scheme using the diffractive imaging has been reported [12] in which the input image is encoded in the diffraction pattern of the image, with RPMs present in the optical path. The decryption is done by using phase retrieval algorithms. Figure 5.3 illustrates the optical set-up required for recording the ciphertexts. The input image is multiplied by an RPM and then is subjected to the FRT operation of order α. The same operation is carried out consecutively for three more RPMs, followed by FRT. Four different diffraction intensities are recorded by translating the RPM M_3 laterally for four different positions. At each hth lateral position this RPM is labeled as M_3^h ($h = 1$–4). The four diffraction patterns denoted by $E^h(\xi, \eta)$ ($h = 1$–4) form the ciphertexts, and can be expressed mathematically as:

$$E^h(\xi, \eta) = \left| \text{FRT}^\alpha \left[\left(\text{FRT}^\beta \left\{ \left[\text{FRT}^\gamma \left(\left\{ \text{FRT}^\omega \left[I(x, y) M_1(x, y) \right] \right\} M_2(\mu_1, \nu_1) \right) \right] \right. \right. \right. \right.$$
$$\left. \left. \left. M_3^h(\mu_2, \nu_2) \right\} \right) M_4(\mu_1, \nu_1) \right] \right|^2 \tag{5.10}$$

The variables α, β, γ, and ω denote the respective FRT orders.

The decryption uses phase retrieval algorithm to retrieve the lost phase and the input image intensity.

The algorithm essentially consists of moving back and forth in the ciphertext domain and an intermediate RPM domain. The RPMs present in the optical path serve as the constraints in the phase retrieval algorithm that

Figure 5.3 Schematic for optical setup for encryption using diffractive imaging. CCD denotes the charged couple device camera.

supply information at each step and help in convergence of the algorithm. The steps for decryption are as follows:

Step 1: Initially, in the first iteration, the wavefront just before the translated RPM M_3 is approximated by a real valued random function, say, $T_n(\mu_2, \nu_2)$. Here, the subscript n refers to the iteration number of the algorithm. The RPM M_3^1 is multiplied with $T_n(\mu_2, \nu_2)$:

$$T_n'(\mu_2, \nu_2) = T_n(\mu_2, \nu_2)M_3^1(\mu_2, \nu_2) \tag{5.11}$$

and is propagated forward using FRT of the order β. The output is again multiplied by the RPM M_4 and fractional Fourier transformed with order α to reach the CCD plane.

$$O_n^1(\xi, \eta) = \mathrm{FrFT}^\alpha \left(\left\{ \mathrm{FrFT}^\beta \left[T_n' \right] \right\} M_4(\mu_3, \nu_3) \right) \tag{5.12}$$

Step 2: At this stage, there is a support constraint to update the quantity $O_n^1(\xi, \eta)$. This constraint is the intensity $E^1(\xi, \eta)$ recorded during the encryption procedure. After applying the constraint, following is obtained:

$$\overline{O_n^1(\xi, \eta)} = \left[E^1(\xi, \eta) \right]^{1/2} \arg\left\{ O_n^1(\xi, \eta) \right\} \tag{5.13}$$

Here *arg{}* represents the argument of the quantity enclosed within {}.
Step 3: $\overline{O_n^1(\xi, \eta)}$ is propagated back to the RPM plane M_3 to get a new updated value of the wavefront just before the RPM M_3:

$$T_n^2(\mu_2, \nu_2) = \left[\mathrm{FRT}^{-\beta} \left(\left\{ \mathrm{FRT}^{-\alpha} \left[\overline{O_n^1(\xi, \eta)} \right] \right\} M_4^*(\mu_3, \nu_3) \right) \right] \left[M_3^1(\mu_2, \nu_2) \right]^* \tag{5.14}$$

Step 4: $T_n^2(\mu_2, \nu_2)$ is used along with $M_3^2(\mu_2, \nu_2)$ and $E^2(\xi, \eta)$ to repeat the above steps to obtain $T_n^3(\mu_2, \nu_2)$, which is then used with $M_3^3(\mu_2, \nu_2)$ and $E^3(\xi, \eta)$ to get $T_n^4(\mu_2, \nu_2)$.
Step 5: The above steps complete a single iteration. Error is calculated between values of $T_n(\mu_2, \nu_2)$ for consecutive iterations and if the error is smaller than a preset threshold then the iteration process stops. If the error exceeds, then the process moves on to $n + 1$ iteration wherein $T_n^4(\mu_2, \nu_2)$ is considered as the wavefront preceding the RPM M_3.

Numerical simulations show that an encrypted image of 512×512 pixels can be decrypted after 2545 iterations of the above phase retrieval algorithm, with the error threshold set as 0.0001 [12]. The RPMs placed in the optical paths along with the order of the FRT serving as the keys. Increasing the number of the recorded diffractive intensity results in easier convergence of the iterative method.

Variants of the diffractive imaging encryption method that uses the phase algorithms have been reported [12–16], which makes the phase retrieval a widely studied tool in the field of optical encryption.

5.3.2 Multiple Image Encryption and Multiplexing Scheme

As another example, phase retrieval has been used to establish a multiple image encryption and multiplexing scheme [36,37]. In this scheme, phase-only functions corresponding to the images which are to be multiplexed are evaluated using modified GS algorithm (MGSA). Phase-only functions refer to complex quantities with amplitude as unity, which would give the input image when subjected to the Fourier or Fresnel transformation. The first step of the multiplexing scheme is to evaluate these phase functions for all the images. The iterative process begins by subjecting the input image I to inverse Fresnel transform.

$$IFrT\left\{I(x,y);\lambda;z\right\} = G(u,v)\exp[i\psi] \tag{5.15}$$

The phase of the output is reserved while the amplitude is substituted by unity:

$$I'(u,v) = \exp[i\psi] \tag{5.16}$$

The function $I'(u,v)$ is Fresnel transformed:

$$FrT\left\{I'(u,v);\lambda;z\right\} = I''(x,y)\exp[i\phi] \tag{5.17}$$

The phase $\exp[i\phi]$ serves as the phase function to be multiplied with the input image in the next iteration step. Hence, the original image $I(x, y)$ is multiplied with this updated phase $\exp[i\phi]$ and is again inverse Fresnel transformed. The iterative process is continued till the error between the original input image $I(x, y)$ and the quantity $I''(x, y)$ is less than a preset threshold. At the end of the iterative process, phase $\exp[i\psi]$ is obtained which gives the original image on Fresnel transformation. Figure 5.4 shows the flowchart explaining the iteration steps for evaluating the phase only mask through MGSA.

Phase functions are obtained in similar fashion for all images. For wavelength multiplexing, different wavelength values for each image are used while implementing the Fresnel transform. Position multiplexing can also be done by using different distance parameters for each image during Fresnel transformation. For a total of n images, the corresponding n phase-only functions can be denoted by $\exp[i\psi_{\lambda_n}]$. The subscript λ denotes the particular wavelength for the nth image used

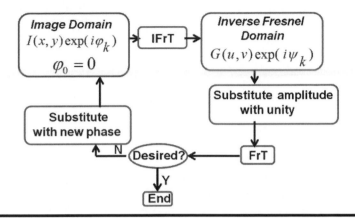

Figure 5.4 **Flowchart showing the steps of MGSA to evaluate phase only mask of a given image.**

in wavelength multiplexing. The phases are then summed and normalized to obtain a single phase only function, which is given by:

$$\psi_T = \arg\left\{ \frac{\sum\limits_{n=1}^{N} \exp[i\psi_{\lambda_n}]}{\left|\sum\limits_{n=1}^{N} \exp[i\psi_{\lambda_n}]\right|} \right\} \tag{5.18}$$

ψ_T serves as the multiplexed ciphertext for n images. For retrieving a particular image, ψ_T is inverse Fresnel transformed using the corresponding wavelength value. Different artifacts can be applied to remove the cross talks in this multiplexing scheme [36].

5.4 Cryptanalysis

As majority of optical cryptosystems are constructed using optical transforms, phase retrieval becomes relevant in these cases to formulate attack algorithms. This section studies such iterative phase retrieval attack algorithms.

5.4.1 Cryptanalysis in DRPE

DRPE was one of the first proposed optical encryption schemes. As mentioned earlier, it consists of a typical 4*f* optical set-up where the input image $I(x, y)$ is multiplied with an RPM R1 and subjected to Fourier transformation using a converging lens. The output is again multiplied with another RPM R2, followed by Fourier transformation. The output is a white stationary noise which serves as the ciphertext [1]. The ciphertext can be expressed mathematically as:

$$E(u,v) = \text{IFT}\left\{\text{FT}\left\{I(x,y)\exp[in(x,y)]\right\}\exp[ib(\alpha,\beta)]\right\} \qquad (5.19)$$

Here, $\exp[in(x,y)]$ and $\exp[ib(\alpha,\beta)]$ are the RPMs R1 and R2, respectively. The functions $n(x,y)$ and $b(\alpha,\beta)$ are random value distributions lying in the interval $[0,2\pi]$.

DRPE has been a widely studied optical cryptosystem and its many variants have been reported. However, the encryption technique was shown to be vulnerable to the known plaintext attack [19]. In a known plaintext attack, the attacker knows the plaintext and the ciphertext and tries to retrieve the keys. This attack is based on the phase retrieval technique, and is described below:

Taking the Fourier transform of both the sides in Equation 5.19,

$$\psi(\alpha,\beta) = \left\{FT\left\{I(x,y)\exp[in(x,y)]\right\}\exp[ib(\alpha,\beta)]\right\} \qquad (5.20)$$

Now if the expression $I(x,y)\exp[in(x,y)]$ is denoted by $G(x,y)$, then Equation 5.20 can be written as:

$$\psi(\alpha,\beta) = FT\left\{G(x,y)\right\}\exp[ib(\alpha,\beta)] \qquad (5.21)$$

Again, considering $FT\left\{G(x,y)\right\} = G(\alpha,\beta)$,

$$\psi(\alpha,\beta) = G(\alpha,\beta)\exp[ib(\alpha,\beta)] \qquad (5.22)$$

Taking modulus of both the sides,

$$|\psi(\alpha,\beta)| = |G(\alpha,\beta)| \qquad (5.23)$$

Equation 5.23 is the key equation that helps construct known plaintext attacks on the DRPE system. It implies that the Fourier transform of the ciphertext can be used to evaluate the amplitude of the complex quantity in the first Fourier domain of the 4f-system of the DRPE. This information can help retrieve the RPM R1. If the first Fourier transformation process (shown in the dashed box in Figure 5.5) is considered, then the quantities known to the attacker are the object domain amplitude $I(x, y)$ and the Fourier domain amplitude $|G(\alpha,\beta)|$ $\left(= |\psi(\alpha,\beta)|\right)$. This is equivalent to the GSA described in Section 5.2.1. Hence $\exp[in(x,y)]$ can be evaluated using the GSA in the first Fourier transformation process of the DRPE.

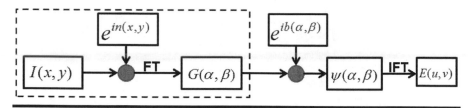

Figure 5.5 Block diagram showing the DRPE. The Fourier transformation in the dashed box is used to implement the GSA to evaluate the phase exp[$in(x, y)$].

Once exp[$in(x, y)$] is known, the conjugate of the other key, RPM R2 can also be evaluated by simple mathematical relation following from Equations 5.19 and 5.20. This conjugate is denoted by $R2'$ and is given by:

$$R2' = \exp[-ib(\alpha, \beta)] = \frac{FT\{I(x, y)R1\}}{\psi(\alpha, \beta)} \tag{5.24}$$

Numerical simulations of the known plaintext attack on DRPE have been shown in Figure 5.6. The simulation platform is MATLAB® (R2015). Initially, two images, shown in Figure 5.6a and b and have been encrypted with the DRPE technique such that the two RPMs used in the process are same for both the cases. Figure 5.6c and d show the corresponding encrypted images. The keys are retrieved using the known plaintext attack on the encrypted image of Figure 5.6a. The retrieved keys are then used to decrypt the image in Figure 5.6b. It can be seen in Figure 5.6e that the retrieved keys can well decrypt the image in Figure 5.6b.

5.4.2 Cryptanalysis in the Asymmetric Cryptosystem

As the DRPE system was shown to be vulnerable to the chosen ciphertext and the known plaintext attacks owing to the linearity of the system. The linearity in the DRPE system arises because the encryption keys and the decryption keys are similar. To remove this linearity the phase truncation Fourier transform (PTFT) based cryptosystems were introduced which fall in the category asymmetric crypto-systems [38]. In these schemes, the encryption keys differ from the decryption keys. This section highlights the phase retrieval based attack systems, namely the specific attacks that are applicable to the PTFT based systems.

In the PTFT-based encryption, the input image $I(x, y)$ is multiplied by an RPM (first encryption key) and subjected to the Fourier transform. The phase of the output is saved as the first private key, while the amplitude is again multiplied by another RPM (second encryption key), and is again Fourier transformed. The amplitude of the output serves as the ciphertext while the phase is reserved as the second private key. Mathematically, the entire encryption process can be summarized as:

$$E(u, v) = PT\left\{IFT\left[\left\{PT\left[FT\left(I(x, y) \times K_1(x, y)\right)\right]\right\} \times K_2(m, n)\right]\right\} \tag{5.25}$$

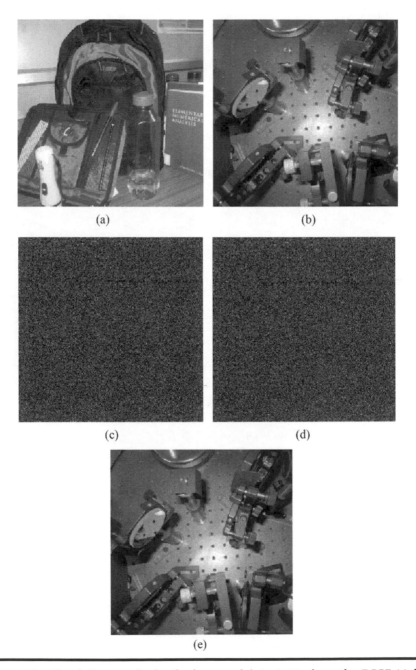

(a)

(b)

(c)

(d)

(e)

Figure 5.6 Simulation results for the known plaintext attack on the DRPE (a) first input image, (b) second input image, (c, d) ciphertexts corresponding to the first and second images respectively, using same RPMs, and (e) image retrieved after applying the keys obtained from known plaintext attack on the first encrypted image.

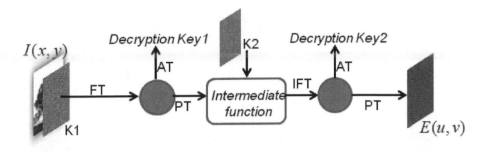

Figure 5.7 Schematic showing the encryption stages in PTFT-based cryptosystem.

Here, PT refers to phase truncation operation. Figure 5.7 shows the encryption schematic for PTFT-based cryptosystem.

Phase retrieval algorithms with different constraints have been used to formulate the specific attacks on these asymmetric cryptosystems [22–24]. In the specific attack, the attacker has the knowledge of one or more encryption keys, the ciphertext and the encryption principle. Knowing these quantities, the attack aims to retrieve the plaintext. As an example, one of the attack methods is discussed here [23].

Step 1: Initially, a random amplitude guess for the plaintext is initiated and is denoted by I_k (for the first guess $k = 0$). This amplitude guess is multiplied with the first key K_1 and then Fourier transformed. The amplitude and the phase parts are separated as follows:

$$G_k(m,n) = \mathrm{PT}\left\{\mathrm{FT}\left[I_k(x,y) \times K_1(x,y)\right]\right\} \tag{5.26}$$

$$P_k(m,n) = \mathrm{PR}\left\{\mathrm{FT}\left[I_k(x,y) \times K_1(x,y)\right]\right\} \tag{5.27}$$

Here PR refers to phase reserve operation.

Step 2: The function $G_k(m,n)$ is multiplied by the second key K_2 and then inverse Fourier transformed. The amplitude and the phase of the output are given by:

$$C_k(u,v) = \mathrm{PT}\left\{\mathrm{IFT}\left[G_k(m,n) \times K_2(m,n)\right]\right\} \tag{5.28}$$

$$B_k(u,v) = \mathrm{PR}\left\{\mathrm{IFT}\left[G_k(m,n) \times K_2(m,n)\right]\right\} \tag{5.29}$$

Step 3: The amplitude of the output is updated with the ciphertext, while the phase is retained. The updated function is Fourier transformed followed by phase truncation.

$$G_k'(m,n) = \mathrm{PT}\left\{\mathrm{FT}\left[E(u,v) \times B_k(u,v)\right]\right\} \tag{5.30}$$

This phase $G'_k(m,n)$ is multiplied with $P_k(m,n)$ and inverse Fourier transformed. The amplitude of the resulting output serves as the upgraded approximation of the plaintext which is to be used in the next iteration step:

$$I_{k+1}(x,y) = \text{PT}\left\{\text{IFT}\left[G'_k(m,n) \times P_k(m,n)\right]\right\} \quad (5.31)$$

The above steps constitute a single iteration of the attack algorithm. The process continues till the error between the actual ciphertext $E(u,v)$ and the function $C_k(u,v)$ reaches a preset threshold. This error is known as the sum square error (SSE) and can be written mathematically as

$$\text{SSE} = 10\log\frac{\displaystyle\sum_{i=1}^{M}\sum_{j=1}^{N}|C_k(u,v) - E(u,v)|^2}{M \times N} \quad (5.32)$$

Figure 5.8 depicts the steps of the algorithm.

Figure 5.9 shows the numerical simulation results of the specific attack carried out on a PTFT-based encrypted image. The plaintext can be well retrieved using the algorithm.

The constraints available to construct the phase retrieval play an important role in the convergence of these attack schemes. Depending on the available information, different algorithms can be formulated. Similar to the above explained specific attack, there are other algorithms have been reported which require the knowledge of both the encryption keys K1 and K2 to breach the system. However, there can be a scenario where the attacker knows only one of the keys K1. A specific attack for such case has been proposed using a combination of HIOA and ERA [24]. As

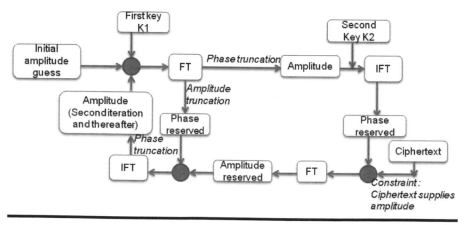

Figure 5.8 Flowchart showing the steps of specific attack on PTFT-based cryptosystem.

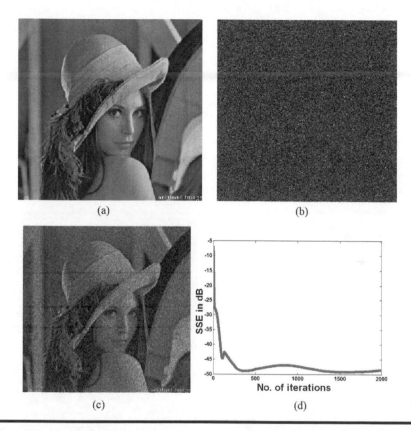

Figure 5.9 (a) Plaintext for PTFT, (b) encrypted image, (c) retrieved image after applying the specific attack, (d) Plot of the SSE in decibels with respect to number of iterations of the applied specific attack.

mentioned in Sections 5.2.2 and 5.2.3, HIOA and ERA use the support and the non-negativity constraints to help the iterative process converge. These constraints can be used in the absence of knowledge of the second key to retrieve the plaintext. As reported in reference [24], such an attack algorithm works in two stages. The aim of the first stage is to obtain the intermediate phase truncated function $Z(u, v)$ without the knowledge of key K2. To achieve this each iterative step consists of 1 cycle of ERA followed by 39 cycles of HIOA. Since the known quantity for this stage is only the ciphertext, therefore, the constraint used is the support, which is evaluated from the inverse Fourier transform of the ciphertext. In the second stage the plaintext is retrieved using $Z(u, v)$ and the key K1 with the GS algorithm set up. Figure 5.10 shows the flowchart of this algorithm.

Figure 5.11 shows the retrieved image using the combination of ERA and HIOA scheme when only the first key K1 was known to the attacker. The attack algorithm consisted of a total of 3000 iterations. As mentioned earlier, each iteration had

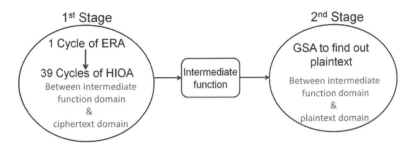

Figure 5.10 **Schematic showing the steps of specific attack on the PTFT-based cryptosystem when only the first encryption key is available to the attacker.**

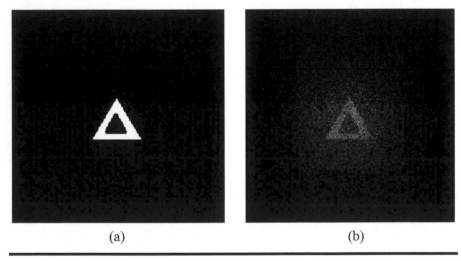

Figure 5.11 **Numerical simulation result for specific attack when only the first encryption key is known to the attacker: (a) plaintext and (b) recovered image.**

1 cycle of ERA and 39 cycles of HIOA. The input image can be well retrieved with the method.

The above discussion shows that the phase retrieval techniques play an important role in the cryptanalysis of optical cryptosystems. Depending on the availability of the constraints, different algorithms are utilized to formulate the attack schemes.

To conclude, phase retrieval based cryptosystems find extensive study in the field of optical security. This chapter discusses few such examples. However, there are many more phase retrieval techniques, like the transport of intensity (TIE) technique which has found application in optical security [39]. The field remains a prospective candidate for formulating newer cryptosystems as well as cryptanalysis methods.

References

1. P. Refregier and B. Javidi, Optical image encryption based on input plane encoding and Fourier plane random encoding, *Opt. Lett.* 20 (1995) 767–769.
2. B. Javidi, A. Carnicer, M. Yamaguchi, T. Nomura, E. Perez-Cabre, M. S. Millan, N. K. Nishchal et al. Roadmap on optical security, *J. Opt.* 18 (2016) 083001.
3. G. Unnikrishnan, J. Joseph, and K. Singh, Optical encryption system that uses phase conjugation in a photorefractive crystal, *Appl. Opt.* 37 (1998) 8181–8186.
4. G. Unnikrishnan, J. Joseph, and K. Singh, Optical encryption by double-random phase encoding in the fractional Fourier domain, *Opt. Lett.* 25 (2000) 887–889.
5. N. K. Nishchal, J. Joseph, and K. Singh, Fully phase encryption using fractional Fourier transform, *Opt. Eng.* 42 (2003) 1583–1588.
6. N. K. Nishchal, J. Joseph, and K. Singh, Securing information encryption using fractional Fourier transform in digital holography, *Opt. Commun.* 235 (2004) 253–259.
7. G. Situ and J. Zhang, Double random-phase encoding in the Fresnel domain, *Opt. Lett.* 29 (2004) 1584–1586.
8. S. K. Rajput and N. K. Nishchal, Fresnel domain nonlinear optical image encryption scheme based on Gerchberg-Saxton phase retrieval algorithm, *Appl. Opt.* 53 (2014) 418–425.
9. Z. Liu, L. Xu, C. Lin, and S. Liu, Image encryption by encoding with a non uniform optical beam in gyrator transform domains, *Appl. Opt.* 49 (2010) 5632–5637.
10. I. Mehra and N. K. Nishchal, Optical asymmetric image encryption using gyrator wavelet transform, *Opt. Commun.* 354 (2015) 344–352.
11. H. Singh, A. K. Yadav, S. Vashisth, and K. Singh, Double phase-image encryption using gyrator transforms and structured phase mask in frequency plane, *Opt. Lasers Eng.* 67 (2015) 145–156.
12. W. Chen, X. Chen, and C. J. R. Sheppard, Optical image encryption based on diffractive imaging, *Opt. Lett.* 35 (2010) 3817–3819.
13. W. Chen, X. Chen, A. Anand, and B. Javidi, Optical encryption using multiple intensity samplings in the axial domain, *J. Opt. Soc. Am. A* 30 (2013) 806–812.
14. Y. Qin, Q. Gong, and Z. Wang, Simplified optical image encryption approach using single diffraction pattern in diffractive-imaging based scheme, *Opt. Express* 22 (2014) 21790–21799.
15. I. Mehra and N. K. Nishchal, Optical asymmetric watermarking using modified wavelet fusion and diffractive imaging, *Opt. Lasers Eng.* 68 (2015) 74–82.
16. A. Fatima, I. Mehra, and N. K. Nishchal, Optical asymmetric cryptosystem using equal modulus decomposition and multiple diffractive imaging, *J. Opt.* 18 (2016) 085701.
17. A. Alfalou and C. Brosseau, Dual encryption scheme of images using polarized light, *Opt. Lett.* 35 (2010) 2185–2187.
18. S. K. Rajput and N. K. Nishchal, Image encryption using polarized light encoding and amplitude and phase truncation in Fresnel domain, *Appl. Opt.* 52 (2013) 4343–4352.
19. S. K. Rajput, D. Kumar, and N. K. Nishchal, Photon counting imaging and polarized light encoding for secure image verification and hologram watermarking, *J. Opt.* 16 (2014) 125406.
20. G. Unnikrishnan, D. S. Monaghan, T. J. Naughton, and T. J. Sheridan, A known-plaintext heuristic attack on the Fourier plane encryption algorithm, *Opt. Express* 14 (2006) 3181–3186.

21. X. Peng, P. Zhang, H. Wei, and B. Yu, Known plaintext attack on optical encryption based on double random phase keys, *Opt. Lett.* 31 (2006) 1044–1046.

22. X. Wang and D. Zhao, A special attack on the asymmetric cryptosystem based on phase-truncated Fourier transforms, *Opt. Commun.* 285 (2012) 1078–1081.

23. X. Wang, Y. Chen, C. Dai, and D. Zhao, Discussion and a new attack of the optical asymmetric cryptosystem based on phase-truncated Fourier transform, *Appl. Opt.* 53 (2014) 208–213.

24. A. Fatima and N. K. Nishchal, Discussion on comparative analysis and a new attack on optical asymmetric cryptosystem, *J. Opt. Soc. Am. A* 33 (2016) 2034–2040.

25. C. Guo, S. Liu, and J. T. Sheridan, Iterative phase retrieval algorithms. Part II: Attacking optical encryption systems, *Appl. Opt.* 54 (2015) 4709–4719.

26. Y. Shechtman, Y. C. Elder, O. Cohen, H. N. Chapman, J. Miao, and M. Segev, Phase retrieval with application to optical imaging: A contemporary overview, *IEEE Signal Process. Mag.* 32 (2015) 87–109.

27. R. W. Gerchberg, A practical algorithm for the determination of phase from image and diffraction plane pictures, *Optik* 35 (1972) 237–246.

28. J. R. Fienup, Reconstruction of an object from the modulus of its Fourier transform, *Opt. Lett.* 3 (1978) 27–29.

29. J. R. Fienup, Phase retrieval algorithm: A comparison, *Appl. Opt.* 21 (1982) 2758–2769.

30. C. Guo, S. Liu, and J. T. Sheridan, Iterative phase retrieval algorithms. I: Optimization, *Appl. Opt.* 54 (2015) 4698–4708.

31. S. K. Rajput and N. K. Nishchal, Fresnel domain nonlinear optical image encryption scheme based on Gerchberg-Saxton phase-retrieval algorithm, *Appl. Opt.* 53 (2014) 418–425.

32. S. K. Rajput and N. K. Nishchal, Optical double image security using random phase fractional Fourier domain encoding and phase-retrieval algorithm, *Opt. Commun.* 388 (2017) 38–46.

33. W. Chen and X. Chen, Interference-based optical image encryption using three-dimensional phase retrieval, *Appl. Opt.* 51 (2012) 6076–6083.

34. W. Chen and X. Chen, Iterative phase retrieval for simultaneously generation two phase-only masks with silhouette removal in interference-based optical encryption, *Opt. Commun.* 331 (2014) 133–138.

35. W. Chen, X. Chen and C. J. R. Sheppard, Optical image encryption based on phase retrieval combined with three-dimensional particle like distribution, *J. Opt.* 14 (2012) 075402.

36. G. Situ and J. Zhang, Multiple image encryption by wavelength multiplexing, *Opt. Lett.* 30 (2005) 1306–1308.

37. H. E. Hwang, H. T. Chang, and W. N. Lie, Multiple-image encryption and multiplexing using a modified Gerchberg-Saxton algorithm and phase modulation in Fresnel-transform domain, *Opt. Lett.* 34 (2009) 3917–3919.

38. W. Qin and X. Peng, Asymmetric cryptosystem based on phase-truncated Fourier transforms, *Opt. Lett.* 35 (2010) 118–120.

39. C. Zhang, W. He, J. Wu, and X. Peng, Optical cryptosystem based on phase-truncated Fresnel diffraction and transport of intensity equation, *Opt. Express* 23 (2015) 8344–8359.

Chapter 6

Security and Cryptography in Images and Video Using Elliptic Curve Cryptography (ECC)

Piyush Raghav and Amit Dua

Contents

DOI: 10.1201/9780429435461-7

113

6.1 Introduction

In today's world, with the rapid growth of technologies, the amount of multimedia content generated has also increased. The generated multimedia data contains images, security footage, biomedical images, videos, etc. These data must be transferred over the Internet where they shouldn't be exposed to any unauthorized user because of the sensitivity of the data. Let's take an example, suppose two people, Alice and Bob, are communicating over a secure line. Eve, an adversary, can tap in the line and can get the information about message M1 and message M2.

Figure 6.1 represents a typical communication scenario in which sender, receiver, and eavesdropper are present, Eve can either intercept and break the cipher or destroy and modify the information. Both attacks are very different and require a different kind of technique. Figure 6.1 shows the scenario when there is no security protocol implemented over communication.

6.1.1 History of Cryptosystem

Cryptography is one of the oldest techniques dated to 1900 BC. Egyptian used the hieroglyphic writing to pass messages in a secure way. Hieroglyphics was a method

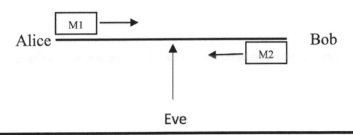

Figure 6.1 A layout of communication and eavesdropping.

to interpret information and message in terms of images. These hieroglyphics known as scribes were meant for certain people in society. Figure 6.2 represents the Egyptian hieroglyphic translation.

The first classical encryption technique known as Caesar cipher was used by Romans and devised by Caesar. Caesar cipher is one of the simplest encryption techniques, in which each letter of a word is replaced by the letter that comes after three units. For example

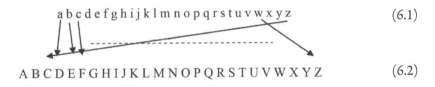

$$a\,b\,c\,d\,e\,f\,g\,h\,i\,j\,k\,l\,m\,n\,o\,p\,q\,r\,s\,t\,u\,v\,w\,x\,y\,z \qquad (6.1)$$

$$A\,B\,C\,D\,E\,F\,G\,H\,I\,J\,K\,L\,M\,N\,O\,P\,Q\,R\,S\,T\,U\,V\,W\,X\,Y\,Z \qquad (6.2)$$

Figure 6.2 Ancient Egyptian Hieroglyph Translation. (Ibn Wahshiyya's translation of the Ancient Egyptian hieroglyph alphabet, Available: https://en.wikipedia.org/ wiki/Egyptian_hieroglyphs#/media/File:Ibn_Wahshiyya%27s_985_CE_translation_ of_the_Ancient_Egyptian_hieroglyph_alphabet.jpg, accessed October 30, 2017.)

Caesar cipher is prone to brute force attack which is very simple; by using 26 keys in the English language, anyone can break the Caesar cipher by putting all the possible combinations, shifting from 1 to 26, and then generating the corresponding English letter. Once the letter forms the word and has some meaning, Caesar cipher is cracked. Caesar cipher was improved by Blaise de Vigenère [2] which works as follows. It uses a word as a secret key by splitting the message into equal size blocks of the key length. It then adds both word a block and a key to get the cipher message in blocks.

Illustration 6.1: This Illustration Shows the Encryption Process of Caesar Cipher

Plain Text: We are learning Caesar cipher
Caesar cipher works on principle of shifting with 3 and it is wrapped around which means after 'z' we move to 'a'.
So by using 6.1 and 6.2, the first letter of plain text substituted with 'w'→'z' similarly 'e'→'h','a'→'d','r'→'u','e'→'h','l'→'o','e'→'h','r'→'u', 'n'→'q','i'→'l','n'→'q','g'→'j','c'→'f','e'→'h','a'→'d','s'→'v','e'→'h','r'→'u', 'c'→'f','i'→'l','p'→'s','h'→'k','e'→'h','r'→'u'.
Plain Text: We are learning Caesar cipher
Cipher Text: zh duh ohuqlqjfhdyhuflskhu

Similarly, classical cryptography consists of monoalphabetic cipher and polyalphabetic substitution cipher which includes the play fair cipher [3] and Hill cipher [4]. However, in today's scenario instead of using classical encryption technique, modern cryptosystems are used which are based upon operations on the finite field.

6.1.2 Modern Cryptosystems

Modern cryptosystems work on the principle of exchanging keys and messages over an insecure network as compared to the classical cryptosystem which uses substitution of words or alphabets based on fixed displacement as in the vigenère cipher. Instead of making channels secure, they encrypt the message and send it over the insecure line so that secure communication without changing the underlying infrastructure is achieved. The following is a general outline for modern cryptosystems which shows the encryption and decryption process. Communication without changing the underlying infrastructure is achieved. The following is a general outline for modern cryptosystems which shows encryption and decryption process.

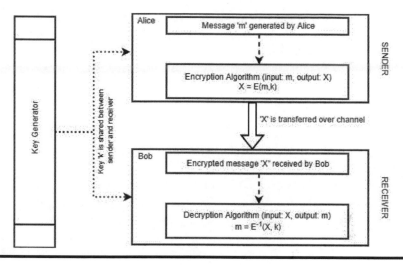

Figure 6.3   Shannon Encryption Model.

Figure 6.3 shows Shannon encryption model, which has the following five components:

1. A plain text message (m)
2. A secret key distribution (k)
3. An encrypted message $X = E(m, k)$
4. A rule to encrypt the message (m) using key (k) to generate a ciphertext X
5. A rule to decrypt ciphertext (X) using key (k) to generate the original message

Figure 6.3 also shows a secret key generator, where the key (k) should be transmitted securely. So, we require a secure channel for this communication; however, the cost of this secure channel is high as there is a tradeoff between communication. The key that we want to send is short as compared to the message. So, sending a short key over a secure channel is better as we are achieving a secure transmission for larger messages.

We will see more powerful modern encryption techniques based upon Shannon theory in the later part of this chapter. In the following section, we will discuss the basis of images and videos.

6.1.3 Images and Videos: A Brief Review

An image is defined as a collection of values, where value denotes the intensity of light in the form of an array or matrix. This matrix could be two dimensional in the case of black and white images or grayscale images, or it may be a three-dimensional matrix, as in case of a color image (RGB image). There is a little difference between black and white and grayscale images. In black and white image, there are only two colors, either black or white; on the other hand, a grayscale image contains values in between 0 to 255 where 0 is completely black and 255 is completely white. For example, an 8-bit grayscale image can have up to 255, or 2^8 shades of black and white, (i.e., 8-bit color depth). A true color or RGB image has a 24-bit color depth which is almost 16 million colors, or 2^{24}. Images can be stored in JPEG, PNG, TIFF, BMP, etc. formats. All these formats differ in terms of compression technique, output size of the compressed image, and visual depth of the compressed image. In image compression lossless compression means an image can be reconstructed accurately from the compressed image. Formats like PNG, TIFF, and BMP support lossless compression while JPEG is lossy compression. Table 6.1 shows the difference in various image formats.

A video, on the other hand, can be defined as a collection of images that form a moving picture. Generally, a term frame rate is associated with videos and is defined as the number of frames captured per second (FPS). The frame rate is essential for generating the illusion of moving pictures. For human perception, the frame rate for movies is 24 FPS while certain movies like "*The Hobbit*" have 48 FPS [5] which makes the movie more real in appearance. Aspect ratio can be

Table 6.1 Comparative Study of Few Popular Image Formats

Image Format	JPEG	PNG	TIFF	BMP
Description	Most common image format, used for transmitting image online	PNG is an upgraded version of GIF, unlike GIF, PNG has more color range than 256 colors as in GIF	Most of the general application like OCR, Scanning, faxing uses this format	Mostly supported windows system
Pros	High color range and small size of image	Many application support, lossless	Lossless and high-quality images	Universal compatibility and efficient compression
Cons	Lossy compression	RGB only support, large file size	Large file size	Large image size
Lossless	No	Yes	Yes	Yes

defined as the size of the video screen with respect to the size of the picture on that screen. Generally, it varies between 4:3 and 16:9.

Like images, videos also have different formats. In terms of video we talk about codecs and containers. While codecs are used for compression and decompression of data, for example, H.265 or H.264, containers are used to pack, transfer, and present this compressed data. For example, 3GP, MP4, and MKV are some popular video containers.

The use of digital images and videos has increased in past decade. With the advent of Internet and increased cyber attacks, the sharing of these data formats has become a challenge. With various kinds of cryptographic attacks, it is a serious problem that needs efficient solutions and techniques. Normal text data encryption techniques can't be directly applied to multimedia data because of a large amount of data and real-time constraints. So, it is necessary to encrypt videos and audio with some efficient real-time algorithm which provides a complete balance among encryption/decryption time, security strength, and size of output file.

6.2 Image Encryption Techniques

Image encryption techniques vary from region selection algorithms to spatial and frequency domain algorithms. Based on complexity, region selection algorithms are divided into two broad categories, one is block selection and other is the pixel-based selection. In the region-based encryption technique, a region of an image is selected for encryption. However, there is one condition for selection of a region, the selected region should be independent or have zero co-variance/similarity with rest of image. This constraint signifies that breaking the encryption is very difficult when the protected region is independent from unprotected region. Selective region techniques are further classified into two categories: one is manual and another is automatic selection. Let's take an example of medical images. In this case, manual selection is appropriate because in medical images the blocks of images are completely independent of each other. As a result, each block is encoded with an image map. Automatic selection techniques are further divided into two main classes, one is block selection and other is pixel selection.

6.2.1 Block Selection Techniques

Block selection technique incorporates the edge detection method. Edge detection includes suitable filters or operators for identifying sharp edges and sudden changes in intensity of images. The simplicity and fast nature of edge detection make them a suitable algorithm. There are several edge detection operators like Sobel, Roberts, and Prewitt. All these operators work in different directions like horizontal edge detection or vertical edge detection.

6.2.1.1 Edge Detection

The image gradient is to find edge strength and direction at location (x, y) of the image, and defined as the vector.

$$\nabla f \equiv \text{grad}(f) \equiv \begin{bmatrix} g_x \\ g_y \end{bmatrix} = \begin{bmatrix} \partial f / \partial x \\ \partial f / \partial y \end{bmatrix} \tag{6.3}$$

The magnitude of vector ∇f is denoted as $M(x, y)$

$$\text{mag}(\nabla f) = \sqrt{g_x + g_y} \tag{6.4}$$

The direction of gradient vector is given by the angle

$$\alpha = \tan^{-1}\left[g_y / g_x \right] \tag{6.5}$$

In edge detection, there are few prominent operators which are generally used for image segmentation process.

Let's see the use of the Sobel operator on a grayscale image.

Figure 6.3 represents a normal grayscale image of moon, Figure 6.4 represents the corresponding histogram of a grayscale moon image. After applying the Sobel

SOME IMPORTANT EDGE DETECTION OPERATORS.

Roberts operator:

$$\begin{bmatrix} -1 & 0 \\ 0 & 1 \end{bmatrix} \begin{bmatrix} 0 & -1 \\ 1 & 0 \end{bmatrix}$$

Prewitt operator:

$$\begin{bmatrix} -1 & -1 & -1 \\ 0 & 0 & 0 \\ 1 & 1 & 1 \end{bmatrix} \begin{bmatrix} -1 & 0 & 1 \\ -1 & 0 & 1 \\ -1 & 0 & 1 \end{bmatrix} \begin{bmatrix} 0 & 1 & 1 \\ -1 & 0 & 1 \\ -1 & -1 & 0 \end{bmatrix} \begin{bmatrix} -1 & -1 & 0 \\ -1 & 0 & 1 \\ 0 & 1 & 1 \end{bmatrix}$$

Sobel operator:

$$\begin{bmatrix} -1 & 2 & -1 \\ 0 & 0 & 0 \\ 1 & 2 & 1 \end{bmatrix} \begin{bmatrix} -1 & 0 & 1 \\ 2 & 0 & 2 \\ -1 & 0 & 1 \end{bmatrix} \begin{bmatrix} 0 & 1 & 2 \\ -1 & 0 & 1 \\ -2 & -1 & 0 \end{bmatrix} \begin{bmatrix} -2 & -1 & 0 \\ -1 & 0 & 1 \\ 0 & 1 & 2 \end{bmatrix}$$

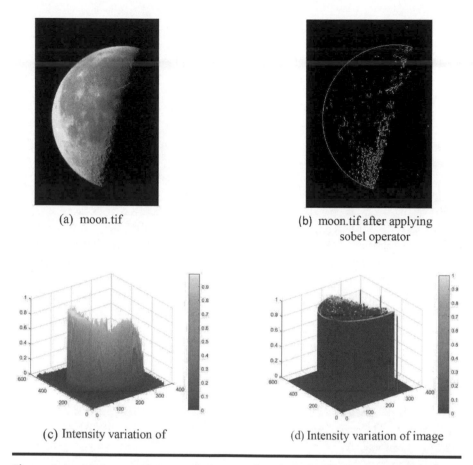

(a) moon.tif

(b) moon.tif after applying
sobel operator

(c) Intensity variation of

(d) Intensity variation of image

Figure 6.4 **(a) A normal grayscale image, (b) edges detected after application of Sobel edge detection operator, (c) histogram of color intensity in normal grayscale image, and (d) histogram of processed image.**

image filter on Figure 6.3, we will get Figure 6.5 where only edges are present and Figure 6.6 shows the corresponding histogram of the filtered image.

The Sobel operator uses two in the center row for image smoothing. The Prewitt operator is simpler to implement than the Sobel operator, but the Sobel operator has better noise-suppression (smoothing) characteristics, which makes it preferable over the Prewitt and Roberts operators.

Edge detection is used in image encryption for classifying significant and insignificant blocks. Similarly, frequency domain wavelet transforms (DWT) and discrete cosine transform (DCT) can be used for identifying the regions. In DWT, the images are decomposed into levels; these levels have sub-bands that consist of the coefficient that defines the original plain image. Therefore, a sub-band which has relatively unique coefficients can be used as a region. Few recent algorithms are discussed below:

Jalesh and Nirmala [6] suggested a hybrid approach having two phases and implementing both image segmentation and image encryption. Their algorithm divides an image into two sub-images, one with edges and one without edges. They achieved it by using canny edge detection algorithm. Once both images are obtained then they are encrypted using crossover and mutation operations. After that, the output is fused together to get a single encrypted image. This method is robust to statistical attack because from histogram analysis, it is shown that the occurrence of each pixel is almost uniform in encrypted image.

Flayh et al. [7] suggested a partial image encryption technique in which only a part of the image is encrypted using secure encryption techniques like advanced encryption standard (AES) and stream cipher. The proposed algorithm works on the principle that most of the information in an image exists in the lower frequency band, which can be used to divide the images into two parts using low pass and high pass filters. The performance parameter they calculated was correlation coefficient, which is equal to one in the case of reconstruction of the image with respect to the original image, and zero in the case of encrypted image and the original image. Because of partial encryption, the time consumed in encryption is also less as compared to those algorithms which use full encryption.

Yekkala et al. [8] proposed a method based on partial encryption of images. Their method was based on adding sufficient noise so that it makes the image unreadable. This method is suitable for both images and videos because it uses the multimedia structure of data. The algorithm works on the assumption that edges in an image contain maximum information. Hence, in this method first edge detection has been carried over bit domain and then encryption is carried out. Each block is represented by the number of bits. If that block contains an edge then the number of bits in that block is greater than a threshold (which is set to identify an edge block), thus that block is identified as an edge block and is encrypted. This bit representation comes from the fact that multimedia structure like most of the images has been encoded as JPEG standard, which internally uses the Huffman table. Once encryption is over the image and bit threshold are transferred over the channel.

Munir [9] proposed a method based on the human visual system that suggests human visual perception is more sensitive to lower frequencies than higher frequencies. Therefore, important information like objects and frames are part of low frequency sub-bands and detailed information is part of a higher frequency sub-band. So, targeting the lower sub-band and encrypting its DCT coefficient ensures the degradation of visual perception of images.

Krishnamoorthi and Malarchelvi [10] suggested a selective encryption technique based on orthogonal polynomial transformation (OPT). The main logic is to de-correlate the pixels from its neighbors. To achieve this task, OPT is used instead of DCT or wavelet transform. DCT and wavelet transform have more computation complexity because of involvement of floating point operation. Once high energy coefficient is segregated from low energy coefficient, a combination of bits shuffling and coefficient shuffling is followed by block shuffling, which is applied to reduce the correlation further.

6.2.2 *Pixel Selection Technique*

Pixel selection technique is one of the most important techniques for region selection. An image is divided into pixels, where each pixel is represented by an 8-bit code. This code is divided into 4-bit least significant bit (LSB) and 4-bit most significant bit (MSB). The division is based on the correlated and uncorrelated information. After this, a pseudo-random arrangement is used to prevent correlated information while keeping the rest of information unencrypted. However, we can use a wavelet transform in a small region followed by Advance Encryption Scheme(AES) in Cipher Feedback (CFB) mode. But this technique is not robust because of scrambling a smaller area. A few recent techniques have been proposed which are discussed below.

Subba Rao et al. [11] proposed a method based on pixel selection technique in which they suggested the use of a pseudo-random sequence to encrypt correlated data. According to human visual sensing (HVS), the MSB of the plane has a high correlation among pixels as compared to LSB plane which contains more of uncorrelated pixels. They used hardware like m-sequence and gold sequence for generating a pseudo-random sequence which is used to encrypt the correlated data.

Steffi and Sharma [12] suggested a method for pixel level encryption. Their method includes the division of the image into 8-bit planes where the visual perception of image degrades from 8th plane to 1st plane. So, encrypting the least significant bit plane can add noise to the image. This naive method is robust to plain text attack because the least significant plane always contains highly uncorrelated data.

Ou et al. [13] proposed two methods which are based on region selection. In the first method, randomly inverting the first two most significant bits of region of interest in wavelet transform domain is carried out during the compression phase, then the bit plane that belongs to the region is upshifted to a maximum value which has the largest magnitude of background coefficient. The efficiency of this process is coming from the inversion of a sign bit of wavelet coefficient and some randomly selected MSBs rather than encrypting all bits. The second method is implied after compression and it is based upon layer mechanism of the JPEG2000 standard to selectively encrypted regions of interest (ROI).

Zhang et al. [14] proposed a chaos-based method, which is actually a confusion diffusion method. However, they removed the confusion step with *expand and shrink strategy* at bit level using a two-dimensional chaotic map. This scheme is better than bit level permutation in terms of computational complexity of confusion diffusion process.

Panduranga and NaveenKumar [15] gives two methods for selective region encryption. The first method is manual region selection and the other is automatic region selection. In the manual region selection technique, an image is divided into blocks and then manually a block is selected. The selected block undergoes encryption process using a map-based partial encryption technique. In the automatic region selection method, the image block is identified using morphological operations and the selected region is then encrypted using map-based encryption.

6.2.3 Performance Parameter

6.2.3.1 Visual Test

Observation is an important aspect of any image encryption technique. This parameter compares the encrypted image with the original image in terms of human visual sensing. A good encryption algorithm must have minimum observable content.

6.2.3.2 Histogram Analysis

To remove any kind of information leakage and aggressive attack, histogram analysis is done which is based on statistical similarity. It expresses the distribution of pixels based on their intensity. Figure 6.4a and b is the histogram representation of moon.jpg; the first histogram gives intensity representation of the whole image while the second histogram represents the intensity at the edges.

6.2.3.3 Information Entropy

It is a measure given by Shannon, which suggests how much information an event contains. The more the information, the more the uncertainty of event.

$$H\left(s\right) = \sum_{i=0}^{2N-1} P(S_i)\log_2 \frac{1}{P(S_i)} \tag{6.6}$$

In the above equation, $P(S_i)$ is the probability of S_i and entropy is in bits.

6.2.3.4 Encryption Quality

Because of encryption, a significant change happens in image pixels. These irregular changes signify the effectiveness of encryption algorithm. Let $E\left(x,y\right)$ and $O\left(x,y\right)$ be the gray level of pixels in the encrypted image and the original image. So, we can define encryption quality as:

$$EQ = \frac{\sum_{L=0}^{255} |H_L(E) - H_L(O)|}{256} \tag{6.7}$$

6.2.3.5 Correlation Analysis

Correlation [16] signifies the relationship between two variables in image encryption; it denotes the relationship between pixels and its neighborhood. Correlation can be defined as:

$$r_{xy} = \frac{\text{Cov}(x, y)}{\sqrt{D(x)} \times \sqrt{D(y)}} \tag{6.8}$$

$$D(x) = \frac{1}{N} \sum_{i=1}^{N} \left(x_j - \frac{1}{N} \sum_{i=1}^{N} x_j \right)^2 \tag{6.9}$$

$$\text{Cov}(x, y) = \frac{1}{N} \sum_{i=1}^{N} \left(x_j - \frac{1}{N} \sum_{i=1}^{N} x_j \right) \left(y_j - \frac{1}{N} \sum_{i=1}^{N} y_j \right) \tag{6.10}$$

where:
r_{xy} is the correlation coefficient of pixel x and y
x, y is the intensity value of two neighboring pixels
N is the number of the pair of pixels used to calculate correlation
$\text{Cov}(x, y)$ is the maximum in original image while it should be minimum in encrypted image

6.2.3.6 Differential Analysis

The major property of any encryption algorithm is that it should be sensitive to any minor changes. So that any change in the original image leads to an entirely new encrypted image. Differential attack is carried out when the changes made in the original image cannot affect the encrypted image.

Mean absolute error (MAE), number of pixel change rate (NPCR) with respect to single pixel change in original image, and unified average changing intensity (UACI) which is a measure of the difference between the average intensity of the original image and encrypted image.

If $E(x, y)$ and $O(x, y)$ are the gray levels of the pixels in $R \times C$ image, then:

$$\text{MAE} = \frac{1}{R \times C} \sum_{x=0}^{C-1} \sum_{y=0}^{R-1} \left| E(x, y) - O(x, y) \right| \tag{6.11}$$

Now, let's say we have two encrypted images E_k and $\overline{E}_k$. So, on these images NPCR is defined as:

$$\text{NPCR}_k = \frac{\sum_{x=0}^{C-1} \sum_{y=0}^{R-1} D_k(x, y)}{R \times C} \times 100\% \tag{6.12}$$

$$D_k(x, y) = \begin{cases} 0, E_k(x, y) = \bar{E}_k(x, y) \\ 1, E_k(x, y) \neq \bar{E}_k(x, y) \end{cases} \tag{6.13}$$

And UACI is defined as:

$$\text{UACI}_k = \frac{1}{R \times C} \times \sum_{x=0}^{C-1} \sum_{y=0}^{R-1} \left[\frac{\left| E_k(x, y) - \bar{E}_k(x, y) \right|}{255} \right] \times 100\% \tag{6.14}$$

It is noted that a large value of NPCR and UACI leads to better encryption algorithm with high sensitivity.

6.2.4 Image Encryption

Encryption of images can be classified into two main categories based on domains in which they are encrypted, spatial and frequency domain.

6.2.4.1 Spatial Domain

This selective encryption technique is based on five principles of advanced encryption standard (AES) algorithm which are: input image, partitioning size, iteration selection, programming usage, and routine determination procedure. Similarly, for biometric images we can use multiple region selections with the RC4 algorithm to protect the uncompressed image. While for JPEG2000 images, a new modern encryption technique is proposed which utilizes the scrambling of bits with respect to some close region followed by AES encryption in cipher feedback block mode (CFB) to scramble the rest of bits. Few proposed spatial domain image encryption techniques are discussed below:

Oh et al. [17] gives image encryption method for medical imaging. Since medical information must require an efficient and robust method for encryption, so they extend the AES into selective encryption algorithm (SEA). In the SEA, a region is selected which is then passed to a Huffman compressor. This is used to remove the number of rounds criteria in AES. Using this compressed data as input in AES, the performance of AES is significantly improved.

Wong and Bishop [18] suggest a way of encrypting an image based on biometric authentication. This method depends upon JPEG2000 extension JPSEC [19] which gives the ability for conditional access to the image. Therefore, this method ensures that different users can see different parts of the image based on their authority.

Kumar and Pateriya [20] suggested a method based on RC4 encryption technique. RC4 works in two phases. First phase: key scheduling algorithm (KSA) and second phase: pseudo-random generation algorithm (PRGA). In KSA, a state vector table from 1 to 256 bytes is generated. After this, they generate a key stream which is used for XORing with the message. PRGA phase is used to generate an output key stream. However, both phases of RC4 have some weakness, like in the second phase the probability of the zero output byte is high. The proposed method modifies the KSA phase in which the initial input key of "x" bytes is divided into two secret keys, which is then used to generate two subkeys and thus ensuring more robustness against attacks known for RC4.

Brahimi et al. [21] gave a novel method for selective image encryption based on JPEG2000 standard. It encrypts only few code blocks based on some closing boundaries. For increasing the security, a permutation of code blocks has been implemented. For encryption, AES is used in CFB mode. JPEG2000 standard is a wavelet-based coding standard. Because of this, an image can be partitioned into sub-rectangular regions called as tiles, wherein each tile a value is encoded through a wavelet transform. Since this method is a partial encryption technique, so in a stream of tiles only those tiles are encrypted which belong to the selected boundary region. This method is suitable for medical imaging.

6.2.4.2 Frequency Domain

Frequency domain techniques deal with encryption by manipulating the coefficients of wavelet transforms of an image. To organize the image ,high pass and low pass band filters are utilized so that every structure has a unique image. In [22] proposed method, wavelet transform is used, followed by fuzzy C-means, randomization of image, and low and high pass filters used on the input image. A particle swarm optimization-based technique can be used with Daubechies domain [23] for protection. The chaotic map technique is used over a low sub-band of DCT transform, this technique is more aligned with HVS images [9]. A few recent techniques are discussed below:

Younis et al. [22] proposed a method for image encryption in the frequency domain, where they implemented a partial image encryption using fuzzy C-means, clustering during the compression phase and in the encryption step, permutation cipher is used. Permutation includes image reversal, row transposition, column transposition, and block or matrix transposition. Fuzzy C-Means (FCM) is different from C-means. In FCM, a point can belong to two or more regions. Vector quantization is used to generate a codebook, the indexes of codewords are used for compression and transmission. Only the important part of the codebook is encrypted with permutation cipher while the least important part is not encrypted.

Metzler et al. [24] proposed a method for selective region encryption using a non-rectangular region. Regions are identified using the edge detection mechanism, then matrix multiplication is carried out in the regions with a key matrix. Because of this multiplication in the matrix domain, the key space is large.

Sasidharan and Philip [25] suggest a fast-partial image encryption scheme using discrete wavelet transform with RC4 stream cipher. Only the lower frequency matrix or approximation matrix is encrypted using a stream cipher.

Because of the partial image encryption, the time taken for encryption is less and they maintain the high level of security by shuffling the rest of the image using a shuffling algorithm.

Taneja et al. [26] suggested a method which is a combination of both spatial domain and frequency domain. In this method, first the Prewitt edge detector is used on the image for identifying the edges. Then divide the image into non-overlapping blocks based upon detected edges. After that, calculate the number of edge denoting pixels (EDP). For identifying the significant blocks set, compare the EDP with the threshold. The significant block is encrypted using a substitution-diffusion based chaotic cipher and the insignificant module is encrypted using DWT, followed by scrambling and inverse DWT that is used to generate a scrambled block.

6.2.5 Video Encryption Parameter

6.2.5.1 Encryption Ratio

It is the ratio of encrypted data with the original data. The value lies between (0,1]. Lesser the value, better the encryption algorithm is.

6.2.5.2 Visual Degradation

This criterion is a measure of distortion of encrypted video with respect to original video. Some sensitive data demands high visual degradation while for some non-sensitive data, only partial visual degradation works out.

6.2.5.3 Compression Friendliness (CF)

Encryption algorithm leads to some challenges in compression. So, a good algorithm makes very little impact on compression by adding very little or no extra information [27]. An algorithm must not increase the size of the encrypted video with respect to original video size.

6.2.5.4 Speed

For the real-time applications like streaming or audio/video (A/V) conferencing, it is desirable to have a highly efficient algorithm which can compute fast to meet the real-time requirement.

6.2.5.5 Format Compliance

Any standard encoder and decoder can be used without any modification in their code to encode and decode the encrypted bitstream.

6.2.5.6 *Cryptographic Security (CS)*

This parameter tells whether the encrypted video is safe from brute force and different plain text-ciphertext attack. For very sensitive and valuable data, this property is important.

6.2.6 Video Encryption

Video encryption is divided into four main categories:
Figure 6.5 represents the various video encryption techniques.

6.2.6.1 *Fully Layered Encryption*

In this class of algorithm, the whole video is first compressed and then encrypted through AES or DES algorithm. The security is high as these algorithms use AES for encryption. But it's a slow process since the whole video undergoes encryption process. Therefore, this technique is not suitable for real-time applications. A few proposed techniques in this class are discussed below:

Naïve Technique: This method [28] suggests to take a whole moving picture expert group (MPEG) bit stream and encrypt it using AES or DES. The main principle is to treat the bit stream as text data and then encrypt it. This method is secure as it is using AES for every bit in a stream. However, this method is slow on big videos and not applicable for real-time applications. But the compression efficiency is intact in this process because the encryption is carried out after compression (Table 6.2).

6.2.6.2 *Permutation-Based Encryption*

In this class of algorithm, the whole video doesn't go for encryption process, instead permutation algorithms are used for scrambling and encrypting the selected

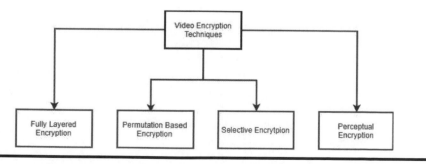

Figure 6.5   Classification of Video Encryption Algorithms.

Table 6.2 Comparative Study of Fully Layered Encryption Techniques

Algorithm Name	Naïve Technique
Visual degradation	High
Encryption ratio	100%
Speed	Slow
Compression friendliness	Satisfied
Format compliance	Unknown
Cryptographic security	Satisfied

part of videos. Some algorithms use a permutation list as part of the secret key. A few techniques in this class are discussed below:

Pure Permutation: This technique is employed when the hardware is decoding a video. This algorithm scrambles bytes within a frame of MPEG stream. But it is vulnerable to known plain text attack by identifying the permutation list that can be generated by comparing known frames with ciphertext [29].

Zig-Zag Permutation: In this technique [30], instead of going to map an 8 * 8 block to 1 * 64 block in a zig-zag manner, we use permutation list-based mapping. Since mapping according to zig-zag and a permutation list leads to the same computational complexity, so this method adds little to no overhead on compression and decompression of video. However, this method is not robust to a known plain text attack. To overcome this attack, two permutation lists are used with a binary coin-flipping sequence method. For every 8 * 8 block, a binary coin is tossed and depending on the outcome a permutation list is used. However, this method now is not robust to ciphertext-only attack.

Huffman Codeword Permutation: This [31] technique combines the compression and encryption phase in MPEG stream. The main aim of this technique is to reduce the computation time by merging compression and encryption phase and maintaining the video compression rate. The secret key is used during the MPEG encoding phase instead of the Huffman codeword list. This step ensures that not all the permutations of the Huffman codeword list can generate a key.

Compression logic based random permutation: This [32] technique used random permutation over a group. Each group contains DCT coefficient of the same frequency regardless of I, P, and B frames (I, P, and B are three major picture types). The random permutation is carried out on the whole video using 64 permutation groups because DCT coefficient can generate 64 groups using 64 frequencies. After this permutation, it is compressed by using standard RLE (run length encoding, in which data is stored in terms

Table 6.3   Comparative Study of Permutation Based Encryption Techniques

Algorithm Name	Pure Permutation	Zig-Zag Permutation	Huffman Codeword	Compression Logic Based Random Permutation
Visual Degradation	High	Unknown	Unknown	Variable
Algorithm Name	Pure permutation	Zig-Zag permutation	Huffman codeword	Compression logic based random permutation
Encryption ratio	100%	100%	Unknown	Variable
Speed	Fast	Fast	Fast	Fast
Compression friendliness	Satisfied	Satisfied	Not satisfied	Satisfied
Format compliance	Unknown	Unknown	Unknown	Satisfied
Cryptographic security	Not satisfied	Not satisfied	Not satisfied	Unknown

of frequency). It is an example of a selective encryption as a small number of blocks are encrypted using the selected permutation group. This method is reliable against brute force attack because of a large keyspace (Table 6.3).

6.2.6.3 Selective Encryption

This class of algorithm selectively encrypts the bytes within a frame. Since it is a class of partial encryption technique, it is fast and computationally not costly. A few techniques in this class are discussed below:

Meyer and Gadegast [33]: This method is used for MPEG stream encryption. Encryption is done using standard RSA or DES algorithm in CBC mode. It deals with four levels of security as follows:

1. Encrypting the header
2. Encrypting all DC and AC lower coefficients
3. Encrypting all I frames, I block in P and B blocks
4. Encrypting the bit stream

If we encrypt the header, then the encryption ratio is very low as compared to encrypting the entire bitstream. The security and computational complexity increase as we move from point "a" to point "d."

Shi and Bhargava [31]: This technique deals with partial encryption at bit level of each DCT coefficient. In this technique, a secret key is used to change DCT coefficient sign bit in MPEG stream. It is computationally fast because of its selective nature and it uses the xor operation between sign bit and secret key. However, this method is vulnerable to plain text attack.

Wu and Kuo [34,35]: This technique is based on energy concentration. The author makes the argument that energy concentration doesn't always mean information concentration in the video. They utilized the technique given by Tang [30] which is the reconstruction of the image by fixing the DC value and recovering the AC coefficient value by choosing plain text attack. They proved that techniques that include orthogonal transform-based compression followed by quantization phase and compression algorithm followed by entropy coder are not a good choice for selective encryption.

Lian et al. [36]: This method is proposed for audio video codec (AVC) scheme. In AVC the data is divided into three main types: intra prediction mode, residue data, and motion vector. Exp-golomb entropy encoding is used to encrypt intra prediction mode, context based adaptive variable length coding is used to encrypt inter macroblocks, and intra macroblock motion vector is encrypted using stream cipher followed by variable length encoding. This scheme is highly sensitive to small changes in the original image; therefore, it is robust against statistical and differential attack (Table 6.4).

Table 6.4　Comparative Study of Selective Encryption Techniques

Algorithm Name	[33,37]	[31,38]	[34,35,39] (MHT)	[34,35,39] (MSI)	[36]
Visual degradation	Variable	High	High	High	High
Encryption ratio	Variable	Unknown	Variable	Low	Unknown
Speed	Variable	Fast	Unknown	Unknown	Fast
Compression friendliness	Satisfied	Satisfied	Satisfied	Satisfied	Unknown
Format compliance	Satisfied over MPEG	Unknown	Not satisfied	Not satisfied	Satisfied
Cryptographic security	Not satisfied	Not satisfied	Not satisfied	Satisfied	Satisfied

6.2.6.4 Perceptual Encryption

This class deals with HVS which states degrade the quality of aural and visual data so that it is barely recognizable in a human visual field. A few techniques in this class are discussed below:

Pazarci et al. [40]: This scheme encrypts the video in RGB space before compression of MPEG2. The method depends upon scrambling in which unauthorized user can have a degraded view. This scrambling is performed prior to MPEG2 compression and thus has few extra overheads on bitstream. The main merit of this scheme is that both encryption and compression phases are entirely different from each other. This scheme is vulnerable to knowing plain text attacks and brute force attacks.

Lian et al. [41,42]: This scheme is proposed for 3D-SPIHT (set partitioning in hierarchal tree) [43] compressed video. Under the controlled quality factor, confusion and diffusion can be implemented by confusing wavelet coefficient, encrypting coefficient sign, and confusing different position of data cubes. This scheme is vulnerable to the chosen plain text attack.

Wang et al. [44]: This scheme is a generalized video encryption algorithm for perceptual encryption for selective encryption of FLC data. FLC data is divided into three main categories:
1. Intra DC coefficients
2. The sign bit of non–intra-AC and DC coefficients
3. The sign bit of residual motion vector

P_{sr}, P_{sd}, and P_{mv} are three control factors that are used, having value in between [0,1] for controlling the quality in three different dimensions, like low-resolution spatial, high-resolution spatial view, and temporal motions. This scheme is robust against known and chosen plain text attack (Table 6.5).

Table 6.5   Comparative Study of Perceptual Encryption Techniques

Algorithm Name	[40]	[41,42]	[44]
Visual degradation	Variable	Variable	Variable
Encryption ratio	Variable	Variable	Variable
Speed	Variable	Variable	Variable
Compression friendliness	Not satisfied	Satisfied	Unknown
Format compliance	Satisfied	Satisfied	Satisfied
Cryptographic security	Not satisfied	Not satisfied	Not satisfied

6.3 Elliptic Curve Cryptography

ECC [45] is a public key cryptography approach over a finite field. It is based on the elliptic curve discrete logarithmic problem, which is NP-hard in nature. ECC is used to create fast, small and efficient cryptographic keys. Instead of using a product of large primes to generate keys in case of AES and DES, ECC uses elliptic curve equations to generate secret keys. Generally, the elliptic curve cryptography equation, defined as elliptic curve over Z_p, $p > 3$, is the set of all pairs $(x, y) \in Z_p$:

$$y^2 = x^3 + ax + b \bmod p \tag{6.15}$$

where $a, b \in Z_p$ and $4a^3 + 27b^2 \neq 0 \bmod p$

Let's take $a = -3$ and $b = 3$, Equation 6.15 will become:

$$y^2 = x^3 - 3x + 3 \tag{6.16}$$

which is represented as:

Figure 6.6 is the graphical representation for Equation 6.16.

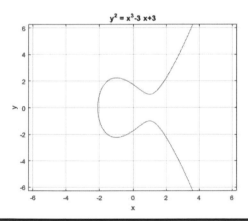

Figure 6.6 Graphical representation of $y^2 = x^3 - 3x + 3$.

Illustration 6.2: This Illustration Shows the Operation on ECC Curve

Operation 1—Summation: Given point P and Q on curve, find $P + Q = R$

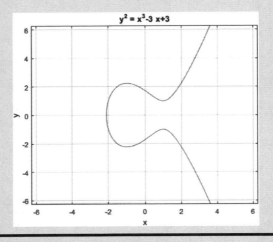

Figure B6.1 **Graphical representation of $y^2 = x^3 - 3x + 3$ with point P and Q.**

Step 1: A line joining P and Q intersect the curve at X which $-R$.

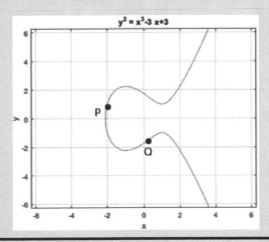

Figure B6.2 **Graphical representation of $y^2 = x^3 - 3x + 3$ with point P, Q, and $-R$.**

Step 2: A mirror image of $-R$ across the x axis gives R.

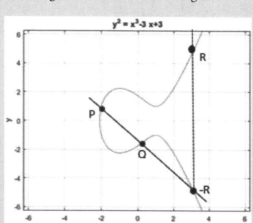

Figure B6.3   Graphical representation of $y^2 = x^3 - 3x + 3$ with point P, Q, $-R$, and its mirror image along X-axis, point R.

The above example signifies the computation efficiency of ECC algorithm with respect to other algorithm where the operations are algebraic and in ECC we can do operations at no cost graphically.

ECC follows closure, associative, identity, and inverse properties of group.

Result 1: Analytical Explanation of Group Operation

Given: $E : y^2 = x^3 + ax + b$, $P = (x_1, y_1)$ and $Q = (x_2, y_2)$
Steps:

1. Find line $L : y = sx + m$ on curve.
   Since line L is on curve E, so it must satisfy it.
   Perform $L = E$

$$(sx + m)^2 = x^3 + ax + b \tag{6.17}$$

$$s^2x^2 + m^2 + 2sxm = x^3 + ax + b \tag{6.18}$$

Now, three solutions exist for Equation 6.18.

$$x_3 = s^2 - x_1 - x_2 \bmod p \tag{6.19}$$

$$y_3 = s(x_1 - x_3) - y_1 \bmod p \tag{6.20}$$

Solving and finding the slope:

$$s = \begin{cases} \dfrac{y_2 - y_1}{x_2 - x_1} \bmod p & \text{if } P \neq Q & \text{Addition} \\[3mm] \dfrac{3x_1^2 + a}{2y_1} \bmod p & \text{if } P = Q & \text{Doubling} \end{cases} \qquad (6.21)$$

Note: This is one of the most important properties that ECC follows, this result will be used in finding the keys.

WORKING OF ECC

Phase 1: Setup
1. Both Alice and Bob agree common ECC equation, let's say:

$$E : y^2 = x^3 + ax + b,$$

And prime elements on this curve (x_p, y_p)

Phase 2: Protocol
1. Alice generates its private key: $a = K_{pt\ A} \in \{2,3,\ldots, \#E - 1\}$ where E is cardinality of group.
2. Bob generates its private key: $b = K_{pt\ B} \in \{2,3,\ldots, \#E - 1\}$ where E is cardinality of group.
3. Alice and Bob generate their public keys using:

$$A = K_{\text{pub}\ A} = a.P = (x_A, y_A) \qquad (6.22)$$

$$B = K_{\text{pub}\ B} = b.P = (x_B, y_B) \qquad (6.23)$$

4. Now both Alice and Bob will generate:

$$a.B = (X_{AB}, Y_{AB}) \qquad (6.24)$$

$$b.A = (X_{AB}, Y_{AB}) \qquad (6.25)$$

5. Message m let's say a video can be encrypted through AES using X_{AB} as a key.

$$C = \text{AES}_{X_{AB}}(m) \qquad (6.26)$$

6. Decryption will be done using the same X_{AB}

$$m = \text{AES}^{-1}{}_{X_{AB}}(C) \qquad (6.27)$$

Note: For calculating $a.P$, $b.P$, $a.B$, and $b.A$ we will use Equation 6.21.

6.3.1 Advantages of ECC Over RSA

The following are the advantages of ECC over RSA.

6.3.1.1 Security

The sub-exponential attack is identified in RSA because of its fast computation of the addition operation. It will not be easy to carry sub-exponential attacks in ECC because of point addition, which is computationally expensive. Therefore, the number of bits required to make RSA key pairs safe is increasing exponentially with respect to the bit required to make key pairing safe in ECC. Jurisic and Menezes [46] studied that to make RSA secure, 1024-bit modulus is required as compared to 160-bit modulus required for ECC (Table 6.6).

Table 6.6   Keys Size Comparison vs. Cracking Time for RSA and ECC

RSA Key Size in Bits	ECC Key Size in Bits	Time to Crack in MIPS-year
512	106	10^4
768	132	10^8
1024	160	10^{11}
2048	210	10^{20}
21000	600	10^{78}

Table 6.7   Comparison of RSA and ECC

Function	ECC-163-bit (in ms)	RSA-1024bit (in ms)
Key generation	3.8	4708.3
Sign	2.1(ECNRA)	228.4
	3.0(ECDSA)	
Verify	9.9(ECNRA)	12.7
	10.7(ECDSA)	

6.3.1.2 Space

Since ECC guarantees to give RSA-like security with low key size, the number of transistors over chip is also less as compared to an RSA encrypted system on chip. However, the bandwidth consumption for both the SoCs (system on chip) will be the same but for a shorter message; ECC SoC performs better because it is fast.

6.3.1.3 Efficiency

ECC and RSA can be modified to run fast by using a smaller exponential in RSA, which can directly impact its security, or by storing the result beforehand in ECC, which directly impacts the space requirement. Certicom, the company behind the ECC, studied the impact of fast ECC and modified RSA (Table 6.7).

Exercise

Exercise 6.1: Hill Cipher—A polygraphic substitution cipher, which uses $m \times m$ invertible matrix in Z_{26} as a secret key. Hill cipher comprises two steps:
Step 1: Encode the message into sequence block of m Z_{26} integers.
Step 2: Separately encrypt each block by using the product with secret matrix.

Recover m and secret key for the following message using known plain text attack.

Message: conversation
Encrypted message: HIARRTNUYTUS

Exercise 6.2: Vigenère cipher—A polyalphabetic substitution cipher, which uses an alphabetic key to encrypt a message. Using vigenère cipher, encrypt the word "*knowledge*" using the key "*books.*"

Exercise 6.3: Data Encryption Algorithm (DES)—A symmetric key algorithm for encryption of electronic data. DES has several modes of operations like ECB, CFB, CBC, OFB, these modes differ in generating ciphertext block from plain text block. Explain all the modes in detail and also sketch the block diagrams for encryption and decryption for each mode.

Exercise 6.4: Show that decryption of b_i and b_{i+1} remains unchanged, if opponent can replace one cipher text block while the decryption of the rest of the block is changed.

Exercise 6.5: Not all DES keys are strong. Weak keys exist if DES_k is an involution where k is a key. Show four weak keys for DES.

Exercise 6.6: Image segmentation uses different kinds of operators for identifying the edges in an image. Write the advantages and disadvantages for each operator and also mention the condition in which the particular operator is used.

Exercise 6.7: Write the advantages and disadvantages for both block selection and pixel selection techniques in images.

Exercise 6.8: Write the conditions in which spatial domain image encryption techniques and frequency domain techniques are used. Give some real-life examples which support your answer.

Exercise 6.9: Write the steps required for surveillance video transfer among two points. Include the steps for encryption, transferring, and decryption of video. Give proper justification for techniques used for the below two scenarios:

Scenario 1: Surveillance video is first stored completely then transferred (non–real-time).

Scenario 2: Surveillance video is encrypted and transferred in real-time with no intermediate data storage unit.

Exercise 6.10: ECC has various advantages over RSA which includes robustness of small key size, faster generation of keys, etc. Discuss the disadvantages of ECC over RSA and give some examples which support your answer.

Bibliography

1. Ibn Wahshiyya's translation of the Ancient Egyptian hieroglyph alphabet. [online]. Available: https://en.wikipedia.org/wiki/Egyptian_hieroglyphs#/media/File:Ibn_Wahshiyya%27s_985_CE_translation_of_the_Ancient_Egyptian_hieroglyph_alphabet.jpg (accessed October 30, 2017).
2. A. A. Soofi, I. Riaz, and U. Rasheed, An enhanced vigenere cipher for data security, *Int. J. Sci. Technol. Res.*, 5(3), 141–145, 2016.
3. B. A. Mohammed Haris, A survey paper on different modification of playfair cipher, *Int. J. Adv. Res. Comput. Sci.*, 8(5).
4. M. Rahman, A. Nordin, A. F. A. Abidin, and M. K. Yusof, Cryptography: A new approach of classical hill cipher, *Int. J. Secur. Appl.*, 7(2), 179–190, 2013.
5. V. Laforet, The hobbit. [online]. Available: https://gizmodo.com/5969817/the-hobbit-an-unexpected-masterclass-in-why-48-fps-fails.
6. K. Jalesh and S. Nirmala, A hybrid approach for enhancing the security of information content of an image, in *Multimedia Processing, Communication and Computing Applications: Proceedings of the First International Conference, ICMCCA*, December 13–15, 2012. P. P. Swamy and D. S. Guru, Eds. New Delhi, India: Springer, 2013, pp. 169–180.
7. N. A. Flayh, R. Parveen, and S. I. Ahson, Wavelet based partial image encryption, in *2009 IEEE International Multimedia, Signal Processing and Communication Technologies*, Aligarh, India, 2009, pp. 32–35.
8. A. K. Yekkala, N. Udupa, N. Bussa, and C. E. V. Madhavan, Lightweight encryption for images, in *2007 Digest of Technical Papers International Conference on Consumer Electronics*, 2007, pp. 1–2.

9. R. Munir, Robustness analysis of selective image encryption algorithm based on arnold cat map permutation, *Proc. 3rd Makassar Int. Conf. Electr. Eng. Informatics*, pp. 1–5, 2012.

10. R. Krishnamoorthi and P. D. S. K. Malarchelvi, Selective combinational encryption of gray scale images using orthogonal polynomials based transformation, *Int. J. Comput. Sci. Netw. Secur.*, 8(5), 195–204, 2008.

11. Y. V Subba Rao, A. Mitra, and S. R. Mahadeva Prasanna, A partial image encryption method with pseudo random sequences, in *Information Systems Security: Second International Conference, ICISS 2006*, Kolkata, India, December 19–21. A. Bagchi and V. Atluri, Eds. Berlin, Germany: Springer, 2006, pp. 315–325.

12. M. A. A. Steffi and D. Sharma, Comparative study of partial encryption of images and video, *Int. J. Mod. Eng. Res.*, 1(1), 179–185, 2011.

13. Y. Ou, C. Sur, and K. H. Rhee, Region-based selective encryption for medical imaging, in *Frontiers in Algorithmics: First Annual International Workshop, FAW 2007*, Lanzhou, China, August 1–3.

14. W. Zhang, K. Wong, H. Yu, and Z. Zhu, A symmetric color image encryption algorithm using the intrinsic features of bit distributions, *Commun. Nonlinear Sci. Numer. Simul.*, 18(3), 584–600, 2013.

15. H. T. Panduranga and S. K. NaveenKumar, Selective image encryption for medical and satellite images, *Int. J. Eng. Technol.*, 5(1), 115–121, 2013.

16. S. Bahrami and M. Naderi, Image encryption using a lightweight stream encryption algorithm, *Adv. Multimed.*, 2012, 1–8, 2012.

17. J.-Y. Oh, D.-I. Yang, and K.-H. Chon, A selective encryption algorithm based on AES for medical information, *Healthc. Inform. Res.*, 16(1), 22, 2010.

18. A. Wong and W. Bishop, Backwards compatible, multi-level Region-of-Interest (ROI) image encryption architecture with biometic authentication, *Int. Conf. Signal Process. Multimed. Appl.*, 324–329, 2007.

19. F. Dufaux, S. J. Wee, J. G. Apostolopoulos, and T. Ebrahimi, JPSEC for secure imaging in JPEG 2000, in *Applications of Digital Image Processing XXVII*, A. G. Tescher, Ed. SPIE, November 2004.

20. P. Kumar and P. K. Pateriya, RC4 enrichment algorithm approach for selective image encryption, *Int. J. Comput. Sci. Commun. Networks*, 2(2), 181–189, 2012.

21. Z. Brahimi, H. Bessalah, A. Tarabet, and M. K. Kholladi, A new selective encryption technique of JPEG2000 codestream for medical images transmission, in *2008 5th International Multi-Conference on Systems, Signals and Devices*, 2008, pp. 1–4.

22. H. A. Younis, T. Y. Abdalla, and A. Y. Abdalla, Vector quantization techniques for partial encryption of wavelet-based compressed digital images, *Iraqi J. Electr. Electron. Eng.*, 5(1), 74–89, 2009.

23. K. Kuppusamy and K. Thamodaran, Optimized partial image encryption scheme using PSO, in *International Conference on Pattern Recognition, Informatics and Medical Engineering* (*PRIME-2012*), 2012, pp. 236–241.

24. R. E. L. Metzler and S. S. Agaian, Selective region encryption using a fast shape adaptive transform, in *2010 IEEE International Conference on Systems, Man and Cybernetics*, 2010, pp. 1763–1770.

25. S. Sasidharan and D. S. Philip, A fast partial encryption scheme with wavelet transform and RC4, *Int. J. Adv. Eng. Technol.*, 1(4), pp. 322–331, 2011.

26. N. Taneja, B. Raman, and I. Gupta, Combinational domain encryption for still visual data, *Multimed. Tools Appl.*, 59(3), 775–793, 2012.

27. A. Kulkarni, S. Kulkarni, K. Haridas, and A. More, Proposed video encryption algorithm v/s other existing algorithms: A comparative study, *arXiv Prepr. arXiv1303.3485*, 65(1), 5, 2013.

28. S. Lian, *Multimedia Content Encryption: Techniques and Applications*. Boston, MA: Auerbach Publications.

29. A. J. Slagell and A. J. Slagell, Known-plaintext attack against a permutation based video encryption algorithm, *Security*, pp. 1–10, 2004.

30. L. Tang, Methods for encrypting and decrypting MPEG video data efficiently, in *Proceedings of the fourth ACM International Conference on Multimedia - MULTIMEDIA'96*, 1996, pp. 219–229.

31. C. Shi and B. Bhargava, A fast MPEG video encryption algorithm, in *Proceedings of the Sixth ACM International Conference on Multimedia - MULTIMEDIA'98*, 1998, pp. 81–88.

32. H. Wang and C. Xu, A new lightweight and scalable encryption algorithm for streaming video over wireless networks. pp. 180–185, 2007.

33. J. Meyer and F. Gadegast, *Security Mechanisms for Multimedia Data with the Example MPEG-1 Video*, Berlin, Germany: Technical University of Berlin, 1995.

34. C. Wu and C.-C. J. Kuo, Fast encryption methods for audiovisual data confidentiality, in *Multimedia Systems and Applications III, Ser. Proc. SPIE*, 2000, pp. 284–295.

35. C. Wu and C.-C. J. Kuo, Efficient multimedia encryption via entropy codec design, in *IS&T/SPIE 13th Annual Symposium on Electronic Imaging, Proceedings of SPIE*, 2001, pp. 128–138.

36. S. Lian, Z. Liu, Z. Ren, and H. Wang, Secure advanced video coding based on selective encryption algorithms, *IEEE Trans. Consum. Electron.*, 52(2), 621–629, 2006.

37. L. Qiao and K. Nahrstedt, A new algorithm for MPEG video encryption, in *Proceedings of The First International Conference on Imaging Science, Systems, and Technology (CISST'97)*, 1997, pp. 21–29.

38. C. Shi and B. Bhargava, An efficient MPEG video encryption algorithm, in *Proceedings Seventeenth IEEE Symposium on Reliable Distributed Systems (Cat. No.98CB36281)*, pp. 381–386.

39. D. W. Gillman and R. L. Rivest, On breaking a Huffman code, *IEEE Trans. Inf. Theory*, 42(3), 972–976, 1996.

40. M. Pazarci and V. Dipcin, A MPEG2-transparent scrambling technique, in *IEEE Transactions on Consumer Electronics*, 48(2), 345–355, 2002.

41. S. Lian, X. Wang, J. Sui, and Z. Wang, Perceptual cryptography on wavelet-transform encoded videos, in *Proceedings of 2004 International Symposium on Intelligent Multimedia, Video and Speech Processing*, 2004, pp. 57–60.

42. S. Lian, J. Sun, and Z. Wang, Perceptual cryptography on JPEG2000 compressed images or videos, in *The Fourth International Conference on Computer and Information Technology, 2004. CIT'04*, pp. 78–83.

43. B. J. Kim, Z. Xiong, and W. A. Pearlman, Low bit-rate scalable video coding with 3-D set partitioning in hierarchical trees (3-D SPIHT), *IEEE Trans. Circuits Syst. Video Technol.*, 10(8), 1374–1387, 2000.

44. C. Wang, H.-B. Yu, and M. Zheng, A DCT-based MPEG-2 transparent scrambling algorithm, *IEEE Trans. Consum. Electron.*, 49(4), 1208–1213, 2003.

45. V. Kapoor, V. S. Abraham, and R. Singh, Elliptic curve cryptography, *Ubiquity*, 2008, 1–8, 2008.

46. A. Jurisic and A. J. Menezes, *Guide to Elliptic Curve Cryptography*, vol.19, pp. 173–193, Springer, 2004.

Chapter 7

Security of Scalable Video Coding: Encryption and Authentication

Zhuo Wei, Swee Won Lo, Yongdong Wu,
Yanjiang Yang, Zheng Yan and Robert H. Deng

Contents

DOI: 10.1201/9780429435461-8

7.1 Scalable Video Coding

Digital video is pervasive and has applications in diversified areas such as remote education, telemedicine, surveillance, IP TV and video-on-demand. In order to cater for heterogeneous networks and various terminal devices, many video coding schemes (e.g., [1,2]) have been designed. However, few of them are widely deployed due to low compression efficiency and/or non-scalability. Fortunately, after at least 20 years of research and experiments, SVC (Scalable Video Coding) [3,4] was finally adopted as an international standard for video coding in 2007. Generally speaking, due to its high improvement in coding efficiency and scalability, SVC is attractive in today's ubiquitous networking environments.

SVC possess the so called "compress once, decompress many times" properties, hence it automatically adapts to network bandwidth as well as capabilities of end user devices. For the sake of scalability, Internet-based multimedia content dissemination increasingly resorts to autonomous proxies to distribute, transcode and aggregate information from content servers to end users, Where multimedia content security play a critical role so as to achieve the following goals: (i) to safeguard end-to-end content authenticity of multimedia streams throughout the entire lifecycle of content delivery; (ii) to enforce end-to-end access control of multimedia streams throughout the entire lifecycle of content generation, delivery and aggregation; (iii) to preserve the content authenticity and confidentiality in the presence of transmission errors and packet losses; and (iv) to extend the above solutions into the mobile computing environment where the end user devices are mobile and resource-constrained and the communication links subject to non-stationary transmission errors and packet losses.

7.1.1 Structure of SVC Bitstream

According to the specification of H.264/SVC standard [3,5], an SVC bitstream consists of one base layer and one or more enhancement layers. The base layer includes the fundamental information of the video while enhancement layers supply more data for video resolution, frame rate and picture quality.

As shown in Figure 7.1, an SVC bitstream is divided into NALUs (Network Abstract Layer Units). Each NALU has a header which includes forbidden zero bit (F), NRI (nal_ref_idc) signalling importance and a NALU type. The NALUs can be classified into Non-VCL NALU and VCL (Video Coding Layer) NALU. A Non-VCL NALU has an auxiliary payload field for decoding (e.g., SVC header in prefix NALU) or facilitating certain system operations (e.g., supplement enhancement information [SEI]), while a VCL NALU has a payload field for the compressed visual data. The VCL NALU has two kinds of structures. One has an SVC header itself, while another is paired with a prefix Non-VCL NALU whose auxiliary payload is an SVC header. The SVC header includes PRID (Priority id), DID (Dependency id), QID (Quality id), TID (Temporal id) indicating three scalability dimensions respectively, which decides the layer of NALU. By ordering NALUs based on PRID, DID, QID and TID in different ways, the SVC bitstream has different representation but the same visual content.

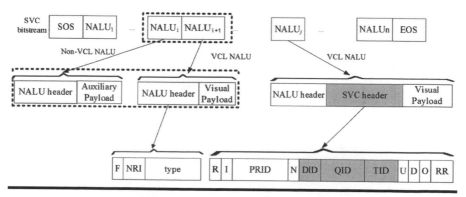

Figure 7.1   **The structure of base layer, enhancement layer and PACSI NALU.**

7.1.2 Scalability

An SVC bitstream consists of a low-quality video sub-bitstream as well as one or more supplement sub-bitstreams. Due to the flexible arrangement of NALUs, SVC provides three kinds of scalabilities, as depicted in Figure 7.2. These scalability properties enable an SVC-aware router to reduce the bit-rate directly without decoding the bitstream so as to meet the requirements of network bandwidth and/or end user devices' capabilities.

There are four temporal layers, two spatial layers, and three quality layers.

Temporal scalability: Temporal enhancement layer defines the various numbers of pictures per second, which is hierarchical P- or B-pictures, and logically organizes the bitstream into a hierarchy of images. The temporal base layer should be coded with highest fidelity since they are used as references for motion-compensated prediction of pictures for all temporal layers; the enhancement layers use a larger quantization parameter because the quality of these pictures influences fewer pictures. Thus, when an SVC-aware router discards some picture (e.g., B-pictures) data directly without decoding the bitstream, it produces a lower bit-rate SVC bitstream.

Spatial scalability: SVC spatial scalability means that its base layer represents a video of low spatial resolution, and the enhancement layers increase the spatial resolution of the video. As there are inter-layer prediction mechanisms for the sake of coding efficiency, a lower layer must be present if a higher layer exists, but the lower layer does not need the higher layers at the decoder side. Therefore, when the highest layer is discarded, the rest of layers are still able to be decoded. This discarding process can be repeated until only one layer remains. In other words, the spatial resolution of an SVC bitstream can be decreased directly without decoding the bitstream.

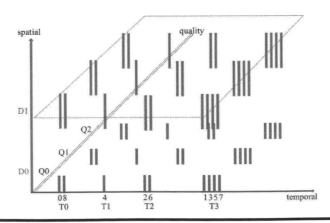

Figure 7.2 An example architecture of H.264/SVC three dimensions.

Quality scalability: Quality scalability means that the quality base layer is coded at a low visual quality, and the quality enhancement layers increase the visual quality of the decoded sequence. Therefore, when the highest quality layer is discarded, the rest of quality layers are still able to be decoded. This discarding process can be repeated until only one quality layer remains.

7.1.3 Security Requirements

When a video stream is disseminated over an open network, an adversary is able to eavesdrop the content. A naive way to thwart the adversary is to treat the video stream as non-structural data, encrypt the bitstream as a whole, and distribute the encrypted bitstream. However, this naive approach is not suitable for secure SVC delivery over heterogeneous networks because the protected bitstream lose the scalability features. Thus, encryption schemes for H.264/SVC should satisfy the following properties:

- Security: Encrypted streams are unperceptive after reconstruction.
- Integrity: An authentication scheme aims to thwart any unauthorized manipulations by verifying the integrity and source of data.
- Scalability: Encrypted streams preserve end-to-end scalability for delivery.
- Format-compliant: Encrypted streams are compliant to the specific syntax of H.264/SVC and are compatible to the standard H.264/SVC decoder.
- Computational complexity: Encryption and decryption should incur limited computational resource and time.
- Compression overhead: Encryption should have no or little effect on compression efficiency.

7.1.4 Architecture

The remainder of this chapter is organized as follows. Section 7.2 gives the analysis and evaluation of scalable video coding. Sections 7.3 and 7.4 describe encryption and authentication schemes for scalable video coding, respectively. We draw a conclusion in Section 7.5.

7.2 Security Analysis and Evaluation of Scalable Video Coding

This Section will figure out the security requirements of scalable video coding from different scalabilities, i.e., encryption and authentication, and analyze the performance of partial encryption algorithms and content-based authentication algorithms.

7.2.1 Confidentiality and Performance Analysis on H.264/SVC Partial Encryption

Scalable video streaming techniques, such as MPEG-4 FGS [6], H.264/SVC [3,4], are widely used in real time content distribution due to their adaptability to a variety of heterogeneous network and platform settings. Accompanying the growth of such techniques is the conflicting requirements between the protection of content confidentiality and the demand for lightweight computation on the content sender and receivers. *Partial encryption* or *selective encryption* is one of the widely adopted approaches to achieve a balance between security and performance. Examples of partial encryption techniques include [7–17]. In contrast to *full encryption* algorithms whereby all content data are encrypted, *partial encryption* algorithms only encrypt those data which are considered important, e.g., the SVC base layers or intra-coded block, and ignore other data. By reducing the amount of encryption operations, partial encryption algorithms aim to reduce the overhead without undermining the security. The argument for the security of partial encryption is that those plaintext data (e.g., enhancement layers) do not leak sensitive information to adversaries as long as they cannot decrypt the base layers.

Unlike several works [18–21] which discusses the security of partial encryption for MPEG-4 SVC, with the focus on the temporal layers, this work systematically investigates the security of partial encryption for H.264/SVC from all three scalability dimensions, i.e., the spatial, quality and temporal scalability. Our experiment results show that partial encryption fails to strike the desired balance because it does not offer the satisfactory security strength for confidentiality protection. To gain more insights, we further investigate the relationship between confidentiality and scalability of H.264/SVC in the light of scalable coding techniques, and conclude that all layers have to be encrypted for confidential video streams.

7.2.1.1 Related Works

In [20], Yu gave an overview of scalable encryption schemes which summarize previous works on selective encryption, format compliant encryption, and progressive encryption on scalable multimedia. At the same time, the article concluded that only a part of the entire bitstream is encrypted while the rest are left in clear. Further, Yu addressed the advantages of scalable encryption for wireless multimedia communication and presented improvement on scalability via progressive encryption. Zhu et al. described in [18] the general requirements and desirable features of an encryption system for scalable multimedia, such as encrypted content leakage (perceptibility), security and scalability, and presented a survey of the current state-of-the-art technologies in scalable encryption and analyzed the performances (leakage, overhead, and complexity) of encryption schemes for scalable multimedia (JPEG2000 and MPEG-4 FGS). The article concluded that naive encryption algorithm is inappropriate for encryption of scalable code stream because scalability is completely removed. Meanwhile, after reviewing selective encryption on JPEG2000 and MPEG-4 FGS, the authors pointed out a selective encryption usually leaks some information of the encrypted content and is insecure, and encryption of the base layer of MPEG-4 FGS alone may be unacceptable in some applications.

In [22], Kunkelmann and Horn gave a brief overview of the concept, desirable feature and possible attacks on multimedia encryption. Before the description of prototype for multimedia encryption, the article introduced the symmetric key encryption (block and stream cipher) and cryptanalysis. They also discussed the desirable requirement, characteristics and attacks of multimedia encryption. In addition, the authors classed them as total encryption, selective encryption, perceptual encryption, joint compression encryption, format compliant encryption, and scalable encryption. For scalable encryption, they reviewed various scalable encryption techniques of JPEG2000 and MPEG-4 FGS and showed that some of them have problems of content leakage if selective encryption is employed. Lian [21] described the partial encryption in which the performance, such as security, encryption efficiency, compression efficiency, and format compliance were analyzed and compared, and showed that some partial encryption schemes were not secure enough due to partitioning and part selection. Meanwhile, he also classified scalable encryption with layered encryption, layered and progressive encryption, progressive encryption and scalable encryption according to the scalable property.

7.2.1.2 Review on Partial Encryption

Partial encryption is to preserve multimedia property (e.g., format-compliance, scalability) by treating different data in a multimedia stream differently according to their importance. The basic idea is that the critical data are encrypted rigorously but the non-critical data are weakly protected or even not protected. The implementation of this idea varies with the scalable media type and the dimension of scalability as described in this section. Scalable video coding includes wavelet-based SVC, MPEG-4 FGS, and H.264/SVC. Based on the granularity of scalability used in the partial encryption schemes, SVC is classified into spatial/quality and temporal levels. In the spatial and quality scalability category, encryption algorithms treat the base layer and the enhancement layers (typically in spatial/quality scalability) differently. For wavelet-based SVC, a sub-band–adaptive approach to scramble surveillance video content (scalable video coding with JPEG XR) is proposed in [7,8], which scrambles DC and LP (low pass) sub-bands, but only inverts the signs of coefficients for HP (high pass) sub-bands and leaves Flex bits sub-bands in the clear. Unlike wavelet-based SVC, MPEG-4 FGS and H.264/SVC bitstreams are composed of a base layer and one or multiple scalable enhancement layers. Partial encryption algorithms for MPEG-4 FGS and H.264/SVC typically apply a strong cipher for the base layer and use selective encryption or even no encryption for the enhancement layers. For instance, in [9] the based layer is encrypted by the Chain and Sum cipher and the sign bits of discrete cosine transform (DCT) coefficients in enhancement layer are masked with a random sequence. The schemes in [23–25] encrypt an H.264/SVC base layer's intra prediction mode, the motion vector difference values and some sign bits of the texture data. Quality scalability can also be achieved using DCT coefficients, whereby low frequency coefficients represent the base layer and the middle or high frequency coefficients represent the enhancement layers. The idea of partial encryption is realized by encrypting DC or low frequency AC coefficients while the high frequency AC coefficient encryption being dismissed. For example, as proposed in [13], the first five coefficients and the subsequent fifteen coefficients are encrypted as the base layer and the middle layer respectively, while the remaining coefficients and high layer are in the clear. On temporal scalability, a compressed video sequence is composed of I, P, and B frames, where the latter two are temporal enhancement layers in scalable video coding. Partial encryption algorithms at the temporal scalability are based on the observation that P frames and B frames are not meaningful when rendered without the corresponding I-frame. Typically, this type of algorithm provides a strong security for I frames while ignoring P and B frame protection. For example, Hong et al. [25] proposed an encryption scheme for temporal scalable video coding whereby the motion vectors and residual coefficients of P or B frames are plaintext. Meanwhile, Li et al. [15] proposed an encryption scheme for H.264/SVC at the NAL level. For all the NAL units, Instantaneous Decoding Refresh (IDR) Picture, Sequence Parameter Set (SPS), and Picture Parameter Set (PPS) are encrypted with a stream cipher. However, the scheme in [15] has no protection over other temporal enhancement NALs.

7.2.1.3 Evaluation of Partial Encryption

In the scalable video experiments to systematically understand the security implication of partial encryption, ten standard benchmark video sequences1 are chosen in order to cover different combinations of video characteristics including motion (fast/slow, an/zoom/rotation), color (bright/dull), contrast (high/low), and object type (vehicle, buildings, people). Bus and Foreman video sequences are of no camera motion while Football and Soccer demonstrate camera panning and zooming with object motion and background texture. Bridge-far and Bridge-close show images with smooth motion. Highway is a sequence of fast motion while Silent is a static sequence except of a person's right hand. Mobile and Hall sequences display a still complex background with foreground motion. All these sequences are encoded with the temporal, spatial and quality enhancement layers. Each GOP (group of picture) includes 16 frames and the I-frame Interval is set as **32**. In the experiments, the base layers of an original SVC video sequence are removed so as to simulate the effect that an adversary acquires no semantic information from a properly encrypted based layer. Then, the remaining SVC enhancement layers are decoded using the default prediction mode and checked as to whether they leak semantic information about the video. A certain weak encryption (e.g., sign encryption) is applied to the enhancement layers. The experiments are implemented with JSVM 9.19 [26].

7.2.1.3.1 Spatial Scalability

The spatial enhancement layer utilizes inter-layer prediction mechanisms [3]. In order to increase compression efficiency, it only transmits the residual signals. In the spatial scalability experiments, we set the frames of the base layer as blank when decoding the enhancement layers. For all ten sequences in testing, I-frames of the enhancement layers are decoded, and they all reveal sufficient texture information of the objects in the sequences. For example, Figure 7.3b illustrates content leakage of enhancement layer for the *Mobile* sequence. The 10 experimental results also indicate some textures are easier to recognize, such as face, non-overlap objects, and the leakage becomes more evident when the video stream (only containing enhancement layers) is played.

7.2.1.3.2 Quality Scalability

When inter-layer prediction for CGS (coarse grain scalability) of H.264/SVC is used, a refinement of texture information is typically achieved by re-quantizing the residual texture signal of the enhancement layer with a smaller quantization step size relative to that used in the reference layer. In the CGS scalability experiments, the images of the reference layer are set as blank, meanwhile, motion vectors are all set as zero. The experiment sets QP (quantization parameter) of the base layer as **34** and sets QP of the enhancement layers from **24** to **32**. Non-overlap texture of images can easily produce leakage in the enhancement layer. QP difference also affects the amount of leakage. Sensitive contents of all ten sequences can be detected if the decoded images of the enhancement layer are continuously played. Figure 7.3c and d show data leakage of *Mobile* for QP **32** and QP **24**. Partial encryption on MGS (medium grain scalability) enhancement layers is not secure either, though the layering techniques are different with CGS. MGS layers are generally parts of CGS as MGS and CGS take the same QP. Each MGS layer is composed of a portion of frequency coefficients of 4×4 DCT to supplement quality enhancement for base layer. We set the transform coefficients with different MGS layers based on the zigzag order (important and unimportant). In our MGS experiments, there are three MGS layers: (1) MGS0: first three coefficients, set other coefficients

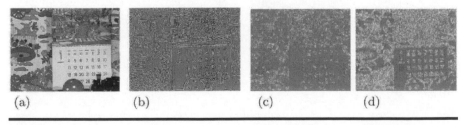

(a)   (b)   (c)   (d)

Figure 7.3 Partial encryption of the mobile sequence: (a) Original stream, (b) Spatial enhancement layer only, (c) CGS with QP 32, and (d) CGS with QP 24.

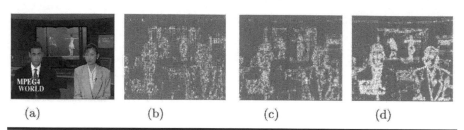

(a) (b) (c) (d)

Figure 7.4 Experiment as MGS scalability layers for News sequence. (a) The original image of base layer; (b) to (d) MGS layers corresponding to images which only contain parts of coefficients of enhancement layers.

with zero; (2) MGS1: the 3rd to the 5th coefficients, set other coefficients with zero; (3) MGS2: the 6th to the 15th coefficients set other coefficients with zero.

Similar to CGS, the QP difference between the enhancement layer and the reference layer affects the amount of disclosure. Moreover, the content of each MGS layer is related to non-zero coefficients which depend on texture feature. For example, Figure 7.4 illustrates the first decoded images corresponding to different MGS layers for *News* sequence. For all the MGS layers, the profile of two speakers is apparent and the dancers on the TV can be easily viewed when being continuously played.

7.2.1.3.3 Temporal Scalability

The temporal enhancement layer depends on inter prediction technique, which uses a range of block sizes from **16 × 16** to **4 × 4** to predict pixels in the current frame from similar regions in previous frames. These previously coded frames may occur before or after the current frame in display. We encode the ten video sequences with four temporal scalability layers, set the images between the temporal layer 0 to the temporal layer 2 as blank, define motion vectors as zero, and then only decode the temporal layer 3. Experimental results indicate that the temporal enhancement layer of the motion sequence scan causes significant information leakage. However, the temporal enhancement layers of static sequences, such as ***Bridge-close***, ***Bridge-far***, generally have less residual and cause small leakage. Figure 7.5a illustrates the 26th frame of the *Hall* sequence in which the person's profile can clearly detected.

7.2.1.4 Summary

The partial encryption may result in multimedia leakage which can be summarized in all three scalabilities.

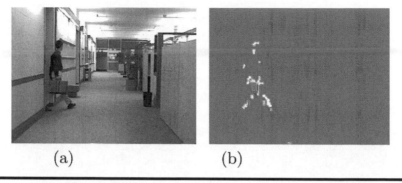

(a)   (b)

Figure 7.5 Experimental results of temporal scalability: (a) Base layer and (b) enhancement layer.

Spatial scalability: In all types of video sequences and an arbitrary QP difference between the reference layer and enhancement layer, the image of spatial scalability always leaks the visual content. The larger the QP difference is, the more content for video sequences are exposed.

- Quality Scalability: Similar to the spatial scalability, the quality scalability is affected by the QP difference. In addition to that, other factors also lead to the exposure.
- Coarse Grain Scalability: The image features, such as texture, shape and edge, lead to –content exposure. The richer the features are, the more data are leaked in the enhancement layers.

Medium Grain Scalability: MGS layers may consist of low frequency, middle frequency, or high frequency DCT coefficients, whose leakage are related to the image features. A richer feature image will contain more non-zero coefficients such that each MGS layer may disclose more information.

Temporal Scalability: The motion feature determines the amount of leakage from the temporal scalability layers. Obviously, more intense motions result in more leakage in the enhancement layers.

7.2.1.5 Conclusion

In this article, we investigate whether partial encryption in H.264/SVC can protect data confidentiality. The experiments show that the unencrypted enhancement layers leak significant context information about the video stream, from all three scalability dimensions. We also analyzed the coding techniques for spatial, quality and temporal scalabilities, and showed that the coding techniques in use determined that those enhancement layers have to be encrypted for the confidentiality purpose, although partial encryption may be sufficient for access control in the sense of deterring unauthorized access to the high quality video.

7.2.2 On Security of Content-Based Video Stream Authentication

This section surveys and classifies existing transform-domain CBA (Content-based authentication) schemes for videos into two categories and points out that, in contrary to CBA for images, there exists a common design flaw in these schemes. We present the principles (based on video coding concept) on how the flaw can be exploited to mount semantic-changing attacks in the transform domain that cannot be detected by existing CBA schemes. We show the attack examples including content removal, modification and insertion attacks. Noting that these CBA schemes are designed at the macro block level, we discuss, from the attacker's point of view, the conditions in attacking content based authenticated macroblocks.

7.2.2.1 The H.264 Video Coding Standard

Most video coding standards including MPEG-2, MPEG-4, and H.264 achieve compression by identifying similarities in the spatial (within frame) and the temporal (between frames) dimensions. In the H.264 standard, a prediction model takes as input a raw video frame and outputs a residual frame. The raw frame is first partitioned into units (each of size 16 × 16 pixels) called macroblocks, which may be further partitioned into 16 (4 × 4) blocks. Given a raw macroblock **Ori**, the prediction model searches for the most perceptually similar macroblock within a searchable region, i.e., neighbouring macroblocks in the same frame (intra prediction) or in adjacent frames (inter-prediction), and uses the most similar macroblock as reference to generate a prediction macroblock **Pred**. The prediction macroblock is (pixel-wise) subtracted from the raw macroblock to obtain the residual macroblock Res as in (1). The residual macroblock is then transformed, quantized and entropy encoded to the bitstream domain.

Figure 7.6 shows the syntax of an H.264 macroblock. In this figure, parameter type indicates whether the macroblock is intra- or inter-predicted. Each (intra/inter) macroblock can be partitioned into sub-blocks of different sizes, which is conveyed by the parameter partition size. For an intra macroblock, prediction mode conveys the Directional Prediction Mode (DPM) indicating the location of reference macroblock(s)

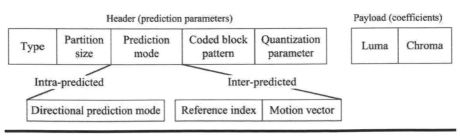

Figure 7.6   The syntax elements of a H.264 macroblock.

and the method of generating prediction macroblock; for an inter macroblock, this parameter conveys the reference frame index pointing to a previously-decoded frame and the Motion Vector (MV) indicating the displacement of the reference macroblocks from the raw macroblock. Coded Block Pattern (CBP) indicates the existence of non-zero coefficients in the macroblock, followed by the QP. We collectively refer to these prediction parameters as the macroblock header. The quantized luma and chroma coefficients are referred to as the macroblock payload.

At the decoder, the decoded macroblock **Dec** is obtained as in (2) after reconstructing the prediction macroblock **Pred***(using the macroblock header) and the residual macroblock **Res***(using the macroblock payload). Note that for a non-tampered macroblock, the quantity α is due to lossy compression and is negligible, and **Dec** is perceptually similar to **Ori**. We can also observe an interdependent relationship between the macroblock header and payload from (2).

$$\text{Encoder} : \text{Res} = \text{Ori} - \text{Pred} \tag{7.1}$$

$$\text{Decoder} : \text{Dec} = \text{Pred}^* + \text{Res}^* = \text{Ori} + \alpha \tag{7.2}$$

7.2.2.2 Common Design Flaw in Existing Content-Based Video Authentication Schemes

The common flaw of existing transform-domain CBA schemes is that the feature extracted is insufficient to truly represent the video semantic. This is because they did not take into account the interdependent relationship between prediction parameters in the macroblock header with the coefficients in the macroblock payload. Nonetheless, attacks performed in the transform domain can change the video semantic, and are also undetectable by the CBA schemes, by exploiting the relationship as follows.

7.2.2.2.1 Exploiting the Flaw in Payload-Protected Schemes

Unlike images where image pixels were directly transformed and quantized [27], a video's macroblock coefficients convey the relationship between the macroblock pixel content and its prediction macroblock, i.e., the residual macroblock **Res**. If an attacker finds an attack prediction macroblock **Pred'** to replace the original prediction macroblock **Pred***, the targeted macroblock **Dec** could be modified to the attacker's desired attack macroblock **Dec'** (see (2)). Hereafter, we base our discussion at the (4 × 4)-block level since it is the smallest coding unit.

To find an attack prediction block, an attacker proceeds as follows. Firstly, the attacker identifies the "searchable region" and the candidate reference blocks that generate the suitable **Pred"** to obtain **Dec'**. In intra-prediction, the searchable region is the four neighbouring blocks (left, top-left, above, and top-right of) the targeted block whereas in inter-prediction, the searchable region is within an area centering on the targeted block [28] to replace **Pred*** with **Pred'**, modify the prediction mode (e.g., DPM, MV and reference frame index) of the targeted block **Dec**.

In some cases, it is possible that a suitable **Pred'** is unavailable. If so, a work-around that indirectly modifies the residual block **Res** without being detected by payload-protected schemes can be performed using the effect of QP. Concretely, at the encoder, a larger QP in forward quantization removes insignificant coefficients; at the decoder, given a set of coefficients, a larger QP in inverse quantization magnifies the residual samples whereas a smaller QP suppresses the samples. If a decoder receives a corrupted QP, inverse quantization results in a different set of coefficients that may misrepresent the residual samples in **Res**. Note that this cannot be detected by payload-protected schemes because the magnifying/suppressing happens during the decoding process, which is only executed after integrity verification. Having different QPs across macroblocks in a frame is not uncommon; macroblock-layer rate control in H.264 has been proven to improve coding efficiency [29] whereas earlier standards (e.g., MPEG-4) and the H.264 High Profile allow different QPs for DC and AC coefficients [30,31].

If the targeted macroblock spans across targeted and non-targeted content, it is more complicated to modify the prediction mode because the attacker needs to find a suitable attack prediction macroblock of the same size that changes only the targeted content while keeping the non-targeted content intact. By modifying the macroblock *partition size*, the targeted macroblock can be partitioned into sub-blocks, such that the targeted content is isolated in a sub-block, and then perform a search for the suitable attack prediction sub-block thereof.

Remarks. Attacks on payload-protected schemes involve replacing the original prediction block with an attack prediction block in order to change the content of a targeted block. Given the searchable region which is constrained in one frame (intra frames) or within the same video (inter frames), arbitrary content insertion attacks cannot be realized. However, content removal and modification attacks are possible as shown in Section 7.2.2.3. We also note that prediction mode parameters such as DPM, MV and reference frame index are encoded differentially between successive blocks. If these parameters are changed, it may affect the corresponding parameter of subsequent (targeted/non-targeted) blocks, causing them to use a wrong/different prediction block for decoding. This may result in error propagation that occurs in the form of visual distortion on the decoded frame. In Section 7.2.2.3, we show an example of such error propagation, and show that the visual distortion can be corrected to a certain degree by either restoring the prediction mode of affected blocks, or by restricting the choice of prediction block to a more suitable one.

7.2.2.2.2 Exploiting the Flaw in Header-Protected Schemes

Although header protected schemes can detect both content-preserving and semantic-changing manipulations; they are more insecure compared to payload-protected schemes. Since the payload represents the residual block with samples that are integers ranging from −255 to +255, an attacker can perform a simple but powerful attack using reverse engineering. Since the verifier has no prior information about the original block, an attacker can replace them with a new block with different content **Dec** and compute the new residual block **Res** such that **Res** = **Dec** − **Pred**, where **Pred** is the original prediction block. The attacker then performs forward transform and quantization to obtain a new set of transform coefficients, replacing the original coefficients in the payload.

7.2.2.2.3 Complying with Watermark Extraction

Apart from ensuring that the transform-domain attacks do not alter the authenticated features, it is also vital for the protection scheme to ensure that the tampered data obeys the watermark extraction rule. Watermark extraction includes: extract location identification and extraction based on extraction rules. Although random extraction locations are deemed vital for security reason [32], we argue that it is more important for copyright protection where the attack objective is to find and destroy the watermark; a successful attack in our approach depends more heavily on complying with the watermark extraction rules. For verification efficiency, existing CBA schemes perform extraction by evaluating either the LSB or zero/non-zero coefficients. Such characteristics can always be engineered in the coefficients or MVs. Since DPMs can be categorized into sets generating similar prediction blocks [33], an attacker can select DPMs within the same set to satisfy the even/odd evaluation.

7.2.2.3 *Attack Examples on Existing CBA Schemes*

In this section, we demonstrate transform-domain attack examples that can be applied on each category of CBA schemes as discussed in Section 7.2.2.2. More specifically, we show content removal and content modification attacks on payload protected schemes, and content insertion attack on header-protected schemes. Our attacks are implemented using the JM reference software [26]. We emulate the attacker's interception and replacement of macroblock stream by modifying the decoder's "read" data. The video sequences used in our attacks are the 352 × 288 News, Bridge and Waterfall sequences [34] and a 384 × 288 surveillance sequence [35], all encoded in IBBBBBBBP format with QP = 28 for intra frames and QP = 30 for inter frames.

7.2.2.3.1 Content Removal Attacks

A content removal attack is the act of replacing an object with its background information. Figure 7.7a shows the first frame of the Bridge sequence. In this example, it is sufficient to modify the DPMs of targeted blocks, i.e., the left pier, to use the background information, i.e., the river, as attack prediction blocks. The result of the removal attack is shown in Figure 7.7b. In this case, QP manipulation is not needed

(a)   (b)

Figure 7.7   Content removal attack on bridge sequence: (a) Original frame and (b) attacked frame.

because the original prediction blocks are obtained from the top of the targeted blocks and they are semantically similar, thus, the residual blocks have samples of small magnitude. Replacing the original prediction blocks with the attack prediction blocks on the left (i.e., the river) replaces the content of the targeted blocks with the content of the attack prediction blocks.

7.2.2.3.2 Content Modification Attacks

Figure 7.8b shows the timing information extracted from a surveillance frame in Figure 7.8a. This timing information is encoded using 16×16 macroblocks, where the upper half of each macroblock covers the timing information (targeted) while the lower half covers the surveillance background (non-targeted). Tampering with the reference frame index will affect *both* the timing information and the surveillance background. By manipulating the *partition size* parameter such that each targeted 16×16 macroblock is partitioned into sixteen 4×4 blocks, the targeted content is isolated from the non-targeted content. The reference frame index of the targeted blocks can then be modified independently without affecting the non-targeted blocks. Figure 7.8c shows the result of this attack; when the attacked frames are inserted into the video sequence, a scrambled timing information is observed.

(a)   (b)   (c)

Figure 7.8   Content replacement attack on a surveillance sequence: (a) Original frame, (b) original timing, and (c) attacked timing.

7.2.2.3.3 Content Insertion Attacks

For completeness, we show an example of content insertion attack on header protected schemes since this attack is not possible on payload-protected schemes. Figure 7.9 shows an example of content insertion attack on header-protected CBA schemes, where the original frame is shown in Figure 7.8a. Taking the samples of arbitrary image of a clock, the residual blocks are obtained by subtracting the original prediction blocks from the samples. The residual blocks are then transformed and quantized, and inserted into the macroblock payload.

7.2.2.4 Summary and Remarks

In summary, we showed that contrary to images, the video header and payload must be simultaneously integrity protected since their interdependency can be exploited by attacks performed in the transform domain. For attacks on payload-protected schemes, DPM, MV and reference frame index affect the generation of prediction block, which when combined with the residual block could semantically change the targeted block. While DPM selects prediction blocks from neighbouring blocks, MV and reference frame index select them from a wider search range. An advanced attacker may modify the macroblock type (intra/inter) and remove or insert bogus prediction mode relevant to the new macroblock type; we leave attacks of such nature as future work. Additionally, the QP is a header parameter that can be used as a workaround to inexplicitly modify the residual block while the partition size can be modified to facilitate search for a suitable prediction block. For attacks on header-protected schemes, it is vital that the distribution of tampered coefficients tallies with the coded block pattern (CBP) in the header, otherwise a decoding error may occur. We acknowledge that authenticating the CBP in the header will impose a higher level of difficulty on the attacks, however, in existing header-protected schemes, this parameter is often left unprotected. In the literature, there are also CBA schemes that authenticate both the payload and the MVs in the header [36–38]. However, as we have shown in the attack examples, these schemes are still vulnerable to attacks such as DPM attacks on intra blocks, reference frame index and/or partition size attacks on

Figure 7.9   Content insertion attack on header-protected CBA schemes.

inter blocks. We also note some interesting observations on H.264/SVC - the scalable extension of H.264/AVC that is used to encode the sequences used in this study. In SVC, a mandatory base layer (BL) that is backward compatible with AVC (Advanced Video Coding) is encoded. Using BL as reference to generate prediction, one or more enhancement layers (ELs) that gradually improve the resolution or quality of the video are encoded. If header-protected CBA schemes are applied on an SVC stream, attacks on the payload of BL and ELs are possible (and powerful). On the other hand, if coefficients-protected CBA schemes are applied, our attacks are applicable to the BL and the effect could propagate to the ELs. Although there are minimal header parameters in the ELs [3], we observe the following important parameters, e.g., the *motion prediction flag* and *residual prediction flag*. For the ELs, a motion prediction flag of "1" indicates that the EL directly uses header parameters of its reference (base) layer; otherwise, it carries its own header parameters. A residual prediction flag of "1," on the other hand, indicates that the EL's payload $\mathbf{R'_{EL}}$ is obtained by subtracting the upsampled BL payload RBL from the payload obtained via AVC-like encoding REL; otherwise, $\mathbf{R'_{EL}} = \mathbf{R_{EL}}$. An advanced attacker could then opt to modify these flags and to manipulate the video semantic. In short, content-based authentication for SVC presents several interesting research problems to be explored.

7.2.2.5 Conclusions

This section shows that existing CBA schemes designed for videos are insecure due to insufficient feature extraction. The overlooked interdependent relationship between the header and payload parameters can be exploited to perform semantic-changing attacks in the transform domain. The semantic-changing attack examples are performed in the transform domain without being detected by the schemes. In addition, the conditions for starting the attack on payload-protected CBA schemes are discussed.

7.3 Encryption of Scalable Video Coding

This section focuses on encryption of scalable video coding, and describes three encryption schemes based on different security requirements. Section 7.3.1 introduces a format-compliant bitstreams encryption scheme which is cost effective; Section 7.3.2 describes an attribute-based encryption scheme for scalable video which helps to achieve access control of video content; Section 7.3.3 gives a partial encryption scheme for scalable video which is suitable for quality and scalable scalabilities.

7.3.1 A Scalable and Format-Compliant Encryption Scheme for H.264/SVC Bitstreams

In this subsection, we will explain the proposed scalable and format-compliant encryption scheme which processes the base layer and enhancement layers in different ways. For the base layer, the scheme encrypts VCL (video coding layer) NALU (Network Abstract Layer Unit) into either SEI (Supplement Enhancement Information) NALU or PACSI (Payload Content Scalability Information) NALU. For an enhancement layer, the scheme replaces a coded slice in scalable extension NALU with an encryption of PACSI NALU. Thus, the proposed encryption scheme preserves SVC scalability and format-compliance. It produces encrypted bitstreams which have the original SVC structure without emulation markers or illegal code words for any standard decoder. The analysis and experiments indicate that the present algorithm is cost-effective and secure against chosen plaintext attack.

7.3.1.1 Structure of NALU

An SVC bitstream is divided into NALUs. Each NALU has a header which includes a forbidden zero bit (F), a 3-bit field signalling importance of the NALU (NRI) and a NUT. As shown in Figure 7.10, the NALUs can be classified into Non-VCL NALU and VCL NALU. A Non-VCL NALU has an auxiliary payload field for

NALU type	Description	SVC class
0	Unspecified	Non-VCL
1	Coded slice of a non-IDR picture	VCL
2-4	Coded slice data partition A, B, C	VCL
5	Coded slice of an IDR picture	VCL
6	Supplemental enhancement information	Non-VCL
7	Sequence parameter set	Non-VCL
8	Picture parameter set	Non-VCL
9	Access unit delimiter	Non-VCL
10	End of sequence	Non-VCL
11	End of stream	Non-VCL
12	Filler data	Non-VCL
13	Sequence parameter set extension	Non-VCL
14	Prefix NALU	Non-VCL
15	Subset sequence parameter set	Non-VCL
16-18	Reserved	Non-VCL
19	Coded slice of an auxiliary coded picture	Non-VCL
20	Coded slice in scalable extension	VCL
21-23	Reserved	Non-VCL
24-27	STAP-A, STAP-B, STAP-16, STAP-24 Aggregation	Non-VCL
28, 29	FU-A, FU-B Fragmentation unit	Non-VCL
30	PACSI: Payload content Scalability Information	Non-VCL
31	Subtype=0 Empty; Subtype=1 NI-MTAP	Non-VCL

Figure 7.10 NALU type of scalable video coding.

decoding (e.g., SVC header in prefix NALU) or facilitating certain system operations (e.g., supplement enhancement information [SEI]), while a VCL NALU has a payload field for the compressed visual data. The VCL NALU has two kinds of structures. One has an SVC header itself, and the other has to form a pair with a prefix Non-VCL NALU whose auxiliary payload is an SVC header. The SVC header includes PRID (Priority id), DID (Dependency id), QID (Quality id), TID (Temporal id) indicating three scalability dimensions respectively, which decides the layer of NALU. By ordering NALUs based on PRID, DID, QID and TID in different ways, the SVC bitstream can have different representations of the same visual content. We are interested in the Non-VCL NALU with type 6, 14, 30 and VCL NALU with types 1, 5, 20. Denote $NALU^{(n)}_i$ as the ith NALU in the bitstream, and let its type be n. We may omit the subscript if the NALU position is not important.

The VCL NALUs of an SVC bitstream are divided into one base layer and several enhancement layers. For the base layer, a non-VCL $NALU_i^{(14)}$ is used to carry the SVC header information for each following VCL $NALU_{i+1}^{(1)}$ or $NALU_{i+1}^5$ as shown in Figure 7.11a. That is, a pair $(NALU_i^{(14)}, NALU_{i+1}^{(1)})$ or $(NALU_i^{(14)}, NALU_{i+1}^{(5)})$ is used together so as to represent the visual content of the base layer.

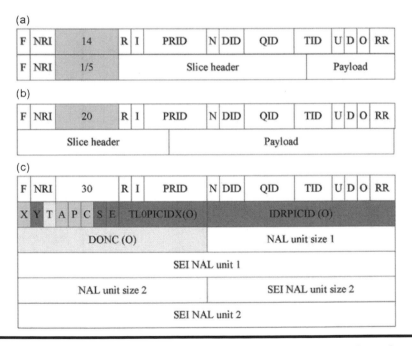

Figure 7.11 The structure of base layer (a), enhancement layer (b) and PACSI NALU (c).

For the enhancement layer, a coded slice NALU[20] shown in Figure 7.11b is used to represent the visual content. PACSI NALU[30] shown in Figure 7.11c consists of an NALU header, SVC NALU header, several flags, and SEI NALUs. A PACSI NALU may include one or more SEI NALUs. NALU[30] may be carried in a single NALU packet or an aggregation packet. If a PACSI NALU[30] is carried in a single packet, its SVC header is the same as that of the non-PACSI NALU$_{i+1}$. But if a PACSI NALU$_i$[30] is carried with other NALUs in an aggregation packet, it must be the first NALU in the aggregation packet, and its SVC NALU header is related to the remaining NALUs in the aggregation packet. Note that NALU[30] must not be fragmented into several packets. Meanwhile, the flags can decide if the field "TL0PICIDX," "IDRPICID," and "DONC" are present.

7.3.1.2 Scalable and Format-Compliant Encryption

In order to ensure format-compliant and security, the proposed scheme creates an encrypted NALU by adjusting the NALU header information and encrypting the NALU visual data according to the NALU type.

7.3.1.2.1 "Root" VCL NALU at Base Layer

A "root" VCL NALU belongs to the base layer, and the TID of its prefix NALU[14] is zero. As it is used as the reference layer of all the other enhancement layers, a "root" VCL NALU must be encrypted to provide the basic protection. To encrypt the "root" NALU, we create a new SEI NALU[6] whose payload type is 5 (user data unregistered message) and replace "root" NALU with the new NALU[6]. The encryption of the visual sample data of the original VCL NALU acts as the payload of SEI NALU[6].

7.3.1.2.2 Temporal Enhancement Layer's NALU at Base Layer

For the temporal enhancement layer NALU[1] or NALU[5] of the base layer following a prefix NALU[14] with TID a 0, a new NALU is constructed as follows. A new PACSI NALU[30] including:

- An NALU header which is the same as that of the original prefix NALU[14].
- An SVC header which is the same as that of the original prefix NALU[14].
- An NALU type which is 6, and its payload type is 5 (i.e., user data unregistered message).
- A payload which is the encryption of the visual data of the original NALU.

7.3.1.2.3 NALU of Quality and Spatial Enhancement Layer

For the NALU[20] of spatial (or quality) enhancement layer with DID a 0 or QID a 0, two NALUs are created as following. A new PACSI NALU[30] including:

- An NALU header which is the same as that of the original NALU[20].
- An SVC header which is the same as that of the original NALU[20].
- An NALU type which is 6, and its payload type is 5 (i.e., user data unregistered message).
- A payload which is the encryption of the visual data of the original NALU.
- A prefix NALU[14] consists of the SVC header of original NALU[20].

7.3.1.2.4 Existing PACSI NALU

According to the SVC specification, a non-protected SVC bitstream may have PACSI NALU[30]. For any of those PACSI NALUs, a new PACSI NALU[30] is constructed as such way, the original NALU[30] is the payload of the new NALU[30].

7.3.1.2.5 Encryption of Payload

Using a secret key which is transmitted under secure socket layer (SSL, http://www.openssl.org) protocol, a stream cipher such as RC4 with Initialization Vector (IV) is used for encryption, where IV should be unique for each message such that the ciphertexts do not repeat themselves even if the corresponding plaintexts are the same. This ensures that the encryption scheme is secure against chosen plaintext attack (CPA). In the encryption scheme, IV is generated as,

$$\mathbf{IV} = F\left(H_n, H_s\right) \tag{7.3}$$

where F is a one-way function such as SHA1, H_n represents the SVC NALU header such as DID, QID, and TID at different scalability layers, and H_s denotes the slice header for each VCL NALU at the same scalability layer. Because the proposed scheme only encrypts the visual sample data, and the header information is in clear text, IV can be deduced from the protected bitstream at the decoder/decryptor side.

In the experiments, the SVC bitstreams are produced by a generator implemented with JSVM 9.19 and stored in the streaming server Live555, while the open SVC decoder is used as the client. Both the server and the client run on PC (2.53 GHz Intel dual-core processor). The test video sequences include football (249 frames), soccer (299 frames), bus (149 frames), mobile (299 frames), and foreman (299 frames), where B/E means base layer B and enhancement layer E. Each GOP1 includes 16 frames and there are 30 frames between two I-frames. In addition, QP of the base layer is 32, and QP of spatial and quality (CGS/MGS) enhancement layers are 30 and 24 respectively.

Table 7.1 states that the overhead introduced by the proposed scheme is between 0.8% and 2.8% of the SVC bitstream, or 2.14% on average.

Table 7.2 illustrates the computation cost results of six SVC sequences, including decoding time of original SVC sequences and encryption/decryption time of our scheme and naive scheme. In the naive scheme, the SVC bitstream is directly encrypted without preserving SVC's format-complaint and scalability. The last column is the decryption overhead of our scheme. With reference to Table 7.2, our proposed encryption scheme is three times slower than the naive scheme. Fortunately,

Table 7.1   Overhead of the Proposed Algorithm

Data Size	Football CGS	Football MGS	Soccer Spatial	Bus MGS	Mobile MGS	Foreman Spatial
Original (bytes)	1 390 808	1 511 335	3 378 146	687 275	1 414 621	689 425
Encryption (bytes)	1 410 150	1 523 372	3 384 273	694 198	1 428 522	695 552
Overhead (bytes)	19 342	35 110	29 285	19 465	39 231	18 749
VCL NALU (number)	598	1196	598	596	1196	598
Overhead per NAL (bytes)	37.34	33.89	48.97	32.66	32.80	31.35
Overhead (%)	1.39	2.32	0.867	2.83	2.77	2.72

Table 7.2   Computation Cost in ms

Test Sequence	Decoding Time	Our Scheme		Naive		Overhead (%)
		enc	dec	enc	dec	dec
Football CGS	7062	117.2	115.82	35.57	34.34	1.64
Football MGS	11 670	128.7	131.60	41.23	39.86	1.13
Soccer spatial	38 477	268.9	271.01	71.37	68.68	0.70
Bus MGS	6577	60.3	61.99	21.85	21.17	0.94
Mobile MGS	13 229	122.7	125.75	38.83	37.81	0.95
Foreman spatial	9365	61.1	62.06	21.86	21.26	0.66

this computation cost is usually acceptable as the last column indicates that the decryption time is smaller than 1.64% of the decoding time.

7.3.1.3 Conclusions

This section presents a novel encryption scheme for SVC bitstreams. The scheme creates new NALUs to replace the original VCL NALUs. Because each new NALU has an SVC NAL header which indicates the scalability information in an SVC bitstream, the encrypted bitstream preserves the SVC scalability. At the same time, since the payload of each new NALU is identified as user data unregistered message, the encrypted bitstream satisfies the SVC specification. The experimental results indicate that the proposed scheme incurs little overhead and has low processing cost.

7.3.2 Efficient Block-Based Transparent Encryption for H.264/SVC Bitstreams

Taking advantage of the inter-layer prediction technique used in H.264/scalable video coding (H.264/SVC), we propose an efficient block-based encryption scheme (BBES) for encrypting H.264/SVC enhancement layers (ELs). BBES operates in three modes, namely, Intra-MB mode, Group-MB mode and 4Group-MB mode. All the three modes are effective in securing ELs, preserve the "adaptation-transparent" property of H.264/SVC, and are format-compliant to the H.264/SVC bitstream format specifications. Moreover, Intra-MB and Group-MB modes also possess the property termed as "transcoding transparency." Experimental results indicate that BBES has low computational complexity and small compression overhead. Thus, BBES is suitable for transparent encryption of H.264/SVC bitstreams in which ELs are encrypted but base layers are left in cleartext.

7.3.2.1 Motivation

The content of an SVC bitstream, such as the content of a video conference, might need to be protected due to commercial, political or security purposes. On the one hand, the protection can be achieved by full bitstream encryption, i.e., encrypting all layers of the SVC bitstream. On the other hand, a pay TV broadcaster does not always intend to prevent unauthorized viewers from receiving and watching a program, but rather intends to promote a contract with non-paying viewers. This can be facilitated by providing a BL version of the broadcasted program for everyone; but only authorized users get access to the full bitstream, (i.e., the BL and the ELs). We focus on this latter scenario that can be accomplished using transparent encryption in which the BL is left in cleartext while all the ELs are encrypted.

A simple way to protect an SVC bitstream is to treat the bitstream as a monolithic non-structured data and encrypt it as a whole. Apparently, this approach destroys the scalable property of the SVC bitstream. Many schemes for encrypting different SVC formats have been proposed in the literature. For examples, secure scalable streaming (SSS) [39] and SSS with error correction codes [40] for general SVC bitstreams, encryption of JPEG XR [7,8], encryption of MPEG-4 fine-grain scalability (FGS) [9,10], and encryption of DWTSB (Discrete Wavelet Transforms subband)-based SVC [11]. Note that above encryption schemes are designed for corresponding SVC formats; hence schemes which are proposed for one SVC format cannot satisfy the requirements on the performance of other SVC formats. For instance, if the scheme of DWTSB-based SVC in [11], which is a selective and scalable encryption for ELs by scrambling of scan patterns, is exploited for protecting H.264/SVC codestreams, the experiments on Foreman sequence indicate that: (1) it causes about 16.6% compression overhead because scrambling destroys the statistical distribution of quantized DCT coefficients; (2) it increases computation overhead, since it must scramble every 4×4 block; (3) it is not transcoding-transparent because encrypted SVC codestream cannot be decrypted again after transcoding, e.g., re-quantization.

7.3.2.2 Proposed Transparent Encryption Scheme

Block-based transparent encryption BBES seamlessly integrates encryption operations into the SVC EL macroblock coding process using secret block permutations. This section first introduces a method for generating secure pseudo-random block permutations and then describes the encryption algorithms. As a result, the rendered video stream appears as random noise to any entity without knowledge of the secret permutations.

7.3.2.2.1 Encryption in Intra-MB and Group-MB Modes

A content sender chooses a secret key k and a string R from NAL header and slice header to encrypt and encode a frame F with n macroblocks, i.e. $F = (B_0; \ldots; B_{n-1})$; the sender carries on the following steps.

Step 1: Compute a pseudo-random macroblock permutation π_n;

Step 2: If in Intra-MB mode, compute a sub-block permutation π_{16}; otherwise choose a parameter m where mB_n, and compute a sub-block permutation π_{16m} and then segment consecutive m macroblocks as one group;

Step 3: Execute the standard SVC frame coding algorithm, except that

– If a macroblock B_i is needed by SVC coding, replace it with macroblock $B_{\pi n(i)}$.

– If a sub-block b_j is needed by SVC coding, either (when in Intra-MB mode) replace it with $b\pi_{16(j)}$, where $\pi_{16(j)}$ is in the same macroblock of b_j; or (when in Group-MB mode) replace it with $\pi_{16m(j)}$.

7.3.2.2.2 Encryption in 4Group-MB Mode

4Group-MB mode is similar to Group-MB mode that reconstructs sub-blocks of MB from different MBs. Essentially, 4Group-MB organizes all the 4×4 sub-blocks into four groups for EL frames based on ***TotalCoeff***, then permutes the sub-blocks within each group. Encryption in this mode proceeds as follows:

> **Step 1**: Compute a macroblock permutation π_n;
>
> **Step 2**: Based on the TotalCoeff of sub-blocks, organize them into four groups:

$$p = \begin{cases} 1 & \text{TotalCoeff} \in [2, 0) \\ 2 & \text{TotalCoeff} \in [2, 4) \\ 3 & \text{TotalCoeff} \in [4, 8) \\ 4 & \text{TotalCoeff} \in [8, 16) \end{cases}$$

> **Step 3**: Let m_p be the number of sub-blocks in Group p, and $n = (\sum_{i=1}^{4} m_p)/16$ Compute a sub-block permutation π_{mp} for each Group p and then segment consecutive m_p sub-blocks as one group;
>
> **Step 4**: Execute the standard CAVLC entropy coding.

7.3.2.3 Experiments and Evaluation

All the three modes of BBES are implemented using JSVM 9.19 [12]. In the experiments, the group of pictures (GOP) size and the intra-period are set as 8 and 16, respectively, and entropy coding selects CAVLC (Context-based adaptive variable length coding). To test the performance of the proposed scheme, we choose ten standard H.264/SVC benchmark video sequences: Bus (150 frames), Foreman (300 frames), Football (260 frames), Soccer (300 frames), Bridge-far (2,100 frames), Bridge-close (2,000 frames), Highway (2,000 frames), Silent (300 frames), Mobile (300 frames) and Hall (300 frames) in the BBES experiments.

7.3.2.3.1 Format Compliance

Except for the coding/decoding order of sub-blocks and macroblocks, BBES encryption and decryption operations are similar to the normal H.264/SVC encoding and decoding operations, respectively; for example, DCT/IDCT (Discrete cosine transform/Invert Discrete cosine transform), quantization/invert quantization, entropy coding/decoding. Hence, a BBES encrypted SVC bitstream complies with the syntax requirement of H.264/SVC. Although a ciphertext frame is incomprehensible without being decrypted, a standard H.264/SVC decoder is able to operate an encrypted bitstream without crashing. This format-compliance property differentiates BBES from the bitstream encryption schemes.

7.3.2.3.2 Computational Cost

The computation cost incurred by BBES is small because BBES uses AES (Advanced Encryption Standard) to generate pseudo-random block permutations and BBES operations are integrated into the standard H.264/SVC coding operations. Note that the encryption speed of AES is very high, e.g., it can encrypt 109 MB/s on a PC with Intel Core 2 1.83 GH processor.

7.3.2.3.3 Compression Overhead

Because permutation used in the scheme reduces the image redundancy, BBES unavoidably introduces some compression overhead. Let the QP of BL be 34; Figure 7.12 shows the compression overhead in Intra-MB, Group-MB and 4Group-MB modes on quality and spatial scalabilities. These figures indicate that compression overhead in Group-MB mode is the highest compared to those in Intra-MB and 4Group-MB modes because this mode has more effect on statistical properties of a frame. Among the three modes, the compression overhead in 4Group-MB mode is the lowest, which is no more than 1%. Note that the increase of compression overhead is almost unavoidable, because compression benefits from information redundancy while encryption reduces redundancy through randomization. Let $\blacktriangle$ QP denote the QP difference between the reference layer and an EL, we analyze the compression overhead of BBES as follows.

7.3.2.3.4 Comparison

Compared with encryption-after-compression, 4Group-MB mode has the least compression overhead. In addition, although Intra-MB which is the simplest scheme has slightly higher compression overhead and Group-MB introduces the highest compression overhead, they trade off with additional properties, e.g., adaptation transparency, format compliance and transcoding transparency. Specifically, row 3 of Table 7.3 indicates that Intra-MB and Group-MB mode can preserve transcoding transparency. Meanwhile, according to rows 4 and 5, BBES can simultaneously possess format-compliance and adaptation transparency properties.

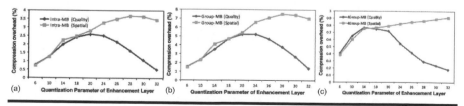

Figure 7.12 Compression overhead of (a) Intra-MB mode, (b) Group-MB, and (c) 4Group-MB.

Table 7.3 Comparison between BBES and Other Schemes

	Encryption-with-Compression		Encryption-after-Compression		BBES		
	Sign Encryption	Sign and DC Encryption [14]	Format-preserved	Adaptation-preserved	Intra-MB	Group-MB	4Group-MB
Transcoding-transparency	No	No	No	No	Yes	Yes	No
Adaptation-transparency	Yes	Yes	No	Yes	Yes	Yes	Yes
Format-compliance	Yes	Yes	Yes	No	Yes	Yes	Yes
Average overhead (%)	No	15	2.35	1.46	2.095	4.12	0.545

Compared with encryption-with-compression, although BBES causes compression overhead while the encryption with-compression scheme has no compression overhead except "Sign&DC" as shown in the last row of Table 7.3, BBES trades off additional properties. Firstly, BBES is more secure than encryption-with-compression because SVC codestreams protected by using encryption-with compression can easily be attacked, exposing sensitive information. Secondly, Intra-MB and Group-MB modes preserve transcoding transparency as shown in row 3 of Table 7.3.

7.3.2.4 Conclusions

Based on the macroblock prediction characteristics of SVC EL coding technique, BBES permutes both macroblock sub-blocks in Intra-MB, Group-MB and 4Group-MB modes using secure pseudo-random block permutations. The analysis and experimental results show that all the three modes in BBES preserve adaptation-transparent property of H.264/SVC. Furthermore, Intra-MB and Group-MB are transcoding-transparent. These properties allow a MANE (Media Aware Network Elements) to directly adapt or transcode encrypted SVC bitstreams for ELs. In addition, BBES is format-compliant and incurs small computational and compression costs. These properties make BBES highly suitable for perceptual/transparent encryption of H.264/SVC bitstreams in applications such as pay-TV broadcasting.

7.4 Authentication of Scalable Video Coding

Many authentication schemes have been proposed for authenticating scalable codestreams and can be classified into three categories: cryptographic authentication, watermarking-based authentication and content-based authentication. Cryptographic authentication techniques, such as digital signature and Message Authentication Code (MAC), are applicable to any digital object, including image [41,42] and video [43–45]. Particularly, for SVC video authentication, Yu [45] proposed to hash each enhancement layer and attach the hash value to the lower layer of the same frame; and Mokhtarian and Hefeeda [46] proposed a packet loss-resilience authentication scheme for H.264/SVC using hash chain and error-correction code. However, proposed schemes are generally very sensitive to content modifications, including content changing manipulations, content-preserving manipulations and bit errors due to transmission or storage noise. Meanwhile, since proposed schemes depend on the structure of layer prediction in order to create a hash chain, their operations are not transparent to users. Furthermore, because proposed schemes had to execute hash functions on each layer, their computation complexity and communication overhead are proportional to the number of layers in a codestream.

Watermarking-based authentication schemes, such as [47,48], embed a reference object (e.g., image or message) into an SVC codestream. Grois and Hadar [49] reviewed recent watermarking-based authentication schemes for SVC. As the reference object and the SVC codestream are mixed together, the embedded reference object will be tampered if the SVC codestream is maliciously tampered. For example, Meerwald and Uhl [50] designed a robust watermarking authentication by embedding the same watermark into both base layer and enhancement layers for quality/ spatial scalabilities; Shi et al. [51] proposed a scalable and credible watermarking algorithm for SVC as part of a copyright protection system; and Park and Shin [52,53] combined encryption and watermarking techniques to achieve authentication and copy protection of H.264/AVC and SVC codestreams. For the sake of robustness and security, watermarking-based authentication schemes must embed the reference object into each layer of an SVC codestream; otherwise the non-watermarked layers can be easily tampered without being detected. However, since most quantized coefficients of enhancement layers are zero, embedding watermarking into each layer is in conflict with the limited embedding capacity.

Content-based authentication schemes ensure the authenticity of video features such as edges, the feature of Matrix transform [54–56], the rotation-invariant feature of Fourier-Mellin transformation [57], and the feature of wavelet domain [58–60]. To authenticate a codestream, a content provider extracts its multimedia features, generates a reference object with the extracted features, and delivers the reference object to end users via a secure channel [61]. Upon receiving the video codestream and the reference object, an end user extracts the video features as the provider did and checks whether the extracted features match those in the reference object. In such schemes, the feature extraction method must be robust against content-preserving manipulations, but sensitive to content-changing manipulations.

7.4.1 A Hybrid Scheme for Authenticating Scalable Video Codestreams

An SVC codestream consists of one base layer and possibly several enhancement layers. The base layer, which contains the lowest quality and resolution images, is the foundation of the SVC codestream and must be delivered to recipients, whereas enhancement layers contain richer contour/texture of images in order to supplement the base layer in resolution, quality, and temporal scalabilities. This paper presents a novel hybrid authentication (HAU) scheme. The HAU employs both cryptographic authentication and content-based authentication techniques to ensure integrity and authenticity of the SVC codestreams. The analysis and experimental results indicate that the HAU is able to detect malicious manipulations and locate the tampered image regions while it is robust to content preserving manipulations for enhancement layers. Although the proposed technique focuses on authenticating H.264/SVC codestreams, it is also applicable to authenticate other scalable multimedia contents such as MPEG-4 fine grain scalability and JPEG2000 codestreams.

7.4.1.1 Motivation

An authentication scheme aims to prevent any unauthorized manipulations by veri-fying the integrity and source of data. In addition to the standard requirements of security, computational efficiency and communication efficiency, an authentication scheme for SVC codestreams should also provide the following properties:

- Robustness: robust or resilient to content-preserving manipulations which do not change the semantic meaning of a codestream.
- Sensitivity: able to detect content-changing manipulations which modify the semantic meaning of a codestream.
- Localization of tampering: able to pinpoint tampered regions if tampering indeed occurred.
- Scalability: preserving the scalability properties of the original SVC codestream. That is, the authentication scheme authenticates an SVC codestream once at the source, but allows verification of the codestream with different scalabilities by various user devices.

7.4.1.2 Hybrid Authentication Scheme of Scalable Video Coding

In an SVC codestream, the base layer consists of the lowest quality/resolution images, and it must be transmitted intact to the receiver in any case. Meanwhile, it is unnecessary to transcode (i.e., re-compress or re-sample) the base layer because it contains the very basic information. Therefore, the base layer can be protected by cryptographic authentication. Meanwhile, higher quality and resolution images are decoded from base layer and enhancement layers, and their content-based features are robust. If features are extracted from the highest quality and resolution images, content-based authentication is suitable for authenticating enhancement layers. Hence, it is reasonable to integrate cryptographic authentication and content-based authentication techniques in order to flexibly authenticate SVC codestreams. Operations of HAU are shown in Figure 7.13, where the provider creates an

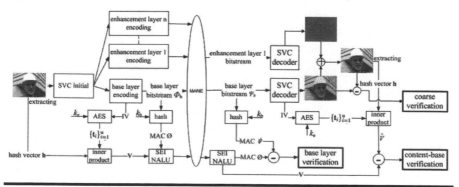

Figure 7.13   Diagram of HAU.

authentication tag for an SVC codestream and the receiver verifies the tag against the received codestream. MANE which receive feedback messages about the terminal capabilities and/or channel conditions, can remove the non-required parts from a scalable bit stream based on its DxQyTz, before forwarding it.

7.4.1.2.1 Authentication Tag Generation

The authentication tag generation process includes MAC generation and feature extraction, where MACs are constructed by taking the encoded image of the base layer and a secret key as inputs, while the features of each frame are extracted from the highest quality and resolution images of SVC bitstreams. Note that if an SVC codestream has spatial enhancement layers, HAU should initially downsample the largest resolution to the same resolution as the base layer, then extract features from the downsampled one. Hence, the length of the feature value is related to the base layer's resolution for each AU (Access Unit).

Message Authentication Codes: With a standard one-way hash function $\mathcal{H}(\cdot)$ for the encoded frame Φ, the provider takes its base layer Φ_b and a key k_b shared by provider and receiver as input to produce MAC φ as:

$$\varphi = \mathcal{H}(k_b, \Phi_b)$$

Feature Extraction: HAU extracts content-based features which are sensitive to content-changing manipulation but robust to content-preserving manipulations in case of large QP. The candidate features include invariant histogram statistics and relation between low frequency DCT coefficients. HAU employs NMF-NMF-SQ (Non-negative matrix factorisation square) hashing to produce content based feature. After obtaining the hash vector h of each AU, pseudorandom weight vectors $\{t_i\}_{i=1}^u$ ($u \leq v$) are generated using AES with the secret key k_e and an initialization vector IV. The k_e is shared by the content sender and receiver and the initialization vector IV consists of scalable information (i.e., temporal identifiers) and slice header of base layer. At last, HAU executes inner product of vector $\mathbf{h}$ and vector t_i to produce $V = \{V_1, V_2, \cdots, V_u\}$.

7.4.1.2.2 Tag Conveyance

It is necessary to deliver the authentication tag (i.e., feature hash V and MAC φ) to the receiver together with the SVC codestream for verification. In HAU, we encapsulate the tag into SVC user data as a new SEI (Supplement Enhancement Information) NALU. The payload type of the new SEI is Unregistered User Data Message so as to preserve SVC format. After receiving the SVC codestream embedded with the tag, the receiver can detect the new SEI based on its UUID

(Universally Unique Identifier) and directly obtain the tag, i.e., NMF-NMF-SQ hash and MAC.

7.4.1.2.3 Tag Verification

After receiving the codestream and obtaining the tag, the receiver performs HAU verification including the base layer verification and enhancement layer verification.

Verification of the Base Layer: For the base layer Ψ_b in a received frame Ψ, HAU first calculates its MAC value ψ as

$$\psi = \mathcal{H}(k_b, \Psi_b)$$

If $\psi = \varphi$, HAU accepts the base. Otherwise, the base layer is considered tampered and HAU directly rejects the base layer and all the enhancement layers of Ψ.

7.4.1.3 Experiments and Comparison

In our experiments, we choose twelve standard benchmark video sequences in order to cover different combinations of video characteristics, including motion (fast/ slow, pan/zoom/rotation), color (bright/dull), contrast (high/low), and object type (vehicle, buildings, people). Bus (150 frames) and Foreman (300 frames) are of less camera motion while Football (260 frames), Container (300 frames) and Soccer (300 frames) demonstrate camera panning and zooming with object motion and background texture. Bridge-far (300 frames) and Bridge-close (500 frames) show images with smooth motion. Highway (1200 frames) is a sequence of fast motion while Silent (300 frames) and News (300 frames) are static sequences except of motion of partial fields. Mobile (300 frames) and Hall (300 frames) sequences display a still complex background with foreground motion. SVC GOP size and Intra period are set to 8; the QPs of enhancement layers are no more than 38 so that the features extracted with NMF-NMF-SQ are stable.

As HAU exploits the characteristics of SVC to ensure its authenticity, it is robust to content-preserving manipulations but sensitive to content-changing manipulations of enhancement layers. However, cryptographic authentication is sensitive to any bit change of SVC and watermarking-based is semi-fragile to content-preserving manipulations. In other words, HAU achieves a good balance between robustness and sensitivity as shown in the second column of Table 7.4. The third column indicates that cryptographic authentication cannot locate tampered areas. Furthermore, the fourth column of Table 7.4 shows that HAU only depends on base layer and content-based features of the highest quality/resolution images, while cryptographic authentication and watermarking-based authentication must involve every layer of SVC to prevent the attacks on unprotected layers. In the fifth column of Table 7.4, cryptographic authentication and watermarking-based authentication

Table 7.4 Comparison with Other H.264/SVC Authentication Schemes

Scheme	Robustness/Sensitivity	Tampered Location	Authentication Operation	Dependence on SVC Structure	Communication Overhead
Cryptographic authentication [10]	Sensitive to any bit change	No	All layer hash	Yes	Quality scalability 2.19% Spatial scalability 2.62%
Watermarking authentication [14]	Semi-fragile	Yes	All layer watermarking	Yes	Quality scalability 8.66% Spatial scalability 2.93%
HAU	Sensitive to base layer change robust to enhancement layers	Yes	Base layer hash content-based features	No	Quality scalability 2.42% Spatial scalability 2.16%

depend on layer prediction relationship of SVC in order to construct hashing chain or embed watermarking. HAU is independent of SVC structure since HAU only considers the authentication of base layer's codestream and content-based features of SVC, hence HAU is transparent to users.

The last column illustrates the communication overhead. In our SVC experiments, GOP size is 8 and encoded SVC sequences have three layers (one base layer and two enhancement layers). The cryptographic authentication [46] appends 960 bytes overhead per GOP (i.e., each frame has 120 bytes overhead). Hence, the average overheads of the scheme [46] are 2.19% and 2.62% of the original codestream for quality and spatial scalability, respectively. In general, HAU produces the smallest communication overhead as shown at the last column of Table 7.4, except the similar communication overhead on quality scalability as that of cryptographic authentication. In addition, HAU's communication overhead is constant, but the overhead of cryptographic authentication [46] and watermarking-based authentication [50] increase with the number of enhancement layers. For example, with GOP size being 8, each frame will carry 40 bytes more overhead [46] when an SVC sequence contains one more enhancement layer.

7.4.1.4 Conclusions

A hybrid authentication scheme was introduced for SVC, named HAU, which processes the base layer and enhancement layers using cryptographic authentication and content-based authentication, respectively. Cryptographic authentication ensures the integrity of the base layer while content-based authentication verifies enhancement layers using extracted features. HAU is secure, SVC format-transparent, light-weight in communication overhead and low computational complexity. The analysis and experiments indicated that HAU is robust to content-preserving manipulations but sensitive to content-changing manipulations.

7.5 Conclusion

This Chapter emphasized the security of scalable video coding. Firstly, it introduced the characteristic of scalable video coding, which consists of temporal, quality, and spatial scalabilities. Then, security requirements were described, i.e., security and integrity. Secondly, it analyzed and evaluated existing encryption and authentication schemes of scalable video and images, and figured out that existing partial encryption and existing content-based authentication algorithms cannot satisfy reality security requirements. Additionally, two encryption schemes were proposed for different scenarios, i.e., bitstream encryption and transparent encryption. Furthermore, a hybrid authentication scheme was designed based on the structure of scalable video coding.

References

1. D. L. Goeckel, Adaptive coding for time-varying channels using outdated fading estimates. *IEEE Transactions on Communications*, 47(6): 844–855, 1999.
2. V. K. Goyal, Multiple description coding: Compression meets the network. *IEEE Signal Processing Magazine*, 18(5): 74–93, 2001.
3. H. Schwarz, D. Marpe, and T. Wiegand, Overview of the scalable video coding extension of the h.264/avc standard. *IEEE Transactions on Circuitsand System for Video Technology*, 17(9): 1103–1120, 2007.
4. M. Wien, H. Schwarz, and T. Oelbaum, Performance analysis of svc. *IEEE Transactions on Circuits and System for Video Technology*, 17(9): 1194–1203, 2007.
5. ITU-T, I. J. 1, Advanced video coding for generic audiovisual services, ITU-T and ISO/IEC JTC 1 Recommendation H.264 and ISO/IEC 14496-10 (MPEG-4) AVC, 2005.
6. W. Li. Overview of fine granularity scalability in MPEG-4 video standard. *IEEE Transactions on Circuits and System for Video Technology*, 11(3): 301–317, 2001.
7. H. Sohn, W. De Neve, and Y. M. Ro. Region-of-interest scrambling for scalable surveillance video using JPEG XR. *ACM Multimedia*, pp. 861–864, 2009.
8. H. Sohn, W. De Neve, and Y. M. Ro. Privacy protection in video surveillance systems: Analysis of subband-adaptive scrambling in JPEG XR. *IEEE Transactions on Circuits and Systems for Video Technology*, 21(2): 170–177, 2011.
9. C. Yuan, B. B. Zhu, Y. Wang, S. Li, and Y. Zhong. Efficient and fully scalable encryption for MPEG-4 FGS. *ISCAS* (2), pp. 620–623, 2003.
10. B. B. Zhu, C. Yuan, Y. Wang, and S. Li. Scalable protection for MPEG-4 fine granularity scalability. *IEEE Transactions on Multimedia*, 7(2): 222–233, 2005.
11. Z. Shahid, M. Chaumont, and W. Puech. Selective and scalable encryption of enhancement layers for dyadic scalable H.264/AVC by scrambling of scan patterns. *ICIP*, pp. 1273–1276, 2009.
12. G. Algin and E. Tunali. Scalable video encryption of H.264 SVC codec. *Journal of Visual Communication and Image Representation (JVCIR)*, 22(4): 353–364, 2011.
13. A. Tosun and W. Feng. Efficient multi-layer coding and encryption of MPEG video streams. *IEEE International Conference on Multimedia and Expo* (I), pp. 119–122, 2000.
14. C. Li, X. Zhou, and Y. Zhong. NAL level encryption for scalable video coding. *PCM*, pp. 496–505, 2008.
15. C. Li, C. Yuan, and Y. Zhong. Layered encryption for scalable video coding. *2nd International Congress on Image and Signal Processing*, pp. 1–4, 2009.
16. W. Zeng and S. Lei. Efficient frequency domain selective scrambling of digital video. *IEEE Transactions on Multimedia*, 5(1): 118–129, 2003.
17. F. Liu and H. Koenig. A survey of video encryption algorithms. *Computer & Security*, 29(1): 3–15, 2010.
18. B. Zhu, M. Swanson, and S. Li. Encryption and authentication for scalable multimedia: Current state of the art and challenges. In *ternet Multimedia Management Systems V*, 5601: 157–170, 2004.
19. X. Liu and A. Eskicioglu. Selective encryption of multimedia content in distribution network: Challenges and new directions. In *2nd IASTED International Conference on Communication, Internet, and Information Technology*, pp. 527–533, 2003.

20. H. Yu. An overview on scalable encryption for wireless multimedia access. *Internet Quality of Service*, 5245: 24–34, 2003.
21. S. Lian. *Multimedia Content Encryption: Techniques and Applications*. Boca Raton, FL: CRC Press, pp. 121–130, 2008.
22. T. Kunkelmann and U. Horn. Video encryption based on data partitioning and scalable coding - A comparison. *IDMS*, pp. 95–106, 1998.
23. T. Stutz and A. Uhl. A survey of h.264 avc/svc encryption, *IEEE Transactions on Circuits and Systems for Video Technology*, 22(3): 325–339, 2012.
24. R. L. Rivest. The RC4 encryption algorithm. RSA Data Security, Inc., March 12, 1992.
25. S.-W. Park and S.-U. Shin. Combined scheme of encryption and watermarking in H. 264/Scalable Video Coding (SVC). In *New Directions in Intelligent Interactive Multimedia*. Springer, Berlin, Germany, pp. 351–361, 2008.
26. Joint scalable video model software, http://ip.hhi.de/imagecomg1/savce/downloads/svc-reference-software.htm.
27. A. Skodras, C. Christopoulos, and T. Ebrahimi. The JPEG 2000 still image compression standard. *IEEE Signal Processing Magazine*, 18(5): 36–58, 2001.
28. Z. Zhao and P. Liang. A statistical analysis of H.264/AVC FME mode reduction. *IEEE Transactions on Circuits and Systems for Video Technology*, 21(1): 53–61, 2011.
29. S. Ma, W. Gao, D. Zhao, and Y. Lu. A study on the quantization scheme in H.264/AVC and its application to rate control. In *Advances in Multimedia Information Processing, PCM*, pp. 192–199, 2004.
30. T. Ebrahimi and C. Horne. MPEG-4 natural video coding - An overview. *Signal Processing: Image Communication*, 15(4–5): 365–385, 2000.
31. I. E. Richardson. *The H.264 Advanced Video Compression Standard*, 2nd ed. Chichester, UK: Wiley, 2010.
32. A. Mansouri, A. M. Aznaveh, F. Torkamani-Azar, and F. Kurugollu. A low complexity video watermarking in H.264 compressed domain. *IEEE Transactions on Information Forensics and Security*, 5(4): 649–657, 2010.
33. J. S. Park and H. J. Song. Selective intra prediction mode decision for H.264/AVC encoders. *World Academy of Science, Engineering and Technology*, 13: 51–55, 2006.
34. Arizona State University: Video trace library. http://trace.eas.asu.edu/index.html.
35. The CAVIAR team: EC funded CAVIAR project/IST 2001 37540. http://homepages.inf.ed.ac.uk/rbf/CAVIAR/.
36. C. Y. Lin and S. F. Chang. Issues and solutions for authenticating MPEG video. In *SPIE International Conference on Security and Watermarking of Multimedia Contents*, Vol. 3657, pp. 54–56, 1999.
37. S. Shahabuddin, R. Iqbal, S. Shirmohammadi, and J. Zhao. Compressed-domain temporal adaptation-resilient watermarking for H.264 video authentication. In *IEEE International Conference on Multimedia and Expo (ICME)*, pp. 1752–1755, 2009.
38. P. Yin and H. H. Yu. A semi-fragile watermarking system for MPEG video authentication. In *IEEE International Conference on Acoustics, Speech, and Signal Processing (ICASSP)*, Vol. 4, pp. IV-3461–IV-3464, 2002.
39. J. G. Apostolopoulos and S. J. Wee. Secure scalable streaming enabling transcoding without decryption. In *Proceedings of the IEEE International Conference on Image Processing*, pp. 437–440, 2001.

40. V. Gergely and G. Fehér. Enhancing progressive encryption for scalable video streams. In *Conference on Information and Communications Technologies*, pp. 51–58, 2009.

41. B. B. Zhu, M. D. Swanson, and S. Li. Encryption and authentication for scalable multimedia: Current state of the art and challenges. In *Proceedings of International Symposium on Information and Communication Technology*, pp. 157–170, 2004.

42. C. Peng, R. H. Deng, Y. D. Wu, and W. Z. Shao, A flexible and scalable authentication scheme for JPEG2000 image codestreams. In *Proceedings of the 11th ACM International Conference on Multimedia*, pp. 433–441, 2003.

43. M. Hefeeda and K. Mokhtarian. Authentication of scalable multimedia streams. In *Handbook on Security and Networks*, Y. Xiao, F. H. Li and H. Chen, Eds. Singapore: World Scientific, pp. 93–125, 2011.

44. Y. D. Wu and R. H. Deng. Scalable authentication of MPEG-4 streams. *IEEE Transactions on Multimedia*, 8(1): 152–161, 2006.

45. H. Yu. Scalable streaming media authentication. In *IEEE International Conference on Communications*, pp. 1912–1916, June 2004.

46. K. Mokhtarian and M. Hefeeda. Authentication of scalable video streams with low communication overhead. *IEEE Transactions on Multimedia*, 12(7): 730–742, 2010.

47. P. Meerwald and A. Uhl. Towards robust watermarking of scalable video. In *Proceedings of the Security, Forensics, Steganography, and Watermarking of Multimedia Contents*, pp. 1–3, 2008.

48. C. C. Wang, Y. C. Lin, S. C. Yi, and P. Y. Chen. Digital authentication and verification in MPEG-4 fine-granular scalability video using bitplane watermarking. In *Proceedings of the International Conference on Image Processing, Computer Vision and Pattern Recognition*, pp. 16–21, 2006.

49. D. Grois and O. Hadar. *Recent Advances in Watermarking for Scalable Video Coding.* Chennai, India: Intech, 2012.

50. P. Meerwald and A. Uhl. Robust watermarking of H.264/SVC-encoded video: Quality and resolution scalability. In *Proceedings of the International Workshop on Digital Watermarking*, pp. 156–169, 2010.

51. F. Shi, S. H. Liu, H. X. Yao, Y. Liu, and S. P. Zhang. Scalable and credible video watermarking towards scalable video coding. In *Proceedings of Pacific Rim Conference on Multimedia*, pp. 697–708, 2010.

52. S. W. Park and S. U. Shin. Combined scheme of encryption and watermarking in H.264/scalable video coding (SVC). In *New Directions Intelligent Interactive Multimedia, Springer, Studies in Computational Intelligence*, Vol. 142, New York: Springer-Verlag, pp. 351–361, 2008.

53. S. W. Park and S. U. Shin. Authentication and copyright protection scheme for H.264/AVC and SVC. *Journal of Information Science and Engineering*, 27(1): 129–142, 2011.

54. S. S. Kozat, R. Venkatesan, and M. K. Mihcak. Robust perceptual image hashing via matrix invariants. In *Proceedings of the International Conference on Image Processing*, pp. 3443–3446, 2004.

55. V. Monga and M. K. Mihcak. Robust and secure image hashing via non-negative matrix factorizations. *IEEE Transactions on Information Forensics and Security*, 2(3): 376–390, 2007.

56. X. D. Lv and Z. J. Wang. Fast Johnson-Lindenstrauss transform for robust and secure image hashing. In *Proceedings of the IEEE 10th Workshop on Multimedia Signal Processing*, pp. 725–729, 2008.

57. A. Swaminathan, Y. Mao, and M. Wu. Robust and secure image hashing. *IEEE Transactions on Information Forensics and Security*, 1(2): 215–230, 2006.
58. R. Venkatesan, S. M. Koon, M. H. Jakubowski, and P. Moulin. Robust image hashing. In *Proceedings of the International Conference on Image Processing*, pp. 664–666, 2000.
59. C. S. Lu and H. Y. M. Liao. Structural digital signature for image authentication: An incidental distortion resistant scheme. *IEEE Transactions on Multimedia*, 5(2): 161–173, 2003.
60. C. W. Tang and H. M. Hang. A feature-based robust digital image watermarking scheme. *IEEE Transactions on Signal Processing*, 51(4): 950–959, 2003.
61. B. B. Zhu and M. D. Swanson. Multimedia authentication and watermarking. In *Multimedia Information Retrieval and Management*, D. Feng, W. C. Siu, and H. Zhang, Eds. New York: Springer-Verlag, pp. 148–177, 2003.

Chapter 8

Compressive Sensing in Color Image Security

Rohit Thanki, Surekha Borra,
Komal Borisagar and Nilanjan Dey

Contents

DOI: 10.1201/9780429435461-9

8.1 Introduction

With the rapid use of social media, exchange of multimedia data is common worldwide. Nowadays, many color images are transmitted and shared over mobile devices and Facebook using the open social media. Sometimes, these color images cannot be transferred due to limited bandwidth of the transmission medium. Also, security of these images is vulnerable when transferred over open networks [1,2]. To solve the above mentioned issues, researchers introduced various approaches based on compression and encryption for multimedia data [1,2].

The model for secure transmission process of an image through a medium is shown in Figure 8.1 [3]. This model consists of two main blocks: encrypter and decrypter. The input image is fed to the encrypter which encrypts the image into a set of symbols. After transmission over a channel, set of symbols is fed to the decrypter, where decryption of the image is performed. The output image is called as decrypted image.

Due to the problems related to limited bandwidth of transmission medium, researchers added a compression process with the encryption following different approaches: encryption+compression approach, compression+encryption approach, and hybrid approach using the CS theory based on compression and encryption [1]. Figure 8.2 shows the basic flow of these approaches. In the encryption+compression approach, first the image is encrypted and then compression of image is performed. In the compression+encryption approach, the image is first compressed then encryption of compressed image is performed. In the hybrid approach, encryption and compression of an image is performed simultaneously. In the first two approaches, encryption of image is performed by various cryptographic approaches such as advanced encryption standard (AES), Rivest Shamir Adleman (RSA), etc., and compression of image is performed by various compression approaches such as Joint Photographic Expert Group (JPEG), JPEG 2000, etc. [1].

The compression approaches used in the first two approaches transforms the input image into its transform coefficients using image processing transform. Then few transform coefficients are neglected which have no significance for image representation. The image is recovered by using the remaining transform coefficients. This recovered image is called as a compressed image. All these approaches were followed and designed based on Shannon-Nyquist sampling criteria. For the recovery of an image using Shannon-Nyquist criteria, the size of transform coefficients

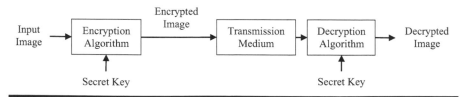

Figure 8.1 Secure transmission process of image through a transmission medium.

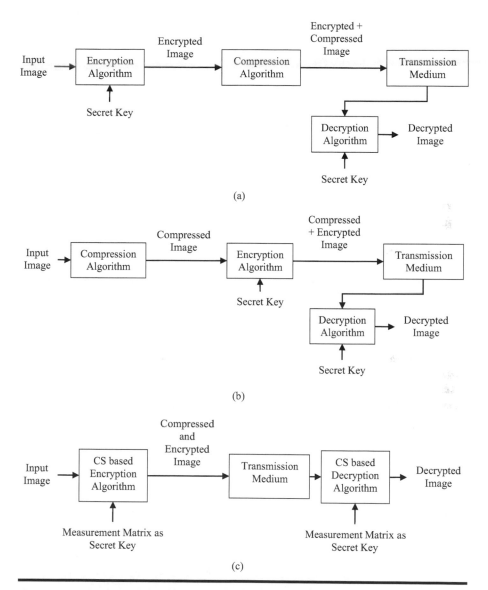

Figure 8.2 Various approaches for security of image using encryption and compression. (a) Encryption + Compression approach (b) Compression + Encryption approach (c) Compressive sensing (CS) based approach.

must be twice or greater than the actual pixel value of image. This is a limitation of Shannon-Nyquist criteria.

To overcome the limitation of Shannon-Nyquist sampling criteria in existing compression approaches, Candes and Donoho introduced new mathematical theory for signal acquisition and compression [4,5]. This mathematical

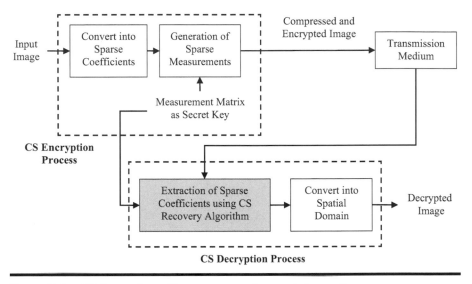

Figure 8.3   CS theory based image encryption and decryption process.

theory is known as compressive sensing, or sampling, (CS) theory. This theory is equally applicable for digital images. This theory states that the image can successfully recover from its few sparse data [4–6]. A necessary condition for CS theory is that the image must be sparse in its own domain. The beauty of this theory is that it simultaneously compresses and encrypts images based on measurement matrix, which may have a binary, Fourier or Gaussian nature. The details of image encryption and decryption based on CS theory are shown in Figure 8.3.

In the CS encryption process, the image is converted into its sparse measurements using sparse coefficients and the measurement matrix. The image in terms of its sparse measurements is called as compressed and encrypted image. The steps for the CS encryption process are given as follows:

Step 1: Convert the image into its sparse coefficients using image transform basis matrix as follows:

$$x_{N \times N} = \Psi_{N \times N} \cdot f_{N \times N} \cdot \Psi'_{N \times N} \tag{8.1}$$

where, x is sparse coefficients of the image, f is the original image, Ψ is transform basis matrix.

Step 2: Generate measurement matrix A with size of $M \times N$. Use A as a secret key and decide the compression factor for the image.

Step 3: Generate the sparse measurements of the image by multiplying sparse coefficients with measurement matrix A.

$$Ef_{M \times N} = A_{M \times N} \times x_{N \times N} \qquad (8.2)$$

where Ef is the compressed and encrypted image in terms of sparse measurements and A is the measurement matrix.

In a CS decryption process, the decryption of an image is taking place from its sparse measurement. The decryption process can be performed using CS recovery algorithms and a measurement matrix. These recovery algorithms are based on linear algebra properties and optimization techniques. There are various types of CS recovery algorithms: L norm minimization and greedy based approach [4–8].

Let Ef be the encrypted image after CS encryption, then the decryption of image Df can be performed using CS recovery algorithm. The sparse coefficients of the image are in transform domain Ψ, the image is decrypted by solving below minimization problem.

$$\min\|f\|_l , Ef = Ax \qquad (8.3)$$

The necessary condition for an image decryption using sparse measurements is that it must satisfy restricted isometric property (RIP). The measurement matrix A of size $M \times N$ obeys the RIP of order K ($K < m$) if measurement matrix A approximately preserves the squared magnitude of any K sparse encrypted image Ef using Equation 8.4.

$$\forall y \; for \; which$$
$$\|y\|_0 \leq k, \qquad (8.4)$$
$$(1 - \delta_K)\|Ef\|^2 \leq \|AEf\|^2 \leq (1 + \delta_K)\|Ef\|^2$$
$$0 < \delta_k < 1$$

The measurement matrix and transform basis matrices are used as secret keys in the CS based encryption process. The chosen criteria of these two matrices depend on various parameters. The measurement matrix must be random, symmetric in nature and easy to generate. The Gaussian distribution shown in Figure 8.4 satisfies all these properties. For transform basis matrix; it must be sparse, real and symmetric. The DFT, DCT, and DWT have sparse property. Therefore, these three transforms are mainly used in CS based encryption process.

Figure 8.4 Gaussian type measurement matrix.

8.2 Related Work

In this section, various techniques based on compression and encryption of images, which are mentioned in Figure 8.2, are described.

The techniques based on first approach are designed and implemented by applying image compression followed by cryptographic based encryption [9–19]. These techniques employ various compression methods such as Slepian-Wolf coding, Huffman coding, Arithmetic coding, Shannon Fano coding, DCT based compression, and DWT based compression. These compression methods may be lossy or lossless. The cryptographic based encryption methods such as binary stream cipher, data encryption standard (DES), RSA, block cipher, etc. are used for encryption of compressed images in these techniques. These encryption methods may be symmetric or asymmetric. Table 8.1 shows the summary of encryption + compression techniques for security of images.

The techniques based on second approach are designed and implemented by applying cryptographic-based encryption followed by image compression to image to get encrypted + compressed image [20–42]. These techniques are designed by various encryption methods such as DES, AES, Bit XOR operation, selective encryption, elliptic curve, etc. These methods are based on symmetric key generation or asymmetric key generation. The image compression methods like DCT, lifting wavelet transform (LWT), SPIHT (Set Partitioning in Hierarchical Trees), JPEG, adaptive compression, etc., are used for compression of encrypted images in these techniques. These methods may be lossy or lossless compression methods. Table 8.2 shows the summary of compression + encryption techniques for security of images.

After invention of CS theory around 2006, researchers introduced this theory in various applications such as image security (image encryption, image watermarking, image hashing, image hiding, and authentication), video security, cloud security scenario, and 5G system security scenario [43]. In the last eight years,

Table 8.1 Summary of Encryption + Compression Techniques for Security of Images

Existing Techniques	Type of Encryption Method	Nature of Key in Encryption Method	Type of Compression Method	Nature of Compression Method	Type of Image
Johnson et al. (2004) [9]	Binary Stream Cipher	Symmetric	Slepian-Wolf Coding	Lossless	Not Mentioned
Liu et al. (2010) [10]	Stream Cipher	Symmetric	Slepian-Wolf Coding	Lossless	Grayscale
Shafinah and Ikram (2011) [11]	RSA and International Data Encryption Algorithm (IDEA)	Symmetric and Asymmetric	ZIP	Lossless	Not Mentioned
Razzaque and Thakur (2012) [12]	Multiplicative Cipher	Symmetric	Discrete Cosine Transform (DCT)	Lossy	Grayscale
Kang et al. (2013) [13]	Stream Cipher	Symmetric	Lossy Scalable Compression	Lossy	Grayscale
Mariselvi and Kumar (2014) [14]	DES	Symmetric	Huffman Coding or Arithmetic Coding	Lossless	Grayscale and Color
Arunkumar and Prabu (2014) [15]	RSA	Asymmetric	Set Partitioning in Hierarchical Trees (SPIHT)	Lossless	Grayscale
Sharma et al. (2014) [16]	Multiple-Parameter Discrete Fractional Fourier Transform (MPDFrFT)	Symmetric	Zig-zaq scan, Huffman, and Run Length Encoding (RLE)	Lossless	Grayscale and Color

(Continued)

Table 8.1 (Continued)   Summary of Encryption + Compression Techniques for Security of Images

Existing Techniques	Type of Encryption Method	Nature of Key in Encryption Method	Type of Compression Method	Nature of Compression Method	Type of Image
Aujla and Sharma (2014) [17]	Random Permutation	Symmetric	Haar Wavelet and Daubechies Wavelet based Compression	Lossy	Grayscale
Kamble and Manwade (2014) [18]	Block Cipher and Blowfish	Symmetric	Linde-Buzo-Gray (LBG) Vector Quantization	Lossy	Not Mentioned
Kale et al. (2014) [19]	RSA and 3D AES	Symmetric and Asymmetric	Shannon Fano	Lossless	Not Mentioned

Table 8.2 Summary of Compression + Encryption Techniques for Security of Images

Existing Techniques	Type of Compression Method	Nature of Compression Method	Type of Encryption Method	Nature of Key in Encryption Method	Type of Image
Wu and Kuo (2005) [20]	Multiple Huffman Tables or QM	Lossless	Stream Cipher	Symmetric	Grayscale
Ou et al. (2006) [21]	DWT, Significance-Linked Connected Component Analysis (SLCCA)	Lossless	AES	Symmetric	Grayscale and Color
Loussert et al. (2008) [22]	DCT	Lossy	Bit XOR Operation	Symmetric	Grayscale
Krikor et al. (2009) [23]	DCT	Lossy	Selective Encryption and Bit Stream Cipher	Symmetric	Color
Hermassi et al. (2010) [24]	Renewing Huffman Coding Tree	Lossless	Stream Cipher	Symmetric	Not Mentioned
Benabdellah et al. (2011) [25]	Faber-Schauder Multi-Scale Transform (FMT)	Lossy	DES or AES	Symmetric	Grayscale, Color, and Medical
Chen et al. (2011) [26]	Entropy Coding	Lossless	Lookup Table	Symmetric	Not Mentioned
Samson and Sastry (2012) [27]	2-D Multilevel Wavelet Transformation	Lossy	Permutation	Symmetric	Grayscale

(Continued)

Table 8.2 (Continued)   Summary of Compression + Encryption Techniques for Security of Images

Existing Techniques	Type of Compression Method	Nature of Compression Method	Type of Encryption Method	Nature of Key in Encryption Method	Type of Image
Samson and Sastry (2012) [28]	Lifting Wavelet Transform	Lossy	Secure Advanced Hill Cipher (SAHC)	Symmetric	Color
Gupta and Silakari (2012) [29]	Curvelet Transformation	Lossy	Elliptic Curve	Symmetric	Color
Kishore et al. (2012) [30]	Slepian-Wolf Coding	Lossless	Bit-wise XOR Operation	Symmetric	Grayscale
Nair et al. (2012) [31]	Arithmetic Coding Technique	Lossless	Bit-wise XOR Operation	Symmetric	Not Mentioned
Alfalou et al. (2013) [32]	Combining Spectral Fusion of pixels according to DCT Properties	Lossless or Lossy	XOR Operation	Symmetric	Grayscale
Tong et al. (2013) [33]	Huffman Coding and NDCT (N-point Discrete Cosine Transform)	Lossless or Lossy	Packed into blocks, Permutation between blocks and diffusion in block	Symmetric	Grayscale
Zhiqianga et al. (2013) [34]	JPEG	Lossless or Lossy	Chaotic Encryption	Symmetric	Grayscale

(Continued)

Table 8.2 (*Continued*)   Summary of Compression + Encryption Techniques for Security of Images

Existing Techniques	Type of Compression Method	Nature of Compression Method	Type of Encryption Method	Nature of Key in Encryption Method	Type of Image
Rahmawati et al. (2013) [35]	DCT, Quantization, Huffman	Lossless or Lossy	Secure Hash Algorithm (SHA) 1	Asymmetric	Grayscale
Sudesh et al. (2014) [36]	Adaptive Compression	Lossless	Milline Transformation	Symmetric	Grayscale
Xiang et al. (2014) [37]	SPIHT	Lossless	Selective Encryption	Symmetric	Grayscale
Goel et al. (2014) [38]	DCT, Huffman	Lossless and Lossy	Dictionary Scrambling	Symmetric	Grayscale
Li and Lo (2015) [39]	JPEG	Lossy	RC4	Symmetric	Grayscale
Challa et al. (2015) [40]	CAN	Lossy	Learning with Errors (LWE) and Public Key	Asymmetric	Grayscale
Tong et al. (2016) [41]	LWT and SPIHT	Lossy and Lossless	Stream Cipher	Symmetric	Grayscale
Kumar and Vaish (2017) [42]	DWT, Singular Value Decomposition (SVD), Huffman	Lossy and Lossless	Stream Cipher	Symmetric	Grayscale

researchers designed approaches using CS theory process with some cryptographic-based encryption techniques applied on grayscale images. Table 8.3 shows the summary of CS based approaches used in combination with cryptographic based encryption techniques to provide security to gray scale images.

There are also CS based encryption methods without using cryptographic based encryption techniques for security of color images [8,52,53]. Nagesh et al. [8] first described color image encryption and decryption process using CS theory. Two methods: Joint R-G-B and Extended Joint R-G-B are proposed for a color image. The DCT is used for generation of encrypted coefficients of each color channels, and TV minimization algorithm is used for decryption of the color image. Zhou et al. [52] described the CS based approach for color astronomical images and ana-lyzed various CS recovery algorithms such as iterative hard thresholding, block TV

Table 8.3 Summary of CS Based Approaches with Combination of Cryptographic Based Encryption Technique for Security of Images

Existing Techniques	Type of Compression Method	Type of Encryption Method	Nature of Key in Encryption Method
Zhou et al. (2014) [44]	CS	Random Pixel Scrambling	Symmetric
Huang et al. (2014) [45]	CS	Arnold Scrambling, Block-wise XOR Operation	Symmetric
Fira (2015) [46]	CS	Substitutions	Symmetric
Zhang et al. (2015) [47]	Random Convolution and Subsampling method based CS	Linear Transform based Encryption	Symmetric
Ahmed et al. (2016) [48]	DCT, Orthogonal Matrix	Partial Encryption	Symmetric
Chen et al. (2016) [49]	Kronecker CS	Elementary Cellular Automata (ECA) Scrambling	Symmetric
Deng et al. (2016) [50]	2D CS	Discrete Fractional Random Transform (DFrRT)	Symmetric
Zhou et al. (2016) [51]	2D CS	Cycle Shift Operation	Symmetric

minimization, and block adaptive sampling TV minimization for decryption of color astronomical images. Singh et al. [53] described how color image is encrypted and decrypted using CS theory process. A color filter array is used to define which channel sparse coefficients are to be sensed by the sensor. Based on these coefficients, the image can be decrypted using CS recovery algorithm.

Most of the existing encryption approaches based on CS are designed using DCT and have less implementations on color images. Thus, in this chapter, image encryption approaches based on CS, DWT and DFT are presented for color images. Measurement matrix A (which is in Gaussian nature) is used as secret key k. The compressed and encrypted color image is generated by various sizes of measurement matrix for individual R-G-B channels of color image. The decryption of color images from these encrypted images is performed by CS recovery algorithm such as orthogonal matching pursuit (OMP) [7]. This approach is analyzed using various image transforms such as DCT [8], DFT, and DWT on various color images that include Landsat satellite images apart from standard images.

Rest of the chapter is organized as follows; Section 8.3 gives the procedure for CS based encryption and decryption of color image. Experimental results and discussion are given in Section 8.4. Finally, the conclusions of the chapter are given in Section 8.5.

8.3 CS Based Encryption Process and Decryption Process for Color Images

In this section, procedure for CS based encryption and decryption of color images is given. At first, the color image is decomposed into individual R, G and B channels. The individual channels are converted into its sparse coefficients using image transform basis matrix. After generating the CS measurements of individual channels using the CS encryption process, they are combined to form an encrypted color image. The decryption of a color image is performed using the CS recovery process. The sparse coefficients of individual channels are extracted using a CS recovery algorithm. The color image is decrypted by applying inverse image transform basis matrix on sparse coefficients of color channels. Figure 8.5 shows the CS based encryption process and CS based decryption process for a color image.

In this chapter, a color image encryption and decryption using CS theory and various image transforms such as DCT, DFT, and DWT are implemented and analyzed. The encryption of a color image is performed using a measurement matrix as a secret key. The decryption of a color image is performed using the measurement matrix and CS recovery algorithm. In all these proposed approaches, a CS recovery algorithm like OMP [7] is used. The reason behind using this algorithm is that its computational time is shorter and easy to be implemented compared to CVX based algorithm. The CVX stands for convex programming. It is optimized based on the modeling system which is developed in MATLAB® for solving complex optimization problems by varying the constraints [54].

The processing steps for existing CS based encryption and decryption processes using DCT for color images is given in Subsection 8.3.1. This approach is designed and implemented by Nagesh in 2009 [8] and modified by Singh in 2014 [52]. In this chapter, this same process is implemented using DCT as well as other two image transforms (DFT and DWT) for color image encryption and decryption.

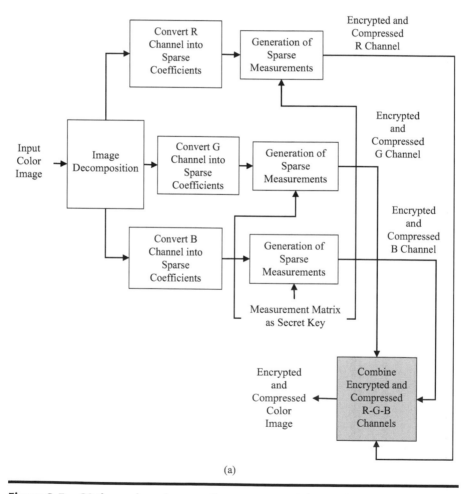

(a)

Figure 8.5   CS theory based encryption process and decryption process for color image. (a) Encryption process.   (*Continued*)

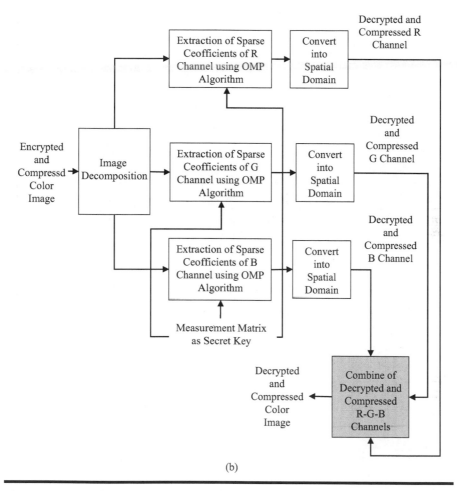

(b)

Figure 8.5 (Continued)   CS theory based encryption process and decryption process for color image. (b) Decryption process.

8.3.1 CS Based Encryption and Decryption Processes Using Image Transform Basis Matrix and Measurement Matrix as a Secret Key

The steps for the CS based encryption and decryption processes using image transform basis matrix and measurement matrix as a secret key for color image are described as follows:

Step 1: Take a color image and decompose it into R channel, G channel and B channel.

Step 2: Generate image transform basis matrices of size equivalent to R channel, G channel and B channel.

Step 3: Convert the value of R channel, G channel and B channels into its sparse coefficients using image transform basis matrix and its inverted version.

$$x_R = \Psi_T \times f_R \times \Psi'_T$$

$$x_G = \Psi_T \times f_G \times \Psi'_T \qquad (8.5)$$

$$x_B = \Psi_T \times f_B \times \Psi'_T$$

where x_R, x_G, and x_B are sparse coefficients of R-G-B channel respectively, Ψ_T is the image transform basis matrix and Ψ'_T is the inverse image transform basis matrix.

Step 4: Generate measurement matrix A using Gaussian distribution with mean = 0 and standard deviation = 1. This matrix A is used as a secret key for the encryption as well as decryption process.

Step 5: Generate CS measurements of R channel, G channel and B channel by multiplying them with their corresponding sparse coefficients and measurement matrix.

$$y_R = A \times x_R$$

$$y_G = A \times x_G \qquad (8.6)$$

$$y_B = A \times x_B$$

where y_R, y_G, and y_B are CS measurements of R-G-B channels respectively, and A is a measurement matrix.

Step 6: Combine CS measurements of individual color channels to get CS measurements of color image, which represent images in encrypted and compressed format. The compressed size and encryption of CS measurements of image depends on the size of measurement matrix.

Step 7: For decryption of a color image, first decompose the encrypted image into CS measurements of R, G and B channels.

Step 8: Feed the CS measurements of R channel, G channel and B channel to OMP algorithm to get extracted sparse coefficients of R channel, G channel and B channel.

$$x'_R = OMP(y_R, A)$$

$$x'_G = OMP(y_G, A) \qquad (8.7)$$

$$x'_B = OMP(y_B, A)$$

where x'_R, x'_G, x'_B are extracted sparse coefficients of R-G-B channel respectively, and OMP is orthogonal matching pursuit algorithm.

Step 9: Obtain the actual values of R channel, G channel and B channel from its extracted sparse coefficients using inverse image transform basis matrices and their original versions.

$$f'_R = \Psi_T \times x'_R \times \Psi'_T$$

$$f'_G = \Psi_T \times x'_G \times \Psi'_T \tag{8.8}$$

$$f'_B = \Psi_T \times x'_B \times \Psi'_T$$

where f'_R, f'_G, f'_B are extracted R-G-B channels of the image respectively.

Step 10: Finally, decrypt color image f' by combining the individual extracted R-G-B channels of the image.

8.4 Experimental Results and Discussion

In this section, the CS based encryption and decryption processes of different color images such as standard images and Landsat satellite image are done and analyzed using various image transform basis matrices such as like DCT, DFT, and DWT. The DCT and DFT basis matrices are generated using the standard DCT [55–59] and DFT equations [55] in MATLAB. The DWT basis matrix is generated using the wavelet matrix described by Yan and Vidakovic [60,61] in MATLAB. The DWT basis matrix is generated using symlet wavelet transform [62]. The implementation of the CS based encryption process and decryption process is done on a laptop: 2 GHz core two Duo processor with 2 GB RAM using MATLAB 2013a software. The information of various test images is described in Subsection 8.4.1. The quality measures for analysis of the proposed technique are discussed in Subsection 8.4.2. The performance analysis of the CS based encryption and decryption process for test images are given in Subsections 8.4.3 and 8.4.4, respectively. Finally, the comparison of approaches are given in Subsections 8.4.5.

8.4.1 Test Color Images

The performance of CS based encryption and decryption varies with different types of color images such as the Goldhill (256×256 pixels) standard image and a Landsat satellite image (256×256 pixels). The Goldhill image is taken from the University of South Carolina SIPI image database [63]. The Landsat satellite image is taken from Landsat image gallery of NASA [64]. These images are shown in Figure 8.6.

 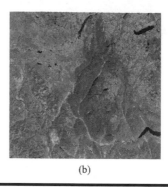

(a)   (b)

Figure 8.6   **Test color images (a) Goldhill (b) Satellite.**

8.4.2 Quality Measures Used for Evaluation of CS Based Encryption and Decryption Processes

The picture quality of CS based encryption and decryption processes is measured by peak Ssignal to noise ratio (PSNR) [2,63–71], structural similarity index measure (SSIM)[66], and compression ratio (CR) [72]. The PSNR measures picture quality of decrypted image with original image. The SSIM is measures similarity of decrypted image with original image. The CR measures compression ratio achieved with CS based encryption. The mathematical equation of PSNR is given as follows:

$$PSNR = 10\log_{10}\left(\frac{255^2}{MSE}\right) \tag{8.9}$$

where MSE is defined as a mean squared error and given by the equation:

$$MSE = \frac{1}{M \times N} \sum_{x=1}^{M} \sum_{y=1}^{N} \{I(x,y) - DI(x,y)\}^2 \tag{8.10}$$

where I and DI are original and decrypted images, respectively. The mathematical equation of SSIM is given below:

$$SSIM = \frac{(2\mu_I\mu_{DI} + C1)(2\sigma_{IDI} + C2)}{\left(\mu_I^2 + \mu_{DI}^2 + C1\right)\left(\sigma_I^2 + \sigma_{DI}^2 + C2\right)} \tag{8.11}$$

where I and DI are original and decrypted images, respectively; μ_I and μ_{I^*} are the corresponding mean value of original and compressed image, respectively;

σ_I and σ_{ID} is the corresponding variance value of original and compressed image, respectively; σ_{IDI} is the covariance of I and DI, $C1$ and $C2$ are positive constant values.

The compression ratio (CR) is found using below equation:

$$CR = \frac{Size_f}{Size_{Cf}} \qquad (8.12)$$

where f is the original image and Cf is the compressed image.

In this chapter, the compression ratio is found between the encrypted image and the original image.

$$CR = \frac{Size_f}{Size_{Ef}} \qquad (8.13)$$

where f is the original image and Ef is the encrypted image.

In this process, the measurement matrix is used as a secret key for generating encrypted and decrypted images. This measurement matrix can be of different types: Fourier, Gaussian, and binary. In this chapter, the Gaussian type measurement matrix is used; it is also responsible for compression in the compressive sensing method. The size of this matrix also decides the compression of image.

The selection of the measurement matrix as a secret key can be done using below equation:

$$k = M \times N \times C \qquad (8.14)$$

where k is the secret key, $M \times N$ is the size of measurement matrix, C is the no. of color channel (here $C = 3$)

8.4.3 Performance Analysis of CS Based Encryption and Decryption Processes for Goldhill Images

In this section, different sizes of encrypted Goldhill images are generated using different sizes of measurement matrices as secret keys. The decryption of these images is performed using the same measurement matrices which are used in encryption and CS recovery OMP algorithm. Figure 8.7 shows the encrypted images and decrypted images using CS based encryption and decryption processes based on DCT coefficients of a Goldhill image. Figure 8.8 shows the results after using DFT coefficients of a Goldhill image instead of DCT. Similarly, Figure 8.9 shows the correponding images when DWT coefficients of the Goldhill image are used. The quality measure values for Goldhill images using CS based encryption and decryption processes are tabulated in Table 8.4.

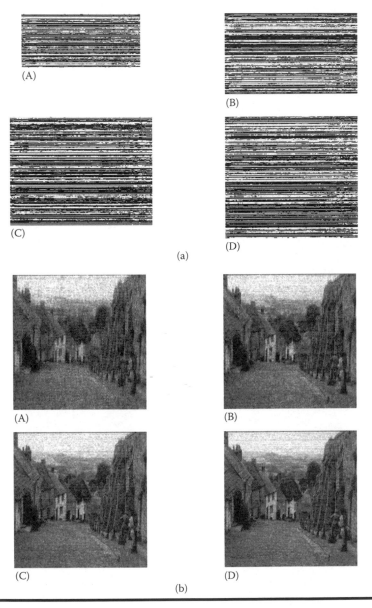

Figure 8.7 Results of CS based encryption and decryption processes using DCT basis matrix. (From Nagesh, P. and Li, B., *Int. Conf. Acoust. Speech Signal Process.*, 1261–1264, 2009; Singh, T. and Singh, M., US Patent No. 8,761,525, US Patent and Trademark Office, Washington, DC, 2014.) (a) Encrypted color image using different secret keys (A) Secret key k = 88320 (B) Secret key k = 118272 (C) Secret key k = 147456 (D) Secret key k = 177408 (b) Decrypted image using different secret keys (A) Secret key k = 88320 (B) Secret key k = 118272 (C) Secret key k = 147456 (D) Secret key k = 177408.

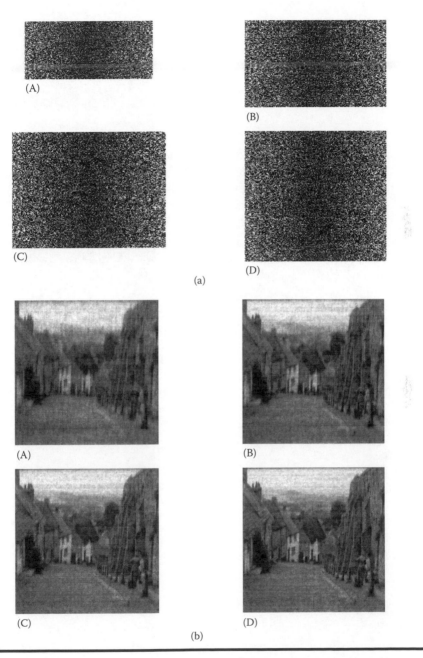

Figure 8.8 Results of CS based encryption and decryption processes using DFT basis matrix (a) Encrypted color image using different secret keys (A) Secret key $k = 88320$ (B) Secret key $k = 118272$ (C) Secret key $k = 147456$ (D) Secret key $k = 177408$ (b) Decrypted image using different secret keys (A) Secret key $k = 88320$ (B) Secret key $k = 118272$ (C) Secret key $k = 147456$ (D) Secret key $k = 177408$.

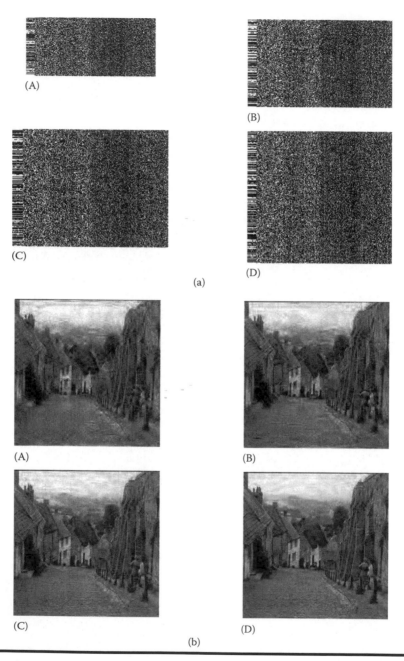

Figure 8.9 Results of CS based encryption and decryption processes using DWT basis matrix (a) Encrypted color image using different secret keys (A) Secret key $k = 88320$ (B) Secret key $k = 118272$ (C) Secret key $k = 147456$ (D) Secret key $k = 177408$ (b) Decrypted image using different secret keys (A) Secret key $k = 88320$ (B) Secret key $k = 118272$ (C) Secret key $k = 147456$ (D) Secret key $k = 177408$.

Table 8.4 Quality Measures Value for CS Based Encryption and Decryption Processes for Goldhill Images

Secret Key k (M×N×C)	Using DCT Basis Matrix [8] [52]		Using DFT Basis Matrix		Using DWT Basis Matrix		Compression Ratio (CR)
	PSNR (dB)	SSIM	PSNR (dB)	SSIM	PSNR (dB)	SSIM	
88320 (115×256×3)	36.12	0.7756	37.05	0.8005	36.81	0.8011	2.22
118272 (154×256×3)	36.73	0.8233	37.95	0.8728	37.56	0.8522	1.66
147456 (192×256×3)	37.27	0.8639	38.40	0.8969	38.38	0.8937	1.33
177408 (231×256×3)	37.75	0.8919	38.90	0.9218	39.18	0.9260	1.11

After obtaining results of CS based encryption and decryption processes for the Goldhill image, below observations are made:

1. The experiment results show that CS based encryption and decryption processes equally performed well for standard images using DCT basis matrix, DFT basis matrix, and DWT basis matrix.
2. The results of DFT and DWT basis matrices are better than results of the DCT basis matrix. This indicates that the performance of the CS encryption and decryption processes using DFT and DWT are better than the existing process using DCT [8,52].
3. The quality of decrypted image increases with size of secret key k.
4. The visual quality of decrypted images shows that some loss has taken place (based on the histogram of decrypted images). This indicates that this approach is lossy.
5. The compression ratio up to 2.22 is achieved using this CS based approach.

8.4.4 Performance Analysis of CS Based Encryption and Decryption Processes for Landsat Satellite Images

In this section, different sizes of encrypted Landsat satellite images are generated using different sizes of measurement matrix as secret keys. The decryption of these images is performed using the same measurement matrix which is used in encryption and CS recovery OMP algorithm. Figures 8.10 through 8.12 shows the encrypted images, decrypted images, and histograms of decrypted images when DCT, DFT and DWT coefficients are used. The quality measures obtained for the Landsat satellite image using CS based encryption and decryption processes are tabulated in Table 8.5.

After obtaining the results of CS based encryption and decryption processes for the Landsat satellite image, the below observation on results are made.

1. The experiment results show that CS based encryption and decryption processes using DCT and DWT basis matrices have not performed well for Landsat satellite images, and hence are not applicable for these kinds of images.
2. The visual quality of decrypted images using DCT basis matrix, DWT basis matrix are not good compared to the visual quality of decrypted images resulting from the DFT basis matrix. This indicates that the results of DFT basis matrix are better than the results of DCT and DWT basis matrices.

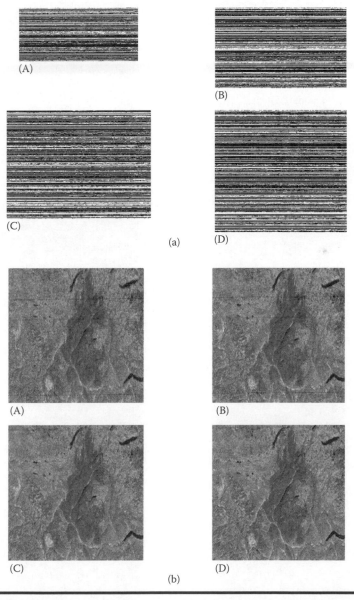

Figure 8.10 Results of CS based encryption and decryption processes using DCT basis matrix. (From Nagesh, P. and Li, B., *Int. Conf. Acoust. Speech Signal Process.*, 1261–1264, 2009; Singh, T. and Singh, M., US Patent No. 8,761,525, US Patent and Trademark Office, Washington, DC, 2014.) (a) Encrypted color image using different secret keys (A) Secret key $k = 216000$ (B) Secret key $k = 288000$ (C) Secret key $k = 360000$ (D) Secret key $k = 432000$ (b) Decrypted image using different secret keys (A) Secret key $k = 216000$ (B) Secret key $k = 288000$ (C) Secret key $k = 360000$ (D) Secret key $k = 432000$.

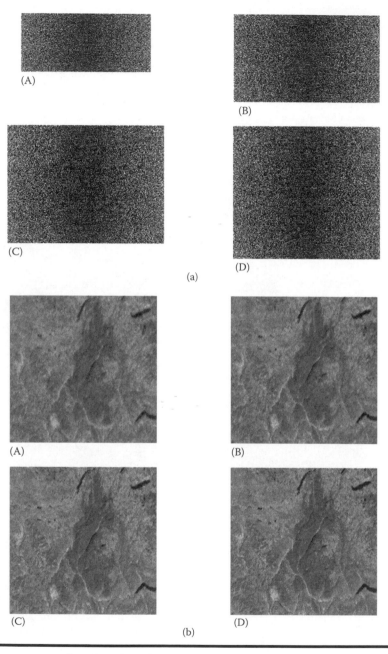

Figure 8.11 Results of CS based encryption and decryption processes using DFT basis matrix (a) Encrypted color image using different secret keys (A) Secret key $k = 216000$ (B) Secret key $k = 288000$ (C) Secret key $k = 360000$ (D) Secret key $k = 432000$ (b) Decrypted image using different secret keys (A) Secret key $k = 216000$ (B) Secret key $k = 288000$ (C) Secret key $k = 360000$ (D) Secret key $k = 432000$.

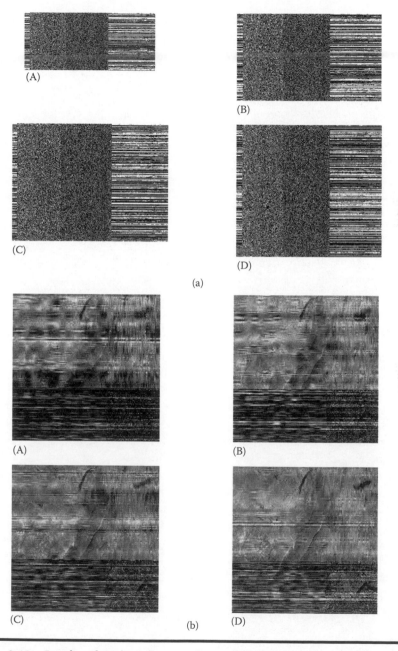

Figure 8.12 Results of CS based encryption and decryption processes using DWT basis matrix (a) Encrypted color image using different secret keys (A) Secret key $k = 216000$ (B) Secret key $k = 288000$ (C) Secret key $k = 360000$ (D) Secret key $k = 432000$ (b) Decrypted image using different secret keys (A) Secret key $k = 216000$ (B) Secret key $k = 288000$ (C) Secret key $k = 360000$ (D) Secret key $k = 432000$.

Table 8.5 Quality Measures Value for CS Based Encryption Process and Decryption Process for Landsat Satellite Images

Secret Key k (M×N×C)	Using DCT Basis Matrix [8] [52]		Using DFT Basis Matrix		Using DWT Basis Matrix		Compression Ratio (CR)
	PSNR (dB)	SSIM	PSNR (dB)	SSIM	PSNR (dB)	SSIM	
216000 (180×400×3)	34.34	0.7007	38.48	0.8201	31.82	0.2990	2.22
288000 (240×400×3)	34.62	0.7506	39.18	0.8776	32.24	0.3591	1.66
360000 (300×400×3)	34.79	0.7729	39.81	0.9147	32.66	0.4477	1.33
432000 (360×400×3)	34.90	0.7864	40.42	0.9399	33.24	0.5373	1.11

8.4.5 Discussion

The test database [63,64] which contains 15 standard color images and 35 Landsat satellite images are used for analysis of a proposed encryption approach. It is observed that the results of DCT and DWT based approaches for Landsat satellite images are not good. This happens since images are acquired remotely by moving sensors from very large distances and have low resolution. It is also observed that the same image transforms effectively work on standard images.

Some researchers [73–75] showed the application of CS theory on Landsat satellite images and color videos. The results obtained using these techniques are not good for data acquired by moving sensor or moving data acquired by steady sensor. The reason behind this situation is that these data are acquired in real time and have real as well as imaginary components. While CS theory using DCT and DWT works effectively on real data, it is observed that there is less effect on imaginary data. On the other hand, the CS theory using DFT effectively works on real as well as imaginary data and hence is good for Landsat satellite images.

8.4.6 Comparison of Presented Process

The presented process using DFT and DWT basis matrices is compared with the Nagesh [8] and Singh [52] processes by various features listed in Table 8.6. While the Nagesh [8] and Singh [52] process used DCT basis matrix, the presented process used DFT and DWT basis matrices. The maximum PSNR value in the Nagesh [8] and Singh [52] processes is 37.75 dB, and in the presented processes it is 40.42 dB.

Table 8.6 Comparison of Presented Process Using DFT Basis Matrix and DWT Basis Matrix with Existing Process Using DCT Basis Matrix [8] [52]

Parameters	Nagesh Process [8] and Singh Process [52]	Presented Process
Applicable for Types of Color Images	Standard Image and Natural Image	Standard Image and Natural Image
Used Transform Basis Matrix	Discrete Cosine Transform (DCT)	Discrete Fourier Transform (DFT) and Discrete Wavelet Transform (DWT)
Maximum PSNR (dB)	37.75	40.42
Maximum SSIM	0.8919	0.9399

The maximum SSIM value in the Nagesh [8] and Singh [52] processes is 0.8919, and in the presented processes it is 0.9399. This indicates that the presented process using DFT and DWT basis matrices performed better than existing processes which used DCT basis matrix [8,52].

8.5 Conclusion and Future Work

This chapter gives study and analysis of CS based encryption and decryption processes for security of different types of color images. The CS based encryption process performs compression of the image simultaneously. The application of the CS theory for image security is discussed. The implementation and analysis of CS based encryption using three different transforms: DCT, DFT, and DWT for various types of color images such as standard and Landsat satellite images are done. A compression ratio of up to 2.22 can be achieved with this process and hence can provide better compression with encryption to a color image. At the same time, the quality of decrypted Landsat satellite images using DCT and DWT are not good. This indicates that this process using DCT and DWT basis matrices are not applicable for images which are acquired using moving sensors.

The results of processes using DFT and DWT basis matrices are compared with the results of an existing process using DCT, which is described by Nagesh in 2009 [8] and Singh in 2014 [52]. It is found from the comparison that CS based encryption and decryption processes using DFT and DWT performed better than using DCT basis matrix in terms of picture quality of the decrypted color images. In the future, this approach can be applied in the security of data in emerging areas such as cloud computing and advanced wireless systems. This approach can also be applied to encryption of medical data in teleradiology applications.

References

1. Setyaningsih, E., Wardoyo, R., 2017. Review of image compression and encryption techniques. *International Journal of Advanced Computer Science and Applications* 8(2): 83–94.

2. Ashour, A., Dey, N., 2017. Security of multimedia contents: A brief. In N. Dey and V. Santhi (Eds.) *Intelligent Technique in Signal Processing for Multimedia Security.* Springer, Cham, Switzerland, pp. 3–14.

3. Ranjan, R., Sharma, R., Hanmandlu, M., 2016. Color image encryption and decryption using Hill Cipher associated with Arnold transform. *Applications and Applied Mathematics: An International Journal* 11(1): 45–60.

4. Candes, E., 2006. Compressive sampling. *Proceedings of the International Congress of Mathematicians, Madrid, Spain* 3: 1433–1452.

5. Donoho, D., 2006. Compressed sensing. *IEEE Transactions on Information Theory* 52(4): 1289–1306.

6. Baraniuk, R., 2007. Lecture notes "Compressive Sensing". *IEEE Signal Processing Magazine* 24(4): 118–124.

7. Tropp, J., Gilbert, A., 2007. Signal recovery from random measurements via orthogonal matching pursuit. *IEEE Transactions on Information Theory* 53(12): 4655–4666.

8. Nagesh, P., Li, B., 2009. Compressive imaging of color images. *2009 IEEE International Conference on Acoustics, Speech and Signal Processing* 1261–1264.

9. Johnson, M., Wagner, D., Ramchandran, K., 2004. On compressing encrypted data without the encryption key. *Proceedings of First Theory of Cryptography Conference, TCC 2004, Cambridge, MA* 491–504.

10. Liu, W., Zeng, W., Dong, L., Yao, Q., 2010. Efficient compression of encrypted grayscale images. *IEEE Transactions on Image Processing* 19(4): 1097–1102.

11. Shafinah, K., Ikram, M., 2011. File security based on pretty good privacy (PGP) concept. *Computer and Information Science* 4(4): 10–28.

12. Razzaque, A., Thakur, N., 2012. An approach to image compression with partial encryption without sharing the secret key. *International Journal of Computer Science and Network Security* 12(7): 1–6.

13. Kang, X., Peng, A., Xu, X., Cao, X., 2013. Performing scalable lossy compression on pixel encrypted images. *EURASIP Journal on Image and Video Processing* 2013(1): 32.

14. MariSelvi, C., Kumar, A., 2014. A modified encryption algorithm for compression of color image. *International Journal of Recent Development in Engineering and Technology* 2(3): 94–98.

15. Arunkumar, M., Prabu, S., 2014. Implementation of encrypted image compression using resolution progressive compression scheme. *International Journal of Computer Science and Mobile Computing* 3(6): 585–590.

16. Sharma, D., Saxena, R., Singh, N., 2014. Hybrid encryption–Compression scheme based on multiple parameter discrete fractional fourier transform with eigen vector decomposition algorithm. *International Journal of Computer Network and Information Security* 6(10): 1–12.

17. Aujla, H., Sharma, R., 2014. Designing an efficient image encryption then compression system with Haar and Daubechies wavelet. *International Journal of Computer Science and Information Technologies* 5(6): 7784–7788.

18. Kamble, Y., Manwade, K., 2014. Secure data communication using image encryption and compression. *International Journal of Advanced Research in Computer and Communication Engineering* 3(12): 8–11.
19. Kale, N., Natikar, S., Karande, S., 2014. Secured mobile messaging for android application. *International Journal of Advance Research in Computer Science and Management Studies* 2(11): 304–311.
20. Wu, C., Kuo, C., 2005. Design of integrated multimedia compression and encryption systems. *IEEE Transactions on Multimedia* 7(5): 828–839.
21. Ou, S., Chung, H., Sung, W., 2006. Improving the compression and encryption of images using FPGA-based cryptosystems. *Multimedia Tools and Applications* 28(1): 5–22.
22. Loussert, A., Alfalou, A., El Sawda, R., Alkholidi, A., 2008. Enhanced system for image's compression and encryption by addition of biometric characteristics. *International Journal of Software Engineering and Its Applications* 2(2): 111–118.
23. Krikor, L., Baba, S., Arif, T., Shaaban, Z., 2009. Image encryption using DCT and stream cipher. *European Journal of Scientific Research* 32(1): 47–57.
24. Hermassi, H., Rhouma, R., Belghith, S., 2010. Joint compression and encryption using chaotically mutated Huffman trees. *Communications in Nonlinear Science and Numerical Simulation* 15(10): 2987–2999.
25. Benabdellah, M., Regragui, F., Bouyakhf, E., 2011. Hybrid methods of image compression–Encryption. *Journal of Communication & Computer Engineering* 1(1): 1–11.
26. Chen, J., Zhou, J., Wong, W., 2011. A modified chaos-based joint compression and encryption scheme. *IEEE Transactions on Circuits and Systems II: Express Briefs* 58(2): 110–114.
27. Samson, C., Sastry, V., 2012. A novel image encryption supported by compression using multilevel wavelet transform. *International Journal of Advanced Computer Science and Applications* 3(9): 178–183.
28. Samson, C., Sastry, V., 2012. An RGB image encryption supported by wavelet-based lossless compression. *International Journal of Advanced Computer and Applications* 3(9): 36–41.
29. Gupta, K., Silakari, S., 2012. Novel approach for fast compressed hybrid color image cryptosystem. *Advances in Engineering Software* 49(1): 29–42.
30. Kishore, P., Nagendra, N., Reddy, K., Murthy, V., 2012. Smoothing and optimal compression of encrypted gray scale images. *International Journal of Engineering Research and Applications* 2(3): 23–28.
31. Nair, A., Sundararaj, G., Perumal, T., 2012. Simultaneous compression and encryption using arithmetic coding with randomized bits. *International Journal of Computer Technology and Electronics Engineering* 2(2): 38–42.
32. Alfalou, A., Brosseau, C., Abdallah, N., Jridi, M., 2013. Assessing the performance of a method of simultaneous compression and encryption of multiple images and its resistance against various attacks. *Optics Express* 21(7): 10253–10265.
33. Tong, X., Wang, Z., Zhang, M., Liu, Y., 2013. A new algorithm of the combination of image compression and encryption technology based on cross chaotic map. *Nonlinear Dynamics* 72(1–2): 229–241.
34. Zhiqianga, L., Xiaoxin, S., Changbin, D., Qun, D., 2013. JPEG algorithm analysis and application in image compression encryption of digital chaos. *Third International Conference on Instrumentation, Measurement, Computer, Communication and Control* 185–189.

35. Rahmawati, W., Saikhu, A., Kompresi, A., 2013. Implementasi Algoritma Penggabungan Kompresi dan Enkripsi Citra dengan DCT dan SHA-1. *Jurnal Teknik POMITS* 2(1): 1–4.
36. Sudesh, Kaushik, A., Kaushik, S., 2014. A two stage hybrid model for image encryption and compression to enhance security and efficiency. *International Conference on Advances in Engineering & Technology Research* 1–5.
37. Xiang, T., Qu, J., Xiao, D., 2014. Joint SPIHT compression and selective encryption. *Applied Soft Computing* 21: 159–170.
38. Goel, N., Raman, B., Gupta, I., 2014. Chaos based joint compression and encryption framework for end-to-end communication systems. *Advances in Multimedia* 2014: 1–10.
39. Li, P., Lo, K., 2015. Joint image compression and encryption based on alternating transforms with quality control. *Visual Communications and Image Processing* 1–4.
40. Challa, R., Kumari, G., Sruthi, P., 2015. Proficient LWE-based encryption using CAN compression algorithm. *2015 Conference on Power, Control, Communication and Computational Technologies for Sustainable Growth* 304–307.
41. Tong, X., Chen, P., Zhang, M., 2017. A joint image lossless compression and encryption method based on chaotic map. *Multimedia Tools and Applications* 76(12): 13995–14020.
42. Kumar, M., Vaish, A., 2017. An efficient encryption-then-compression technique for encrypted images using SVD. *Digital Signal Processing* 60: 81–89.
43. Zhang, Y., Zhang, L., Zhou, J., Liu, L, Chen, F., He, X., 2016. A review of compressive sensing in information security field. *IEEE Access* 4: 2507–2519.
44. Zhou, N., Zhang, A., Zheng, F., Gong, L., 2014. Novel image compression-encryption hybrid algorithm based on key-controlled measurement matrix in compressive sensing. *Optics & Laser Technology* 62: 152–160.
45. Huang, R., Rhee, K., Uchida, S., 2014. A parallel image encryption method based on compressive sensing. *Multimedia Tools and Applications* 72(1): 71–93.
46. Fira, M., 2015. Applications of compressed sensing: Compression and encryption. *2015 E-Health and Bioengineering Conference (EHB)* 1–4.
47. Zhang, Y., Wong, K., Zhang, L., Wen, W., Zhou, J., He, X., 2015. Exploiting random convolution and random subsampling for image encryption and compression. *Signal Processing: Image Communication* 39(20): 202–211.
48. Ahmed, J., Khan, M., Hwang, S., Khan, J., 2016. A compression sensing and noise-tolerant image encryption scheme based on chaotic maps and orthogonal matrices. *Neural Computing and Applications* 2016: 1–5.
49. Chen, T., Zhang, M., Wu, J., Yuen, C., Tong, Y., 2016. Image encryption and compression based on kronecker compressed sensing and elementary cellular automata scrambling. *Optics & Laser Technology* 84: 118–133.
50. Deng, J., Zhao, S., Wang, Y., Wang, L., Wang, H., Sha, H., 2017. Image compression–Encryption scheme combining 2D compressive sensing with discrete fractional random transform. *Multimedia Tools and Applications* 76(7): 10097–10117.
51. Zhou, N., Pan, S., Cheng, S., Zhou, Z., 2016. Image compression–Encryption scheme based on hyper-chaotic system and 2D compressive sensing. *Optics & Laser Technology* 82: 121–133.
52. Singh, T., Singh, M., 2014. US Patent No. 8,761,525. US Patent and Trademark Office: Washington, DC.

53. Zhou, W. Li, Y., Liu, Q., Wang, G., Liu, Y., 2014. Fast compression and reconstruction of astronomical images based on compressed sensing. *Research in Astronomy and Astrophysics* 14(9): 1207.
54. Michael, G., Boyd, S., Ye, Y., 2011. CVX users' guide Paper. Stanford University, Stanford, CA.
55. Jain, A., 1989. *Fundamentals of Digital Image Processing.* Prentice-Hall: Englewood Cliffs, NJ.
56. Parah, S., Sheikh, J., Dey, N., Bhat, G., 2017. Realization of a new robust and secure watermarking technique using DC coefficient modification in pixel domain and chaotic encryption. *Journal of Global Information Management* 25(4): 80–102.
57. Bhattacharya, T., Dey, N., Chaudhuri, S.R., 2012. A session based multiple image hiding technique using DWT and DCT. *arXiv preprint arXiv: 1208.0950.*
58. Dey, N., Das, P., Roy, A.B., Das, A., Chaudhuri, S.S., 2012. DWT-DCT-SVD based intravascular ultrasound video watermarking. *In Information and Communication Technologies (WICT), 2012 World Congress on* 224–229.
59. Dey, N., Biswas, D., Roy, A.B., Das, A., Chaudhuri, S.S., 2012. DWT-DCT-SVD based blind watermarking technique of gray image in electrooculogram signal. *In Intelligent Systems Design and Applications (ISDA), 2012 12th International Conference on* 680–685.
60. Vidakovic, B., 1999. *Statistical Modeling by Wavelets.* Wiley: New York.
61. Yan, J., 2009. Wavelet matrix. Report. Department of Electrical and Computer Engineering, University of Victoria, BC, Canada.
62. Thanki, R., Borisagar, K., Borra, S., 2017. *Advance Compression and Watermarking Technique for Speech Signals.* Springer, Cham, Switzerland.
63. The University of South Carolina SIPI Image Database: http://sipi.usc.edu/database/database.php, Last access date: August 30, 2017.
64. Landsat satellite image Database: https://landsat.visibleearth.nasa.gov/ and http://sipi.usc.edu/database/database.php, Last access date: August 30, 2017.
65. Mrak, M., Grgic, S., Grgic, M., 2003. Picture quality measures in image compression systems. *In EUROCON 2003, Computer as a Tool, The IEEE Region 8* 1: 233–236.
66. Wang, Z., Bovik, A., Simoncelli, E., 2004. Image quality assessment: From error visibility to structural similarity. *IEEE Transactions on Image Processing* 13: 600–612.
67. Borra, S., Lakshmi, H., Dey, N., Ashour, A., Shi, F., 2017. Digital image watermarking tools: State-of-the-art. *Frontiers in Artificial Intelligence and Applications* 296: 450–459.
68. Thanki, R., Kothari, A., 2017. Digital watermarking: Technical art of hiding a message. In S. Bhattacharyya, H. Bhaumik, S. De and G. Klepac (Eds.) *Intelligent Analysis of Multimedia Information.* IGI Global, Hershey, PA, pp. 431–466.
69. Dey, N. and Santhi, V. Eds., 2017. *Intelligent Techniques in Signal Processing for Multimedia Security.* Springer, Cham, Switzerland.
70. Dey, N., Roy, A.B., Dey, S., 2012. A novel approach of color image hiding using RGB color planes and DWT. *arXiv preprint arXiv: 1208.0803.*
71. Bhattacharya, T., Dey, N., Chaudhuri, S.R., 2012. A novel session based dual steganographic technique using DWT and spread spectrum. *arXiv preprint arXiv: 1209.0054.*
72. Bhojani, D., 2013. Design and performance analysis of digital video compression and watermarking using transform domain techniques. Access online: ir.inflibnet.ac.in.

73. Divekar, A., Ersoy, O., 2010. Theory and applications of compressive sensing. Report. Purdue University, Lafayette, IN.

74. Feng, W., Feng-wei, C., Wang, J., 2015. Reconstruction technique based on the theory of compressed sensing satellite images. *The Open Electrical & Electronic Engineering Journal* 9: 74–81.

75. Thanki, R., Vedvyas, D., Borisagar, K., 2017. Review and comparative evaluation of compressive sensing for digital video. *Proceedings of the 5th International Conference on Advanced Computing, Networking, and Informatics (ICACNI 2017), Goa.*

Chapter 9

Secure Threshold Attribute-Based Signcryption with Constant Number of Pairings

Y. Sreenivasa Rao and Nishant Doshi

Contents

DOI: 10.1201/9780429435461-10

217

9.1 Introduction

Over the last decade, Attribute-Based Encryption (ABE) [1–3] has become an elegant solution to the problem of providing fine grained access control over encrypted data. In this public key encryption, public keys are attributes, and private keys and ciphertexts are generated based on some policies (a.k.a. access policies) over attributes. If the policy is embedded in user secret key, such ABE is called as Key-Policy ABE (KP-ABE) [1,3]. The complementary encryption is called as Ciphertext-Policy ABE (CP-ABE) [2,4] wherein the policy is encoded in ciphertext. Following the introduction of ABE, the notion of digital signature was soon extended to the attribute-based framework. In Attribute-Based Signature (ABS) [5], a message is signed under a policy or an attribute set using a signing key associated with an attribute set or a policy, respectively. Encryption offers confidentiality and signature provides authenticity. To achieve these two functionalities in a single primitive, Gagné et al. [6] suggested an Attribute-Based Signcryption (ABSC), called threshold ABSC (tABSC), which is a logical combination of ABE and ABS. They use threshold policies to encrypt and sign messages. Subsequently, various ABSC schemes [5,7–9] have been proposed realizing expressive policies like monotone Boolean formulae. However, tABSC schemes remain attractive for many applications such as body area network security [10], authenticated key agreement [11] etc.

The existing tABSC schemes [6,10–12] have been cryptanalysed as follows. In [13], the authors showed that the scheme [10] cannot resist private key forgery attack, in the sense that an adversary can impersonate the trusted key server and generate private keys for any set of attributes, thus totally break the scheme. In [14], the authors presented a concrete forgery attack on the tABSC scheme [6]. The attack can make use of some keys to construct any other legal keys and at last totally break the scheme. It can be seen that the tABSC [11] cannot provide message confidentiality in existing security model. This is due to the fact that the construction [11] has not employed any of the standard signcryption techniques such as Sign-then-Encrypt, Encrypt-then-Sign and logical combination of signature and encryption. Besides, the number of expensive pairing computations in [6,10,11] is linear in $e + s$, where e (resp. s) is the number of encryption (resp. signing) attributes. In turn, constructing efficient tABSC scheme with strong security notion is a crucial problem. Belguith et al. [12] proved that their scheme is IND-CCA2 secure; that is, given a cipher-text for the message msg_b randomly chosen from $\{msg_0, msg_1\}$, no polynomial time adversary (with an access to unsigncrypt oracle) can determine from which message msg_0 or msg_1 the ciphertext is computed, i.e., $msg_b = msg_0$ or $msg_b = msg_1$, with a non-negligible advantage. However, the tABSC in [12] is not even IND-CPA secure, i.e., any adversary can decide wether $msg_b = msg_0$ or $msg_b = msg_1$ with certainty, with-out querying the unsigncrypt oracle. This follows from the subsequent argument. The adversary obtains the challenge ciphertext of msg_b after submitting $\{msg_0, msg_1\}$ to the challenger that is of the form $CT = (C_1, C_2, C_3, \sigma_1, \sigma_2, \sigma_3, P_{A_S,S}(\gamma), B_1)$, where $\sigma_3 = h_0^{\mathcal{H}(msg_b)}$. Note here that h_0 is a public parameter and $\mathcal{H}(\cdot)$ is a publicly known hash function. The adversary first guesses $msg_b = msg_0$ and checks whether $\sigma_3 \stackrel{?}{=} h_0^{\mathcal{H}(msg_0)}$. If this verification passes, $msg_b = msg_0$; otherwise, $msg_b = msg_1$. This vio-lates the IND-CPA security of the tABSC scheme proposed in [12]. This description exhibits that the existing tABSC schemes [6,10–12] are not secure, thereby not suit-able for practical applications. So, we study the problem of designing secure tABSC scheme with low computation cost.

9.1.1 Our Contribution

In this chapter, we focus on constructing a secure tABSC scheme with a *constant* number of pairing evaluations, to be precise only 7. This makes our scheme effi-cient from a computation point of view. We also target to realize *public verifiability*, which enables any intermediate party to check the ciphertext's integrity and sender authenticity without knowledge of the underlying message and secret keys. This reduces unnecessary overload on the decryptor for unsigncrypting invalid cipher-texts. The security notion of the message confidentiality of our tABSC scheme will be discussed in indistinguishability of ciphertexts under selective encryption attri-bute set and adaptive chosen ciphertext attack (IND-sEA-CCA2 security) model by assuming the interactability of the decision bilinear Diffie-Hellman (DBDH) problem. And the ciphertext unforgeability will be argued through existential unforgeability under selective signing attribute sets and an adaptive chosen mes-sage attack (EUF-sSA-CMA security) model assuming the hardness of the compu-tational Diffie-Hellman (CDH) problem.

Chapter Organization. The rest of the chapter is organized as follows: The necessary mathematical and cryptographic background is reviewed in Section 9.2. Definition and security notions of threshold attribute-based signcryption are dis-cussed in Section 9.3. In Section 9.4, we will present our tABSC scheme with a constant number of pairings and its security proofs. Section 9.5 is dedicated to discuss the performance of our proposed scheme. Finally, the chapter is concluded in Section 9.6.

9.2 Background

We begin cryptographic preliminaries by describing some important notations that are required for an unambiguous presentation of the paper.

9.2.1 Notation

$\mathbb{N}$	: set of all natural numbers
$[n]$	: set $\{1, 2, \ldots, n\}$ of first n natural numbers, for any $n \in \mathbb{N}$
$z \xleftarrow{R} X$	: z is randomly chosen from X according to uniform distribution
$\mathbb{Z}_p$	: the set of integers modulo p
$\mathbb{Z}_p^*$	: $\mathbb{Z}_p \setminus \{0\}$
$\text{Prob}[E]$	: probability of an event F happening
PPT	: probabilistic polynomial time

9.2.2 Lagrange Interpolation

Every $\delta - 1$ degree polynomial $f(x)$ (over $\mathbb{Z}_p$) can be reconstructed from any δ distinct points $(x_1, f(x_1)), (x_2, f(x_2)), \ldots, (x_\delta, f(x_\delta))$ as described below.

$$f(x) = \sum_{i \in \Omega} f(i) \cdot \Delta_{i,\Omega}(x)$$

where $\Omega := \{x_1, x_2, \ldots, x_\delta\}$ and $\Delta_{i,\Omega}(x) := \prod_{j \in \Omega, j \neq i} (x - j / i - j)$ which is the Lagrange coefficient of i in Ω. Hence, given any δ different polynomial values, one can compute $f(y)$ for any $y \in \mathbb{Z}_p$. Note that if only $\delta - 1$ different polynomial values are given, the other polynomial values are unconditionally secure.

9.2.3 Bilinear Pairings in Prime Order Groups

A bilinear group generator takes as input a security parameter κ and outputs a description of a prime order bilinear group, $\Sigma := [p, \mathbb{G}, \mathbb{G}_T, g, e]$, where

- p is a prime number with $p \in \Theta(2^\kappa)$,
- $(\mathbb{G}, \cdot)$ and $(\mathbb{G}_T, \cdot)$ are cyclic groups of the same order p, and g is a generator of $\mathbb{G}$,
- $e : \mathbb{G} \times \mathbb{G} \to \mathbb{G}_T$ is a bilinear mapping or (bilinear) pairing satisfying
  a. $\forall g, h \in \mathbb{G}$ and $x, y \in \mathbb{Z}_p$, we have $e(g^x, h^y) = e(g, h)^{xy}$,
  b. $\exists g \in \mathbb{G}$ such that $e(g, g)$ is distinct from the identity element in $\mathbb{G}_T$,
  c. There is a polynomial (in κ) time algorithm to compute every $e(g, h)$, where $g, h \in \mathbb{G}$.

9.2.4 Hardness Assumptions

Decision Bilinear Diffie-Hellman Assumption The DBDH problem is defined as follows: given $\Sigma, \Gamma_1 := g^a \in \mathbb{G}, \Gamma_2 := g^b \in \mathbb{G}, \Gamma_3 := g^c \in \mathbb{G}$ for unknown $a, b, c \in \mathbb{Z}_p^*$ and $Z \in \mathbb{G}_T$, to decide whether $Z = e(g, g)^{abc}$ or Z is a random element of $\mathbb{G}_T$.

We say that the DBDH assumption holds in Σ if the advantage $Adv_A^{DBDH} := | Prob[1 \leftarrow A(\Sigma, \Gamma_1, \Gamma_2, \Gamma_3, e(g, g)^{abc})] - Prob[1 \leftarrow A(\Sigma, \Gamma_1, \Gamma_2, \Gamma_3, Z)]|$ of every PPT algorithm A in solving DBDH problem is negligible.

Computational Diffie-Hellman Assumption The CDH is defined as follows: given $\Sigma, \Gamma_1 := g^a \in \mathbb{G}, \Gamma_2 := g^b \in \mathbb{G}$ for unknown $a, b \in \mathbb{Z}_p^*$, to compute $g^{ab} \in \mathbb{G}$.

We say that the CDH assumption holds in $\mathbb{G}$ if the advantage $Adv_A^{CDH} := Prob[g^{ab} \leftarrow A(\Sigma, \Gamma_1, \Gamma_2)]$ of every PPT algorithm A in solving CDH problem is negligible.

9.3 Definition and Security Notions of Threshold Attribute-Based Signcryption

9.3.1 Threshold Attribute-Based Signcryption Definition

The tABSC scheme comprises the following five algorithms (as shown in Figure 9.1). In this construction, the threshold value need not be the same for all the executions.

Setup(κ, U) A Central trusted Authority (CA) executes this algorithm to initialize the system. The system setup algorithm takes as input the security parameter $\kappa \in \mathbb{N}$ and the attribute universe U, and creates the system public parameters

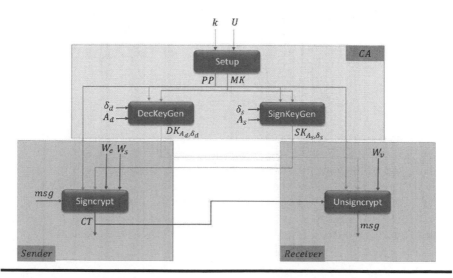

Figure 9.1 Architecture of threshold attribute-based signcryption.

$\mathcal{PP}$ together with the system master key $\mathcal{MK}$. The public parameters $\mathcal{PP}$ include a description of the message space $\mathcal{M}$. The attribute universe U is union of both signing attribute universe U_s and encryption/decryption attribute universe U_e. That is, $U = U_s \cup U_e$.

DecKeyGen$(\mathcal{PP}, \mathcal{MK}, A_d, \delta_d)$ This decryption key generation algorithm is executed by CA to compute a decryption key $\mathcal{DK}_{A_d, \delta_d}$ for a set $A_d \subset U_e$ ($|A_d| \geq \delta_d$) of decryption attributes and a threshold δ_d.

SignKeyGen$(\mathcal{PP}, \mathcal{MK}, A_s, \delta_s)$ The signing key generation algorithm is executed by CA to compute the signing key $\mathcal{SK}_{A_s, \delta_s}$ for a set $A_s \subset U_s$ of signing attributes and a threshold δ_s. Note that $|A_s| \geq \delta_s$.

Signcrypt$(\mathcal{PP}, \mathcal{SK}_{A_s, \delta_s}, W_e, W_s, msg)$ A signcrypting party executes this algorithm with the input $\mathcal{PP}$, a message $msg \in \mathcal{M}$, signing key $\mathcal{SK}_{A_s, \delta_s}$ for the attribute set A_s, an encryption attribute set $W_e \subset U_e$ and a signing attribute set $W_s \subseteq A_s$ with $|W_s| \geq \delta_s$. It produces a ciphertext CT. The encryption attribute set W_e and the signing threshold δ_s are included in CT.

Unsigncrypt$(\mathcal{PP}, CT, W_v, \mathcal{DK}_{A_d, \delta_d})$ This algorithm is executed by ciphertext receivers with the input $\mathcal{PP}, CT$, a signature verification attribute set W_v and a decryption key $\mathcal{DK}_{A_d, \delta_d}$ of a decryption attribute set A_d. It will correctly recover the message msg only if $|A_d \cap W_e| \geq \delta_d$ and the ciphertext CT contains a valid signature corresponding to W_v. Otherwise, it outputs $\perp$, indicating that either the ciphertext is not valid or the ciphertext cannot be decrypted.

Definition 9.1. *The tABSC scheme is correct if it satisfies the following property:*

$$
\begin{array}{l|l}
\textbf{Setup}\,(\kappa, U) \rightarrow (\mathcal{PP}, MK) & \\
\textbf{DecKeyGen}\,(\mathcal{PP}, \mathcal{MK}, A_d, \delta_d) \rightarrow \mathcal{DK}_{A_d, \delta_d} & \Rightarrow \textbf{Unsigncrypt} \\
\textbf{SignKeyGen}\,(\mathcal{PP}, \mathcal{MK}, A_s, \delta_s) \rightarrow \mathcal{SK}_{A_s, \delta_s} & (\mathcal{PP}, CT, W_v, \mathcal{DK}_{A_d, \delta_d}) = msg \\
\textbf{Signcrypt}\,(\mathcal{PP}, \mathcal{SK}_{A_s, \delta_s}, W_e, W_s, msg) \rightarrow CT & \\
W_v = W_s \text{ and } |A_d \cap W_e| \geq \delta_d &
\end{array}
$$

9.3.2 Security Definitions

We define here the message confidentiality and ciphertext unforgeability which are essential security notions of attribute-based signcryption.

Message Confidentiality We define the security notion of message confidentiality in tABSC through indistinguishability of ciphertexts under selective encryption attribute set and adaptive chosen ciphertext attack (IND-sEA-CCA2 security). This security notion is defined by the following game $Game_{tABSC}^{IND\text{-}sEA\text{-}CCA2}$ played between a challenger $\mathcal{C}$ and an adversary $\mathcal{A}$.

Commit. $\mathcal{A}$ sends an encryption attribute set $W_e^* \subset U_e$ to $\mathcal{C}$.

Setup Phase. $\mathcal{C}$ gets $[\mathcal{PP},\mathcal{MK}] \leftarrow$ Setup (κ,U) and sends $\mathcal{PP}$ to $\mathcal{A}$.

Query Phase 1. $\mathcal{A}$ adaptively issues the following queries a polynomial number of times.

- *DecKey Query:* $\mathcal{A}$ gives a decryption attribute set $A_d \subset U_e$ and a threshold δ_d such that $|A_d \cap W_e^*| < \delta_d$, and obtains $\mathcal{DK}_{A_d,\delta_d} \leftarrow$ DecKeyGen $(\mathcal{PP},\mathcal{MK},A_d,\delta_d)$ from $\mathcal{C}$.
- *SignKey Query:* $\mathcal{A}$ sends a signing attribute set $A_s \subset U_s$ with a threshold δ_s, and receives $\mathcal{SK}_{A_s,\delta_s} \leftarrow$ SignKeyGen $(\mathcal{PP},\mathcal{MK},A_s,\delta_s)$ from $\mathcal{C}$.
- *Unsigncrypt Query:* $\mathcal{A}$ submits $[CT,W_v,A_d,\delta_d]$ to $\mathcal{C}$ and gets back the output of Unsigncrypt $(\mathcal{PP},CT,W_v,\mathcal{DK}_{A_d,\delta_d})$, where $\mathcal{DK}_{A_d,\delta_d} \leftarrow$ DecKeyGen $(\mathcal{PP},\mathcal{MK},A_d,\delta_d)$.

Challenge. $\mathcal{A}$ outputs two equal length messages $msg_0^*,msg_1^* \in \mathcal{M}$ and a signing attribute set $W_s^* \subset U_s$. $\mathcal{C}$ selects a random bit $\mu \in \{0,1\}$ and sends the challenge ciphertext $CT^* \leftarrow$ Signcrypt $(\mathcal{PP},\mathcal{SK}_{A_s,\delta_s},W_e^*,W_s^*,msg_\mu^*)$ to $\mathcal{A}$, where $W_s^* \subseteq A_s$ with $|W_s^*| \geq \delta_s$ and $\mathcal{SK}_{A_s,\delta_s} \leftarrow$ SignKeyGen $(\mathcal{PP},\mathcal{MK},A_s,\delta_s)$.

Query Phase 2. $\mathcal{A}$ continues to adaptively issue DecKey, SignKey and Unsigncrypt queries, as in Query phase 1, but with the restrictions that $\mathcal{A}$ cannot issue an Unsigncrypt query $[CT^*,W_s^*,A_d,\delta_d]$ such that $|A_d \cap W_e^*| \geq \delta_d$.

Guess. $\mathcal{A}$ outputs its guess $\mu' \in \{0,1\}$ for μ. and wins the game if $\mu' = \mu$.

The advantage of $\mathcal{A}$ in this game is defined to be $Adv_\mathcal{A}^{IND-sEA-CCA2} := |\text{Prob}[\mu' = \mu] - 1/2|$.

Remark 1. In the above game, it is not necessary for $\mathcal{A}$ to issue signcryption queries because he can obtain the signing key for any signature attribute set, and hence he can signcrypt on his own.

Definition 9.2. *The tABSC scheme is said to be IND-sEA-CCA2 secure if all PPT adversaries have at most a negligible advantage in Game$_{tABSC}^{IND-sEA-CCA2}$.*

Ciphertext Unforgeability This security notion is defined through existential unforgeability under selective signing attribute set and adaptive chosen message attack (EUF-sSA-CMA security). The following game $Game_{tABSC}^{EUF-sSA-CMA}$ played between a challenger $\mathcal{C}$ and an adversary $\mathcal{A}$ captures EUF-sSA-CMA security.

Commit. $\mathcal{A}$ submits a signing attribute set $W_s^* \subset U_s$ to $\mathcal{C}$.

Setup Phase. $\mathcal{C}$ obtains $[\mathcal{PP},\mathcal{MK}] \leftarrow$ Setup(κ,U) and gives $\mathcal{PP}$ to $\mathcal{A}$.

Query Phase. $\mathcal{A}$ adaptively issues the following queries a polynomial number of times.

- *DecKey Query:* $\mathcal{A}$ gives a decryption attribute set $A_d \subset U_e$ and a threshold δ_d, and obtains $DK_{A_d,\delta_d} \leftarrow \text{DecKeyGen}(PP, MK, A_d, \delta_d)$ from $\mathcal{C}$.
- *SignKey Query:* $\mathcal{A}$ sends a signing attribute set $A_s \subset U_s$ with a threshold δ_s such that $|A_s \cap W_s^*| < \delta_s$, and then receives $SK_{A_s,\delta_s} \leftarrow \text{SignKeyGen}(PP, MK, A_s, \delta_s)$ from $\mathcal{C}$.
- *Signcrypt Query:* $\mathcal{A}$ submits $[msg, W_e, W_s]$ to $\mathcal{C}$ and gets back a ciphertext $CT \leftarrow \text{Signcrypt}(PP, SK_{A_s,\delta_s}, W_e, W_s, msg)$, where $SK_{A_s,\delta_s} \leftarrow \text{SignKeyGen}(PP, MK, A_s, \delta_s)$ with $W_s \subseteq A_s, |W_s| \geq \delta_s$.

Forgery. $\mathcal{A}$ returns a ciphertext $CT^* := [W_e^*, \ldots]$.

$\mathcal{A}$ wins the game if the ciphertext $CT^* := [W_e^*, \ldots]$ is valid and was not obtained from a Signcrypt query. That is, $\text{Unsigncrypt}(PP, CT, W_v, DK_{W_e^*,|W_e^*|}) = msg^* \neq \bot$ and $\mathcal{A}$ did not issue a Signcrypt query $[msg^*, W_e^*, W_s^*]$.

The advantage of $\mathcal{A}$ in this game is defined to be $Adv_{\mathcal{A}}^{EUF-sSA-CMA} := \text{Prob}[\mathcal{A} \text{ wins}]$.

Remark 2. In the above game, it is not necessary for $\mathcal{A}$ to issue unsigncryption queries because he can obtain the decryption key for any decryption attribute set, and hence he can unsigncrypt on his own.

Definition 9.3. *The tABSC scheme is said to be EUF-sSA-CMA secure if all PPT adversaries have at most a negligible advantage in $\text{Game}_{tABSC}^{EUF-sSA-CMA}$.*

9.3.3 Symmetric-Key Encryption

A symmetric-key encryption scheme Π_{SE} with key space $\mathcal{K}$ and message space $\mathcal{M}$ consists of two PPT algorithms, $SE\text{-}Enc$ and $SE\text{-}Dec$, where $SE\text{-}Enc(k, m)$ maps a key $k \in \mathcal{K}$ and a message $m \in \mathcal{M}$ to a ciphertext ct and $SE\text{-}Dec(k, ct)$ recovers the message m from the ciphertext ct using the key k.

Definition 9.4. *A one-time symmetric-key encryption scheme Π_{SE} is said to be semantically secure if for any PPT adversary $\mathcal{A}$, the advantage*

$$\left| \text{Prob}\left[\breve{i} = i \quad : \quad \begin{array}{c} (m^{(0)}, m^{(1)}) \leftarrow \mathcal{A}(1^{\kappa}) \\ i \xleftarrow{R} \{0,1\}, k \xleftarrow{R} \mathcal{K} \\ ct \leftarrow SE\text{-}Enc(k, m^{(i)}) \\ \breve{i} \leftarrow \mathcal{A}(ct) \end{array} \right] - \frac{1}{2} \right|$$

of $\mathcal{A}$ is at most negligible.

9.3.4 Key Derivation Function

A key derivation function [15] is an algorithm that produces cryptographically secure secret keys from input of an initial keying material. Part of the bits or keys output by the key derivation function should not leak information on the other generated bits. A key derivation function with the output length τ, denoted by KDF, takes as input an instance from a keying source, and outputs a string of τ bits, that is, $KDF(I) \in \{0,1\}^{\tau}$, where I denotes an initial secret key obtained from keying source.

Definition 9.5. *The key derivation function with the output length τ, KDF is secure if for any PPT adversary $\mathcal{A}$, the advantage $|\mathrm{Prob}[\mathcal{A}(KDF(I)) = 1] - \mathrm{Prob}[\mathcal{A}(R) = 1]|$ of $\mathcal{A}$ is at most negligible, where I denotes an initial secret key obtained from keying source and R is chosen uniformly at random from $\{0,1\}^{\tau}$.*

9.4 Proposed tABSC Scheme

In this section, we propose a tABSC scheme and prove its security in a standard model.

9.4.1 Description of the Scheme

The proposed tABSC scheme is detailed in the following algorithms.

$\mathbf{Setup}(\kappa, U)$ This algorithm takes as input the security parameter κ and an attribute universe description $U := U_s \cup U_e$, and creates the system public and secret parameters as follows.

■ Select secure bilinear pairing parameters $\Sigma := [p, \mathbb{G}, \mathbb{G}_T, g, e]$ such that $\mathbb{G} = \langle g \rangle$, where g is a generator of the group $\mathbb{G}$.
■ Sample $a, b \xleftarrow{R} \mathbb{Z}_p^*$ and set $g_1 := g^a, g_2 := g^b$ and $Y := e(g_1, g_2)$.
■ Choose $z_i \xleftarrow{R} \mathbb{Z}_p^*$ and set $h_i := g^{z_i}$ for each $i \in U_s$.
■ Select $t_i \xleftarrow{R} \mathbb{Z}_p^*$ and set $k_i := g^{t_i}$ for each $i \in U_e$.
■ Pick $h_0, k_0, \xi_1, \xi_2, \xi_3, u_0, u_1, \ldots, u_\ell \xleftarrow{R} \mathbb{G}$.
■ Choose $H_1 : \{0,1\}^* \to \{0,1\}^{\ell}$ and $H_2 : \{0,1\}^* \to \mathbb{Z}_p^*$ from appropriate families of collision-resistant hash functions.
■ Define a function $\mathcal{W} : \{0,1\}^{\ell} \to \mathbb{G}$ by $\mathcal{W}(\theta) := u_0 \prod_{i=1}^{\ell} u_i^{\theta_i}$, where $\theta := (\theta_1, \ldots, \theta_\ell) \in \{0,1\}^{\ell}$.
■ Let $\Pi_{SE} := (SE\text{-}Enc, SE\text{-}Dec)$ be a one-time symmetric-key encryption scheme with key space $\mathcal{K} := \{0,1\}^{\tau}$ and message space $\mathcal{M} := \{0,1\}^*$. Let KDF be the key derivation function with the output length τ.

The system public parameters $\mathcal{PP}$ are set as

$$\mathcal{PP} := [\Sigma, g_2, Y, \{h_i\}_{i \in U_s}, \{k_i\}_{i \in U_e}, h_0, k_0, \xi_1, \xi_2, \xi_3, u_0, \{u_i\}_{i=1}^\ell, H_1, H_2, \mathcal{W}, \Pi_{SE}, KDF, \mathcal{M}, U]$$

The system master secret key $\mathcal{MK}$ is set as $\mathcal{MK} := a$.

DecKeyGen$(\mathcal{PP}, \mathcal{MK}, A_d, \delta_d)$ This algorithm takes as input $\mathcal{PP}, \mathcal{MK}$, a set $A_d \subset U_e$ of decryption attributes and a threshold δ_d, and computes the decryption key $\mathcal{DK}_{A_d, \delta_d} := [\delta_d, \{D_i, i \in A_d\}]$ as follows.

■ Let f_d be a random polynomial of degree $\delta_d - 1$ such that $f_d(0) = a$. Compute $D_i := g_2^{f_d(i) + t_i} k_0^{-t_i}$ for each $i \in A_d$.

SignKeyGen$(\mathcal{PP}, \mathcal{MK}, A_s, \delta_s)$ This algorithm takes as input $\mathcal{PP}, \mathcal{MK}$, a set $A_s \subset U_s$ of signing attributes and a threshold δ_s, and computes the signing key $\mathcal{SK}_{A_s, \delta_s} := [\delta_s, \{S_i, i \in A_s\}]$ as follows.

■ Let f_s be a random polynomial of degree $\delta_s - 1$ such that $f_s(0) = a$. Compute $S_i := g_2^{f_s(i) + z_i} h_0^{-z_i}$ for each $i \in A_s$.

Signcrypt$(\mathcal{PP}, \mathcal{SK}_{A_s, \delta_s}, W_e, W_s, msg)$ This algorithm takes as input $\mathcal{PP}$, an encryption attribute set $W_e \subset U_e$, a signing attribute set $W_s \subset A_s$ with $|W_s| \ge \delta_s$, the signing key $\mathcal{SK}_{A_s, \delta_s}$ and a message $msg \in \mathcal{M}$. Then it caries out the following steps.

■ Sample $\alpha, \gamma \xleftarrow{R} \mathbb{Z}_p^*$ and set
■ $\mathfrak{m} := SE\text{-}Enc\left(KDF(Y^\alpha \| W_e \| W_s), msg\right)$
■ $C := g^\alpha, C_i := k_i^\alpha, \forall i \in W_e$
■ $\sigma_i := S_i \cdot \mathcal{W}(\theta)^\alpha, \forall i \in W_s$, where $\theta = H_1(\mathfrak{m} \| W_e \| W_s \| \delta_s)$
■ $ct := [\mathfrak{m}, C, \{C_i : i \in W_e\}]$ and $\sigma := \{\sigma_i : i \in W_s\}$
■ $C_e := (\xi_1^\beta \xi_2^\gamma \xi_3)^\alpha$, where $\beta = H_2(ct \| \sigma \| W_e \| W_s \| \delta_s)$
■ The ciphertext is $CT := [W_e, ct, \sigma, C_e, \gamma, \delta_s]$.

Unsigncrypt$(\mathcal{PP}, CT, W_v, \mathcal{DK}_{A_d, \delta_d})$ Given $\mathcal{PP}, CT$, a verification attribute set $W_v \subset U_s$ and $\mathcal{DK}_{A_d, \delta_d}$, this algorithm proceeds as follows.

■ Choose a set $\Omega_s \subset W_v$ of signature attributes of size (at least) δ_s, compute $\beta = H_2(ct \| \sigma \| W_e \| W_v \| \delta_s), \theta = H_1(\mathfrak{m} \| W_e \| W_v \| \delta_s)$ and check whether

$$e(g, C_e) \overset{?}{=} e(C, \xi_1^\beta \xi_2^\gamma \xi_3) \tag{9.1}$$

$$e\left(g, \prod_{i \in \Omega_s} \sigma_i^{\Delta_{i,\Omega_s}(0)}\right) \cdot e\left(h_0 \cdot g_2^{-1}, \prod_{i \in \Omega_s} h_i^{\Delta_{i,\Omega_s}(0)}\right) \overset{?}{=} Y \cdot e(C, \mathcal{W}(\theta))^{\sum_{i \in \Omega_s} \Delta_{i,\Omega_s}(0)} \tag{9.2}$$

If any one of these two equations does not hold, output $\perp$. Otherwise, execute the subsequent steps. Now, $W_v = W_s$.

- If $|A_d \cap W_e| < \delta_d$, then output $\perp$.
- Otherwise, choose a decryption attribute set $\Omega_d = A_d \cap W_e$ of size (at least) δ_d and then compute

$$
e\left(C, \prod_{i \in \Omega_d} D_i^{\Delta_{i,\Omega_d}(0)}\right) \cdot e\left(k_0 \cdot g_2^{-1}, \prod_{i \in \Omega_d} C_i^{\Delta_{i,\Omega_d}(0)}\right) = Y^{\alpha} \tag{9.3}
$$

- Recover the correct message $msg = SE \text{-} Dec\left(KDF(Y^{\alpha} \| W_e \| W_v), \mathfrak{m}\right)$.

Lemma 9.1 *The proposed tABSC scheme is correct.*

Proof. Assume the hypothesis of Definition 9.1. Since $W_v = W_s$, we have $\theta = H_1(\mathfrak{m} \| W_e \| W_s \| \delta_s)$ and $\beta = H_2(ct \| \sigma \| W_e \| W_s \| \delta_s)$. Hence,

$$
e(g, C_e) = e\left(g, (\xi_1^{\beta} \xi_2^{\gamma} \xi_3)^{\alpha}\right) = e\left(g^{\alpha}, \xi_1^{\beta} \xi_2^{\gamma} \xi_3\right) = e(C, \xi_1^{\beta} \xi_2^{\gamma} \xi_3)
$$

and

$$
e\left(g, \prod_{i \in \Omega_s} \sigma_i^{\Delta_{i,\Omega_s}(0)}\right) \cdot e\left(h_0 \cdot g_2^{-1}, \prod_{i \in \Omega_s} h_i^{\Delta_{i,\Omega_s}(0)}\right)
$$

$$
= e\left(g, \prod_{i \in \Omega_s} (g_2^{f_s(i)+z_i} h_0^{-z_i} \mathcal{W}(\theta)^{\alpha})^{\Delta_{i,\Omega_s}(0)}\right) \cdot e\left(h_0 \cdot g_2^{-1}, \prod_{i \in \Omega_s} h_i^{\Delta_{i,\Omega_s}(0)}\right)
$$

$$
= e\left(g, g_2^{\sum_{i \in \Omega_s} f_s(i) \cdot \Delta_{i,\Omega_s}(0)}\right) e\left(g, \prod_{i \in \Omega_s} (\mathcal{W}(\theta)^{\alpha})^{\Delta_{i,\Omega_s}(0)}\right)
$$

$$
= e\left(g, g_2^{f_s(0)}\right) e\left(g^{\alpha}, \mathcal{W}(\theta)^{\sum_{i \in \Omega_s} \Delta_{i,\Omega_s}(0)}\right)
$$

$$= Y \cdot e\big(C, \mathcal{W}(\theta)\big)^{\sum_{i \in \Omega_s} \Delta_i, \Omega_s (0)}$$

Since $f_s(0) = a$. This establishes the correctness of Equations 9.1 and 9.2. Similarly, one can verify the correctness of Equation 9.3. Finally,

$$SE\text{-}Dec\big(KDF(Y^\alpha \| W_e \| W_v), \mathfrak{m}\big) = SE\text{-}Dec\big(KDF(Y^\alpha \| W_e \| W_s), \mathfrak{m}\big) = msg.$$

9.4.2 Security Analysis

Theorem 9.1. *Suppose the key derivation function KDF is secure and the one-time symmetric-key encryption scheme Π_{SE} is semantically secure. Assume H_1 and H_2 are collision-resistant hash functions. If a PPT adversary is able to break IND-sEA-CCA2 security of tABSC scheme with advantage ϵ in standard model, then there is a PPT algorithm $\mathcal{B}$ that can break the DBDH assumption with advantage $(\epsilon/2)(1-(q/p))$, where q is the number of unsigncryption queries requested by the adversary in the game $Game_{tABSC}^{IND\text{-}sEA\text{-}CCA2}$.*

Proof. Suppose an adversary $\mathcal{A}$ has advantage ϵ in breaking IND-sEA-CCA2 security of our tABSC scheme. We build an algorithm $\mathcal{B}$ that breaks the DBDH assumption with advantage $(\epsilon/2)(1-(q/p))$. Suppose $\mathcal{B}$ is given the DBDH problem instance $[\Sigma, \Gamma_1 := g^a, \Gamma_2 := g^b, \Gamma_3 := g^c, Z]$, where $\Sigma := [p, \mathbb{G}, \mathbb{G}_T, g, e]$. Note that $\mathcal{B}$ does not know explicitly the values $a, b, c \in \mathbb{Z}_p^*$. Now, $\mathcal{B}$ interacts with $\mathcal{A}$ and responds to all the queries requested by $\mathcal{A}$ as follows.

Commit. $\mathcal{A}$ sends an encryption attribute set $W_e^* \subset U_e$ to $\mathcal{B}$.
Setup Phase. $\mathcal{B}$ computes the public parameters as follows.
– Set $g_1 := \Gamma_1, g_2 := \Gamma_2$ and $Y := e(\Gamma_1, \Gamma_2)$.
– For each $i \in U_s$, select $\hat{z}_i \xrightarrow{R} \mathbb{Z}_p^*$ and set $h_i := g^{\hat{z}_i} \Gamma_1^{-1}$; i.e., z_i is implicitly defined as $z_i := \hat{z}_i - a$
– For each $i \in U_e$, pick $\hat{t}_i, v_i \xleftarrow{R} \mathbb{Z}_p^*$ and set

$$k_i := \begin{cases} g^{t_i}, & \text{if } i \in W_e^*; \\ g^{t_i} \cdot \Gamma_1^{-v_i}, & \text{if } i \notin W_e^*. \end{cases}$$

Here t_i is implicitly defined as

$$t_i := \begin{cases} \hat{t}_i, & \text{if } i \in W_e^*; \\ \hat{t}_i - a v_i, & \text{if } i \notin W_e^*. \end{cases}$$

- Choose $\eta, v, w_1, w_2 \xleftarrow{R} \mathbb{Z}_p^*$ and set $h_0 := g^{\eta}$ and $k_0 := \Gamma_2\left(g^{w_2}\right)^{1/vw_1}$.
- Pick $\varrho_1, \varrho_2, \varrho_3, \tau_2, \tau_3 \xleftarrow{R} \mathbb{Z}_p^*$ and set $\xi_1 := \Gamma_1 \cdot g^{\varrho_1}, \xi_2 := (\Gamma_1)^{\tau_2} \cdot g^{\varrho_2}, \xi_3 := (\Gamma_1)^{\tau_3} \cdot g^{\varrho_3}$.
- For each $i \in \{0, 1, 2, \ldots, \ell\}$, select $\pi_i \xleftarrow{R} \mathbb{Z}_p^*$ and then set $u_i := g^{\pi_i}$
- Choose $H_1 : \{0,1\}^* \to \{0,1\}^{\ell}$ and $H_2 : \{0,1\}^* \to \mathbb{Z}_p^*$ from appropriate families of collision-resistant hash functions.

Finally, $\mathcal{B}$ gives the public parameters

$$\mathcal{PP} := [\Sigma, \delta, g_2, Y, \{h_i\}_{i \in U_s}, \{k_i\}_{i \in U_e}, h_0, k_0, \omega_1, \omega_2, \omega_3, u_0, \{u_i\}_{i=1}^{\ell}, H_1, H_2, \mathcal{W}, \Pi_{SE}, KDF, \mathcal{M}, U] \text{ to } \mathcal{A}.$$

These parameters have the same distribution as in the real construction from $\mathcal{A}$' view.

Query Phase 1. $\mathcal{A}$ adaptively issues the following queries.
- *DecKey Query:* The simulation of this query is analogous to the simulation of the Extract query described in the security proof of (t, t)-ABS small universe scheme [16]. That is, when $\mathcal{A}$ submits $[A_d, \delta_d]$ as input for decryption key DK_{A_d, δ_d}, $\mathcal{B}$ responds as in [16].
- *SignKey Query:* For any request of signing key query on $[A_s, \delta_s]$, $\mathcal{B}$ chooses $r_1, r_2, \ldots, r_{\delta_s - 1} \xleftarrow{R} \mathbb{Z}_p^*$ and implicitly defines $f_s(x) := a + r_1 x + r_2 x^2 + \cdots + r_{\delta_s - 1} x^{\delta_s - 1}$. For each $i \in A_s$, it sets $S_i := (\Gamma_2)^{\hat{z}_i} g^{-\eta \hat{z}_i} (\Gamma_1)^{\eta} \prod_{j=1}^{\delta_s - 1} (\Gamma_2)^{r_j i^j}$. The signing key $SK_{A_s, \delta_s} := [\delta_s, \{S_i, i \in A_s\}]$ will be given to $\mathcal{A}$. It is not difficult to see that the signing key simulated by $\mathcal{B}$ is a well-formed key in $\mathcal{A}$'s point of view.
- *Unsigncrypt Query:* When $\mathcal{A}$ asks for a Unsigncrypt query on the input $[CT, W_v, A_d, \delta_d]$, where $CT := [W_e, ct := [\mathsf{m}, C, \{C_i : i \in W_e\}], \sigma := \{\sigma_i : i \in W_s\}, C_e, \gamma, \delta_s,$ $\mathcal{B}$ checks Equations 9.1 and 9.2, and $|A_d \cap W_e| \geq \delta_d$ If any one of these three tests does not hold, it outputs $\bot$. Otherwise, if $|A_d \cap W_e^*| < \delta_d$, then $\mathcal{B}$ obtains the decryption key DK_{A_d, δ_d} by performing DecKey query for the tuple $[A_d, \delta_d]$ and returns the output of $\text{Unsigncrypt}(\mathcal{PP}, CT, W_v, DK_{A_d, \delta_d})$ to $\mathcal{A}$. If $|A_d \cap W_e^*| \geq \delta_d$, $\mathcal{B}$ cannot execute the DecKey query and then it responds as follows. First $\mathcal{B}$ computes $\beta = H_2(ct \| \sigma \| W_e \| W_v \| \delta_s)$, and checks whether $\beta + \gamma \tau_2 + \tau_3 = 0$ which happens with probability at most $1/p$. If so, it aborts (we refer to this event as *abort*) and outputs a random bit. Else if $C := g^{\alpha}$, $\mathcal{B}$ can compute Y^{α} as

$$e\left(C_e \cdot C^{-(\beta \varrho_1 + \gamma \varrho_2 + \varrho_3)}, \Gamma_2^{(\beta + \gamma \tau_2 + \tau_3)^{-1}}\right) = Y^{\alpha}$$

where $\beta = H_2(ct \| \sigma \| W_e \| W_v \| \delta_s)$. Now, $\mathcal{B}$ returns $msg = SE\text{-}Dec$ $(KDF(Y^{\alpha} \| W_e \| W_v), \mathsf{m})$ to $\mathcal{A}$.

Challenge. $\mathcal{A}$ outputs two equal length messages $msg_0^*, msg_1^* \in \mathcal{M}$ and a signing attribute set $W_s^* \subset U_s$. $\mathcal{B}$ selects a random bit $\mu \in \{0, 1\}$ and signcrypts msg_{μ}^* under the challenge encryption attribute set W_e^* and signing attribute set W_s^* in the following way.

- Set $C := \Gamma_3 = g^c$, $\mathfrak{m} := SE\text{-}Enc\left(KDF(Z \| W_e^* \| W_s^*), msg_\mu^*\right)$, for each $i \in W_e^*, C_i := (\Gamma_3)^{\bar{t}_i}$ and $ct^* := [\mathfrak{m}, C, \{C_i : i \in W_e^*\}]$
- Choose a signing attribute set $A_s \subset U_s$ and a threshold $\delta_s \in \mathbb{N}$ such that $W_s^* \subset A_s$ and $|W_s^*| \geq \delta_s$, and generate a signing key $\mathcal{SK}_{A_s,\delta_s} := [\delta_s, \{S_i, i \in A_s\}]$ by running a SignKey query on $[A_s, \delta_s]$.
- For each $i \in W_s^*$, set $\sigma_i := S_i \cdot (\Gamma_3)^{\pi_0 + \sum_{i=1}^{\ell} \theta_i \pi_i}$, where $\theta := (\theta_1, \ldots, \theta_\ell) = H_1(\mathfrak{m} \| W_e^* \| W_s^* \| \delta_s)$, $\sigma^* := \{\sigma_i : i \in W_s^*\}$
- Compute $\beta^* = H_2(ct^* \| \sigma^* \| W_e^* \| W_s^* \| \delta_s$ and $\gamma^* = -(\beta^* + \tau_3)/\tau_2$, and set

$$C_e := (\Gamma_3)^{\beta^* \varrho_1 + \gamma^* \varrho_2 + \varrho_3},$$

Then $\mathcal{B}$ gives $CT^* := [W_e^*, ct^*, \sigma^*, C_e, \gamma^*, \delta_s]$ as a challenge ciphertext to $\mathcal{A}$. It can be seen that if $Z = e(g,g)^{abc}$, then the challenge ciphertext CT^* is a valid signcryption of the message msg_μ^* under the encryption attribute set W_e^* and signature attribute set W_s^*. If Z is a random element in $\mathbb{G}_T$, then CT^* is independent of μ in $\mathcal{A}$'s view.

Query Phase 2. Again $\mathcal{A}$ issues a second series of queries, and $\mathcal{B}$ responds to these queries as in query phase 1. But, in this phase, $\mathcal{A}$ cannot ask an Unsigncrypt query $[CT^*, W_s^*, A_d, \delta_d]$ satisfying $|A_d \cap W_e^*| \geq \delta_a$.

Guess. $\mathcal{A}$ outputs its guess $\mu' \in \{0,1\}$ for μ.

If $\mu' = \mu$ then $\mathcal{B}$ outputs 1, indicating that $Z = e(g,g)^{abc}$. Otherwise, $\mathcal{B}$ outputs 0, indicating that Z is a random element of $\mathbb{G}_T$. The calculation of $\mathcal{B}$'s advantage in breaking the DBDH assumption follows from arguments analogous to those of the proof of Theorem 2 in [9]. Hence, $\mathcal{B}$ can break the DBDH assumption with advantage $(\epsilon/2)(1 - (q/p))$.

Theorem 9.2. *Assume H_1 and H_2 are collision-resistant hash functions. Suppose the one-time symmetric-key encryption scheme Π_{SE} is semantically secure and the key derivation function KDF is secure. If a PPT adversary is able to break EUF-sSA-CMA security of our tABSC scheme with advantage ϵ in standard model, then there is a PPT algorithm $\mathcal{B}$ that can break the CDH assumption with advantage $\epsilon/(8(\ell+1)q)$, where q is the number of signcryption queries requested by the adversary in the game $Game_{tABSC}^{EUF\text{-}sSA\text{-}CMA}$ and ℓ is the size of the output of the hash function H_1.*

We can prove Theorem 9.1 stated above following the same line of proving Theorem 3.31 in [16] and the ideas in proof of Theorem 9.2, and so we omit the details.

9.5 Efficiency Analysis

The following table summarizes the notations used for efficiency analysis.

$|U|$: size of the attribute universe

$|\mathbb{G}|$ (resp. $|\mathbb{G}_T|$ and $|\mathbb{Z}_p|$) : size of an element of the group $\mathbb{G}$ (resp. $\mathbb{G}_T$ and $\mathbb{Z}_p$)

ℓ : size of the output of hash function

$|A_s|$ (resp. $|A_d|$) : size of the signing (resp. decryption) attribute set

$|W_e|$ (resp. $|W_e|$) : number of signing (resp. decryption) attributes used in signcryption

$|\mathfrak{m}|$: size of the ciphertext of one-time symmetric-key encryption scheme

δ_s (resp. δ_d) : number of required signing (resp. decryption) attributes during unsigncryption

In our tABSC scheme, the size of the system public parameters is $(|U| + \ell + 7)|\mathbb{G}| + |\mathbb{G}_T|$. The size of signing key and decryption key depend on the number of attributes held by a user. Precisely, the signing key size is $|A_s| \cdot |\mathbb{G}|$ and the decryption key size is $|A_d| \cdot |\mathbb{G}|$. The size of the ciphertext depends on both the signing and decryption attributes used in signcryption. To be specific, the ciphertext size is $(|W_s| + |W_e| + 2)|\mathbb{G}| + |\mathbb{Z}_p| + |\mathfrak{m}|$. These communication costs are presented in Table 9.1.

Our signing key generation algorithm executes $2|A_s|$ number of exponentiations to compute a signer's key and the decryption key generation algorithm carries out $2|A_d|$ number of exponentiations to compute a unsigncryptor's key. Our signcryption algorithm performs $|W_s| + |W_e| + 5$ number of exponentiations to compute the signcrypted ciphertext. To recover the original message, our unsigncrytpion algorithm needs $\delta_s + \delta_d + 5$ number of exponentiations and only 7 pairing computations. Table 9.2 summarizes the computation cost of our tABSC scheme.

The proposed tABSC scheme realizes strong security notions, IND-sEA-CCA2 security for message confidentiality and EUF-sSA-CMA security for ciphertext unforgeability, with constant number of pairings. As described in the

Table 9.1 Communication Cost of Proposed tABSC Scheme

Scheme	Public Parameters Size	Sign. Key Size	Dec. Key Size	Ciphertext Size
Proposed	$(|U| + \ell + 7)|\mathbb{G}| + |\mathbb{G}_T|$	$|A_s| \cdot |\mathbb{G}|$	$|A_d| \cdot |\mathbb{G}|$	$(|W_s| + |W_e| + 2)|\mathbb{G}| + |\mathbb{Z}_p| + |\mathfrak{m}|$

Table 9.2 Computation Cost of Proposed tABSC Scheme

Scheme	SignKeyGen	DecKeyGen	Signcrypt	Unsigncrypt	
	Exp.	Exp.	Exp.	Exp.	Pairings
Proposed	$2|A_s|$	$2|A_d|$	$|W_s|+|W_e|+5$	$\delta_s + \delta_d + 5$	7

Introduction section, the existing tABSC schemes [6,10–12] are not secure in these security models. In sum, to the best of our knowledge, this is the first work that attempts to build a secure tABSC scheme with constant number of pairings.

9.6 Conclusion

In this chapter, we presented an efficient and secure tABSC scheme with constant number of pairings, by employing the threshold ABS scheme [16] as a building block. Our scheme can handle any threshold access policy to sign and encrypt messages. We proved that our scheme is selectively secure in the standard model. The security of our scheme relies on standard complexity assumptions, namely DBDH and CDH assumptions. Only 7 pairing evaluations are required to unsigncrypt the ciphertext which makes our scheme efficient from computation point of view.

References

1. A. Sahai and B. Waters. Fuzzy identity-based encryption. In *Advances in Cryptology–EUROCRYPT 2005*, pages 457–473. Springer, Berlin, Germany, 2005.
2. B. Waters. Ciphertext-policy attribute-based encryption: An expressive, efficient, and provably secure realization. In *Public Key Cryptography–PKC 2011*, volume 6571 of Lecture Notes in Computer Science, pages 53–70. Springer, Berlin, Germany, 2011.
3. Y. S. Rao and R. Dutta. Computational friendly attribute-based encryptions with short ciphertext. *Theoretical Computer Science*, 668:1–26, 2017.
4. N. Doshi and D. C. Jinwala. Fully secure ciphertext policy attribute-based encryption with constant length ciphertext and faster decryption. *Security and Communication Networks*, 7(11):1988–2002, 2014.
5. Y. S. Rao and R. Dutta. Efficient attribute-based signature and signcryption realizing expressive access structures. *International Journal of Information Security*, 15(1):81–109, 2016.
6. M. Gagné, S. Narayan, and R. Safavi-Naini. Threshold attribute-based signcryption. *International Conference on Security and Cryptography for Networks*, pages 154–171. Springer, Berlin, Germany, 2010.
7. J. Liu, X. Huang, and J. K. Liu. Secure sharing of personal health records in cloud computing: Ciphertext-policy attribute-based signcryption. *Future Generation Computer Systems*, 52:67–76, 2015. Special Section: Cloud Computing: Security, Privacy and Practice.

8. Y. S. Rao. A secure and efficient ciphertext-policy attribute-based signcryption for personal health records sharing in cloud computing. *Future Generation Computer Systems*, 67:133–151, 2017.

9. Y. S. Rao. Attribute-based online/offline signcryption scheme. *International Journal of Communication Systems*, 30(16):e3322, 2017.

10. C. Hu, N. Zhang, H. Li, X. Cheng, and X. Liao. Body area network security: A fuzzy attribute-based signcryption scheme. *IEEE Journal on Selected Areas in Communications*, 31(9):37–46, 2013.

11. H. Zheng, J. Qin, J. Hu, and Q. Wu. Threshold attribute-based signcryption and its application to authenticated key agreement. *Security and Communication Networks*, 9(18):4914–4923, 2016.

12. S. Belguith, N. Kaaniche, M. Laurent, A. Jemai, and R. Attia. Constant-size threshold attribute based signcryption for cloud applications. In *SECRYPT 2017: 14th International Conference on Security and Cryptography*, volume 6, pages 212–225, Madrid, Spain, July 2017. Scitepress.

13. C. Wang, X. Xu, Y. Li, and D. Shi. Integrating ciphertext-policy attribute-based encryption with identity-based ring signature to enhance security and privacy in wireless body area networks, *International Conference on Information Security and Cryptology*, pages 424–442. Springer International Publishing, Cham, Switzerland, 2015.

14. C. J. Wang, J. S. Huang, W. L. Lin, and H. T. Lin. Security analysis of Gagne et al.'s threshold attribute-based signcryption scheme. In *2013 5th International Conference on Intelligent Networking and Collaborative Systems*, pages 103–108, September 2013.

15. H. Krawczyk. Cryptographic extraction and key derivation: The HKDF scheme. In *CRYPTO*, volume 6223, pages 631–648. Springer, Berlin, Germany, 2010.

16. M. Gagné, S. Narayan, and R. Safavi-Naini. Short pairing-efficient threshold-attribute-based signature, *International Conference on Pairing-Based Cryptography*, pages 295–313. Springer, Berlin, Germany, 2013.

Chapter 10

Multimedia Contents Encryption Using the Chaotic MACM System on a Smart-display

Rodrigo Méndez-Ramírez, Adrian Arellano-Delgado, Miguel Angel Murillo-Escobar and César Cruz-Hernández

Contents

DOI: 10.1201/9780429435461-11

10.1 Introduction

Embedded systems (ES) are used to develop and integrate a large number of electronic devices for wired and wireless communication. Audio and video applications with graphic interfaces in smart displays have been increasing such as in Liquid Cristal Display (LCD) monitors, tablets, and smart-phones. It is indispensable that the use of output data allows the designer to observe the behavior of the systems and validate in a smart-display [1]. Indeed, the smart display is one device able to adapt its behavior and its structure following the semantic of data output produced by the development of some application by using internal hardware peripherals of ES. Depending on the application, it is more convenient and economical to use some communication protocol that allows the use of fewer communication lines in the internal peripherals of an ES, where the link is secure [2]. The Inter-Integrated Circuit (I2C) protocol was created by Philips Semiconductors [3,4], and the Serial Peripheral Interface (SPI) protocol was created by Motorola Inc. [5]. Both types of protocols coexist in modern digital electronic systems, and probably these protocols will continue complementing each other in the future because they are inexpensive of implementation [6].

The SPI protocol allows communication between peripherals and electronic devices. The mode of connection of these devices can be assigned in master and slave modes. The SPI protocol has been adopted by many manufacturers of integrated circuits (ICs) in wired and wireless communications since SPI protocol requires fewer communication lines and low cost of implementation. Recently, the literature reports some applications of the SPI protocol in ES with secure link [7].

On the other hand, modern cryptography reports different encryption techniques, for example in images encryption by using algorithms such as Triple Data Encryption Algorithm (3DES), Advanced Encryption Standard (AES), International Data Encryption Algorithm (IDEA) [8], by using chaotic maps and hyperchaotic systems to encrypt information for different applications such as secure e-mail communication [9], chaos-based cryptosystems on Digital signal processing (DSP) [10,11], and experimental networks synchronization via plastic optical fiber [12], Red, Green, and Blue (RGB) image encryption algorithms based on chaos [13,14], and recently one cryptosystem based in chaos where the SPI protocol is encrypted [7], among others.

To implement chaotic systems in an ES, we need robust processors based on DSPs or Field Programmable Gate Arrays (FPGA) due their robust architectures, and their more processing capacity [15]. In this sense, the microcontrollers in ESs represent an economical alternative for encryption applications based on chaos for generating pseudo-random sequences [16,17]. The Digital signal controller referred to as dsPIC microcontrollers are also an alternative for implementation at low cost. In addition, the architecture and the properties for DSP allow the performance of mathematical calculations with precision. These microcontrollers gather the sufficient conditions as central part of ES [18]. For example, reported studies using dsPIC microcontrollers are: the processing of multiple messages with dsPIC and Digital-to-Analog Converters (DACs) [19], and a flexible pseudo-random number generator for tinnitus treatment implemented on a dsPIC [20].

Currently, some smart display manufacturers are Microchip, Display Tech, Winstar, New Haven Displays, and RBID Prototypes. The compact smart displays are represented with Thin Film Transistor (TFT) LCD displays and touch screen (TS) modules with the purpose to implement a friendly interface for the end user, e.g., tablets, smartphones, smart-tvs, and monitors. Some manufacturers of TFT LCD controllers are Himax, Solomon Systech, Renesas SP, Sitronix, and Ilitek. One touch screens are featured in the resistive and capacitive versions, some TS manufacturers are Thinktouch, CJ Touch, Neoser, Stone Technology, and Multi-Inno Technology. The smart-display is controlled by an ES, where the main part is implemented depending the applications to reproduce multimedia contents such as video, image, and audio in which the multimedia contents depend of the performance of the main processor, e.g., microprocessor, microcontrollers, DSP, FPGA. The same case happens with the quality of TFT LCD displays that depend of the response time, brightness, and pixel structure.

The Mikromedia is the developer of compact smart displays with TFT LCD boards interface, where main parts are microcontrollers of 8-, 16-, and 32-bits PIC Microchip microcontrollers. Also, Mikroelektronika presents the development of smart displays using Tiva, Xmega, FT90X, and STM32 microcontrollers [21]. The Mikromedia smart displays features with integrated modules such as stereo MP3 codec, TFT 320 × 240 touch screen display, accelerometer, USB connector, audio connector, MMC/SD card slot, 8 Mbit flash memory, 2 × 26 connection pads, etc.

In this study, we present the design and experimental implementation of one chaotic encryption and decryption algorithm applied to SPI communication protocol with studies for the acquisition, processing, and reconstruction of digital images. The implementation of the ES was developed in Mikromedia smart displays for dsPIC33EP microcontrollers at a low cost for implementation. For the design of the encryption and decryption stages, we use the novel Méndez-Arellano-Cruz-Martínez (MACM) Chaotic System (CS) in combination with Deoxyribonucleic Acid (DNA) sequences, and two diffusion and confusion methods to hide the information. The SPI protocol properties are used to establish the link and achieve synchronization for the Mikromedia dsPIC33EP smart displays. For the digital applications in image and audio interface, we proposed a MACM OS where three experimental tests are conducted: sensitivity of secret keys, MACM CS animation, and MP3 audio file transference. The experimental results are accomplished using the TFT LCD of the Mikromedia dsPIC33EP smart-display. In addition, statistical tests are carried out on the obtained cryptogram to prove that the SPI protocol generates Pseudo-random (PR) sequences.

This chapter is organized as follows. Section 10.2 presents the ES design for generating PR sequences. Section 10.3 describes the transmission process for the encryption of a message. Section 10.4 presents statistical tests to prove that the cryptogram exhibits PR sequences. Section 10.5 describes the reception process for the decryption of a message. Section 10.6 presents three experimental tests to prove the performance of the chaotic cryptosystem proposed in the ES. Section 10.7 presents the main conclusions of this work. Finally, Appendix A describes one DNA sequence matrix used for the algorithms of the proposed chaotic cryptosystem.

10.2 Description of Embedded Chaotic Cryptosystem

In this section, we present the properties of the SPI protocol, the hardware description of the ES, the generation of PR sequences based on a discrete chaotic map, and the sensibility test regarding the key definition.

10.2.1 SPI Protocol

The SPI protocol is used for communication of the ES because it has an easy configuration, fast serial data bus transmission, and low quantity lines for connecting other peripherals (ICs, or devices). Many microcontrollers and microprocessors manufacturers have adopted the SPI protocol to be implemented directly by hardware using one to three dedicated ports. The data transmission communication protocol is full duplex and the operation modes are master or slave. The SPI protocol specifies four wires connected to external pins. One of these pins is the master-output to slave-input (MOSI), and it is used to connect from master to slave devices. This pin is also referred to as serial data output (SDO). The pin master-input to slave-output (MISO) is used to connect from master to slave devices. In addition, this pin is referred as serial data input (SDI). The pin serial clock (SCK) is used to synchronize the data transfer from master to slave (or slaves) devices. The slave select (SS) is the pin that selects from master to slave devices [5].

The dsPICs devices feature SPI modules. This SPI module is configured with internal registers that mainly consist of 16-bit shift register. This shift register (SPIzSR,

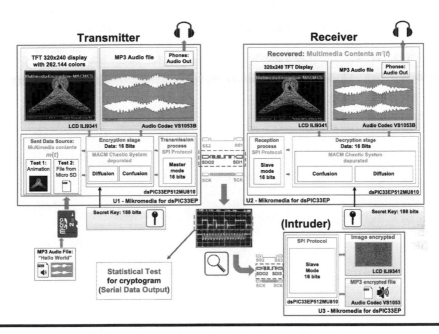

Figure 10.1   Block diagram of the embedded cryptosystem.

where z indicates the number of the SPI module) is used for shifting data in and out from the buffer register (SPIzBUF). The control register (SPIzCON) configures the SPI module. The statistical register (SPIzSTAT) shows the status conditions of the operations of the SPI module, where the flag SPIRBF allows verification if the reception of a word with 16 bits from another external device is accomplished [22].

In this study, we propose the SPI protocol configuration with 16 bits using two smart-displays Mikromedia for dsPIC33EPs. To program the dsPIC33EPs we use the Mikroc Pro for the dsPIC compiler [23]. Figure 10.1 shows the complete block diagram of the embedded chaotic cryptosystem to transmit and receive encrypted messages using the SPI protocol. The dsPIC33EP transmitter (configured in master-mode) first processes the initial message $m(t)$ with confidential information. This message is encrypted and transmitted using the SPI protocol. The other dsPIC33EP is mainly considered as a receiver. Finally we propose one simple graphic interface to identify all processes in smart-display.

10.2.2 Hardware Description of Implemented ES

The benefits of the TFT LCD and dsPIC microcontrollers are used to obtain and prove the results by using the SPI communication protocol with multimedia contents. Table 10.1 shows the hardware description assigned to the ES to connect: unit, smart display with the dsPIC description, mode and port-number of the SPI protocol used, and its function.

Table 10.1 Hardware Description of the Embedded Cryptosystem

Unit	IC Description	SPI Mode/Port	Function
U1	Mikromedia for dsPIC33EP	Master/SPI2	Transmitter
U2	Mikromedia for dsPIC33EP	Slave/SPI1	Receiver
U3	Mikromedia for dsPIC33EP	Slave/SPI1	Intruder

10.2.3 Generating PR Sequences

The first stage of the digital encryption system is implemented using the novel MACM CS in 3-dimension in the transmitter [24],

$$
\begin{cases}
\dot{x} = -ax - byz, \\
\dot{y} = -x + cy, \\
\dot{z} = d - y^2 - z,
\end{cases}
\tag{10.1}
$$

where $a, b, c, d \in \Re^+$, with b and d as the bifurcation parameters. The nonlinear MACM system (10.1) is chaotic with $a = 2$, $b = 2$, $c = 0.5$, and $d = 4$. Eulers discretization is considered to obtain the Discretized Version (DV) of the MACM CS (10.1), the parameters a, b, c, d, and the state variables x, y, z are changed by α_1, $\beta_1, \gamma_1, \delta_1$, and x_1, y_1, z_1; respectively. The MACM CS in DV is represented as follows,

$$
\begin{cases}
x_{1(n+1)} = x_{1(n)} + \tau(-\alpha_1 x_{1(n)} - \beta_1\, y_{1(n)} z_{1(n)}), \\
y_{1(n+1)} = y_{1(n)} + \tau(-x_{1(n)} + \gamma_1 y_{1(n)}), \\
z_{1(n+1)} = z_{1(n)} + \tau(\delta_1 - y_{1(n)}^2 - z_{1(n)}).
\end{cases}
\tag{10.2}
$$

where τ is the step size and n is the iteration number that represents the time in discrete version in the transmitter U1. The numerical algorithm of MACM in DV is reproduced in U1 considering $\tau = 0.004$, and the initial conditions $x_{1(0)} = 0.5$, $y_{1(0)} = 0.1$, and $z_{1(0)} = 0.1$.

We proposed one depurated MACM CS in DV to improve the heterogeneity in the concentration and dispersion of chaotic data, where the values of states $x_{1(n)}$, $y_{1(n)}$, and $z_{1(n)}$ are converted to values between 0 and 1. The three first integer numbers in the states $x_{1(n)}$, $y_{1(n)}$, and $z_{1(n)}$ are removed to let only the decimal numbers on MACM CS in DV (10.2), and we obtain the depurated MACM CS in DV,

$$
\begin{cases}
x_{1m(n)} = (20 + x_{1(n)})1000 - floor((20 + x_{1(n)})1000), \\
y_{1m(n)} = (20 + y_{1(n)})1000 - floor((20 + y_{1(n)})1000), \\
z_{1m(n)} = (20 + z_{1(n)})1000 - floor((20 + z_{1(n)})1000),
\end{cases}
\tag{10.3}
$$

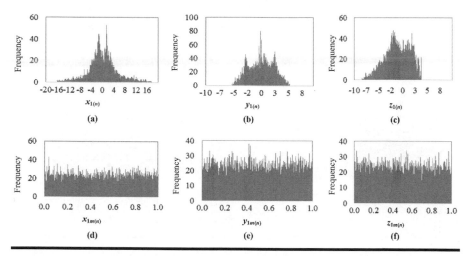

Figure 10.2 Histograms: (a) state $x_{1(n}$, (b) state $y_{1(n}$, and (c) state $z_{1(n}$ of MACM CS in DV standard (10.2), and (d) state $x_{1m(n}$, (e) state $y_{1m(n}$, and (f) state $z_{1m(n}$ of MACM CS in DV depurated (1.3).

where $x_{1m(n)}$, $y_{1m(n)}$, and $z_{1m(n)} \in [0,1]$ are the states variables of the depurated chaotic map, and the subscript m denotes that the MACM CS in DV standard (10.1) was modified. Two depurated chaotic maps with similar features are reported in [7,14,13,25]. In order to obtain the improved data distribution of the MACM CS in DV depurated (10.3) with respect to the MACM CS in DV standard (10.2), Figure 10.2 shows the histogram with the data distribution by using $n = 20000$, where the data distribution is clearly improved.

Experimental implementation of the CSs in DV (10.2), and (10.3) using the smart display Mikromedia for dsPIC33EP are conducted, similar implementation of MACM CS in DV (10.2) using smart display is reported in [7].

Figure 10.3a shows the phase plane of the states $x_{1(n)}$ versus $z_{1(n)}$ projected on the TFT LCD of U1, where the data concentration and dispersion of the strange attractor is homogeneous. Figure 10.3b shows the phase plane $x_{1m(n)}$ vs $z_{1m(n)}$ with the depurated attractor on U1, where there is a change in the data dispersion of the MACM CS in DV depurated (10.3).

Finally the states $x_{1m(n)}$, $y_{1m(n)}$, and $z_{1m(n)}$ of the MACM CS in DV depurated (10.3) are considered to generate two PR sequences in the encryption and decryption stages and each number of the PR sequences is generated in one iteration n for U1 and U2 algorithms.

10.2.4 Secret Key Definition

The secret key is symmetric, it is defined by initial conditions and parameters of the MACM CS in DV standard (10.2), and of the MACM CS in DV

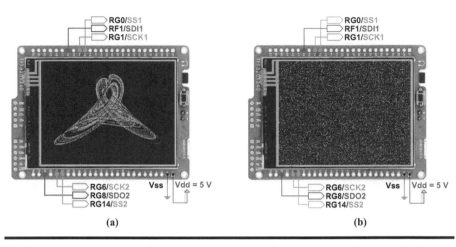

Figure 10.3 **Representation of CSs (10.2) and (10.3), and pins description of Mikromedia for dsPIC33EP: (a) phase plane representation** $x_{1(n}$ **vs** $z_{1(n}$ **of MACM CS in DV standard (10.2) projected in TFT LCD display, and (b) [hase plane representation** $x_{1m(n}$ **vs** $z_{1m(n}$ **MACM CS in DV depurated (10.3) projected in TFT LCD display.**

depurated (10.3). The key must be secure, i.e., it should be subject to a value greater than 2^{100} according with [26].

We used the standard IEEE-754 with extension AN575 to 32 bits for the numerical representation of dsPICs, as reported in [27]. Table 10.2 shows the numerical representation of floating point formats with operating intervals that dsPICs microcontrollers use as standard, where *eb* is a biased exponent, *e* is the exponent or characteristic, $f*$ is the fraction or mantissa, and $|A*|$ is the decimal number.

According to the intervals of Table 10.2, there are a maximum 0xFF7FFFFF and 0×01000000 minimum in the hexadecimal base. The maximum interval represented in the decimal base is 4286578687 which is equivalent to subtracting 232 less 223, the result is 231. By performing the calculations representation of 7 numbers is $2^{31} + 2^{31} + 2^{31} + 2^{31} + 2^{31} + 2^{31} + 2^{31} = 2^{217} > 2^{100}$. The space of keys can be represented in numerical base. We proposed the following hexadecimal notation as key: FF7F FFFF FF7F FFFF FF7F FFFF FF7F FFFF FF7F FFFF FF7F FFFF FF7F FFFF.

Table 10.2   Microchip Standard IEEE-754 for 32 Bits

	eb	*e*	$|A*|f*$	*Decimal*
Max	$0 \times FF$	128	7FFFFF	6.805646930E + 38
Min	0×01	− 128	000000	1.17549435E − 38

Notation of microchip standard IEEE-754 for 32 bits is used to build the key space by using the parameters and initial conditions of the MACM CS in DV standard (10.2). Table 10.3 shows the secret key for 155 bits, where the float decimal and hexadecimal notations are used.

The secret key is built with one slight variation of the parameters and initial conditions of the MACM CS in DV standard (10.2). Table 10.4 shows the set of three keys using parameters and different initial conditions of the MACM CS in DV standard (10.2).

Table 10.3 Notation of Secret Key of the MACM CS in DV Standard (1.2)

	Initial Condition			*Parameter*			
	$x_{1(0)}$	$y_{1(0)}$	$y_{1(0)}$	α_1	β	γ_1	δ_1
Float decimal	1.2345678	0.1234567	0.7654321	2.0	2.0	0.5	4.0
Float 32 bits IEEE	3F9E 0651	3DFC D6DE	3F43 F35C	4000 0000	4000 0000	3F00 0000	4080 0000

Table 10.4 Set of Secret Keys of the MACM CS in DV Standard (1.2)

Keys	*Initial Condition*			*Parameter*			
	$x_{1(0)}$	$y_{1(0)}$	$y_{1(0)}$	α_1	β_1	γ_1	δ_1
K_1	1.2345678	0.1234567	0.7654321	2.0	2.0	0.5	4.0
	3F9E 0651	3DFC D6DE	3F43 F35C	4000 0000	4000 0000	3F00 0000	4080 0000
K_2	1.2345678	0.1244567	0.7654321	2.0	2.0	0.5	4.0
	3F9E 0651	3DFC D1A0	3F43 F35C	4000 0000	4000 0000	3F00 0000	4080 0000
K_3	1.2345678	0.1234567	0.7654321	2.0	2.0	0.5	4.1
	3F9E 0651	3DFC D6DE	3F43 F35C	4000 0000	4000 0000	3F00 0000	4083 3333

10.3 Transmission Process

This section describes the transmission process of confidential multimedia message $m(t)$, which is divided into three stages: acquisition process, encryption stage, and transmission of encrypted message. Figure 10.4 illustrates the description of the transmission process.

10.3.1 Acquisition Process

The conversion result of message $m(t)$ is contained in one register of 16 bits defined as REG1. We define the vector A as the equivalent of REG1 where each element is expressed as a_k, with $k = 1, 2, ..., 16$,

$$A = [a_1, a_2, a_3, a_4, ..., a_{16}], \tag{10.4}$$

where $a_k \in [0,1]$. The elements a_{1-16} of REG1 represent the data with the intervals of 0 to 65535 possibilities where the data can represent audio and image contents.

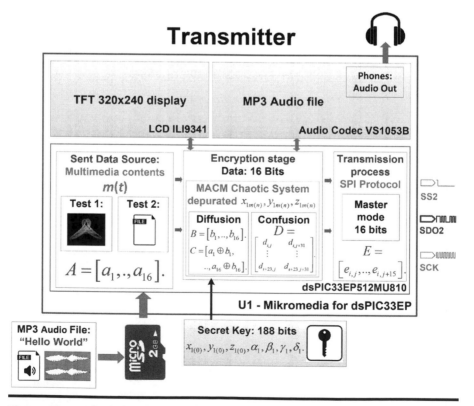

Figure 10.4   Block diagram of the transmitter.

In traditional signal processing, in order to not lose information, the Nyquist-Shannon theorem tells us that in uniformly sampling a signal we must sample at least twice [28,29]. The message size directly depends on the maximum frequency f_{max} of message $m(t)$, and sampling frequency f_s that the algorithm of U1 can process. These frequencies are related as follows:

$$f_s \geq 2 f_{max} \tag{10.5}$$

An anti-aliasing filter is required at the inputs of the analog channels of U1, where the cut-off frequency of this filter f_c has to be fixed such that

$$f_{max} < f_c < f_s \tag{10.6}$$

For the audio processing, we recommended to check the conversion rate of the internal analog to digital converter (ADC) of U1, similar consideration are reported in [7]; however in this study we are only considering the encryption of proposed multimedia digital contents as examples.

10.3.2 Encryption Stage

The message encryption considers two subprocesses: diffusion and confusion. We describe these methods using the states of the MACM CS in DV depurated (10.3).

10.3.2.1 Diffusion Method

The diffusion method consists of hiding the information of message $m(t)$ using a logic operation over the elements of vector A. We use the 3rd state $z_{1m(n)}$ of the MACM CS in DV depurated (10.3) with a numerical arrangement to generate values from 0 to 65535. The result is described by

$$O_{ex(U1)} = z_{1m(n)} 2^k = [(20 + z_{1(n)})1000 - floor((20 + z_{1(n)})1000)]2^k \tag{10.7}$$

Also, (10.7) can be defined as vector B with 16 equivalent elements

$$B = [b_1, b_2, b_3, b_4, ..., b_{16}] \tag{10.8}$$

The OR-EX logic operation is calculated with each element of vectors A and B. The information of vector A is hidden, and the results are defined by vector C,

$$C = [a_1 \oplus b_1, a_2 \oplus b_2, ..., a_{16} \oplus b_{16}] = [c_1, c_2, ..., c_{16}]. \tag{10.9}$$

10.3.2.2 Confusion Method

This method consists in building a matrix with PR numbers extracted from a DNA database. The construction of the DNA matrix is described in Appendix A. The elements of Table 10.14 shows the DNA sequences with the details of positions; this matrix has dimension $r \times s$, where r represents the rows and s represents the columns. The elements show disordered positions from 1 to higher values of k. These disordered elements are considered as one sequence. For each row r of Table 10.14, the sequence of k elements is repeated two times.

For this process, the same elements of matrix in Table 10.14 are considered for the DNA sequence matrix referred to as D. This matrix consists of $r = 24$ sequences of $s = 32$ elements,

$$
D = \begin{pmatrix}
d_{1,1} & d_{1,2} & \cdots & d_{1,s} \\
d_{2,1} & d_{2,2} & \cdots & d_{2,s} \\
\vdots & \vdots & \ddots & \vdots \\
d_{r,1} & d_{r,2} & \cdots & d_{r,s}
\end{pmatrix}
\tag{10.10}
$$

The confusion algorithm consists of permuting the position of $k = 16$ elements of vector C. We calculate a numerical arrangement from states of the MACM CS in DV depurated (10.3), and these states define the initial coordinates to obtain from (10.10) a new vector with 16 new permuted positions. The initial coordinates are described by

$$
\begin{cases}
i = x_{1m(n)}r = [(20 + x_{1(n)})1000 - floor((20 + x_{1(n)})1000)]r, \\
j = y_{1m(n)}\dfrac{s}{2} = [(20 + y_{1(n)})1000 - floor((20 + y_{1(n)})100)]\dfrac{s}{2},
\end{cases}
\tag{10.11}
$$

where i, j are integers and the subscripts and define the rows and columns of matrix D, respectively. The initial coordinates of $d_{i,j}$ allow the finding of the initial position of a sequence up to the complete 16 positions with the last referred to as $d_{i,j+15}$,

$$
D = \begin{pmatrix}
d_{i,j} & d_{i,j+1} & \cdots & d_{i,j+31} \\
d_{i+1,j} & d_{i+1,j+1} & \cdots & d_{i+1,j+31} \\
\vdots & \vdots & \ddots & \vdots \\
d_{i+23,j} & d_{i+23,j+1} & \cdots & d_{i+23,j+31}
\end{pmatrix}
\tag{10.12}
$$

Finally, the confusion process is calculated using (10.12), and the result is contained in the new row vector E. The first element e_j of vector E contains the first element c_1 of vector C that is referred to as the first position of the element $d_{i,j}$ of vector D

until 16 elements are completed, the last element c_{16} corresponding to the element e_{j+15} that is referred to as the position $d_{i,j+15}$ of vector D,

$$E = [c_1, c_2, ..., c_{16}] = [d_{i,j}, d_{i,j+1}, ..., d_{i,j+15}] = [e_j, e_{j+1}, ..., e_{j+15}]. \qquad (10.13)$$

10.3.3 Transmission of Encrypted Messages

The encryption algorithm is processed on U1. The encrypted information of $m(t)$ is contained in the row vector E, where the 16 elements are equivalent to one word of 16 bits, and when this word is transmitted it corresponds to one iteration n.

Now, Table 10.1 shows the SPI configuration mode of U1 and U2. U1 is connected with U2 using the pins: SS2 connected with SS1, SDO2 connected with SDI2, and SCK, which is the common clock to synchronize the smart display Mikromedia dsPIC33s. Finally, the word contained in vector E is transmitted iteration-by-iteration n from U1 to U2.

10.4 Cryptogram

In this section, we describe the statistical tests to prove the hypothesis that $m(t)$ is secure from the observer stand point. In order to show whether the proposed algorithm reproduces PR sequences, we performed the statistical tests to the cryptogram extracted from U1.

Figure 10.5 shows the block diagram of the ES where an intruder intervenes in the SPI protocol by using an external Mikromedia for dsPIC33EP U3. U1 is connected with U3 using the pins: SS2 connected with SS1, SDO2 connected with SDI1, and SCK is the common clock to synchronize the dsPIC33EPs. The rebuilt encrypted message $m(t)$ is obtained, but the intruder cannot read the data.

10.4.1 Statistical Tests

We present test results of the behavioral analysis of the sequence generator obtained from the proposed encryption algorithm. Here, we consider encrypted binary sequences with length $n = 20000$ bits generated from U1. The binary sequence is read and stored by a computer, then we calculate the statistical tests using MATLAB®. We performed statistical tests to check whether the encrypted algorithm generates sufficiently secure PR sequences [30,31]. Table 10.5 shows the results of five basic tests [32].

In addition, Table 10.6 shows the Federal Information Processing Standards (FIPS) 140-1 statistical test for randomness in encrypted binary sequences with length $n = 20000$ bits generated from U1 [32]. Figure 10.6 shows graphical results of FIPS 140-1 by using histogram in poker and runs tests.

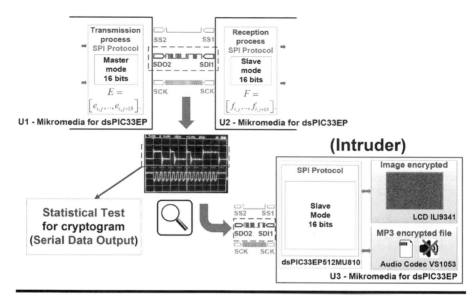

Figure 10.5   Block diagram to obtain the cryptogram.

Table 10.5   Five Statistical Basic Test

Test	Proposed	Interval Required	Parameter
Frequency X_1	2.4642	< 3.8415	—
Serial X_2	2.5486	< 5.9915	—
Poker X_3	5.80798	< 14.0671	$m = 3$
	22.7872	< 24.9958	$m = 4$
	42.7919	< 44.9853	$m = 5$
Runs X_4	5.8263	< 9.4877	$k = 3$
	6.288	< 12.5916	$k = 4$
	6.7137	< 15.5073	$k = 5$
Autocorrelation X_5	1.4144	$-1.96 < X_5 < 1.96$	—

Table 10.6   FIPS 140-1 Randomness Results

Test	Proposed		Interval Required	Parameter
Monobit	9889		$9654 < n1 < 10346$	$n1$ is the number of 1s
Poker	22.7872		$1.03 < X3 < 57.4$	$m = 4$
	Block	*Gap*		
	2523	2444	[2267–2733]	$i = 1$
	1235	1254	[1079–1421]	$i = 2$
Runs	615	675	[2267–2733]	$i = 3$
	316	301	[1079–1421]	$i = 4$
	160	149	[2267–2733]	$i = 5$
	74	90	[1079–1421]	$i = 6$
Long run	*Block*	*Gap*		
	0	0	< 34	

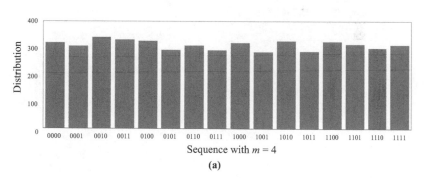

(a)

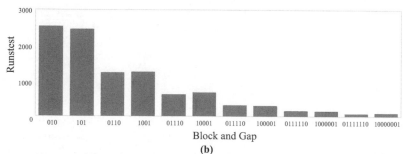

(b)

Figure 10.6   Graphical results of FIPS 140-1: (a) Poker test for $m = 4$ and (b) Runs test for $1 \le i \le 6$.

These results demonstrate that the proposed encryption algorithm successfully passes all the statistical tests and the algorithm can generate PR sequences.

10.5 Receiver Process

This section describes the reception process for the reconstruction of $m'(t)$. The reception process is similar to the transmission process of Section 10.3, but the diffusion and confusion processes are performed in inverted stages. The processes are divided into three stages: reception of encrypted message, decryption process, and the digital representation of the recovered message, see Figure 10.7.

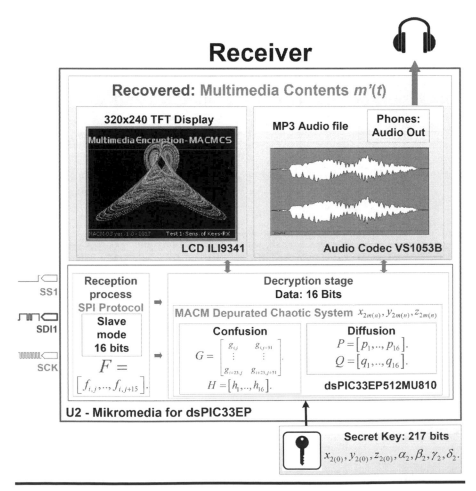

Figure 10.7   Block diagram of the receiver.

10.5.1 Reception of the Encrypted Message

We use the properties of the SPI protocol to synchronize U1 with U2. The Mikromedia dsPIC33 U2 is always waiting for the first word of 16 bits that contained the 16 elements of vector E from U1, which is the first iteration n. First, the SPI configuration of U2 is in slave-mode, because it is waiting for the encrypted message from U1, then, the SPI configuration changes to master-mode because the decrypted message $m'(t)$ is transmitted to U5.

The decryption algorithm of U2 is configured to constantly check if the word of 16 bits from U1 is successfully received. We consider $z = 1$ in the configuration of the SPI module on U2. The flag SPIRBF of the internal register SPI1STAT, allows verification on whether reception of a word with 16 bits from U1 is accomplished. Finally, the vector F contains the reception of the encrypted message,

$$F = [f_j, f_{j+1}, f_{j+2}, ..., f_{j+15}]. \tag{10.14}$$

10.5.2 Decryption Stage

We use the same proposed methods with the same features as in the encryption stage of Section 10.3.2, but in reverse order. The secret key is symmetric, and therefore it is mandatory that the U2 algorithm contains the same initial condition and parameters of the MACM in DV standard (10.2). These subsections are described as follows.

10.5.2.1 Reverse Process of Confusion Method

To generate PR sequences we use the MACM CS in DV standard (10.2), and the MACM CS in DV depurated (10.3), but the notation of states variables is changed to differentiate the transmission and reception stages. We define the state variables $x_{2(n)}, y_{2(n)}, z_{2(n)}$, and parameters $\alpha_2, \beta_2, \gamma_2, \delta_2$ of the new MACM CD in DV used in this stage as,

$$\begin{cases} x_{2(n+1)} = x_{2(n)} + \tau(-\alpha_2 x_{2(n)} - \beta_2 y_{2(n)} z_{2(n)}), \\ y_{2(n+1)} = y_{2(n)} + \tau(-x_{2(n)} + \gamma_2 y_{2(n)}), \\ z_{2(n+1)} = z_{2(n)} + \tau(\delta_2 - y_{2(n)} - z_{2(n)}) \end{cases} \tag{10.15}$$

The depurated states are referred as $x_{2m(n)}, y_{2m(n)},$ and $z_{2m(n)}$. The initial coordinates are described as follows,

$$\begin{cases} l = x_{2m(n)} v = [(20 + x_{2(n)})1000 - floor((20 + x_{2(n)})1000)]v, \\ u = y_{2m(n)} \dfrac{w}{2} = [(20 + y_{2(n)})1000 - floor((20 + y_{2(n)})1000)]\dfrac{w}{2}. \end{cases} \tag{10.16}$$

where l and u are integers, the subscripts $l = \{0 \le x_{2m(n)} \le 1\}$ with $l \in [1,v]$, and $u = \{0 \le y_{2m(n)} \le 1\}$ with $u \in [1,w]$ define the rows and columns respectively to determine the positions of the elements for the new DNA matrix G. This matrix contains the same elements as matrix D (10.10). The initial coordinates $g_{l,u}$ allow the finding of the initial position of a sequence until 16 positions are completed and the last position is referred to as $g_{l,u+15}$,

$$G = \begin{pmatrix} g_{l,u} & g_{l,u+1} & \cdots & g_{l,u+31} \\ g_{l+1,u} & g_{l+1,u+1} & \cdots & g_{l+1,u+31} \\ \vdots & \vdots & \ddots & \vdots \\ g_{l+23,u} & g_{l+23,u+1} & \cdots & g_{l+23,u+31} \end{pmatrix} \qquad (10.17)$$

The vector F contains $m(t)$, and the confusion process is calculated using Equations 10.14 through 10.17. We obtain the new row vector H. The first element h_u of vector H contains the first element f_j of vector F, and the last element f_{j+15} is referred to as h_{u+15},

$$H = [f_j, f_{j+2}, ..., f_{j+15}] = [g_{l,u}, g_{l,u+1}, ..., g_{l,u+15}] = [h_u, h_{u+1}, ..., h_{u+15}] \quad (10.18)$$

10.5.2.2 Reverse Process of Diffusion Method

This method uses the MACM CS in DV standard (10.15), and one state $z_{2m(n)}$ of the MACM CS in DV depurated (10.16). We calculated a numerical arrangement to generate values from 0 to 65535 and the result is defined by

$$O_{ex(u2)} = z_{2m(n)} 2^k = [(1.3 + z_{2(n)})1000 - floor((1.3 + z_{2(n)})1000)]2^k, \quad (10.19)$$

where the vector P defines the 16 equivalent elements,

$$P = [p_1, p_2, ..., p_{16}] \qquad (10.20)$$

The OR-EX logic operation is calculated on each element of vector H with respect to vector P. Finally, the decrypted message $m'(t)$ is found and the data are contained in the vector Q,

$$Q = [h_1 \oplus p_1, h_2 \oplus p_2, ..., h_{16} \oplus p_{16}] = [q_1, q_2, ..., q_{16}] \qquad (10.21)$$

10.5.3 Transmission of Recovered Message

Once the decrypted message is recovered, we configured the second SPI protocol using U2 to receive the data in 16 bits. The hardware of Mikromedia U2 is configured for SPI port 1 in slave mode. Figure 10.6 showed the block diagram where the recovered message $m'(t)$ is showed on the display LCD for image encryption cases, and the MP3 file audio is reproduced by using the audio codec of U2 for digital audio encryption cases.

10.6 Experimental Results

In this section, we present the results of the experiment to transmit and recover confidential multimedia messages from U1 to U2. We propose the design of a simple Operative System (OS) based in MACM CS to represent the friendly graphic interface for final users in the encryption and decryption process in the transmitter U1, and the receiver U2 in real-time. Three kinds of test are developed to determine the performance of the proposed MACM OS: sensitivity of secret keys, animation of one phase plane of the MACM CS, and MP3 Audio File.

10.6.1 Proposal of Simple Operative System Based in Chaos

One simple OS is conducted using the software and hardware tools of the smart displays U1 and U2. The proposed OS is based in the digital cryptosystem where the MACM CS is used. The graphic interface and the control of proposed MACM OS are designed considering the manage of multimedia contents for final users. Specific routines are developed in the design of the proposed OS, e.g., tests identification, transmitter and receiver recognition, image control for animations and text, stored of files using inner memory, audio-digital control, among others.

The smart displays are programed by using some libraries of the Micro C Pro dsPIC compiler, e.g., TFT, MMC, MP3, and SPI libraries routines [23].

The internal hardware used for the proposed OS using the Mikromedia smart displays U1 and U2 is as follows:

- TFT LCD display ILI9341. The display has one resolution of 320242. The color control is represented in 16-bits format with 65536 colors combination, the color representation is divided in 5 bit for red, 6 bits for green, and 5 bits for blue. The control bus of the ILI9341 is in parallel, and its implementation is carried out using 8 bits for data bus and 5 bits for the bus control.
- Audio codec VS1053B. The audio codec allows to reproduce digital audio files for the standards format as MP3, Ogg, ACC, MIDI, WMA, among others. Its configuration is conducted using the SPI protocol in 8 bits slave mode. The messages processed and reproduced by the VS1053B are obtained by the headphones audio-out.
- Slot for Micro SD Card. The Micro SD Cards supports files in FAT16 format until 32 GBs for stored. Also, its configuration is conducted using the SPI protocol.

■ USB connection. The smart-displays U1 and U2 are programmed with boot-loader USB Human Interface Device (HID); this means that is not necessary to use an external programer. The power of U1 and U2 is through USB connection, or directly from external Vdd = 5V, and Vss = 0 V.

■ Memory. We use the internal memory of the dsPIC33EP512MU810 to manage multimedia contents stored in memory-block segments. In this version, 20KB are used to manage data from external devices as SD Card or internal devices; for example, to store animation, pictures, etc.

The inner communication of the audio codec VS1053B and Slot for SD Card is linked with the port 2 of the SPI protocol. The smart display has other devices linked in the SPI port 2, but in this version these devices are disabled. Figure 10.8 shows the simple description of the proposed MACM OS.

The main functions of MACM OS are described as follows:

■ Graphic mode. The "Graphic Interface" represents images and animation contents on TFT LCD ILI93141 of U1 and U2, the TFT Dot library is used to draw one pixel on TFT LCD where X and Y axis coordinates, and color are considered as parameters represented in REG1 format where 6 bytes or 48 bits represent the data of one pixel. The "Text Interface" allows to verify the status of the use of software and hardware process applications of U1 or U2.

■ Mode operation. "TX" refers to transmitter in U1, and "RX" refers to receiver in U2.

■ Test number. Three tests are referred to as valid the performance of the proposed MACM OS.

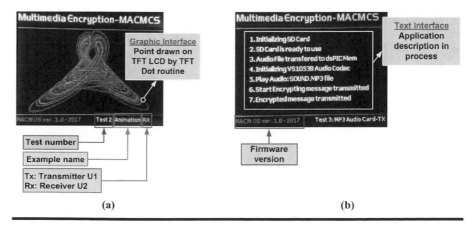

(a)   (b)

Figure 10.8   Description of MACM OS to reproduce multimedia contents: (a) function description of MACM OS, reproduction of decrypted image, and (b) applications description for the file encryption process using MACM OS.

- Example name. For this version we considered a brief description of the proposed examples.
- Firmware version. We presented the first version for educational purposes, which means: version 1.0, year 2017. This version contemplates always display the text description of the MACM OS functions.

The performance of the proposed examples using the interface of MACM OS are calculated in the next section.

10.6.2 Experimental Results on the ES

One animation was considered for the experimental tests to reproduce the chaotic oscillator MACM in DV; similar CSs are referred in Equations 10.3 and 10.15, and it is defined by

$$
\begin{cases}
x_{3(n+1)} = x_{3(n)} + \tau(-\alpha_3 x_{3(n)} - \beta_3 y_{3(n)} z_{3(n)}), \\
y_{3(n+1)} = y_{3(n)} + \tau(-x_{3(n)} + \gamma_3 y_{3(n)}), \\
z_{3(n+1)} = z_{3(n)} + \tau(\delta_3 - y_{3(n)}^2 - z_{3(n)}),
\end{cases} \tag{10.22}
$$

where $x_{3(n)}$, $y_{3(n)}$, $z_{3(n)}$ are the state variables, and the values of $\alpha_3 = 2$, $\beta_3 = 2$, $\gamma_3 = 0.5$, and $\delta_3 = 4$ are referred to as parameters. We use the initial conditions $x_{3(n)} = y_{3(n)} = z_{3(n)} = 1$, and step size $\tau = 0.015$ as example for the next subsections. The initial conditions and the step size τ of the chaotic oscillator (10.22) is totally independent of the cryptosystem based in MACM CS proposed in Section 10.3 and 10.5. The next sections show the performance of the encryption and decryption algorithms to characterize the animation of (10.22) as message $m_1(t)$.

10.6.2.1 Time Complexity of the Algorithms

The time complexity (TC) is estimated by counting the number of elementary operations performed for the algorithms of U1, where an elementary operation takes a fixed amount of time to perform the running time of one iteration n [33]. In order to determine the performance of the proposed ES using TC for image and audio digital applications, we calculated the number of iterations n that U1 generates in 1 second. The TC of U1 is calculated with the time period referred to as $T_{Q(U1)}$, and it is the reciprocal of the frequency referred to as $f_{Q(U1)}$:

$$
f_{Q(U1)} = \frac{1}{T_{Q(U1)}} \tag{10.23}
$$

The encryption algorithm is implemented on U1. The TC of U1 is calculated using (10.23). Table 10.7 shows the experimental results of encrypted algorithm to

Table 10.7   Time Complexity of U1

Process	Algorithm	$T_{Q(U1)}(\mu s)$	$f_{Q(U1)}(Hz)$	Denotation
Multimedia content	Chaotic Oscillator MACM in DV	108	9259	A
Data encryption 48 bits	TFT Dot function to drawn one pixel on the TFT LCD	480	2083	$B \to C \to D$
Transmission	Encrypted message for 6 bytes	4	250000	E
Total		**592**	**1689**	-

reproduce the DV of MACM oscillator (10.22) in U1. The algorithm is designed to encrypt one pixel using the TFT Dot function, where three words in REG1 format are considered to represent one dot using 48 bits or 6 bytes.

According to Table 10.7, the algorithm of U1 presents TC = 592 μs and $f_{Q(U1)} = 1689$ Hz. For our study, we considered $f_{Q(U1)}$ as $n = 1689$ iterations per second.

In the case of U2, we need the minor TC in all processes; the configuration of U2 is accelerated with the modification of the internal PPL. This allows processing to be faster in the decryption algorithm. Therefore, the TC of U2 must be less than that of U1

$$T_{Q(U1)} > T_{Q(U2)} \tag{10.24}$$

Table 10.8 shows the experimental results of the decryption algorithm.

Table 10.8   Time Complexity of U2

Process	Algorithm	$T_{Q(U2)}(\mu s)$	Denotation
Reception	Encrypted message	4	F
Decryption stage 6 bytes	Decryption of pixel: X, Y coordinates, and color	480	$G \to H \to P$
Transmission of recovered message	Draw one pixel on the TFT LCD	25	Q
Total		**509**	—

According to the results shown in Tables 10.7 and 10.8, the TC of $T_{Q(U1)}$ is higher than $T_{Q(U2)}$. The condition (10.24) to synchronized U1 and U2 is fulfilled.

Now, the next sections show experimental results of the proposed test and the necessary conditions to obtain the multimedia contents encrypted and descripted in U1 and U2, respectively, considering the symmetric master keys. Two kinds of messages are considered to carry out three experimental tests on the ES. The first message is referred to as $m_1(t)$ and the second message is referred to as $m_2(t)$. Their examples are described in next sections. The recovered massages of $m_1(t)$ and $m_2(t)$ are referred to as $m'_1(t)$ and $m'_2(t)$, respectively.

10.6.2.2 First Test: Sensitivity of Secret Keys

The sensitivity test is carried out using the secret keys K_1, K_2, and K_3 in the Table 10.4. The secret keys are entered by directly programming the algorithms of U1 and U2, but the secret keys can be registered using touch-screen routines or external keyboard connected to dsPICEP33s U1 and U2. Table 10.9 shows the combination of secret keys K_1, K_2, and K_3 to carry out the sensitivity test. The message $m_1(t)$ is reproduced using the initial conditions and parameters proposed in the animation (10.22) where the MACM OS is used to represent the phase plane $x_{3(n)}$ vs $z_{3(n)}$ as example.

Figure 10.9 shows the result of the sensitivity test among the set of three secret keys. We conclude that the definition of secret key supports the hypothesis that its construction of 217 bits is secure because for slight variations of the initial conditions and parameters of secret keys, the result of the recovered message $m'_1(t)$ is different than the original message $m_1(t)$ for different secret keys; similar results are reported in Liu et al. (2016).

10.6.2.3 Second Test: Animation of the Chaotic Oscillator as Message $m_1(t)$

We use the initial conditions and parameters of MACM chaotic oscillator described in Equation 10.22 to reproduce $m_1(t)$. For this test we use the MACM OS, the same secret key K_1 is considered for U1 and U2, and the results of messages recovered

Table 10.9   Sensitivity Test Secret Keys on the Smart-Displays

Case	Secret Key on U1	Secret Key on U2
1	K_1	K_1
2	K_1	K_2
3	K_1	K_3

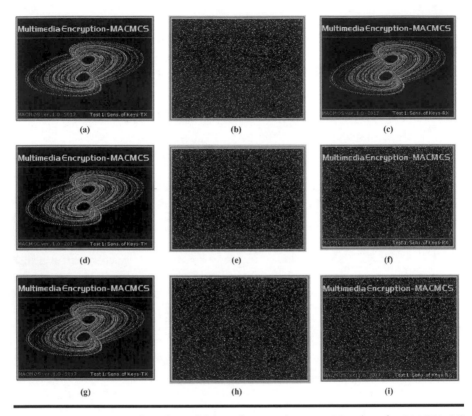

Figure 10.9 **Test results of sensitivity of secret keys on ES using the MACM OS and the phase plane of $x_{3(n)}$ vs $y_{3(n)}$. Case 1: (a) original $m_{1(t)}$, (b) cryptogram, (c) reception of $m_1'(t)$, Case 2: (d) original $m_1(t)$, (e) cryptogram, (f) reception of $m_1'(t)$, and Case 3: (g) original $m_1(t)$, (h) cryptogram, and (i) reception of $m_1'(t)$.**

$m_1'(t)$ is shown in Figure 10.10a. The K_2 is entered in U2, and K_1 is conserved in U1, where the Figure 10.10b shows the animation (10.22) encrypted in U2.

Tables 10.8 and 10.9 showed the algorithms performance of this example using graphic interface mode in the MACM OS. Therefore, according the graphic-processing capacity of U1 and U2, the proposed MACM OS support 1689 pixels per second considering the animation of MACM chaotic oscillator (10.22).

10.6.2.4 Third Test: MP3 Audio File as Voice Message $m_2(t)$

We propose to manage external block-memory segments where the multimedia contents are stored. An external Micro SD card is considered to store one file where the multimedia contents are loaded from Micro SD Slot of U1. The MP3 audio file with the information "Hello World" is stored in the Micro SD with the name: SOUND.MP3. Table 10.10 shows the characteristics of SOUND.MP3 file.

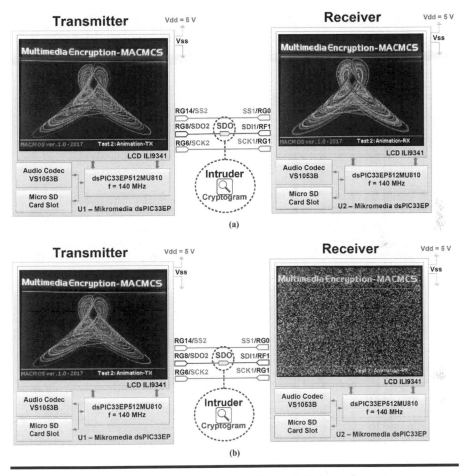

Figure 10.10 Animation of the chaotic oscillator (1.22) used as message $m_1(t)$: (a) animation recovered in U2 using same K_1 in U1 and U2, and (b) animation encrypted in U2 using K_1 in U1, and K_2 used in U2.

Table 10.10   Characteristics of MP3 Audio File: SOUND.MP3

Property	Value
Size	17.8 KB (18240 bytes)
File format	MPEG 1 Layer 3 File
Audio	160 kbps
Sample Rate	32000 Hz
Configuration	Stereo
Time length	0:00:00.865 s

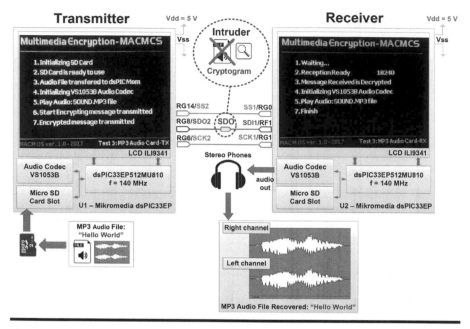

Figure 10.11 Test results on the MACM OS using external Micro SD Card to encrypt MP3 audio file.

Cubase 5 professional audio software is used to obtain the voice recorder MP3 audio file. Figure 10.11 shows the block diagram where the MACM OS is configured in "Text Interface" to show the encryption process of MP3 file in U1, and decryption process to recover the MP3 data file in U2. In order to resume the process, Table 10.11 shows the steps with the processes description in U1, and the Table 10.12 describe the process in U2.

Now, the package according the size of file $m_2(t)$ is sent. In this stage, the intruder can read or copy the encrypted message, it is impossible to identify the format, the MP3 file has one format according to the standard, and it is impossible to reproduce the file using one MP3 player.

Finally, the $m_2'(t)$ MP3 audio file was recovered; this message has the same audio characteristics of the original audio file. We conclude that MACM OS allows to encrypt, decrypt, and transfer data from U1 to U2 6250 times per second for data with structure of 16 bits (or 2 bytes).

Table 10.11   Description of the Processes to Encrypt the MP3 File in U1

Step	Process	Description
1	Initializing SD Card	We configured the SPI port 2 only to use the MMC library.
2	SD Card ready to use	The file SOUND.MP3 is loaded from external Micro SD card.
3	Audio file transfer to dsPIC Mem	The MP3 audio file is transferred to dsPIC memory.
4	Initializing VS1053B Audio Codec	Now, the SPI port 2 is configured to control audio coded VS1053B.
5	Play Audio: SOUND. MP3 file	MP3 file is reproduced by using audio out VS1053B.
6	Start encryption of the Message	MP3 file was encrypted using the inner memory of dsPIC33, and the SPI port 2 is configured to transmit data package.
7	Encrypted message transmitted	The encrypted message $m_2(t$ was satisfactorily transmitted.

Table 10.12   Description of the Processes to Encrypt the MP3 File in U1

Step	Process	Description
1	Waiting...	SPI port 1 of U2 was configured in slave-mode to wait the data link from U1.
2	Reception Ready (file size in bytes)	The complete encrypted message $m_2'(t)$ is received by using the inner dsPIC33 U2 memory.
3	Message Received is decrypted	Message $m_2'(t)$ was decrypted byte to byte by using the inner dsPIC33EP memory.
4	Initializing VS1053B Audio Codec	We use SPI port 2 to control the audio coded VS1053B.
5	Play Audio: SOUND. MP3 file	MP3 file is reproduced by using the audio out of VS1053B.
6	Finish	The complete process was conducted.

10.7 Conclusions

We proposed the design and experimental implementation of chaotic encryption algorithm by using the communication protocol SPI 16-bit on smart-displays to acquire, process, encrypt, transmit, synchronize, receive, decrypt, and reproduce multimedia contents with one friendly graphic interface, where MACM OS was implemented. Three kinds of tests were carried out to prove the message performance in the ES: sensitivity secret key, animation of MACM chaotic oscillator, and MP3 audio file transferred. The cryptogram was subjected to statistical test generating PR sequences. This algorithm can be used in an integrated circuit (IC) and smart-displays that has the standard SPI protocol.

The numerical results were verified with Mikroc Pro for the dsPIC compiler that includes the properties of standard IEEE-754, AN575 of 32 bits into the dsPICs. The quality of message depends on the processing capacity of the smart display. The Mikromedia for dsPIC33EP smart display is easy to install and it has a low cost implementation because the system costs less than 99 USD.

In future work, we will test with other multimedia contents and apply the encrypted and decrypted algorithms with other communication protocols such as I2C, USB-CAN, or Ethernet with larger quantity of bits using other smart displays, with more processing capacity.

Acknowledgments

This work was supported by the CONACYT, México, under Research Grant 166654.

References

1. Feredj, M. 2016. A smart display component model for embedded systems modeling and simulation. *2016 SAI Computing Conference* 452–457.
2. Barr, M. and Massa, A. 2006. *Programming Embedded Systems: With C and GNU Development Tools*. 2nd edition. Newton, MA: O'Reilly Media.
3. Philips Semiconductors, 1995. The I2C-bus and how to use it. http://www.i2cbus.org/fileadmin/ftp/i2c_bus_specification_1995.pdf (accessed November 10, 2016).
4. Philips Semiconductors, 2003. AN10216-01 I2C Manual. http://www.nxp.com/documents/application_note/AN10216.pdf (accessed November 10, 2016).
5. Motorola, Inc., 2003. SPI Block Guide V03.06. Document Number S12SPIV3/D.
6. Oudjida, A.K., Berrandjia, M.L., Tiar, R. et al. 2009. FPGA implementation of I2C & SPI protocols: A comparative study. *16th IEEE International Conference Electronics, Circuits, and Systems*, 507–510.
7. Méndez-Ramírez, R., Arellano-Delgado, A., Cruz-Hernández, C., Abundiz-Pérez, F., and Martínez-Clark, R. 2018. Chaotic digital cryptosystem by using SPI protocol and its dsPICs implementation. *Front Inform Tech* 19:165–179.

8. Muhaya, F.B., Usama, M., and Khan, M.K. 2009. Modified AES using chaotic key generator for satellite imagery encryption. *Emerg Intell Comput Technol Appl* 5754:1014–1024.

9. Aguilar-Bustos, A.Y., Cruz-Hernández, C., López-Gutiérrez, R.M. et al. 2010. Hyperchaotic encryption for secure e-mail communication. In R. Chbeir, Y. Badr, A. Abraham, A.-E. Hassanien (Eds.), *Emergent Web Intelligence: Advanced Information Retrieval* (pp. 471–486). London, UK: Springer.

10. Guglielmi, V., Pinel, P., Fournier-Prunaret, D. et al. 2012. Chaos-based cryptosystem on DSP. *Chaos Soliton Fract* 42:2135–2144.

11. Rhouma, R., and Belghith, S. 2011. Cryptanalysis of a chaos-based cryptosystem on DSP. *Commun Nonlinear Sci Numer Simulat* 16:876–884.

12. Arellano-Delgado, A., López-Gutiérrez, R.M., Cruz-Hernández, C. et al. 2012. Experimental network synchronization via plastic optical fiber. *Opt Fiber Technol* 19:93–108.

13. Murillo-Escobar, M.A., Cruz-Hernández, C., Abundiz-Pérez, F. et al. 2015. A RGB image encryption algorithm based on total plain image characteristics and chaos. *Signal Process* 109:119–131.

14. Liu, W., Sun, K., and Zhu, C. 2016. A fast image encryption algorithm based on chaotic map. *Opt Lasers Eng* 84:26–36.

15. Azzaz, M.S., Tanougast, C., Sadoudi, S. et al. 2013. A new auto-switched chaotic system and its FPGA implementation. *Commun Nonlinear Sci* 18:1792–1804.

16. Murillo-Escobar, M.A., Cruz-Hernández, C., Cardoza-Avendaño, L., and Méndez-Ramírez, R. 2017. A novel pseudorandom number generator based on pseudo randomly enhanced logistic map. *Nonlinear Dynam* 86:1–19.

17. Méndez-Ramírez, R., Cruz-Hernández, C., Arellano-Delgado, A., and López-Gutiérrez, R.M. 2016. Degradation analysis of generalized Chuas circuit generator of multi-scroll chaotic attractors and its implementation on PIC32. *IEEE 2016 Future Technologies Conference*, 1034–1039.

18. Di Jasio, J. 2008. *Programming 32-bit Microcontrollers in C. Exploring the PIC32*. Burlington, MA: Newnes.

19. Siddiqui, R.A., Grosvenor, R.I., Prickett, P.W. 2015. DsPIC-based advanced data acquisition system for monitoring, control and security applications. *12th International Bhurban Conference on Applied Sciences and Technology*, 293–298.

20. Uriz, A.J., Aguero, P.D., Moreira, J. et al. 2016. Flexible pseudorandom number generator for tinnitus treatment implemented on a dsPIC. *IEEE Lat Am T* 14: 72–77.

21. Mikroelektronika, 2017. Smart-display, Mikromedia for dsPIC33EP. http://www.mikroe.com/ (accessed October 26, 2017).

22. Microchip Technology Inc., 2012. dsPIC33EP512MU810 Data Sheet. http://ww1.microchip.com/downloads/en/DeviceDoc/70616g.pdf (accessed October 26, 2017).

23. Mikroelektronika, 2016. MikroC Pro for dsPIC compiler, ver. 7.0.1. http://www.mikroe.com/ (accessed October 26, 2017).

24. Méndez-Ramírez, R., Arellano-Delgado, A., Cruz-Hernández, C., and Martínez-Clark R. 2017. A new simple chaotic Lorenz-type system and its digital realization using a TFT touch-screen display embedded system. *Complexity* 2017:1–13.

25. Murillo-Escobar, M.A., Cruz-Hernández, C., Abundiz-Pérez, F. et al. 2015. A robust embedded biometric authentication system based on fingerprint and chaotic encryption. *Expert Syst App* 42:8198–8211.

26. Alvarez, G., Li, S. 2006. Some basic cryptographic requirements for chaos-based cryptosystems. *Int J Bifurcat Chaos* 16:2129–2151.
27. Microchip Technology Inc., 1997. AN575 IEEE 754 Compliant Floating Point Routines. http://denethor.wlu.ca/cp316/PIC_documentation/AN575.pdf (accessed November 10, 2016).
28. Nyquist, H. 1928. Certain topics in telegraph transmission theory. *AIEE Trans* 47:617–644.
29. Shannon, C. 1949. Communication in the presence of noise. *Proceedings IRE* 37:10–21.
30. Fúster, A., Hernández, L., Montoya, F. et al. 2012. Criptografía, Protección de Datos y Aplicaciones-guía para estudiantes y profesionales. *Alfaomega, Ra-ma* 133–157.
31. Yalcin, M.E., Suykens, J.A.K., and Vandewalle J. 2004. True random bit generation from a double-scroll attractor. *IEEE Trans Circ Syst I* 51:1395–1404.
32. Menezes, A.J., Van Oorschot, P.C., and Vanstone, S.A. 1996. *Handbook of Applied Cryptography*. Boca Raton, FL: CRC Press.
33. Sipser, M., 2006. *Introduction to the Theory of Computation*. 2nd edition. Boston, MA: Thomson Course Technology.
34. National Center for Biotechnology Information, 2016. GenBank U.S. National Library of Medicine. http://www.ncbi.nlm.nih.gov/genbank/ (accessed November 10, 2016).
35. Cornish-Bowden, A., 1985. Nomenclature for incompletely specified bases in nucleic acid sequences: Recommendations 1984. *Nucleic Acids Res* 13:3021–3030.

Appendix A: DNA Sequence Matrix

The DNA sequence matrix was used in the confusion process and inverse confusion process. The DNA sequences can be obtained from MATLAB functions *getgenbank* and *randseq(N)* or the information can be directly requested by accessing *genbank* [34]. In this paper, the DNA matrix was performed using the MATLAB functions. Table 10.13 shows one sequence of four nucleotides referred to as *Ad*, *Cy*, *Gu*, and *Th* to represent the difference with the vectors and variables used in previous sections that represents the base of a DNA strand [35].

Table 10.13   Binary Representation of Nucleotides

Nucleotide	Description	Binary Number
Ad	Adenine	$(00)_2$
Cy	Cytosine	$(01)_2$
Gu	Guanine	$(10)_2$
Th	Thymine	$(11)_2$

For the design of the elements of the DNA matrix, we considered pairs of nucleotides to represent the k positions, e.g., the pair of nucleotides Ad (adenine) and Th (thymine) represents binary position $(0011)_2$. This means that the pair $AdTh$ represents the position 3. The elements determine positions from 1 to the higher value of $k = 16$, because the SPI protocol was configured in 16 bits. These elements are disordered, and cannot be repeated.

Numerical arrangements of 16 DNA pairs represent one sequence for the DNA matrix. We performed 24 sequences of DNA referred to as $r = 24$ rows, and $s = 32$ columns. The sequences were twice repeated according the design of algorithms for encryption and decryption. The results of the DNA sequences were contained on matrixes D and G.

Initially, the data have 16 elements contained in the vectors C and F. The chaotic DHMs (1.2), and (1.16) define the initial coordinates i, j, and l, u. We evaluate these coordinates on the matrixes D and G to determine a DNA sequence with 16 new positions. The new positions of these elements were contained in the vectors E and H. Finally, the complete information of these DNA sequences were defined for D and G in the matrix of Table 10.14.

Table 10.14 Binary Representation of Nucleotides

5	10	0	13	2	7	4	11	6	1	8	9	15	14	3	12	5	17	0	13	2	7	4	11	6	1	8	9	15	14	3	12
14	5	12	9	4	7	8	10	11	3	1	15	13	2	0	6	5	5	12	9	4	7	8	10	11	3	1	15	13	2	0	6
10	5	9	2	7	3	13	4	14	6	8	11	1	15	12	0	5	5	9	2	7	3	13	4	14	6	8	11	1	15	12	0
13	7	5	10	0	9	8	11	2	4	6	14	15	6	3	12	7	13	5	10	0	9	8	11	2	4	6	14	15	6	3	12
11	13	12	8	14	9	4	7	5	2	3	6	14	3	15	10	13	4	12	8	14	9	4	7	5	2	3	6	14	3	15	10
5	4	2	15	11	12	7	8	1	0	1	5	6	1	5	6	9	13	2	15	11	12	7	8	1	0	1	5	6	1	5	6
14	13	15	5	10	3	11	12	7	9	0	6	13	4	14	18	4	13	9	5	10	3	11	12	7	9	0	6	13	4	14	10
7	9	11	14	15	6	5	3	3	4	9	1	7	13	4	3	13	9	11	14	15	6	5	3	3	4	9	1	7	13	4	2
3	4	5	6	11	8	6	1	1	12	2	0	0	13	7	2	9	4	4	6	11	8	6	1	1	12	2	0	0	13	7	9
8	7	6	5	13	12	8	2	4	15	13	5	5	7	8	9	4	7	8	5	13	12	8	2	4	15	13	5	5	7	8	15
2	4	8	6	7	9	3	0	12	3	11	6	6	4	2	15	7	4	1	6	7	9	3	0	12	3	11	6	6	4	2	4
3	15	1	13	3	8	8	5	9	14	0	8	8	10	3	12	3	15	11	13	3	8	8	5	9	14	0	8	8	10	3	14
10	5	13	7	12	13	13	2	8	15	10	9	13	6	8	2	5	12	7	13	12	13	13	2	8	15	10	9	13	6	8	7
6	12	7	0	9	13	13	6	2	10	1	8	14	9	0	14	12	5	3	0	9	13	13	6	2	10	1	8	14	9	0	7
4	5	0	5	6	13	14	3	11	0	6	15	7	1	5	4	0	12	8	5	6	13	14	3	11	0	6	15	7	1	5	3
1	0	6	15	10	5	5	9	2	10	8	4	12	11	4	11	6	0	11	15	10	5	5	9	2	10	8	4	12	11	4	11

(Continued)

Table 10.14 (Continued) Binary Representation of Nucleotides

	0	1	2	3	4	5	6	7	8	9	10	11	12	13	14	15
0	0	1	2	3	4	5	6	7	8	9	10	11	12	13	14	15
15	15	14	13	12	11	10	9	8	7	6	5	4	3	2	1	0
12	12	6	14	8	0	2	4	10	11	13	15	9	1	7	3	5
1	1	3	5	7	9	11	13	15	0	2	4	6	8	10	12	14
2	2	0	6	4	8	14	12	3	10	1	7	5	9	11	15	13
7	7	15	11	9	13	5	3	14	12	4	6	8	10	2	0	1
13	13	5	10	3	8	9	6	2	0	15	14	7	1	11	12	4
9	9	6	15	11	0	10	4	13	2	1	8	14	12	3	7	5

Chapter 11

Medical Image Encryption

Padmapriya Praveenkumar and
Amirtharajan Rengarajan

Contents

DOI: 10.1201/9780429435461-12

11.1 Overview

Data handling and manifesting are the inevitable sectors of communications. Especially, e-governance of Telemedicine turns out to be essential to avert unwanted situations due to hackers and thereby to provide cheap, fast and efficient health care governance to the rural population of the nation. Due to the hi-tech development in Information Communication Technology (ICT) in the recent decades, the privacy and security issues persist, which needs to be addressed with precision.

In this era of ICT, multimedia tools have been used to share the Electronic Patients Record (EPR) among the entitled users. As EPR has the detailed medical information of an individual and it needs to be accessible only by the concerned persons. Intended unauthorised access will be done by wicked people, which may lead to anti-social activity. At the same time, patient information should be readily available whenever required by authorised users for authenticated purposes in providing telemedicine consultation and telediagnosis.

Data breaches in healthcare are alarmingly costlier and frequent. They continue to put patient record at risk. The Sixth Annual Benchmark Study on Privacy and Security of Healthcare data by Ponemon Institute, on May 2016 reveals that majority of the healthcare organisations experience multiple data breaches [1]. Nearly 90% of the healthcare organisations had a data breach in the past two years.

Identity theft resource centre (ITRC) on August 16, 2016, reveals that 217 breaches were from medical/healthcare organisations, where the number of breaches over all the sectors was 384 [3]. Undoubtedly, the security and easy availability of EPRs needs a critical attention owing to the heavy utilisation and storage of confidential medical case studies. The Government of India has planned to set up National e-Health Authority (NeHA) as a part of Digital India flagship initiative to maintain standards for Health Electronic Record (HER) to be followed by various healthcare service providers in India for the portability and easy sharing of medical data [1,2].

Personalized Health and Care 2020 by the Department of Health has suggested a plan to integrate EPR [3] and make it possible for every individual to access their online health records securely by 2018 [4]. This real-time data availability helps the diagnosis in telemedicine through integrated care [5]. By 2021, the estimated market value to implement Internet of Things (IoT) has been estimated to reach USD 661.74 billion to provide integrity and authentication. The Health Insurance Portability and Accessibility Act (HIPAA) have requested measures and authentication schemes to regulate the secure access of patient health records [6]. Hence, there is a need to develop a system which protects and to provide security solutions to EPR when transmitted and shared over public channels. There is also a significant requirement in developing a system that manages and effectively handles EPR, and to integrate the peers involved in telemedicine in an authenticated network [7–9].

11.2 Digital Imaging and Communications in Medicine (DICOM)

Medical image security plays a vital role as the sensitive and significant patient information is communicated over public channels. Health Insurance Portability and Accountability Act (HIPAA) by the federal government made it mandatory to all the hospitals to take appropriate measures in safeguarding the medical health records [10].

To afford suitable and straightforward accessing between the peers involved in transmission and reception of medical records, Picture Archiving and Communication System (PACS) with HIPAA started a format called as Digital Imaging and Communications in Medicine (DICOM). Then after this introduction, slowly all the medical imaging devices started adopting DICOM format [11–13].

It supports various modalities for integrating and maintaining health records of patients.

Each medical image has its information and characteristics. The unique identifiers decide the templates of these individual medical images, and it should be registered under National Electrical Manufacturers Association (NEMA).

The medical images have information objects called Service Object Pairs (SOP) which helps in DICOM exchanging. The procedure used in DICOM is robust, and each command transmission needs to be acknowledged. The sender device will not transmit the command until the receiver compatibility is verified [14,15]. Then it includes transfer syntax to include compression of the information before communicating. To check the compatibility of the end device, DICOM conformance document is maintained which includes the SOP and transfer syntax. This document holds the entire specification details about the modality adopted.

Functionalities of PACS: Supporting various modalities of imaging systems, developing a communication medium for the trans-reception of EPR, building a network to provide images for interpretation and reviewing and designing a storage unit for keeping the images and reports [1–4].

11.3 Electronic Medical Record (EMR)/ Electronic Patient Record (EPR)

Electronic patient record (EPR) (patient)/EMR (Hospital) is the digitised sensitive information about patient health information. It also provides the information about the authentication and the accessing information at each level. It gives details about age, sex, patient name, scan images, lab reports, disease detail, diagnosis information, insurance details, doctor's name, hospital name etc. Hence, it is very much essential and significant requisite to provide utmost security to the private details of the patient [16–20]. Based on the sensitivity of the EPR the storage system of that can be decided. It can be a centralised storage system or an individual network storage system based on the modalities. While transmitting EPR over the public channel for diagnosis purpose, access should be restricted to avoid modification, deletion, duplication and tampering of EPR.

The mandatory information in DICOM needed for diagnosis is referred to as Region of Interest (ROI), and the other information is referred to as Non-Region of Interest (NROI). This ROI and NROI vary from patient to patient based on their clinical complaints [21,22].

11.4 Modalities of DICOM

Modality refers to the complete information about the image and the non-image under diagnosis [23] as in Table 11.1.

11.5 Image Analysis

The three requirements of any crypto algorithm are Confidentiality, Integrity and Authentication (CIA). To achieve a better-encrypted image, the encryption algorithm must produce a different image pixel values as compared to the original input image. With the developed encryption algorithm, image analysis has to be carried out to prove the randomness and sternness of the cipher image [24,25]. To obtain the better cryptic effect, shuffling, permutation, rotation, substitution, transposition, confusion and diffusion are the various techniques adopted in any fashion to produce the non-intelligible ciphertext. To prove the robustness of the image encryption algorithm, image analysis has been broadly classified into the statistical and differential analysis.

11.5.1 Statistical Attack Analysis

Statistical attack analysis determines the statistical complexity relationship between the pixels in the original and the encrypted images. The encryption algorithm

Table 11.1 Modalities in Maintaining EPR

Image Modality	Non-image Modality
CR—computed radiography	ST—stand alone object (overlay, curve, modality look up table (LUT), ROI LUT
CT—computed tomography	Basic study description
MR—magnetic resonance, enhanced MR	Gray scale presentation
NM—nuclear medicine	Stored print
DX—digital X-ray	Enhanced MR
US—ultrasound, multiframe	Raw data
XA—X-ray angiography	RT—radiation therapy (dose, structure, plan)
XF—X-ray fluoroscopy	WF—wave form (audio, ECG)
RT—radiation therapy image	SR—structured report (text, enhanced text, comprehensive, key-based, mammography)
PET—positron emission tomography	
DR—digital radiography	
MG—mammography	
IO—intra oral	
VL—visible light (endoscopy, microscopic, slide, photographic)	

should always withstand the statistical attack which can be analyzed by various techniques like Histogram Analysis, Pixel Distribution Analysis, Information Entropy: Local and Global, Key Sensitivity, Key Space Analysis, Chi-Square Test, Histogram Deviation Analysis and Deviation from Ideality Analysis.

11.5.1.1 Histogram Analysis

Visual assessment is the first examining metric in any encryption scheme. The histogram represents the graphical measure of plotting the pixel values at each intensity level typically. For an accurately random cipher image, it is evident that the histogram should be uniformly flat over the entire range of pixel values and should differ entirely from the histogram of the original input image over visual evaluation.

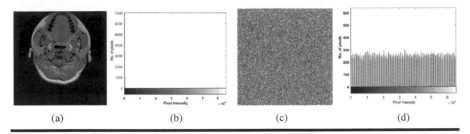

| (a) | (b) | (c) | (d) |

Figure 11.1   (a) Original DICOM, (b) Histogram of (a), (c) Encrypted image of (a) and (d) Histogram of (c).

Figure 11.1a and 11.1c represents the original and the encrypted images, respectively. Figure 11.1b represents the histogram of Figure 11.1a, respectively. From the visual assessment of Figure 11.1d, it is clear that there exists no relationship between the plain and the cipher images.

11.5.1.2 Correlation Analysis

According to Pearson's correlation analysis, correlation coefficient determines the linear relationship and the correlation between the adjacent image pixels in all the directions (x, y and z) in the encrypted image. Table 11.2 provides the correlation relation between the image pixels. The estimated value close to zero indicates that there exists no correlation between the adjacent pixels in the encrypted cipher image.

11.5.1.3 Pixel Distribution Analysis

The correlation coefficient analysis can be carried out diagrammatically using pixel distribution analysis for vertical, horizontal and diagonal directions for the adjacent pixels in original and in encrypted image respectively. The correlation coefficients (Q_{12}) were calculated,

$$Q_{uv} = \frac{COV(u,v)}{\sqrt{W(u)}\,\sqrt{W(v)}}$$

Table 11.2   Pearson's Correlation Coefficient Analysis

Correlation Coefficient between Adjacent Pixels in Cipher Image	Robustness of the Cipher
−0.0 to 0.3	Weak
0.3 to −0.7	Moderate
0.7 to −1	Strong

where:

$$W(u) = \frac{1}{P} \sum_{k=1}^{P} \left(u_k - \frac{1}{P} \sum_{k=1}^{P} u_k \right)^2$$

$$W(v) = \frac{1}{P} \sum_{g=1}^{P} \left(v_g - \frac{1}{P} \sum_{g=1}^{P} v_g \right)^2$$

$$COV(u,v) = \frac{1}{P} \sum_{l=1}^{m} \left[u_l - E(u) \right] \left[v_l - E(v) \right]$$

$$E(u) = \frac{1}{J} \sum_{j=1}^{J} u_j$$

where u, v are the adjacent pixels in the image considered, and P denotes the number of pixels. From Figure 11.2a and 11.2b the pixels were concentrated in the original image whereas in the encrypted image the pixels were uniformly distributed over the entire region considering horizontal direction.

11.5.1.4 Information Entropy: Local and Global

Conventional global Shannon entropy is used to measure the uncertainty in the cipher image using the equation,

$$G(E) = -\sum_{j=1}^{P} P(E_u) \log_2 P(E_u)$$

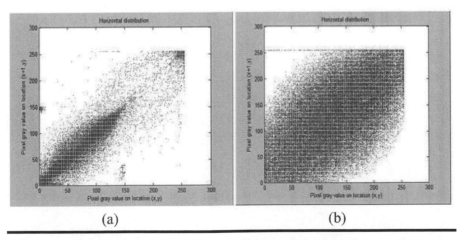

(a)　　　　　　　　　　　　　(b)

Figure 11.2　Pixel distribution analysis of adjacent pixels in the horizontal direction (a) original image input and (b) cipher image.

where, $P(E_u)$ is the probability of occurrence the pixel E_u in the image histogram.

Consider an image of bit depth 'I' and intensity levels 'J', then the entropy lies in the interval $[0, J]$. To be highly uncertain, the estimated value should be closer to J.

Though global Shannon entropy aims at measuring the uncertainty of the complete encrypted image, it fails to address the same for the image blocks in the cipher image. The weakness of Global entropy measure has been addressed by Local entropy measure. It can be estimated, using Local entropy by considering all the non-overlapping blocks and determine the mean of global Shannon entropy over all the blocks.

11.5.1.5 Key Sensitivity Analysis

Key plays an essential role in deciding the efficiency and the sternness of the proposed encryption system. The techniques used to transfer the keys to the recipients and the safe storage of it decides the CIA component of the algorithm. Even a single bit change in the key parameter in decryption end should result in an utterly absurd image. Original Key used in encryption side K=@#45%^&GHtyui23450_9gkjhf GYUOIKJ9(*7nbhjJKILOEFDA**9**, a single bit change in LSB (least significant bit) of the original key K=@#45%^&GHtyui23450_9gkjhfGYUOIKJ9(*7nbhjJKILO EFDA**8**, should result in a completely different random image.

11.5.1.6 Key Space Analysis

Key space defines the number of keys and rounds it is involved in diffusion, confusion and shuffling process of an encryption algorithm. The larger the key size and number of rounds involved, the more randomness and complexity will be introduced in the encrypted image.

11.5.1.7 Chi-Square Tests

The uniform distribution of pixels in the encrypted image can be studied from the histogram by analysing chi-square test. It is estimated using,

$$\chi^2 = \sum_{i=0}^{255} \frac{\left(\left(\begin{matrix} \text{pixel value in the encrypted} \\ \text{image histogram} \end{matrix} \right) - \left(\begin{matrix} \text{Actual expected pixel values} \\ \text{in the encrypted image} \\ \text{histogram} \end{matrix} \right) \right)^2}{\text{Actual expected pixel values in the encrypted image histogram}}$$

where 'i' represents the intensity level, the actual expected value for a 256×256 encrypted image pixel values form the histogram is 256. From the chi-square distribution table, the critical theoretical values have to compared with estimated probability value for the various levels of significance (e.g., 5%, 1% etc.) and the hypothesis. If the estimated values lie below the critical values, then it justifies that the encrypted histogram has uniform pixel distribution.

11.5.1.8 Histogram Deviation

It measures the variation in the pixels between the original and encrypted image histogram. It can be estimated using

$$H_D = \left(\frac{\frac{i_0 + i_{255}}{2} + \sum_{j=1}^{254} i_j}{a \times b} \right)$$

where i_j represents the amplitude of the difference at a pixel value j, $a \times b$ represents the row and the column of the encrypted image. The higher the estimated value, the better will be the encryption algorithm.

11.5.1.9 Irregular Deviation

It estimates the difference between the original and the encrypted image by estimating the mean difference in the histograms. It can be calculated as

$$I_D = \left(\frac{\sum_{j=0}^{255} \mathrm{MH}(j)}{a \times b} \right)$$

where $\mathrm{MH}(j)$ represents the histogram deviation and is given as the difference between the Mean Histogram value from Histogram deviation. $a \times b$ represents the image size. Lower the estimated value; better will be the encryption algorithm.

11.5.1.10 Deviation from Ideality

It is a measure, which helps in reducing the deviation of the encrypted image from the ideal case. It can be estimated using

$$\mathrm{HI}_E = \begin{cases} \dfrac{a \times b}{256} & 0 \leq E_i \leq 255 \\ 0 & \text{otherwise} \end{cases}$$

$$I = \frac{\sum_{c_0=0}^{255} |\mathrm{HI}(E) - H(E)|}{a \times b}$$

where HI(E) and $H(E)$ represents the histograms of the ideal and actual encrypted image. The lower the computed value, the better will be the encryption algorithm.

11.5.2 Differential Attack Analysis

Differential attack analysis determines the difference in the pixel values of the encrypted images by making a one-bit change in the image pixel of the original image.

11.5.2.1 NPCR and UACI

Number of Pixel Changing Rate (NPCR) and Unified Average Changing Intensity (UACI) are the most commonly used measures in Differential attack analysis. It can be done by analysing the two encrypted images. One from the original input plain image and the second one from the plain image by making a single bit change. They are calculated using Equations

$$\text{NPCR} = \sum_{o,p} \frac{E(o, p)}{a \times b} \times 100\%$$

$$\text{UACI} = \frac{1}{a \times b}\left[\sum_{o,p} |\frac{E_1(o, p)\ E_2(o, p)}{255}|\right] \times 100\%$$

where $E(o, p)$ equals the same image size of E_1 and E_2

$$E(o, p) = \begin{cases} 0 & \text{if } E_1(o, p) = E_2(o, p) \\ 1 & \text{if } E_1(o, p) \neq E_2(o, p) \end{cases}$$

The estimated UACI should lie between the lower and the upper significance level and the NPCR value should lie above the critical value to resist the differential attacks as in Tables 11.3 and 11.4.

11.5.3 Attack Analysis

To validate and to prove the robustness and the sternness of the encryption algorithm, various attack analysis have to be carried out. This section discusses three types of attacks namely cropping attack, noise attack and chosen plain text attack.

11.5.3.1 Cropping Attack

In cropping attack, some random blocks or uniform blocks of the encrypted images are cropped intentionally (1%, 5% etc.) and it is given as input to

Table 11.3   Theoretical UACI Critical Value for Various Significance Levels

Significance level	Theoretical UACI critical value
$U^{*-}_{0.05}$	33.2824%
$U^{*-}_{0.01}$	33.2255%
$U^{*-}_{0.001}$	33.1594%
$U^{*+}_{0.05}$	33.6447%
$U^{*-}_{0.01}$	33.7016%
$U^{*-}_{0.001}$	33.7677%

Table 11.4   Theoretical NPCR Critical Value for Various Significance Levels

Significance Level	Theoretical UACI Critical Value
$N^{*}_{0.05}$	99.5693%
$N^{*}_{0.01}$	99.5527%
$N^{*}_{0.001}$	99.5341%

the decryption algorithm. At the receiver end, the decrypted image recovery determines the resistant against various attacks purposely caused by the intruders over a public medium which validates the strength and immune power of the proposed encryption algorithm. Real time example includes CCTV image transmission through internet gateway when hacked by an intruder, the security algorithm at the receiver end should estimate the input image to some extent.

11.5.3.2 Noise Attack Analysis

In real time scenario, during diagnosis of the medical records, the encrypted medical image will be passed through a communication channel to exchange data between peers. This section discusses various communication channels like AWGN (Additive White Gaussian Noise), Rayleigh and Rician.

Color Noises: Color noises arise due to the power spectrum of noise signals. Each color noise has its property. With the Power Spectral Density (PSD) of noise, various noises can be generated.

Communication Channels: AWGN channel is the one which adds white Gaussian noise to it. Rayleigh channel makes the fading of the input signal amplitude which is based on the Rayleigh distribution parameter.

Rician channel provides multipath to the applied input signal and in that one of the signal path will be shortened or extended based on rician distribution. The channel output can be estimated using Signal to Noise Ratio (SNR), Bit Energy to PSD of Noise (Eb/N0) and Signal Energy to PSD of noise (ES/N0).

System noises: Gaussian noise model is a statistical model, whose Probability Density Function (PDF) is equal to the Gaussian distribution function. Poisson noise is a noise an electronic noise created by poisons distribution function. Salt and pepper noise is an impulse noise created due to the sudden disturbances in the image input. Colored noises and system noises can be added to the encrypted medical images and passed over the communication channels. At the receiver end, the image recovery decides the withstanding capacity of the encryption algorithm.

11.5.3.3 Chosen Plaintext Attack

Any encryption algorithm which can withstand chosen plaintext attack, it should naturally withstand plain and cipher text attack also. The equation to estimate the attack is done by the bit XOR operation of two cipher images obtained from two everyday images equals to the bit XOR operation between the two plain images

$$\begin{pmatrix} \text{Cipher image1 (MXN)} \\ \text{XOR Cipher Image2 (MXN)} \end{pmatrix} = \begin{pmatrix} \text{Plain image1 (MXN)} \\ \text{XOR Plain Image2 (MXN)} \end{pmatrix}$$

The cipher image output depends on the number of rounds involved in each stage of the encryption algorithm. If the equation is satisfied by the proposed algorithm, then it is prone to chosen plaintext attack by the intruder else it will resist against this attack.

11.6 Encryption Techniques in DICOM

Electronic Patient Record (EPR) has been implemented in many developing countries which refer to the systematic collection and storage of health information about patients in digital format. It includes medical history, personal details and billing information of the patients. Attacks like an interruption, interception, modification, and fabrication of health records have been identified as the root cause for the failure of telemedicine projects.

Maintaining EPR is the fundamental role for the successful implementation of Telemedicine application in urban areas to improve the health care quality. Confidentiality, Integrity, Authentication (CIA), reliability, availability and privacy are the key features of any telemedicine diagnosis. Department of Health Services, New Delhi, elaborated the various ethical issues while maintaining and sharing EPR in real time scenario [8].

Department of Community Medicine, New Delhi, differentiates EMR and HER and also elaborates on the challenges in customising the EMR as it provides efficient use of digitised data, which provides the chance for doctors to efficiently diagnose the diseases in due course of treatment.

In this regard, Bhattacharya et al. [9] Indian Institute of Information, Technology & Management, Gwalior, provides the security solutions in accessing EPR by employing RSA and DES algorithms. Sugandh [26], co-founder of Iam wire, a digital tech incubator, recommended a secured cloud-based storage of digitised EPR to enhance life-saving in emergency situations. Pradeep kumar et al. [12], Erode, Tamil Nadu addressed the DCT and DWT based watermarking schemes on medical records to provide identity and privacy to EPR. Lavanya et al. [11] MIT, Chennai, proposed a joint encryption and watermarking scheme to provide integrity to patients medical record by considering the NROI of the EPR. Saroj Kanta Mishra et al. [13], Sanjay Gandhi Postgraduate Institute of Medical Sciences (SGPGIMS), Lucknow, and Rajesh [14], Indian Institute of Management, Ahmedabad, provides the challenges, solutions, merits and demerits of telemedicine in India.

To overcome the challenges faced by EPR access, a secured cloud-based structure for sharing EPR among peers using Attribute-Based Encryption (ABE) was carried out by Sangeetha et al. [15], where the details of the patients were encrypted and stored on semi-trusted cloud servers. In their work, the cloud-based security has been divided into Personal Domain (PSDs) to provide privacy to patients to authenticate the users in hospitals and related healthcare providers.

When the EPR is loaded on the cloud servers, flexible access, security, and privacy have to be provided by the servers. To curtail these issues, improved Shamir secret sharing encryption was proposed by Sangeetha et al. [16] to enhance the integrity and the authenticity of the secured cloud environment.

To establish a secure communication between authenticated stakeholders in e-health care, the conventional methods employed are steganography, cryptography and watermarking. The traditional security algorithms employed in the current medical applications are Advanced Encryption Standard (AES) and Data Encryption Standard (DES) Norcen et al. [27]. However, the same algorithms cannot be used for accessing EPR due to its large capacity and size.

To provide integrity to EPR data, watermarking integrated with steganography was proposed by Zaz et al. [28] and Coatrieux et al. [29]. To minimize the computational complexity and the time involved in executing the algorithms on EPR, many researchers are attracted to develop selective image encryption schemes without compromising the security aspects [30].

Secured medical data sharing and handling is a primary objective in IoT platform for various medical applications. Ibrahim Mashal et al. [18] and Debasis Bandyopadhyay et al. [19] proposed the end-end communication using IoT architecture and the related security issues in interconnecting the smart devices and the protocols used to provide confidentiality and authentication of the stakeholders involved in communication.

Sharma et al. [20] provide the methodology to protect EPR by employing ROI and NROI based watermarking and embedding schemes. Further, the identity of the patient has also been verified using MD5 Hash and Rivest-Shamir-Adleman (RSA) algorithms to enhance the robustness of the system. Also, Hamming error correction code has been applied to the encrypted medical data to resist the channel noise.

Method 1: 2D Chaotic based gray scale DICOM image encryption
Read DICOM image
Using key permute the DICOM sequence
Using two different initial seed values generate chaotic sequence 1 and 2
Bit XOR the sequences with two different key values
Concatenate the Bit XOR sequence outputs
Use this sequence for diffusing the image pixel values in the diffused image to produce the final encrypted output as in Figure 11.3.

Method 2: 3D Chaotic based RGB DICOM image encryption
Read RGB DICOM Image
Divide into R, G and B planes as in Figure 11.4.
Generate a 3D chaotic map using initial seed generator
Using the generated sequences, position of the pixels in the individual planes are scrambled
Concatenate the planes and apply transformation
Concatenated image is then divided into blocks and sorting is done based on the scrambled pixel values
Then scrambling of the blocks is carried out using the chaotic sequences to generate the final encrypted image

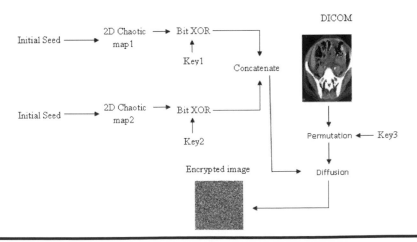

Figure 11.3   Chaotic key diffusion sequence based image encryption.

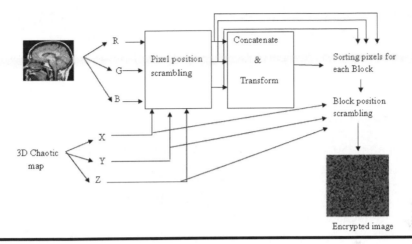

Figure 11.4   Pixel and block based chaotic image encryption.

11.6.1 *Watermarking and Embedding Techniques in DICOM*

The impact of design and methodology selection with improved assurance in medical records optimised communication, and clear medical terminologies have been analysed by Soderstrom et al. [31]. A cloud-based EPR using Fuzzy has been implemented by Liu and Weng et al. [22] and Chen et al. [32]. Here, a binary tree and attribute-based encryption schemes had been developed to encrypt the medical records of the patients before storing it in the cloud environment. This helps in securing the EPR and maintains it privacy.

A reversible encrypted data hiding scheme by employing ROI and NROI of DICOM image has been carried out by Liu et al. [23] and Cyganek et al. [24]. In this scheme encryption followed by substitution-based data hiding has been employed to protect the EPR and to measure its tolerance against tamper.

Hazzaa et al. [33], introduced a Discrete Wavelet Transform based digital watermarking technique. In this technique, patient details are embedded as a watermark in the original image to restrict any unauthorised access of the EPR when transmitted. Tieu et al. [34] provided a review on protection of EPR and its related security issues and solutions to protect it from unauthorised access and alterations has been carried out by Mancy et al. [35] to improve the data protection level in EPR sharing.

Method 1: QR based secret sharing in DICOM
- Get the secret input
- Apply QR (quick response) to it
- Initial seed is used to generate chaotic maps and then concatenate to form multiple chaotic maps

- Using the generated chaotic sequences, perform pixel and block scrambling on the secret QR
- Read the input DICOM
- Perform shuffling, permutation and diffusion operation based on the sequence generated from the individual maps
- To the diffused image, embed the QR watermarking as in Figure 11.5, to produce the final encrypted image.

Method 2: QR based watermarking in RGB DICOM

- Watermarking will be implemented for authentication and embedding for data integrity.
- Quick response (QR) codes are widely used in various products for ownership identification.
- In the proposed scheme, QR code-based visible watermarking will be done on the encrypted NROI image
- The NROI section of DICOM image will carry the 25 × 25 QR code as a watermark, the size of which can be decided based on medical image payload.
- LSB substitution has been adopted as simple data embedding on the spatial domain for greater imperceptibility.

In the encrypted NROI, the pixel bits which were present before the insertion of 25 × 25 QR code image coefficients will be embedded in the LSBs of the other sections of the DICOM image to avoid data loss. Here QR code is generated using patient and doctor's name which will be watermarked as in Figure 11.6a. The sample results are shown in Figure 11.6 (b–h).

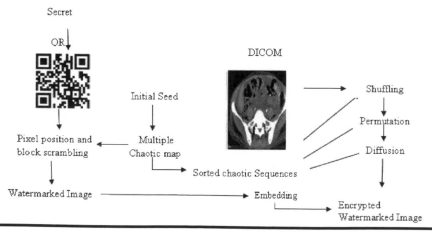

Figure 11.5   QR based secret sharing in DICOM.

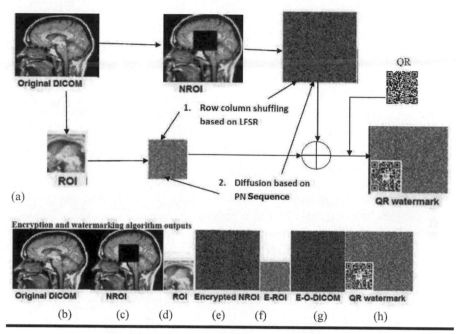

Figure 11.6 **(a) QR based watermarking in RGB DICOM (b) original DICOM, (c) NROI, (d) ROI, (e) encrypted NROI, (f) encrypted ROI, (g) encrypted output DICOM, and (h) QR watermark in NROI.**

11.6.2 Cryptographic Techniques in DICOM

Diagnostic medical equipment such as Magnetic Resonance Imaging Scanner (MRI) and Computer Tomography Scanner (CT) play a crucial role in recording the clinical status of a patient diagnosed or suspected with organ abnormality due to chronic diseases. For the treatment of malignant or benign tumours on the brain or other significant parts of human body, MRI images have a noticeable role in assisting the medical practitioners during diagnosis.

The Electronic Patient Record (EPR) in various modalities is a collection of the status report obtained through these MRI or CT scanners. Security of such patient records requires a critical attention as the number of patients reported with abnormalities is, unfortunately, rapidly increasing every day. Presently such patient records are being stored in a compact disk (CD) storage medium and handed over to the concerned patients in most of the scanning centres attached to hospitals. Hence, chances for the unauthorised access to medical records are on the higher side.

For enhanced EPR security, the digitised legal patient record which carries the sensitive health information of patient must be encrypted with a stringent procedure. Digital Imaging in Communication in Medicine (DICOM) is one of the predominantly used formats for representing the medical information all over the world [1]. The proposed system secures the acquired DICOM images of patients from MRI/CT scanner and embeds the patient details. Firstly, the medical image is divided into ROI and NROI based on the diagnosis. The NROI of the EPR will be watermarked with patient and hospital details (visible/non-visible) to yield a high level of authentication.

Method 1: LSIC – Rubik's – DNA Triple layered HASH based cryptographic technique

In this regard, the provision of security elements such as CIA to EPR storage will be carried out.

A simple but efficient encryption algorithm integrating Latin Square Image Cipher (LSIC) and Rubik's algorithm to achieve high throughput considering the massive arrival of medical images.

MD5 Hash is a favorite Hash function used to generate Hash values to verify the integrity of a data unit. In the proposed scheme, hash value will be generated using the following equations.

$$F\ (B, C, D) = [B\ \&\ C(|\ (\sim B\ \&\ \sim D))] \tag{1}$$

$$G\ (B, C, D) = [B\ \&\ D\ (|\ (C\ \&\ \sim D))] \tag{2}$$

$$H\ (B,C,D) = B^{\wedge}C^{\wedge}D \tag{3}$$

$$I\ (B,C,D) = C^{\wedge}(B\ |\!\!\sim D) \tag{4}$$

where &, ~, ^ and | represents the AND, NOT, XOR and NOT operations respectively.

Further, ROI will be divided into bit blocks, and bit XOR operation will be performed between the ROI and the hash value.

Concatenate ROI and NROI to form the final encrypted image as in Figure 11.7.

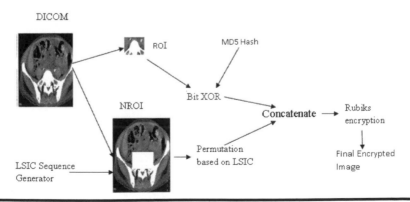

Figure 11.7   Triple layered HASH based cryptographic technique.

Method 2: DNA and Chaos-based encryption in DICOM
- Read the DICOM image from the storage unit.
- Divide the image into two blocks of equal size and perform DNA addition and subtractions using Tables 11.5 and 11.6.
- Compute the discrete logistic sequence by the following equation $Xn + 1 = rXn \, 1 - Xn$
- Select the DNA rules using the chaotic sequence to perform DNA encoding and decoding

Perform Discrete Gould Transform (DGT) using the matrix given below

$$g_r, mo = (-1)^{m+o} \left(\frac{r!}{(m-o)!(r-m+o)!} \right)$$

where $m, o = 0, 1 \dots K{-}1$ and r is a positive Integer. Compute DGT matrix for the required order and Perform XOR operation between the DGT output and encoded result to produce the final encrypted image as in Figure 11.8.

Table 11.5 DNA Operations

+	T	C	G	A	–	T	C	G	A
T	T	C	G	A	T	G	C	T	A
C	A	T	C	G	C	C	T	A	G
G	G	A	T	C	G	T	A	G	C
A	C	G	A	T	A	A	G	C	T

Source: Rehman, A.U. et al., *Multimed. Tools Appl.*, 74, 4655–4677, 2015.

Table 11.6 DNA Encoding and Decoding Using Chaotic Sequences Derived from Rehman et al.

S. No	Interval of Chaotic sequence	Encoding	Decoding
1	0.10–0.15, 0.20–0.25, 0.35–0.40, 0.80–0.85, 0.55–0.60	GATC	CTAG
2	0.01–0.05, 0.50–0.55, 0.60–0.65, 0.85–0.90, 0.95–0.99	AGCT	GTAC
3	0.15–0.20, 0.25–0.30, 0.40–0.45, 0.65–0.70, 0.75–0.80	CATG	TCGA
4	0.051–0.10, 0.30–0.35, 0.45–0.50, 0.70–0.75, 0.90–0.95	ACGT	TGCA

Source: Rehman, A.U. et al., *Multimed. Tools Appl.*, 74, 4655–4677, 2015.

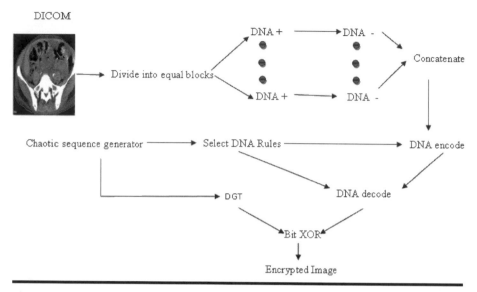

Figure 11.8   DNA and Chaos-based image encryption.

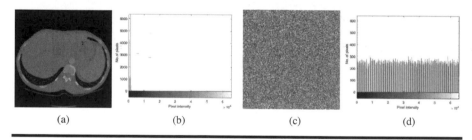

<table>
<tr><td>(a)</td><td>(b)</td><td>(c)</td><td>(d)</td></tr>
</table>

Figure 11.9   (a) Original DICOM, (b) histogram of (a), (c) DNA-Chaos-DGT encrypted output of (a) and (d) histogram of (c).

The sample result outputs are shown in Figure 11.9a–d.

The proposed algorithm can be implemented on a medical image of any arbitrary size. Metrics like UACI, NPCR, correlation coefficients, global, local entropies and chi-square tests can be estimated as in Table 11.7 to validate the quality of image encryption algorithms.

Table 11.7 Metrics Computation Considering Five Test Images

Test Images	Chi Squared Γ^2	Vertical Correlation	Diagonal Correlation	Horizontal Correlation	Global Shanon Entropy	Local Shanon Entropy	NPCR	UACI
MR-1	264.9297	−0.0226	0.0017	0.0312	7.9970	7.6438	99.61	33.46
MR-2	265.4531	0.0458	0.0098	0.0487	7.9961	7.7213	99.621	33.45
MR-3	265.6548	−0.0045	0.8451	0.0354	7.9812	7.7921	98.456	33.56
CT-1	266.9345	0.0548	0.5668	0.0435	7.9932	7.7891	99.456	33.67
CT-2	267.5865	0.05656	0.9921	0.0936	7.9917	7.7126	99.532	32.58

11.7 Summary

■ Allows secure transmission and sharing of EPR to provide security, confidentiality and patient's privacy across the globe
■ To integrate the peers involved in telemedicine in an authenticated network.
■ To provide cryptic solutions for EPR transceiving through wireless channels
■ To develop encryption schemes for the authenticated access by all the stakeholders like doctors, hospitals, patients, scan centres and insurance agencies

References

1. http://www.ihe.net
2. http://medical.nema.org
3. http://www. OTechimg.com/
4. http://www.ringholm.com/docs/02030_en.htm
5. Heywood J. How developments in technology and data in the NHS are improving outcomes for patients. *Blog Civil Service*. Gov.uk. December 14, 2014.
6. DesRoches CM, Campbell EG, Rao SR, Donelan K, Ferris TG, Jha A, Kaushal R et al., Electronic health records in ambulatory care—A National Survey of Physicians. *New England Journal of Medicine* 2008; 359: 50–60.
7. HIPAA basics: Medical privacy in the electronic age from the privacy rights clearinghouse. www.privacyrights.org
8. Ozair FF, Jamshed N, Sharma A, Aggarwal P. Ethical issues in electronic health records: A general overview. *Perspectives in Clinical Research* 2015; 6: 73–76.
9. Bhattacharya M, Pal K, Ghosh G, Mandal SS. Generation of novel encrypted code using cryptography for multiple level data security for Electronic Patient Record. *Bioinformatics and Biomedicine (BIBM), IEEE International Conference on,* Washington, DC, 2015; pp. 916–921.
10. http://www.iamwire.com/2013/10/startup-promote-electronic-health-records-india
11. Lavanya NV. Watermarking patient data in encrypted medical images. *Sadhana* 2012; 37: 723.
12. Pradeepkumar G, Usha S. Effective watermarking algorithm to protect Electronic Patient Record using image transform. *International Conference on Information Communication and Embedded Systems (ICICES)* 2013; 1030–1034.
13. Mishra SK, Kapoor L, Singh IP. Telemedicine in India: Current scenario and the future. *Telemedicine and e-Health.* 2009; 15: 568–575.
14. Chandwani RK, Dwivedi YK. Telemedicine in India: Current state, challenges and opportunities. *Transforming Government: People, Process and Policy* 2015; 9: 393–400.
15. Sangeetha D, Vaidehi V. A secure cloud based Personal Health Record framework for a multi owner environment. *Annales des Telecommunications/Annals of Telecommunications* 2016; 1–10 (Article in Press).

16. Sangeetha D, Vaidehi V. An improved cloud-based privacy preserving approach for secure PHR access. *Network Security and Communication Engineering: Proceedings of the 2014 International Conference on Network Security and Communication Engineering (NSCE 2014)* 2015; 25–26.
17. Sheetal K, Sood SK. Secure authentication scheme for IoT and cloud servers. *Pervasive and Mobile Computing* 2015; 24: 210–223.
18. Mashal I, Alsaryrah O, Chung T-Y, Yang C-Z, Kuo W-H, Agrawal DP. Choices for interaction with things on Internet and underlying issues. *Ad Hoc Networks* 2015; 28: 68–90.
19. Bandyopadhyay D, Sen J. Internet of things: Applications and challenges in technology and standardization. *Wireless Personal Communications* 2011; 58: 49–69.
20. Sharma A, Singh AK. Ghrera SP. Robust and secure multiple watermarking for medical images. *Wireless Personal Communications* 2017; 92: 1611–1624.
21. Söderström E, Eriksson N, Åhlfeldt RM. Managing healthcare information: Analyzing trust. *International Journal of Health Care Quality Assurance* 2016; 29: 786–800.
22. Liu Z, Weng J, Li J, Yang J, Fu C, Jia C. Cloud-based electronic health record system supporting fuzzy keyword search. *Soft Computing* 2016; 20: 3243–3255.
23. Liu Y, Qu X, Xin G. A ROI-based reversible data hiding scheme in encrypted medical images. *Journal of Visual Communication and Image Representation* 2016; 39: 51–57.
24. Cyganek B, Graña M, Krawczyk B, Kasprzak A, Porwik P, Walkowiak K, Woźniak M. A survey of big data issues in electronic health record analysis. *Applied Artificial Intelligence* 2016; 30: 497–520.
25. Rehman AU, Liao XF, Kulsoom A, Abbas SA. Selective encryption for gray images based on chaos and DNA complementary rules. *Multimedia Tools and Applications* 2015; 74: 4655–4677.
26. http://www.mnhs.org/preserve/records/docs_pdfs/Instrumental_MHSReport Final_Public_v2.pdf
27. Norcen R, Podesser M, Pommer A, Schmidt HP, Uhl A. Confidential storage and transmission of medical image data. *Computers in Biology and Medicine* 2003; 33: 277–292.
28. Zaz Y, El Fadil L, El Kayyali M. Securing EPR data using cryptography and image watermarking. *International Journal of Mobile Computing and Multimedia Communications* 2014; 4: 76–87.
29. Coatrieux G, Maitre H, Sankur B, Rolland Y, Collorec R. Relevance of watermarking in medical imaging. *International Conference on Information Technology Applications in Biomedicine* 2000; 9–10.
30. Kanso A, Ghebleh M. An efficient and robust image encryption scheme for medical applications. *Communications in Nonlinear Science and Numerical Simulation* 2015; 24: 98–116.
31. Söderström L, Hagborg A, von Konrat M, et al. World checklist of hornworts and liverworts. *PhytoKeys*. 2016; 59: 1–828. doi:10.3897/phytokeys.59.6261.
32. Chen TL, Liao YT, Chang YF, Hwang JH. Security approach to controlling access to personal health records in healthcare service. *Security and Communication Networks* 2016; 9: 652–666.

33. Hazzaa HM, Ahmed SK. Watermarking algorithm for medical images authentication. *4th International Conference on Advanced Computer Science Applications and Technologies* 2015; 7478751: 239–244.

34. Tieu L, Sarkar U, Schillinger D, Ralston JD, Ratanawongsa N, Pasick R, Lyles CR. Barriers and facilitators to online portal use among patients and caregivers in a safety net health care system: A qualitative study. *Journal of Medical Internet Research* 2015; 17: 4847.

35. Mancy L, Maria Celestin Vigila S. A survey on protection of medical images. *International Conference on Control Instrumentation Communication and Computational Technologies* 2015; 7475331: 503–506.

WATERMARKING

Chapter 12

Watermarking Techniques for Copyright Protection of Texts in Document Files

Surekha Borra, Rohit Thanki and Nilanjan Dey

Contents

DOI: 10.1201/9780429435461-14

12.1 Introduction

With the rapid use of the internet and other social media, exchange of document is common between any two persons or between two organizations. The document file is usually generated using different software such as Latex, Microsoft Word, and many others available on the computer. Some of the document generation software provide additional features such as watermark insertion on generation of secure document file. The process of watermark insertion into a document file is called document watermarking process [1–14].

The watermarking is defined as the "process of insertion of secure information into host data". The secure information often called a watermark can be any logo, text information or any other identity of the owner. Since the watermarking is generally designed for digital content, it is referred to as digital watermarking [1–14]. The host data can be different as per the requirement of the owner. The host data may be a text, image, audio, or video.

Figure 12.1 shows the generalized steps in the watermarking system. It contains mainly three modules: watermark embedder, transmission medium and watermark detector. The embedder module inserts the watermark into the host data. The inputs of this module are: host data, private key and watermark. The watermarked data is the output of the module. The detector module detects the watermark from the watermarked data. While the general inputs to this module are watermarked data and secret key, the output of the module is an extracted watermark.

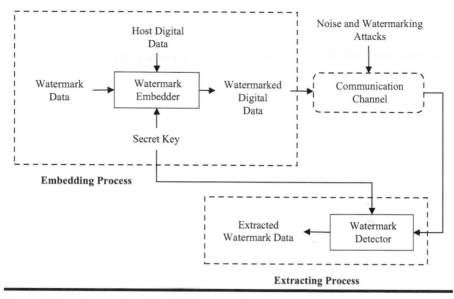

Figure 12.1 Generalized block diagram of watermarking.

The watermarking techniques are divided with respect to host data, robustness, perceptual quality and watermark extraction [5,14,15–17]. According to host data, watermarking is divided into four types: text watermarking, video watermarking, image watermarking and audio watermarking. According to robustness, watermarking is divided into three types: robust watermarking, fragile watermarking and semi-fragile watermarking. The robust watermarking can extract a watermark even if the watermarked data is corrupted or modified by any attacks. The fragile watermarking cannot extract the watermark if watermarked data is corrupted or modified. The semi fragile watermarking can extract some, but not all, the watermarks. Based on the perceptual quality of the Human Visual System (HVS), watermarking can be divided up as visible and invisible watermarking. With invisible watermarking, the watermark is seen visibly by naked human eye in contrast to invisible watermarking. The watermark extraction can be achieved in two ways: blind watermarking and non-blind watermarking. In blind watermarking, extraction of watermark data is performed without the knowledge of the host data. In non-blind watermarking, extraction of watermark data is performed with the help of host data.

Any requirements of watermarking [5,14,15–17] depend on several factors such as application and type of host data to be watermarked. The general requirements of any watermarking scheme are given below:

■ *Imperceptibility*: The watermark embedded in the host must be imperceptible both statistically and perceptually from the host data.

- *Robustness*: The watermarking scheme must provide various levels of robustness against any manipulations or attacks that change the characteristics of the watermarked data.
- *Security*: The watermarking scheme must provide security against unauthorized or imposters from detecting and modifying the embedded watermark in the host data. The secret keys are to be used for security and must ensure that only authorized owners are able to extract or modify the watermark.
- *Capacity*: It is the number of watermark bits a watermarking scheme can insert into a host data. The capacity ratio in watermarking is calculated [18] as:

$$\text{Capacity}(\%) = (\text{Size of Watermark Data}/\text{Size of Host Data}) \times 100 \quad (12.1)$$

The various applications of watermarking [3] are given below:

- *Copyright Protection*: For copyright protection, the watermark is embedded into owner data to generate copyrighted owner data. This watermark is extracted whenever required and is used for proving his/her ownership when an imposter has modified the copyrighted data.
- *Fingerprinting*: For identification of illegal copies, the user can use a fingerprinting technique. In this application, the owner can use multiple watermarks for multiple customers.
- *Copy Protection*: The watermark information can directly control illegal copies of data [19]. In this application, the watermark has copy-prohibit bits which provides protection against illegal copies.
- *Broadcast Monitoring*: The watermark can be used in commercial advertisements and in TV broadcast monitoring [20].
- *Data Authentication*: Fragile watermarks [21] can be used to check the authenticity of the data and is used to indicate where the host data is modified or corrupted.
- *Medical Safety*: The watermark data such as patient's information can be embedded into a medical image for the protection of medical image.
- *Data Hiding*: The watermarking scheme can be used for transmission of secret information.

Document watermarking is an important type of text watermarking. Any document watermarking scheme should be easy to implement, imperceptible, robust and applicable for various types of text formats. The document watermarking scheme should have high information capacity [22] and it is dependent on the text size, language, the grammar used in the text, rules and its features [23].

Nowadays, many companies and agencies are transferring their important documents over the open access network. During transmission, the files may be modified, corrupted and/or stolen by an impostor or attacker. This is a threat to the copyright protection of Intellectual Property (IP). The document watermarking scheme is one proved solution for this problem.

This chapter is an overview of document watermarking techniques. Further, applications of some document watermarking schemes for Indian language text is provided. The chapter is organized such that Section 12.2 gives basic document watermarking process along with the classification. Section 12.3 presents the state-of-the-art document watermarking techniques. Section 12.4 gives various tools for document watermarking. The challenges and future direction for document watermarking are given in Section 12.5.

12.2 Document Watermarking

The document watermarking is an important area of research. A variety of related watermarking schemes have been proposed in the past two decades. These schemes are based on the text images, synonyms, pre-supposition, syntactic tree, noun-verbs, words, sentences, acronyms, typo errors etc. [23,24]. The basic document watermarking is generally achieved in two stages: watermark embedding and watermark extraction as shown in Figure 12.2.

For a digital document D, a watermark w, and modification function σ, secret key K, a watermark embedding scheme X embeds a watermark w to the digital document D using below equation:

$$D' = X(D,w,K,\sigma) \tag{12.2}$$

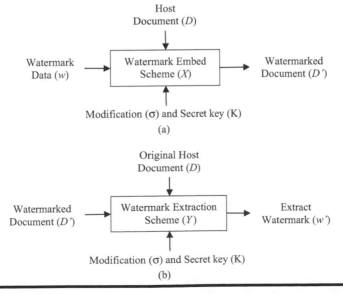

Figure 12.2 **(a) Embedding process (b) Extraction process for document data.**

The basic watermarking scheme for document watermarking is explained by Cox [4]; it is a spread-spectrum scheme in which host document size is greater than the watermark size. In this scheme the watermark data is spread all over the host data. The watermark data is inserted into every important text of host document data using a modification function. This scheme is known as additive watermarking where a pseudo-random noise sequence is inserted as a watermark pattern, and watermark data is extracted by correlation of this noise sequence.

The text line in the document is considered as a text character $D = \{D_1, D_2 \ldots D_M\}$ and watermark is considered as a watermark bit $w = \{w_1, w_2 \ldots w_N\}$, where $N \geq M$. The modification function modifies or shuffles watermark bits before inserting them into the text of host document. This function also provides security to watermark bits before they are embedded into the host document D. The modified watermark bits are inserted into the text of the host document using linear embedding operations such as XOR, as given in Equations 12.3 and 12.4. The other linear embedding operations may be additive operation and multiplicative operation. In additive operation, the watermark data is added to the host data in order to generate watermarked data. In multiplication operation, the watermark data is multiplied with host data to generate watermarked data.

$$\sigma(w) = \{w_1', w_2', \ldots, w_N'\} \tag{12.3}$$

$$D' = D \oplus K \times \sigma(w) = \{D_1 \oplus Kw_1', D_2 \oplus Kw_2', \ldots, D_N \oplus Kw_N'\} \tag{12.4}$$

The watermark extraction extracts a watermark w from the piece of the watermarked documents D' in two ways: non-blind scheme and blind scheme. In the non-blind scheme, extraction requires knowledge of the text of the original document D. In the blind scheme, extraction do not required knowledge of the text of the original document D.

$$Y(D, D', w, K, \sigma) = \textit{Authenticated if } w \textit{ is extracted from } D' \tag{12.5}$$

$$Y(D, D', w, K, \sigma) \neq \textit{Unauthenticated if } w \textit{ is extracted from } D' \tag{12.6}$$

In any document watermarking scheme, the secret key plays an important role in providing the security. As per Kerckhoffs' principle [25,26], a programmer assumes that the impostor knows every information except secret key. All document watermarking techniques create its own secret key from random number generator. This secret key is needed at the embedding side as well as at the extraction side. The secret key is a discrete random number and is uniformly distributed. The secret key can be public or private. The public key is transmitted over open network for extraction of watermark data from the watermarked document file. The private key is only transmitted to authorized user who has rights to access watermark information from the watermarked document file. The basic methods use symmetric key algorithms (i.e., DES, AES) and public key algorithms (i.e., RSA) for generation of a secret key. In the image based approach, secret keys are randomly generated using a random noise generator or pseudorandom number generator.

The existing document watermarking schemes are designed based on: images, contents, structures, and zero-watermarking [27–29]. The description of each such approach is given in the following:

12.2.1 Image Based Approach

In this approach, the document file is taken as host data and watermark is embedded into it. The document watermarking is a difficult task as it is very sensitive and has less watermark capacity. The document file is treated as an image in this approach. Various schemes proposed by researchers under this category are dependent on imperceptible modification of text spacing, letter spacing, baselines shifting, modification of serifs, Kerns etc. [27,28]. Image based document watermarking approaches are classified per its embedding characteristics such as line, word or character shifting, fixed partitioning of the image into blocks, boundary modifications, modification of character features, run-length patterns and halftone images. These schemes are discussed in the next section.

12.2.1.1 Line, Word or Character Shifting

The line-shifting scheme changes the text information in the document image by exchanging text sentences upward or downward according to the watermark bits. This scheme is a non-blind approach because original text information is required for extraction of the watermark. The word or character shifting scheme changes the text information in the document image by moving word or character horizontally based on the binary watermark bit. This scheme is performed in both blind and non-blind modes. Figure 12.3 shows an example of line shifting technique.

12.2.1.2 Fixed Partitioning of the Image into Blocks

This approach embeds text information of the document into fixed portions of the images. In this approach, the document image is partitioned into blocks, and then some of the features such as statistics or invariants of the pixel are extracted for embedding text information. In this approach, document file is treated as an image. Then find region of interest (ROI) in the document image where less important information lies. This ROI is divided into fixed size blocks and watermark data is inserted into these blocks. If a document file image is divided into blocks of size 8 × 8, then the watermark logo is inserted into 8 × 8 blocks of document file image using additive watermarking approach in order to generate watermarked document. This approach is widely used in watermarking of document files which are in terms of images.

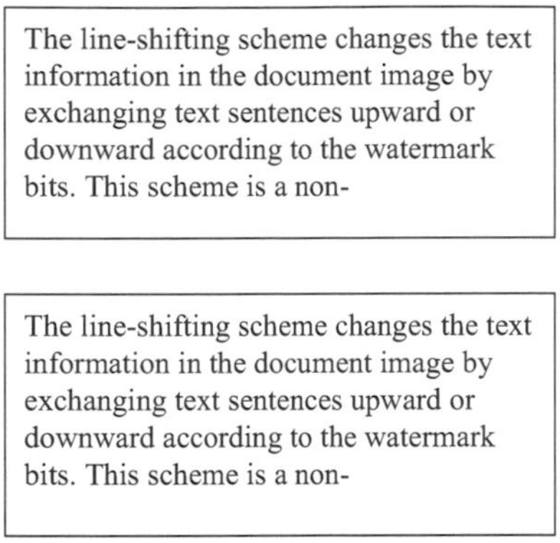

> The line-shifting scheme changes the text
> information in the document image by
> exchanging text sentences upward or
> downward according to the watermark
> bits. This scheme is a non-

> The line-shifting scheme changes the text
> information in the document image by
> exchanging text sentences upward or
> downward according to the watermark
> bits. This scheme is a non-

Figure 12.3   Example of line shifting technique.

12.2.1.3 Boundary Modifications

This approach embeds the watermark into the connected boundary of the character. A fixed set of five-pixel patterns pair's, which are dual to each other, are used for
embedding of watermark bits. In this approach, first pair pattern is found from the
centre foreground pixel, and other patterns are required as additional information
for detection of the watermark. It means that pixels in one pattern affect the pixel
positions in the second pattern. This property eases the extraction of watermark
data without the knowledge of original host document. This approach is non-blind
and is used for document images which have connected components.

12.2.1.4 Modification of Character Features

This approach extracts local features from document images for watermark data
embedding. These features are modified according to the watermark bits to generate a watermarked document file. This approach first finds neighborhood blocks of
the text in the portion of the image using connected component analysis and makes
different blocks based on its spatial closeness. Then each bonding blocks of each
block are partitioned into two sets [30]. The average horizontal width of a character
is taken as a feature which is calculated by vertical run lengths and is less than a
predefined threshold and average value. Then two operations that involve making
fat and thin characters are performed by changing the lengths of the character. For
watermark bit 1 embedding, the operation like "make a fat character" is applied to
character of set 2 partition blocks. For watermark bit 0 embedding, the operation
like "make a thin character" is applied to character of set 1 partition blocks. For
extraction of the watermarking extraction of line bounding of text block, partitioning process of text block, and grouping process of text block are required. The
character width is detected from the partitions block and added with each set. If
the difference of the character width is greater than the predefined threshold value

then the watermark bit 1 is detected, otherwise watermark bit 0 is detected. This scheme is used for embedding the watermark into a grayscale scanned document image. The approach provides security against distortions occurring due to point and scan process in the document. The robustness test of a scheme which is based on this approach needs to be further investigated.

12.2.1.5 Modification of Run-Length Patterns

This approach inserts a watermark into facsimile document image run-lengths, which has 1728 pixels in each horizontal line. According to bits in watermark sequences, each run length of text character pixels is encoded using the Huffman coding approach and is increased or decreased in one pixel. Based on predefined rules, the bits of watermark are embedded in the boundaries of the run lengths of text characters [31].

12.2.1.6 Modification of Halftone Images

This approach is used for watermarking halftone images which are found on printed material such as books, newspapers and printed documents and is not suitable for any other types of documents. The approach embeds watermark data during the half-toning process. For generation of a half-tone image, two different dither matrices are used in the halftoning process to encrypt the watermark data. These two matrices are applied in accordance to watermark bit values [32].

12.2.2 Content Based Approach

In this approach, a text character in the document file is used to embed watermark bits into it. This approach can be classified based on syntactic, semantic and structure. The various sentence characteristics such as structure of sentences, grammar rules, synonyms, various types of text structure, text position changes and important text content objects are used in embedding bits of watermark. This approach is used for natural language watermarking where it includes changes in the syntax or the semantics of text, structure of the text, grammar, text position exchanging and so on. There are many schemes using this approach and a few are discussed in the next section.

12.2.3 Syntactic Based Approach

The text information contains various sentences, words, and characters. The sentences in document files have different grammar and syntactic structures. In this approach, syntactic transformations are applied on structure of text to embed watermark data. Here, first a syntactic tree is constructed and transformation is then applied on text to embed the watermark without changing properties of the

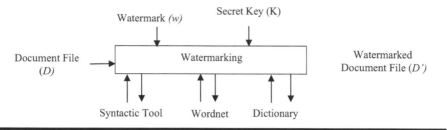

Figure 12.4 Syntactic sentence based document watermarking approach.

sentences in the document. The language processing algorithms are used to find syntax structures of the text while changing the watermark bits [23]. Figure 12.4 shows the syntactic based document watermarking approach. The syntactic tree can be constructed using various tools such as syntactic tool, wordnet, and dictionary.

12.2.4 Semantic Based Approach

The semantic structures of text in the document are used for embedding watermarks in this approach. The text information contents have various characteristics (e.g., verbs, spelling, different grammar rules and structure of sentences, etc.), which are used for embedding the watermark data in the text of the document. This approach depends on the language and has limited applicability for document watermarking. The scheme based on this approach uses natural language processing schemes to analyze text formation and to perform a transformation on it.

12.2.5 Structure Based Approach

This approach is recently used for document watermarking. In this approach, the text structure is used to embed the watermark data. A document watermarking scheme, which is based on double letter occurrences in text information, is chosen for watermark data embedding [33]. The algorithm in [33] uses a combination of encryption, steganography and watermarking for the protection of text in the document file.

12.2.6 Zero Watermarking Based Approach

The original text in documents can be modified by advanced techniques on the computer so that researchers can develop new watermarking approaches with higher imperceptibility capacity. This watermarking approach is known as a Zero Watermarking approach where no watermark bit is embedded into the text of the document. The approach is to find bit stream from the text's features to generate watermark information. This approach does not modify the text in the document but generates watermark information from the document texts which is to be registered by a Certifying Authority (CA). This approach is mainly used for tamper

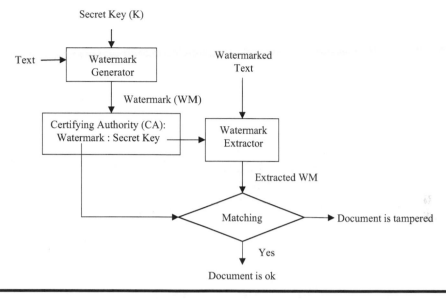

Figure 12.5   Zero watermarking based document watermarking approach.

identification of the document. Figure 12.5 shows the basic flow of the zero water-marking based document watermarking approach.

In a figure, first, the watermark is generated using text information and a secret key. This generated watermark and secret key can be certified by CA. The watermark extractor extracts watermark information from the watermarked text using the blind-extraction approach. Finally, a comparison of the extracted water-mark with the original watermark is made for the decision about tampering of the document.

12.3 Attacks on Document Watermarking

The watermarking attacks play an important role in checking performance and comparison of different watermarking techniques. The standard watermarking attacks used for any watermarking scheme are given by Voloshynovskiy [34]. These attacks are divided into various types: removal attacks, geometric attacks, crypto-graphic attacks and protocol attacks. The watermarking attacks such as noise addi-tion, filtering, compression, and geometric attacks can be applied on watermarked text image. The attacks modeled [35] for document watermarking is given below:

12.3.1 Collusion Attacks

If an impostor has obtained multiple watermarked documents copies, the impostor tries to extract watermark data, even if impostor knows nothing about the algorithm.

Usually, these attacks that rely on possession of many watermarked documents are known as collusion attacks.

12.3.2 Removal Attacks

There are two scenarios in dealing with these attacks. In the first scenario, an impostor who has knowledge about watermark inserting steps and private key explores the weakness of the inserting algorithm without the knowledge of watermark extraction. An imposter identifies the distortions occurring in the text of documents which the extractor cannot compensate and then applies a masking attack to remove the watermark data from the watermarked content. In the second scenario, an imposter has no knowledge of watermark embedding but tries to get watermark by exploring the knowledge of watermark extraction. An imposter may apply iterative modifications on a watermarked document in the attempt to gain the watermark data.

12.3.3 Syn Attack and Birthday Attack

These attacks depend on the structure of the sentence and are a synonym substitution for destroying text watermark information in watermarked content.

12.3.4 Holliman-Memon and Parity Attack

Holliman and Memon [30] defined counterfeiting attacks for watermark techniques that operates block independently. One can transfer a watermark from one watermark image to another image irrespective of the knowledge of detection algorithms and secret keys.

12.4 Document Watermarking Schemes

The document watermarking started around 1993. After that, many watermarking schemes are designed and proposed for text protection in documents. The description of various watermarking schemes is given below.

12.4.1 Image Based Document Watermarking Schemes

The algorithms are designed for hiding the watermarks in scanned documents. The text which is in the form of an image is used as watermark, and hence is called "image based" document watermarking. Often, the spatial properties of text image are modified by watermark data. Alternately, transform domains, additive noise, and other techniques can be used to the text image modification.

The scheme based on text document images is proposed by Kim et al. [36]. They used space statistics of interword to insert watermark information based on the preprocessing system which relies on white spaces between cover document texts. The shifting of the text character was conducted to insert a watermark bit (0 or 1) in this scheme. Wan et al. [37] proposed a document watermarking scheme with high payload capacity. The interword spaces are used in this scheme to embed watermark data. This approach maximized embedding payload capacity. Huang and Yan [38] implemented a different scheme for text as a binary image. The sine wave characteristics of spaces of interword in the line texts are used to insert the watermark bit. The sampling points of interword spaces are used in construction of sine watermark, and this watermark data is inserted in terms of sine wave with in-phase sampled sine wave of the line text. Puhan et al. [39] have proposed text authentication scheme using binary document images. In this scheme, the document image is divided into nonoverlapping blocks and then is inserted with the hash value of watermark in each block of image. The watermark bits which are extracted pixel-wise provide robustness against various text attacks such as Holliman-Memon parity.

In Afrakhteh et al. [40] scheme, the watermark data is inserted into partitions of the host image. The embedding of a watermark image is performed by multiplying with a gain factor which ranges from 0 to 1. The watermark extraction is performed using normalization for achieving better accuracy. In this scheme, watermark data could be extracted by an impostor. This scheme is not applicable for text image which is prone to attacks such as Rotation, Scaling and Cropping (RSC). Du and Zhao [41] developed a scheme using Human Visual System (HVS) for color text documents. In this scheme, the lower four bits of each character of RGB components are used for inserting watermark bits. The watermark data is converted into an encrypted vector by using Huffman encoding and is then is segmented into 12 bits for embedding 4 bits. The watermark insertion process is performed in a repetition manner for the whole text in the document. The average capacity of this scheme is around 8.6 bit rate.

Xia et al. [42] proposed two Chinese documents watermarking schemes. In the first scheme, spacing of the text character is used to insert bit 1 or 0. The spacing of text characters is calculated using pixel numbers between the characters and is grouped into two groups. If the length of group space is greater than average space of character bit 1 is embedded; otherwise, bit 0 is embedded. In the second scheme, boundary of each character is used for calculation of character height with respect to horizontal reference line. Watermark bits are inserted by shifting position of characters upper or lower the reference line. This scheme provides more payload capacity but less robust against copy attacks. Yazdani et al. [43] designed a scheme for watermarking Persian text documents. In this scheme, the Persian letters like 'ح، چ، ج' which have curved characteristics is taken from the document file. The watermark bits are embedding by shifting specific pixels in the selected text for embedding watermark bit 1 while shifting of text is not performed for

Table 12.1 Comparison of Image Based Document Watermarking Schemes

Schemes	Payload Capacity	Processing Time	Text Modification Rate
Kim et al. [36]	Intermediate	Higher	Higher
Huang and Yan [37]	Intermediate	Higher	Higher
Wan et al. [38]	Intermediate	Higher	Higher
Puhan et al. [39]	Higher	Lower	Higher
Afrakhteh et al. [40]	Higher	Lower	Intermediate
Du and Zhao [41]	Higher	Lower	Lower
Xia et al. [42]	Higher	Higher	Intermediate
Yazdani et al. [43]	Intermediate	Intermediate	Lower

watermark bit 0. This scheme is also applicable for Arabic text. This scheme provides more capacity and robustness compared to other existing schemes.

All the above schemes for document watermarking used text document as a binary image. The major limitations being: high false detection and poor quality of original text. Table 12.1 shows the comparison of image-based document watermarking schemes based on payload capacity, processing time and text modification rate.

12.4.2 Content Based Document Watermarking Schemes

The characteristics of the text in the document are used by the watermarking scheme to embed the watermark data in content-based schemes. Few schemes in the literature use natural language processing for document watermark. These schemes are based on analysis of text's syntactic/semantic/structure such as structure of sentence, synonyms, grammar rules punctuation, etc. In a natural language processing-based scheme, algorithms modify the semantics/syntax/ordering preserving the meaning of the sentence.

Atallah et al. [44] designed syntactic structure-based scheme for embedding watermark bits. In this scheme, a key is used for security of watermark bits before embedding. The syntax tree is generated by analysis of the sentence. Then the watermark bit is embedded into text using predefined assigned criterion and by modification of syntax tree transformation. Chiang et al. [45] focused on a Chinese language document and presented a semantic approach in which the character of text is divided into segments and then using a secret key, user texts are selected. Finally, the replacement of semantics is performed.

Liu et al. [46] used the same approach for a Chinese language document. The neural network with syntactic structure is used for generation of a syntax tree. The texts in the sentence are segmented using the Chinese language tool AutoTag.

Another semantic-based approach is proposed by Topkara et al. [47] by enhancements of synonym replacements. This algorithm improves payload capacity as well as reduces the modification rate in the watermarked document. Vybornova and Macq [48] proposed document watermarking using presuppositions to insert watermark data to secure the document. In this scheme, sentences are transformed using presupposition triggers after analysis of the text in a sentence. To insert the watermark bit, sequences are forced to have even presuppositions indicating '1' and odd presuppositions indicating '0'.

Kim [49] used a syntax tree-based scheme for Korean language documents. In this scheme, the first syntactic tree is generated by analysis of the text. By using this tree, the embedded locations are selected using target constituents and movement of targets. This scheme is only applicable for Korean and Turkish language text. Meral et al. [50] proposed a scheme for watermark data embedding using binary changes on Wordnet and syntax tree dictionary. This algorithm is implemented using morpho-syntactic tools. The watermark bits are embedded by changing adverbs, conjuncts, and by replacement of verbs. Further, the sentences are modified in forward or backward direction according to embedded bit 1 or 0. This scheme has the low capacity: embed half to one bit per one sentence.

Mail et al. [51] implemented and proposed another scheme that generates watermark data from the text content. This scheme is used for web page security. In this scheme, grammatical rules are used to get the watermark data. A user ID combination, conjunctions count, verbs modal and pronouns obtained from the sentence are used in the formation of a secret key, which is to be registered at Certifying Authority (CA) securely after applying AES encryption algorithm on it. This scheme has more imperceptibility, but is less robust compared to other natural language watermarking schemes.

Another content-based document watermarking research work is proposed by Halvani et al. [52]. Four approaches are designed using lexical or syntactic transformation for watermark data embedding process. These schemes are specifically designed for documents with German language text. In the first approach, watermarks are inserted based on enumeration modulation and syntactic transform. The second approach is based on conjunction modulation of constituent movement. The third approach used prefix expansion based on negation modifications of the text. The fourth scheme used lexical transform which embeds watermark bits by modification of words or repeated characters. A document watermarking scheme combining watermarking with RSA encryption is presented by Lew and Woo [53]. This scheme uses semantic technique to implement embedding process and includes Pseudo-Random Number Generators (PRNG) to generate secret key to achieve better results [24].

An advanced reversible document watermarking scheme using prediction error techniques and context collation is described by Fei and Tang [54], for Chinese text to resolve the semantics ambiguity during synonyms replacement. The novelty of scheme is that original text can be obtained after extraction of watermark data from the watermarked text.

Table 12.2 Comparison of Content Based Document Watermarking Schemes

Schemes	Payload Capacity	Processing Time	Text Modification Rate
Atallah et al. [44]	Lower	Intermediate	Higher
Chiang et al. [45]	Lower	Intermediate	Higher
Liu et al. [46]	Lower	Intermediate	Higher
Topkara et al. [47]	Lower	Intermediate	Higher
Vybornova and Macq [48]	Lower	Intermediate	Higher
Kim [50]	Lower	Intermediate	Higher
Meral et al. [50]	Lower	Intermediate	Higher
Mali et al. [51]	Lower	Intermediate	Lower
Halvani et al. [52]	Lower	Intermediate	Higher
Lew and Woo [53]	Lower	Intermediate	Higher
Fei and Tang [54]	Lower	Intermediate	Higher

The content-based document watermarking schemes are based on natural language processing, which is a complex task because all languages have different characteristics and it does not have enough support for semantic or syntactic manipulation. Table 12.2 shows the comparison of content-based document watermarking schemes based on payload capacity, processing time and text modification rate.

12.4.3 Structure Based Document Watermarking Schemes

In these schemes, text properties or text formatting is modified by watermark bits. There are many schemes based on this approach. The watermark data is embedded into the layout of the text by making use of some properties of text such as extensions of the letter, line and word spaces, shape of characters, curvelet letters, diacritics of letters etc.

Jalil and Mrirza [24,55] have proposed two schemes for embedding watermark data in terms of image in a document by preserving the content of sentence. In the first scheme, the algorithm converts text into an image before integrating the alphabet of original text features to get a secret key, which is further used for extraction of watermark information from the document text to ownership authentication of document. The second scheme uses image-plus-text based watermark data for improvement of robustness of scheme.

A watermarking scheme based on structure and format of the Arabic language text is proposed by Gutub et al. [56]. The Arabic text characters' extension is used to insert watermark bits based on 'Kashiba' extension approach so that it does not affect text property. In this scheme, the length of Kashiba letters are increased according to the watermark bits inserted into it. Here, a key is used during watermark insertion to make the original watermark secure. This scheme is used for e-text authentication. Jaseena and John [57] improved the Jalil scheme by introducing the encryption method for security of watermark data. In this scheme, watermark data is encrypted before inserting into the text.

Por et al. [58] proposed Unicode space characters-based text hiding scheme for protection of the document (Microsoft Word). It uses spaces between inter-word and between intersentence, line ending and ending spaces of paragraph to insert watermark bit. Normal space characters and Unicode characters are used to encrypt watermark data. The scheme increases the space between characters and paragraphs in the document and provides robustness against attacks due to statistical analysis on Unicode characters.

Ruia and Jinqiaob [59] proposed a scheme based on format and structure of the text, which uses mixed language text such as Chinese and English for multiple watermarking. This scheme utilizes Microsoft Word for implementation of the watermark embedding process. Jaiswal and Patil [60] have described a scheme using text document properties. This scheme is proposed for watermarking of web pages based on HyperText Markup Language (HTML). A HEX code watermark is constructed using Unicode and are used to get the HTML tag which is embedded into the source code of the HTML web page. This scheme provides good imperceptibility but is less robust.

Mir [61] developed a hybrid scheme that applies and analyses a hashing algorithm on both semantics and syntactics to obtain watermark data. The scheme is applied to the security of web pages. Table 12.3 shows the comparison of structure-based document watermarking schemes based on payload capacity, processing time and text modification rate.

12.4.4 Zero Watermarking Based Schemes

All the schemes discussed in the previous sections introduce distortions in the text; therefore, new research has taken place in document watermarking area that achieves high imperceptibility without affecting text property in the document. Zero watermarking is proposed for avoiding distortions in the text. In this scheme, watermarks are not physically embedded in the text. The scheme extracts the bit sequences from text's features to generate the watermark to construct watermark.

The zero watermarking scheme is proposed by Jalil et al. [62] where a keyword is used to determine the features of text. Based on the keyword and author texts, the number of letters after and before the keywords are stored as variables. The keyword is inserted as a prefix into the text watermark. This watermark is saved with

Table 12.3 Comparison of Structure Based Document Watermarking Schemes

Schemes	Payload Capacity	Processing Time	Text Modification Rate
Jalil and Mrirza [24,55]	Lower	Higher	Intermediate
Gutub et al. [56]	Lower	Higher	Higher
Jaseena and John [57]	Intermediate	Higher	No Distortion
Por et al. [58]	Intermediate	Medium	Higher
Ruia and Jinqiaob [59]	Lower	Higher	No Distortion
Mir [61]	Intermediate	Medium	Intermediate
Jaiswal and Patil [60]	Higher	Medium	No Distortion

CA for tamper identification. Another tamper detection scheme is also proposed by Jalil et al. [63] where word length is used in the generation of watermark data. In this scheme, a word with more than four letters is chosen for watermark embedding. The first character of each word is considered for generating the watermarked document file.

Yingjie et al. [64] proposed a watermarking scheme for a Chinese text document file. Kuang and Xu [65] proposed a word frequency based watermarking scheme, where the sentence of a document is divided into words and textural features of words are extracted. The watermark data is generated using a timestamp and extracted features. In this scheme, a hash value/SHA-1/MD5 value of watermark is registered instead of an actual watermark. Another watermarking scheme described by Kaur and Babbar [66] is based on multiple appearances of words in the watermark pattern. The pattern is generated by choosing the first letter from multiple appearances of words. The combination of these patterns is to get the watermark data which is registered with CA.

Qi and Liu [67] described entropy frequency-based techniques to watermark Chinese documents. In this scheme, the different portion of speech information and expected text value are used to generate watermark data which is registered with CA. This scheme claimed to achieve high robustness. Another zero watermarking scheme based on double letters technique is proposed by Prasannakumar and Balachandrudu [68]. In this scheme, an image is converted into text before constructing the watermark key. Then to generate the final watermark key, merging of host image and watermark is done. The chaotic based zero watermarking for protection against automated attack is proposed by He and Gui [69]. This scheme provides high imperceptibility and new research directions for design of automated attacks.

Table 12.4 Comparison of Zero Watermarking Schemes

Schemes	Payload Capacity	Processing Time	Text Modification Rate
Jalil et al. [62,63]	Intermediate	Higher	No Modification
Yingjie et al. [64]	Lower	Medium	No Modification
Kuang and Xu [65]	Lower	Medium	No Modification
Kaur and Babbar [66]	Lower	Higher	No Modification
Qi and Liu [67]	Lower	Higher	No Modification
Prasannakumar and Balachandrudu [68]	Lower	Higher	No Modification
Ba-Alwi et al. [70]	Lower	Higher	No Modification

Ba-Alwi et al. [70] presented a third-order Markov model based zero watermarking to create a watermark by analysing the document. The model has chosen three unique letters for generation of a pattern. These patterns are converted into the sequence at Markov model output. The secure watermark data is generated by applying MD5 hashing algorithm.

All the zero watermarking schemes provide high imperceptibility without affecting textual characteristics in the document. But these are limited to a few applications where fragility is required. Table 12.4 shows the comparison of zero watermarking schemes based on payload capacity, processing time and text modification rate.

12.4.5 Other Schemes

There are other schemes proposed by various researchers without using the above approaches. Cheng et al. [71] described polymorphism watermarking which combines multiple existing schemes in improving the robustness andto overcome each others weaknesses. Abdullah and Waheb [72] proposed a document watermarking scheme using the z-axis of text. This scheme mainly targets object based text environment. Qadir and Ahmad [73] gave a scheme for document watermarking for document transfer from sender to receiver. Alatter and Alatter [74] used a spread spectrum approach to get an encrypted sequence of watermark data using Bose–Chaudhuri–Hocquenghem (BCH) error codes. This scheme treated the text as an image. The watermarked text is generated using word-shift and line-shift operation. Table 12.5 shows the comparison of other watermarking schemes based on payload capacity, processing time and text modification rate.

Table 12.5 Comparison of Other Watermarking Schemes

Schemes	Payload Capacity	Processing Time	Text Modification Rate
Abdullah and Wahab [72]	Lower	Lower	Lower
Qadir and Ahmad [73]	Higher	Lower	Higher
Alattar and Alattar [74]	Lower	Intermediate	Higher

12.5 Tools for Document Watermarking

A variety of tools are available for watermarking of text documents on the internet and computer. These tools generate watermarked text documents using some predefined secret key and document watermarking algorithms. The image watermarking tools are described by Le et al. [75] and can be applicable when text is treated as an image. The summary of tools used for document watermarking is given in Table 12.6.

12.6 Performance Analysis for Document Watermarking Scheme

The performance of any document watermarking scheme can be analyzed using various parameters such as detection error, watermarking capacity and invisibility [35], watermark performance evaluation, robustness, and security. The description of these evaluation parameters is given below.

12.6.1 Detection Error Analysis

This analysis checks the performance of detection algorithm and can be calculated using two errors: false positives and false negatives for detection of watermark bit. The false positive error occurs when the detector detects incorrect watermark. The false negative error occurs when the does not detector the watermark.

12.6.2 Watermarking Capacity Analysis

This analysis estimates the size of watermark bits that can be embedded into the host text documents.

Table 12.6 Various Tools for Document Watermarking

Tool Name	Information about Tool	Characteristics of Tool
Syntactic [76]	This tool contains 21 different syntactic tools.	• This tool is used for Turkish document watermarking. • Out of 21 tools, 7 syntactic tools are effectively used for watermarking.
Siotra Watermark [77]	Available at: http://www.softsea.com/review/Siotra-Watermark.html, Published by http://www.softsea.com/review/Siotra-Watermark.html	• The size of the tool is 860.5 kB and used for watermarking of images • Applicable for image-based text watermarking.
Batch Watermark Creator [78]	Available at: www.easy-tools.net	• The size of the tool is 3.36 MB • User-defined parameters-based software • Applicable for image-based text watermarking.
Easy Watermark Creator [79]	Available at: http://www.easyimagetools.com/products/watermark/easy-watermark-creator.html Published by: Easy Image Tools Group.	• The size of the tool is 7.80 MB • Applicable for image-based text watermarking.
Watermarklt [80]	Available at: http://watermarkit.software.informer.com/ Published by: Salo Strom Software	• The size of the tool is 978 kB • Applicable for image-based text watermarking.
Winwatermark [81]	Available at: http://downloads.tomsguide.com/WinWatermark,0301-21094.html Published by: Kozasoft Design Studio	• The size of the tool is 4.84 MB • Applicable for image-based text watermarking.
Vidlogo [82]	Available at: http://download.cnet.com/VidLogo/3000-2170_4-10429620.html published by: GeoVid	• The size of the tool is 15.78 MB • Applicable for image-based text watermarking • Processing speed is higher compared to other tools.

12.6.3 Analysis of Invisibility

The watermark insertion decreases the quality of text information. Therefore, during implementation and analysis of any document watermarking scheme, invisible watermark must be considered for analysis of the scheme.

12.6.4 Watermark Performance Evaluation

Some charts, variables, and constants are used for evaluation of the performance of the document watermarking scheme. Table 12.7 lists different graphs and its corresponding variables and constants for the document watermarking scheme [35]. The ROC curve depends on two detection errors: false positive and false negative. It plots the relationship between False Positive Error (FPE) on the y-axis and False Negative Error (FNE) of the x-axis.

12.6.5 Watermark Robustness Evaluation

The robustness and invisibility are most important parameters used for evaluation of watermark embedding scheme. The watermark robustness is affected by two factors: structure of watermark data and the embedding approach. A document watermarking system should be a compromise between robustness and imperceptibility and must be evaluated and tested under benchmark conditions.

12.6.6 Watermark Security Evaluation

The security analysis of a document watermarking scheme is a very complicated task and can be performed based on various focal points described by Zhou in [35]. The evaluation can be done using quality measures such as Mean Squared Error (MSE), Peak Signal to Noise Ratio (PSNR), Structural Similarity Index Measure (SSIM) and

Table 12.7 Different Charts with Corresponding Variables and Constants [33]

Chart Type	Parameter Values			
	Visual Quality	Robustness	Watermarking Attacks	Watermark Bits
Robustness vs. Attack	Static	Dynamic	Dynamic	Static
Robustness vs. Visual Quality	Dynamic	Dynamic	Static	Static
Attack vs. Visual Quality	Dynamic	Static	Dynamic	Static

many others [83] by treating the text as an image. The Certimark, Optimark, and StirMark are some benchmark tools used to evaluate document watermarking schemes [33,35,75]. Nowadays, researchers are using detection error rate for evaluation of a document watermarking scheme and to find the accuracy of the watermarking scheme [84].

12.7 Application of Document Watermarking for Indian Language Text

In this section, application of document watermarking for Indian language text is demonstrated. Here, two standard image-based watermarking schemes namely Least Significant Bit (LSB) approach [85] and spread-spectrum approach [4] are used for watermarking of Indian language text. The Indian language text is first scanned and then converted into an image. The watermark data is also Indian language text and is also treated as an image. In LSB approach, the least significant bit is modified according to watermark text bits to generate watermarked text image. In spread spectrum approach, the bits of host text are modified by two Pseudo Random Noise (PN) sequences according to watermark text bits. Figures 12.6 and 12.7 shows

साहित्यनो संदर्भ योरस क्रीसमां अरबी संख्या द्वारा मुખ્ય ટેક્સ્टमां ઉલ્લેખ કરવો જોઈએ. પ્રશસ્તિ-સિક્વન્સ સિસ્ટમનો ઉપયોગ કરો અને દરેક પેપર અથવા પ્રકરણના અંતમાં ક્રમાંકિત સંદર્ભોની યાદીમાં, મથાળા સંદર્ભો હેઠળ. સામગ્રી, સ્વરૂપ અને વિરામચિહ્નની બાબતમાં, જો વોલ્યુમ એડિટરએ કોઈ એક વિશિષ્ટ શૈલીની પસંદગી ન વ્યક્ત કરી હોય, તો લેખકોએ સૌથી યોગ્ય શૈલી પસંદ કરવી જોઈએ અને તેનો ઉપયોગ સતત રીતે કરવો જોઈએ.	
(a) Host Text Document	(b) Watermark Text
साहित्यनो संदर्भ योरस क्रीसमां अरबी संख्या द्वारा मुખ્ય ટેક્સ્टमां ઉલ્લેખ કરવો જોઈએ. પ્રશસ્તિ-સિક્વન્સ સિસ્ટમનો ઉપયોગ કરો અને દરેક પેપર અથવા પ્રકરણના અંતમાં ક્રમાંકિત સંદર્ભોની યાદીમાં, મથાળા સંદર્ભો હેઠળ. સામગ્રી, સ્વરૂપ અને વિરામચિહ્નની બાબતમાં, જો વોલ્યુમ એડિટરએ કોઈ એક વિશિષ્ટ શૈલીની પસંદગી ન વ્યક્ત કરી હોય, તો લેખકોએ સૌથી યોગ્ય શૈલી પસંદ કરવી જોઈએ અને તેનો ઉપયોગ સતત રીતે કરવો જોઈએ.	
(c) Watermarked Text Document	(d) Extracted Watermark Text

Figure 12.6 **Results of document watermarking for Indian language text using LSB approach. (a) Host text document (b) Watermark text (c) Watermarked text document (d) Extracted watermark text.**

સાહિત્યનો સંદર્ભ ચોરસ ફ્રેંસમાં અરબી સંખ્યા દ્વારા મુખ્ય ટેક્સ્ટમાં ઉલ્લેખ કરવો જોઈએ. પ્રશસ્તિ- સિલ્વન્સ સિસ્ટમનો ઉપયોગ કરો અને દરેક પેપર અથવા પ્રકરણના અંતમાં ક્રમાંકિત સંદર્ભોની યાદીમાં, મશ્યાળા સંદર્ભો હેઠળ. સામગ્રી, સ્વરૂપ અને વિરામચિહ્નની બાબતમાં, જો વોલ્યુમ એડિટરએ કોઈ એક વિશિષ્ટ શૈલીની પસંદગી ન વ્યક્ત કરી હોય, તો લેખકોએ સૌથી યોગ્ય શૈલી પસંદ કરવી જોઈએ અને તેનો ઉપયોગ સતત રીતે કરવો જોઈએ.

(a) Host Text Document

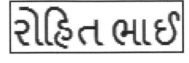

(b) Watermark Text

સાહિત્યનો સંદર્ભ ચોરસ ફ્રેંસમાં અરબી સંખ્યા દ્વારા મુખ્ય ટેક્સ્ટમાં ઉલ્લેખ કરવો જોઈએ. પ્રશસ્તિ- સિલ્વન્સ સિસ્ટમનો ઉપયોગ કરો અને દરેક પેપર અથવા પ્રકરણના અંતમાં ક્રમાંકિત સંદર્ભોની યાદીમાં, મશ્યાળા સંદર્ભો હેઠળ. સામગ્રી, સ્વરૂપ અને વિરામચિહ્નની બાબતમાં, જો વોલ્યુમ એડિટરએ કોઈ એક વિશિષ્ટ શૈલીની પસંદગી ન વ્યક્ત કરી હોય, તો લેખકોએ સૌથી યોગ્ય શૈલી પસંદ કરવી જોઈએ અને તેનો ઉપયોગ સતત રીતે કરવો જોઈએ.

(c) Watermarked Text Document

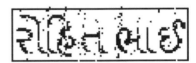

(d) Extracted Watermark Text

Figure 12.7 Results of document watermarking for Indian language text using spread-spectrum approach (a) Host text document (b) Watermark text (c) Watermarked text document (d) Extracted watermark text.

the application of document watermarking for Gujarati text which is an Indian language. In LSB approach, the size of the host text and watermark text are same, but the size of the watermark text is less in spread-spectrum approach.

12.8 Challenges in Document Watermarking

The document watermarking schemes uses watermark image or digital signature for the protection of text in the document and uses text documents interword spaces, text features and other parameters which are of normal usage. The watermark data is easily extracted by using reformatting, conversion, and copying from the watermarked text. The natural languages-based scheme changes the original content of the text. Therefore, it is not applicable for legal documents, official letters and other important documents of the owner. The zero watermarking-based schemes provides higher imperceptibility, but it is a complicated and difficult task to implement.

Most of the document watermarking in the literature is done considering text documents as binary images. These schemes add more distortions in original text documents. Also, the watermark data can be corrupted by various operations such as compression and other image processing operations. The lower robustness, less security, less imperceptibility and less applicability for text language are found as weaknesses in existing document watermarking schemes. Also it was found that there are very few schemes proposed for Indian text document protection. The image watermarking benchmarking tools are not applicable for text watermarking system when text is not treated as an image. There is no standard watermarking tool available for document watermarking. Future research can focus on these topics. This chapter also brushed upon some common watermarking attacks: retyping attacks, shots screen attacks, and printing attacks.

References

1. Hartung, F., Kutter, M. 1999. Multimedia watermarking techniques. *Proceedings of the IEEE* 87(7): 1085–1103.
2. Bender, W., Gruhl, D., Morimoto, N., Lu, A. 1996. Techniques for data hiding. *IBM Systems Journal* 35(3–4): 313–336.
3. Langelaar, G., Setyawan, I., Lagendijk, R. 2000. Watermarking of digital image and video data–A state of art review. *IEEE Signal Processing Magazine* 17: 20–46.
4. Cox, I., Kilian, J., Shamoon, T., Leighton, F. 1997. Secure spread spectrum watermarking for multimedia. *IEEE Transactions on Image Processing* 6(12): 1673–1687.
5. Borra, S., Lakshmi, H., Dey, N., Ashour, A., Shi, F. 2017. Digital image watermarking tools: State-of-the-art. *Frontiers in Artificial Intelligence and Applications* 296: 450–459.
6. Borra, S., Swamy, G., 2013. Sensitive digital image watermarking for copyright protection. *International Journal of Network Security* 15(2): 95–103.
7. Borra, S., Swamy, G., 2012. Visual secret sharing based digital image watermarking. *International Journal of Computer Science* 9(3): 312–317.
8. Borra, S., Swamy, G., 2011. A spatial domain public image watermarking. *International Journal of Security and Its Applications* 5(1): 1–11.
9. Ashour, A., Dey, N., 2017. Security of multimedia contents: A brief. *Intelligent Technique in Signal Processing for Multimedia Security* 3–14. Springer, Cham, Switzerland.
10. Parah, S., Sheikh, J., Dey, N., Bhat, G., 2017. Realization of a new robust and secure watermarking technique using DC coefficient modification in pixel domain and chaotic encryption. *Journal of Global Information Management* 25(4): 80–102.
11. Pal, A., Dey, N., Samanta, S., Das, A., Chaudhuri, S., 2013. A hybrid reversible watermarking technique for color biomedical images. *Computational Intelligence and Computing Research, 2013 IEEE International Conference on* 1–6. IEEE.
12. Chakraborty, S., Maji, P., Pal, A.K., Biswas, D., Dey, N., 2014. Reversible color image watermarking using trigonometric functions. *In Electronic Systems, Signal Processing and Computing Technologies (ICESC), 2014 International Conference on* 105–110. IEEE.
13. Banerjee, S., Chakraborty, S., Dey, N., Pal, A.K. and Ray, R., 2015. High payload watermarking using residue number system. *International Journal of Image, Graphics and Signal Processing*, 7(3): 1.
14. Thanki, R., Kothari, A., 2016. Digital watermarking: Technical art of hiding a message. *Intelligent Analysis of Multimedia Information* 431–466. IGI Global, Hershey, PA.

15. Wolfgang, R., Podilchuk, C. 1999. Perceptual watermarks for digital images and video. *Proceedings of the IEEE* 87(7): 1277–1281.
16. Katzenbeisser, S., Petitcolas, F. 2000. *Information Hiding Techniques for Steganography and Digital Watermarking.* Artech House, Norwood, MA.
17. Irena, O. 2012. *Multimedia Signals and Systems.* Springer Science & Business Media, Boston, MA.
18. Alotaibi, R., Elrefaei, L. 2015. Arabic text watermarking: A review. *International Journal of Artificial Intelligence and Applications* 6(4): 1–16.
19. Anderson, R., Petitcolas, F. 1998. On the limits of steganography. *IEEE Journal of Selected Areas of Communication* 16: 474–481.
20. Kalker, T., Depovere, G., Haitsma, J., Maes, M. 1999. A video watermarking system for broadcast monitoring. *Processing of SPIE Electronic Imaging'99, Security and Watermarking of Multimedia Contents,* San Jose, CA, 102–112.
21. Wolfgang, R., Delp, E. 1999. Fragile watermarking using the VW2D watermark. *Processing of SPIE Electronic Imaging'99, Security and Watermarking of Multimedia Contents,* San Jose, CA, 3657: 204–213.
22. Alginahi, M., Muhammad, K., Omar, T. 2014. An enhanced Kashida-based watermarking approach for increased protection in Arabic text-documents based on frequency recurrence of characters. *International Journal of Computer and Electrical Engineering* 6: 381–392.
23. Jalil, Z., Mirza, A. 2009. A review of digital watermarking techniques for text documents. *International Conference on Information and Multimedia Technology,* 230–234. IEEE.
24. Jalil, Z., Mirza, A. 2010. An invisible text watermarking algorithm using image watermark. *Innovations in Computing Sciences and Software Engineering,* T. Sobh, K. Elleithy (Eds.). Springer, New York, 147–152.
25. Kerckhoffs, A. 1883. La Cryptographie Militaire. *Journal Des Sciences Militaires,* IX: 5–83, 161–191.
26. Charles, C. 2002. Homeland Insecurity. *The Atlantic Monthly,* 290 (2).
27. Ranganathan, S., Ali, A., Kathirvel, K., Mohan, M. 2010. Combined text watermarking. *International Journal of Computer Science and Information Technologies* 1(5).
28. Kaur, M., Mahajan, K. 2015. An existential review on text watermarking techniques. *International Journal of Computer Applications* 120(18): 29–32.
29. Al-Maweri, N., Ali, R., Adnan, W., Ramli, A., Rahman, S. 2016. State-of-the-art in techniques of text digital watermarking: Challenges and limitations. *Journal of Computer Sciences* 12(2): 62–80.
30. Holliman, M., Memon, N. 2000. Counterfeiting attacks and block wise independent watermarking techniques. *IEEE Transactions on Image Processing* 9(3): 432–441.
31. Brassil, J., O'Gorman, L. 1996. Watermarking document images with bounding box expansion. *Proceedings of 1st International Workshop on Information Hiding,* Newton Institute, Cambridge, UK, 227–235.
32. Katsavounidis I., Jay Kuo, C. 1997. A Multiscale error diffusion technique for digital half-toning. *IEEE Transactions on Image Processing* 6(3): 483–490.
33. Jalil, Z., Jaffar, M., Mirza, A. 2011. A novel text watermarking algorithm using image watermark. *International Journal of Innovative Computing, Information and Control* 7(3).
34. Voloshynovskiy, S., Pereira, S., Thierry, P. 2001. Attacks on digital watermarks: Classification, estimation based attacks and benchmarks. *IEEE Communications Magazine* 118–126.

35. Zhou, X., Wang, S., Xiong, S., Yu, J. 2010. Attack model and performance evaluation of text digital watermarking. *Journal of Computers* 5(12): 1933–1941.
36. Kim, Y., Moon, K., Oh, I. 2003. A text watermarking algorithm based on word classification and interword space statistics. *Proceedings of the 7th International Conference on Document Analysis and Recognition* 775–779.
37. Wan, I., Gilani, S., Shah, S. 2006. Utilization of maximum data hiding capacity in object-based text document authentication. *Proceedings of the International Conference on Intelligent Information Hiding and Multimedia Signal Processing* 597–600.
38. Huang, D., Yan, H. 2001. Interword distance changes represented by sine waves for watermarking text images. *IEEE Transactions on Circuits and Systems for Video Technology* 11(12): 1237–1245.
39. Puhan, N., Ho, A., Sattar, F. 2007. Erasable authentication watermarking in binary document images. *Proceedings of the 2nd International Conference on Innovative Computing, Information and Control*, 288.
40. Afrakhteh, M., Ibrahim, S., Salleh, M. 2010. Printed document authentication using watermarking technique. *Proceedings of the 2nd International Conference on Computational Intelligence, Modelling and Simulation*, Bali, 367–370.
41. Du, M., Zhao, Q. 2011. Text watermarking algorithm based on human visual redundancy. *Advances in Information Sciences and Service Sciences* 3: 229–235.
42. Xia, Z., Wang, S., Sun, X., Wang, J. 2013. Print-scan resilient watermarking for the Chinese text image. *International Journal of Grid and Distributed Computing* 6: 51–62.
43. Yazdani, V., Doostari, M., Yazdani, H. 2013. A new method to Persian text watermarking using curvaceous letters. *Journal of Basic and Applied Scientific Research* 3: 125–131.
44. Atallah, M., Raskin, V., Crogan, M., Hempelmann, C., Kerschbaum, F. 2001. Natural language watermarking: Design, analysis and a proof-of concept implementation. *Proceedings of the 4th International Workshop on Information Hiding* 185–199.
45. Chiang, Y., Chang, L., Hsieh, W., Chen, W. 2004. Natural language watermarking using semantic substitution for Chinese text. *In: Digital Watermarking*, Kalker, T., I. Cox and Y. Ro (Eds.). Springer, Berlin, Germany, 129–140.
46. Liu, Y., Sun, X., Wu, Y. 2005. A natural language watermarking based on Chinese syntax. *Proceedings of the 2nd International Conference on Advances in Natural Computation*, 958–961.
47. Topkara, U., Topkara, M., Atallah, M., 2006. The hiding virtues of ambiguity: Quantifiably resilient watermarking of natural language text through synonym substitutions. *Proceedings of the 8th Workshop on Multimedia and Security*. Geneva, Switzerland, 164–174.
48. Vybornova, O., Macq, B. 2007. Natural language watermarking and robust hashing based on presuppositional analysis. *Proceedings of the IEEE International Conference on Information Reuse and Integration*, Las Vegas, NV, 177–182.
49. Kim, M. 2008. Text watermarking by syntactic analysis. *Proceedings of the 12th WSEASE International Conference on Computers*, Greece, 904–909.
50. Meral, H., Sankur, B., Zsoy, A., Günger, T., Sevinç, E. 2009. Natural language watermarking via morphosyntactic alterations. *Computer Speech and Language* 23: 107–125.
51. Mali, M., Patil, N., Patil, J. 2013. Implementation of text watermarking technique using natural language watermarks. *Proceedings of the International Conference on Communication Systems and Network Technologies*, Gwalior, India, 482–486.

52. Halvani, O., Steinebach, M., Wolf, P., Zimmermann, R. 2013. Natural language watermarking for German texts. *Proceedings of the 1st ACM Workshop on Information Hiding and Multimedia Security*, France, 193–202.

53. Lew, C., Woo, C. 2013. Design and implementation of text based watermarking combined with pseudo-random number generator (PRNG) for cryptography application. *Proceedings of the 12th International Conference on Applied Computer and Applied Computational Science*, Wseas LLC.

54. Fei, W., Tang, X. 2013. Reversible text watermarking algorithm using prediction-error expansion method. *Proceedings of the International Conference on Computer, Networks and Communication Engineering*, Atlantis Press, Amsterdam, the Netherlands.

55. Jalil, Z., Mirza, A. 2010. Text watermarking using combined image-plus-text watermark. *Proceedings of the 2nd International Workshop on Education Technology and Computer Science*. Wuhan, China, 11–14.

56. Gutub, A., Al-Haidari, F., Al-Kahsah, K., Hamodi, J. 2010. Utilizing 'Kashida' extensions in Arabic language electronic writing. *Journal of Emerging Technologies in Web Intelligence* 2: 48–55.

57. Jaseena, K., John, A. 2011. Text watermarking using combined image and text for authentication and protection. *International Journal of Computer Applications* 20: 8–13.

58. Por, L., Wong, K., Chee, K. 2012. Unispach: A text-based data hiding method using unicode space characters. *Journal of Systems and Software* 85: 1075–1082.

59. Ruia, X., Jinqiaob, C. 2013. A multiple watermarking algorithm for texts mixed Chinese and English. *Procedia Computer Science* 17: 844–851.

60. Jaiswal, R., Patil, N. 2013. Implementation of a new technique for web document protection using unicode. *Proceedings of the International Conference on Information Communication and Embedded Systems*, Chennai, India, 69–72.

61. Mir, N. 2014. Copyright for web content using invisible text watermarking. *Computers in Human Behavior* 30: 648–653.

62. Jalil, Z. Mrirza, A., M. Sabir 2010. Content based zero-watermarking algorithm for authentication of text documents. *International Journal of Computer Science and Information Security* 7: 212–217.

63. Jalil, Z. Mrirza, A., Jabeen, H. 2010. Word length based zero-watermarking algorithm for tamper detection in text documents. *Proceedings of the 2nd International Conference on Computer Engineering and Technology*, Chengdu, China, 378–382.

64. Yingjie, M. Tao, G., Zhihua, G., Liming, G. 2010. Chinese text zero-watermark based on sentence's entropy. *Proceedings of the International Conference on Multimedia Technology*, Ningbo, China, 1–4.

65. Kuang, Q., Xu, X. 2011. A new zero-watermarking scheme based on features extraction for authentication of text. *Journal of Convergence Information Technology* 6: 155–165.

66. Kaur, S., Babbar, G. 2013. A zero-watermarking algorithm on multiple occurrences of letters for text tampering detection. *International Journal of Computer Science & Engineering* 5: 294–301.

67. Qi, X., Liu, Y. 2013. Cloud model based zero-watermarking algorithm for authentication of text document. *Proceedings of the 9th International Conference on Computational Intelligence and Security*, Leshan, China, 712–715.

68. Prasannakumar, K., Balachandrudu, K. 2013. Text watermarking using combined image and text. *International Journal of Engineering Research and Technology* 2: 3812–3818.

69. He, L., Gui, X. 2013. An active attack on chaotic based text zero-watermarking. *Proceedings of the IEEE Conference Anthology*, China, 1–4.

70. Ba-Alwi, F, Ghilan, M., Al-Wesabi, F. 2014. Content authentication of English text via internet using zero watermarking technique and Markov model. *International Journal of Applied Information Systems* 7: 25–36.

71. Cheng, Y., Zhang, J., Liu, X., Li, Q., Chen, Z. 2013. Research on polymorphism in digital text watermarking. *Proceedings of 5th International Conference on Intelligent Networking and Collaborative Systems, Xi'an*, 166–172.

72. Abdullah, M., Wahab, F. 2008. Key based text watermarking of e-text documents in an object based environment using z-axis for watermark embedding. *World Academy of Science, Engineering and Technology* 46: 199–202.

73. Qadir, M., Ahmad, I. 2006. Digital text watermarking: Secure content delivery and data hiding in digital documents. *IEEE Aerospace and Electronic Systems Magazine* 21: 18–21.

74. Alattar, A., Alattar, O. 2004. Watermarking electronic text documents containing justified paragraphs and irregular line spacing. *Proceedings of the Security, Steganography and Watermarking of Multimedia Contents, SPIE*, 685–685.

75. Le, T., Nguyen, K., Le, H. 2010. Literature survey on image watermarking tools, watermark attacks and benchmarking tools. *2010 Second International Conferences on Advances in Multimedia*, 67–73.

76. Meral, H. M., Sevinc, E., Ünkar, E., Sankur, B., Özsoy, A. S., & Güngör, T. 2007. Syntactic tools for text watermarking. In *Electronic Imaging 2007, International Society for Optics and Photonics*, 6505.

77. http://www.softsea.com/review/Siotra-Watermark.html, 17/5/2017

78. www.easy-tools.net, 17/5/2017

79. http://www.easyimagetools.com/products/watermark/easy-watermark-creator.html, 17/5/2017

80. http://watermarkit.software.informer.com/, 17/5/2017

81. http://downloads.tomsguide.com/WinWatermark,0301-21094.html, 17/5/2017

82. http://download.cnet.com/VidLogo/3000-2170_4-10429620.html, 17/5/2017

83. Kutter, M., Petitcolas, F. 1999. A fair benchmark for image watermarking systems. *Electronic Imaging' 99, Security and Watermarking of Multimedia Contents*, 3657, 1–14.

84. Muharemagic, E., Furth, B. 2006. Survey of watermarking techniques and applications. *Multimedia Watermarking Techniques and Application*, Kirovski D. (Ed.). Auerbach Publications, CRC Press, Boca Raton, FL. 91–130.

85. Chan, C., Cheng, L. 2004. Hiding data in images by simple LSB substitution. *Pattern Recognition* 37: 469–474.

Chapter 13

VLSI Implementation of Video Watermarking for Secure HEVC Coding Standard

Amit M. Joshi

Contents

DOI: 10.1201/9780429435461-15

13.1 Introduction

The growth in technology has changed the scenario of data transmission of the multimedia communication. The transfer of data is now faster and requiring less effort to make duplication. The use of Internet has enabled a simple way of exchanging data in society, science, business and entertainment industry. The data (that is audio, speech, image or video etc.) can be transmitted very rapidly on WWW [1]. Video is the common multimedia object which is exchanged immensely over the networks. It has been shared through various devices as digital television, mobile phones and PDA.

The challenges in the field of data integrity and ownership have roused with great concern worldwide. This provides a real challenge for the originator to prevent any misuse or malpractice. The owner wants to ensure that there should not be any unauthorized access without any prior permission. One of the solutions would be to restrict the access of the content with help of encryption techniques. However, encryption methods are non reliable for overall protection. They are no longer secure after the decryption. There is a difficulty even to trace back illegal user. There will be a dilemma to resolve the problem where two users simultaneously claim for the same object as shown in Figure 13.1.

The following questions may require a justified answer.

1. Who is the originator of the content?
2. How can we prove the ownership?
3. Is there any tampering happen with original content?
4. Where was the content created?
5. Who has tampered the content?
6. Where shall the owners go to complain if he finds illegal copy of his/her content?

There should be some proof that can be generated as court evidence to resolve such kind of ownership problem. With access of various editing tools, the content

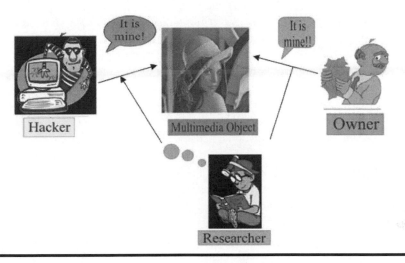

Figure 13.1 Problem of ownership. (From Mohanty, S.P., *Watermarking of Digital Images*, PhD thesis, Department of Electrical Engineering, Indian Institute of Science, Bangalore, India, 1999.)

of video is able to be copied and disseminated in large amount. The traditional protection schemes are not well suited longer for video security. The field of digital watermarking is used to address the authentication issues of any multimedia object. We have discussed video watermarking in this chapter.

13.1.1 Motivation

The idea of watermarking is quite ancient, almost 700 years ago. It was used to authorize the product by their paper manufacturers.

In software watermarking, the algorithm runs on a PC which helps for watermarking in video and afterwards it would be distributed. However, the main drawback of such delay when the video is captured and the watermark gets inserted is, if any attacker could attack the video before the embedding of the watermark, then it can create an issue of ownership for originator.

The development of the watermarking system is in demand mainly due to concerns over Intellectual Property Right (IPR). HEVC (high efficienty video coding) based real-time watermarking could mitigate such issues if the watermark is inserted at the time of capturing the video.

For uncompressed watermarking, the bit stream is decoded in partial way in order to insert the watermark and then once again encoded for a secure bit-stream generation. The watermark is embedded with compression standard in compressed domain watermarking. The chapter focuses on hardware implementation of video watermarking based on HEVC standard. Thus, the delay is getting reduced between capturing and embedding the watermark which is the shortcoming of software watermarking. The hardware module of our scheme supports integer arithmetic, so it can be adapted to HEVC encoder to produce a real-time secure bit stream. The parallel data path architecture of the watermark embedding unit is designed to reside as a crucial part of the forward encoder path.

The tentative flow of the sections are as follows: Section 13.2 contains the basic background theory of video watermarking. The desired features which are required for real time video watermarking are discussed. Related works for hardware implementation of video watermarking are elucidated. Section 13.3 emphasizes the fundamental concept of HEVC video coding. Section 13.4 describes the proposed video watermarking algorithm. The steps involved during watermark embedding process and watermark extraction process will be explained. Section 13.5 highlights the implementation of our secure watermarking system. The architectures of Integer DCT (discrete cosine transform) are also explained. Section 13.6 analyzes the proposed video watermarking with results on MATLAB® and a hardware platform. The hardware results of proposed schemes are covered with field programmable gate array (FPGA) and application specific integrated circuit (ASIC) implementation. Finally, the conclusion is derived in Section 13.7 along with the scope of further work.

13.2 Background and Related Work

The video is used to exchange frequently in today's multimedia world. Therefore maximum chances of copyright infringement can occur for video media content [3]. Video is considered as a collection of frames where individual frame is considered as a one still image [4]. Earlier, watermarking algorithms were targeted for software platforms [5]. The design of any watermarking schemes require several features such as invisibility, blind detection and robustness. The computational complexity is crucial factor for VLSI implementation [6]. There has been a shortage of real-time watermarking scheme which are targeted for hardware platform. Shoshan et al. [7] and Li et al. [8] mentioned various challenges along with their applications for hardware implementation.

Petitjean et al. [9] described new video watermarking schemes for DSP and VLIW processor that was extended later to hardware implementation. However, the algorithm on MPEG standard required some fractal coding method with floating point arithmetic. This method cannot be applied directly to real-time application because of computationally intensive process.

Brunton and Zhao [10] designed spatial domain video watermarking for real-time application. The algorithm used the concept of pixel change detection in incoming video frame and further targeted it to programmable hardware. The algorithm was demonstrated for spatial domain, thus provided less robustness and was not suited to filtering and compression attacks.

Jeong et al. [11] proposed a robust watermarking scheme to insert an invisible watermark with Haar wavelet. The algorithm was having some issues regarding the artifacts that affects perceptual property of watermarked video.

ElAraby et al. [12] demonstrated a video watermarking with FPGA implementation where pseudo random sequence (as a watermark) is embedded at low value to DCT. The method was used to add an invisible watermark in each frame of a video. The method was not suitable for any compression standard and was based on uncompressed video.

De Strycker et al. [13] illustrated real-time watermarking for the broadcast monitoring. The algorithm was implemented on Trimedia processor at 4 BOPS. A pseudo random value is embedded to input stream while watermarking. The watermark embedding process uses the uncompressed video and the correlation is applied during extraction process. The algorithm has large computational complexity which avoids the real time implementation.

Maes et al. [14] implemented the Millennium watermarking scheme for DVD copyright protection. The algorithm uses an additional security level with encryption along with watermark embedding. The system was memory hungry, this avoids the integration with custom hardware of consumer devices.

Mathai et al. [15] presented video watermarking using JAWS (just another watermarking system) method for VLSI (very large scale integrated circuit) implementation. The concept uses FFT, filtering process and floating data path to have transformation at the receiver end. The algorithm again was based on uncompressed video and not suited for compression standard.

Tsai and Wu [3] designed the spatial and transform domain-based spread spectrum-based watermarking. A VLSI architecture is designed to be integrated in the MPEG encoder. However, the floating point data path design limits its scope in real time applications.

Vural et al. [16] designed a traceable watermarking scheme using wavelet where the watermark is embedded at lower frequency components of every frame of a video. The pseudo random generator was used for a frame selection for watermark embedding. A watermark helps to have a secure transmission at the encoder end. The retrieval of the watermark follows the blind process. The algorithm was based on wavelet transformation whereas the most standards have DCT. Therefore, an integration of a watermark embedding module is not compatible with video standard.

Mohanty and Kougianos [17] suggested a real-time visible watermarking scheme for video broadcasting. VLSI architecture was proposed and FPGA prototyping was done to suite the MPEG-4 standard. However, the algorithm uses the perceptual watermark concept which has limited practical applications.

Roy et al. [18] developed a semi fragile as well as invisible watermark embedding process for video authentication purpose. The scheme was designed for MJPEG compression. The algorithm has floating point arithmetic for DCT computation. Floating point DCT was used which makes it is not suited for HEVC standard.

Joshi et al. [19] has developed an efficient watermark embedding process. The algorithm was tragated H.264 standard which covers invisible and blind video watermarking. It was noted that all schemes were developed for MPEG or H.264 video compression standard. Few of them are not at all used for video compression standard. The proposed HEVC based algorithm uses an AC prediction concept during watermarking process. It has following features such as (1) integer arithmetic involvement which reduces the computational complexity, and (2) the detection of a scene change concept is used, where bit planes of the same watermark are embedded at different frames of a scene to have greater robustness.

13.3 HEVC Video Coding Standard

The coding method and bit-stream structure for compression of video are described in a document called video coding standards. A set of tools are defined by video coding standards for doing the compression. All the design techniques of decoding are not included in the standards. The consumers have very much flexibility in selecting among various manufacturers. A working group, Motion Pictures Experts Group (MPEG), with the International Organization for Standardization (ISO), and Video Coding Experts Group (VCEG) with Telecommunication Sector of the International Telecommunications Union (ITU-T), have developed a series of video standards either independently or jointly. The common standard developed by ISO are MPEG-4, MPEG-2 and MPEG-1. ITU-T develops H.263, H.262, H.261. H.264/AVC (advanced video coding) or MPEG-4 Part-10 video coding was developed by VCEG and Joint Video Team (JVT). High Efficiency Video Coding (HEVC) is designed by the Joint Collaborative Team on Video Coding (JCT-VC).

The H.265/MPEG or HEVC includes almost all the features of previous standard H.264/MPEGAVC while putting emphasis on HD video coding ad parallel processing. HEVC attains very high bit-rate for the same visual quality. HEVC has following important features: (1) It achieves very high compression, (2) high throughput for HD video, (3) low power consumption, (4) highly parallel architecture, and (5) easier streaming of HD video to mobile devices.

Most popular formats for video compression are MPEG-X (ISO standard) and H.264-x formats (ITU-T standard), which are based on DCT [20].

13.4 Blind and Robust Video Watermarking Algorithm

Proposed algorithm uses Integer DCT and can be easily integrated with HEVC. It involves the integer arithmetic which results in the improvement of real time performance. It uses the prediction concept for estimation of the AC coefficients of the middle block using nearby blocks DC co-efficient values.

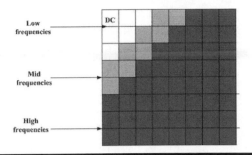

Figure 13.2 **Frequency distribution of 8 × 8 sub block. (From Lam, E.Y. and Goodman, J.W., *IEEE Trans. Image Process.*, 9, 1661–1666, 2000.)**

In the case of a frame of the video (or still image), there exists an intra correlation between the neighboring values of the pixel. Each frame is divided into chunka of block with size 3 × 3 where every block contains 8 × 8 sub block (total 64 pixels). This process generates total of nine blocks as shown in Figure 13.2. The value of AC coefficient of the central block (5th block) is predicted using the value of adjacent block DC co-efficient. The watermark is embedded in low frequency values to have greater robustness. The common signal processing attacks and low pass filter tend to change the low frequency components much lesser than middle or high frequency components. In a sub block of 8 × 8 DCT, the left most corner coefficients are the low frequency values that carry a DC component and 5 AC components as shown in Figure 13.2.

The DC component is not used while applying a watermark because it would introduce visual distortion. Five top most AC values $AC_{(0,1)}$, $AC_{(0,2)}$, $AC_{(1,1)}$, $AC_{(2,0)}$, and $AC_{(1,0)}$ of low frequencies are considered for watermarking.

13.4.1 Steps for Embedding of the Watermark

The input is uncompressed video and original watermark is an image. After completion of process, the watermarked video is generated. The watermark unit is part of the HEVC encoder.

Step 1: The detection of scene change from video is determined using histogram difference as follows in Equation 13.1:

$$H = \sum_{k=1}^{N} \sum_{i=0, j=0}^{N} (P_1(i,j,k) - P_2(i,j,k+1))^2 \qquad (13.1)$$

P_1 and P_2 are consecutive frames of a particular video. N total pixels of a frame.
Step 2: An 8 bit original watermark is divided various planes which are LSB to MSB (least significant to most significant bit) (total 8 planes) using bit plane slice method. Each plane is considered as an watermark.

Step 3: These bit planes (which are known as watermark) are inserted in various frames for a particular scene. It has an edge that if any distortion happens then it would not hamper whole watermark, but the other parts of the watermark still is able to be extracted from remaining frames.

Step 4: Every frame from a scene is again further divided into 8×8 size of blocks. For every block, Integer 2D DCT is computed which resulted in one DC and other 63 AC values.

Step 5: The prediction of AC values for a middle block (5th block) is performed with surrounding blocks DC value as shown in Figure 13.3. The prediction process uses Equations 13.2 through 13.6 as follows:

$$AC_{(0,1)} = p1 * (DC_4 - DC_6) \tag{13.2}$$

$$AC_{(1,0)} = p1 * (DC_2 - DC_8) \tag{13.3}$$

$$AC_{(0,2)} = p2 * (DC_4 - DC_6 - 2 * DC_5) \tag{13.4}$$

$$AC_{(2,0)} = p2 * (DC_2 + DC_8 - 2 * DC_5) \tag{13.5}$$

$$AC_{(1,1)} = p3 * (DC_1 + DC_9 - DC_3 - DC_7) \tag{13.6}$$

where, $p_1 = 9/64$, $p_2 = 1/32$, $p_3 = 3/128$.

The prediction process involves constants k_1, k_2, and k_3 which carries the denominator value in terms of 2^N here N is a natural number. This has an advantage as it requires only shift operation, thereby avoiding the division requirement. The hardware implementation of shifter is simpler in comparison to divisor. The developed watermarking is based on integer arithmetic that is adapted to integer DCT. The algorithm outperforms the others in terms of

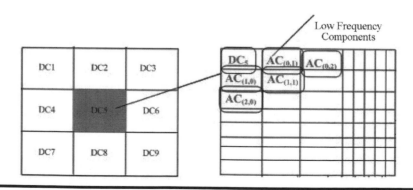

Figure 13.3   Prediction of central block with adjacent blocks. (From Küçüktunç, O. et al., *Comput. Vis. Image Underst.*, 114, 125–134, 2010.)

computational complexity. Existing algorithms have floating point structure, which degrades the performance in real-time system.

Step 6: The watermark in terms of Δ value is inserted in predicted AC values to generate new AC values as in Equation (13.7). The value of Δ ranges from 1 to 5. The particular value of Δ has to be chosen as per requirement of robustness against the quality of the frame.

If watermark bit $= 1$ then, set

$$AC_i \geq AC_i + \Delta$$

else

$$AC_i < AC_i' - \Delta \tag{13.7}$$

Step 7: Once the watermark is embedded, then Int IDCT (Integer Inverse DCT) of each block is executed to have watermark. Again all frames are accumulated to have secure embedded video.

13.4.2 Watermark Extraction Process

The retrieval of the algorithm is blind. The generated secure watermarked video is used while extraction process. The output of retrieving process is an extracted watermark.

Step 1: Secure watermarked video uses scene change detection method again, The various frames are gathered of a particular scene.

Step 2: Every frame which is extracted from a scene is separated into 8×8 blocks to calculate the Integer DCT for a block.

Step 3: AC value of 5th block is predicted once again with DC values of the adjacent blocks as per Equations (13.2) through (13.6) which were used earlier in the embedding process.

Step 4: The watermark bit is found by comparing the original AC value and estimated AC value as shown in (13.8).

If

$$AC_i \geq AC_i'$$

Watermark bit $= 1$

Else

$$\text{Watermark bit} = 0; \tag{13.8}$$

Step 5: Each watermark bit helps to have the bit planes.

Step 6: The bit planes are combined to have extracted watermark image.

13.5 Implementation of Proposed Secure HEVC

Our secure system uses Integer DCT based watermarking to be used in HEVC. Therefore, the hardware implementation of Integer DCT and watermarking process are discussed in this section.

13.5.1 Implementation of Integer DCT Algorithm

In HEVC standard, 2-D integer transform is computed with the help of separable property where a 1-D horizontal transform (row wise) is calculated first, followed by a 1-D vertical (column wise) transform calculation. The process flow is shown in Figure 13.4.

1-D 8×8 Integer DCT matrix is defined as C_f in Equation (13.9).

$$
C_f = \frac{1}{8}
\begin{bmatrix}
8 & 8 & 8 & 8 & 8 & 8 & 8 & 8 \\
12 & 10 & 6 & 3 & -3 & -6 & -10 & -12 \\
8 & 4 & -4 & -8 & -8 & -4 & 4 & 8 \\
10 & -3 & -12 & -6 & 6 & 12 & 3 & -10 \\
8 & -8 & -8 & 8 & 8 & -8 & -8 & 8 \\
6 & -12 & 3 & 10 & -10 & -3 & 12 & -6 \\
4 & -8 & 8 & -4 & -4 & 8 & -8 & 4 \\
3 & -6 & 10 & -12 & 12 & -10 & 6 & -3
\end{bmatrix}
\tag{13.9}
$$

The above matrix is used for integer DCT calculation in our proposed system.

13.5.2 Butterfly Structure of 8 Point 1-D Forward DCT

1-D transform is evaluated via fast butterfly structure and is implemented with three different stages. Three stages data flow diagram of 1-D DCT algorithm is shown in Figure 13.5 (where X is input vector and Y denotes the output vector

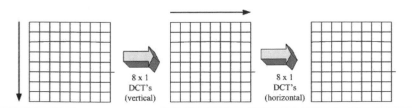

Figure 13.4 Implementation of 2-D DCT with separable property. (From Chen, Z. et al., *J. Vis. Commun. Image Represent.*, 17, 264–290, 2006.)

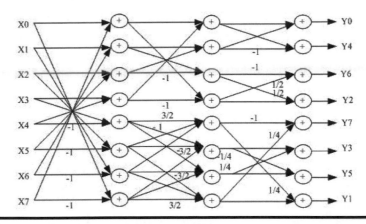

Figure 13.5 1-D Integer DCT module using butterfly diagram. (From Krishnan, T. and Oraintara, S., Fast and lossless implementation of the forward and inverse mdct computation in mpeg audio coding. In *Circuits and Systems, IEEE International Symposium on* (*ISCAS 2002*), Vol. 2, 2002.)

with transformed values). The butterfly method is multiplier-less and can be implemented with integer arithmetic only. The different stages of structure are shown in Table 13.1. With help of this stage-wise process, 8×8 block transform is implemented with simple operation as additions/subtractions and shifts only. Here $\gg 1$ stands for right operation by shift one bit and $\gg 2$ stands for similarly right shift by 2 bits.

Table 13.1 Butterfly Structure of Forward DCT

Stage 1	Stage 2	Stage 3
a0 = X0 + X7	b0 = a0 + a3	Y0 = b0 + b1
a1 = X1 + X6	b1 = a1 + a2	Y2 = b2 + (b3 ≫ 1)
a2 = X2 + X5	b2 = a0 − a3	Y4 = b0 − b1
a3 = X3 + X4	b3 = a1 − a2	Y6 = (b2 ≫ 1) − b3
a4 = X0 − X7	b4 = a5 + a6 + ((a4 ≫ 1) + a4)	Y1 = b4 + (b7 ≫ 2)
a5 = X1 − X6	b5 = a4 − a7 − ((a6 ≫ 1) + a6)	Y3 = b5 + (b6 ≫ 2)
a6 = X2 − X5	b6 = a4 + a7 − ((a5 ≫ 1) + a5)	Y5 = b6 − (b5 ≫ 2)
a7 = X3 − X4	b7 = a5 − a6 + ((a7 ≫ 1) + a7)	Y7 = −b7 + (b4 ≫ 2)

Source: Liang, J. and Tran, T.D., *Signal Processing, IEEE Transactions on*, 49, 3032–3044, 2001.

Here, the input of first stage carries 8-bit integer value. The output of first stage adders consist of 9-bit in which one bit carry is generated after addition block. The output of second stage adders consist of 11 bits. The final transformed outputs are 12-bit integer values. Here, carry-look ahead adder or subtracter is used for addition or subtraction respectively.

13.5.3 8 Point 1-D Inverse Integer DCT Algorithm

With the help of C_f^T matrix, 1-D IDCT algorithm is applied to compute the values. 1-D Inverse Integer transforms is also calculated using fast butterfly operations as denoted in Table 13.2. (where Y is input vector and X is transformed output vector). The hardware implementation for 8 point 1-D Integer Inverse DCT module is similar as 1-D Integer forward DCT algorithm as shown in Figure 13.6. It follows similar kind of butterfly diagram of stage-wise. Proposed architecture of 1-D IDCT algorithm also includes three stages same as DCT. The proposed 8 point 1-D IDCT transform can also be implemented with help of addition/subtraction and shifting operations only. The inclusion of addition/subtraction operation generates one bit carry at every instance. The carry-look ahead adder or subtracter is used to perform addition or subtraction operation respectively.

Table 13.2 Butterfly Structure of Inverse DCT

Stage 1	Stage 2	Stage 3
a0 = Y0 + Y4	b0 = a0 + a6	X0 = b0 + b7
a4 = Y0 − Y4	b2 = a4 + a2	X1 = b2 + b5
a2 = (Y2 >> 1) − Y6	b4 = a4 − a2	X2 = b4 + b3
a6 = (Y6 >> 1) + Y2	b6 = a0 − a6	X3 = b6 + b1
a1 = −Y3 + Y5 − Y7 + (Y7 >> 1)	b1 = a1 + (a7 >> 2)	X4 = b6 − b1
a3 = Y1 + Y7 − Y3 + (Y3 >> 1)	b7 = −(a1 >> 2) + a7	X5 = b4 − b3
a5 = −Y1 + Y7 + Y5 + (Y5 >> 1)	b3 = a3 + (a5 >> 2)	X6 = b2 − b5
a7 = Y3 + Y5 + Y1 + (Y1 >> 1)	b5 = (a3 >> 2) − a5	X7 = b0 − b7

Source: Liang, J. and Tran, T.D., *Signal Processing, IEEE Transactions on,* 49, 3032–3044, 2001.

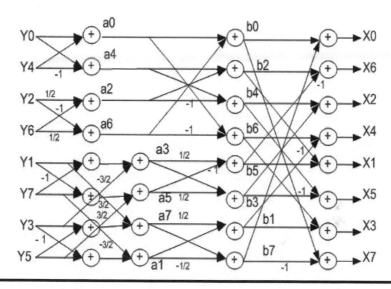

Figure 13.6 **1-D Inverse Integer DCT module using butterfly diagram. (From Krishnan, T. and Oraintara, S., Fast and lossless implementation of the forward and inverse mdct computation in mpeg audio coding. In *Circuits and Systems, IEEE International Symposium on (ISCAS 2002)*, Vol. 2, 2002.)**

13.6 Proposed 2-D Integer DCT Architecture

Incoming frames are extracted from input video and are stored subsequently in memory. Every frame is further separated in 8 × 8 non overlapping blocks. 2-D Integer DCT has been applied on these 8 × 8 image blocks using the separable property. All these 8 × 8 blocks are stored in ROM, so that each column can be accessed from a block at every positive edge of the clock cycle. The proposed VLSI architecture for 2-D Integer DCT module is defined in Figure 13.7.

Both (Horizontal and Vertical) process of 1-D DCT calculation are similar. The bit width for data path of each pipeline stage of these architectures is different and also the number of bits to represent each sample. Each addition would generate a carry bit which increases the data representation width. Both 1-D DCT modules are designed with similar approach.

The parallel architecture of 2D DCT is developed to remove the possibility of any stall states. 1-D transform is calculated with fast butterfly structure which has three different stages. A single 8 × 8 block produces total 64 pixels of 8-bit data width and are stored in SRAM (static RAM). Each column is operated with DCT calculation

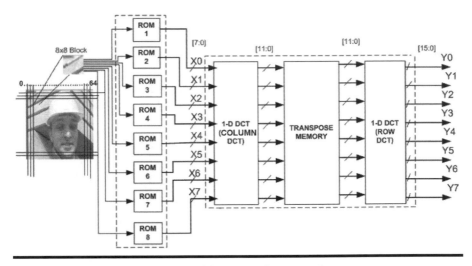

Figure 13.7   2-D integer DCT architecture of proposed system.

on each positive edge of the clock from SRAM. Thus, around 9 clocks are desired to process every 8 × 8 block with initial latency of one clock for column processing. Eight elements are provided to the transpose memory as shown in Figure 13.8.

The values of column processing from 1-D DCT are stored in transpose memory horizontally and read through row processing vertically. Then 2-D DCT values are generated and stored in internal block RAM for further watermark embedding process.

In our algorithm, we have implemented 8 × 8 DCT block using transpose memory. The method is multiplier-less and uses 56 adders/subractors. The design is implemented on Vertex 2 pro and maximum operating frequency is around 367 MHz.

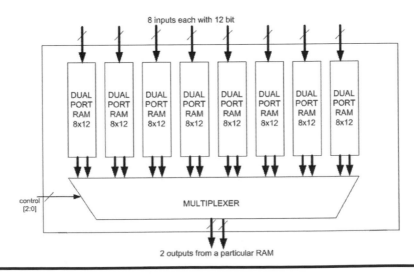

Figure 13.8   Proposed transpose memory block.

13.7 Watermark Embedding Unit

Our proposed video watermarking has two main functional units: One is the watermark insertion unit and another is the watermark generation unit. These units operate in parallel because they are independent of each other and are able to fetch data at the same time, therefore the performance of overall system is improved. VLSI architecture of our watermarking scheme is developed as shown in Figure 13.9, by parallel execution to enhance the real time performance.

13.7.1 Watermark Insertion Unit

It has two step process operating separately. In first step, a frame is transformed from spatial to frequency domain using 2D Integer DCT. The second step involves the prediction module where AC values estimation is performed using DC value of adjacent blocks. The values are fetched from RAM1 and helpful for AC prediction concept as shown in Figure 13.9. The combination of adder/sub-tractor and multiplier along with shifter helped to predict AC values after one clock delay. Estimated AC values are then being compared to original values. The embedding rule suggest that a quantity delta (which may be from 1 to 5) is going to be added with predicted values in order to get watermarked frames.

13.7.2 Watermark Generation Unit

It is useful for the generation of a watermark bit which helps to be embedded in every 24 × 24 block. A watermark is considered in the form of one image (8 bit per pixel) and shared memory is used to store the binary values of pixels. After reading

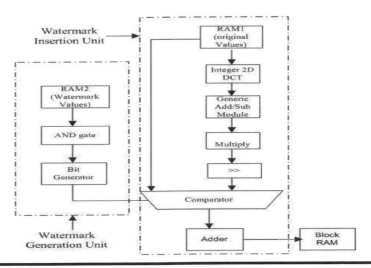

Figure 13.9   Proposed watermark embedding unit.

the first value read from memory, bitwise AND is carried out with each pixel value of the watermark and stored 8-bit register value. The register is initialized with 10000000. Then right shift logical operation is done for subsequent clock cycle to store 01000000 and again bitwise AND is done with a same value of pixel from the watermark. Same way, a logical right shift of stored value is performed for the next seven subsequent cycles. Every time, bitwise AND is performed with same pixel of watermark. This process creates a weight of a plane (Bit plane 8 to Bit plane 1).

Now as a example, consider original value of a pixel is as 202 (i.e., binary **11001010**).

> MSB plane: **1**1001010 and **1**0000000: The output gets generated as 10000000.
> Second plane: 1**1**001010 and 0**1**000000: The output gets generated as 01000000.
> Third plane: 11**0**01010 and 00**1**00000: The output gets generated as 00000000.
> Fourth plane: 110**0**1010 and 000**1**0000: The output gets generated as 00000000.
> Fifth plane: 1100**1**010 and 0000**1**000: The output gets generated as 00001000.
> Sixth plane: 11001010 and 00000100: The output gets generated as 00000000.
> Seventh plane: 110010**1**0 and 000000**1**0: The output gets generated as 00000010.
> LSB plane: 1100101**0** and 0000000**1**: The output gets generated as 00000000.

The is useful to generate a watermark bit with respect to the weight of the bit plane. If the outcome of a plane is greater than zero then a bit for watermarking is 1 else a bit is 0. Finally, the extracted watermark image is generated with assembling all the bit planes.

13.8 Results and Analysis

The proposed watermarking algorithm is initially simulated by MATLAB to validate the performance. The architecture of proposed system is subsequently implemented on hardware to measure the real-time performance. The hardware performance of proposed algorithm is demonstrated with FPGA prototyping and ASIC Implementation. FPGAs have high speed processing and reconfigurability. Therefore, the proof of concept is verified by FPGA. ASIC implementation is an efficient approach to having a small and dedicated watermarking module as an integral part of portable consumer devices for example camcorder, mobile camera, digital camera or any other similar multimedia devices. This is helpful to embed the real-time watermarking in terms of custom hardware, which is available at electronic appliances and inserts the watermark when video is being captured. The proposed algorithm may be used as an embedding unit which should be an integral part of HEVC encoder. The choice of the hardware implementation either on FPGA or as ASIC chip depends mainly on power requirement, cost and speed. The results are first endorsed on MATLAB platform to verify the essential requirements for ownership verification method. Later on, the proposed algorithm is realized on hardware platform.

Original Video Watermark

Figure 13.10   Frame of video and original watermark.

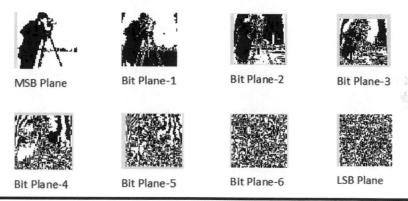

MSB Plane   Bit Plane-1   Bit Plane-2   Bit Plane-3

Bit Plane-4   Bit Plane-5   Bit Plane-6   LSB Plane

Figure 13.11   Different bit planes of watermark.

13.8.1 Specification

The original video is considered as "Forman.avi" which consist of 300 frames of each (720×576 size) size. The original watermark is taken as "Lena" image (24×30 size). First frame of the original video and the watermark both are shown as Figure 13.10.

The original watermark (which is "Cameraman" image) is further divided in various bit planes (MSB Plane to LSB Plane) as in Figure 13.11. Each one of the planes is treated as one watermark. The First part (MSB Plane) is going to be inserted on first frame, the second is embedded in second frame and so on finally last plane (LSB Plane) is in eighth frame of a scene. This way the different parts of original watermark are distributed among the chunk of eight frames which provides the robustness against the temporal attacks also. This has main advantage that some part of watermark can be still retrieved if some frames are lost due to one or multiple attacks.

13.8.2 Software Implementation

13.8.2.1 Performance Measurement

Normalized Correlation is important parameter to evaluate the performance. It helps to calculate the similarity between retrieved and original watermark as in Equation 13.10.

$$NC(w, w') = \frac{\sum_{m=1}^{N-1} \sum_{n=1}^{M-1} (w(m,n) \times w'(m,n))}{\sqrt{\sum w(m,n)^2 \times \sum w'(m,n)^2}}. \tag{13.10}$$

here, $w(m, n)$ = original watermark, $w'(m, n)$ = extracted watermark.

The another qualified parameters are also measured as MSE (mean squared error) or PSNR (peak signal to noise ratio) to evaluate the robustness and transparency of the proposed algorithm. MSE is a vital parameter to estimate the robustness whereas PSNR helps to measure the quality of the watermarked frame which may be degraded during watermarking process. However, PSNR and MSE are inversely related to each other. PSNR and MSE are expressed as in Equations 13.11 and 13.12.

MSE is calculated by squared difference between the watermarked and original frame as in Equation (13.11)

$$MSE = \frac{1}{P \times Q} \sum_{m=0}^{P-1} \sum_{n=0}^{Q-1} [I(m,n) - I_w(m,n)]^2 \tag{13.11}$$

where, $I_w(m, n)$ = watermarked frame and $I(m, n)$ = original frame, P, Q = size of the frame.

PSNR is defined as in Equation (13.12)

$$PSNR = 10 \times \log \frac{S_{max}^2}{MSE} \tag{13.12}$$

MSE is also computed as above Equation 13.11. S_{max} is maximum value of pixel of the gray image. S_{max} is considered as 255 for our 8 bit per pixel gray level image.

Table 13.3 defines various scenario where watermark is extracted if single or multiple frames are lost because of temporal attacks. Temporal attacks occur at time axis which include swapping, averaging and dropping of frames etc. In case

Table 13.3   Frame Dropping Attacks

Missing Plane	Retrieved Watermark	Missing Plane	Retrieved Watermark	Missing Plane	Retrieved Watermark
Plane 2	NC = 0.9307 MSE = 0.5138	MSB Plane	NC = 0.8456 MSE = 0.9876	LSB Plane	NC = 0.9920 MSE = 0.1006
Plane 3 and LSB	NC = 0.9906 MSE = 0.2962	Plane 1 and Plane 2	NC = 0.8314 MSE = 1.6825	Plane 5 and Plane 6	NC = 0.9934 MSE = 0.1578

any one plane is missed because of any attacks which can be LSB plane, then defines that a plane of multiple $8l + 1$ (where $l = 0, 1, 2...$) frames is either lost or corrupted. The proposed system would still able to retrieve the watermark in such scenarios. Similarly, any other planes are also lost when there is high probability of recovering watermarks from remaining frames.

The proposed algorithm has the ability to extract the watermark with high NC (0.80 or more) or worst cases where up to three frames are totally lost at the same time. For a particular frame, the watermark insertion process along with its effect on resultant frames are demonstrated in Table 13.4. The performance evaluation of proposed watermarking is defined with MSE, PSNR and NC of few frames (Frame 45, Frame 95, and Frame 145) as shown in Table 13.4. MSE is measured, also NC is computed particular frame, also NC is computed particular frame.

13.8.2.2 Security

The security depends on payload capacity. According to the prediction method, five watermark bits are inserted in every 24×24 block of every frame. Therefore, a total of 3600 (720×5) bits are added in each of the frames. The watermark image

Table 13.4 Watermark Embedding on Selected Frames

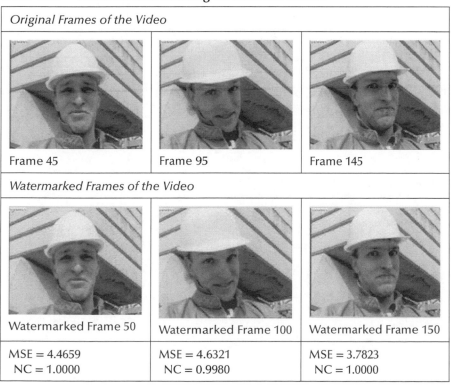

Original Frames of the Video		
Frame 45	Frame 95	Frame 145
Watermarked Frames of the Video		
Watermarked Frame 50	Watermarked Frame 100	Watermarked Frame 150
MSE = 4.4659 NC = 1.0000	MSE = 4.6321 NC = 0.9980	MSE = 3.7823 NC = 1.0000

("Lena" image in our case) is divided in different 8 bit planes. Each plane is inserted on every eight frames, this way a total payload of every GOP (group of picture) would be 28,800 (3600 × 8) bits. This huge payload is enough to be useful in ownership verification application.

13.8.3 FPGA Based Hardware Implementation

VLSI architecture of our watermarking system is developed to have optimized performance with high speed, low power and less area. The proposed system is designed using verilog HDL. Integer DCT and watermark embedding units have been evaluated using functional simulation on Modelsim software. The system has been synthesized on SPARTEN 3A FPGA family and the results of the same are reported in Tables 13.5 and 13.6 for hardware utilization and device utilization respectively.

The speed and power performance of our scheme is noted in Table 13.7. The power is calculated with Xilinx Xpower tool. The values are estimated power by tool without any constraint.

Table 13.5   Hardware Utilization Reports of Secure HEVC

Components	BELs	Registers	Adder/ Subtracter	Multiplier	Total
Integer 2D DCT	2845	534	43	0	3422
Watermark embedding unit	714	221	10	3	948

Table 13.6   Device Utilization Reports of Secure HEVC Reports

Resources	Integer 2D DCT	Watermark Embedding Unit
Slice (Total 16840)	1503 (9%)	619 (3%)
Slice FFs (Total 33280)	362 (1%)	167 (0%)
input LUTs (Total 33280)	2610 (9%)	1299 (3%)
Bounded IOBs (Total 519)	108 (21%)	60 (11%)
GCLKS (Total 24)	1 (4%)	1 (4%)

Table 13.7   Timing Reports of Secure HEVC Modules

Modules	Frequency (MHz)	Minimum Period	Power (μW)
Integer 2D DCT	39.29	25.45	0.112
Watermark embedding unit	30.68	32.59	0.111

Table 13.8   Synthesis Results for Secure HEVC Modules

Modules	Area (um²)	Power (mW)
Integer 2D DCT	30115.00	255.19
Watermark embedding unit	1043.00	6.691
Total	31158.00	261.88

13.8.4 ASIC Implementation

The performance of secure HEVC is measured for custom hardware with cost, power dissipation and utilization of resources.

13.8.4.1 Hardware Cost

Both, Integer DCT and watermark embedding unit are synthesized with Design Complier of synopsys with Farday 0.18 μm technology. The resultant area are reported in Table 13.8. The watermark embedding unit occupies 3.35% area. The custom IC of the watermark embedding chip is capable of providing the security of HEVC encoder with the expanse of a relatively small area. The device such as HEVC video encoder is huge enough and would have room for a watermarking unit in order to have the facility of ownership verification. The obtained values of area justify the simplicity of our watermarking algorithm.

13.8.4.2 Power Consumption

The power consumption for HEVC modules is also calculated by Design Complier (0.18 μm) and is noted in Table 13.8. The total power consumption of HEVC encoder including watermarking unit is around 261.88 mW using recursive DCT method. Whereas, the watermarking unit consumes power of only 6.691 mW which is (2.5%) for the overall encoding system. This guarantees that the inclusion of the watermark embedding unit does not have much overhead of power consumption for the overall system. The power consumption will not be affected even for high resolution video. The watermarking system operated on 8 × 8 blocks of a frame at a time irrespective of any resolution of frame of a video. The overall performance is not dependent on resolution of frame but depends only on the number of frames which are to be watermarked.

13.8.5 Comparison with Related Work

Previous works were mainly based on uncompressed or older compression standards. Petitjean et al. [9] realized MPEG-2 standard-based watermarking that uses general

DCT method. The floating point arithmetic used in the algorithm increases computational complexity of architecture and degrades the real-time performance. Vural et al. [16] developed watermarking with wavelet based frequency domain, but all video coding standards use DCT for its transformation. Mohanty and Kougianos [17] designed visible watermarking architecture for MPEG-4, however floating data path restricts its real-time performance. This avoids the integration with HEVC standard as it is based on integer arithmetic. Roy [18] suggested DCT MJPEG based video watermarking. The method was used to embed the semi-fragile watermark where the watermark gets destroyed against severe attacks. The method required large computational due to involvement of floating point operation.

The proposed algorithm provides enough robustness against various attacks and is helpful for ownership. The proposed watermarking implementation is compared in a similar video-based ASIC implementation in Table 13.9. The results show the comparable values for our proposed watermarking system.

13.9 Conclusion

The chapter includes a blind and invisible video watermarking scheme for latest HEVC standard. The watermarking unit would be a integral of HEVC secure encoder to generate the bit stream. The proposed algorithm is validated against different signal processing, temporal attacks and geometric attacks. The algorithm provides excellent results against all types of attack. Efficient architectures of a watermarking system are designed and subsequently implemented on hardware. The hardware performance of our system is checked on FPGA and ASIC implementation. The obtained results validate the real-time watermarking performance. The system has integer arithmetic to reduce computational complexity. The efficiency has been verified with area and speed using hardware utilization, device utilization and a timing reports. The comparison with related work reveals that the hardware implementation of proposed system has better results compare to all existing algorithms. The results of the proposed algorithm in terms of power and area suggest that a custom IC of proposed scheme can be integrated easily with HEVC encoder without much overhead and this would help in security of video being captured in real-time.

13.10 Future Work

The algorithm proposed in this chapter has used a gray image as an watermark. However, the algorithm can be extended to have a color image as a watermark. Biometric watermark has more significance in the security system for various applications. Fingerprints and iris scan can be used as a watermark which present the unique identity of the person. The extracted watermark is compared with the person's identity and the ownership problem can easily be resolved. In this chapter, the

Table 13.9 Comparison with Related ASIC Implementation

Research Work	Petitjean [9]	Vural [16]	Mohanty [17]	Roy [18]	Proposed Secure System
Watermark type	Robust	Invisible—robust	Visible	Invisible semi fragile	Invisible—robust
Domain	Fractal	DWT	DCT	DCT	Integer DCT
Standard	MPEG-2	MPEG	MPEG-4	MJPEG	HEVC
Frame size	512 × 512	512 × 512	320 × 240 × 3	640 × 480	720 × 486
Results	6 μs for FPGA (50 MHz), 78 μs for Pentium III, 118 us for VLIW (250 MHz)	NA	100 MHz	0.18 μm technology, 10 mW, 40 MHz	0.18 μm, 3.75 mm², 70.25 mW, 140 MHz

different bit planes of the image are used as individual watermarks and are inserted in the particular frames of a particular scene. The bit planes can be also used for an error correction/detection code to increase the level of robustness.

Bibliography

1. A. Joshi, V. Mishra, and R. Patrikar. Real time implementation of integer dct based video watermarking architecture. *International Arab Journal of Information Technology (IAJIT)*, (12), 2015.

2. S. P. Mohanty. *Watermarking of Digital Images*. PhD thesis, Department of Electrical Engineering, Indian Institute of Science, Bangalore, India, 1999.

3. T.-H. Tsai and C.-Y. Wu. An implementation of configurable digital watermarking system in mpeg video encoder. In *Consumer Electronics, 2003. ICCE. 2003 IEEE International Conference on*, pp. 216–217. IEEE, 2003.

4. A. M. Joshi, R. M. Patrikar, and V. Mishra. Design of low complexity video watermarking algorithm based on integer dct. In *Signal Processing and Communications (SPCOM), 2012 International Conference on*, pp. 1–5. IEEE, 2012.

5. C. H. Wu, Y. Zheng, W. H. Ip, C. Y. Chan, K. L. Yung, and Z. M. Lu. A flexible H.264/AVC compressed video watermarking scheme using particle swarm optimization based dither modulation. *AEU-International Journal of Electronics and Communications*, 65(1):27–36, 2011.

6. J. P. Uyemura. *Introduction to VLSI Circuits and Systems*. John Wiley & Sons, 2002.

7. Y. Shoshan, A. Fish, X. Li, G. Jullien, and O. Yadid-Pecht. VLSI watermark implementations and applications. *International Journal Information Technologies & Knowledge*, 2(4):379–386, 2008.

8. X. Li, Y. Shoshan, A. Fish, G. Jullien, and O. Yadid-Pecht. Hardware implementations of video watermarking. In *International Book Series on Information Science and Computing*, pp. 9–16. Sofia, Bulgaria: Institute of Information Theories and Applications FOI ITHEA, 2008.

9. G. Petitjean, J.-L. Dugelay, S. Gabriele, C. Rey, and J. Nicolai. Towards real-time video watermarking for system-on-chip. In *Multimedia and Expo, 2002. ICME'02. Proceedings. 2002 IEEE International Conference on*, Vol. 1, pp. 597–600. IEEE, 2002.

10. A. Brunton and J. Zhao. Real-time video watermarking on programmable graphics hardware. In *Electrical and Computer Engineering, 2005. Canadian Conference on*, pp. 1312–1315. IEEE, 2005.

11. Y.-J. Jeong, K.-S. Moon, and J.-N. Kim. Implementation of real time video watermark embedder based on haar wavelet transform using fpga. In *Future Generation Communication and Networking Symposia, 2008. FGCNS'08. Second International Conference on*, Vol. 3, pp. 63–66. IEEE, 2008.

12. W. S. ElAraby, A. H. Madian, M. A. Ashour, and A. M. Wahdan. Hardware realization of DC embedding video watermarking technique based on FPGA. In *Microelectronics (ICM), 2010 International Conference on*, pp. 463–466. IEEE, 2010.

13. L. De Strycker, P. Termont, J. Vandewege, J. Haitsma, T. Kalker, M. Maes, and G. Depovere. Implementation of a real-time digital watermarking process for broadcast monitoring on a trimedia VLIW processor. In *Vision, Image and Signal Processing, IEE Proceedings*, Vol. 147, pp. 371–376. IET, 2000.

14. M. Maes, T. Kalker, J.-P. Linnartz, J. Talstra, F. G. Depovere, and J. Haitsma. Digital watermarking for dvd video copy protection. *Signal Processing Magazine, IEEE*, 17(5):47–57, 2000.

15. N. J. Mathai, D. Kundur, and A. Sheikholeslami. Hardware implementation perspectives of digital video watermarking algorithms. *Signal Processing, IEEE Transactions on*, 51(4):925–938, 2003.

16. S. Vural, H. Tomii, and H. Yamauchi. Video watermarking for digital cinema contents. In *Proceedings of the 13th European Signal Processing Conference*, pp. 303–304, 2005.

17. S. P. Mohanty and E. Kougianos. Real-time perceptual watermarking architectures for video broadcasting. *Journal of Systems and Software*, 84(5):724–738, 2011.

18. S. D. Roy, X. Li, Y. Shoshan, A. Fish, and O. Yadid-Pecht. Hardware implementation of a digital watermarking system for video authentication. *Circuits and Systems for Video Technology, IEEE Transactions on*, 23(2):289–301, 2013.

19. A. M. Joshi, V. Mishra, and R. M. Patrikar. FPGA prototyping of video watermarking for ownership verification based on H.264/AVC. *Multimedia Tools and Applications*, 75(6):3121–3144, 2016.

20. S. Lian, Z. Liu, Z. Ren, and H. Wang. Commutative encryption and watermarking in video compression. *Circuits and Systems for Video Technology, IEEE Transactions on*, 17(6):774–778, 2007.

21. E. Y. Lam and J. W. Goodman. A mathematical analysis of the DCT coefficient distributions for images. *Image Processing, IEEE Transactions on*, 9(10):1661–1666, 2000.

22. O. Küçüktunç, U. Güdükbay, and Ö. Ulusoy. Fuzzy color histogram-based video segmentation. *Computer Vision and Image Understanding*, 114(1):125–134, 2010.

23. Z. Chen, J. Xu, Y. He, and J. Zheng. Fast integer-pel and fractional-pel motion estimation for H.264/AVC. *Journal of Visual Communication and Image Representation*, 17(2):264–290, 2006.

24. T. Krishnan and S. Oraintara. Fast and lossless implementation of the forward and inverse mdct computation in mpeg audio coding. In *Circuits and Systems, 2002. ISCAS 2002. IEEE International Symposium on*, Vol. 2, pp. II–181. IEEE, 2002.

25. J. Liang and T. D Tran. Fast multiplierless approximations of the dct with the lifting scheme. *Signal Processing, IEEE Transactions on*, 49(12):3032–3044, 2001.

Chapter 14

Data Hiding in Compressed Images and Videos

Shaohui Liu

Contents

DOI: 10.1201/9780429435461-16

14.1 Introduction

With the development of digital media technology, the security and privacy concerns are growingly given much attention in research and industrial areas. For example, data sharing and cultural challenges in modern cloud computing platform may contain sensitive information. In social network platform, such as Facebook, Wechat, the faithfulness and authentication of transmitted media files and messages are critical for forensic or verification in practical applications. Actually, these problems can be partially solved by combing encryption and information hiding technologies. Information hiding originated in the 1990s, and then it entered a new stage of rapid development in the following decades. However, when it comes to the late 2000s, the development momentum of information hiding is waning due to the limited application areas, transparent to the users and weak surveyability compared the modern Artificial Intelligence (AI) techniques, such as image, video and related techniques. Although AI has drawn a lot of attention in these years and achieves success in many application fields, here comes the security and privacy issue. Thus, the information hiding (after that will be called as data hiding) may enter its second stage of development and application. In this chapter, we will review the development and techniques and give some guidance for further development.

First, we give a simple example of hiding a logo into the LSB (least significant bit plane) of host Lena image. Figure 14.1 shows the result image by hiding the binary logo VILAB OF HIT image into the LSB of the Lena image. Figure 14.2 is the Lena image with size 256×256. Then it can be decomposed into 8 bitplanes shown in Figure 14.2. From this Figure, it is easily to see that the importance of bitplane is increasing with the number of the bitplane. The first bitplane is the least significant bitplane (sometimes it is called as LSB), and the 8th bitplane is the most significant bitplance (it is called as MSB). In addition, the first few bitplanes look like random noise. Hence, these bit-planes are usually used to hide messages. For example, message can be represented as binary form and then reshaped as the same size as the bit-plane of host image,

Figure 14.1 The illustration of LSB hiding: hiding a logo image into Lena image.

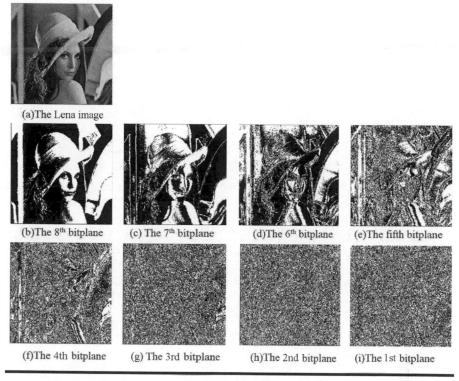

(a)The Lena image

(b)The 8ᵗʰ bitplane   (c) The 7ᵗʰ bitplane   (d)The 6ᵗʰ bitplane   (e)The fifth bitplane

(f)The 4th bitplane   (g) The 3rd bitplane   (h)The 2nd bitplane   (i)The 1st bitplane

Figure 14.2   The bit-plane decomposition of the 8-bit gray Lena image.

the hiding processing is simple achieved by replacing the first bitplane of host image with the reshaped binary message bit-plane.

In this example, the original Lena image is called the cover signal or host signal. The logo is called a message or information. The hiding procedure is carried by using one information bit to replace the LSB (least significant bit) of one pixel. Thus, the hiding scheme does not consider the relationship among these pixels and takes each pixel as an independent hiding unit. One hiding unit means that one hiding scheme can hide at least one bit information by modifying its attributes in this unit not referring any other units. In the same hiding scheme, all hiding units with the same information bits have the same attributes. This is equivalent to partitioning the hiding units into equivalent classes according to their attributes. For example, if each hiding unit hides one bit, then all hiding units are partitioned into two equivalent classes where bit 1 is for one and bit 0 if for another one. Similarly, if each hiding unit hides two bits, there are 4 equivalent classes. When you operate the hiding unit to hide two bits, what you only need to do is to choose an element in the equivalent class to minimize the distortion between that element and the hiding unit.

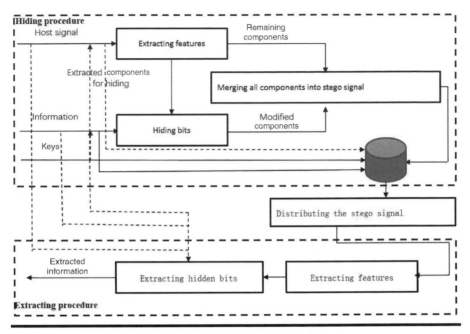

Figure 14.3 **The general hiding framework: hiding and extracting procedures.**

According to the development of the data hiding technique, the general hiding framework can be depicted in Figure 14.3. From Figure 14.3, the hiding processing can be divided into two parts: hiding and extracting. The key places will be described in the next section.

From Figure 14.3, the host signal can be any format signal which are called as cover signal or host signal or cover source, such as audio, image, video, 3D point cloud model, binary executable program, TCP/IP (Transmission Control Protocol/Internet Protocol) NTFS (New Technology File System) packet, NTFS, documents and so on whatever else you can think.

Although the hiding procedure is very similar in different application domain, there are some differences in different branches of data hiding. The first taxonomy of data hiding is proposed by Petitcolas in [1] and then by Liu [2]. Actually, according to the latest development, its related research area can be expanded further. Figure 14.4 shows the taxonomy of data hiding and its related researches.

From Figure 14.4, data hiding means that someone hides some message bits into the cover source to produce the stego source. However, different application environments have different requirements. As a result, there are different branches. Most of branches are the same as the beginning of data hiding research. But with the development of techniques, some new ideas are proposed to deal with new situations. For example, steganography requires generally the security, especially the capability of resisting steganalysis. But in some special application, it is not so important. For example, hiding personal information into medical images does not require the capability of resisting

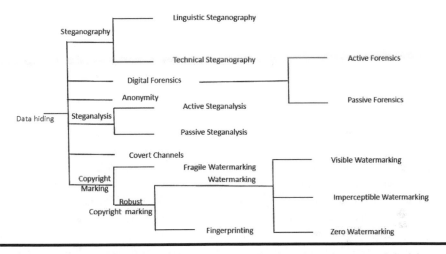

Figure 14.4 A classification of data-hiding techniques based on [1]. Digital forensics and steganalysis are on against steganography. The digital forensics focuses mainly on the intrinsic properties of all kinds physically things, such as imaging conditions, lighting, shadow, reflection, sensor, noise patterns, file format and so on. The steganalysis focuses mainly on detecting the steganography channel and estimating the key and hidden message and so on.

steganalysis. In this case, it requires the capability of perfect recovery after extracting the personal information. In this chapter, we call all hiding methods including watermarking and steganography as data hiding except where specified clearly.

The rest of this chapter is organized as follows. Section 14.2 introduces the hiding space in cover sources, and especially introduces the JPEG compress and H.264 video compression. Sections 14.3 and 14.4 introduce the non-inversible and reversible data hiding, and the classical hiding strategies are reviewed. In the Section 14.5, we give a hiding strategy combing different hiding methods to decrease the distortion. The conclusion will be given in the Section 14.6.

14.2 Hiding Space

The main goal of data hiding is to communicate a secret message without making it apparent that a secret or message is being discovered by surficial observation. This can be achieved by hiding information in ordinary-looking objects, such as many cover sources mentioned in the Section 14.1. Then these ordinary-looking objects with hidden message are communicated in public channels.

From Figure 14.3, the hiding procedure determines the extracting procedure. The keys in data hiding can be used in many places, such as extracting the components to be hidden bits, encrypting the message bits or permuting the elements of cover signal. The keys are secretly kept in a database maintained by the owner of a hiding application platform; they will be used to authenticate the hidden message once someone argues the hiding message. The hidden message is usually encrypted by keys to improve the security. However, whatever message it is, it will be represented by binary bits. In a practical hiding system, the size of message bits and the related hiding parameters are usually hidden in the cover signal with message bits.

There are many places used as hiding spaces in a cover signal. Moreover, different cover signals have different hiding places. Following, we summarize the potential hiding places into four categories.

The first is to append message bits to the end of file. It's just like the idea of some viruses. However, it does not alter the cover signal data. Hence, some application software neglects it; other intent receivers can extract the expected message.

The second category is the reservation places in some standard format. For example, the reservation fields in TCP/IP packet, the reservation extra bits in BITMAP format when the number of bytes in each row pixels is not an integer multiple of 4 and so on. These reservation fields do not deliberately design for data hiding but are used as hiding places. The hiding procedure is to pad reserved field with message bits.

The third category is the few least significant components in cover signal. These components are not important to understanding the cover signal from the viewpoint of application. Thus, the hiding procedure is to replace these components with message bits.

The fourth category is the relationship between any two objects in a cover signal. It is noted that these two objects belong to one hiding unit. For example, one hiding unit includes A and B objects, suppose A and B represent the two pixels value, if A is larger than B, then this hiding unit means that bit 1 is hidden, otherwise the bit 0 is hidden. This relationship includes many different specific implementations, such as the magnitude of transform coefficients, motion vector, variable length coding (VLC: Variable-Length Coding) pairs, even the space interval between words and lines, and the size of fonts in documents.

Actually, the message bits only include bit 0 and bit 1. Whether cover signal has been hidden with a message or not, we can always perform the extracting procedure based on the corresponding hiding procedure. However, if cover signal does not hide any message or using error parameters or keys, extracted messages could be meaningless; contrarily, if cover signal does hide message, then extracted message should be comprehensible. Hence, for each hiding unit of signal in an extracting procedure, the extracting procedure is equivalent to classify all hiding units into two equivalence classes, where one corresponds to the bit 0 and another corresponds to the bit 1. For example, watermarking is a branch of data hiding, all cover signals can be partitioned into two classes, and one is that the signal has watermark and another is that the signal does not have a watermark. Specifically, the range of all 8-bit gray pixel values is [0, 255], then we can partition this set into two equivalent classes: the set of all even numbers and the set of all odd numbers. Then the hiding strategy can be designed simply as the set of all even numbers indicate the hidden bit 0, and otherwise the hidden bit 1. Once the size of the message bits is known, then the hidden message can be easily extracted by using correct keys.

Although there are many cover signals, digital images, audios and videos are the most common cover signals in data hiding research community. Following, we will give a short introduction for image, audio and video.

Digital image is one of most commonly used cover signals. Due to the large size of raw pixels, still image coding is proposed to decrease the communication bandwidth and storage size of images. Since the mid-1980s, the ITU and ISO have been working together to develop a joint international standard for the compression of still images. It is JPEG which is officially called the ISO/IEC international standard 10918-1: digital compression and coding of continuous-tone still images or the ITU-T Recommendation T.81 in 1992. Although in the beginning of data hiding, BITMAP images were used as cover images, JPEG images are used more commonly in practical applications. As a result, data hiding in JPEG became more popular. Following, JPEG is introduced.

The JPEG standard has both lossy and lossless encoding of still images. The lossy coding is based on DCT (Discrete Cosine Transform) and it is the baseline of JPEG. Moreover, this baseline is most commonly used in many applications. The basic process of JPEG is shown in Figure 14.5 Another lossless encoding is

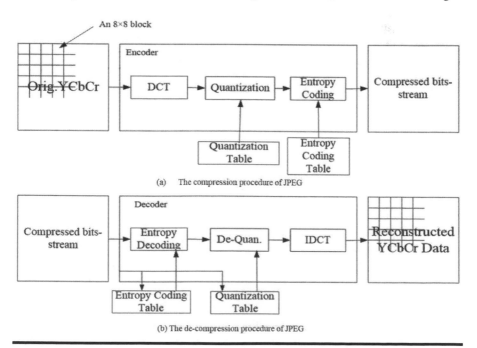

(a)   The compression procedure of JPEG

(b) The de-compression procedure of JPEG

Figure 14.5   The illustration of JPEG compression and decompression.

based on a predictive coding and meets the requirement of lossless storage, such as medical images. From the algorithmic point of view, JPEG has four distinct modes of operation: sequential DCT-based mode, progressive DCT-based mode, lossless mode, and hierarchical mode. In this chapter, only sequential DCT-based mode and lossless mode are considered. The other two modes are seldom used.

In the sequential DCT-based mode, a RGB image is first transformed into YCbCr color space, and then partitioned into non-overlap blocks with size 8×8 pixels of each channel. Then each block are transformed by 2-D DCT from left to right and top to bottom. The transformed block is further quantized by 8×8 quantization matrix. Then, the quantized DCT coefficients are scanned by zigzag order into 64 coefficients $d(i), i = 01,2,...,63$, and represented as VLC pairs. Finally, the VLC pairs are entropy encoded and output as part of the compressed bit stream. It should be noted that each 8×8 block is treated independently.

Actually, the 2-D forward and inverse DCT of 8×8 block are defined as:

$$D(u,v) = \frac{1}{4}C(u)C(v)\sum_{x=0}^{7}\sum_{y=0}^{7}I(x,y)[\frac{\pi}{8}(x+\frac{1}{2}u)]cos[\frac{\pi}{8}(y+\frac{1}{2}v)] \qquad (14.1)$$

$$I(x,y) = \frac{1}{4}\sum_{u=0}^{7}\sum_{v=0}^{7}D(u,v)cos[\frac{\pi}{8}(x+\frac{1}{2}u)]cos[\frac{\pi}{8}(y+\frac{1}{2}v)] \qquad (14.2)$$

where u, v are the horizontal and vertical spatial frequency independently, and $0 \leq u$, $v \leq 7$, $I(x,y)$ is the pixel value at coordinates (x,y) in one 8×8 block,

$$C(u)C(v) = \begin{cases} \frac{1}{\sqrt{2}}, & u = v = 0 \\ 1, & otherwise \end{cases}$$

It is obvious that $d(u+8v)$ is the $(u+8v)^{th}$ DCT coefficient of the block.

The quality of compressed image is controlled by adjusting the quality factor to modify the 8×8 quantization matrix Q according to the following equation:

$QuanTable$
$$= \begin{cases} round(StdQuanTable \cdot (2-0.02 \cdot QualityFactor)), & QualityFactor >= 50 \\ round(StdQuanTable \cdot (50 / QualityFactor)), & QualityFactor < 50 \end{cases}$$

$$(14.3)$$

where the *StdQuanTable* is shown in Figure 14.6 for luminance components. And the chrominance quantization table is shown in Figure 14.7. It is obvious that larger quality factor leads to less quantization step and better compressed quality.

$$
StdQuanTab\ le =
\begin{pmatrix}
16 & 11 & 10 & 16 & 24 & 40 & 51 & 61 \\
12 & 12 & 14 & 19 & 26 & 58 & 60 & 55 \\
14 & 13 & 16 & 24 & 40 & 57 & 69 & 56 \\
14 & 17 & 22 & 29 & 51 & 87 & 80 & 62 \\
18 & 22 & 37 & 56 & 68 & 109 & 103 & 77 \\
24 & 35 & 55 & 64 & 81 & 104 & 113 & 92 \\
49 & 64 & 78 & 87 & 103 & 121 & 120 & 101 \\
72 & 92 & 95 & 98 & 112 & 100 & 103 & 99
\end{pmatrix}
$$

Figure 14.6 The standard illumination quantization table, corresponding to the quality factor 50.

$$
StdQuanTable =
\begin{pmatrix}
17 & 18 & 24 & 47 & 99 & 99 & 99 & 99 \\
18 & 21 & 26 & 66 & 99 & 99 & 99 & 99 \\
24 & 26 & 56 & 99 & 99 & 99 & 99 & 99 \\
47 & 66 & 99 & 99 & 99 & 99 & 99 & 99 \\
99 & 99 & 99 & 99 & 99 & 99 & 99 & 99 \\
99 & 99 & 99 & 99 & 99 & 99 & 99 & 99 \\
99 & 99 & 99 & 99 & 99 & 99 & 99 & 99 \\
99 & 99 & 99 & 99 & 99 & 99 & 99 & 99
\end{pmatrix}
$$

Figure 14.7 The standard chrominance quantization table, corresponding to the quality factor 50.

At the same quality factor, elements in chrominance quantization matrix are larger than those in luminance quantization matrix. The principle of designing these two quantization matrix is based on the fact that HVS (human visual system) is more sensitive to luminance than chrominance.

After the forward DCT, each of the 64 DCT coefficients is quantized by the quantization matrix Q (it can be represented as $Q(u,v)$, $0 \leq u,v \leq 7$):

$$
QD(u,v) = round\left(\frac{D(u,v)}{Q(u,v)} \right) \tag{14.4}
$$

where $QD(u,v)$ is quantized index of the DCT coefficient $D(u,v)$, and the $Q(u,v)$ is the quantization step obtained from the quantization table Q. This quantization will lead to many zeros. Hence, a small amount of 64 DCT coefficients are non-zero coefficients after quantization. It is the idea of compression. There existing systems hide bits with JPEG-compressed images. In general, they operate by modifying some subset of the quantized coefficients by ±1 to hide bits. ±1 hiding is also equivalent to equivalent partition mentioned above.

However, the quantization step is usually large; ±1 hiding will lead to large distortion. Hence, one can modify the quantization matrix (usually using much small quantization step) and then adjust the quantized index to decrease the distortion caused by hiding.

The QD is the quantized index matrix, then it is scanned by zig-zag order shown in Figure 14.8 into one dimension array, and represented as (Run, Level) VLC pairs. And finally, a form of lossless encoding (Huffman or arithmetic coding) is used to compress the VLC. In this stage, (Run, Level) can be modified to hide bits, and the statistical model in arithmetic coding was used to hide bits. It is called as model-based steganography.

The HVS is more sensitive to luminance than chrominance. In JPEG there are at least two places to indicate this. The first is the chrominance data is downsampled into the quarter of luminance data. The second is the quantization table with larger quantization steps in chrominance as shown in Figures 14.6 and 14.7. Thus hiding equivalent quantities of bits in chrominance, as opposed to luminance, causes significantly more distortion and hence more detectable. For this reason, the majority of data hiding systems hide information bits in luminance data.

The lossless mode is another commonly used, especially in medial environment and hence in data hiding. In the lossless coding mode, the coding is spatial-based coding instead of DCT-based coding. It is like the way of coding DC coefficients in the sequential DCT-based coding mode. Each pixel is first predicted from the coded pixels and the predictive error is coded.

The predictive process is shown in the Figure 14.9. $I(x, y)$ is the current pixel, and the upper and left pixels had been coded. Then a predicted pixel value $\hat{I}(x, y)$

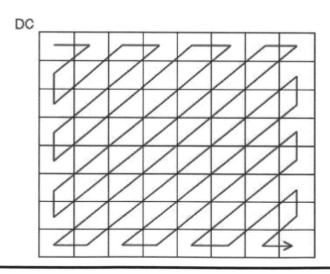

Figure 14.8　The zig-zag scan order in JPEG.

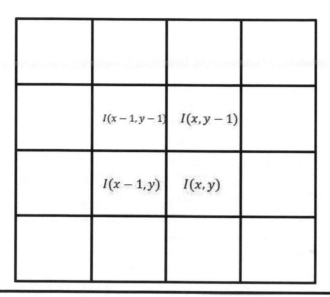

Figure 14.9 The illustration of prediction.

of pixel $I(x,y)$ is obtained according to its coded neighbor pixels $I(x-1,y-1)$, $I(x,y-1)$, $I(x-1,y)$. There are 7 modes:

$$\hat{I}(x,y) = I(x-1,y-1)$$
$$\hat{I}(x,y) = I(x,y-1)$$
$$\hat{I}(x,y) = I(x-1,y)$$
$$\hat{I}(x,y) = I(x-1,y) + I(x,y-1) - I(x-1,y-1)$$
$$\hat{I}(x,y) = I(x-1,y) + (I(x,y-1) - I(x-1,y-1))/2$$
$$\hat{I}(x,y) = I(x,y-1) + (I(x-1,y) - I(x-1,y-1))/2$$
$$\hat{I}(x,y) = (I(x,y-1) - I(x-1,y))/2$$

(14.5)

In the coding, the predicted error is the $I(x,y) - \hat{I}(x,y)$ which is coded with either Huffman coding or arithmetic coding. This predictive way is very similar with the intra-prediction in video coding which will be introduced in the following. The data hiding is performed by modifying the predictive error or histogram shifting in Sections 14.3 and 14.4.

Video compression plays an important role in modern communication. Nowadays, there are three organizations to standardize video coding standard.

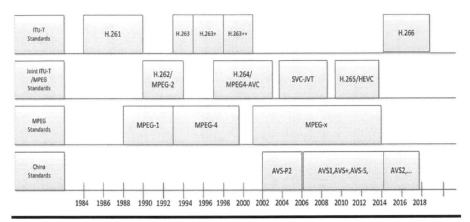

Figure 14.10 **The international standard organizations and their standards. The x-axis is the time table for different video coding standards.**

They have developed a series of standards shown in Figure 14.10. From MPEG1 to MPEG 4, H.261 to H.265, there are many video coding standards. All are based on hybrid coding framework which is shown in Figure 14.11. Following, we introduce it by taking H.264 as an example.

In Figure 14.11, there exist many components. Among them, the intra-frame prediction, motion estimation, transform/quantization, de-blocking filter and entropy coding are the most important components. The intra-frame prediction just likes the prediction in lossless mode in JPEG. The distinction is that the number of predictive mode is much larger than modes in JPEG. Different predictive modes only affect the

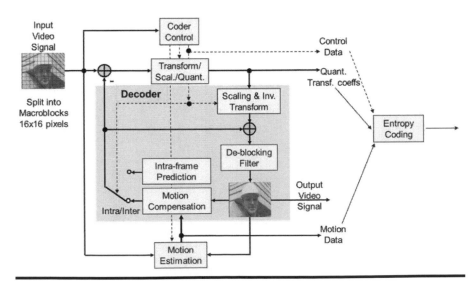

Figure 14.11 **The hybrid coding framework in video coding.**

accuracy of predictive value hence it only leads to slightly increase the size of compressed bit stream. Thus data hiding schemes prefer to hide bits by modifying the optimal predictive mode to sub-optimal predictive mode. The second component is the motion estimation which finds the best matching in the coded frame for the current block. The displacement in horizontal and vertical direction is called as motion vector. Like the intra-prediction, motion vector is another component which is often used to hide bits. The third component is the transform and quantization. It is similar to the corresponding one in JPEG. Thus, it is also often used to hide bits. The last component is the entropy coding. The most common two kinds of entropy coding are CAVLC (Context-based Adaptive Variable Length Coding) and CABAC (Context-based Adaptive Binary Arithmetic Coding). It is noted that CAVLC and CABAC are supported in H.264, however, CAVLC is removed from the latest standard H.265/HEVC (High Efficiency Video Coding). In data hiding, researchers often hide bits by equivalent partitions of entropy coding tables in compressed video and audio. In addition, video coding has a common organization structure. It is shown in Figure 14.12.

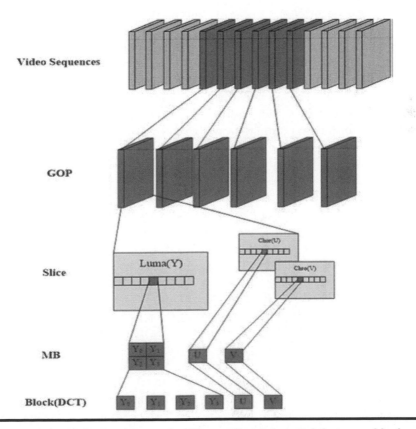

Figure 14.12 **The basic structure in video coding. It is noted that some blocks are different in different standards.**

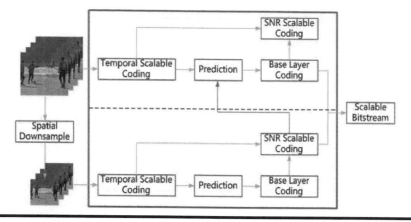

Figure 14.13   The basic structure in scalable video coding.

Another video coding standard is the scalable video coding which is an extension of general video coding, such as H.264 and H.265. Figure 14.13 shows the SVC framework of H.264. The SVC of H.265 has the similar structure.

A SVC bit stream can provide three types scalability, namely temporal, spatial and quality scalability. In this paper, we mainly focus on spatial and quality scalability for hiding and encryption. For spatial scalability, SVC introduces three prediction mechanisms including inter-layer motion prediction, inter-layer residual prediction and inter-layer intra-prediction. Following, the most appropriate places for hiding information bits will be analyzed in these three prediction mechanisms.

The first mechanism is inter-layer motion prediction where the motion vector in base layer will be upsampled as the motion vector in enhancement layer, but the reference layer macroblock and the enhancement layer macroblock are inter-coded. It is obvious that we do not know whether macroblocks in the enhancement layer are inter-coded or not when we are coding macroblocks in base layer. If motion vectors in base layer are modified to hide information bits, they may be discarded by enhancement decoding. Thus, motion vectors are not appropriate for hiding bits in this case. The second one is inter-layer residual prediction which is employed for all inter-coded macroblocks in base layer and enhancement layer. The residual signal in base layer is upsampled as the prediction for the residual signal of the enhancement layer macroblock. It is obvious that the decoding of macroblocks of the enhancement layer must use the residual signal of the base layer. Thus we can hide or encrypt the residual signal of the base layer. And encryption of base layer leads to encryption of enhancement layer. The third mechanism is inter-layer intra-prediction which is employed for enhancement layer macroblock and its reference layer (base layer) is intra-coded. Therefore, the decoding of the enhancement layer requires the decoding of base layer. Modifying the information of intra-coded block can achieve the destination of higher layer detection and encryption.

14.3 Non-reversible Hiding

Non-reversible hiding means that the hiding procedure causes quality degeneration of the cover signal. Of course, the degeneration is usually perceptual neglected. General speaking, the non-reversible hiding has better robustness than reversible hiding. Moreover, stego signal often has better quality in non-reversible hiding than reversible hiding. In non-reversible hiding, there are two common used hiding methods: quantization-based and spread spectrum-based.

Figure 14.14 shows the basic principle of quantization-based data hiding. Where Δ is the quantization step, and b_i is the decision boundary, y_i is the reconstruction level. Basically speaking, the odd/even of quantized index is the hidden bit. Of course the design of the hiding scheme is to determine how to hide the information to achieve less distortion and more secure.

Spread spectrum in communication is used to improve the security of the transmitted message. Spread spectrum-based data hiding uses sequences to modulate the information bits to improve the security and robustness of data hiding. It is commonly used particularly in watermarking. The hiding and extracting procedures are defined as:

■ Hiding:

$$I' = I + \alpha \cdot W \tag{14.6}$$

■ Extracting:

$$I' \cdot W = (I + \alpha \cdot W) \cdot W = I \cdot W + \alpha \parallel W \parallel^2 \approx \alpha \parallel W \parallel^2 \tag{14.7}$$

where I is the feature vector extracted from the cover signal, W is the sequence modulated by information bit, α is the hiding strength, I' is the stego feature vector. In the extracting, if suppose the W has been normalized, namely, $\parallel W \parallel^2 = 1$, then thresholding α will extract the hidden bit in each hiding unit.

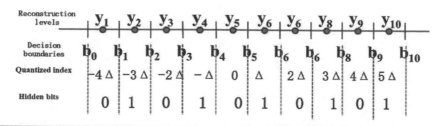

Figure 14.14   The illustration of quantization-based data hiding.

Whenever it is non-reversible or reversible data hiding, the hiding can be summarized as:

Given a set H in which each element is a hiding unit of cover signal, then the general hiding strategy can be divided into three steps.

- Step 1. Constructing an equivalence relation on H, generally speaking, the equivalence relation can be the capacity of a hiding unit;
- Step 2. Establishing the set of equivalence classes based on the equivalence relation, and the set of all equivalence classes of H forms a partition of H;
- Step 3. Hiding message bits equivalence-class by equivalence-class. In each equivalence class, user can permute the embedding order of hiding units to improve the security of the data hiding scheme.

Following we give several data hiding schemes.

14.3.1 LSB-like Hiding

Although many different data hiding are proposed, spatial domain hiding algorithms, especially LSB hiding algorithm mentioned in Section 14.1, are always research hot topic due to theirs low complexity and high capacity. From the first LSB schemes [3–5] by A.Z. Tirkel to Patchwork [6] by Bender et al. and PK [7] by Pitas and Nikolaidis, and later some sophisticated schemes [8–10], most of them are based on fixed bits substitution.

Suppose the subset of hiding units, pixels set in LSB hiding, $\{p_0, p_1, \cdots, p_n\}$, information bits $M = \{m_0, m_1, \cdots, m_n\}$, $m_i \in 0,1$, the function $LSB(p_i)$ means the LSB of p_i, then the LSB hiding:

- LSB hiding:

$$p_i' = \begin{cases} p_i, & LSB(p_i) = m_i \\ p_i \pm 1, & LSB(p_i) \neq m_i \end{cases} \tag{14.8}$$

- LSB extracting:

$$m_i = LSB(p_i') \tag{14.9}$$

After the first LSB [3] substitution algorithm, related algorithms focus on how to improve the quality of steg image. Wang et al. [11] proposed to use genetic algorithm to search the optimal substitution matrix, which made the error by substitution be least. But genetic algorithm is time-consuming, and the obtained matrix is not optimal. Hence, Chang et al. [12] used dynamic programming to search the substitution matrix, it remarkably decrease the search time. Chan et al. [13] also provided an improved moderate-bitplane hiding scheme based on Wangs work [8]. Later, optimal adjustment process [9] was used to decrease the error by a few LSB bitplanes substitution and improve greatly the quality of the steg image. Recently, Mielikainen [10] presented an improved LSB algorithm, each hiding unit includes two pixels, one pixel LSB is the first message bit, and the second message bit is hidden by a function of these two pixel values. It can decrease the probability of change of LSB, therefore it improves the quality of the steg image. In fact, the extracting procedure of LSB is the result of modulus 2, moreover a few LSBs substitution is equivalent to modulus the power of 2. Hence, LSB based on modulus operation was proposed in 2003 [14], and use the similar strategy in [9] to improve the quality of the steg image. Wang et al. [15] proposed an improved version, which partitioned all pixels into two parts according to a predefined threshold, and then those pixels with larger pixel values hid more bits according to method [14]. Based on it, Chang et al. [16] used dynamic programming in [12] to search optimal substitution matrix and then hid message by optimal measure in [14].

In [17], the author decreased the expected number of modifications per pixel from 0.5 to 0.375. And Li further extended the method to generalized LSB matching in [18]. In these methods, the ± 1 operator is random to break the statistical characteristic of the original LSB hiding: $0 \leftrightarrow 1, 2 \leftrightarrow 3, \ldots, 254 \leftrightarrow 255$. The original LSB hiding leads to the equal distribution these pixel pairs. Thus, well-known F3, F5 hiding methods use this strategy to enhance the security.

Another hiding strategy uses predictive error to hide information bits.

First a hiding unit comprises two pixels (p_i, p_{i+1}), the difference $d \in [-255, 255]$ for 8-bit images. Then the interval $[-255, 255]$ is partitioned into 6 disjoint sub-intervals with width $8,8,16,32,64,128$, the kth interval is $R_k = [l_k, u_k]$. For example the first two subintervals are $[0,7]$ and $[8,15]$. The length of information bits can be hidden into R_k is $log_2(u_k - l_k + 1)$. Suppose its decimal number of information bits is b, then:

■ Hiding:

$$(p'_i, p'_{i+1}) = \begin{cases} (p_i - \lceil \frac{m}{2} \rceil, p_{i+1} + \lfloor \frac{m}{2} \rfloor), & d \text{ is an odd number} \\ (p_i - \lfloor \frac{m}{2} \rfloor, p_{i+1} + \lceil \frac{m}{2} \rceil), & d \text{ is an even number} \end{cases} \quad (14.10)$$

where $d = p_{i+1} - p_i$,

$$d' = \begin{cases} l_k + b, & d >= 0 \\ -(l_k + b), & d < 0, \end{cases} \quad (14.11)$$

and $m = d' - d$.

■ Extracting:

$$b = \begin{cases} d' - l_k, & d' >= 0 \\ b = -d' - l_k, & d' < 0 \end{cases} \quad (14.12)$$

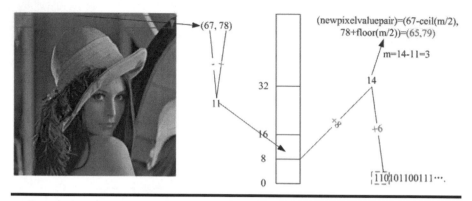

Figure 14.15 **The illustration of hiding using difference.**

Figure 14.15 shows the example which hides information bits 110 into a hiding unit $(p_i, p_{i+1}) = (67, 78)$, then the resulting hiding unit becomes $(65, 79)$.

There are many methods to design a hiding unit. The basic idea is to get one difference by predictive methods in image or video coding.

14.3.2 *Hiding in Non-compressed Media*

Hiding in non-compressed media usually uses mathematic transform, such as discrete Fourier transform (DFT), DCT [19], discrete wavelet transform (DWT) [20,21], singular value decomposition (SVD), to transform the cover signal into transformed domain [22], and then modify features to hide information bits. These mathematic transforms usually have their integer version, namely integer DCT, integer DWT and so on. Integer transform is more suitable for high-capacity data hiding, and float transform is more suitable for high-robustness data hiding.

14.3.3 *Hiding in Compressed Media*

Multimedia has a large amount size compared with text; hence, most media are compressed media. Hiding in compressed media is more useful but more difficult [23–25]. The compression has removed redundant space in cover signal so the representation is more compact and formatted. Moreover, compressed media requires the hiding scheme is format-compatible. There are two types of hiding strategies: one is first decompressing the media into spatial domain, and then information bits are hidden by methods like equation (14.8) and (14.10) 14.3.1 and 14.3.2. But it is time-consuming, another is first to decompress partially the cover signal and then modify the syntax elements to hide information bits [26] just like those methods in 3.1 and 3.2.

Of course, it is more convenient that information bits are hidden while compressing the cover signal. Moreover, one can use the original cover signal to design hiding strategy to decrease the distortion due to compression and data hiding in this case.

14.3.4 Hiding in Encrypted Media

In some cases, compression and encryption are performed at the same time [27–31]. Data hiding is still useful.

In general, the framework of combining image compression and encryption is illustrated in Figure 14.16. Namely compression and encryption are independently operated in general applications [32,33]. Once an image has been encrypted then it is very hard to process this encrypted image because the statistics characteristic of the image have been interrupted by encryption. Hence, most of techniques proposed so far to deal with image security try to apply some cryptographic primitives on the compressed image. The common case is partial encryption [27], where an encryption algorithm is used to encrypt only part of the compressed image or video to avoid the huge amount of operations because of the low speed of the encryption algorithm. From Figure 14.16, plain image and encrypted image exist simultaneously in the public domain. the public domain means that all data in this domain can be accessed by parties. Users do not control the transferred data. Obviously, it faces the risk of leakage of private information. Hence, one can first encrypt and then compress the image, such as shown in Figure 14.17 in [34]. Of course, you can hide information bits during this process.

In compressed video, we can do the similar operation by combining the encryption and data hiding operations. Figure 14.18 shows the framework in [35].

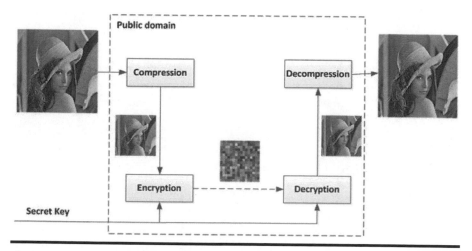

Figure 14.16 **The general compression and encryption.**

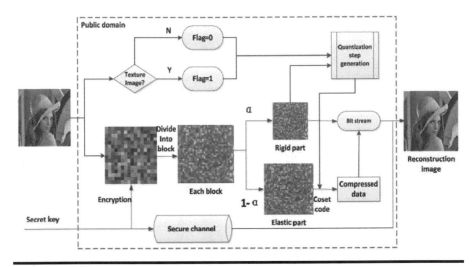

Figure 14.17   The framework combing the encryption and compression.

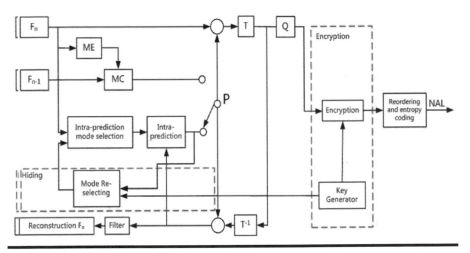

Figure 14.18   The framework combing the encryption and data hiding in compressed domain.

14.4 Reversible Data Hiding

Reversible hiding is sometimes called as lossless hiding which recovers perfectly the cover signal after extracting the hidden bits. The most basic principle is to compress or preprocess the cover signal and then the saved space is used to hide bits. Once the hidden bits are extracted, the cover signal is decompressed or post-processed to recover the cover signal. Most reversible data hiding schemes are based on this idea. However, if the cover signal has been a compressed signal, it is very different to hide bits by this strategy. Thereafter, researchers invented many other comprehensive reversible data hiding schemes. There are two commonly used strategies. One is histogram-shifting and another is difference expansion hiding. Following, we will review the principles.

14.4.1 Difference Expansion Hiding

The first well-known reversible data hiding is the difference expansion hiding at 2003. The hiding unit includes two pixels which are usually neighbor pixels. Otherwise, the expanded difference becomes relative larger and causes large modification for the two pixels. This is different from the non-reversible data hiding by modifying the difference. Suppose the pixel values are p_i, p_{i+1}, then the difference d is $p_{i+1} - p_i$, it is represented in binary form: $d = (d_k \cdots d_2 d_1 d_0)_2$, the information bit is m_i, then:

■ Hiding:

$$(p_i', p_{i+1}') = (\lfloor \frac{p_i + p_{i+1}}{2} \rfloor \pm \lfloor \frac{d'}{2} \rfloor, \lfloor \frac{p_i + p_{i+1}}{2} \rfloor \mp \lfloor \frac{d'}{2} \rfloor) \tag{14.13}$$

where, $d' = (d_k \cdots d_2 d_1 d_0 m_i)_2$.
■ Extracting:

$$d' = p_{i+1}' - p_i' = (d_k \cdots d_2 d_1 d_0 m_i)_2, \tag{14.14}$$

m_i is the extracted bit.
■ Recovering:

$$d = (d_k \cdots d_2 d_1 d_0)_2, \; p_i = \lfloor \frac{p_i' + p_{i+1}'}{2} \rfloor \mp \lfloor \frac{d}{2} \rfloor, \; p_{i+1} = \lfloor \frac{p_i' + p_{i+1}'}{2} \rfloor \pm \lfloor \frac{d}{2} \rfloor \tag{14.15}$$

Suppose (p_i, p_{i+1}) be $(108,115)$, then $d = 7 = (111)_2$, the information bit is 0. Then $d' = (1110)_2 = 14$, thus $p_i' = 111 - 7 = 104$, $p_{i+1}' = 111 + 7 = 118$. The extracting is straightforward. The recovering is also simple: $p_i = 111 - 3 = 108$, $p_{i+1} = 111 + 3 = 115$.

Later, this scheme is extended into other domain and hiding units and it is considered as a special case of generalized integer transform [36]. But the basic idea is not changed. It also can be used in compressed domain. The difference is that the hiding unit are other elements in compressed domain rather than the pixels values.

14.4.2 Histogram-Shifting Hiding

This scheme is based on the statistical histogram of an image. First a peak value $hist_p$ in the 256-dimensional histogram $hist$ is located, and then shifting the left and right side histogram at that peak point hides information bits. It is noted that the original scheme only shifts one place, thus the capacity equals the number of pixels falling into the two adjacent histogram bins.

■ Hiding: the peak point $hist_p$ in histogram $hist$, then

$$I'(x,y) = \begin{cases} I(x,y)-1, & I(x,y) < hist_p \\ I(x,y)+1, & I(x,y) > hist_p \end{cases} \tag{14.16}$$

Then pixels whose value equal $hist_p - 2$ or $hist_p + 2$ is modified to hide information bits, namely

$$hist_p - 2 \leftrightarrow hist_p - 1, hist_p + 2 \leftrightarrow hist_p + 1. \tag{14.17}$$

■ Extracting: According to the hiding rule, all pixels whose value equal $hist_p - 2$, $hist_p - 1$, $hist_p + 1$ and $hist_p + 2$ may contain bits. The extracting procedure is just the reverse processing as the hiding.
■ Recovering: changing all pixels by $hist_p - 1 \rightarrow hist_p - 2$ and $hist_p + 1 \rightarrow hist_p + 2$, then

$$I(x,y) = \begin{cases} I'(x,y)+1, & I'(x,y) < hist_p \\ I'(x,y)-1 & I'(x,y) > hist_p \end{cases} \tag{14.18}$$

then the original image has been recovered.

14.5 A New Hiding Strategy

Nowadays, there are many hiding schemes. The basic idea must belong to domains mentioned above. Most hiding schemes consider non-reversible hiding or reversible hiding independently. The effect of hiding can be evaluated from the less distortion and the high security. The security will be discussed in the next section. The distortion caused by hiding always increases with hiding more and more bits. Is it possible to decrease the distortion when hiding more bits? Namely, can we hide some bits into the stego signal to decrease the distortion by using another hiding scheme after hiding bits into the cover signal using one hiding scheme? It means that these two hiding schemes have the complementary effect.

We think this strategy is possible. Let me consider the combination of non-reversible and reversible hiding schemes. First, if the first round hiding is non-reversible hiding, then the second round hiding may decrease the distortion by comprehensive designing. Of course, the first round hiding can be reversible hiding. But it is much better to consider the two hiding functions before performing hiding. Even the same reversible hiding scheme is again applied to the stego signal, it is possible to decrease the distortion if the scheme is designed carefully.

The second strategy is just like matrix coding. First suppose the hiding unit *hunit* comprises n elements, there are also K mutual orthogonal sequences Q_i, where $Q_i = q_1 q_2 \cdots q_n$, $q_j \in \{1,-1\}, 1 \leq i \leq K, 1 \leq j \leq n$. Information bits $M = (m_1, m_2, \cdots)$, $m_i \in \{-1,1\}$. The general hiding and extracting are defined except the processing of overflow as following:

■ Hiding:

$$
hunit' = \begin{cases}
hunit + Q_j, & hunit \cdot Q_j^T >= \mid \alpha Q_j Q_j^T \mid \\
hunit + m_i \cdot \alpha \cdot Q_j, & \mid hunit \cdot Q_j^T \mid < \mid \alpha Q_j Q_j^T \mid \\
hunit - Q_j, & hunit \cdot Q_j^T \leq - \mid \alpha Q_j Q_j^T \mid
\end{cases} \tag{14.19}
$$

■ Extracting: According the hiding rule, the extracted bit m_i is:

$$
m_i = \frac{hunit \cdot Q_j^T}{\mid hunit \cdot Q_j^T \mid}, \text{only if} \mid hunit \cdot Q_j^T \mid < 2 \mid \alpha Q_j Q_j^T \mid \tag{14.20}
$$

■ Recovering: Actually, it can be easily extended into reversible hiding because it is similar to the histogram-shifting.

The third strategy is coset coding. Under the constrain of minimizing the distortion, the hiding chooses the most suitable hiding unit in the coset to replace the current data hiding unit.

We combine non-reversible and reversible hiding together to decrease the distortion. Actually, when we consider the distortion caused by non-reversible, we can decrease the distortion by reversible hiding. However, this complementation effect should be careful designed when combining non-reversible and reversible hiding algorithms.

Taking the hiding in the prediction mode of HEVC (High Efficiency Video Coding) as an example, we simple hide bits into these modes by modifying the mode according to bits. There are 34 modes in HEVC. Actually, this modification does not change the syntax and subsequent processing. In the practical implementation, the exact predication mode is very time-consuming so most of codec uses some heuristic rule to search the sub-optimal mode. In this meaning, the hiding in prediction modes is reasonable by changing the optimal mode to sub-optimal mode. Following Table shows the results for Traffic and Nebuta sequence. Actually if the same rule is used again, then the bit-rate does not double due to the effect of complement. Moreover, the quality is not affected by this hiding at the cost of increasing the bit-rate (Figure 14.9 and Table 14.1).

These complement hiding strategies can be used in many places. Especially in loss compression standards.

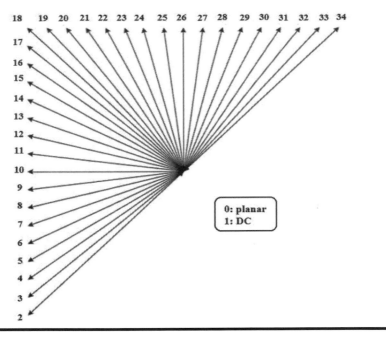

Figure 14.19 The 34 prediction mode in HEVC.

Table 14.1 The Bit-Rate of Hiding Bits in Prediction Mode

Sequence	Fast Mode Decision	Sub-optimal Mode Decision	Hiding Bits
Traffic	0.162%	0.852%	1.034%
Nebuta	0.024%	0.495%	0.863%

14.6 Security Discussions

The cover signals must be modified by hiding bits and hence they must be distorted except zero watermarking which just likes hash algorithms. Hence, the degree of distortion is critical for security. In data hiding, the steganalysis is usually used as the tool to evaluate the security of data hiding schemes [37–44]. However, there are no public test tools. Most steganalysis tools are used in some private places. From the research view of point, the closed systems are not tested utterly by steganalysis. However, there are some general criteria to design more secure hiding schemes after research and development of data hiding for many years.

First rule is to permute the cover signal or hiding units by key before hiding. For example, 2D Arnold Transform Mapping. Thus, the non-intent receiver does not know the key and does not extract the hidden bits. Of course, it looks like to permuting the information bits. However, there is a distinct difference that the permutation of cover signal affects the capacity of hiding.

Second rule is that the hiding should keep the statistical characteristic unchanged as much as possible. Most of modern steganalysis detects the existence of data hiding by analyzing the statistical characteristics [45]. Thus, most data hiding schemes by padding reserved fields with information bits are not secure in abnormal attributes detection. This rule is particularly important in hiding bits in compressed images, audios and videos because these formats have explicit characteristics, such as the distribution of predictive mode, transform coefficients, motion vectors.

Third rule is that the hiding should hide firstly bits into hiding units with less distortion and then hide bits into hiding units with more distortion. At this time, the total distortion caused by hiding will be less than ones caused by other hiding strategies. The small distortion means usually more secure.

These days, AI (artificial intelligence) is a hot research topic. It is worth thinking that how to develop data hiding in this era of AI. Most research of AI includes huge data and needs a cloud computing platform. Thus data hiding can be used to provide some privacy protection mechanism for data in cloud platform. Take deep learning as an example, there are many models which are obtained by many experts efforts in deep learning. It is very helpful for encourage technology innovation if inventors of each model can be traced by technical measures. Actually, data hiding provides the potential technical measures to verify, authenticated even protect these models.

Social service platforms have been popular. Many media files are exchanged and processed, the authentication of media files can be achieved by robust data hiding schemes. Thus designing robust data hiding scheme is a potential research topic.

Another potential direction is to design data hiding schemes for the latest new media standards, such as HEVC, JPEG-X, 3D video codec and so on.

14.7 Conclusions

This chapter introduces the data hiding in compressed image and video. First, it gives the JPEG compression standard and the basic hybrid coding framework of video coding standards, such as MPEG1, MPEG2, MPEG4, H.264 and HEVC and so on. Then it reviews the potential hiding space and methods in compression domain. Following it gives the basic reversible data hiding strategies in images and videos. It also gives the further research directions and potential applications.

References

1. F. A. P. Petitcolas, Anderson R. J., Kuhn M. G. Information hiding–A survey. *Proceedings of the IEEE* 87 (1999) 1062–1078.
2. H. Cheng, Li X. B. Partial encryption of compressed images and videos. *IEEE Transactions on Signal Processing* 48 (8) (2000) 2439–2451.
3. A. Z. Tirkel, Rankin G. A., Schyndel R. M. V. Electronic watermark. *Proceedings of International Conference Digital Image Computing, Technology and Applications* (1993) 666–672.
4. R. G. V. Schyndel, Tirkel A. Z. Osborne C. F. A digital watermark. *Proceedings of IEEE International Conference Image Processing* 2 (1994) 86–90.
5. R. G. V. Schyndel, Tirkel A. Z., Osborne C. F. A two dimensional watermark. *Proceedings International Conference Digital Image Computing, Technology and Applications* (1995) 378–383.
6. W. Bender, Gruhl D., Morimot N., Lu A. Techniques for data hiding. *IBM Systems Journal* 35 (3–4) (1996) 313–336.
7. N. Nikolaidis, Pitas I. Copyright protection of images using robust digital signatures. *Proceedings of IEEE International Conference on Acoustics Speech and Signal Processing* (1996) 2168–2717.
8. R. Z. Wang, Lin C. F., Lin J. C. Hiding data in images by optimal moderately-significant-bit replacement. *IEE Electronics Letters* 36 (25) (2000) 2069–2070.
9. C. K. Chan, Cheng L. M. Hiding data in images by simple LSB substitution. *Pattern Recognition* 37 (3) (2004) 469–474.
10. J. Mielikainen. LSB matching revisited. *IEEE Signal Processing Letters* 13 (5) (2006) 285–287.
11. R. Z. Wang, Lin C. F., Lin J. C. Image hiding by optimal LSB substitution and genetic algorithm. *Pattern Recognition* 34 (3) (2001) 671–683.
12. C. C. Chang, Hsiao J. Y., Chan C. S. Finding optimal least-significant-bit substitution in image hiding by dynamic programming strategy. *Pattern Recognition* 36 (7) (2003) 1583–1595.
13. C. K. Chan, Cheng L. M. Improved hiding data in images by optimal moderately-significant-bit replacement. *IEE Electronics Letters* 37 (16) (2001) 1017–1018.
14. C. C. Thien, Lin J. C. A simple and high-hiding capacity method for hiding digit-by-digit data in images based on modulus function. *Pattern Recognition* 36 (12) (2006) 2875–2881.
15. S. J. Wang. Steganography of capacity required using modulo operator for embedding secret image. *Applied Mathematics and Computation* 164 (1) (2006): 99–116.
16. C. C. Chang, Chan C. S., Fan Y. H. Image hiding scheme with modulus function and dynamic programming strategy on partitioned pixels. *Pattern Recognition* 39 (6) (2006) 1155–1167.
17. X. L. Li, Yang B., Cheng D. F., Zeng T. Y. A generalization of LSB matching. *IEEE Signal Processing Letters* 16 (2) (2009) 69–72.
18. S. Liu, Yao H., Zhang S., Gao W. A progressive quality hiding strategy based on equivalence partitions of hiding units. *LNCS Transaction on Data Hiding and Multimedia Security* 6 (2011) 58–82.
19. H. T. Hu, Hsu L. Y. Robust, transparent and high-capacity audio watermarking in DCT domain. *Signal Processing* 109 (2015) 226–235.

20. M. Ali, Ahn C. W., Pant M., Siarry P. An image watermarking scheme in wavelet domain with optimized compensation of singular value decomposition via artificial bee colony. *Information Sciences* 301 (2015) 44–60.

21. C. Li, Zhang Z., Wang Y., Ma B., Huang D. Dither modulation of significant amplitude difference for wavelet based robust watermarking. *Neurocomputing* 166 (2015) 404–415.

22. Z. Shao, Duan Y., Coatrieux G., Wu J., Meng J., Shu H. Combining double random phase encoding for color image watermarking in quaternion gyrator domain. *Optics Communications* 343 (2015) 56–65.

23. Y. X. Liu, Liu S. Y., Zhao H. G. et al. A data hiding method for H.265 without intra-frame distortion drift. *Intelligent Computing Methodologies* (2017) 642–650. Cham, Switzerland, Springer.

24. J. Wang, Wang R., Xu D., Li W. An information hiding algorithm for HEVC based on angle differences of intra prediction mode. *JSW* 10 (2) (2015) 213–221.

25. L. P. Van, De Praeter J., Van Wallendael G., De Cock J., Van de Walle R. Out-of-the-loop information hiding for HEVC video. *ICIP* (2015) 3610–3614.

26. S. D. Lin, Shie S.-C., Guo J. Y. Improving the robustness of DCT-based image watermarking against JPEG compression. *Computer Standards & Interfaces* 32 (2010) 54–60.

27. W. Liu, Zeng W., Dong L., Yao Q. Efficient compression of encrypted grayscale images. *IEEE Transactions on Image Processing* 19 (4) (2010) 1097–1102.

28. X. G. Kang, Xu, X. Y., Peng A. J., Zeng W. J. Scalable lossy compression for pixel-value encrypted images. *IEEE Data Compression Conference 2012* Snowbird, Utah (2012).

29. X. G. Kang, Peng A. J., Xu X. Y., Cao X. C. Performing scalable lossy compression on pixel encrypted images. *EURASIP Journal on Image and Video Processing* 32 (2013) 1–6.

30. G. C. Zhang, Liu S. H., Jiang F., Zhao D. B., Gao W. An improved image compression scheme with an adaptive parameters set in encrypted domain. *Visual Communications and Image Processing* (2013) 1–6.

31. Q. Su, Niu Y., Zhao Y., Pang S., Liu X. A dual color images watermarking scheme based on the optimized compensation of singular value decomposition. *AEU-International Journal of Electronics and Communications* 67 (2013) 652–664.

32. S. A. Parah, Sheikh J. A., Hafiz A. M., Bhat G. M. Data hiding in scrambled images: A new double layer security data hiding technique. *Computers & Electrical Engineering* 40 (2014) 70–82.

33. S. Liu, Paul A., Zhang G., Jeon G. A game theory-based block image compression method in encryption domain. *Journal of Supercomputing* (2015). doi:10.1007/s11227-015-1413-0.

34. S. Liu, Rho S., Jifara W., Jiang F., Liu C. A hybrid framework of data hiding and encryption in H.264/SVC. *Discrete Applied Mathematics* (2016). doi:10.1016/j.dam.2016.06.028.

35. A. M. Alattar. Reversible watermark using the difference expansion of a generalized integer transform. *IEEE Transactions on Image Processing* 13 (2014) 1147–1156.

36. F. Huang, Qu X., Kim H. J., Huang J. Reversible data hiding in JPEG images. *IEEE Transactions on Circuits and Systems for Video Technology* 26 (9) (2016) 1610–1621.

37. Y. Zhang, Liu F. L., Yang C. F. et al. Steganalysis of content-adaptive JPEG steganography based on Gauss partial derivative filter bank. *Journal of Electronic Imaging* 26 (1) (2017) 013011.

38. J. Gan, Liu J., Luo X., Yang C., Liu F. Reliable steganalysis of HUGO steganography based on partially known plaintext. *Multimedia Tools and Applications* (2017) 1–21. doi:10.1007/s11042-017-5134-7.

39. K. Tasdemir, Kurugollu F., Sezer S. Spatio-temporal rich model based video steganalysis on cross sections of motion vector planes. *IEEE Transactions on Image Processing* 25 (7) (2016) 3316–3328.

40. P. Wang, Cao Y., Zhao X. et al. A steganalytic algorithm to detect DCT-based data hiding methods for H.264/AVC videos. *ACM Workshop on Information Hiding and Multimedia Security* (2017) 123–133.

41. Y. Cao, Zhao X., Feng D. Video steganalysis exploiting motion vector reversion-based features. *IEEE Signal Processing Letters* 19 (1) (2012) 35–38.

42. Y. Ren, Zhai L., Wang L. et al. Video steganalysis based on subtractive probability of optimal matching feature. *ACM Workshop on Information Hiding and Multimedia Security* (2014) 83–90.

43. K. Wang, Zhao H., Wang H. Video steganalysis against motion vector-based steganography by adding or subtracting one motion vector value. *IEEE Transactions on Information Forensics Security* 9 (5) (2014) 741–751.

44. Y. Zhao, Zhang H., Cao Y. et al. Video steganalysis based on intra prediction mode calibration. *International Workshop on Digital-forensics and Watermarking* (*IWDW*) (2015).

45. X. F. Song, Liu F. L., Yang C. F. et al. Steganalysis of adaptive JPEG steganography using 2D gabor filters. *Proceedings of ACM Workshop on Information Hiding and Multimedia Security* (2015) 15–23.

Chapter 15

Robust Image Watermarking Based on Multiple-Criteria Decision-Making

Musab Ghadi, Lamri Laouamer, Laurent Nana
and Anca Pascu

Contents

DOI: 10.1201/9780429435461-17

15.1 Introduction

With the advancement of computerized businesses and network technologies a huge amount of digital data (like images, audios, videos) are transmitted via public networks. This rapid development of the digital technology makes it easy to access, distribute and share digital data between users. Images are among the most common data shared between users. Providing security for these images and their content is an essential need. Many systems and applications require transmission of digital images in secure way. As example, we can cite biometric, telemedicine, copyright protection and remote sensing image systems.

Confidentiality, availability, and reliability are the three main conditions required to achieve image security. The confidentiality involves that only authorized users can access image data. The availability involves access to image data in normal scheduled conditions of access. The reliability involves two requirements: integrity verification and content authentication. The integrity involves proof that the image data has not been altered or modified by non-authorized users. The authentication involves proof of the image origins and its attachments to one generator [1].

Watermarking has been used efficiently to verify the reliability of images by asserting their authenticity. It involves hiding a watermark w in the original image I (the result is the image denoted Iw) such that an attacker cannot remove, modify, or replace the watermark w in Iw. Watermarking can be achieved in the spatial domain by modifying or modulating the spatial pixels of the original image with the watermark pixels. It can also be achieved in the frequency domain by modifying or modulating the coefficients of the frequency representation of the original image with those of the watermark [2].

Any watermarking model needs to provide strong security against removal or modification of the watermark w. Indeed, during their transfer, watermarked images may be subject to different attacks aiming to alter the watermark. The watermarking system should ensure that, even in case of attack, the watermark w extracted from the watermarked image will be identical or close to its original form as much as possible. As well, watermarking systems aim to preserve high visual watermarked image (high watermark imperceptibility), less storage space and a high watermark embedding rate [3]. Generally, watermarking systems based on spatial domain such as Least Significant Bit (LSB) achieve less robustness with low memory usage and high embedding rate, while watermarking systems based on frequency domain such as Discrete Cosine Transform (DCT) or Discrete Wavelet Transform (DWT) achieve high imperceptibility and high robustness, but with high memory usage and low embedding rate [1,3,4].

Designing an efficient watermarking system in terms of high imperceptibility and high robustness, less memory usage, and a high embedding rate can be achieved by analyzing the spatial image features. Texture property, color representations, brightness/darkness, and the boundary of gray-scale image pixels are a set of image characteristics that can provide efficient solutions to achieve images authentication [5–9]. All of these characteristics, which have significant correlation with Human Visual System (HVS), are intangible and uncertain because there is no precise meaning or real standard of these characteristics [10].

The texture feature quantifies the perceived texture of the host image by calculating a set of metrics in image processing. Image texture is a spatial property. It gives information about the spatial arrangement of intensities or color in overall image or selected regions of an image.

Texture can be defined as an entity consisting of mutually related pixels and group of pixels. Texture property has many different dimensions and there is no standard method for the texture representation that is adequate for all of its dimensions. Analyzing image texture helps for objects detection, image segmentation, image classification and also for image security. Two main approaches are used for analyzing image texture: structural approach and statistical approach [11].

For the design of watermarking systems, the principles of HVS confirm that embedding watermarks in strongly textured locations leads to high imperceptibility and robustness. Indeed, modifications in highly textured blocks in host images due to embedding of the watermark are less sensitive to the human eye [5].

The color feature deals with the degree of sensitivity of each color space of the host image to the human eyes. Many studies in the literature confirmed that analyzing RGB image in means of HVS requires to convert it into another color space such YCbCr, which contains the luminance (Y component), the chrominance blue (Cb) and chrominance red (Cr). The luminance is very close to the gray scale of the original RGB image. It expresses the most information in the image. The chrominance refers to the color components and they express the details of the host image. In means of HVS characteristics, the human eyes are more sensitive to the luminance component and are less sensitive to the Cb component [6]. For designing a watermarking system, hiding a watermark in Cb component will be more appropriate in terms of imperceptibility and robustness, since the human eye will not be able to easily detect the modification or change in the embedded image. But the difficulty is deciding the amount of bits that can be embedded in the Cb component without extreme deficiency in perceptual quality and robustness of watermarked image.

The brightness/darkness is a relative property of the host image that depends on the visual perception of the user. It expresses the amount of energy output by a source of light and it can be measured by calculating the mean intensity of pixels (higher intensity expresses higher brightness) [12]. For the design of a watermarking system, hiding a watermark in high brightness or darkness regions of a host image will be more appropriate in terms of imperceptibility and robustness, since the human eye will not be able to easily detect the modification or change in the embedded image.

The gray-scale ambiguity problem is related to the varying of gray-scale values of neighboring pixels in the host image. This variation in pixel values of neighbored regions has imperfect perceptibility due to the deficiency of contrast. Then, it make it hard to exactly bound the gray scale values of a given image [8]. In terms of HVS, the uncertainty and vague gray-scale values may adversely affect the image's contrast, then it may weaken the perceptual quality of the image. Therefore, embedding a watermark in vague and uncertain gray-scale values could lead to bad perceptual quality of the image.

The degrees of randomness or regularity of gray-scale intensities have to be measured and compared to characterize the texture, color representations, brightness/darkness, and varying of gray-scale values. Many processing techniques like computational intelligence and knowledge discovery techniques are applied to analyze these characteristics [6–9]. The associations between the deduced image's characteristics and the techniques mentioned provide efficient solutions for objects detection, image classification, segmentation, and image authentication.

The computational intelligence techniques (like genetic algorithm, artificial neural network, rough sets and Multi-Criteria Decision Making (MCDM)) and the knowledge discovery approaches (i.e. image classification/clustering, image mining and frequent pattern) are used to solve the imprecision of the image's characteristics and exploit them to achieve image authentication through the identification of interesting locations for embedding the watermark.

This chapter presents how the texture problem can be analyzed using one of the MCDM methods in order to identify highly textured blocks within a host image to hold the watermark with high imperceptibility, high robustness and low memory usage. The problem of identification of textured regions in an image can be considered as a decision-making problem where a set of partitioned blocks of the host image is a set of possible alternatives to be evaluated using a set of criteria (texture features) to select which of them are more appropriate to hold the watermark. The first order histogram features can be used as set of criteria to achieve the evaluation process. Hence, a decision matrix can be built and Technique for Order of Preference by Similarity to Ideal Solution (TOPSIS) can be applied to rank all alternatives and select the best alternative for embedding watermark.

This chapter is organized as follows. Background related to the principles of texture analysis and decision-making theory is presented in Section 15.2. Intelligent systems based image watermarking is then presented in Section 15.3. Section 15.4 introduces TOPSIS based watermarking approaches with the experiment results and the comparative study. The chapter ends with the conclusion and open issues in Section 15.5.

15.2 Background and Principles

15.2.1 Texture Analysis of Digital Images

The texture of digital images can be defined through four statistical features that are related to the HVS. These features are Direct Current (DC), skewness, kurtosis, and entropy. Analyzing these features helps to identify the most suitable locations within host images for inserting watermarks with high imperceptibility and high robustness against different attacks. The analysis of these features is discussed below.

1. **DC coefficient**. The result of transforming spatial pixels of image's block sized 8 × 8 into frequency domain by applying 2D-DCT is a matrix sized 8 × 8. The first element is the DC coefficient and the rest are 63 AC coefficients. The DC coefficient expresses the average energy and the mean brightness of the processed block. In the case of texture analysis, a high DC coefficient block is more textured than a low DC coefficient block [13]. Furthermore, embedding a watermark in a high DC coefficient block means embedding weak pixels under a strong background. This means that any change in the high DC coefficient block will be more imperceptible and will be more robust against different attacks [13]. The DC coefficient of a given block of size *NN* is directly obtained in spatial domain without need to 2D-DCT process. The DC coefficient is calculated using Equation 15.1.

$$DC = \frac{1}{\sqrt{N \times N}} \sum_{x=1}^{N-1} \sum_{y=1}^{N-1} f(x, y) \tag{15.1}$$

where a partitioned block is represented as a function *f*(*x, y*) of two space variables *x* and *y* (*x* = *0,1,...,N–1; y* = *0,1,...,N–1*).

2. **Skewness**. It characterizes the degree of asymmetry of distribution of gray-level intensities around the mean [14]. In the case of texture analysis, the skewness describes three cases. (a) The symmetrical distribution, where the processed image is neither dense toward black nor toward white. The mean value of the gray-level intensities is equal to the median and then the skewness value is zero. (b) The negative distribution, where the histogram distribution of the processed image is dense toward the high gray-level intensities (dense toward the white). In this case, the median is greater than the mean and the value of skewness is usually negative. (c) The positive distribution, where the histogram distribution of the processed image is dense toward the low gray-level intensities (dense toward the black). In this case, the median is less than the mean and the value of skewness is usually positive. Based on these cases, highly negative or positive distribution expresses much information in the processed image and its textured nature. While, the symmetrical distribution expresses untextured nature.

The skewness feature of a given block in size $N \times N$ is obtained by computing the intensity-level of all pixels in that block $h(i)$ ($i = 0,1,...,255$) and computing the density of occurrence of the intensity levels $P(i)$ ($i = 0,1,...,255$). The skewness value is calculated using Equation 15.2.

$$skewness = \sigma^{-3} \sum_{i=0}^{255} (i - \mu)^3 \times P(i) \tag{15.2}$$

where $P(i) = h(i)/(N \times N)$, $\mu = \sum_{i=0}^{255} i \times P(i)$ is the mean value of block pixels, and $\sigma = \sqrt{\sum_{i=0}^{255} (i - \mu)^2 P(i)}$ is the square root of the variance.

3. **Kurtosis**. It measures the flatness of the gray-level intensities around the mean [14]. In the case of texture analysis, the kurtosis value of the processed image expresses the amount of image's information through two cases: (a) If the distribution of gray-level intensities around the mean is peaky, this means that the surface of the processed image follows the dense gray-scale value, and then the information content would be significantly low. (b) If the distribution of the gray-level intensities around the mean is flat, this shows that the surface of the processed block has much information and is textured [14]. The kurtosis feature of a given block of size $N \times N$ is obtained using Equation 15.3.

$$kurtosis = \sigma^{-4} \sum_{i=0}^{255} (i - \mu)^4 \times P(i) - 3 \tag{15.3}$$

4. **Entropy**. It expresses the uniformity of the distribution of the gray-level intensities along the processed block. In the case of texture analysis, the entropy value is used as a good indicator to the magnitude of the processed block's information. If the gray-level intensities of the processed block are distributed randomly, this means that the block combines dispersant pixels' values and the entropy value is high. In contrary, if the gray-level intensities of the processed block are distributed uniformly, this means that the block combines harmonious (similar) pixels' values and the entropy value is low. In the context of texture analysis, high entropy's block has much information than low entropy's block and is more textured. Furthermore, based on the principles of HVS, embedding watermarks in high entropy blocks is more suitable than embedding in low entropy blocks, since any change in a high entropy block will be less sensitive to the human eyes and then it will be more robust against different attacks [14]. The entropy feature of a given block of size $N \times N$ is obtained using Equation 15.4.

$$entropy = -\sum_{i=0}^{255} P(i)\log_2[P(i)] \tag{15.4}$$

15.2.2 Decision-Making Theory

This section presents a general overview of MCDM problems and the main steps for solving such types of problems using various MCDM methods. This section also provides a brief description of some MCDM methods.

15.2.2.1 General Overview of Decision-Making Problems

Decision-making is the study of solving the problems that are characterized as a choice among many alternatives to find the best one based on different criteria and decision-maker's preferences. The importance of this study comes due to the difficulty to deal with traditional paradigm for analyzing decision making which is based on uni-dimensional and only one criterion to make a decision. Many problems in our life involve multiple objectives and criteria. These problems are related to the fields of engineering, industry, commercial, and human resource management.

MCDM is a branch of Operational Research (OR) field whose aim is to provide solutions for many complex decision-making problems. Some of these problems are related to high imprecise/uncertainty information and conflicting objectives. MCDM is divided into two categories: Multi-Objective Decision Making (MODM) and Multi-Attribute Decision Making (MADM). MODM relates to an infinite or numerous number of alternatives. It assumes a simultaneous evaluation with regard to a set of objectives that are optimized to a set of criteria in order to find the best alternative. In contrast, MADM is based on evaluation of a relative predetermined number of alternatives characterized by criteria; the evaluation process searches for how well the alternatives satisfy the objectives. Weighting the importance of selected criteria and assigning preference for alternatives are taken into account in MADM [15]. In this chapter MCDM methods refer to MADM category.

15.2.2.2 General Steps of MCDM Methods

There are many MCDM methods proposed in the literature to solve problems that are characterized as a choice among alternatives. All of these methods implement the same steps to solve the decision-making problem [15]. These main steps of any MCDM method are illustrated in the following:

Step 1: Defining the problem, the alternatives and the criteria.

This step involves the analysis of the decision-making problem to define the multiple conflicting criteria, different measurement among the criteria and the possible alternatives.

Step 2: Assigning criteria weights.

Most of MCDM methods require that attributes be assigned weights of importance. Usually, these weights are normalized so that their sum is one. This step manages the priorities of the criteria by assigning them proper weights. These weights show the relative importance of the selected criteria. The weights of the different criteria may be assigned by mutual consultation, pair wise comparison between criteria or by establishing a hierarchy of priorities using the Analytic Hierarchy Process (AHP).

Several equations are used to normalize the values. Some often used equations are presented in 15.5 through 15.7.

$$r_{ij} = \frac{x_{ij}}{\sqrt{\sum_{i=1,j=1}^{m,n} x_{ij}^2}}, i = 1,...,m; j = 1,...,n \tag{15.5}$$

$$r_{ij} = \frac{x_{ij} - min_j}{max_j - min_j}, i = 1,...,m; j = 1,...,n \tag{15.6}$$

$$r_{ij} = \frac{x_{ij}}{max_j}, i = 1,...,m; j = 1,...,n \tag{15.7}$$

where m is the number of alternatives, n is the number of criteria and x_{ij} is the score of alternative A_i when it is evaluated in terms of decision criterion C_j.

Step 3: Construction of the evaluation matrix.

An MCDM problem can be expressed in a matrix format. A decision matrix A is an $(m \times n)$ matrix in which the element x_{ij} indicates the score of alternative A_i when it is evaluated in terms of decision criterion C_j, $i = 1,2,...,m$ and $j = 1,2,...,n$.

It is also assumed that the decision maker has determined the weights of relative performance of the decision criteria (denoted as W_j, for $j = 1,2,...,n$). This information is summarized in the following matrix.

$$
A = \begin{array}{c} \\ A_1 \\ A_2 \\ \vdots \\ A_m \end{array}
\begin{array}{cccc} C_1 & C_2 & \cdots & C_n \end{array}
\begin{bmatrix}
x_{11} & x_{12} & \cdots & x_{1n} \\
x_{21} & x_{22} & \cdots & x_{2n} \\
\vdots & \vdots & \ddots & \vdots \\
x_{m1} & x_{12} & \cdots & x_{mn}
\end{bmatrix}
$$

Criteria

Step 4: Selecting the appropriate method.

In this step, the decision maker is responsible to select a proper MCDM method for selecting the preferred alternative. Based on the matrix illustrated in step 3, the MCDM method is used to determine the suitable alternative A^* with the highest degree of desirability with respect to all relevant criteria.

Step 5: Ranking the alternatives.

In the final step, the set of alternatives are ranked and the first ranked alternative with the highest value based on user's preferences is selected as an optimal solution.

15.2.2.3 General Description of Some MCDM Methods

Different methods are proposed in the literature to solve the problem of multicriteria decision making. This section provides an abstract description for some of these methods.

15.2.2.3.1 Weighted Sum Method (WSM)

WSM is a simple and most widely used MCDM. Basically, the WSM method starts by converting the intangible values into comparable values and then obtains the normalized decision matrix R $(r_{ij}, i = 1,...,m$ and $j = 1,...,n)$ according to Equations 15.8 and 15.9. Equation 15.8 is used if the jth criterion is a benefit criterion and Equation 15.9 is used if the jth criterion is a non-benefit criterion.

$$r_{ij} = x_{ij}/r_j^* \qquad (15.8)$$

$$r_{ij} = r_j^-/x_{ij} \qquad (15.9)$$

where x_{ij} is the score of alternative i with respect to criterion j, r_j is the maximum value of r in column j and r_j^- is the minimum value of r in column j.

Afterward, the WSM method uses the additive aggregation of the criteria according to Equation 15.10 to calculate the score for each alternative.

$$A_i = \sum_{j=1}^{n} r_{ij} \times w_j \qquad (15.10)$$

where w_j is the criterion weight.

Based on the final scores, decision maker can rank all alternatives to select the best one, which has the maximum score value. Equation 15.11 presents the calculus of the best alternative A^*.

$$A^* = max(A_i) : i = 1, 2,..., m \qquad (15.11)$$

15.2.2.3.2 Weighted Product Method (WPM)

This method is similar to WSM, but instead of addition the main mathematical operation is the product. Each alternative is compared with other alternatives by multiplying a number of ratios for each criterion. Each ratio is raised to the power of the relative weight of the corresponding criterion. Equation 15.12 is used to compare two alternatives (A_p and A_q).

$$R(A_p/A_q) = \Pi_{j=1}^{n}(x_{pj}/x_{qj})^{w_j} \qquad (15.12)$$

where n is the number of criteria, w_j is the weight of the jth criteria, x_{pj} is the actual value of the pth alternative in terms of the jth criterion, and x_{qj} is the actual value of the qth alternative in terms of the jth criterion.

If the resulted ratio of $R(A_p/A_q)$ is greater than or equal to one, this indicates that the alternative A_p is more desirable than alternative A_q. The alternative which is more desirable than all other alternatives is the best one.

15.2.2.3.3 Analytic Hierarchy Process (AHP)

AHP is another MCDM method designed to solve complex problems involving multi-criteria. The advantage of AHP is that it is designed to handle situations in which the subjective judgments of individuals constitute an important part of the decision process. Initially, the AHP method starts by developing an hierarchy representation of the problem in terms of the overall goal, the decision criteria and the alternatives. Then, the relative weight for each decision criterion is specified in terms of its contribution to the achievement of the overall goal. The pairwise comparisons are used in AHP methods to rate the relative preferences for two criteria and then to assign proper weight for each criterion. Subsequently, the relative priorities of alternatives are determined, where both qualitative and quantitative information can be compared by using informed judgments to derive weights and priorities. The output of the AHP is a prioritized ranking indicating the overall preference for each of the decision alternatives.

15.2.2.3.4 Technique for Order of Preference by Similarity to Ideal Solution (TOPSIS)

The TOPSIS method is a simple ranking method for solving the problems of large number of discrete alternatives [16]. It has the ability to allocate the scores to each alternative based on its geometric distance from the positive and negative ideal solutions. The closest alternative (the shortest geometric distance) to the positive ideal solution and the farthest (the longest geometric distance) to the negative ideal alternative is the best alternative among all alternatives. TOPSIS method assumes that we have m alternatives and n attributes/criteria, as well as the score of each alternative with respect to each criterion. Let x_{ij} the score of alternative i with respect to criterion j and $X = (x_{ij})_{(m \times n)}$ the decision matrix. The TOPSIS method uses the following steps to find best alternative:

Step 1: Constructing the normalized decision matrix

This step transforms various dimensional attributes into non-dimensional attributes to allow comparisons across criteria. Different normalization methods are proposed in the litterature to transform decision matrix $X = (x_{ij})_{(m \times n)}$ into a normalized matrix $R = (r_{ij})_{(m \times n)}$, where each attribute value in decision matrix is transformed into a value between [0–1] according to one of Equations 15.5 through 15.7.

Step 2: Constructing the weighted normalized decision matrix

The TOPSIS method assumes a weight value w_j for each criterion j, where $\sum_{j=1}^{n} w_j = 1$. Then, each column of the normalized decision matrix R is multiplied by its associated weight w_j. This step results in a new matrix V, where each element r_{ij} in matrix R is transformed using Equation 15.13.

$$V_{ij} = w_j \times r_{ij}, i = 1,...,m; j = 1,...,n \tag{15.13}$$

Step 3: Determining the positive ideal and negative ideal solutions

In this step, two artificial alternatives A^+ (the positive ideal alternative) and A^- (the negative ideal alternative) are defined. The choice of positive ideal solution is presented in Equation 15.14 and the choice of negative ideal solution is presented in Equation 15.15.

$$
\begin{aligned}
A^+ &= \{v_1^+,...,v_n^+\}, \\
v_j^+ &= \{(max(v_{ij}) if \ j \in J),(min(v_{ij}) if \ j \in J^-), \\
&(i = 1,...,m; j = 1,...,n)\}
\end{aligned}
\tag{15.14}
$$

$$
\begin{aligned}
A^- &= \{v_1^-,...,v_n^-\}, \\
v_j^- &= \{(min(v_{ij}) if \ j \in J),(max(v_{ij}) if \ j \in J^-), \\
&(i = 1,...,m; j = 1,...,n)\}
\end{aligned}
\tag{15.15}
$$

where J is associated with benefit attribute, which offers an increasing utility with its higher values, and J^- associated with cost criteria.

Step 4: Calculating the separation measures for each alternative

In this step, the separation measurement relative to the positive ideal alternative is performed by calculating the distance between each alternative in V and the positive ideal alternative A^+ using Euclidean distance as illustrated in Equation 15.16.

$$S_i^+ = \sqrt{\sum_{j=1}^{n}(v_j^+ - v_{ij})^2}, i = 1,...,m; j = 1,...,n \qquad (15.16)$$

Similarly, the separation measurement relative to the negative ideal alternative is performed by calculating the distance between each alternative in V and the negative ideal alternative A^- using Euclidean distance as illustrated in Equation 15.17.

$$S_i^- = \sqrt{\sum_{j=1}^{n}(v_j^- - v_{ij})^2}, i = 1,...,m; j = 1,...,n \qquad (15.17)$$

Step 5: Calculating the relative closeness to the ideal solution C_i^+

In this step, the closeness of A_i to the positive ideal solution A^+ is calculated using Equation 15.18.

$$C_i^+ = \frac{S_i^-}{S_i^+ + S_i^-}, i = 1,...,m; 0 < C_i^+ < 1 \qquad (15.18)$$

In this case, $C_i^+ = 1$ if $V_i = A^+$ and $C_i^+ = 0$ if $V_i = A^-$. Afterward, a set of alternatives can be ranked in preference order according to the descending order of C_i^+. Then, the alternative with C_i^+ closest to 1 indicates the best alternative with highest performance.

15.3 Intelligent Systems Based Image Watermarking

Decision making for multimedia data watermarking is another multi-criteria problem. Many perspectives in using MCDM in the field of multimedia data watermarking require to consider it as subject of interest for the interested researchers.

For the purpose of comparative study between the proposed image watermarking model based on MCDM method and other intelligent systems based image watermarking, this section presents some of these systems.

The authors of [6] proposed a semi-blind image watermarking approach that combined frequent pattern mining and digital watermarking to provide a significant contribution in images authentication. The proposed approach is based on extracting the maximal frequent pattern among all frequent patterns of the host image. The frequent patterns are defined through features including DC, skewness, kurtosis and entropy, which are used to discriminate between the robust blocks and the fragile blocks. Initially, the host image is partitioned into 8×8 blocks, then all of these blocks are represented in a transaction database, where each block is represented as one transaction. The transaction database combines the features values for each block. After that, the transactions database is transformed into a Boolean database based on some thresholds. Once the Boolean database is constructed, the Apriori algorithm is applied to extract the maximal patterns. The maximal pattern among all patterns has a certain user-defined minimum support, and it is used to define the most robust blocks for secret data embedding. The experiments results showed that the perceptual quality of watermarked image in terms of Peak Signal-to-Noise Ratio (PSNR) reached 43.5 dB and the Bit Error Rate (BER) of embedded watermark due to different attacks did not exceed 20%.

In [7] the authors proposed a semi-blind image watermarking approach based on Formal Concept Analysis (FCA) method. The FCA is another data analysis method used to examine the relationships between different features with the HVS. FCA manipulates the features and the image blocks to find the set of all the blocks that share a common subset of features and the set of all features that are shared by one of the blocks. The result of this manipulation is a set of formal concepts, each consists of an extent (a set of blocks) and an intent (a set of features). The constructed formal concepts give an indication about the set of blocks that satisfy the maximum number of features. These blocks are considered as the strongly visual significant blocks and are used for embedding watermarks with least noticeable quality distortion of the host image and maximum robustness against different attacks. The imperceptibility in terms of PSNR reached 45.5 dB, while the BER did not exceed 11%.

The authors of [8] used the HVS characteristics and rough set theory to design a semi-blind image watermarking system in the frequency domain. The rough set theory is applied to solve two intangible problems that are related to the HVS in terms of perceptual quality of watermarked image and robustness of embedded watermark. These problems are the ambiguity of varying gray-scale values of neighboring pixels in host images and the statistical redundancy in conventional DWT. The rough set technique approximates the coefficients of one sub-band of DWT into upper and lower sets, then the selected sub-band of DWT is represented as a reference image. The singular value of a watermark is embedded in the singular value of a reference image. The imperceptibility of the watermarked image in terms of PSNR reached 52.7 dB and the BER of the embedded watermark due to different attacks did not exceed 13%.

In [17] the authors based on genetic algorithm proposed a new image watermarking model. The textured blocks within the host image are identified with means to the HVS for embedding watermarks. The singular values of each of the processed image's blocks are utilized to find the activity factor using a weight parameter α. The high activity factor blocks which involve a good visual masking effect are selected for embedding the watermark. The embedding process is carried out in the DC coefficients and the embedding intensity parameter β is considered to control the degree of image quality. The genetic algorithm is applied in this model to optimize the α and β parameters, which reflect both the robustness and the perceptual quality of the watermarked image. A fitness function of genetic algorithm considers the resulted imperceptibility and robustness ratios against different attacks to find approximately the optimal value of α and β. The quality of the watermarked image under different capacity thresholds ranged 31–46 dB in average and the similarity between the original watermark and the extracted watermark ranged 83%–93%.

In [18] the authors built a blind image watermarking approach based on the inter-block prediction and visibility thresholds in discrete cosine transform (DCT) based on Back Propagation Artificial Neural Network (BPANN). The BPANN is applied to draw a connection between the DCT coefficients of adjacent blocks, where increasing the value of one DCT coefficient according to the other could improve the imperceptibility and robustness rates. The inequality relationship between the real and the predicted values is exploited to insert the watermark bit with least visual distortion and maximum robustness. The minimum perceptual threshold (Just-Noticeable Difference [JND]), minimum clearance and adequate offset are set of parameters used to preserve the limit distortion and to decide the embedding strength. The imperceptibility in terms of the PSNR reached 40 dB, while the BER ranged 15%–43%.

In [19] the authors proposed a blind image watermarking approach using the Artificial Bee Colony (ABC) technique. The correlation between DCT coefficients of adjacent blocks is exploited to define the visual significant locations in the host image for embedding watermarks with maximum robustness and less image quality distortion. Indeed, the difference value between the coefficients of adjacent blocks defines the texture property of host image blocks. The ABC technique is used as a meta-heuristic optimization method for optimizing the watermark embedding process. The goal of this optimization is to achieve the maximum level of robustness and a lower level of noticeable image distortion. A new fitness function is proposed to optimize the embedding parameters in order to provide required convergence for the optimum values of robustness and imperceptibility. The imperceptibility ratio ranged 39.7–46.7 dB, while the BER ranged between 1%–50%.

The authors of [20] proposed a blind image watermarking approach based on Fuzzy Inference System (FIS). The FIS is used to calculate the orthogonal moments of the host image and to calculate the quantization factor for each moment. The orthogonal moments of the spatial pixels represent the fine information of the host image that is correlated to HVS. The generated quantization factors of orthogonal moments are used to control the embedding strength of the watermark. The genetic algorithm optimized these factors to find the maximum amount of watermark bits that can be added to the image without causing noticeable visual distortion. The imperceptibility ratio reached 40 dB, while the BER ranged between 19%–35%.

In [21] the authors proposed a blind image watermarking approach based on FIS and BPANN algorithm. The FIS and BPANN algorithm are integrated in this approach to optimize the intensity factor (α), which is used to balance between the robustness and the imperceptibility rates. By manipulating the texture and brightness characteristics of DCT coefficents, the FIS constructed a basis for selecting the high textured and high luminance blocks in the host image for holding watermark. While, the BPANN optimized weight factor of embedding process to improve the robustness and imperceptibility ratios. The DCT coefficients of the selected blocks are used as a training data for centroid method based BPANN to find the optimum weight factor for the embedding process. Using centroid method based BPANN enhanced the robustness and imperceptibility ratios. The imperceptibility ratio reached 47 dB, while the Normalized Correlation (NC) between the original watermark and the extracted watermark ranged 73%–100%.

15.4 Image Watermarking Based on TOPSIS Method

Texture property is one of the important spatial characteristics of a host image that has high significant relations with HVS. Analyzing this property can help to identify highly textured blocks within host images to hold the watermark with high imperceptibility, high robustness and low memory usage. The various features that are often used to analyze the texture property are intangible and uncertain because there is no formal, mathematical definition of texture and there is no precise level for each feature to distinguish between textured and untextured blocks within a host image. Hence, MCDM methods can help for decision making for image watermarking through solving this uncertainty problem and identifying highly textured blocks.

Deciding whether partitioned blocks of an image are textured or not can be presented as a decision-making problem where the set of partitioned blocks are considered as the set of possible alternatives that need to be evaluated using texture features as the set of criteria. A decision matrix is built and the TOPSIS method is applied to rank all possible alternatives based on the closeness to the ideal solution (the highest texture). A percentage of alternatives having the highest closeness values (including the best one) is selected for watermark embedding.

In this section, two robust image watermarking approaches based on the TOPSIS method are presented. The first approach [22] is a semi-blind image watermarking and the second one [23] is a blind image watermarking. These approaches use four features/criteria (skewness, kurtosis, entropy, and DC coefficient) to analyze the texture nature of each partitioned block (alternatives) of the host image. Then, the TOPSIS method is used to rank all partitioned blocks based on their texture magnitude. Afterward, the proposed approaches select 10% of highly textured blocks to embed the watermark. This procedure enhances the ability to prove the origins of the host image even with geometric attacks (like cropping, rotation, affine transformation, and translation).

The two approaches share the texture analysis phase, but they differ in the implementation of embedding and extraction procedures. The texture analysis of an image is based mainly on the TOPSIS method to identify the highly textured blocks, which are more appropriate for embedding watermarks. The texture analysis phase is presented in the next subsection. It is followed by the presentation of the proposed embedding and extraction procedures.

The pseudo-code of the proposed TOPSIS method based image watermarking is presented in algorithm (1).

Algorithm 1 *The pseudo-code of the proposed model*

1. **preliminary**: defining the set $k = \{k_1,\ldots,k_n\}$ as texture features (the criteria) and defining the weight vector WV
2. **input**: host image I sized $M \times M$ (assuming M is multiple of 64) and watermark image w sized $L \times L$
3. partitioning I into $L \times L$ blocks, results by m blocks, $m = M/L \times M/L$
4. **for** each feature k_j, $j = 1,\ldots,n$ **do**
5.   **for** each block (b_i), $i = 1,\ldots,m$ **do**
6.   define x_{ij} score of alternative b_i with respect to criterion k_j
7.   **end for**
8. **end for**
9. constructing the decision matrix $X = (x_{ij})_{m \times n}$
10. applying the TOPSIS method to rank all blocks based on closeness value (texture amount)
11. selecting top 10% of highest ranked blocks as preferable to hold the watermark
12. embedding watermark (I, w)
13. extracting watermark (I_{wa}, w)

15.4.1 Texture Analysis Using TOPSIS Method

In aims to solve the problem of detecting highly textured locations in a host image, the TOPSIS method can be applied to evaluate all possible alternatives based on defined criteria and to rank them based on the closeness to ideal solution. This approach also provides a practical way to measure the importance and the effect of each of the used features on the results of texture analysis by using diverse weight vectors. The texture analysis using the TOPSIS method uses the following steps.

Step 1: Initially, the host image of size $M \times M$ is partitioned into a set of non-overlapping $L \times L$ blocks (alternatives) based on the size of watermark. The host image must be in gray scale and its bit depth equals 8 (all pixels are ranged from 0 to 255).

Step 2: The texture features including DC, skewness, kurtosis and entropy are calculated for each partitioned block using Equations 15.1 through 15.4.

Step 3: Building the decision matrix X, where the blocks $\left(b_1,\ldots,b_{(M/L \times M/L)}\right)$ of the host image represent the set of alternatives and the texture features

(DC, skewness, kurtosis and entropy) represent the set of attributes (criteria). The entries of this matrix are the numerical values of intangible attributes of all alternatives. An example of a decision matrix is illustrated as follows.

$$
X = \begin{array}{c} \text{alternatives/criteria} \\ b_1 \\ b_2 \\ \vdots \\ bM/64 \times M/64 \end{array}
\begin{array}{cccc} DC & skewness & kurtosis & entropy \end{array}
\begin{bmatrix} 271.3 & -1.86 & 3.18 & 4.81 \\ -45.69 & -0.12 & -0.60 & 4.80 \\ \vdots & \vdots & \vdots & \vdots \\ -131.2 & 1.36 & 4.61 & 6.2 \end{bmatrix}
$$

Step 4: Applying the TOPSIS method on a decision matrix to rank all blocks based on closeness to the ideal solution C_i^+. Through this step, the proposed model uses Equation 15.6 as the normalization method rather than Equation 15.5 or 15.7, because the numerical scales of DC, skewness and kurtosis features could be negative or positive, and the goal of the normalization step is to normalize all numerical values into positive values in range [0–1]. This in fact, allows a comparison of the given attributes. On the other hand, the proposed model suggests to assign multiple Weight Vectors (WV) to evaluate the performance of the proposed model under different cases. Five WVs are defined as follows: the first vector assigns same weight to all features, while each of the other vectors assign high weight value to one of the used features, such as following:

– $WV1 =< \frac{1}{4}, \frac{1}{4}, \frac{1}{4}, \frac{1}{4} >$ assigns the same weight values for all features.

– $WV2 =< \frac{3}{4}, \frac{1}{12}, \frac{1}{12}, \frac{1}{12} >$ assigns high weight value for DC coefficient and others have same weight value.

– $WV3 =< \frac{1}{12}, \frac{3}{4}, \frac{1}{12}, \frac{1}{12} >$ assigns high weight value for skewness feature and others have same weight value.

– $WV4 =< \frac{1}{12}, \frac{1}{12}, \frac{3}{4}, \frac{1}{12} >$ assigns high weight value for kurtosis feature and others have same weight value.

– $WV5 =< \frac{1}{12}, \frac{1}{12}, \frac{1}{12}, \frac{3}{4} >$ assigns high weight value for entropy feature and others have same weight value.

Analyzing the performance of the proposed approach using different WVs makes it possible to measure the significance of each feature by comparing the obtained results through all cases. In addition, this suggestion introduces a way to define which WV is more preferable for texture analysis process and may be recommended to other researchers.

Step 5: Selecting the top 10% of highest closeness blocks as the preferred blocks for embedding watermark with high imperceptibility and high robustness.

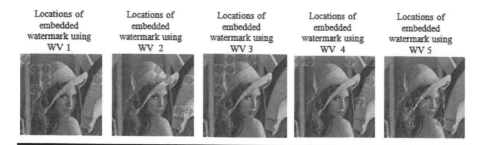

| Locations of embedded watermark using WV 1 | Locations of embedded watermark using WV 2 | Locations of embedded watermark using WV 3 | Locations of embedded watermark using WV 4 | Locations of embedded watermark using WV 5 |

Figure 15.1 Locations of highly textured blocks corresponding to different weight vectors.

Figure 15.1 presents the locations of highly textured blocks corresponding to the WVs, and the distribution of those blocks within the host image increases the opportunity of the proposed model to prove the origin of image even after different attacks and especially after cropping attack.

Table 15.1 illustrates the index of the top 10% of highly textured blocks that are more close to the ideal solution using five WVs. These blocks are arranged descending from the closest to the ideal solution towards the farthest from the ideal solution.

From Table 15.1, we can find the set of blocks that are frequently selected with different WVs and we can exactly define which block is frequently selected with most WVs. The blocks which have indexes {26,24,11,10,1} are frequently selected as highly textured blocks with five WVs, and the block which has index *24* is the most textured block among all other alternatives. Thus, we can state that block which has index *24* is the highest textured block among all other blocks. As well, the weight vectors *WV1, WV3* worked well by identifying most or even all of frequently textured blocks mentioned above. This, in turn, gives a way to define the importance of each of the used criteria.

Table 15.1 Indexes of Top 10% of Highly Textured Blocks Selected Using Five WVs

WV No.	Goes to the Closest Block					
WV 1	26	24	11	10	1	19
WV 2	47	48	22	24	13	21
WV 3	5	26	18	11	3	10
WV 4	2	39	6	1	24	8
WV 5	36	30	43	54	51	38

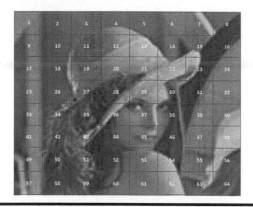

Figure 15.2   A partitioning Lena image into non-overlapping 64 × 64 blocks.

Figure 15.2 presents a partitioning of the Lena image into *64 × 64* non-overlapping blocks, and Figure 15.3 presents the blocks that are frequently selected in the proposed model as the most textured.

The efficiency of using the TOPSIS method in designing image water-marking is measured from the time complexity and the memory space requirements. The time complexity is calculated based on the number of operations of the computing stages performed in the TOPSIS method and the memory space is measured from the memory used by the data structure contained in the TOPSIS method. In the TOPSIS method, the size of the decision matrix is $m \times n$. The complexity value resulting from the calculation of score values of normalization and weighting is $O(m \times n)$. The complexity of calculation of positive and negative ideal solutions is $O(m \times n)$, and the complexity of calculation of geometric distance to ideal solutions is $O(mlog(n))$. The algorithmic complexity of calculation of the closeness values is $O(m)$ and that of the ranking of results is $O(mlog(m))$. Therefore, the total time complexity of the proposed approach is $O(m \times n)$.

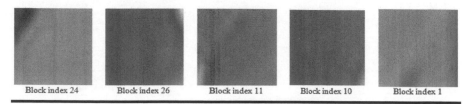

| Block index 24 | Block index 26 | Block index 11 | Block index 10 | Block index 1 |

Figure 15.3   Texture nature of the selected frequent blocks in the proposed model.

15.4.2 Approach 1: Semi-blind Image Watermarking Using Spatial Pixels

The first image watermarking approach starts by applying the texture analysis phase to identify the top 10% of highly textured blocks for the watermark embedding process. Then, it uses the linear interpolation technique to achieve watermark embedding in the original image I and uses the inverse form of linear interpolation to extract the attacked watermark from the attacked watermarked image I_{wa}. This approach is semi-blind watermarking, because it requires the original watermark for the watermark extraction procedure.

The general framework of the first approach is illustrated in Figure 15.4 and the embedding and extraction procedures are presented in the following subsections.

Figure 15.4 shows that the original image is partitioned into a set of non-overlapping blocks and the decision matrix is built and processed by the TOPSIS method to identify the top 10% of highly textured blocks for embedding watermark. The embedding procedure takes place using linear interpolation and the result is watermarked image I_w. Then, the I_w and the indexes of textured blocks are transmitted via communication medium to the receiver side. The receiver extracts the embedded watermark to verify the image origins. He supposes

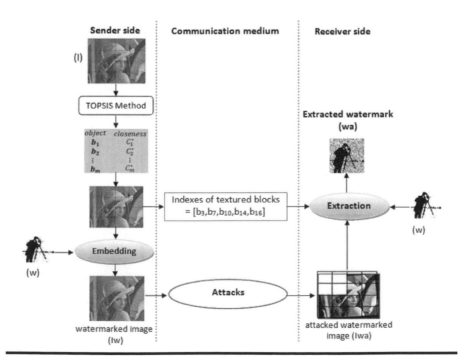

Figure 15.4   General framework of approach 1.

that he received an attacked image due to different attacks in the communication medium. The extraction process using inverse form of linear interpolation takes place to extract the attacked watermark. Measuring the similarity between the original watermark and the extracted attacked watermark proves image authenticity.

15.4.2.1 Watermark Embedding Process

The watermark is embedded in the selected blocks using linear interpolation technique proposed in [24]. This technique is useful because it provides the ability to manage a trade-off between imperceptibility and robustness by selecting proper interpolation factor. Equation 15.19 presents the linear interpolation technique, and algorithm (2) presents the pseudo-code of the watermark embedding process.

15.4.2.2 Watermark Extraction Process

After the embedding process, the obtained watermarked image I_w will be sent to the receiver via public networks and it will be exposed to different kind of attacks. Therefore, the received image is an attacked watermarked image I_{wa} and the extraction process must be applied to prove the origin of image by extracting the set of attacked watermarks w_a from I_{wa}. The inverse form of the linear interpolation technique, presented in Equation 15.20, is applied and the pseudo-code of attacked watermark extraction process is illustrated in algorithm (3).

Algorithm 2   *The pseudo-code of embedding watermark*

1. **input:** host image *I* of size $M \times M$, the selected textured blocks by the TOPSIS method *B*, original watermark image *w* of size $L \times L$, and interpolation factor $t = 0.99$
2. dividing *I* into $L \times L$, the result is *n* blocks
3. **for** $i \leftarrow 1$ to *n* **do**
4.   **if** $block_i \in$ the set of textured blocks *B*, $block_i \in I$ **then**

$$block_{iw} \leftarrow (1-t)w + t \times block_i : t \in\,]0-1[\qquad (15.19)$$

5.   **end if**
6. **end for**
7. **output:** watermarked image (I_w)

Algorithm 3 *The pseudo-code* *of extraction watermark*

1. **input**: attacked watermarked image I_{wa} of size $M \times M$, the original watermark image w of size $L \times L$, the selected textured blocks by the TOPSIS method B, and interpolation factor t
2. dividing I_{wa} into $L \times L$, the result is n blocks
3. **for** $k \leftarrow 1$ to n **do**
4.   **if** $block_k \in$ the set of textured blocks B **then**

$$w_a \leftarrow (1/t)w - ((1-t)/t) \times block_k : t \in]0-1[\quad (15.20)$$

5.   **end if**
6. **end for**
7. **output**: set of attacked watermarks (w_a)

15.4.3 *Approach 2: Blind Image Watermarking Using Spatial Pixels*

The second image watermarking approach also starts by applying the texture analysis phase to identify the top 10% of highly textured blocks for the watermark embedding process. Then, it uses the closeness value of each of the selected blocks to achieve embedding and extraction procedures. As well, it uses the maximum closeness value to define a public key α for a blind watermarking. The value of the public key is calculated according to Equation 15.21. The general framework of approach 2 is illustrated in Figure 15.5 and the embedding and extraction procedures are presented in following subsections.

$$\alpha \leftarrow max(closeness) / 100 \times w \quad (15.21)$$

where w is the original watermark.

Figure 15.5 shows that the original image is partitioned into set of non-overlapping blocks and the decision matrix is built and processed by TOPSIS method to identify the top 10% of highly textured blocks for embedding watermark. The maximum closeness and the original watermark are used to generate the public key α and then the embedding procedure takes place using closeness value of each of the selected blocks and the original watermark. The result is the watermarked image I_w. I_w, α and the indexes of textured blocks are transmitted via communication medium to the receiver. The receiver extracts the embedded watermark to verify the image origins. The receiver supposes that he received an

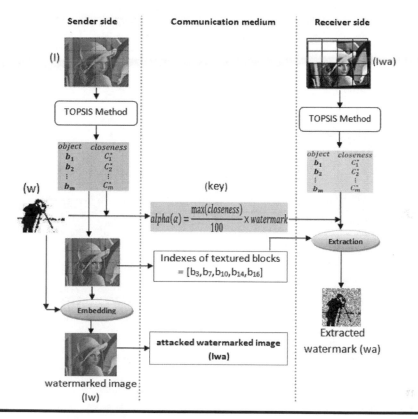

Figure 15.5   General framework of approach 2.

attacked watermarked image I_{wa} due to different attacks in the communication medium. It starts by partitioning I_{wa} into a set of non-overlapping blocks and the decision matrix is built and processed using the TOPSIS method to find the closeness value of each of the attacked textured blocks. The extraction process takes place using α and the closeness value of the attacked textured blocks. The result is the attacked watermark image w_a. The similarity between the original watermark and the extracted attacked watermark is measured to ensure image authenticity.

15.4.3.1 Watermark Embedding Process

A new embedding technique is proposed in this approach using the closeness coefficients of the selected textured blocks. Equation 15.22 presents the embedding equation, and algorithm (4) presents the pseudo-code of the watermark embedding process.

Algorithm 4 *The pseudo-code of embedding watermark*

1. **input**: the host image *I* of size $M \times M$, the indexes of selected textured blocks *B*, the closeness values of *B*, and the original watermark image *w* of size $L \times L$
2. dividing *I* into $L \times L$, the result is *n* blocks$_I$
3. **for** $s \leftarrow 1$ to *n* **do**
4.   **if** block$_I$ (*s*) $\in$ the set of textured blocks *B* **then**

$$block_{Iw}(s) \leftarrow block_I(s) + closeness(block_I(s)) / 100 \times w \quad (15.22)$$

5.   **end if**
6. **end for**
7. **output**: watermarked image (I_w)

15.4.3.2 Watermark Extraction Process

Once watermark embedding is done, the extraction Equation in 15.23 is applied to extract the watermarks from the attacked watermarked image. Initially, the receiver runs the texture analysis phase to find the closeness values of the attacked textured blocks and the extraction process uses these closeness values and the public key alpha (α) to extract the attacked watermark. The pseudo-code of the attacked watermarks extraction process is illustrated in algorithm (5).

As illustrated in Equation 15.23, the extraction procedure is blind. Indeed, the receiver uses only the public key alpha (α) to extract the attacked watermark without any knowledge about the original watermark or the original image. As well, the public key alpha (α) used in the extraction process is not fixed. For each host image, a new key is generated. This increases the robustness of the watermarking process against brute force attacks.

15.4.4 Experiment Results for Proposed Watermarking Approaches

The proposed watermarking approaches have been tested by embedding a binary 64×64 watermark in high textured blocks of gray-scale host images sized 512×512. The experiment results have been analyzed on three gray-scale images (Lena, Boat, and Airplane) to show the perceptual quality of watermarked images (imperceptibility of embedded watermark) and the robustness of an embedded watermark against different image processing attacks. The attacks are classified into three categories including geometric (like rotation, cropping, scaling, translation

---

Algorithm 5   *The pseudo-code of the extraction watermark*

1. **preliminary**: defining the set $k = \{k_1, \ldots, k_n\}$ as texture features and defining the weight vector WV
2. **input**: attacked watermarked image I_{wa} of size $M \times M$, the indexes of selected textured blocks B, and alpha α
3. partitioning I_{wa} into $L \times L$ blocks, results are m blocks$_{Iwa}$, $m = M/L \times M/L$
4.   **for** each feature k_t, $t = 1, \ldots, n$ **do**
5.   **for** each block$_{Iwa}(s)$, $s = 1, \ldots, m$ **do**
6.   define $x_{s,t}$ score of alternative block$_{Iwa}(s)$ with respect to criterion k_t
7.   **end for**
8. **end for**
9. constructing the decision matrix $X = (x_{s,t})_{m \times n}$
10. applying the TOPSIS method to find the closeness values of all partitioned blocks
11.   **for** each block$_{Iwa}$ (s), $s = 1, \ldots, m$ **do**
12.   **if** block$_{Iwa}$ $(s) \in$ the set of textured blocks B **then**

$$w_a \leftarrow \alpha \times 100 \,/\, closeness(block_{Iwa}(s)) \qquad (15.23)$$

13.   **end if**
14. **end for**
15. **output**: set of attacked watermarks (w_a)

---

and affine transformation), non-geometric (like JPEG compression, median filtering, Gaussian noise, sharpening and histogram equalization) and hybrid. The performance of the proposed system in terms of imperceptibility and robustness is measured using well-known metrics including PSNR, mean Structure SIMilarity (mSSIM) and BER [3].

15.4.4.1 Perceptual Quality Analysis

The host images and the two used watermark images are presented in Figure 15.6. As well, Figure 15.6 presents the perceptual quality of the watermarked images with reference to the original images in terms of PSNR and mSSIM.

The perceptual quality results in Figure 15.6 show that the PSNR and mSSIM in approach 1 range 54.86–57.40 dB and 0.98–0.99 respectively, while the PSNR

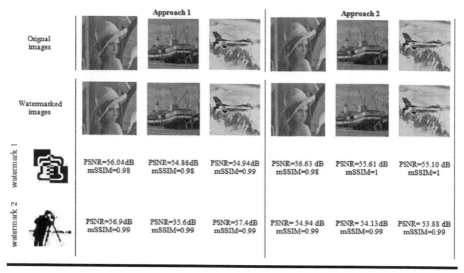

Figure 15.6   Perceptual quality in terms of PSNR and SSIM (in case of water-marked Lena, Boat, Airplane images).

and mSSIM in approach 2 range 53.88–56.63 db and 0.98–1 respectively. These results ensure the efficiency of the proposed approaches through embedding water-mark in a host image with low quality degradation of the original image and high imperceptibility of the embedded watermark to the human eye.

15.4.4.2 Robustness Analysis

The robustness of watermarks against different geometric, non-geometric and hybrid attacks is also evaluated in the proposed approaches. These attacks include: JPEG compression, cropping, rotation, translation, removing lines (RML), scaling, affine transformation, median filtering, adding noise, histogram equalization, and sharpening. Nineteen different attacks (a1–a19) as listed in Table 15.2, are used to test the robustness of watermarks. The consequence of applying these attacks on the Lena image is illustrated in Figure 15.7. StirMark Benchmark v.4 [25] and MATLAB® (v. R2016a) are used to apply these attacks on the watermarked images. The presentation of these attacks is available in [26].

Table 15.3 summarizes BER results of the extracted watermarks against different attacks in the two approaches and for the three images. This experiment uses WV_1: $WV_1 = \langle 1/4,\ 1/4,\ 1/4,\ 1/4 \rangle$ as input for TOPSIS method.

The results in Table 15.3 show that the BER results against all non-hybrid attacks (a1–a15) for each approach are very convergent for the three image. The BER results in approach 1 range 3.4%–4.8% and in approach 2 range 0%–1.7%. Against hybrid attacks (a16–a19) the proposed approaches achieve good robustness,

Table 15.2   Attacks Scenario

Attack Id	Attack's Name and Factor	Attack Id	Attack's Name and Factor
a1.	JPEG compression (quality factor (QF) = 20)	a11.	crop (25%) left up corner (white)
a2.	Gaussian noise (variance = 0.001, mean = 0)	a12.	crop (50%) bottom (white)
a3.	salt & pepper (noise density = 0.01)	a13.	affine transformation (2)
a4.	Speckle noise (variance = 0.01, mean = 0)	a14.	remove lines (RML) (10)
a5.	median filtering (3 × 3)	a15.	translation vertically (10)
a6.	scaling (25%) shrink image from 512 × 512 to 256 × 256	a16.	rotation (counterclockwise 5°) + crop (25%) left up corner
a7.	rotation (counterclockwise 45°)	a17.	histogram equalization + resize (256 × 256)
a8.	Gaussian noise (variance = 20, mean = 0)	a18.	rotation (counterclockwise 5°) + crop (25%) left up corner + histogram equalization
a9.	sharpening	a19.	Gaussian noise (variance = 0.001, mean = 0) + rotation (counterclockwise 5°) + sharpen
a10.	crop (10%) center (white)		

where BER ranges 0%–3.9%. In both approaches the robustness against rotation (counterclockwise 45°) is the worst, the BER reaches 4.8% in the approach 1% and 1.7% in approach 2.

Furthermore, Table 15.3 shows that the BER results using approach 2 are more interesting than the achieved BER results in approach 1. This can be explained due to the convergent value of the resulting closeness value of the selected textured blocks in the case of original image and in the case of attacked watermarked image in approach 2.

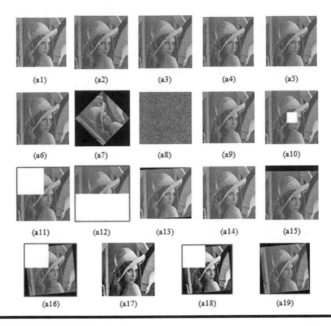

Figure 15.7 Consequences of applying nineteen different attacks (a1–a19) on Lena image.

Generally, the mentioned BER results ensure the ability of the proposed watermarking approaches to extract the watermark robustly from the attacked watermarked images.

15.4.5 Comparative Study

To prove the efficiency of the proposed watermarking system in preserving high perceptual quality of watermarked image and high robustness against different attacks, this section presents comparative study between the proposed approaches and other proposed watermarking models in terms of PSNR and BER. The considered models in the comparative study are not based on MCDM methods, but most of them are based on intelligence techniques.

Figure 15.8 presents PSNR comparison between the proposed approaches and other proposed models presented in [3,6,8,18] in the case of the Lena image and using watermark 1.

Figure 15.8 shows the efficiency of the proposed approaches over other models by achieving higher PSNR. The achieved PSNR in the other models did not exceed 53 dB, while it exceeded 55 dB in the proposed approaches.

On the other hand, the performance of the proposed approaches in terms of robustness is also evaluated comparing with other proposed models. Table 15.4 presents BER

Table 15.3   BER Results Against Different Attacks (in case of Lena, Boat, and Airplane images)

Attack Id	Attacks	Approach 1			Approach 2		
		Lena	Boat	Airplane	Lena	Boat	Airplane
a1.	JPEG compression (quality factor (QF) = 20)	3.5	3.5	3.5	0	0	0
a2.	Gaussian noise (variance = 0.001, mean = 0)	3.5	3.6	3.5	0	0	0
a3.	salt & pepper (noise density = 0.01)	3.5	3.6	3.5	0	0	0
a4.	speckle noise (variance = 0.01, mean = 0)	3.6	3.6	3.5	0.01	0.58	0
a5.	median filtering [3 × 3]	4.01	3.6	3.5	0.027	1.09	0.80
a6.	scaling (25%) shrink image from 512 × 512 to 256 × 256	3.6	3.6	3.5	0	0	0
a7.	rotation (counterclockwise 45°)	4.8	3.99	3.7	0.02	0.73	1.69
a8.	Gaussian noise (variance = 20, mean = 0)	4	4.1	4.06	0	0	0.02
a9.	sharpening	4	3.6	3.5	0.035	0	0
a10.	crop (10%) center (white)	3.7	3.6	3.5	0	0	0

(Continued)

Table 15.3 (*Continued*) BER Results Against Different Attacks (in case of Lena, Boat, and Airplane images)

Attack Id	Attacks	Approach 1			Approach 2		
		Lena	Boat	Airplane	Lena	Boat	Airplane
a11.	crop (25%) left up corner (white)	3.44	3.6	3.4	0.006	0	0.006
a12.	crop (50%) bottom(white)	3.6	3.6	3.4	0.19	0.15	1.09
a13.	affine transformation (2)	3.8	3.7	3.6	0	0	0.09
a14.	remove lines (RML) (10)	3.5	3.4	3.6	0.024	0	0
a15.	translation vertically (10)	3.9	3.7	3.6	0.12	0	0.19
a16.	rotation (counterclockwise 5°) + crop (25%) left up corner	3.4	3.8	3.4	0.58	0	1.7
a17.	histogram equalization + resize (256 × 256)	3.5	3.8	3.8	0	0.73	1.7
a18.	Rotation (counterclockwise 5°) + crop (25%) left up corner + histogram equalization	3.4	4.0	3.4	0.62	0	1.09
a19.	Gaussian noise (variance = 0.001, mean = 0) + rotation (counterclockwise 5°) + sharpen	3.9	3.7	3.5	0	0	1.08

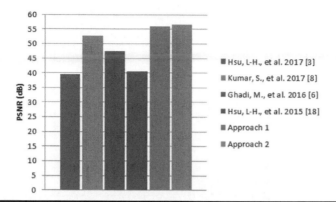

Figure 15.8 PSNR comparison (in case of gray-scale Lena image).

comparison between the proposed approaches and the models presented in [3,6,18] against different attacks in the case of the Lena image and using watermark 1.

The mentioned results in Table 15.4 show that approach 2 achieved the lowest BER values compared with other proposed models against all tested attacks. The BER in approach 2 is ranged 0%–0.62% against attacks a1-a15. As well, Table 15.4 shows that the achieved BERs using approach 1 against some attacks are lower compared with the proposed models in [3,6,18]. As an example, the achieved BER using approach 1 is lower than the achieved BER in model [3] against attacks a1, a3, a4 and a10. On the other hand, Table 15.4 shows that the BER results in the proposed model in [6] are slightly lower than the achieved BER in the proposed approach 1 against some attacks (a1, a3, a4, a6, a7–a11, a13 and a15) and the proposed model in [3] achieved lower BER than the proposed approach 1 against attacks a2, a5, a6 and a7. Additionally, the achieved BER in model [18] is lower than the BER in approach 1 against a1 and a6.

15.5 Conclusion and Open Issues

Many problems in various applications in our life involve choosing the best alternative among many possible alternatives. The decision-making in these problems can be done using MCDM methods. These methods can be used to rank all possible alternatives after evaluation process based on a set of criteria and preferences provided by the decision-maker. Selecting the highly textured locations within host image based on texture property is important to build a robust watermarking model. Nevertheless, it is a complex problem due particularly to the imprecision of texture properties. In this chapter, one of the MCDM methods named TOPSIS is used to solve the imprecision of the image's texture properties in order to build a robust image watermarking model. In the proposed model, a decision matrix composed of many alternatives (partitioned blocks) and four criteria (texture properties)

Table 15.4 Comparison of BER for Different Attacks Scenarii

Attack Id	Attack's Name and Factor	Model of L-Y. Hsu et al. [3]	Model of M. Ghadi et al. [6]	Model of L-Y. Hsu et al. [18]	Approach 1	Approach 2
a1.	JPEG compression (quality factor (QF) = 20)	13.21	3.4	1.98	3.5	0
a2.	Gaussian noise (variance = 0.001, mean = 0)	2.17	5.2	9.25	3.5	0
a3.	Salt & pepper (noise density = 0.01)	11.65	3.4	16.5	3.5	0
a4.	speckle noise (variance = 0.01, mean = 0)	11.04	3.4	×	3.6	0.01
a5.	median filtering (3 × 3)	3.05	5.1	4.0	4.01	0.03
a6.	scaling (25%) shrink image from 512 × 512 to 256 × 256	1.83	3.4	2.1	3.6	0
a7.	rotation (counterclockwise 45°)	1.23	3.4	8.01	4.8	0.02
a8.	Sharpening	×	3.4	×	4.0	0.04
a9.	crop (10%) center (white)	×	3.4	×	3.7	0
a10.	crop (25%) left up corner (white)	12.31	3.3	12.6	3.4	0
a11.	crop (50%) bottom (white)	×	3.3	×	3.6	0.19
a12.	Rotation (counterclockwise 5°) + crop (25%) left up corner	×	7.9	×	3.4	0.58
a13.	histogram equalization + resize (256 × 256)	×	3.3	×	3.5	0
a14.	Rotation (counterclockwise 5°) + crop (25%) left up corner + histogram equalization	×	5.4	×	3.4	0.62
a15.	Gaussian noise (variance = 0.001) + rotation(counterclockwise 5°) + sharpen	×	3.3	×	3.9	0

is built. The TOPSIS method is applied to rank all alternatives based on the defined criteria. The alternatives with the highest score are used for watermark embedding. Two watermarking approaches are proposed: the first one is semi-blind and based on linear interpolation technique. The second approach exploits the closeness values of the TOPSIS method to build a public key for blind watermarking and also uses the closeness values of highly textured blocks to achieve watermark embedding and extraction. The results in terms of perceptual quality and robustness against different attacks are presented and compared with other watermarking models to prove the efficiency of the proposed approaches. For future directions, one proposal is to investigate other MCDM methods for solving the problem of texture property in order to evaluate the possible benefits in the watermarking process.

References

1. Roy, S., Kumar Pal A., 2017. A blind DCT based color watermarking algorithm for embedding multiple watermarks. *International Journal of Electronics and Communications* 72:149–161.
2. Khalili, M., 2015. DCT-Arnold chaotic based watermarking using JPEG-YCbCr. *International Journal for Light and Electron Optics* 126(23):4367–4371.
3. Hsu, L-Y., Hu, H-T., 2017. Robust blind image watermarking using crisscross inter-block prediction in the DCT domain. *Journal of Visual Communication and Image Representaion* 46:33–47.
4. Vaidya, P., Mouli, C., 2017. A robust semi-blind watermarking for color images based on multiple decompositions. *Multimedia Tools and Applications* 76(24): 25623–25656.
5. Lihua, G., Yuanjian, Z., 2006. Robust watermark using the auxiliary information. *Proceedings of the 4th International Conference on Communications, Circuits and Systems* 1:6–10.
6. Ghadi, M., Laouamer, L., Nana, L., Pascu, A., 2016. A robust associative watermarking technique based on frequent pattern mining and texture analysis. *Proceedings of the 8th International ACM Conference on Management of computational and collective Intelligence in Digital Ecosystems, ACM* 73–81.
7. Ghadi, M., Laouamer L., Nana, L., Pascu, A., 2017. A robust watermarking system based on formal concept analysis and texture analysis. *Proceedings of the 30th International Florida Artificial Intelligence Research Society Conference, AAAI* 682–687.
8. Kumar, S., Jain, N., Fernandes, S.L., 2017. Rough set based effective technique of image watermarking. *Journal of Computational Science* 19:121–137.
9. Ghadi, M., Laouamer, L., Nana, L., Pascu, A., 2016. Fuzzy rough set based image watermarking approach. *Proceedings of the 2nd International Conference on Advanced Intelligent Systems and Informatics* 533:234–245.
10. Sen, D., Pal, S., 2009. Generalized rough sets, entropy, and image ambiguity measures. *IEEE Transactions on Systems, Man, and Cybernetics* 39(1):17–28.
11. Materka, A., Strzelecki, M., 1998. Texture analysis methods–A review. *Technical University of Lodz, Institute of Electronics, COST B11 Report, Brussels* 9–11.
12. Sirkaya-Turk, E., Uysal, M., Hammit, W.E., Vaske, J.J., 2011. *Research Methods for Leisure, Recreation and Tourism.* Prentice Hall, Upper Saddle River, NJ.

13. Su, Q., Chen, B., 2017. Robust color image watermarking technique in the spatial domain. *Soft Computing* 1–16.
14. Das, A., 2015. *Guide to Signals and Patterns in Image Processing: Foundations, Methods and Applications*. Springer International Publishing, Cham, Switzerland.
15. Cristobal, S., Ramon, J., 2012. *Multi Criteria Analysis in the Renewable Energy Industry*. Springer-Verlag, London, UK.
16. Huang, C-L., Yoon, K., 1981. *Multi Attribute Decision Making: Methods and Applications*. Springer-Verlag, Berlin, Germany.
17. Han, J., Zhao, X., Qiu, C., 2016. A digital image watermarking method based on host image analysis and genetic algorithm. *Journal of Ambient Intelligence and Humanized Computing* 7:37–45.
18. Hsu, L-Y., Hu, H-T., 2015. Blind image watermarking via exploitation of inter-block prediction and visibility threshold in DCT domain. *Journal of Visual Communication and Image Representation* 32:130–143.
19. Abdelhakim, A., Saleh, H., Nassar, A., 2017. A quality guaranteed robust image watermarking optimization with artificial bee colony. *Expert Systems with Applications* 72:317–326.
20. Papakostas, G.A., Tsougenis, E.D. Koulouriotis, D.E., 2016. Fuzzy knowledge-based adaptive image watermarking by the method of moments. *Complex & Intelligent Systems* 2:205–220.
21. Jagadeesh, B., Kumar, R. P., Reddy, C. P., 2016. Robust digital image watermarking based on fuzzy inference system and back propagation neural networks using DCT. *Soft Computing* 20:3679–3686.
22. Ghadi, M., Laouamer, L., Nana, L., Pascu, A., 2017. A joint spatial texture analysis/watermarking system for digital image authentication. *Paper Presented in the 12th IEEE International Workshop on Signal Processing Systems*.
23. Ghadi, M., Laouamer, L., Nana, L., Pascu, A., 2017. A robust watermarking technique in spatial domain using closeness coefficients of texture. *Paper Presented in the 8th International Conference on Information, Intelligence, Systems and Applications*.
24. Benhocine, A., Laouamer, L., Nana, L., Pascu, A., 2008. A new approach against color attacks of watermarked images. *Proceedings of the 8th International IEEE Conference on Intelligent Information Hiding and Multimedia Signal Processing* 969–972.
25. Petitcolas, F., Anderson, R., Kuhn, M., 1998. Attacks on copyright marking systems. *Proceedings of 2nd Workshop on Information Hiding, Lecture Notes in Computer Science, Springer* 1525:218–238.
26. Ghadi, M., Laouamer, L., Nana, L., Pascu, A., 2016. A novel zero-watermarking approach of medical images based on Jacobian matrix model. *Security and Communication Networks* 9(18):5203–5218.

Chapter 16

The Role of Image Fusion and Watermarking Techniques in Medical Imaging

Ch. Hima Bindu

Contents

DOI: 10.1201/9780429435461-18

16.1 Introduction to Medical Imaging

Medical imaging is the process of creating human body images with various medical scanners for clinical purposes. These reports are providing radiologists and physicians for detection and treatment of disorders and diseases. Medical imaging is projection of non-invasive methods to look inside the body [20]. It replaces the need for surgery and allows medical professionals to view various organs and areas. Moreover, medical imaging is mostly helpful to follow-up a disease already diagnosed and/or treated. With enhanced human services arrangement and expanding accessibility of medical equipment, the quantity of worldwide imaging-based techniques is expanding impressively. Powerful, safe, and quality imaging plays a vital role for much decision making and can diminish unnecessary techniques.

Throughout the years, medicinal imaging has turned into a key part in the early recognition, conclusion and treatment. At times medical imaging is the initial step in preventing the spread of disease through early detection and much of the time makes it conceivable to cure. Computer Tomography (CT) imaging, Magnetic Resonance Imaging (MRI), Mammography, Positron Emission Tomography (PET), Nuclear Medicine (NM) imaging, Ultrasound (US) imaging and X-beam imaging are generally essential imaging reports for diagnosis. That has the added benefits of decreasing the amount of time a patient has to remain in the hospital and reduces the costs associated with surgery and other hospital expenses.

After a disease has been analyzed, imaging is frequently used to take after the course of disease treatment and to screen the development. Medicinal imaging is being utilized more frequently to design exact computer assistance models which enable specialists to manage correct radiation treatment of disease. CT and MRI are both especially great at imaging delicate tissue structures, and in this way are remarkable for distinguishing and diagnosing.

Medical imaging for medical purposes involves a group which incorporates the administration of radiologists, radiographers (X-beam technologists), sonographers (ultrasound technologists), therapeutic physicists, attendants, biomedical architects, and other supporting staff to take care about the health of the patients. Proper utilization of medical imaging requires a multidisciplinary approach. The benefits of medical imaging are extensive, and include:

- Rapid and accurate diagnosis
- More evidence-based decision-making
- More personalized treatment
- Fewer complications during and after surgery
- Faster recovery following surgery
- Increased understanding of the effect of treatments on diseases
- Less repeat of sickness
- Decreased mortality and grimness

For the patient, these advantages convert into a healthy life, longer life span, and substantially less time to get back into a routine life than would be required something else.

16.2 Introduction to Image Fusion

The process of combining two or more images of a scene into a single image, which is more informative and more suitable for visual perception or computer processing, is called image fusion. The benefit of image fusion is more spatial and temporal coverage with reduced uncertainty, enhanced reliability and robustness of system performance [31]. The preliminary requirements of image fusion are: fused image should exhibit all relevant information of the source images; second, the fusion process should not initiate any artifact or noise in the resultant fused image.

The MRI and CT medical images provide structural and anatomical information of the body with high resolution. PET images provide functional information with low spatial resolution, with this it gives unsatisfactory results for morphological analysis. Fusion of anatomical and functional tomography images is useful for more informative analysis. It leads to qualitative detection and quantitative determination of the data. Recently, the fusion of MRI-CT, PET-MRI and PET-CT imaging created new era in the clinical applications and analysis [33]. Numerous fusion algorithms on multi source medical images have been proposed for various applications like MRI-CT image fusion for edge preservation technique, MRI-PET image fusion for retina models, CT-PET image fusion for tissue identification etc.

16.2.1 Types of Fusion Techniques

Image fusion techniques are categorized depending on the fusion process and application as follows [22].

- Multi View Fusion
- Multi Focus Fusion
- Multi Temporal Fusion
- Multi Modal Fusion

16.2.1.1 Multi View Fusion

In this fusion method the images of the same modality are taken at the same time but from different viewpoints. The aim of this method is to produce corresponding information from different views. For many applications single view images of the scene are adequate. The fusion process depends upon number of views to be fused. Different views will clearly contain more information about the scene, but will require extended data acquisition and processing times. This fusion method provides higher isotropic resolution than in any of the unprocessed individual views [30].

Many image processing techniques give better results from the availability of multiple views such as interpolation, enhancement, segmentation, object recognition and in monitoring and surveillance applications. A multi view fusion example [30] is given in Figure 16.1. Real time 3-D echocardiography permits the acquisition and visualization of the beating heart in 3-D. In this the fusion is based on the wavelet sub bands.

16.2.1.2 Multi Focus Fusion

Multi focus image fusion is fusion of the images with different focal length but identical view points of same scene. The variable focal length of a camera will produce images out of focus or in focus. Due to the limited depth of focus of optical lenses in CCD devices, it is often not possible to get an image that contains all relevant

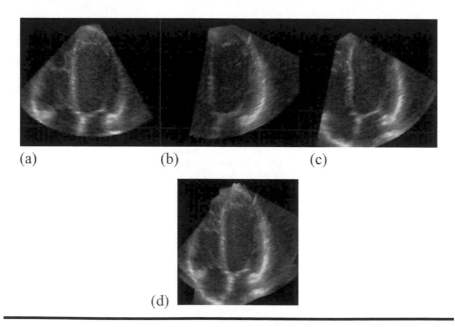

(a)   (b)   (c)

(d)

Figure 16.1   Multi view image fusion example, shows representative 2D slices of Echocardiography images (a)–(c) 3 single-view 4-chamber images (d) fused image.

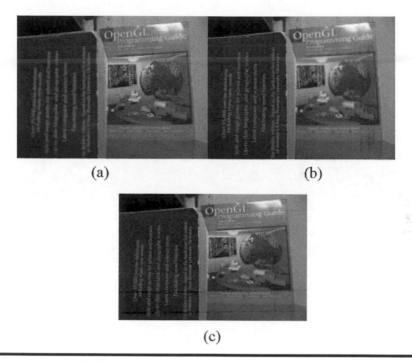

(a)   (b)

(c)

Figure 16.2   Multi focus image example (a), (b) multi focused images and (c) fused image.

objects in focus. To obtain an image with every object in focus, a fusion process is needed to fuse the images taken from the same view point under different focal settings [23].

The process of multi focus image fusion is to decide which portions of each image are in better focus than their respective counterparts in the associated images and then combine these regions to give better focused image [24]. This method has both spatial [25] and transform [26] domain approaches. The existing techniques are probabilistic method [26], PCA method [27], multi scale method [28] and multi resolution methods [29]. The following Figure 16.2 shows the fusion of multi focus images.

16.2.1.3 Multi Temporal Fusion

Multi temporal fusion is, fusion of same scene taken at different times to detect changes among them. The purpose of this process is to identify the changes in the image that are captured at different times and give out a fused image with more details. The application areas are in satellite imagery, medical imagery, and different general applications [23]. The resultant image shows the variation among the captured input images at different times. The following Figure 16.3 shows fusion of multi temporal fusion technique.

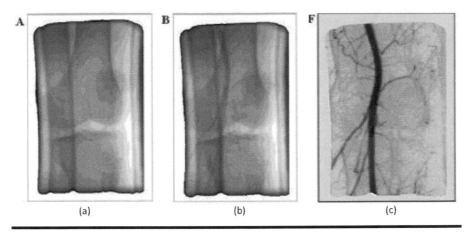

(a)   (b)   (c)

Figure 16.3 Example of multi temporal fusion of digital subtraction angiography.

16.2.1.4 Multi Modal Fusion

Multi modal fusion is fusion of different modes of scanner or capturing device images. In this process the rest of the parameters are constant. The resultant image should provide more complete and accurate description of the same scene [23]. This is also named as multi source image fusion. Images of various scanners are PET, CT, MRI, visible, infrared, ultraviolet etc. The image information varies according to the scanner working principle. The following Figures 16.4 through 16.6 show fusion of multi modal images of various scenes.

The benefits of multi-sensor or multi modal image fusion include [21]:

■ Effective range of operation: multiple sensors that operate under different operating conditions can be employed to extend the effective range of operation.

■ Extended temporal and spatial coverage: different sensors that differ in temporal resolution and spatial resolution can increase the spatial coverage and temporal coverage respectively.

■ Increased reliability: the fusion of multiple measurements can reduce noise and then improve the reliability of the measured quantity.

■ Reduce uncertainty: combined information of multiple scanners can reduce the uncertainty related with the sensing or decision process.

■ Compact representation of information: fusion leads to compact representations. For example, in medical applications, instead of storing imagery from several sensors, it is comparatively more efficient to store the fused information.

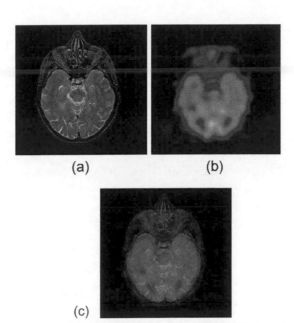

Figure 16.4 Multi modal medical imaging example: (a) MRI image, (b) PET image, and (c) fused image.

Figure 16.5 Multi modal fusion of spectral images: (a) Visible band image, (b) infrared band image, and (c) fused image.

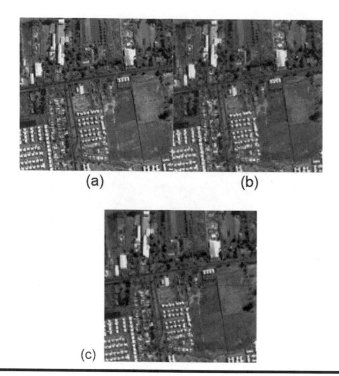

(a)   (b)

(c)

Figure 16.6 Multi model satellite imaging example: (a) Multi spectral image, (b) panchromatic image, and (c) fused image.

16.3 Introduction to Watermarking

Digital watermarking is watermarking of digital objects instead of physical objects. In digital watermarking an important image is hided/ watermarked into unimportant image. The important image is treated as watermark and unimportant image is called as cover image. The watermark image posses secured data. The cover image protects the watermark image details through embedding process. It indeed leads to secured data transmission [43].

The image watermarking process splits the in two ways: embedding and extraction. The embedding process inserts the watermark image into the cover image with unpredicted way of approach. The watermark extraction process applies inverse of embedding process to extract the watermark image from the watermarked image.

The embedded process inserts a watermark onto the cover image and the watermark detector detects the presence of watermark signal. The whole process is the way of inserting and extracting watermarks. The watermark key has a one-to-one correspondence with the watermark signal. The process of watermark is confidential and known to only authorized customers to detect the watermark. Henceforth the computerized watermarking methods have to be strong to both noise and security attacks [42].

16.3.1 Features of Digital Watermarking

The main features of digital watermarking techniques are very attractive, since it provides the following main features [36–38]. The watermarking process embeds the secured information into the cover image directly in such a way that it need not requires additional bandwidth [39–40].

- Imperceptibility
- Robustness
- Inseparability
- Security

16.3.2 Applications of Watermarking

There is a wide range of applications with the digital watermarking process [36, 41]. Some of the applications are listed below:

- Security/Defense
- Medial communication
- Copyright Protection
- Broadcasting
- Satellite/Space communications

16.3.3 Watermarking Techniques

Digital watermarking techniques are categorized into three ways based on various parameters. These are shown in the following Figure 16.7. Each of the techniques is having their own applications.

The first category of embedding is further classified into spatial or transform domain based on existence of image domain. The second category, extraction leads to blind and nonblind classification. Here, the extraction process deals with usage of embedding end details. If details are carried it's called blind, otherwise nonblind. The last category depends on visibility or nonvisibility of watermark image in watermarked image. This process is shown in Figure 16.8.

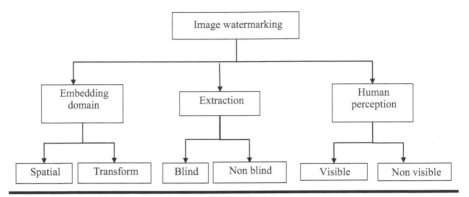

Figure 16.7   Classification of watermarking techniques.

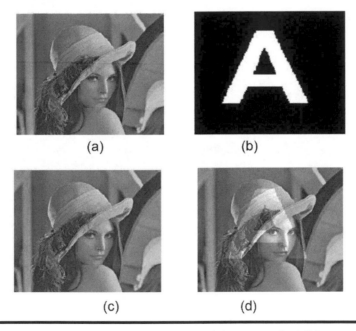

Figure 16.8   (a) Original image, (b) watermark image, (c) invisible watermarked image, and (d) visible watermarked image.

16.4 Applications of Watermarking Technique in Medical Imaging

This section discusses the role of image watermarking in medical imaging. The author focuses on multiple image processing techniques like image fusion and image watermarking on a single platform. The given example addresses both integration and content security of clinical data. In clinical diagnosis, the physician looking for more and more medical images of the patient for accurate treatment.

The first part of the section has focused on fusion of multimodal medical images with fusion rule. The final fused image must contain more information than individual images alone. A second part has dealt with reversible and robust watermarking. The watermarked image consists of fused image and other clinical reports of the patient. With this, the data is stored securely and a single image has been transmitted instead of multiple images. At the receiver end, the patient's reports could be extracted effectively.

16.4.1 Integration of Patient Clinical Database Using Watermarking for Content Security and e-Diagnosis

In the field of medical or bio informatics the storage and process of medical data plays a vital role. Today's digital era is solving the problem of maintaining and collecting the patient's data records. So, it is giving scope to introduce medical image processing techniques. With the advent of medical imaging, multiple images can be effectively stored and processed. Indeed, image watermarking supports this feature to handle multiple data with integrity, authenticity and effective handling. This paper work discusses the fusion and watermarking to handle more patient records with more security.

Image fusion is the combination of more than one image into single image that gives more information. Normally medical images are MRI, CT, and PET [1, 4]. The image fusion is based on two types of domains: In the spatial domain it is directly on pixel values; in the frequency domain it is on coefficient values. The spatial domain techniques are Brovey method, PCA etc. the frequency domain techniques are DWT (Discrete Wavelet Transform), DCT (Discrete Cosine Transform), etc [2, 4–5].

Image watermarking is one of the research areas for providing better security of data. Watermarking provides more security, especially for color images. The process of watermarking defines embedding of watermark image into the host image for safety and integrity. The watermarked image is invisible and robust without affecting the image quality [3, 11–12]. The color image watermarking is better than gray level images for visual perception and clear analysis.

In present days there is a need to exchange the data over the internet, but the problem is with data authenticity, integrity and confidentiality over the internet [14]. Luo (2003) worked on DICOM (Digital Imaging & Communications in Medicine) format images to avoid occurrence of mistakes in medical practices [17]. Coatrieux (2006) reviewed the role of image watermarking in health care systems for protection, secure sharing and handling of medical images [15]. Imen (2009) proposed dermatology control using reversible watermarking techniques. He also evaluated image visual quality with effective locating of tampered regions [16]. Kavitha (2013) discussed the use of watermarking on various medical images. Javier (2014) worked for his doctorial degree on medical database content security with the use of watermarking [17].

The next sections are organized as follows. Sections 16.2 and 16.3 are the basic concept preliminaries and proposed work, respectively. Experimental results are marked in Section 16.4, and finally Section 16.5 is the conclusion.

16.4.1.1 Preliminaries

16.4.1.1.1 Discrete Wavelet Transform

This preliminaries section discusses the useful transformation techniques for proposed work. DWT is one of the important transform domain techniques in the various field of digital image processing. DWT transformed image holds four subbands like approximation, Vertical, Horizontal and Diagonal bands. These are named as LL, LH, HL, and HH respectively. DWT is more advanced over Fourier Transform and short-term Fourier Transform. Fourier Transform does not provide both time and frequency information simultaneously, however, short-term Fourier Transform provides both time and frequency content but window size is fixed. These are the disadvantages of FT and STFT [4, 9, 12].

$$f(t) = \sum_{m,n} c_{m,n} \psi_{m,n}(t) \tag{16.1}$$

Where $\psi_{m,n}(t) = 2^{-m/2} \psi(2^{-m}t - n)$, is a wavelet function, m and n are integers. There exist very special choices of ψ such that $\psi_{m,n}(t)$ constitutes an ortho normal basis, so that the wavelet transform coefficient can be obtained by an inner calculation:

$$c_{m,n} = \langle f, \psi_{m,n} \rangle = \int \psi_{m,n}(t) f(t) dt \tag{16.2}$$

In order to develop a multiresolution analysis, a scaling function ϕ is needed, together with the dilated and translated parameters of $\phi_{m,n}(t) = 2^{-m/2} \phi(2^{-m}t - n)$. The signal $a_{m,n}$ can be decomposed in its coarse part and details of various sizes by projecting it onto the corresponding spaces. Therefore, the approximation coefficients $a_{m,n}$ of the function f at resolution 2^m and wavelet coefficients $c_{m,n}$ can be obtained:

$$a_{m,n} = \sum_{k} h_{2n-k} a_{m-1,k} \tag{16.3}$$

$$c_{m,n} = \sum_{k} g_{2n-k} a_{m-1,k} \tag{16.4}$$

Where h_n is a low pass FIR filter and g_n is a high pass FIR filter. To reconstruct the original signal, the analysis filter can be selected from a biorthogonal set which have a related set of synthesis filters. These synthesis filters $\tilde{h}$ and $\tilde{g}$ can be used to perfectly reconstruct the signal using the reconstruction formula

$$a_{m-1,l}(f) = \sum_n \left| \tilde{h}_{2n-1} a_{m,n}(f) + \tilde{g}_{2n-1} c_{m,n(f)} \right| \qquad (16.5)$$

Equations 16.3 and 16.4 are implemented by filtering and down sampling. Conversely Equation 16.5 is implemented by an initial up sampling and a subsequent filtering. The process of decomposition is shown in Figure 16.9. The process of decimation clearly mentioned in the following figure: the size of the original image is N×N after decomposition along the row and column wise the size of the resultant sub bands are: N/2×N and N/2×N/2, respectively. Finally, original image split into four sub-images each of size N/2 by N/2.

DWT is a very vast topic. Detail of wavelets is given in [29, 30]. Two commonly used abbreviations are DWT and IDWT. DWT stands for Discrete Wavelet Transformation. It is the transformation of sampled data, e.g. transformation of values in an array, into wavelet coefficients. IDWT is Inverse Discrete Wavelet Transformation: The inverse procedure that converts wavelet coefficients into the original sampled data. Here we will discuss the case of square images. Let's saywe have an image N by N.

The image filtered with high and low-pass filters along the rows and the results of each filter are down-sampled by two. Later, this time the image is filtered with high- and low-pass filters along the columns. Now these are again down sampled by two. The whole process is shown in Figures 16.10 to 16.11.

The multilevel decomposition of the image into various sub-bands along the LL sub-band is shown in the Figure 16.12. Here the process is recursively performed on LL sub-band for n-levels.

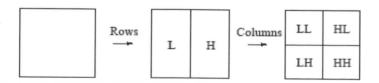

Figure 16.9 **One level DWT.**

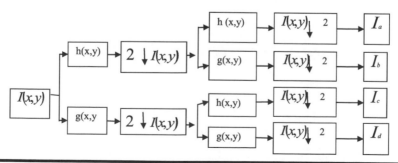

Figure 16.10 **Decomposition step of the image.**

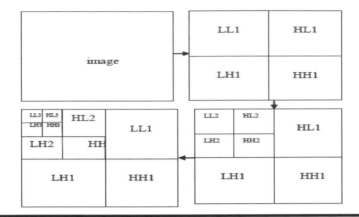

Figure 16.11 Multilevel DWT decomposition.

Figure 16.12 Example of multilevel decomposition.

16.4.1.1.2 Discrete Cosine Transform

Similarly, DCT (Discrete Cosine Transform) is another important transform domain technique (shown in Figure 16.13). It is mainly applicable for image compression, image watermarking and image fusion [5, 12]. The image is transformed into DCT domain using the following equations:

DCT transform:

$$F(k,l) = \alpha(k)\alpha(l) = \sum_{m=0}^{N-1} \sum_{n=0}^{N-1} f(m,n)\cos\left[\frac{(2m+1)\pi k}{2N}\right]\cos\left[\frac{(2n+1)\pi l}{2N}\right]$$

Inverse DCT transform:

$$f(m,\mathrm{n}) = \sum_{m=0}^{N-1} \sum_{n=0}^{N-1} \alpha(k)\alpha(l)F(k,l)\cos\left[\frac{(2m+1)\pi k}{2N}\right]\cos\left[\frac{(2n+1)\pi l}{2N}\right] \quad (16.6)$$

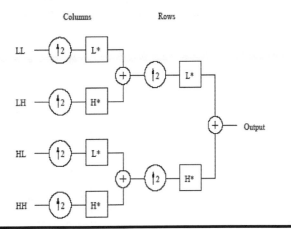

Figure 16.13 Inverse transform.

Scaling coefficients are:

$$
\alpha(k) = \begin{cases} \sqrt{\dfrac{1}{N}} & \text{if } k = 0 \\[3mm] \sqrt{\dfrac{2}{N}} & \text{if } k \neq 0 \end{cases}
$$

$$
\alpha(l) = \begin{cases} \sqrt{\dfrac{1}{N}} & \text{if } l = 0 \\[3mm] \sqrt{\dfrac{2}{N}} & \text{if } l \neq 0 \end{cases}
$$

(16.7)

Here $f(m,n)$ is the input image with mXn size.

16.4.1.2 Example Model Work Flow

The proposed idea of the author is to divide the work into two sessions: first session deals with multiple image fusion and final session deals with watermarking of fused images and other patient records (like photo, OP information, ECG reports etc.) into single image. The author tries to explore the new way of combining multiple techniques, which could be useful and extendable for effective image processing. The following session explains the fusion and watermarking process respectively in Figures 16.14 through 16.16.

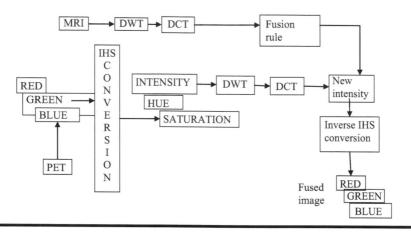

Figure 16.14   Proposed image fusion method.

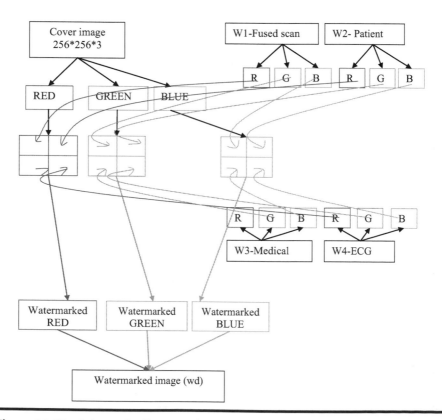

Figure 16.15   Schematic diagram of proposed watermark embedding process.

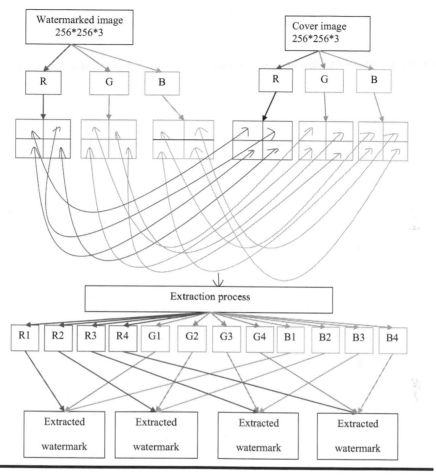

Figure 16.16   Schematic diagram of proposed watermark extraction process.

16.4.1.2.1 Image Fusion

Image fusion carries with DWT [4, 9], DCT [5, 12]. Here MRI provides soft tissue information and PET image provides blood cells information. An individual image does not provide maximum information. After fusion process to obtain fused image it contains soft tissue information and also blood information.

1. Read the MRI (ip1) and PET (RGB) (ip2) color image with same size. The PET (RGB) color image converted to HSI (hue, saturation and intensity) model. We can process only the intensity component while hue and saturation components remain unchanged.

2. Apply one level DWT on MRI (ip1) and intensity component (i) of PET color image to attain one low frequency co-efficient and three high frequency coefficients.

$$1 - DDWT \quad (ip\ 1) \in (LL, LH, HL, HH) \tag{16.8}$$

$$1 - DDWT \quad (i) \in (LL1, LH1, HL1, HH1) \tag{16.9}$$

3. Apply DCT on wavelet co-efficient of MRI (*LL, LH, HL, and HH*) and intensity component of PET image (*LL1, LH1, HL1, and HH1*).
4. Apply the following fusion rule:

Compute spatial frequency of two image DCT coefficients. Apply the following functional conditions to get fused coefficients [8].

$$F_{LL1} = \begin{cases} f_{LL(x,y)} & SF_{DCT(LL)} > SF_{DCT(LL1)} + TH \\ f_{LL1(X,Y)} & SF_{DCT(LL)} < SF_{DCT(LL1)} + TH \\ \dfrac{(f_{LL} + f_{LL1})}{2} & otherwise \end{cases} \tag{16.10}$$

Apply the same rule for F_{LH1}, F_{HL1} & F_{HH1} also.
5. Apply Inverse DCT on fused $F_{LL1}, F_{LH1}, F_{HL1}$ & F_{HH1} coefficients respectively.
6. Apply Inverse DWT on output of step 5 to get new intensity component image.
7. Finally the fused color image is a combination of new intensity component of PET image and unchanged components of hue and saturation.

16.4.1.2.2 Image Watermarking

The second part of proposed algorithm is image watermarking. This can effectively reduce the total information size by embedding multiple reports into a single cover image. The cover image inhabits the multiple patient reports and transfers to the destination for further processing. At the receiver end all the images are extracted effectively with lossless. The whole procedure is split into the embedding process and extraction process, one is at the transmission side and the other one is at the receiver end. The following sections discuss the watermarking embedding and extraction process.

16.4.1.2.2.1 Watermark Embedding Process
1. Read the color cover image (*IN*) (256*256*3) and four color watermark images (*W1, W2, W3, and W4*) (128*128*3). Out of four one is fused scan image and other three are clinical reports of patient (like patient photo, medical record, ECG report).

2. The Red (*inr*), Green (*ing*), and Blue (*inb*) components of cover image are divided into four equal parts. Each part size is 128*128.
3. The embedding process is given below:
   The red components of four watermark images embedding into red component of cover image with scaling factor α to obtain new red component (*fr*). Where $\alpha = 0.005$.

$$rr1 = inr(1:m/2,1:n/2) + (\alpha^* rw1) \tag{16.11}$$

$$rr2 = inr(1:m/2,n/2+1:n) + (\alpha^* rw2) \tag{16.12}$$

$$rr3 = inr(m/2+1:m,1:n/2) + (\alpha^* rw3) \tag{16.13}$$

$$rr4 = inr(m/2+1:m,n/2+1:n) + (\alpha^* rw4) \tag{16.14}$$

$$fr(1:m/2,1:1/2) = rr1 \tag{16.15}$$

$$fr(1:m/2,n/2+1:n) = rr1 \tag{16.16}$$

$$fr(1:m/2+1:m,1:n/2) = rr1 \tag{16.17}$$

$$fr(m/2+1:m,n/2+1:n) = rr1 \tag{16.18}$$

The same procedure is applicable for green and blue components to obtain new a green (*fg*) and a new blue component (*fb*).

4. Finally a watermarked image (*wd*) can be obtained by combining the above three new (red, green and blue) components.

The whole process of embedding is shown in Figure 16.15.

16.4.1.2.2.2 Watermark Extraction Process

1. Consider watermarked image (*wd*). The watermarked image having three components (red, green, and blue). The red (*inwr*), green (*inwg*), and blue (*inwb*) components are divided in to four equal parts. Each part having same size.
2. The extraction of watermark image is given below:
   To extract the red components of four watermark images (*rwe1, rwe2, rwe3, and rwe4*) by following equations.

$$rwe1 = ((inwr(1:m/2,1:n/2)) - (inr(1:m/2,1:n/2)).\,/\,\alpha \tag{16.19}$$

$$rwe2 = ((inwr(1:m/2, n/2+1:n)) - (inr(1:m/2, n/2+1:n))./\alpha \quad (16.20)$$

$$rwe3 = ((inwr(m/2+1:m, 1:n/2)) - (inr(m/2+1:m, 1:n/2))./\alpha \quad (16.21)$$

$$rwe4 = ((inwr(m/2+1:m, n/2+1:n)) - (inr(m/2+1:m, n/2+1:n))./\alpha \quad (16.22)$$

The same process applies on both green and blue components of watermarked and cover images to extract four green (*gwe1, gwe2, gwe3, and gwe4*) and blue (*bwe1, bwe2, bwe3, and bwe4*) components.

3. Finally watermark (w1) can be obtained by combining (*rwe1, gwe1, and bwe1*) components, similarly watermark (w2) with (*rwe2, gwe2, and bwe2*) components, watermark (w3) with the combination of (*rwe3, gwe3, and bwe3*) components and watermark (w4) also with (*rwe4, gwe4, and bwe4*) components.

16.4.1.3 Experimental Results

This section deals with types of images, their features, software details and performance metric used for quality analysis. The work used in PET and MRI images. The input image dimensions of MRI and PET are 256×256 and 256 * 256 * 3 pixels respectively. The PET and MRI images are inregister. The medical scan images are collected from [19]. The input and output images of fusion rule is displayed in Figures 16.17 and 16.18 and performance results are tabulated in Table 16.1.

The fused color images were used as one of the watermark images. The other images are, Lena as patient photo, electrocardiogram (ECG) image (downloaded from net), and medical record (created by author). The host/cover image, watermark: embedding and extraction images are displayed in Figures 16.19 through 16.22.

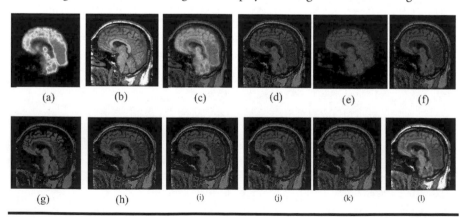

Figure 16.17   New mild Alzheimer's disease images: (a) PET scan, (b) MRI scan, (c) ground truth image, and (d–l) output image of various algorithms listed in Table 16.1.

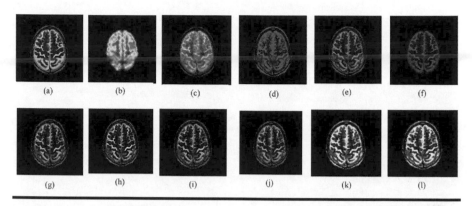

Figure 16.18 New mild Alzheimer's disease images: (a) PET scan, (b) MRI scan, (c) ground truth image, (d–l) output image of various algorithms listed in Table 16.1.

Table 16.1 Performance Metric Values of Fusion Methods with PSNR (Peak Signal to Noise Ratio) and MSE (Mean Squared Error)

Figures	Parameters	PSNR (db)	MSE
New Mild Alzheimer's disease images (Figure 4.9)	DWT and SF	43.4645	0.4599
	DSWT	43.4864	0.4241
	PCA	47.6211	0.4012
	Brovey	52.8826	0.3348
	IHS and PCA	53.0583	0.3215
	DWT and PCA	55.3214	0.2334
	DWT and PCA with SF	59.2578	0.1589
	Ref. [20]	64.7244	0.0748
	Proposed method	67.5575	0.0114
New Mild Alzheimer's disease images (Figure 4.10)	DWT and SF	46.4746	0.0260
	DSWT	56.7172	0.0692
	PCA	58.1331	0.0500
	Brovey	62.2149	0.0174
	IHS and PCA	62.5289	0.0182
	DWT and PCA	62.7243	0.0174
	DWT and PCA with SF	63.3078	0.0152
	Ref. [20]	63.4051	0.0148
	Proposed method	63.9120	0.0115

Figure 16.19   Watermark embedding process: (a) Color cover image, (b–e) color watermark images: Patient photo, medical record, and fused scan image, ECG record respectively.

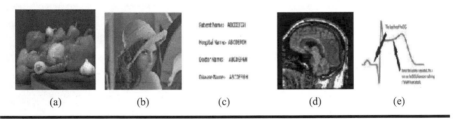

Figure 16.20   Watermark extraction process: (a) Color Watermarked image, (b–e) Extracted watermark images: Patient photo, medical record, and fused scan image, ECG record respectively.

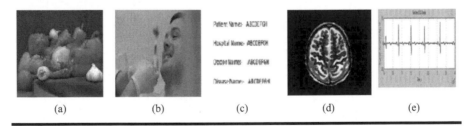

Figure 16.21   Watermark embedding process: (a) Color cover image, (b–e) color watermark images: Patient photo, medical record, and fused scan image, ECG record respectively.

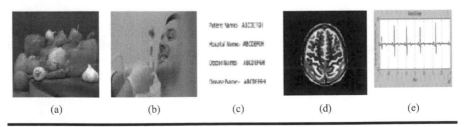

Figure 16.22   Watermark extraction process: (a) Color watermarked image, (b–e) Extracted watermark images: Patient photo, medical record, and fused scan image, ECG record respectively.

The experimental results are verified with PSNR (Peak Signal to Noise Ratio) [3, 6] and MSE (Mean Squared Error) [7]. These values prove the strength of the proposed work. The highest PSNR value means the host image and watermarked image both are identically same for human perception.

16.4.1.3.1 Fusion Results

The following figure and table addressing the results of proposed fusion process and the results are compared with existing techniques. The existing methods results are collected from [34] reference.

The performance of the fusion process is compared with various standard algorithms and existing techniques. The details are tabulated in Table 16.1.

16.4.1.3.2 Watermark Results

The following figures and Table 16.2 are addressing the proposed watermarking process on various patient databases. Figures 16.19 through 16.21 are embedding process results and Figures 16.20 through 16.22 are extraction process results. The database includes the patient photo, patient disease record, fused scan report and ECG report. The ECG signals are downloaded from [35].

16.4.1.3.3 Watermark Results with Noise

The following Figures 16.23 and 16.24 are showing the extracted watermark images in the presence of salt and pepper noise with various densities like 0.1, 0.001 etc.

Table 16.2 The Image Watermarking Performance Results in Terms of PSNR and MSE

Parameters	PSNR (db's)	MSE
Ref. [9]	45.0833	2.0172
Proposed method (Figures 16.19 and 16.20)	49.7155	0.6943
Proposed method (Figures 16.21 and 16.22)	50.6625	0.5583

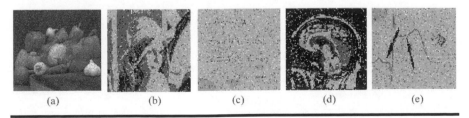

(a) (b) (c) (d) (e)

Figure 16.23 Salt and pepper noise (density = 0.1) (a) watermarked images, (b–e) extracted watermark images.

(a)	(b)	(c)	(d)	(e)

Figure 16.24   Salt and pepper noise (density = 0.001) (a) watermarked images, (b–e) extracted watermark images.

Table 16.3   The Measures Results in Terms of PSNR and MSE after Attacks

			Proposed Method	
Figures	*Noise*	*Density*	*PSNR (db's)*	*MSE*
Figure 4.15	Salt and pepper	0.1	14.6763	2.2154e+003
Figure 4.16	Gaussian noise	0.01	20.4297	588.9992

When the watermarked image is travelling through channels it is affected by various noises. Hence, the author proves the robustness of the proposed algorithm (Table 16.3).

16.5 Summary

This section summarised the novel approach in watermarking process by carrying various medical databases in a single image instead of various images. Thus, this chapter showed that multiple images can be embedded into a single image for an easy and short way of transmission. The effectiveness of the technique was also verified under various noises. Nearly five patient image databases were embedded and transmitted effectively. This can be extendable by transmitting various other medical scan images, iris image, biometric image etc.

References

1. N. Kausar, A. Majid, and S. G. Javed. A novel ensemble approach using individual features form multi-focus image fusion, *Computers and Electrical Engineering*, (2016), 1–13.
2. M. Haribabu, C.H. Bindu, and K.S. Prasad. Multimodal medical image fusion of MRI—PET Using wavelet transform, *IEEE International Conference MANCApps*, (2012), 127–130.
3. A. Roček, K. Slavíček, O. Dostál, and M. Javorník. A new approach to fully-reversible watermarking in medical imaging with breakthrough visibility parameters, *Biomedical Signal Processing and Control*, 29 (2016), 44–52.

4. J. Agarwal and S. S. Bedi. Implementation of hybrid image fusion technique for feature enhancement in medical diagnosis, *Human-centric Computing and Information Sciences*, 5(3) (2015), 1–17.
5. L. Cao et al., Multi-focus image fusion based on spatial frequency in discrete cosine transform domain, *IEEE Signal Processing Letters*, 22(2) (2015), 220–224.
6. R. Gharbia et al., Fusion of multi-spectral and panchromatic satellite images using principal component analysis and fuzzy logic, *FUZZ-IEEE, 2014*, July 6–11, China, pp. 1118–1222.
7. N. Makbol and B. E. Khoo. Robust blind image watermarking scheme based on Redundant Discrete Wavelet Transform and Singular Value Decomposition, *AEU - International Journal of Electronics and Communications*, 67(2) (2013), 102–112.
8. M. AlShaikh, L. Laouamer, L. Nana, and A. Pascu. A novel CT scan images watermarking scheme in DWT transform coefficients, *Journal of Computer Science and Network Security*, 16(1) (2016), 62–71.
9. M. Abdipour and M. Nooshyar. Multi-focus image fusion using sharpness criteria for visual sensor networks in wavelet domain, *Computers and Electrical Engineering*, 51 (2016), 74–88.
10. J. Du, W. Li, K. Lu, and B. Xiao. An overview of multi-modal medical image fusion, *Neurocomputing*, 215 (2016), 3–20.
11. A. K. Shaw and S. Majumder. Multiresolution SVD and pixel-wise masking BasedImage watermarking, Conference on Control, Instrumentation, Energy, & Communication *CIEC*, 2016, IEEE, pp. 193–196.
12. T. T. Takore, P. R. Kumar, and G. L. Devi. A modified blind image watermarking scheme based on DWT, DCT and SVD domain using GA to optimize robustness, *International Conference on Electrical, Electronics, and Optimization Techniques*, 2016, IEEE, pp. 2725–2729.
13. C. He, Q. Liu, H. Li, and H. Wang. Multimodal medical image fusion based on IHS and PCA, *Procedia Engineering*, 7 (2010), 280–285.
14. K. Kavitha. Survey on digital watermarking on medical images, *Journal of Advanced Computer Research*, 3(13) (2013), 330–335.
15. G. Coatrieux. A review of image watermarking applications in healthcare, *28th IEEE EMBS Annual International Conference*, August 30 to September 3, 2006, New York, IEEE, pp. 4691–4694.
16. I. F. Kallel, Control of dermatology image integrity using reversible watermarking, *Wiley Periodicals*, 19 (2009), 5–9.
17. X. Luo and Q. Cheng. Health information integrating and size reducing, *Nuclear Science Symposium Conference Record*, October 2003, IEEE, pp. 3014–3018.
18. F. C. Javier, Watermarking services for medical database content security, PhD thesis Department of ITI, Telecom, Bretagne, 2015.
19. http://www.med.harvard.edu/AANLIB/home.html
20. World Health Organization. http://www.who.int/diagnostic_imaging/en/
21. E. Fernandez Canga. Image fusion, M Engg thesis, University of Bath, Signal & Image Processing Group, 2002.
22. J. Flusser, F. Sroubek, and B. Zitova. Image fusion: Principles, methods, and applications, *EUSIPCO* 2007, pp. 1–60.
23. L. Yang, B. L. Guo, W.Ni, "Multimodality Medical Image Fusion Based On Multiscale Geometric Analysis Of Contourlet Transform", Neuro Computing, December 2008, pp. 203 – 211.
24. Y. Yang. A novel DWT based multi-focus image fusion method, *Procedia Engineering*, 24 (2011), 177–181.

25. V. Aslantas and R. Kurban. Fusion of multi-focus images using differential evolution algorithm, *Expert System with Applications*, 37 (2010), 8861–8870.

26. A. C. Wang and P. Zhao. Multi-focus image fusion with the double-density dual-tree DWT, *IEEE Conference on Image and Signal Processing*, 4 (2008), 371–374.

27. J. Yonghong. Fusion of landsat TM and SAR images based on principal component analysis, *Remote Sensing Technology and Application*, 13(1) (1998), 46–49.

28. S. Mukhopadhyay and B. Chanda. Fusion of 2d gray scale images using multi-scale morphology, *Pattern Recognition*, 34(12) (2001), 1939–1949.

29. V. S. Petrovic and C. S. Xydeas. Gradient-based multi-resolution image fusion, *IEEE Transaction Image Processing*, 13(2) (2004), 228–237.

30. K. Rajpoot, J. Alison Noble, V. Grau, C. Szmigielski, and H. Becher. *Multiview RT3D Echocardiography Image Fusion*, Springer-Verlag, Berlin Germany, 2009, pp. 134–143.

31. Guest Editorial, Image fusion: Advances in the state of the art, *Information Fusion*, 8 (2007), 114–118.

32. G. G. Bhutada, R. S. Anand, and S. C. Saxena. Edge preserved image enhancement using adaptive fusion of images denoised by wavelet and curvelet transform, *Digital Signal Processing*, 21 (2011), 118–130.

33. C. H. Bindu, and K. S. Prasad. Performance analysis of multi source fused médical images using multi resolution transform, *International Journal of Advanced Computer Science and Applications*, 3(10) 2012, 54–62.

34. M. Haribabu, C. H. Bindu, and K. S. Prasad. A new approach of medical image fusion using discrete wavelet transform, *ACEEE, IJSIP*, 4 (2013), 21–25.

35. ECG Data collected from this Weblink: https://www.google.co.in/search?biw=1024 &bih=588&tbm=isch&sa=1&ei=OuIPWqyKBMHsvgTe3rqYDA&q=ecg+signals& oq=ecg+signals&gs_l=psyab.3..0j0i24k1l3.5388.7822.0.8089.11.11.0.0.0.0.255.1511. 0j6j2.8.0....0...1.1.64.psyab..3.8.1511...0i67k1j0i30k1.0._YQCuyzxUPc

36. Alper Koz, "Digital Watermarking Based on Human Visual System", The Graduate School of Natural and Applied Sciences, thesis, The Middle East Technical University, pp. 2–8, Sep 2002.

37. J. J. K. O'Ruanaidh, W. J. Dowling, and F. M. Boland, Watermarking digital images for copyright protection, *IEE Proceedings-Vision, Image and Signal Processing*, 143(4) (1996), 250–254.

38. B. Jellinek, Invisible watermarking of digital images for copyright protection, PhD thesis, University of Salzburg, pp. 9–17, 2000.

39. C. Pik-Wah, Digital video watermarking techniques for secure multimedia creation and delivery, PhD thesis, The Chinese University of Hong Kong, pp. 7–15, 2004.

40. D. Anand and U. C. Niranjan. Watermarking medical images with patient information, in *Proceedings of the 20th Annual International Conference of the IEEE Engineering in Medicine and Biology Society*, 20(2) (1998), 703–706.

41. A. Nikolaidis, S. Tsekeridou, A. Tefas, and V. Solachidis. A survey on watermarking application scenarios and related attacks, *IEEE international Conference on Image Processing*, 3 (2001), 991–993.

42. M. Haribabu, C. H. Bindu, and K. V. Swamy. A secure & invisible image watermarking scheme based on wavelet transform in HSI color space, *Elsevier Procedia Computer Science*, 93 (2016), 462–468.

43. N. A. Kumar, M. Haribabu, and H. Bindu. Novel image watermarking algorithm with DWT-SVD, *International Journal of Computer Applications (IJCA)*, 106(1) (2014), 12–17.

Chapter 17

Watermarking Techniques and Its Applications in Tele-Health: A Technical Survey

Sriti Thakur, Amit Kumar Singh, SP Ghrera
and Mayank Dave

Contents

DOI: 10.1201/9780429435461-19

17.1 Introduction

Recently, tele-health services not only facilitate the transmission of essential medical information over open channel but also incorporate exchanges between the patient and the doctor at distant locations [1–5]. Presently, tele-health applications are very promising and have great potentials at the international level [1,2]. It refers to the use of recent information and communication technologies to meet the needs of society, patients, healthcare professionals, healthcare providers as well as policy makers [1–3]. However security requirements in terms of reliability, availability and confidentiality of medical patient information are the most challenging problems in the implementation of dependable tele-health management systems [1,3,5]. In addition to this, medical identity theft is a growing and a dangerous offense in recent times [1,2]. Therefore, the validity of the medical information is of prime concern as they form the basis of inference for diagnostic purposes [1]. Figure 17.1 shows the major security requirements for electronic patient record (EPR) documents/watermark(s) [6]. Research concluded that efficient watermarking techniques are proving to be a counter measure in mitigating the above mentioned issues. It is the process of embedding watermark information/data into cover media in such a way that the hidden watermark information can be detected or extracted later to make an assertion about the authenticity and/or originality of the media [1]. According to the recent literature [6], the digital watermark

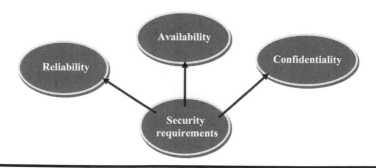

Figure 17.1 Major security requirements. (From Mohanty, S.P. et al., *IEEE Consum. Electron. Mag.*, 6, 83–91, 2017.)

Table 17.1 Difference between Closely Related Concepts

Digital Watermarking	Steganography	Cryptography	Digital Rights Management (DRM)
It secures the owner of digital data instead of digital data itself.	It deals with covert transformation of an object so that only the communicating parties understand the hidden message.	It is known as secret writing and deals with protecting the digital data transmitted over an unsecured channel.	It is concerned with the prevention of unauthorized access of digital content therefore; only authorized person can access it.
The purpose behind it is concealment of a scrambled message into a digital signal without causing distortion.	The objective behind steganography is hiding a message for a communication intended at one to one basis.	It modifies the message so that it becomes unintelligible/ non-interpretable for unintended receivers.	It attempts to encrypt the digital content in a manner to make it undecipherable, further a secret key is required for decryption.
The watermark embedding process requires learned skill and should be done in a way which is not visible through human eyes.	An important concern with it is the bandwidth that the hidden message occupies.	Authentication of the sender is a concerning issue in this particular case.	It does not guarantee owner protection against false declaration of possession.

is identified as a visible, invisible, public, private, perceptual, and bit stream watermark. The different types of watermarks are important according to the application needs. The concept of digital watermarking is better than other closely related techniques such as steganography, cryptography, and digital rights management (DRM) [1,6,7] as shown in Table 17.1.

The rest of the chapter is structured as follows: Section 17.2 provides the important characteristics of digital watermarks. Potential applications of digital watermarking are reported in Section 17.3. Section 17.4 provides the generic structure of watermarking embedding and extraction process. Section 17.5 presents the spatial and transform domain watermark embedding techniques. Vital performance measures of digital watermarking techniques are presented in Section 17.6. Section 17.7 presents the watermarking attacks. A brief literature review of current state-of-the-art tele-health applications are provided followed by the potential challenges and fruitful solutions in Section 17.8. Section 17.9 provides summary of the chapter.

17.2 Important Characteristics of Digital Watermarks

The desirable characteristics of digital watermarks are explained below [1,6,8,9]. Further, the important characteristics of digital watermark are presented in Figure 17.2.

- **Robustness** – it is a measure of the capability of the concealed watermark to resist valid or image-processing transformations, such as intentional or unintentional attacks. Intentional attacks are aimed towards destroying the watermark, whereas unintentional attacks do not carry out any kind of alteration.
- **Fragility** – it is a measure which is indicative of the content authenticity. Fragile and semi-fragile are the important consideration in this study. Fragile watermarks are aimed towards achieving complete integrity verification. Semi-fragile watermarks find their utilization for the detection of any unauthorized modification but allowing some image-processing transformations.
- **Imperceptibility** – it is a measure of visual perceptibility of watermark. In other words, it is a measure which gives the extent to which the original and watermarked images are similar to each other.
- **Embedding capacity** – it is defined as the amount of information that a watermark can embed in a multimedia cover.
- **Security** – in the context of watermarking, security implies that the removal, alteration or any such modifications to a watermark becomes difficult without causing any damage to the cover image. Security in watermarking is application-specific and may vary from application to application.
- **Computational complexity** – it refers to the cost associated with the insertion and detection of digital watermarks into/from the cover media. Computational cost varies with the requirement of applications. Some

Figure 17.2   Major characteristics of digital watermark(s).

applications demand the embedding process to be faster whereas other applications focus on making the time involved in extraction process to be lengthy. The implementation cost should ideally be zero [6].

- **Key restrictions** – research concluded that unrestricted-key and restricted-key are placed on the ability to access the watermark/secret information. The selection of key length greatly depends on security as well as applications.
- **False positive rate** – it is the probability that it will recognize an un-watermark portion of data as containing a watermark. This error further depends on applications.
- **Tamper resistance** – it is a measure which verifies the integrity and authenticity of a digital watermarking system. Tamper resistant watermarks are sensitive to any kind of content modification, replacement and alteration, thus fulfilling in providing reliability and content validation.

17.3 Potential Applications of Digital Watermarking

Recently, digital watermarking has potential use in tele-health, e-governance, chip and hardware protection, military, digital cinema, copyright protection and content authentication. [1,6,8,9]. The popular applications of digital marking are depicted in Figure 17.3.

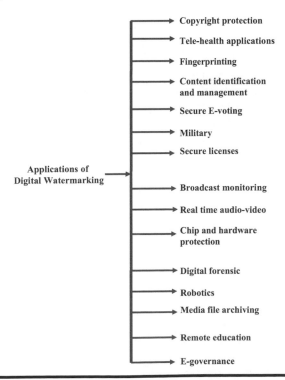

Figure 17.3   Major applications of digital watermarking.

17.4 Generic Structure of Watermarking Embedding and Extraction Process

The generic structure of the watermarking embedding and extraction process is presented in detail in [6,10]. Figure 17.4 shows the embedding and extraction process. The encoder accepts two inputs in the form of an input image (I) and a watermark (W_m). The output is produced as an image containing the watermark (I_o). The watermarked image (I_o) is the product of the function $E(I, W_m)$

$$I_o = E(I, W_m) \tag{17.1}$$

Similarly, the decoder accepts test image (I_t) and original image (I) as input and produces the output in the form of extracted watermark (W_e). Therefore, the extracted watermark(s) is the product of the function $D(I_t, I)$.

$$W_e = D(I_t, I) \tag{17.2}$$

Finally, the original watermark(s) is compared with possibly distorted extracted watermark(s).

17.5 Spatial and Transform Domain Techniques of Embedding Watermarks

The digital image watermarking techniques can be categorized into two important domain methods as spatial and transform domain techniques [1].

The spatial domain techniques are straight forward and computationally simple. However, the techniques are not robust against attacks. Research concluded that the transform domain techniques are robust for various attacks. However, these techniques are computationally expensive. Some of the popular spatial and transform domain techniques are discussed in Tables 17.2 and 17.3, respectively. Further, important spatial and transform domain techniques are depicted in Figure 17.5.

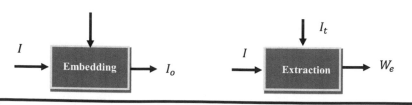

Figure 17.4 Watermark embedding and extraction process.

Table 17.2 Common Spatial Domain Watermarking Techniques

S. No.	Spatial Domain Technique	Description	Major Advantages
1.	Least substitution bit (LSB)	The information hiding in the sequential binary numbers is done by swapping the LSB of every element with one bit of the secret message [11].	It is known to have easy implementation along with higher embedding capacity.
2.	Patchwork	This technique involves the use of a pseudorandom generator which produces the locations of the cover image which hosts the watermark [11].	It offers low computational complexity.
3.	Correlation-based technique	As the name suggests, this spatial domain technique harnesses correlation properties of additive pseudorandom noise patterns.	This technique can be implemented to multiple-bit watermarks.
4.	Spread spectrum	It tries to resolve the issue of inserting watermark(s) into the prominent regions of the spectrum and at the same time retaining the fidelity.	Dispersion of the watermark(s) right through the image spectrum guarantees security against watermarking attacks.

Table 17.3   Common Transform Domain Watermarking Technique

S. No.	Transform Domain Technique	Description	Major Advantages
1.	Discrete cosine transform (DCT)	It divides an image into low, high and middle frequency coefficients. Further, researchers can embed the secret/ watermark information into selected coefficients of the DCT image.	– The time and space (volume) required by DCT is less. – It has excellent energy compaction property.
2.	Discrete wavelet transform (DWT)	It divides an image into a set of four non-overlapping multi-resolution sub-bands.	– Most popular method as it provides the space frequency localization, multi-resolution and multi-scale analysis etc.
3.	Singular value decomposition (SVD)	Divides an image into ortho-normal and diagonal parts. Singular values appear in descending order in the diagonal parts of an image.	Singular values are unique, stable and exhibit excellent energy compaction properties.
4.	Karhunen-Loeve transform (KLT)	The KL transform is a reversible linear transform that takes the advantage of statistical properties of a vector representation and optimally de-correlates the input data.	The de-correlation property of KL transform eradicates the requirement for cross channel smoothing.
5.	Discrete Fourier transform (DFT)	It decomposes an image into a set of orthogonal functions and converts the spatial intensity of the image into its frequency domain.	DFT employs phase modulation in place of magnitude components for data hiding which yields better robustness against noise attacks. However, it shows poor energy compaction property.

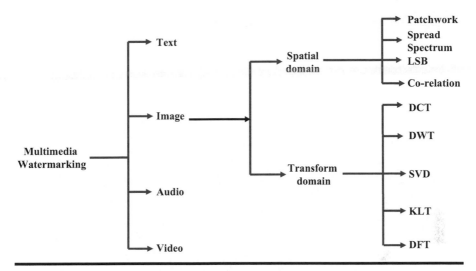

Figure 17.5 Watermarking techniques in spatial and transform domain.

17.6 Vital Performance Parameters in Digital Watermarking

Researchers are using various parameters for evaluating the performance of water-marking algorithms/systems. Some of the important parameters are introduced as follows [1,12]:

17.6.1 Peak Signal to Noise Ratio (PSNR)

It is a ratio of maximum possible power of a signal to the power of corrupting noise. It is used for measuring the quality of the watermarked images. Ideally PSNR value greater than 28 is considered tolerable for watermarking systems. Therefore, the higher the value of PSNR the more imperceptible it is (similar to original image).

$$\text{PSNR} = 10 \log \frac{(255)^2}{\text{MSE}} \tag{17.3}$$

The mean squared error (MSE) is defined as

$$\text{MSE} = \frac{1}{X \times Y} = \sum_{k=1}^{l=1} \sum_{k=1}^{l=1} (P_{kl} - Q_{kl})^2 \tag{17.4}$$

where $X \times Y$ = size of the cover image/watermarked image, P_{kl} = pixel of the original image, and Q_{kl} = pixel of the watermarked image.

17.6.2 Normalized Correlation (NC)

The normalized correlation (NC) determines the differences and the similarities between the original and extracted watermark (s) images. The value of NC ranges between 0 and 1 and preferably it should be 1. Generally, NC value of 0.7 is considered to be acceptable [9]. It is defined as

$$
NC = \frac{\sum_{k=1}^{X} \sum_{l=1}^{Y} \left(Q_{\text{original } kl} \times Q_{\text{recovered } kl} \right)}{\sum_{k=1}^{X} \sum_{l=1}^{Y} Q_{\text{original } kl}^{2}}
\tag{17.5}
$$

where $Q_{\text{original } kl}$ = pixel of the original watermark, $Q_{\text{recovered } kl}$ = pixel of the extracted watermark.

17.6.3 Bit Error Rate (BER)

The bit error rate (BER) is a ratio of number of incorrectly decoded bits to total number of bits [1]. Ideal acceptable value of bit error rate is 0.

$$
BER = \frac{\text{Number of incorrectly decoded bits}}{\text{Total number of bits}}
\tag{17.6}
$$

17.6.4 Weighted Peak Signal to Noise Ratio (WPSNR)

Recently, weighted peak signal to noise ratio (WPSNR) provides a superior quality metric than PSNR for measuring the quality of the watermarked images. It introduces noise visibility function (NVF), which is an arbitrary texture-masking function with a permissible value ranging between 0 for test image with extreme textured areas and 1 for test image with visually clear flat areas. The WPSNR is defined as

$$
WPSNR = \frac{255^2}{NVF \times MSE}
\tag{17.7}
$$

where $NVF = NORM\left\{ 1/1 + \delta^2_{\text{block}} \right\}$

NVF is a normalization function where "δ" is luminance variance of the blocks used in calculations [13].

17.6.5 Structural Similarity Index (SSIM)

It is one of the recent performance parameters enabling measurement of the perceptual quality between watermarked image and original image, or how similar the two images are to each other. Permissible value of SSIM ranges between –1 and 1, where value equal to 1 is indicative of the two images (watermarked image and original image) to be similar [1,14,15].

$$a(m,n) = \frac{2\mu_m \mu_n + C_1}{\mu_m^2 + \mu_n^2 + C_1} \tag{17.8}$$

$$b(m,n) = \frac{2\sigma_m \sigma_n + C_2}{\sigma_m^2 + \sigma_n^2 + C_2} \tag{17.9}$$

$$c(m,n) = \frac{\sigma_{mn} + C_3}{\sigma_m \sigma_n + C_3} \tag{17.10}$$

The variables $a(m, n)$, $b(m, n)$, and $c(m, n)$ are three different functions and are called luminance comparison function, contrast comparison function and structure comparison function, respectively. Further C_1, C_2, and C_3 are defined as constants and selected as positive values.

17.7 Watermarking Attacks

Attacks with respect to digital watermarking are defined as any ill-intentioned action carried out to perform illicit embedding, deletion and revealing of a (valid or invalid) watermark [16]. An attack is considered to be successful if it harms the watermark beyond permissible limits while maintaining the perceptual quality of the attacked data [17]. Mainly it can be divided into two parts as intentional and unintentional attacks. In first, attackers maliciously try to hinder the functionality of the watermark(s) for fulfilling his/her motives, e.g., geometric attacks, cryptographic attacks, and protocol attacks. However, in second, attacker has no malicious intent behind hindering the functionality of the watermark, e.g., image processing attacks. In addition, some important attacks are categorized and discussed in detail in Table 17.4 (Figure 17.6).

Table 17.4 Watermarking Attacks

S. No.	Attacks	Description	Major Examples
1.	Image-processing attacks	These attacks come under unintentional attacks as there is no malicious intent behind it.	Filtering, re-modulation, JPEG coding distortion and JPEG 2000 compression.
2.	Geometric attacks	These kinds of attacks are not aimed towards removal of data rather they attempt in perceptually harming the digital content.	Linear transformation, clipping, scaling, rotation, perspective projection, warping, bending, template and collage.
3.	Cryptographic attacks	These attacks try to foil the security techniques involved in protecting a watermark and often have high computational cost associated with them, therefore they find less usage.	Oracle attack and collusion attack.
4.	Protocol attacks	The main motive behind such attacks is to get an idea about the watermark instead of modifying or removing it. This in turn can make the attacker claim the ownership of cover and watermarked image.	Copy attack and invertible attack.
5.	Other intentional attacks	These comprises of attacks which try to challenge the authenticity of the rightful possession of an entity.	Rescanning, printing, re-watermarking, IBM attack, forgery attack, unzign and stirmark attacks.

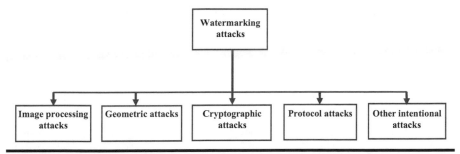

Figure 17.6 Important watermark attacks. (From Mohanty, S.P., Digital water-marking: A tutorial review. http://www.csee.usf.edu/smohanty/research/Reports/WMSurvey1999Mohanty.pdf, 1999.)

17.8 Recent State-of-the-Art Watermarking Techniques for Tele-Health Applications

In [18], Ustubioglu and Ulutas proposed a secure medical image watermarking technique using fusion of modified difference expansion and least significant bit (LSB). Initially, the medical cover image is divided into different blocks and the watermark information is embedded only in the border pixels of the cover image. Further, the method can detect tampered regions with finer precision and it does not depend on the size of the region of interest (ROI) portion of the cover. Experimental results demonstrated that the performance in terms of PSNR and (true positive rate) TPR is found superior than other similar existing methods [19–24].

Parah et al. developed a blind watermarking technique using intermediate significant bit (ISB) for e-healthcare applications [25]. Two different watermarks are embedded into the same cover media for content authentication at receiver end. Further, security of the watermark data is enhanced by using non-linear dynamics of chaos. The imperceptibility, robustness, localization analysis and tamper detection and of the work is found to be suitable for e-medical applications.

Sharifara and Ghaderi proposed a robust and secure watermarking technique in DWT (discrete wavelet transform) domain [26]. In this method, the cover image is divided into region of interest (ROI) and region of non-interest (RONI). Both ROI and RONI portions are transformed using DWT. However, the encrypted watermark(s) (using public key) information is embedded into the RONI portion of the cover. The performance of the method is determined by PSNR and SSIM.

Further, region-based blind watermarking is proposed by Shih et al. [27]. This method embeds the watermark information in RONI portion of the cover image using particle swarm optimization (PSO). First, the RONI portion of the cover is transformed by DWT and the singular vector of the selected DWT sub-band is determined by singular wave decomposition (SVD). Finally, the singular vector is further transformed by DCT and the middle frequency DCT component is considered for the watermark embedding. Experimental results demonstrated that the method is imperceptible and has good embedding capacity. In [28], Gao et al. developed a blind watermarking technique for medical images. In the first step, the segmented ROI and RONI portion of the cover medical image is determined and the feature-bit matrix generated from the ROI is embedded into the LSBs of the RONI portion for detection of tampered regions at the receiving end. Experimental results demonstrated that the relative contrast error (RCE), PSNR and SSIM performance of the proposed method is acceptable for medical image applications. In [29], the author proposed a fragile watermarking technique using logistic map. The generated binary watermark information and absolute difference (as determined by cover image pixel and element of the key) are embedded into the cover image. Experimental results have shown that the method offered very low false detection rate with excellent PSNR performance. Further, results demonstrated that performance in terms of PSNR, false-negative rate (FNR), and false positive rate (FPR) of the proposed method is found better than other techniques [30,31]. The technique explained in [32] exploits a pixel-based watermarking using combination of DWT and SVD for telemedicine application. The proposed technique also determined the ROI and RONI portion of the cover medical image and ROI information is embedded into the RONI portion of the cover image using bit replacement method. Results indicated that the method is better than other similar state-of-the-art techniques [33–36]. Further, Khor et al. [37] proposed a segmented ROI and RONI based watermarking technique in which the ROI information is embedded into the RONI least significant bits of the cover medical image using hash-256 and JPEG compression. The result indicated that the elapsed time of the watermark embedding and authentication is better than other similar research in [38].

In [39], Lei et al. introduced an integer wavelet transform (IWT) based intelligent dual watermarking technique for the purpose of content authentication and copyright protection. Further, artificial bee colony (ABC) algorithm was used to create a balance between watermark conflicting requirements. These requirements include robustness, imperceptibility and embedding capacity. The robust and fragile watermarks are embedded into the selected sub-bands of the IWT cover image. The low frequency coefficients of IWT are transformed by SVD before embedding the robust watermark into the considered sub-band. Experimental results demonstrated that the method is imperceptible, robust and secure for various attacks. The technique explained in [40] exploits a just noticeable distortion (JND) based medical image watermarking technique in DCT (disrete cosine ransform) domain. The low frequency components (as obtained by DCT) of the cover image is considered for the watermark embedding. Further, imperceptibility is enhanced by using Chou's JND method [41]. Experimental results reveal that the NC performance of the proposed method is better than other reported technique [42].

A robust and reversible watermarking technique using combination of DWT and SVD for telemedicine application is proposed in [43]. Initially, DWT is applied on the ROI portion of the cover medical image and SVD is applied on the selected

DWT sub-band of the ROI cover image. The watermark information is embedded into the selected SVD block ("U" matrix) of the considered DWT sub-band. Further, EPR watermark encoded by error correction code is embedded into the RONI portion of the cover. The performance of the method is evaluated extensively and found superior than other state-of-the-art techniques [44,45]. Further, a robust and secure region-based watermarking technique for tele-ophthalmology application is introduced by Pandey et al. [46]. The multiple watermarks are embedding into the non-region of interest (NROI) portion of the cover image. The EPR watermark information is modified with ROI (generation hash using SHA-512) portion before embedding into the RONI portion of the cover. Experimental results demonstrated that the method is robust and highly secure against common attacks including Checkmark attacks. Further, visual quality and robustness performance of the method is better than other existing method [45].

Arsalan et al. [47] proposed a blind medical image watermarking technique using integer wavelet transform (IWT) and genetic programming. The concept of companding is introduced for the watermark embedding. Experimental results demonstrated that the performance (in terms of PSNR and SSIM) of the proposed method is found better than the technique reported in [48]. In [49], Liu et al. also proposed a region (ROI and RONI) based secure and blind medical image watermarking technique. In the first step, hash value (using MD5) of the ROI of the cover image is generated and combined with RONI portion and border area of the image. The watermark information is embedded into the LSB plane of the ROI portion of the cover. The proposed method offered better performance than other similar existing methods [50–53].

For security of the patient data as well as the important parts of the image, Mantos and Maglogiannis reported a watermarking method in [54]. Initially, the hash value of the sensitive information (as considered from DICOM file) and ROI portion of the cover image are evaluated and both hash information are encrypted by cryptographic key. Further, the encrypted information is embedded into the ROI portion of the cover using LSB technique. Furthermore, information needed to extract the ROI before embedding is to be found in the RONI portion of the cover. The method is secure and highly imperceptible. However, the method is computationally expensive.

For copyright protection and authentication of medical information Anusudha et al. [55] also reported a combination of encryption and watermarking techniques for healthcare applications. Two different watermark information are embedded into the selected sub-bands of the DWT cover medical image. The energy of the DWT sub-band is determined before the secret watermark information is embedded into the selected sub-bands. The method is tested for various kinds of attacks. Further, the method uses the power of DNA sequence and exploits the capability of GA to find the optimal solution at the encryption stage. In [56], the authors have proposed a secure watermarking technique in DWT-SVD domain. The transformed cover image is obtained by DWT and SVD which is applied on the selected sub-bands. The ROI and RONI portion of all four sub-bands are determined before applying any transforms. SVD is applied only on the RONI portion of the selected DWT cover sub-bands. In this method, the watermark data (hash, logo and EPR) is embedded into the higher singular value of the RONI portion of selected DWT sub-bands of the cover image. Experimental results in terms of robustness, imperceptibility and tamper localization showed the suitability of the method for tele-medicine applications. In [57], Amri et al. developed a lossless compression based watermarking technique. The technique addresses the problem of large volume of medical data which consumed higher bandwidth during the transmission. The performance of the method is evaluated in terms of number of bits per pixel, SSIM and PSNR, and is found to have a higher compression ratio at acceptable image quality. The work presented in [58] addresses the issues related to robustness of the water-marking techniques against salt and pepper noise. This method also embeds the encoded electronic patient record (EPR) watermark information (by ROI pixels) in RONI portion of the cover image using LSB, channel coding and noise filtering schemes. The imperceptibility performance of the method is evaluated using PSNR SSIM, and the accuracy of the extracted watermark is assessed in terms of bit error rate (BER). Parah et al. [59] reported a robust watermarking technique in DCT domain. Two different ways of watermark embedding are used in the method. In the first method, the watermark(s) is embedded in the cover image whereas in the second, the watermark(s) information is embedded only in the RONI portion of the cover image. The performance of the method is evaluated for different attacks and the results demonstrated an improved performance in terms of robustness and payload. DWT and SVD based robust dual watermarking technique is reported in [60]. Further, the performance of the method is extensively evaluated with different types of error correcting codes (ECCs). Experimental analysis of the hybrid technique showed improved robustness for various kinds of attacks at acceptable visual quality of the image. In addition to this, Singh et al. [61] developed a robust and secure watermarking technique in DWT domain. The watermark is embedded only in the selective wavelet coefficients using secure spread-spectrum scheme. A strong threshold criterion is considered for the watermark embedding. Further, the robustness of the method is improved by using Bose, Ray-Chaudhuri, Hocquenghem (BCH) error correction code. The method is extensively evaluated and found robust and imperceptible for various image processing attacks. Furthermore, performance of the proposed method is found superior to other state-of-the-art techniques [62,63]. For medical image authentication Thabit and Khoo [23] reported a region-based watermarking technique in transform domain. In this method, the watermark information is generated from the ROI portion of the cover image and the generated information is embedded into the RONI portion of the image. Extensive analysis of the work demonstrated that the method is robust and imperceptible for important image processing attacks.

In [24], authors also proposed a region based watermarking technique in transform domain. However, the hash value and recovery data of ROI and EPR information is embedded into the RONI portion of the cover image using IWT. The results indicated that the method is not only robust for various attacks but also accurately detects and localize tampered regions inside ROI. In [64], a robust and automatic ROI detection framework is proposed for watermarking application. Experimental results demonstrated the detection method is robust against numerous attacks. Lu et al. [65] proposed a secure and region-based watermarking technique for healthcare applications. In this method, the cover image is divided into ROI and RONI portions and two different encrypted watermark information are embedded into both regions of the cover image. The performance of the method is extensively evaluated in terms of PSNR and SSIM and is found superior to other state-of-the-art techniques [66]. Further, region-based blind watermarking technique with tamper detection is proposed in [67]. Two different watermarks are generated and embedded into the ROI and RONI portion of the cover image. Embedding capacity, PSNR and SSIM performance of the method is found better than other similar existing techniques [68,69]. Lei et al. [70] developed a blind image watermarking method in DWT-SVD domain. Initially, the cover medical image is divided into different sub-blocks and each sub-block is transformed by DWT followed by SVD. Encrypted watermark bits are embedded into selected singular vector of the wavelet coefficients by quantization using reversible dither modulation. In this proposed study, differential evolution is applied to design the quantization steps optimally for controlling the strength of the watermark. The experimental results show the superiority of the proposed method as compared to other similar techniques [71–76] in terms of PSNR and MSSIM. In [77], the authors have used secure and region based dual watermarking using combination of transform (DWT-SVD) and spatial domain (LSB) techniques. Three different watermarks are generated such as ROI LSB, EPR information and logo, which are embedded into the selected DWT sub-bands of RONI portion of the cover medical image. The selected DWT sub-band of the RONI portion of cover is further transformed by SVD before the watermark(s) embedding. Simulation results demonstrate the efficiency of the proposed method in providing security solution for telemedicine applications. Sparse Coding (SC) based robust watermarking technique is reported in [78]. In the first step, ROI portion of the selected cover and EPR watermark is concatenated and sparse coding is applied on the concatenated watermark. Further, the encoded watermark is embedded into the singular vector of the RONI portion of cover image. Simulation results have shown that the method is imperceptible and robust against various attacks.

In [79], a medical image watermarking technique using fusion of wavelet and KL (Karhunen-Loeve) transform is proposed. The cover image is decomposed by DWT and KLT (Karhunen-Loeve transform),which is applied on the selected DWT coefficients. The generated watermark as obtained by SHA-1 hash function, EPR data and logo image is embedded into the cover image. The watermark information is encoded by turbo code before embedding into the cover image. The performance of the method is evaluated in terms of PSNR, WPSNR, and NC and is found suitable for medical applications. A region based fragile watermarking technique is developed in [80]. The method first divides the cover image into three different portions as ROI, RONI and border pixels. The authentication data and ROI information are embedded into the border pixels. Then, recovery information of ROI is embedded into the RONI portion of the cover image. Performance of the method is extensively evaluated in terms of various important parameters such as PSNR, WPSNR, MSSIM, and total perceptual error (TPE). From the results it is evident that the method is suitable for medical applications. A reversible dither modulation and region based secure watermarking method in transform domain (DWT and SVD) is reported in [81]. Initially, concatenated vertices of ROI, hash of ROI (using SHA-256), identification code and logo image are combined and the watermark information is generated. The generated watermark is further encrypted by AES and the encrypted watermark is embedded into a singular vector of the DWT cover image. Simulation results demonstrated that the method offered good balance between major performance parameters.

In [82], the performance of the genetic algorithm (GA) and particle swarm optimization (PSO) based blind watermarking techniques is investigated. Experimental results demonstrated that the embedding capacity, PSNR, bpp and SSIM performance of the proposed method is found superior than the other state-of-the-art techniques [83–86]. Further, it is evident that the GA outperforms PSO in terms of temporal cost. The work presented in [20] addresses the issues related to health data distribution and management issues. In this technique, author have reported a region based blind and fragile watermarking technique in which the ROI hash value and encrypted EPR information is embedded into the cover medical image. From the experimental evaluation it is evident that the method is efficient and suitable for healthcare applications.

DWT and SVD based robust watermarking technique is reported in [87]. In this technique, the watermark information is directly embedded into the singular vector of the selected DWT sub-bands of the cover image. In this way, the technique required less SVD computations. Further, simulation analysis illustrated that the method is robust for numerous attacks. In [88], a region-based high capacity and robust watermarking technique is reported. The hash value of ROI along with encoded EPR is embedded into the RONI portion of the cover medical image. The EPR watermark is encoded by class dependent coding scheme (CDCS) before the embedding into the cover media. Experimental results have shown that the method is able to withstand a variety of attacks.

The summary of the above state-of-the-art medical image watermarking is presented in Table 17.5.

Table 17.5 Summary of Recent State-of-the-Art Watermarking Techniques for Tele-Health Applications

Ref No.	Proposed Objectives	Techniques to Achieve Objectives	Type of Watermarking Technique	Performance Evaluations	Size of the Cover/ Watermark Image(s)	Other Important Considerations
[18]	Secure medical image watermarking with high accuracy.	ROI and RONI MDE LSB SHA-256	Reversible	PSNR = 44dB (X-ray) Determined up to 99% of tampered area. Average TPR = 99.29 (Size of the tampered region = 1.43%).	Tested for different sizes of cover image up to 1024 × 1024 (X-ray)/1 K–64 K (EPR).	– The performance of algorithm is independent of ROI size of medical cover. – Tamper localization capability is tested for different experiments.
[25]	High capacity watermarking technique.	PTB conversion ISBS Checksum Chaotic encryption	Reversible	For medical imagery Avg PSNR = 46.3698, Avg SSIM = 0.9827, For standard images Avg PSNR = 46.3684 Avg SSIM = 0.98864	Divisible by 4 × 4 block/total capacity = 0.75 bits per pixel (bpp.)	– Subjective and objective. – Analysis used to determine the perceptual quality.

(Continued)

Table 17.5 (*Continued*)   Summary of Recent State-of-the-Art Watermarking Techniques for Tele-Health Applications

Ref No.	Proposed Objectives	Techniques to Achieve Objectives	Type of Watermarking Technique	Performance Evaluations	Size of the Cover/ Watermark Image(s)	Other Important Considerations
[26]	Secure and high capacity watermarking technique.	Region based DWT	Non-blind	PSNR = 42.453 dB SSIM = 0.9891 Max capacity = 48422 pixels	256 × 256/32 × 32	– Medical images of two modalities considered – 194 CTI and 68 MRI.
[27]	Region based watermarking in transform domain.	PSO DWT SVD DCT	Reversible and fragile	PSNR = 57.33 Q = 0.99 Bit = 52,000 Used area = 9968	500 × 300/52,000 bits	– ROI is lossless. – Watermark embedding is done into RONI. – Complexity of the method is evaluated.
[28]	Secure region based watermarking with contrast enhancement.	Otsu's method AE LWT	Reversible	RCE = 0.5164, PSNR = 30.45 dB, SSIM = 0.9829, Rate = 0.076, Time = 14.58	512 × 512/-	– The segmentation algorithm does not necessitate any parameter assignment.

(Continued)

Table 17.5 (*Continued*) Summary of Recent State-of-the-Art Watermarking Techniques for Tele-Health Applications

Ref No.	Proposed Objectives	Techniques to Achieve Objectives	Type of Watermarking Technique	Performance Evaluations	Size of the Cover/ Watermark Image(s)	Other Important Considerations
[29]	Secure watermarking technique.	Logistic map based chaotic encryption Hamming weight method	Blind	PSNR = 51.177 (max for cameraman), Comparative analysis for Leena image PSNR = 51.14 FNR = 0.00018 FPR = 0.00012	256 × 256/-	– The proposed technique was employed on four standard gray scale images.
[32]	Self-authentication pixel based watermarking.	Identified the regions BSFE DWT SVD Bit replacement technique Tamper detection algorithm	Blind	PSNR = 33 dB Accuracy < 80% FAR = 0% FRR = 85%	256 × 256/-	– X-ray image was selected from IRMA dataset. – Accuracy of the method highly depends on no. of altered pixels.

(Continued)

Table 17.5 (Continued) Summary of Recent State-of-the-Art Watermarking Techniques for Tele-Health Applications

Ref No.	Proposed Objectives	Techniques to Achieve Objectives	Type of Watermarking Technique	Performance Evaluations	Size of the Cover/ Watermark Image(s)	Other Important Considerations
[37]	Robust and secure watermarking.	Identified the regions SHA-256	——	PSNR = 48dB Elapsed time = 0.342 sec (ROI-DR)	One ROI pixel consists of 8 bits, which is four pairs of bits.	– Different ultrasound images are considered. – Using segmentation technique. – Less memory consumption.
[39]	Intelligent image watermarking.	IDWT SVD QIM non-linear chaotic map ABC algorithm	Robust and fragile	Max PSNR = 37 dB (Leena) NC = 1 (original watermark) best objective value = 0.011848	512 × 512 / 64 × 64	– Suitable for copyright protection and content authentication. – Objective function = f (fidelity, robustness, capacity).
[40]	Robust and higher imperceptible watermarking.	Bit threshold map Chou's JND model DCT	——	PSNR = 44.99 dB (max) NC = 0.99 (max)	512 × 512/128 × 128	– Robust against checkmark attacks.

(Continued)

Table 17.5 (Continued)   Summary of Recent State-of-the-Art Watermarking Techniques for Tele-Health Applications

Ref No.	Proposed Objectives	Techniques to Achieve Objectives	Type of Watermarking Technique	Performance Evaluations	Size of the Cover/Watermark Image(s)	Other Important Considerations
[43]	Robust and secure multiple watermarking.	DWT SVD ECCs	Blind	Avg PSNR, WPSNR and SSIM value is 46.2128, 53.5685, and 0.9749 dB respectively. NCC = 1(Max) and BER = 0.	1024 × 1024/32 × 32, EPR = 1022 bits	– Also tested for color images. – Dataset of mammogram images is considered.
[46]	Robust and secure watermarking for tele-ophthalmology.	Region based DWT SVD SHA-512	Robust	PSNR = 54.26 dB, NC = 0.87 BER = 0	1024 × 1024/512 × 512	– Also robust for checkmark attacks. – Management of EPR data is considered.
[47]	Secure watermarking.	CDF IWT Histogram processing GP	Reversible	PSNR = 56.79 dB SSIM = 0.9984 (max for hand image)	256 × 256/0.75 bpp (196608 bits).	– Embedding method is generic in nature. – Method is capable to determine the tradeoff between imperceptibility and payload using GP.

(Continued)

Table 17.5 (*Continued*) Summary of Recent State-of-the-Art Watermarking Techniques for Tele-Health Applications

Ref No.	Proposed Objectives	Techniques to Achieve Objectives	Type of Watermarking Technique	Performance Evaluations	Size of the Cover/ Watermark Image(s)	Other Important Considerations
[49]	Secure watermarking using encrypted image.	Identified the regions Image encryption LSB substitution	Reversible	PSNR = 131.02, SSIM = 0.9999 (Max–recovered image) PSNR = 113.55 SSIM = 0.9999 (Max–decrypted image) embedding rate = 0.05	512 × 512/size of ROI = 14,416 payload bits.	– Using image database of CIP.
[54]	Secure medical data hiding using cryptography.	Identified the regions, LSB AES	Reversible	PSNR = 107.1503 dB MSE = 0.0828 computational complexity = $O(x*n)$ For images of size 512 × 512, insertion rate = 0.25 bpp, mean execution time for embedding and extraction is 697.4 and 403.4 milliseconds, respectively.	512 × 512/insertion of 0.25 bits per pixel.	– Using AES with a key size = 128 bits.

(Continued)

Table 17.5 (*Continued*)   Summary of Recent State-of-the-Art Watermarking Techniques for Tele-Health Applications

Ref No.	Proposed Objectives	Techniques to Achieve Objectives	Type of Watermarking Technique	Performance Evaluations	Size of the Cover/ Watermark Image(s)	Other Important Considerations
[55]	Secure DNA information using watermarking and cryptography.	DWT logistic map function DNA conversion rules GA	Blind	PSNR = 56.42, NC = 1 Entropy = 7.99, NPCR = 0.99 UACI = 0.33 Correlation co-efficient for: Horizontal = 0.0020 Vertical = 0.0009 Diagonal = −0.0016	256 × 256/-	– Iterative method for optimum performance.
[56]	Combining crypto-watermarking method for medical data security.	SVD DWT AES-CBS	Blind	PSNR = 36.6125 dB (max) NC = 1.00 (for Hash)	2048 × 2048 (max)	– Medical images of 3 modalities were used (MRI, X-ray, and US).

(*Continued*)

Table 17.5 (Continued) Summary of Recent State-of-the-Art Watermarking Techniques for Tele-Health Applications

Ref No.	Proposed Objectives	Techniques to Achieve Objectives	Type of Watermarking Technique	Performance Evaluations	Size of the Cover/ Watermark Image(s)	Other Important Considerations
[57]	Watermarking with high compression rate.	TIFF/ JLS Lossless compression Square-square mesh decimation Zero-padding Nearest-neighbor and cubic interpolation Interpolation with B- spline function	Blind	Avg PSNR = 46.79 (max), Avg SSIM = 0.9974	—	– Two different databases consist of 30 images. – Method achieved high compression rate.
[58]	Robust watermarking for salt and pepper attack using MRI images.	Identified the regions Spatial domain repetition noise filtering	Robust	PSNR = 47.88 dB SSIM = 0.9747 BER = 0 (salt and pepper density = 1%) (max for DB5) Embedded bits = 51720	256 × 256/51.712 (kbit)	– Using 179 brain MRI images for experimental purpose.

(Continued)

Table 17.5 (Continued) Summary of Recent State-of-the-Art Watermarking Techniques for Tele-Health Applications

Ref No.	Proposed Objectives	Techniques to Achieve Objectives	Type of Watermarking Technique	Performance Evaluations	Size of the Cover/ Watermark Image(s)	Other Important Considerations
[59]	Region based robust watermarking.	Identified the regions, DCT	Blind	PSNR > 40 dB NAE = 0.0092 and 0.0130 BER = 0.20 (Watermark) NCC = 0.9978 At K = 10 BER = 1.47 (EPR) NCC = 0.9863 SSIM = 0.009857 at K = 10 SSIM = 0.9627 at K = 20	512 × 512/32 × 32 and 47 × 47 EPR = 1024 bits	– Embedding done only in RONI portion.
[60]	Robust and imperceptible dual watermarking.	DWT SVD ECCs	Non-blind	PSNR = 35 NC = 0.9912	512 × 512/256 × 256 and 20 characters as EPR	– Excellent analysis of different ECCs.
[61]	Robust and secure dual watermarking.	DWT Spread spectrum	Blind	Gain factor = 1.0, PSNR = 31.92 dB, BER = 0.0472 NC > 0.7 BER = 0	512 × 512/different size of image watermark and 8 characters of EPR data	– Selected bits are used for embedding.

(Continued)

Table 17.5 (Continued)   Summary of Recent State-of-the-Art Watermarking Techniques for Tele-Health Applications

Ref No.	Proposed Objectives	Techniques to Achieve Objectives	Type of Watermarking Technique	Performance Evaluations	Size of the Cover/ Watermark Image(s)	Other Important Considerations
[23]	Secure watermarking in hybrid domain.	Identified the regions SLT IWT	Reversible	PSNR = 51.823 dB	$512 \times 512 \times 8$ bits/ patient's information = 1000 bits	– Robust against unintentional attacks. – The tampered area in the ROI is detect and recovered.
[24]	Watermarking technique for ROI tamper detection and recovery.	Identified the regions IWT	Robust	Avg PSNR = 49.41 dB Avg WPSNR = 50.23 dB Avg MSSIM = 0.9856 Avg TPE = 0.0302	225×225 Size of ROI = 114×93 Different size of ROI is selected according to the size of cover image	– Experimental evaluation was carried out on 20 (each) medical images of (CT scan, MRI, ultrasound and PET scan) modalities.

(Continued)

Table 17.5 (Continued) Summary of Recent State-of-the-Art Watermarking Techniques for Tele-Health Applications

Ref No.	Proposed Objectives	Techniques to Achieve Objectives	Type of Watermarking Technique	Performance Evaluations	Size of the Cover/ Watermark Image(s)	Other Important Considerations
[64]	Robust ROI detection for watermarking.	Morphological reconstruction morphological opening by reconstruction filtering Gaussian low pass filter in frequency domain	Robust	Mean of CA = 63.7% (Max) database 8	—	– The proposed method was implemented on ten databases that comprised of 746 medical images with square as well as non-square dimensions.
[65]	Robust and high capacity medical image watermarking.	Identified the regions using Otsu's algorithm DWT Logistic chaotic map Arnold transform DCT	Semi-fragile	PSNR = 63.6916 SSIM = 0.9993 and NC = 0.9974 at quantization step = 8	512 × 512/4 bytes	– The method provides lower error rate.

(Continued)

Table 17.5 (Continued)   Summary of Recent State-of-the-Art Watermarking Techniques for Tele-Health Applications

Ref No.	Proposed Objectives	Techniques to Achieve Objectives	Type of Watermarking Technique	Performance Evaluations	Size of the Cover/ Watermark Image(s)	Other Important Considerations
[67]	Secure medical image watermarking with tamper detection.	Identified the regions Prediction error expansion Sorting techniques MD5 algorithm Huffman coding	Reversible	Size of ROI = 8.01% PSNR = 98.5473 SSIM = 0.9999 (Embedding capacity) bpp = 0.6783	4096 × 3328/ First watermark = 35260 bits Second watermark = 9523014 bits	– Enhanced embedding capacity without overflow and underflow problem.
[70]	Secure watermarking through scrambling method.	IWT RDM SVD DE	Reversible	PSNR = 48.47 (Avg NC) NCA = 0.9612 MSSIM = 0.9934 Fit = 0.9612 P_{fpp} = 0 (approx) Capacity = 0.05 bpp BER = 0 (for JPEG quality factor <80)	512 × 512/ Text watermark– 64 × 64. Image watermark– (logo) 64 × 64.	– The false positive error is inversely proportional to NC value and watermark length. – The value of maximum generation (G) is taken to be 80 and the DE optimization factors are selected as D = 30, F = 0.2, CR = 0.4.

(Continued)

Table 17.5 (*Continued*) Summary of Recent State-of-the-Art Watermarking Techniques for Tele-Health Applications

Ref No.	Proposed Objectives	Techniques to Achieve Objectives	Type of Watermarking Technique	Performance Evaluations	Size of the Cover/ Watermark Image(s)	Other Important Considerations
[77]	Secure watermarking with tamper localization.	Identified the regions DWT-SVD LSB	Reversible	Max PSNR = 34.1107 dB (X-ray), BER = 0 NC = 0.973 (for JPEG compression quality factor = 100) RONI max capacity = 2,882,154 bits (MRI) ROI max capacity = 2,823,848 bits (X-ray), Total execution time <700 seconds (block size 8 × 8)	2048 × 2048/ hospital logo (4,050 bits)and EPR(19,584 bits)	– Three different medical images are considered.
[78]	Robust and imperceptible watermarking through sparse coding.	Identified the regions SVD	Robust	PSNR = 22.6943 dB for addition attack NC > 0.8	512 × 512/256 × 256	– Robust for various attacks.

(*Continued*)

Table 17.5 (*Continued*)   Summary of Recent State-of-the-Art Watermarking Techniques for Tele-Health Applications

Ref No.	Proposed Objectives	Techniques to Achieve Objectives	Type of Watermarking Technique	Performance Evaluations	Size of the Cover/ Watermark Image(s)	Other Important Considerations
[79]	Robust and imperceptible medical image watermarking.	DWT KLT FIS SHA-1 Turbo code	Robust	Without attack PSNR = 56.8716 WPSNR = 67.7058 NC = 1 approx (for most of the attacks)	512 × 512/-	– Enhanced the integration rate.
[80]	Watermarking technique with high accuracy.	Identified the regions Block based SHA-1 for ROI	Fragile	Average value of PSNR = 55.47 dB, WPSNR = 56.42 dB, MSSIM approx = 0.9612 and TPE = 0.0301	480 × 512/ Size of ROI = 208 × 216 Bit depth = 16	– 100 images of bit depth 8, 12, and 16 are considered.
[83]	High capacity intelligent watermarking.	interpolation-error algorithm GA PSO	Reversible	For GA / PSO Capacity = 87,415 (GA)/87,390(PSO), PSNR = 49.005 (GA)/49.008911(PSO) BPP = 0.99777(GA)/ 0.99782(PSO) SSIM = 0.3332(GA)/ 0.98566(PSO)	512 × 512/-	– Using modified interpolation-error method.

(Continued)

Table 17.5 (*Continued*)   Summary of Recent State-of-the-Art Watermarking Techniques for Tele-Health Applications

Ref No.	Proposed Objectives	Techniques to Achieve Objectives	Type of Watermarking Technique	Performance Evaluations	Size of the Cover/ Watermark Image(s)	Other Important Considerations
[20]	Robust and imperceptible watermarking.	Identified ROI AES SHA-256 Arithmetic coding	Blind-fragile	Avg PSNR = 44.8029 dB, avg WPSNR = 45.8453 dB, avg MSSIM = 0.9786, avg TPE = 0.0322	Three different size of cover up to 512 × 512/- varying sizes of ROI used = (5%– 30% of the original image's pixels)	– 430 medical images with different size, format, and bit-depth are considered.
[87]	Computationally low and robust watermarking.	DWT SVD	Robust	PSNR = 51.14 Efficiency = 2.107 (embedding) Efficiency = 1.086 (extraction) NC = 0.9994	256 × 256/128 × 128	– Using C# for implementing the method. – Robust against different attacks.

(*Continued*)

Table 17.5 (Continued)   Summary of Recent State-of-the-Art Watermarking Techniques for Tele-Health Applications

Ref No.	Proposed Objectives	Techniques to Achieve Objectives	Type of Watermarking Technique	Performance Evaluations	Size of the Cover/Watermark Image(s)	Other Important Considerations
[88]	Robust and high capacity watermarking with tamper detection.	Identified the regions CDCS SHA-256	Reversible	PSNR = 41.54 dB (max) using CDCS PSNR = 42.27 BER = 3 (max-under attack)	512 × 512/ 270 characters for offset value = 4	– Robustness and imperceptibility is dependent on offset value.

Abbreviations: PSNR: peak signal to noise ratio, MSE: mean squared error, NC: normalized correlation, SSIM: structural similarity index, RCE: relative contrast error, NRMSE: normalized root mean squared error, BER: bit error rate, WPSNR: weighted peak signal to noise ratio, EPR: electronic patient record, ROI: region of interest, RONI: region of non interest, NROI: non-region of interest, bpp: bits per pixel, MDE: modified difference expansion, LSB: least significant bit, PTB: pixel to block, ISBS: intermediate significant bit substitution, GP: genetic programming, GA: genetic algorithm, PSO: particle swarm optimization, DWT: discrete wavelet transform, SVD: singular value decomposition, ECC: error correcting code, DCT: discrete cosine transform, LBPROT: local binary pattern rotation invariant, SIFT: scale invariant feature transform, AE: arithmetic encoding, LWT: lifting wavelet transformation, AWGN: additive white Gaussian noise, BSE: background suppression and foreground enhancement, FAR: false acceptance rate, FRR: false rejection rate, TALLOR: tamper localization and lossless recovery, TALLOR-RS: tamper localization and lossless recovery with ROI segmentation, SHA: secure hash algorithm, IDWT: integer discrete wavelet transform, QIM: quantization index modulation, ABC: artificial bee colony, JND: just noticeable distortion, AES: advanced encryption standard, IWT: integer wavelet transform, Pfpp probability of false positive or negative error, CDF: cohen-Daubechies-Fauraue, CDCS: class dependent coding scheme, TPE: total perceptual error, and TPR: true positive rate.

17.8.1 Potential Issues in Existing Medical Image Watermarking Techniques

In view of the above discussion, robustness, security, embedding capacity, imperceptibility and embedding/extraction time are considerable factors in the area of medical image watermarking. However, most of the watermarking techniques are improving some of the above mentioned factors and compromising with other factors. Further, potential researchers are using region-based robust and secure watermarking techniques. However, watermark payload is dependent on size of the ROI portion of the cover and this portion is lossless only. Some methods are very secure; however, the techniques are computationally complex.

17.8.2 Existing Solutions for the Potential Issue/Challenges

- Researchers have presented a combination of **watermarking and cryptography** techniques. These techniques enhanced the security of the watermark(s)/secret information [18,20,25,26,39,46,47,49,54–56,67,70,80,88].
- In [23,24,32,40,43,60,61,65,67,77,79,87] the authors have proposed **wavelet-based** watermarking techniques. These techniques enhanced the robustness of the watermark against various kinds of attacks.
- In [82], authors have proposed a watermarking technique using GA. The GA-based watermarking achieved the optimal balance between major performance parameters of general watermarking systems. Further, authors proved that GA outperforms PSO in terms of temporal cost.
- In [23,44,54,65,67,77,80] authors have presented region-based dual watermarking in which watermark information is embedded into both regions. The dual watermarking techniques enhanced the security, embedding capacity and reduced the bandwidth requirements for tele-health applications.
- In [20,27,37,49,57,67,80,81,88], the authors have developed a watermarking technique using lossless compression techniques. These techniques achieved lossless recovery of medical information which is very important in accurate diagnosis.
- In [18], authors have used modified difference expansion and least significant bit (LSB). This method can detect tampered regions with finer precision and does not depend on the size of the ROI portion of the cover.
- In [88], the authors have developed a watermarking technique using CDCS which enhanced the embedding capacity.
- In [20], authors have developed a watermarking technique using SHA-256 for hashing, AES for encryption and arithmetic coding for lossless compression, simultaneously.
- In [78], the authors have developed a watermarking technique using sparse coding. The imperceptibility and robustness of the technique is enhanced through sparse coding.

17.9 Summary

In this chapter, we have introduced various state-of-the-art watermarking techniques for tele-health applications. In addition to these basic concepts of digital watermarking techniques, major characteristics of the watermarks, recent applications, important spatial and transform domain techniques, various vital performance parameters and watermarking attacks are provided in brief. Then, a detailed review of existing medical image watermarking techniques along with their potential issues and existing solutions is provided. Finally, the brief summary of the reported techniques has been tabulated.

References

1. Singh, A.K., Kumar, B., Singh, G. and Mohan, A. (2017) *Medical Image Watermarking: Techniques and Applications* (*Multimedia Systems and Applications*), Springer, New York.
2. Chauhan, D.S., Singh, A.K., Kumar, B. and Saini, J.P. (2017) Quantization based multiple medical information watermarking for secure e-health, *Multimedia Tools and Applications*, 1–13, doi:10.1007/s11042-017-4886-4.
3. Giakoumaki, A., Perakis, K., Tagaris, A. and Koutsouris, D. (2006) Digital watermarking in telemedicine applications - Towards enhanced data security and accessibility, In: *Proceedings of the 28th Annual International Conference of the IEEE Engineering in Medicine and Biology Society*, New York City, pp. 6328–6331.
4. Chao, H.M., Hsu, C.M. and Miaou, S.G. (2002) A data-hiding technique with authentication, integration, and confidentiality for electronic patient records, *IEEE Transactions on Information Technology in Biomedicine*, 6(1), 46–53.
5. Giakoumaki, A., Pavlopoulos, S. and Koutsouris, D. (2006) Multiple image watermarking applied to health information management, *IEEE Transactions on Information Technology in Biomedicine*, 10(4), 722–732.
6. Mohanty, S.P., Sengupta, A., Guturu, P. and Kougianos, E. (2017) Everything you want to know about watermarking: From paper marks to hardware protection: From paper marks to hardware protection, *IEEE Consumer Electronics Magazine*, 6(3), 83–91.
7. Singh, A.K., Kumar, B., Singh, S.K., Ghrera, S.P. and Mohan, A. (2016) Multiple watermarking technique for securing online social network contents using Back Propagation Neural Network, *Future Generation Computer Systems*, pp. 1–16, doi:10.1016/j.future.2016.11.023.
8. Singh, A.K., Kumar, B., Dave, M., Ghrera, S.P. and Mohan, A. (2016) Digital image watermarking: Techniques and emerging applications, In: *Handbook of Research on Modern Cryptographic Solutions for Computer and Cyber Security*, IGI Global, Hershey, PA, pp. 246–272.
9. Singh, A.K., Dave, M. and Mohan, A. (2014) Wavelet based image watermarking: Futuristic concepts in information security, *Proceedings of the National Academy of Sciences, India Section A: Physical Sciences*, 84(3), 345–359.
10. Mohanty, S.P. (2015) *Nanoelectronic Mixed-Signal System Design*, McGraw-Hill Education, New York.
11. Katzenbeisser, S. and Petitcolas, F. (2000) *Information Hiding Techniques for Steganography and Digital Watermarking*, Artech House, Norwood, MA.

12. Boato, G., Conotter, V. and De Natale, F.G. (2007) GA-based robustness evaluation method for digital image watermarking, In: *International Workshop on Digital Watermarking*, pp. 294–307, Springer, Berlin, Germany.

13. Thakkar, F.N. and Srivastava, V.K. (2017) A blind medical image watermarking: DWT-SVD based robust and secure approach for telemedicine applications, *Multimedia Tools and Applications*, 76(3), 3669–3697.

14. Hore, A. and Ziou, D. (2010) Image quality metrics: PSNR vs. SSIM, In: *20th International Conference on Pattern Recognition*, IEEE, Istanbul, Turkey, pp. 2366–2369.

15. Nyeem, H., Boles, W. and Boyd, C. (2014) Digital image watermarking: Its formal model, fundamental properties and possible attacks, *EURASIP Journal on Advances in Signal Processing*, 1, 135.

16. Voloshynovskiy, S., Pereira, S., Pun, T., Eggers, J.J. and Su, J.K. (2001) Attacks on digital watermarks: Classification, estimation based attacks, and benchmarks, *IEEE Communications Magazine*, 39(8), 118–126.

17. Mohanty, S.P. (1999) Digital watermarking: A tutorial review. http://www.csee.usf.edu/smohanty/research/Reports/WMSurvey1999Mohanty.pdf.

18. Ustubioglu, A. and Ulutas, G. (2017) A new medical image watermarking technique with Finer Tamper Localization, *Journal of Digital Imaging*, 1–16, doi:10.1007/s10278-017-9960-y.

19. Kulkarni, M.B. and Patil, R.T. (2012) Tamper detection and recovery in medical image with secure data hiding using reversible watermarking, *International Journal of Emerging Technology and Advanced Engineering*, 2(3), 370–373.

20. Das, S. and Kundu, M.K. (2013) Effective management of medical information through ROI-lossless fragile image watermarking technique, *Computer Methods and Programs in Biomedicine*, 111(3), 662–675.

21. Liew, S.C., Liew, S.W. and Zain, J.M. (2013) Tamper localization and lossless recovery watermarking scheme with ROI segmentation and multilevel authentication, *Journal of Digital Imaging*, 26(2), 316–325.

22. Woo, C.-S., Du, J., Pham, B., Multiple watermark method for privacy control and tamper detection in medical images, In: *Proceedings of the APRS Workshop on Digital Image Computing Pattern Recognition and Imaging for Medical Applications*, 2005.

23. Thabit, R. and Khoo, B.E. (2015) Medical image authentication using SLT and IWT schemes, *Multimedia Tools and Applications*, 1(76), 309–332.

24. R. Eswaraiah and E. Sreenivasa Reddy (2015) Robust medical image watermarking technique for accurate detection of tampers inside region of interest and recovering original region of interest, *IET Image Processing*, 9(8), 615–625.

25. Parah, S.A., Ahad, F., Sheikh, J.A. and Bhat, G.M. (2017) Hiding clinical information in medical images: A new high capacity and reversible data hiding technique, *Journal of Biomedical Informatics*, 66, 214–230.

26. Sharifara, A. and Ghaderi, A. (2017) Medical Image Watermarking using 2D-DWT with Enhanced security and capacity, arXiv preprint arXiv: 1703.05778.

27. Shih, F.Y., Zhong, X., Chang, I.C. and Satoh, S.I. (2017) An adjustable-purpose image watermarking technique by particle swarm optimization, *Multimedia Tools and Applications*, 1–20, doi:10.1007/s11042-017-4367-9.

28. Gao, G., Wan, X., Yao, S., Cui, Z., Zhou, C. and Sun, X. (2017) Reversible data hiding with contrast enhancement and tamper localization for medical images, *Information Sciences*, 385–386, 250–265.

29. Trivedy, S. and Pal, A.K. (2017) A logistic map-based fragile watermarking scheme of digital images with tamper detection, *Iranian Journal of Science and Technology, Transactions of Electrical Engineering*, 41(2), 103–113.

30. Chang, C.C., Chen, K.N., Lee, C.F. and Liu, L.J. (2011) A secure fragile watermarking scheme based on chaos-and-hamming code, *Journal of Systems and Software*, 84(9), 1462–1470.

31. Hsu, C.S. and Tu, S.F. (2010) Probability-based tampering detection scheme for digital images, *Optics Communications*, 283(9), 1737–1743.

32. Bakthula, R., Shivani, S. and Agarwal, S. (2017) Self authenticating medical X-ray images for telemedicine applications, *Multimedia Tools and Applications*, 1–18. doi:10.1007/s11042-017-4738-2.

33. Tan, C.K., Ng, J.C., Xu, X., Poh, C.L., Guan, Y.L. and Sheah, K. (2011) Security protection of DICOM medical images using dual-layer reversible watermarking with tamper detection capability, *Journal of Digital Imaging*, 24(3), 528–540.

34. Eswaraiah, R. and Reddy, E.S. (2014) Medical image watermarking technique for accurate tamper detection in ROI and exact recovery of ROI, *International Journal of Telemedicine and Applications*, p. 13. doi:10.1155/2014/984646.

35. Memon, N.A., Chaudhry, A., Ahmad, M. and Keerio, Z.A. (2011) Hybrid watermarking of medical images for ROI authentication and recovery, *International Journal of Computer Mathematics*, 88(10), 2057–2071.

36. Wu, J.H., Chang, R.F., Chen, C.J., Wang, C.L., Kuo, T.H., Moon, W.K. and Chen, D.R. (2008) Tamper detection and recovery for medical images using near-lossless information hiding technique, *Journal of Digital Imaging*, 21(1), 59–76.

37. Khor, H.L., Liew, S.C. and Zain, J.M. (2017) Region of interest-based tamper detection and lossless recovery watermarking scheme (ROI-DR) on ultrasound medical images, *Journal of Digital Imaging*, 30(3), 328–349.

38. Liew, S.C. (2011) Tamper localization and recovery watermarking schemes for medical images in PACS, Doctoral dissertation, Universiti Malaysia Pahang.

39. Lei, B., Zhao, X., Lei, H., Ni, D., Chen, S., Zhou, F. and Wang, T. (2017) Multipurpose watermarking scheme via intelligent method and chaotic map, *Multimedia Tools and Applications*, pp. 1–23. doi:10.1007/s11042-017-4743-5.

40. Seo, H.U., Wei, Q., Kwon, S.G. and Sohng, K.I. (2017) Medical image watermarking using bit threshold map based on just noticeable distortion in discrete cosine transform, *Technology and Health Care*, (Preprint), pp. 1–9.

41. Chou, C.H. and Li, Y.C. (1995) A perceptually tuned subband image coder based on the measure of just-noticeable-distortion profile, *IEEE Transactions on Circuits and Systems for Video Technology*, 5(6), 467–476.

42. Liu, J.L., Lou, D.C., Chang, M.C. and Tso, H.K. (2006) A robust watermarking scheme using self-reference image, *Computer Standards & Interfaces*, 28(3), 356–367.

43. Thakkar, F.N. and Srivastava, V.K. (2016) A blind medical image watermarking: DWT-SVD based robust and secure approach for telemedicine applications, *Multimedia Tools and Applications*, 3(76), 3669–3697.

44. Parah, S.A., Sheikh, J.A., Ahad, F., Loan, N.A. and Bhat, G.M. (2015) Information hiding in medical images: A robust medical image watermarking system for E-healthcare, *Multimedia Tools and Applications*, 8(76), 10599–10633.

45. Singh, A.K., Kumar, B., Dave, M. and Mohan, A. (2015) Multiple watermarking on medical images using selective discrete wavelet transform coefficients, *Journal of Medical Imaging and Health Informatics*, 5(3), 607–614.

46. Pandey, R., Singh, A.K., Kumar, B. and Mohan, A. (2016) Iris based secure NROI multiple eye image watermarking for teleophthalmology, *Multimedia Tools and Applications*, 75(22), 14381–14397.

47. Arsalan, M., Qureshi, A.S., Khan, A. and Rajarajan, M. (2017) Protection of medical images and patient related information in healthcare: Using an intelligent and reversible watermarking technique, *Applied Soft Computing*, 51, 168–179.

48. Xuan, G., Yang, C., Zhen, Y., Shi, Y.Q. and Ni, Z. (2004) Reversible data hiding using integer wavelet transform and companding technique, In: *International Workshop on Digital Watermarking*, pp. 115–124.

49. Liu, Y., Qu, X. and Xin, G. (2016) A ROI-based reversible data hiding scheme in encrypted medical images, *Journal of Visual Communication and Image Representation*, 39, 51–57.

50. Zhang, X. (2011) Reversible data hiding in encrypted image. *IEEE Signal Processing Letters*, 18(4), 255–258.

51. Hong, W., Chen, T.S. and Wu, H.Y. (2012) An improved reversible data hiding in encrypted images using side match, *IEEE Signal Processing Letters*, 19(4), 199–202.

52. Zhang, X. (2012) Separable reversible data hiding in encrypted image, *IEEE Transactions on Information Forensics and Security*, 7(2), 826–832.

53. Lavanya, A. and Natarajan, V. (2012) Watermarking patient data in encrypted medical images, *Sadhana*, 37(6), 723–729.

54. Mantos, P.L. and Maglogiannis, I. (2016) Sensitive patient data hiding using a ROI reversible steganography scheme for DICOM images, *Journal of Medical Systems*, 40(6), 156.

55. Anusudha, K., Venkateswaran, N. and Valarmathi, J. (2016) Secured medical image watermarking with DNA codec, *Multimedia Tools and Applications*, 2(76), 2911–2932.

56. Al-Haj, A. and Mohammad, A. (2017) Crypto-watermarking of transmitted medical images, *Journal of Digital Imaging*, 30(1), 26–38.

57. Amri, H., Khalfallah, A., Gargouri, M., Nebhani, N., Lapayre, J.C. and Bouhlel, M.S. (2017) Medical image compression approach based on image resizing, digital watermarking and lossless compression, *Journal of Signal Processing Systems*, 87(2), 203–214.

58. Mousavi, S.M., Naghsh, A., Manaf, A.A. and Abu-Bakar, S.A.R. (2017) A robust medical image watermarking against salt and pepper noise for brain MRI images, *Multimedia Tools and Applications*, 76(7), 10313–10342.

59. Parah, S.A., Sheikh, J.A., Ahad, F., Loan, N.A. and Bhat, G.M. (2017) Information hiding in medical images: A robust medical image watermarking system for E-healthcare, *Multimedia Tools and Applications*, 76(8), 10599–10633.

60. Singh, A.K., Kumar, B., Dave, M. and Mohan, A. (2015) Robust and imperceptible dual watermarking for telemedicine applications, *Wireless Personal Communications*, 80(4), 1415–1433.

61. Singh, A.K., Kumar, B., Dave, M. and Mohan, A. (2015) Multiple watermarking on medical images using selective discrete wavelet transform coefficients, *Journal of Medical Imaging and Health Informatics*, 5(3), 607–614.

62. Kumar, B., Singh, H.V., Singh, S.P. and Mohan, A. (2011) Secure spread-spectrum watermarking for telemedicine applications, *Journal of Information Security*, 2(2), 91–98.

63. Kumar, B., Anand, A., Singh, S. P. and Mohan, A. (2011) High capacity spread-spectrum watermarking for telemedicine applications, *World Academy of Science, Engineering and Technology*, p. 79.

64. Mousavi, S.M., Naghsh, A. and Abu-Bakar, S.A.R. (2015) A heuristic automatic and robust ROI detection method for medical image warermarking, *Journal of Digital Imaging*, 28(4), 417–427.

65. Jianfeng, L., Meng, W., Junping, D., Qianru, H., Li, L. and Chin-Chen, C. (2015) Multiple watermark scheme based on DWT-DCT quantization for medical images, *Journal of Information Hiding and Multimedia Signal Processing*, 6(3), 458–472.

66. Qi, X. and Xin, X. (2011) A quantization-based semi-fragile watermarking scheme for image content authentication, *Journal of Visual Communication and Image Representation*, 22(2), 187–200.

67. Liu, Y., Qu, X., Xin, G. and Liu, P. (2015) ROI-based reversible data hiding scheme for medical images with tamper detection, *IEICE Transactions on Information and Systems*, 98(4), 769–774.

68. Al-Qershi, O.M. and Khoo, B.E. (2011) Authentication and data hiding using a reversible ROI-based watermarking scheme for DICOM images, *Journal of Digital Imaging*, 24(1), 114–125.

69. Al-Qershi O.M. and Khoo, B.E (2009) Authentication and data hiding using a reversible ROI-based watermarking scheme for DICOM images, In *Proceedings of International Conference on Medical Systems Engineering (ICMSE)*, pp. 829–834. World academy of science, Engineering and Technology (WASET).

70. Lei, B., Tan, E.L., Chen, S., Ni, D., Wang, T. and Lei, H. (2014) Reversible watermarking scheme for medical image based on differential evolution, *Expert Systems with Applications*, 41(7), 3178–3188.

71. Kumsawat, P., Attakitmongcol, K. and Srikaew, A. (2005) A new approach for optimization in image watermarking by using genetic algorithms, *IEEE Transactions on Signal Processing*, 53(12), 4707–4719.

72. Coatrieux, G., Pan, W., Cuppens-Boulahia, N., Cuppens, F. and Roux, C. (2013) Reversible watermarking based on invariant image classification and dynamic histogram shifting, *IEEE Transactions on Information Forensics and Security*, 8(1), 111–120.

73. Hwang, H.J., Kim, H.J., Sachnev, V. and Joo, S.H. (2010) Reversible watermarking method using optimal histogram pair shifting based on prediction and sorting, *KSII Transactions on Internet and Information Systems (TIIS)*, 4(4), 655–670.

74. Kamstra, L. and Heijmans, H.J. (2005) Reversible data embedding into images using wavelet techniques and sorting, *IEEE Transactions on Image Processing*, 14(12), 2082–2090.

75. Pan, W., Coatrieux, G., Cuppens, N., Cuppens, F. and Roux, C. (2010) An additive and lossless watermarking method based on invariant image approximation and Haar wavelet transform, *2010 Annual International Conference of the IEEE Engineering in Medicine and Biology*, IEEE, Buenos Aires, Argentina, pp. 4740–4743.

76. Sachnev, V., Kim, H.J., Nam, J., Suresh, S. and Shi, Y.Q. (2009) Reversible watermarking algorithm using sorting and prediction, *IEEE Transactions on Circuits and Systems for Video Technology*, 19(7), 989–999.

77. Al-Haj, A. (2014) Secured telemedicine using region-based watermarking with tamper localization, *Journal of Digital Imaging*, 27(6), 737–750.

78. Tareef, A., Al-Ani, A., Nguyen, H. and Chung, Y.Y. (2014) A novel tamper detection-recovery and watermarking system for medical image authentication and EPR hiding, *36th Annual International Conference of the IEEE Engineering in Medicine and Biology Society (EMBC)*, Chicago, IL, pp. 5554–5557.

79. Hajjaji, M.A., Bourennane, E.B., Ben Abdelali, A. and Mtibaa, A. (2014) Combining Haar wavelet and Karhunen Loeve transforms for medical images watermarking, *BioMed Research International*, p. 15.

80. Eswaraiah, R. and Reddy, E.S. (2014) Medical image watermarking technique for accurate tamper detection in ROI and exact recovery of ROI, *International Journal of Telemedicine and Applications*, p.13. doi:10.1155/2014/984646.

81. Priya, R.L., Belji, T. and Sadasivam, V. (2014) Security of health imagery via reversible watermarking based on differential evolution, *International Conference on Medical Imaging, m-Health and Emerging Communication Systems (MedCom)*, Greater Noida, India, pp. 30–34.

82. Naheed, T., Usman, I., Khan, T.M., Dar, A.H. and Shafique, M.F. (2014) Intelligent reversible watermarking technique in medical images using GA and PSO, *Optik-International Journal for Light and Electron Optics*, 125(11), 2515–2525.

83. Luo, L., Chen, Z., Chen, M., Zeng, X. and Xiong, Z. (2010) Reversible image watermarking using interpolation technique, *IEEE Transactions on Information Forensics and Security*, 5(1), 187–193.

84. Xuan, G., Shi, Y.Q., Yang, C., Zheng, Y., Zou, D. and Chai, P. (2005) Lossless data hiding using integer wavelet transform and threshold embedding technique, *IEEE International Conference on Multimedia and Expo*, IEEE, Amsterdam, the Netherlands, pp. 1520–1523.

85. Tian, J. (2003) Reversible data embedding using a difference expansion, *IEEE Transactions on Circuits and Systems for Video Technology*, 13(8), 890–896.

86. Lee, S., Yoo, C.D. and Kalker, T. (2007) Reversible image watermarking based on integer-to-integer wavelet transform, *IEEE Transactions on Information Forensics and Security*, 2(3), 321–330.

87. Lai, C.C. and Tsai, C.C. (2010) Digital image watermarking using discrete wavelet transform and singular value decomposition, *IEEE Transactions on Instrumentation and Measurement*, 59(11), 3060–3063.

88. Dhavale, S.V. and Patnaik, L.M. (2010) High capacity, robust lossless EPR data hiding using CDCS with ROI tamper detection, *International Journal of Recent Trends in Engineering and Technology*, 3(2), 51–54.

References for Advance/Further Reading

Singh, A.K., Kumar, B., Singh, G. and Mohan, A. (2017) *Medical Image Watermarking: Techniques and Applications (Multimedia Systems and Applications)*, Springer, New York.

Chauhan, D.S., Singh, A.K., Kumar, B. and Saini, J.P. (2017) Quantization based multiple medical information watermarking for secure e-health, *Multimedia Tools and Applications*, 1–13. doi:10.1007/s11042-017-4886-4.

Singh, A.K., Kumar, B., Singh, S.K., Ghrera, S.P. and Mohan, A. (2016) Multiple watermarking technique for securing online social network contents using Back Propagation Neural Network, *Future Generation Computer Systems*, pp. 1–16, doi:10.1016/j.future.2016.11.023.

Singh, A.K., Kumar, B., Dave, M., Ghrera, S.P. and Mohan, A. (2016) Digital image watermarking: Techniques and emerging applications, In: *Handbook of Research on Modern Cryptographic Solutions for Computer and Cyber Security*, IGI Global, Hershey, PA, pp. 246–272.

Singh, A.K., Dave, M. and Mohan, A. (2014) Wavelet based image watermarking: Futuristic concepts in information security, *Proceedings of the National Academy of Sciences, India Section A: Physical Sciences*, 84(3), 345–359.

Katzenbeisser, S. and Petitcolas, F. (2000) Information hiding techniques for steganography and digital watermarking, Artech House.

Key Terminology and Definitions

PSNR—Peak Signal to noise ratio (PSNR) is used for measuring the quality of the watermarked images.

NC—Normalized correlation (NC) is performance parameter used to measure the similarities and differences between the original and extracted watermark(s) images.

BER—The Bit error rate (BER) is a used to determine the ratio of number of incorrectly decoded bits to total number of bits.

SSIM—Structural Similarity Index (SSIM) is one of the recent performance parameters which measure the perceptual quality between watermarked image and original image, or how similar the two images are to each other.

WPSNR—is a performance parameter which measures the quality of the watermarked images through an arbitrary texture masking function called as visibility function (NVF).

Databases

- Ultrasound database [online]. Available at: http://splab.cz/en/download/database/ultrasound
- Osirix.2014.OSIRIX DICOM image library [online]. Available at: http://www.osirix-viewer.com/resources/diacom-image-library/

STEGANOGRAPHY

Chapter 18

Utilization of Small S-Boxes for Information Hiding

Majid Khan and Syeda Iram Batool Naqvi

Contents

DOI: 10.1201/9780429435461-21

Digital steganography exploits the usage of cover information to obnubilate mystery data such that it is vague to a human spectator. The mystery data can be covered in substance, for example, picture, sound, or video. This section gives a novel picture steganographic strategy to obnubilate shading mystery picture in shading spread picture using minute nonlinear part to be specific supersession boxes (S-boxes) predicated on multiplicative group of nonzero elements of Galois field of order 16 i.e., $\mathbb{Z}_{17}^{*}$, symmetry group S_4 and least significant bits (LSBs). The amalgamation of these two techniques will improve the security of the information embedded. This mixed method will perfect the desiderata, for example, limit, security and heartiness for secure data transmission over an open channel. A comparative examination is made to demonstrate the practicality of the proposed strategy by first and second order texture analysis, mean squared error (MSE), root mean squared error (RMSE), mean absolute error (MAE), average difference (AD), normalized absolute error (NAE), maximum difference (MD), enhancement error (EME), peak signal to noise ratio (PSNR), structure contents (SC), normalized cross-correlation (NCC), universal image quality index (UIQI) and structural similarity index metric (SSIM). We researched the data disguising technique using the picture execution parameters like first order and second order texture characteristics. The stego pictures are attempted by transmitting them and the embedded data are strongly removed by the authority. There is no visual change between the stego picture and the cover picture. The examinations showed the high concealment of the recommended display even with tremendously goliath estimate mystery picture.

18.1 Introduction

Because of copyright infringement, forging, falsification, and misrepresentation, transmitting the computerized information in open systems such as the internet which is not reliably shielded. Consequently, for securing the mystery information numerous methodologies are forward for ensuring key advanced information [1]. Cryptographic techniques are utilized for transmitting the coded information scrambled by cryptosystems and utilized for coded correspondence. The pointless manifestation of the scrambled information may draw interested programmers.

This classified information can be secured by utilizing data concealing methods, such as watermarking and steganography, which shrouds the secret data into a cover data and creates a stego object.

Watermarking is utilized for screen checking, copyright guard, following exchange and comparative exercises. Conversely, steganography is utilized basically for secret correspondence. This system modifies a cover media to veil an incognito message. Subsequently, it can cover up the extreme presence of disguised correspondences. For further security, a cryptographic system is utilized before implanting procedure [2].

In World War-II, the Microdot procedure was produced by the Germans. Data, particularly photos, were lessened in size until it was the span of a written period. Very hard to catch; an ordinary spread message was sent over an unreliable channel with one of the periods on the paper containing shrouded data [3]. Today steganography is generally utilized on computers with computerized information being the carriers and digital network protocol being the high speed transmission channels.

Steganography is broadly classified in to spatial and frequency domain techniques. The spatial domain techniques involve encoding at the LSB level. Least Significant Bit Substitution (LSBS) [4] is the most commonly used stenographic technique. The basic concept of LSBS includes the embedding of secret data at the bits which having minimum weight so that it will not affect the value of theoriginal pixel. In frequency domain, we find a way to hide information in areas of the image which is scarcely visible to compression, cropping, and image processing. In this chapter, we combine S-boxes which are the most important object of symmetric cryptography along with information hiding schemes, namely steganography, to provide protection against digital security terrorizations.

The chapter is organized as follows. In Section 18.2, algorithm for the construction of small S-boxes is given. The application of proposed schemes of S-boxes is then utilized in image hiding given in Section 18.3. In order to validate the suggested information hiding technique, statistical analyses were performed in Section 18.4. Finally, we conclude our proposed idea along with some future recommendations.

18.2 Construction of Nonlinear Component of Block Ciphers (S-Box)

By designing nonlinear component for block cipher namely S-box, it is quite important to find structures which have the best cryptographically excellent characterisitcs. In order to construct a best nonlinear component, first select a mapping, say $T : M \rightarrow M$ defined as follows:

$$x \mapsto \begin{cases} a^m \bmod 17, & \text{if } x < 16, \\ 0, & \text{if } x = 16, \end{cases} \tag{18.1}$$

where $x = a^m$ (mod 17) and $m \in M = \{0,1,2,...,16\}$. Its is understood that a is a primitive element in $\mathbb{Z}_{17}^*$ which is responsible to generate the set $\mathbb{Z}_{17}^*$ of order 16.

18.2.1 Proposed Small Nonlinear Component

We take all invertible elements produced in Equation 18.1 and element 16 is mapped to 0. The multiplicative inversion operation in the construction of S-box is the inversion in $\mathbb{Z}_{17}^*$ with the extension $16 \mapsto 0$. We define the following function $I(x)$ in $\mathbb{Z}_{17}^*$ corresponding to this multiplicative inversion step [5–14]:

$$I(x) = \begin{cases} x^{-1}, & \textit{if } x < 16 \\ 0, & \textit{if } x = 16. \end{cases} \tag{18.2}$$

We decompose the affine transformation step in proposed S-box construction into two linear transformations L_i $(i = 1,2)$, two affine transformations K_i $(i = 1,2)$ and one inversion function $I(x)$ given as follows:

$$S(x) = K_2 \circ L_2 \circ I \circ K_1 \circ L_1, \tag{18.3}$$

where matrices used in linear and affine transformations are given below:

$$L_1 = \begin{bmatrix} 1 & 1 & 0 & 1 \\ 1 & 0 & 1 & 1 \\ 0 & 1 & 1 & 1 \\ 1 & 1 & 1 & 0 \end{bmatrix}, L_2 = \begin{bmatrix} 0 & 1 & 1 & 1 \\ 1 & 1 & 1 & 0 \\ 1 & 1 & 0 & 1 \\ 1 & 0 & 1 & 1 \end{bmatrix}, \tag{18.4}$$

$$K_1 = [\ 1 \quad 1 \quad 0 \quad 1\ ]^T, K_2 = [\ 1 \quad 0 \quad 1 \quad 1\ ]^T. \tag{18.5}$$

Now applying permutations of S_4 on Equation 18.5, we have

$$S - box = S_4(S(x)) = S_4(K_2 \circ L_2 \circ I \circ K_1 \circ L_1). \tag{18.6}$$

There are total 72 S-boxes in total due to three distinct S-boxes were obtained from $\mathbb{Z}_{17}^*$ by using Equation 18.6 and then we apply S_4 permutations on each S-box. We take only three from 72 S-boxes for our projected applications. The proposed S-boxes are presented in Tables 18.1 through 18.3.

Table 18.1   The Proposed S-Box-1

7	0	3	13
1	6	2	8
14	15	10	5
12	4	9	11

Table 18.2 The Proposed S-Box-2

14	0	15	6
5	11	10	2
9	12	8	4
3	1	7	13

Table 18.3 The Proposed S-Box-3

13	0	12	15
8	5	4	6
3	11	2	9
7	1	14	10

18.3 Proposed Algorithm for Steganography Based on Small S-Boxes

In this section, we will discuss three different cases of information hiding techniques, mainly steganography based, on our three proposed S-boxes.

18.3.1 Steganography Based on S-Box-1

We take a color image for secret media and cover media. The color secret image is converted to binary value where each pixel has 8-bit value. We divide our S-box-1 into four small blocks with four distinct values and used these small blocks to allocate encoded values for pixels in secret image using corresponding blocks. The small blocks of S-box-1 are shown in Table 18.4.

Secondly, we need to select the color component where to embed the secret than take a pixel with 8-bits value which is further distributed into four blocks of two bits (see Figure 18.1). Each of these two bits block take values from respective blocks (Blocks-1,2,3,4) in the order of initial part from Block-1, second part from Block-2, third part from Block 3 and fourth part from Block 4 respectively (see Figure 18.2).

18.3.1.1 Embedding Bit into Cover Image

In this phase, we have inserted values obtained from each block by bit division into cover image. We converted values of blocks into four bits binaries and placed these four binaries in LSBs of cover image consecutively. First we take

Table 18.4 Division of S-Box-1 into Four Blocks of Size 2 × 2

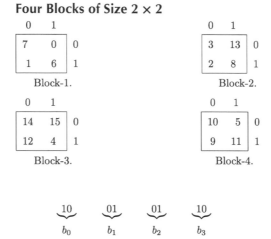

	0	1	
	7	0	0
	1	6	1

Block-1.

	0	1	
	3	13	0
	2	8	1

Block-2.

	0	1	
	14	15	0
	12	4	1

Block-3.

	0	1	
	10	5	0
	9	11	1

Block-4.

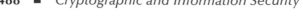

$$\underbrace{10}_{b_0} \quad \underbrace{01}_{b_1} \quad \underbrace{01}_{b_2} \quad \underbrace{10}_{b_3}$$

Figure 18.1 Bit division of secret image pixel.

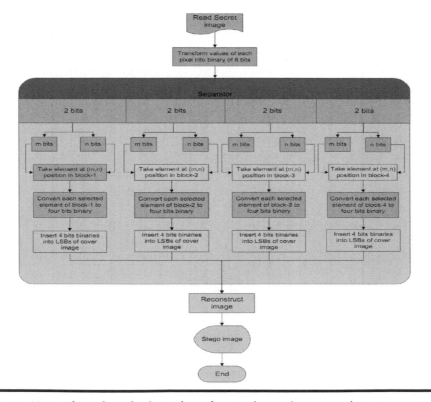

Figure 18.2 Flow chart for insertion of secret image into cover image.

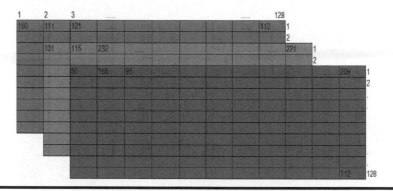

Figure 18.3 Secret image in 3-D view of size 128 × 128.

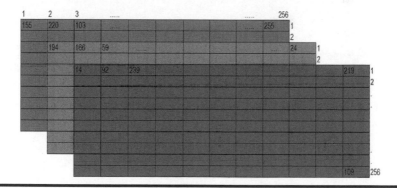

Figure 18.4 Cover image in 3-D view of size 256 × 256.

1001 1011	Replace by 1 binaries	1001 0001
155	⟹	145
1101 1100	Replace by 3 binaries	1101 0011
220	⟹	211
0110 0111	Replace by 15 binaries	0110 1111
103	⟹	111
1111 1111	Replace by 9 binaries	1111 1001
255	⟹	249

Figure 18.5 Bit insertion into cover image (for red layered).

the pixels one by one from the cover media and then place 4 bits binaries of LSBs obtained from respective blocks into the cover image (see Figures 18.3 through 18.5).

After getting the new pixel values, we form the stego image. The pixel values for red component 145, 211, 111, 249 are place into the position of the previous values.

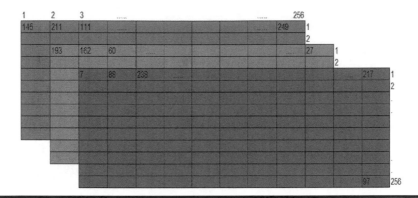

Figure 18.6   Stego image in 3-D view of size 256 × 256.

Similarly we performed these operations for green and blue component of the cover image. The resulting stego image in components form is given in Figure 18.6.

The stego image contains the secret image but we cannot identify the secret image. The variations of pixels varies from 0 to 15 which is a negligible amount due to information carriers in digital image. The pixels or colors will not change in large amounts with these proposed insertions (see Figure 18.7). Notice, the difference between the stego-images is barely distinguishable by the human eye.

18.3.2 Steganography Based on S-Box-2

In this case, we divide our anticipated S-box-2 into two horizontal blocks and each block consists of eight different values belonging from S-box-2 (see Table 18.5) and used these small blocks to allocate encoded values for pixels in a secret image using corresponding blocks. In the next stage, we have performed our experimentation

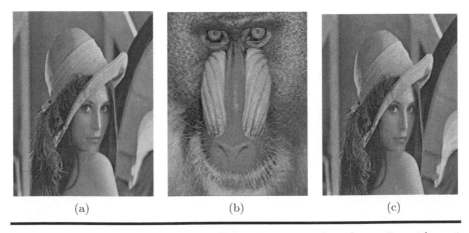

(a)   (b)   (c)

Figure 18.7   (a) Cover (Lena image) of size 256 × 256, (b) Baboon (Secret image) of size 128 × 128, (c) Stego (Lena image) size 256 × 256.

**Table 18.5   Division of S-Box-2
into Two Equal Parts**

00	01	10	11	
14	0	15	6	0
5	11	10	2	1

Block-1.

00	01	10	11	
9	12	8	4	0
3	1	7	13	1

Block-2.

$\underbrace{1001}$	$\underbrace{0110}$
b_0	b_1
$\underbrace{101}$	$\underbrace{101}$
c_0	c_1

Figure 18.8   Bit division of secret image pixel into two four bits blocks and XOR operations to each 4 bits blocks.

on steganographic media which consists of secret and cover media. The color secret media (data/image) is converted to binary value where each pixel has 8-bit values.

Also, we have to choose the shading part where to insert the code, then bring a pixel with 8-bits esteem which is further dispersed into two pieces of four bits (see Figure 18.8). Each of these four bit pieces is XOR to three bits so as to take values from segment (Blocks-1,2) in the sequence of starting part from Block-1, second part from Block-2 individually (see Figure 18.9).

For instance, we have 101 and 101 binary bits after applying XOR operations on each 4 bits. In the first three bit binaries i.e., 101, first two bits 10 represents column and 1 represent row of the blocks. For example 101 represent 2 and in second block we mapped 101 to 13 respectively.

18.3.2.1 Embedding Bit into Cover Image

In this phase, we have inserted values obtained from each block by bit division into the cover image. We converted values of blocks into four bits binaries and placed these four binaries in LSBs of the cover image consecutively. First we take the pixels one by one from the cover media and then place 4 LSBs from each of the two horizontal blocks serially (see Figures 18.10 through 18.12).

After getting the new pixel values, we form the stego image. The pixel values for green component 197, 168, 21 and 104 are placed into the position of the previous values. Similarly we performed these operations for the green and blue component of the cover image. The resultant stego image is given in Figure 18.13.

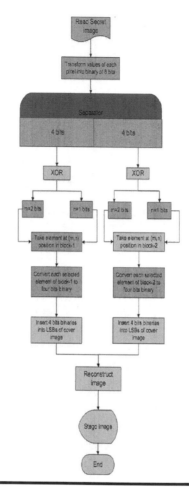

Figure 18.9 Flow chart for insertion of secret image into cover image.

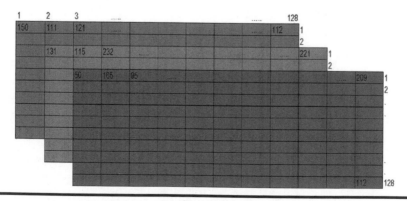

Figure 18.10 Secret image in 3-D view of size 128 × 128.

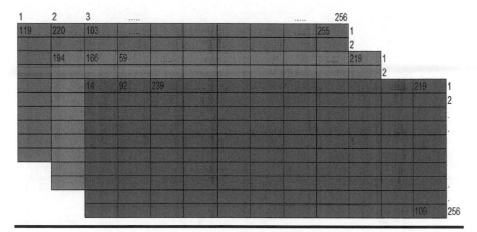

Figure 18.11 Cover image in 3-D view of size 256 × 256.

$$\underbrace{1100\,\overbrace{0011}}_{194} \quad \text{Replace by 5 binaries} \quad \underbrace{1100\,\overbrace{0101}}_{197}$$

$\underbrace{1100\,\overbrace{0011}}$	Replace by 5 binaries	$\underbrace{1100\,\overbrace{0101}}$
194	$\Longrightarrow$	197
$\underbrace{1101\,\overbrace{1100}}$	Replace by 8 binaries	$\underbrace{1010\,\overbrace{1000}}$
166	$\Longrightarrow$	168
$\underbrace{0110\,\overbrace{0111}}$	Replace by 5 binaries	$\underbrace{0001\,\overbrace{0101}}$
59	$\Longrightarrow$	21
$\underbrace{1111\,\overbrace{1111}}$	Replace by 8 binaries	$\underbrace{1101\,\overbrace{1000}}$
219	$\Longrightarrow$	104

Figure 18.12 Bit insertion into cover image (for green layer).

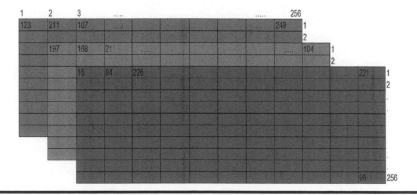

Figure 18.13 Stego image in 3-D view of size 256 × 256.

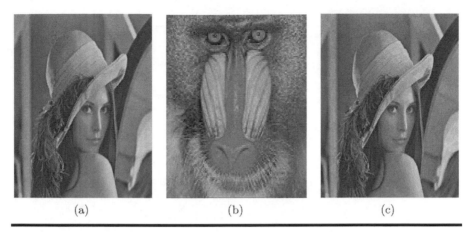

(a)   (b)   (c)

Figure 18.14 (a) Cover (Lena image) of size 256 × 256, (b) Baboon (Secret image) of size 128 × 128, (c) Stego (Lena image) size 256 × 256.

The stego image hides the secret image, yet we cannot distinguish the secret image. The variations of the pixels of cover image is varied in four bit binary which is an insignificant portion of pixel value because of data conveys implies LSBs of pixels (see Figure 18.14).

18.3.3 Steganography Based on S-Box-3

The method projected on S-box-3 is fundamentally based on division of S-box-3 into two vertical small blocks with eight distinct values and used these small blocks to allocate encoded values for pixels in s secret image using corresponding blocks. The vertical blocks of S-box-3 are given in Table 18.6.

Secondly, we need to select the color component to embed the secret, then take a pixel with 8-bits value which is further distributed into two blocks of four bits (see Figure 18.15). Each of these four bit blocks is XOR to three bits in order to take values from respective blocks (Blocks-1,2) in the order of initial part from Block-1, second part from Block-2 respectively (see Figure 18.16).

Table 18.6   Division of S-box-3 into Two Equal Parts

0	1		0	1	
13	0	00	12	15	00
8	5	01	4	6	01
3	11	10	2	9	10
7	1	11	14	10	11
Block-1			Block-2		

$$\underbrace{1001}_{} \qquad \underbrace{0110}_{}$$
$$b_0 \qquad\qquad b_1$$
$$\underbrace{101}_{} \qquad \underbrace{101}_{}$$
$$c_0 \qquad\qquad c_1$$

Figure 18.15   Bit division of secret image pixel into two four bits blocks and XOR operations to each 4 bits block.

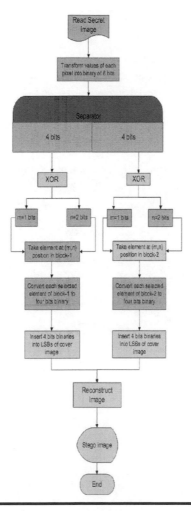

Figure 18.16   Flow chart for insertion of secret image into cover image.

For instance, we have 101 and 101 binary bits after applying XOR operations on each 4 bits. In first three bit binaries i.e., 101, first two bits 10 represents row and 1 represent column of the blocks. For example 101 represent 5 and in second block we mapped 101 to 9 respectively.

18.3.3.1 Embedding Bit into Cover Image

In this phase, we have inserted values obtained from each blocks by bit division into cover image. We convert values of blocks into four bits binaries and placed these four binaries in LSBs of cover image consecutively. First we take the pixels one by one from the cover media and then place 4 (Figures 18.17 through 18.19).

After getting the new pixel values, we form the stego image. The pixel values for red component 145, 211, 111, 249 are place into the position of the previous values. Similarly we performed these operations for green and blue component of cover image. The resultant stego image is given in Figure 18.20.

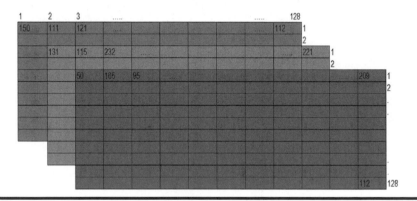

Figure 18.17　Secret image in 3-D view of size 128 × 128.

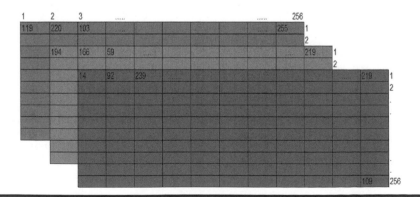

Figure 18.18　Cover image in 3-D view of size 256 × 256.

$\overbrace{0000\,1110}$	Replace by 3 binaries	$\overbrace{0000\,0011}$
14	$\Longrightarrow$	3
$\overbrace{1101\,1100}$	Replace by 14 binaries	$\overbrace{0101\,1110}$
92	$\Longrightarrow$	94
$\overbrace{1110\,1111}$	Replace by 1 binaries	$\overbrace{1110\,0001}$
239	$\Longrightarrow$	225
$\overbrace{1101\,1011}$	Replace by 10 binaries	$\overbrace{1101\,1010}$
219	$\Longrightarrow$	218
$\overbrace{0110\,1101}$	Replace by 1 binaries	$\overbrace{0110\,0001}$
109	$\Longrightarrow$	97

Figure 18.19   Bit insertion into cover image (for blue layer).

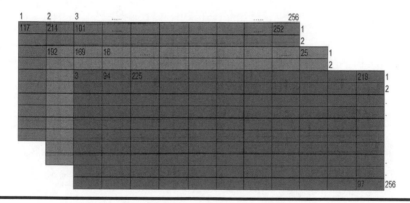

Figure 18.20   Stego image in 3-D view of size 256 × 256.

The stego image contains the secret image, but we cannot identify the secret image. The changes of the pixel values will be varied from 0 to 15 which is a negligible amount of pixel value due to information carries means LSBs of pixels. So the pixels or colors will not be change in large amount.

18.4 Performance Analysis

It is notable that numerous steganographic algorithms have been effectively broke down with the assistance of factual examination and a few measurable assaults which have been formulated on them. In this way, a perfect steganographic algorithm ought to be vigorous against any statistical attacks. To demonstrate the strength of the proposed picture steganographic technique, we have performed factual investigation by ascertaining first order texture analysis:

mean, standard deviation, skewness, kurtosis; second order texture analysis: entropy, energy, correlation, homogeneity and contrast; simple statistics errors: mean squared error, root mean squared error, absolute differences, maximum difference, normalized absolute difference, enhancement error; correlation based analysis: structure content, normalized cross correlation and finally, we will talk about the human visual framework examination which incorporates all inclusive picture quality file and structure similitude file metrics for the cover and stego pictures separately [19].

18.4.1 First Order Texture Features

First-order texture measures are determined from the original image values. They do not consider the connections with neighborhood pixels. Histogram-based approach to composition analysis is in light of the intensity esteem focuses on all or part of an image spoke to as a histogram. Characteristics received from this approach incorporate moments such as mean, standard deviation, skewness, and kurtosis. The histogram of intensity levels will be a straightforward outline of the measurable data of the image and individual pixels will be utilized to compute the gray-level histogram. Along these lines, the histogram contains the first-order measurable data about the picture (or sub picture). These measurements are defined as follows [15]:

$$\text{Mean} = \mu_k = \frac{\sum_{i=0}^{M-1}\sum_{i=0}^{N-1} I_k(i,j)}{M \times N},$$

$$\text{Standard Deviation} = \sigma_k = \sqrt{\frac{\sum_{i=0}^{M-1}\sum_{i=0}^{N-1} \left(I_k(i,j)-\mu\right)^2}{M \times N}},$$

$$\text{Skewness} = \gamma_1 = \frac{\sum_{i=0}^{M-1}\sum_{i=0}^{N-1} \left(I_k(i,j)-\mu\right)^3}{M \times N \times \sigma^2},$$

$$\text{Kurtosis} = \gamma_2 = \frac{\sum_{i=0}^{M-1}\sum_{i=0}^{N-1} \left(I_k(i,j)-\mu\right)^4}{M \times N \times \sigma^4} - 3.$$

The proposed system will be likewise assessed, built with respect to first order texture features like mean, standard deviation, skewness and kurtosis to authenticate the effect on the image in case of replacement of bits. Here, we lead an investigation

Table 18.7   First Order Texture Analysis for Steganographic Based on S-Box-I

	Cover Image			Stego Image		
	Red	*Green*	*Blue*	*Red*	*Green*	*Blue*
Mean	0.574219	0.304688	0.171875	0.578125	0.300781	0.175781
Standard Deviation	0.495429	0.461177	0.378011	0.494826	0.459496	0.38138
Skewness	−0.300201	0.848678	1.73946	−0.316386	0.868817	1.70357
Kurtosis	1.09012	1.72025	4.02573	1.1001	1.75484	3.90216

Table 18.8   First Order Texture Analysis for Steganographic Based on S-Box-II

	Cover Image			Stego Image		
	Red	*Green*	*Blue*	*Red*	*Green*	*Blue*
Mean	0.566406	0.300781	0.175781	0.566406	0.304688	0.199219
Standard Deviation	0.496541	0.459496	0.38138	0.496541	0.461177	0.400195
Skewness	−0.267999	0.868817	1.70357	−0.267999	0.848678	1.50612
Kurtosis	1.07182	1.75484	3.90216	1.07182	1.72025	3.26839

Table 18.9   First Order Texture Analysis for Steganographic Based on S-Box-III

	Cover Image			Stego Image		
	Red	*Green*	*Blue*	*Red*	*Green*	*Blue*
Mean	0.589844	0.3164406	0.179688	0.59375	0.304688	0.1875
Standard Deviation	0.492825	0.465984	0.384679	0.492094	0.461177	0.391077
Skewness	−0.365321	0.789526	1.66861	−0.381771	0.848678	1.66128
Kurtosis	1.13346	1.62335	3.78427	1.14575	1.72025	3.5641

between cover image and the stego-image in light of statistical alteration. The after effect of the execution parameters prior and then after the implanting procedure are ascertained and precise in (see Tables 18.7 through 18.9). The image parameters are an estimation of the safety for the stego-system. Minimizing parameters distinction is one of the fundamental targets in order to get rid of statistical attacks.

From the Tables 18.7 through 18.9, it is seen that there is no significant difference between the mean, standard deviation, skewness and kurtosis between the cover image and the stego image. This study shows that the magnitude of change in the stego image based on image parameters is small from a cover image. These analysis confirmed the reliability of the proposed information hiding scheme.

18.4.2 Second Order Texture Features

The second order features depends on gray level co-occurrence matrix (GLCM) [15] and it is a standout among the most prominent strategies for pixel variety measurements. A portion of the second order factual features are entropy, contrast, homogeneity, energy and correlation of the gray level pixels, characterized as [16]:

1. **Entropy**: This statistic measures the disorder or complexity of an image. The entropy is large when the image is not texturally uniform and many GLCM elements have very small values. Complex textures tend to have high entropy. Entropy is strongly, but inversely correlated to energy.

2. **Angular second moment**: This statistic is also called uniformity second moment. It measures the textural uniformity that are pixel pair repetitions. It detects disorders in textures.

3. **Inertia**: This statistic measures the spatial frequency of an image and is the difference moment of GLCM. This measure is also called contrast. It is the difference between the highest and the lowest values of a contiguous set of pixels.

4. **Inverse difference moment**: Inverse difference moment is the local homogeneity. It is high when local gray level is uniform and inverse GLCM is high. Inverse difference moment weight value is the inverse of the contrast weight. It measures image homogeneity as it assumes larger values for smaller gray tone differences in pair elements. It is more sensitive to the presence of near diagonal elements in the GLCM.

5. **Correlation**: Correlation is a measure of gray tone linear-dependencies in the image, in particular, the direction under investigation is the same as vector displacement. Correlation reaches it maximum regardless of pixel pair occurrence, as high correlation can be measured either in low or in high energy situations. The five common texture features are given as follows:

$$\text{Entropy} = -\sum_{i=0}^{N_g-1}\sum_{i=0}^{N_g-1} P_{i,j} \log P_{i,j},$$

$$\text{Angular second moment} = \sum_{i=0}^{N_g-1}\sum_{i=0}^{N_g-1} P_{i,j}^2,$$

$$\text{Inertia} = \sum_{i=0}^{N_g-1} \sum_{i=0}^{N_g-1} (i-j)^2 P_{i,j},$$

$$\text{Inverse difference moment} = \sum_{i=0}^{N_g-1} \sum_{i=0}^{N_g-1} \frac{P_{i,j}}{1+(i-j)^2},$$

$$\text{Correlation} = \frac{\sum_{i=0}^{N_g-1} \sum_{i=0}^{N_g-1} ijP_{i,j} - \mu_x \mu_y}{\sigma_x \sigma_y},$$

where $P_{i,j}$ is the (i, j) th entry of the normalized co-occurrence matrix, N_g is the number of gray levels of an image, μ_x, μ_y, σ_x and σ_y are the means and standard deviations of the marginal probabilities $P_x(i)$ and $P_y(j)$ obtained by summing up the rows or the columns of matrix $P_{i,j}$ respectively (Tables 18.10 through 18.12).

18.4.3 Image Quality Measures

Image quality measures are key for most picture handling applications. Any picture and feature procurement framework can utilize the quality metric to modify itself consequently for getting enhanced quality pictures. It can be utilized to pose as a viable rival and assess picture handling systems and algorithms.

Picture quality measures prevail to convey quantitative information on the dependability of extracted images. Commonly, the nature of an image combination system will be assessed utilizing numerical procedures which endeavor to measure loyalty utilizing image to image examinations; a few image quality measurements have been created to foresee the unmistakable contrasts between cover and stego images. This work is taking into account the way that concealing data in

Table 18.10   Second Order Texture Analysis for Steganographic System-I

	Cover Image			Stego Image		
	Red	*Green*	*Blue*	*Red*	*Green*	*Blue*
Contrast	0.357274	0.374341	0.341988	0.363067	0.377068	0.359574
Homogeneity	0.87546	0.873758	0.879416	0.871784	0.872185	0.870501
Entropy	7.27854	7.57291	7.05544	7.28795	7.4984	7.07227
Correlation	0.926586	0.932406	0.861158	0.924661	0.931912	0.855571
Energy	0.141417	0.100946	0.17250	0.139518	0.100174	0.163683

Table 18.11 Second Order Texture Analysis for Steganographic System-II

	Cover Image			Stego Image		
	Red	Green	Blue	Red	Green	Blue
Contrast	0.372687	0.392816	0.365273	0.384053	0.399004	0.3799381
Homogeneity	0.872453	0.871262	0.874949	0.868679	0.869308	0.869657
Entropy	7.2911	7.58133	7.07945	7.29576	7.5216	7.08361
Correlation	0.923453	0.929416	0.853858	0.920758	0.928464	0.848844
Energy	0.138624	0.0999494	0.169877	0.138927	0.0990417	0.165287

Table 18.12 Second Order Texture Analysis for Steganographic System-III

	Cover Image			Stego Image		
	Red	Green	Blue	Red	Green	Blue
Contrast	0.776379	0.752543	0.761933	0.822595	0.79784	0.807721
Homogeneity	0.827889	0.836525	0.834285	0.816972	0.827534	0.822203
Entropy	7.76992	7.86391	7.72703	7.77383	7.84679	7.74232
Correlation	0.92185	0.90929	0.888301	0.91677	0.903984	0.882108
Energy	0.0892355	0.0758187	0.0851768	0.085572	0.073779	0.0804689

computerized media obliges changes of the sign properties that present some type of debasement, regardless of how little; these degradations can go about as marks that could be used to uncover the presence of a hidden message. Image quality measurements are sorted into six groups as per the kind of data they are utilizing. The classifications utilized are:

1. Pixel difference-based measures
2. Correlation-based measures
3. Human visual system-based measures

In this section, we will discuss pixel difference-based measures, correlation-based measures and human visual system-based measures. The pixel difference-based measures were derived based on pixel to pixel error such as mean squared error (MSE), root mean squared error (RMSE), average difference (AD), maximum difference (MD), mean absolute error (MAE), peak signal to noise ratio (PSNR), enhancement error (EME) and mutual information (MI). The correlation based measures includes normalized cross correlation (NCC), structure content (SC) and universal image quality index (UIQI), structural similarity index metric (SSIM) are included in human visual system (HVS)-based measures. The pixel difference-based, correlation-based and human visual system-based measures defined as follows [16]:

18.4.3.1 Mean Squared Error (MSE)

The mean squared error (MSE) is the simplest, and the most widely used, full-reference image quality measurement. Similarity is determined by computing the error between the stego image and the reference cover image.

$$MSE = \frac{1}{M \times N} \sum_{i=1}^{M} \sum_{j=1}^{N} (C(i, j) - S(i, j))^2,$$

where $M \times N$ is the size of the image. The parameters $C(i, j)$ and $S(i, j)$ refer to the pixels located at the ith row and the jth column of original image and stego image due to the imbedding of the secret information [19].

18.4.3.2 Root Mean Squared Error (RMSE)

To evaluate the proposed stegosystem, this method is tested on the color Lena image of 256×256 pixels as shown in Figure 18.7a. The stego image result is shown in Figure 18.7c. To find the accuracy of the results and the robustness of the steganographic system, a root mean square of error is calculated. These criteria provide the error between the cover image and stego image. The rms value can be described by the following relation [16]:

$$RMSE = \sqrt{\frac{1}{M \times N} \sum_{i=1}^{M} \sum_{j=1}^{N} (C(i, j) - S(i, j))^2},$$

where the $C(i, j)$ is the pixel intensity of the cover image, $S(i, j)$ is the pixel intensity of the stego image. The row and column numbers of these two images are defined by $M \times N$.

18.4.3.3 Mean Absolute Error (MAE)

MAE is the average of absolute difference between the reference signal and test image. It is given by the equation

$$MAE = \frac{1}{M \times N} \sum_{i=1}^{M} \sum_{j=1}^{N} |C(i, j) - S(i, j)|.$$

18.4.3.4 Average Difference (AD)

AD is simply the average of difference between the reference signal and the test image and it is given by the equation

$$AD = \frac{1}{M \times N} \sum_{i=1}^{M} \sum_{j=1}^{N} (C(i, j) - S(i, j)).$$

18.4.3.5 Maximum Difference (MD)

MD is the maximum of the error signal (difference between the stego and cover image)

$$MD = Max|C(i, j) - S(i, j))|.$$

18.4.3.6 Peak Signal to Noise Ratio (PSNR)

The PSNR is evaluated in decibels and is inversely proportional the Mean Squared Error. It is given by the equation

$$MSE = 10\log_{10} \frac{255^2}{\sqrt{255}}.$$

18.4.3.7 Enhancement Error (EME)

A number of blind-reference metrics have been proposed during the last decade. EME (enhancement error) has been developed by Agaian et al. [17,18] give an absolute score to each image on the basis of image contrast processed with Fechner's Law relating contrast to perceived brightness or the well-known entropy concept. The following equation gives us the EME formula

$$EME = \frac{1}{M \times N} \sum_{i=1}^{M} \sum_{j=1}^{N} 20\log_2 \frac{\max(I(i, j)}{\min(I(i, j)}$$

where the image is divided into $M \times N$ blocks, $\max(I(i, j)$, $\min(I(i, j)$ are the maximum and minimum values of the pixels in each block of the enhanced image.

18.4.3.8 Structure Content (SC)

It is one of the correlation based measures. It means the closeness between two digital images which can be quantified in terms of correlation function. This metrics measures the similarity between two images. The structural content metric is based on the following equation:

$$SC = \frac{\sum_{i=1}^{M}\sum_{j=1}^{N}(C(i,j))^2}{\sum_{i=1}^{M}\sum_{j=1}^{N}(S(i,j))^2},$$

where $C(i,j)$ is the (i,j)th pixel value of cover image, $S(i,j)$ is the pixel value of stego image.

18.4.3.9 Normalized Cross Correlation (NCC)

The Normalized Cross Correlation (NCC) metric is used to show the amount of deflection in the stego image with respect to the cover image after insertion of the message. NCC is applied to evaluate the performance of various existing methods which is given by the following equation

$$NCC = \frac{\sum_{i=1}^{M}\sum_{j=1}^{N}C(i,j)\times S(i,j)}{\sum_{i=1}^{M}\sum_{j=1}^{N}(C(i,j))^2}.$$

This measure measures the similarity between two images, hence in this sense it's complementary to the difference-based measures.

18.4.3.10 Human Visual Systems (HVS) Based Measures

A noteworthy accentuation in late research has been given to a more profound investigation of the Human Visual System (HVS) highlights. Specialists expect that fusing information of the HVS and human recognition into target quality appraisal algorithms could expand their precision. This HVS-based FR worldview has been the prevailing worldview throughout the previous three decades. The fundamental introduced is that humans don't see pictures as signs in a high-dimensional space, yet are occupied with different properties of those pictures, for example, brightness, contrast, shape and texture of objects, orientations, smoothness, etc. Since the affectability of the HVS is distinctive for various parts of pictures, it bodes well to represent these sensitivities while influencing an examination between the test and the reference to flag.

There are a great deal of HVS attributes that may impact the human visual recognition on picture quality. In spite of the fact that HVS is excessively mind boggling, making it impossible to completely comprehend with show psychophysiology implies, the joining of even an improved model into target measures purportedly prompts a superior relationship with the reaction of the human spectators. Human Visual System (HVS) has been broadly presented to the common visual condition, and an assortment of confirmation has demonstrated that the HVS is exceptionally adjusted to extricate helpful data from normal scenes. Two HVS based picture quality measures are given beneath [19]:

Universal Image Quality Index (UIQI) Let $x = \{x_i, i = 1,2,\ldots\ldots,N\}$ and $y = \{y_i, i = 1,2,\ldots\ldots\ldots,N\}$ be the cover and stego images. The proposed quality index is defined as:

$$Q = \frac{4\sigma_{xy}\,\overline{x}\overline{y}}{(\sigma_x^2 + \sigma_y^2)(\overline{x}^2 + \overline{y}^2)},$$

where

$$\overline{x} = \frac{1}{N}\sum_{i=1}^{N}x_i, \quad \overline{y} = \frac{1}{N}\sum_{i=1}^{N}y_i, \quad \sigma_x^2 = \frac{1}{N-1}\sum_{i=1}^{N}(x_i - \overline{x})^2, \quad \sigma_y^2 = \frac{1}{N-1}\sum_{i=1}^{N}(y_i - \overline{y})^2,$$

$$\sigma_{xy} = \frac{1}{N-1}\sum_{i=1}^{N}(x_i - \overline{x})(y_i - \overline{y}).$$

The dynamic range of Q is [0,1]. The best value $Q = 1$, is achieved when $x_i = y_i$, $i = 1,2,\ldots,n$. The UIQI can also be defined as the product of three components:

$$Q = Q_1 \times Q_2 \times Q_3$$

where

$$Q_1 = \frac{\sigma_{xy}}{\sigma_x \sigma_y},$$

$$Q_2 = \frac{2\overline{x}\overline{y}}{\overline{x}^2 + \overline{y}^2},$$

$$Q_3 = \frac{2\sigma_x \sigma_y}{\sigma_x^2 + \sigma_y^2},$$

where first term defines the degree of correlation between x and y with dynamic range between $[-1,1]$, second term measures how close the luminance is between x and y range is $[0,1]$ and third term measures how similar the contrasts of the image x and y are.

18.4.3.11 Structural Similarity Index Metric (SSIM)

The structural similarity index matrix (SSIM) is a technique for measuring the similarity between two pictures. The SSIM record is a full reference metric; as such, the measuring of picture quality focused around an introductory uncompressed or without distortion picture as reference. The SSIM metric is figured on different windows of a picture. The measure between original and marked images of size is given below [19]:

$$SSIM(X,Y) = \frac{(2\mu_x\mu_x + c_1)(\sigma_{xy} + c_2)}{(\mu_x^2 + \mu_y^2 + c_1)(\sigma_x^2 + \sigma_y^2 + c_2)}.$$

The error comparison between a cover image and stego image are shown in the Tables 18.13 through 18.15. These results indicate the presence of secret information in the stego image. These tables additionally concludes that the stego image is of better quality if MAE, MSE, RMSE, AD, NAE and EME values are less while the high value of PSNR means that the stego image is most similar to the original image. It is hard

Table 18.13 Simple Statistics Errors for Cover and Stego Images for Steganographic System-I

	Image Color Components		
	Red	*Green*	*Blue*
MSE	14.6721	13.0356	13.6659
RMSE	3.83042	3.61049	3.69674
PSNR	36.4659	36.9795	36.7744
MAE	3.00061	2.84267	2.87642
AD	0.554657	0.561356	0.409073
MD	19	15	20
NAE	0.0166466	0.028655	0.0272485
EME (Cover image)	7.87436	19.4497	11.7173
EME (Stego image)	8.34606	20.9805	12.7009

Table 18.14 Simple Statistics Errors for Cover and Stego Images for Steganographic System-II

	Image Color Components		
	Red	Green	Blue
MSE	25.8806	21.7254	27.3693
RMSE	5.0873	4.66105	5.23156
PSNR	34.0011	34.7611	33.7552
MAE	3.93118	3.57509	4.0278
AD	−0.537994	−0.58934	−0.755493
MD	28	28	29
NAE	0.0218192	0.0361022	0.0382225
EME (Cover image)	8.15026	18.8942	12.4686
EME (Stego image)	8.47044	19.8622	12.9848

Table 18.15 Simple Statistics Errors for Cover and Stego Images for Steganographic System-III

	Image Color Components		
	Red	Green	Blue
MSE	26.6135	25.9582	27.5116
RMSE	6.29393	6.07933	6.44295
PSNR	32.1524	32.4537	31.9491
MAE	4.67821	4.49437	4.81732
AD	−0.664719	−0.69764	−1.10873
MD	40	36	37
NAE	0.0303843	0.0403222	0.0515037
EME (Cover image)	16.1939	14.9457	18.2867
EME (Stego image)	17.5367	16.6970	19.2368

for the human eyes to distinguish between the cover image and stego image when the PSNR ratio is larger than 30dB. The values of MD for image color components simply indicates the presence of hidden data in stego image pixels. The values of MD equals zero for no secret information in athe stego image or, in other words, the stego image is not generated from the cover image by apply the proposed steganographic technique.

The value of normalized cross correlation is equal to one for same images i.e., the outcome of proposed technique on cover image with itself and the hidden data length equals to zero. That means the minimum value of normalized cross correlation value equals zero; in other words, that means there is no hidden data in the image. When the value of normalized cross correlation is greater than one that means the two images (cover image, stego image) are not identical; in other words, the stego image is carrying hidden data (secret message), and the hidden data lengths are greater than zero (see Tables 18.16 through 18.18). As it can be seen

Table 18.16 Correlation Based Image Quality Measures for Steganographic System-I

	Image Color Components		
	Red	Green	Blue
SC	1.00593	1.00926	1.00561
NCC	0.996841	0.994891	0.996658

Table 18.17 Correlation Based Image Quality Measures for Steganographic System-II

	Image Color Components		
	Red	Green	Blue
SC	0.994433	0.990126	0.93674
NCC	1.00243	1.00412	1.00561

Table 18.18 Correlation Based Image Quality Measures for Steganographic System-III

	Image Color Components		
	Red	Green	Blue
SC	0.993695	0.918738	0.912193
NCC	1.00249	1.00322	1.00718

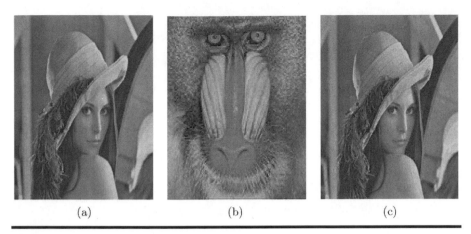

Figure 18.21 (a) Cover (Lena image) of size 256 × 256, (b) Baboon (Secret image) of size 128 × 128, (c) Stego (Lena image) size 256 × 256.

from Figures 18.21a and 18.21c, while the two images seem similar to each other, in fact they are different in the structure. The analyses of cover and stego images with respect to structure content reveals that two images under study seem to be the same for human eyes but in fact they are not, and these values represents the similarity factor between cover and stego images (see Tables 18.19 through 18.21).

The universal image quality index split the judgment of similarity between cover image (C) and stego image (S) into three comparisons: Luminance, Contrast and Structural Information. SSIM estimates "Perceived change in structural information". It computes the similarity between two images of common size. The value of UIQI

Table 18.19 Human Visual System Based Image Quality Measures for Steganographic System-I

	Image Color Components		
	Red	*Green*	*Blue*
UIQI	0.833114	0.848125	0.841500
SSIM	0.937995	0.944472	0.937726

Table 18.20 Human Visual System Based Image Quality Measures for Steganographic System-II

	Image Color Components		
	Red	*Green*	*Blue*
UIQI	0.80084	0.833829	0.78798
SSIM	0.919597	0.930689	0.911057

Table 18.21 Human Visual System Based Image Quality Measures for Steganographic System-III

	Image Color Components		
	Red	*Green*	*Blue*
UIQI	0.846898	0.863393	0.859568
SSIM	0.912866	0.918783	0.912193

and SSIM varies between 1 and −1. The closer the highest positive value denotes change in two images and −1 shows totally mismatch. The UIQI and SSIM are considered as more consistent and accurate than MSE and PSNR. As MSE and PSNR are adequate for image closeness measure just when the images vary by essentially expanding contortion of a certain sort. In any case, they neglect to catch image quality when they are utilized to gauge across contortion sorts. SSIM is a broadly utilized technique for estimation of image quality. It meets expectations precisely and can quantify better across distortion types when differentiated with MSE and PSNR. The numerical values of UIQI and SSIM are close to one which clearly indicates that the suggested technique is highly secure for transferring secret information in a information carrier and the two images seem similar to each other but actually they are different in the structure.

18.5 Conclusion

In this chapter, we have utilized the small S-boxes that take into account Galois field $\mathbb{Z}_{17}^*$, symmetry group S_4 and LSB to get a protected stage image. The proposed system has been utilized for applications that oblige high-volume insertions with strength against certain statistical attacks. The present system is an endeavor to recognize the prerequisites of a decent information concealing algorithm. Our results show that the LSB insertion utilizing small S-boxes are superior to straightforward LSB insertion. The image resolution doesn't change much and is unimportant when we embed the message into the image and the image is secured. In this manner, it is unrealistic to harm the data by unapproved personnel. This segment concentrates on the methodology, like increasing the security of the secret embedded information and reducing the distortion rate. This idea can be easily implemented in audio and video steganography.

Acknowledgment

The author of the present chapter, Dr. Majid Khan, Department of Applied Mathematics & Statistics, Institute of Space Technology, Islamabad, Pakistan is highly thankful to Vice Chancellor Engr. Imran Rahman, Institute of Space Technology, Islamabad, Pakistan, for providing an excellent atmosphere for research and development.

References

1. A. D. Ker, Steganalysis of LSB matching in grayscale images, *IEEE Signal Processing Letters*, 12(2005):441–444.
2. C. Chang, T. D. Kieu, A reversible data hiding scheme using complementary embedding strategy, *Information Sciences*, 180(16)(2010):3045–3058.
3. T. Jamil, Steganography: The art of hiding information is plain sight, *IEEE Potentials*, 15(1999):1.
4. C. K. Chan, L. M. Chang, Hiding data in image by simple LSB substitution, *Pattern Recognition*, 37(2003):469–471.
5. M. Khan, T. Shah, A copyright protection using watermarking scheme based on nonlinear permutation and its quality metrics, *Neural Computing and Applications*, 26(2015):845–855.
6. M. Khan, T. Shah, S. I. Batool, A new implementations of chaotic S-boxes in CAPTCHA, *Signal, Image and Video Processing*, 10(2016):293–300.
7. M. Khan, T. Shah, A novel construction of substitution box with Zaslavskii chaotic map and symmetric group, *Journal of Intelligent & Fuzzy Systems*, 28(2015):1509–1517.
8. M. Khan, T. Shah and S. I. Batool, A color image watermarking scheme based on affine transformation and S_4 permutation, *Neural Computing and Applications*, 25(2014):2037–2045.
9. M. Khan, T. Shah, A novel image encryption technique based on Hénon chaotic map and S_8 symmetric group, *Neural Computing and Applications*, 25(2014):1717–1722.
10. M. Khan, T. Shah, A construction of novel chaos base nonlinear component of block cipher, *Nonlinear Dynamics*, 76(2014):377–382.
11. M. Khan, T. Shah, An efficient construction of substitution box with fractional chaotic system, *Signal Image and Video Processing*, 9(2015):1335–1338.
12. M. Khan, T. Shah, H. Mahmood, M. A. Gondal, An efficient method for the construction of block cipher with multi-chaotic systems, *Nonlinear Dynamics*, 71(2013):493–504
13. M. Khan, T. Shah, M. A. Gondal, An efficient technique for the construction of substitution box with chaotic partial differential equation, *Nonlinear Dynamics*, 73(2013):1795–1801.
14. M. Khan, T. Shah, H. Mahmood, M. A. Gondal and I. Hussain, A novel technique for constructions of S-Boxes based on chaotic Lorenz systems, *Nonlinear Dynamics*, 70(2012):2303–2311.
15. M. Khan, T. Shah, S. I. Batool, A new approach for image encryption and watermarking based on substitution box over the classes of chain rings, *Multimedia Tools and Applications*, 76(2017):24027–24062.
16. M. Khan, Z. Asghar, A novel construction of substitution box for image encryption applications with Gingerbreadman chaotic map and S_8 permutation, *Neural Computing and Applications*, 29(2018):993–999.
17. S. S. Agaian, K. P. Lentz, and A. M. Grigoryan, A new measure of image enhancement, In *IASTED 2000: Proceedings of the International Conference on Signal Processing and Communication*, pages 19–22, 2000.
18. S. S. Agaian, K. Panetta, and A. Grigoryan, Transform based image enhancement with performance measure, *IEEE Transactions on Image Processing*, 10(2001):367–381.
19. M. Khan, T. Shah, A novel statistical analysis of chaotic S-box in image encryption, *3D Research* 5(2014):16.

Chapter 19

Secure and Robust ECG Steganography Using Fractional Fourier Transform

Gajanan K. Birajdar, Vishwesh A. Vyawahare and Mukesh D. Patil

Contents

DOI: 10.1201/9780429435461-22

19.1 Introduction

Digital information in the form of audio, image and video is shared over the Internet due to the availability and efficiency of global computer networks for the communication of digital information. Due to powerful computing hardware and easy to use software that can capture, store, edit and share the information, there is a rise in variety of applications in entertainment, education institutes, newspaper and magazines and medicine fields. At the same time, because of these powerful hardware and software editing tools, it is easy to modify original contents by the malicious attacker. The issue of individual's data privacy and security is attracting attention.

Advances in the medical field have increased dramatically due to the development of bio-medical devices for the diagnosis of diseases facilitating remote healthcare monitoring [1]. In remote healthcare applications, patient's electrocardiogram (ECG) is continuously monitored and in case of any abnormal cardiac activity, emergency alerts can be sent to doctors. Patient's ECG signal and other physiological recordings are collected and sent to the hospital server through the Internet using the patient's personal digital assistant (PDA). In addition to diagnostic data, patient's personal information and medical records are also sent. To prevent information theft and to secure this information, steganography techniques are employed as per the Health Insurance Portability and Accountability Act (HIPPA).

The idea of embedding the secret information in a cover medium and extraction at the receiver end stimulated great interest among the researchers. These methods are called steganography techniques. Steganography is the art of concealing secret data in the cover medium which is imperceptible and undetectable to the attacker. *Cover* medium refers to the medium used to carry the embedded bits. *Stego* refers to the cover with embedded data and inserted data bits are called *payload* or *embedding capacity. Imperceptibility* is undetectablility of the secret data in stego signal [2].

Steganography results in irreversible degradation to the cover ECG sample. Therefore, an ECG steganography technique must have the following desirable properties: (a) stego ECG must have minimum distortion while maintaining the diagnostic capability (b) bit error rate at the receiver must be minimum (c) identification of the bits/coefficients for embedding the secret information in order to introduce minimum degradation in stego ECG.

Steganography using ECG signal is proposed in this chapter as ECG data is collected frequently in healthcare systems along with temperature, glucose level and blood pressure. Besides, the volume of ECG data is also large. Therefore, ECG is the suitable choice for embedding patient's secret information. The presented approach follows HIPPA of 1996 which provides access of patient data and records to authorized persons only [3].

**HEALTH INSURANCE PORTABILITY AND
ACCOUNTABILITY ACT (HIPPA)**

In remote patient health monitoring (e-healthcare applications), ECG data
from the patient's device is transmitted to the hospital server over the Internet.
Exchange of information using Internet adds security and privacy concern
of secret information. As per HIPPA, the privacy and confidentiality of a
patient must be maintained when information is sent through the Internet
and patient information must be retrieved by the authorized individual only.
Also, the stored data must be secured on the hospital server.

HIPPA includes who is covered, what information is protected, and how
protected health information can be used and disclosed. [3,4]. The technical safeguard emphasizes two primary concerns: (a) patient privacy: patient's
personal information and medical history and its authorized access and
(b) security: secret data security when transmitted over internet and stored
on the hospital server.

19.1.1 Electrocardiogram (ECG) Signal

An electrocardiogram reveals heart's electrical activity in rhythmic pattern measured in terms of beats per minute (bpm) used to study cardiac pathology for analysis of different arrhythmia. The ECG signal is collected using skin electrodes and
consists of Q, R, S, P, T waves and a QRS complex. It begins with P wave following
the QRS complex, U and T waves. The amplitude and time duration of ECG waveforms carry important information of the type of heart disease including normal
and abnormal functioning of the heart. Figure 19.1 illustrates one cycle of a normal
electrocardiogram pattern.

The ECG activity monitoring and collection device originates huge amount
of data depending on the sampling rate, number of bits and number of sensors.
For the ECG signal, the sampling rate deviates from 125 to 1024 Hz. Every data
sample can be characterized using 8 to 16 bit binary number representation.
Number of electrodes (number of sensors) may vary from 10 to 12 to collect
the sample. Considering the minimum values of all three parameters, 750 KB
of ECG data is generated in one minute (45 MB per hour). Maximum values
of these parameters result in 11.79 MB ECG signals in one minute (707.4 MB
per hour) [5]. Such a large amount of data is present as a cover medium in ECG
steganography.

In this chapter, a new secure and robust approach is proposed to assure secure
transmission of patient's confidential data using patient electrocardiogram reading. Input ECG signal is converted into frequency domain by applying fractional

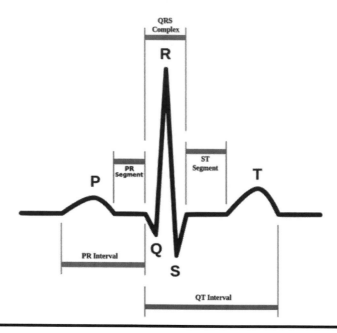

Figure 19.1 **Normal electrocardiogram signal.**

Fourier transform. Patient's secret information is embedded in fractional Fourier transform coefficients using least significant bit embedding approach. The technique has two major advantages: (1) steganography is used to conceal patient's secret data inside the ECG sample using encryption. Incorporating encryption techniques permit authorized individuals to extract and read patient's confidential medical records and history. (2) Additionally, in order to enhance robustness of the method and to reduce bit error rate, Hamming error correction coding is employed. Mean squared error, mean absolute error, signal to noise ratio, peak signal to noise ratio, percentage residual difference, bit error rate, relative root mean squared error and fractional Fourier percentage residual difference are computed to validate the proposed algorithm.

The chapter is organized as follows. Various state-of-the-art ECG steganography techniques are briefly described and compared in Section 19.2. Fractional Fourier transform based ECG steganography architecture and algorithm is proposed in Section 19.3. Detailed embedding and extraction steps of the secret data in the ECG signal is also illustrated. Fractional Fourier transform and its use in steganography is explained in Section 19.4. Proposed algorithm is evaluated using eight different parameters and experimental results are presented in Section 19.5. Architecture of a typical ECG steganography method employed in e-healthcare application is also illustrated. Finally, Section 19.6 concludes the chapter.

19.2 Related Work

In the last decade, various approaches have been proposed to secure and protect patient's confidential information using electrocardiogram (ECG) stagenography. Transform domain steganography is a popular choice because of its robustness against steganography attacks (steganalysis) and substantial embedding capacity [6]. This section briefly reviews state-of-the-art ECG steganography approaches (It should be noted that the ECG watermarking techniques are not discussed here).

Special ranger numbers (2.1475×10^9) of ECG signals are exploited for embedding and extraction of patient's secret information with very low PRD (Percentage residual difference) of watermarked ECG [7]. The method was robust in terms of identifying locations of embedded bits. A wavelet-based ECG steganography approach was introduced in [4,8,9] by combining encryption and scrambling methods to protect patient's confidential records. After five-level discrete wavelet transform (DWT) decomposition, the secret data is embedded using variable bit length least significant bits (LSB) insertion (1 to 5 LSB bits).

In transform domain ECG steganography, wavelet transform is widely used for information hiding. A DWT-SVD (singular value decomposition) based robust ECG steganography algorithm is presented using BCH (Bose–Chaudhuri–Hocquenghem) codes in [10]. Secret information is embedded in high frequency band of DWT, as this band is not significant during the diagnosis stage. Input *1-D* ECG signal is converted into *2-D* matrix before DWT decomposition. A similar approach is proposed without BCH codes for e-Healthcare applications [11]. Improved DWT-SVD based ECG steganography approach is demonstrated in [12] and compared to the method in [10]. After converting input ECG into *2-D* matrix, DWT decomposition is applied. The secret data is embedded in a specified sub-band (HH-sub-band) by replacing the singular values of the *2-D* ECG signal by the singular values of the secret information using dynamic location selection approach.

Use of a continuous ant colony optimization (CACO) is proposed [13] to enhance imperceptibility and robustness of DWT-SVD based steganography algorithm. To acquire multiple scaling factors (MSF), CACO based optimization problem is formulated and solved in order to reduce deterioration in the ECG stego signal. Reversible ECG steganography is presented using histogram shifting and thresholding approach [14]. Integer-to-integer DWT is applied over the ECG signal for reversibility and high capacity information hiding.

To provide high security to patient's secret information, the input data is encrypted using Advanced Encryption Standards (AES) before embedding into LSB of DWT coefficients [15]. High peak signal to noise ratio (PSNR) is achieved using the proposed method. A low capacity reversible ECG steganography for secure transmission of patient's data is proposed in [16]. The characteristics of the Hamming code and matrix coding are utilized for secret message insertion in the ECG signal. Same approach is extended for EMG (Electromyography) data embedding with minimum distortion using different hamming codes including $(3,1),(7,4),(15,11),(31,26)$.

Complete extraction of the embedded data at the receiver is presented using integer wavelet transform based ECG steganography [17–19]. Rest of the approach is similar to [4] including XOR ciphering and scrambling matrix embedding of data in wavelet coefficients. Curvelet transform based ECG steganography is proposed by choosing the curvelet coefficients around zero values for embedding [20,21]. Selection of these coefficients deteriorates the ECG signal least and ensures imperceptibility of the secret information. The method [20] has zero bit error rate and PSNR decreases as secret data size increases.

Discrete wavelet transform, discrete cosine transform (DCT) and discrete Fourier transform (DFT) are explored for ECG steganography using quantization based information hiding [6]. ECG signal is first decomposed using 7-level Haar DWT and secret data is embedded using coefficient quantization. Two methods, high-capacity but lossy and reversible ECG data hiding approaches are proposed [22] using the coefficient alignment. The first method is robust and capable of large information hiding capacity. Local linear predictor (LLP) based reversible ECG data hiding algorithm is presented in [23]. Input ECG signal is divided into three parts and three different predictors are used for each part. Higher payload is obtained and scrambling process incorporated to protect ECG signal and to enhance information security.

As described above, all the ECG data hiding algorithms are classified into two categories. First type includes transform based techniques (DWT, DCT and DFT) which are widely studied with high embedding capacity. Second category involve methods that embed the secret information directly in the ECG signal. These methods are less robust and have low embedding capacity. Also, very few approaches are concerned with data security and the corresponding encryption technique as described in [4,16,17,20,23].

Robustness is another critical and significant characteristic of the steganography technique, as it is important to recover the patient's information at the receiver side with zero bit error rate. Different methods including [16,20,23] recovers the secret data with zero bit error rate at the receiver. Reconstruction of the ECG signal without any loss (reversible approach) is proposed in [14,16,22,23]. Fractional Fourier transform is a generalization of the classical Fourier transform and used in various signal and image processing applications. This chapter presents fractional Fourier transform based secure and robust ECG data hiding techniques with zero bit error rate. Secret information of the patient is encrypted using XOR encryption to increase the security. Additionally, Hamming code is applied to enhance the robustness of the proposed approach and lowering the bit error rate at the receiver (extraction side). Table 19.1 summarizes different ECG steganography techniques.

Table 19.1 Various ECG Steganographic Techniques

Method	Transform	Security Analysis	Capacity	PRD (%)	Comments
[4]	Wavelet	Yes	2.4 kB	0.32	59 ECG samples including normal, VF and VT samples used for analysis
[7]	LSB of ECG signal	Yes	2.5 kB	0.0678	Simple and efficient method
[10]	DWT-SVD	No	—	0.000059	Use of BCH error-correcting codes to improve robustness
[12]	DWT-SVD	No	3500 bits	0.0031	Dynamic location selection approach with error rates less than 0.6%
[13]	DWT-SVD	No	3.07 kB	0.06	Continuous ant colony optimization (CACO) is employed to improve robustness
[14]	IWT	No	324.3 kB for 30 min	0.2241	Use of IWT for reversible operation
[16]	Hamming code	Yes	66.67 kB	0.1286	Reversible approach
[17]	IWT	Yes	2.4 kB	0.2934	Faster and low loss of information
[20]	FDCT	Yes	512 Bytes	0.0132	Zero bit error rate
[6]	DWT, DCT & DFT	No	32 bits	—	DWT is better compared DCT and DFT in terms of SNR and RMSE
[22]	ECG coefficients	No	40 kB	0.4388	Robust and reversible technique
[23]	LLP	Yes	7.9 BPS	2.1179e+03	High capacity reversible approach

19.3 Fractional Fourier Transform Based ECG Steganography

ECG steganography hides the information in cover ECG sample. Proposed fractional Fourier transform based ECG steganography architecture consists of two major steps: (a) embedding algorithm and (b) extraction algorithm. Embedding algorithm is used to ensure secure information insertion and to hide the data with minimum degradation in the cover ECG.

The electrocardiogram sample is subjected to a fractional Fourier transform resulting in transform coefficients. The embedding step hides the patient's secret information into these coefficients. In order to reconstruct the stego ECG signal, inverse fractional Fourier transform is applied. At the receiver side, the patient's data is retrieved using the stego ECG. This data can be extracted only by authorized person using the encryption key. Sample data consisting of patient personal data and medical records is depicted in Figure 19.2.

To secure secret information and to not allow unauthorized access, shared key based encryption algorithm is employed. XOR ciphering technique is employed with ASCII shared key, which acts as a security key. XOR encryption is simple to implement and has low complexity. Additionally, to reduce bit error rate and in turn to enhance robustness of the approach, Hamming block coding is used. Hamming encoder and decoder with the codeword length n and the message length k is used.

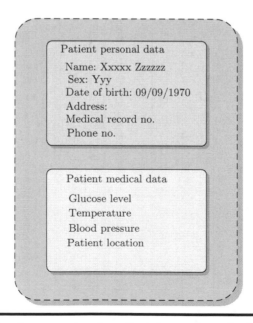

Figure 19.2   Patient's personal and medical data to be embedded.

19.3.1 Embedding Algorithm

Figure 19.3 illustrates different steps of information embedding in ECG sample. The embedding technique consists of the following steps:

- *Patient's secret information pre-processing:* First step in pre-processing includes collecting patient's information stored as text file, $msg = \{c_1, c_2, c_3, ..., c_k\}$ where k represents total number of characters in text message followed by its conversion into binary form. After obtaining the data in binary form, $d_s = \{b_1, b_2, b_3, ..., b_m\}$, in second step XOR ciphering is applied using a shared key resulting in encrypted data $d_{cip} = \{b_1, b_2, b_3, ..., d_m\}$. This key is common for embedding as well as the extraction stage. In the last step of pre-processing, encrypted data is encoded using the Hamming error correcting code $d_{enc} = \{b_1, b_2, b_3, ..., b_n\}$.
- *Forward fractional Fourier transform:* In this experiment, a 1-D ECG signal from MIT-BIH normal and arrhythmia database is used as the carrier. Fractional Fourier transform is applied over this ECG sample resulting in transform coefficients $F_{coef} = \{c_1, c_2, c_3, ..., c_j\}$ with fractional order α.
- *Embedding algorithm:* The secret bit b_i is extracted from the input data stream and least significant bit of transform coefficient $b_{LSB} = c_{i_{LSB}}$ is replaced by data bit.
- *ECG stego reconstruction:* In this last stage, stego ECG signal is reconstructed by applying inverse fractional Fourier transform over the resultant embedded coefficients $F_{stego} = F^{-1}(c_1, c_2, c_3, ..., c_j)$. The inverse transform step transforms frequency domain signal into time domain signal. The reconstructed stego ECG will be similar to original ECG sample. The detailed embedding algorithm is shown in Algorithm 1.

Algorithm 1   Embedding algorithm.

Input: Msg, ECG, Key, FractOrd, k, n
Output: ECGSteg
  1. *ECG:* Cover ECG signal
  2. *Key:* Encryption key

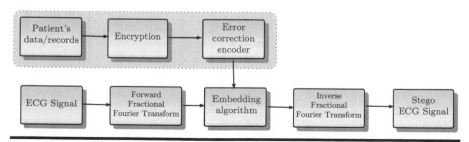

Figure 19.3   ECG embedding algorithm architecture.

3. *FractOrd:* Fractional order α
4. *Msg:* Secret text data
5. *Len:* Size of secret data bits
6. *Samp:* Number of ECG samples
7. *b:* Secret data in binary
8. *k, n:* Hamming encoder and decoder parameters
9. $b_{bin} \leftarrow$ Txt2Bin(*Msg*)
10. $b_{enc} \leftarrow$ Key (b_{bin})
11. $b_{tns} \leftarrow$ Hamming (b_{enc}, k, n)
12. **for** i=1 to *Samp* **do**
13. $C_{ecg} \leftarrow F^{\alpha}$ (ECG)
14. bits $\leftarrow$ LSB(C_{ecg})
15. bits $\leftarrow b_{tns}$
16. LSB(C_{emb}) $\leftarrow$ bits
17. $C_{steg} \leftarrow F^{-\alpha}(C_{emb})$
18. **end for**
19. ECGStego $\leftarrow C_{steg}$

19.3.2 Extraction Algorithm

Figure 19.4 shows architecture of the secret data extraction process from stego ECG signal. In order to correctly obtain the secret information from the stego ECG, the receiver requires: (1) shared key, (2) secret length and (3) transform order.

Forward fractional Fourier transform is performed over received stego ECG to generate transform coefficients. In next step, using the shared key and secret length the extraction step obtains the secret bit. Next, the extracted binary secret bits are decoded using Hamming error correction decoder. Finally, the receiver uses the same shared key for decryption of the secret data.

19.4 Fractional Fourier Transform

The Fractional Fourier Transform (FrFT) is a generalization of Fourier transform and belongs to the class of 1-D time-frequency characterization of a signal [24,25]. FrFT transformation has been popularly utilized in various applications including signal processing [26–32]. Fractional Fourier transform is a linear operator corresponding to signal rotation by an angle ϕ and has different kind of mathematical definitions.

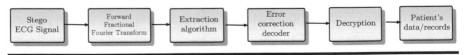

Figure 19.4 ECG extraction algorithm steps.

ECG signal (time-domain) can be represented in multiple FrFT domains by varying the order α. The case of $\alpha = 1$ corresponds to the rotation angle of $\pi/2$ that is equivalent to a classical Fourier transform. $\phi = 0$ corresponds a identity operator. The fractional order α ranges between $[0,1]$ and signal is characterized between time and frequency plane.

The continuous FrFT of any signal $x(t)$ with fractional order α is defined in Equation 19.1,

$$F^{\alpha}[x(t)] = \int_{-\infty}^{\infty} x(t)\mathbf{K}_{\alpha}(u,t)dt \qquad (19.1)$$

where α is the transform order (fractional) and $\mathbf{K}_{\alpha}(u,t)$ is the transform kernel and is given by:

$$\mathbf{K}_{\alpha}(u,t) = \begin{cases} \sqrt{\dfrac{1 - j\cot\phi}{2\pi}}\ exp\left(j\dfrac{t^2 + u^2}{2}\cot\phi - jutcsc\phi \right), & \phi \neq n\pi \\ \delta(t - u), & \phi = 2n\pi \\ \delta(t + u), & \phi = (2n \pm 1)\pi \end{cases} \qquad (19.2)$$

where u represents the αth fractional domain, $\phi = \alpha(\pi/2)$ is a rotation angle in the phase plane.

Fractional Fourier transform is a time-frequency analysis tool processing useful properties for time-varying signals. The FrFT achieves rotation of input signal in the time-frequency plane by any angle and FrFT based steganography approaches are robust and can provide better confidentiality considering both time and frequency domain.

In fractional Fourier transform, when the order α is close to 0, the transformed signal being dominant in the time domain. Whereas, for order $\alpha = \pi/2$, the transformation signal is dominantly in the frequency domain. The FrFT transform coefficients progresses from time domain to frequency domain when the transform order α varies from 0 to 1 exhibiting the characteristics in both domains. Embedding data in the ECG sample using fractional Fourier transform exploits peculiarities of both spatial and transform domain steganography algorithms. During the experimentation stage, α is varied from $0.1 - 0.95$ and we observed better performance of all the evaluation metrics in the range $0.75 - 0.95$. In this study, α is varied from $0.75 - 0.95$ and different evaluation metrics are computed.

19.5 Results and Discussions

To verify performance of the proposed fractional Fourier transform based ECG steganography algorithm, this section presents the performance analysis using different metrics. Description of the database used for the experimentation is described in the Subsection 19.5.1. In Subsection 19.5.2, eight different performance metrics used to assess the algorithm performance are discussed. Experimental results are reported in 19.5.3 with discussion. Subsection 19.5.4 illustrates embedding capacity performance along with security analysis. Finally, Subsection 19.5.5 demonstrates typical application of ECG steganography in e-healthcare applications.

19.5.1 Experimental Database

Presently, three internationally recognized ECG recording databases are available (i) Massachusetts Institute of Technology-Beth Israel Hospital (MIT-BIH) database, [33] (ii) American Heart Association (AHA) database and (iii) European ST-T ECG database [6]. In this chapter a proposed scheme is evaluated using MIT-BIH ECG database. From the MIT-BIH ECG database two different types of ECG signal are used for the experimentation. The first set of ECG samples consist of 5 normal ECG samples from MIT-BIH normal sinus rhythm database. Each sample was one minute long with 128-Hz sampling frequency. Second set of ECG samples involves 5 samples from MIT-BIH arrhythmia database. Each sample was of one minute duration with 360-Hz sampling frequency and a 12- bit binary representation.

19.5.2 Performance Evaluation Parameters

Embedding data in ECG using steganography approach deteriorates cover ECG sample. To evaluate the performance of the algorithm, one needs to compare the cover signal and the watermarked signal. To assess and demonstrate the efficacy the presented fractional Fourier transform based ECG steganography technique, eight different performance evaluation parameters are computed. These parameters are briefly summarized below.

■ **Mean squared error (MSE)**: MSE represents the average of the squares of error between the cover ECG and the stego ECG signals. Lower the value of MSE higher the similarity and better quality. It is computed as,

$$MSE = \frac{1}{N} \sum_{i=1}^{N} [Ec_i - Es_i]^2 \qquad (19.3)$$

where, Ec is original ECG signal, Es is stego ECG signal and N represents number of ECG samples.

■ **Mean absolute error (MAE):** MAE represents the absolute error between the cover ECG and the stego ECG signals. Low MAE values depicts high similarity between cover and stego ECG and therefore better quality. It is expressed as,

$$MSE = \frac{1}{N} \sum_{i=1}^{N} | Ec_i - Es_i |$$ (19.4)

■ **Signal to noise ratio (SNR):** Signal to noise ratio is expressed in terms of the decibel (dB) and is defined as,

$$SNR = 10 log_{10} \frac{\sum_{i=1}^{N} Ec_i^2}{\sum_{i=1}^{N} (Ec_i - Es_i)^2}$$ (19.5)

Higher the SNR, better the imperceptibility of stego ECG sample.

■ **Peak signal to noise ratio (PSNR):** It is the ratio of maximum amplitude of the cover ECG signal to the mean squared difference between cover and stego ECG samples (noise). Higher PSNR means better imperceptibility and quality. PSNR is evaluated using the following equation,

$$SNR = 20 log_{10} \left(\frac{\max [Ec_i]}{\sqrt{\frac{1}{N} \sum_{i=1}^{N} [Ec_i - Es_i]^2}} \right)$$ (19.6)

Percentage residual difference (PRD): PRD is employed to measure the distance between the cover ECG sample and the stego ECG signal. Lower the value of PRD better the imperceptibility. PRD is computed as,

$$PRD = \sqrt{\frac{\sum_{i=1}^{N} (Ec_i - Es_i)^2}{\sum_{i=1}^{N} Ec_i^2}} \times 100$$ (19.7)

■ **Bit error rate (BER):** BER represents the data loss due to the steganography process and is defined as the ratio between total number of bits of the secret data correctly recovered and the total number of bits embedded in the cover ECG. BER increases as the number of bits correctly recovered increases (increases the data loss). BER is given as,

$$BER = \frac{B_{Rec}}{B_{Emb}} \times 100 \tag{19.8}$$

Where, B_{Rec} is the number of bits of secret data correctly recovered and B_{Emb} is the total number of bits embedded in the cover ECG sample.

■ **Relative root mean squared error (rRMSE)**: Relative RMSE is given by the following equation,

$$rRMSE = \sqrt{\frac{1}{N} \sum_{i=i}^{N} \left(\frac{Ec_i - Es_i}{Ec_i} \right)^2} \tag{19.9}$$

For better performance of ECG steganography method, lower value of rRMSE is expected.

■ **Fractional Fourier percentage residual difference (FrFPRD)**: In order to estimate the distortion in the transform domain due to secret data embedding, a new measure FrFPRD using Fractional Fourier transform is proposed. FrFPRD is expressed as,

$$FrFPRD = \sqrt{\frac{\sum_{i=1}^{N} (Fc_i - Fs_i)^2}{\sum_{i=1}^{N} Fc_i^2}} \times 100 \tag{19.10}$$

Where, Fc_i is the original fractional Fourier transform coefficient and Fs_i is the fractional Fourier transform coefficient of stego ECG signal.

19.5.3 Results

The embedding algorithm as described in Section 19.3 is applied to normal and arrhythmia electrocardiogram signals from the MIT-BIH database to hide secret input data. Figure 19.5 depicts all the samples from each category. In Figure 19.5a–e shows five normal ECG samples whereas (i)–(m) shows five arrhythmia electrocardiogram signals. Different performance measures are evaluated and summarized in the Tables 19.2 and 19.3.

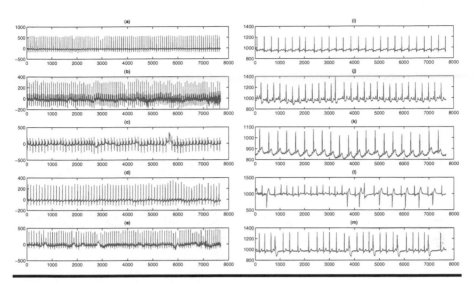

Figure 19.5   Normal and arrhythmia ECG samples.

Table 19.2   Performance Parameters of Steganographic Technique for Normal ECG Samples

	MSE	MAE	SNR (dB)	PSNR (dB)	PRD	BER	RRMSE	FrFPRD
Sample 1	0.234	0.202	37.98	72.63	0.4513	0	0.0855	0.0276
Sample 2	0.238	0.228	37.47	71.47	0.4283	0	0.0953	0.0378
Sample 3	0.231	0.269	37.83	71.83	0.4105	0	0.0995	0.0410
Sample 4	0.225	0.215	38.24	72.37	0.4903	0	0.0703	0.0201
Sample 5	0.227	0.220	39.63	70.73	0.5013	0	0.0692	0.0199

Table 19.3   Performance Parameters of Steganographic Technique for Arrhythmia ECG Samples

	MSE	MAE	SNR (dB)	PSNR (dB)	PRD	BER	RRMSE	FrFPRD
Sample 1	0.241	0.220	44.38	74.52	0.440	0	0.0738	0.0304
Sample 2	0.238	0.243	46.24	72.95	0.4158	0	0.0814	0.0403
Sample 3	0.254	0.216	45.39	72.38	0.3905	0	0.0895	0.0390
Sample 4	0.247	0.227	45.78	73.28	0.4893	0	0.0793	0.0235
Sample 5	0.235	0.214	44.83	73.29	0.4930	0	0.0634	0.0209

Tables 19.2 and 19.3 shows the experimental results for five normal and arrhythmia ECG signals respectively. Eight different evaluation metric are computed and tabulated using the fractional order (α) 0.95. Higher values of SNR (maximum 45.78 dB) and PSNR (maximum 74.52 dB) are reported using the proposed algorithm. Also, FrFPRD is minimum indicating low distortion because of the fractional Fourier transform. Additionally, all the bits are correctly recovered at the receiver indicating zero bit error rate. For both ECG types, MSE and MAE values are lower (average MSE = 0.24, average MAE = 0.22) indicating superior performance of the steganography approach.

Figure 19.6a–f shows two samples from normal ECG database before and after embedding the information. Figure 19.6a and b illustrates two original ECG samples, whereas Figure 19.6c and d shows corresponding stego ECG samples. For better understanding, these images are magnified and displayed in Figure 19.6e and f. As it can be seen, the deterioration because of the embedding process in minimum achieving high imperceptibility (Figure 19.7).

Probability density function (pdf) plots of original and stego ECG signals are also investigated in this study. Figures 19.8 and 19.9 shows pdf plots of original and stego ECG signals from normal MIT-BIH ECG database for two samples. It is evident from these figures, that the difference between the original and stego ECG signal is small and they are indistinguishable. It also shows that, stego ECG signal can be used for diagnoses with minimum distortion (Figures 19.10 and 19.11).

In this experiment, amplitude component is employed for secret data hiding instead of phase component of fractional Fourier transform. Importance of phase and amplitude in the Fourier transform has been studied [34,35] and it is revealed that Fourier phase is more important than the Fourier amplitude [36]. Additionally, major features can be recovered using phase component than amplitude [37] as by modifying amplitude information high frequencies of the Fourier spectrum are emphasized (Fourier amplitude of natural images is mostly concentrated in the low-frequency region). The result is enhanced edge information (high frequency).

As fractional Fourier transform has various definitions and its corresponding implementation with different computational complexities. Here, FrFT is obtained using Eigen decomposition method because of its low computational complexity $O(NlogN)$ which is equivalent to DFT [28,38].

The fractional order value (α) plays an important role in evaluating the performance of the method. Various performance metric are computed by varying α in the range $0.75 - 0.95$. Figures 19.12 through 19.15 show MSE, MAE, SNR and PSNR plots for five normal ECG samples using $\alpha = \{0.75, 0.80, 0.85, 0.90, 0.95\}$

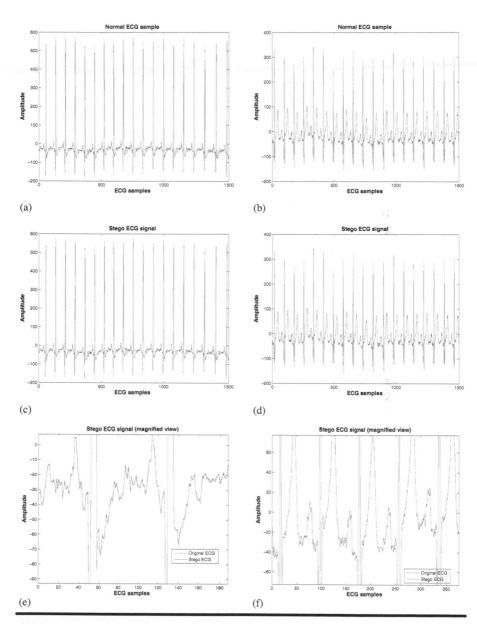

Figure 19.6 Original and stego ECG using normal ECG samples. (a) Original normal ECG signal (b) Original normal ECG signal (c) Stego ECG (d) Stego ECG (e) Magnified view of stego and original ECG (f) Magnified view of stego and original ECG.

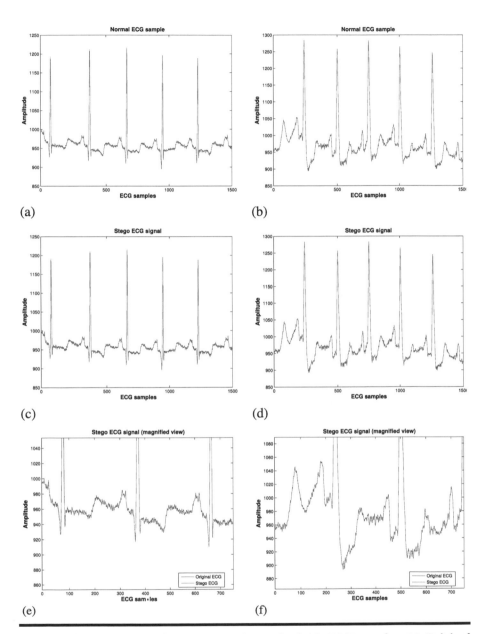

Figure 19.7 Original and stego ECG using arrhythmia ECG samples. (a) Original normal ECG signal (b) Original normal ECG signal (c) Stego ECG (d) Stego ECG (e) Magnified view of stego and original ECG (f) Magnified view of stego and original ECG.

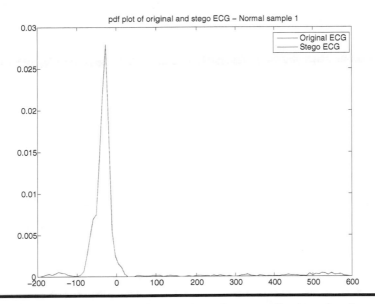

Figure 19.8 Pdf plot of original and stego electrocardiogram signal – Normal ECG sample 1.

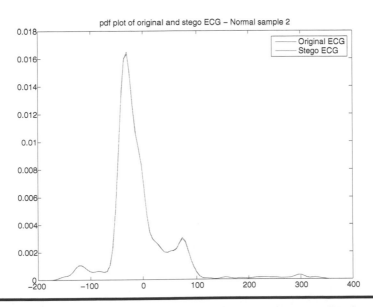

Figure 19.9 Pdf plot of original and stego electrocardiogram signal – Normal ECG sample 2.

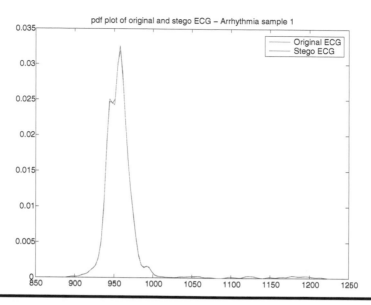

Figure 19.10   Pdf plot of original and stego electrocardiogram signal – Arrhythmia ECG sample 1.

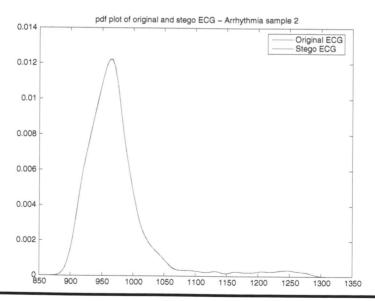

Figure 19.11   Pdf plot of original and stego electrocardiogram signal – Arrhythmia ECG sample 2.

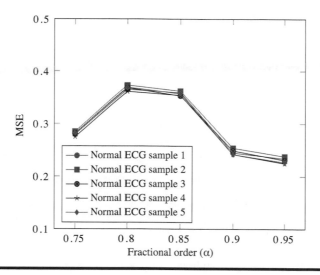

Figure 19.12   Effect of fractional order (α) on mean squared error (MSE) for various normal ECG samples.

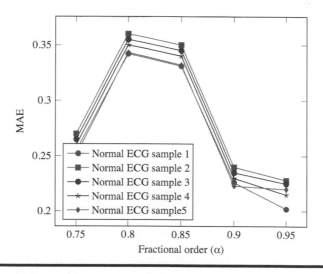

Figure 19.13   Effect of fractional order (α) on mean absolute error (MAE) for various normal ECG samples.

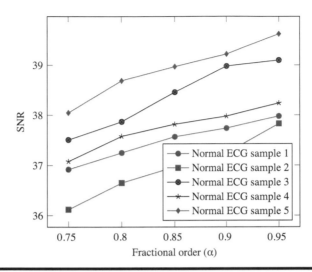

Figure 19.14   Effect of fractional order (α) on signal to noise ratio (SNR) for various normal ECG samples.

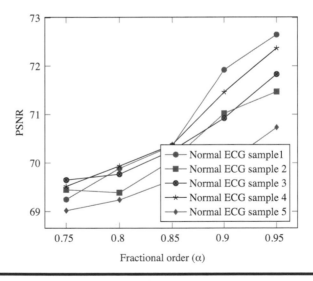

Figure 19.15   Effect of fractional order (α) on peak signal to noise ratio (PSNR) for various normal ECG samples.

values. Lower values of MSE and MAE are achieved at higher values of α, which is desirable. Whereas, higher α value produces better SNR and PSNR. Similar trend is observed in arrhythmia ECG database. Figures 19.16 through 19.19 depict results for MSE, MAE, SNR and PSNR for five arrhythmia samples using different α values.

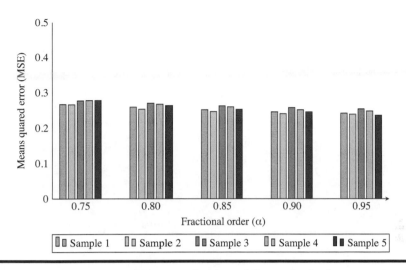

Figure 19.16   Mean squared error evaluation of five arrhythmia stego ECG samples for different fractional order (α).

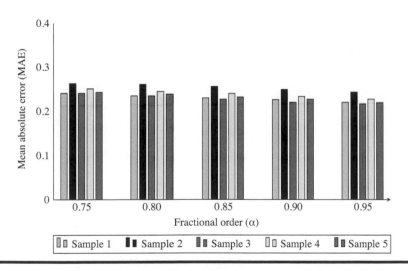

Figure 19.17   Mean absolute error evaluation of five arrhythmia stego ECG samples for different fractional order (α).

As it is seen from Figures 19.12 through 19.19, average variation in all the parameters ranges from 2% to 5% only (which is very small) when α is varied between 0.75 and 0.95. Additional flexibility in terms of α is achieved here without much variation in the performance parameter.

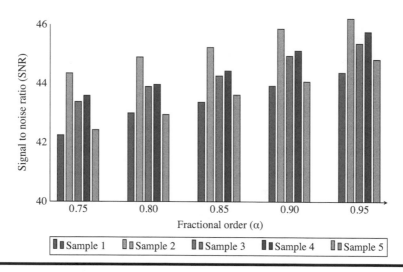

Figure 19.18 Signal to noise ratio of five arrhythmia stego ECG samples for different fractional order (α).

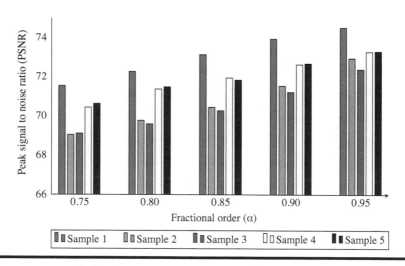

Figure 19.19 Peak signal to noise ratio of five arrhythmia stego ECG samples for different fractional order (α).

19.5.4 Security and Embedding Capacity Analysis

Three different parameters are shared between transmitter and receiver:

■ The encryption key
■ FrFT transform order
■ Secret length

When any unauthorized person tries to access the data with variation in any of the shared parameter will results in extraction of incorrect data. For the correct data generation, all three parameters should be known at the decoder side. Transform order is utilized as the key to the secret information extraction, as with wrong transform order it is difficult to reconstruct the original secret information. These parameters are never transmitted over the unsecured internet channel and stored at the transmitter and receiver.

The number of bits that can be inserted in the ECG sample is called the embedding capacity. In the proposed scheme, each of the FrFT coefficients is embedded one secret data bit. Total number of bits that can be inserted is computed as,

$$c = t_{Sam} \times f_s \times 2 \tag{19.11}$$

where, t_{Sam} is ECG samples time period in seconds, f_s ECG sampling frequency and c is embedding capacity. Increase in ECG cover sample time increases the embedding capacity.

The proposed FrFT based ECG steganography approach is compared with existing state-of-the-art ECG steganography algorithms. Table 19.4 shows comparison of FrFT based ECG steganography method with other existing techniques. For fair comparison only transform based ECG steganography algorithms are considered. As evident from the Table 19.4, the proposed method has FrPRD less than all other methods except [10]. Also, the presence of XOR encryption enhances

Table 19.4   Comparison of Fractional Fourier Transform Based ECG Steganography Method with Other Existing Techniques

Method	Transform	Security Analysis	Capacity	PRD (%)
[4]	Wavelet	Yes	2.4 kB	0.32
[10]	DWT-SVD	No	—	0.000059
[12]	DWT-SVD	No	3500 bits	0.0031
[13]	DWT-SVD	No	3.07 kB	0.06
[14]	IWT	No	324.3 kB for 30 min	0.2241
[17]	IWT	Yes	2.4 kB	0.2934
[20]	FDCT	Yes	512 Bytes	0.0132
[6]	DWT, DCT & DFT	No	32 bits	—
Proposed	Fractional FT	Yes	5400 Bytes	0.0199

security levels. In terms of embedding capacity, the method is capable of embedding 5400 bytes of data (one second ECG sample) which is higher compared to [4,12,17].

19.5.5 Application of ECG Steganography in eHealthcare Systems

Recent advancements in biomedical devices has accelerated interest in wearable sensors and its commercial applications in remote health monitoring system and fitness monitoring. Typical architecture of remote patient health monitoring systems, which is termed as eHealthcare system, is shown in the Figure 19.20 to observe, examine and record of patients physiological parameters. In the eHealthcare

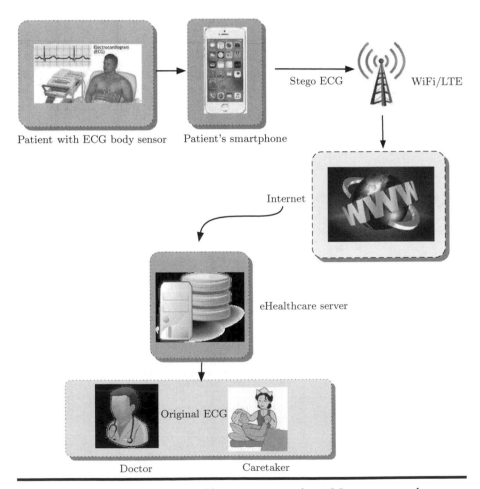

Figure 19.20   Schematic of eHealthcare system using ECG steganography.

applications, information and communication technologies are introduced to enhance the health care system remotely [39]. The difficulties like waiting in a queue and traveling time can be easily resolved using the eHealthcare system, which aids patient's in-home health care services. e-Health combines three different fields: medical informatics, public health and business to provide health services and information using the Internet.

As shown in the eHealthcare architecture, an ECG sample is collected using wearable body sensor (additionally other signals like blood pressure and glucose level can also be collected and transmitted), the sensor observations are transmitted to the patient's smartphone using Bluetooth. ECG steganography is implemented in the smartphone to embed patient secret data and other physiological information in the cover ECG signal. Stego ECG signal is finally transmitted to the eHelathcare server (or hospital server) through internet with minimum overhead bits.

At the eHealthcare server, the stego ECG is received and the original ECG along with patient's data is stored for future use. Only authorized doctors and administrative persons, including caretaker, having the secret key are entitled to view the ECG signal and to access secret information. The architecture illustrated can also be used for different applications like medical data sharing between two hospitals. Presented methods ensure high level security with minimum deterioration in the ECG signal.

19.6 Summary

Secure and robust ECG steganography technique to embed patient's personal and medical records based on fractional Fourier transform is presented in this chapter. In order to enhance security and to allow authorized access to the patient's personal data, XOR encryption is used. The method is evaluated using eight different performance metrics on two database: (a) normal MIT-BIH ECG and (b) Arrhythmia MIT-BIH ECG. The proposed technique introduces minimum distortion in the stego ECG. The scheme achieves zero bit error rate, high security, high capacity and low complexity. It is observed that the method is imperceptible, extracts all the information with zero error rate and the stego ECG signal can be used for diagnosis. Use of the fractional order parameter adds flexibility in the approach without significant variation in the system performance. Architecture of ECG steganography based eHealthcare system is also presented.

References

1. F. Hu, M. Jiang, M. Wagner, and D.-C. Dong. Privacy-preserving tele-cardiology sensor networks: Toward a low-cost portable wireless hardware/software codesign. *IEEE Transactions on Information Technology in Biomedicine*, 11(6):619–6127, 2007.

2. S. Katzenbeisser and F. Petitcolas (Eds.). *Information Hiding Techniques for Steganography and Digital Watermarking*. Artech House,, Norwood, MA, 1st ed., 2000.

3. W.-B. Lee and C.-D. Lee. A cryptographic key management solution for HIPAA privacy/security regulation. *IEEE Transactions on Information Technology in Biomedicine*, 12(1):34–41, 2008.

4. A. Ibaida and I. Khalil. Wavelet-based ECG steganography for protecting patient confidential information in point-of-care systems. *IEEE Transactions on Biomedical Engineering*, 60(12):3322–3330, 2013.

5. R. Horspool and W. Windels. An LZ approach to ecg compression. In *Proceedings on IEEE Seventh Symposium on Computer-Based Medical Systems*, pages 71–76. IEEE, 1994.

6. S.-T. Chen, Y.-J. Guo, H.-N. Huang, W.-M. Kung, K.-K. Tseng, and S.-Y. Tu. Hiding patients confidential data in the ECG signal viaa transform-domain quantization scheme. *Journal of Medical Systems*, 38(6):54, 2014.

7. A. Ibaida, I. Khalil, and D. Al-Shammary. Embedding patients confidential data in ECG signal for healthcare information systems. In *2010 Annual International Conference of the IEEE Engineering in Medicine and Biology*, pages 3891–3894, IEEE, August 2010.

8. D. Awasthi and S. Madhe. Analysis of encrypted ECG signal in steganography using wavelet transforms. In *2015 2nd International Conference on Electronics and Communication Systems (ICECS)*, pages 718–723, IEEE, February 2015.

9. D. Awasthi and S. Madhe. Evaluation of wavelet based ECG steganography system by using percentage residual difference (PRD) measurements. In *2015 International Conference on Communications and Signal Processing (ICCSP)*, pages 559–563, IEEE, April 2015.

10. S. E. Jero and P. Ramu. A robust ECG steganography method. In *2016 10th International Symposium on Medical Information and Communication Technology (ISMICT)*, pages 1–3, IEEE, March 2016.

11. D. Meghani and S. Geetha. ECG steganography to secure patient data in an e-healthcare system. In *Proceedings of the ACM Symposium on Women in Research 2016*, WIR'16, pages 66–70, ACM, 2016.

12. S.E. Jero, P. Ramu, and S. Ramakrishnan. Discrete wavelet transform and singular value decomposition based ECG steganography for secured patient information transmission. *Journal of Medical Systems*, 38(10):132, 2014.

13. E. Jero, P. Ramu, and R. Swaminathan. Imperceptibility-robustness tradeoff studies for ECG steganography using continuous ant colony optimization. *Expert Systems with Applications*, 49(Supplement C):123–135, 2016.

14. W. Wu, B. Liu, W. Zhang, and C. Chen. Reversible data hiding in ECG signals based on histogram shifting and thresholding. In *2015 2nd International Symposium on Future Information and Communication Technologies for Ubiquitous HealthCare (Ubi-HealthTech)*, pages 1–5, IEEE, May 2015.

15. S. Singh and V. Kumar. Securing patient's confidential data in ECG steganography using advanced encryption standards. In *Communication and Computing Systems*, pages 821–826. CRC Press, Boca Raton, FL.

16. H.-J. Shiu, B.-S. Lin, C.-H. Huang, P.-Y. Chiang, and C.-L. Lei. Preserving privacy of online digital physiological signals using blind and reversible steganography. *Computer Methods and Programs in Biomedicine*, 151(Supplement C):159–170, 2017.

17. K. PremChandran and K. Krishnakumar. ECG steganography using integer wavelet transform. In *2015 International Conference on Computer Communication and Informatics (ICCCI)*, pages 1–5, IEEE, January 2015.

18. C.A. Liji, K.P. Indiradevi, and K.K. Anish Babu. Integer-to-integer wavelet transform based ECG steganography for securing patient confidential information. *Procedia Technology*, 24(Supplement C):1039–1047, 2016.

19. S. S. Patel and S. V. Sankpal. Secure patients data transmission using XOR ciphering encryption and ECG steganography. In *2016 International Conference on Electrical, Electronics, and Optimization Techniques (ICEEOT)*, pages 1311–1315, IEEE, March 2016.

20. S.E. Jero, P. Ramu, and S. Ramakrishnan. ECG steganography using curvelet transform. *Biomedical Signal Processing and Control*, 22(Supplement C):161–169, 2015.

21. S. E. Jero and P. Ramu. Curvelets-based ECG steganography for data security. *Electronics Letters*, 52(4):283–285, 2016.

22. C.-Y. Yang and W.-F. Wang. Effective electrocardiogram steganography based on coefficient alignment. *Journal of Medical Systems*, 40(3):66, 2015.

23. H. Wang, W. Zhang, and N. Yu. Protecting patient confidential information based on ECG reversible data hiding. *Multimedia Tools and Applications*, 75(21):13733–13747, 2016.

24. A. Mcbride and F. Kerr. On namias's fractional fourier transforms. *IMA Journal of Applied Mathematics*, 39(2):159–175, 1987.

25. V. Namias. The fractional order fourier transform and its application to quantum mechanics. *IMA Journal of Applied Mathematics*, 25(3):241–265, 1980.

26. J. Lang. Image encryption based on the reality-preserving multiple-parameter fractional fourier transform and chaos permutation. *Optics and Lasers in Engineering*, 50(7):929–937, 2012.

27. P. Singh, B. Raman, and M. Misra. A secure image sharing scheme based on svd and fractional fourier transform. *Signal Processing: Image Communication*, 57(Supplement C):46–59, 2017.

28. D. Bhalke, C. Rama Rao, and D. Bormane. Automatic musical instrument classification using fractional fourier transform based- MFCC features and counter propagation neural network. *Journal of Intelligent Information Systems*, 46(3):425–446, 2016.

29. X.J. Zhang, Y. Shen, S.Y. Li, and H.Y. Zhang. Medical image registration in fractional fourier transform domain. *Optik-International Journal for Light and Electron Optics*, 124(12):1239–1242, 2013.

30. T. Nagashima, G. Cincotti, T. Murakawa, S. Shimizu, M. Hasegawa, K. Hattori, M. Okuno et al. Peak-to-average power ratio reduction of transmission signal of all-optical orthogonal time/frequency domain multiplexing using fractional fourier transform. *Optics Communications*, 402(Supplement C):123–127, 2017.

31. L.-L. Tang, C.T. Huang, J.-S. Pan, and C.-Y. Liu. Dual watermarking algorithm based on the fractional fourier transform. *Multimedia Tools and Applications*, 74(12):4397–4413, 2015.

32. M.-Y. Zhai. Seismic data denoising based on the fractional fourier transformation. *Journal of Applied Geophysics*, 109(Supplement C):62–70, 2014.

33. G. Moody and R. Mark. The impact of the MIT-BIH arrhythmia database. *IEEE Engineering in Medicine and Biology Magazine*, 20(3):45–50, 2001.

34. A. W. Lohmann, D. Mendlovic, and G. Shabtay. Significance of phase and amplitude in the fourier domain. *Journal of the Optical Society of America A*, 14(11):2901–2904, 1997.

35. A. Oppenheim and J. Lim. The importance of phase in signals. *Proceedings of the IEEE*, 69(5):529–541, May 1981.

36. T. Alieva and M. Calvo. Image reconstruction from amplitude-only and phase-only data in the fractional fourier domain. *Optics and Spectroscopy*, 95(1):110–113, 2003.

37. L. Gao, L. Qi, E. Chen, X. Mu, and L. Guan. Recognizing human emotional state based on the phase information of the two dimensional fractional fourier transform. In *Pacific-Rim Conference on Multimedia* pages 694–704. Springer, Berlin, Germany, 2010.

38. C. Candan, M.A. Kutay, and H.M. Ozaktas. The discrete fractional Fourier transform. *IEEE Transactions on Signal Processing*, 48(5):1329–1337, 2000.

39. H. Oh, C. Rizo, M. Enkin, and A. Jadad. What is ehealth (3): A systematic review of published definitions. *Journal of Medical Internet Research*, 7(1):1–10, 2005.

Chapter 20

Visual Secret Sharing Scheme for (*k, n*) Threshold-Based on QR Code with Multiple Decryptions

Song Wan, Yuliang Lu, Xuehu Yan,
Yongjie Wang and Chao Chang

Contents

DOI: 10.1201/9780429435461-23

20.1 Introduction

A secret sharing scheme is a method of encoding a secret image into a number of shares where each share reveals no information about the secret image. Only qualified shares can reconstruct the secret message [1]. Visual cryptography (VC), also called visual secret share (VSS), is a kind of secret sharing scheme [2–5] where the secret image can be recovered by stacking the qualified number of shares based on the human visual system (HVS) without any computation. Similarly as secret sharing, VSS [6] can overcome the problem of storing a secret in a single information-carrier, which would be damaged and lost easily by splitting and encoding a secret into a number of shares. While less than the qualified number can reveal nothing of the secret image by inspecting their shares; unfortunately, it would suffer from pixel expansion and codebook (basic matrices) design [7]. Based on this, VSS by random grids (RG) which could avoid pixel expansion and has no codebook needed was investigated. Nevertheless, in RG-based VSS, it would affect the visual quality of the recovered secret image as the background becomes darker when more shares are stacked together. XOR-based VSS is an alternative approach to solve the problem of RG-based VSS [8]. Better image quality can be obtained as well, by applying the XOR-based VSS schemes. XOR-based VSS would be useless when light-weight computation device isn't available. Through integrating both the conventional RG-based and XOR-based VSS together, the secret image can be recovered by HVS without any computation, and also could be revealed with better or lossless visual quality for a general k out of n mechanism by XOR when light-weight device is available [9]. However, as each share in VSS looks like a random pattern of pixels, it will raise suspicion and increase the likelihood of attracting the attention of potential attackers. Furthermore, the alignment is also an important issue for VSS recovery.

QR code [10] has recently become a popular used two-dimensional barcode with the advantages of larger contents and error correction capability. Even if it is dirty, we may be able to read it since it has error correcting capability. Also, the appearance of QR code is similar to the share of VSS. Based on the above advantages, the technology of combining QR code and VSS can be applied in many scenes, such as transferring secret information via public channels [11].

Recently, many researchers have proposed some schemes combining the technologies of QR code and VSS. Jonathan and Yan [12] presented a scheme that uses a QR code to authenticate the shares. It attempts to embed the verification information into the recovered secret in the form of a QR code. In their scheme, the QR code can be used as the secret transport mechanism which along string of alphanumeric characters can be embedded into the barcode. Wang et al. [13] proposed a scheme by embedding QR codes into given shares to prevent cheating. They search the best region of a given share where the QR code could be embedded into so as to keep the visual quality of the revealed secret and the embedding will not affect the secret revealing too much. However, the shares are random in the schemes above, which may attract suspicion of encryption, due to embedding QR codes into VSS shares.

Chow et al. [14] proposed a secret sharing scheme for $(n,n)(n \geq 3)$ threshold-based on XOR operation by distributing and encoding the information of a QR code containing a secret message into a set of QR codes. Each QR code share is a valid QR code that can be recognized by a QR code reader. The secret message can be recovered by first XORing the light and dark modules contained in the encoding region of all the n QR code shares and adding the function patterns. Nevertheless, the scheme needs a computational device with XOR ability and a QR code reader for secret recovery as well as is only for cases (n, n) where n is equal to or greater than 3.

Now, we assume that there is a scenario as follows. A treasure map is encrypted into 3 shadow images and distributed to 3 associated participants. The treasure map can be recovered by stacking any 2 or more shadow images by human visual system without cryptographic computation. The treasure is stored in the wild; they don't have any computational device to perform the decryption, i.e., VSS may be a good choice. On the roadmap to the designation, they should pass an unsafe area with inspection. QR code may not attract suspicion of secret encryption. Our scheme can be applied in the scenario.

In this article, we propose a novel scheme which deeply integrates the error correction mechanism of QR code with the theory of VSS. The proposed scheme which has the abilities of stacking and XOR recovery generates the bits corresponding to shares generated by VSS from a secret bit in the processing of encoding QR code. Each share is a valid QR code that can be scanned and decoded by a QR code reader. The secret image can be recovered by stacking k or more shares based on HVS without any computation, and also could be revealed with better or lossless visual quality for a general k out of n QR code shares by XOR when a light-weight device is available. As a result, when recovering the secret image we can choose one way to recover the secret image due to the different application scenarios and don't need QR code readers as well, as n can be equal to 2 for (k,n) threshold. Since each QR code can be recognized, it means that the shares may not be suspected if distributed via public channels and will reduce the likelihood of attracting the attention of potential attackers. Based on this, the proposed scheme can be applied in the scenario above.

The remainder of the paper is organized as follows. The introduction to the QR code and VSS are presented in Section 20.2. The secret algorithm is described in Section 20.3. Section 20.4 demonstrates the simulation results and analyses. Finally, Section 20.5 concludes this paper.

20.2 Background

20.2.1 QR Codes

QR code which was invented by the Denso Wave [15] Corporation in 1994 is defined as a two-dimensional barcode. The standard [10] defines forty sizes of QR code symbol versions which range from versions 1 to 40. A QR code is divided into modules and each QR code symbol version is comprised of a different number of modules. Each version has four modules more than the previous one. For example, Version 1 is made up of 21 × 21 modules while version 2 is made up of 25 × 25 modules. Each QR code has three Finder Patterns which are located in the lower left, upper left and upper right corner. They are used to recognize the QR code and detect the position of the symbol. Alignment Patterns that only occur from version two up to forty permit QR code readers to compensate for image distortion. The higher the version is, the more Alignment Patterns exist. A quiet zone which is the blank area around the QR code is necessary for reading the QR code. It should have the same reflectance value as the light modules, because the QR code readers could not distinguish between the Finder Patterns and the dark background.

The data in a QR code is encoded into the binary numbers of "1" and "0" based on Reed-Solomon codes that used for error detection and correction. The bit stream which is generated by message data encoded is divided into a sequence of codewords that are 8 bits inlength. There are four different error correction levels (L ~ 7%, M ~ 15%, Q ~ 25%, H ~ 30%). The error correction [16,17] is used for recovering the QR code in the event that parts of the symbol are dirty or destroyed. So, the QR code can also be recognized when other information is embedded into it. The recovery capacity of QR code will be improved by using the higher error correction levels, but it will increase the amount of data to be encoded. It means that a larger QR code version may be required when using a higher error correction level to encode the same message.

Based on the QR code version and error correction level, the codewords are divided into a large number of error correction blocks and corresponding error correction codewords are generated for each block. The number of error correction blocks, data codewords and error correction codewords depend on the QR code version and error correction level. In [10], the error correction codeword for each block is given as (c,k,r). Here, c is the total number of codewords, k is the number of data codewords and r is the error correction capacity which represents the maximum number of codewords that can be altered per block. It means that if more than r codewords per block contain errors, the QR code would not be decoded. To minimize the possibility that localized damage will cause the QR code to become undecodable, the codewords from the blocks are encoded in an interleaved manner, with the error correction codewords appended to the end of the data codewords sequence. The data codewords and error correction

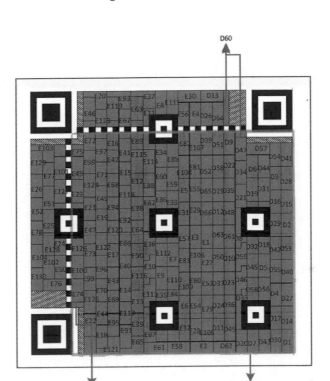

Figure 20.1 Data and error correction codewords arrangement for QR code version 7 with error correction level H.

codewords arrangement for QR code version 7, with an error correction level of H, is shown in Figure 20.1.

The maximum number of codewords that can be altered in QR code can be referred to as l. As a codeword equals eight modules in the QR code structure, we define the n is equal to $8l$. If a QR code need to be decoded correctly, we must make sure that the codewords altered per block can't be more than r and the total codewords altered in QR code need to be equal to or less than l. In [18] of our previous work, it can be concluded that the codewords of QR code can be modified in data region, which can reach the maximum number of codewords that can be altered. In order to make sure that the three identical finder patterns of QR code could not be altered so that it does not affect the appearance of QR codes, we define the data, which is the blue region as shown in Figure 20.1, that could be modified is from the coordinate of (7,7) to the right down corner of the QR code. The altered region can be a rectangle from the coordinate of $(7, p - j)$ to the right down corner while the value of j can be determined by the error correction capacity of the QR code so that the codewords altered can reach the maximum error correction capacity. The range of j will be as follow:

$$\left\lfloor \frac{n}{p-7} \right\rfloor - 1 \le j \le \left\lfloor \frac{n}{p-7} \right\rfloor + 1 \tag{20.1}$$

Here, the coordinate of the right down corner is (p, p), $(p - 7)$ represents the number of lines in the blue region.

D1-D13	Data Block 1
D14-D26	Data Block 2
D27-D39	Data Block 3
D40-D52	Data Block 4
D53-D66	Data Block 5
E1-E26	Error Correction Block 1
E27-E52	Error Correction Block 2
E53-E78	Error Correction Block 3
E79-E104	Error Correction Block 4
E105-E130	Error Correction Block 5

20.2.2 Visual Cryptography

Visual cryptography scheme (VCS) was first introduced by Naor and Shamir [2]. The idea is to split a secret image into n images that called shares and afterwards using the OR-operation to stack some of these shares, the original image will be revealed. In a general (k, n) threshold VCS, a secret image is divided into n random shares (also called shadows) which respectively reveals nothing about the secret. The n shares are distributed to n associated participants. Stacking any k or more shares can visually reveal the secret image based on HVS without any computation, but any $k - 1$ or less shares cannot recover the secret [3]. Better or lossless visual quality can be obtained as well, by applying the XOR-based VSS schemes with a light-weight device [9]. In an $(2, 2)$ RG-based VCS, the secret is encrypted into two random shares of the secret image. Although some contrast [19] loss appears, the recovered image is clearly identified. In an $(2, 2)$ XOR-based VCS, the secret image is recovered lossless and can be recognized as the same with the original secret image with light-weight device.

In general, the visual quality of the recovered secret image is evaluated by contrast in VCS. It means that when contrast is equal to zero, the recovered secret image couldn't be recognized as the original secret image, while the reconstructed secret image can be recognized as the original secret image when contrast is greater than zero. The larger the contrast, the better the visual quality. Some definitions used in this paper are presented.

Symbols $\otimes$ and $\oplus$ denote the Boolean OR and XOR operations. The binary secret image S is shared among n shadow images and the reconstructed secret image S' is reconstructed from t $(2 \leq t \leq n)$ shadow images. Here 1 denotes black pixels, 0 denotes white pixels.

The probability of pixel color is transparent or white (0) and the same for the probability of pixel color is opaque or black (1) for a certain pixel a in binary image A with size of M × N. AS_0(resp., AS_1) is the white (resp., black) area of original secret image A defined as $A_0 = \{(i, j) \mid A(i, j) = 0, 1 \leq i \leq M, 1 \leq j \leq N\}$ (resp., $A_1 = \{(i, j) \mid A(i, j) = 1, 1 \leq i \leq M, 1 \leq j \leq N\}$)

Definition 1 (Contrast): *The visual quality, which will decide how well human eyes could recognize the recovered image, of the recovered secret image S' corresponding to the original secret image S is evaluated by contrast defined as follows* [9,20]

$$\alpha = \frac{P_0 - P_1}{1 + P_1} = \frac{P(S'[AS_0] = 0) - P(S'[AS_1] = 0)}{1 + P(S'[AS_1] = 0)} \tag{20.2}$$

In this paper, contrast which is defined in Definition1 would be applied to evaluate the visual quality of the recovered secrete image and it is also widely used in VC related schemes. Where α denotes contrast, P_0 (resp., P_1) is the appearance probability of white pixels in the recovered image S' in the corresponding white (resp., black) area of original secret image S, that is, P_1 is the wrongly decrypted probability corresponding to the black area of original secret image S and P_0 is the correctly decrypted probability corresponding to the white area of original secret image S.

Definition 2 (Visually recognizable) [9,20]: *The recovered secret image S is recognizable as original secret image S by $\alpha > 0$ when $t \geq k$.*

Based on Definition 2, we can recognize the recovered secret image as the original secret image by $\alpha > 0$, while the revealed secret image couldn't be recognized as the original secret image if $\alpha = 0$.

VSS can be applied in many scenes, such as, social computing security, authentication and identification, watermarking [21], information hiding and transmitting passwords etc. In this paper, we use the so-called $(2,2)$ scheme. One (k,n) RG-based applied in our article and the algorithmic steps are described in Algorithm 1[22].

Algorithm 1 (k, n) RG-based VSS

Input: A M × N binary secret image S, the threshold parameters (k, n)

Output: n shadow images $SC_1, SC_2, ... SC_n$

Step 1: For each position
$(i, j) \in \{(i, j) \mid 1 \leq i \leq M; 1 \leq j \leq N\}$ repeat Steps 2–6.

Step 2: Select $b_1, b_2, ... b_k \in \{0, 1\}$ randomly.

Step 3: If $S(i, j) = b_1 \oplus b_2 ... b_k$, go to Step 5; else go to Step 4.

Step 4: Randomly select $p \in \{1, 2, ..., k\}$ flip $b_p = \overline{b_p}$ (that is $0 \rightarrow 1$ or $1 \rightarrow 0$).

Step 5: Select $b_{k+1}, b_{k+2}, ... b_n \in \{0, 1\}$ randomly.

Step 6: Randomly rearrange $b_1, b_2, ... b_n$ to $SC_1(i, j), SC_2(i, j), ... SC_n(i, j)$.

Step 7: Output the n shadow images $SC_1, SC_2, ... SC_n$.

20.3 Proposed Visual Secret Sharing Based on QR Codes (VSSQR) Scheme

In this section, we propose a novel scheme which deeply integrates the error correction mechanism of QR code with the theory of VSS. The errors can be corrected by the error correcting code which uses the strict mathematical relations of information bits and then checks bits to locate the wrong positions, so that the QR code can be correctly decoded while manipulated some of the codewords but still maintaining a QR code symbol. In this paper, the scheme proposed is for (k, n) threshold which will be referred to as VSS based on QR code. The scheme proposed is to use the highest level of QR code error correction. According to the different application scenarios, two different recovered ways of the secret image are given.

20.3.1 The Proposed Scheme

The idea behind VSSQR is to generate the bits corresponding to shares by VSS from a secret bit in the processing of encoding QRs. The information of n QR codes is altered in the range of the error correction mechanism, in order to generate n QR code shares which contain the information of n shadow images. Each share is a valid QR code that can be scanned and decoded by a QR code reader. The secret image could be revealed by HVS without any computation based on stacking when no light-weight computation device. On the other hand, if the light-weight computation device is available the secret image can be revealed with better visual quality based on XOR operation and could be lossless revealed when sufficient shares are collected. But any $k-1$ or less shares cannot recover the secret with the abilities of stacking and XOR decryptions.

The QR code shares generation architecture of the proposed scheme is illustrated in Figure 20.2, the corresponding algorithmic steps are described in detail in Algorithm 2.

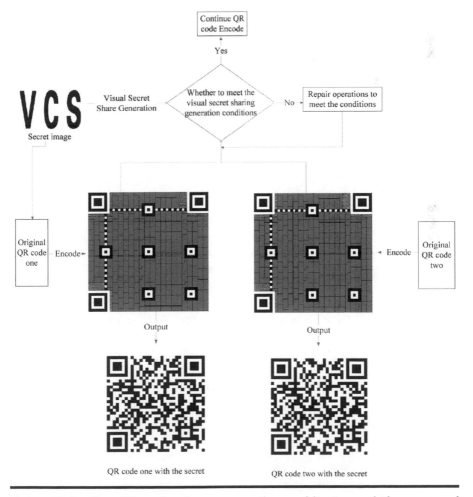

Figure 20.2 The QR code shares generation architecture of the proposed scheme.

Algorithm 2   The proposed scheme

Input: A M × N binary secret image S, Original QR_1 message, Original QR_2 message... Original QR_n message, the threshold parameters (k, n)

Output: QR code shares SC_1, SC_2,... SC_n

Step 1: Turn left and right the secret image, then rotate it 90 degrees anticlockwise.

Step 2: S is divided into 2n regions, denoted as:

$A[1]: (i_1, j_1) \in \{(i_1, j_1) \mid 1 \leq i_1 \leq N; 1 \leq j_1 \leq \lfloor M/2n \rfloor\}$

$A[2]: (i_2, j_2) \in \{(i_2, j_2) \mid 1 \leq i_2 \leq N; \lfloor M/2n \rfloor \leq j_2 \leq \lfloor M/n \rfloor\}$

$A[2n]: (i_{2n}, j_{2n}) \in \{(i_{2n}, j_{2n}) \mid 1 \leq i_{2n} \leq N; \lfloor (2n-1)M/2n \rfloor \leq j_{2n} \leq M\}$

Step 3: Let $Q_1, Q_2, ... Q_n$ denote the regions of QR_1.., QR_n with the same size of S in the processing QR codes from the coordinate of $(7, 7)$ to the right down corner of QR code, and $Q_x(i, j)$ indicates the encoded bits corresponding to QR_x message. In the encoding processing of QR_1 message, QR_2 message... QR_n message for each position $(i, j) \in \{(i, j) \mid 1 \leq i \leq N; 1 \leq j \leq M\}$, repeat Steps 4–5.

Step 4: For the regions of A[x] and A[n + x], randomly select (k–1) processing QR codes from $Q_1, Q_2, ... Q_n$ excluding Q_x, denoted as $Q_{i_1}(i, j), Q_{i_2}(i, j), ... Q_{i_{k-1}}(i, j)$.

Step 5: If $S(i, j) \neq Q_x(i, j) \oplus Q_{i_1}(i, j) \oplus Q_{i_2}(i, j) ... \oplus Q_{i_{k-1}}(i, j)$, $Q_x(i, j) = Q_x(i, j)$.

Step 6: Output the n QR code shares $SC_1, SC_2, ... SC_n$.

Algorithm 2 takes one secret image S and n original QR code messages as the input and outputs n QR code shares $SC_1, SC_2, ... SC_n$. Each QR code share is a valid QR code which will gain the original message when decoded by a QR code reader. The secret recovery of the proposed scheme can be based on stacking or XOR operation, and the secret image can be revealed in the encoding regions by any k or more QR code shares.

20.3.2 Performance Analyses

From the above steps, in Step 1 the data generation when encoded before data mask is stored in an array module from left to right while the pixels of image shown are from top to bottom, so that the secret image preprocessing as Step 1 can be shown correctly while embedded in QR code. Step 2 divides the processed secret image into 2*n* regions, A[1], A[2],... A[2n]. The reason can be described as follows:

1. In [18] of our previous work, it can be concluded that the number of code-words which can be modified in the error correction region is equal to or less than that in the data region, so that we can reach the maximum modified codewords number in the data region. The maximum altered region can be a rectangle from the coordinate of $(7, j)$ to the right down corner and the value of j can be determined by Equation 20.1 in Section 20.2. The maximum altered region can reach one third of the blue region as shown in Figure 20.1. So, the QR code can be correctly decoded.

2. To make sure that k out of n QR code shares can reveal each part of the original secret, we need to divide the original secret into 2*n* regions that each QR code takes two pieces of the 2*n* regions, denoted as A[x] and A[n + x]. In this cases, the reconstructed secret image could reveal the original whole secret.

3. Due to the characteristics and basic design principles of QR code, the QR code can be correctly decoded when we altered the region of A[x] and A[n + x], where the altered region can be controlled to satisfy the error correction mechanism. The bigger value of n, the capacity of embedding secret will be bigger.

In Step 3, select the regions of QR$_1$.., QR$_n$ with the same size of S from the process-ing QR codes at the same locations, denoted as $Q_1, Q_2 \ldots Q_n$, and $Q_x(i, j)$ indicates the encoded bits corresponding to QR$_x$ message. S is divided into 2n regions, so Q_x has the same divided regions as S. If the regions of both A[x] and A[n + x] need to be altered, we only modify the bits in the two regions of Q_x while preserving Q_y, $(y = 1, 2, \ldots x - 1, x + 1, \ldots n)$. For the regions of A[x] and A[n + x], select $(k - 1)$ QR codes which selected from the rest of the processing QR codes which refer to $Q_1, Q_2, \ldots Q_n$ that exclude Q_x randomly, as $Q_{i_1}(i, j), Q_{i_2}(i, j), \ldots Q_{i_{k-1}}(i, j)$ in Step 4. Check $S(i, j)$ and the result by XORing $Q_x(i, j)$ and $Q_{i_1}(i, j), Q_{i_2}(i, j), \ldots Q_{i_{k-1}}(i, j)$ are the same or not, if not, the bit of $Q_x(i, j)$ will be altered in Step 5. For each position $(i, j) \in \{(i, j) | 1 \le i \le N; 1 \le j \le M\}$, repeat Steps 4 and 5, then output the QR code shares in Step 6.

In such a way, the proposed approach can satisfy the error correction mechanism in the QR code, which is applicable to all QR code versions. Although the capacity of embedding a secret is different for different QR code versions, the approach is the same. In our article, we just list some typical examples to test the efficiency of the proposed approach.

20.4 Experimental Results and Analyses

In this section, the effectiveness of the proposed scheme is evaluated by our experiments. Four versions of QR codes are used: QR code version 17 with error correction level H, QR code version 26 with error correction level H, QR code version 27 with error correction level H and QR code version 30 with error correction level H. Several secret images are used: original binary secret image 1 with size of 60×60 as shown in Figure 20.3a, original binary secret image 2 with size of 90×90 as shown in Figure 20.4a, original binary secret image 3 with size of 110×110 as shown in Figure 20.5a, original binary secret image 4 with size of 110×110 as shown in Figure 20.6a, to test the efficiency of the proposed scheme.

20.4.1 Image Illustration

In our experiments, the simulation environment of the proposed scheme is Python language. (2,2) threshold with QR code version 17 and image 1, (2,2) threshold with QR code version 30 and image 2, (2,3) threshold with QR code version 27 and image 3, (3,3) threshold with QR code 26 and image 4 are used to do the test of the proposed scheme.

Figure 20.3 shows the simulation results of the seventeen version, 17-H, QR barcode with 85×85 modules. Original QR_1 message "Information and secret!" while

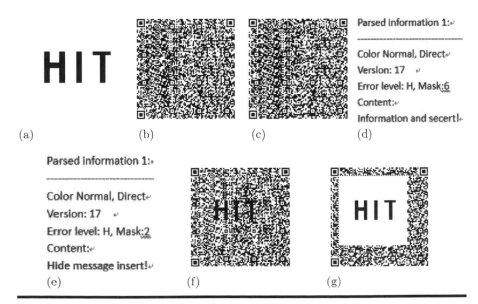

Figure 20.3 The results of QR code version 17 with error correction level H by (2,2) VSSQR scheme proposed. (a) Secret image 1 *S* (b) QR share SC_1 (c) QR share SC_2 (d) The decoding information for SC_1 (e) The decoding information for SC_2 (f) Reconstructed QR code by stacking, *Sr* (g) Reconstructed QR code by XORing, Sr_1.

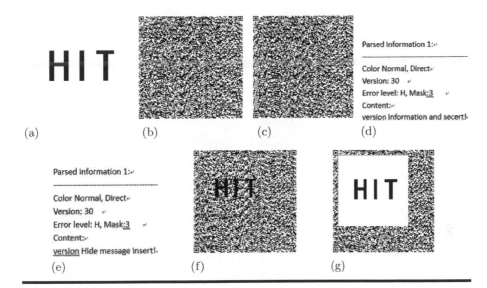

Figure 20.4 **The results of QR code version 30 with error correction level H by (2,2) VSSQR scheme proposed. (a) Secret image 2 *S* (b) QR share *SC₁* (c) QR share *SC₂* (d) The decoding information for *SC₁* (e) The decoding information for *SC₂* (f) Reconstructed QR code by stacking, *Sr* (g) Reconstructed QR code by XORing, *Sr₁*.**

original QR_2 message is "Hide message insert!". Figure 20.3b–c shows the QR code shares resulting from the proposed VSSQR scheme, SC_1, SC_2. Figure 20.3d–e show the decoding information for SC_1, SC_2, which are random noise-like. We can see that the shares are valid QR codes, which can be decoded by any standard decoding software into the original messages. Figure 20.3f shows the reconstructed QR code, Sr, which is recovered by stacking two QR code shares. The secret message can be seen directly from the reconstructed QR code. Figure 20.3g shows the revealed QR code, Sr_1, which is recovered by XORing two QR code shares with a light-weight device. We can see that the secret message can be recovered lossless.

Figure 20.4 shows the results of the thirty version, 30-H, QR barcode with 137×137 modules. Original QR_1 message is "version Information and secret!" while Original QR_2 message is "version Hide message insert!". Figure 20.4b–c show the QR code shares resulting from the proposed VSSQR scheme, SC_1, SC_2, which are random noise-like. Figure 20.4d–e show the decoding information for SC_1, SC_2. Figure 20.4f shows the reconstructed QR code, Sr, which is recovered by stacking two QR code shares. Figure 20.4g shows the revealed QR code, Sr_1, which is recovered by XORing two QR code shares with light-weight device. We can see that the secret message can be recovered lossless.

Figure 20.5 shows the results of the twenty-seven version, 27-H, QR barcode with 125×125 modules. The contents of cover QR codes will be different to verify the universality. Figure 20.5b–d show the QR code shares resulting from the proposed VSSQR scheme, SC_1, SC_2, SC_3, which are random noise-like. Figure 20.5e–g

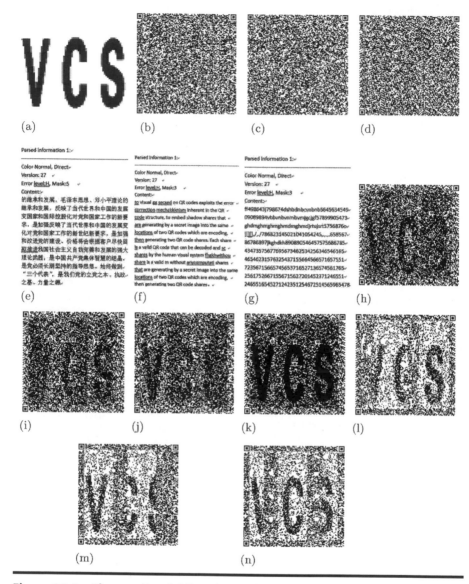

Figure 20.5 The results of QR code version 27 with error correction level H by (2,3) VSSQR scheme proposed. (a) Secret image 3 S **(b)** QR share SC_1 **(c)** QR share SC_2 **(d)** QR share SC_3 **(e)** The decoding information for SC_1 **(f)** The decoding information for SC_2 **(g)** The decoding information for SC_3 **(h)** Reconstructed image $SC_1 \otimes SC_3$ **(i)** Reconstructed image $SC_2 \otimes SC_3$ **(j)** Reconstructed image $SC_1 \otimes SC_2$ **(k)** Reconstructed image $SC_1 \otimes SC_2 \otimes SC_3$ **(l)** Reconstructed image $SC_2 \otimes SC_3$ **(m)** Reconstructed image $SC_1 \otimes SC_2$ **(n)** Reconstructed image $SC_1 \otimes SC_3$.

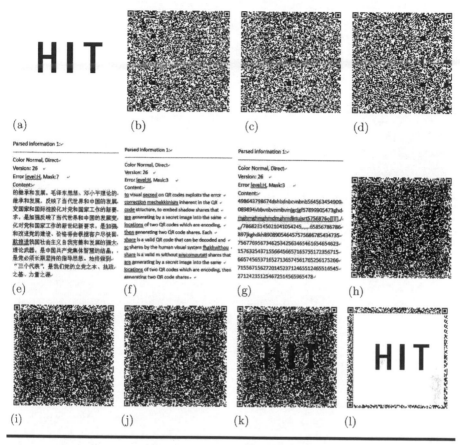

Figure 20.6 **The results of QR code version 26 with error correction level H by (3,3) VSSQR scheme proposed. (a) Secret image 4 S (b) QR share SC_1 (c) QR share SC_2 (d) QR share SC_3 (e) The decoding information for SC_1 (f) The decoding information for SC_2 (g) The decoding information for SC_3 (h) Reconstructed image $SC_1 \otimes SC_3$ (i) Reconstructed image $SC_2 \otimes SC_3$ (j) Reconstructed image $SC_1 \otimes SC_2$ (k) Reconstructed image $SC_1 \otimes SC_2 \otimes SC_3$ (l) Reconstructed image $SC_1 \otimes SC_2 \otimes SC_3$.**

show the decoding information for SC_1, SC_2, SC_3. Figure 20.5h–k show the reconstructed QR code by stacking any t ($2 \leq t \leq 3$) QR code shares, from which better visual of the reconstructed secret will be gained by stacking more shadow images. Figure 20.5l–n show the reconstructed QR code by XORing a general k out of n QR code shares. Compared with the reconstructed QR code by stacking the same QR code shares, it can be seen that better visual quality of the reconstructed secret can be gained.

Figure 20.6 shows the results of the twenty-six version, 26-H, QR barcode with 121×121 modules. The contents of cover QR codes will be different to verify the universality. Figure 20.6b–d shows the QR code shares resulting from the proposed

VSSQR scheme, SC_1, SC_2, SC_3, which are random noise-like. Figure 20.6e–g show the decoding information for SC_1, SC_2, SC_3. Figure 20.6h–k show the reconstructed QR code by stacking any $t(2 \leq t \leq 3)$ QR code shares. Figure 20.6h–j shows the reconstructed secret image with any less than 3 shadow images by stacking, from which there is no information could be recognized. Figure 20.6k shows the reconstructed secret image with 3 shadow images by stacking, the secret message can be seen directly based on HVS. Figure 20.6l shows the revealed QR code which is recovered by XORing three QR code shares with light-weight device. The secret message can be seen that it is recovered lossless.

20.4.2 Visual Quality of the Revealed Secret Images

In this section, the contrast [7,19] in Definition 1 is used to evaluate the visual quality of the recovered secret image. Some original binary secret images which are shown in Figures 20.3a and 20.5a are used to do the experiments of contrast. The size of secret images used will be changed to satisfy the needs of different QR code versions. Average contrast of the proposed (2,2) and (3,3) threshold for the binary secret image 1 as shown in Figure 20.3a with the abilities of stacking and XOR lossless recovery, and the proposed (2,3) threshold for binary secret image 2 as shown in Figure 20.5a with abilities of stacking and XOR recovery are shown in Table 20.1. Where t is the number of revealed shadow images.

From Table 20.1, the results indicate that:

1. It means that the recovery is lossless when the contrast reaches the maximum 1.
2. Better visual of the reconstructed secret will be gained by stacking more shadow images and the contrast based on XOR operation is greater than stacking in the propose scheme.
3. In the experiments of contrast with (2,3) threshold, the contrast of the revealed secret image will be different with the different original messages of the cover QR codes. The more similar the original messages of the cover QR codes are, the higher the contrast of the revealed secret image will be gained. The contrast of the recovered secret image will achieve the highest when the original messages of the cover QR codes are the same but not the empty due to the algorithm of VSS.
4. In the experiments of contrast with (3,3) threshold, the contrast is smaller than that in (2,2) threshold due to the algorithm of VSS.

The original messages of the cover QR codes can be the same but not empty. If the contents of the cover QR codes are empty, the QR code shares couldn't be decoded correctly. In the (3,3) threshold, the QR code shares generated will show the part of secret images directly when the contents of the cover QR codes are the same. Although it can improve the contrast of the recovered secret image in this case, it couldn't achieve our purpose of reducing the likelihood of attracting the attention of potential attackers.

Table 20.1   Contrast of the Proposed Scheme with Stacking (OR) and XOR Recovery

(k, n)	Average Contrast(AND)			Average Contrast(XOR)	
	QR code version	t = 2	t = 3	t = 2	t = 3
(2,2)	7	0.51612		1	
	14	0.50994		1	
	17	0.53430		1	
	20	0.52090		1	
	25	0.51230		1	
	27	0.51262		1	
	30	0.52110		1	
	35	0.51066		1	
(2,3)	7	0.15248	0.28263	0.27978	
		0.28677	0.51330	0.50903	
	14	0.17699	0.29571	0.28777	
		0.29244	0.50883	0.50090	
	18	0.17228	0.31554	0.30914	
		0.28786	0.51172	0.50089	
	21	0.17867	0.30907	0.30948	
		0.2967	0.51195	0.50212	
	25	0.18181	0.31070	0.30180	
		0.29218	0.51031	0.50332	
	27	0.15601	0.26285	0.26432	
		0.20927	0.37368	0.36804	
		0.29236	0.50957	0.50176	
	30	0.16952	0.29836	0.29810	
		0.28538	0.50674	0.50082	
	35	0.17129	0.29513	0.29569	

(Continued)

Table 20.1 (*Continued*) Contrast of the Proposed Scheme with Stacking (OR) and XOR Recovery

(k, n)	Average Contrast(AND)			Average Contrast(XOR)	
	QR code version	$t = 2$	$t = 3$	$t = 2$	$t = 3$
		0.29385	0.51093	0.50233	
(3,3)	7		0.26299		1
	15		0.28066		1
	19		0.25957		1
	22		0.27799		1
	26		0.25948		1
	29		0.27278		1
	33		0.28326		1
	40		0.28255		1

Based on the contrast as shown in Table 20.1, the secret image can be revealed with better visual quality or lossless recovery based on XOR operation when sufficient shares are collected with light-weight computation device. The experimental results of the contrast verify the validity of the proposed scheme.

20.4.3 Analysis

The encoded data before data mask is stored in an array module of QR code from left to right. The coordinate of $(0,0)$ represents the top left corner of the array module. The three identical finder patterns which are made up of 7×7 modules are used to recognize the QR code and to determine the rotational orientation of the symbol, so we define the data which are blue regions as shown in Figure 20.1 that could be modified is from the coordinate of $(7,7)$ to the right down corner of QR code.

In the experiments, (2,3) threshold with $k \leq t \leq n$ is applied as an example shown in Figure 20.5. The QR code version 27 with error correction level H is used and the data regions which can be modified is a rectangle from the coordinate of $(7,7)$ to $(125,125)$. Based on the Algorithm 2 above, the region modified of QR code is divided into six regions matching the secret image. The region of A[1] is from the coordinate of $(7,7)$ to $(117,25)$, the region of A[2] is from the coordinate of $(7,25)$ to $(117,43)$, the region of A[3] is from the coordinate of $(7,43)$ to $(117,61)$, the region of A[4] is from the coordinate of $(7,61)$ to $(117,79)$, the region of A[5] is from the coordinate of $(7,79)$ to $(117,97)$, the region of A[6] is from the coordinate of $(7,43)$

to (117,117). The processing QR_1 will be altered in the region of A[1] and A[4], the processing QR_2 will be altered in the region of A[2] and A[5] while the processing QR_3 will be altered in the region of A[3] and A[6]. According to the principle of the error correction mechanism [18] in the QR code and the tests, the cover QR codes above can be recognized correctly with the data of rectangular region altered completely. As the secret image with the size of 110 × 110 pixels, we divide the secret image into six regions that matching the QR codes regions, A[1]... A[6]. QR code shares will be generated according to the proposed scheme as steps above. This means that the QR code shares can be recognized correctly in any case and the secret image can be recovered by stacking two or three QR code shares without any computation. On the other hand, if the light-weight computation device is available, the secret image can be revealed with better visual quality based on XOR operation and could be lossless revealed when sufficient shares are collected.

As a result, in the experiments, through looking up Figures 20.3 through 20.6, the following conclusions are obtained:

1. When $t < k$ shadow images are collected, there is no information of the secret image could be recognized, which shows the security of the proposed scheme.
2. When t ($k \leq t \leq n$) shadow images are reconstructed by stacking, the secret image could be recognized. When k shadow images are reconstructed by XORing, the secret image can be revealed with better visual quality or lossless revealed.
3. The secret image can be recovered by stacking k or more shares based on the human visual system without any computation and QR code readers. In addition, the secret image can also be revealed with better visual quality based on XOR operation and could be lossless revealed when sufficient shares are collected with light-weight computation device.
4. The scheme proposed can reach (k,n) VSS threshold with the abilities of stacking and XOR lossless recovery.

20.4.4 Compared with Related Schemes

In the section, we compare the proposed scheme with other related schemes especially Jonathan and Yan's scheme [12] and Wang et al.'s scheme [13], and Chow et al.'s scheme [14].

Jonathan and Yan [12] presented a scheme that uses a QR code to authenticate the shares. The basic idea is to embed the verification information into the recovered secret in the form of a QR code. In this way, when cheating is suspected, the QR code wouldn't verify the invalid share after it is used to recover the secret. The reason is that the QR code wouldn't be guessed or that after a cheater has used his own share, the QR code may not even be recovered as part of the secret. Additionally, an extended form of this secret sharing is presented which embeds the QR code as part of the cover image. In their scheme, the QR code can be used as

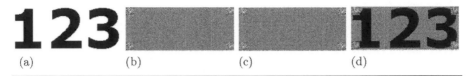

Figure 20.7 An example of Jonathan and Yan's scheme. (a) Original secret (b) Share one with embeded (c) Share two with embedded (d) Recovered secret.

the secret transport mechanism which along string of alphanumeric characters can be embedded into the barcode.

An example of the scheme proposed can be seen as Figure 20.7. The shares are random in the scheme above, which may attract suspicion of encryption, due to embedding QR codes into VSS shares.

Wang et al. [13] proposed a scheme which embedding QR code into VC shares for authentication. The basic idea is to embed QR codes into given shares to prevent cheating. They search the best region of a given share where the QR code could be embedded into so as to keep the visual quality of the revealed secret and the embedding will not affect the visual cryptography secret revealing too much. The contribution of the scheme proposed is to authenticate the VC shares using a QR code by embedding it into the similar regions of the VC share, the embedding could not affect the VC secret revealing too much. An example of the scheme proposed can be seen as Figure 20.8. The shares are random so that we cannot get any information in the scheme above, which may attract suspicion of encryption, due to embedding QR codes into VSS shares. Also, the QR code embedded may be hard to extract.

The schemes proposed above is to embed QR codes into VC shares which can achieve the purpose of authentication. Unfortunately, it may attract suspicion of encryption. Our scheme proposed is to embed VC shares into cover QR codes which may reduce the likelihood of attracting the attention of potential attackers. Each output share can be scanned and decoded utilizing a QR code reader. The secret image can be revealed with the abilities of stacking and XOR lossless recovery.

Figure 20.9 shows the results of QR code version 4 with error correction level H by Chow et al.'s scheme [14] proposed. Figure 20.9a–c shows the cover QR codes, (d–f) shows the resulting QR code shares that can be decoded correctly,

Figure 20.8 An example of Wang et al.'s scheme. (a) Secret revealing using QR code (b) A VC share embedded with QR code having the string "AUT" (c) A VC share embedded with QR code having the URL "http://www.aut.ac.nz."

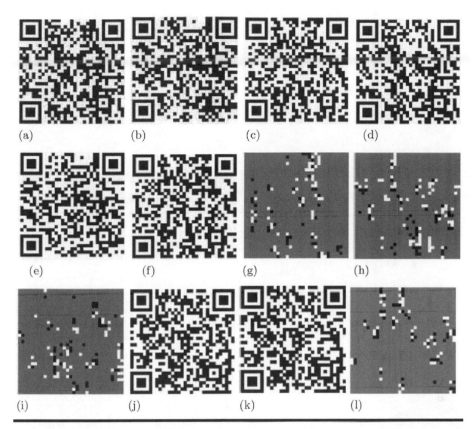

Figure 20.9 **The results of QR code version 4 with error correction level H by Chow, et al.'s scheme proposed. (a) Cover image C₁ (b) Cover image C₂ (c) Cover image C₃ (d) QR share S₁ (e) QR share S₂ (f) QR share S₃ (g) Difference image between C₁ and S₁ (h) Difference image between C₂ and S₂ (i) Difference image between C₃ and S₃ (j) Original qr code with secret message secret S (k) Reconstructed QR code S′ (l) Difference image between S and S′.**

(g–i) shows the respective difference images between the cover QR codes and the resulting QR code shares. Figure 20.9j shows the original QR code containing the secret message while the reconstructed secret QR code which can be decoded as the same with the original message is shown in Figure 20.9k. Figure 20.9l shows the differences between the reconstructed secret QR code and the secret QR code.

Figure 20.10 shows the results of QR code version 4 with error correction level H by our scheme proposed. Figure 20.10a shows the secret image. Figure 20.10b–c shows the QR code shares resulting from the proposed VSSQR scheme, SC_1, SC_2. Figure 20.10d–e shows the decoding information for SC_1, SC_2, which are random noise-like. We can see that the shares are valid QR codes which can be decoded by

Figure 20.10 **The results of QR code version 4 with error correction level H by our scheme proposed. (a) Secret image *S* (b) QR share *SC₁* (c) QR share *SC₂* (d) The decoding information for *SC₁* (e) The decoding information for *SC₂* (f) Reconstructed QR code by stacking, *Sr* (g) Reconstructed QR code by XORing, *Sr₁*.**

any standard decoding software into the original messages. Figure 20.10f shows the reconstructed QR code, *Sr*, which is recovered by stacking two QR code shares. The secret message can be seen directly from the reconstructed QR code. Figure 20.10g shows the revealed QR code, *Sr₁*, which is recovered by XORing two QR code shares with a light-weight device. The secret message can be seen that it is recovered lossless.

We can see that Chow et al.'s scheme distributes and encodes the information of a QR code containing a secret message into a set of QR codes so as to reduce the likelihood of attracting the attention of potential attackers. Each QR code share is a valid QR code that can be recognized by a QR code reader. However, the secret can only be recovered by XORing the light and dark modules contained in the encoding region of all the *n* QR code shares and adding the function patterns with a computational device and a QR code reader as well as is only for cases (*n*, *n*) where *n* is equal to or greater than 3.

Compared with the Chow et al.'s scheme above, there are some superior performances as follows. It can be seen that the secret could be revealed with abilities of stacking and XOR lossless recovery by the VSSQR scheme proposed. When stacking two QR code shares which can be decoded correctly, it can be seen directly by HVS without any computational device. On the other hand, the secret image can be also recovered based on XOR operation with lossless recovery when two shares are collected with light-weight computation device.

Based on the two means of recovery above, we don't need any QR code readers. In addition, *n* can be equal to 2 by our scheme proposed.

20.4.5 Extensions

The proposed scheme can be extended through the following methods:

1. Firstly, the secret information can be encoded into a QR code. Secondly, the information of *n* cover QR codes is altered in the range of the error correction mechanism, in order to distribute and encode the information of the secret QR code into *n* QR code shares that *n* can be equal to 2. Lastly, each share is a valid QR code that can be scanned and decoded by a QR code reader.
2. The secret QR code could be revealed without any computation devices based on stacking when no light-weight computation device is available. On the other hand, the secret QR code can be revealed based on XOR operation if the light-weight computation device is available. The reconstructed secret QR code, which can be revealed with multiple decryptions, can be decoded as another QR code correctly by any standard decoding software.

Recently, the extended scheme proposed to use the highest level of QR code error correction which is (2,2) the visual secret sharing threshold. Two versions of QR code are used: QR code version 20 with error correction level H which is used as the secret QR code, QR code version 39 with error correction level H which is used as the cover QR code, to test the efficiency of the proposed extended scheme.

Figure 20.11 shows the results of QR code version 39 with error correction level H by our extended scheme proposed. Figure 20.11a shows the secret QR code. Figure 20.11b–c show the QR code shares resulting from the proposed extended scheme, SC_1, SC_2. Figure 20.11d–f show the decoding information for S, SC_1, SC_2, which are random noise-like. Although Figure 20.11e–f have a little artifact, we can see that the shares are valid QR codes which can be decoded by any standard decoding software into the original messages. Figure 20.11g shows the reconstructed QR code, Sr, which is recovered by stacking two QR code shares. Figure 20.11h shows the revealed QR code, Sr_1, which is recovered by XORing two QR code shares. The secret QR code can be seen in the right down region of the reconstructed QR codes as shown in Figure 20.11g–h. Figure 20.11i–j shows the reconstructed secret QR codes, Sr_2, Sr_3, which are extracted from the reconstructed QR codes as shown in Figure 20.11g–h. The decoding information for Sr_2 and Sr_3 are shown in Figure 20.11k–l. It can be seen that the revealed secret QR codes can be decoded correctly which are the same as the original secret QR code. The secret QR code can be revealed by stacking and XOR operation, which can be decoded as another QR code correctly by a QR code reader. We will do more research and analysis about the extended scheme proposed in the future.

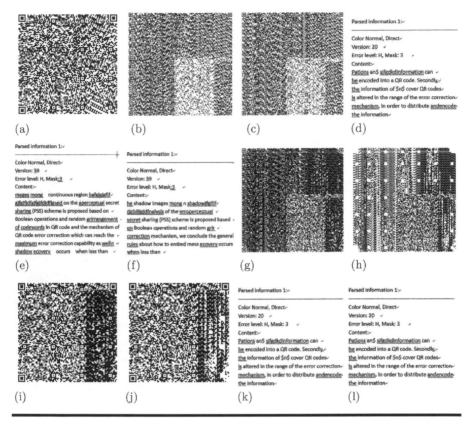

Figure 20.11 The results of QR code version 39 with error correction level H by our extended scheme proposed. (a) Secret image QR code (b) QR share SC_1 (c) QR share SC_2 (d) The decoding information for S (e) The decoding information for SC_1 (e) The decoding information for SC_2 (g) Reconstructed QR code by stacking, Sr (h) Reconstructed QR code by XOR, Sr_1 (i) The secret QR code by stacking, Sr_2 (j) The secret QR code by XORing, Sr_3 (k) The decoding information for Sr_2 (l) The decoding information for Sr_3.

20.5 Conclusion and Future Work

This paper presents a novel VSS scheme using QR code. In this scheme, a secret image is distributed and encoded into n QR code shares. The proposed scheme exploits the error correction mechanism in the QR code structure, to generate the bits corresponding to shares by VSS from a secret bit in the processing of encoding QRs. Each share is a valid QR code which contains original information when scanned. So, it reduces the likelihood of attracting the attention of potential attackers if distributed via public channels. When recovering the secret image, we do not need any computational devices and QR code readers by stacking k or more shares based on the human visual system. The secret image could also be revealed with better or lossless visual quality with sufficient shares collected by XOR when a light-weight device is available. It satisfies (k, n) threshold and the abilities of stacking and XOR lossless recovery. Thus, the proposed scheme could be applied in different situations whether the light-weight device is available or not. Experiments are conducted to show the efficiency of the scheme proposed. Comparisons with related schemes show the superior performances of the proposed scheme.

Acknowledgments

The authors would like to thank the anonymous reviewers for their valuable discussions and comments. This work is supported by the National Natural Science Foundation of China (Grant Number 61602491).

References

1. Beimel, A.: Secret-sharing schemes: A survey. In: *Coding and Cryptology 3rd International Workshop*. (2011) pp. 11–46.
2. Naor, M., Shamir, A.: Visual cryptography. *Lecture Notes in Computer Science* **950**(9) (1999) 1–12.
3. Yang, C.N.: New visual secret sharing schemes using probabilistic method. *Pattern Recognition Letters* **25**(4) (2004) 481–494.
4. Wang, Z., Arce, G.R., Di Crescenzo, G.: Halftone visual cryptography via error diffusion. *IEEE Transactions on Information Forensics and Security* **4**(3) (2009) 383–396.
5. Weir, J., Yan, W.Q.: *A Comprehensive Study of Visual Cryptography*. Springer, Berlin, Germany (2010).
6. Wang, D., Yi, F., Li, X.: On general construction for extended visual cryptography schemes. *Pattern Recognition* **42**(11) (2009) 3071–3082.
7. Yan, X., Wang, S., Li, L., El-Latif, A.A.A., Wei, Z., Niu, X.: A new assessment measure of shadow image quality based on error diffusion techniques. *Journal of Information Hiding and Multimedia Signal Processing (JIHMSP)* **4**(2) (2013) 118–126.
8. Wang, D., Zhang, L., Ma, N., Li, X.: Two secret sharing schemes based on boolean operations. *Pattern Recognition* **40**(10) (2007) 2776–2785.
9. Yan X., Wang S., El-Latif A.A., et al.: Visual secret sharing based on random grids with abilities of AND and XOR lossless recovery. *Multimedia Tools & Applications* **74**(9) (2015) 3231–3252.
10. ISO/IEC JTC 1/SC: Information technology – automatic identification and data capture techniques – QR code 2005 bar code symbology specification (2006).
11. Snyder, A.J.: Visual cryptography and secret image sharing. *Pattern Recognition Letters* **34**(3) (2012) 283–291.
12. Weir, J., Yan, W.: Authenticating Visual Cryptography Shares Using 2D Barcodes. In: *Digital Forensics and Watermarking: 10th International Workshop, IWDW 2011*, Berlin, Germany (2012) pp. 196–210.

13. Wang, G., Liu, F., Yan, W.Q.: 2D Barcodes for visual cryptography. *Multimedia Tools and Applications* **75**(2) (2016) 1223–1241.

14. Chow, Y.W., Susilo, W., Yang, G., Phillips, J.G., Pranata, I., Barmawi, A.M.: Exploiting the error correction mechanism in QR codes for secret sharing. *Australasian Conference on Information Security and Privacy.* Springer International Publishing, Cham, Switzerland (2016).

15. Denso, W.I.: http://www.qrcode.com. (2002)

16. Yan X., Guan S., Niu X.: Research on the Capacity of Error-Correcting Codes-Based Information Hiding. In: *International Conference on Intelligent Information Hiding and Multimedia Signal Processing, IEEE Computer Society* (2008) pp. 1158–1161.

17. Saito, K., Morii, M.: Efficient decoding of qr code using error correcting capability: Decoding method using erasure error correction and the ability. *Technical Report of IEICE ISEC* **111** (2011) 79–84.

18. Wan, S., Lu, Y., Yan, X. et al.: High capacity embedding methods of QR code error correction. In: *International Wireless Internet Conference.* Springer, Cham, Switzerland (2016) pp. 70–79.

19. Yan, X., Wang, S., Niu, X.: Threshold progressive visual cryptography construction with unexpanded shares. *Multimedia Tools & Applications* **75**(14) (2016) 1–18.

20. Yan, X., Chen, G., Yang, C.N., Cai, S.R.: Random girds-based threshold visual secret sharing with improved contrast by boolean operations. In: *Digital-Forensics and Watermarking: 13th International Workshop,* IWDW 2014, Taipei, Taiwan, October 1–4, 2014. Springer International Publishing, Cham, Switzerland (2015) pp. 319–332.

21. Lee, S., Yoo, C.D., Kalker, T.: Reversible image watermarking based on integer-to-integer wavelet transform. *IEEE Transactions on Information Forensics and Security* **2**(3) (2007) 321–330.

22. Yan, X., Liu, X., Yang, C.N.: An enhanced threshold visual secret sharing based on random grids. *Journal of Real-Time Image Processing* (2015) 1–13.

Chapter 21

Steganography Based on Interpolation and Edge Detection Techniques

Ki-Hyun Jung

Contents

DOI: 10.1201/9780429435461-24

21.1 Introduction

As interest of information security has increased, it becomes the first consideration to prevent illegal access in security systems. Data hiding technique is one of the methods for secret communication and data security. In data security, it is very important to transmit data safely because multimedia data is easy to copy or destroy by unauthorized persons through the Internet.

Security systems are very important to prevent internal data from being intercepted by unauthorized person. Cryptography and data hiding methods are prominent techniques to solve copyright protection of multimedia contents. Data hiding, which is also called information hiding and includes watermarking and steganography, involves concealing the secret data within innocuous cover multimedia objects like text, audio, image, and video [1–17]. Data hiding is the art of hiding the secret data in the cover objects whereas cryptography is about protecting the contents of the secret data. As the spread of multimedia contents is increased rapidly, data hiding techniques have become important recently. In general, security systems are divided into three parts—cryptography, steganography, watermarking—as shown in Figure 21.1.

Steganography is the art and science of embedding secret data within other information without the existence of the hidden secret data. Recently, data hiding techniques have become important in a number of application areas. The subject of information hiding encompasses a vast array of secret communication methods where the purpose is to hide information in ways that prevent the detection of the hidden messages and even conceal their very existence [1–28].

For example, many digital images, audio, and video now include distinguishing yet imperceptible marks that contain a hidden copyright notice or serial number to help preventing unauthorized copying. There are both irreversible and reversible data hiding techniques, depending on what happens to the original image after

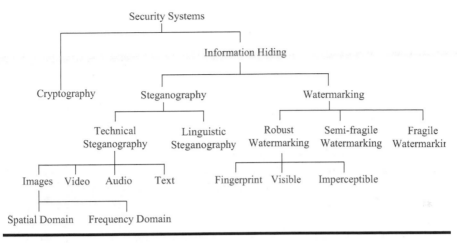

Figure 21.1 Classification of security systems.

recovering the data from the stego-image. Irreversible data hiding is called steganography or data hiding for short.

The embedding model shown in Figure 21.2 is based on the results of the discussions at the Information Hiding Workshop [16]. In steganography, it can be classified into a reversible data hiding method and irreversible data hiding method whether the cover object can be recovered on the receiver side. The message *secret* to be embedded is hiding in the cover object cover by using the function f_E and a secret key. The output object secret containing the secret data will be extracted by the operation f_E^{-1} and the secret key optionally on the receiver side. The extracted

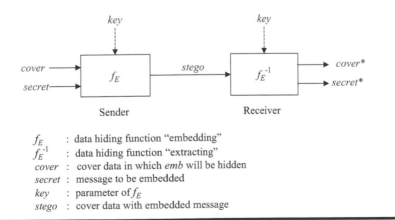

f_E : data hiding function "embedding"
f_E^{-1} : data hiding function "extracting"
cover : cover data in which *emb* will be hidden
secret : message to be embedded
key   : parameter of f_E
stego : cover data with embedded message

Figure 21.2 Data hiding model.

secret data secret* is equal to the input secret data. In the embedding model; it is called as a reversible data hiding method if the cover* can be also recovered.

In data hiding, the well-known steganography methods are least significant bit (LSB) substitution and pixel-value differencing (PVD). LSB substitution replaces the least significant bit with a secret bit stream. LSB matching is either added or subtracted randomly from the pixel value of the cover data when the embedding bit does not match. The revised LSB matching was proposed to improve by lowering the number of modifications. The PVD offers imperceptibility by calculating the difference of two consecutive non-overlapping pixels. Wu et al. took advantage of both the pixel-value differencing technique and the base decomposition scheme. Lee et al.'s method embedded in a cover image using tri-way pixel-value differencing compressed by JPEG2000 on a secret image. In reversible data hiding, it can be classified into five groups shown in Figure 21.3, i.e., quantization based, histogram modification based, expansion based and compressed based, and dual image based methods. Recently dual image based reversible data hidings are presented where two similar stego-objects are generated [18–69].

Reversible data hiding methods allow data to be embedded inside a digital media and later retrieved as required, leaving an exact original image. It is mainly used for content authentication of multimedia data due to the emerging demand for it in various fields, where the original host signal is crucial in order to make the right decision. Reversible data hiding methods can be classified into three types: spatial domain, frequency domain, and compressed domain. Most spatial domain reversible data hiding methods are developed based on difference expansion (DE) and histogram modification. Many data hiding techniques in frequency domain also tried to improve the embedding capacity or have a high image quality.

Recently, interpolation techniques are used in the field of data hiding. Interpolation techniques are important in digital image processing and it is

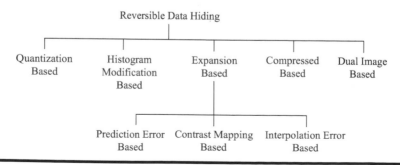

Figure 21.3 Classification of reversible data hiding.

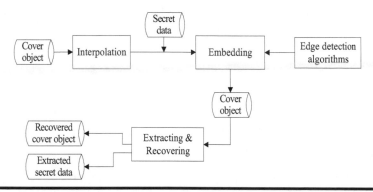

Figure 21.4 **Reversible data hiding model using interpolation and edge detection techniques.**

worthwhile to use in data hiding to improve the embedding capacity and the visual image quality. The block diagram of interpolation and edge detection based reversible data hiding is shown in Figure 21.4. Jung and Yoo proposed first a reversible data hiding method based on the neighboring mean interpolation, which improved the embedding capacity and image quality [29]. It utilized interpolation and edge detection algorithms in data hiding. Lee and Huang improved Jung and Yoo's method using the interpolation by neighboring pixels [30]. Hu and Li proposed the interpolation by maximizing the difference values between neighboring pixels [31]. Lu used Jung and Yoo's method to enlarge a cover image to conceal in virtual predicted pixels and re-encoded the secret message to rearrange the value before embedding, and Yang et al. modified Jung and Yoo's method to improve image quality [32]. There are other kinds of works utilizing interpolation techniques. Some works used the interpolation error to increase the embedding capacity and are based on image interpolation to detect smooth and complex regions for high image quality. The hybrid data hiding method uses interpolation scheme and histogram modification technique to provide high capacity and good visual quality. These methods are a different type of data hiding in the aspect that interpolation techniques are used to divide into smooth and edge areas and hybrid data hiding techniques based on interpolation are introduced. There are many works that continue to be introduced, but are still based on similar techniques [30,31,33–50].

Figure 21.5 shows a flowchart of data hiding methods using interpolation and edge detection techniques. Firstly, a cover image is generated by image interpolation method like the nearest neighbor interpolation and bilinear interpolation methods, where the size of the generated cover image is scaling up than the source image. This is very easy to calculate unknown pixel values late, as exact values can be obtained using neighbor pixel values from the neighbor pixel values.

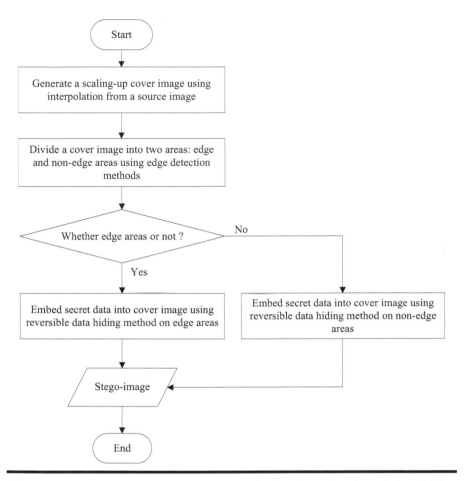

Figure 21.5   Flowchart of interpolation and edge detection based data hiding methods.

When edge detection techniques are used, how many bits can be embedded? It came from basic idea that it is difficult to discriminate the distortion in edge areas even though the embedding bits are larger than smooth areas.

The cover image is easily calculated from the original image and used as the source for the data hiding method. An edge detection algorithm is then applied to divide the cover image into edge and non-edge areas, as more secret data can be embedded in edge areas, plus a different data hiding method is used when embedding the secret data in edge and non-edge areas.

In this chapter, reversible data hiding methods using image interpolation techniques and edge detection techniques are described.

The rest of this chapter is organized as follows. In Sections 21.2 and 21.3, interpolation and edge detection techniques are explained. Important properties of data hiding and performance analysis measurements are treated in Section 21.4. The previous interpolation and edge detection based reversible data hiding methods are described in Section 21.5. The conclusions are presented in Section 21.6.

21.2 Interpolation Techniques

Interpolation techniques are the problem of approximating the value of a function for a non-given point in some space [70]. Image interpolation techniques have many applications which are as old as computer graphics and image processing field [71–82]. There is generally a trade-off between speed and degree to which the visual artifacts are reduced. The capability of digitally interpolating images to a higher resolution with a good image quality is important in many applications of electronic imaging. Plus, the sharpness of edges and freedom from artifacts are two critical factors in the perceived quality of an interpolated image, along with ease of computation. The nearest neighbor method finds the closest corresponding pixel in the source image for each pixel in the destination image pixel. Yet, nearest neighbor interpolation suffers from normally unacceptable aliasing effects when enlarging and reducing images. Meanwhile, bilinear interpolation determines the grey level from the weighted average of the four closest pixels to the specified input coordinates and assigns that value to the output coordinates. Although this method generates an image with a smoother appearance than nearest neighbor interpolation, the grey level values are altered in the process, resulting in blurring or a loss of image resolution. Therefore, due to these changes in the grey level values, any image classification process must be performed before the interpolation. As such, bilinear interpolation requires 3 to 4 times the computation time of the nearest neighbor method. There is also a great variety of methods, like B-spline, cubic, bi-cubic, Lagrange, and Gaussian interpolation.

21.2.1 Nearest Neighbor Interpolation

Nearest neighbor interpolation, also known as proximal interpolation, is a simple method of multivariate interpolation in one or more dimensions [70]. Nearest neighbor is the basic algorithm and it requires the least processing time of all the interpolation algorithms which has the effect of simply making each pixel bigger.

While the nearest neighbor interpolation method is simple to implement, it often produces undesirable artifacts, such as the distortion of straight edges in images with a high resolution. Smoother results can be obtained by using more sophisticated techniques, such as cubic convolution interpolation. Yet, the price paid for smoother approximations is an additional computational burden.

The basis function associated to nearest neighbor interpolation is the simplest of all, since it is made of a square pulse. It satisfies the partition on unity, provided a slight asymmetry is introduced at the edges of the square pulse.

21.2.2 Bilinear Interpolation

For general purpose image processing, a bilinear interpolation approach that uses the gray levels of the four nearest neighbors is usually adequate. The bilinear interpolation technique considers the closest 2×2 neighborhood of known pixel values surrounding the unknown pixel. Then, it takes a weighted average of these 4 pixels to reach its final interpolated value. This results in much smoother looking images than nearest neighbor. Bilinear interpolation determines the grey level from the weighted average of the four closet pixels to the specified input coordinates and assigns that value to the output coordinates. Although this method generates an image with a smoother appearance than nearest neighbor interpolation, the grey level values are altered in the process, resulting in blurring or a loss of image resolution. Therefore, due to the changes in the grey level values, any image classification process must be performed before the interpolation. Thus, bilinear interpolation requires 3 to 4 times the computation time of the nearest neighbor interpolation method.

21.2.3 Bi-cubic Interpolation

The bi-cubic interpolation technique goes one step beyond bilinear by considering the closest 4×4 neighborhood of known pixels that will total 16 pixels. Since these are at various distances from the unknown pixel, closer pixels are given a higher weighting in the calculation. Bi-cubic algorithm produces noticeably sharper images than the previous two methods, and is perhaps the ideal combination of processing time and output quality. For this reason, it is a standard in many image editing programs, printer drivers, and in-camera interpolation.

21.2.4 Higher Order Interpolation

There are many other interpolators which take more surrounding pixels into consideration and are thus also much more computationally intensive. These algorithms include spline and sinc functions, and retain the most image information after an interpolation. They are therefore extremely useful when the image requires multiple rotations or distortions in separate steps. However, for single-step enlargements or

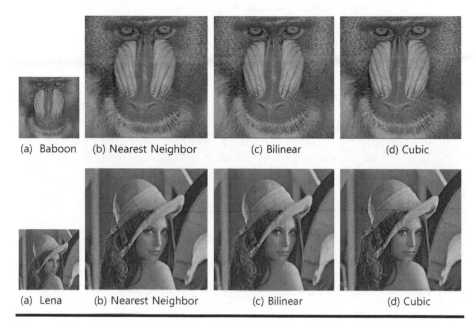

(a) Baboon (b) Nearest Neighbor (c) Bilinear (d) Cubic

(a) Lena (b) Nearest Neighbor (c) Bilinear (d) Cubic

Figure 21.6 Result images of some interpolation techniques. (a) Baboon (b) Nearest Neighbor (c) Bilinear (d) Cubic (a) Lena (b) Nearest Neighbor (c) Bilinear (d) Cubic.

rotations, these higher-order algorithms provide diminishing visual improvement as processing time is increased [82].

For 256 × 256 gray images, results of interpolation techniques are shown in Figure 21.6.

21.3 Edge Detection Techniques

Edge detection techniques are an important topic in digital image processing. Edges are usually considered an important feature of images and widely applied to high level applications such as image compression, region segmentation, pattern recognition, image retrieval, data hiding and so on. Detecting edge boundaries is based on changes in the pixel intensity, and several basic schemes such as Sobel, Roberts, Prewitt, Laplacian, and Canny have been proposed [83–89].

Edge detectors are a collection of very important local image pre-processing methods used to locate changes in the intensity function; edges are pixels where this function changes abruptly. Calculus describes the changes of continuous functions using derivatives; an image function depends on two variables—coordinates in the image plane—and so operators describing edges are expressed using partial derivatives. A change of the image function can be described by a gradient that points in the direction of the largest growth of the image function.

An edge is a property attached to an individual pixel and is calculated from the image function behavior in the neighborhood of that pixel. As such, an edge is a vector variable with two components, magnitude and direction, where the edge magnitude is the length of the gradient, while the edge direction gives the direction of maximum growth of the function, e.g., from black to white. Edge detection techniques can be used to divide into smooth and edge areas in data hiding to decide the embedding bits.

The gradient magnitude $|G|$ and gradient direction ∂ are continuous image functions calculated as Equations 21.1 and 21.2.

$$|G| = \sqrt{(G_x)^2 + (G_y)^2} \tag{21.1}$$

$$\partial = \tan^{-1} \frac{G_y}{G_x} \tag{21.2}$$

The Sobel is the baseline historical "standard" and still frequently used in published research. Meanwhile, the Canny is a modern "standard," in the sense that papers describing new edge detectors often compare the results to those of the Canny.

A variety of approaches for edge detection have been proposed for different purposes in different applications. Among the earliest works on edge detection are the Sobel, Prewitt, Roberts, and Laplacian edge detectors, all of which use convolution masks to approximate the first or second derivative of an image. Plus, an optimal filter for edge detection, referred to as the Canny edge detector, has also been proposed. The three performance criteria defined for optimal edge detection are good detection, good localization, and a unique answer for a true edge.

Let a 3×3 convolution window be defined as shown in Figure 21.7, where w_i is the intensity levels of each pixel, where $i = 1, 2, \ldots, 9$.

21.3.1 Sobel Edge Detector

With the Sobel edge detector, the task of edge detection is fulfilled by performing a 2D spatial gradient convolution operation on an image using the following two convolution masks (kernels) K_x and K_y, as shown in Figure 21.8, to estimate the gradients G_x and G_y in the horizontal and vertical directions respectively.

w_1	w_2	w_3
w_4	w_5	w_6
w_7	w_8	w_9

Figure 21.7 3 × 3 convolution window.

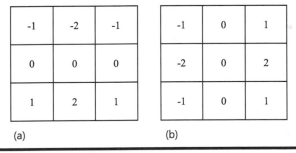

-1	-2	-1
0	0	0
1	2	1

(a)

-1	0	1
-2	0	2
-1	0	1

(b)

Figure 21.8 Masks for Sobel edge detector (a) Convolution mask K_x (b) Convolution mask K_y.

Here, G_x and G_y are computed as Equations 21.3 and 21.4 respectively.

$$G_x = (-1)w_1 + (-2)w_2 + (-1)w_3 + 1w_7 + 2w_8 + 1w_9 \tag{21.3}$$

$$G_y = (-1)w_1 + 1w_3 + (-2)w_4 + 2w_6 + (-1)w_7 + 1w_9 \tag{21.4}$$

Instead of Equation 21.1, the gradient magnitude G can also be computed using Equation 21.5 to increase the speed of computation.

$$|G| = |G_x + G_y| \tag{21.5}$$

Finally, the gradient magnitude has a threshold. The Sobel edge detector is a simple and effective approach for finding edges in an image. However, it is sensitive to noise in the image. Moreover, the detected edges are thick, which may not be suitable for certain applications where a detector of the outmost contour of an object is required.

21.3.2 Prewitt Edge Detector

Similar to the Sobel edge detector, the Prewitt operator approximates the first derivative. The gradient is estimated in eight (for a 3 × 3 convolution mask) possible directions and the convolution result of greatest magnitude indicate the gradient direction. Larger masks are also possible.

Operators approximating the first derivative of an image function are sometimes called compass operators, due to their ability to determine the gradient direction. Here, only the first two 3 × 3 only tasks are presented for each operator, shown in Figure 21.9, as the others can be created by simple rotation.

The direction of the gradient is given by the mask giving the maximal response. This is also the case for all the following operators approximating the first derivative.

Here, G_x and G_y are computed as Equations 21.6 and 21.7 respectively.

$$G_x = (-1)w_1 + 1w_3 + (-1)w_4 + 1w_6 + (-1)w_7 + 1w_9 \tag{21.6}$$

$$G_y = 1w_1 + 1w_2 + 1w_3 + (-1)w_7 + (-1)w_8 + (-1)w_9 \tag{21.7}$$

The gradient magnitude G is also computed as shown in Figure 21.9.

As with the Sobel operator, each point in the image is convolved with both masks, and the maximum determines the output. The Prewitt operator likewise produces an edge magnitude image.

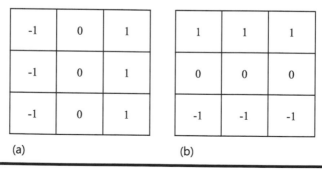

(a)   (b)

Figure 21.9 Masks for Prewitt edge detector (a) Convolution mask K_x (b) Convolution mask K_y.

0	0	-1
0	1	0
0	0	0

-1	0	0
0	1	0
0	0	0

(a) (b)

Figure 21.10 Masks for Roberts edge detector. (a) Convolution mask K_x (b) Convolution mask K_y.

21.3.3 Roberts Edge Detector

The Roberts operator is one of the oldest operators, and is very easy to compute, as it only uses the 3 × 3 neighborhood of the current pixel. Its convolution masks are shown in Figure 21.10.

Thus, the magnitude of the edge is computed as Equations 21.8 and 21.9 respectively.

$$G_x = (-1)w_3 + 1w_5 \qquad (21.8)$$

$$G_y = (-1)w_1 + 1w_5 \qquad (21.9)$$

21.3.4 Laplacian Edge Detector

The Laplacian operator is very popular and approximates the second derivative, which only gives the gradient magnitude. This is approximated in digital images by a convolution sum, and a 3 × 3 mask is often used (Figure 21.11).

-1	-1	-1
-1	8	-1
-1	-1	-1

Figure 21.11 Mask for Laplacian edge detector.

Since it is a second derivative, the Laplacian produces an abrupt zero-crossing at an edge. The Laplacian is a linear, shift-invariant operator, and its transfer function is zero at the origin of the frequency space. Thus, a Laplacian-filtered image has a zero mean gray level.

21.3.5 Canny Edge Detector

The Canny edge detector was devised as an optimal edge detector, and satisfies all three performance criteria: minimizing the detection of false edges and missing actual edges, minimizing the distance between detected and actual edges, and minimizing multiple responses to an actual edge, i.e. ensuring there is only one response for an actual edge point.

Using these criteria, the Canny edge detector was designed with a multi-stage process, where the first step filters out noise in the image using a Gaussian smoothing filter, as shown in Figure 21.12. The second step locates the edge strength in the smoothed image by computing the image gradient, thereby helping to indicate where the edges are. A two-dimensional first derivative operator, such as Sobel, can also be employed to highlight the maximum of the first derivative where the edges are located. The final step then thins down the edges by tracking along the edge in the edge direction and sets any pixel that is not at the maximum to be zero, which is called non-maximum suppression. A pixel set at zero is not regarded as an edge. The whole tracking process is controlled using two thresholds: low and high. If the magnitude is below the low threshold, the pixel is considered as a non-edge. If the magnitude is between the two thresholds, the pixel is set to be zero, except when there is a path from an edge pixel to a pixel whose magnitude is above the low threshold.

For 512 × 512 gray images, results of edge detection techniques are shown (Figure 21.13).

Edge detection algorithms can distinguish edge and smooth areas and hide larger amounts of secret data. And it is possible to avoid attacks that occur when hiding uniform secret data such as least significant bits replacement algorithms.

2	4	5	4	2
4	9	12	9	4
5	12	15	12	5
4	9	12	9	4
2	4	5	4	2

Figure 21.12   Mask for Gaussian noise removal.

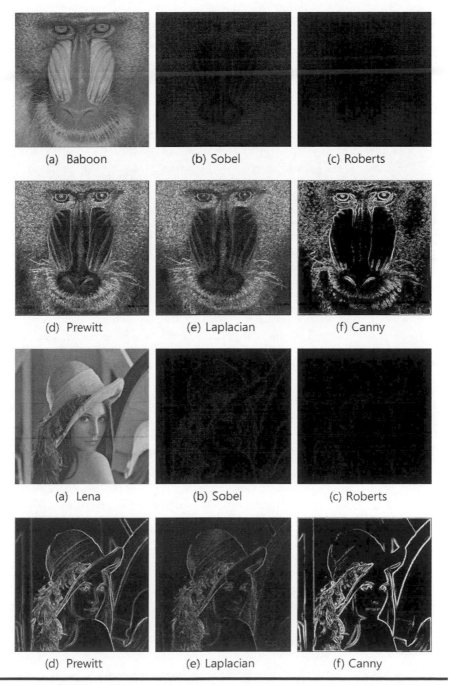

Figure 21.13 Result images of edge detection techniques. (a) Baboon (b) Sobel (c) Roberts (d) Prewitt (e) Laplacian (f) Canny (a) Lena (b) Sobel (c) Roberts (d) Prewitt (e) Laplacian (f) Canny.

21.4 Data Hiding Properties and Performance Analysis

The key to successful data hiding is finding the holes that are not suitable for exploitation. A further challenge is to fill these holes with data in a way that remains invariant to a large class of host signal transformations. The trade-offs exist between the quantity of embedded data and the degree of immunity to host signal modification. By constraining the degree of host signal degradation, a data hiding method can operate with either a high embedded data rate or high resistance to modification, yet not both. As one increases, the other must decrease. While this can be shown mathematically for some data hiding systems, such as a spread spectrum, it would seem to hold true for all data hiding systems. In any system, the bandwidth can be traded for robustness by exploiting redundancy. The quantity of embedded data and degree of host signal modification vary from application to application. Consequently, different techniques are employed for different applications. From the information hiding point of view, reversible data embedding hides information in a digital image in such a way that an authorized party can decode the hidden information and also restore the image to its original, pristine state.

All data hiding techniques have certain properties that are dictated by the intended application, and the most important properties are robustness, undetectability, invisibility, security, complexity, and capacity.

21.4.1 Data Hiding Properties

21.4.1.1 Robustness

Robustness determines the behavior of the algorithm in the case of data distortions introduced through standard and malicious data processing. Embedded information is said to be robust if its presence can be reliably detected after the image has been modified, yet not destroyed beyond recognition. Without robustness, embedded secret data can be easily removed, making it useless in a legal procedure.

Examples of modification include linear and nonlinear filters, such as blurring, sharpening, and median filtering, lossy compression, contrast adjustment, gamma correction, re-coloring, re-sampling, scaling, rotation, small nonlinear deformations, noise adding, cropping, printing, copying, scanning, D/A and A/D conversion, pixel permutation in small neighborhoods, color quantization as in palette images, skipping rows and columns, adding rows and columns, frame swapping, frame averaging and temporal averaging etc. Robustness does not include attacks on the embedding scheme based on knowledge of the embedding algorithm or the availability of the detector function.

21.4.1.2 Undetectability

Undetectability is typically required for secure covert communication. Embedded information is undetectable if the image with embedded data is consistent with the source model from which the image is drawn.

For example, if a data hiding method uses the noise component of a digital image to embed a secret message, it should avoid making statistically significant changes to the noise in the carrier. Thus, the concept of undetectability is inherently tied to the statistical model of the cover-object source. However, in the case an attacker has a more detailed model of the source signal, they may be able to detect the presence of a hidden message.

21.4.1.3 Invisibility

Invisibility is based on the properties of the human visual system or human audio system. Embedded information should not introduce any perceptible artifacts, meaning that an average human subject should be unable to distinguish between carriers that contain hidden information and those that do not. This problem can be solved by applying human perceptual modeling in the embedding process. A commonly accepted experimental arrangement that is frequently used in psychovisual experiments is a blind test, where large numbers of carriers with and without hidden information are randomly presented, and then the subjects are asked to identify which cover-objects contain hidden information. As a result, it has been successfully demonstrated that subjects cannot distinguish carriers with a close to 50% ratio of hidden information. Thus, a blind test can be used to determine the visibility of artifacts caused by data embedding schemes.

21.4.1.4 Security

An embedding algorithm is said to be secure if the embedded information cannot be removed beyond reliable detection by targeted attacks based on full knowledge of the embedding algorithm and detector, except the secret key, and knowledge of at least one carrier with a hidden message. Here is introduced the concept of a secure black-box public detector and secure public detector. A secure black-box public detector is a message detector implemented in tamper-proof hardware. It is assumed that the box cannot be reverse-engineered, and the secret key used to read the hidden messages is wired in the black-box and cannot be recovered. The availability of the black-box should not enable an attacker to recover the secret key or remove the hidden information from the carrier. Here, it is also assumed that the attacker has full knowledge of the embedding algorithm and inner workings of the detection function. Of course, any embedding technique that has a secure black-box public detector must also be secure in the sense defined above. However, at present, it is not clear if a secure black-box public detector can really be built, as attacks on a general class of data embedding techniques that use linear correlators have recently been described. In contrast, a secure public detector is an even stronger concept, where all details of the detector are publicly known. If such a detector can be built, it would have many applications and could be implemented in software rather than tamper-proof hardware. As such, it would enable the building of intelligent internet browsers capable of filtering images containing certain marks and the automatic display of copyright information with every image etc. Special care would have to be taken to overcome a so-called mosaic attack. Yet, so far, no secure public detectors exist.

However, the above requirements are mutually competitive and cannot be clearly optimized at the same time. Thus, if the intention is to hide a large message inside an image, it is impossible to achieve both absolute undetectability and robustness, meaning there has to be a trade-off. Conversely, if robustness to serious distortion is the key issue, the message to be hidden cannot be too long.

21.4.2 Performance Evaluation

Image is used mainly in the formation hiding methods because it can be easily expanded to different data formats. The common performance measurements are the embedding capacity and visual image quality. Sometimes, time complexity and histogram analysis are used to compare more details.

1. Embedding capacity limit: what is the maximal amount of information that can be embedded?
2. Visual image quality: what is the visual quality between the original cover object and the stego-object?
3. Complexity: what is the algorithm complexity?

A new method must be considered a trade-off between the embedding capacity and the image quality since there is correlation with each other. At least, the image quality is to be maintained more than 30 dB.

21.4.2.1 Embedding Capacity

The embedding bits or bpp (bits per pixel) are used to measure the embedding capacity. For the size of width W and height H for a cover image, *bpp* is given as follows.

$$\text{bpp} = \frac{1}{2} \times \frac{E}{W \times H}, \qquad E = \{\text{the total payload bits}\} \qquad (21.10)$$

A high value of bpp indicates the proposed method has a high embedding capacity.

21.4.2.2 Image Quality

In image quality analysis, the peak signal-to-noise ratio (PSNR) and the universal Q index are used to measure an image quality. The PSNR of the gray image is calculated by comparing the cover image and dual stego-images for each pixel value p in a position (i, j).

$$PSNR = 10\log_{10} \frac{255^2}{MSE}, \qquad MSE = \sum_{i=1}^{W \times H} \frac{\left(p'_{ij} - p_{ij}\right)^2}{W \times H} \qquad (21.11)$$

A universal image quality index is also used to demonstrate the quality of the stego-image. A universal image quality Q index is based on statistical measurements of the visual quality of stego-images. The Q index is based on statistical measurements, where the equation is defined as follows:

$$Q = \frac{4 \cdot \theta_{xy} \cdot M_x \cdot M_{x'}}{\left(\theta_x^2 + \theta_y^2\right)\left(M_x^2 + M_{x'}^2\right)} \qquad (21.12)$$

Each factor is calculated by Equation 21.13. The value of Q index is ranged $[-1, 1]$, where two images are similar each other as close to 1 and unrelated if the value is close to -1.

$$M_x = \frac{1}{W \times H} \sum_{i=0}^{W-1} \sum_{j=0}^{H-1} p_{ij} \qquad M_{x'} = \frac{1}{W \times H} \sum_{i=0}^{W-1} \sum_{j=0}^{H-1} p'_{ij}$$

$$\theta_x^2 = \frac{1}{W \times H} \sum_{i=0}^{W-1} \sum_{j=0}^{H-1} (p_{ij} - M_x)^2 \qquad \theta_y^2 = \frac{1}{W \times H} \sum_{i=0}^{W-1} \sum_{j=0}^{H-1} (p'_{ij} - M_{x'})^2$$

$$\theta_{xy}^2 = \frac{1}{W \times H} \sum_{i=0}^{W-1} \sum_{j=0}^{H-1} (p_{ij} - M_x)(p'_{ij} - M_{x'}) \qquad (21.13)$$

21.5 Data Hiding Techniques

In this section, some data hiding techniques are described to illustrate how interpolation and edge detection algorithms apply to data hiding techniques. For a cover image C with $W \times H$ size, let a pixel value be p. A stego-image S with a pixel value p' is represented as shown in Figure 21.14. Assume that a scaling-up factor is $k=2$ to simplify the previous algorithms.

$P_{(i,j)}$	$P_{(i,j+1)}$	$P_{(i,j+2)}$
$P_{(i+1,j)}$	$P_{(i+1,j+1)}$	$P_{(i+1,j+2)}$
$P_{(i+2,j)}$	$P_{(i+2,j+1)}$	$P_{(i+2,j+2)}$

(a)

$P'_{(i,j)}$	$P'_{(i,j+1)}$	$P'_{(i,j+2)}$
$P'_{(i+1,j)}$	$P'_{(i+1,j+1)}$	$P'_{(i+1,j+2)}$
$P'_{(i+2,j)}$	$P'_{(i+2,j+1)}$	$P'_{(i+2,j+2)}$

(b)

Figure 21.14 Pixel values of a cover image and stego-image (a) Cover pixels (b) Stego pixels.

21.5.1 Neighbor Mean Interpolation Based Data Hiding Method

Neighbor mean interpolation and three directional pixel value differencing method was proposed to calculate the mean value of neighboring pixel values and embedding secret data [29]. New pixels are calculated by Equation 21.14 for a parameter $k = 2$ when cover pixels and stego pixels are given as Figure 21.15.

$$
\begin{pmatrix} p'(i, j+1) \\ p'(i+1, j) \\ p'(i+1, j+1) \end{pmatrix} = \begin{pmatrix} \dfrac{p(i, j) + p(i, j+1)}{2} \\ \dfrac{p(i, j) + p(i+1, j)}{2} \\ \dfrac{p(i, j) + p'(i, j+1) + p'(i+1, j)}{3} \end{pmatrix} \tag{21.14}
$$

The neighbor mean interpolation (NMI) method uses a neighboring pixel value to calculate the mean, and then the calculated mean value is inserted into a pixel that has not been allocated yet. In general, we can get more high-resolution pixels when neighboring pixel values are referenced in order to calculate a value that is to be allocated, but time complexity is higher when the number of referenced pixels is higher. The scaling up method decides what application to which it should be applied.

Figure 21.15 shows an example of how to process the neighbor mean interpolation. The resulting image is scaled two times more. The pixel $p'(0,0)$ and $p'(2,2)$ are the same value with $p(0,0)$ and $p(2,2)$ respectively. In the case of $i < j$, $p'(0,1)$ is calculated from the $\{p(0,0) + p(0,2)\}/2$ operation. When $i > j$, $p'(1,0)$ is the result of $\{p(0,0) + p(2,0)\}/2$. Finally, $p'(1,1)$ can be derived from $\{p(0,0) + p'(0,1) + p'(1,0)\}/3$.

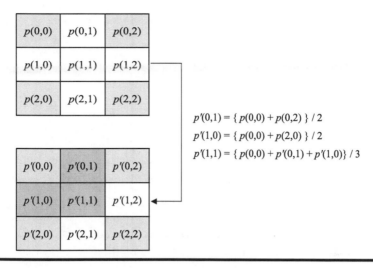

Figure 21.15   An example of the two-time scaling up process on the NMI method.

Embedding algorithm uses the difference value of three neighboring pixel values to decide the length of embedding bits. Before embedding secret bits, difference value $d_t (1 \leq t \leq 3)$ is calculated and the number of embedding bits $n_t (1 \leq t \leq 3)$ is decided as following Equations 21.15 and 21.16.

$$
\begin{pmatrix} d_1 \\ d_2 \\ d_3 \end{pmatrix} = \begin{pmatrix} p'(i, j+1) - p'(i, j) \\ p'(i+1, j) - p'(i, j) \\ p'(i+1, j+1) - p'(i, j) \end{pmatrix}
\tag{21.15}
$$

$$
n_t = \log_2 |d_t|, \ 1 \leq t \leq 3
\tag{21.16}
$$

The n_t – sized secret bits are converted to decimal value b and it can be embedded into three pixels in respective. Finally, a new pixel value $p'' = p' + b$ is obtained by the addition operation.

Figure 21.16 shows the example of 2 × 2 sub-block for four pixel values $(p(0,0), p(0,1), p(1,0), p(1,1)) = (100, 92, 156, 112)$. $p'(0,1) = (100+92)/2 = 96$, $p'(1,0) = (100+156)/2 = 128$, and $p'(1,1) = (96+128)/2 = 112$ are calculated. Next, three difference values $d_1 = 96 - 100 = -4, d_2 = 128 - 100 = 28$, and $d_3 = 112 - 100 = 12$ are obtained to determine the size of embedding bits. The size of embedding bits $n_1 = 2$, $n_2 = 4$, and $n_3 = 3$ are reduced as results. Finally, new four pixel values $(p'(0,0), p'(0,1), p'(1,0), p'(1,1)) = (100, 98, 138, 119)$ are obtained.

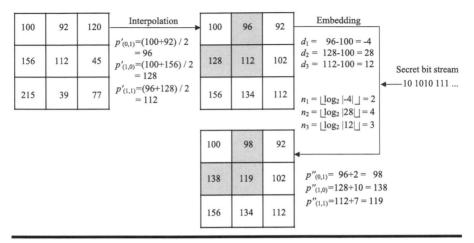

Figure 21.16   Example of NMI based data hiding method.

21.5.2 *Interpolation by Neighboring Pixel Based Data Hiding Method*

Interpolation by neighboring pixels was proposed to improve neighbor mean interpolation based data hiding method [30].

$$
\begin{pmatrix}
p'(i,\, j+1) \\
p'(i+1,\, j) \\
p'(i+1,\, j+1)
\end{pmatrix}
=
\begin{pmatrix}
\dfrac{\left[p(i,\, j) + \dfrac{p(i,\, j) + p(i,\, j+1)}{2} \right]}{2} \\[4mm]
\dfrac{\left[p(i,\, j) + \dfrac{p(i,\, j) + p(i+1,\, j)}{2} \right]}{2} \\[4mm]
\dfrac{p'(i,\, j+1) + p'(i+1,\, j)}{2}
\end{pmatrix}
\tag{21.17}
$$

Difference value $d_t (1 \le t \le 3)$ is calculated by Equation 21.18 where $p_{\max} = \max\big(p(i,\, j),\ p(i,\, j+1),\ p(i+1,\, j),\ p(i+1,\, j+1) \big)$ is used. The number of embedding bits $n_t (1 \le t \le 3)$ is obtained by Equation 21.16 that is applied the same as NMI method.

$$
\begin{pmatrix}
d_1 \\
d_2 \\
d_3
\end{pmatrix}
=
\begin{pmatrix}
p_{\max} - p'(i,\, j+1) \\
p_{\max} - p'(i+1,\, j) \\
p_{\max} - p'(i+1,\, j+1)
\end{pmatrix}
\tag{21.18}
$$

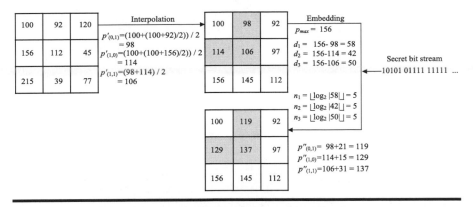

Figure 21.17   Example of INP based data hiding method.

For example, $(p(0,0), p(0,1), p(1,0), p(1,1)) = (100, 92, 156, 112)$ are also given. In first, $p'(0,1) = \left(100 + \frac{100+92}{2}\right)/\ 2 = 98$, $p'(1,0) = \left(100 + \frac{100+156}{2}\right)/2 = 114$, and $p'(1,1) = (98+114)/2 = 106$ are calculated. Next, three difference values $d_1 = 156-98 = 58$, $d_2 = 156-114 = 42$, and $d_3 = 156-106 = 50$ are calculated for $p_{max} = 156$. And the size of embedding bits $n_1 = 5$, $n_2 = 5$, and $n_3 = 5$ are determined by using Equation 21.16. Finally, new pixel values $(p'(0,0), p'(0,1), p'(1,0), p'(1,1)) = (100, 119, 129, 137)$ are obtained for the secret bits $10101_2 = 21, 01111_2 = 15$, and $11111_2 = 31$ (Figure 21.17).

21.5.3 Interpolation by Maximizing the Difference Values between Neighboring Pixel Based Data Hiding Method

Data hiding based on interpolation by maximizing the difference values between neighboring pixels was presented to improve Lee and Huang's method in 2015 [31]. The interpolation equation is defined as Equation 21.19 where p_{max} is used.

$$\begin{pmatrix} d_1 \\ d_2 \\ d_3 \end{pmatrix} = \begin{pmatrix} p'(i, j+1) - p_{min} \\ p'(i+1, j) - p_{min} \\ p'(i+1, j+1) - p_{min} \end{pmatrix} \tag{21.19}$$

Next, three difference values d_t $(1 \leq t \leq 3)$ are calculated using the min value of four pixels p_{min} and the number of embedding bits n_t $(1 \leq t \leq 3)$ are decided. In Equation 21.20, $p_{min} = \min(p(i, j), p(i, j+1), p(i+1, j), p(i+1, j+1))$ can be calculated.

$$\begin{pmatrix} d_1 \\ d_2 \\ d_3 \end{pmatrix} = \begin{pmatrix} p'(i, j+1) - p_{min} \\ p'(i+1, j) - p_{min} \\ p'(i+1, j+1) - p_{min} \end{pmatrix} \tag{21.20}$$

$$n_t = \log_2 d_t, \qquad 1 \le t \le 3 \tag{21.21}$$

Finally, new pixel values p'' are calculated by Equation 21.22 (Figure 21.18).

$$\begin{pmatrix} p''(i,\ j+1) \\ p''(i+1,\ j) \\ p''(i+1,\ j+1) \end{pmatrix} = \begin{pmatrix} \max(p'(i,\ j),\ p'(i,\ j+2)) - b_1 \\ \max(p'(i,\ j),\ p'(i+2,\ j)) - b_2 \\ \min(p'(i,\ j+1),\ p'(i+1,\ j)) - b_3 \end{pmatrix} \tag{21.22}$$

Four pixel values $(p(0,0), p(0,1), p(1,0), p(1,1)) = (100, 92, 156, 112)$ are given for example. First, $p_{\max} = 156$ can be calculated and new three pixels by the interpolation technique. $p'(0,1) = \left(156 + \frac{100+92}{2}\right)/2 = 126$, $p'(1,0) = \left(156 + \frac{100+156}{2}\right)/2 = 142$, and $p'(1,1) = (126+142)/2 = 134$ are calculated. Next, three difference values $d_1 = 126 - 92 = 34$, $d_2 = 142 - 92 = 50$, and $d_3 = 134 - 92 = 42$ are obtained for $p_{\min} = 92$. The size of embedding bits $n_1 = 5$, $n_2 = 5$, and $n_3 = 5$ are determined by using Equation 21.21. Finally, new pixel values $(p'(0,0), p'(0,1), p'(1,0), p'(1,1)) = (100, 79, 141, 95)$ are obtained for the secret bits $10101_2 = 21$, $01111_2 = 15$, and $11111_2 = 31$.

As mentioned above, data hiding methods using interpolation and edge detection techniques have been introduced, but they show a similar pattern. In other words, previous data hiding schemes are applied to the enlarged images by the interpolation method. And then edge detection algorithms are used to divide into edge and smooth areas. It is possible to embed different lengths of secret data and be less distorted to the human visual system.

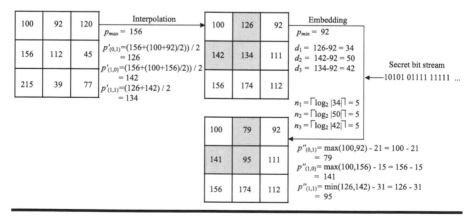

Figure 21.18 Example of IMNP based data hiding method.

21.6 Conclusions

In this chapter, reversible data hiding methods based on interpolation and edge detection techniques have been described. The interpolation method has the advantage of hiding more secret data through image enlargement and could apply various application techniques. The edge detection method also distinguished between edge and smooth areas that could be less distortion to the human eye. Many algorithms have been presented since the introduction to interpolation and edge detection based data hiding techniques, but most of the algorithms have been applied that were previously introduced in other data hiding techniques.

Some advantages of interpolation and edge detection based data hiding methods are:

1. Various existing data hiding techniques can be applied after various interpolation algorithms were used.
2. Embedding capacity can be increased by using interpolated image before concealing secret data without distortion to the human visual system.
3. Although irreversible data hiding techniques are used, it can provide reversibility depending on which interpolation and edge detection data hiding algorithms are used.
4. Image quality can be improved because most interpolation methods use neighboring pixel values.
5. Embedding bits are different depending on edge or smooth area, it makes the proposed method difficult to detect on steganalysis attacks.
6. With additional functions like authentication, forgery detection is possible by using the correlation between interpolation pixels.

In summary, some works have been increasingly presented in interpolation and edge detection techniques based reversible data hiding methods, but there is still room to improve regarding the trade-off between the embedding capacity and the visual image quality. In the future, a new hybrid data hiding method based on interpolation and edge detection techniques will be introduced and used to communicate over the Internet to the public.

Acknowledgments

This research was supported by Basic Science Research Program through the National Research Foundation of Korea (NRF) funded by the Ministry of Education (NRF-2015R1D1A1A01058019).

References

1. A. Khan, A. Siddiqa, S. Munib, S.A. Malik, A recent survey of reversible watermarking techniques, *Information Sciences* 279 (2014) 251–272.
2. M.S. Subhedar, V.H. Mankar, Current status and key issues in image steganography: A survey, *Computer Science Review* 13(14) (2014) 95–113.
3. A. Cheddad, J. Condell, K. Curran, P.M. Kevitt, Digital image steganography: Survey and analysis of current methods, *Signal Processing* 90 (2010) 727–752.
4. A. Nissar, A.H. Mir, Classification of steganalysis techniques: A study, *Digital Signal Processing* 20 (2010) 1758–1770.
5. N.F. Johnson and S. Jajodia, Exploring steganography: Seeing the unseen, *Computer Practices* 31(2) (1998) 26–34, 31(2).
6. R.J. Anderson and F.A.P. Petitcolas, On the limits of steganography, *IEEE Journal on Selected Areas in Communications* 16 (1998) 474–481.
7. F.A.P. Petitcolas, R.J. Anderson, M.G. Kuhn, Information hiding–A survey, *Proceedings of the IEEE, Special Issue on Protection of Multimedia Content* 87(7) (1999) 1062–1078.
8. W. Bender, D. Gruhl, N. Morimoto, A. Lu, Techniques for data hiding, *IBM Systems Journal* 35(3) (1996) 313–336.
9. M. Swanson, M. Kobayashi, A. Tewfik, Multimedia data embedding and watermarking technologies, *Proceedings of the IEEE* 86(6) (1998) 1064–1087.
10. C. Cox, J. Killian, T. Leighton, T. Shamoon, Secure spread spectrum communication for multimedia, Technical Report, N.E.C. Research Institute (1995).
11. A. Shizaki, J. Tanimoto, M. Iwata, A digital image watermarking scheme withstanding malicious attacks, *IEICE Transactions on Fundamentals of Electronics, Communications and Computer Sciences* 83(10) (2000) 2015–2022.
12. F. Hartung, M. Kutter, Multimedia watermarking techniques, *Proceedings of the IEEE* 86(6) (1998) 1079–1107.
13. R.J. Anderson, Information hiding, *Proceedings of the First International Information Hiding Workshop*, LNCS 1174 (1996) 207–226.
14. B. Pfitzmann, Information hiding terminology, *Proceedings of the First International Information Hiding Workshop*, LNCS 1174 (1996) 347–350.
15. R.Z. Wang, C.F. Lin, J.C. Lin, Image hiding by optimal LSB substitution and genetic algorithm, *Pattern Recognition* 34(3), (2001) 671–683.
16. J. Zollner, H. Federrath, H. Klimant, A. Pfitzmann, R. Piotraschke, A. Westfeld, G. Wicke, G. Wolf, Modeling the security of steganographic systems, *2nd Workshop on Information Hiding* 1525 (1998) 345–355.
17. K.H. Jung, A survey of interpolation-based reversible data methods, *Multimedia Tools and Applications* 77(7) (2018) 7795–7810.
18. J. Mielikainen, LSB matching revisited, *IEEE Signal Processing Letters* 13 (2006) 285–287.
19. N.I. Wu, K.C. Wu, C.M. Wang, Exploring pixel-value differencing and base decomposition for low distortion data embedding, *Applied Soft Computing* 12 (2012) 942–960.
20. Y.P. Lee, J.C. Lee, W.K. Chen, K.C. Chang, I.J. Su, C.P. Chang, High-payload image hiding with quality recovery using tri-way pixel-value differencing, *Information Sciences* 191 (2012) 214–225.

21. Z. Ni, Y.Q. Shi, N. Ansari, W. Su, Reversible data hiding, *IEEE Transactions on Circuits and Systems for Video Technology* 16(3) (2006) 354–361.
22. L.C. Huang, L.Y. Tseng, M.S. Hwang, A reversible data hiding method by histogram shifting in high quality medical images, *Journal of Systems and Software* 86 (2013) 716–727.
23. H. Luo, F.X. Yu, H. Chen, Z.L. Huang, H. Li, P.H. Wang, Reversible data hiding based on block median preservation, *Information Sciences* 181 (2011) 308–328.
24. Z. Zhao, H. Luo, Z.M. Lu, J.S. Pan, Reversible data hiding based on multilevel histogram modification and sequential recovery, *AEU-International Journal of Electronics and Communications* 65(10) (2011) 814–826.
25. D.M. Thodi, J.J. Rodriguez, Expansion embedding techniques for reversible watermarking, *IEEE Transactions on Image Processing* 16(3) (2007) 721–730.
26. C.F. Lee, H.C. Chen, Adjustable prediction-based reversible data hiding, *Digital Signal Processing* 22(6) (2012) 941–953.
27. X. Li, B. Yang, T. Zeng, Efficient reversible data watermarking based on adaptive prediction-error expansion and pixel selection, *IEEE Transactions on Image Processing* 20(12) (2011) 3524–3533.
28. X. Li, J. Li, B. Li, B. Yang, High-fidelity reversible data hiding scheme based on pixel-value-ordering and prediction-error expansion, *Signal Processing* 93 (2013) 198–205.
29. K.H. Jung, K.Y. Yoo, Data hiding method using image interpolation, *Computer Standards & Interfaces* 31(2) (2009) 465–470.
30. C.F. Lee, Y.L. Huang, An efficient image interpolation increasing payload in reversible data hiding, *Expert System Applications* 39(8) (2012) 6712–6719.
31. J. Hu, T. Li, Reversible steganography using extended image interpolation technique, *Computers and Electrical Engineering* 46 (2015) 447–455.
32. C.N. Yang, S.C. Hsu, C. Kim, Improving stego image quality in image interpolation based data hiding, *Computer Standards & Interfaces* 50 (2017) 209–215.
33. A. Giannoula, N.V. Boulgouris, D. Hatzinakos, K.N. Plataniotis, Watermark detection for noisy interpolated images, *IEEE Transactions on Circuits and Systems* 53(5) (2006) 359–363.
34. L. Luo, Z. Chen, M. Chen, X. Zeng, Z. Xiong, Reversible image watermarking using interpolation technique, *IEEE Transactions on Information Forensics and Security* 5(1) (2010) 187–193.
35. L. Zhang, X. Wu, An edge-guided image interpolation algorithm via directional filtering and data fusion, *IEEE Transactions on Image Processing* 15(8) (2006) 2226–2238.
36. K.H. Jung, K.Y. Yoo, Data hiding using edge detector for scalable images, *Multimedia Tools and Applications* 71 (2014) 1455–1468.
37. T.C. Lu, Interpolation-based hiding scheme using the modulus function and re-encoding strategy, *Signal Processing* 142 (2018) 244–259.
38. G.P.V. Sabeen, M.K. Sajila, M.V. Bindiya, A two stage data hiding scheme with high capacity based on interpolation and difference expansion, *Procedia Technology* 24 (2016) 1311–1316.
39. A. Malik, G. Sikka, H.K. Verma, An image interpolation based reversible data hiding scheme using pixel value adjusting feature, *Multimedia Tools and Applications* 76 (2017) 13025–13046.
40. T.C. Lu, An interpolation-based lossless hiding scheme based on message recoding mechanism, *Optik* 130 (2017) 1377–1396.

41. T.C. Lu, C.C. Chang, Y.H. Huang, High capacity reversible hiding scheme based on interpolation, difference expansion and histogram methods, *Multimedia Tools and Applications* 72 (2014) 417–435.

42. T.C. Lu, M.C. Lin, C.C. Huang, K.M. Deng, Reversible data hiding based on image interpolation with a secret message reduction strategy, *International Journal of Computer & Software Engineering* 1 (2016) 102–112.

43. L. Liu, T. Chen, S. Zhu, W. Hong, X. Si, A reversible data hiding method using improved neighbor mean interpolation and random-block division, *Information Technology Journal* 13 (2016) 2374–2384.

44. Y.Y. Tsai, J.T. Chen, Y.C. Kuo, C.S. Chan, A generalized image interpolation-based reversible data hiding scheme with high embedding capacity and image quality, *KSII Transactions on Internet and Information Systems* 8(9) (2014) 3286–3301.

45. X.T. Wang, C.C. Chang, T.S. Nguyen, M.C. Li, Reversible data hiding for high quality images exploiting interpolation and direction order mechanism, *Digital Signal Processing* 23 (2013) 569–577.

46. W. Hong, T.S. Chen, Reversible data embedding for high quality images using interpolation and reference pixel distribution mechanism, *Journal of Visual Communication and Image Representation* 22 (2011) 131–140.

47. Y.T. Chang, C.T. Huang, C.F. Lee, S.J. Wang, Image interpolating based data hiding in conjunction with pixel-shifting of histogram, *The Journal of Supercomputing* 66(2) (2013) 1093–1110.

48. Y.Y. Tsai, Y.H. Huang, R.J. Lin, C.S. Chan, An adjustable interpolation-based data hiding algorithm based on LSB substitution and histogram shifting, *International Journal of Digital Crime and Forensics* 8(2) (2016) 48–61.

49. M. Kumar, S. Agrawal, Reversible data hiding based on prediction error expansion using adjacent pixels, *Security and Communication Networks* 9(16) (2016) 3703–3712.

50. K.H. Jung, K.Y. Yoo, Steganographic method based on interpolation and LSB substitution of digital images, *Multimedia Tools and Applications* 74 (2015) 2143–2155.

51. T.C. Lu, C.Y. Tseng, J.H. Wu, Dual imaging-based reversible hiding technique using LSB matching, *Signal Processing* 108 (2015) 77–89.

52. T.C. Lu. J.H. Wu, C.C. Huang, Dual-image-based reversible data hiding method using center folding strategy, *Signal Processing* 115 (2015) 195–213.

53. C.F. Lee. Y.L. Huang, Reversible data hiding scheme based on dual stego-images using orientation combinations, *Telecommunication Systems* 52(4) (2013) 2237–2247.

54. B. Jana, High payload reversible data hiding scheme using weighted matrix, *Optik* 127 (2016) 3347–3358.

55. M. Tang, J. Hu, W. Song, S. Zeng, Reversible and adaptive image steganographic method, *AEU–International Journal of Electronics and Communications* 69(12) (2015) 1745–1754.

56. J.Y. Hsiao, K.F. Chan, J.M. Chang, Block-based reversible data embedding, *Signal Processing* 89 (2009) 556–569.

57. A.M. Alattar, Reversible watermark using the difference expansion of a generalized integer transform, *IEEE Transactions on Image Processing* 13(8) (2004) 1147–1156.

58. C.C. Chang, H.W. Tseng, A steganographic method for digital images using side-match, *Pattern Recognition Letters* 25(12) (2004) 1431–1437.

59. C.L. Tsai, H.F Chiang, K.C Fan, C.D Chung, Reversible data hiding and lossless reconstruction of binary images using pair-wise logical computation mechanism, *Pattern Recognition* 38(11) (2005) 1993–2006.

60. K.H. Jung, A survey of reversible data hiding methods in dual images, *IETE Technical Review* 33(4) (2016) 441–452.
61. X. Liao, Q.Y. Wen, J. Zhang, A steganographic method for digital images with four-pixel differencing and modified LSB substitution, *Journal of Visual Communication and Image Representation* 22(1) (2011) 1–8.
62. C.M. Wang, N.I. Wu, C.S. Tsai, M.S. Hwang, A high quality steganographic method with pixel-value differencing and modulus function, *Journal of Systems and Software* 81 (2008) 150–158.
63. H.C. Wu, N.I. Wu, C.S. Tsai, M.S. Hwang, Image steganographic scheme based on pixel-value differencing and LSB replacement methods, *IEE Processing Visualization, Image Signal Processing* 152 (2005) 611–615.
64. J. Marin, F.Y. Shih, Reversible data hiding techniques using multiple scanning difference value histogram modification, *Journal of Information Hiding and Multimedia Signal Processing* 5(3) (2014) 451–460.
65. H.C. Huang, F.C. Chang, Hierarchy-based reversible data hiding, *Expert Systems with Applications* 40(1) (2013) 34–43.
66. S.W. Weng, J.S. Pan, Reversible watermarking based on eight improved prediction modes, *Journal of Information Hiding and Multimedia Signal Processing* 5(3) (2014) 527–53316.
67. D.C. Wu, W.H. Tsai, A steganographic method for images by pixel-value differencing, *Pattern Recognition Letters* 24 (2003) 1613–1626.
68. K.C. Chang, P.S. Huang, T.M. Tu, C.P. Chang, Image steganographic scheme using try-way pixel-value differencing and adaptive rules, *Intelligent Information Hiding and Multimedia Signal Processing* 2 (2007) 449–452.
69. J. Tian, Reversible data embedding using a difference expansion, *IEEE Transactions on Circuits and Systems for Video Technology* 13(8) (2003) 890–896.
70. Wikipedia, https://en.wikipedia.org/
71. T.M. Lehmann, C. Gonner, K. Spitzer, Survey: interpolation methods in medical image processing, *IEEE Transactions on Medical Imaging* 18(11) (1999) 1049–1075.
72. P. Thevenaz, T. Blu, M. Unser, Interpolation revisited, *IEEE Transaction on Medical Imaging* 19(7) (2000) 739–758.
73. C.R. Appledorn, A new approach to the interpolation of sampled data, *IEEE Transactions on Medical Imaging* 15 (1996) 369–376.
74. E. Maeland, On the comparison of interpolation methods, *IEEE Transactions on Medical Imaging* 7(3) (1988) 213–217.
75. H.S. Hou, H.C. Andrews, Cubic splines for image interpolation and digital filtering, *IEEE Transactions on Acoustics, Speech, and Signal Processing*, 26(6) (1987) 508–517.
76. R.G. Keys, Cubic convolution interpolation for digital image processing, *IEEE Transactions on Acoustics, Speech, and Signal Processing*, 29(6) (1981) 1153–1160.
77. J.A. Parker, R.V. Kenyon, D.E. Troxel, Comparison of interpolating methods for image re-sampling, *IEEE Transactions on Medical Imaging* 2 (1983) 31–39.
78. M. Unser, A. Aldroubi, M. Eden, Fast B-splines transforms for continuous image representation and interpolation, *IEEE Transactions on Pattern Analysis and Machine Intelligence* 13 (1991) 277–285.
79. M. Unser, P. Thevenaz, L. Yaroslavsky, Convolution-based interpolation for fast, high-quality rotation of images, *IEEE Transactions on Image Processing* 4 (1995) 1371–1381.
80. R.R. Schultz, R.L. Stevenson, A Bayesian approach to image expansion for improved definition, *IEEE Transactions on Image Processing* 3(3) (1994) 233–242.

81. X. Li, M. T. Orchard, New edge-directed interpolation, *IEEE Transactions on Image Processing* 10(10) (2001) 1521–1527.
82. Cambridge in Color, http://www.cambridgeincolour.com/tutorials/image-interpolation.htm.
83. J.F. Canny, A computational approach to edge detection, *IEEE Transactions on Pattern Analysis and Machine Intelligence* 8(6) (1986) 679–698 8(6).
84. L.S. Davis, A survey of edge detection techniques, *Computer Vision Graphics and Image Processing* 4(3) (1975) 248–270.
85. D. Geman, Stochastic model for boundary detection, *Image Vision Computing* 5(2) (1987) 61–65.
86. R. Nevatia, A color edge detection and its use in scene segmentation, *IEEE Transactions on System and Man, and Cybernetic* 7(11) (1977) 802–826.
87. C.C. Chang, T.S. Chen, Y. Lin, An efficient edge detection scheme of color image, *Proceedings of the Fifth Joint Conference on Information Science* 2 (2000) 448–455.
88. P. Tsai, C.C. Chang, Y.C. Hu, An adaptive two-stage edge detection scheme for digital color images, *Real Time Imaging* 8(4) (1985) 329–343.
89. Y.H. Yu, C.C. Chang, A new edge detection approach based on image context analysis, *Image and Vision Computing* 24(10) (2006) 1090–1102.

Chapter 22

Steganography and Medical Data Security

Rukiye Karakis and Inan Guler

Contents

22.1 Introduction

Today, advances in information and communication technologies have changed the policies about medical information (MI) security. Electronic personal health information may include patient personal data, clinical and diagnosis reports, medications, past medical history, histological and pathological findings, immunizations, laboratory data, radiology and biological signals such as EEG, ECG, or EMG reports [1–3]. For this reason, patient personal data are at risk on the local or

DOI: 10.1201/9780429435461-25

wide networks because of cyber-attacks. If financial data or credit cards are stolen, credit cards can be easily cancelled or prevented identity theft. Once medical data is stolen, it's difficult to retrieve. It can be sold to uninsured people for obtaining some drugs or medical equipment. Furthermore, medical data modified or destroyed may cause a life-threatening situation for patient [1,4–7].

Until recently, MI systems in hospitals contained only textual data. However, medical images have to be digitized and archived because of the requirement of transferring patients' all data to the digital environments. The modality of medical images can be X-ray, ultrasound, computer tomography (CT), magnetic resonance imaging (MRI), etc. Digital Imaging and Communications in Medicine (DICOM) standard is used to handle medical images into a picture archiving and communication system (PACS) [1,8–10].

Medical images are formed with patient, study, series and image steps into DICOM. Each patient may have multiple studies, each study can have one or more series of images, and each series contains one or more images. DICOM file differs from the other image file formats such as JPEG, BMP which do not contain information in the file header. However, DICOM format has both a header and binary data of image. The header includes the metadata of image (data type, bit format, modality, image size, etc.), patient information (name, ID, birth date, age, gender, weight, and address, etc.), the properties of study and exam, acquisition parameters, information of physician and radiology center [8–11]. Image viewer software such as MRIcron, MRIcro, MicroDicom, 3DSlicer, dicom2, ezDICOM, ImageMagick, AMIDE, Medcon/XMedcon, ImageJ, dicom2pgm, Offis dcmtk displays both the image data and the header of DICOM. These softwares can be easily obtained via the Internet.

There are two major problems about medical images in DICOM file format, which are DICOM images size, and patient personal data security in DICOM header. Each DICOM image is a file ranging in size from 1MB to100MB. The amount of disk space required to store medical images increases between 10% and 20% each year [9]. For this reason, compression algorithms are used to reduce the size of medical images that occupy petabyte space within the PACS. There are two major categories of compression algorithms which are lossy and lossless. Lossless compression method allows the original data to be retrieved from the compressed data and its compression ratio is 2:1 or 3:1. Lossy compression method cannot recover the original data. The compression rate of lossy can be 10:1 to 50:1 and even more. However, radiological diagnosis can be affected by losses in medical images that compressed with lossy compression. For this reason, lossless compression methods such as run length coding (RLE), Huffman, Lempel-Ziv-Welch (LZW) and JPEG 2000 are preferred for reducing image size [1,9].

Patient personal data in DICOM file header has to be secured over the destruction, modification, and illegal copying. Security tools such as virtual private networks (VPNs), firewalls, access and user control services, antivirus and other software, cryptography techniques (symmetric, asymmetric, or hashing encryption), and electronic signatures ensure the confidentiality, reliability and availability of MI system. Furthermore, steganography techniques have been proposed to protect patient information in medical image [1,6–7].

Steganography embeds a secret message within text, image, or video file [1,12]. In literature, different file such as hypertext markup language (HTML), extensible markup language (XML), or executable (.EXE) file are also used as cover object to carry message [12]. The major goals of steganography are to increase capacity of the secret message, to enhance the imperceptibility and to robust against steg-analysis [1,6–7,12].

In literature, steganography techniques are used to embed and extract the hidden message with or without a stego-key. Image steganography techniques, involved in this chapter, can be categorized as spatial domain or transform domain. Transform domain techniques (Discrete Cosine Transform [DCT], Discrete Fourier Transform [DFT], and Discrete Wavelet Transform [DWT]) are complex, so that they increase computational complexity and time. Nevertheless, transform domain techniques are robust against steg-attacks such as compression, filtering, and geometric distortion. Spatial domain techniques (LSB [least significant bit] embedding, palette sorting, fixed quantization, histogram shifting methods, and etc.) are so simple and fast. However, these methods are not robust against steg-attacks [1,12].

Steganography techniques in medical data use medical images (X-ray, MRI, CT, PET [positron emission tomography], ultrasound [US], angiogram, etc.) or biological signals (ECG, EMG, EEG etc.) as cover object to embed patient information [1,6–7,13–16]. The steganography methods for medical images can be identified as three categories [10,17–40]. The first approach is LSB based classical image steganography techniques in spatial domain [7,10,32–40]. The LSB method sequentially embeds the secret message' bits in the least significant bits of pixels' gray level values of the cover image. In the LSB method, the imperceptibility and embedding capacity are high. For this reason, the LSB method is generally preferred if hidden message is combined with patient privacy data, doctors' comment, and biological signals in medical image steganography application. However, this method is vulnerable to steg-analysis, so that the embedding message has to be secured by encryption and lossless compression.

The second group method hides information within regions of non-interest (RONI) of the medical images not to affect the patient diagnosis [7,17–23]. RONI based steganography can be performed within spatial or transform domain. A disadvantage of these methods is the capacity of hidden message that is directly related to RONI area size that include black background [7].

The third technique is reversible steganography in medical images. The purpose of the reversible steganography techniques is to reconstruct the original cover image [7,24–31]. In these methods, patient personal data is hidden in spatial domain or transform domain. Imperceptibility of reversible data hiding techniques is related to the capacity of the embedded message [7,24–31].

This chapter is organized as follows. We describe medical information systems, the details of PACS and DICOM in Section 22.2. We next present medical steganography technique formulations and demonstrate their performance on medical images in Section 22.3. We then give the comparison metrics of medical image steganography in Section 22.4. Finally, we conclude this chapter and future research directions in Section 22.5.

22.2 Medical Information (MI) Systems

Today, the development of computer systems has affected the healthcare industry. The electronic health record (EHR) of a patient is a systematic collection of personal health information from birth to the time after death. These records are collected in healthcare institutions, insurance companies, clinical researches, and epidemiological studies. In EHR systems, all health processes of patients should be recorded with respect to unique registration numbers. All patient information can be accessed quickly and easily from anywhere. Requests should be transferred from the systems and the results should be seen. Furthermore, patient appointments and its management procedures should be performed.

In EHR systems, all patient records with or without numerical data should be secured. For this reason, MI security is ensured by strict ethics and rules defined in medical standards and guidelines for both the health professionals and patients. The essential standard is ISO27799 that provide guidelines for the protection of medical information according to the definitions in the ISO17799/ISO27002 standards. Some countries use their own health information management policies such as The Health Insurance Portability and Accountability Act (HIPAA) in the USA, the Code of Federal Regulations number 45 (CFR 45) in Australia, the Europe's Directive 95/46/EC. HIPAA includes the steps for health plans with healthcare providers to protect medical images of patients. The Europe's Directive 95/46/EC ensures the security of processing patient data. Furthermore, The CFR 45 defines the detailed rules for sensitive patient data [1,6].

The MI system has to ensure three mandatory characteristics which are confidentiality, reliability and availability. Confidentiality means that information is available to authorized users, entities, or processes. Reliability includes authenticity and integrity where authenticity is the corroboration that correct patient information is from the right source, and integrity is that the property data has not been modified or deleted by unauthorized people. Availability ensures that authorized users are able to access information at any time when needed. Security tools are used in the EHR systems to ensure the confidentiality and integrity of information within computer systems that are or are not connected to a network. Confidentiality can be threatened by means of revealing or redirecting of information in computer systems. In data transmission, medical files can be illegally copied by a malicious hacker. Furthermore, injection attacks, Trojan horses, and capturing database permissions can directly affect the confidentiality of MI systems. For this reason, access control and secure transmission protocols in standalone desktop or portable devices should be established to prevent confidentially threats. In addition, firewalls can be used in open networks and the data can be encrypted while being transferred.

Reliability can be damaged by production, destruction, and modification of medical files. For this reason, it is necessary to define who has the authority to erase, record, and modify data. Antivirus software and firewalls should be used to protect the system from attacks. Furthermore, the integrity of the data can be assured with digital signatures while transferring. Availability can be interrupted due to disablement on the file management system, destruction hard-disk, or alteration data [1,6,7]. The MI system should ensure data handling rules such as access and auditing.

In health information systems (HIS), firewalls, virtual private networks, and encryption are used to ensure MI security. However, security tools and firewalls have limits and they can be exploited by pirates. Furthermore, encrypted medical data is sensitive to bit errors during transmission and encryption which increase the operating and running cost of medical data. In addition, the file headers of medical data can be easily captured in plain text format [1,4,6,7]. Another problem in HIS is that medical data can be recorded manually by mistake. For this reason, steganography can be used as an alternative to encryption.

22.2.1 Picture Archiving and Communication System (PACS)

PACS manages the software and platforms to acquire, store, distribute, and retrieve the medical images. It integrates with radiology and hospital information systems, as shown in Figure 22.1 [9]. PACS consists of main server and workstations which uses images from the main server or provides images to main server on local area network (LAN) or wide area network (WAN).

The main server manages operations such as recording, retrieving, and backing up images. Radiology workstations provide the image retrieving, processing, and demonstrating. In PACS, patient information can be easily obtained through hospital and radiology information systems. Web servers are required to communicate over the Internet. For this reason, the web address (URL: Uniform Resource Locator) is given to the images in the PACS and all the images can be accessed by querying in the PACS archive [8].

PACS should have to overcome high recording capacity of the medical images. Hence, the system disk capacity should be increased when requested. PACS should have high process capacity to synchronize with medical imaging devices. The system service should be reliable, unlimited, and uninterrupted. It has to have high bandwidth and fast data communication between servers and clients [8,9].

In PACS, compression algorithms, which are lossless and lossy, reduce the size of medical images that occupy petabyte data space. Lossless compression methods, which enable the retrieval of the data, compress at a ratio of 2:1 or 3:1. Lossy compression methods which make it impossible to recover the data can compress 10:1 to 50:1 and more. Nevertheless, a lossy compressed image can affect the radiological

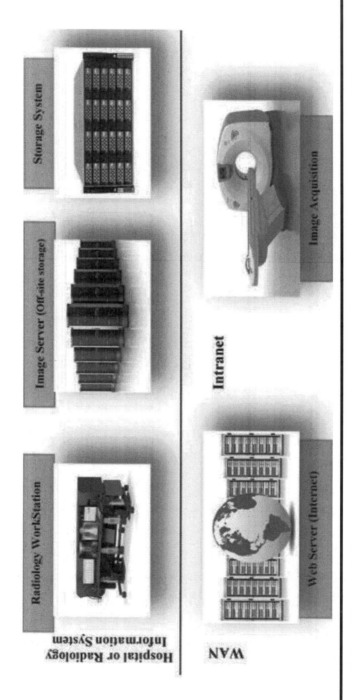

Figure 22.1   PAC Systematic Scheme.

assessment according to health standards. For this reason, lossless compression methods (Run Length Encoding [RLE], Huffman, LZW, and JPEG 2000 etc.) are preferred to decrease data sizes [1,8,9].

22.2.2 Digital Imaging and Communications in Medicine (DICOM)

In PACS, medical images are stored in DICOM file format. DICOM includes definitions for different devices, software, and platforms that are compatible with each other in PACS. DICOM has been constituted in 1983 by the American College of Radiology (ACR) and the National Electrical Manufacturers Association (NEMA). The first aim of the committee was to make the digital medical imaging system independent of the device manufacturers. In 1985, the first version of ACR-NEMA with many errors was published as a guideline. The second version of ACR-NEMA was announced to compensate the errors within ACR-NEMA 1.0 in 1988. PACS has used DICOM 3.0 standard due to the widespread use of computer networks since 1993. Today, updates and changes of DICOM are in progress, and the most recent version is released in 2008. DICOM is developed using NEMA standard (PS3) and ISO standard (12052: 2006) by information technology manufacturers, users and organizations in the field of medical imaging and healthcare [1,7–11].

The DICOM file differs from image file formats (JPEG, BMP, PNG etc.) which do not include information in the file header. However, the DICOM file consists of file header and pixel data of image in two parts. The file header contains information about patient personal data (name, surname, identification number, address, birth date, weight), institute, expert's data, study, series and image properties (type, format, size etc.) [7–11]. In DICOM, patient images consist of patient, study, series, and image steps. Accordingly, each patient can have multiple studies. Each study has one or more series of images. Each series contains one or more images of the patient.

The DICOM file has 4 different fields. These are: preamble with a 128 byte that is free space description field, prefix indicating that the file is a DICOM file, data elements that includes DICOM tags with data, and pixel data [7–11]. DICOM files are read and written by hexadecimal number. In the DICOM file, data such as characters, integers, decimal numbers, and date are stored in double number length using 27 basic data types. In DICOM, a data dictionary is created to read and write data. In the dictionary, the data is placed sequentially. Each data element has a tag, value representation (VR), value length (VL), and value field (VF) [7–11]. Figure 22.2 shows the properties of the DICOM data element.

As shown in Figure 22.2, the tag in each data element is described with a pair of numbers (group, element). For example, patient name and birth date are represented in the tag as Patient Name (0010,0010), and Patient Birth Date (0010, 0030). 0010 is the group number, 0010 and 0030 are the element properties.

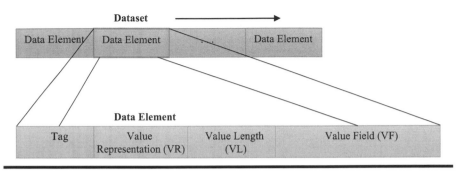

Figure 22.2   The properties of DICOM data element.

Table 22.1   Sample Essential Data Element Properties in the DICOM Header

Attribute Name	Tag Data (group, element)	Type	Attribute Description
Patient's Name	(0010,0010)	2	Patient's full name
Patient ID	(0010,0020)	2	Patient's identification number
Patient's Birth Date	(0010,0030)	2	Patient's birth date
Patient's Sex	(0010,0040)	2	Patient's Gender M: Male F: Female O: Other
Study Instance UID	(0020,000D)	1	The unique identifier number of the study
Study Date	(0008,0020)	2	Start date of study
Study Time	(0008,0030)	2	Start time of study
Study ID	(0020,0010)	2	Identification number generated by user or device
Modality	(0008,0060)	1	Describing images in the series
Series Instance UID	(0020,000E)	1	The unique identifier number of the series
Series Number	(0020,0011)	2	The number defined for series

In Table 22.1, the essential data element properties in the DICOM file header are given. The VR includes an abbreviated name consisting of 2 characters and a description of the name, the length of the data, and a description of the characters.

DICOM files with headers are easily viewed via commercial or free software such as MRIcron, MRIcro, MicroDicom, 3DSlicer, dicom2, ezDICOM, ImageMagick, AMIDE, Medcon/XMedcon, ImageJ, dicom2pgm, Offis dcmtk etc. For this reason, patient's personal information in the DICOM file header must be secured against steg-attack according to the personal rights of the patient.

22.3 Medical Steganography Techniques

Steganography, which is developed as an alternative to cryptology, hides the secret data in a media file such as image, text, or video. Medical steganography techniques use medical images or biological signals as cover objects to embed patient information, health reports, medical images, and biological signals [1,6,7,13–16]. In medical steganography, the first studies are related to tamper detection and authentication [13]. Tamper detection aims to prevent possible attacks from hostile people with respect to the concealment of the patient information into the medical images or biological signals. Authentication ensures the security of transferring patient data through Internet. In recent studies of this field, patient's different data such as medical images, biological signals, health reports, patient's information are combined into one file format to ensure the data security, and to reduce of data repository and transmission capacity [1,41–47].

Medical steganography consists of two stages which are embedding and extracting message, respectively. The embedding message operation is performed with Equation 22.1 [12,48–50].

$$Em : C \oplus K \oplus M \to \tilde{C} \tag{22.1}$$

where:

C is cover medical image
$\tilde{C}$ is stego medical image
K is an encryption stego-key
M is the message
Em also represents the embedded message

The extracting message stage is performed using Equation 22.2 [12,48–50].

$$Ex\big(Em(c,k,m)\big) \approx m, \forall c \in C, k \in K, m \in M \tag{22.2}$$

Where Ex denotes the extracted message.

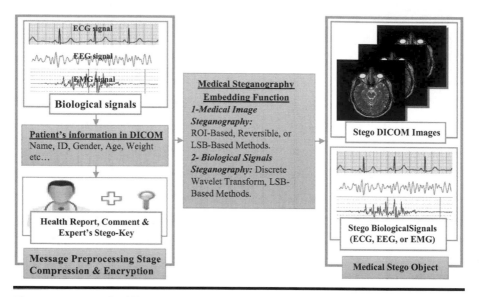

Figure 22.3   Embedding message into medical images or biological signals.

The embedding message stage is shown in Figure 22.3. The patient's information into DICOM file header, biological signals, health report, and/or expert's comment compose of the embedding message. The secret message is encoded by the encryption algorithm using a stego-key to ensure the security and it is alternatively compressed to decrease the message capacity and the complexity against attacks. Lossless compression algorithms, which are Huffman, LZW and RLE compression etc., should be used to prevent data loss according to health standards.

In medical steganography, a cover object can be medical images or biological signals. The embedding message methods for medical images can be categorized into LSB-based, ROI (region of interest)-based, and reversible steganography [4,6,7]. In literature, the steganography methods of biological signals are discrete wavelet transform and LSB-based steganography [54]. The medical steganography techniques are developed based on imperceptibility, robustness, and capacity. If the message contains patient's information obtained from the DICOM file header, this information is deleted from the header after the message is hidden. If the cover objects are medical images, the embedding process should be simultaneously executed with all DICOM files in order to increase computational efficiency [1].

In the extracting message stage, medical stego object and a stego-key are required to obtain a message, as shown Figure 22.4. Firstly, the message is gathered by using the medical steganography method. Secondly, this meaningless message is decrypted and/or decompressed. The extracted message can only be accessed by authorized persons with a stego-key.

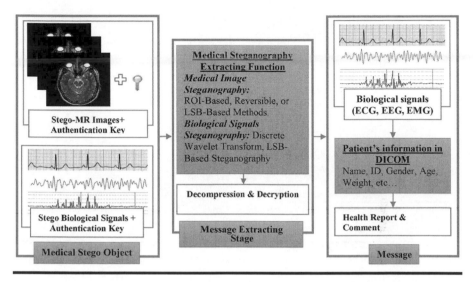

Figure 22.4   Extracting message from medical images or biological signals.

This chapter focuses on the medical image steganography. For this reason, the details of these methods are given below.

22.3.1 LSB-Based Steganography

The least significant bit (LSB)-based steganography is essential image steganography technique in spatial domain [7,10,32–40]. The embedding process of LSB steganography is described by Equation 22.3 [48–50].

$$Yi = 2\left|\frac{X_i}{2}\right| + m_i \tag{22.3}$$

where:

m_i is the i-th message bit
x_i is the i-th gray value of selected pixel
Y_i is the gray value of pixel after embedding message

In LSB technique, the message can be embedded sequentially or randomly in the gray values of cover image pixels. In sequential LSB, the LSBs of pixel are altered by the message bits starting from the beginning or the end of the cover image, as shown in Figures 22.5 and 22.6.

In Figure 22.6, the stego image's histogram differs according to the cover image's histogram when different LSBs of the pixels are used to embed message bits. Hence, the imperceptibility of the LSB steganography using 3rd and 4th LSB bits of pixels reduces against the steg-attacks, as shown in Figure 22.6 [51].

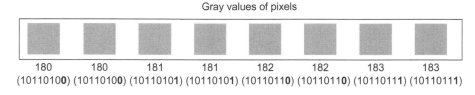

Gray values of pixels

180	180	181	181	182	182	183	183
(10110100)	(10110100)	(10110101)	(10110101)	(10110110)	(10110110)	(10110111)	(10110111)

Message bits of A: **01000001**

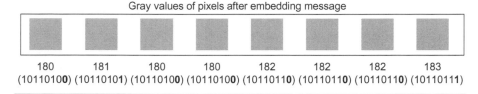

Gray values of pixels after embedding message

180	181	180	180	182	182	182	183
(10110100)	(10110101)	(10110100)	(10110100)	(10110110)	(10110110)	(10110110)	(10110111)

Figure 22.5 Embedding the secret message' bits in LSBs of pixel's gray values.

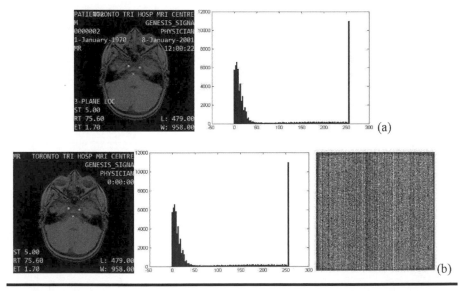

Figure 22.6 Cover and stego images, histograms, and difference images between cover and stego images, (a) cover image, (b) stego image by 1st LSB.
(Continued)

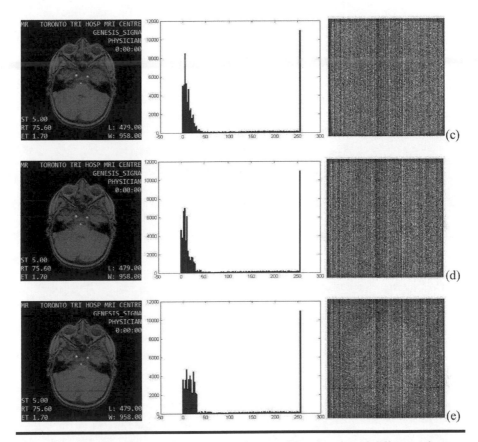

Figure 22.6 (Continued)   Cover and stego images, histograms, and difference images between cover and stego images, (c) stego images by 2nd LSB, (d) stego image by 3rd LSB, (e) stego image by 4th LSB bit. (From Micro Dicom Viewer Software Website, Available: http://www.microdicom.com/component/jdownloads/send/2-images/1-mr.html, November 19, 2017.)

In sequential LSB steganography, the embedding capacity of DICOM series for one patient is: Image Height * Image Width * Number of Frames* Bytes per Pixel. We have 512 × 512 pixels in each DICOM frame, 200 frames, 2 bytes per pixel, so that we can embed 512 * 512 * 200 * 2=104 857 600 bits. More LSBs of the DICOM image's pixels may be used to increase the embedding message capacity.

If the message combines with patient personal information, health report, and biological signals (EEG, ECG, EMG etc.), there are two ways to solve the embedding message capacity problem. First, the features of biological signals for the diagnosis or treatment are extracted manually or by signal processing methods and these features are embedded in the DICOM images. In the second method, the embedding message is compressed by lossless compression methods [1]. Then it is

Message Length	Patient Personal Information	Diagnosis Report	Information of EEG Signal File Header	Size of Segmented Signal	Segmented Signal Data

Figure 22.7 The embedding message for each DICOM file. (From Karakış, R. et al., *Comput. Biol. Med.*, 67, 172–183, 2015; From Karakış, R., A fuzzy logic-based steganography application for MRI AND EEG data of epilepsy, PhD Thesis, Gazi University, Informatics Institute, Ankara, 2015.)

sequentially segmented and hidden in each file of the DICOM series. The generated message for each DICOM file includes: the length of message, patient personal information, diagnosis report, the information of biological signal file header (time points, sampling intervals, starting time, number of electrodes etc.), the size of segmented biological signal data, and segmented biological signal, as shown in Figure 22.7 [1,52].

However, the sequential LSB method is vulnerable to steg-analysis, so that embedding message has to be secured by encryption. Furthermore, LSBs of pixels should be selected randomly for embedding process by using histogram, pixel value differences, statistical values, similarity, or fuzzy logic [1,52]. Four methods selecting random LSBs of pixels are mentioned the following.

The first method embeds the message starting from the center of the image to protect the message against steg-attacks such as rotation, scaling, or translation. For this reason, the image moments, which give the different information about images, can be used in order to obtain the center of images (x_0, y_0). The zeroth order image moment that is the mass of image is defined in Equation 22.4 [16].

$$m_{00} = \sum_{x=0}^{M-1} \sum_{y=0}^{N-1} f(x, y) \tag{22.4}$$

Where f represents the image matrix whose size is $M \times N$. The first and second order image moments are given in Equation 22.5 and 22.6, respectively [16].

$$m_{10} = \sum_{x=0}^{M-1} \sum_{y=0}^{N-1} x.f(x, y) \tag{22.5}$$

$$m_{01} = \sum_{x=0}^{M-1} \sum_{y=0}^{N-1} y.f(x, y) \tag{22.6}$$

The first and second order image moments (m_{10} and m_{01}) can be used to find the center of the image (x_0, y_0) which is defined in Equation 22.7 [16].

$$x_0 = \frac{m_{10}}{m_{00}}, y_0 = \frac{m_{01}}{m_{00}} \tag{22.7}$$

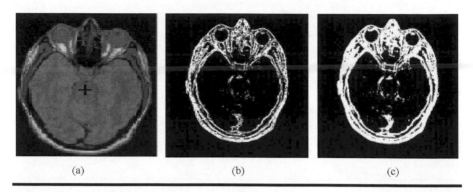

Figure 22.8 (a) selection the center of image, (b) selection pixels with 3 × 3 window (*k* = 3), (c) selection pixels with 5 × 5 window (*k* = 5). (From Raul, R.-C. et al., *Electronics, Communications and Computers, CONIELECOMP '07, 17th International Conference on*, 32–37, 2007.)

Statistical values such as mean, standard deviance, or variance can be used to select the pixels to embed message. For instance, the variance values of pixel are calculated in the block with $k \times k$ size of the pixels starting from the center of image, and then the possible pixels are determined according to a threshold value defined by user, as shown in Figure 22.8. The variance formula is given in Equation 22.8 [16].

$$\sigma^2 = \frac{1}{k^2} \sum_{x=0}^{k-1} \sum_{y=0}^{k-1} \left(f(x,y) - \mu \right)^2$$

$$\mu = \frac{1}{k^2} \sum_{x=0}^{k-1} \sum_{y=0}^{k-1} f(x,y) \tag{22.8}$$

In the second method, RGB (R: Red, G: Green, B: Blue) values of medical image can be converted into YCbCr (Y: Luminance, Cb: Chrominance Blue, Cr: Chrominance Red) color space with Equation 22.9. The bits of the message are replaced with the pixel LSBs of Cb and Cr components. After embedding the message, YCbCr color components of medical image are converted into RGB space to generate the stego-medical image. It secures the message against steg-attacks such as image compression, motion blur, erosion, multiplicative, averaged, dilated, salt and pepper noise, and Gaussian noise, as shown in Figure 22.9 [37].

$$\begin{pmatrix} Y \\ Cb \\ Cr \end{pmatrix} = \begin{pmatrix} 0.299 & 0.587 & 0.114 \\ -0.168636 & 0.232932 & -0.064296 \\ 0.499813 & -0.418531 & -0.081282 \end{pmatrix} \begin{pmatrix} R \\ G \\ B \end{pmatrix} \tag{22.9}$$

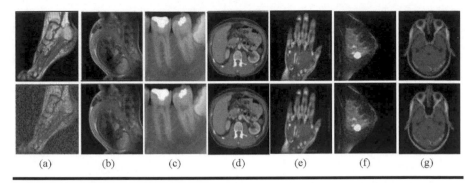

(a)   (b)   (c)   (d)   (e)   (f)   (g)

Figure 22.9 **Steg attacks (a) 40% salt and pepper, (b) 9% JPEG, (c) compressed, (d) erode, (e) Gaussian, (f) averaged, (g) motion blur. (From Koley, S. et al., *IJIGSP*, 3, 18–31, 2014.)**

In the third method, similarity values of pixels determine randomly the LSBs of pixels to embed message. Initially, the gray level differences of each color component ($\Delta R = \left| L_{R_1} - L_{R_2} \right|$, $\Delta G = \left| L_G - L_{G_2} \right|$, $\Delta B = \left| L_{B_1} - L_{B_2} \right|$) between neighboring pixels of the image in the 3×3 window are calculated. Euclidean norm, which measures the color distance using these gray level differences, is defined in Equation 22.10 [1,52].

$$d_{i,j} = \frac{1}{\sqrt{3}}(\Delta R^2 + \Delta G^2 + \Delta B^2) \tag{22.10}$$

Secondly, color similarity is measured using an exponential function of distance [53–54]. It is represented in Equation 22.11 [1,52].

$$C_k(x_i, x_j) = \exp\left(\frac{-d_{ij}^q}{D_n}\right) \tag{22.11}$$

Where D_n is the normalization coefficient, and it is defined by user. Thirdly, local similarity values with the 3×3 window for each pixel are obtained by using Equation 22.12 [1,52].

$$S_k = \frac{1}{8}\sum_{n=1}^{9} C_{k,n} \ for \ k \neq n \tag{22.12}$$

The local similarity values of image higher than a threshold value (*Th*) are chosen to embed the message bits. In this method, it is possible to select random LSB, but it includes the parameters (D_n and *Th*) to be obtained by trial and error, and Euclidean norm are not efficient to determine the perceptual color proximity. For this reason, similarity values of the medical images may be determined by fuzzy logic.

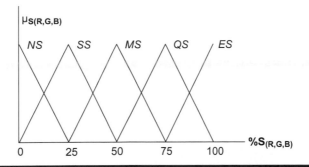

Figure 22.10   Five triangular fuzzy sets to fuzzify the gray level differences of pixels. (From Karakış, R. et al., *Comput. Biol. Med.,* **67, 172–183, 2015; From Karakış, R., A fuzzy logic-based steganography application for MRI AND EEG data of epilepsy, PhD Thesis, Gazi University, Informatics Institute, Ankara, 2015.)**

In fourth method based on fuzzy logic (FL), the gray level differences $(\Delta R + \Delta G + \Delta B)$ between neighbor pixels in a 3 × 3 window are first calculated for each color component [9]. These gray level differences of pixels are fuzzified by fuzzy sets with linguistic values which can be triangular, trapezoid, or Gaussian. Figure 22.10 shows the five triangular fuzzy sets (Not Similar: NS, Slightly Similar: SS, Moderately Similar: MS, Quite Similar: QS, and Exactly Similar: ES). The fuzzy sets can be at the interval [3–7]. However, three fuzzy sets may obtain same similar values for image pixels and seven fuzzy sets may increase the computational time [1,52].

In fuzzification stage, the membership values of the pixels are obtained with fuzzy sets. Fuzzy rules, which are specific for each problem and defined by experts, are used to compute the fuzzy output with respect to the fuzzified gray level differences of pixels for each color component. The fuzzy rules for similarity may be as follows:

Rule 1: If ΔR is Zero and ΔG is Large and ΔB is Medium, Then P_1 and P_2 are MS,
Rule 2: If ΔR is Large and ΔG is Zero and ΔB is Zero, Then P_1 and P_2 are QS,
Rule 3: If ΔR is Large and ΔG is Large and ΔB is Zero, Then P_1 and P_2 are SS,
and so on.

In defuzzification stage, the similar values as output are obtained by a defuzzification function such as center-average method, centroid method, mean-max, center of sums, center of largest area etc. The center-average defuzzification method is given in Equation 22.13 [1,54].

$$
C = \frac{\displaystyle\sum_{j=1}^{z} S_j \mu_{prem}^{j}(L)}{\displaystyle\sum_{j=1}^{z} \mu_{prem}^{j}(L)}
\tag{22.13}
$$

where:

Z is the number of the rules

S_j is the center of similarity value in the *jth* rule

$\mu_{prem}^j(L)$ is defined in Equation 22.14 [1,54].

$$\mu_{prem}^j(L) = \mu_R^j(L_{\Delta R})\mu_G^j(L_{\Delta G})\mu_B^j(L_{\Delta B}) \qquad (22.14)$$

In the last stage, the local similarity values of neighboring pixels are obtained by Equation 22.12. The coordinates mean similarity values of the neighboring pixels are used to replace the LSBs of the message. Figure 22.11 indicates the cover and stego images generated by similarity and FL based LSB methods.

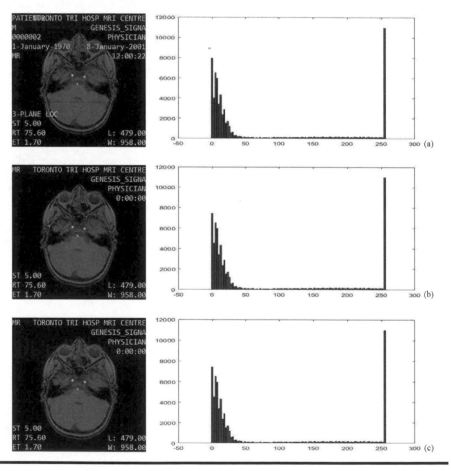

Figure 22.11 Cover and stego images (a) Cover image and its histogram, (b) Stego image of the similarity based LSB algorithm and its histogram, (c) Stego image of the FL based LSB algorithm and its histogram. (From Micro Dicom Viewer Software Website, Available: http://www.microdicom.com/component/jdownloads/send/2-images/1-mr.html, November 19, 2017.)

As shown in Figure 22.11, LSB based steganography in spatial domain has high imperceptibility and capacity.

22.3.2 RONI Based Steganography

The RONI based steganography methods hide information within RONI of medical images not to affect the patient diagnosis or treatment [7,17–23]. The border pixels or background of the medical image can be identified as RONI. It is difficult to generalize the RONI selection because the ROIs in the image are independent of the image modality. Furthermore, since each patient has a different head shape, the same ROIs cannot be selected from the images. For this reason, ROIs selection may be manually performed to personalize by a doctor using a rectangle, ellipse, or polygon tool of the DICOM viewer software. RONI should have no relevance the diagnosis, and it should have the capacity to embed message [17,22].

RONI based steganography can be performed within spatial or transform domain, as it can be shown in Figure 22.12. First, medical images are segmented as ROI and RONI. Second, the detail parameters of the embedding function are

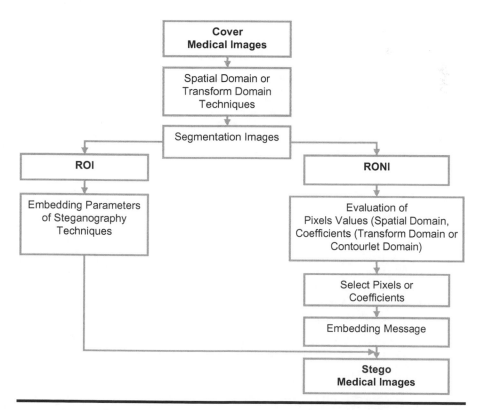

Figure 22.12   The flowchart of ROI-based steganography techniques.

hidden in the ROI not to affect the diagnosis. Third, the message is embedded into determined coefficients in transform domain or pixels in spatial domain according to the embedding function. Finally, stego image are constituted using ROI and RONIs of medical images.

In spatial domain, the border-pixels of medical images which is RONI can be automatically or semi-automatically selected by rectangle, contourlet method, or threshold values. If the rectangle frame is used to obtain RONI, its information (coordinates, width and height etc.) should be embedded in the medical image to extract the hidden message. Furthermore, background of medical image can be automatically segmented using a threshold value. Thresholding methods can be categorized into histogram shape based, clustering based, entropy based, object attribute based, the spatial, and local methods, respectively [58]. The clustering based methods are clustered the gray level values of pixels in background and foreground regions. The entropy based methods use the entropy of the image's background and foreground. Especially, these two methods can be used to determine RONI and ROIs of the medical images [55]. For instance, Otsu thresholding method, which is a clustering based methods, find an optimum threshold by means of minimizing the weighted sum within class variances of the foreground and background pixels in an image. Its formulation is defined in Equation 22.15. [19,55].

$$T_{opt} = \arg \max \left\{ \frac{P(T)[1 - P(T)][m_f(T) - m_b(T)]^2}{P(T)\sigma_f^2(T) + [1 - P(T)]\sigma_f^2(T)} \right\} \qquad (22.15)$$

where:
$P(T)$ is probability function of image
m_f and m_b are the mean of the foreground and background
σ_f^2 and σ_b^2 are foreground and background's variances [55].

The optimal threshold value (T_{opt}) determines ROI and ROIs of medical images and the LSBs of image pixels in this region are used to embed message bits, as shown in Figure 22.13. However, the threshold value of stego image may be different in the extracting stage, because the embedding process changes the gray level values of the pixels. For this reason, the optimal threshold value may be combined with the message before embedding.

RONI based steganography in spatial domain is vulnerable to copy-attacks. For this reason, the message can be embedded into coefficients of frequency domain instead of spatial domain to ensure the robustness against copy-attacks. In frequency domain, DCT gives an image which is a sum of sinusoids at different magnitudes and frequencies. It is widely used in lossy compression of audio or image, because the essential information of the image is in a few coefficients of DCT. The formulation of the two-dimensional (2D) DCT with a $M \times N$ image is defined in Equations 22.16 and 22.17 [12].

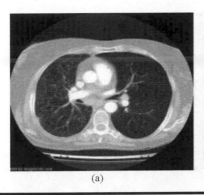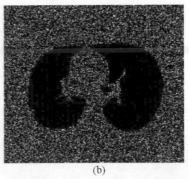

(a)   (b)

Figure 22.13   (a) Stego images by threshold-based ROI algorithm, (b) difference image between cover and stego images. (From Memon, N. A. and Gilani S.A.M., *Int. J. Comput. Math.*, 88, 265–280, 2011.)

$$T_{pq} = \alpha_p \alpha_q \sum_{m=0}^{M-1} \sum_{n=0}^{N-1} F_{mn} cos \frac{\pi(2m+1)p}{2M} cos \frac{\pi(2n+1)q}{2N} \qquad (22.16)$$

$$\alpha_p = \left\{ \begin{array}{l} 1/\sqrt{N}, p=0 \\ \sqrt{2/M}, 1 \le p \le M-1 \end{array} \right\}, \alpha_q = \left\{ \begin{array}{l} 1/\sqrt{N}, q=0 \\ \sqrt{2/N}, 1 \le q \le N-1 \end{array} \right\} \qquad (22.17)$$

where:
p is $0 \le p \le M - 1$, and
q is $0 \le q \le N - 1$.

The DCT coefficients of the cover medical image are replaced by the message bits and then quantization is performed. Inverse 2D-DCT returns the stego-medical image into space domain [12].

DWT is another transform technique that obtain both frequency and temporal information of a 2D image. It is especially used for compression and denoising of image. DWT decompose the image into low and high frequencies in multiple levels of resolution with filters such as Haar, Daubechies Biorthogonal, Symlets etc. In DWT, the high-pass filter H determines the detail coefficients and the low-pass filter L represents the approximation coefficients of the medical image. The decomposition stage is repeated until a number of levels, as shown in Figure 22.14. Two level decomposition of the 2D-DWT generates four sub-bands which are LL (approximation), LH (horizontal), HL (vertical) and HH (diagonal). The LL sub-bands contains the lowest resolution with a half-sized of the medical image, but it has the most information to reconstruct the medical image. The other sub-bands are the vertical, horizontal and diagonal details of the medical images. The DWT of medical image $f(x, y)$ with $M \times N$ size is represented in Equations 22.18 and 22.19 [56].

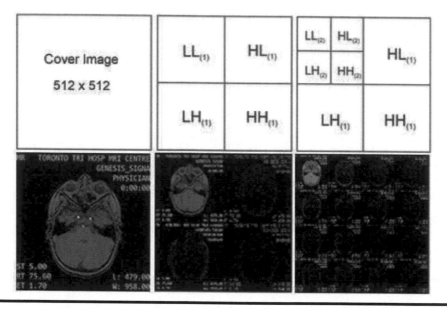

Figure 22.14 DWT decomposition process with low and high-pass filters of two and three levels resolution.

$$W\varphi(j_0, m, n) = \frac{1}{\sqrt{MN}} \sum_{x=0}^{M-1} \sum_{y=0}^{N-1} f(x, y)\varphi j_{0,m,n}(x, y) \qquad (22.18)$$

$$W_\psi^i(j, m, n) = \frac{1}{\sqrt{MN}} \sum_{x=0}^{M-1} \sum_{y=0}^{N-1} f(x, y)\psi j_{0,m,n}(x, y) \qquad (22.19)$$

where:

$W_\varphi(j_0, m, n)$ coefficients give the approximation of medical image as j_0 is an arbitrary starting scale

$W_\psi^i(j, m, n)$ coefficients add the horizontal, vertical and diagonal details for $j > j_0$ [56]. In RONI based steganography with DWT, ROI and RONIs of the medical image are first defined, as shown in Figure 22.15. Secondly, DWT decomposes the medical image into the LL, LH, HL and HH sub-bands. The coefficients of LH, HL and HH sub-bands are used to embed message bits because LL coefficients have approximate values of the image. After embedding the message, the stego medical image is reconstructed by all the information from high-pass and low-pass filters.

The contourlet transform is better than wavelet transform in determining edges and contours of an image. For this reason, RONI based steganography can be performed by contourlet transform that decomposes the image intolow and high frequency sub-bands, respectively. For each sub-band, directional decomposition

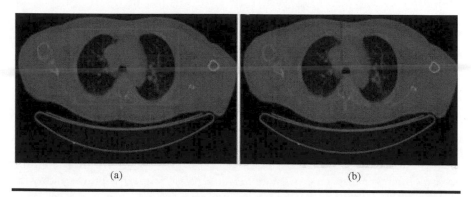

(a)   (b)

Figure 22.15 **(a) Cover image with ROI, (b) stego image after embedding message. (From Acharya, U.R. et al., *Comput. Biol. Med.*, 33, 303–310.)**

is ensured by directional filter banks and then directional sub-bands generate the image with multiple scales, as shown in Figure 22.16. [18]. Before embedding the message, ROI and RONIs of medical images are first obtained according to a rectangle frame or a thresholding value. Secondly, the coefficients of the low-pass sub-band (I_l) in the medical image, which is obtained by the contourlet transform, are replaced by the message bits. If the message capacity is high, the detail sub-bands should be preferred to embed message for the imperceptibility [18].

A disadvantage of these methods is the capacity of a hidden message that is directly related to RONI area size. RONIs of medical images generally include black background, so that it can be easily captured by copy-attacks. However, they may contain gray-level areas of interest if medical image is segmented as background, brain, skull or tumor, etc. Segmentation may increase the embedding message capacity, and ROI-based steganography in transform domain can be robust when the embedding process is performed by wavelet or contourlet transform.

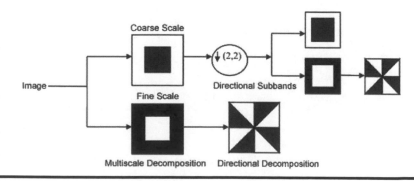

Figure 22.16 **Decomposition with contourlet transform. (From Rahimi, F. and Rabbani, H., *BioMed. Eng. OnLine*, 10, 1–18, 2011.)**

22.3.3 Reversible Steganography

The third technique is reversible steganography in medical images. Reversible steganography techniques are preferred for image authentication and copyright protection applications. The aim in these methods is to restore the original cover image without any deterioration after the hidden message is extracted from stego image [7,24–31]. In this method, patient personal data is hidden in spatial domain using histogram shifting, statistical differences of pixels' gray level values, or contrast mapping. In transform domain, the message is embedded into wavelet coefficients or discrete cosine coefficients of medical images [7]. The reversible methods have high message capacity, visual quality, and low complexity. Furthermore, the embedding message method should be implemented in all images in order to prevent copy-attacks. It should preserve the details of medical images, and not leave any salt and pepper noise. The embedding methods comply with the sparse histogram of intensity levels in medical images. Some reversible methods need a location map to restore stego images, but it can increase the complexity in large medical image or video series. For this reason, reversible methods should not be dependent on the location map [29]. In this chapter, we give the following details of three reversible techniques.

The first method is performed by histogram shifting. A zero point and a peak point is obtained according to an image's histogram, as shown in Figure 22.17. A zero-point means that the grayscale value of any pixel is not found in the image, and a peak point is the maximum number of pixels' gray scale value in the image. The pixel selection for embedding is performed one or multiple pairs of maximum and minimum points at the interval [0, 255]. For an MXN image, pseudo code of one pair reversible embedding is given as follows [25].

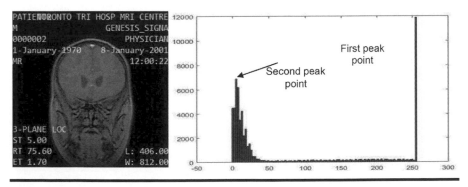

Figure 22.17 Histogram of medical cover image. (From Micro Dicom Viewer Software Website, Available: http://www.microdicom.com/component/jdownloads/send/2-images/1-mr.html, November 19, 2017.)

1. Generate image histogram $H(x)$.
2. Find the maximum point $h(a)$ and minimum point $h(b)$ at the interval $[0, 255]$.
3. If $h(b)>0$, set $h(b) = 0$, and add the coordinates information of $h(b)$ in the embedding message bits.
4. Shift the histogram to the right by adding 1 to the pixel's gray scale values.
5. Scan the gray scale values of maximum point. If the embedding message bit is 1, add 1 to the gray scale value of pixels. If it is 0, not to change the pixel's value [25].

The embedding capacity of one pair reversible method is restricted by $h(a)$. For this reason, multi pair reversible embedding may be used if the embedding capacity is too much. The pseudo code of multi pair reversible embedding is given below.

1. Generate image histogram $H(x)$.
2. Find three minimum point $h(b_1)$, $h(b_2)$, $h(b_3)$ and three maximum point $h(a_1)$, $h(a_2)$, $h(a_3)$ at the interval $[0, 255]$.
3. Apply the above pseudo code steps 3 to 5 for each pair.

In the extracting stage of histogram shifting reversible method, maximum and minimum points (a, b) are first obtained from the image histogram. Secondly, the embedding message bits are gathered from the gray level values of pixels with respect to the maximum point. If the gray level value is $a + 1$, message bit is 1. If the gray level value is a, message bit is 0. Thirdly, the pixel value is subtracted by 1, and if there is the coordinates information of $h(b)$ into extracted message bits, its value is changed. Finally, stego image is obtained from the cover image without any distortion [25].

In second method with histogram shifting, the image is first divided into blocks (4×4 or 16×16 etc.) to determine the optimum threshold value k instead of the finding the multi maximum and minimum points of image histogram. In each block, the number of the maximum and minimum point pairs (p_i: peaks, z_i: zeros) can be defined by user, and all pairs should not decrease both image and perceptual qualities. The embedding stage with the pairs in blocks can be performed as follows [15].

1. $p_i>z_i$, the pixel's gray values between z_i+1 and p_i are decreased by 1 to shift the histogram to the left. If the message bit is 1, the pixel's gray values as p_i-1 are increased by 1, otherwise they are not changed.
2. $z_i>p_i$, the pixel's gray values between p_i+1 and z_i+1 are increased by 1. If the message bit is 1, the pixel's gray values as p_i-1 are increased by 1, otherwise they are not changed.

In the extracting message stage, the image is divided into the blocks. The message with the pairs in blocks can be detected as follows [15].

1. $p_i>z_i$, if the pixel's gray value is p_i, the message bit is 0. If the pixel's gray value is p_i-1, the message bit is 1. In order to reverse original image, the pixel's gray values between z_i *and* p_i-2 are increased by 1.

2. $z_i>p_i$, if the pixel's gray value is p_i, the message bit is 0. If the pixel's gray value is p_i+1, the message bit is 1. In order to reverse original image, the pixel's gray values between p_i+2 *and* z_i are decreased by 1 [15].

In third method with histogram shifting, the medical image with MxN is first divided into u × v blocks. Secondly, the difference values of blocks are computed by dividing blocks into A and B zone which are marked by "+" and "−", respectively. The difference value is formulated in Equation 22.20 [29].

$$\alpha = \frac{1}{n}\sum_{i=1}^{n}(a_i - b_i) \tag{22.20}$$

where:

n is the number of pixel pairs

a_i and b_i are marked pixels by "+" and "−", respectively

Thirdly, a new difference image is constructed by using difference values of blocks. An optimal threshold is calculated separately for positive and negative blocks of the difference image with Equations 22.21 and 22.22, respectively [29].

$$k_{p-h} = \left[\frac{\alpha_{max-p} - \alpha_{zero} + 1}{Partition\ Level}\right], k_{N-h} = \left[\frac{\alpha_{zero} - \alpha_{min-N} + 1}{Partition\ Level}\right] \tag{22.21}$$

$$k = k_{p-h} + \left|mod(k_{p-h}, 2)\right|, k = \left(k_{N-h} + \left|mod(k_{n-h}, 2)\right|\right)* -1 \tag{22.22}$$

Where α_{zero} is the center coordinate of the 0. α_{max-p} and α_{min-N} is the maximum difference value of the positive blocks and the minimum difference value of the negative blocks, respectively. Partition level is a value by defined user, which depend on α_{max-p}, α_{min-N} and α_{zero}. For instance, $\alpha_{max-p} = 2.45$ and $\alpha_{zero} = 0$ or $\alpha_{min-N} = -2.45$ and $\alpha_{zero} = 0$, partition level can be 3 [29].

Fourthly, message is embedded with the positive and negative blocks of medical image according to partition level, the difference value(α), and histogram shifting with k. If the partition level is set to 3, the message hiding stage in the positive blocks is performed as follows [29].

1. The difference value (α) is between 0 and k. If the message bit is "1", the histogram of the positive block is shifted the right with k. In the other case, no shifting is performed.

2. The difference value (α) is between k and $2k$. If the message bit is "1", the histogram of the positive block is shifted the right with $2k$. In the other case, the histogram of the positive block is shifted the right with k.
3. The difference value (α) is between $2k$ and $3k$. If the message bit is "1", the histogram of the positive block is shifted the right with $3k$. In the other case, the histogram of the positive block is shifted the right with $2k$.

If the partition level is set to 3, the message hiding in the negative blocks is performed as follows.

1. The difference value (α) is between 0 and $-k$. If the message bit is "1", the histogram of the negative block is shifted the left with k. In the other case, no shifting is performed.
2. The difference value (α) is between $-2k$ and $-k$. If the message bit is "1", the histogram of the negative block is shifted the left with $2k$. In the other case, the histogram of the negative block is shifted the left with k.
3. The difference value (α) is between $-3k$ and $2k$. If the message bit is "1", the histogram of the negative block is shifted the left with $3k$. In the other case, the histogram of the negative block is shifted the left with $2k$.

The shifted histogram may be caused of overflow/underflow problem for the medical images which are recorded with sign or unsigned bit. To solve the overflow/underflow problem, utilization rate should be computed by using intensity rate, underflow/overflow rate, and bit depth of the medical images. In medical images with high bit depth such as 16 bit, there is only underflow problem, so that the histogram should be shifted left by the value of underflow to overcome this problem [29].

In the extracting of the third method, the block size, partition level, the length of the message, and the value of overflow/underflow for shifting histogram have to be known. Firstly, the histogram of image is shifted by the value of overflow/underflow. Secondly, the image is divided into the blocks whose difference values are calculated by using Equation 22.20. The difference values give a difference image. Thirdly, optimal threshold is found by Equations 22.23 and 22.24 [29].

$$k_{p-h} = \left\lceil \frac{\alpha_{max-p} - \alpha_{zero} + 1}{Partition\ Level * 2} \right\rceil, k_{N-h} = \left\lceil \frac{\alpha_{zero} - \alpha_{min-N} + 1}{Partition\ Level * 2} \right\rceil \quad (22.23)$$

$$k = k_{p-h} + \left| mod(k_{p-h}, 2) \right|, k = \left(k_{N-h} + \left| mod(k_{N-h}, 2) \right| \right) * -1 \quad (22.24)$$

The threshold value (k) is used obtain message bits according to the difference values. In positive area, if the difference value is in the zone 0, the message bit is extracted as 0 and the difference value is shifted left. If the difference value is in zone 1, the message bit is extracted as 1 and the difference value is shifted left. On the other hand, shifting is performed to the right both zone 0 and zone 1. This extracting process gives us the message and original image as defined cover image [29].

Imperceptibility of reversible data hiding techniques is so high with respect to low capacity of embedding message. Hence, these methods cannot be efficient, if hidden message includes patient information such as biological signal, doctor's comment, and report [7,24–31].

22.4 Comparison Metrics of Medical Image Steganography

In literature, the difference between the cover and stego images are analyzed to evaluate the embedding process by using the different comparison methods which are MSE (mean square of error), PSNR (peak signal-to-noise ratio), SSIM (structural similarity measure), UQI (universal quality index), and correlation coefficient (*R*). The first is commonly used MSE function which is the average of the squares of the errors. It is given in Equation 22.25.

$$MSE = \frac{1}{MN} \sum_{i=0}^{M-1} \sum_{j=0}^{N-1} \left(S(x_i, x_j) - C(x_i, x_j) \right)^2 \qquad (22.25)$$

where:
   x and y are the image coordinates
   M and N represent the dimensions of the image
   $S(x, y)$ and $C(x, y)$ symbolize the stego and cover medical images, respectively.

Peak signal-to-noise ratio (PSNR), which is an approximation to human perception, is used to measure the image distortion. The signal is the cover medical image's data, and the noise is the embedded message in the stego medical image. The PSNR function is represented in Equation 22.26. The unit of PSNR is decibel (dB) which is a logarithmic scale and take a value from 0 and infinity. However, if PSNR values below 30 dB, it indicates high degradation, so that the hidden message is perceptible. For this reason, PSNR values should be higher than 40 dB and above to ensure high imperceptibility [12].

$$PSNR = 10 \log \left(\frac{C_{max}^2}{MSE} \right) \qquad (22.26)$$

C_{max}^2 indicates the maximum value of the image. In literature, its default value is 255 for 8 bit images. However, when the images' gray level values are lower than 255, the square of C is taken. The default value in this case increases PSNR value while it should be less. For this reason, C should be considered the largest value of the image [12].

MSE and PSNR are inconvenient to express Human Visual System (HVS). In literature, UQI, and SSIM are proposed to measure the quality of steganography process according to HVS [57–58]. SSIM is a perceptual metric using image quality degradation as perceived change in structural information. In SSIM, structural information which indicates the structure of patterns in the scene of image, is not related to the average luminance and contrast that can be vary across in scene. The similarity between two image signals can be measured by the comparisons of luminance ($l(x,y)$), contrast ($c(x,y)$), and structure ($s(x,y)$). First, the luminance and contrast measurements of each signals are calculated by using the mean intensity (μ_x, μ_y) and the standard deviation (σ_x, σ_y). Second, the comparisons of the luminance, contrast and structure are obtained by these measurements values. Luminance comparison is given in Equation 22.27 [58].

$$I(x, y) = \frac{(2\mu_x\mu_y + c_1)}{\mu_x^2\mu_y^2 + c_1} \quad (22.27)$$

Where $c_1 = (k_1 L)^2$ is the constant to ensure stability when $\mu_x^2 + \mu_y^2$ is very close to zero. L is dynamic range of pixel values that is 255 for 8-bit gray scale images and $k_1 \ll 1$ is a small constant [58].

The contrast comparison is shown in Equation 22.28.

$$c(x, y) = \frac{(2\alpha_{xy} + c_2)}{\alpha_x^2 + \alpha_y^2 + c_2} \quad (22.28)$$

Where $c_2 = (k_2 L)^2$ and $k_2 \ll 1$ are constant [58].

The structure comparison that is correlated with luminance subtraction and variance normalization, is given in Equation 22.29.

$$s(x, y) = \frac{(\alpha_{xy} + c_3)}{(\alpha_x\alpha_y + c_3)} \quad (22.29)$$

SSIM combines the luminance, contrast, and structure comparisons with respect to Equation 22.30.

$$SSIM(x, y) = [I(x, y)c(x, y)s(x, y)] = \frac{(2\mu_x\mu_y + c_1)(2\alpha_{xy} + c_2)}{(\mu_x^2 + \mu_x^2 + c_1)(\alpha_x^2 + \alpha_x^2 + c_2)} \quad (22.30)$$

UQI index is derived from the equation of SSIM where assume as $c_1 = c_2 = 0$. UQI evaluates the luminance and contrast degradation in the image scenes [57–58]. The formulation of UQI index is shown in Equation 22.31.

$$UQI(x, y) = \frac{(4\mu_x\mu_y 2\alpha_{xy})}{(\mu_x^2 + \mu_y^2)(\alpha_x^2 + \alpha_y^2)} \qquad (22.31)$$

Correlation coefficient (R) compares the cover and stego images by using Equation 22.32 [59].

$$R = \frac{\sum^{M}\sum^{N}(S_{MN} - \bar{S}) - (C_{MN} - \bar{C})}{\sqrt{\left(\sum^{M}\sum^{N}(S_{MN} - \bar{S})^2\right)\left(\sum^{M}\sum^{N}(C_{MN} - \bar{C})^2\right)}} \qquad (22.32)$$

Where $\bar{S}$ and $\bar{C}$ are the mean intensity values of the pixels in stego image and cover images, respectively [59].

22.5 Conclusion

In MI systems, medical data can be obtained by cyber-attacks. Encryption and steganography is generally used to secure medical data. In medical steganography application, patient personal data (name, birthdate, weight, address etc.) from a DICOM file header are embedded in spatial or transform domain, and these data can be only extracted by authority with a stego-key. Medical steganography techniques categorized into LSB based, RONI based and reversible steganography. LSB based method in spatial domain, which has high imperceptibility and embedding capacity, replaces sequentially or randomly the message' bits by the LSBs of image pixels' gray level values. RONI based steganography within spatial or transform domain, which has capacity problem, is used borders or black background of medical image to embed message. Reversible steganography method in spatial or transform domain, which has capacity problem, reconstruct original image without distortion after extracting message.

Especially, the capacity of embedding message and robustness are essential problem for medical steganography application. If a hidden message is combined with patient personal data, doctors' comment, diagnosis report, and biological signals, RONI- based and reversible steganography techniques may not be efficient due to high capacity. For this reason, LSB based steganography with lossless compression and encryption can ensure the confidentiality of the patient's information, and to reduce data repository. However, steganography techniques have to be robust against attacks. ROI-based steganography techniques in transform domain with DWT or contourlet transform can be performed both to embed and to secure messages. Furthermore, if the RONI based method uses both ROI and RONIs of medical image to embed the message without affecting diagnosis or treatment, it can solve the capacity problem. Similarly, if reversible steganography techniques can find optimal threshold values in blocks of image, it can embed more message bits.

In the future, DICOM medical file format, which includes the file header of the image with patient's personal data and the pixels' data, may be combined with the health reports, and other biological signals according to health standards in a new DICOM version.

References

1. Karakış, R., Güler, I., Çapraz, İ., Bilir, E. (2015). A novel fuzzy logic-based image steganography method to ensure medical data security, *Computers in Biology and Medicine*, 67: 172–183.
2. Electronic Health Record, http://en.wikipedia.org/wiki/Electronic_health_record (November 19, 2017).
3. Electronic Health Records Overview http://www.himss.org/files/HIMSSorg/content/files/Code%20180%20MITRE%20Key%20Components%20of%20an%20EHR.pdf (November 19, 2017).
4. Coatrieux, G., Maitre, H., Sankur, B., Rolland, Y., Collorec, R. (2000). Relevance of watermarking in medical imaging, Information Technology Applications in Biomedicine, *Proceedings 2000 IEEE EMBS International Conference on*, 250–255.
5. https://www.benton.org/headlines/medical-data-has-become-next-cybersecurity-target (November 19, 2017).
6. Nyeem, H., Wageeh Boles, W., Colin Boyd, C. (2013). A review of medical image watermarking requirements for teleradiology, *Journal of Digital Imaging*, 26: 326–343.
7. Coatrieux, G., Lecornu, L., Sankur, B., Roux, C. (2006). A review of image watermarking applications in healthcare, Engineering in Medicine and Biology Society, EMBS '06, *28th Annual International Conference of the IEEE*, 4691–4694.
8. About DICOM, The National Electrical Manufacturers Association (NEMA), http://medical.nema.org/Dicom/about-DICOM.html (November 19, 2017).
9. Haidekker, M. (2011). Image storage, transport, and compression, *Advanced Biomedical Image Analysis*, 386–412.
10. Kuang, L.-Q., Zhang, Y., Han, X. (2009). Watermarking image authentication in hospital information system, *Information Engineering and Computer Science, 2009*, 1–4.
11. Oosterwijk, H. (2010). The DICOM standard, overview and characteristics, http://www.ringholm.com/docs/02010_en.htm (November 19, 2017).
12. Cheddad, A., Condell, J., Curran, K., McKevitt, P. (2010). Digital image steganography: Survey and analysis of current methods, *Signal Processing*, 90: 727–752.
13. Navas, K. A., Sasikumar, M. (2007). Survey of medical image watermarking algorithms, *SETIT 2007 fourth International Conference: Sciences of Electronic, Technologies of Information and Telecommunications*, TUNISIA, 1–6.
14. Golpira, H., Danyali, H. (2010). Reversible blind watermarking for medical images based on wavelet histogram shifting, *IEEE International Symposium on Signal Processing and Information Technology* (ISSPIT), 31–36.
15. Fallahpour, M., Megias, D., Ghanbari, M. (2011). Reversible and high-capacity data hiding in medical images, *IET Image Processing*, 5(2): 190–197.

16. Raul, R.-C., Claudia, F.-U., Trinidad-Bias, G.J. (2007). Data hiding scheme for medical images, *Electronics, Communications and Computers, CONIELECOMP '07, 17th International Conference on*, 32–37.

17. Ravali, K., Kumar, A.P., Asadi, S. (2011). Carrying digital watermarking for medical images using mobile devices, *International Journal of Computer Science Engineering and Technology*, 1(7): 366–369.

18. Rahimi, F., Rabbani, H. (2011). A dual adaptive watermarking scheme in contourlet domain for DICOM images, *BioMedical Engineering OnLine*, 10(53): 1–18.

19. Memon, N.A., Gilani, S.A.M. (2011). Watermarking of chest CT scan medical images for content authentication, *International Journal of Computer Mathematics*, 88 (2): 265–280.

20. Zain, J.M., Fauzi A.R.M., Aziz A.A. (2006). Clinical evaluation of watermarked medical images, *Proceedings of the 28th IEEE EMBS Annual International Conference*, New York, 5459–5462.

21. Shukla, A., Singh, C. (2014). Medical image authentication through watermarking, *International Journal of Advanced Research in Computer Science & Technology*, 2(2): 292–295.

22. Nyeem, H., Boles, W., Boyd, C. (2015). Content-independent embedding scheme for multi-modal medical image watermarking. *BioMedical Engineering OnLine*, 14(7): 1–19.

23. Fatemizadeh, E., Maneshi, M. (2012). A new watermarking algorithm based on human visual system for content integrity verification of region of interest, *Computing and Informatics*, 31: 877–899.

24. Huang, S.-C., Lin, M.-S. (2010). A high-capacity reversible data-hiding scheme for medical images, *Journal of Medical and Biological Engineering*, 30(5): 289–296.

25. Ni, Z., Shi, Y.Q., Ansari, N., Su W. (2006). Reversible data hiding, *IEEE Transactions on Circuits and Systems for Video Technology*, 16: 354–362.

26. Tseng, H.W., Hsieh, C.P. (2008). Reversible data hiding based on image histogram modification, *The Imaging Science Journal*, 56: 271–278.

27. Lin, C.C., Tai W.L., Chang, C.C. (2008). Multilevel reversible data hiding based on histogram modification of difference images, *Pattern Recognition*, 41: 3582–3591.

28. Huang, L.-C., Tseng, L.-Y., Min-Shiang Hwang, M.-S. (2012). The study on data hiding in medical images, *International Journal of Network Security*, 14(6): 301–309.

29. Huang, L.-C., Tseng, L.-Y., Hwang, M.-S. (2013). A reversible data hiding method by histogram shifting in high quality medical images, *Journal of Systems and Software*, 86: 716–727.

30. Lou, D.-C., Hu, M.-C., Liu, J.-L. (2009). Multiple layer data hiding scheme for medical images, *Computer Standards & Interfaces*, 31: 329–335.

31. Tan, C.-K., Changwei Ng, J., Xu, X., Poh, C.L., Guan, Y.L., Sheah, K. (2011). Security protection of DICOM medical images using dual-layer reversible watermarking with tamper detection capability, *Journal of Digital Imaging*, 24(3): 528–540.

32. Zaim J.M., Istepanian R.S.H. Digital watermarking in wireless telemedical environment, 1–3, http://umpir.ump.edu.my/928/1/13_JMZ_digital.pdf. (November 19, 2017).

33. Pandey, V., Singh, A., Shrivastava, M. (2012). Medical image protection by using cryptography data-hiding and steganography, *International Journal of Emerging Technology and Advanced Engineering*, 2 (1): 106–109.

34. Mortazavian, P., Jahangiri, M., Fatemizadeh, E. (2004). A low-degradation steganography model for data hiding in medical images, *Proceeding of the Fourth IASTED International Conference Visualization, Imaging, and Image Processing*, 914–920.

35. Viswanathan, P., Venkata Krishna, P. (2009). Text fusion watermarking in medical image with semi-reversible for secure transfer and authentication, *2009 International Conference on Advances in Recent Technologies in Communication and Computing*, 585–589.

36. Navas, K.A., Sasikumar, M., Sreevidya, S. (2007). A benchmark for medical image watermarking, *Systems, Signals and Image Processing, 2007 and 6th EURASIP Conference focused on Speech and Image Processing, Multimedia Communications and Services, 14th International Workshop on*, 237–240.

37. Koley, S., Pal, K., Ghosh, G., Bhattacharya, M. (2014). Secure transmission and recovery of embedded patient information from biomedical images of different modalities through a combination of cryptography and watermarking, *International Journal of Image, Graphics and Signal Processing*, 3: 18–31.

38. Li, Y., Li, C.-T., Wei, C.-H. (2007). Protection of mammograms using blind steganography and watermarking, *Information Assurance and Security, IAS 2007. Third International Symposium on*, 496–500.

39. Doğan, F., Güzeldereli, E.A., Çetin, Ö. (2013). Medikal görüntü içerisine tıbbi bilgilerin gömülmesi için yeni bir yaklaşım, *Sakarya University Journal of Science*, 17(2): 277–286.

40. Öksüzoğlu, S. (2009). Data hiding application for radiographic images (Radyografik Görüntülere Veri Gizleme Uygulaması), *13th National Congress and Exhibition of Electrical-Electronics-Computer and Biomedical Engineering (Elektrik-Elektronik-Bilgisayar ve Biyomedikal Mühendisliği 13. Ulusal Kongresi ve Fuarı)*.

41. Miaou, S.-G., Hsu, C.-M., Tsai, Y.-S., Chao, H.-M. (2000). A secure data hiding technique with heterogeneous data-combining capability for electronic patient records, *Engineering in Medicine and Biology Society. Proceedings of the 22nd Annual International Conference of the IEEE*, 1: 280–283.

42. Nambakhsh, M.S., Ahmadian, A., Zaidi, H. (2011). A contextual based double watermarking of PET images by patient ID and ECG signal, *Computer Methods and Programs in Biomedicine*, 104(3): 418–425.

43. Giakoumaki, A., Pavlopoulos, S., Koutsouris, D. (2006). Secure and efficient health data management through multiple watermarking on medical images, *Medical and Biological Engineering and Computing*, 44(8): 619–631.

44. Nambakhsh, M.S., Ahmadian, A., Ghavami, M., Dilmaghani, R.S., Karimi-Fard. S. (2006). A novel blind watermarking of ECG signals on medical images using EZW algorithm, *Proceedings of the 28th IEEE-EMBS Annual International Conference*, New York, 3274–3277.

45. Anand, D., Niranjan, U.C. (1998). Watermarking medical images with patient information, *Engineering in Medicine and Biology Society, 1998, Proceedings of the 20th Annual International Conference of the IEEE*, 2: 703–706.

46. Acharya, U.R, Subbanna Bhat, P., Kumar, S., Min, L.C. (2003). Transmission and storage of medical images with patient information, *Computers in Biology and Medicine*, 33(4): 303–310.

47. Acharya, U.R., Niranjan, U.C., Iyengar, S.S., Kannathal, N., Min, L.C. (2004). Simultaneous storage of patient information with medical images in the frequency domain, *Computer Methods and Programs in Biomedicine,* 76(1): 13–19.

48. Li, B., He, J., Huang, J., Shi, Y.Q. (2011). A survey on image steganography and steganalysis, *Journal of Information Hiding and Multimedia Signal Processing,* 2(2): 142–172.

49. Johnson, N.F., Katzenbeisser, S.C., Chapter 3. A survey of steganographic techniques. http://www.artechhouse.com/uploads/public/documents/chapters/petitcolas035-ch03.pdf. (November 19, 2017).

50. Hamid, N., Yahya, A., Ahmad, R.B., Al-Qershi, O.M. (2012). Image steganography techniques: An overview, *International Journal of Computer Science and Security (IJCSS),* 6(3): 168–187.

51. Micro Dicom Viewer Software Website. Available: http://www.microdicom.com/component/jdownloads/send/2-images/1-mr.html. (November 19, 2017).

52. Karakış, R. (2015). A fuzzy logic-based steganography application for MRI AND EEG data of epilepsy, PhD Thesis, Gazi University, Informatics Institute, Ankara.

53. Demirci, R. (2007). Similarity relation matrix-based color edge detection, *AEU-International Journal of Electronics and Communications,* 61: 469–477.

54. Elmas, Ç., Demirci, R., Güvenç, U. (2013). Fuzzy diffusion filter with extended neighborhood, *Expert Systems with Applications,* 40: 866–872.

55. Sezgin, M., Sankur, B. (2004). Survey over image thresholding techniquesand quantitative performance evaluation, *Journal of Electronic Imaging* 13(1): 146–165.

56. Gonzales, R., Woods, R.E. (2008). *Digital Image Processing,* Prentice Hall, Upper Saddle River, NJ.

57. Structural similarity, http://en.wikipedia.org/wiki/Structural_similarity (April 23, 2015). (November 19, 2017).

58. Wang, Z., Bovik, A.C. (2002). A universal image quality index, *IEEE Signal Processing Letters,* 9(3): 81–84.

59. Neto, A.M, Victorino, A.C., Fantoni, I., Zampieri, D.E., Ferreira, J.V., Lima, D.A., (2013). Image processing using Pearson's correlation coefficient: Applications on autonomous robotics. https://hal.inria.fr/file/index/docid/860912/filename/Image_Processing_Using_Pearsona_s_Correlation_Coefficient_-_Applications_on_Autonomous_Robotics_final.pdf. (November 19, 2017).

FORENSICS IV

Chapter 23

Digital Visual Media Forensics

Raahat Devender Singh

Contents

DOI: 10.1201/9780429435461-27

Truth will ultimately prevail where there is pains taken to bring it to light.

—George Washington

23.1　Introduction to the Forensic Applications of Images and Videos

As unbiased and unmediated proofs of occurrence of events, photographs and videos are an especially privileged kind of evidence. In this section, we discuss the origin and history of the forensic applications of photographic and video evidence, so as to better understand how they came to be the significant and compelling sources of information they are today.

23.1.1　Photographic Evidence: Origin and History

Photographs have had a 174 year-long history of sustained forensic use, the origin of which can be traced back to the early nineteenth century, i.e., almost as soon as the invention of photography itself. When French inventor Joseph Nicéphore Niépce created the world's first permanent camera and made a photograph in 1826 or 1827, several attempts were made to commercialize the process of photography. It was only after the invention of daguerreotype cameras by French photographer and artist Louis-Jacques-Mandé Daguerre, that it became possible to mass-produce cameras, and as soon as these cameras became publically available in 1839, photography's potential for the documentation and identification of criminal classes was recognized. Earliest instances of photographic documentation of prisoners dates back to 1843–1844 in Belgium and 1851 in Denmark. By 1848, police in Liverpool and Birmingham were photographing criminals, and by the mid 1850s, English and French authorities had begun encouraging their law enforcement agencies to photograph prisoners, mostly to prevent escapes and document recidivism.

By the 1870s, photographs had become a widely accepted means of forensic identification; professional photographers were being employed to take posed portraits, also known as portraitures, of criminals. However, despite their widespread use, portraitures were not standardized using the same lighting, scale, and angles, and were thus futile for identification purposes, a fact that was first realized in 1888 by Alphonse Bertillon, a French police officer and biometrics researcher. Bertillon then suggested anthropological studies of profiles and full-face shots (aka mug shots) for reliable documentation and identification of criminals.

Photographs were finding similar utility for the documentation of crime scenes and scenes of accidents as well. The earliest documented instance in that regard can be found in an 1852 American photographic journal that described an accident in which the victim's lawyer used pictures taken at the scene of the accident, and which from their realism explained the entire event much more clearly than any sort of oral description could.

Over time, with advancements in photography and camera manufacturing techniques, photographs (of people, objects, and events) became a generally accepted form of evidence, both inside and outside the justice system.

23.1.2 Video Data as Evidence and the Impact of CCTV

A photograph captures a single moment in time, which essentially makes it an arrested representation of reality. A video on the other hand, presents a record of an event over a period of time, which makes it a much more potent forensic evidence that still photographs.

In the olden days, video evidence was hard to come by. But in the modern world with ubiquitous surveillance and a plethora of digital multimedia capture devices where hardly any event of significant worth escapes the watchful eye of a camera, video data has emerged as a truly indispensable source of information. During a criminal trial for instance, video evidence, when available, is regarded as a particularly inculpatory kind of evidence. Unlike other forensic evidence like DNA and fingerprints, which are circumstantial in nature and require further inference, videos provide a first-hand account of an event, and its realism makes us confident in its authority as a witness.

23.1.2.1 Video Evidence: Origin Story

The first documented instance of use of video footage during a criminal trial was the Rodney King case of 1991. On the night of March 3, 1991, King, a taxi driver in Los Angeles, was assaulted by Los Angeles Police Department officers following a high-speed car chase. A witness named George Holliday videotaped much of the beating from his balcony and sent the footage to a local news station (Figure 23.1).

The footage was used during the ensuing trial in 1992 where the officers were charged with assault with a deadly weapon and use of excessive force. Despite the video evidence, the jury failed to convict the officers and they were acquitted of the charges brought against them. Within hours of the acquittals, angry LA citizens

Figure 23.1   A snapshot from Holliday's video showing LAPD offices assaulting King. (Courtesy of PBS, Arlington, TX.)

erupted in a riot that lasted for six days and claimed the lives of 63 people while injuring over 2,000 more.

23.1.2.2 CCTV and Surveillance

Today, the term *large-scale surveillance* has become synonymous with Closed Circuit Television (CCTV), and though CCTV surveillance had begun as early as the mid 20th century in minor capacities in the UK and US, the idea of widespread surveillance is not that recent. It was first posited in 1869, when an article in the journal *Legal Purposes of Photography*, suggested that when photographic techniques were "perfected," all of the streets and alleys of cities should be swept by surveillance cameras. The author expected these cameras to capture images of anyone rioting or disturbing the peace, which could then be used as evidence during subsequent legal proceedings.

In its early days, diffusion of CCTV was limited, and most of the systems were small-scale, locally funded, and were set up as the result of individual entre-preneurship, often on the part of a local police officer. The expansion of CCTV may very well have continued in a gradual manner, had it not been for the events of February 1993 in Merseyside, England, which put CCTV surveillance in the spotlight. On February 12, 1993, James Patrick Bulger, a two-year-old boy from Kirkby, Merseyside, disappeared from the New Strand Shopping Centre in Bootle, where he had been shopping with his mother. After he was reported as missing, the authorities examined the tapes from several CCTV cameras installed within and around the shopping centre, one of which showed Bulger being led out of the building by two ten-year-old boys, Robert Thompson and Jon Venables, who then tortured and murdered him later that day (Figure 23.2).

These images led to the apprehension of the culprits and eventually, to the conceptualization of open-street CCTV; ever since then, there has been a steady increase in its expansion as a surveillance and investigation tool.

(a)   (b)

Figure 23.2 Snapshots from CCTV footage (a) showing Bulger being abducted by Thompson (above Bulger) and Venables (holding Bulger's hand), and (b) the two abductors. (Courtesy of BBC News, London, UK.)

Today, use of video evidence in civil and criminal litigations seems to have become a matter of routine. There have been numerous cases over the past years where video evidence has been instrumental in the discovery of truth and dispensation of justice; some of the most notable instances include the David Copeland (London Nail Bomber) case of 1999, 7/7 London Bombings of 2005, 2008 Mumbai Attacks, 2011 England Riots, Boston Marathon Bomber case of 2013, 2015 Paris Attacks, 2016 Brussels Bombings, 2016 Nice Attack, and the more recent 2017 Manchester Arena Bombing, 2017 London Bridge Attack, and 2017 Barcelona Attacks.

Video evidence has proved to be equally beneficial for the exposition of social injustices. Whether it is a video of child soldiers or police torture of prisoners, or footage of human rights violations or wildlife abuse, video evidence can accomplish a lot from instigating inquiries and investigations to expediting cases in court. For instance, footage of the 2012 Houlah Massacre in Syria called attention to the incident and led the United Nations (UN) to call for a special inquiry to conduct an investigation. Video evidence played a critical role in the Endorois Welfare Council's human rights violation case against the Kenyan government in 2009. Similarly, videos documenting human rights violations and war crimes during the Sri Lankan Civil War in 2014 were used by UN to initiate several investigations.

All these and numerous other cases are demonstrative of the fact that when used in an evidentiary capacity, photographs and videos can be incredibly compelling (consider for instance, the O.J. Simpson civil trial of 1997, where pictures of him clad in Bruno Magli shoes served as the key piece of evidence that led the jury to find him liable for the deaths of his ex-wife Nicole Brown Simpson and her friend Ronal Goldman, two years after he was acquitted of murder on both counts). In a world where visual evidence holds such power over our decision-making faculties, we need to be absolutely certain that this evidence is in actuality what it purports to be, because as influential as photographs and videos are, the picture they paint may not always be an exact replication of reality.

23.2 Visual Evidence and the Fallacy of Infallibility

Visual evidence, especially digital visual evidence, is exceedingly pliable, and is therefore highly prone to misrepresentation; by simply altering the contents displayed by a photograph or a video, one can effectively alter the reality it depicts.

Frivolous malice aside, the act of distorting the visual truth presented by a photograph or video is almost always motivated by the desire to satisfy a personal, political, or social agenda, and contrary to popular belief, it is not a recent trend. Instances of photo manipulation began to emerge within half a century of the invention of photography itself. Shown below are some of the earliest known examples of image tampering (Figures 23.3 and 23.4).

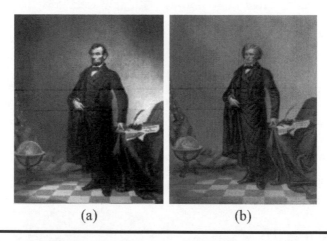

(a) (b)

Figure 23.3   **(a) This iconic portrait of Abraham Lincoln (c.1860) was found to be a composite of Lincoln's head and South Caroline politician John Calhoun's body (b). (Courtesy of W.J. Mitchell, MIT Press, Cambridge, MA.)**

(a) (b)

Figure 23.4   **In this doctored photograph (a) a commissar was removed from the original picture (b) after falling out of favor with Stalin (c.1930). (Courtesy of Fourandsix Technologies Inc., San Jose, CA.)**

The previous examples demonstrate pre-digital era tampering, i.e., when photos were on film. In those days, content manipulation was a task that could only be performed by trained photographers in specialized photo labs. Today in the digital age, amid the astonishing miscellanea of high-resolution digital cameras, powerful personal computers, and sophisticated content editing software such as Adobe Photoshop, Adobe Lightroom, Phantasmagoria, and PhotoScape, we have come to realize that digital images can be altered without any significant effort, even by novice individuals with menial skills and malice aforethought. Figures 23.5 through 23.7 depict some instances of tampered digital images that surfaced in the media and information world in the more recent times.

All these examples of content manipulation bear witness to the fact that while a picture is often believed to be worth a thousand words, those words may not always be true. Moreover, in the wake of widespread proliferation of powerful video editing software like Adobe Premier, Lightworks, and Video Edit Magic, we have become aware of the fact that the issue of content infidelity is not just limited to the domain of digital images; the integrity of video data too cannot be taken for granted any more. In the past, due to the inherent complexity of video processing and the general unavailability of high-tech video processing tools, we were less hesitant about accepting videos as truthful representations of reality. This however, is no longer the case.

The instances of missing footage as witnessed in case of the July 2005 police shooting of Charles de Menezes in London and in the 2013 murder case of Kendrick Johnson in Georgia, US, to the infamous cases of footage tampering that came to

(a)   (b)

Figure 23.5 In July 2012, Austria's largest newspaper Kronen Zeitung (Krone) published a photograph of a family fleeing a bombed-out neighborhood in war-torn Aleppo, Syria (a), which was soon discovered to be a fake; its background had been changed from the original European press photo agency picture (b), in which there was no visible bomb-damage within the scene. (Courtesy of Fourandsix Technologies Inc., San Jose, CA.)

(a)   (b)

Figure 23.6 Covering a solidarity march through Paris by world leaders after the Charlie Hebdo terrorist attacks in January 2015, Israeli ultra-Orthodox Jewish newspaper HaMevaser published a photo of the march (a) in which prominent female world leaders had been removed from the original picture (b). Orthodox Jewish publications have a policy against printing photos of women, but this picture attracted particular condemnation for virtually eliminating important women from the world stage. (Courtesy of Fourandsix Technologies Inc., San Jose, CA.)

(a)   (b)

Figure 23.7 After Dylann Roof was identified as the shooter responsible for the Emmanuel African Methodist Episcopal Church massacre in Charleston, South Carolina, on June 17, 2015, evidence of Roof's white supremacist associations began to emerge. Among the evidence was a photo from Roof's own website (a) which showed him wearing a jacket with patches representing former apartheid-era Rhodesian and South African flags (both of which are popular symbols among white supremacist factions). Later, a manipulated version of this photo (b) began appearing on Facebook and certain blogs, in which these patches had been replaced with a patch representing Barack Obama's campaign logo, as if to insinuate that Roof was an Obama supporter. (Courtesy of Fourandsix Technologies Inc., San Jose, CA.)

light during the trail of Srebrenican war criminal Radovan Karadžić in 2006 and again in the Sandra Bland custodial death case in 2015, shed light on the very tangible threat that evidence tampering poses in our society today.

Our dependence on images and videos to the extent where our perception of reality is strongly linked to their contents, and where we expect this content to serve as objective proof of occurrence of events in numerous aspects of our day to day lives, compels us to verify the trustworthiness and integrity of this content, before using it as evidence for making critical decisions or judgments with long-term consequences. As Bertrand Russell once said, "In all affairs it's a healthy thing now and then to hang a question mark on the things you have long taken for granted." After all, digital images and videos are just data, there is no reason why they should not be treated as such.

23.3 Indispensability of Visual Evidence and the Need for Authentication

One of the most prominent weaknesses of digital data is its inherent vulnerability to inconspicuous manipulations, and though this flaw has diminished the unwavering trust we once had in the legitimacy of digital visual evidence, the usefulness of this evidence in today's world is simply ineluctable. Digital images and videos have demonstrated their evidential utility on countless occasions throughout the world; for us to dismiss their worth on the grounds of vulnerability would be ill-advised.

Therefore, in situations where dependence on photographic or video evidence is unavoidable, and where reliance on a distorted version of reality could have dangerous implications, it becomes paramount to first examine the authenticity and integrity of the given visual data. This data must demonstrably be an accurate reflection of the events of interest to be considered *evidence* in the true sense of the word, and the scientific chain of investigation that helps make a definitive decision regarding content trustworthiness is known as Digital Visual Media Forensics.

23.4 Digital Visual Media Forensics

As forensic evidence, digital images and videos are not above reproach, but the testimony they provide can be difficult to impeach, which is why, whenever visual evidence of any sort is used as a means to convey important information, it is crucial to first substantiate this information. Since subjective inspection may fail to provide the desired degree of conviction regarding content fidelity, specialized forensic techniques have to be relied upon, which are provided by digital visual media forensics (DVMF), a branch of digital forensics that deals with the recovery and repair, scientific examination and investigation, comparison, and in-depth evaluation and interpretations of photographic or video evidence, mostly in legal

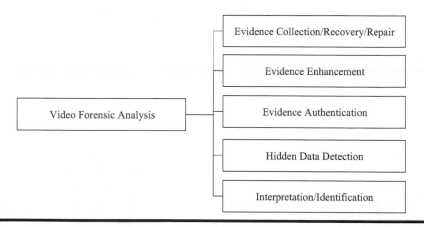

Figure 23.8   Primary tasks constituting the process of digital visual media forensic analysis.

matters, so as to ascertain the integrity and legitimacy of the evidence with a high degree of scientific certainty. DVMF aims at the accomplishment of four primary tasks, as illustrated in Figure 23.8. In the upcoming sub-sections, we explore these primary objectives of digital visual media forensics in more detail.

23.4.1 Evidence Collection, Recover, and Repair

Forensic analysis of digital visual evidence begins with the collection of the evidence (i.e., image or video) from the storage media (such as a magnetic hard disk drive, an optical disk, or a flash drive) of a source device (which could be any kind of acquisition device such as a surveillance camera, a cell phone, a police bodycam or dashcam, or a personal video camera or camcorder). Evidence collection is performed by either the responding officers or the crime scene investigators, who then submit it to the forensic analyst for examination. The analyst extracts the data from the source media or device and prepares it for further processing.

The process of evidence extraction may involve additional recovery/repair operations in case the source media or device is suffering from some sort of damage, which could occur due to natural factors like heat, misuse, everyday wear and tear, and environmental conditions of the crime scene, or due to intentional tampering by the offender; successful recovery of the evidence is subject to the exact circumstances and extent of damage.

In case of small-scale events (such as an isolated case of robbery-homicide), and in the absence of any noticeable damage to the recording device or the source media, evidence collection poses no significant challenges. But in case of large-scale events, especially in the presence of multiple recordings of the same event, the sheer amount of available data can complicate the process of evidence collection and analysis considerably. Consider for instance, the aftermath of the Vancouver riots that occurred in British Columbia after the 2011 Stanley Cup Finals, in which law enforcement agencies had to sift through more than 5,000 hours of video recordings for the identification of suspects. It took them over 4 years to examine all the available footage and bring a total 887 criminal charges against 301 suspects.

23.4.2 Forensic Evidence Enhancement

Evidence enhancement is one of the most frequent tasks performed during forensic analysis of digital images and videos. In most circumstances, high quality photographs or video recordings of the event in question are not available, in which case it becomes the responsibility of the forensic analyst to enhance the quality of the available evidence, so that the details of the event depicted in it become more apparent to the investigators, attorneys, jurors, and judges; content enhancement operations are generally authorized by the court itself.

In a scenario where a camera is the sole witness to a crime, apprehension of the culprit might rely entirely on the intelligibility of the visual evidence. Visual content enhancement played an instrumental role in the identification of the perpetrator who kidnapped and murdered 11-year-old Carlie Brucia on February 1, 2004 in Florida. Footage from a security camera at the parking lot of a car wash (scene of abduction) showed Brucia being approached by a man in his late 20s to early 30s (later identified as 37-year-old Joseph Peter Smith), who then grabbed her by the arm, steered her towards a parked car, and drove off. In an effort to find Brucia and her abductor, the FBI joined forces with NASA researchers, who used advanced image processing technology to enhance the quality of the security footage by reducing image jitter. Upon significant enhancement of the footage, they were able to provide clearer images of the abductor's face, the tattoos on his forearms, and even the nametag on his uniform. Smith was eventually convicted and sentenced to death.

This however, was an isolated incident since most investigations do not have the luxury of receiving help from NASA. Nevertheless, evidence enhancement, to the extent performed by image and video processing specialists, plays a crucial role in successful culmination of investigations and legal trials. The most commonly employed evidence enhancement techniques include brightness and contrast adjustments, noise reduction, color correction, image sharpening, harsh lighting enhancement, video stabilization, frame rate adjustment, masking or redacting (a process that helps obscure faces or other areas of an image or video that may need to be concealed in order to protect a witness, victim, or a law enforcement officer), zooming/cropping certain regions of an image/video frame, image reconstruction to counteract the effect of motion blur, sub-titling and time-coding, background noise suppression, frequency equalization (a process that makes speech more intelligible by isolating or enhancing the frequency band containing most speech content, i.e., 200–5000 Hz), selective amplification, and leveling (a process by which faint sounds in the video recording are boosted by compressing or leveling the signal so that the dynamic range of the audio is reduced).

Every evidence enhancement operation that is applied to an image or video must be constructed in a precise and careful manner so as to ensure that the given content remains a true and accurate representation of the actual scene at all times. The analyst must in no way change the recorded data but only enhance what is already present. Another important consideration is the fact that it is not possible to obtain the same kind of enhancement results for every image or video recording; the extent of achievable enhancement is affected by factors such as the initial quality of the image/video, technical parameters of the content acquisition device, environmental conditions prevalent at the time of recording, and the amount of compression involved.

23.4.3 Evidence Authentication

Authentication of visual evidence is the cardinal responsibility of the forensic analyst. In a world where our perception of reality is directly influenced by the contents of images and videos, the perils of unreliable evidence are not hard to fathom, which is why it becomes important to ascertain the credibility of this evidence, a task that is accomplished by answering the following questions:

1. *Where* is the image or video coming from?
2. *Has* the image or video been processed after acquisition, and if yes, *how?*

While the first question relates to *Source Identification* or *Evidence Provenance*, the second question relates to *Content Authentication and Tamper*[1] *Detection*. In order to substantiate the given visual evidence, we must first determine its origin (i.e., establish provenance) and then validate its contents, and the key to doing both is the Locard's Exchange Principle, which states that, "Every contact leaves a trace." Formulated by Dr. Edmond Locard in 1910, this exchange principle is one of the foremost principles of all disciplines of forensic science.

23.4.3.1 The Concept of Identifying Traces

Every operation that is applied to a digital image or video, and which changes its existent composition in some way, leaves behind subtle evidence of its occurrence. This evidence, which is generally referred to as a *forensic artifact* or a *forensic fingerprint*, is unique to every content processing operation (innocuous or otherwise) and therefore serves as an *identifying trace* for that operation. But these traces are not

---

[1] While "tampering" refers to the deliberate alteration of composition of something in a way that would render it harmful, a "forgery" refers to something that is falsely made with the intent to deceive. Despite the subtle difference in meaning, in the context of digital visual media forensics, these terms are used synonymously.

always superficial and may not lend themselves to discernment via mere subjective examination of the visual content. Their revelation is essentially contingent on the forensic analyst's ability to examine in detail the underlying characteristics and attributes of the given image or video. Identifying traces facilitate source identification as well as content authentication and tamper detection.

23.4.3.2 Source Identification and Evidence Provenance

The first step towards visual evidence authentication is to establish conclusively that the image or video in question was captured using the device it is claimed to have been captured with, and that it did not undergo any unauthorized transfers from one media to another without the knowledge of the investigators and forensic analysts involved with the investigation. The forensic process whereby the given visual content is linked to a particular acquisition device is known as *Source Camera Identification* (SCI).

All SCI techniques rely on the successful detection of certain identifying traces, which are furnished by the components of the digital content acquisition device itself. Every component of an image/video acquisition device affects the characteristics of the resulting content in a uniquely distinct manner. This implies, for instance, that not only will a video captured by a CCTV camera exhibit characteristics dissimilar from that recorded by a cell phone, but that the characteristics of videos recorded by different kinds of CCTV cameras will also be dissimilar.

Variations in the manner by which each image/video acquisition device impacts the characteristics of the respective acquired content exist due to the presence, or absence, of certain components in the acquisition device, and due to the differences in the processes by which these components were manufactured and implemented. Upon exhaustive investigation of these variations, particulars of the acquisition device and the content generation process can be inferred, which then facilitate source identification. An example of such a variation is *sensor noise*, which is a unique kind of noise that every camera introduces in every image or video it records. Sensor noise patterns vary from camera to camera, but remain consistent across all the content recorded by a particular camera.

Furthermore, since a digital image/video acquisition process essentially follows a pipeline structure, each component of the acquisition process can interfere with, or even wipe out, the traces introduced by the previous component, and since the characteristics of an earlier stage of content generation may not always be present in the final content, the forensic analyst can determine the origin of the given content based not only on the *presence* of identifying traces but also based exclusively on the *non-existence* of anticipated traces. This non-existence of traces, or presence of *inconsistent traces*, is suggestive of the fact that the given content has undergone some sort of post-production modification. Specialized source camera identification is discussed in detail in Section 23.6.

23.4.3.3 Content Authentication and Tamper Detection

Once the origin of the given image/video is definitively ascertained, the next step is to validate the integrity and legitimacy of its contents by determining if they are a truthful representation of the event of interest, and that the contents have not been altered from the time the image/video was recorded to the time it was presented for authentication. Forensic techniques that help discover the presence of semantic manipulations in digital images and videos are collectively referred to as *Forgery* or *Tamper Detection Techniques*.

Every operation that a digital image or video undergoes after it has been generated is referred to as a post-production operation, and all such operations influence the underlying characteristics of the digital content and modify its existent configuration, which in turn causes the attributes of the affected image/video to demonstrate behavior that deviates from the normal behavior exhibited by the attributes of an unmodified image/video. Every tamper detection technique relies on the successful detection of these deviations and uncharacteristic behavior, which act as identifying traces and facilitate discrimination between authentic content and content that has undergone some sort of post-production modification. Specialized tamper detection techniques are discussed in further detail in Section 23.8.

23.4.3.4 Evidence Enhancement and Evidence Tampering

Every evidence enhancement operation is technically a content modification operation because it ultimately changes the attributes of the digital visual content in question, and since both evidence enhancement and evidence tampering are characterized by eventual content modification, it becomes important to distinguish the two, especially from a forensic standpoint.

While the primary function of evidence enhancement operations is to *improve* the quality of the image/video and *emphasize* vital scene details so that they become easier to comprehend and interpret, tampering is a malevolent operation which is performed with the specific intent to alter the *meaning* conveyed by the given image/video by changing the events depicted in it, a process that ultimately renders the evidence harmful for decision-making purposes.

23.4.4 Hidden Data Detection

Another important task related to forensic analysis of photographic and video evidence is to detect the presence of hidden data within the content under consideration. The art of hiding secret data within a cover medium for the purpose of covert communication is known as *steganography*, and the challenge of detecting such data is referred to as *forensic steganalysis*. The primary aim of forensic steganalysis is to discern the presence of hidden data within the given image or video file, with the additional requirement of recovering the hidden data content.

The key to steganalysis is the same as in the case of source identification and tamper detection, which is that any process that alters the pre-existing configuration of an image or video file, introduces certain abnormalities in the content features. These abnormalities, if successfully detected, can be used as evidence of presence of hidden data.

In forensic steganalysis, the analyst may encounter one of two extreme scenarios. In the first scenario, the analyst has some level of suspicion that two parties are communicating covertly, whereas in the second scenario, the analyst may have some additional information about this covert communication, for instance, the algorithm that has been used for steganography. Depending on the scenario at hand, there are two methods of conducting steganalysis: *universal* or *blind steganalysis*, where the analyst needs to deploy a system capable of detecting all forms of steganography, and *specific* or *targeted steganalysis,* where the analyst can exploit the available background information to perform a more focused analysis.

23.4.4.1 Specific or Targeted Steganalysis

Targeted steganalysis approaches work under the premise that the algorithm used to embed the secret data (i.e., steganography algorithm) is known to the analyst. The steganalysis algorithm is therefore specifically designed to detect those abnormalities that the corresponding steganography algorithm is known to introduce. For instance, a common steganography technique is to embed secret data in the Least Significant Bit (LSB) of the given content, primarily because LSB data appears random to a human observer regardless of the presence or absence of any secret data. An effective way to detect such patterns is to perform statistical analyses of the LSB data, which help in the discovery of hidden patterns that arise when any change is made to the LSB data.

The advantage of using targeted steganalysis approaches is that their results are highly accurate. The disadvantage however, is that they have a limited scope of applicability; in real-life scenarios, information regarding the steganography algorithm used is mostly unavailable.

23.4.4.2 Universal or Blind Steganalysis

The techniques that fall under this category of steganalysis attempt to discover the presence of hidden data by either performing visual, structural, and statistical analyses, or by employing supervised learning approaches.

1. **Visual Analysis Methods**

   These methods aim at performing steganalysis through visual inspection, either with the naked eye or with the help of some automated processes. When performed with the naked eye, visual analysis methods can succeed only when the secret data is hidden in relatively smooth areas of the image or video frame with nearly equal pixel values. However, when visual analysis is performed with the help of automated processes, the odds of successful steganalysis are greatly increased. For instance, instead of examining the given image *as is*, it is much more beneficial to first decompose it into individual bit-planes. A bit-plane consists of a single bit of memory for each pixel in an image, and is the typical storage place where steganography applications embed the secret data. Any abnormalities in the appearance of the least significant bit-plane is indicative of the existence of hidden data.

2. Structural Analysis Methods

Such methods attempt to expose any modifications in the format of the given image or video file. For instance, a steganography technique may append hidden data past an image's end-of-file marker. An image that has been modified in such a manner is interpreted by the operating system just as if it were the original carrier file. The two files appear identical because none of the image's actual data bits have been altered, and so, the hidden data embedded past the end-of-file marker is simply ignored by the operating system. But the presence of this hidden data can be revealed by conducting suitable structural analysis of the given files, for instance, by examining them manually with a hex editor.

3. Statistical Analysis Methods

This category of steganalysis approaches aim at detecting minute modifications in the statistical behavior of the given image or video file. Such steganalysis methods are cumbersome and time consuming, since a variety of approaches may have been used to embed secret data into the given file, and each of these approaches may have modified the carrier file in a different way. The contemporary research in statistical steganalysis methods is centered around determining statistics such as *means, variances, skewness, kurtosis*, and *chi-square tests*, which help measure the amount of redundant information and/or deviation from the expected file characteristics.

4. Supervised Learning Based Approaches

In supervised learning based steganalysis approaches, classifiers are trained to distinguish *non-stego* or *cover objects* (i.e., objects that do not contain any hidden data) from *stego-objects* (i.e., objects that contain hidden data). Generally speaking, a *classifier* is a mathematical algorithm that determines which of a set of categories the new observation belongs to. This determination is based on a training set of data, which contains observations (or instances) whose category membership is already known. In the context of steganalysis, the classifier is trained to distinguish various objects of the suspicious file based on the variations in certain object features that are believed to undergo alteration during the data hiding/embedding process. Some of the most commonly used features are based on *wavelet image decompositions, image quality metrics, controlled perturbations, moment functions*, and *histogram characteristic functions*. The most frequently used classifiers include *multivariate regression,*

Fisher Linear Discriminant (FLD), Support Vector Machines (SVMs), and *Artificial Neural Networks (ANNs).*

Due to the inherent complications of their methods of operation, this category of steganalysis techniques are often rendered inapt in most practical scenarios. For instance, features used to train the classifier require careful selection, and in the absence of any systematic rule for feature selection, empirical trial and error methods are often employed. Moreover, some classifiers have several parameters (such as type of kernels, training conditions, learning rate) that require precise setting, which makes the whole process even more difficult and error-prone.

23.4.4.3 Caveats of Blind Steganalysis

In a real-life forensic scenario, blind steganalysis methods could face the following complications:

- The image or video file under consideration may or may not have any data hidden in it in the first place.
- Most blind steganalysis methods are only capable of detecting the presence of an anomaly in the given file, and are more often than not, unable to extract the hidden data successfully.
- The hidden data may have been encrypted before being embedded in the carrier file. In such a scenario, the hidden data thus extracted will be in the form of a cipher text, which may or may not be decipherable, depending on the strength of the encryption algorithm used.
- It may also happen that due to some similarity in the characteristics of the suspicious file and those of an anomaly, the steganalysis method triggers a false alarm.
- The suspicious file may have had noise or some other irrelevant data encoded in it, which reduces the stealth aspect (i.e., makes it easier to detect the presence of hidden data) but makes steganalysis very time-consuming.
- Unless the hidden data can be successfully detected, completely recovered/extracted, and decrypted (if encrypted), it is often not possible to make sure whether or not the file under consideration actually contained any hidden data. The best outcome in such a scenario is a probability that the file may have something hidden within it. In the absence of any concrete proof, this information alone is of little value.

23.4.4.4 Steganalysis Tools

Aside from the general steganalysis methods discussed previously, forensic steganalysis can be performed with the help of several potent and effective open-source tools such as StegDetect, StegExpose, Virtual Steganographic Laboratory (VLS), StegSecret, and StegSpy, and other commercial steganalysis tools such as Steganography Analyzer Signature Scanner (StegAlyzerSS) and CANVASS.

23.4.5 Identification and Interpretation

The process of digital visual media forensics generally ends with identification of various scene elements depicted in the image or video in question and interpretation of their meaning in relation to the scene.

23.4.5.1 Object Identification

During this phase of forensic analysis, operations like object detection, tracking, and highlighting are performed. Preliminary object detection is followed by specialized analyses that help make positive identification of people (suspects, witnesses, or victims), or inanimate objects (such as license plates, nametags, house numbers, names of buildings and streets) depicted in the image/video. Basic object identification techniques include facial mapping (which involves comparing one facial image to other facial images to find a match), videogrammetry (which is a process used to take measurements of video objects, for instance, to estimate the height of a perpetrator), and identification of other distinguishing features such as tattoos and scars.

Aside from these basic identification techniques, there are some other subjective inspection methods, such as forensic gait analysis and behavioral pattern analysis, whose forensic contributions cannot be overlooked since they often provide invaluable clues as to the identity of the person of interest in the image or video in question.

23.4.5.2 Evidence Interpretation

During a trial, visual evidence is often left to speak for itself, since it is expected to present to the court all the facts it contains within itself. This however, could be troublesome as it may lead to judgments based on speculative assessment of an overall incorrect interpretation of the evidence.

Consider for instance, the Claudia Muro case from October 2003. Muro, a Peruvian immigrant woman working as a nanny in Florida, was accused by her employers of aggravated child abuse. The key evidence against Muro was a hidden nanny cam video, which showed her violently shaking the 5-month-old baby girl and repeatedly slamming her in the playpen. In light of this incriminating evidence, Muro was convicted. But even after being sent to jail, Muro refused to take the plea bargain and kept insisting that the video was misleading. After much deliberation, the case was reopened in March 2006, and upon re-examination of the video evidence by several forensic experts, it was discovered that the nanny cam had actually recorded less than 5.5 frames per second, which made gentle motions seem violent when the video was played back at normal frame rate. Muro was finally acquitted, after spending 29 months in jail for a crime she did not commit.

This case is demonstrative of how the slightest misinterpretation of even a single aspect of visual evidence can lead to horrific miscarriage of justice. Correct interpretation of evidence is therefore of unquestionable importance.

Please note that as far as evidence interpretation is concerned, the only obligation of the forensic analyst is to interpret the events depicted in the given evidence; whether or not those events hold any probative value is for the courts to decide.

23.5 Variants of Digital Visual Media Forensics

So far, our discussion about digital visual media forensics was confined to a very general setting where we made no assumptions regarding whether or not the forensic analyst has any access to the components of the content acquisition process, or to any *a priori* knowledge vis-à-vis the processing history of the given content. If we keep these factors under consideration, digital visual media forensics can be classified according to the scheme presented in Figure 23.9.

23.5.1 Active and Passive Forensics

Active Forensics: Active forensics is a variant of digital visual media forensics wherein certain identifying traces are deliberately inserted into the digital content during an earlier stage of its production. These traces are either embedded directly into the content (such as a watermark), or are attached to the content in the form of metadata (such as a hash or a signature). Active forensic approaches are implemented directly in the content acquisition device, and the components of the content generation process cannot be inferred until the identifying traces are appended to or embedded into the content.

Passive Forensics: In this variant of digital visual media forensics, the analyst has no control whatsoever over the digital content generation process or the type and/or appearance of the identifying traces. The analyst is completely

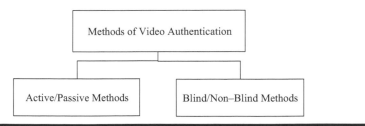

Figure 23.9 Categories of digital visual media forensic techniques.

oblivious to the particulars of the content generation process and to the processing history of this content, and is restricted to authenticating the given image/video by examining the characteristics and features it exhibits. The identifying traces that passive forensic approaches generally rely on are of two kinds: device characteristics and processing artifacts.

1. **Device Characteristics**

   Due to the inherent dissimilarities in the operation of different acquisition devices, every device leaves a distinct and uniquely identifiable trace on the content it generates. Upon close inspection, these traces, which are also referred to as *device characteristics*, enable the forensic analyst to make inferences about the acquisition device itself.

   Variations between the characteristics of different acquisition devices primarily occur because different camera manufacturers use different components in their devices, and sometimes, they adjust certain recording parameters of their devices, which also differ from camera to camera. Certain variations can also be caused due of unavoidable technological defects such as sensor imperfections.

2. **Processing Artifacts**

   Processing artifacts refer to those traces that are introduced into the digital image or video by various post-production content processing operations it may undergo during its lifetime. Every content processing operation leaves a unique trace or fingerprint on the given content (for instance, the artifacts introduced by an image denoising operation are different from those introduced by a brightness adjustment operation). Each artifact thus serves as a means for the detection and revelation of a particular content processing operation.

   Although both active and passive forensic approaches rely on the appropriate discernment of identifying traces, the method whereby these traces get introduced into the given content differs in each case. While in case of active forensics, these traces are appended to or embedded into the data *deliberately*, in case of passive forensics, these traces are introduced by the *intrinsic characteristics* of the content generation process (i.e., device characteristics) or the various *post-production operations* the content undergoes after it is generated (i.e., processing artifacts).

23.5.2 Blind and Non-Blind Forensics

Blind Forensics: A digital visual media forensic approach is called blind if the forensic analyst examines the integrity and legitimacy of the given image or video without the help of any kind of *a priori* knowledge about the acquisition device, the content generation process, the nature of the original scene captured by the image or video, or any of the post-production processing operations that the image or video may have been subjected to. Such approaches try to infer the identity of the acquisition device or the post-production content modification operations by detecting the identifying traces that may be present (or absent) in the given content.

Non-Blind Forensics: In contrast to blind forensics, non-blind forensic approaches use additional background knowledge about the identity and characteristics of the acquisition process and/or information about the processing history of the content. Non-blind forensic approaches also use identifying traces that are inserted into the content at the time of its creation.

While the non-blind nature of these approaches helps overcome some of the uncertainty the analyst might encounter regarding the given content's provenance or its post-production processing history, such methods lack utility in most real-life forensic scenarios, primarily because in such scenarios, the image or video in question is the only available piece of evidence and any additional background information is generally unavailable.

23.6 Source Identification and Evidence Provenance

The source of the image or video in question has as much to do with its trustworthiness as the legitimacy of its contents; determination of its origin is thus an essential first step towards evidence authentication. The topic of source identification and evidence provenance was introduced in a general sense in Section 23.4.3.2; in the upcoming sub-sections, we analyze it in further detail.

23.6.1 Source Camera Identification (SCI)

The underlying operational premise for all source identification techniques is that an image or video captured by a particular acquisition device will display certain characteristics that are exclusive to that device because of its (proprietary) content generation pipeline and the unique hardware components it uses, regardless of the actual contents of the image or video, and since these characteristics differ from device to device, they can act as identifying traces that help link a particular image or video to a specific acquisition device. The most potent device characteristic is *noise*, and so, by matching the noise patterns of the given image or video (i.e., *test noise patterns*) against the noise patterns of the acquisition device under consideration (i.e., *reference noise patterns*), the content in question can be linked to the given device. Source identification can either be performed in a blind manner or a non-blind manner.

Non-blind SCI: In this case, the analyst either has access to the acquisition device or is aware of its identity. If the acquisition device is available at the time of forensic examination, the analyst can use that device to estimate its noise characteristics and compare them with the noise characteristics exhibited by the given image or video to see if they match. If the source device is unavailable but the analyst knows about the identity of the device that is suspected of being the source device, another set of images or an earlier video recorded by that device can be used to estimate the reference noise pattern for that device, which can then be matched against the noise characteristics of the given image or video. For instance, if the video under examination is a surveillance footage recorded by a certain CCTV camera (whose identity is known), and if that camera is unavailable at the time of investigation, then another video recorded by the same CCTV camera at some earlier point in time can be used to estimate reference noise characteristics for that camera. **Blind SCI:** If the analyst is uncertain of the identity of the acquisition device, or if no other image or video captured by that same device exists or is available at the time of examination, then the process of source camera identification becomes a bit more complicated, because now the analyst must identify the source camera in a blind manner. The most commonly used approach in such a circumstance is to train a machine-learning based classification algorithm to categorize the available test noise patterns and infer the identity of the source device. We learn more about blind SCI in Section 23.6.4; first, we study the various non-blind device-linking methods.

It is important to note at this point that though acquisition devices generally encode the device related information and recording parameters, such as camera model, date and time of file creation/access/modification, image/video resolution, video frame rate, and compression details as *metadata*, this information is easy to modify and/or remove. It is therefore advisable to refrain from relying solely on this data for forensic purposes and utilize other artifacts obtained from alternative sources as well; we explore such artifacts in the upcoming sub-sections.

23.6.1.1 Image/Video Acquisition Pipeline

In order to understand how and why different acquisition devices leave unique traces on the content they capture, we first need to acquire a basic understanding of a typical image/video acquisition pipeline. Figure 23.10 illustrates the flow of data within a standard digital camera.

Acquisition of the digital visual data begins with light passing through the camera lens and possibly through a filter (which is generally used to remove infrared or ultra-violet light). Color cameras contain an additional Color Filter Array (CFA), which is placed over the sensor to generate different color channels. An RGB Bayer

Figure 23.10 **A typical digital image/video acquisition pipeline.**

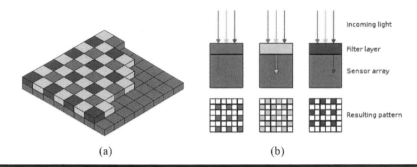

Figure 23.11 Color image acquisition process. (a) represents a Bayer mosaic; each two-by-two cell contains two green, one blue, and one red filter, and (b) illustrates how each filter allows only one wavelength of the incoming light—red, green, or blue, to pass through to any given pixel, allowing only one color to be recorded at each pixel location. (Courtesy of Wikimedia Commons.)

Pattern, also known as a Bayer filter mosaic, is the most commonly used CFA. It is a 2×2 array that contains alternative rows of red and green, and green and blue filters (Figure 23.11a). A demosaicing (aka debayering or demosaicking) algorithm then reconstructs a full color image using the incomplete color samples output from a CFA-overlaid sensor; this process is known as CFA interpolation or color reconstruction. An alternative CFA configuration is the CMYK subtractive color model; it is relatively lesser known and is only available in very few high-end sensors.

The incoming light waves (of variable attenuation) pass through the CFA and reach the imaging sensor, which converts them into signals that constitute the captured image. A typical imaging sensor is either a silicon CCD (Charge Coupled Device) or CMOS (Complementary Metal Oxide Semiconductor). The captured image then undergoes several processing operations, such as aperture correction, gamma correction, white balancing, sharpening, and compression.

Though the aforementioned camera components and processing operations represent standard phases in a digital camera pipeline, the precise manner in which each component operates or processes the data varies from manufacturer to manufacturer, and may even vary between different camera models manufactured by the same company. What remains universal however is that each component of the digital camera operates in an imperfect manner, which causes it to introduce certain inconsistencies in the image or video it acquires, and since these inconsistencies are inimitable, they act as unique identifying characteristics or artifacts that can be used to trace the given image or video back to the camera that captured it.

23.6.2 *Classes of Source Camera Identification*

Source camera identification entails identification of the model and/or manufacturer of the device that produced the image or video in question (a task generally referred to as *source model identification* or *device class identification*), and identification of the exact device that produced the image or video in question (a task generally referred to as *individual source identification* or *specific device identification*).

23.6.2.1 Source Model or Device Class Identification

In order to identify the model and/or manufacturer of the camera used to capture the image or video in question, the forensic analyst takes advantage of the variations in component technologies and processing techniques used by different camera manufacturers. Optical distortions caused by different type of camera lenses, variations in the sizes of the imaging sensors, the choice of CFA, or the respective demosaicing algorithm employed within a particular camera, all serve as identifying traces that can be quantitatively characterized to perform source model identification.

Now, since several camera models and brands use common components produced by a few manufacturers, and since different models of a brand use similar image/video processing algorithms, reliable identification of a source camera-model necessitates that the analyst characterizes and analyzes those specific features that differ from one camera model to another; these features have been examined below.

1. **CFA and Demosaicing Algorithms**

   The choice of CFA and the particulars of the demosaicing algorithm used in a particular camera, are responsible for some of the most pronounced dissimilarities between content captured by different camera-models. The demosaicing algorithm that creates the final color image/video frame from three separate color channels is basically a kind of *interpolation*. Interpolation, a process used to estimate new pixel values from existing values, inevitably introduces certain correlations or interdependencies amongst neighboring pixels in an image or video frame. Based on the nature of correlations present in the given image/video frame, the presence of a particular demosaicing algorithm can be identified, which can then help identify the camera-model that was used to capture the image/video in question.

2. **Lens Distortions**

   Digital cameras with spherical lenses introduce radial distortions in the images or frames of the videos they capture. Radial distortions refer to the phenomenon that causes straight lines in object space to be rendered as curved lines (Figure 23.12).

   Radial distortions are most prominent when the widest angle, i.e., shortest focal length, is selected either with a fixed or a zoom lens. Though such distortions seldom affect the quality of the image or video, they have a substantial impact on the geometry of solid objects present in the scene, which is why camera manufacturers try to counterbalance their effect by adjusting several parameters during image formation. This process yields unique artifacts, which can be utilized for camera-model identification.

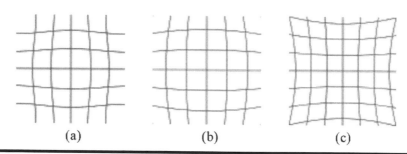

(a)   (b)   (c)

Figure 23.12   Types of radial distortions (a) Pincushion distortion, (b) Barrel distortion, and (c) Moustache distortion.

23.6.2.2 Individual Source or Specific Device Identification

Individual source identification aims to identify the exact device that was used to capture the given image or video, and because of the level of specificity involved, this kind of identification requires the analyst to make use of far more specialized forensic features than those used during source model identification. These features primarily originate due to:

- Hardware defects and imperfections
- Faults arising due to inhomogeneity in the camera manufacturing process
- Effects of operating and environment conditions
- Abnormalities caused by a noisy sensor
- Aberrations produced by a faulty lens or dust present on the lens

All these artifacts are transient by nature, i.e., they tend to vary with time and the prevalent operating conditions, and are therefore not consistently reliable. Various device-dependent features used during specific device identification have been discussed below.

1. **Imaging Sensor Imperfections**

    Sensor imperfections introduce certain systematic errors in the images or video frames they record, and these errors reveal themselves across all the content acquired by that sensor, irrespective of the actual scene content. These errors or artifacts, namely *pixel defects* and *pattern noise*, can be used as forensic features to link the image or video in question to a specific acquisition device.

    a. **Pixel Defects:** Unique traces introduced by defective pixels, such as hot, cold/dead pixels, and pixel traps, can be used to determine the identity of the source camera. Hot pixels refer to those individual pixels on the sensor that have higher than normal charge leakage and thus appear brighter than they should (Figure 23.13a), whereas cold/dead pixels refer to those pixels that are permanently damaged and do not receive any power (Figure 23.13b). Pixel traps are an interference with the charge transfer process; it results in either a partial or whole bad line, which can either be all white or all black.

As forensic artifacts, pixels defects are not very reliable or potent. One immediate problem with them is that most cameras have the ability to detect these defects and correct them by post-processing their images on-board. Reliable source identification therefore requires us to turn to a more consistent as well as persistent artifact.

b. Pattern Noise: Pattern noise, also known as *sensor noise*, is the name given to the unique uncorrelated pattern of noise that every digital camera introduces in every image or video that it captures. This noise is the result of inhomogeneity of the CCD or CMOS sensors used in the camera, which arises due to the variations in the sensitivities of the silicon wafers used in these sensors. Pattern noise follows the hierarchy illustrated in Figure 23.14.

Fixed Pattern Noise (FPN) can be defined as the difference between the maximum and minimum measured values for all active pixels in an image or video frame, and is caused by the dark currents in digital cameras. Dark current refers to the rate at which electrons accumulate in each pixel due to thermal

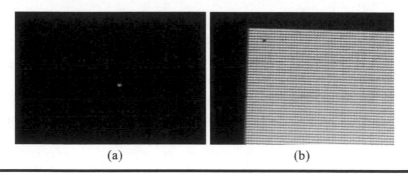

     (a)   (b)

Figure 23.13 (a) A uniformly dark image with a hot pixel, and (b) an enlarged region of an image demonstrating a dead pixel. (Courtesy of Wikimedia Commons.)

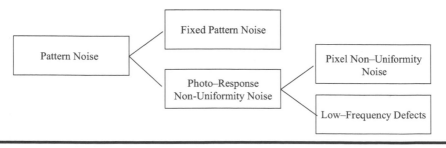

Figure 23.14 Hierarchy of pattern noise.

action. FPN is typically measured with the sensor in darkness, which is why it is also known as *Dark Signal Non-Uniformity* (DSNU).

Photo-Response Non-Uniformity (PRNU) noise is a combination of *Pixel Non-Uniformity* (PNU) noise, which arises due to different pixels having different sensitivity to light, and *low frequency defects*, which are caused by light refracting on particles on or near the camera and optical surfaces, and also on the zoom settings of the camera. We study pattern noise-based SCI in greater detail in Section 23.6.3.

2. Sensor Dust Characteristics

Sensor dust characteristics are somewhat exclusive to cameras that offer interchangeable lenses, such as Digital Single-Lens Reflex (DSLR) cameras. Basically, sensor dust problem arises when the sensor area is exposed to dust and moisture when the lens of the camera is removed. This causes a unique dust pattern to appear on the surface of the sensor, which can then be used for two purposes: to distinguish images/videos captured by cheaper consumer level cameras from those captured by DSLR cameras, and to link an image/video to a specific DSLR camera.

Although the notion of using sensor dust artifacts to link the image or video in question to a particular DSLR camera seems viable to some extent, the transient nature of these artifacts brings into question their dependability; as soon as the sensor surface gets cleaned, the entire process of sensor dust-based device linking is rendered futile.

23.6.3 Pattern Noise-Based Source Camera Identification

In order to use pattern noise as a distinguishing feature for camera identification, the analyst must first extract test noise pattern from the image or video in question and compare that with the reference noise pattern obtained from a particular camera to see if they match. Now, the reference pattern noise must ideally be extracted from a uniformly lit scene before it undergoes any non-linear operation, which implies that the image or video frame must essentially be *raw*. This raw sensor data however, is not available to the analyst in a real-life scenario, who, in the absence of any direct methods of noise extraction, must then rely on some alternative approach to obtain an *estimation* of pattern noise.

The simplest way to estimate pattern noise (which we refer to as PRNU for the sake of simplicity) for a specific camera is to average multiple images (or video frames) captured by that camera. Ideally, the most precise estimates of reference PRNU are obtained with the help of flat-field images or frames of a flat-field video (i.e., images/frames of an approximately uniform illumination which are devoid of any scene content, such as pictures of a wall or cloudless sky). Having said that, in case acquisition of flat-field images or a flat-field video is impossible or infeasible for some reason, one can use images or videos of natural scenes (recorded by that device) to estimate PRNU just as well.

When the images or video frames being used for noise estimation display a lot of scene details, the process of image/frame averaging can become quite time-intensive, which is why it is recommended that the scene details be removed using an appropriate denoising filter to obtain noise residuals for the images/video frames (Equations 23.1 and 23.2), and average those residuals to obtain the final noise estimate, i.e., reference PRNU (Equation 23.3).

$$\bar{I}_k = F(I_k) \tag{23.1}$$

$$W_k = I_k - \bar{I}_k \tag{23.2}$$

$$N_{\text{ref}} = \frac{1}{N} \sum_{k=1}^{N} W_k \tag{23.3}$$

Here, F denotes the denoising filter, I_k denotes the kth image or frame and $\bar{I}_k$ denotes the denoised version of this image/frame; W_k denotes the noise residue for the kth image/frame. N_{ref} is the reference PRNU (which is basically just average noise residue).

Using the same method described above, N_{test} (i.e., test PRNU) is estimated using the image or video in question, which is then correlated with N_{ref} to measure the degree of similarity between the two, using Equation 23.4.

$$\text{corr}\left(N_{\text{ref}}, N_{\text{test}}\right) = \frac{\left(N_{\text{test}} - \overline{N_{\text{test}}}\right) \cdot \left(N_{\text{ref}} - \overline{N_{\text{ref}}}\right)}{\left\|N_{\text{test}} - \overline{N_{\text{tests}}}\right\| \cdot \left\|N_{\text{test}} - \overline{N_{\text{tests}}}\right\|} \tag{23.4}$$

Here, $\overline{N_{\text{ref}}}$ and $\overline{N_{\text{test}}}$ denote means of N_{ref} and N_{test}, respectively.

If the correlation thus obtained is above a pre-determined threshold, the image or video in question is established to have been recorded by the camera under consideration. In case the given image/video is to be linked to one of several possible cameras, the camera whose reference PRNU is most correlated with the test PRNU is established to be the source camera. Note that in this case too, a threshold is still required because it is not necessary for any one of the given cameras to be the source camera.

23.6.3.1 Limitations of PRNU-Based SCI

Although the PRNU-based camera identification method discussed above has been shown to be quite efficacious in the literature, it suffers from two significant limitations. First, PRNU calculations are highly sensitive to synchronization. Even the slightest geometric transformation, such as rotation, scaling, or cropping of the given image/video frame causes desynchronization, which may lead to erroneous detection results. Second, PRNU calculations are often unreliable when the content in question has undergone compression.

The first limitation can be overcome by computing *normalized correlation coefficient* instead of *correlation* between test and reference PRNU (Equation 23.5). This helps neutralize the effects of mild geometric transformations.

$$\text{NCC}\left(N_{\text{ref}},\ N_{\text{test}}\right) = \frac{\left(N_{\text{test}} - \overline{N_{\text{test}}}\right) \cdot \left(N_{\text{ref}} - \overline{N_{\text{ref}}}\right)}{\sqrt{\overline{N_{\text{test}} - \overline{N_{\text{test}}}}^2 \cdot \overline{N_{\text{ref}} - \overline{N_{\text{ref}}}}^2}} \tag{23.5}$$

The second limitation can be overcome by modifying the noise pattern estimation process to make it more robust and effective, as explained in the following sub-section.

23.6.3.2 Modified Noise Pattern Estimation: SPN Based Analysis

By modifying the noise pattern estimation process, the accuracy and dependability of source camera identification techniques can be improved significantly. More specifically, instead of PRNU, we suggest working with Sensor Pattern Noise (SPN). Reference and test SPN are estimated using the same method as outlined in Equations 23.1 and 23.2; the only modifications are made to Equation 23.3, which now becomes:

$$\text{SPN}_{\text{ref}} = \frac{\sum_{k=1}^{N} W_k \overline{I}_k}{\sum_{k=1}^{N} \left(\overline{I}_k\right)^2} \tag{23.6}$$

Here, I_k denotes the kth image or video frame and $\overline{I}_k$ is the denoised version of this image/frame; W_k denotes the noise residue for the kth image/frame. Test SPN (SPN_{test}) is then estimated in a similar manner. (Correlation and NCC between reference and test SPN can be calculated using Equations 23.4 and 23.5, but with reference and test SPN instead of PRNU.)

As a forensic feature, SPN is quite efficacious and robust. Not only is it a unique characteristic of every digital camera, it also remains highly consistent within every image or video frame recorded by that camera. It is distributed evenly across all pixel of the image/frame, which is why it survives even the harshest of compressions. Furthermore, it remains completely unaffected by environmental conditions such as humidity and temperature variations.

Note that in the digital visual media forensics literature, PRNU and FPN are sometimes collectively referred to as SPN. The terms PRNU and SPN are sometimes used synonymously as well.

23.6.4 *Blind Source Camera Identification*

All the source camera identification methods discussed previously require the analyst to either have access to the suspected acquisition device, or in the very least, have access to another set of images or a video recorded by the same device at some previous moment in time. If none of these criteria can be fulfilled, the analyst must infer the identity of the source camera in a completely blind manner, which is generally done with the help of a *machine-learning based classifiers*. Some commonly used classifiers include *SVMs, k-Nearest Neighbors algorithm (k-NN), neural networks, naïve Bayes*, and *decision trees*.

Blind source camera identification is performed in two phases. Phase 1 is the *Training Phase*, during which the classifier is taught to differentiate the noise characteristics of one acquisition device from those of another, and put different test images/videos into different categories according to the characteristics they display. Training requires the help of certain distinguishing features, which are extracted from a training dataset that contains numerous images and/or videos captured by a certain number of acquisition devices. The classifier is trained to distinguish images and videos acquired by different cameras based on the features these images/videos exhibit.

After the training phase comes Phase 2, i.e., the *Testing Phase*. Once the classifier has been trained to categorize noise patterns into different classes (where each class represents an acquisition device), it is presented with a test image or video whose origin has to be determined. The classifier examines the characteristics of the test image or the frames of the test video, and based on the distinguishing features, tries to extrapolate the identity of the device that is most likely to have generated them, i.e., it essentially classifies the test data as belonging to one of the classes it was taught about during training.

Recent innovations in the machine-learning domain have led to significant improvements in the accuracy and precision of machine-learning based source identification techniques. But in spite of such innovations, these techniques still suffer from several operational constraints, the most significant among which is the cost and time-intensive nature of such techniques. This in turn bounds the classifier to be trained on a very limited number of camera models, thus restricting the scope of applicability of these techniques.

23.7 Integrity Verification and Content Authentication

Once the task of evidence provenance is complete, the next challenge is content authentication. The forensic analyst must determine, with a high degree of certainty, whether the contents of the image/video have undergone any kind of unauthorized modification from the time the image or video was created to the time it was submitted for forensic examination, and ascertain that the events depicted in the evidence are an accurate representation of what really occurred. We begin the discussion about content authentication with an analysis of some rudimentary active-non-blind forensic methods.

23.7.1 Content Authentication: Active-Non-Blind Methods

Active-non-blind content authentication methods, as the name implies, require the assistance of certain identifying traces that are either attached to or embedded into the content at the time of its creation (or later by some authorized individual). The most commonly employed methods of active-non-blind content authentication are illustrated in Figure 23.15.

23.7.1.1 Timestamp Analysis Based Authentication

Overlaid timestamps are amongst the most preliminary defenses against content manipulation. An overlaid timestamp is a sequence of characters embedded onto the images or video frames that identify when a certain event occurred (and was subsequently captured by the camera), usually giving date and time of day, sometimes accurate to a small fraction of a second.

23.7.1.2 Limitations of Timestamp Based Authentication

Timestamp based authentication is a very primitive solution to a challenge as elaborate and consequential as establishing the trustworthiness of digital content, and while it may be considered to be a precursory method of authentication, its results must not be accepted as an absolute proof of content reliability, primarily because not only are timestamps *prone to inaccuracies* (which can occur if the internal clock of the camera is inaccurate, or due of failure to pay attention to daylight saving

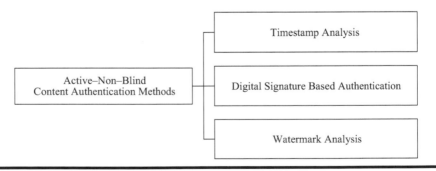

Figure 23.15 Various techniques used to perform active-non-blind content authentication. Note that in the present discussion about timestamps, we limit our attention to the analysis of timestamps that are overlaid onto the image/video itself; timestamps that are stored as a part of the image/video file's metadata are a topic of discussion in Section 23.7.2.2.

in countries where it is applicable), but they are *susceptible to tampering* as well (timestamps can be superimposed from one image/frame onto another).

23.7.1.3 Digital Signatures and Watermarks for Content Authentication

A digital signature is an encrypted translation of a succinct representation of the data under consideration. It primarily consists of key information regarding the data and some kind of unique identification of the data producer in the form of a condensed bit-stream. The process of watermarking on the other hand, consists of embedding content integrity information as well as unique identification of the content producer into the data content itself.

23.7.1.4 Limitations of Digital Signature and Watermark Based Content Authentication

Although the digital signature technology has been shown to be quite proficient for the purposes of content confidentiality and integrity verification, it is rendered ineffective in the content authentication domain, primarily because of the following limitations:

- Digital signature schemes are computationally intensive and therefore suffer from scalability issues. While within a controlled environment, digital signature based schemes can be effective for tamper detection, they do not adjust well to the necessities of a large-scale media domain.
- The external security token that digital signatures rely on is quite easy to remove, which implies that such techniques work only if preservation of this token is in the interest of all the parties involved (which is not the case when the possibility of tampering exists).
- Digital signatures are extremely fragile and even innocuous operations such as lossy compression, noise removal, contrast or brightness enhancement, color adjustments, cropping, geometric operations like rotation, and local changes to data (such as blackening out a logo) are capable of destroying or damaging the signatures.
- Digital signatures rely heavily on the technology they are based on; in today's age of transient technology, such techniques end up with a very short shelf-life.
- Generation, verification, and deployment of digital signature based content authentication schemes are not only time-intensive processes but they incur great costs as well. Both these factors impose severe restrictions on the practical feasibility of such schemes.

Though digital watermarking technology has some utility in the copyright protection domain, its content authentication properties are very limited; it suffers from the following shortcomings:

- Watermarking based content authentication works for only those images or videos that have already been watermarked. This restriction, along with the fact that most digital cameras do not contain a watermark embedding module, results in a very limited scope of applicability of such schemes.
- A damaged watermark is not always indicative of tampering; completely harmless content modification operations, such as lossy compression, noise removal, contrast or brightness enhancement, color adjustments, cropping, and local changes to data (such as blackening out a logo), also have a negative impact on the integrity of watermarks.
- Some watermarks have been shown to degrade the visual quality of the digital content.
- Watermarking techniques do not possess the ability to resist willful attempts to remove the watermark. Generation of a counterfeit watermark is also not a difficult endeavor.
- Watermarking based schemes do not allow for the possibility of independent third-party verification, since the only people capable of detecting watermarks are the content producers or owners themselves. Such lack of independent verification may be unacceptable in certain sensitive situations, for instance, during a criminal trial.

23.7.2 Passive-Blind Methods for Content Integrity Verification

Digital content integrity verification is a crucial component of digital visual media forensics, and active-non-blind methods that we examined in the previous sections are largely unsuitable for this task, primarily because the operation of these methods is contingent upon certain pre-embedded identifying traces, which are generally unavailable in a realistic forensic scenario. In order to ensure a widely effective scope of applicability, the task of integrity verification must ideally be performed using self-reliant schemes that base themselves upon the inspection of inherent details of the given content and clues regarding content integrity provided thereby.

23.7.2.1 Hash Value Analysis

A *hash* (aka hash code, hash value, or digest) is a distinctive identifier that can be assigned to a file, a group of files, or a portion of a file, and is created using the file's contents and structure with the help of a standard mathematical algorithm. Hash-based verification is a process that helps ascertain that the given file has not been corrupted in any way. The process of integrity verification is quite straightforward: the given file's hash value is compared to a previously calculated hash value of the same file. If the two values match, the file is assumed to be unmodified.

The most commonly used hash algorithms are the 5th generation of the *Message Digest Algorithm*, commonly known as *MD5* and the *Secure Hash Algorithm* 1 or *SHA1*. Although there are newer algorithms (for instance, *MD6*), MD5 remains the premier balance of security and popular cross-platform support.

Although hash value analysis is a very simple strategy for file integrity verification, some fundamental limitations may cause it to produce misleading results. For instance, an altered hash value does not necessarily indicate content modification; sometimes even the simplest of acts like opening and resaving a file (with no content change) might alter the hash value of the file. Hash value analysis is also not a dependable strategy for the detection of deliberate content tampering because these values can be altered manually (with the help of programs such as Hash Manager). A forger can use such a program to change the hash values of the tampered image or video file to what it was before the file was tampered.

23.7.2.2 Metadata Analysis

Metadata, which is generally described as *data about data*, provides detailed information about a digital material, such as file name, file extension, file size, hash value, date created, date last accessed, and date last modified. In case of image and video files, metadata may also include details about the software or equipment used to capture the content, including the user settings in effect at the time the content was created and saved.

A computer can generally provide information about the dates and times when the file was last modified, accessed, and first created in the form of MAC dates, but since this information is stored by the computer's operating system, it can become erroneous due to several reasons such as user errors, viruses, file transfers, or deliberate modification with the help of specialized software, such as File Multi Tool 6 and BulkFileCanger. It is therefore prudent for the forensic analyst to rely on another, more dependable and resilient source of metadata, preferably one located within the target file. Metadata inconsistencies must always initiate an exhaustive series of authentication tests.

23.7.2.3 Hex Editor Analysis

Hex editors allow one to examine and modify any bit of the data individually. (*Hex* stands for hexadecimal). Changing this information alters the file's hash value, but examining this data can provide valuable information regarding the integrity of the digital file. For instance, a forensic analyst can use this kind of analysis to ascertain if two seemingly identical copies of a given file are truly identical (because even if the files *seem* to perfect copies of each other, their hex values can reveal even the slightest pixel-level differences between them).

23.8 Passive-Blind Methods of Tamper Detection

The forensic solutions we have reviewed so far were general purpose methods that were aimed at providing rudimentary content authentication services; they were preliminary techniques that could allude to the possibility of tampering in the given content, but were essentially incapable of actually detecting or locating said tampering. In order to conclusively reveal the presence of a forgery in the given image or video, specialized passive-blind tamper detection techniques need to be employed. Regardless of their actual manner of operation, all these techniques work under the common principle that in the absence of any post-production content modification operation, the underlying characteristics of the digital data exhibit a certain level of consistency or uniformity, and any damage (either partial or complete) to this consistency must be regarded with suspicion. In the words of Sherlock Holmes, "We must look for consistency. Where there is a want of it we must suspect deception." The passive-blind nature of these techniques further ensures their applicability in a wide range of real-life forensic scenarios where the analyst may have little to no information vis-à-vis the processing history of the image or video in question.

Before we discuss the various passive-blind tamper detection schemes documented in the literature, we take a quick look at all known kinds of image and video forgeries.

23.8.1 Kinds of Forgeries in Digital Images and Videos

Digital images and videos are known to suffer from several different kinds of visual forgeries. These forgeries can be categorized according to the scheme presented in Figure 23.16.

Intra-frame forgeries are those kinds of visual manipulations that involve direct alteration of the contents of an image or video frame, whereas *inter-frame forgeries*, which are sometimes referred to as *inter-frame copy-paste forgeries*, are those kinds of forgeries which alter the pre-established sequence of frames in a video.

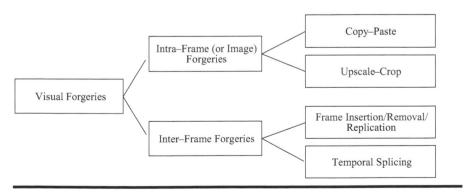

Figure 23.16   Categorization of visual forgeries.

23.8.1.1 Copy-Paste Forgeries

Copy-paste forgeries, aka copy-move forgeries, involve insertion or removal of an object or region into or from an image or a set of frames. Such forgeries are also referred to as *partial manipulation* since only a small region of the image/frame is modified while the rest of the image/frame remains unaffected. Figure 23.17 presents some examples of copy-paste forgeries.

In case of an object-removal forgery, once a particular object (or region) is removed from the image or video frames in question, a technique known as *inpainting* is used to repair the missing or tainted regions in a manner that maintains visual coherence and plausibility within the tampered image/video. Inpainting can be performed in one of two ways:

1. **Temporal Copy and Paste (TCP):** In case of TCP inpainting, tampered regions are filled-up using similar pixels from the surrounding regions of the same frame or with the help of the most coherent blocks from the frames adjacent to the affected frames.
2. **Exemplar Based Texture Synthesis (ETS):** In case of ETS inpainting, the missing regions are filled-in with the help of sample textures.

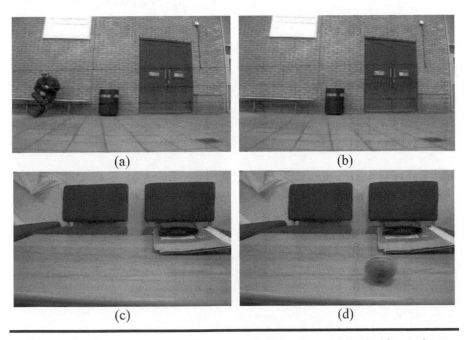

(a) (b)

(c) (d)

Figure 23.17 (a) and (c) represent sample frames from original videos whereas (b) and (d) represent samples frames from the tampered versions of these videos. (Original Videos Courtesy of SULFA, Tampered Video in (d) Courtesy of PU Dataset.)

TCP is a far more preferable video inpainting scheme than ETS, primarily because ETS treats each video frame separately, which makes it difficult to preserve temporal consistency among successive frames after inpainting, whereas TCP uses pixel information from the frames that precede and succeed the inpainted frames, which helps maintain a certain level of visual consistency throughout the tampered video when it is played back as a sequence.

23.8.1.2 Upscale-Crop

Upscale-crop forgeries entail cropping an image or set of video frames in order to eliminate scene content present at the extremities of said image or frames, and enlarging the cropped image/frames so that they match their original resolution. Figure 23.18 exemplifies such forgeries.

Another kind of intra-frame forgery[2] is green-screening, which is also known as blue-screen compositing or chroma key compositing (see Figure 23.19).

(a)

(b)

(c)

(d)

Figure 23.18 **(a) and (c) represent sample video frames, which are cropped to eliminate objects at the extremities of the frames and then enlarged to match their original resolutions, thereby producing the tampered frames (b) and (d), respectively. (Original Videos Courtesy of SULFA.)**

---

[2] It is important to note that although green–screening currently finds application in areas such as weather forecasting and movie production, and has not yet emerged as a means of performing intentional tampering, it has the potential to become a potent forgery technique in the near future. It is therefore prudent to keep this technique under the forensic radar.

Figure 23.19 (a) and (c) represent sample frames from videos depicting people engaged in various activities in front of a green screen, while (b) and (d) represent frames from a new video where the green screen has been replaced by other background or surrounding details. (Courtesy of Imgur and WorldPress.)

23.8.1.3 Frame-Insertion/Removal/Replication

Frame-insertion (or removal) forgeries involve insertion (or removal) of a set of frames into (or from) a video sequence. In a frame-replication or duplication forgery, a set of frames are copied and inserted at another temporal location within the same video (see Figure 23.20).

Such forgeries are among the most unconvoluted methods of event falsification; by removing a handful of frames from a video sequence, one can easily remove all evidence of occurrence of a particular event. Similarly, by moving a set of frames from one temporal location to another within a video, one can falsify the occurrence of an event during a time period in which it did not actually occur.

23.8.1.4 Temporal Splicing

Temporal splicing is another kind of inter-frame forgery wherein frames of two or more separate source videos are combined to create a new fraudulent video. The primary difference between temporal splicing and a frame-insertion forgery is that while temporal splicing is an *inter-video forgery* (i.e., the frames being inserted into

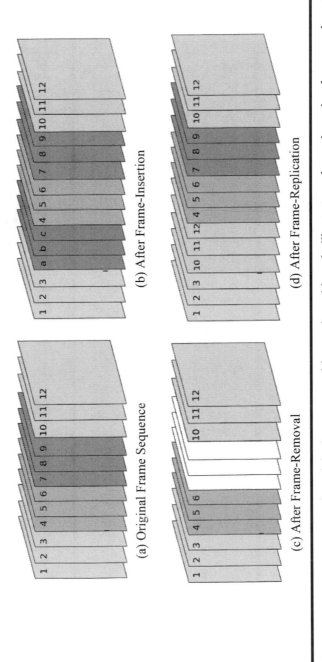

Figure 23.20 (a) represents the original sequence of frames in a video, (b) illustrates a frame-insertion forgery, where frames a, b, and c have been inserted into the video. (c) illustrates a frame-deletion forgery, where frames 7, 8, and 9 (denoted in white) have been removed from the video, and (d) illustrates a frame-replication forgery, where frames 10, 11, and 12 have been replicated at another location within the video.

the video are taken from another video), frame-insertion is an *intra-video forgery* (i.e., the frames being inserted into the video come from the same video).

23.8.2 Specialized Tamper Detection Techniques

In the upcoming sections, we will learn about various passive-blind image and video forgery detection techniques that have been specifically designed to detect the kinds of visual forgeries we examined in the previous section. These techniques have been categorized according to the scheme presented in Figure 23.21.

23.8.2.1 Detection of Frame-Insertion/Removal/Replication

In the upcoming sub-sections, we examine the various forensic artifacts that help detect the presence of such forgeries.

1. **Sensor Artifact Based Techniques**
   Image/video acquisition devices generally leave unique identifiable traces in the content they record. We discussed in Section 23.6 that such traces are mainly used during source camera identification, but some researchers have shown them to be utile for the task of tamper detection as well. Sensor artifact (or sensor noise) based tamper detection techniques basically operate by determining if all the frames of the given video were captured by the same camera, depending on whether or not they exhibit similar noise patterns.
   Read Out Noise: A CCD camera introduces read out noise in every frame it records, and this noise follows a consistent pattern over the entire video sequence. In case a video is suffering from frame-insertion forgery (where the frames being inserted were captured using a different camera), variations in the noise patterns between the frames can be used as an evidence of forgery. This scheme was suggested in De et al. (2006).

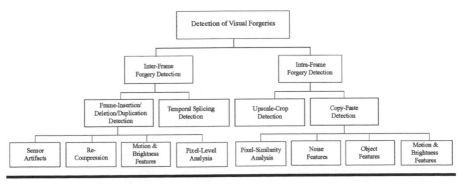

Figure 23.21   Categorization of various tamper detection techniques.

Sensor Pattern Noise: SPN is another unique noise artifact that can be used for the detection of forgeries. By comparing reference SPN of the source camera with test SPN estimated from the given video, frame-replication and frame-insertion forgeries can be detected; in case of a frame-replicated video, reference and test SPN are highly correlated (because of the presence of identical content in the replicated sets of frames), whereas in case of a frame-inserted video, correlation between reference and test SPN is quite low (on account of presence of foreign frames, i.e., frames that originate from a device other than the one used to capture the given video). This method was suggested in Mondaini et al. (2007).

Photon Shot Noise: Presence of foreign frames can also be detected by examining variations in the photon shot noise patterns in different frames of the video in question, as suggested in Kobayashi et al. (2010).

2. **Recompression Detection Based Techniques**

This category of forensic techniques draws inspiration from the chain of events involved in the creation of a typical inter-frame forgery, according to which, any alterations in the pre-established sequence of frames in the given (compressed) video requires the forger to first extract individual frames from this video, then perform the forgery (say frame-removal), and finally combine the altered series of frames to create a new video. This final step is essentially a re-encoding process, which involves a certain amount of compression. This compression is actually a *recompression* since it is in addition to the initial compression that the video underwent when it was first created. Since recompression is an unavoidable consequence of tampering in the compressed domain, it can be treated as an evidence of post-production content modification. Some of the earliest known inter-frame tamper detection schemes detected forgeries in compressed videos by detecting the presence of recompression artifacts.

Discrete Cosine Transform (DCT) Coefficients: When a compressed video undergoes frame-insertion or frame-removal followed by recompression, its pre-established GOP structure gets desynchronized (GOP structure refers to the arrangement of I, P, and B-frames in a compressed video), which causes the DCT coefficients of the video frames to diverge from their usual distribution patterns. Presence of such deviations serves as an evidence of recompression, and subsequently, of inter-frame tampering. DCT coefficient irregularities have been used for detecting frame-insertion/removal forgeries in Wang and Farid (2006, 2009), Su and Xu (2010), Su et al. (2011), Milani et al. (2012), Xu et al. (2012), Sun et al. (2012).

Block Artifact Strength: Block based lossy video encoding schemes, such as MPEG, quantize coefficients in neighboring pixel blocks of a frame separately, which introduces visible artifacts along the block boundaries, known as block artifacts or blocking artifacts. According to Luo et al. (2008), these block artifacts persist even after the video is recompressed after some of its frames are removed. Therefore, by detecting (and quantifying) the degree of change in the Block Artifact Strength (BAS) of the recompressed video as compared to when the video was singly-compressed, presence of frame-removal forgeries can be revealed.

Variation of Prediction Footprint: The authors in Vázquez-Padín et al. (2012) proposed a novel and robust forensic feature called Variation of Prediction Footprint (VPF), which demonstrably appears in only those P-frames of recompressed video sequences that were I-frames when this video was first compressed. VPF was later used for the detection of recompression and inter-frame tampering in Labartino et al. (2013), Gironi et al. (2014), Sitara and Mehtre (2017).

3. **Motion and Brightness Features Based Techniques**

Although recompression artifacts can often provide valuable clues regarding the processing history of the video in question, to state that their presence is always indicative of tampering would be rather unwise, simply because perfectly authentic digital content that we come across in our day to day lives has often undergone multiple post-production compressions. All the tamper detection techniques we reviewed in the previous section relied much too heavily on the forensic evidence offered by recompression artifacts, and consequently failed to differentiate tampered videos from harmlessly recompressed ones.

Since recompression artifacts do not offer conclusive evidence of tampering in realistic forgery scenarios, alternative forensic artifacts have to be relied upon; these are discussed next.

Motion Compensated Edge Artifacts (MCEA): MCEAs are unique artifacts that have been shown to appear in videos that are compressed with the help of coding algorithms that utilize block based motion-compensated frame prediction (such as MPEG-2). During motion-compensated frame prediction, successive video frames are decoded with the help of previously decoded frames, which causes consecutive video frames to become dependent on one another. Inter-frame forgeries destroy such dependencies or correlations, thereby causing the existent block boundary artifacts in the video frames to become even more prominent. This increase in block boundary artifacts, which is referred to as MCEA, can help detect the presence of inter-frame forgeries. MCEAs have been used as discriminating features for the detection of videos suffering from frame-removal forgeries in Su et al. (2009), Dong et al. (2012).

Motion/Prediction Residue: At the time of its creation, a video exhibits an enormous amount of temporal redundancy, which the video encoder takes advantage of by predicting certain frames from other frames. Prediction residual or prediction error, which is the difference between the original video frame and frame predicted by the video encoder, follows a particular pattern for a series of consecutive frames in a natural video. These patterns are established when the video is first acquired, compressed, and saved. If this video is subjected to post-production tampering that affects its frame sequence in any way, the pre-established residual patterns get disrupted, which results in certain statistical abnormalities that can be discovered via suitable analyses. Such abnormalities have been used as forensic features in Stamm et al. (2012), Shanableh (2013), Kancherla and Mukkamal (2012), Liu et al. (2014), Kang et al. (2015), Aghamaleki and Behrad (2016a, 2016b), Yu et al. (2016), Mathai et al. (2016), Singh and Aggarwal (2017a).

Optical Flow and Brightness Variance: Optical flow, which refers to the pattern of apparent motion of objects, surfaces, and edges among successive video frames, is yet another utilitarian forensic feature that enables detection of inter-frame forgeries. In an authentic video, optical flow variations between successive frames remain more or less consistent but in case the pre-established frame sequence is disturbed, optical flow starts exhibiting certain irregularities, which once detected, can serve as the fingerprint of tampering. Optical flow has been used as a forensic feature in Chao et al. (2013), Zheng et al. (2014), Kingra et al. (2017), Singh and Aggarwal (2017a).

Velocity Field Consistency: Velocity field refers to the displacement between neighboring video frames caused by time separation. While velocity field follows a consistent pattern in an authentic video, the authors in Wu et al. (2014) demonstrated that an inter-frame tampering such as frame-removal or frame-replication causes the velocity field sequences to exhibit discernible irregularities, thereby enabling detection of said tampering.

4. **Pixel-Level Analysis Based Techniques**

   Pixel-correlation analysis is among the most instinctive methods for the detection of frame-duplication forgeries. Frame-duplication forgeries basically involve replication of a set of frames at another temporal location within the same video, which implies that the final tampered video essentially contains multiple instances of the same set of frames. Due to the presence of identical frames, pixel-correlations among consecutive frames of such a video become abnormally high. Note that certain amount of pixel-correlation is always present among successive frames of a natural video (because in order to create the illusion of continuous motion, adjacent frames of a video have to be somewhat alike), this correlation is not nearly as high as that present in a frame-replicated video. This forensic methodology has been used in several works (Wang and Farid 2007a, 2007b, Lin et al. 2011, Lin and Chang 2012, Bestagini et al. 2013a, Li and Huang 2013, Yang et al. 2016, Liu and Huang 2017, Ulutaş et al. 2017a, 2017b, Huang et al. 2017, Wei et al. 2017).

23.8.2.2 Detection of Temporal Splicing

Temporal slicing is the process of merging the frames of two or more separate videos to create a new fraudulent video. If the source videos have different frame rates, they must be temporally interpolated before they can be spliced together. This is done with the help of an operation called *Frame Rate Up-Conversion* (FRUC) or *frame interpolation*, which is a process whereby new frames are created with the help of existing ones and are inserted into the given video, thus increasing its frame rate. Techniques that detect temporal splicing basically try to detect FRUC.

The authors in Bestagini et al. (2013b) demonstrated that frame interpolation, when performed with the help of motion compensation, introduces certain discernible artifacts, which can be used as the evidence of presence of FRUC. FRUC also introduces periodic artifacts in the inter-frame similarity sequences of up-converted videos, which can be used for the detection and identification of interpolated frames, as suggested in Bian et al. (2014a, 2014b).

When a new frame is generated by merging two different frames, certain amount of blurring occurs, especially in those pixels that lie at the boundaries of the objects in the frames. This suggests that the intensity of edges of a particular object is lower in the interpolated frame as compared to the intensity of edges of the same object in the original frames (i.e., those that were used to generate the interpolated frame). Furthermore, since the interpolated frames are interleaved periodically into the original video, reduction in intensities of object edges in an up-converted video will exhibit certain periodicity along its temporal dimension. The presence of this periodicity can thus serve as the evidence of presence of interpolated frames, as proposed in Yao et al. (2016). FRUC has also been observed to introduce discernible periodic artifacts in the texture regions of the affected (interpolated) frames. The scheme suggested in Xia et al. (2016) relies on the detection of such artifacts.

23.8.2.3 Detection of Copy-Paste Forgeries

Copy-paste aka copy-move forgeries involve insertion or removal of objects into or from video frames or images. Forensic techniques that detect such forgeries either search for evidence of presence of duplicate regions in an image or video frame (which occurs when inpainting is performed), or search for artifacts that emerge when an object or region is removed from an image or video frame.

1. **Pixel Similarity and Correlation Based Techniques**

   Copy-paste detection techniques that belong to this category detect similarities or correlations among regions of the same frame (or image) or among regions of consecutive video frames, which in theory should be devoid of any similarities, mainly because they have different origins or time/place associated with their lineage.

   Pixels in neighboring regions of an image or video frame typically demonstrate certain amount of similarity (due to spatial redundancy), but when this similarity surpasses a certain pre-determined threshold, the image or video frame is classified as a forgery. Another way of utilizing inter-pixel correlations to detect copy-paste forgeries is to identify and highlight those regions of the given image or frame that exhibit uncharacteristically high or abnormally low pixel-correlations, as compared to other regions of the image/frame. Such methods generally train a machine-learning model to identify those regions of the image or video frame that demonstrate abnormal pixel-correlations. The techniques proposed in Fridrich et al. (2003), Popescu and Farid (2004), Bayram et al. (2005), Jing and Hongbin (2006), Luo et al. (2006), Li et al. (2007), Wang and Farid (2007b), Huang et al. (2008), Huang and Long (2008), Lin et al. (2009), Fan et al. (2009), Das et al. (2012), Bestagini et al. (2013a), Lin and Tsay (2014), Singh and Aggarwal (2017b) examine pixels similarities/correlations to detect copy-pasted regions in images/videos.

2. **Noise Residue and Sensor Pattern Noise Based Techniques**
   Another popular strategy used to identify identical regions within images or video frames is to examine the correlations between noise residue (or sensor pattern noise) components in image/frames (noise residue for every image/frame is calculated by subtracting the actual image/frame from its denoised version). This strategy is based on the principle that correlation between noise residue in regions that have been copy-pasted demonstrate a significant deviation from the norm and detecting this deviation leads to the detection of the forged region. Noise features have been used for the detection of copypaste forgeries in Gou et al. (2007), Chen et al. (2008), Hsu et al. (2008), Mahdian and Saic (2009), Dirik and Memon (2009), Goodwin and Chetty (2010), Pandey et al. (2014), Singh and Aggarwal (2017b).

3. **Object Feature Based Techniques**
   In case of videos, the presence of a copy-paste forgery can be revealed with the help of those artifacts that arise after an object has been removed from the scene. One of the most prominent artifacts of object-removal is the ghost shadow artifact, which arises when moving objects are removed from a video frame. In order to detect these ghost artifacts, video frames are first segmented into static background and moving foreground. The moving foreground is used to construct a foreground mosaic and an Absolute Difference Frame (ADI). The presence of any discrepancy between the foreground mosaic and the ADI is considered to be an evidence of forgery. This scheme was suggested in Zhang et al. (2009). Another similar concept was used in Richao et al. (2014); it was based on the observation that object-based manipulations leave certain splicing traces in video frames, which emerge as discernible inconsistencies near the object boundaries within the frames.

   Another way to detect a copy-paste forgery is by identifying physically improbable trajectories of any solid objects in the video. This method was suggested in Conotter et al. (2012), and it works by first creating a 3D model of the parabolic trajectories of objects in free flight and its corresponding 2D projection onto the image plane, and then weeding out any geometric inconsistencies.

4. **Motion and Brightness Features Based Techniques**
   Motion and brightness features not only help detect inter-frame forgeries, but provide valuable clues regarding the presence of copy-paste forgeries as

well. By extracting motion residue from successive frames and looking for any inconsistencies therein, presence of identical regions within frames can be revealed; use of this principle was demonstrated in Chen et al. (2015) and Yao et al. (2017). Optical flow inconsistencies among different regions of a suspicious frame can also help detect copy-paste forgeries, as proposed in Bidokhti and Ghaemmaghami (2015). In images, copy-paste forgeries can be detected by searching for pixels with identical intensity patterns, as suggested in Langille and Gong (2006).

23.8.2.4 Detection of Upscale-Crop

Upscale-crop forgeries can be detected by looking for traces of *resampling* (specifically, up-sampling), which is required to enlarge the cropped frames so that the resolution of the affected frames matches that of the rest of the un-tampered frames of the video.

When the extremities of a frame are cropped out, pixels at those locations are lost forever. Now, when this cropped frame needs to be enlarged, new pixels are required, which are generated with the help of existing pixels through a process known as *pixel interpolation*. This process of interpolation introduces certain correlations among pixel values, which are greater than the naturally existing correlations found in an authentic image or the frames of an authentic video. These abnormalities in pixel correlations can be detected by analyzing variations in the correlation properties of reference and test SPN estimated from the upscaled frames, as done in the case of Hyun et al. (2013), or in magnitudes of Fast Fourier Transform (FFT) or Discrete Fractional Fourier Transform (DFrFT) coefficients of autocorrelation sequences of variance signals for n^{th} order signal derivatives, as suggested in Singh and Aggarwal (2017c). The authors in Singh and Aggarwal (2017c) also suggested plotting autocorrelation sequences for reference and test SPN for the given video to detect superfluous noise added to hide the traces of resampling.

In case of images, the mere presence of resampling or interpolation artifacts is sometimes construed as evidence of tampering. The techniques proposed in Gallagher (2005), Popescu and Farid (2005), Prasad and Ramakrishnan (2006), Kirchner (2008, 2009), Poilpré et al. (2008), Mahdian and Saic (2008a, 2008b), all detected image tampering via interpolation detection.

23.8.2.5 Detection of Green-Screening

Green-screening is not yet regarded as a proper forgery technique, but the ability to detect its presence is nonetheless crucial from a forensics point of view. The green-screening detection technique presented in Xu et al. (2012) was based on the observation that unlike natural videos, the background and foreground scenes in a composite video exhibit distinct statistical distributions of DCT coefficients, mainly because they are produced using different encoders (or are encoded with different settings). Therefore, by measuring the degree of similarity (or lack thereof) between the background and foreground regions of the video in question, it can be classified as natural or composite.

23.9 Anti-Forensics and Counter Anti-Forensics

In the previous sub-sections, we explored several image and video forgery detection techniques, all of which were ultimately dependent on certain identifying traces various content modification operations inevitably leave behind, thus serving as evidence of tampering. This begs the question: *What would happen is a forger deliberately hid the evidence of manipulation by eliminating or minimizing the presence of these traces?* This question leads us to another aspect of digital visual media forensics, i.e., the domain of *anti-forensics and counter anti-forensics.*

23.9.1 *Image and Video Anti-Forensics*

An anti-forensic technique is a forgery technique that has been specifically designed to thwart the digital investigation process by modifying the content alteration operation in such a way that any evidence of the alteration remains hidden and highly difficult to detect or locate by even the most potent tamper detection techniques. For instance, in order to hide the evidence of recompression in a digital image, a forger could add *dither* or *dither+blur* to the DCT coefficients of a compressed JPEG image. Dither is a kind of noise that removes the quantization artifacts produced by compression whereas dither+blur removes both quantization artifacts and blocking artifacts produced by compression. The process of using dither or dither+blur to remove the evidence of JPEG compression is known as *Anti-JPEG Compression or Anti-Forensic Dithering.* When a JPEG image undergoes anti-JPEG compression, traces of the previous compression get destroyed, thereby causing double-compressed JPEG image to exhibit characteristics of a singly-compressed image.

Anti-forensic techniques are equally beneficial for falsifying the *origin* of an image. One of the most commonly used source identification features is the image's quantization table (a quantization table, also known as a quantization matrix, helps transform a continuous signal into its discrete version and is used during the quantization step of a digital image creation process). Since most digital cameras and content editing software use proprietary quantization tables while performing JPEG compression, these tables can serve as identifying traces that help link an image to a specific camera or a content editing software. If a forger adds dither to the image's DCT coefficients before recompressing it using quantization tables associated with another device, the origin of the image can be falsified, all the while prohibiting the introduction of recompression artifacts that could make the forensic analyst aware of such a forgery. This strategy was suggested in Stamm et al. (2010a, 2010b) and Stamm and Liu (2011a).

In contrast to image anti-forensics, the domain of video anti-forensics has made very limited headway. In Stamm and Liu (2011b), the authors suggested an anti-forensic technique that was specifically aimed at fooling the frame-insertion/removal detection technique presented in Wang and Farid (2006). This was done by creating fake DCT coefficient abnormalities, which then interfered with the actual abnormalities introduced by frame-insertion/removal. This technique was later extended in Stamm et al. (2012).

23.9.2 Image and Video Counter Anti-Forensics

Counter anti-forensic techniques are specialized techniques that aim at detecting anti forensically created forgeries. Innovations in the domain of counter anti-forensics are vital because they are our only line of defense against clever forgeries that are immune to detection by even the most effective forensic solutions.

The key to success in the counter anti-forensics domain is the same old Locard's Exchange Principle, i.e., *every contact leaves a trace*. It has been demonstrated in Valenzise et al. (2011a, 2012b), Liu and Kang (2014), Su et al. (2015) that all anti-forensic operations have a tendency to leave behind their own detectable traces. For instance, while it is possible to destroy the evidence of a previous JPEG compression using anti-JPEG compression, the end results cannot be achieved without degrading the quality of the tampered image. This loss in quality can serve as the evidence of an anti-forensic manipulation. Furthermore, since anti-forensic techniques introduce their own artifacts into the content, a forger may have to make a compromise between completely eliminating the artifacts of the content manipulation operation and introducing new artifacts of the anti-forensic operation; inconsistencies caused by such a trade-off can be taken advantage of during the development of counter anti-forensic solutions.

23.10 Summary

Through the ages, photographs and videos have risen as indispensable sources of information with high evidentiary value, but amid the relentless march of technology, we have come to realize that though this information may be compelling, it may not always mean what it seems to mean. Subsequently, in a sensitive situation where dependence on visual evidence is unavoidable, it becomes crucial to verify the validity and credibility of this evidence, before we confer upon it our unmitigated trust.

This chapter was dedicated to the comprehensive assessment of the field of digital visual media forensics, which is a chain of scientific inquiry that supports digital image and video authentication and integrity verification. We began the discussion with a brief account of the origin and history of digital photographs and videos in regards to their role as forensic evidence, followed by an overview of some of the most notable instances of use of visual evidence during investigations and trials. We then examined the inherent frailty of digital evidence with the help of some illustrative examples, which led us to the discussion about the necessity of digital visual media forensics and the basic tasks associated therewith, including the concepts of evidence collection/recovery/repair, evidence enhancement and authentication, hidden data detection, and evidence identification and interpretation. We studied the concept of identifying traces and examined the various methods by which such traces can be used during source camera identification, integrity verification, content authentication, and tamper detection. We also explored the variants of digital visual media forensics, i.e., active/passive forensics and blind/non-blind forensics. The chapter concluded with an analysis of the domains of anti-forensics and counter anti-forensics.

References and Resources

3 witnesses identify Kasab, court takes on record CCTV footage. *The Economic Times.* 2009. https://economictimes.indiatimes.com/news/politics-and-nation/3-witnesses-identify-kasab-court-takes-on-record-cctv-footage/articleshow/4665196.cms (accessed September 13, 2017).

Adams, C. 2016. Expert opinion and evidence of human identity, in *Forensic Evidence in Court: Evaluation and Scientific Opinion.* Hoboken, NJ: John Wiley & Sons.

Aghamaleki, J.A. and Behrad, A. 2016a. Malicious inter-frame video tampering detection in MPEG videos using time and spatial domain analysis of quantization effects, *Multimedia Tools and Applications* 1: 1–7.

Aghamaleki, J.A. and Behrad, A., Vol. 1, 2016b. Inter-frame video forgery detection and localization using intrinsic effects of double compression on quantization errors of video coding, *Signal Processing and Image Communications* 47: 289–302.

Avcibas, I., Kharrazi, M., Memon, N. et al. 2005. Image steganalysis with binary similarity measures, *EURASIP Journal on Applied Signal Processing* 17: 2749–2757.

Bayram, S., Avcibas, I., Sankur, B. et al. 2005. Image manipulation detection with binary similarity measures, *13th European Signal Processing Conference*, Antalya, Turkey, pp. 752–755.

Bayram, S., Sencar, H.T., and Memon, N. 2005. Source camera identification based on CFA interpolation, *IEEE International Conference on Image Processing*, Genoa, Italy.

Bayram, S., Sencar, H.T., and Memon, N. 2006. Improvements on source camera-model identification based on CFA interpolation, *International Conference on Digital Forensics.*

Best Practices for Administrative Metadata, 2010. Champaign, IL: University Library, University of Illinois.

Best Practices for Technical Metadata, 2010. Champaign, IL: University Library, University of Illinois.

Bestagini, P., Battaglia, S., Milani, S. et al. 2013b. Detection of temporal interpolation in video sequences, *IEEE International Conference on Acoustics, Speech and Signal Processing*, Vancouver, Canada.

Bestagini, P., Milani, S., Tagliasacchi, M. et al. 2013a. Local tampering detection in video sequences, *15th IEEE International Workshop on Multimedia Signal Processing*, Pula, Italy, pp. 488–493.

Bian, S., Luo, W., and Huang, J. 2014a. Exposing fake bit rates video and estimating original bit rates, *IEEE Transaction on Circuits, Systems and Video Technology* 24(12): 2144–2154.

Bian, S., Luo, W., and Huang, J. 2014b. Detecting video frame-rate up-conversion based on periodic properties of inter-frame similarity, *Multimedia Tools and Applications* 72(1): 437–451.

Bidokhti, A. and Ghaemmaghami, S. 2015. Detection of regional copy/move forgery in MPEG videos using optical flow, *International Symposium on Artificial Intelligence and Signal Processing*, Mashhad, Iran, pp. 13–17.

Blackwell, V. 2013. Kendrick Johnson footage released; expert finds it "highly suspicious". *CNN*. https://edition.cnn.com/2013/11/21/justice/kendrick-johnson-surveillance-videos/index.html (accessed September 15, 2017).

Böhme, R. and Kirchner, M. 2013. Counter-Forensics: Attacking image forensics, *Digital Image Forensics*, New York: Springer, pp. 327–366.

Brady, E. 2016. The photos that sent O.J. Simpson spiraling. *USA Today Sports*. https://www.usatoday.com/story/sports/2016/06/02/photos-sent-oj-simpson-spiraling/84911596/ (accessed September 15, 2017).

Bucktin, C. 2013. Boston bomber caught on CCTV: FBI close in on suspect seen dropping bag in street. *Mirror*. https://www.mirror.co.uk/news/world-news/boston-marathon-bomber-caught-cctv-1838523 (accessed September 14, 2017).

CANVASS. https://commons.erau.edu/cgi/viewcontent.cgi?article=1126&context=adfsl (accessed January 3, 2018).

Cao, G., Zhao, Y., Ni, R. et al. 2010. Anti-forensics of contrast enhancement in digital images, *12th ACM Workshop on Multimedia and Security*, Rome, Italy, pp. 25–34

Chao, J., Jiang, X., and Sun, T. 2013. A novel video inter-frame forgery model detection scheme based on optical flow consistency, *Digital Forensics and Watermarking* 7809: 267–281.

Chen, M., Fridrich, J., and Goljan, M. 2007. Digital imaging sensor identification (further study), *Proceedings of SPIE*.

Chen, M., Goljan, M., and Lukas, J. 2008. Determining image origin and integrity using sensor noise, *IEEE Transactions on Information Forensics and Security* 3(1): 74–90.

Choi, K.S., Lam, E.Y., and Wong, K.K.Y. 2006. Source camera identification using footprints from lens aberration, *Proceedings of SPIE*, Vol. 6069.

Conotter, V., O'Brien, J.F., and Farid, F. 2012. Exposing digital forgeries in ballistic motion, *IEEE Transactions on Information Forensics and Security* 7(1): 283–296.

Cowan, R. 2005. Row over "blank" CCTV tapes at station. *The Guardian*. https://www.theguardian.com/uk/2005/aug/23/politics.brazil (accessed September 15, 2017).

Cox, I.J., Miller, M.L., and Bloom, J.A. 2002. *Digital Watermarking*. Burlington, MA: Morgan Kaufmann Publishers.

Das, S., Darsan, G., Shreyas, L. et al. 2012. Blind detection method for video inpainting forgery, *International Journal of Computer Applications* 60(11): 33–37.

De, A., Chadha, H., and Gupta, S. 2006. Detection of forgery in digital video, *10th World Multi Conference on Systems, Cybernetics and Informatics*, France, pp. 229–233.

Dearden, L. and Bulman, M. 2017. London attack: CCTV video shows terrorists laughing while planning atrocity at Ilford gym. *The Independent*. http://www.independent.co.uk/News/uk/home-news/london-attack-cctv-video-terrorists-ilford-gym-before-borough-market-stabbing-ummah-fitness-centre-a7778666.html (accessed September 14, 2017).

Deeming Sri Lanka execution video authentic, UN expert calls for war crimes probe. *UN News Centre*. 2010. http://www.un.org/apps/news/story.asp?NewsID=33423#. WnmVrVNubow (accessed September 15, 2017).

Dirik, A.E. and Memon, N. 2009. Image tamper detection based on demosaicing artifacts, *IEEE International Conference on Image Processing*, Cairo, Egypt, 429–432.

Dirik, E, Sencar, H., and Memon, N. 2008 , pp. 539–552. Digital single lens reflex camera identification from traces of sensor dust, *IEEE Transaction on Information Forensics and Security* 3(3): 539–552.

Dong, Q., Yang, G., and Zhu, N. 2012. A MCEA based passive forensics scheme for detecting frame-based video tampering, *Digital Investigation* 9: 151–59.

Edmond Locard. http://aboutforensics.co.uk/edmond-locard/

Fan, N., Jin, C., and Huang, Y. 2009. A pixel-based digital photo authentication framework via demosaicking inter-pixel correlation, *11th ACM Workshop on Multimedia and Security*, New York, pp. 125–130.

Fan, W., Wang, K., Cayere, F. et al. 2013. A variational approach to JPEG anti-forensics, *IEEE 38th Inernational Conference on Acoustics, Speech, and Signal Processing*, Vancouver, Canada, pp. 3058–3062.

Fridrich, J., Soukal, D., and Lukas, J. 2003. Detection of copy–move forgery in digital images, *Digital Forensic Research Workshop, IEEE Computer Society*, Cleveland, OH, pp. 55–61.

Gallagher, A.C. 2005. Detection of linear and cubic interpolation in jpeg compressed images, *2nd Canadian Conference on Computer and Robot Vision*, Washington, DC, pp. 65–72.

Geradts, Z.J., Bijhold, J., Kieft, M. et al. 2001. Methods for identification of images acquired with digital cameras, *Proceedings of SPIE*, Vol. 4232.

Gironi, A., Fontani, M., Bianchi, T. et al. 2014. A video forensic technique for detecting frame deletion and insertion, *IEEE International Conference on Acoustics, Speech, and Signal Processing*, Florence, Italy, pp. 6267–6271.

Golijan, M. and Fridrich, J. 2008. Camera identification from scaled and cropped images, *SPIE Electronic Imaging, Forensics, Security, Steganography, Watermarking of Multimedia Contents*.

Goodwin, J. and Chetty, G. 2011. Blind video tamper detection based on fusion of source features, *IEEE International Conference on Digital Image Computing Techniques and Applications*, Noosa, Australia, pp. 608–613.

Gou, H., Swaminathan, A., and Wu, M. 2007. Noise features for image tampering detection and steganalysis, *IEEE International Conference on Image Processing*, San Antonio, TX, pp. 97–100.

Gou, H., Swaminathan, A., and Wu, M. 2007. Robust scanner identification based on noise features, *Proceedings of SPIE*, Vol. 6505.

Granados, M., Kim, K., Tompkin, J. et al. 2012. How not to be seen: Object removal from videos of crowded scenes, *Computer Graphics Forum, EUROGRAPHICS*.

Hales, J. 2013. *Criminal Evidence*. 8th ed. Belmont, CA: Wadsworth Publishing.

Hannavy, J. ed. 2008. *Encyclopedia of Nineteenth-Century Photography*, Abingdon, UK: Routledge.

Hirsch, R. 2000. *Seizing the Light: A History of Photography*, New York City: McGraw-Hill.

Hopkins, N. and Hall, S. 2000. David Copeland: A quiet introvert, obsessed with Hitler and bombs. *The Guardian.* https://www.theguardian.com/uk/2000/jun/30/uksecurity.sarahhall (accessed September 13, 2017).

Hsu, C.-C., Hung, T.-Y., Lin, C.-W. et al. 2008. Video forgery detection using correlation of noise residue, *10th IEEE Workshop on Multimedia Signal Processing.* Cairns, Australia, pp. 170–174.

Huang, C.C., Zhang, Y., and Thing, V.L.L. 2017. Inter-frame video forgery detection based on multi-level subtraction approach for realistic video forensic applications, *2nd International Conference on Signal and Image Processing*, Singapore.

Huang, H., Guo, W., and Zhang, Y. 2008. Detection of copy–move forgery in digital images using sift algorithm, *IEEE Pacific-Asia Workshop on Computational Intelligence and Industrial Application*, Washington, DC, pp. 272–276.

Huang, Y. and Long, Y. 2008. Demosaicking recognition with applications in digital photo authentication based on a quadratic pixel correlation model, *IEEE Conference on Computer Vision and Pattern Recognition*, Anchorage, AK, pp. 1–8.

Hyun, D.-K., Ryu, S.-J. Lee, H.-Y. et al. 2013. Detection of upscale-crop and partial manipulation in surveillance video based on sensor pattern noise, *Sensors* 13: 12605–12631.

Ibrahim, A. 2007. Steganalysis in computer forensics, *Australian Digital Forensics Conference*, p. 10.

Independent Commission on the Los Angeles Police Department. 1991. Chapter 1, The Rodney King beating, *Report of the Independent Commission on the Los Angeles Police Department*, DIANE Publishing.

Jaeger, L. 2005. *Police and Forensic Photography*, The Oxford Companion to the Photograph, Oxford, UK: Oxford University Press.

James, S.H., Nordby, J.J., and Bell, S. 2014. *Forensic Science: An Introduction to Scientific and Investigative Techniques*, 4th ed., Boca Raton, FL: Taylor & Francis Group.

Jing, W. and Hongbin, Z. 2006. Exposing digital forgeries by detecting traces of image splicing, *8th International Conference on Signal Processing*, Guilin, China, pp. 16–20.

Kancherla, K., and Mukkamal, S. 2012. Novel blind video forgery detection using Markov models on motion residue, *Intelligent Informatics and Database Systems* 7198: 308–315.

Kang, X., Liu, J., Liu, H. et al. 2015. Forensics and counter anti-forensics of video inter-frame forgery, *Multimedia Tools and Applications* 75: 1–21.

Khanna, N., Mikkilineni, A.K., Chu, G.T.-C. et al. 2007. Forensic classification of imaging sensor types, *Proceedings of SPIE*, Vol. 6505.

Kharrazi, M., Sencar, H.T., and Memon, N. 2004. Blind source camera identification, *IEEE International Conference on Image Processing*, Singapore.

Kingra, S., Aggarwal, N., and Singh, R.D. 2017. Inter-frame forgery detection using motion and brightness gradients, *Multimedia Tools and Applications* 1–20.

Kirchner, M. 2008. Fast and reliable resampling detection by spectral analysis of fixed linear predictor residue, *10th ACM workshop on Multimedia and security*, New York, pp. 11–20.

Kirchner, M. 2009. On resampling detection in re-compressed images, *IEEE Workshop on Information Forensics and Security*, pp. 21–25.

Kobayashi, M., Okabe, T., and Sato, Y. 2010. Detecting forgery from static-scene video based on inconsistency in noise level functions, *IEEE Transactions on Information Forensics and Security* 5(4): 883–892.

Kurosawa, K., Kuroki, K., and Saitoh, N. 1999. CCD fingerprint method, *IEEE International Conference on Image Processing*, Kobe, Japan.

Labartino, D., Bianchi, T., de Rosa, A. et al. 2013. Localization of forgeries in MPEG-2 video through GOP size and DQ analysis, *IEEE 15th International Workshop on Multimedia Signal Processing*, Pula, Italy, pp. 494–499.

Langille, A. and Gong, M. 2006. An efficient match-based duplication detection algorithm, *3rd Canadian Conference on Computer and Robot Vision*, Washington, DC.

Li, F. and Huang, T. 2013. Video copy-move forgery detection and localization based on structural similarity, *3rd International Conference on Multimedia Technology*, Guangzhou, China, pp. 63–76.

Lin, C.-S. and Tsay, J.-J. 2014. A passive approach for effective detection and localization of region-level video forgery with spatio-temporal coherence analysis, *Digital Investigation* 1(2): 120–140.

Lin, G.-S. and Chang, J.-F. 2012. Detection of frame duplication forgery in videos based on spatial and temporal analysis, *International Journal of Pattern Recognition and Artificial Intelligence* 26(7).

Lin, G.-S., Chang, J.-F., and Chuang, C.-H. 2011. Detecting frame duplication based on spatial and temporal analyses, *6th IEEE International Conference on Computer Science and Education*, SuperStar Virgo, Singapore, pp. 1396–1399.

Lin, H.-J., Wang, C.-W., and Kao, Y.-T. 2009. Fast copy–move forgery detection, *WSEAS Transactions on Signal Processing* 5(5): 188–197.

Liu, H., Li, S., and Bian, S. 2014. Detecting frame deletion in H.264 video, *10th International Conference on Information Security Practice and Experience*, Fuzhou, China, pp. 262–270.

Liu, J. and Kang, X. 2014. *Anti-Forensics of Video Frame Deletion*. http://www.paper.edu.cn/download/downPaper/201407-346 (accessed December 13, 2017).

Liu, Y. and Huang, T. 2017. Exposing video inter-frame forgery by Zernike opponent chromaticity moments and coarseness analysis, *Multimedia Systems* 23(2): 223–238.

London riots: Police release more CCTV suspect images. *BBC News*. 2011. http://www.bbc.com/news/uk-england-london-14479707 (accessed September 14, 2017).

Longand, Y. and Huang, Y. 2006. Image based source camera identification using demosaicing, *IEEE Multimedia Signal Processing*, Vancouver, Canada.

Lukas, J., Fridrich, J., and Goljan, M. 2006. Digital camera identification from sensor pattern noise, *IEEE Transactions on Information Forensics and Security* 1(2): 205–214.

Luo, W., Huang, J., and Qiu, G. 2006. Robust detection of region-duplication forgery in digital image, *18th International Conference on Pattern Recognition, IEEE Computer Society*, Washington, DC, pp. 746–749.

Luo, W., Wu, M., and Huang, J. 2008. MPEG recompression detection based on block artifacts, *SPIE Security, Forensics, Steganography, and Watermarking of Multimedia Content*.

Lyu, S. and Farid, H. 2006. Steganalysis using higher-order image statistics, *IEEE Transaction on Image Forensics and Security* 1(1): 111–119.

Mahdian, B. and Saic, S. 2008. Blind authentication using periodic properties of interpolation, *IEEE Transactions on Information Forensics and Security* 3(3): 529–538.

Mahdian, B. and Saic, S. 2008. Detection of resampling supplemented with noise inconsistencies analysis for image forensics, *International Conference on Computational Sciences and its Applications*, Perugia, Italy, pp. 546–556.

Mahdian, B. and Saic, S. 2009. Using noise inconsistencies for blind image forensics, *Image Vision Computing* 27(10): 1497–1503.

Mathai, M., Rajan, D., and Emmanuel, S. 2016. Video forgery detection and localization using normalized cross-correlation of moment features, *IEEE Southwest Symposium on Image Analysis and Interpretation*, Santa Fe, NM.

Milani, S., Bestagini, P., Tagliasacchi, M. et al. 2012. Multiple compression detection for video sequences, *14th IEEE International Workshop Multimedia Signal Processing*, Banff, AB, pp. 112–117.

Mnookin, J.L. 1998. The image of truth: Photographic evidence and the power of analogy, *Yale Journal of Law & the Humanities* 10(1): 1–13.

Mondaini, N., Caldelli, R. Piva, A. et al. 2007. Detection of malevolent changes in digital video for forensic applications, *SPIE Conference on Security, Steganography and Watermarking of Multimedia Contents* 6505(1).

Montaldo, C. 2017. The murder of Carlie Brucia. *ThoughtCo*. https://www.thoughtco.com/the-murder-of-carlie-brucia-971024 (accessed September 16, 2017).

Morris, B., Clement, N., and Jason, B. 2005. Police and Tube firm at odds over CCTV footage of innocent Brazilian's shooting. *The Independent*. http://www.independent.co.uk/news/uk/crime/police-and-tube-firm-at-odds-over-cctv-footage-of-innocent-brazilians-shooting-307649.html (accessed September 15, 2017).

Muir, J. and Hosea, L. 2012. Syria crisis: Houla massacre leaves 90 dead. *BBC News*. http://www.bbc.co.uk/news/world-middle-east-18216176 (accessed September 15, 2017).

Nanny cleared of violently shaking baby, *ABC News*. 2006. http://abcnews.go.com/GMA/LegalCenter/story?id=1749672 (accessed September 23, 2017).

Navarro, M. 2017. Los cinco de Cambrils comprando cuchillos en el bazar chino [The five of Cambrils buying knives in the Chinese bazaar]. *La Vanguardia*. http://www.lavanguardia.com/politica/20170824/43775507992/atentado-barcelona-cambrils-cuchillos-bazar-chino.html (accessed September 14, 2017).

Newson, A., Almansa, A., Fradet, M. et al. 2014. Video inpainting of complex scenes, *SIAM Journal of Imaging Sciences* 7(4): 1993–2019.

Pandey, R.C., Singh, S.K., and Shukla, K.K. 2014. Passive copy-move forgery detection in videos, *IEEE 5th International Conference on Computer and Communication Technology*, Allahabad, India, pp. 301–306.

Paris attacks suspect Abdeslam "caught on CCTV" in French petrol station. *BBC News*. 2016. http://www.bbc.com/news/world-europe-35286647 (accessed September 14, 2017).

Photo tampering throughout history. http://pth.izitru.com/

Poilpré, M.-C., Perrot, P., and Talbot, H. 2008. Image tampering detection using Bayer interpolation and jpeg compression, *1st International Conference on Forensic Applications and Techniques in Telecommunications, Information, and Multimedia and Workshop*, Brussels, Belgium, pp. 1–5.

Popescu, A. 2005. Statistical tools for digital image forensics, PhD dissertation, Department of Computer Science, Darthmouth College, Hanover, NH.

Popescu, A. and Farid, H. 2004. Exposing digital forgeries by detecting duplicated image regions, Technical Report TR2004-515, Hanover, NH: Department of Computer Science, Dartmouth College.

Popescu, A. and Farid, H. 2005. Exposing digital forgeries by detecting traces of re-sampling, *IEEE Transactions on Signal Processing* 53(2): 758–767.

Prasad, S. and Ramakrishnan, K.R. 2006. On resampling detection and its application to image tampering, *IEEE International Conference on Multimedia and Exposition*, Toronto, Canada, pp. 1325–1328.

PU Dataset. http://pudataset.puchd.ac.in:8080/jspui/handle/123456789/22.

Rayner, G. 2017. Manchester suicide bombing: How the worst UK terror attack since 7/7 unfolded. *Financial Review.* http://www.afr.com/news/world/europe/manchester-suicide-bombing-how-the-worst-uk-terror-attack-since-77-unfolded-20170524-gwbsl5 (accessed September 14, 2017).

Report into the London terrorist attacks on 7 July 2005. Intelligence and Security Committee, *BBC News*. 2006. https://www.gov.uk/government/uploads/system/uploads/attachment_data/file/224690/isc_terrorist_attacks_7july_report.pdf (accessed September 13, 2017)

RFC 1321 – The MD5 Message-Digest Algorithm, 1992. Internet Engineering Task Force.

RFC 3174 - US Secure Hash Algorithm 1 (SHA1). 2001.

Rhodes, H.T.F. 1956. *Alphonse Bertillon: Father of Scientific Detection*, New York: Abelard-Schuman Ltd.

Richao, C., Gaobo, Y., and Ningbo, Z. 2014. Detection of object-based manipulation by the statistical features of object contour, *Forensic Science International* 236: 164–169.

Roberts, L. 2011. History of video surveillance and CCTV. http://www.wecusurveillance.com/cctvhistory (accessed September 3, 2017).

Rocha, A. Scheirer, W., Boult, T. et al. 2011. Vision of the unseen: Current trends and challenges in digital image and video forensics, *ACM Computing Surveys* 43 (4), 26.

S. Chen, S. Tan, B. Li, and J. Huang. 2015. Automatic detection of object-based forgery in advanced video, *IEEE Transactions on Circuits, Systems and Video Technology*, Vol. 99.

Scott, C.C. 1938. Photography in criminal investigations. *Journal of Criminal Law & Criminology* 29: 383–419.

Seelow, S. 2016. Attaque de Nice: un projet « mûri depuis plusieurs mois » et plusieurs complices [Attack in Nice: A project "matured for several months" and several accomplices], *Le Monde.* http://www.lemonde.fr/societe/article/2016/07/22/nice-cinq-suspects-mis-en-examen-pour-association-de-malfaiteurs-terroriste-criminelle_4972976_3224.htm (accessed September 14, 2017).

Shanableh, T. 2013. Detection of frame deletion for digital video forensics, *Digital Investigation* 10: 350–360.

Shaw, S. 1999. Overview of watermarks, fingerprints, and digital signatures, *JISC Technology Applications Programme Report*, pp. 1–20.

Singh, R.D. and Aggarwal, N. 2017. Video content authentication techniques: A comprehensive survey, *Multimedia Systems*, 1–30.

Singh, R.D. and Aggarwal, N. 2017a. Optical flow and prediction residual based hybrid forensic system for inter-frame tampering detection, *Journal of Circuits, Systems & Computers* 26(7).

Singh, R.D. and Aggarwal, N. 2017b. Detection and localization of copy-paste forgeries in digital videos, *Forensic Science International* 281: 75–91.

Singh, R.D. and Aggarwal, N. 2017c. Detection of upscale-crop and splicing for digital video authentication, *Digital Investigation* 21: 31–52.

Sitara, K. and Mehtre, B.M. 2017. A comprehensive approach for exposing inter- frame video forgeries, *IEEE 13th International Colloquium on Signal Processing & its Applications*, Batu Ferringhi, Malaysia.

Smith, D.J. 1994. *The Sleep of Reason: The James Bulger Case*. London, UK: Century Arrow Books.

Stamm, M., Lin, W.S., and Liu, K.J.R. 2012. Temporal forensics and anti-forensics for motion compensated video, *IEEE Transaction on Information Forensics and Security*, Vol. 7.

Stamm, M.C. and Liu, K.J.R. 2010. Wavelet-based image compression anti-forensics, *17th IEEE International Conference on Image Processing*, Hong Kong, China, pp. 1737–1740.

Stamm, M.C. and Liu, K.J.R. 2011a. Anti-forensics of digital image compression, *IEEE Transaction on Information Forensics and Security* 6(3): 1050–1065.

Stamm, M.C. and Liu, K.J.R. 2011b. Anti-forensics for frame deletion/addition in MPEG video, *IEEE International Conference on Acoustics Speech and Signal Processing*, Prague, Czech Republic, pp. 1876–1879.

Stamm, M.C., Lin, W.S., and Liu, K.J.R. 2012. Temporal forensics and anti-forensics for motion compensated video, *IEEE Transaction on Information Forensics Security* 7(4): 1315–1329.

Stamm, M.C., Tjoa, S.K., Lin, W.S. et al. 2010a. Anti-forensics of JPEG compression, *IEEE International Conference on Acoustics Speech and Signal Processing*, Dallas, TX, pp. 1694–1697.

Stamm, M.C., Tjoa, S.K., Lin, W.S. et al. 2010b. Undetectable image tampering through JPEG compression anti-forensics, *IEEE International Conference on Image Processing*, Hong Kong, China, pp. 2109–2112.

StegAlyzerSS. http://www.sarc-wv.com/products/stegalyzerss/ (accessed January 3, 2018).

StegDetect. http://www.outguess.org/detection.php (accessed January 3, 2018).

StegExpose. https://isc.sans.edu/forums/diary/Steganography+in+Action+Image+Steganography+StegExpose/21803/ (accessed January 3, 2018).

StegSecret. http://stegsecret.sourceforge.net/ (accessed January 3, 2018).

StegSpy. http://www.spy-hunter.com/stegspydownload.htm (accessed January 3, 2018).

Su, P.-C., Suei, P.-L., Chang, M.-K. et al. 2015. Forensic and anti-forensic techniques for video shot editing in H. 264/AVC, *Journal of Vision Communication and Image Representation* 29: 103–113.

Su, Y. and Xu, J. 2010. Detection of double-compression in MPEG-2 videos, *2nd International Workshop on Intelligent System and Applications*, Vol. 1. Wuhan, China, pp. 22–25.

Su, Y., Nie, W., and Zhang, C. 2011. A frame tampering detection algorithm for MPEG videos, *6th IEEE Joint Int. Information Technology and Artificial Intelligence Conference*, Chongqing, China, pp. 461–464.

Su, Y., Zhang, J., and Liu, J. 2009. Exposing digital video forgery by detecting motion-compensated edge artifact, *International Conference on Computer Intelligence and Software Engineering*, Vol. 1. Wuhan, China, pp. 1–4.

Sun, T., Wang, W., and Jiang, X. 2012. Exposing video forgeries by detecting mpeg double compression, *IEEE International Conference Acoustics, Speech, and Signal Processing*, Kyoto, Japan, pp. 1389–1392.

Surrey University Library for Forensic Analysis (SULFA). http://sulfa.cs.surrey.ac.uk/.

Sutcu, Y., Bayram, S., Sencar, H.T. et al. 2007. Improvements on sensor noise based source camera identification, *IEEE International Conference on Multimedia & Expo*, Beijing, China.

Swaminathan, A., Wu, M., and Liu, K.J.R. 2006. Non-intrusive forensics analysis of visual sensors using output images, *IEEE International Conference on Image Processing*, Toulouse, France.

The investigation of the Srebrenica videos made by Belgrade journalist. *The Hague.* 2010. http://www.sense-agency.com/icty/the-investigation-of-the-srebrenica-videos-made-by-belgrade-journalist.29.html?news_id=12234 (accessed September 15, 2017).

Tsai, M.-J. and Wu, G.-H. 2006. Using image features to identify camera sources, *IEEE International Conference on Acoustics, Speech, and Signal Processing*, Toulouse, France.

Ulutaş, G., Üstübioğlu, B., Ulutaş, M. et al. 2017a. Frame duplication/mirroring detection method with binary features, *IET Image Processing* 11(5): 333–342.

Ulutaş, G., Üstübioğlu, B., Ulutaş, M. et al. 2017b. Frame duplication detection based on BoW model, *Multimedia Systems* 1–19.

Valenzise, G., Nobile, V., Tagliasacchi, M. et al. 2011b. Countering JPEG anti-forensics, *IEEE 18th International Conference on Image Processing*, Brussels, Belgium, pp. 1949–1952.

Valenzise, G., Tagliasacchi, M., and Tubaro, S. 2011a. The cost of jpeg compression anti-forensics, *IEEE International Conference on Acoustics, Speech and Signal Processing*, Prague, Czech Republic, pp. 1884–1887.

Vazquez-Padín, D., Fontani, M., Bianchi, T. et al. 2012. Detection of video double encoding with GOP size estimation, *IEEE International Workshop on Information Forensics Security*, Tenerife, Spain, pp. 151–156.

Video as evidence: Field guide, *WITNESS*, Brooklyn, NY.

Virtual Steganographic Laboratory for Digital Images (VSL). http://vsl.sourceforge.net/ (accessed January 3, 2018).

Wang, W. and Farid, H. 2006. Exposing digital forgeries in video by detecting double MPEG compression, *8th Workshop Multimedia Security*, New York, pp. 37–47.

Wang, W. and Farid, H. 2007a. Exposing digital forgeries in interlaced and deinterlaced video, *IEEE Transaction on Information and Forensics Security* 2(3): 438–449.

Wang, W. and Farid, H. 2007b. Exposing digital forgeries in video by detecting duplication, *9th ACM workshop on Multimedia and Security*, ACM Press, New York, pp. 35–42.

Wang, W. and Farid, H. 2009. Exposing digital forgeries in video by detecting double quantization, *11th Workshop Multimedia Security*, New York, pp. 39–48.

Wei, W., Fan, X, Song, H. et al. 2017. Video tamper detection based on multi-scale mutual information, *Multimedia Tools and Applications*, Vol. 1, 1–18.

What happened at each location in the Brussels attacks. *The New York Times.* 2016. https://www.nytimes.com/interactive/2016/03/22/world/europe/brussels-attacks-graphic.html (accessed September 14, 2017).

Wolthusen, S. 1998. On the limitations of digital watermarks: A cautionary note, *World Multiconference on Systems, Cybernetics, and Information*, Vol. 4. Orlando, FL, pp. 489–495.

Worland, J. 2015. Sandra Bland arrest video appears edited. *Time.* http://time.com/3967329/sandra-bland-video-continuity/ (accessed September 15, 2017).

Wu, Y., Jiang, X., Sun, T. et al. 2014. Exposing video inter-frame forgery based on velocity field consistency, *IEEE International Conference on Acoustic, Speech and Signal Processing*, Florence, Italy, pp. 2693–2697.

Xia, M., Yang, G., Li, L. et al. 2016. Detecting video frame rate up-conversion based on frame-level analysis of average texture variation, *Multimedia Tools and Applications* 72(1): 1–23.

Xu, J., Su, X., and You, X. 2012. Detection of video transcoding for digital forensics, *International Conference on Audio, Language, and Image Processing*, Shanghai, China, pp. 160–164.

Xu, J., Yu, Y., Su, Y. et al. 2012. Detection of blue screen special effects in videos, *International Conference on Medical Physics and Biomedical Engineering*, Beijing, China, pp. 1316–1322.

Yang, J., Huang, Y.T., and Su, L. 2016. Using similarity analysis to detect frame duplication forgery in videos, *Multimedia Tools and Applications* 75(4): 1793–1811.

Yao, Y., Shi, Y., Weng, S., and Guan, B. 2017. Deep learning for detection of object-based forgery in advanced video, *Symmetry* 10(1).

Yao, Y., Yang, G., Sun, X. et al. 2016. Detecting video frame-rate up-conversion based on periodic properties of edge-intensity, *Journal of Information Security and Applications* 26: 39–50.

Yu, L., Wang, H., Han, Q. et al. 2016. Exposing frame deletion by detecting abrupt changes in video streams, *Neurocomputing* 205: 84–91.

Zhang, J., Su, Y., and Zhang, M. 2009. Exposing digital video forgery by ghost shadow artifact, *1st ACM Workshop on Multimedia in Forensics*, New York, pp. 49–54.

Zheng, L., Sun, T., and Shi, Y.-Q. 2014. Inter-frame video forgery detection based on block-wise brightness variance descriptor, *13th International Workshop on Digital Forensics and Watermarking*, Taipei, Taiwan.

Chapter 24

Review of Image Tampering Detection Techniques

V. T. Manu and B. M. Mehtre

Contents

DOI: 10.1201/9780429435461-28

24.1 Introduction

There has been a tremendous rise in the rate of cyber crimes related to multimedia content in recent times with the advancement of technology. Multimedia content, especially digital images on the internet have always been the target of visual content manipulation attacks due to the ease of modification with the availability of powerful image manipulation programs. Malicious visual content manipulation, also known as image tampering, has become common. Digital images have become the part and parcel of information sharing on the internet in a plethora of forms like memes, infographics and photos by citizen-photojournalists. Concerns over the trustworthiness of such images have become alarmingly high with their quick proliferation.

Image tampering detection is a sub problem of image forensics. Tamper detection, along with integrity verification and source identification, help accomplish the task of evidence authentication. Evidence authentication is in itself one of the major tasks of image forensics.

Copy-move attack is the most common image tampering technique and has been around for many years. This forgery technique is synonymous with region duplication and cloning, as they share more or less similar modus operandi. It involves copying of an image region and pasting within the same. The attack is mostly done to conceal something in the image while exploiting the fact that certain parameters of the image remain the same, thereby, making it difficult for the analyzer to distinguish if the image is tampered or not. An example of this attack is presented in Figure 24.1a, wherein a region showing a tree is copied and pasted side by side.

Image splicing or mosaicing which is the next common type of tampering, involves copy pasting of image regions from different images to create a new image. An example of this attack is presented in Figure 24.1b, wherein the imagery of a helicopter and a shark belonging to different images are combined together to give a feel that a shark is attacking a man climbing down on a ladder from the helicopter.

(a)   (b)

Figure 24.1   Examples of images which are subjected to a copy-move and splicing attacks. (a) Copy-move attack: The trees in the foreground of the image are clones of each other. (b) Image splicing attack: The imagery of the helicopter and the shark belong to different images, they have been combined together to give a feel that a shark is attacking a man climbing down a ladder from a helicopter.

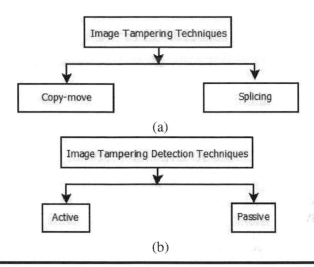

Figure 24.2 **Classifications of tampering and detection techniques: (a) common image tampering techniques, classified as copy-move and splicing; (b) tampering detection techniques classified as active and passive based on the availability of prior-image information.**

Image tampering detection techniques are plenty and are broadly classified into two based on of the availability of prior image information: active and passive. Active methods are those which use prior image information for detection of tampering. Passive or blind methods do not use prior image information. Considering the infeasibility of active techniques in most real crime investigation scenarios, blind techniques have gained more attention. These techniques do not depend on the availability of prior image information. Blind methods attempt to identify certain properties which are intrinsic to the test file, the variation of which may indicate a tampering activity (Figure 24.2).

Our focus in this chapter is on copy-move and splicing as they are the most common forms of image tampering techniques. We also discuss the various classification of them based on the detection mechanism like keypoint based, texture based, etc. A special section is devoted to the common copy-move detection pipeline. The latest works in image tampering detection using deep learning and big data are discussed, followed by suggestions on the future directions in this area.

24.2 Copy-move Forgery Detection

Copy-move forgery/tampering detection essentially involves looking for identical regions in the image based on some kind of matching. Based on this, we may generalize the steps in a copy-move tampering detection system as discussed below.

24.2.1 Copy-move Forgery Detection Pipeline

Almost all the copy-move detection techniques have at least six components [1] and are represented in Figure 24.3.

1. *Image preprocessing*: The image has to be converted to grayscale or any other color models that suits the algorithm to improve the discerning power
2. Most of them follow either of the two below approaches
   a. *Key-point detection*: Identify the pixels that stand out and better represents the regions in the input image.
   b. *Block tiling*: Split the image into sub-blocks which are overlapping or non-overlapping having a particular geometrical property. In some cases it can be done adaptively as well.

   Recently, researchers combined both of these techniques to come up with hybrid approaches so that the benefits of both are achieved.
3. *Feature extraction*: Feature vectors are computed for every keypoint or block corresponding to the method opted in the previous step.
4. *Feature matching*: Done by searching every feature vector for appropriate nearest neighbors within the set of features obtained.
5. *Filtering*: Done to reduce the false positives by setting a threshold value in classifying the features by removing weak matches.
6. *Post processing*: Preserves the matches having a common property.

24.2.1.1 Comparison Between Keypoint and Block Tiling Based Methods

In a given image, the 'interest points' are computed at characteristic locations like corners, blobs, and T-junctions [2]. The most important property is their repeatability. This means we are able to reliably locate the same interest points under various viewing conditions. This is followed by the representation of its neighborhood by a feature vector. In essence, the components of keypoints are detectors and descriptors. The Harris detector is believed to be the pioneering work in keypoint detection, which featured a combined corner and edge detection scheme [3]. The keypoint detection algorithms commonly used in the literature employ a concept called scale-space representation. This idea was proposed by [4] and [5] and considered

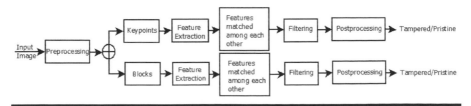

Figure 24.3   A representation of a generic copy-move forgery detection pipeline.

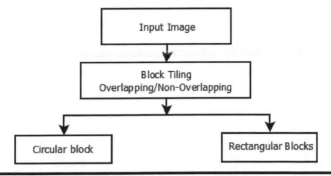

Figure 24.4 The process of block-tiling an image into rectangular and circular blocks.

to be seminal works. Scale-space representation essentially treats an image under consideration into different scales followed by the use of a Gaussian or similar filter to identify points which are dominant among its neighbors in these scales.

In block-based methods an image is divided into fixed-size sub images which may be either overlapping or non-overlapping as shown in Figure 24.4. These shapes can be either rectangular or circular. This is done to make comparisons between them for similarity.

Once a feature is represented as a vector, we compare them to identify similar members among them. But this could be an expensive task with respect to computation time. To avoid unnecessary comparisons, the commonly used method is to row-sort the feature vector lexicographically so that similar vectors come closer to each other.

As discussed in the previous Section 24.2.1, there are two different approaches for copy-move attack detection – key point detection and block tiling. There are three observations while comparing both these approaches:

- The feature size of block tiling methods is high, but it has better space and time complexity compared to keypoint detection methods.
- Keypoint detection methods are suitable when scaling and rotation operations are done to the copied areas.
- Sometimes, keypoint generation fails in the suspected regions due to several reasons like post-processing applications.

24.2.2 Detection Techniques

We can divide the detection techniques as keypoint based, block based, combination of keypoint as well as block based (hybrid) and transformation based. An illustration of the classification of copy-move detection techniques are presented in Figure 24.5.

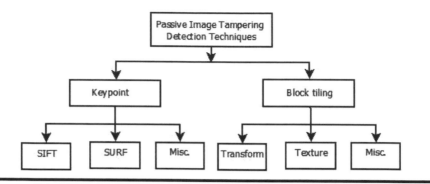

Figure 24.5 **Classification of copy-move tampering detection techniques based on keypoint and block tiling.**

24.2.2.1 Keypoint Based Detection

24.2.2.1.1 SIFT Keypoint Based Approaches

Checking if a copy-move attack has occurred by recovering geometric transformation used to perform region duplication is done in [6]. In [7], a comparative study of various copy-move forgery detection algorithms is presented. It also involves the comparisons of various processing steps like matching, filtering, detection of outliers, estimation of affine transformation with performance evaluations.

Affine transformation property preservation in copy-moved regions are used in [8]. Keypoints are clustered, followed by testing that the keypoints qualify for collinearity. The decision is further fortified by testing if the ratio of distances between corresponding keypoints are preserved in the cloned regions. The work addresses copy-move forgered areas in multiple locations within an image.

The work, [9], initially segments the test image, followed by a keypoint extraction scheme. The matching is done as a two step process. First step involves feature extraction, patch matching and transformation. In the next step, new correspondence is obtained and new transform matrices are obtained in an iterative fashion. Finally, the estimated matrix is refined using an EM-based algorithm to confirm that copy-move forgery exists.

The work in [10] uses a rotation-invariant feature extracted densely on images. It offers superior performance at the cost of a longer processing time caused due to the feature matching. This problem was countered by an approximate nearest-neighbor search called PatchMatch which is robust towards scale changes and rotations to a great extent.

SIFT-based framework depend highly on parameters whose values are often determined through experiments. Also, these values are only applicable to a few images, which limits their application. To address this issue, [11] uses Particle Swarm Optimization (PSO) algorithm for generating customized parameter values for the input images, which are used for copy-move forgery detection under the SIFT-based framework.

The work [12] introduces a concept called SIFT-Symmetry, that combines the SIFT with symmetry-based matching for image tampering detection in case of reflection attacks.

An improvised keypoint based approach is proposed in [13] by trying to improve the discerning power of keypoints having low contrast, reduce the computational complexity of clustering process and the non-uniform distribution of the keypoints. Initially, to acquire uniformly distributed keypoints, keypoint selection is done with respect to region instead of contrast. To achieve this, detection of keypoints and processes of selection are separately performed. The combination of contrast and density of each keypoint is employed to choose the keypoints by non-maximum value suppression. Later, the opponent SIFT descriptor is used to improve the discerning power of keypoints by the addition of color related information. Finally, clustering overhead is reduced by an optimized J-Linkage algorithm. This optimization is achieved by altering the initial cluster computation and affine transformation hypotheses.

24.2.2.1.2 SURF Keypoint Based Approaches

The SURF (Speeded Up Robust Features) [4] consists of a keypoint detector and descriptor. In [14], the keypoints are generated using Fast-Hessian Detector which is based on the Hessian matrix for a particular image pixel. The keypoint descriptor is formed from the wavelet responses in a particular neighborhood of the keypoint and Haar wavelet responses are used for orientation assignment.

The work in [15] extracts interest points, finding possible correspondences between them. Based on geometric constraints, they are clustered into regions with respect to correspondent points. This is followed by a multi-scale representation of the image. The groups generated over various scales are analyzed using a descriptor. This is done to decrease the search space of duplicated regions and leads to the construction of a detection map. The final verdict is made depending on a voting procedure among these detection maps.

24.2.2.1.3 Keypoint Based Approaches: Miscellaneous

A hybrid method is presented [16] in which the comparison is based on triangles. Given an input image, the interest points are generated, followed by modeling the objects as a set of connected triangles. The triangles are then matched with respect to inner angles, color representations, and local feature vectors extracted from the vertices. The images used in their work are presented in Figure 24.6.

Yet another hybrid keypoint based work is discussed in [17] which uses an interest point detector called KAZE in combination with SIFT for extracting more feature points. Multiple region duplication is achieved by an improved matching algorithm that use the n-best matched features. False matches are reduced by

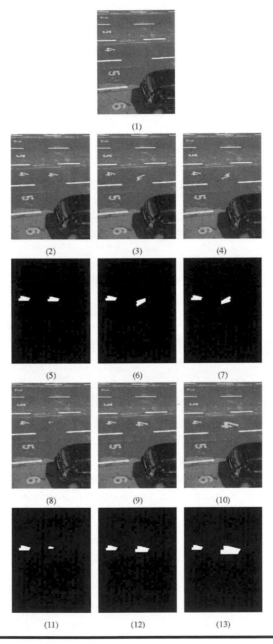

Figure 24.6 Copy-moved images with various rotation and scaling operations from [1] dataset. (1) pristine image. Images (2) to (4) are subjected to copy-move attacks rotations 0° (simple translation), 30° and 210°. Images (8) to (10) are images with copy-move attacks with scale factors 0.5, 1.25 and 1.75. Images from (5) to (7) and (11) to (13) are the expected results of the corresponding images above them.

segmentation. An iteration strategy is employed for the estimation of transformation matrices and determining if forgery is present or not.

In [18] the authors have used image signature tools which were used in MPEG-7. These tools, which were originally used for content-based image retrieval, are modified to be used to detect copy-move forgeries.

The work in [19] uses a combination of SIFT keypoints and Zernike moments. SIFT keypoints are generated on the entire input image and Zernike moments supplements the areas where the SIFT keypoints are missed.

A mixed moment approach is used in [20] to improve the robustness of copy-move forgery detection. They used exponential-fourier moments and histogram moments, which they called mixed moments. They claim to improve robustness towards translations, rotations, scalings and mixing of these operations. It is claimed to work on post processing like brightness and contrast adjustments.

A combination of Dyadic Wavelet Transform (DyWT) and SIFT are used in [21]. DyWT is applied on an input image to decompose it into four parts LL, LH, HL, and HH. SIFT is applied on the LL image, which carried more information regarding the input image. This procedure ensures obtaining more keypoint extraction, which is required for matching to identify the copy-moved regions.

A texture based copy-move detection is proposed in [22]. The proposed method is a block-based approach. The input image is divided into overlapping blocks and feature vectors for each block are extracted using texture descriptors called LBP operators. The rest of the matching of the descriptors is carried out on similar lines with the general copy-move forgery pipeline discussed earlier.

A summarization of keypoint based methods are provided in Table 24.1.

24.2.2.2 Block Based Approaches

Localization and detection of copyrotatemove (CRM) manipulations using Zernike moments is discussed in [28] over small overlapping image blocks. A block matching scenario depending on locality sensitive hashing is employed and it exploits the phase differences of Zernike moments in a feature-based error reduction approach.

The authors in [29] divide an input image into fixed-size overlapping blocks and apply 2D-DCT on each of these blocks followed by quantization. Each of these quantized blocks are then further divided into nonoverlapping sub-blocks for applying singular value decomposition (SVD) on each of them. Copy-move forged areas are found out by matching. The results reveal that they are able to detect multiple copy-moves and accurate localization of these areas. They claim that it is robust towards postprocessing operations like Gaussian blur, JPEG compression and combined operations.

In [30], an input image is split into sub blocks and mapped to log-polar coordinates. These are then represented with a dimensionality reduced feature vector. Similar regions are searched by comparing the feature vectors.

Table 24.1   Keypoint Based Works Used for Copy-Move Forgery Detection

SI	Authors	Keypoint
1	Amerini et al. [8]	SIFT [23]
2	Li et al. [11]	SIFT
3	Ardizzone et al. [1]	SIFT, SURF [4] and Harris [24]
4	Cozzolino et al. [12]	PatchMatch [25]
5	Wenchang et al. [13]	SIFT
6	Kee et al. [26]	KAZE [27], SIFT
7	Warif et al. [14]	SIFT
8	Jin and Wan [15]	SIFT
9	Silva et al. [15]	SURF [4]
10	Manu and Mehtre [10]	SIFT
11	Bo et al. [14]	SURF

In [31], the input image is split into blocks of fixed sizes. Discrete cosine transform (DCT) coefficients are computed on each of them to represent the corresponding block. It is then represented as circular blocks. Four features are extracted from these blocks in order to perform dimensionality reduction of each block. Lexicographic sorting and subsequent matching is done based on a threshold for finding the copy-moved regions.

24.2.2.2.1 Hybrid Methods

In this section, the combination of block and keypoint based approaches are discussed, which we call hybrid methods.

The work [32], uses the adaptive detection of keypoints which are supposed to cover the complete image based on a uniqueness metric. A filtering algorithm effectively prunes the wrongly matched regions. The entire procedure is repeated along with adjusting the keypoints density depending on the information achieved.

The work [33] combines various properties of copy-move detection techniques and model the scenario on a multiscale behavior knowledge space. This encodes the output combinations of these techniques as a priori probability considering multiple scales of the training data. The conditional probabilities of missing entries are accurately estimated using generative models. Finally various techniques are proposed that exploit the multi-directionality to generate a detection map using a machine learning based decision-making method.

24.2.2.2.2 Transformation Based

In [34], a multi-radius polar complex exponential transform (PCET) is used by extracting rotational invariant and multi-scale features. Lexicographical order matching algorithm optimized using minimum heap is applied to get a approximate match which is later refined using radius ratio and position information.

Most of the existing block matching copy-move forgery detection algorithms fails if the perpetrator blurs the edges of the tampered region(s). In order to solve this issue, the authors of [35] uses stationary wavelet transform (SWT) helps in identifying the noise, between the blocks of an image, caused due to blurring. SVD is used to represent the blocks and a colour-based segmentation is used to attain blur invariance.

A block matching related work is presented in [36] which utilizes polar representation to get the representative features for each block. The main feature used is the frequency of each block based on Fourier transform. It is experimentally found to be tolerant to post-processing operations such as rotation, scaling, application of Gaussian blur, brightness alteration, JPEG compression and noise addition.

The authors of [37] proposes a framework for the performance enhancement of tampering localization by incorporating possibility maps. First of all, statistical feature-based and copy-move forgery detectors are chosen and improvised, followed by adjusting their results to produce tampering possibility maps. After investigating the properties of possibility maps and comparing various fusion methods, the tampering possibility maps are integrated to obtain the final forgery localization results.

The work in [38] uses log-polar fast Fourier transform (LPFFT) on image blocks as an approximation to log-polar Fourier transform (LPFT) making it computational efficient as its computation only involves 1-D Fourier transformation and interpolations. Areas of tampering are located based on the similarity of LPFFT among different blocks. It is robust towards rotation and scaling.

The work [39] is based on a multiple classifier one. They assume that by combining the results of a set of forensic tools the performance will be superior than a single tool.

The work [40] is based on a Markov features. These features are used to capture the inter block and intra block variations in the DCT coefficients of the sub-image blocks. Further, discrete wavelet transform (DWTs) are computed to find similar discrepancies in scale spaces. The feature vector constructed out of these are dimensionality reduced to fed into a SVM for classifying if the images are tampered or not.

A summary of these sections are given in Table 24.2

24.2.2.2.3 Texture Based Methods

Texture based analysis is becoming so popular in recent time in copy-move forgery detection research as the regions involved in the forgery may be textured, thereby making the artifacts of tampering invisible for the viewers.

Table 24.2 Block-based and Other Works Used for Copy-move Forgery Detection

Sl	Authors	Feature Used
1	Ryu et al. [28]	Zernike moments
2	Fadl and Semary [36]	Polar coordinate representation & Fourier Transforms
3	Mahmood et al. [41]	Local binary pattern
4	Lee [42]	Gabor
5	Lee et al. [43]	Histogram of orientated gradients

Local binary pattern variance (LBPV) on the low approximation components of the stationary wavelets is employed in [41]. Circular regions are considered in order to tackle the possibility of post processing so as to improve performance. The proposed technique is evaluated on images with postprocessing like translation, flipping, blur, rotation, scaling, color reduction, brightness alteration and multiple forged regions.

Another texture based method in the category of block based approach is discussed in [42]. Gabor filter is applied to each overlapping block of the input image, followed by computing a histogram of orientated Gabor magnitude (HOGM). The features are generated by reduction for similarity measurement and are sorted lexicographically.

A similar texture-block based method is presented in [43]. HOG is applied on the input image. Features based on statistics are extracted, followed by its reduction so as to ease the similarity measurement. These are then sorted lexicographically for identification of duplicated areas.

In Table 24.3 another classification of hybrid methods are summarized.

Table 24.3 Copy-move Detection Using Hybridizing Keypoint and Block Based Approaches as Well as Transformation Domains

Sl	Authors	Approach
1	Zandi et al. [32]	Hybrid
2	Christlein et al. [9]	Multiple
3	Ferreira et al. [33]	Hybrid
4	Wo et al. [34]	Transform
5	Dixit et al. [35]	Transform
6	Li et al. [37]	Transform

24.2.3 *Image Splicing Detection*

Splicing localization in images becomes a challenging problem when a perpetrator uses postprocessing operations like resizing or blurring to remove its traces. In the paper [44], a partial blur type inconsistency model is used to address such issues. They use a block-based image partitioning scheme and a local blur type detection feature is extracted from the local blur kernels. The image blocks are grouped into out-of-focus or motion blur depending on this feature to create invariant blur type regions. To improve the precision of region boundaries a fine splicing localization is applied. Variations in blur type are used to identify the inconsistencies for splicing localization.

In [45], a 2-D noncausal Markov model is proposed with model parameters considered as the discriminative features to differentiate the spliced images from pristine. The model is applied in the BDCT domain and the discrete Meyer wavelet transform domain. The cross-domain features are treated as the final discriminative features used for classification using a support vector machine.

In [46], blocking and blur artifacts are quantified and the classification of images as tampered or not, is done based on the standard deviations of the entropy histograms and block DCT. The result of this work is illustrated in Figure 24.7.

24.2.3.1 *Texture Based Methods*

The detection accuracy of passive splicing detection methods can be improved by using textural features based algorithms. A grey level co-occurrence matrices called TF-GLCM, is proposed in [47]. Unlike the traditional GLCM the difference BDCT arrays are used to capture the textural information and the spatial relationship between image pixels. The discriminable properties contained in the GLCM are described by six textural features along with statistical moments mean and standard deviation. A support vector machine is employed for classification purpose.

In [48], the local binary pattern (LBP) operator is used to model magnitude components of two-dimensional arrays obtained by applying multisize block discrete cosine transform (MBDCT) on test images. Bins of histograms computed from LBP codes are considered as the discriminative features for image-splicing detection using a SVM after being dimensionality reduced with a kernel PCA.

The work [49] is based on LBP and DCT to detect copy-move and splicing forgeries. The chrominance component of the input image is extracted and 2D DCT in LBP space is applied to obtain discriminative localized features to be used in a support vector machine for forgery classification.

A steerable pyramid transform (SPT) and LBP based work is presented in [50]. Initially, the test color image is converted into YCbCr color space and SPT transform is applied on chrominance channels Cb and Cr to yield a number of multi-scale and multi-oriented subbands. Then, the texture is described in each SPT subband using LBP histograms. They are then concatenated to produce a

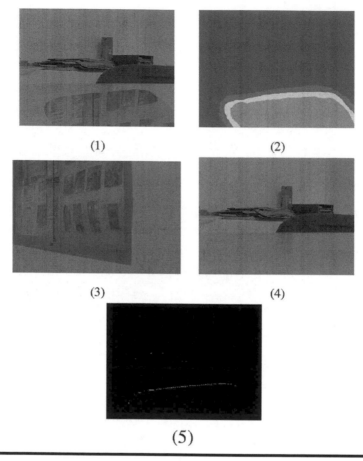

Figure 24.7 Results of the proposed algorithm in [2] (1) spliced image; (2) mask image provided by the dataset creators; (3) image from which a portion is copied; (4) image on which the portion that is copied is pasted; (5) splicing boundary correctly detected as white pixels.

feature vector to fed into a support vector machine for images into forged or authentic (Table 24.4).

24.2.3.2 Latest Works That Detect Real World Image Splicing

The works in [51] tries to investigate the potential for applying the latest state-of-the-art in image splicing detection in the realm of Web and social media images. A real-world dataset of forged images are also presented which are collected from various Web sources.

In the work nicknamed as Splicebuster [52] the authors use the co-occurrence based features to follow an anomaly detection approach, learning a model for the

Table 24.4   Latest Image Splicing Detection Algorithms

Sl	Authors	Peculiarity
1	Bahrami et al. [44]	Block based, blur type identification
2	Zhao et al. [45]	BDCT, Discrete Meyer wavelet transform and support vector machine
3	Zampoglou et al. [51]	Web images, social media images
4	Cozzolino et al. [52]	Despite the obvious loss of reliability due to the lack of an adequate training set, a very good performance can be obtained in most cases of interest.

features based on the same image under analysis. In a first supervised scenario, the user is required to select a tentative training set to learn the model parameters, while in the unsupervised scenario, segmentation and model learning are pursued jointly by means of the expectation-maximization (EM) algorithm.

The work [53] takes two assumptions. The first one is that the scene is static. The second one is that the image blur is due to camera motion. It uses Transformation Spread Function (TSF) and Point Spread Function (PSF) in blur estimation. The inconsistency in motion blur, which depends on the depth of the corresponding scene point, its position in the image, and also camera motion are used to expose the existence of splicing.

A summary of splicing methods are listed in Figure 24.4.

24.3 Decision Fusion Based Image Forgery Detection

So far in this work we have seen various methods of combining features to obtain better representation that will help in analysis. The final step which makes the tamper detection more reliable is its ability to confidently distinguish a tampered image from pristine. In other cases, this confidence and reliability should be there in identifying the tampered regions within the image. Therefore, decision making problem is crucial in image tampering detection. To foster the decision making problem, various clues or decisions has to be combined based on certain criteria. This section deals with a few works in this direction.

Dempster-Shafer evidence [54] based framework is presented in [55]. Based on this theory uncertainty about answers from the tools and lack of availabilities of prior- probabilities are taken care of.

The work [56] proposes a method to evaluate the trustworthiness of a images. It combines feature level and the decision level fusions. Dempster-Shafer evidence theory and an improvised least square methods are used to resolves conflicts on fusion.

The authors in [57] came up with two frameworks, one based on Dempster-Shafers theory of evidence and the other based on fuzzy theory respectively. This help to perform the fusion of heterogeneous, incomplete or conflicting outputs of forensic algorithms.

In the work [58], instead of using Dempsters original rule of combination, they use feature fusion method to resolve the problem of evidence conflicts.

The authors in [59] proposes a statistical fusion framework based on Discriminative Random Fields (DRF) to integrate multiple cues suitable for forgery detection, such as double quantization artifacts and camera response function inconsistency.

24.4 Deep Learning and Big Data Based Image Tampering Detection

Deep learning techniques form a class of machine learning algorithms which uses cascade of multiple layers of nonlinear processing units for feature extraction, transformation and learning. The learning may be either supervised or unsupervised based on the problem to be addressed.

The work in [60] utilizes a convolutional neural network (CNN). This is then used to learn hierarchical representations for image forgery detection in an automatic approach. The weights of the first layer of the network are initially set to basic high-pass filters. These are used for computing residual maps in spatial rich model (SRM). They acts as a regularizer to efficiently reduce the effect of image contents. They also capture the subtle artifacts formed due to tampering activity. The pre-trained CNN acts as a patch descriptor for extracting dense features from the input images. The fused features are fed into a SVM for classification.

Deep Matching and Validation Network (DMVN) which is a new deep CNN architecture is proposed in [61]. Instead of feature representation, raw images are used to create deep learned representations. The DMVN is end-to-end optimized for generating probability estimates and masks for segmentation. Their method has the ability to detect image splicing and localization of tampering.

In [62] a technique that utilizes a fully convolutional network (FCN) is used to localize image splicing. First a single-task FCN (SFCN) was evaluated and trained only on the surface label. But, it provided a coarse localization output in certain cases. Therefore, the use of a multi-task FCN (MFCN) that utilizes two output branches for multi-task learning was proposed.

A universal forensic approach for image tampering detection with the help of deep learning is described in [63]. Specifically, a new convolutional network architecture capable of learning tampering detection features directly from training data in an automatic approach is proposed. In their current implementation, CNN learns features that capture image contents than tamper detection features. In order to overcome this issue, a novel convolutional layer which is particularly designed to suppress image contents and adaptively learn tampering detection features is developed. The authors demonstrate that the proposed approach can automatically learn the detection of multiple image forgeries without depending on pre-selected features or other preprocessing.

The authors of [64] propose two approaches to identify and localize image tampering by fusing resampling features and deep learning. In the former approach, Radon transform of resampling features are generated on overlapping patches of the input image. A heatmap is created using deep learning classifiers and Gaussian conditional random field models. The locations of tampering in the image regions are located by a random walker segmentation approach. In the latter approach, resampling features generated on overlapping image patches are passed through a Long short-term memory (LSTM) based network for classification and used for localization of tampering.

The work [65] demonstrates the effect of tampering on the performance of automatic face recognition, and also proposes an algorithm to classify face images as pristine or retouched with high accuracy. A supervised deep Boltzmann machine algorithm is proposed to detect retouching by using facial parts to learn discriminative features for the classification of face images as pristine or not.

In [66] a composite manipulation detection method is mentioned based on CNNs. It learns the statistical change due to the manipulation through the proposed CNN architecture and classify the manipulated image. The proposed technique is effective since it learns integrated image of composite manipulation and extracts characteristic distinguished from original image.

24.5 Future Directions in Image Tampering Detection

Image tampering detection systems are far from mature to use in real-world scenarios. To make such systems to overcome this challenge, image forensics algorithms has to be integrated with a reverse image search algorithm. Image phylogeny is an evolving branch of study of how images evolve from other images and it strives to establish relationships among them using tree structures. This helps to reveal the origin of images and subsequent changes undergone till the point it was subjected to a forensic investigation. The relationship between different objects or sources that were used to create the doctored image is represented by a tree structure. This idea is inspired by the concept of phylogenetic trees in biology. They find many applications like tracking copyright infringement perpetrators, hinting at child pornography content creators, and investigating on online harassment using images.

The paper [67] aims at automatically detecting the structure of relationships between images, properly reconstructing the information about their history, and grouping them into distinct trees based on processing history. A novel algorithm is proposed that automatically processes different image sets containing related images, and outputs corresponding phylogeny trees.

Identifying if the digital objects came from the same source or from various sources is essentially addressed as a clustering problem. The related objects fall into same clusters and the rest fit into different clusters. In [68], the problem of identifying these clusters in the sets of semantically similar images are done before the tree reconstruction by combining manifold learning and spectral clustering.

Decision fusion based image forensics methods has to be developed to improve the real-world efficiency.

24.6 Conclusions

We have classified image tampering techniques based on the way they are performed and presented the latest and dependable works in each of these. A common observation about the image tampering detection methods is that most them are designed to perform well on specific datasets than on real cases. We have attempted to give a future direction for image forensics research by carrying out research in the overlapping areas of image forensics and relationship establishment between different sources that were used to create the doctored image, for better real-world usability. Also, there should be decision fusion methods that fuse clues from different sources.

The realm of image forensics is becoming more challenging due to the volume of data, hybrid attack methods, multi-sensor acquisition, its variety of application areas and fast paced development of anti-forensics activities.

References

1. V. Christlein, C. Riess, J. Jordan, C. Riess, and E. Angelopoulou. An evaluation of popular copy-move forgery detection approaches. *Information Forensics and Security, IEEE Transactions on*, 7(6):1841–1854, 2012.
2. H. Bay, T. Tuytelaars, and L. Van Gool. SURF: Speeded up robust features. In *Computer vision–ECCV 2006*, pp. 404–417. Springer, Berlin, Germany, 2006.
3. C. Harris and M. Stephens. A combined corner and edge detector. In *Proceedings of the Fourth Alvey Vision Conference*, pp. 147–151, Manchester, UK, August 1988.
4. J. Babaud, A. P Witkin, M. Baudin, and R. O. Duda. Uniqueness of the gaussian kernel for scale-space filtering. *IEEE Transactions on Pattern Analysis and Machine Intelligence*, 8(1):26–33, 1986.
5. T. Lindeberg. Feature detection with automatic scale selection. *International Journal of Computer Vision*, 30(2):79–116, 1998.
6. I. Amerini, L. Ballan, R. Caldelli, A. Del Bimbo, and G. Serra. A sift-based forensic method for copy–move attack detection and transformation recovery. *IEEE Transactions on Information Forensics and Security*, 6(3):1099–1110, 2011.
7. V. Christlein, C. Riess, J. Jordan, C. Riess, and E. Angelopoulou. An evaluation of popular copy-move forgery detection approaches. *IEEE Transactions on Information Forensics and Security*, 7(6):1841–1854, 2012.

8. V. T. Manu and B. M. Mehtre. Copy-move tampering detection using affine transformation property preservation on clustered keypoints. *Signal, Image and Video Processing*, Vol. 12, 1–8, 2017.

9. J. Li, X. Li, B. Yang, and X. Sun. Segmentation-based image copy-move forgery detection scheme. *IEEE Transactions on Information Forensics and Security*, 10(3):507–518, 2015.

10. D. Cozzolino, G. Poggi, and L. Verdoliva. Efficient dense-field copy–move forgery detection. *IEEE Transactions on Information Forensics and Security*, 10(11):2284–2297, 2015.

11. S. Wenchang, Z. Fei, Q. Bo, and L. Bin. Improving image copy-move forgery detection with particle swarm optimization techniques. *China Communications*, 13(1):139–149, 2016.

12. N. B. A. Warif, A. W. A. Wahab, M. Y. Idna Idris, R. Salleh, and F. Othman. Siftsymmetry: A robust detection method for copy-move forgery with reflection attack. *Journal of Visual Communication and Image Representation*, 46 (Supplement C): 219–232, 2017.

13. G. Jin and X. Wan. An improved method for sift-based copy–move forgery detection using non-maximum value suppression and optimized j-linkage. *Signal Processing: Image Communication*, 57(Supplement C):113–125, 2017.

14. X. Bo, W. Junwen, L. Guangjie, and D. Yuewei. Image copy-move forgery detection based on surf. In *Multimedia Information Networking and Security (MINES), 2010 International Conference on*, pp. 889–892, Nanjing, China, November 2010.

15. E. Silva, T. Carvalho, A. Ferreira, and A. Rocha. Going deeper into copy-move forgery detection: Exploring image telltales via multi-scale analysis and voting processes. *Journal of Visual Communication and Image Representation*, 29(Supplement C):16–32, 2015.

16. E. Ardizzone, A. Bruno, and G. Mazzola. Copy–move forgery detection by matching triangles of keypoints. *IEEE Transactions on Information Forensics and Security*, 10(10):2084–2094, 2015.

17. F. Yang, J. Li, W. Lu, and J. Weng. Copy-move forgery detection based on hybrid features. *Engineering Applications of Artificial Intelligence*, 59(Supplement C):73–83, 2017.

18. P. Kakar and N. Sudha. Exposing postprocessed copy–paste forgeries through transform-invariant features. *IEEE Transactions on Information Forensics and Security*, 7(3):1018–1028, 2012.

19. Z. Mohamadian and A. A. Pouyan. Detection of duplication forgery in digital images in uniform and non-uniform regions. In *2013 UKSim 15th International Conference on Computer Modelling and Simulation*, Cambridge, UK, pp. 455–460, April 2013.

20. L. Zhong and W. Xu. A robust image copy-move forgery detection based on mixed moments. In *2013 IEEE 4th International Conference on Software Engineering and Service Science*, pp. 381–384, May 2013.

21. M. F. Hashmi, V. Anand, and A. G. Keskar. Copy-move image forgery detection using an efficient and robust method combining un-decimated wavelet transform and scale invariant feature transform. *AASRI Procedia*, 9:84–91, 2014. 2014 AASRI Conference on Circuit and Signal Processing (CSP 2014).

22. R. Davarzani, K. Yaghmaie, S. Mozaffari, and M. Tapak. Copy-move forgery detection using multiresolution local binary patterns. *Forensic Science International*, 231(1):61–72, 2013.

23. D. G. Lowe. Distinctive image features from scale-invariant keypoints. *International Journal of Computer Vision*, 60(2):91–110, 2004.

24. C. Harris and M. Stephens. A combined corner and edge detector. In *Alvey Vision Conference*, vol. 15, pp. 147–151. Manchester, UK, 1988.

25. C. Barnes, E. Shechtman, A. Finkelstein, and D. B. Goldman. Patchmatch: A randomized correspondence algorithm for structural image editing. *ACM Transactions on Graphics*, 28(3):24–1, 2009.
26. E. Kee, J. F. O'brien, and H. Farid. Exposing photo manipulation from shading and shadows. *ACM Transactions on Graphics*, 33(5):165–171, 2014.
27. P. Fernández Alcantarilla, A. Bartoli, and A. J. Davison. Kaze features. In *European Conference on Computer Vision*, pp. 214–227. Springer, Heidelberg, Germany, 2012.
28. S.-J. Ryu, M. Kirchner, M.-J. Lee, and H.-K. Lee. Rotation invariant localization of duplicated image regions based on zernike moments. *IEEE Transactions on Information Forensics and Security*, 8(8):1355–1370, 2013.
29. J. Zhao and J. Guo. Passive forensics for copy-move image forgery using a method based on dct and svd. *Forensic Science International*, 233(1):158–166, 2013.
30. S. Bravo-Solorio and A. K. Nandi. Automated detection and localisation of duplicated regions affected by reflection, rotation and scaling in image forensics. *Signal Processing*, 91(8):1759–1770, 2011.
31. Y. Cao, T. Gao, L. Fan, and Q. Yang. A robust detection algorithm for copy-move forgery in digital images. *Forensic Science International*, 214(1):33–43, 2012.
32. M. Zandi, A. Mahmoudi-Aznaveh, and A. Talebpour. Iterative copy-move forgery detection based on a new interest point detector. *IEEE Transactions on Information Forensics and Security*, 11(11):2499–2512, 2016.
33. A. Ferreira, S. C. Felipussi, C. Alfaro, P. Fonseca, J. E. Vargas-Muñoz, J. A. dos Santos, and A. Rocha. Behavior knowledge space-based fusion for copy–move forgery detection. *IEEE Transactions on Image Processing*, 25(10):4729–4742, 2016.
34. Y. Wo, K. Yang, G. Han, H. Chen, and W. Wu. Copy–move forgery detection based on multi-radius pcet. *IET Image Processing*, 11(2):99–108, 2016.
35. R. Dixit, R. Naskar, and S. Mishra. Blur-invariant copy-move forgery detection technique with improved detection accuracy utilising swt-svd. *IET Image Processing*, 11(5):301–309, 2017.
36. S. M. Fadl and N. A. Semary. Robust copy-move forgery revealing in digital images using polar coordinate system. *Neurocomputing*, 265(Supplement C):57–65, 2017.
37. H. Li, W. Luo, X. Qiu, and J. Huang. Image forgery localization via integrating tampering possibility maps. *IEEE Transactions on Information Forensics and Security*, 12(5):1240–1252, 2017.
38. Q. Wu, S. Wang, and X. Zhang. Log-polar based scheme for revealing duplicated regions in digital images. *IEEE Signal Processing Letters*, 18(10):559–562, 2011.
39. D. Cozzolino, F. Gargiulo, C. Sansone, and L. Verdoliva. *Multiple Classifier Systems for Image Forgery Detection*, pp. 259–268. Springer, Heidelberg, Heidelberg, Germany, 2013.
40. Z. He, W. Lu, W. Sun, and J. Huang. Digital image splicing detection based on markov features in dct and dwt domain. *Pattern Recognition*, 45(12):4292–4299, 2012.
41. T. Mahmood, A. Irtaza, Z. Mehmood, and M. Tariq Mahmood. Copy–move forgery detection through stationary wavelets and local binary pattern variance for forensic analysis in digital images. *Forensic Science International*, 279(Supplement C):8–21, 2017.
42. J.-C. Lee. Copy-move image forgery detection based on gabor magnitude. *Journal of Visual Communication and Image Representation*, 31(Supplement C):320–334, 2015.
43. J.-C. Lee, C.-P. Chang, and W.-K. Chen. Detection of copy–move image forgery using histogram of orientated gradients. *Information Sciences*, 321(Supplement C):250–262, 2015; Security and privacy information technologies and applications for wireless pervasive computing environments.

44. K. Bahrami, A. C. Kot, L. Li, and H. Li. Blurred image splicing localization by exposing blur type inconsistency. *IEEE Transactions on Information Forensics and Security*, 10(5):999–1009, 2015.

45. X. Zhao, S. Wang, S. Li, and J. Li. Passive image-splicing detection by a 2-d non-causal markov model. *IEEE Transactions on Circuits and Systems for Video Technology*, 25(2):185–199, 2015.

46. V. T. Manu and B. M. Mehtre. Blind technique using blocking artifacts and entropy of histograms for image tampering detection. In *Second International Workshop on Pattern Recognition*, Vol. 10443, p. 104430T. International Society for Optics and Photonics, Bellingham, Washington, 2017.

47. X. Shen, Z. Shi, and H. Chen. Splicing image forgery detection using textural features based on the grey level co-occurrence matrices. *IET Image Processing*, 11(1):44–53, 2016.

48. Y. Zhang, C. Zhao, Y. Pi, S. Li, and S. Wang. Image-splicing forgery detection based on local binary patterns of dct coefficients. *Security and Communication Networks*, 8(14):2386–2395, 2015.

49. A. Alahmadi, M. Hussain, H. Aboalsamh, G. Muhammad, G. Bebis, and H. Mathkour. Passive detection of image forgery using dct and local binary pattern. *Signal, Image and Video Processing*, 11(1):81–88, 2017.

50. G. Muhammad, M. H. Al-Hammadi, M. Hussain, and G. Bebis. Image forgery detection using steerable pyramid transform and local binary pattern. *Machine Vision and Applications*, 25(4):985–995, 2014.

51. M. Zampoglou, S. Papadopoulos, and Y. Kompatsiaris. Detecting image splicing in the wild (web). In *Multimedia & Expo Workshops (ICMEW), 2015 IEEE International Conference on*, pp. 1–6. IEEE, 2015.

52. D. Cozzolino, G. Poggi, and L. Verdoliva. Splicebuster: A new blind image splicing detector. In *2015 IEEE International Workshop on Information Forensics and Security (WIFS)*, pp. 1–6, November 2015.

53. M. P. Rao, A. N. Rajagopalan, and G. Seetharaman. Harnessing motion blur to unveil splicing. *IEEE Transactions on Information Forensics and Security*, 9(4):583–595, 2014.

54. J. Gordon and E. H. Shortliffe. The dempster-shafer theory of evidence. *Rule-Based Expert Systems: The MYCIN Experiments of the Stanford Heuristic Programming Project*, 3:832–838, 1984.

55. M. Fontani, T. Bianchi, A. De Rosa, A. Piva, and M. Barni. A framework for decision fusion in image forensics based on dempster–shafer theory of evidence. *IEEE Transactions on Information Forensics and Security*, 8(4):593–607, 2013.

56. D. Hu, X. Zhang, Y. Fan, Z.-Q. Zhao, L. Wang, X. Wu, and X. Wu. On digital image trustworthiness. *Applied Soft Computing*, 48:240–253, 2016.

57. M. Fontani, A. Costanzo, M. Barni, T. Bianchi, A. De Rosa, and A. Piva. Two decision fusion frameworks for image forensics. In *Annual GTTI Meeting*, Taormina, Italy, 2011.

58. D. Hu, L. Wang, Y. Zhou, Y. Zhou, X. Jiang, and L. Ma. D-s evidence theory based digital image trustworthiness evaluation model. In *2009 International Conference on Multimedia Information Networking and Security*, Vol. 1, pp. 85–89, IEEE, Hubei, China, November 2009.

59. Y. F. Hsu and S. F. Chang. Statistical fusion of multiple cues for image tampering detection. In *2008 42nd Asilomar Conference on Signals, Systems and Computers*, pp. 1386–1390, Pacific Grove, CA, October 2008.

60. Y. Rao and J. Ni. A deep learning approach to detection of splicing and copy-move forgeries in images. In *Information Forensics and Security (WIFS), 2016 IEEE International Workshop on*, pp. 1–6. IEEE, 2016.

61. Y. Wu, W. Abd-Almageed, and P. Natarajan. Deep matching and validation network - an end-to-end solution to constrained image splicing localization and detection. *CoRR*, abs/1705.09765, 2017.

62. R. Salloum, Y. Ren, and C.-C. Jay Kuo. Image splicing localization using a multi-task fully convolutional network (mfcn). *arXiv preprint arXiv:1709.02016*, 2017.

63. B. Bayar and M. C. Stamm. A deep learning approach to universal image manipulation detection using a new convolutional layer. In *Proceedings of the 4th ACM Workshop on Information Hiding and Multimedia Security*, pp. 5–10. ACM, New York, 2016.

64. J. Bunk, J. H. Bappy, T. Manhar Mohammed, L. Nataraj, A. Flenner, BS Manjunath, S. Chandrasekaran, A. K. Roy-Chowdhury, and L. Peterson. Detection and localization of image forgeries using resampling features and deep learning. In *Computer Vision and Pattern Recognition Workshops (CVPRW), 2017 IEEE Conference on*, pp. 1881–1889. IEEE, 2017.

65. A. Bharati, R. Singh, M. Vatsa, and K. W. Bowyer. Detecting facial retouching using supervised deep learning. *IEEE Transactions on Information Forensics and Security*, 11(9):1903–1913, 2016.

66. H. Y. Choi, H. U. Jang, D. Kim, J. Son, S. M. Mun, S. Choi, and H. K. Lee. Detecting composite image manipulation based on deep neural networks. In *2017 International Conference on Systems, Signals and Image Processing (IWSSIP)*, pp. 1–5, Poznan University of Technology, Poznan, Poland, May 2017.

67. Z. Dias, S. Goldenstein, and A. Rocha. Toward image phylogeny forests: Automatically recovering semantically similar image relationships. *Forensic Science International*, 231(1):178–189, 2013.

68. M. A. Oikawa, Z. Dias, A. de Rezende Rocha, and S. Goldenstein. Manifold learning and spectral clustering for image phylogeny forests. *IEEE Transactions on Information Forensics and Security*, 11(1):5–18, 2016.

Chapter 25

Blockchain Security for Wireless Multimedia Networks

Ankit Songara, Lokesh Chouhan and Pankaj Kumar

Contents

DOI: 10.1201/9780429435461-29

25.1 Introduction

In the upcoming years, most of the devices will be connected wirelessly, which also increases the risk of attacks like a DDoS (distributed denial of service) attack. Satoshi Nakamoto in 2008 described the bitcoin design. As the "Internet of Things" technology is emerging day by day, devices under this technology are also increasing in large numbers. Technology has increased rapidly from bluetooth low energy (BLE), radio frequency identification (RFID), to sensor technology, mobile devices, actuators, and global positioning system (GPS) devices. Internet of things (IoT) can play a huge role in making a city or home "smart" (Biswas and Muthukkumarasamy, 2016). The future of connected devices lay in the hands of IoT technology. But, with the increase in the "things" under IoT, concerns on securing these things also increased (Lee and Kim, 2017). Traditional security methods are highly expensive as well as centralized. On the other hand, a new emerging technology, popularly known as the blockchain, is totally decentralized. The blockchain is the technology behind the security of the first crypto currency, i.e., bitcoin. In addition to its decentralized nature, the blockchain is transparent, persistent, and secure. The blockchain can be considered as the future of not only IoT security but also in other fields, such as cryptography of multimedia networks which contains text, audio files, images or videos. As the IoT is growing up, sensors and devices are becoming more and more vulnerable to attacks and threats. In IoT, participants have to rely greatly on the administrator or the central authority of the network. Administrator is all powerful; he/she can delete or modify the data without any restrictions. Transactions made are not totally secure; data can be easily manipulated by any third party. When it comes to money, people trust a third party to complete a transaction successfully without any hindrance.

Blockchain is a technology that can overpower the current security measures in IoT. By using mathematics and cryptography techniques, blockchain provides an open decentralized database of every transaction, creating a record whose authenticity can be verified by the entire community. All the details of every transaction are recorded with full visibility to everyone on the blockchain network. The blockchain is better suitable for IoT because it is distributed, transparent, persistent, and secure. Every transaction is added to the blockchain providing historic transaction data and latest added blocks contain the fingerprints to the previously added block, therefore, the transaction gets more secure as more blocks are added. Overall, blockchain technology can help us fill the security gaps in an IoT enabled network because it is not only reliable but also secure as blockchain practically makes it impossible to modify a historic transaction (Pierro, 2017).

25.2 Issues with Centralized Network Scheme

A centralized system implies that a central body controls the network. It acts as an agent for all kind of communications in the network. Most of the instant messaging systems are built on central network scheme. Though we cannot disagree that centralization has its benefits, but it also comes with several disadvantages. Some of the mare listed below:

- Failure: The probability of complete failure is quite high as compared to a decentralized system. Since the control is in the hands of a single body, even a natural disaster can disrupt the whole system or cause the complete shutdown. This can result in the loss of information gathered within the network.
- Diversity: A centralized system uses one single operating system for the whole network. Though, this can be an advantage for some users, however, it reduces the diversity in the network and prevents some users to access the network.
- Security: One of the major drawbacks of a centralized system is its security. A centralized system is always an easy target than a decentralized system. If a malicious user is able to hack into the central server then it can take control of every client connected to it, hence the whole network will be compromised. Systems running in multiple locations with different operating systems provide better security than a single centralized system.

25.3 What is Bitcoin?

Bitcoin is an online digital decentralized cryptocurrency. It was first proposed in the year 2008 by Satoshi Nakamoto. In bitcoin, transactions are being issued by users to transfer bitcoins from one account to another. The security of bitcoin is run by a huge network called a blockchain. Basically, blockchain is where bitcoins reside. Bitcoins are created through mining and the users who do mining are called miners. If *A* has to send money to *B* then he/she has to send it to the bank. The bank here acts as the middleman. While in decentralized currency, like bitcoin, there is no middleman, there is no government in between *A* and *B*. Once bitcoin is transferred or exchanged, then that transaction is verified by a miner. When the miners verify some certain number of transactions then they will get some bitcoins as their reward for mining. Miners use their computers to mine bitcoins by making their computers solve a difficult math problem. These bitcoins can be used to purchase video games, gifts, books, servers etc.

25.3.1 Bitcoin Advantages

Bitcoin's use has gone up in the past few years because of the features it provides. Some major advantages of using bitcoin transactions are:

1. *Cheap and Fast Transactions*: Bitcoin wallets provide faster transactions with minimal transactional fees. Just like we store cash in our regular wallets, we can store bitcoins in bitcoin wallets. Bitcoins can be transferred from one account to another without any transactional fees.
2. *Decentralized*: Bitcoin is a decentralized currency, i.e., no central authority has any control over the bitcoin exchange transactions. Users can only read the history but cannot modify it. If a malicious entity wants to modify any transaction, it has to take control over 51% of the nodes. Hence making it secure.
3. *Use of Keys*: Bitcoin transactions are signed using private keys creating a certificate which is then verified using public keys. These private keys are stored in bitcoin wallets. These private keys are used for sending or receiving bitcoins from or to an account. Figure 25.1 describes the process of making a transaction on

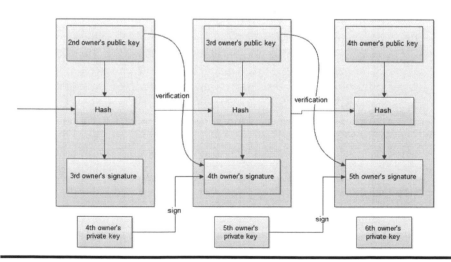

Figure 25.1   Chain of Bitcoin transactions.

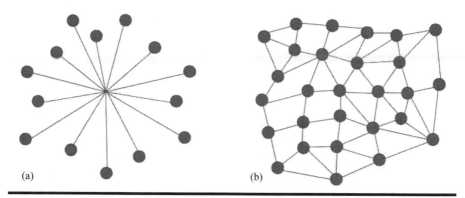

(a) (b)

Figure 25.2 (a) Centralized vs (b) Distributed networks.

bitcoin network. Cryptography of blocks includes a set of Public-Private key. A private key is used to sign the hash of the previous transaction and a public key is used to verify it. Algorithms like SHA-2(SHA-256) are used to generate a hash. The task of the miners is to decode this hash and figure out the actual code hidden behind it. The miner who does it first wins the race.

Figure 25.2a shows a centralized system, where nodes collect all the data from their surroundings and send it to a central authority.

The problem with this kind of infrastructure is that if the central authority is attacked and crashed then the whole system will go down. On the other hand, Figure 25.2b shows a distributed peer-to-peer connected network. If some of the nodes fail the system as a whole will survive.

25.4 Concept of Blockchain

Blockchain technology is not a single working technique. It is a combination of several techniques which makes it suitable for any network. Integrating cryptography, encryption algorithms, mathematics, with peer-to-peer network and distributed consensus property makes a better blockchain and solves the traditional problem of distributed synchronization of any database.

25.4.1 Properties of Blockchain

The key elements of blockchain technology can be categorized as:

1. **Distributed:** The traditional systems involve central authorities whose task is to verify and validate movements on the network. Distribution is a basic property of blockchain, which means that blockchain does not have to rely

on any centralized authority or node for any kind of permission. Data can be stored, updated and recorded distributedly.

2. **Transparency:** The reason why blockchain is trustworthy is its transparent nature. Every node on the network can see the recorded data. Whenever any update takes place in the network, it is distributed among all the nodes on the network hence making it public and transparent.

3. **Immutable:** All the data recorded on blockchain is reserved forever and cannot be altered until and unless someone takes control over more than 51% of nodes at the same time, which is almost impossible. Since everyone on the network has the same copy of the ledger, if someone tries to manipulate any data present on the network, every node on the network will get notified about it. For example, suppose there is a box containing money is kept in a place where no one is watching over it. Chances of it getting stolen are quite high. Instead, if the box is kept in a place where everybody is keeping an eye on it then the chances of getting it stolen? Less!

4. **Anonymous nature:** Blockchain technology solves the problem of trust between nodes to nodes, so transferring of data and transactions can be anonymous. The transactions can take place even if we only know the other node's blockchain address.

5. **Open Source:** Most of the blockchain process is open to everyone, i.e., records are public and people can also make use of blockchain technology to create other applications of their choice. Also, the more number of blocks in a chain makes it more invulnerable and secure from the attacks (Figure 25.3). Hence, as the number of blocks keeps on adding in the blockchain, the difficulty level for compromising the network also becomes high.

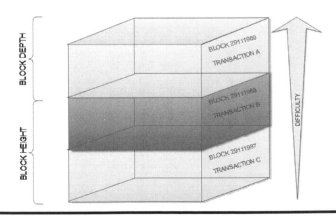

Figure 25.3 Difficulty level increases with addition of blocks.

25.4.2 Working with Blockchain

The blockchain technology is basically built on three technologies:

25.4.2.1 Cryptographic Keys

25.4.2.2 Peer-to-Peer Network

25.4.2.3 The Blockchain Protocol

The result of combining above technologies is a digital interactions system that does not require any trusted third party. The work of securing digital relationships is implicit—supplied by the elegant, simple, yet robust network architecture of blockchain technology itself.

How above-mentioned technologies work together in making a digital relationship secure is explained in the following section.

Cryptographic keys: The most important elements of blockchain are private keys and public keys. Let's take an example by assuming two people as shown in Figure 25.4, A and B wish to transact some data over the Internet. Both A and B have their own private key and a public key (Figure 25.5).

Figure 25.4   User A and user B.

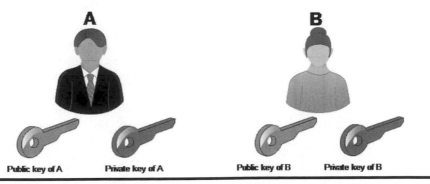

Figure 25.5   User A and B with respective key pairs.

Figure 25.6 **Combinations of private key and public is used to generate a digital signature.**

The main purpose is to create a secure digital identity reference using this component of blockchain technology. Identity is based on possession of a combination of private and public cryptographic keys.

As shown in Figure 25.6, by combining these private keys and public keys, an extremely useful and powerful digital signature can be created. And in turn, this digital signature is used to provide strong control of ownership of the data.

Peer-to-peer network: Cryptography does provide strong control of ownership but it is not enough to make the digital relationships secure. Authentication problem is solved using cryptographic keys, but we also need some kind of authorization. In blockchain it is done using distributed network.

The key benefit of a distributed network is that nodes witness every transaction that takes place on the network. It can be better understood using an example; suppose we have a very big hall with a hundred people in it and there are thousands of cameras installed to capture or record every move of the people. Now, if one person in the hall gives something to another one, it is going to be recorded in the cameras' memory. Similarly, in blockchain, there are nodes on the network which act as validators, like the cameras in the example provided. These nodes reach a consensus state that they have witnessed a transaction at the same time on the blockchain. They use some mathematical verification for this purpose.

This explains one thing, that the size of the network matters and is important to make itself secure. More the number of nodes on the network, more secure the network will be. The process starts with person A taking its private key and making an announcement that he/she is sending some money and attach it to person B's public key.

A block is then created using a time stamp, digital signature and other relevant information which is then broadcasted to every node on the network. Verification process gets initiated to verify the block. As soon as the block gets verified, it is added to the blockchain. Figure 25.7b tells us about the process flow of the working of blockchain. Now, what happens if two miners find the solution at the very same time? Who gets the chance to add the block to the chain? Well, the answer is quite simple; the miner who

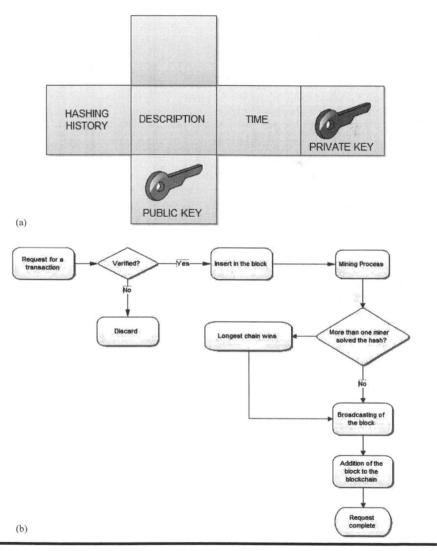

Figure 25.7   (a) Contents of a block. (b) Process flow of blockchain.

spends more computational power will have higher priority. If there are two chains available in which a block can be added, then it gets appended to the longest chain. And the next blocks will continue to be added in the longest thereafter. This is what happens when a bitcoin fork occurs.

The blockchain protocol: We saw in the previous example that many cameras are used to record people's activity in the hall. But the question is: why there are a thousand cameras installed to record one person's activity? How are they benefited when they are spending their computing power to give service to the people they don't know?

Blockchain answers this question by taking into account one more process called *mining.*

For open, public blockchains mining is used. In blockchains, when nodes offer their computing power for servicing the network, a reward is provided to one of them in terms of some bitcoins. Nodes who serve the network create and maintain a chain of history of transactions of every bitcoin. To achieve this, they have to solve *proof-of-work* mathematical problems. So basically, they use their computation power whether to agree upon a valid transaction or to reject invalid blocks.

When the majority of the miners agree with the same decision, they add a new block to the blockchain. This block will be time stamped and can also have data and messages in it. Chain of blocks in a blockchain will look something like what is shown in Figure 25.8. Now the interesting thing about blockchain is that we can design our own blockchain with our own rules and permissions. We can set up properties of our blockchain on our own terms.

For example, there can be different blockchains for different types of organizations or even for different tasks. We can develop two completely different blockchains with a completely different set of rules for

a. An organization where only images need to be secured.
b. An organization where we have to keep a record of everything such as in healthcare systems.

The verification process needs not be same for all the blockchains. Any needed new rules can be added.

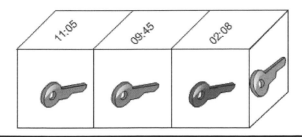

Figure 25.8 Blockchain consisting of blocks with their timestamp and keys.

25.5 Structure of a Block in Blockchain

A block holds a set of data which contains all the necessary information to verify a transaction and connect the current block to the previous block in the blockchain. Blocks size is measured simply in bytes. Generally, a block contains a hash of the previous block that was added to the blockchain before the current one, a hash of current block, timestamp and some other information as depicted in the figure provided (Figure 25.9).

> *Main data:* Depending upon the service for which a blockchain is built for, main data can differ. For example bank records, transaction records, contracts or Internet of things data records.
>
> *Hash:* When a transaction executes on blockchain, it is first hashed to a code and thereafter it is broadcast to every other node. Since each block can contain thousands of transaction records, blockchain makes use of the *Merkel tree function* for generating a hash value, which is also known as Merkel tree root. This final hash value is then recorded in the hash of the current block (or the block header). By using Merkel tree function computing resources can be reduced tremendously.
>
> *Timestamp:* It contains the time of block generation.
>
> *Other Information:* User-defined information, block's signature or nonce value.

25.5.1 Bitcoin's Block

The main way to identify a block in a blockchain is through its hash (block header hash) (Table 25.1).

The block header is calculated using the SHA-256 algorithm. A block header is calculated by each and every node as a part of verification process. Above table shows the information about fields and size of the respective fields in a bitcoin's

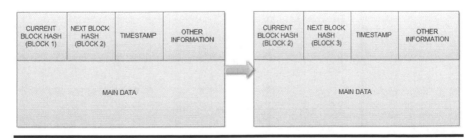

Figure 25.9 Two blocks connected with each other, block 1 contains the hash of block 2.

Table 25.1   Structure of a Bitcoin Block

Size	Field Content
4 Bytes	Version
32 Bytes	Hash of previous block
32 Bytes	Merkel Root
4 Bytes	Timestamp
4 Bytes	Difficulty target for the block
4 Bytes	Nonce Counter

block. The size of a block header in bitcoin is 80 bytes which contain a hash version (4 bytes) of the previous block (32 bytes), i.e., block 10's hash if the current block's number is 11, a hash of the current block (32 bytes), timestamp (4 bytes), difficulty target (4 bytes), nonce (4 bytes). Next information is the number of transactions and transactions themselves. Depending upon its type, a transaction usually takes more than 250 bytes. Multi-signature transactions take a lot of space because of the several conditions. An average block in a blockchain contains around 500 transactions.

There were five standard types of bitcoin transactions when it was first written. There are also some non-standard transactions. Most popular transactions among all the transactions are TX_PUBKEY and TX_PUBKEYHASH, i.e., pay to public key and pay to public hash address respectively (Table 25.2).

The former transaction is commonly used in earlier mining software—software which does not include P2PKH and later allows the user to send or receive bitcoins to a single bitcoin address. This transaction contains P2PKH script which is solved using digital signature and public key. The ScriptPubKey and ScriptSig for a transaction are shown below:

Table 25.2   Types of Transactions

S.no	Transaction Type
1	Pay To Public Key
2	Pay To Address
3	Pay To Script Hash
4	Multi-Signature Transaction
5	OP_Return Meta Coin
6	Non-Standard

```
<ScriptPubKey=OP_DUP OP_HASH160<Public KeyHash> OP_EQUAL
OP_CHECKSIG
ScriptSig= <Signature><Public Key>
```

Execution of The ScriptPubKey and ScriptSig takes place in the following manner:

```
Validation=<Signature><Public Key>OP_DUP OP_HASH160<Public
KeyHash> OP_EQUAL OP_CHECKSIG
```

If the result of the above statement is 1 then it shows that the transaction is valid. The process executes from left to right and addition in stack takes place in *Last In First Out* order.

First, the signature is pushed into the stack, then the public key is pushed on top of the stack. The top is duplicated by the OP_DUP operator and Hash 160 function does the hashing of the top item (public key) in the stack. It turns the public key into a hash. The OP_EQUAL operator is used to check whether the hashed values of public key are equal. Verification of the signature is done by the OP_CHECKSIG operator.

25.5.2 Genesis Block

Genesis block of a blockchain is the first block in a chain. Nowadays, it is also called as block 0, although early versions named it as block 1. Every cryptocurrency has a genesis block. Since it's the first block created, every block after the genesis block can trace back to it and its previous ancestor bocks using the linkage in the block header. Meaning, if we start from any block and move in a backward direction, we will eventually find ourselves at genesis block. Each node knows the hash of genesis block, its time of creation and the only transaction it contains. Table 25.3, shows the hash details about the genesis block (block 0) of a blockchain. Since it is the first ever block created, hence, its height is zero. The timestamp will be the time when it was created.

Table 25.3   Hashes of Blocks After a Transaction

Hashes	
Hash	2866f114d3c5ec5ab073f90179223cf6e70a6f7bf6908bbe1583cc6d591c33ad
Previous Block	00000000000000000000000000000000000000000000000000000000000000000000
Next Block Hash	75a11da44c802486bc6f65640aa48a730f0f684c5c07a42ba3cd1735eb3fb070
Merkle Root	828c5202934ead693783ea3f0e9da029999b541822c0e80eb92f35008dad82b3

We can see in Table 25.3, the hash of the genesis block is an alphanumeric hash. And the hash of the next bock is also in alphanumeric form. On the other hand, hash of the previous block is 0 as there is no previous block to this genesis block. By applying the cryptographic algorithm again we get the Merkel root.

25.5.3 Merkle Trees

A summary of all the transaction in the block is kept in each block of blockchain using *Merkle tree* (Figure 25.10a). A Merkle tree or a binary hash tree is a tree which

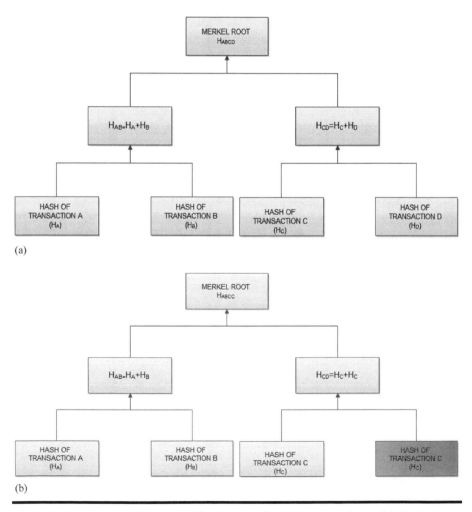

Figure 25.10 (a) Merkel tree with even number of transactions. (b) Merkel tree with odd number of transactions.

contains cryptographic hashes. A Merkle tree is usually upside down having root at the top and leaves at the bottom. In bitcoin, Merkle trees produce a digital fingerprint for the complete set of transactions. It provides an efficient way to verify whether a transaction exists in the block or not. A binary hash tree is formed by recursive and continuous hashing of a pair of nodes. It is done until only one hash is left, which is also known as root or Merkle root. In bitcoin, the SHA-256 cryptographic algorithm is used twice.

$$H_A = SHA\text{-}256(SHA\text{-}256(TRANSACTION\ A))$$

$$H_{AB} = SHA\text{-}256(SHA\text{-}256(H_A + H_B))$$

This process keeps on going until only one node is left at the top of the tree and this last node is known as Merkle root. Since it is a binary tree, it requires an even number of nodes. If an odd number of nodes (transactions) are present, the last hash is duplicated to make the leaf nodes even, making it a balanced tree as shown in the Figure 25.10b. The same method is used to summarize any number of transactions.

In bitcoin, it will have hundreds to thousands of transactions in a block. All of them are summarized to generate a 32 bytes hash. The efficiency of Merkle tree decreases as more number of nodes are added. As the scale increases, the Merkle path to prove that a transaction is included in a bock also increases slowly.

25.6 Terminology

25.6.1 Proof-of-Work

Proof-of-work is data which is quite difficult to generate but can be easily verified. It is a race or a kind of competition among the miners to find the hash. Although the chance of finding the correct hash is very low when a miner actually finds out the correct hash, it is awarded some reward in terms of bitcoins.

Consider an example, when people are talking to each other they convey some meaning to each other. Suppose there are two people, *Ankit* and *Prateek,* sitting on a dinner table. Ankit says "Pass me the pepper", here Ankit knows what he asked is to receive the pepper shaker. When Prateek hear these words he also understands the same meaning. So Ankit and Prateek both understand the correct meaning of the said statement. This is called consensus, i.e., agreeing on the same point.

With money, it remains same but consensus should not include just the two parties. For X to receive some money in exchange for some services or goods, not only X should recognize that whatever is given to him is money, but he should also have the assurance that everyone else also recognizes it as such.

The process of calculating a proof-of-work is called *mining*. Each block contains a random value, *Nonce*, in the block header. By changing the nonce value, proof-of-work has to generate a value which should make the block header hash value smaller than a *difficulty target*. In order to make a network accept the block, miners have to complete a proof of work which covers every single data in the block. Because of the very low possibility of generation, it is almost impossible to predict which node on the network will generate next block.

The two main purposes of mining can be states as:

1. To verify whether a transaction is a legitimate transaction or not or to avoid the double spending problem.
2. For a generation of new digital currency by awarding miners for performing a task.

So, an attack on a network using proof-of-work can be quite expensive. One would require more money and resources than what he gets after stealing. Although, if someone is able to take control over 51% or more nodes at the same time then the network will be compromised.

25.6.2 Proof-of-Stake

Proof-of-stake is a little different from proof-of-work. In a proof-of-stake network nodes do not spend their computational power and resources or solving some mathematical problem. Instead of this, nodes place a bet on the blocks. When a block is attached to the chain, whichever node had put a bet on it gets the reward. If a block is a dishonest one and some node had placed a bet on it the node gets a penalty. Whatever amount the node had put gets deducted from their balance. Placing these bets do not require high computational power. A node must have some stake to get rewarded. This makes the network fat, cheaper and more efficient.

In proof-of-work, if someone tries to be dishonest with the network, there is no counteraction to stop them from being dishonest. On the other hand, in proof-of-stake, dishonest nodes get a penalty. Although proof-of-stake does give us some benefits it also has some problems. First of all, a node must have some digital currency in its balance or else it cannot place any bets. For example, is the minimum balance required to place a bet is 1,000 ETH (1,000 ethers), then the nodes having less than this amount will not get a chance to place a bet. So, nodes having more than the minimum amount will get richer and below this threshold, poor remain poor. After a period of time, this gap between poor and rich will get bigger and only rich nodes will get to control the network.

25.6.3 Smart Contracts

A smart contract is an important part of blockchain technology. A smart contract is a digital contract that can execute itself. It may consist of a transaction that is triggered by a certain event. The main purpose of smart contracts is to eliminate the requirement of any third party completely. Before these smart contracts were included, the traditional way to send or receive funds was to approach a third party. With the inclusion of smart contracts, the transactions are programmed to be executed once a certain condition is met without any human intervention. Below is an extract code of a smart contract.

```
function payOut(address _recipient, uint _amount) returns (bool) {
  if (msg.sender != owner || msg.value > 0 || (payOwnerOnly &&
_recipient != owner))
  throw;
  if (_recipient.call.value(_amount)()) {
  PayOut(_recipient, _amount);
  return true;
  } else {
  return false;
  }
}
```

These smart contracts contain a certain set of instructions which may further be directed to perform some calculations, store information or make the transaction from one account to another.

Smart contract code acts like terms and conditions which, once uploaded to blockchain, cannot be altered. This gives you the assurance that the code will do exactly what it has been programmed for. Smart contracts give strength to blockchain, for example, instead of creating a different blockchain for every application, it can be done by creating one blockchain with different smart contracts for every application. Smart contracts also allow you to create smaller subcontracts. Suppose you have two smart contracts, one contains the ownership of your actual currency (let's say INR) and another contains the ownership of real estate. You can create a new smart contract which acts as an escrow for the two previous contracts. You can program the third contract in a way which allows it to purchase real estate without any third intermediate agency.

25.7 Blockchain Technology and Multimedia World

Although the blockchain technology was proposed for its unique way of handling transactions that includes money, it can also be used for far more.

25.7.1 Blockchain in Photography Industry

By now some of the photo agencies are using blockchain technology for licensing and payments. As the blockchain contains only data, it is easy to include a photo in its digital format and some relevant information. The first of all the uses of blockchain in the photography industry is to secure copyright images or any information. Since, in a blockchain once data is created it cannot be changed, a photo will always be associated with its actual owner without the possibility of any kind of dispute.

One more application of blockchain in this field is to build an image registry which will contain information about every photo and its owner along with its copyright proof.

By securely storing the original images into the blockchain, it can be used to keep the original image intact without alteration. Later these images can be used to detect any kind of modifications by comparing an image to its unaltered original. This technology can be used in photojournalism, where manipulation of images is a big issue.

Companies Like Ascribe, Mediachain and Blinded are working on how blockchain can secure a multimedia world whether it is music, image or video. Using blockchain, photographers can monetize all of their photographs by controlling rights and make a better living.

25.7.2 Blockchain in Music Industry

OPUS is an ethereum powered blockchain startup which might be the first decentralized platform for music. The company solves the issue of music ownership and sharing. Its platform can track in a complete decentralized way. OPUS encrypts the music tracks and stores them permanently through an interplanetary file system (IPFS). Users can listen to songs using smart contracts which contains hashes and decryption keys. The process is very simple: Store the songs permanently on the blockchain, make them protected and give the keys to the users who have rights to access the music.

25.8 Applications of Blockchain

25.8.1 Cloud Storage

Till now cloud storage providers are using centralized service, which means users have to trust these providers. Additionally, using giant servers is quite expensive and demands high maintenance. The data on the servers needs to be updated and refreshed frequently. On the other hand, blockchain can change the whole idea of cloud storage by introducing decentralization in it. This creates a system which is transparent and contains peer-to-peer connections, making it almost impossible to hack. For example, Storj is a cloud storage which works on the concept of the blockchain, this helps in reducing security loopholes and dependency. It uses spare storage in people's hard drive to store the data. The data is encrypted and spread throughout its network.

25.8.2 *Financial Service*

Current financial sectors like banking act as a central authority to send or receive money. These intermediate bodies are needed for the smooth flow of transactions; however, this costs time and money and we cannot ignore the security of these bodies. With blockchain technology, there will be no need for any central bodies. It will make the transactions cheaper, efficient and transparent. By using smart contracts users will be able to send and receive money without any human interference. Additionally, blockchain technology can make a difference in simplifying and speeding up cross-border payments. Transferring value is slow and expensive using traditional methods. However, blockchain can speed up this process by eliminating middle parties and agents. Moreover, blockchain also reduces the cost of remittance and provides guaranteed security.

25.8.3 *Blockchain and Internet of Things (IoT)*

The major concern of IoT devices is their security. With millions of devices connected with each other, it is quite difficult to maintain the security of the data they are sharing. Blockchain technology is the key to settle security of IoT devices along with reliability and privacy issues. The cryptography used in blockchain technology can make data on devices more private. The blockchain is also tamper proof and no single point attack will work. Also, it prevents these devices from a man-in-the-middle attack. It is autonomous, decentralized and efficient on trustless networks, and that is what makes it a fundamental element for IoT solutions. Simply put, it is cost-effective, builds trust and accelerates transactions.

Other sectors where blockchain can be useful:

- Assets Management
- Insurance industries
- Real Estate
- Healthcare
- Music
- Supply chain
- Digital Notary
- Digital identities
- Digital Voting

25.9 Case Study 1

25.9.1 Blockchain-Based Healthcare Using IoT

We all know that what IoT technology has brought us. There are a lot of possibilities when it comes to combining IoT with other technologies. Integrating blockchain with IoT in healthcare is one of these possibilities. The blockchain is used for securing sensitive data of patients. And IoT devices can be used to collect data from various sources in near real time. Blockchain can also be used for secure access to the data and exchange between organizations.

25.9.1.1 Introduction

According to Gartner, there will be more than 20 billion connected things by 2020. These many devices can be of great help and provide better insights into different fields like smart homes, cities, agriculture, healthcare, transportation, supply chain etc. With this many devices, we can collect a large number of data for analysis and decision making. However, we have to provide a system that is capable of withholding the huge amount chunks of data without any failure (Ekblaw, 2018). Also, this system should be able to provide safe and secure access to the data.

In context to healthcare, these devices can be either wearable devices like smart watches and smart bands or nonwearable devices yet connected to patients like smart tablets, smartphones etc. Or neither wearable nor connected to patients, yet can affect their health like a thermometer for measuring room temperature. All these devices must be connected to the Internet for sending and receiving the data. Using IoT in healthcare helps in numerous ways, such as doctors checking the patient's condition in real time and making a better decision without running any tests.

Gathered data can be collected in Electronic Health Records (EHR) for analysis and diagnostics.

Patient and the chosen doctor should be given permission to personalize the EHR. Patients should not be allowed to change the historical data present in EHR. Current healthcare institutes use centralized systems which can be hacked into by other parties and sensitive data can be lost. Also, interoperability difficulties between different institutes and medical centers make it even more challenging to share data. One way to store the sensitive data is by using blockchain. And by combining big data and IoT it is possible to collect and exchange the data between healthcare institutes securely. Additionally, using the concept of the blockchain, the patient will be in full control of his/her EHR and makes it harder for anyone to steal the data.

25.9.1.2 Blockchain and IoT in Healthcare

Devices which can monitor patient's health and are connected to the Internet can solve many problems and save a lot of time. When a doctor examines any patient, he must note the data measured by him. It is very possible that he may forget to write something or make a mistake and write down something which is not accurate. When we are using connected devices, all the data can be transferred directly to his EHR. As the patient checks in the hospital, the real time in his EHR can be used for examination, saving both time and money. Also, wearable devices can be used to provide data 24/7 about a specific part of the human body which can be used by doctors or researchers for a better understanding of diseases. It can also be used in prediction of the patient's health and help in the prevention of deterioration before it happens. IoT monitoring devices can collect a huge volume of data and automatically update the data in EHR without any third-party intervention. Because of the blockchain's immutability feature, patients' data cannot be changed and modified. Complete health and checkup history of patients will be preserved. Results will be available as long as people having the right credentials are accessing it. This cost of transferring information from one medical institute to another will decrease and auditing will be easier. Electronic healthcare records must provide a complete 360-degreeview of a patient from a healthcare perspective. This one is a complex problem in itself. In a medical institute there are a lot of tests generating lots of different types of data (numeric data, images, text etc). Another problem is a centralized system, which makes it harder for institutes to collaborate with one another and exchange data. On the other hand, blockchain is new technology with lots of opportunities; however, it would be difficult to store this much amount of medical data on blockchain. Replication of data would be expensive. Along with this, storage itself is a problem for blockchain technology. To solve this, we can make use of Big Data technology for storing and processing of the data collected. Or we can combine big data tools as the storage and blockchain technology for securing the stored data. The combination of blockchain and big data tools—BlockchainDB—can be used. After storing the data in the database, we can keep it as a transaction in the blockchain. This way blockchain will act as an index layer. Smart contracts can be created in such a way that they can tell the doctors if the patient's condition gets worse. Smart contracts can also be programmed such that doctors can get secure access to the wearable devices a patient has on his body. This provides real-time care and support to the patient. These smart contracts can also be used to notify the doctor about what medication is being given to which patient and alarm the doctor if the patient is getting wrong medicines. Blockchain working as an access or index layer can prevent third parties from stealing patients' data (Figure 25.11).

25.9.1.3 Conclusion

The case study presents how adding blockchain and IoT in healthcare can improve it. Whether it is about collecting data from various nodes, storing the collected data or monitoring patient's health, this can be done by integrating blockchain and IoT.

Figure 25.11   A blockchain healthcare example which can be implemented.

The current drawback of blockchain is its storage capacity. Since IoT devices generate a huge amount of data, it is not possible for blockchain to accommodate all the data in its storage; however, using big data tools like BlockchainDB will sort this problem out. This way using blockchain overall cost will be reduced and collaboration and interoperability between healthcare institutes will also be improved. Blockchain provides us a distributed, resilient system and the ability to exchange data on a trustless network. Additionally, smart contracts automate everything saving large amount process time.

25.10   Case Study 2

25.10.1   *Digital Voting System Using Blockchain*

25.10.1.1 *Introduction*

Digital voting has already been implemented but governments are too slow to adapt it. Despite the technology we have currently which protects the data, maintains confidentiality, privacy, and integrity of the data, the digital voting technology still encounters some problems regarding data leaks and fraud voting. For this issue to be resolved we need a more secure process and blockchain technology just seems fine for the digital voting process. Blockchain provides a way to prevent data modifications and keeps transactions private. But blockchain is not enough on its own to solve other concerns in digital voting like, how to know if the person is eligible to provide vote, how to be sure that the person giving his valuable vote will not be influenced by external bodies and how to be sure that the people taking votes are not tampering it. Blockchain, as the process behind bitcoin, makes altering of a transaction computationally expensive, providing integrity. Likewise, blockchain's mining process is also distributed. These two features of blockchain make sure to hold and store the voting records preventing integrity loss. Although the anonymity provided by bitcoin is good, but it might not help much in hiding identities of voters. Suppose we give an address to every candidate participating in voting within a blockchain, but one can still track the transactions and can find out which address belongs to which candidate. For a successful digital voting system, one or more mechanisms are required other than blockchain.

Privacy: Most people do not feel comfortable about telling which party they have voted for, for both their safety and privacy. Privacy in the digital voting system must not only look after keeping the votes not related to the voters, but also not disclosing any personal information about any voter. This demands high cyber security, which can be done using two systems: a system for voting and another one for verification. Using the verification system, we can be assured that the address has all the valid information and it has not been used previously for voting which assures single vote per person. The verification system will provide a *vote*. This vote or token will have a digital signature attached to it making it a verified and authorized entry for the voting system. From thereon, the voting system will keep track of all the transactions happening in every booth. It will hold on and evaluate the transactions until the end, after which it will complete all the transactions. This works similar to miners in the blockchain network.

Interim Results: Bitcoin blockchain is suitable for this kind of voting because of its anonymous nature of transactions. However, it will not hide the interim results until the end of the voting process. For each ballot, a separate public and private key should be used. A user's device, using user account's private key, will be used to encrypt the address of the voted candidate. Then it will encrypt this encrypted address with the public key of the ballot, which means without the private key it cannot be read. Lastly, the whole transaction will be encrypted with the private key of the account. Now, who is going to take responsibility for the ballot's private key? Until this key is secret, no one is able to view votes for the candidates, but can view which address has sent votes. One way to keep the key secret is by splitting it among the candidates, making it of no use unless they combine all the parts. At the end of the voting process, candidates must give their respective keys for the results.

Proposed framework: It will include a *voting registration server* whose job is to validate the interested users, *a voting server*, a user app (Figure 25.12). The voting server mentioned here is a distributed and the public can view all the transactions. The voter registration server is a kind of verification system; its basic task is to verify the voter's identity. The *voter app* is an application used by the voters to cast their vote. The voter registration server will not store any address sent by the voting server and the voting server does not have permission to access the voting registration server. All three bodies will have a pair of public-private keys which will be used to verify the transmission of messages. A unique key pair will be generated by vote organizers for every position and the public key will be shared with every registered voter. Voters will get one vote or token and a signature per elected position. When a vote is cast, transactions will be transmitted

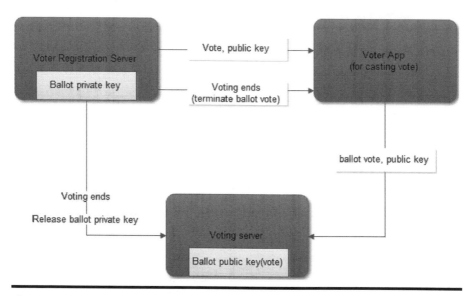

Figure 25.12 Voting framework based on blockchain.

to the voting server. This transaction contains candidate's ID encrypted with public key related to the position. A hash of this transaction is sent back to the voting server. After the voting process is over, the private key is used to decrypt the vote. This key is the one that was split earlier and was distributed among the candidates. By combining all the portions of the key, results can be declared.

25.10.1.2 Conclusion

By combining blockchain encryption and using a key at the end of the process, integrity and secrecy both are preserved. Furthermore, blockchain makes it impossible to modify the votes once they are cast. And by using the private key for decryption at the end of the process, one will not be able to know any results in between the voting process.

25.11 Summary

There can be a lot of applications of blockchain technology, and not all of them are just about digital currencies, mining or payments. In the near future, it is quite possible that most of the transactions will become decentralized and support blockchain technology. Till now, government and banks have been our main authorities for making transactions and moving money. With the deployment of the blockchain, it can bring the control back to the users. Blockchain future looks bright in the finance market. Blockchain will revolutionize many industries, from banks to photography. Who does not need an extra layer of security? Blockchain can be adopted by major central banks and cryptographically secured money will be used worldwide. This new technology has the capability to decrease the cyber risks and vulnerabilities by offering a unique identity through public ledger. Car rental companies can make use of blockchain and smart contracts for providing better service to the users. Once the authentication of the user is completed and payment is received, rentals can be allowed. Similarly, a refrigerator in your home with sensors attached can make use of smart contracts and blockchain for managing automated transactions like tracking its warranty, ordering depleted supplies and paying for them, or upgrading its software. Blockchain has already been implemented by many startups and major companies. As time passes, we will see more and more innovative ideas about blockchain.

Bibliography

Ahram, T., Sargolzaei, A., Sargolzaei, S., Daniels, J., and Amaba, B. (2017). Blockchain technology innovations, *2017 IEEE Technology & Engineering Management Conference (TEMSCON)*, Santa Clara, CA, pp. 137–141.

Akamai: How to Protect Against DDoS Attacks–Stop Denial of Service. (2016). https://www.akamai.com/us/en/resources/protect-against-ddos-attacks.jsp [Accessed September 29, 2017] and research directions. CoRR abs/1608.00771.

Anon, (n.d.). Blockchain use cases–IBM Blockchain. [online] Available at: https://www.ibm.com/blockchain/use-cases/ [Accessed November 25, 2017].

Antonopoulos, M. (2014). *Mastering Bitcoin: Unlocking Digital Cryptocurrencies*, 1st ed. Sebastopol, CA: O'Reilly Media, 2014.

ascribe. (n.d.). Artists & Creators|ascribe. [online] Available at: https://www.ascribe.io/ [Accessed November 15, 2017].

Aste, T., Tasca, P., and Di Matteo, T. (2017). Blockchain technologies: The foreseeable impact on society and industry. *Computer*, 50(9), 18–28.

Bhowmik, D. and Feng, T. (2017). The multimedia blockchain: A distributed and tamper-proof media transaction framework. *Digital Signal Processing (DSP), 2017 22nd International Conference on* (pp. 1–5) doi:10.1109/ICDSP.2017.8096051.

BigchainDB. (2018). Features & use cases. [online] Available at: https://www.bigchaindb.com/features/.

Biswas, K. and Muthukkumarasamy, V. (2016). Securing smart cities using blockchain technology, *2016 IEEE 18th International Conference on High Performance Computing and Communications; IEEE 14th International Conference on Smart City; IEEE 2nd International Conference on Data Science and Systems (HPCC/SmartCity/DSS)*, Sydney, Australia, 2016, pp. 1392–1393.

Bitcoin.org. (n.d.). Merkle tree–Bitcoin glossary. [online] Available at: https://bitcoin.org/en/glossary/merkle-tree [Accessed October 14, 2017].

Blockchain Pilot For A Leading Oil And Gas Firm: A Learning Journey. (n.d.). [ebook] Available at: http://www.fintricity.com/wp-content/uploads/2017/04/Blockchain-Case-Study-Oil-Gas.pdf [Accessed October 12, 2017].

Blockchain.com. (2018). Blockchain. [online] Available at: https://www.blockchain.com/ [Accessed September 17, 2017].

Blockgeeks. (2017). 17 blockchain applications that are transforming society. [online] Available at: https://blockgeeks.com/guides/blockchain-applications/ [Accessed November 25, 2017].

Cbsnews.com. (2018). Hacker demonstrates how voting machines can be compromised. [online] Available at: https://www.cbsnews.com/news/rigged-presidential-elections-hackers-demonstrate-voting-threat-old-machines/ [Accessed October 10, 2017].

Christidis, K. and Devetsikiotis, K. (2016). Blockchains and smart contracts for the internet of things. *IEEE Access*, 4, 2292–2303.

CIO India. (2016). Five uses of blockchain beyond Bitcoin. [online] Available at: http://www.cio.in/feature/five-uses-blockchain-beyond-bitcoin [Accessed October 11, 2017].

Clack, C. D., Bakshi, V. A., and Braine, L. (2016). Smart contract templates: Foundations, design landscape and research directions. arXiv preprint arXiv:1608.00771.

Conoscenti, M., Vetrò, A., and De Martin, J. C. (2017). Peer to peer for privacy and decentralization in the internet of things, *2017 IEEE/ACM 39th International Conference on Software Engineering Companion (ICSE-C)*, Buenos Aires, pp. 288–290.

Crosby, M., Pattanayak, P., Verma, S., and Kalyanaraman, V. (2016). Blockchain technology: Beyond bitcoin. *Applied Innovation*, 2, 6–10.

Ekblaw, A. (2018). *A Case Study for Blockchain in Healthcare: "MedRec" Prototype for Electronic Health Records and Medical Research Data*. [ebook] Available at: http://dci.mit.edu/assets/papers/eckblaw.pdf [Accessed October 9, 2017].

En.wikipedia.org. (n.d.). Electronic voting by country. [online] Available at: https://en.wikipedia.org/wiki/Electronic_voting_by_country [Accessed November 25, 2018].

Eris Industries Documentation—Blockchains. [online] Available: https://docs.erisindustries.com/explainers/blockchains/ [Accessed March 15, 2016].

Faculty of Technical Sciences, U. (2017). A case study IoT and blockchain powered healthcare M. Simic. [online] Slideshare.net. Available at: https://www.slideshare.net/MilosSimic/a-case-study-io-t-and-blockchain-powered-healthcare-m-simic [Accessed November 25, 2017].

Gartner.com. (2017). Gartner says 8.4 billion connected "things" will be in use in 2017, up 31 percent from 2016. [online] Available at: https://www.gartner.com/en/newsroom/press-releases/2017-02-07-gartner-says-8-billion-connected-things-will-be-in-use-in-2017-up-31-percent-from-2016.

Gartner.com. (2016). Gartner says 6.4 billion connected. [online] Available at: http://www.gartner.com/newsroom/id/3165317.

Greenfield IV, R. (2017b). Explaining how proof of stake, proof of work, hashing and blockchain work together. Medium [online] Available at: https://medium.com/@robertgreenfieldiv/explaining-proof-of-stake-f1eae6feb26f [Accessed November 25, 2017].

Greenspan, G. (2015). Ending the bitcoin vs blockchain debate. Available: http://www.multichain.com/blog/2015/07/bitcoinvsblockchain-debate/.

Gupta, M. (2016). Blockchain use cases. [online] Slideshare.net. Blockchain.com. (n.d.). Bitcoin Block #0. Available at: https://www.blockchain.com/en/btc/block-index/14849 [Accessed November 26, 2017].

HuffPost. (2017). 5 blockchain applications that are shaping your future. [online] Blockchain.com. (n.d.). Bitcoin Block #0. Available at: https://www.blockchain.com/en/btc/block-index/14849 [Accessed November 25, 2017].

Iot.ieee.org. (2017). IoT and blockchain convergence: Benefits and challenges - IEEE Internet of Things. [online] Available at: https://iot.ieee.org/newsletter/january-2017/iot-and-blockchain-convergence-benefits-and-challenges.html [Accessed November 25, 2017].

It Still Works|Giving Old Tech a New Life. (n.d.). The disadvantages of a centralized network scheme. [online] Available at: https://itstillworks.com/disadvantages-centralized-network-scheme-12213044.html [Accessed November 25, 2017].

Jin, T., Zhang, X., Liu, Y., and Lei, K. (2017). BlockNDN: A bitcoin blockchain decentralized system over named data networking, *2017 Ninth International Conference on Ubiquitous and Future Networks (ICUFN)*, Milan, pp. 75–80.

Jovanovic, D. (2017a). Blockchain case studies – Medium. [online] Available at: https://medium.com/@dejanjovanovic_24152/blockchain-case-studies-2271d37d3ed [Accessed November 2017].

Kshetri, N. (2017). Can blockchain strengthen the internet of things? *IT Professional*, 19(4), 68–72.

Lee, J. H. and Kim, H. (2017). Security and privacy challenges in the internet of things [Security and privacy matters]. *IEEE Consumer Electronics Magazine*, 6(3), 134–136.

Maksimović, M. and Vujović, V. (2015). *Folia Medica Faculatis Medcinae Univiversitatis Saraeviensis*, 50(1), 23–28.

Maksimović, M., Vujović, V., and Perišić, B. (2016). Do It Yourself solution of Internet of Things Healthcare System: Measuring body parameters and environmental parameters affecting health. *Journal of Information Systems Engineering & Management*, 1(1), 25–39.

McConaghy, T., Marques, R., Müller, A., De Jonghe, D., McConaghy, T. T., McMullen, G., Henderson, R., Bellemare, S., and Granzotto, A. (2016). BigchainDB: A scalable blockchain database, June 8, 2016, ascribe GmbH, Berlin Germany, https://www.bigchaindb.com/whitepaper/bigchaindb-whitepaper.pdf.

Moinet, A., Darties, B., and Baril, J. (2017). Blockchain based trust & authentication for decentralized sensor networks. [ebook] Available at: https://arxiv.org/pdf/1706.01730.pdf [Accessed November 25, 2017].

Nakamoto, S. (2008). Bitcoin: A peer-to-peer electronic cash system. Available: https://bitcoin.org/bitcoin.pdf.

Nakamoto, S. (2009). Bitcoin: A peer-to-peer electronic cash system. Consulted.

NASDAQ.com. (2017). What could blockchain technology mean for photography? [online] Available at: https://www.nasdaq.com/article/what-could-blockchain-technology-mean-for-photography-cm802750 [Accessed October 11, 2017].

Noizat, P. (n.d.). *Blockchain Electronic Vote*. [ebook] Available at: https://www.weusecoins.com/assets/pdf/library/blockchain-electronic-vote.pdf [Accessed November 24, 2017].

Ober, M., Katzenbeisser, S., and Hamacher, K. (2013). Structure and anonymity of the bitcoin transaction graph. *Future Internet*, 5(2), 237–250.

Omanović-Mikličanin, E. (2015). The future of healthcare: Nanomedicine and internet of nano things. Conference paper. *1st Conference on Medical and Biological Engineering*, Sarajevo, Bosnia and Herzegonia.

Onystok, J. (2017). Photography and the art of blockchain technology. [online] Blockchain WTF. Available at: https://blockchain.wtf/2017/06/blog/photography-art-blockchain/ [Accessed November 19, 2017].

Peck, M. E. (2017). Blockchain world–Do you need a blockchain? This chart will tell you if the technology can solve your problem. *IEEE Spectrum*, 54(10), 38–60.

Pepijn, D. (2017). With smart controls and contracts, blockchain tech is bridging the real and virtual worlds. [online] The Next Web. Available at: https://thenextweb.com/contributors/2017/07/31/smart-controls-contracts-blockchain-tech-bridging-real-virtual-worlds/ [Accessed November 25, 2017].

PetaPixel. (2016). Blockai uses the bitcoin blockchain to protect your copyright. Blog entry by Avery Wong July 25, 2016. [online] Available at: https://petapixel.com/2016/07/25/blockai-uses-bitcoin-blockchain-protect-copyright/ [Accessed November 25, 2017].

Pierro, M. D. (2017). What is the blockchain? *Computing in Science & Engineering,* 19(5), 92–95, 2017.

Ross, S. (2017). How does a blockchain prevent double-spending of Bitcoins? [online] Investopedia. Available at: http://www.investopedia.com/ask/answers/061915/how-does-block-chain-prevent-doublespending-bitcoins.asp [Accessed September 28, 2017].

Simic, M., Sladic, G., and Milosavljević, B. (2017). A case study IoT and blockchain powered healthcare. Conference paper. *The 8th PSU-UNS International Conference on Engineering and Technology (ICET–2017),* Novi Sad, Serbia.

Singh, S. and Singh, N. (2016). Blockchain: Future of financial and cyber security, *2016 2nd International Conference on Contemporary Computing and Informatics (IC3I),* Noida, pp. 463–467.

Szabo, N. (1994). Smart contracts. Available: http://szabo.best.vwh.net/smart.contracts.html.

Szabo, N. (1997). The idea of smart contracts. Available: http://szabo.best.vwh.net/smart_contracts_idea.html.

The Economist Case Study: Blockchain-based digital voting system. (n.d.). [ebook] Available at: http://www.economist.com/sites/default/files/ualr.pdf [Accessed October 27, 2017].

Thecityuk.com. (n.d.). Case Study: Blockchain | TheCityUK. [online] Available at: https://www.thecityuk.com/research/retail-financial-services-bringing-real-benefits-to-europes-customers/case-study-blockchain/ [Accessed November 25, 2017].

Thoughts of a Bohemian blog. (2015). Photography and blockchain technology. Blog entry by P. Melcher November 25, 2015. [online] Available at: http://blog.melchersystem.com/photography-blockchain-technology/ [Accessed November 8, 2017].

Tufekci, Z. (2016). Opinion. The election won't be rigged. But it could be hacked. [online] Nytimes.com. Available at: https://www.nytimes.com/2016/08/14/opinion/campaign-stops/the-election-wont-be-rigged-but-it-could-be-hacked.html [Accessed October 12, 2017].

Vujović, V. (2015). Development of a custom data acquisition system based on internet of things. *International Scientific Conference "UNITECH 2015",* Gabrovo, Bulgaria, pp. I339–I343.

Webopedia.com. (n.d.). What is centralized network? Webopedia definition. [online] Available at: https://www.webopedia.com/TERM/C/centralized_network.html [Accessed November 26, 2017].

Chapter 26

Copy-Move Image Forgery Detection Using Redundant Keypoint Elimination Method

Zahra Hossein-Nejad and Mehdi Nasri

Contents

DOI: 10.1201/9780429435461-30

26.1 Introduction

Information security means the protection of information and information systems from unauthorized activities, which include access, use, disclosure, reading, copying or recording, tampering, changing, and manipulation. The main concepts in information security are information confidentiality, integrity, and availability. Integrity means preventing unauthorized change of information and detecting the change in case of unauthorized manipulation of information. Integrity is violated when information is changed in an unauthorized way not only during transfer but also in use or storage. Today, the development of image processing and image editing software such as Adobe Photoshop®, and Photo Editor has caused created image forgery, and these images ultimately cause limitations in the information security system (Huang et al. 2008; Birajdar and Mankar 2013). In this chapter, while reviewing the methods of copy-move forgery detection, a method is presented that has a high accuracy in detecting forged areas. The Scale Invariant Feature Transform (SIFT) algorithm is one of the most common methods of forgery detection based on keypoints. One of the disadvantages of SIFT is the extraction of inappropriate keypoints, which cause an increased FP-rate and interference in the forgery areas detection. In this chapter, to solve the mentioned problem, the Redundant Keypoint Elimination Method-SIFT (RKEM-SIFT) is used to extract keypoints of the image by eliminating the redundant keypoints, which increases the accuracy of matching. To evaluate the performance of the proposed method, the MICC-F220 standard database is used to show the results of the experiments: the effectiveness of the proposed method in comparison with the classical methods.

26.2 Methods for Detecting Forgery in Digital Images

Many methods are used for forgery detection in digital images, which, in general, can be divided into two active and passive methods (Warif et al. 2016), each of which are described below.

26.2.1 Active Methods

In active methods, additional information is required to identify forged areas. Two examples of this method are digital signature and digital watermarks (Ustubioglu et al. 2016). Digital watermarking is a method to confirm the authenticity of the image. In this method, an invisible digital code is embedded in the image content before it is transmitted or shared. This code must be in such a way that it is not identifiable by the eye and only authorized persons are able to extract the data. In addition, the signal of this code should not be erased due to the usual processing on the image. Watermarking has many applications, the most important of which is forgery protection. This method can be used for a variety of purposes, including multimedia indexing, broadcast monitoring, fingerprinting, and quality assessment. However, these methods require a special hardware or software to insert the correct code into the image. Moreover, watermarking should be done at the time of recording, which would limit the method to equipped digital cameras.

A digital signature is a kind of asymmetric encryption. When a message is sent from an insecure channel such as the Internet, a digital signature that is valid can give the recipient the assurance that the letter is not fake and the sender has signed the letter.

26.2.2 Passive Methods

In passive methods, there is no more need for additional information to identify forged areas, and these methods are widely used to identify the forged region (Lee et al. 2015). Passive techniques, in addition to determining whether the images are authentic or not, can also detect the area that has been forged. Furthermore, in passive methods, without any watermarking, the received image is only used to evaluate its accuracy. Most of the passive methods used to detect forgery first train the features extracted from the training image set, and then categorize the features. The set of passive digital-image forgery methods can be separated into five categories using image processing tools and its analysis, which will be explained below (Qureshi and Deriche 2014).

26.2.2.1 Format-Based Methods

The format-based methods are another type of forgery detection method. The main task of these techniques is based on the JPEG (Joint Photographic Experts Group) image format. Detection of forgery in compressed images is very difficult; to detect forgery in such images JPEG quantization, JPEG blocking, and double JPEG methods exist (Ansari et al. 2014).

26.2.2.2 Camera-Based Methods

Digital images may be obtained from various imaging devices such as various cameras, scanners, and computer graphics imaging technology. In order to determine the integrity and accuracy of the given images, the devices should be identified. These effects are signed with an inherent kind of fingerprint of imaging devices, which can be used for detecting the image resources. Imaging sensors used in photographic devices identify various flaws and generated noise in pixels (Dixit and Gupta 2016). The sensor noises are because of the flaws, fixed pattern noise (FPN) and photo response non-uniformity (PRNU). FPN and PRNU are two parameters that are named "noise patterns."

26.2.2.3 Physical Based Methods

Various pictures are taken under different illuminations. When various pieces of images are combined to create a forgery image, the illumination condition conformity from unique photos are so difficult even with sophisticated editing tools. Therefore, light incompatibility detection can be used for different parts of the pictures to detect manipulation. The main advantage of this method is that hiding the effects of incompatibility in different light conditions is difficult due to digital manipulation (Ansari et al. 2014).

26.2.2.4 Geometry-Based Methods

In valid (real) images, the main point (camera center projection on the image) is at the nearest center of the image, but when a person or object is forged in the image, the main point will also be changed. The difference in the estimations of the main point across the image is used as the evidence of manipulation (Dixit and Gupta 2016).

26.2.2.5 Pixel-Based Methods

In this method, the main assumption is that, if any manipulation is correctly applied, the statistical correlation of the image changes at the pixel level although the manipulation is not visibly recognizable. The pixel correlation is directly or indirectly analyzed at the pixel level, which provides a special form of manipulation. Four techniques for detecting the different forms of manipulation at the pixel level include resampling, image statistical features, image splicing and copy-move forgery (Dixit and Gupta 2016).

26.3 Categorizing Pixel-Based Approaches

In general, the pixel-based forgery type can be divided into three categories: image splicing, images retouching, and copy-move forgery (Qazi et al. 2013; Sadeghi et al. 2017).

> **Image splicing** involves combining parts of two or more images together and creates a new image. This is one of the most common methods of forgery in digital images, an example of which is shown in Figure 26.1.
>
> **Retouching images** increases the quality of images. This type of forgery is widely used in editing the magazine's images, an example of which is shown in Figure 26.2.
>
> **Copy-move forgery:** In this type of forgery, some parts (object or individual) are copied from the image and pasted to the other area of the same image or the other image with or without (geometric transformation) manipulation. This method is one of the most common types of forgery that has attracted many researchers in recent years. An example of this type of forgery is shown in Figure 26.3.

The types of copy-move forgery are described in the next section.

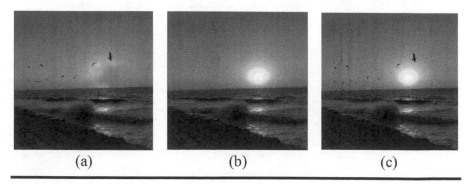

| (a) | (b) | (c) |

Figure 26.1 Example of splicing images, (a) original image, (b) original image, (c) spliced image.

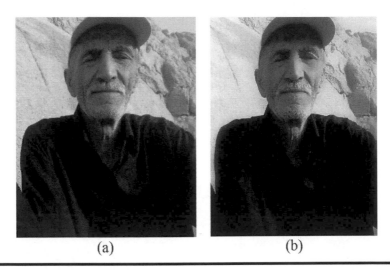

(a)   (b)

Figure 26.2   Example of retouching images, (a) original image, (b) retouching image.

(a)   (b)

Figure 26.3   Example of copy-move forgery images, (a) original image, (b) forgery image.

26.4 Types of Copy-Move Forgery

Given the widespread use of the copy-move technique for forgery digital images, this kind of forgery can be divided into three categories according to the approach of the images, whose steps are examined below (Sudhakar et al. 2016).

■ **The foreground object of the image copied and pasted on the same:**
In this kind of forgery, some objects are commonly added to pictures (images). Figure 26.4 shows an example of this forgery in the picture.

- **The background of the image is used to hide some of the object or region of the image itself:**
  The pluurpose of this kind of forgery is to hide one or more objects from the image, performed by using the image background and copying it to the desired objects. Figure 26.5 shows an example of this forgery.
- **The foreground or background portion of the other image copied and pasted to the new image:**
  This kind of forgery includes adding or removing some of the picture (image) information. In this method, some parts of the image are added or copied to the main image. Figure 26.6 shows an example of this forgery.

In the following section, the copy-move forgery detection (CMFD) methods are described.

(a)

(b)

Figure 26.4 **Example of copy-move forgery images, (a) original image, (b) forged image.**

(a)

(b)

Figure 26.5 **Example of copy-move forgery images, (a) original image, (b) forged image.**

(a)   (b)

Figure 26.6 **Example of copy-move forgery images, (a) original image, (b) forged image.**

26.5 Classification of CMFD Methods

In general, CMFD methods are divided into two categories: block-based methods and keypoint-based methods (Han et al. 2016). Each of these methods is described in the following subsections.

26.5.1 Block-Based Methods

In block-based methods, the image is first divided into square or circle blocks of the same size, which may or may not overlap each other. Then, the features of each block are identified, and the similar blocks are matched in order to identify the areas of copy-move, and finally, proper filters and methods can be used to improve the precision of the forgery areas, for eliminating mismatches (Moradi-Gharghani and Nasri 2016; Mahmood et al. 2015).

26.5.1.1 Feature Extraction Methods

Generally, the feature extraction techniques in block-based methods include frequency transform (Lucchese and Cortelazzo 2000), texture and intensity (Lin et al. 2009), moment invariant (Mahdian and Saic 2007), log polar transform (Wu et al. 2010) and dimension reduction (Zhang and Wang 2009). The details of the feature extraction techniques are discussed as follows.

- Frequency Transform
  Frequency transform is the most common method of the feature extraction technique in block-based methods, which is robust to noise, rotation and translation. The Fourier transform (Shao et al. 2012), fast Walsh-Hadamard Transform (FWHT) (Bin et al. 2013), Discrete Wavelet Transform (DWT) (Zhang et al. 2008), Dyadic Wavelet Transform (DyWT) (Muhammad et al. 2012) are some examples of frequency transformation techniques. The DCT are widely used in CMFD because of its robustness to noise addition and JPEG compression (Warif et al. 2016).
- Texture and Intensity
  Texture and intensity exists in natural scenes such as grass, cloud, tree, and the image properties such as smoothness and coarseness represent the texture contents. Texture and intensity can be utilized as features to extract in forgery image. In CMFD, the patterns, colors, and brightness in images are considered as features in this category; patterns are robust to geometric distortion.
- Moment invariant
  Moment invariant is another type of the feature extraction method, which is invariant due to changes in rotation, translation and scale. Despite the mentioned benefits, moment invariant is not appropriate for detecting small tampered regions (Warif et al. 2016).
- Log Polar Transform
  Log Polar transform is another kind of feature extraction technique, which is invariant to rotation, translation and scale. The Fourier Mellin Transform (FMT) is a kind of Log Polar which is limited to the rotation up to 10 degrees (Bayram et al. 2009).
- Dimension Reduction
  The dimension reduction technique is commonly used with domain features to reduce the dimensionality of the image and improve the complex. The Singular Value Decomposition (SVD) (Zhang and Wang 2009) and Locally Linear Embedding (LLE) (Junhong 2010) are samples of these techniques.

26.5.1.2 Matching Techniques

Matching is the process of determining the correspondence between two or more features in images. The matching techniques for block-based methods can be divided into three categories: sorting, correlation, and Euclidean distance. The details of each type of matching techniques are discussed as follows.

- Sorting
  The sorting technique is used in CMFD algorithms for matching the similar block pairs. Usually, after sorting the feature matrix, the search is usually performed through in it to put similar vectors near each other and make the matching faster and simpler. Lexicographical, KD-Tree, and Radix are

samples of sorting techniques that are widely lexicographical and are used to match block-based approaches (Warif et al. 2016).

■ Correlation
In this method, the degree of similarity between the blocks is calculated and the maximum similarities are determined as the similar cases. Usually, the correlation coefficients are used to determine the forged areas after sorting (Peng et al. 2011; Wang et al. 2012; Gan and Zhong 2014). However, the correlation coefficients can be used independently and without sorting in block-based matching methods (Warif et al. 2016).

■ Euclidean distance
Euclidean distance measures the intervals (distances) between the blocks and matches the similar blocks. The Euclidean distance, similar to correlation, is used to determine the manipulated areas after the sorting process (Ryu et al. 2010; Zhong and Xu 2013).

26.5.2 Keypoint-Based Methods

In the method of detecting areas of copy-move forgery based on keypoints, it is not necessary to split the image into blocks. In these methods, the feature points are first detected. Then, a descriptor is created for each of the identified features and, finally, the matching process is performed to identify the areas of forgery.

26.5.2.1 Feature Extraction Algorithms

The feature extraction techniques in keypoint-based methods include, Harris algorithm (Harris and Stephens 1988), Scale Invariant Feature Transform (SIFT) (Lowe 2004), Speed Up Robust Features (SURF) (Bay et al. 2006) and Mirror reflection Invariant Feature Transform (MIFT) (Guo et al. 2009). The details of the feature extraction techniques are discussed as follows.

■ Harris Algorithm
Harris detector was proposed by Chris Harris and Stephens in 1988. This detector uses the Gaussian window to identify the corner, and then, using the Taylor expansion, moves the window in all directions and examines the intensity value in all directions. This identifier is changeable relative to scale (Harris and Stephens 1988).

■ SIFT Algorithm
The SIFT algorithm was introduced by Low in 2004. The feature detection step in this algorithm consists of three phases: extracting the scale space extrema, improving the accuracy of localization, eliminating the unstable extrema, and, at the end, allocation of orientation to each created feature. The features obtained from this algorithm are constant against scale and rotation and are robust in changing viewpoint and illumination variations (Lowe 2004).

- SURF Algorithm

  The SURF algorithm was proposed by Bay et al. in 2006. SURF uses quick measurements of Hessian's matrix to detect features and the distribution-based descriptor to describe features. This algorithm is the developed version of SIFT in terms of speed, but is less accurate (Bay et al. 2006).

- MIFT Algorithm

  The MIFT algorithm was proposed by Guo et al. (2009). This algorithm is similar to SIFT at the features extraction stage, but is improved at the stage of descriptors, which is constant relative to mirror reflection. This algorithm is constant against scale changes, rotation and mirror reflection and is robust against viewpoint variations.

26.5.2.2 Matching Techniques

The similarity of the feature points in the image can be measured using the nearest neighbor and clustering techniques; each technique of matching is described in the following.

- Nearest Neighbor: The nearest neighbor technique calculates the similarity between feature points' distance from each keypoint relative to each other. Then the distance of the keypoints less than the predetermined threshold is matched. The nearest neighbor techniques for the keypoint-based approach are divided into four types: Best Bin First, 2NN, g2NN, and others where the g2NN method is suitable for multiple copy-move forgery detection (Amerini et al. 2011; Fan et al. 2016).

- Clustering: In clustering techniques, similar objects are placed in the same category (cluster) and different objects are placed in a different category. The Hierarchical Agglomerative Clustering (HAC) is a common example of the clustering technique in CMFD (Amerini et al. 2013).

  Next section concludes both methods (block-based and keypoint-based methods) to CMFD.

26.5.2.3 Comparison of Methods for CMFD

Block-based methods for CMFD are suitable for cases of the compression JPEG, but is not suitable for geometric distortion (scale change, rotation, angle, affine and translation), and they have a high computational complexity (Li et al. 2014). Their computational complexity has led to a widespread use of keypoint-based methods, including the SIFT algorithm (Amerini et al. 2011; Sadeghi et al. 2017). SIFT is one of the keypoint-based methods for detecting forgery, which is constant against scale and rotation changes and is also stable against intensity, affine, and noise distortions. But this algorithm has some disadvantages:

detecting redundant keypoints and the existence of some mismatches that increase the positive rate of error (Lowe 2004). The following is an analysis of the amendments made to the SIFT algorithm to improve the precision of detection of forged areas. In Fan et al. (2016), using T-Linkage clustering has improved the matching function in SIFT and ultimately has led to an increase in the precision of the correct identification of the forged areas. In Mursi et al. (2017), Principle Component Analysis (PCA) is used to reduce the dimension of the feature vector in SIFT, and the Density-Based Spatial Clustering of Applications with Noise (DBCAN) clustering is used to eliminate mismatches and to reduce the false positive rate. In Amerini et al. (2013), SIFT first identifies keypoints and uses the J-Linkage clustering algorithm to reduce the false positive rate. Since no method is provided for removing redundant keypoints in SIFT with regard to the identification of forged areas, redundant keypoints are eliminated using RKEM-SIFT (redundant keypoint elimination method-SIFT) (Hossein-Nejad and Nasri 2017), which reduces the matching time as well as the false positive rate.

The organization of the rest of this chapter is as follows. In Section 26.5 RKEM-SIFT algorithm is described. In Sections 26.6 and 26.7, the CMFD by the proposed RKEM-SIFT, experiment and results are reviewed, respectively. Finally, this chapter is concluded in Section 26.8.

26.6 RKEM-SIFT Method

In RKEM-SIFT (Hossein-Nejad and Nasri 2017), after identifying the SIFT keypoints in each image, the distance of the keypoints from each other is initially calculated. Then when the distances between two different keypoints are less than a certain threshold value, the redundant keypoint is removed based on the redundancy index (RI), and the other one is maintained in the image keypoints. RKEM is presented in order to reduce the redundant keypoints in the SIFT algorithm and improve the matching precision. The details of the method are described in the following.

26.6.1 Extraction of Scale Space Extrema

The first step of the process of feature extraction in the RKEM-SIFT algorithm according to the classic SIFT, is identification of situations of the image that are independent of changes in the image scale. For this purpose, stable features of the image are extracted on different scales with the use of "scale space." Scale space is the display of image structures on different scales consisting of a series of Gaussian images and Difference of Gaussian (DOG) images, arranged in different layers called octaves (Lowe 2004). Figure 26.7 shows the created scale space. In the following, process the created scale space are discussed in detail.

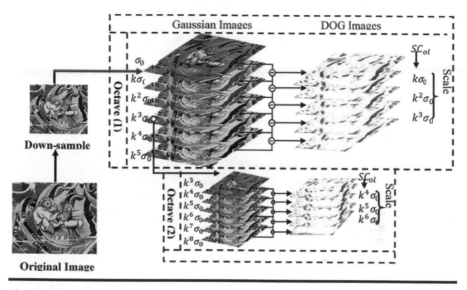

Figure 26.7   Scale space SIFT.

First, in order to increase the number of stable features of the image, image dimensions are doubled using linear interpolation, and considered as the first level image in the first octave. Then, the first level image is convolved in an iterative manner with a Gaussian kernel to create Gaussian scale space images in each octave (the left column images in Figure 26.7). Therefore, the Gaussian scale space images are created using Equation 26.1

$$L\left(x,y,\sigma\right) = G\left(x,y,\sigma\right) \otimes I\left(x,y\right)$$
(26.1)

In this equation, $I(x, y)$ is the image function, $G(x, y, \sigma)$ is the Gaussian kernel and represents the convolution operator. G represents the Gaussian function calculated according to Equation 26.2.

$$G(x,y,\sigma) = \frac{1}{2\pi\sigma^2} e^{-(x^2-y^2)/2\sigma^2}$$
(26.2)

The parameter σ indicates the scale of each image and its initial value is equal to $\sigma_0 = 1/6$ and by using a fixed parameter. Then, DOG images are calculated using the differential between two adjacent Gaussian images according to Equation 26.3 (the images of the right column in Figure 26.7).

$$D(x,y,\sigma) = L(x,y,k\sigma) - L(x,y,\sigma)$$
(26.3)

In this equation, $L(x, y, \sigma)$ is the Gaussian image with the σ scale, and $L(x, y, k\sigma)$ is the Gaussian image with the $k\sigma$ scale in each octave. As can be seen in Equation 26.3,

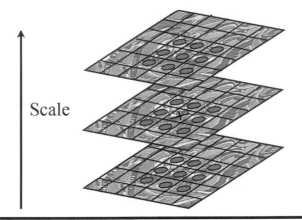

Figure 26.8 Extraction of extrema of DOG images by examining each pixel (marked with) with its 26 neighbours.

the scale of the smaller image is considered as the scale of the DOG image. After creating each octave, the Gaussian image whose scale is twice the initial scale is selected, and its dimensions are split by resampling and considered as the initial image of the next octave and the process is repeated. The purpose of creating the scale space is extraction of features that are independent of the scale. So, in order to extract the middle stable positions of DOG image in each octave, they are compared with its eight neighbouring pixels on its scale in addition to the nine upper scale and nine lower scale neighbourhood pixels in the DOG images. In addition, its extrema values (maximum or minimum) are stored as candidates as can be seen in Figure 26.8. At this stage, the scale parameter is selected for each extracted feature based on the scale of the DOG image. After this stage, the unstable extrema should be removed, as described in the next subsection.

26.6.2 Improving the Accuracy of Location and Removal of Unstable Extrema

During this process, the features with low-contrast and features that are on the edge will be deleted. The algorithm determines the exact locations of keypoints by interpolation of the adjacent data of each keypoint. Interpolation is done using the expansion of the quadratic Taylor series from the difference Gaussian scale space function $D(x, y, \sigma)$ over candidate keypoint. This Taylor expansion is calculated according to Equation 26.4.

$$D(X) = D + \frac{\delta D^T}{\delta X} X + \frac{1}{2} X^T \frac{\delta^2 D}{\delta X} X \qquad (26.4)$$

D and its derivatives are evaluated the keypoint and $X = (x, y, \sigma)$ is the offset of this point. In order to determine the position of extremum, Equation 26.4 is derived with respect to x and set equal to zero as a result, is obtained according to Equation 26.5.

$$\hat{X} = -\left(\frac{\delta^2 D}{\delta X^2}\right)^{-1}\frac{\delta D}{\delta X} \tag{26.5}$$

Then, the value of the offset $\hat{X}$ is examined. If it is larger than 0.5, the position of the candidate keypoint varies and interpolation is done for this point. Otherwise, the offset is added to the candidate keypoint and the size of the function is expressed in this extremum position using Equation 26.6.

$$D(\hat{X}) = D + \frac{1}{2}\frac{\partial D^2}{\partial X}\hat{X} \tag{26.6}$$

Thus, the location of the feature in the sub-pixel size is calculated and its exact scale is estimated. The absolute value of the function in the extremum position $|D(\hat{X})|$ is considered as the contrast of each feature and used for the removal of unstable features. In accordance with the proposal of Lowe, features whose contrast value is less than a pre-defined threshold value ($T_c = 0.03$) are unstable and sensitive to noise and thus must be removed. At this stage, after removing these low-contrast features, it is needed to remove the features that are on the edge, as they are sensitive to noise and small changes in their neighbourhood (Lowe 2004). For this purpose, the ratio between the eigenvalues of the Hessian matrix is used to detect and remove the points on the edge. The Hessian matrix is the matrix of second order partial derivatives in respect to x and y, estimated according to Equation 26.7.

$$H = \begin{bmatrix} D_{xx} & D_{xy} \\ D_{yx} & D_{yy} \end{bmatrix} \tag{26.7}$$

In this equation, D_{xx} is the second derivative of the candidate point with respect to x on the DOG images, D_{xy}, D_{xy} and D_{yx} are the second derivative of the candidate points with respect to x, y on the DOG image, and D_{yy} is the second derivative of the candidate points with respect to y on the DOG image. It is assumed that α is the larger and β is the smaller magnitude eigenvector of the Hessian matrix. Therefore, the ratio of these Eigenvalues can be obtained according to Equation 26.8.

$$r = \frac{\alpha}{\beta} \tag{26.8}$$

Based on Lowe's basic SIFT algorithm, the points for which r is greater than 10 should be deleted.

26.6.3 Assignment of Orientation for Each Feature

At this stage, an orientation parameter is determined for each of the extracted features from the previous. The process of allocation of orientation starts by selecting a circular window around each feature in the corresponding Gaussian image. Afterwards, size values and direction of the gradient are calculated for the pixels within the area, and, ultimately, a histogram is created as the histogram of orientation. Moreover, the directions related to the maximum of the histogram column and the directions that are 80% maximum are considered as the direction related to the extracted features.

26.6.4 Removal of Unnecessary Keypoints

In this part, removal of the redundant keypoints method is explained consisting of three different steps according to Figure 26.9 after identifying the SIFT keypoints in each image, the distance of the keypoints from each other is initially calculated. Then, when the distances between two different keypoints are less than a certain threshold value, the redundant keypoint is removed based on the redundancy index (RI), and the other one is maintained in the image keypoints.

First, Manhattan distance is calculated between each keypoint and all other keypoints in each image, according to Equation 26.9.

$$d_1\left(p_m, p_n\right) = \sum_{i=1}^{l}\left|p_m(i) - p_n(i)\right| \tag{26.9}$$

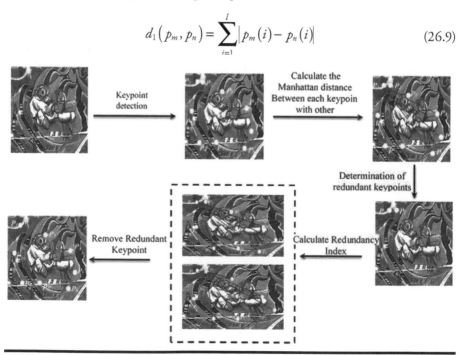

Figure 26.9   Flowchart of RKEM-SIFT.

In this equation, $p_m(i)$ and $p_n(i)$ is the ith coordinate of keypoint p_m and p_n respectively, and l is the dimension of the keypoints in the image. Moreover, sum of distances between each keypoint and all other keypoints in the image is stored according to Equation 26.10

$$SD\left(p_m\right) = \sum_{j=1}^{N} d\left(p_m, p_j\right) \qquad (26.10)$$

In this equation, N is the number of keypoints in the image, and $d\,(p_m, p_j)$ is the distance between keypoint p_m and keypoint p_j based on Equation 26.9. The RI of keypoint pm is defined according to Equation 26.11. Then, a threshold value is selected to remove redundant keypoints and in finally, if the distance between keypoints (except for the distance of each keypoint from itself) is less than the threshold value, one of these keypoints, which its sum distance value is smaller (RI is higher) is removed.

$$RI(p_m) = \frac{1}{SD\left(p_m\right)} \qquad (26.11)$$

26.7 Description of the Proposed CMFD Method Based on RKEM-SIFT

In this section, we concentrate on RKEM-SIFT for CMFD. According to the Figure 26.10, the proposed method is composed of four main steps: feature extraction using the RKEM-SIFT algorithm, the matching process using the g2NN criteria, the keypoint clustering and forgery detection using the agglomerative hierarchical clustering algorithm and removal of mismatches using RANSAC (random sample consensus).

26.7.1 Image Features Extraction

In this stage, features and descriptors are computed by applying the RKEM-SIFT algorithm on the image for CMFD. More details of which are described in Section 26.5.

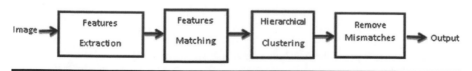

Figure 26.10 Flowchart of the proposed method.

26.7.2 Keypoints Matching

There are various methods for keypoints matching, where 2NN and generalized 2NN (g2NN) (Amerini et al. 2011) are widely used in image forgery. In the 2NN method, the Euclidean distance of each keypoint descriptor is calculated relative to the descriptors of other keypoints, and then the keypoint whose distance from the first nearest neighbor to its second nearest neighbor, according to Equation 26.12, is less than the threshold is matched. The method is not suitable for the copy-move forgery when an object is copied more than once in the image. The g2NN method iterates the 2NN method between until this ratio is greater than the threshold value which this value according to (Amerini et al. 2011), is set to 0.5. This method is applicable to multiple copies.

$$\frac{d_1}{d_2} \langle T \tag{26.12}$$

26.7.3 Clustering

In this stage, the hierarchical agglomerative clustering is used to identify copied areas. In this clustering, each matching point is first considered as distinct clusters, and during the repetitive process at each stage, the Euclidean distance between all clusters is calculated, and, ultimately, the clusters with the most similarity are merged to form one cluster. Linkage methods on the clusters and the cut-off threshold value have an important effect on identifying the forging areas and herein we, according to paper (Amerini et al. 2011), use Ward's linkage method with the threshold value 2.2.

26.7.4 Removal of Mismatches

The random sample consensus (RANSAC) algorithm introduced in 1981 by Fischler is one of the most applicable methods for remove of mismatches in the image (Fischler and Bolles 1981). In the following, the details of this algorithm are described.

First stage: First, it is required to choose a proper model according to the transformation model because of the variations of the reference and sensed images. The needed matched points for calculation of different transformation parameters are according to Equation 26.13.

$$q = \frac{p}{2} \tag{26.13}$$

where:
q is the least possible matched points needed for calculation of the parameters of the transformation
p is the parameters number in each transformation model

In the affine transformation, three matching points need to be chosen randomly in order to calculate the transformation parameters according to Equations 26.14 and 26.15.

$$
\begin{bmatrix} x_1 & y_1 & 1 \\ x_2 & y_2 & 1 \\ x_3 & y_3 & 1 \end{bmatrix} \begin{bmatrix} a \\ b \\ c \end{bmatrix} = \begin{bmatrix} x_1' \\ x_2' \\ x_3' \end{bmatrix} \tag{26.14}
$$

$$
\begin{bmatrix} x_1 & y_1 & 1 \\ x_2 & y_2 & 1 \\ x_3 & y_3 & 1 \end{bmatrix} \begin{bmatrix} d \\ e \\ f \end{bmatrix} = \begin{bmatrix} y_1' \\ y_2' \\ y_3' \end{bmatrix} \tag{26.15}
$$

In these relations, $(x_1, y_1), (x_2, y_2$ and (x_3, y_3) are the coordinates of the matching points in duplicated region, and $(x_1', y_1'), (x_2', y_2')$ and (x_3', y_3') are the coordinates of the matching points in the other duplicated region and f, e, c, b, a are the parameters of the transformation model.

Second stage: To choose the best model, three random matching points (in the affine transformation) are chosen to calculate the transformation parameters and the transformation model is accordingly calculated in each iteration, according to Equation 26.16.

$$
\begin{bmatrix} a & b & c \\ d & e & f \\ 0 & 0 & 0 \end{bmatrix} \begin{bmatrix} x_1 \\ y_1 \\ 1 \end{bmatrix} = \begin{bmatrix} x_1' \\ y_1' \\ 1 \end{bmatrix} \Rightarrow
$$

$$
\begin{cases} x_1' = ax_1 + by_1 + c \\ y_1' = ax_1 + ey_1 + f \end{cases} \tag{26.16}
$$

where:

$a, b, c, d, e,$ and f are the transformation parameters

(x_1, y_1) is the matching point coordinates in the duplicated region in the image

(x_1', y_1') is the other duplicated region in the image coordinates of the transformation model

the transformation model could be written as HP_e in which H is the transformation parameters and P_e is the matching points in the duplicated region in the image.

Third stage: After calculating the transformation model parameters, for each matching point in the duplicated region in the image, the distance (P, HP_e) is calculated in the other duplicated region in the image. If this distance is less than the threshold, this matching point is accurately matched; otherwise, the matched point image is deleted, and the tolerance error is empirically determined.

Fourth stage: In each iteration, the number of points that have been matched accurately is calculated. If the number of points that are accurately matched is more than the desired value, or reaches the predetermined maximum number of iterations, the algorithm stops. At the end, all the matching points, based on the transformation model that has the largest number of accurate matchings, are again calculated.

26.8 Experiment and Results

In this section, the functions of the proposed methods are evaluated by the MICC-F220 dataset (Amerini et al. 2011). The MICC-F220 dataset consists of 220 images where 110 are tampered and 110 are original. To investigate the effectiveness of the proposed methods, they are also compared with the method presented in Fridrich et al. (2003), Popescu and Farid (2004) and Amerini et al. (2011). In the following, evaluation criteria and simulation results are presented.

26.8.1 Evaluation Criteria

In order to evaluate the proposed method, three common evaluation criteria, i.e. the True Positive Rate (TPR) according to Equation 26.17, False Positive Rate (FPR) according to Equation 26.18 and precision according to Equation 26.19 are used. As the TPR and precision are higher and FPR is lower, those two are more suitable.

$$\text{TPR} = \frac{T_P}{N} \tag{26.17}$$

$$\text{FPR} = \frac{F_P}{M} \tag{26.18}$$

$$\text{Precision} = \frac{T_P}{T_P + F_P} \tag{26.19}$$

where:
T_P is the number of forgery images that are correctly identified as forgery
N is the number of forgery images
F_P is the number of original images that are detected as forgery
M is the number of original images.

26.8.2 Examining the Performance of the Proposed Method by the MICC-F220 Database

In this section, using images from the MICC-F220 database, we investigate the performance of the proposed method on CMFD images, the result of which can be seen in Figure 26.11 and Table 26.1.

As Figure 26.11 shows, by the removal of the redundant keypoints, the proposed method reduces mismatches and ultimately increases the accuracy of CMFD. According to Table 26.1, it is seen that method (Fridrich et al. 2003) based on DCT and method (Popescu and Farid 2004) based on PCA have acceptable TPR but not acceptable FPR. The low performance of these two methods comes from the forging areas in this database. Scale and translation changes renders these methods inappropriate for identifying forgery areas with geometric distortions. The proposed method has better performance compared to that of (Amerini et al. 2011) as it reduces mismatches, which ultimately reduces FPR. The proposed method has more precision compared to other methods, showing its better performance in detecting the areas of copy-move forgery.

Figure 26.11 Copy-move image forgery detection. (a) forgery detection by Amerini method [36], (b) forgery detection by the proposed method, (c) forgery detection by Amerini method [36], (d) forgery detection by the proposed method.

Table 26.1   Copy-Move Forgery Detection Results of Different Methods by Classic Criteria

Method	TPR (%)	FPR (%)	Precision
Fridrich et al. (2003)	89	84	0.514
Popescu and Farid (2004)	87	86	0.494
Amerini et al. (2011)	100	8	0.925
Proposed method	100	3	0.970

26.9 Conclusion

In this chapter, while introducing forgery detection methods, we dealt with a more precise examination of the problem of copy-move forgery as one of the most important and common types of forgery. For this purpose, two general classifications, including keypoint-based and block-based methods were examined. By examining these methods, it was concluded that keypoint-based methods have better performance. Hence, in this section, a keypoint-based method is used. In this chapter, a keypoint-based method based on redundant keypoint removal in the SIFT algorithm was used to identify forged areas. The experiments were carried out by MICC-F220 database (Amerini et al. 2011). The results of the experiments were evaluated using standard evaluation criteria and compared with classical methods. The results thereof proved the better efficiency and capability of the proposed method in detecting forged areas.

Exercises

Examine the types of areas that can be tampered with in copy-move forgery.

Examine which type of copy-move forgery each of the methods (keypoint-based and block-based) is used more.

Check the performance of the proposed method by adding Gaussian noise with the standard deviations 3, 4, and 5 on MICC-F220 images.

Check the performance of the proposed method by adding different JPEG transforms to MICC-F220 images.

References

Amerini, I., Ballan, L., Caldelli, R., Del Bimbo, A., Del Tongo, L., Serra, G. 2013. Copy-move forgery detection and localization by means of robust clustering with J-Linkage. *Signal Processing: Image Communication* 28 (6): 659–669.

Amerini, I., Ballan, L., Caldelli, R., Del Bimbo, A., Serra, G. 2011. A SIFT-based forensic method for copy–move attack detection and transformation recovery. *IEEE Transactions on Information Forensics and Security* 6 (3): 1099–1110.

Ansari, M. D., Ghrera, S., Tyagi, V. 2014. Pixel-based image forgery detection: A review. *IETE Journal of Education* 55 (1): 40–46.

Bay, H., Tuytelaars, T., Van Gool, L. 2006. Surf: Speeded up robust features. 9th European Confernece on Computer Vision–*ECCV, Austria.* pp. 404–417.

Bayram, S., Sencar, H. T., Memon, N. 2009. An efficient and robust method for detecting copy-move forgery in Acoustics, Speech and Signal Processing. IEEE 12th *International Conference on Computer Vision,* pp. 1053–1056.

Bin, Y., Xingming, S., Xianyi, C., Zhang, J., Xu, L. 2013. An efficient forensic method for copy–Move forgery detection based on DWT-FWHT. *Radioengineering* 22 (4).

Birajdar G. K., Mankar, V. H. 2013. Digital image forgery detection using passive. *Digital Investigation* 10 (3): 226–245.

Dixit A., Gupta, R. 2016. Copy-move image forgery detection a review. *International Journal of Image, Graphics and Signal Processing* 8 (6): 29.

Fan, Y., Zhu, Y.-S., Liu, Z. 2016. An improved SIFT-based copy-move forgery detection method using T-linkage and multi-scale analysis. *Journal of Information Hiding and Multimedia Signal Processing* 7 (2): 399–408.

Fischler, M. A., Bolles, R. C. 1981. Random sample consensus: A paradigm for model fitting with applications to image analysis and automated cartography. *Communications of the ACM* 24 (6): 81–395.

Fridrich, A. J., Soukal, B. D., Lukáš, A. J. 2003. Detection of copy-move forgery in digital images. *In Proceedings of Digital Forensic Research Workshop*, August 2003, Cleveland, OH, USA.

Gan, Y., Zhong, J. 2014. Image copy-move tamper blind detection algorithm based on integrated feature vectors. *Journal of Chemical and Pharmaceutical Research* 6 (6): 1584–1590.

Guo, X., Cao, X., Zhang, J., Li, X. 2009. Mift: A mirror reflection invariant feature descriptor. *In Asian Conference on Computer Vision* pp. 536–545.

Huang, H., Guo, W. and Zhang, Y. 2008. Detection of copy-move forgery in digital images using in Computational Intelligence and Industrial Application. *IEEE* 2: 272–276.

Han, Q., Yu, L., Niu, X. 2016. Feature point-based copy-move forgery detection: Covering the non-textured areas. *Multimedia Tools and Applications* 75 (2): 1159–1176.

Harris, C., Stephens, M. 1988. A combined corner and edge detector. *In Alvey Vision Manchester, UK* 10 (50): 10–5244.

Hossein-Nejad, Z., Nasri, M. 2017. RKEM: Redundant keypoint elimination method in image registration. *IET Image Processing* 11 (5): 273–284.

Junhong, Z. 2010. Detection of copy-move forgery based on one improved LLE method in advanced computer control (ICACC). *2nd International Conference on IEEE* pp. 547–550.

Lee, J.-C., Chang, C.-P., Chen, W.-K. 2015. Detection of copy–move image forgery using histogram of orientated gradients. *Information Sciences* 321: 250–262.

Li, L., Li, S., Zhu, H., Wu, X. 2014. Detecting copy-move forgery under affine transforms for image forensics. *Computers & Electrical Engineering* 40 (2): 1951–1962.

Lin, H.-J., Wang, C.-W., Kao, Y.-T. 2009. Fast copy-move forgery detection, *WSEAS Transactions on Signal Processing* 5 (5): 188–197.

Lowe, D. G. 2004. Distinctive image features from scale-invariant keypoints. *International Journal of Computer Vision* 60 (2): 91–110.

Lucchese, L., Cortelazzo, G. M. 2000. A noise-robust frequency domain technique for estimating planar roto-translations. *IEEE Transactions on Signal Processing* 48 (6): 1769–1786.

Mahdian, B., Saic, S. 2007. Detection of copy–move forgery using a method based on blur moment invariants. *Forensic Science International* 171 (2): 180–189.

Mahmood, T., Nawaz, T., Ashraf, R., Shah, M., Khan, Z., Irtaza, A., Mehmood, Z. 2015. A survey on block based copy move image forgery detection techniques in emerging technologies (ICET). *International Conference on Emerging Technologies, IEEE* pp. 1–6.

Moradi-Gharghani, H., Nasri, M. 2016. A new block-based copy-move forgery detection method in digital images in communication and signal processing (ICCSP). *International Conference on ICCSP, IEEE* pp. 1208–1212.

Muhammad, G., Hussain, M., Bebis, G. 2012. Passive copy move image forgery detection using undecimated dyadic wavelet transform. *Digital Investigation* 9 (1): 49–57.

Mursi, M. F. M., Salama, M. M., Habeb, M. H. 2017. An improved SIFT-PCA-based copy move image forgery detection method. *International Journal of Advanced Research in Computer Science and Electronics Engineering (IJARCSEE)* 6 (3): 23–28.

Peng, F., Nie, Y.-Y., Long, M. 2011. A complete passive blind image copy-move forensics scheme based on compound statistics features. *Forensic Science International* 212 (1): e21–e25.

Popescu, A., Farid, H. 2004. Exposing digital forgeries by detecting duplicated image regions. Department Computer Science, Dartmouth College, Technology Report TR2004-515.

Qazi, T., Hayat, K., Khan, S. U., Madani, S. A., Khan, I. A., Kołodziej, J., Li, H., Lin, W., Yow, K. C., Xu, C. Z. 2013. Survey on blind image forgery detection. *IET Image Processing* 7 (7): 660–670.

Qureshi, M. A., Deriche, M. 2014. A review on copy move image forgery detection techniques in systems, signals & devices (SSD). *11th International Multi-Conference on SSD, IEEE* pp. 1–5.

Ryu, S.-J., Lee, M.-J., Lee, H.-K. 2010. Detection of copy-rotate-move forgery using zernike moments. *Information Hiding* 6387: 51–65.

Sadeghi, S., Jalab, H. A., Wong, K., Uliyan, D., Dadkhah, S. 2017. Keypoint based authentication and localization of copy-move forgery in digital image. *Malaysian Journal of Computer Science* 30 (2): 117–133.

Shao, H., Yu, T., Xu, M., Cui, W. 2012. Image region duplication detection based on circular window expansion and phase correlation. *Forensic Science International* 222 (1): 71–82.

Sudhakar, K., Sandeep, V., Kulkarni, S. 2016. Redundant sift features via level sets for fast copy move forgery detection in signal and information processing. *International Conference on IEEE* pp. 1–4.

Ustubioglu, B., Ulutas, G., Ulutas, M., Nabiyev, V. V. 2016. A new copy move forgery detection technique with automatic threshold determination. *AEU-International Journal of Electronics and Communications* 70 (8): 1076–1087.

Wang, T., Tang, J., Zhao, W., Xu, Q., Luo, B. 2012. Blind detection of copy-move forgery based on multi-scale autoconvolution invariants. *In Chinese Conference on Pattern Recognition* pp. 438–446. Berlin, Germany: Springer.

Warif, N. B. A., Wahab, A. W. A., Idris, M. Y. I., Ramli, R., Salleh, R., Shamshirband, S., Choo, K. K. R. 2016. Copy-move forgery detection: Survey, challenges and future. *Journal of Network and Computer Applications* 75: 259–278.

Wu, Q., Wang, S., Zhang, X. 2010. Detection of image region-duplication with rotation and scaling tolerance. *Computational Collective Intelligence Technologies and Applications* pp. 100–108. Berlin, Germany: Springer.

Zhang, J., Feng, Z., Su, Y. 2008. A new approach for detecting copy-move forgery in digital images, in communication systems. *11th IEEE Singapore International Conference on* pp. 362–366.

Zhang, T., Wang, R.-D. 2009. Copy-move forgery detection based on SVD in digital image in image and signal processing. *2nd International Congress on IEEE* pp. 1–5.

Zhong, L., Xu, W. 2013. A robust image copy-move forgery detection based on mixed moments in software engineering and service science (ICSESS). *4th IEEE International Conference on* pp. 381–384.

Chapter 27

Anti-Forensics for Image and Video Tampering: A Review

K. Sitara and B. M. Mehtre

Contents

DOI: 10.1201/9780429435461-31

27.1 Introduction

Fast proliferation of multimedia capturing devices and related editing software tools have made its recording and tampering easier than ever before. Videos and images submitted in the court of law are acceptable as evidence provided its integrity and authenticity are validated scientifically. Video tampering is a process of malicious alteration of video content with the intention of concealing objects, events or changing the meaning conveyed by the video [1]. Malicious image editing is known as image tampering. Multimedia forensics deals with multimedia content analysis for identifying the traces of tampering thereby arriving at the conclusions regarding its origin and authenticity. These technologies aim at revealing the history of digital contents by identifying the acquisition device which captured the data, integrity validation of its content and retrieval of relevant information from them. Editing operations performed on a signal will leave some traces which can be identified for reconstructing the possible alterations and classify the signal as tampered (forged/doctored) or not. The terms forgery and tampering are used interchangeably.

Anti-forensic or counter forensic techniques are those which are designed to mislead forensic analysis by erasing or falsifying fingerprints (tamper traces or artifacts) left by editing operations. Anti-forensic tools and techniques are also used as privacy protection measures. Just as the fact that digital editing processes leave traces, anti-forensic techniques also leave its traces. Knowing this, researchers have come up with methods for countering anti-forensics. Those techniques designed to reveal the traces of anti-forensic activities are called counter anti-forensic techniques.

Multimedia covers many advanced technologies like interactive content. The focus of this chapter is limited to video and imaging technologies. In the literature, there exist several methods for detecting forgeries in video and images which can be classified into two categories: Active and Passive. Active techniques use a known subtle trace such as digital signature or watermarking for forgery detection. This trace is either embedded at the time of recording or is extracted during recording time and reinserted into the content or its header. Any change in this embedded content indicates that the file is forged. The major drawback is that it requires hardware which supports this facility. Whereas passive techniques use the content under examination for verifying its integrity and authenticity without the help of external descriptors such as meta-data. These techniques exploit the existence of fingerprints left by editing operations in digital content or acquisition process. Studies reveal that many of these techniques may still be fooled with the application of anti-forensic methods.

A perpetrator must balance the trade-off between complete removal of forgery traces and introduction of new evidence from anti-forensic manipulations. The workflow diagram that a counterfeiter/perpetrator may follow for attaining imperceptible forgery is given in Figure 27.1. The Figure shows that an image or video is first subjected to content manipulation by the perpetrator, followed by the application of forensics techniques to detect traces of tampering. If such traces are present,

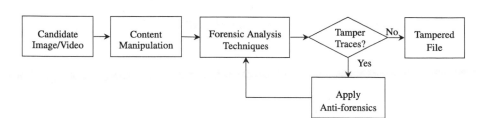

Figure 27.1   Work-flow diagram for attaining imperceptible forgery.

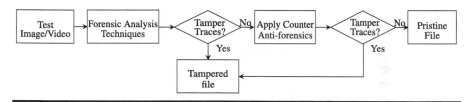

Figure 27.2   Work-flow diagram for successful forgery detection.

anti-forensics techniques are performed on the forged file to hide or remove them. This anti-forensically modified file can undergo further forensic analysis for finding the new tamper traces. The perpetrator may perform forensic analysis for finding the tamper traces followed by hiding or removing them till he/she gains sufficient confidence that the there are no identifiable traces left. The aforementioned activity can be observed as a loop in the diagram with the exit condition as the absence of tamper traces, which is an ideal condition hard to achieve in practical scenario.

On the other hand, investigators must maintain a trade-off between the accuracies of forgery detection and anti-forensics. The work-flow diagram for attaining successful forgery detection is given in Figure 27.2. The image or video under investigation (test image/video) needs to undergo forensic analysis for tamper detection. Generally, the presence of artifacts in any form indicate a probable forgery and its absence a genuine case. Considering the anti-forensic perspective, a forensic investigator should examine the possibility of any anti-forensic techniques been applied in the seemingly genuine case. As shown in the diagram, if tamper traces are found to be absent, counter anti-forensic techniques have to be adopted for finding the anti-forensic tamper traces.

The study on anti-forensics should be encouraged for the development of counter anti-forensic techniques. The literature in image and video tampering detection have limitations which will give rise to anti-forensic techniques that can be applied against them. Anti-forensic methods are also advancing with advances in digital forensics. This raises the question "How reliable are these forensic technqiues against a counterfeiter who is aware of their existence?" [2]. In this chapter, we present a survey on anti-forensic techniques that can be applied either on passive image or on passive video tampering detection methods. The methods used for countering anti-forensics are also discussed.

27.2 Anti-Forensics in Digital Image Tampering

The two most common techniques in image tampering are copy-move and splicing. Image tampering process in which the image regions used to execute forgery are taken from the same image is called copy-move forgery. If the image region used for tampering is taken from a different image, then it is called image splicing. A detailed overview of various image tamper detection methods in the literature is given in [3–7]. These surveys provide discussions on the features used, their advantages and limitations, and open challenges in tamper detection. To create high quality forged images, several types of tampering techniques (like resampling, compression, contrast enhancement, median filtering, blurring, sharpening, geometric and affine transformations) may be applied simultaneously. This makes it difficult for the tamper detection methods to categorize such images as forged. These operations conceal visual traces and destroy the forensically significant statistical fingerprints. When a small candidate region is down-scaled with a scaling factor like 0.25, it is very difficult to detect forgery.

Examples of imperceptible copy-move forged images with post processing operations from the CoMoFoD dataset [8] are shown in Figure 27.3. One pristine

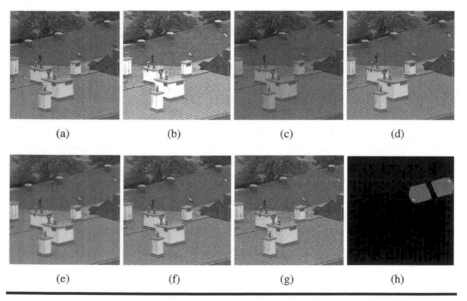

(a)	(b)	(c)	(d)
(e)	(f)	(g)	(h)

Figure 27.3 An example of visually imperceptible copy-move forgery with post-processing operations from the CoMoFoD dataset [8]. (a) Original image; (b) to (g) are copy-move forged images with translation and post-processing; (b) Brightness change with (lower bound, upper bound) = (0.01, 0.8); (c) Contrast adjustments with (lower bound, upper bound) = (0.01, 0.8); (d) Colour reduction (intensity levels per each colour channel = [32, 64, 128]); (e) Image blurring with $\mu = 0$ and $\sigma^2 = 0.005$; (f) JPEG compression with quality factor 30; and (g) Noise addition with averaging filter 5×5; (h) the mask image showing candidate regions of copy-move forgery.

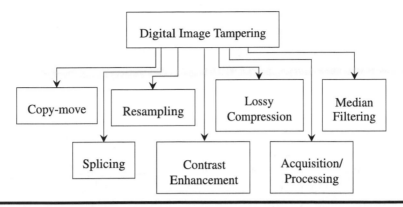

Figure 27.4   Sub categories of image tampering on which anti-forensic approaches are discussed in Section 27.2.

image from the dataset is given in Figure 27.3a. Copy-move forged images after applying post processing operations like brightness change, contrast adjustments, colour reduction, image blurring, JPEG compression and noise addition are shown in Figure 27.3b–g respectively. Figure 27.3h is the mask image showing candidate regions of copy-move forgery.

Bohme and Kirchner [9] described various anti-forensic approaches on image forensics. The sub categories of image tampering on which anti-forensic approaches are discussed in this section is shown in Figure 27.4.

27.2.1 Copy-Move Forgery

Traditional copy-move detection algorithms usually employ a partition based approach as the image region used to perform forgery is a part of the test image itself. The methods that use partitions which are equal in size can be classified as block-based approaches and other as nonblock-based [6]. In block division, the image will be divided into overlapping or non-overlapping blocks for feature extraction. The detection accuracy depends on feature selection. These features are extracted from the spatial domain or transform domain.

The methods in [10,11] that used spatial domain features from the colour space and bit-plane slices have got good accuracy. They failed when the image is JPEG compressed or when the image region used to execute forgery underwent geometric or affine transformations. Therefore, these can be used as anti-forensics towards the methods in [10,11].

The transform domain techniques obtain its features from Discrete Cosine Transform (DCT), Discrete Wavelet Transform (DWT), Fourier transform Curvelet Transform or from statistical techniques such as principal component analysis (PCA).

Cao et al. [12] used block-wise DCT coefficients for representing specific blocks and lexicographically sorted them for checking the similarity measure on the basis of some predefined threshold value. A DWT-based method that uses phase correlation for copy-move detection is presented in [13]. However, these techniques exhibit poor performance when the copied region is slightly scaled or rotated.

To make the tamper detection system robust to affine transformations, a part of the literature is based on keypoint based approaches. Among these, Scale invariant feature transform (SIFT) keypoint [14] based detectors are more robust. SIFT based approaches such as [15–22] in the literature are robust to compression, illumination and affine transformation attacks. But these methods are challenged by SIFT keypoint manipulations in candidate regions of forgery. This can be achieved in either of two ways: (1) altering the keypoint's neighbourhood so that the keypoint descriptors of its corresponding points in cloned areas do not match anymore (2) direct removal of keypoints in cloned regions. The anti-forensic techniques proposed for SIFT-based copy-move detectors discussed in [23,24] utilized the latter category. In [23], the authors used warping attacks in watermarking to introduce local warping in cloned image regions for reducing the detection accuracy of SIFT-based approaches. But warping attacks will contribute a bending effect on edges that would be visible. In [24], keypoints are removed by manipulating its neighbouring pixels using the following attacks: Gaussian Smoothing (GS), Collage and Removal with Minimum Distortion (RMD) [25]. GS is performed to flatten the local pixel intensity values for reducing the potential keypoints by decreasing their contrast values that are slightly above the SIFT threshold. In Collage attack, the original image patch will be substituted with a new patch where the new patch should be similar to the original. It is chosen from a database based on some similarity measure and it should be free from keypoints. The basic idea behind an RMD attack is to compute a small patch that when added on to a keypoint's neighbourhood will result in keypoint removal. Attack strength increases with increases in patch size. Obtaining the coefficients of this patch is considered as a constrained optimization problem as it should reduce the contrast around concerned keypoints with minimum visual distortion. In an attempt to delete existing keypoints, one attack may contribute new keypoints. To delete such keypoints, attacks were performed in an iterative fashion. Costanzo et al. [26] extended [24] using two supports (square region around keypoint) of increasing size. At first, an image is attacked with 8×8 support. For further keypoint removal, the resultant image is attacked with 10×10 support. Fake keypoints are then re-introduced for hiding traces of keypoint removal in [26,27].

Anti-forensic approaches using keypoint removal will leave traces in manipulated image regions. Absence or abnormal reduction of keypoints in high-variance textured image regions is the clue for forensic investigator to infer the anti-forensic activity. Costanzo et al. [26] proposed three detectors for identifying the removed and re-inserted SIFT keypoints. The first detector made use of two simple observations: (1) SIFT keypoints lie in proximity of corners, (2) keypoint removal attacks work on small neighbourhoods around the targeted keypoints by preserving as much image content as possible. SIFT keypoint algorithm discards candidate keypoints having low contrast neighbourhood. Hence, keypoints are concentrated in high variance image regions. The second detector utilized this observation. The authors used a Support Vector Machine (SVM) as last detector for discriminating authentic and forged images.

Copy-move forgery detection techniques [15–20,28–30] exhibit poor performance in smooth/uniform regions. Hence, image editing using such regions will work as an anti-forensic technique here.

27.2.2 Splicing Forgery

The spliced image regions have different background and lighting conditions. Therefore, it is relatively harder to make the boundaries of spliced region imperceptible in forged images. The presence of sharp edges (or changes) between different regions and their surroundings in the concerned image constitute valuable clues of splicing.

Boundary-based splicing detectors [31,32] utilized irregular modifications at splicing boundaries. The work by Fang et al. [31] is based on the consistency of colour division in surrounding pixels of splicing boundary. In [32], a method that relies on human visual system (HVS) is proposed. Splicing correlation between the boundary and fixation points produced by the visual fixation algorithm is used.

Johnson and Farid [33] proposed splicing detectors based on light inconsistencies. When different image regions are combined as a single-spliced image, direction of light discriminates the splicing region. When the light effects on original and spliced regions are same or in the same direction, it functions as an anti-forensic technique on the splicing detector in [33].

Mahdian and Saic [34] proposed a splicing detector based on noise inconsistencies. The authors used high-resolution wavelet coefficients for noise estimation. The detection rate of this technique is affected by low noise ratio. The variance of isolated regions is another factor that affects detection performance.

Most of the detectors [31–34] developed for image splicing forgery are highly sensitive to noise and blurring. These post processing operations hide the splicing traces from the forged image which can be treated as anti-forensics. Blurred image splicing localization based on the partial blur type inconsistency is proposed in [35]. After estimating local blur kernels from image blocks, its blur types (motion and out-of-focus) are identified to detect regions with different blur models.

27.2.3 Resampling Forgery

In image resampling, the original size of the image or image region is up-sampled or down-sampled to create meaningful forgery. Interpolation algorithms are applied on images to create smooth and visually appealing resampled images. Interpolation is the process of finding pixel values at intermediate pixel locations which are not present in its original version. Image regions might be resampled for blending the forgery region with its new neighbouring objects. These resampled regions may not contribute an exact match with the original image region before resampling. Thus, it forms an anti-forensic approach on block matching based copy-move forgery detection methods. The counter method on this anti-forensics is to apply resampling detector on suspicious image regions or on entire image in small blocks. Table 27.1 provides information regarding resampling detection methods and their anti-forensic approaches. The second and third columns provide information on features used and anti-forensic approaches that can be applied on a particular method respectively.

Popescu and Farid [36] identified that interpolation process for creating resampled images will introduce linear dependences between adjacent pixels. The linear correlation between a pixel and its neighbours are computed. The expectation/maximization (EM) algorithm is employed to estimate probability of correlation. Based on the resampling parameters, one can find a set of samples which are correlated in the same way as their neighbours. In resampled images, the correlation probability map, called p-map, tends to exhibit periodic peaks in Fourier domain. As [36] requires high computation due to EM algorithm, Kirchner replaced the EM algorithm using linear filter in [37] and linear row and column predictors in [38]. He extended his work in [37] to address resampling detection in recompressed images [39]. The fourier spectrum of p-map is normalized with its median filtered version and 0-ed out all non-maximum frequency components in a window of size W to find the peaks of resampling. All frequency components at frequencies $(k/8, l/8), (k, l) \in \{-4,...,4\}^2$ are removed to avoid JPEG peaks due to blocking artifacts.

Gallagher [40] exploited the periodicity in second derivatives of interpolated images. He proved that when a signal is resampled, the variance of its second derivative has a periodicity equal to the sampling rate. The discrete Fourier transform (DFT) of the variance signal is computed to examine peaks in it. In [41], the authors exploited the periodicity in second derivative of the interpolated signal by analyzing it in the frequency domain from a binary signal created from the zero-crossing of the second derivative. Mahdian and Saic identified that the variance of nth order derivatives of interpolated images exhibit periodic patterns [42,43], which is a generalization of the concept in [40]. The periodicity of the variance signal is investigated using radon transformation to make the detector robust to affine transformations. After finding traces of resampling using radon transformation, Mahdian and Saic [44] divided the input image into homogeneous blocks based on noise for identifying blocks with locally added noise. Birajdar and Mankar [45] proposed a resampling detector based on the autocovariance sequence of zero-crossings of second difference of the input image. In [46], resampling detection is performed using texture classification.

The resampling detection algorithms fail when the image is downsampled to half its size. In this scenario, alternate rows and columns will be deleted and hence no rows or columns will be a linear combination of its neighbours. Also, the noise and blocking artifacts generated by lossy compressions like JPEG affect resampling detection.

Table 27.1   Features Used and Anti-Forensic Approaches on Image Resampling Detectors

Method	Features Used	Anti-Forensic Approach
Popescu and Farid [36]	Linear dependence estimated using periodic patterns in p-map estimated with EM algorithm	Noise and blocking artifacts due to compression
Kirchner and Matthias [37]	Linear filter	Noise and blocking artifacts due to compression; Geometric transformation
Kirchner and Matthias [38]	Linear row and column predictors	Noise and blocking artifacts due to compression
Kirchner and Gloe [39]	Fourier spectrum of p-map normalized to its median filtered version	Resampling rate peak overlapping with blocking artifacts
Gallagher [40]	DFT of variance of second derivative	Noise and blocking artifacts due to compression; rotation and skewing
Prasad and Ramakrishnan [41]	Zero-crossing of the second derivative	Noise and blocking artifacts due to compression; rotation and skewing
Mahdian and Saic [42,43]	Radon transformation of second derivative	Noise and blocking artifacts due to compression
Mahdian and Saic [44]	Radon transformation of second derivative and noise inconsistencies	Noise
Birajdar and Mankar [45]	Zero-crossings of the second difference	Noise and blocking artifacts due to compression; Rescaling with rotation
Hou et al. [46]	Local linear transform texture	Rotation and skewing
Su et al. [47]	Blind deconvolution of non-overlapping blocks with trained SVM classifier	Blurred images
Feng et al. [48]	Normalized energy density of frequency spectrum of second-derivative	Noise

High compression ratio may introduce more noisy pixels. Block-based lossy compression techniques will introduce sharp transitions at block boundaries between neighbouring blocks. This blocking artifacts will introduce periodic peaks which when coincides with that of resampling leads to the failure of algorithms. This paves the way for anti-forensic approaches on the methods in [36,38–44]. Using a high compression rate will help in hiding the periodic patterns of actual resampling with that from blocking artifacts. The noise introduced by compression will also function as anti-forensics as it decreases the detection performance of these algorithms. The method in [40] fails when the original image is resampled with an interpolation factor of 2 where the phase of variance signal is preserved. Also, it fails when the resampled region is rotated or skewed.

Su et al. [47] proposed method for resampling detection using blind deconvolution which requires prior knowledge for refining the output kernel. The image is divided into non-overlapping blocks and blind deconvolution is performed. The output kernels are given to an SVM classifier. This method fails when the resampled image is blurred. Feng et al. [48] utilized normalized energy density in small windows of second-derivative of the input image in the frequency spectrum to extract 19-D feature vector for SVM. Its performance decreases with increase in noise.

Generally, the resampling detectors perform well on low order interpolation function (like linear or cubic interpolation). But the performance decreases with increases in order of interpolation function. Hence, using windowed sinc interpolator is another anti-forensic approach.

Kirchner and Bohme [49] proposed three anti-forensic techniques for hiding resampling traces. The first technique is to perform a post processing operation on a resampled image with a non-linear filter (like median filter). The usage of non-linear filters will destroy the periodic dependencies due to resampling. Secondly, the systematic similarity (constant sequence of discrete lattice position mapping from original to target image) is destroyed using geometric distortion. The quality loss is mitigated using Sobel filters. Dual-path approach is the last attack which is a combination of median filtering and geometric distortion. The resampled image is decomposed into low and high frequency components. The high frequency components will undergo geometric distortion and edge modulation where edge information is taken from the resampled image before median filtering. This is added to the low frequency components for obtaining the anti-forensic image. From their studies, it is mentioned that of the three, dual-path is the strongest anti-forensic technique on resampling detection.

27.2.4 Contrast Enhancement Forgery

Contrast is an important factor in image quality. Contrast manipulations involve non-linear pixel mappings that introduce artifacts in the image's histogram. Stamm and Liu [50–52] proposed contrast enhancement (CE) detectors that make use of the gaps and peaks in histograms. Anti-forensic approach to these detectors is proposed in [53]. The idea is to add noise to the pixels that contribute the peaks and gaps in the histogram and also to those in its adjacent bins.

A Modified Contrast Enhancement based Forensics (MCEF) method based on Fuzzy Fusion for detecting post-processing activity is presented in [54]. The authors also proposed two anti-forensic schemes: CE trace hiding attack and CE trace forging attack. CE trace hiding attack is performed by integrating local random dithering in pixel value mapping. CE trace forging attack counterfeit the peak/gap artifacts in the gray level histogram of a target pixel region by modifying the histogram. Feature selection methods in conjunction with fuzzy fusion approach is then used for tamper detection.

27.2.5 Lossy Compression

Stamm et al. [55–57] discussed anti-forensic techniques for hiding traces of compression from an image. When a JPEG image is decompressed, the recovered coefficients will be multiples of q (quantization factor). If the histograms of DCT coefficients of block-wise DCT of an image contains gaps and peaks corresponding to a previous q, then it indicates that the image has underwent a previous JPEG compression [58]. It arises due to rounding and truncation errors (inverse DCT and mapping to eligible value range). An anti-forensic approach to remove quantization artifacts by adding noise to each quantized DCT coefficient is proposed in [56]. Unquantized DCT coefficients are modeled using Laplacian distribution. To restore the shape of DCT histogram of a never-compressed image, its coefficients are redistributed by adding noise according to the conditional probability functions of each peak and DCT frequency band. The concept is applied to the distribution of each subband's wavelet coefficients in [55] for anti-forensics to wavelet based image compression detection.

Fan et. al [59] proposed a JPEG anti-forensic procedure composed of four steps: total variation (TV)-based deblocking in the spatial domain, perceptual DCT histogram smoothing based on an adaptive local dithering signal model, second round TV-based deblocking and decalibration. Total variation (TV)-based deblocking removes JPEG blocking artifacts and plausibly fill gaps in the DCT histogram, so as to facilitate histogram smoothing. Discrete cosine transform (DCT) quantization artifacts removal will introduce unnatural noise and blocking artifacts. Hence, a second round of TV-based deblocking and regularization is applied. The resultant image is processed by the decalibration operation. The authors in [60] improved [59] for achieving better tradeoff between image visual quality and forensic undetectability. It consists of four stages: perceptual DCT histogram smoothing, denoising operation, TV-based deblocking, and decalibration operation. The authors proposed two denoising algorithms based on (1) TV by solving the constrained minimization problem and (2) a normalized weighted function that depends on the similarity between two pixels. In [59], energy variations along horizontal and vertical directions are taken. Whereas in [60], TV-based deblocking takes the combined effect of energy variations along horizontal, vertical and diagonal directions.

Another JPEG anti-forensic approach that uses deblocking, smoothing with dither, and de-calibration operation is proposed in [61]. Least Cuckoo Search (LCS) algorithm based noise artifact estimation is performed for adding it to the JPEG compressed image during the deblocking and de-calibration operation. Histogram deviation (HD) fitness function is used for selecting the optimal noise-like signal. After deblocking, gaps in the histogram are filled using histogram smoothing which will add noise utilizing a signal dithering model without altering the DCT coefficient distribution. The noise and blocking artifacts thus introduced is again deblocked and regularized using another round of LCS-HD-based deblocking. LCS-HD-based de-calibration is applied over the resultant image for better visual quality.

Double JPEG compression may lead to blocking artifacts due to pixel discontinuities at block boundaries. An anti-forensic approach to the blockiness detector [58] using a combination of median filter and additive Gaussian noise is proposed in [57].

Jiang et al. [62] proposed a noise level based method for detecting JPEG anti-forensics. It does not perform well in textured images. Zeng et al. [63] resolved this using the L_2 norm of the noise level of an image and the noise level of its compression residual (CR). The noise present in the test image is estimated from image patches using the method in [64]. JPEG compression usually removes high frequency components and preserves low frequency component in an image. CR tends to be zero in weak textured areas. Gaussian noise addition will contaminate it in forged images. The anti-forensic dither and Gaussian noise in weak textured regions makes the noise level of CR an effective feature in revealing the traces of JPEG anti-forensic.

Valenzise et al. [65] estimated noisiness by means of TV for JPEG recompression detection robust to JPEG anti-forensics in [55–57]. The test image is re-compressesed at different quality factors for analyzing TV of the re-compressed images. Fan et al. [66] proposed anti-forensics on [65] with less image quality degradation using the quantization noise in the DCT domain.

27.2.6 Median Filtering

Median filtering (MF) is a nonlinear image processing operation. Therefore, it is effective in hiding the traces of different types of image manipulation. The median filtering in overlapping windows characterize high probability of adjacent pixels being similar. That is, the pixel values in an MF image at certain neighourhood may originate from the same pixel of original image. The difference between adjacent pixels will be zero at these positions, termed as streaking artifact. In [67,68], streaking artifact is utilized for MF detection. Chen et al., [69] utilized the statistics of difference domain, extracting the Global and Local Feature (GLF) set comprised of Global Probability Features (GPF) and Local Correlation Features (LCF) which are used for classification by SVM. In [70], second order Local Ternary Patterns (LTP) is used for detecting MF.

The anti-forensic approaches for countering MF detectors modified the pixel value difference distribution. In [71], this distribution of an unaltered and MF image are modeled using Generalized Gaussian Distribution (GGD) whose parameters are learned by simple regression. A method for estimating the plausible pixel value difference distribution of an unaltered image from an MF is presented. Using this estimated distribution as target, noise distribution is estimated for adding it in to the MF image so that the resultant distribution will shift to the plausible one.

MF anti-forensics is formulated as an ill-posed inverse problem in [72]. This optimization problem consists of convolution term, fidelity term and prior term. The convolution term uses a convolution kernel for the approximation of MF process. The fidelity term is for keeping the processed image close to the MF image. Using GGD, the prior term regularizes the pixel value derivative of the obtained image so that its distribution resembles original. In [73], random noise is added to high textured blocks for deceiving MF detectors. In [74], an optimization framework that maintains peak signal-to-noise ratio while reducing the cost of features that detect MF is presented.

In [75], MF anti-forensic technique robust to MF detectors in [67,69,70] is formulated as an optimization problem constrained by a difference of anisotropic and isotropic TV regularization. It ensures minimal changes in the spatial characteristics of an MF image. The squared L_2 norms of the differences between anti-forensically modified (AFM) and MF images and that between AFM and unfiltered images are taken as the features.

27.2.7 Image Acquisition or Processing Chain

Local dependencies between pixel values in different colour channels of colour images have attracted the interest of forensic investigators [76]. A method for synthetic creation or restoration of a colour filter array (CFA) fingerprint in digital images is presented in [77]. This attack is used for concealing the traces of manipulation that disrupted the CFA pattern.

Another important feature in image tampering detection is sensor pattern noise (SPN) which arises due to sensor defects in the image acquisition device. Stable parts of the sensor noise, which emerges from variations in the hardware manufacturing process and sensor wear-out, leave traces that are unique for each individual sensor. This noise pattern is useful to link (parts of) images with acquisition devices, by extracting a sensor fingerprint from the photo response non-uniformity (PRNU). A simpler correlation detector was proposed in [78]. An anti-forensic for this is presented in [79]. The flat-field frame holds the PRNU component of SPN. Assuming that the counterfeiter has access to the primary acquisition device, he/she can extract the SPN of the camera. Then, counterfeiting an image involves two steps: (1) suppression of original SPN and (2) insertion of a counterfeit SPN. If the counterfeiter has no access to the acquisition device, an estimate can be created from the publicly available images of the same make and model camera. The risk of failure increases when the forensic investigator performs a triangle test with the same images [80].

27.3 Anti-Forensics in Digital Video Tampering

Video forgeries can be classified into inter-frame and intra-frame forgeries. In inter-frame forgeries, the frame as a whole is tampered to execute forgery. Whereas in intra-frame forgeries, only regions of frames are tampered. Inter-frame video forgeries are of the following four types:

1. **Frame deletion** is the process in which a sequence of frames in a video are removed for concealing objects or events in the video. Example, the presence of a person in the recorded field of view (FOV) can be removed by deleting the frames corresponding to it.
2. **Frame insertion** is the process in which a sequence of frames from one video are taken and pasted in another video. This is usually done to fill the gap of frame deletions so that the duration (number of frames) in a video segment remains overall the same as other segments. In surveillance systems, the recordings are usually stored as video segments of particular duration or file size. The recordings of a whole day (24×7) is not saved as a single video file.
3. **Frame duplication** forgery is executed by copying a sequence of frames from one video and pasting them at another location in the same video. This can be executed for two reasons. First, for filling the gap of deletion as explained in frame insertion to create a meaningful forgery. Example, consider the scenario where a person stole a precious item in the FOV. He can remove his presence and the frames corresponding to the event by deleting those frames. Then to fill the gap of deletion, he can use the frames recorded at some other instance of time. These replicated frames can be static without any event in it or may contain an event (like some other person or group of persons entering and leaving the FOV) to confuse the viewers. Second, for creating an event at particular sensitive instance of time. An example would be, frames corresponding to an event that a person entering and leaving the room can be replicated for fabricating an allegation against the victim.
4. **Frame shuffling** forgery is a particular case of frame duplication where the order of the frames are rearranged randomly so that the new sequence of frames thus formed will never follow the order of its original sequence. This kind of forgery is successful with static surveillance systems. In dynamic scenes, changing the order of frames will disturb the follow of objects in the scene (can be detected visibly). Hence, for meaningful forgery that are visually imperceptible, frame shuffling is performed in static surveillance systems.

The pictorial representation of inter-frame forgeries are shown in Figure 27.5. A sequence of 9 frames in an original video is given in Figure 27.5a. Figure 27.5b represents frame insertion forgery, where the frames in blue colour are the newly added frames taken from a different video. As insertion is performed without deleting any frames from the original video, it will cause the shifting of frames in forged video after the inserted frames according to the number of frames inserted. The 4th frame in original will now appear at the 7th position and so on. The actual positions of these shifted frames in the original are written inside the frames. Figure 27.5c shows frame deletion where the frames outlined with dotted lines correspond to deleted frames. Frame deletion causes the shifting of 7th frame to the 4th position. Figure 27.5d shows frame duplication where frames 1 to 3 are copied

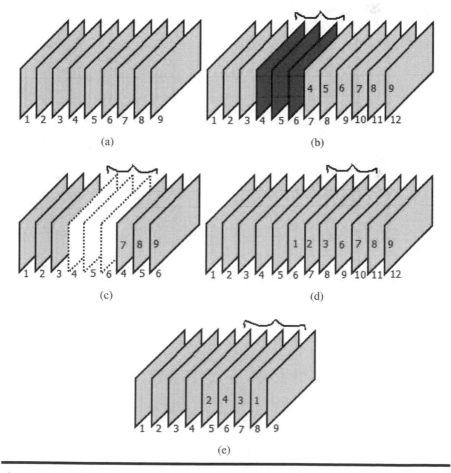

Figure 27.5 Pictorial representation of video inter-frame forgery. (a) Original Video Sequence; (b) Frame Insertion; (c) Frame Deletion; (d) Frame Duplication and (e) Frame Shuffling.

and replicated after the 5th frame. As frame duplication is performed without deleting any frames from the replicated positions, 6th frame in original will now appear at the 9th position and so on. Frame shuffling is shown in Figure 27.5e where frames 5 to 8 in the original sequence are replaced with the frames from 1 to 4 after rearranging them.

Intra-frame forgeries consist of region duplication (copy-move) and region splicing forgeries at frame level. In region duplication, small portions (blocks or regions) of frames from a sequence are copied and pasted at another frame position in the same video. In splicing, frame regions or objects taken from one video are inserted into another video. The pictorial representation of intra-frame forgeries are shown in Figure 27.6. The 3D-planes in the figures correspond to frame sequence where x and y denote frame size and t is the duration of video. Region duplication forgery is shown in Figure 27.6a with blue coloured frame regions which are copied from the video and pasted at a later frame sequence in the same video. Region splicing is indicated with brown coloured frame regions in Figure 27.6b which correspond to the inserted frame regions from a different video.

The detailed reviews of video tamper detection methods in the literature are presented in [1,81]. In [82], an overview of various video forensic methods is presented. A detailed description of anti-forensic techniques are not there in these works.

A part of the literature on video tampering detection is focusing on video recompression detection. The basic assumption is that a video will undergo compression at least twice if it is tampered. Due to storage constraints, videos are saved in compressed format. To edit its contents, it need to be decompressed. After

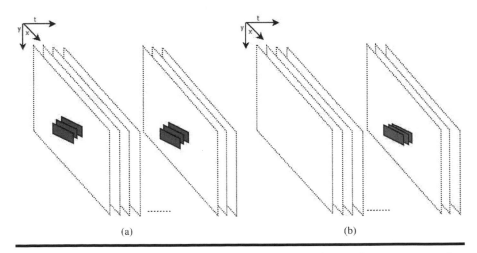

(a)   (b)

Figure 27.6 Pictorial representation of video intra-frame forgery. (a) Region duplication forgery – indicated in blue are small frame regions copied from a video and pasted at a later sequence of frames in the same video; (b) Region splicing – indicated in brown are the frame regions inserted from a different video.

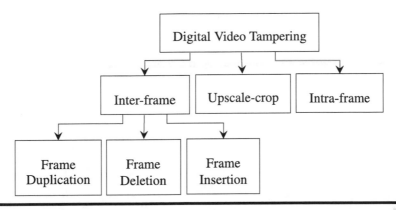

Figure 27.7 Sub categories of video tampering on which anti-forensic approaches are discussed in Section 27.3.

editing, it will undergo another compression for storage. The methods discussed in [83–87] classify videos as tampered if they underwent double or multiple compressions. As a video can undergo double compression even without modifying its contents, performing forgery classification based on this concept is not correct. Examples are videos appearing in YouTube, Facebook etc. These platforms apply compression algorithms on uploaded compressed videos without modifying its contents for ease of operation. Unless the content of a video is altered, it cannot be classified as a tampered video. Hence, anti-forensic approaches for these methods are not discussed in this section. The sub categories of video tampering on which this section discussed the anti-forensic approaches is shown in Figure 27.7.

27.3.1 Inter-Frame Video Forgeries

Up-scale crop forgery can be considered as an anti-forensic approach against frame insertion, deletion, duplication and shuffling. It helps the counterfeiter to perform video tampering without performing any of the traditional inter-frame or intra-frame forgeries. Up-scale crop forgery enables the perpetrator in removing any unwanted criminal activities that happened on the border regions of the surveillance FOV. In such videos, the outer frame regions are cropped so that activities at the border of frames are removed. These cropped frames are up-scaled so that they can have the same resolution as that of original untouched frames in the video. With small up-scale factors, these forgeries may not be detected with inter-frame forgery detection methods. If they detect, then it will have two tamper locations, one at the beginning and another at the end of the up-scale cropped frames. Inter-frame forgery detection methods will confuse it for frame insertion. Assuming that the frames at suspicious locations are dissimilar in frame insertion, the methods in [88,89] use thresholding approach for insertion detection. As the candidate frames of forgery are taken from the same video, this is violated.

The counter method for upscale-crop forgery detection is presented in [90–92]. Hyun et al., [91] utilized resampling detection method in [40] and SPN for upscale-crop forgery detection. Its performance is poor in compressed and static surveillance videos. Later, they modified the work using scaling invariance of the minimum average correlation energy, Mellin radial harmonic (MACE-MRH) correlation filter to reliably unveil traces of upscaling in videos [90]. Two different MACE-MRH correlation filters are designed from a reference SPN for distinguishing normal and upscale-cropped sequences. Singh and Aggarwal [92] utilized SPN and pixel correlation for upscale-crop forgery detection. They used Discrete Fractional Fourier Transform (DFrFT) domain for extracting resampling artifacts due to pixel correlations with a modified Gallagher method.

27.3.1.1 Frame Duplication Forgery

Frame duplication is typically detected using the repetition of a statistical property. The method in [93] tries to find out whether the velocity field intensity (VFI) of a sequence of frames under suspicion (query clip) is repeated elsewhere in the video. The video is partitioned into small clips or segments of size (number of frames in the clip) equal to the size of the query clip. The correlation of colour histogram differences between adjacent frames in the query clip and other small segments of the video is used in [94]. The correlation of Singular Value Decomposition (SVD) feature of frame segments with suspicious frame sequence is used in [95]. The correlation and root mean squared error (RMSE) of mean and residues in frame sub blocks are utilized in [96]. Wang et al., [88] used optical flow sequence for duplication detection. The distance between the query clip and other segments in the video is obtained by computing the l_2-norm of differences between optical flow values. These methods fail when the duplicated frames are shuffled before pasting. Frame shuffling can be considered as an anti-forensic approach on frame duplication detection as authors usually exploit features extracted from the repetition of frame sequence in the exact same order.

In [93], the authors tackled frame shuffling by finding the frame correlation of all possible frame combinations of the query clip and other segments of the same size as that of the query clip in the video. The correlations obtained between the frame correlation sequences of query clip and other segments are used for classifying the video as forged with shuffled frames or not. It acts as a counter anti-forensic towards frame shuffling.

Other anti-forensic approaches to frame duplication detection are upscale-crop forgery and synthetic zooming. Consider an example for upscale-crop forgery where a sequence of frames corresponding to an event need to be deleted. If the upscale-cropped frames used to hide an event in the video are created from a future or past sequence of frames in the same video, then it has to be detected as frame duplication. The up-scaling and cropping processes will disturb the underlying statistical properties of the frame sequence. Hence, the methods for frame duplication detection [88,93–96] which exploit repetition of statistical properties will fail. Examples and details regarding synthetic zooming is given in Section 27.3.2.

27.3.1.2 Frame Deletion Forgery

Su et al., [97] and Dong et al., [98] used Motion Compensated Edge Artifact (MCEA) for frame deletion detection. MCEA occurs in video codecs that use block-based motion-compensated prediction. Within a Group of Pictures (GOP), when the distance of a frame from its last I-frame (Intra-coded frames) increases, it will increase the high frequency artifacts in its block boundaries. Su et al., [99] utilized periodic artifacts in the DCT coefficients of P-frames (Predicted) and B-frames (Bi-directional predicted) in MPEG recompressed videos. Liu et al., [100] used the periodic artifacts caused by Sequence of Average Residual of P-frames (SARP) of H.264 encoded videos in the time and frequency domains. Gironi et al., [101] utilized Variation of Prediction Footprint (VPF) for detecting frame deletion and insertion forgeries. It occurs when an I-frame is converted to P-frame as part of frame deletion or insertion. These P-frames will contain more intra macroblocks (I-MB) and less skipped macroblocks (S-MB) compared to its neighbouring P-frames. Being an I-frame in first compression, it contains more details than its neighbouring P-frames which cannot be coded with predicted macroblocks (P-MB) and S-MBs in second compression after editing. All these methods work with fixed GOP structure videos only. Hence, removal of frames by removing an entire GOP or groups of GOP will not get detected which can be used as an anti-forensic approach on these methods.

Kang et al., [102] improved the method in [100] by analyzing the magnitudes of P-frame prediction error. They analyzed an anti-forensic method that explicitly increases the P-frame prediction error of the forged sequence. They also came up with a method for countering this approach by estimating the actual prediction error for comparing it with the prediction error obtained from the video under investigation.

27.3.1.3 Frame Insertion Forgery

Stamm and Liu [103] discussed an anti-forensic approach for frame deletion and insertion detection presented in [104]. When frames are shifted from one GOP to another, it will introduce periodic spikes in the DFT of P-frame prediction error [104]. The anti-forensic operation [103] modifies the MPEG encoding process for converting the P-frame prediction error sequence to a target sequence. This will remove the temporal fingerprint from P-frame prediction error sequence. The error value of a given P-frame is increased to the target by changing the frame's predicted value in a manner that increases the prediction error. The motion vectors (MV) of the selected MBs of those P-frames are set to 0 for obtaining new prediction errors.

Stamm et al. [105] discussed methods for frame insertion and deletion detection in fixed and variable GOP structure videos. They utilized periodic increase in prediction error for codecs having fixed GOP structure and energy detector for variable GOP. The authors utilized the anti-forensic approach discussed in [103]. They also proposed a counter anti-forensic technique which will detect the unusual MVs with zeros by comparing the MVs of video under investigation with its estimated true MVs.

In [106], the absolute differences between the frames before and after applying deblocking filters is used for frame insertion and deletion detection in H.264 videos. The authors discussed an anti-forensic approach by recording the MB types and quantization indices of the frames at intended tamper positions in the video. These recordings are used as reference for adjusting the MB types and residuals of the edited video so that it appears genuine. The authors then countered this anti-forensic technique using the de-blocking filter of H.264/AVC and relationship of Quantization Parameter (QP) to video bitrate. If the actual QP value extracted from the video under investigation is different from the one that is stored, then it indicates tampering.

27.3.2 Frame Upscale-crop Forgery

A simple anti-forensic approach on upscale-crop forgery detectors in [90–92] is synthetic zooming. That is, instead of performing upscale-crop with a fixed scale factor on all frames, the scale factor can be incremented gradually. Then, the resulting frames resemble those recorded during camera zooming operation. For example, consider an event occurring near the border of field of view (FOV) needs to be deleted. The perpetrator can perform upscale-crop forgery in those frames. If he is in a situation that he has to use a large scale factor (>1.3, quarter portion of the frame will be removed after upscale-cropping) for removing the event, then it may be noticeable while watching the video. Rapid scale change at immediate neighbouring frames (frame that precedes and follows upscaled frames) with large scale factor will introduce visible artifacts. To avoid this, the frames preceding and following the event can be upscaled with variable (gradually decreasing) scale factor for smooth upscaling. With the availability of video editing tools like Adobe Premier Pro, one can easily perform such synthetic zooming.

Figure 27.8 shows video frames of a two-storey building. The frames created using Adobe Premiere Pro for mimicking those recorded during natural camera zooming are shown in Figure 27.8. The frames in Figure 27.8a–f are the original frames from 2 to 102 in a pristine video with frame gap of 20 frames recorded by us. The corresponding synthetically zoomed frames created using Adobe Premiere Pro is shown in Figure 27.8g–l respectively. The frame gap is introduced for visible understanding of zooming. With a frame rate of 25 fps, the change of content in successive frames is very less. In edited frames, you can see that the intended FOV of the ground floor is completely removed. Hence, the activities happening on the ground floor will be completely missing in an edited surveillance video. This helps the perpetrator in removing his/her presence without performing any state of the art inter-frame or intra-frame forgeries.

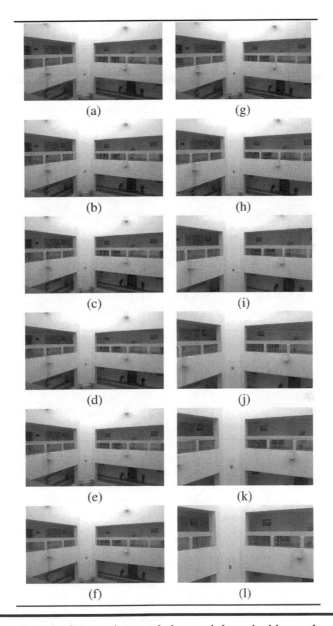

Figure 27.8 Sample frames from pristine and forged videos of a two-storey building. (a) to (f) are the original frames from 2 to 102 in a pristine video with frame gap of 20 frames from our dataset. (g) to (l) are its corresponding synthetically zoomed (upscale-cropped) frames using Adobe Premiere Pro. Intended FOV of ground floor is completely removed by synthetic zooming.

If the frame sequence corresponding to an event needs to be deleted completely, then perpetrators can perform frame duplication with synthetic zooming. That is, a sequence of frames from former or later instances of time can be copied and pasted for filling the gap of deletion. These copied frames can be processed for synthetic zooming before or after pasting it to the new location. It works as an anti-forensic approach to frame duplication detection as the synthetic zoomed frames will no longer share any statistical properties with their original frame sequence.

27.3.3 Intra-frame Forgery

Kobayashi et al., [107] proposed a method for detecting forged regions in digital videos based on the inconsistencies of noise characteristics. When frame region patches from one video are placed into a different video, it affects the underlying noise characteristics. The noise characteristics, being an intrinsic properties of the camera, may not be useful when the forgery patch is taken from the same video or is recorded using another camera of the same make and model. For a particular make and model, the noise characteristics may be the same. Also, compression is another factor which affects proper noise estimation. These form the anti-forensics for [107].

Wang and Farid [108] proposed methods for region tamper detection using spatial and temporal correlations in de-interlaced videos and motion between fields in interlaced videos. This method is highly sensitive to compression. Hence, high compression ratio will work as an anti-forensic technique.

Subramanyam and Emmanuel [109] proposed methods for detecting spatial and temporal region duplication forgery. Histogram of Oriented Gradients (HOG) features extracted from blocks in each frame are matched against the HOG features extracted from the rest of the blocks in the spatial and temporal domains. The temporal region duplication is detected based on the assumption that a region is replicated onto a sequence of frames in a GOP in the spatially collocated area. And this gives high correlation in the collocated area. Region tampering in a real scenario will be created with region patches taken from a continuous sequence of frames. This itself is an anti-forensic approach. The temporal correlation of blocks in these regions will be similar to that of non-tampered blocks.

27.4 Conclusions and Future Work

From this study on anti-forensic techniques for image and video tampering, it is inferred that forensic methods for discovering digital evidence will be under attack. Hence, before losing its credibility, multimedia forensics has to anticipate the existence of anti-forensics and come up with new countermeasures. The investigator should always assume that the forger has performed anti-forensic techniques on the image or video under investigation for hiding the traces of tampering. Forensics investigators can counter anti-forensics using multiple forensic detectors or hybrid combinations of them. This makes it difficult for the counterfeiter to hide tamper traces which can deceive all forensic methods in the literature. The decision on authenticity and integrity of digital evidence should be taken based on forensic and counter anti-forensic analysis. An ensemble of forensic and counter anti-forensic techniques using a machine-learning approach may be used for this purpose.

Multimedia forensic researchers should approach forgery detection problems in a game theoretic perspective, so that the future proposals may have a security evaluation framework on how resistant it is towards various anti-forensic techniques. Researchers should concentrate on anti-forensics and its corresponding counter anti-forensics for preventing the potential misuse of the digital evidence. The challenges posed by cryptography in multimedia forensics is alarming with multimedia systems adopting security measures based on it. In this regard, cryptanalysis know-how is becoming a prerequisite for forensic investigators. Like the traditional digital forensics procedures, multimedia forensics may also suffer from considerable time consumption. Developing special hardware for multimedia forensics is expected to accelerate forensic analysis procedures. Though such hardware already exists and are in use for system forensics, there are hardly any in multimedia forensics. In this era of hardware becoming cheaper this may not be a major issue. Even an other solution to think of is cloud or fog computing based multimedia forensics solutions offered as a service.

References

1. K. Sitara and B. M. Mehtre. Digital video tampering detection: An overview of passive techniques. *Digital Investigation*, 18:8–22, 2016.
2. M. Kirchner and R. Böhme. Tamper hiding: Defeating image forensics. In *Information Hiding: 9th International Workshop, IH 2007, Saint Malo, France*, 326–341. Springer, Berlin, Germany, 2007.
3. G. K. Birajdar and V. H. Mankar. Digital image forgery detection using passive techniques: A survey. *Digital Investigation*, 10(3):226–245, 2013.
4. A. Piva. An overview on image forensics. *ISRN Signal Processing*, 2013: 496701, 22p, 2013.
5. T. Qazi, K. Hayat, S. U. Khan, S. A. Madani, et al. Survey on blind image forgery detection. *IET Image Processing*, 7(7):660–670, 2013.
6. W. Nanda, N. Diane, S. Xingming, and F. K. Moise. A survey of partition-based techniques for copy-move forgery detection. *The Scientific World Journal*, 2014: 975456, 13p, 2014.
7. T. M. Shashidhar and K. B. Ramesh. Reviewing the effectivity factor in existing techniques of image forensics. *International Journal of Electrical and Computer Engineering (IJECE)*, 7(6):3558–3569, 2017.
8. D. Tralic, I. Zupancic, S. Grgic, and M. Grgic. CoMoFoD-New database for copy-move forgery detection. In *Proceedings ELMAR-2013, 55th international symposium*, Zadar, Croatia, pp. 49–54, IEEE, 2013.
9. R. Böhme and M. Kirchner. Counter-forensics: Attacking image forensics. In H. T. Sencar and N. Memon (Eds.) *Digital Image Forensics: There Is More to a Picture than Meets the Eye*, 327–366. Springer, New York, 2013.

10. W. Luo, J. Huang, and G. Qiu. Robust detection of region-duplication forgery in digital image. In *18th International Conference on Pattern Recognition (ICPR'06)*, Hong Kong, China, 746–749. IEEE Computer Society, 2006.

11. E. Ardizzone and G. Mazzola. Detection of duplicated regions in tampered digital images by bit-plane analysis. In *Image Analysis and Processing – ICIAP 2009: 15th International Conference Vietri sul Mare, Italy, September 8–11, Proceedings*, 893–901. Springer, Berlin, Germany, 2009.

12 Y. Cao, T. Gao, L. Fan, and Q. Yang. A robust detection algorithm for copy-move forgery in digital images. *Forensic Science International*, 214(1):33–43, 2012.

13. A. N. Myna, M. G. Venkateshmurthy, and C. G. Patil. Detection of region duplication forgery in digital images using wavelets and log-polar mapping. In *International Conference on Computational Intelligence and Multimedia Applications (ICCIMA 2007)*, Sivakasi, India, 371–377. IEEE, 2007.

14. D. G. Lowe. Distinctive image features from scale-invariant keypoints. *International Journal of Computer Vision*, 60(2):91–110, 2004.

15. X. Pan and S. Lyu. Region duplication detection using image feature matching. *IEEE Transactions on Information Forensics and Security*, 5(4):857–867, 2010.

16. X. Pan and S. Lyu. Detecting image region duplication using SIFT features. In *2010 IEEE International Conference on Acoustics, Speech and Signal Processing*, 1706–1709, 2010.

17. I. Amerini, L. Ballan, R. Caldelli, A. Del Bimbo, and G. Serra. A SIFT-based forensic method for copy-move attack detection and transformation recovery. *IEEE Transactions on Information Forensics and Security*, 6(3):1099–1110, 2011.

18. J. Li, X. Li, B. Yang, and X. Sun. Segmentation-based image copy-move forgery detection scheme. *IEEE Transactions on Information Forensics and Security*, 10(3): 507–518, 2015.

19. G. Jin and X. Wan. An improved method for SIFT-based copy move forgery detection using non-maximum value suppression and optimized J-Linkage. *Signal Processing: Image Communication*, 57(Supplement C):113–125, 2017.

20. N. B. A. Warif, A. W. A. Wahab, M. Y. I. Idris, R. Salleh, and F. Othman. SIFT-symmetry: A robust detection method for copy-move forgery with reflection attack. *Journal of Visual Communication and Image Representation*, 46(Supplement C): 219–232, 2017.

21. S. Wenchang, Z. Fei, Q. Bo, and L. Bin. Improving image copy-move forgery detection with particle swarm optimization techniques. *China Communications*, 13(1):139–149, 2016.

22. E. Ardizzone, A. Bruno, and G. Mazzola. Copy–move forgery detection by matching triangles of keypoints. *IEEE Transactions on Information Forensics and Security*, 10(10):2084–2094, 2015.

23. R. Caldelli, I. Amerini, L. Ballan, G. Serra, M. Barni, and A. Costanzo. On the effectiveness of local warping against SIFT-based copy-move detection. In *2012 5th International Symposium on Communications, Control and Signal Processing*, 1–5, May 2012.

24. I. Amerini, M. Barni, R. Caldelli, and A. Costanzo. Counter-forensics of SIFT-based copy-move detection by means of keypoint classification. *EURASIP Journal on Image and Video Processing*, 2013(1):18, 2013.

25. T.-T. Do, E. Kijak, T. Furon, and L. Amsaleg. Deluding image recognition in SIFT-based CBIR systems. In *Proceedings of the 2nd ACM Workshop on Multimedia in Forensics, Security and Intelligence*, 7–12, ACM, New York, 2010.

26. A. Costanzo, I. Amerini, R. Caldelli, and M. Barni. Forensic analysis of SIFT keypoint removal and injection. *IEEE Transactions on Information Forensics and Security*, 9(9):1450–1464, 2014.

27. I. Amerini, M. Barni, R. Caldelli, and A. Costanzo. SIFT keypoint removal and injection for countering matching-based image forensics. In *Proceedings of the First ACM Workshop on Information Hiding and Multimedia Security*, 123–130, ACM, New York, 2013.

28. T. Zhang and R. D. Wang. Copy-move forgery detection based on SVD in digital image. In *2009 2nd International Congress on Image and Signal Processing*, 1–5, 2009.

29. G. Li, Q. Wu, D. Tu, and S. Sun. A sorted neighborhood approach for detecting duplicated regions in image forgeries based on DWT and SVD. In *2007 IEEE International Conference on Multimedia and Expo*, 1750–1753, 2007.

30. B. Mahdian and S. Saic. Detection of copy move forgery using a method based on blur moment invariants. *Forensic Science International*, 171(2):180–189, 2007.

31. Z. Fang, S. Wang, and X. Zhang. Image splicing detection using color edge inconsistency. In *2010 International Conference on Multimedia Information Networking and Security*, 923–926, 2010.

32. Z. Qu, G. Qiu, and J. Huang. Detect digital image splicing with visual cues. In *Information Hiding: 11th International Workshop, IH 2009, Darmstadt, Germany, June 8–10, 2009*, 247–261. Springer, Berlin, Germany, 2009.

33. M. K. Johnson and H. Farid. Exposing digital forgeries by detecting inconsistencies in lighting. In *Proceedings of the 7th Workshop on Multimedia and Security*, 1–10. ACM, New York, 2005.

34. B. Mahdian and S. Saic. Using noise inconsistencies for blind image forensics. *Image and Vision Computing*, 27(10):1497–1503, 2009.

35. K. Bahrami, A. C. Kot, L. Li, and H. Li. Blurred image splicing localization by exposing blur type inconsistency. *IEEE Transactions on Information Forensics and Security*, 10(5):999–1009, 2015.

36. A. C. Popescu and H. Farid. Exposing digital forgeries by detecting traces of resampling. *IEEE Transactions on Signal Processing*, 53(2):758–767, 2005.

37. M. Kirchner. Fast and reliable resampling detection by spectral analysis of fixed linear predictor residue. In *Proceedings of the 10th ACM Workshop on Multimedia and Security*, 11–20. ACM, New York, 2008.

38. M. Kirchner. Linear row and column predictors for the analysis of resized images. In *Proceedings of the 12th ACM Workshop on Multimedia and Security*, 13–18. ACM, New York, 2010.

39. M. Kirchner and T. Gloe. On resampling detection in re-compressed images. In *2009 First IEEE International Workshop on Information Forensics and Security (WIFS)*, 21–25, 2009.

40. A. C. Gallagher. Detection of linear and cubic interpolation in JPEG compressed images. In *The 2nd Canadian Conference on Computer and Robot Vision (CRV'05)*, 65–72, 2005.

41. S. Prasad and K. R. Ramakrishnan. On resampling detection and its application to detect image tampering. In *2006 IEEE International Conference on Multimedia and Expo*, 1325–1328, 2006.

42. B. Mahdian and S. Saic. On periodic properties of interpolation and their application to image authentication. In *Third International Symposium on Information Assurance and Security*, 439–446, 2007.

43. B. Mahdian and S. Saic. Blind authentication using periodic properties of interpolation. *IEEE Transactions on Information Forensics and Security*, 3(3):529–538, 2008.

44. B. Mahdian and S. Saic. Detection of resampling supplemented with noise inconsistencies analysis for image forensics. In *2008 International Conference on Computational Sciences and Its Applications*, 546–556, 2008.

45. G. K. Birajdar and V. H. Mankar. Blind method for rescaling detection and rescale factor estimation in digital images using periodic properties of interpolation. *AEU-International Journal of Electronics and Communications*, 68(7):644–652, 2014.

46. X. Hou, T. Zhang, G. Xiong, Y. Zhang, and X. Ping. Image resampling detection based on texture classification. *Multimedia Tools and Applications*, 72(2):1681–1708, 2014.

47. Y. Su, X. Jin, C. Zhang, and Y. Chen. Hierarchical image resampling detection based on blind deconvolution. *Journal of Visual Communication and Image Representation*, 48(Supplement C):480–490, 2017.

48. X. Feng, I. J. Cox, and G. Doerr. Normalized energy density-based forensic detection of resampled images. *IEEE Transactions on Multimedia*, 14(3):536–545, 2012.

49. M. Kirchner and R. Bohme. Hiding traces of resampling in digital images. *IEEE Transactions on Information Forensics and Security*, 3(4):582–592, 2008.

50. M. Stamm and K. J. R. Liu. Blind forensics of contrast enhancement in digital images. In *2008 15th IEEE International Conference on Image Processing*, 3112–3115, 2008.

51. M. C. Stamm and K. J. Liu. Forensic detection of image tampering using intrinsic statistical fingerprints in histograms. In *Proceedings: APSIPA ASC 2009: Asia-Pacific Signal and Information Processing Association, 2009 Annual Summit and Conference*, 563–572.

52. M. C. Stamm and K. J. R. Liu. Forensic estimation and reconstruction of a contrast enhancement mapping. In *2010 IEEE International Conference on Acoustics, Speech and Signal Processing*, 1698–1701, 2010.

53. G. Cao, Y. Zhao, R. Ni, and H. Tian. Anti-forensics of contrast enhancement in digital images. In *Proceedings of the 12th ACM Workshop on Multimedia and Security*, 25–34, ACM, New York, 2010.

54. B. S. Rao. A fuzzy fusion approach for modified contrast enhancement based image forensics against attacks. *Multimedia Tools and Applications*, 77(5): 5241–5261, 2018.

55. M. C. Stamm and K. J. R. Liu. Wavelet-based image compression anti-forensics. In *2010 IEEE International Conference on Image Processing*, 1737–1740, 2010.

56. M. C. Stamm, S. K. Tjoa, W. S. Lin, and K. J. R. Liu. Anti-forensics of JPEG compression. In *2010 IEEE International Conference on Acoustics, Speech and Signal Processing*, 1694–1697, 2010.

57. M. C. Stamm, S. K. Tjoa, W. S. Lin, and K. J. R. Liu. Undetectable image tampering through JPEG compression anti-forensics. In *2010 IEEE International Conference on Image Processing*, 2109–2112, 2010.

58. Z. Fan and R. L. de Queiroz. Identification of bitmap compression history: JPEG detection and quantizer estimation. *IEEE Transactions on Image Processing*, 12(2):230–235, 2003.

59. W. Fan, K. Wang, F. Cayre, and Z. Xiong. JPEG anti-forensics with improved tradeoff between forensic undetectability and image quality. *IEEE Transactions on Information Forensics and Security*, 9(8):1211–1226, 2014.

60. G. Singh and K. Singh. Improved JPEG anti-forensics with better image visual quality and forensic undetectability. *Forensic Science International*, 277:133–147, 2017.

61. P. M. Shelke and R. S. Prasad. An improved anti-forensics JPEG compression using least cuckoo search algorithm. *The Imaging Science Journal*, 66(3):169–183, 2018.

62. Y. Jiang, H. Zeng, X. Kang, and L. Liu. The game of countering JPEG anti-forensics based on the noise level estimation. In *2013 Asia-Pacific Signal and Information Processing Association Annual Summit and Conference*, 1–9, 2013.

63. H. Zeng, J. Yu, X. Kang, and S. Lyu. Countering JPEG anti-forensics based on noise level estimation. *Science China Information Sciences*, 61(3):032103, 2017.

64. X. Liu, M. Tanaka, and M. Okutomi. Noise level estimation using weak textured patches of a single noisy image. In *2012 19th IEEE International Conference on Image Processing*, 665–668, 2012.

65. G. Valenzise, V. Nobile, M. Tagliasacchi, and S. Tubaro. Countering JPEG anti-forensics. In *2011 18th IEEE International Conference on Image Processing*, 1949–1952, 2011.

66. W. Fan, K. Wang, F. Cayre, and Z. Xiong. JPEG anti-forensics using non-parametric DCT quantization noise estimation and natural image statistics. In *Proceedings of the First ACM Workshop on Information Hiding and Multimedia Security*, 117–122, ACM, New York, 2013.

67. H. D. Yuan. Blind forensics of median filtering in digital images. *IEEE Transactions on Information Forensics and Security*, 6(4):1335–1345, 2011.

68. M. Kirchner and J. Fridrich. On detection of median filtering in digital images. In *Media Forensics and Security II*, volume 7541. International Society for Optics and Photonics, 2010.

69. C. Chen, J. Ni, and J. Huang. Blind detection of median filtering in digital images: A difference domain based approach. *IEEE Transactions on Image Processing*, 22(12):4699–4710, 2013.

70. Y. Zhang, S. Li, S. Wang, and Y. Q. Shi. Revealing the traces of median filtering using high-order local ternary patterns. *IEEE Signal Processing Letters*, 21(3):275–279, 2014.

71. Z. H. Wu, M. C. Stamm, and K. J. R. Liu. Anti-forensics of median filtering. In *2013 IEEE International Conference on Acoustics, Speech and Signal Processing*, 3043–3047, 2013.

72. W. Fan, K. Wang, F. Cayre, and Z. Xiong. Median filtered image quality enhancement and anti-forensics via variational deconvolution. *IEEE Transactions on Information Forensics and Security*, 10(5):1076–1091, 2015.

73. D. T. Dang-Nguyen, I. D. Gebru, V. Conotter, G. Boato, and F. G. B. De Natale. Counter-forensics of median filtering. In *2013 IEEE 15th International Workshop on Multimedia Signal Processing (MMSP)*, 260–265, 2013.

74. M. Fontani and M. Barni. Hiding traces of median filtering in digital images. In *2012 Proceedings of the 20th European Signal Processing Conference (EUSIPCO)*, 1239–1243, 2012.

75. S. Sharma, A. V. Subramanyam, M. Jain, A. Mehrish, and S. Emmanuel. Anti-forensic technique for median filtering using L1-L2 TV model. In *2016 IEEE International Workshop on Information Forensics and Security (WIFS)*, 1–6, 2016.

76. A. C. Popescu and H. Farid. Exposing digital forgeries in color filter array interpolated images. *IEEE Transactions on Signal Processing*, 53(10):3948–3959, 2005.

77. M. Kirchner and R. Böhme. Synthesis of color filter array pattern in digital images. In *Media Forensics and Security*, volume 7254. International Society for Optics and Photonics, 2009.

78. J. Lukáš, J. Fridrich, and M. Goljan. Detecting digital image forgeries using sensor pattern noise. In *Security, Steganography, and Watermarking of Multimedia Contents VIII*, volume 6072. International Society for Optics and Photonics, 2006.

79. T. Gloe, M. Kirchner, A. Winkler, and R. Böhme. Can we trust digital image forensics? In *Proceedings of the 15th ACM International Conference on Multimedia*, MM'07, 78–86. ACM, New York, 2007.

80. M. Goljan, J. Fridrich, and M. Chen. Sensor noise camera identification: Countering counter-forensics. In *Media Forensics and Security II*, volume 7541, pages 75410S. International Society for Optics and Photonics, 2010.

81. R. D. Singh and N. Aggarwal. Video content authentication techniques: A comprehensive survey. *Multimedia Systems*, 24(2):211–240, 2018.

82. S. Milani, M. Fontani, P. Bestagini, M. Barni, A. Piva, M. Tagliasacchi, and S. Tubaro. An overview on video forensics. *APSIPA Transactions on Signal and Information Processing*, 1:e2, 2012.

83. D. Vazquez-Padin, M. Fontani, T. Bianchi, P. Comesaña, A. Piva, and M. Barni. Detection of video double encoding with GOP size estimation. In *2012 IEEE International Workshop on Information Forensics and Security (WIFS)*, 151–156. IEEE, 2012.

84. W. Wang and H. Farid. Exposing digital forgeries in video by detecting double quantization. In *Proceedings of the 11th ACM Workshop on Multimedia and Security*, 39–48. ACM, New York, 2009.

85. J. Xu, Y. Su, and Q. Liu. Detection of double MPEG-2 compression based on distributions of DCT coefficients. *International Journal of Pattern Recognition and Artificial Intelligence*, 27(01):1354001, 2013.

86. X. Jiang, W. Wang, T. Sun, Y. Q. Shi, and S. Wang. Detection of double compression in MPEG-4 videos based on markov statistics. *IEEE Signal Processing Letters*, 20(5):447–450, 2013.

87. A. V. Subramanyam and S. Emmanuel. Pixel estimation based video forgery detection. In *2013 IEEE International Conference on Acoustics, Speech and Signal Processing*, 3038–3042. IEEE, 2013.

88. W. Wang, X. Jiang, S. Wang, M. Wan, and T. Sun. Identifying video forgery process using optical flow. In *International Workshop on Digital Watermarking*, 244–257. Springer, Berlin, Germany, 2013.

89. J. Chao, X. Jiang, and T. Sun. A novel video inter-frame forgery model detection scheme based on optical flow consistency. In *International Workshop on Digital Watermarking*, 267–281. Springer, Berlin, Germany, 2012.

90. D.-K. Hyun, S.-J. Ryu, H.-Y. Lee, and H.-K. Lee. Detection of upscale-crop and partial manipulation in surveillance video based on sensor pattern noise. *Sensors*, 13(9):12605–12631, 2013.

91. D.-K. Hyun, M.-J. Lee, S.-J. Ryu, H.-Y. Lee, and H.-K. Lee. Forgery detection for surveillance video. In J. S. Jin, C. Xu, and M. Xu (Eds.) *The Era of Interactive Media*, 25–36. Springer, New York, 2013.

92. R. D. Singh and N. Aggarwal. Detection of upscale-crop and splicing for digital video authentication. *Digital Investigation*, 21:31–52, 2017.

93. K. Sitara and B. M. Mehtre. A comprehensive approach for exposing inter-frame video forgeries. In *2017 IEEE 13th International Colloquium on Signal Processing its Applications (CSPA)*, 73–78, 2017.

94. G.-S. Lin, J.-F. Chang, and C.-H. Chuang. Detecting frame duplication based on spatial and temporal analyses. In *Computer Science & Education (ICCSE), 2011 6th International Conference on*, 1396–1399. IEEE, 2011.

95. J. Yang, T. Huang, and L. Su. Using similarity analysis to detect frame duplication forgery in videos. *Multimedia Tools and Applications*, 75(4):1793–1811, 2016.
96. V. K. Singh, P. Pant, and R. C. Tripathi. Detection of frame duplication type of forgery in digital video using sub-block based features. In *International Conference on Digital Forensics and Cyber Crime*, 29–38. Springer, Cham, Switzerland, 2015.
97. Y. Su, J. Zhang, and J. Liu. Exposing digital video forgery by detecting motion-compensated edge artifact. In *Computational Intelligence and Software Engineering, 2009. International Conference on*, 1–4. IEEE, 2009.
98. Q. Dong, G. Yang, and N. Zhu. A MCEA based passive forensics scheme for detecting frame-based video tampering. *Digital Investigation*, 9(2):151–159, 2012.
99. Y. Su, W. Nie, and C. Zhang. A frame tampering detection algorithm for MPEG videos. In *2011 6th IEEE Joint International Information Technology and Artificial Intelligence Conference*, volume 2, 461–464, 2011.
100. H. Liu, S. Li, and S. Bian. Detecting frame deletion in H.264 video. In *Information Security Practice and Experience: 10th International Conference, ISPEC 2014, Fuzhou, China, May 5–8, 2014*, 262–270. Springer International Publishing, Cham, Switzerland, 2014.
101. A. Gironi, M. Fontani, T. Bianchi, A. Piva, and M. Barni. A video forensic technique for detecting frame deletion and insertion. In *2014 IEEE International Conference on Acoustics, Speech and Signal Processing (ICASSP)*, 6226–6230, 2014.
102. X. Kang, J. Liu, H. Liu, and Z. J. Wang. Forensics and counter anti-forensics of video inter-frame forgery. *Multimedia Tools and Applications*, 75(21):13833–13853, 2016.
103. M. C. Stamm, W. S. Lin, and K. J. R. Liu. Temporal forensics and anti-forensics for motion compensated video. *IEEE Transactions on Information Forensics and Security*, 7(4):1315–1329, 2012.
104. W. Wang and H. Farid. Exposing digital forgeries in video by detecting double MPEG compression. In *Proceedings of the 8th Workshop on Multimedia and Security*, 37–47. ACM, 2006.
105. M. C. Stamm and K. J. R. Liu. Anti-forensics for frame deletion/addition in MPEG video. In *2011 IEEE International Conference on Acoustics, Speech and Signal Processing (ICASSP)*, 1876–1879, 2011.
106. P.-C. Su, P.-L. Suei, M.-K. Chang, and J. Lain. Forensic and anti-forensic techniques for video shot editing in H.264/AVC. *Journal of Visual Communication and Image Representation*, 29(Supplement C):103–113, 2015.
107. M. Kobayashi, T. Okabe, and Y. Sato. Detecting video forgeries based on noise characteristics. In *Advances in Image and Video Technology: Third Pacific Rim Symposium, PSIVT 2009, Tokyo, Japan, January 13–16, 2009*, 306–317. Springer, Berlin, Germany, 2009.
108. W. Wang and H. Farid. Exposing digital forgeries in interlaced and deinterlaced video. *IEEE Transactions on Information Forensics and Security*, 2(3):438–449, 2007.
109. A. V. Subramanyam and S. Emmanuel. Video forgery detection using HOG features and compression properties. In *2012 IEEE 14th International Workshop on Multimedia Signal Processing (MMSP)*, 89–94, 2012.

BIOMETRICS

Chapter 28

Securing Biometrics Using Data Hiding Techniques

Mehul S. Raval, Vaibhav B. Joshi and Jignesh S. Bhatt

Contents

Biometric systems are widely used for person authentication. Uniqueness and permanence of biometrics are driving this choice. However, conventional biometric systems have several vulnerable points which can be attacked. In order to improve security, the chapter propose creation of a data hiding layer over biometric system. The basic idea is to authenticate biometric templates before passing it to underlying systems. Initially the chapter explores fragile watermarking for protection but it has several shortcomings. This motivates use of reversible data hiding in which content regains its originality after watermark removal. The reversible data hiding also facilitates joint framework with cryptography to provide simultaneous privacy and

DOI: 10.1201/9780429435461-33

authentication for biometrics. The chapter uses fingerprint as a biometric modality to demonstrate several important case studies. With rapid growth in technology and digitization, personal data is available on the Internet. A strong user authentication mechanism [1] is required to prevent illegal access, e.g., a key based cryptographic system. A decryption key is used to establish user authenticity. However cryptographic keys are long and random, and they are difficult to memorize, e.g., 128 bits for the advanced encryption standard (AES) [2,3]. As a result, these keys are stored in a computer or a smart card and released based on alternative authentication mechanism (e.g., password). A password by ordinary users is very simple and it can be easily guessed or broken by dictionary attacks [4]. Thus, multimedia data protected by a cryptographic algorithm are only secure as a password.

Following are major problems with password based user authentication:

1. Some users store passwords at easy and accessible locations.
2. Most people use the same password across different applications. An impostor on finding this fact can access multiple applications with the same password.
3. In a multiuser case where the same password is available with many users it is very difficult to nail a culprit who caused security breach.

Many limitations of a password based mechanism indicate a need for a better and robust user authentication mechanism. As a result biometric based authentication [5–7] became popular. They establish an identity based on the physical and behavioral characteristics of an individual. Many countries, and recently even India, have started using biometrics like fingerprints and iris on a large scale through the Unique Identification Authority of India (UIDAI) [8]. Advantages of a biometric trait for human identification are as follows: (1) They are inherently more reliable as they cannot be lost or forgotten; (2) biometric traits are difficult to copy, share, and distribute; (3) they require presence of the person at point of data collection; and (4) they are difficult to forge.

A typical biometric system has four imporant modules. Their functions are as follows:

1. A sensor module captures biometric data. For example, a fingerprint sensor images ridge, minutiae and valley structure of a finger.
2. Feature extraction module which pulls out salient points from a sample. For example, position and orientation of minutiae points, local ridge and valley singularities in a fingerprint image.
3. Matcher module compares extracted and stored features to generate a matching score. For example, number of matching minutiae between the input and the stored fingerprints are determined and a score is reported. It also encapsulates a unit which rolls out identification decision.
4. System database module stores biometric templates of enrolled users.

Each module of a system is connected by a communication channel. Some channels are internal to a system e.g., channel between feature extractor and a matcher module. Some communication channels are external e.g., channel connecting matcher subsystem to database. Such external channels are vulnerable to malicious manipulations.

Various attacks on a biometric system are summarized as follows [9]:

1. *Circumvention:* An attacker gains access to the system bypassing the matcher module. An intruder can violate privacy and modify biometric information of a user.
2. *Repudiation:* A legitimate user may turn hostile, misuse the system and later claim that it had been circumvented by an intruder. For example, a bank clerk who can change financial records of a customer and then claim it has been done by an intruder.
3. *Collusion:* A system administrator or superuser may collaborate with an external party to modify the biometric system. It allows illegal access to the external and malicious party.
4. *Coercion:* A legitimate user is forced or coerced by an external entity to forcefully grant access privileges for the system.
5. *Denial of Service (DoS):* An attacker modulates system resources such that access to a legitimate user is denied. For example, a fingerprint server can be flooded with large number of fake queries, overloading and preventing it from processing genuine requests. This leads to large numbers of false negatives and increases in the input queue.

In fact it has been shown that a biometric system has eight vulnerable points [10] that can be attacked to manipulate the system. The authors in [6,11–13] extended an eight point model to 22 vulnerable points in a biometric system. The above discussed attacks can be executed as follows to exploit vulnerable points [10]:

1. By presenting a fake biometric at a sensor.
2. Illicitly intercepting features of a legal biometric trait(s) and then resubmission to get illegal access. This is known as a replay attack.
3. By overriding feature extraction process.
4. By stealing templates from the database and submit it for matching.
5. Modifying software to produce artificially low or high scores or change threshold for a successful match with an illegal template.
6. (i) Tampering a stored biometric template; (ii) associating a malicious template with already enrolled user; (iii) enrolling a malicious user.
7. Injecting a malicious template in the database.
8. Overriding judgment given by a decision module.

Usually an attack is initiated by threat agents [13]. Their goal is to compromise a biometric system to gain unauthorized access. The adversary's offensive are categorized as follows [12]: (1) administration or insider; (2) non-secure infrastructure;

(3) biometric overtness. With increasing threat, biometric template protection becomes even more crucial. The next section describes alternatives available to protect biometric system.

28.1 Securing Biometric Systems

In [14] authors suggested use of biometric cryptosystem, wherein biometric and cryptography are combined for template protection and matching in the encrypted domain. Unlike classical cryptographic techniques, biometric cryptosystem is flexible and adapts to changes in the template during enrollment and matching. Another approach of protecting a template using fuzzy vault is proposed in [15]. The main idea behind fuzzy vault is to encode biometric features using a secret key and a polynomial function. A match in the polynomial domain poses a challenge to recognition accuracy. Authors in [15–18] provide different fuzzy vault schemes for different biometric modalities. Similarly [19,20] suggested robust watermarking techniques [21] to hide features of one biometric modality into other.

In [10] authors suggested a use of *cancelable biometrics*. A key based transform is applied to a biometric template which randomly change structure, rendering it useless for template matching. An inverse transform yields an original form which can be subsequently used for matching. With cancelable biometric techniques one can regenerate an alternative template from the biometric trait using different keys. Recently, researchers are also using cancelable biometrics with visual cryptography. This combination provides revocability as well as privacy protection to a biometric template [22].

All methods discussed above secure biometric templates by either encrypting or concealing them. They do not provide authentication to a biometric template stored in the database or protect their transfer through s communication channel in a biometric system. Further, these methods cannot identify tampering [23] of a biometric template. This may allow success for DoS attacks and also make biometric systems prone to unauthorized template injection into the database.

Apart from cryptosystem and invertible transformation based methods, watermarking [24] also provides an effective solution for biometric data security and authentication [25]. Biometrics watermarking are broadly classified as 'sample watermarking' where a biometric template works as a host or cover and 'template embedding' where a biometric template is used as a watermark in cover data [26]. Recently researchers are using watermarks generated from different biometric modalities. In [27] authors embed two watermarks into a cover image generated from an iris and fingerprint template. The method secured two biometric modalities used in the multimodal biometric system. In [28] authors embedded features of one biometric modality into other. Therefore, all methods [26–29] are classified under the *template embedding* category. They provide template security by concealing one biometric into other and act as an alternative mechanism for biometric authentication.

Fragile watermarking can also build an authentication layer on top of a biometric system. Authors [30] proposed a fragile watermarking technique to detect the tampered part of a fingerprint images in database. In [31], authors proposed chaotic watermarking and steganography [32] to protect biometric data. In the communication channel, encryption and watermarking keys provide security and robustness to a biometric data. Authors in [33] used fragile watermarking to check integrity of a database. The authors used singular value decomposition (SVD) and least significant bit (LSB) plane for embedding the watermark. SVD is popular for watermarking applications because it uses optimal basis for representation derived from the data. In [29], block-based fragile watermarking is used to detect tampered fingerprint and protect multiple vulnerable points.

Authors in [34] proposed a biometric sample-dependent watermark generation and embedding to protect the communication channel between sensor and feature extractor. The method calculated features a sample and embeds them as watermark. At feature extractor, watermark and the sample features are matched to check its integrity. The methods [29–31,33,34] are classified as 'sample watermarking'. The steganographic technique [35] is also used to hide eigen coefficients of face into fingerprint images. Similarly [19,20,36] suggested robust watermarking to hide features of one biometric modality into other.

28.2 Existing Research Gaps

The authors of this chapter argue that watermarking can create an additional security layer on a biometric system. A template will be authenticated by the watermarking subsystem and selected ones are sent to biometric system. In case template does not pass authentication test by the watermarking subsystem, it will be rejected. Usually a robust watermark is used for copyright protection. However, authentication requires a watermark to be fragile i.e., it will be sensitive to manipulation on the biometric template.

Early watermarking approaches in biometrics use one trait as a watermark into another. This is a useful idea for robust watermarking. But such schemes are vulnerable to concurrent attacks at many points [5]. Watermarking degrades biometric template's fidelity and it will change system accuracy. This introduces a constraint that a watermark should not change biometrics accuracy [26].

Based on above literature survey, the following points summarize research gaps in current techniques:

■ All the watermarking methods discussed above can secure one or at most two vulnerable points [10] of a biometric authentication system.
■ Insertion of watermark changes a biometric template which impacts recognition performance of the biometric system [10]. A possible solution to avoid this effect is to embed the watermark without affecting the feature extraction or use *reversible watermarking* technique [26,37].

■ All the watermarking methods discussed above do not provide privacy protection to biometric templates.

■ The methods do not use watermarking in conjunction with encryption to provide privacy protection and authentication.

Among biometric traits like iris, palm print, retina, signature; fingerprint has been the longest serving, most successful and popular trait for human identification [6]. Hence this chapter will use fingerprint as a biometric modality to discuss various case studies in later sections.

Privacy protection is also a key requirement as every person has unique and limited biometric traits. It is achieved by using a key based invertible algorithm. It randomizes data so that direct information extraction is useless. Therefore, it is necessary to use encryption in conjunction with watermark to enhance privacy and security [9]. Watermarking provides authentication and encryption delivers privacy protection. This means that a watermark must regain its original form after its removal. This necessitates use of reversible data hiding (RDH) as discussed in the next section.

28.3 Reversible Data Hiding Techniques

In the case of reversible data hiding, a *cover* regains its original form after removal of the watermark. Reversible data hiding techniques are classified as follows: (1) difference expansion (DE) [38–42]; (2) histogram modification [43–45]; and (3) lossless compression [46–48].

Initially RDH was developed using the lossless compression technique [46–48]. In these schemes cover image I is losslessly compressed to generate space for watermark embedding. The maximum embedding capacity achieved in these techniques is different in the size of I and compressed image I_C i.e., $I - I_C$. Therefore, compression algorithm decides performance of these methods. In [48], authors proposed to compress a bit-plane with minimum redundancy. Moving one step ahead in [46], Celik et al., suggested the LSB compression method which increased compression. Also embedding in LSB results in a perceptually appealing watermarked image.

Difference expansion based reversible data hiding was first proposed by Tian [42]. For a pixel pair (x_0, x_1), their integer average is defined as $l = \lfloor (x_0 + x_1)/2 \rfloor$ and difference is defined as $h = x_1 - x_0$. To embed one watermark bit $m \in \{0,1\}$, the difference h is expanded as $h^* = 2h + m$, and the watermarked pixel pair (y_0, y_1) is generated as $y_0 = l - \lfloor h^*/2 \rfloor$ and $y_1 = l + \lfloor (h^* + 1)/2 \rfloor$. Further simplification generates the relation between (x_0, x_1) and (y_0, y_1) as below:

$$\begin{cases} y_0 = 2x_0 - \lceil (x_0 + x_1)/2 \rceil \\ y_1 = 2x_1 - \lceil (x_0 + x_1)/2 \rceil + m \end{cases} \tag{28.1}$$

At decoder one can extract watermark bit m as the LSB of $y_1 - y_0$. The original pixel pair (x_0, x_1) can be recovered as $x_0 = l' - \lfloor h'/2 \rfloor$ and $x_1 = l' + \lceil h'/2 \rceil$, where $l' = \lfloor (y_0 + y_1)/2 \rfloor$ and $h' = \lfloor (y_1 - y_0)/2 \rfloor$.

Among all three techniques, DE based techniques provide the greatest data hiding capacity with low distortion. Tian [42] proposed a integer-to-integer transformation based DE technique. The variants of this technique are other forms of integer-to-integer transformation [38,49,50], location map reduction [51,52] and prediction-error expansion (PE) [53–56]. Among these extensions, the PE-based method has attracted considerable attention since it has the potential to exploit spatial redundancy. In PE, correlation of a larger neighbourhood is exploited to improve its performance.

Ni et al., [45] proposed histogram shifting (HS) based RDH which embedded watermarks by modifying the image histogram. To have a idea about HS based technique, consider a 8-bit gray-scale image I. For an integer $a \in [1, 253]$, the watermark is embedded into I as follows to get the watermarked image I_W.

$$
I_{W_{i,j}} = \begin{cases}
I_{i,j} - 1 & \text{if} : I_{i,j} < a \\
I_{i,j} - m & \text{if} : I_{i,j} = a \\
I_{i,j} + m & \text{if} : I_{i,j} = a+1 \\
I_{i,j} + 1 & \text{if} : I_{i,j} > a
\end{cases} \tag{28.2}
$$

where, (i, j) is a pixel location and $m \in \{0, 1\}$ is the watermark bit. From Equation 28.2 one can easily see that maximum modification applied to each pixel value is 1 which results into very good peak signal to noise ratio (PSNR) between I_W and I.

At the receiver side, the watermark can be extracted as:

- If $I_{W_{i,j}} < a - 1$, pixel does not contain watermark and its original pixel value is $I_{W_{i,j}} + 1$.
- If $I_{W_{i,j}} \in \{a - 1, a\}$, the pixel carries the watermark bit. Extract $m = a - I_{W_{i,j}}$ with original value as a.
- If $I_{W_{i,j}} \in \{a + 1, a + 2\}$, the pixel carries the watermark bit extracted as $m = I_{W_{i,j}} - (a + 1)$ and its original value is $a + 1$.
- If $I_{W_{i,j}} > a + 2$, pixel does not contain watermark and the original value is $I_{W_{i,j}} - 1$.

In [57] Lee et al., suggested improvement by using the histogram of the difference image in place of original image. The method outperforms Ni et al., in terms of embedding capacity as well as visual quality. Recently [43,44], proposed extension of both Ni et al., and Lee et al., schemes.

28.4 Data Hiding Techniques for Biometric Authentication

28.4.1 Semi-Fragile Watermarking

Authors in [58] proposed a multiple semi-fragile watermark based technique to protect vulnerable points at the sensor and matcher system. Some manipulations on biometric templates are completely harmless, e.g., storing biometrics in lossy compression format like JPEG 2000 [59] to conserve space, or a mild rotation in a test template captured at sensor. The watermark should not treat such changes as malicious and be resistive to them. At the same time the watermark should be sensitive enough to detect malicious manipulations like copy attack. The copy attack is a malicious manipulation applied to negate the effect of the watermarking system [60]. The copy attack attempts to estimate the watermark used with a cover. On successful estimation of the watermark, an attacker would add a fake or illegal cover. Thus a watermarking system will be spoofed and will declare fake content to be authenticated. Therefore, a watermark should also be able to identify malicious and non-malicious attacks. A semi-fragile watermark satisfies both of the above requirements and it is showcased through some of the results discussed in this section. It is robust to non-malicious manipulation and sensitive to malicious ones.

The scheme in [58] uses two watermarks to secure database and sensor. Watermark W_1 is used for database authentication and it is resistive to lossy compression. It is derived using block based singular values (SVs) of a fingerprint image. W_1 establish linkages between the watermark and fingerprint image. Watermark W_2 is used to secure feature matcher subsystem. It is computed using second and third order moments of the fingerprint image. W_2 is resistive to mild affine transformation i.e., rotation up to $\pm 10°$ and lossy compression to incorporate practical aspects of the biometric fingerprint system. The watermarking method not only protects the database – the image dependent watermark makes it robust against copy attack.

Fingerprint images from FVC2002 [61], FVC2004 [62] and FVC2006 [63] databases have been used for experimentation. The filter bank based fingerprint matching system [12] is used for testing watermarking algorithm. Figure 28.1 show samples of original and watermarked fingerprint images, respectively. It can be seen from Figure 28.1 that two watermarks remains perceptually transparent in the fingerprint image. Two watermarks perform authenticity checks at the database and sensor. Table 28.1 shows the effect of different attacks on the database. Table 28.2 shows the effect of different attacks on a query fingerprint at sensor. A distortion in an extracted watermark is measured using bit error rate (BER), which is a ratio of total bit difference between extracted and computed watermark to total the number of watermark bits. In Tables 28.1 and 28.2 CR represents compression ratio.

Watermark W_1 is robust to *JPEG* 2000 compression which is treated as a non-malicious manipulation. The resultant average BER for this attack is very low. Every other attack i.e., histogram equalization (Hseq), Gaussian noise *GN* and

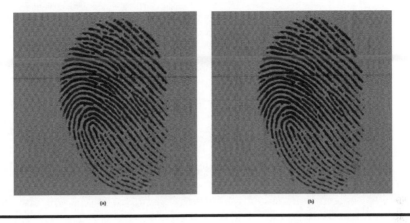

Figure 28.1 (a) Original image, and (b) watermarked image.

Table 28.1 Average BER for Different Attacks on W_1

Attacks	Average BER	Decision
No attack	0.0000	Authentic
JPEG2000 (CR = 5)	0.0066	Authentic
Hseq	0.4602	Unauthentic
GN ($\mu = 0$, $\sigma = 1$)	0.5001	Unauthentic
Copy attack	0.2053	Unauthentic

Table 28.2 Average BER for Different Attacks on W_2

Attacks	Average BER	Decision
No attack	0.0000	Authentic
JPEG2000 (CR = 5)	0.0004	Authentic
Rotation of −5°	0.0470	Authentic
Rotation of +5°	0.0360	Authentic
Up scaling by 2	0.0014	Authentic
Down scaling by 2	0.0030	Authentic
GN ($\mu = 0$ $\sigma = 1$)	0.4700	Unauthentic
Copy attack	0.6300	Unauthentic

copy attack results into significantly large distortion and BER. Similarly W_2 which is derived from higher order moments are restive to non-malicious manipulations of *JPEG* 2000, mild rotation up to 5° and scale change. The watermark exhibits resistivity to these non-malicious manipulations. At the same time W_2 is very sensitive to malicious attempts of noise addition and copy attack. The BER for such attacks are very high. Thus watermarks are semi-fragile in nature as it rolls out authentication for non-malicious attempts and declares template unauthentic for malicious attacks. This proves usefulness of scheme in identifying different attacks and its protection to database and sensor.

Table 28.3 shows the average Euclidean distance between fingerprint images and its watermarked version for 100 images from [61,62] calculated using very well known fingerprint matching algorithms proposed in [64]. It also shows distance between watermarked and any other image in the database. It can be observed that watermark does change the structure of the fingerprint that results in a finite distance between original and watermarked fingerprint. However, this distance is less than the distance between a watermarked and any other fingerprint in the database. It means that biometric system accuracy is unlikely to be impacted by watermarking.

The method requires the selection of threshold to decide malicious and non-malicious manipulations. In the present case threshold is set at 400 to balance probability of false positive (Pfp) and false negative (Pfn). Figure 28.2 also highlights that watermark changes inherent characteristics of a fingerprint image which is not acceptable in many situations. This makes the method unfit for template protection. Thus, watermarking schemes must be reversible in nature.

28.4.2 Initial Attempts at RDH Biometric Authentication

The method discussed in Section 28.4.1 secure multiple vulnerable points, but watermark is irreversible and affects biometric accuracy. Therefore, an improvement using the reversible data hiding technique [65] is covered in this section. Fingerprint dependent watermark W_1 authenticates the database and shields it against the copy attack. The second watermark W_2 verifies fingerprint captured by the sensor and foil replay attack. W_2 is derived from the higher order

Table 28.3 Average Euclidean Distance (for 100 images)

Average Distance Between Watermarked and Original Fingerprint Image	Average Distance Between Watermarked and Fake Fingerprint Image	Threshold
140.5677	994.6301	400

Source: From FVC2002, Fingerprint database: Fvc2002, bias.csr.unibo.it/fvc2002/databases.asp, 2002; From FVC2004, Fingerprint database: Fvc2004, bias.csr.unibo.it/fvc2004/databases.asp, 2004.

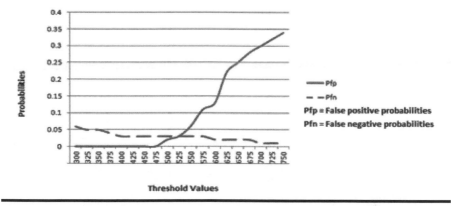

Figure 28.2 Probability of false positive and false negative after watermark embedding.

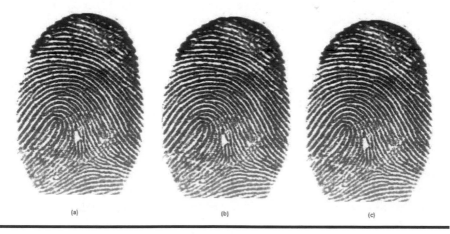

Figure 28.3 (a) Original image (b) watermarked image, and (c) recovered image from [61].

moments of the fingerprint. Following are the results of experimentation with method in [65].

Figure 28.3 shows original, watermarked and recovered fingerprint images respectively. It can be observed that perceptually the watermarked fingerprint is similar to original. Table 28.4 shows effect of histogram equalization and copy attack on database as well as on query fingerprints from the sensor. It can be seen from Table 28.4 that watermarks cannot survive histogram equalization and copy attack. Their structure changes and therefore, the fingerprint cannot regain its originality. This signals that manipulation and fingerprint is not used for further processing. It is easy to visualize that reversible watermark provides authentication at multiple vulnerable points of the fingerprint system without affecting native recognition accuracy.

Table 28.4   BER under Different Attacks on Fingerprints in the Database (Average of 200 images)

Attacks	Average BER (W_1)	Average BER (W_2)	Reversibility	Decision
No attack	0.00	0.00	Yes	Authentic
Hseq	0.45	0.47	No	Unauthentic
Copy attack	0.55	0.58	No	Unauthentic

Source: From FVC2002, Fingerprint database: Fvc2002, bias.csr.unibo.it/fvc2002/databases.asp, 2002; From FVC2004, Fingerprint database: Fvc2004, bias.csr.unibo.it/fvc2004/databases.asp, 2004.

28.4.3 Reversible Data Hiding with Privacy Protection

The use of reversible watermarking with multiple watermarking is shown in [65]. The method is resistive to replay and copy attack. It is sensitive to manipulation and it rejects manipulated template. Unlike semi-fragile method [58] it does not segregate between malicious and non-malicious manipulations of watermark though the method secures multiple points. As seen earlier, privacy protection is also one of the important requirements. Loss of biometrics to an impostor can create an alter-ego. This means that privacy of biometrics should be protected. This chapter section studies the method which provide simultaneous authentication and privacy protection.

As an improvement, a scheme with commutativity between reversible watermarking and encryption has been proposed in [66]. Due to commutative property, one can embed and extract a watermark in either a plain or encrypted fingerprint image; irrespective of the order in which encryption or watermarking is applied. The encryption and the watermarking keys are shared using secret key sharing mechanism. The biometric database consists of encrypted and watermarked fingerprint images. After successful authentication, watermarking is inverted to get back the plain fingerprint. The proposed scheme protects many of the vulnerable points [5] of a biometric authentication system. Also native recognition accuracy remains unaffected due to reversible watermarking.

The 8 bit fingerprint images with 500 dpi resolution and size 512×512 are selected for experimentation. The $2^8 \times 1$ multiplexer is used for image encryption and decryption. Hence, random numbers are generated in the range $[0, 255]$ and thus probability of brute force P_b is $1/(256!)$ which is close to zero. Figure 28.4a and b show the original fingerprint image and its watermarked version; while Figure 28.4c and d show encrypted and decrypted versions of the watermarked image. The watermarking method is reversible in nature, thus native fingerprint authentication accuracy remains unaffected. This means there is no change in the receiver operation characteristics (ROC) of the fingerprint authentication system.

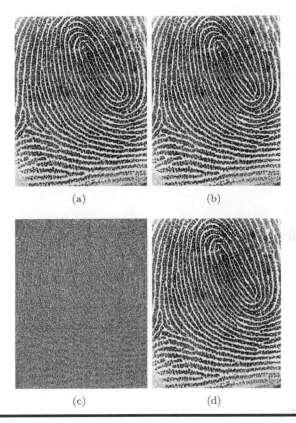

Figure 28.4 Reversible data hiding with privacy protection (a) original image, (b) plain watermarked image, (c) encrypted watermarked, and (d) decrypted watermarked image.

Due to commutative property, watermarking the plain fingerprint secures the sensor. The watermarked and encrypted image I_{WE} is stored in the database. The flexibility of extracting the watermark from the decrypted image secures the communication channel. Hence, the single watermarking scheme is used for securing multiple vulnerable points i.e., sensor, database and communication channel of a fingerprint authentication system. Table 28.5 shows sensitivity of a watermark at different vulnerable points. It shows that method is sensitive against any manipulation and it declares the fingerprint image as unauthentic due to high bit error rate.

28.4.4 *Improved Reversible Data Hiding Technique*

Methods discussed in [66] provide commutativity between reversible watermarking and encryption. However, it has a poorly designed reversible watermarking subsystem as:

Table 28.5   BER at Different Vulnerable Points

Attacks	BER Sensor	BER Database	BER Channel
Histogram equalization	0.47	0.48	0.48
Laplacian filtering ($\alpha = 0.2$)	0.50	0.53	0.52
Average filtering (3×3)	0.49	0.52	0.48
Gaussian noise ($\mu = 0$ and $\sigma = 0.01$)	0.49	0.48	0.48

1. Watermarking method is non-blind in nature due to requirement of the original watermark at receiver.
2. The probability of the watermark substitution increases when all fingerprints are *marked* using the same watermark. This probability can be lowered by using unique watermark for each fingerprint but then watermark management becomes a major issue.
3. Watermark is embedded only in LSB planes of an image which cannot detect tampering in most significant bit (MSB) planes.
4. The key space is relatively small (2^8)! and may succumb to brute force search.

High probability of watermark substitution leads to unauthorized data insertion in fingerprint database and MSB tampering is one of the ways to apply DoS attacks. Therefore, [66] is improved by strengthening authentication. This makes the method robust against unauthorized data insertion and it can also detect tampering in MSBs to avoid DoS attacks.

In the present section we study a method with such improvements. The method uses image dependent watermarks which makes it secure against watermark substitution. Also the entire image contributes in either watermark computation or its embedding. Hence, tampering of any image part can be easily detected. The method under study use symmetric key cryptograpy which is more robust and secured compared to the multiplexer based encryption in [66]. The results of our investigations are as follows.

Fingerprint images with 500 dots per inch (dpi) and size 512×512 are selected for experiments [62]. The even random integer during encryption falls in $[0,512)$ and therefore P_b is $\frac{1}{2}(2097152)$. Figures 28.5 and 28.6 show sample of original fingerprints and their watermarked version which is generated using integer wavelet transform (IWT). Figure 28.7 shows encrypted versions of the watermarked image. The encrypted version mildly retains the shape of the fingerprint as a high frequency *HH* band of IWT is left untouched during the processing. However, it is also clear from Figure 28.7 that the encrypted image does not retain any intelligible information and it is useless for further processing.

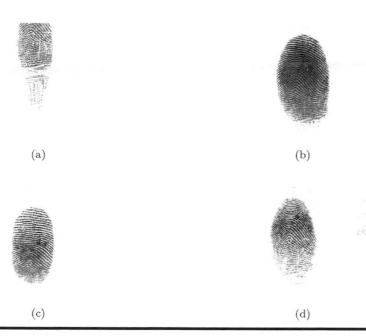

Figure 28.5 Original image; (a) img1, (b) img2, (c) img3, and (d) img4. (From FVC2004, Fingerprint database: Fvc2004, bias.csr.unibo.it/fvc2004/databases. asp, 2004.)

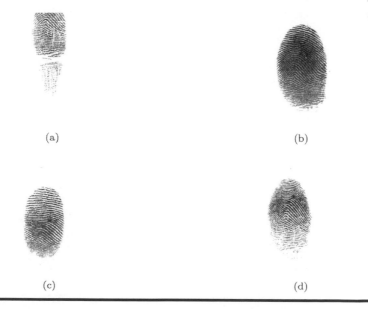

Figure 28.6 Watermarked image corresponding to Figure 28.5(a) wm_img1, (b) wm_img2, (c) wm_img3, and (d) wm_img4.

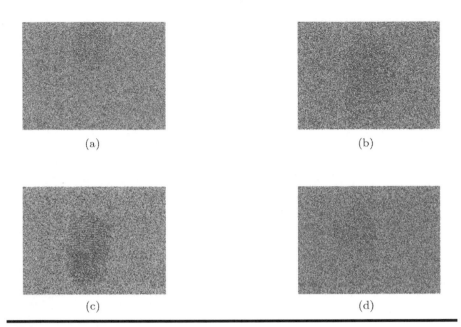

Figure 28.7 Encrypted watermarked image corresponding to Figure 28.5; (a) enc_img1, (b) enc_img2, (c) enc_img3, and (d) enc_img4.

This fact has been established with the following experimentation. Figure 28.8 shows two sample fingerprint images and their corresponding *HH* band. In order to check quantum of information that is revealed by *HH* band, minutia are extracted from fingerprint and *HH* band images. These minutia are extracted using a standard fingerprint minutiae viewer provided by the National Institute of Standards and Technology (NIST) [67]. One can see from the Figure 28.8c and d that core fingerprint matching features, i.e., minutia from *HH* band, are very noisy. Hence, *HH* band is used for watermark generation and it is left untouched during watermarking.

Another experiment is performed to establish that using an encrypted image (cf. Figure 28.7) to query the fingerprint database will not yield the match. The matching is performed using a well-known filter bank based fingerprint matching algorithm [64]. The Euclidean distance (ED) between plain and its corresponding database fingerprint is *zero* for all four cases. The ED between query and output image is very large in the case of encrypted images, as shown in Table 28.6.

Table 28.7 shows BER of the [65] and the method as discussed in the current section. It can be seen from Table 28.7 that method [66] fails to detect change in the watermark and does not capture any error due to watermark substitution. However, the method discussed in this section detects change in watermark structure.

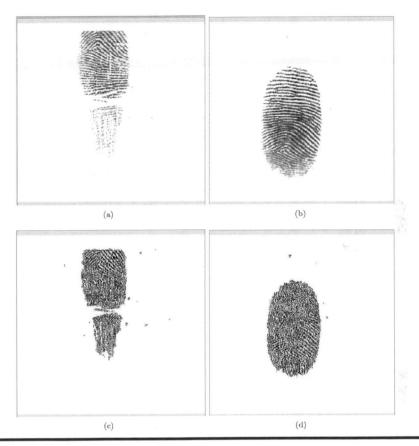

Figure 28.8 Fingerprint minutiae points extracted from plain fingerprint image and corresponding *HH* bands.

Table 28.6 Encrypted Fingerprint Matching

Query Image	Output Image	ED
enc_img1	img1	2334
enc_img2	img1	2437
enc_img3	img3	1998
enc_img4	img3	2410

Table 28.7   BER against Watermark Substitution

Image	Method in [66]	Method Section 28.4.4
img1	0	0.1956
img2	0	0.2035
img3	0	0.2215
img4	0	0.2563
Average	0	0.1856

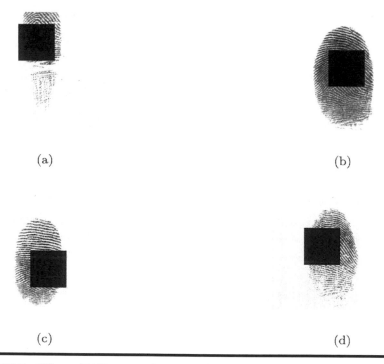

(a)   (b)

(c)   (d)

Figure 28.9   Effect of MSB tampering on (a) img1, (b) img2, (c) img3, and (d) img4.

Figure 28.9 shows the visual effect of MSB tampering on a fingerprint image. It can be seen that major portion of the fingerprint from which features are extracted has been corrupted. Table 28.8 show the BER against MSB tampering. It should be noted that method in [66] fails to capture MSB tampering while the method in the current section captures this manipulation.

Table 28.8 BER against MSB Tampering

Image	Method [66]	Method Section 28.4.4
img1	0	0.3412
img2	0	0.3251
img3	0	0.3178
img4	0	0.3549
Average	0	0.3059

28.5 Conclusion

The central goal of this chapter is to study security of conventional biometric systems. It is evident that biometrics are extensively used for person verification or identification. The chapter covers the study of vulnerable points in a biometric system which can be exploited to gain illegal access. It has been shown that there are eight vulnerable points that have been extended to 22 points. The chapter reviewed various alternative to secure a biometric system like cryptosystem, fuzzy vault, and fragile watermarking.

The authors of this chapter presented the use of watermarking for improving security and sealing vulnerable points in a biometric system. It is essentially a two-layered architecture with the watermarking layer residing on top of a biometric system. The watermarking is used as an authentication mechanism. Initial semi-fragile techniques [58] secured multiple points but it was using irreversible watermarks affecting the biometric system accuracy. It also required the threshold to segregate malicious and non-malicious attacks.

The constraint on watermarks to keep the structure of cover intact motivated use of RDH [65]. The method secured multiple points without changing the ROC of a biometric system. However, the method could not provide privacy. The method developed in [66] is one such attempt to bring privacy and authentication together. The method created commutativity between watermarking and encryption. A reversible watermarking creates authentication layer and encryption provides privacy protection. However, the scheme has several security flaws as discussed in Section 28.4.4. This leads to study of the scheme as discussed in Section 28.4.4. The core idea is to use an image dependent watermark. It is derived from using high frequency coefficients and inserted into low-frequency-high-energy image coefficients. The initial results showcase that method is resistive to MSB tampering and watermark substitution.

Thus, it has been showcased through study of various schemes that commutative and reversible data hiding schemes are the best alternatives to secure multiple vulnerable points with privacy protection.

Acknowledgment

The authors are thankful to the Board of Research in Nuclear Science (BRNS), Department of Atomic Energy, Goverment of India for the grant to carry out this research work.

References

1. A. K. Jain and A. Kumar. Biometrics of next generation: An overview. In *Second Generation Biometrics*, 49–79, Springer, Berlin, Germany, 2010.
2. National Institute of Standards and Technology Federal Information Processing Standards (NIST FIPS) Pub. 197: Advanced encryption standard (aes), Federal Information Processing Standards, US Department of Commerce/nist, November 26, 2001. available from the nist website.
3 W. Stallings and M. P. Tahiliani. *Cryptography and Network Security: Principles and Practice*, volume 6. Pearson, London, UK, 2014.
4. D. V. Klein. Foiling the cracker: A survey of, and improvements to, password security. In *USENIX 2nd Security Workshop*, 5–14, Boston, MA, 1990.
5. A. K. Jain, A. Ross, and S. Prabhakar. An introduction to biometric recognition. *IEEE Transactions on Circuits and Systems for Video Technology*, 14(1):4–20, 2004.
6. A. Jain, R. Bolle, and S. Pankanti. *Biometrics: Personal Identification in Networked Society*, volume 479. Springer Science & Business Media, New York, 2006.
7. R. M. Bolle, J. Connell, S. Pankanti, N. K. Ratha, and A. W. Senior. *Guide to Biometrics*. Springer Science & Business Media, New York, 2013.
8. Uidai project., Aadhar Authentication, https://www.uidai.gov.in/authentication/authentication-overview/authentication-en.html, access: June 2012.
9. A. K. Jain, A. Ross, and S. Pankanti. Biometrics: A tool for information security. *IEEE Transactions on Information Forensics and Security*, 1(2):125–143, 2006.
10. N. K. Ratha, J. H. Connell, and R. M. Bolle. Enhancing security and privacy in biometrics-based authentication systems. *IBM Systems Journal*, 40(3):614–634, 2001.
11. B. Cukic and N. Bartlow. Biometric system threats and countermeasures: A risk based approach. In *Proceedings of the Biometric Consortium Conference (BCC 05)*, 237–246, IEEE, 2005.
12. A. K. Jain, K. Nandakumar, and A. Nagar. Biometric template security. *EURASIP Journal on Advances in Signal Processing*, 2008:113, 2008.
13. C. Roberts. Biometric attack vectors and defences. *Computers & Security*, 26(1):14–25, 2007.
14. U. Uludag, S. Pankanti, S. Prabhakar, and A. K. Jain. Biometric cryptosystems: Issues and challenges. *Proceedings of the IEEE*, 92(6):948–960, 2004.
15. U. Uludag, S. Pankanti, and A. K Jain. Fuzzy vault for fingerprints. In *International Conference on Audio-and Video-Based Biometric Person Authentication*, 310–319. Springer, Berlin, Germany, 2005.
16. Y. C. Feng and P. C. Yuen. Protecting face biometric data on smartcard with reed-solomon code. In *Computer Vision and Pattern Recognition Workshop, 2006. CVPRW'06 Conference on*, 29. IEEE, 2006.

17. M. R. Freire, J. Fiérrez, and J. Ortega-Garca. Cryptographic key generation using handwritten signature. In *Proceedings of SPIE-The International Society for Optical Engineering*. Society of Photo-Optical Instrumentation Engineers, 588–595, Bellingham, WA, 2006.

18 L. Leng and A. B. J. Teoh. Alignment-free row-co-occurrence cancelable palmprint fuzzy vault. *Pattern Recognition*, 48(7):2290–2303, 2015.

19. M. Khan, L. Xie, and J. Zhang. Robust hiding of fingerprint-biometric data into audio signals. In *Proceedings International Conference on Biometrics, Advances in Biometrics*, 702–712. Springer, Berlin, Germany, 2007.

20. M. Khan, L. Xie, and J. Zhang. Robust hiding of fingerprint-biometric data into audio signals. In *Proceedings International Conference on Biometrics*, Advances in Biometrics, 702–712. Springer, Berlin, Germany, 2007.

21. M. S. Raval, P. P. Rege, and S. K. Parulkar. Secure and robust watermarking technique. In *TENCON 2012-2012 IEEE Region 10 Conference*, 1–6. IEEE, 2012.

22. H. Kaur and P. Khanna. Biometric template protection using cancelable biometrics and visual cryptography techniques. *Multimedia Tools and Applications*, 75(23):16333–16361, 2016.

23. M. S. Raval, M. Joshi, P. Rege, and S. Parulkar. Image tampering detection using compressive sensing based watermarking scheme. In *Proceedings of MVIP 2011*, IEEE, 16–21, 2011.

24. M. S. Raval and P. P. Rege. Scalar quantization based multiple patterns data hiding technique for gray scale images. *GVIP Journal*, 5(9):55–61, 2005.

25. V. B. Joshi, M. S. Raval, P. P. Rege, S. K. Parulkar et al. Multi-stage VQ based exact authentication for biometric images. *Computer Society of India Journal of Computing*, 2(1–2):R3–25, 2013.

26. J. Hämmerle-Uhl, K. Raab, and A. Uhl. Watermarking as a means to enhance biometric systems: A critical survey. In *International workshop on Information Hiding*, 238–254. Springer, Berlin, Germany, 2011.

27. M. Paunwala and S. Patnaik. Biometric template protection with DCT-based watermarking. *Machine Vision and Applications*, 25(1):263–275, 2014.

28. L. R. Haddada, B. Dorizzi, and N. E. Ben Amara. A combined watermarking approach for securing biometric data. *Signal Processing: Image Communication*, 55:23–31, 2017.

29. C. Li, Y. Wang, B. Ma, and Z. Zhang. Multi-block dependency based fragile watermarking scheme for fingerprint images protection. *Multimedia Tools and Applications*, 64(3):757–776, 2013.

30. M. M. Yeung and S. Pankanti. Verification watermarks on fingerprint recognition and retrieval. *Journal of Electronic Imaging*, 9(4):468–476, 2000.

31. M. K. Khan, J. Zhang, and L. Tian. Protecting biometric data for personal identification. In *Chinese conferences on Biometric recognition Advances in Biometric Person Authentication*, 629–638. Springer, Berlin, Germany, 2004.

32. M. S. Raval. A secure steganographic technique for blind steganalysis resistance. In *Advances in Pattern Recognition, 2009. ICAPR'09. Seventh International Conference on*, 25–28. IEEE, 2009.

33. D. Wang, J. Li, and X. Wen. Biometric image integrity authentication based on svd and fragile watermarking. In *Image and Signal Processing, 2008. CISP'08. Congress on*, volume 5, 679–682. IEEE, 2008.

34. R. Huber, H. Stögner, and A. Uhl. Semi-fragile watermarking in biometric systems: Template self-embedding. In *International conference on Computer Analysis of Images and Patterns*, 34–41. Springer, Berlin, Germany, 2011.

35. A. K. Jain and U. Uludag. Hiding biometric data. *IEEE Transactions on Pattern Analysis and Machine Intelligence*, 25(11):1494–1498, 2003.

36. Y. Chung, D. Moon, K. Moon, and S. Pan. Hiding biometric data for secure transmission. In *International Conference on Knowledge-Based Intelligent Information and Engineering Systems KES 2005*, 1049–1057. Springer, Berlin, Germany, 2005.

37. V. B. Joshi, M. S. Raval, S. Mitra, P. P. Rege, and S. K. Parulkar. Reversible watermarking technique to enhance security of a biometric authentication system. In *Computer Vision, Pattern Recognition, Image Processing and Graphics, 2013 Fourth National Conference on*, 1–4. IEEE, 2013.

38. A. M. Alattar. Reversible watermark using the difference expansion of a generalized integer transform. *IEEE Transactions on Image Processing*, 13(8):1147–1156, 2004.

39. D. Coltuc. Improved embedding for prediction-based reversible watermarking. *IEEE Transactions on Information Forensics and Security*, 6(3):873–882, 2011.

40. I.-C. Dragoi and D. Coltuc. Local-prediction-based difference expansion reversible watermarking. *IEEE Transactions on Image Processing*, 23(4):1779–1790, 2014.

41. D. M. Thodi and J. J. Rodriguez. Prediction-error based reversible watermarking. In *International Conference on Image Processing ICIP*, volume 3, 1549–1552. IEEE, 2004.

42. J. Tian. Reversible data embedding using a difference expansion. *IEEE Transactions on Circuits and Systems for Video Technology*, 13(8):890–896, 2003.

43. X. Li, B. Li, B. Yang, and T. Zeng. General framework to histogram-shifting-based reversible data hiding. *IEEE Transactions on Image Processing*, 22(6):2181–2191, 2013.

44. X. Li, W. Zhang, X. Gui, and B. Yang. Efficient reversible data hiding based on multiple histograms modification. *IEEE Transactions on Information Forensics and Security*, 10(9):2016–2027, 2015.

45. Z. Ni, Y.-Q. Shi, Nirwan Ansari, and Wei Su. Reversible data hiding. *IEEE Transactions on Circuits and Systems for Video Technology*, 16(3):354–362, 2006.

46. M. U. Celik, G. Sharma, A. M. Tekalp, and E. Saber. Lossless generalized-LSB data embedding. *IEEE Transactions on Image Processing*, 14(2):253–266, 2005.

47. J. Fridrich, M. Goljan, and R. Du. Lossless data embedding: New paradigm in digital watermarking. *EURASIP Journal on Applied Signal Processing*, 2002(1):185–196, 2002.

48. J. J. Fridrich, M. Goljan, and R. Du. Invertible authentication. *Security and Watermarking of Multimedia Contents*, 3:197–208, 2001.

49. D. Coltuc. Low distortion transform for reversible watermarking. *IEEE Transactions on Image Processing*, 21(1):412–417, 2012.

50. X. Wang, X. Li, B. Yang, and Z. Guo. Efficient generalized integer transform for reversible watermarking. *IEEE Signal Processing Letters*, 17(6):567–570, 2010.

51. L. Kamstra and H. J. A. M. Heijmans. Reversible data embedding into images using wavelet techniques and sorting. *IEEE Transactions on Image Processing*, 14(12):2082–2090, 2005.

52. S. Weng, Y. Zhao, J.-S. Pan, and R. Ni. Reversible watermarking based on invariability and adjustment on pixel pairs. *IEEE Signal Processing Letters*, 15:721–724, 2008.

53. X. Li, B. Yang, and T. Zeng. Efficient reversible watermarking based on adaptive prediction-error expansion and pixel selection. *IEEE Transactions on Image Processing*, 20(12):3524–3533, 2011.

54. L. Luo, Z. Chen, M. Chen, X. Zeng, and Z. Xiong. Reversible image watermarking using interpolation technique. *IEEE Transactions on Information Forensics and Security*, 5(1):187–193, 2010.
55. D. M. Thodi and J. J. Rodríguez. Expansion embedding techniques for reversible watermarking. *IEEE Transactions on Image Processing*, 16(3):721–730, 2007.
56. H.-T. Wu and J. Huang. Reversible image watermarking on prediction errors by efficient histogram modification. *Signal Processing*, 92(12):3000–3009, 2012.
57. S.-K. Lee, Y.-H. Suh, and Y.-S. Ho. Reversible image authentication based on watermarking. In *IEEE International Conference on Multimedia and Expo*, 1321–1324, 2006.
58. M. V. Joshi, V. B. Joshi, and M. S. Raval. Multilevel semi-fragile watermarking technique for improving biometric fingerprint system security. In *Intelligent Interactive Technologies and Multimedia*, 272–283. Springer, Berlin, Germany, 2013.
59. M. A. Joshi, M. S. Raval, Y. H. Dandawate, K. R. Joshi, and S. P. Metkar. *Image and Video Compression: Fundamentals, Techniques, and Applications*. CRC Press, Boca Raton, FL, 2014.
60. M. Kutter, S. Voloshynovskyy, and A. Herrigel. Watermark copy attack. In *Proceedings of SPIE Security and Watermarking of Multimedia*, vol. 3971, San Jose, CA, 1–10, 2000.
61. FVC2002. Fingerprint database: Fvc2002. bias.csr.unibo.it/fvc2002/databases.asp, 2002.
62. FVC2004. Fingerprint database: Fvc2004. bias.csr.unibo.it/fvc2004/databases.asp, 2004.
63. FVC2006. Fingerprint verification competition: Fvc2006. bias.csr.unibo.it/fvc2006/, 2006.
64. A. K. Jain, S. Prabhakar, L. Hong, and S. Pankanti. Filterbank-based fingerprint matching. *IEEE Transactions on Image Processing*, 9(5):846–859, 2000.
65. V. B. Joshi, M. S. Raval, D. Gupta, P. P. Rege, and S. K. Parulkar. A multiple reversible watermarking technique for fingerprint authentication. *Multimedia Systems*, 22(3):367–378, 2016.
66. V. B. Joshi, D. Gupta, and M. S. Raval. A commutative encryption and reversible watermarking for fingerprint image. In *14th International Workshop on Digital-Forensics and Watermarking*, 323–336. Springer, Cham, Switzerland, 2015.
67. NIST. Fingerprint minutiae viewer. https://www.nist.gov/services-resources/software/fingerprint-minutiae- viewer-fpmv, 2017.

Chapter 29

Secure Biometric Modalities for Effective Communication

Sandhya Tarar

Contents

DOI: 10.1201/9780429435461-34

29.1 Introduction

29.1.1 Biometric Systems

A few decades back, if you had asked security experts about the usage of biometrics as a means of mainstream authentication security, majority would have not agreed. They were apprehensive about the application areas of biometrics. Only a few could have predicted the huge scale and enormous growth and larger scope of this mode of security. The motivation behind choosing biometric technology is that it has an edge over traditional authentication modalities like login id, passwords or names. Because these techniques are only based on establishing personal identity and providing the proof of ownership, whereas the former is entirely focused on exact identification like "who are they"?

Biometrics is a quantitative measurement of biological features of an individual. The usage of biometrics is to uniquely identify an individual based upon biological characteristics like their face, fingerprint, voice, iris etc. Biometric systems are used as a means of secure communication in multiple applications ranging from Mobile phones, Surveillance cameras (CCTV etc), forensics, secured data storage (Cloud), automobile industry (car security system) to national/international airports and research areas like computer vision, Internet of things and many more like this. In order to provide security to any critical information these biometric traits are used.

Biometric techniques are playing a crucial role in laying the foundation of a comprehensive series of highly secure identification method and designing of individual verification systems. With every instance of a breach in security, transaction fraud increases and the need of the hour is to have in place a more secure personal verification and identification technology.

29.2 Classification of Biometrics

There are different types of biometric systems: physiological and behavioral biometrics. Physiological biometrics consist of physical features like fingerprint, iris, face, ear, palm etc. while behavioral represents speech, DNA, etc.

29.2.1 Human Identification

Researchers underlined the need of identification and various other factors that are collectively required for individualistic human identification in 1990s. Also, various other identification parameters such as codes, names, token-based and knowledge-based biometrics can be used for identification. As far as biometric identification is concerned, iris, palm, face and fingerprint based recognition methods can be used to ensure the security of systems. A broad classification is discussed in the following sections.

29.2.2 Face Based Identification

It has been observed that human identification based on a face is an effective security technique. It's an accurate method to identify an individual and offers significant benefits over traditional identification methods and other biometrics, like fingerprint. It is undoubtedly more reliable than fingerprint identification because it is harder to clone and not as easy as in the case of fingerprints. However, with this enhanced security, it cannot be denied that the complexity of a face-based identification system is higher than fingerprint. Researchers have discussed different issues associated with face identification-based security as a problem of rotation detection of multi view faces. Width first search tree, vector boosting algorithm and sparse granular features are the popular techniques used. Some methods based on empirical evaluation may be employed in case of face recognition for the designing of specific training and testing sets, such as experimental settings in Facial Recognition Technology (FERET) and Face Recognition Grand Challenge (FRGC).

29.2.3 Palm Identification

A palm print based authentication system uses the palm as a means of secure authentication. This technique may include cancellable biometric concept which is designed for transforming the palm image into a feature representation of lower dimensions. Cancellable biometric design can be done with the random number generation methods. Pseudo random data is being generation with wavelet based palm print features. Research done by Purdue University shows that majority of people appreciated the use of this secure method. Besides, the human hand can be divided into different parts associated with fingers and then the confidence value of each of them can be calculated. Then a support vector data description is reduced by putting it in place. The calculated confidence is then compared with the threshold value and, if it is higher than that, to maintain the symmetry, confidence of other fingers is also raised.

29.2.4 Iris Based Identification

Iris based identification can use different steps right from iris image acquisition, image enhancement, feature extraction and feature matching, which can be used for gender identification. Iris coding techniques like Discrete Cosine Transform (DCT), novel patch encoding methods have been devised by researchers for making iris based identification effective. Probability statistical analysis is used to predict equal error rates in worst case scenarios to model for matching and non-matching algorithms. Guo et al. discussed that if iris pattern is compromised that will lead to the breach of security provided by the iris-based security system. The concept of cancellable biometrics is useful in this case; transformation of the iris image is stored rather than storing the original image. Different techniques like gray-combo, bin-combo, gray-salt and bin-salt can be used to design the cancellable biometric, i.e. transformed image. Another method which is used in iris based security is the Bayesian method, which is used to deform pattern matching since the matching process depends on MAP estimation and the type of deformation. Correlation filter is used to recognize same pattern class and its design. Fast fourier transformation can be used to enhance the images and improve the quality of the iris templates.

29.2.5 Fingerprint Based Identification

Fingerprint identification is the most popular biometric among the researchers because of its easy to use characteristic. Fingerprint recognition has some positives like legibility, i.e. this is a biometric which is highly universal because mostly people have legible fingerprints. Having a high degree of reliability as it is unique in nature, fingerprints are formed at a very early stage of life and remain structurally unchanged during the whole life and can be measured accurately. Thus, fingerprint recognition is a widely used biometric and used as a secure means of communication. Fingerprint identification uses different steps like normalization, image enhancement, binarization, thinning, minutia extraction and minutia matching. High quality image acquisition is a pre-requisite for a high quality fingerprint identification system. In order to acquire high quality images, various quality improvement techniques like fourier transformation, fast fourier transformation, enhancement through gabor filters, mace filters and wavelet transformation, are among the most widely used methods [24]. Gabor filters are the ones which have optimal joint resolution in both frequency as well as spatial domain. Figure 29.1 represents different methods for human identification.

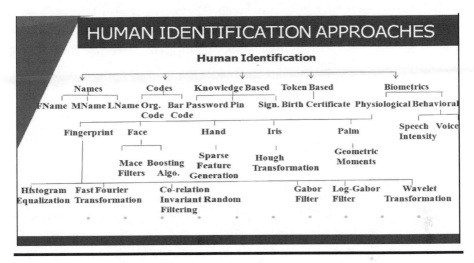

Figure 29.1 Human identification approaches.

29.3 Advantages and Disadvantages of Biometrics

29.3.1 Advantages

1. Biometric based security provides unmatched security over other traditional methods like passwords, token based, knowledge based etc.
2. It's a way of unique identification. i.e. no two fingerprints can be the same.
3. There is no need to remember the detail of security data like in other traditional methods.
4. Security through biometrics is less prone to be breached by software or online hackers.
5. Easy to use and socially acceptable.

29.3.2 Challenges

1. Major drawback of using biometrics as a means of secure communication is that if it is stolen once it is compromised for forever since it is unchanged for life.
2. In case of fingerprints, it is not so hygienic to use it for scanning because of its proneness towards viruses/germs.
3. During a long span of time biometrics can change. For example, face gets aged and can carry wrinkles etc.
4. In case of face recognition, twins might have identical faces. Thus, it's very difficult to differentiate and identify them.

29.4 Uni-modal versus Multimodal Biometrics

Selection of biometric identification system is critically important before pre-deployment as to whether it should be uni-modal or multimodal system. There are positives and negatives associated with each of them; however, in cases where high accuracy and security is a primary concern, multimodal biometric is an obvious choice. These systems are the best suited solution for industries with high security and privacy. Multimodal provides higher security because two biometric credentials are used in order to authenticate, while in uni-modal systems its only one credential. That is the reason why multimodal biometric identification has an edge over uni-modal identification and traditional authentication.

There are a few characteristics that support the deployment of multimodal biometrics like reliable authentication, high accuracy, high security, acceptance of user and vulnerability. Multimodal biometrics provide reliable authentication and it allows a higher degree of assurance of correct verification and accurate authentication. In multimodal biometrics, multiple biological characteristics are taken into consideration and each one adds additional evidence for authenticity of an individual. For example, gaits of two persons can be similar because of the same family/background because sometimes people from the same family may depict the similar behavior/patterns of movements and the security based upon gaits might not be as accurate as with multimodal or may lead to false recognition. In such a case, multimodal biometrics always has an edge over uni-modal since it can extract more information which is unique in nature, i.e. if gait and iris biometrics are used together, the recognition rate will increase because it is impossible that two people will have similar gait/iris characteristics.

Security is another critical parameter which gets improved with the use of multimodal biometric because multiple patterns are involved and a system can preserve higher threshold settings and a decision on the required security can be made. It depends on the degree of security required; if the security requirement is critical then two or more biometrics can be taken into consideration and if security is marginal then only one biometric is sufficient in order to indentify an individual. For enhanced security, up to three biometric can be taken into consideration so that even if the identification system fails for some reason, another biometric can be used and chances of any error or probability of admitting an imposter can be reduced significantly.

Spoofing is another challenge for any security system. It is one of the biggest threat's for biometric systems and can lead to a vulnerable situation. Spoofing is a result of breaking down the security and pretending to be someone else which leads to an unauthorized access and thus a breach of security. Researchers used an artificial biometric database and tested for its authentication vulnerability and exhibited that they got matched for more than 50% data. In order to avoid these scenarios, liveness detection is a good choice where blood flow, pulse and temperature can be taken into consideration in the case of a fingerprint as a biometric.

Multimodal biometric is helpful in these sorts of situations to bridge the gap created by artificial data.

As far as accuracy is concerned, it can be measured in terms of image acquisition errors and matching errors. The causes of image acquisition errors are failure to acquire the actual impression of an image, failure to enroll and matching errors, which are the result of false non match rate and false match rates. As discussed earlier, uni-modal biometric uses only a single biometric trait in order to indentify an individual while multimodal biometrics use multiple traits. Thus, if there is some issue regarding the identification of an individual like sweat on the fingerprint or common behavioral traits of son and father, uni-modal biometric is not able to provide the correct authentication at times. In these sorts of cases, multimodal biometrics ensures authentic identification and provides a higher degree of security. User acceptance is also very high with multimodal biometrics; this is evident because multiple countries are using multimodal biometrics-based authentication for an individual. In systems, where security and accuracy are of critical importance, multimodal biometrics-based systems have become pervasive.

29.5 Multimodal Biometric: Benefits and Limitations

Inaccuracy of traditional authentication modalities and inadequate efficacy of uni-modal biometric systems leads to the necessity of multimodal based security systems to provide better recognition and accurate authentication.

Privacy is a serious concern in multimodal biometrics-based systems. The design of these systems must ensure that there should not be any threat of personal or information privacy. It's a vital aspect of any security system. All collected personal information should be used for its intended purpose only.

In areas where security is a prime concern, a single error can create a chaotic picture or disturb things, for example, in healthcare or the financial sector. Moreover, all the countries (developed and developing) are using multimodal based identification systems to identify their citizens uniquely and provide them benefits given from the government.

29.6 Watermarking of Biometric Data

Concealing the information into a document in the form of text or image to verify the authenticity or the identity is called as digital watermarking (shown in Figure 29.2). Verifying the authenticity has become challenging with the overflowing content shared online. Digital watermarking poses a solution to such a serious problem in order to protect their materials from being duplicated without their permission. It motivates the separation among copies of the same data in an indistinguishable manner. Major benefits of this technique are its robustness and its invisibility without

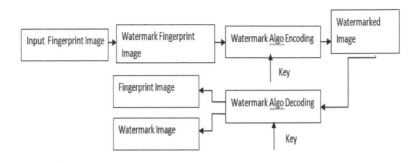

Figure 29.2   Block diagram for fingerprint watermarking.

degrading the data quality of an image. These days, modern sensors have high resolution for the contactless acquisition of required information from different biometrics. However, the biggest challenge is the privacy protection assurance for scanned latent fingerprints which is an individual's private information. To protect the personal information and ensuring the privacy of a person, an encryption method can be used. However, using compression and encryption/decryption, the quality of the original image can be reduced up to a certain level. Thus, there is a technique required where, without compromising the quality of an image, privacy can be achieved at its highest level (shown in Figure 29.3).

The watermarking technique applied on fingerprint images is used to ensure the security of data and comes under the widespread publicly accepted security mechanism. As biometric security is getting higher public acceptance than ever before, digital watermarking is playing a crucial role in security domains. A balance between identification efficiency and security of fingerprint impressions is required to provide efficient security results. Different methods like text watermarking and image watermarking and others are used as security mechanisms, however, because of the need to maintain the trade-off between identification efficacy and system's complexity. In order to improve the performance of a recognition system, watermarking techniques are used widely and provide

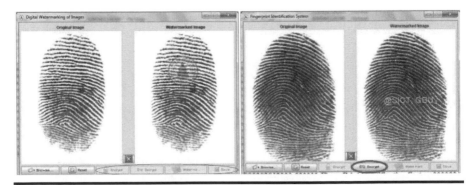

Figure 29.3   Fingerprint images after image and text watermarking.

impressive results in real life. During the process of watermarking, text and image watermarks can be used in order to provide the protection to person-related data [36]. Image and text watermarking of an image can be done in the following ways. Following algorithms can effectively address the security concerns and are used to improve the recognition performance without compromising the fingerprint quality.

29.6.1 Image Watermarking

Process for Image Watermarking:

1. A fingerprint image is captured with fingerprint scanner and stored. It is kept in BufferedImage where its pixels, RGB colors and other characteristics are preserved.
2. Extract image data and calculate the values of different characteristics by using BufferedImage.
3. Color model object and Raster object are two parts of an image which is an object of BufferedImage.
4. Color model is used to extract pixel data of an image and translates it into color component i.e. red, green and blue in a computer. A rectangular array of pixels is represented by the Raster.
5. Sample values are stored in a Databuffer and to locate a sample value, a sample model can be used. Raw image data and samplemodel which describes organization of data in the buffer is held by a Databuffer.
6. Map Graphics object to a Graphics 2D object and then image is drawn on the screen.
7. SetComposite method is used, which specifies the combination of pixels, and is combined with already available pixels present in the background. Transparency of the shape is controlled by setting the alpha value which is related with composite rule. Transparency value is measured in the form of Opaque and by default it is 1.0f.
8. Then draw the image by using Graphics 2D and the watermarked BufferedImage is saved.

29.6.2 Text Watermarking

1. A fingerprint image is captured with a fingerprint scanner and stored. It is kept in BufferedImage where its pixels, RGB colors and other characteristics are preserved.
2. Extract image data and calculate the values of different characteristics by using BufferedImage.
3. Color model object and Raster object are two parts of an image which is an object of BufferedImage.
4. Color model is used to extract pixel data of an image and translates it into color components i.e. red, green and blue in a computer. A rectangular array of pixels is represented by the Raster.

5. Sample values are stored in a Databuffer; to locate a sample value, a sample model can be used. Raw image data and samplemodel which describes organization of data in the buffer is held by a Databuffer.

6. Map Graphics object to a Graphics 2D object and then the image will be drawn on the screen.

7. SetComposite method is used which specifies the combination of pixels combined with already available pixels present in the background. Transparency of the shape is controlled by setting the alpha value which is related with composite rule. Transparency value is measured in form of Opaque and by default it is 1.0f.

8. Then draw the text/string by using Graphics 2D and watermarked BufferedImage is saved.

9. In digital transactions and transmissions, biometrics offers an accurate, secure, efficient, flexible and cost effective communication model. On the other hand, there is a serious drawback that transmitted data can be compromised or duplicated very easily without the possibility of any deformations in the image or without introducing any anomalies or quality degradations and digital watermarking posses an effective solution because after watermarking original data is not accessible to everyone and It is not easy to tamper the watermarked data. In order to make any changes in the data or information, one must get the permission from the owner of that data, which is the reason why this topic is attracting researchers from throughout the world. Fingerprint digital watermarking is an electronic method to embed the text or image on fingerprints. Fingerprint identification is a significant method to provide the security to data or information. Watermarks may be in the form of text or images and used to provide protection to data from getting compromised and hence plays a significant role in secure systems. The broad classification of watermarking techniques can be as follows: image watermarking which is embedding an image over the data needs to be protected, video watermarking is a technique used to watermark the videos, audio watermarking is watermarking audio signal and text watermarking is to watermarked text over the data that needs to be protected. Another classification is based upon visibility of watermarks and it can be divided into further three categories as visible watermark, invisible robust watermark, and invisible fragile watermark. In visible watermarking, the watermark is visible on the image or information it is embedded upon. Traditionally, watermarked information is either text or logo and it is used to identify the owner of the media. The invisible robust watermark is not visible on the data and having equal brightness and intensity as original data. In un-watermarked content it is easy to create watermarks that are robust in nature or imperceptible; however, to design robust and imperceptible watermarks is not easy and very challenging. In invisible fragile watermarking, if any modification or alteration would be there in data or image, it will destroy the watermark and breach of security can be identified [38]. Digital watermarking can be classified as

source based and destination based watermarking. Source watermarking is required for ownership identification or authentication and is used where multiple copies of data are distributed and a unique watermark is used to recognize the owner and prevent the data from getting it compromised. In case of illegal reselling/distributing of data/information, destination based watermarking can be used. Hence, fingerprint watermarking is considered as an effective and accurate method to eliminate the issues regarding the security of data. In order to enhance the privacy of fingerprint data, watermarking techniques are an effective tool. It is kept in BufferedImage where its pixels, RGB colors and other characteristics are preserved. In this process, extract image data and calculate the values of different characteristics by using BufferedImage. Then Color model object and Raster object are two parts of an image that is an object of BufferedImage. The Color model is used to extract pixel data of an image and translates it into color components i.e., red, green and blue in a computer. A rectangular array of pixels is represented by the Raster. After this, sample values are stored in a Databuffer and to locate a sample value, a sample model can be used. Raw image data and samplemodel which describes organization of data in the buffer is held by a Databuffer (Figure 29.3).

29.7 Mosaicking on Biometrics

29.7.1 Fingerprint Quality Improvement by Using Mosaicking Technique

29.7.1.1 Introduction

It is evident that security systems and forensics are the main application areas of biometrics. Sometimes, it has been observed and found that it is not necessary to capture the fingerprints in a complete or perfect shape and size from the crime scenes or even from the scanners. Sometimes it is about the angle used to scan the image, carelessness of using the image acquisition devices, environment, climate conditions, injury on the fingertip or sweating that makes image acquisition of low quality or incomplete in nature. With the wrong angle, only a limited portion is being captured and that is the time when it becomes very complicated to use this as a measure of security. It is very difficult to identify an individual based on partial/incomplete impression. Mosaicking is the solution to this sort of condition where impartial data is being captured by image acquisition device. Also, it is a popular area of investigation among the researchers these days.

This method is used to provide authentic access and security to the data needs to be protected. Fingerprint mosaicking algorithms provides accurate and precise solution and address the issues related with biometric security and ensuring no loss in the quality of fingerprint impression and high performance can be achieved [38].

Two stages of fingerprint verification i.e. enrollment stage and authentication stage are the components of fingerprint identification systems. In the enrollment stage, fingerprint images are captured and saved in the database. Multiple images of the same fingerprint are stored during image acquisition stage so that the image from every angle can be captured, which can be used to ultimately design the composite image from various impressions and used in the future for verification of authentic user. In the authentication stage, stored fingerprint impressions are matched against the query template. Various applications used by commercial, financial and other sectors use solid state sensors. And solid state sensors are known for the acquisition of limited amount of ridges and valleys from the fingertip impression. This limited information acquired from fingertips is not sufficient for effective authentication. Thus, the performance of fingerprint identification system will get affected because the overlap region captured from the query image and stored impression is small and consists of fewer numbers of ridges and minutia which increase the false rejection or genuine acceptance rates [37].

Fingerprint mosaicking is a perfect solution for this problem and it is designed in the form of a composite image by combining multiple impressions and this composite image of fingerprint is generated more information and requires less space rather than storing multiple impressions which is used to improve matching efficiency by reducing matching time.

Another reason of reduced acquisition performance of sensors is that they cover the small amount of area, which is why it does not provide sufficient information about the fingerprint impressions that is required. This also creates a negative impact over the identification efficiency. Fingerprint mosaicking is a technique used to create an approximation of an image from multiple dab images. These images are captured while user dabs (presses) the fingertip on the image acquisition device. If the rolled image is created from these dabbed images and after merging them, it improves fingerprint area and low quality fingerprint impressions.

Mosaicking can be classified as touch based and touchless based mosaicking. When the images are collected through the sensors where the fingerprint comes in the physical contact of a scanner. The fingertip actually needs to be swiped on the screen of sensors and then mosaicking will take place and composite template is created. Another type of mosaicking is touchless based where fingerprint acquisition is done without physical contact. Rather than using the sensors to swipe the fingers, cameras and CCD are used to acquire the image. This way of image acquisition is used to avoid image deformations which are the results of non-uniform pressure, dirt or any other reason like this and provides better results than touch based image acquisition (Figure 29.4).

The outcome of both matching process is compared and will be analyzed. An algorithm is demonstrated in following steps:

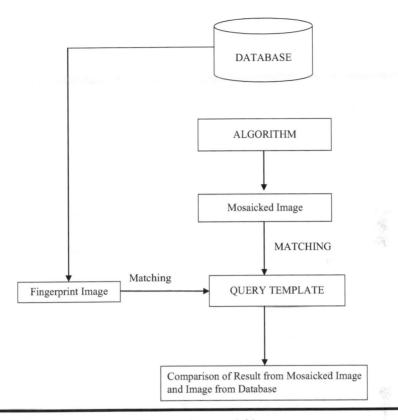

Figure 29.4   Block diagram of fingerprint mosaicking process.

29.7.1.2 *Fingerprint Mosaicking Algorithm*

1. Two or more fingerprints of an image are acquired by acquisition devices to create a composite image.
2. Then apply fast fourier transformation (FFT) and calculate conjugate of the result after FFT. Afterwards, calculate the parameters like height and width of images after mosaicking.
3. After mosaicking, load the image for further processing and save the mosaicked image in the database.
4. Then minutia extraction of mosaicked fingerprint image will take place.
5. Minutia extraction of query image will get processed.
6. Then comparing both the images and matching algorithm will check the efficacy of the process.
7. Performance analysis of the process.

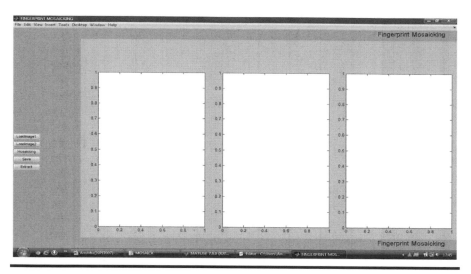

Figure 29.5   GUI interface.

29.7.1.3 Experimental Results

The following screenshots are representing the process of fingerprint mosacking:

1. Graphical User Interface (Figure 29.5).
2. Fingerprint images are loaded (Figure 29.6).
3. Mosaicked Image is generated (Figure 29.7).

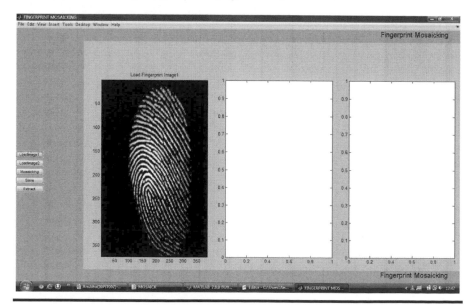

Figure 29.6   Loading fingerprint image in the axes.

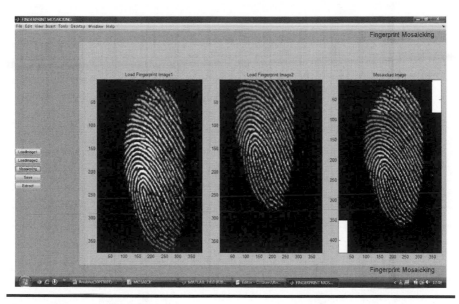

Figure 29.7   Mosaicked image.

4. After mosaicked image generation, it is saved in the database for matching process (Figure 29.8).
5. For template matching another GUI is called (Figure 29.9).
6. Query image and stored image are being compared and for that image is fetched from the database (Figure 29.10).

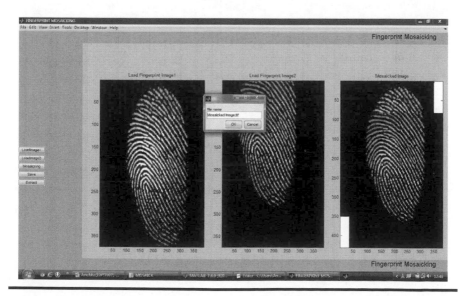

Figure 29.8   Saving the mosaicked image.

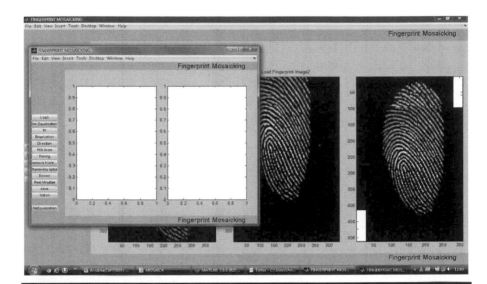

Figure 29.9   GUI for matching.

Figure 29.10   Fingerprint image loaded for matching.

7. Histogram equalization of loaded fingerprint image is done (Figure 29.11).
8. FFT is performed on the image generated (Figure 29.12).
9. Binarization of the fingerprint image is done, i.e. it is being converted in the form of 0 and 1 (Figure 29.13).

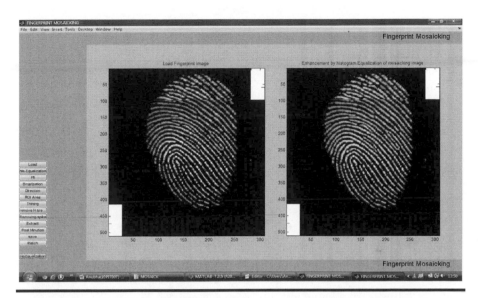

Figure 29.11   Histogram equalized image.

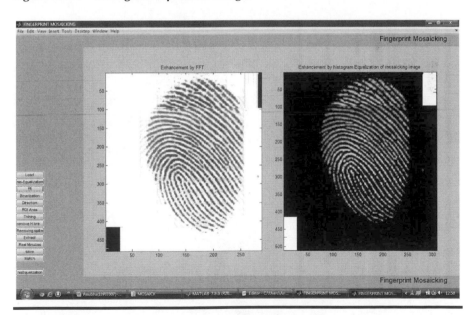

Figure 29.12   First fourier transformed fingerprint image.

10. Ridge direction is found (Figure 29.14).
11. Region of interest (ROI) is calculated (Figure 29.15).
12. Thinning of the ridges is done (Figure 29.16).
13. H-Breaks are removed after thinning process (Figure 29.17).

Figure 29.13   Binarization of image.

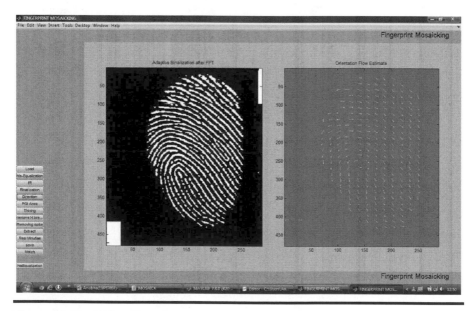

Figure 29.14   Ridge direction.

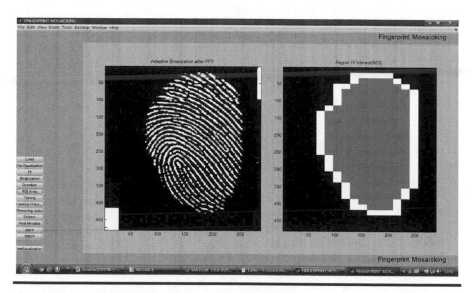

Figure 29.15　ROI image.

Figure 29.16　Thinning image.

Figure 29.17   H-breaks removed fingerprint image.

Figure 29.18   Spikes removal image.

14. Spikes are deleted from the fingerprint image that can create a false impression of ridge existence (Figure 29.18).
15. Minutiae extraction is done (Figure 29.19).
16. False minutiae that exist in the above image are removed and real minutiae that are helpful in matching process are extracted (Figure 29.20).

Figure 29.19   Minutiae extracted image.

Figure 29.20   Real minutiae extracted image.

17. Save the minutiae extracted image in the database (Figure 29.21).
18. Matching procedure is called to match query template with stored image (Figure 29.22).
19. Output of matching process (Figure 29.23).

Figure 29.21 Image saved in database.

Figure 29.22 Matching of fingerprint templates.

29.7.2 Fingerprint Quality Improvement with the Help of Discrete Wavelet Transformation

29.7.2.1 Image Enhancement Approach

In the fingerprint identification process, de-noising is a critical issue. There are different de-noising methods used to make fingerprint image soothing or noise free. Most of them are used to make image distortion free. Usually, noise/distortion

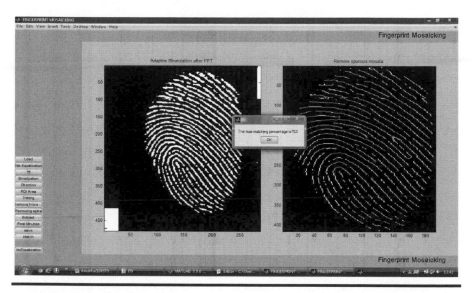

Figure 29.23 Matching result.

has a different frequency than the original signal captured from fingerprint data. Fingerprint image enhancement process is used to increase the intensity of the complete image and then normalize it with the mapping of certain threshold value. An image enhancement algorithm is used for the same purpose. So, the segmentation process is required to keep the fingerprint in the frame of specified region [37]. For this purpose fingerprint image decomposition is used in a non-overlapping manner. This type of decomposition and analysis of variance involved is used for separation of foreground and background portions which include ridges and furrows, respectively. The following steps are taken into account for image enhancement:

1. **Normalization**
2. **Wavelet Decomposition**
3. **Noise Removal from each block**
4. **Match with threshold value**
5. **Reconstruction of image**

Ridge orientation (direction) and frequency are issues of primary concern. Ridge orientation is a major characteristic used for fingerprint identification [37]. As far as frequency domain is considered, fingerprint ridges and furrows are responsible to form a wave that is sinusoidal in nature with certain frequency, direction, angles, and is critical for identification systems in terms of accuracy. It is evident from the research done in this area that to efficiently analyze the frequency spectrums of the signals and for their appropriate application, discrete wavelet transformation (DWT) can be used. A finite impulse response (FIR) filter which is low pass in nature is depicted by a scaling filter and defined as an orthogonal wavelet.

Wavelets are defined by the wavelet function Ψ (t) (i.e. the mother wavelet) and scaling function $\Phi(t)$, the father wavelet in the time domain [10].

Image filtering is necessary for image smoothing and noise removal. Since a low pass filter is used to decrease the disparity between pixel values, thus an orthogonal wavelet low pass FIR filter is used for noise removal/image smoothing. The general formula for filter will be:

$$F(t) = 1\ ; \ \textit{if} \quad f < (\text{threshold} - \omega)$$

$$F(t) = 0\ ; \ \textit{if} \quad f > (\text{threshold} - \omega)$$

where:

f is representing the filter

ω is representing the wavelength of wavelet

threshold value is used for wavelet co-efficient thersholding

Among different types of wavelet transforms, DWT is critically sampled and most widely used [5,11].

The following dilation and wavelet equations are used to represent a multi-resolution framework: also scaling function and wavelets are represented through it.

$$\varphi(t) = \sqrt{2} \sum_{1}^{n} ho(n)\varphi\,(2t - n)$$

$$\Psi i(t) = \sqrt{2} \sum_{1}^{n} hi(n)\varphi\,(2t - n)$$

where:

$i = 1, 2$

$hi(n), n \in \mathbb{Z}$

$\varphi(t)$ is representing as scaling function and $\Psi i(t)$ is representing wavelet after dilation while hi is depicting as filters of digital filter bank. If $hi(n)$ satisfy the perfect reconstruction conditions given below and if $\varphi(t)$ is sufficiently regular, then the dyadic dilations and translations of $\Psi i(t)$ form a tight frame for $L^2(R)$.

Researchers discussed about the expansive wavelet transform that oversample the time and frequency by some factor, in this case it is 2. The transform has intermediate scales as one scale between each pair of scales of the critically sampled DWT. The wavelet frame has two generators (t); where $i = 1, 2$ that means the spectrum of the first wavelet is concentrated between the spectrum of the second wavelet and the spectrum of its dilated versions i.e. $\Psi i(t)$ is concentrated between $\Psi 2(t)$ and $\Psi 2(2t)$. The second wavelet is translated by integer multiples of one half rather than whole integers.

Now our objective is simple to develop a set of filters that generate a tight wavelet frame and to achieve this we will find the conditions on the filters. Low pass filter h0 is considered for Z transform. If we consider that $P(n)$ and $Q(n)$ are the values of input and output signals correspondingly then the Z transform will be

$$Q(Z) = \sum_{k=0}^{n} q(n)\, Z^{-k}$$

After rearrangements,

$$Q(n) = \sum_{k=0}^{n} q[k]\delta[n-k] \rightarrow Q[Z] = \sum_{0}^{n} q[k](Z^{-1})^{k}$$

This derives that the low pass filter ho is not a factor of a maximally flat linear phase filter and ho is a finite impulse response filter in this case and h0 and h1 are anti-symmetric. $\delta[n-k]$ represents time delayed impulses that are added up from $k = 0$ to n.

The process for noise removal for fingerprint images uses the structure like this:

1. Decompose the image into some blocks.
2. Denoise each block with the discrete wavelet transform
3. Reconstruct the fingerprint image

In this chapter, construction of wavelets will depend on vanishing moments. Vanishing moments are features of wavelets.

29.7.2.2 An Algorithm for Image Enhancement: Normalization – To Normalize an Image

1. Calculate the iterative fast fourier transformation then consider its square for every fragment of power spectrum.
2. Normalize it by fragment size and total energy.
3. Apply Gabor filter to filter the distorted portion of image.
4. Image quality value can be calculated by the sum of the two dimensional filtered spectrum of each and every fragment of an image.
5. For each image, identify the highest image quality fragment.
6. Convert this image quality to normalized image quality to make equivalence.
7. Weight Image quality by square of average grey values.
8. Cross check each fragment of image for image quality if uneven distribution appear, adjust image quality accordingly.
9. Scale the image.

29.7.2.3 Results after Algorithm Implementation (Figure 29.24)

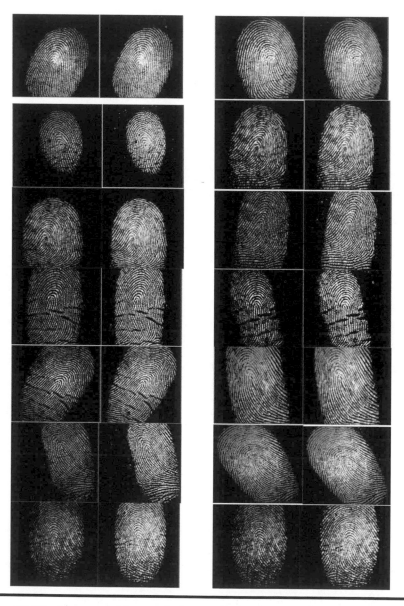

Figure 29.24 Fingerprint images before and after image enhancement.

(Continued)

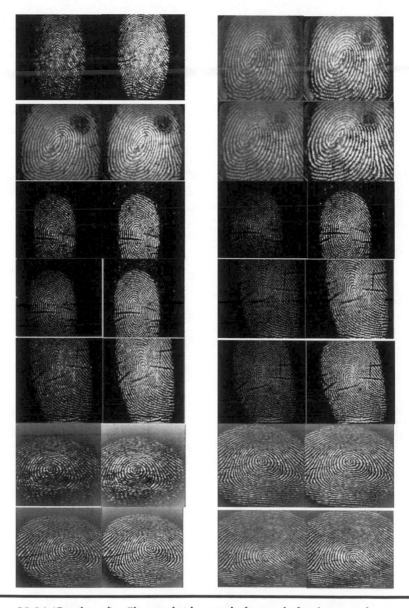

Figure 29.24 (Continued) **Fingerprint images before and after image enhancement.**

(Continued)

Figure 29.24 (Continued) Fingerprint images before and after image enhancement.

29.8 Conclusion

This chapter describes and discusses different aspects of security provided by biometrics. Broadly discussed security techniques are fingerprint watermarking and fingerprint mosaicking.

Extraction of minutia plays a critical role in order to calculate the reliability of fingerprint identification systems. Precision of minutia extraction process is directly proportional to the reliability of the security system. This chapter proposed an algorithm that constructs the mosaicked template by integrating the multiple impressions of same image and creating a composite image out of it. Extracted minutia points are used for matching purposes to establish a result whether the identity of the user is verified or not. The mosaicking algorithm discussed in the chapter depicts the creation of a composite image from multiple dabbed images and addresses effectively the problem of inefficiencies and inaccuracies encountered because of partially acquired fingerprint images that may result in an ineffective recognition. Also discussed was a process to deal with broken ridges/false minutia and their removal to provide improved security of the system.

Bibliography

1. Ailisto, H. L. (2004). A review of fingerprint image enhancement methods. *International Journal of Image and Graphics*, 3 (3): 401–424.
2. Simoncelli, E. P., Freeman, W. T., Adelson, E. H., and Heeger, D. J. (1992) Shiftable multiscale transforms. *IEEE Transactions on Information Theory*, 38 (2): 587–607.
3. Almansa, A. and Lindeberg, T. (2000). Fingerprint enhancement by shape adaptation of scale-space operators with automatic scale selection. *IEEE Transactions on Image Processing*, 9 (12): 2027–2042.
4. Amayeh, G. B. (2009). Improving hand based verification through online finger template update based on fused confidences. *IEEE Transactions on Pattern Recognition*, 978–984.
5. Ang, R. S. (2002). Systematic methods for the computation of the directional fields and singular points of fingerprints. *IEEE Transactions on Pattern Analysis and Machine Intelligence*, 24 (7): 905–919.
6. Beveridge, J. R. (2009). Factors that influence algorithm performance in the face recognition grand challenge. *Computer Vision and Image Understanding*, 113 (6): 750–762.
7. BhattaCharya, A. K. (2001). A modified texture filter for satellite images. *Asian Conference on Remote Sensing*, pp. 78–84.
8. Bian, Z. Z. (2002). Knowledge-based fingerprint postprocessing. *International Journal Pattern Recognition Artificial Intelligence*, 16 (1): 53–67.
9. Blotta, E. and Moler, E. (2004). Fingerprint image enhancement by differential hysteresis processing. *Forensic Science International*, 141(2–3): 109–113.
10. Boer, J. B. (2001). Indexing fingerprint database based on multiple features. *Proceedings of Workshop on Circuits, Systems, and Signal Processing*, pp. 58–66, 25–27 Nov 2003, Veldhoven, the Netherlands.

11. Bolle, R. M. and Pankanti, S. (2000). Evaluation techniques for biometrics-based authentication systems (FRR). *Proceedings of International Conference on Pattern Recognition (ICPR)*, 2: 2831–2837, 3–7 Sept. 2000, Barcelona, Spain.

12. Bolle, R. C. (2002). Biometrics perils and patches. *Transaction of Pattern Recognition*, 35 (12): 2727–2738, October 2001, Exploratory Computer Vision Group, IBM Thomas J. Watson Research Center, Yorktown Heights, NY 10598, USA.

13. Cappelli, R. D. (2001). Modeling plastic distortion in fingerprint images. *Advances in Pattern Recognition*, March 11–14, 369–376. Berlin, Germany: Springer, March 11–14, 2001, Springer-Verlag Berlin, Heidelberg.

14. Chang Huang, H. A. (2007). High-performance rotation invariant multiview face detection. *IEEE Transaction on Pattern Analysis and Machine Intelligence*, 671–686, IEEE Transactions.

15. Chikkerur, S. G. (2005). Minutia verification in fingerprint images using steerable wedge filters. *IEEE Transaction on Pattern Recognition and Machine Intelligence*, 45–51, IEEE Transactions.

16. Clarke, R. (1994). Human identification in information systems: Management challenges and public policy issues. *Information Technology & People*, 7 (4): 6–37, 4–7 December 1994, Canberra.

17. Dass, S. (2004). Markov random field models for directional field and singularity extraction in fingerprint images. *IEEE Transactions on Image Processing*, 13 (10): 1358–1367, IEEE Transactions.

18. Dodis, Y. R. (2004). Fuzzy extractors: How to generate strong keys from biometrics and other noisy data. *Proceedings of International Conference Theory and Applications of Cryptographic Techniques*, pp. 523–540. Berlin, Germany: Springer, 2–6 May 2004, Interlaken, Switzerland.

19. Eswara, R. B. (2007). Texture classification by simple patterns on edge direction movements. *International Journal of Computer Science and Network Security*, 7 (11): 220–225.

20. Farina, A. Z. (2001). Fingerprint minutiae extraction from skeletonized binary images. *Transaction of Pattern Recognition*, 32 (5): 877–889.

21. Fayyaz, A. M. (2004). Fingerprint identification and verification system using minutia matching. *National Conference on Emerging Technologies*, 2: 141–146, 4–6 December, Karachi, Pakistan.

22. Feng, Y. C. (2010). A hybrid approach for generating secure and discriminating face template. *IEEE Transactions on Information Forensics and Security*, 201–212.

23. Galy, N. C. (2007). A full fingerprint verification system for a single line sweep sensor. *IEEE Sensor Journal*, 7 (7): 1054–1065.

24. Zaidi, S., Singh, S. K., and Tarar, S. (2015). To evaluate the performance of fingerprint enhancement techniques. *India Conference (INDICON), 2015 Annual IEEE*.

25. Ghosal, S. U. (2000). Learning partitioned least squares filters for fingerprint enhancement. *IEEE Workshop on Applications of Computer Vision*, pp. 2–7.

26. Gonzalez, R. C. (2002). *Digital Image Processing*. Upper Saddle River, NJ: Prentice Hall.

27. Gonzalez, R. C. (2004). *Digital Image Processing using MATLAB*. New Delhi, India: Pearson Education and Dorling Kindersley Publishing.

28. Guo, G. J. (2008). Iris extraction based on intensity gradient and texture difference. *IEEE Workshop on Applications of Computer Vision*, pp. 211–216.

29. Hadhoud, M. M. (2007). An adaptive algorithm for fingerprints image enhancement using gabor filter. *Proceedings of IEEE*, pp. 77–89.

30. Hong, L. W. (1998). Fingerprint image enhancement: Algorithm and performance evaluation. *Transactions on Pattern Analysis and Machine Intelligence*, 20 (8): 777–789.
31. Hong, L. W. (2000). Fingerprint image enhancement: Algorithm and performance evaluation. *IEEE Transaction of Pattern Analysis and Machine Intelligence*, 20: 670–781.
32. Huang, Z. Q. (2001). Fingerprint image enhancement based on MRF with curve accumulation. *Proceeding of SPIE*, 4552: 45–50.
33. Jain, A. H. (2000). Biometrics: Promisingfrontiers for emerging identification market. *ACM Communications*, 43: 91–98.
34. Jain, A. H. (2002). On-line fingerprint verification. *IEEE Transaction on Pattern Analysis and Machine Intelligence*, 19 (4): 302–314.
35. Jain, A. P. (2004). Biometrics: A grand challenge. *Proceedings of International Conference on Pattern Recognition*, 2: 935–942.
36. Tarar, S. and Kumar, E. (2013). Fingerprint image enhancement: Iterative fast fourier transform algorithm and performance evaluation. *International Journal of Hybrid Information Technology SERSC, South Korea*, 6 (4), 11–20.
37. Tarar, S., Kumar, A., and Kumar, E. (2012). A fingerprint watermarking algorithm to enhance the privacy of fingerprint data. *WSEAS Transactions on Information Science and Applications*, 9 (8): 231–240.
38. Tarar, S. and Kumar, E. (2014). Fingerprint mosaicking algorithm to improve the performance of fingerprint matching system, *Computer Science and Information Technology*, 2 (3): 142–151.

Chapter 30

Application of Video-Based Face Recognition for Mobile Security Using Machine Learning Techniques

Emir Kremić and Abdulhamit Subasi

Contents

DOI: 10.1201/9780429435461-35

30.1 Introduction

With an increasing dependence on smartphones, mobile phones went beyond communication's purpose. Nowadays, smartphones are used to implement a wide range of daily tasks such as: banking, shopping, ordering food, etc. Moreover, mobile phones are becoming more complex to meet consumer's needs (Zualkernan, Aloul, Shapsough, Hesham, & El-Khorzaty, 2017).

The smartphone is a pervasive device used to simplify daily activities, such as storing personal information related to credit cards, user passwords, e-mail addresses or other credentials which may increase the severity and risk of identity theft (Sidek, Mai, & Khalil, 2014).

In this era, the reliability of real–time personal identification in mobile devices is a crucial requirement. The automatic identification of individuals built on their physical characteristics is called as biometric authentication, such as keystroke, voice, iris, gait, face and fingerprint. Although biometric identification systems can eliminate the limitations relevant to the use of passwords, they are vulnerable to spoofing attacks (Jain, Nandakumar, & Ross, 2016; Jain, Ross, & Nandakumar, 2011). Actually, gait and keystroke identification techniques are not very secure in terms of identification accuracy. Similarly, a face which is exposed as an artificial mask, a voice which might be imitated, a fingerprint which might be falsified by a gummy fingerprint, and an iris which might be duplicated by means of contact lenses, are also not robust against falsifications (Sidek et al., 2014). Recently, face recognition based on video was proposed as a potential biometric identification technique due to the robustness (Kremić & Subasi, 2016).

Mobility is a significant element of mobile biometrics. In order to keep personal information on mobile devices, for improved security the feasibility of person identification techniques on mobile devices is imperative. To confirm voters in elections, to identify customers in financial institutions, or to identify automobile drivers are possible by recognizing video-based biometric applications. In order to protect private information and individual identity against unauthorized access, these applications need to be consistent, reliable, and easy to implement for identification (Sidek et al., 2014). Nowadays, mobile devices and applications are increasing quickly, and the necessity for security in storing business and personal data or accessing web data is to use innovative biometric authentication techniques. In addition, traditional mobile login methods, like numerical or graphical passwords, and face recognition are vulnerable to passive attacks. Biometric characteristics such as voice recognition, iris scans, or fingerprints etc. can be changed easily and replaced if they are stolen. Video-based biometric authentication system can eliminate this problem (Kremić & Subasi, 2016).

Facial recognition from video is focused on the analysis and retention building that are the skills for self-learning and training in future artificial models of human recognition systems. The intention of this chapter is to syndicate the area of theory and practice. The model denoted and developed for face recognition from video for the mobile phone is implemented on an Android platform. The system is designed to work for *client–server* architecture. Research in the field of pattern recognition, machine learning, artificial intelligence, etc., are enabling us to apply and use such a novel mobile application development system. Such application does not aggregate the subject of machine learning, nor pattern recognition for video to still image face recognition, yet it combines the skills of software development integrated into smart applications by extending the human security as a future model of authentication. Such a problem does not only include achieving higher accuracy, but it involves building a stable model that will be referenced for its extended version in future development.

A very common verification method applied on mobile phone is the *Personal Identification Number (PIN)*. In this chapter, we present the work related to the implementation face authentication. Therefore, we will stress on theoretical approaches, accuracy of the methods and implementation. The aim is to present the client–server model for video to still image that works on Android Samsung Galaxy Note 10.1, as well on Samsung Galaxy S. Even biometry inherits advantages over the traditional model. The problem of ensuring the security and integrity of biometric data is critical (Alhussain, Drew, & Alfarraj, 2010). Individuals have a good sense for recognizing and identifying known faces. However, humans are not proficient when they are transacting a multifarious number of faces that are unfamiliar. Even today, video recognition is not a fully solved problem in face recognition. A great deal of aforementioned research related to biometric has examined the fusion of modalities at score and decision levels (Mian, 2011). Actually, Woodrow W. Bledsoe, back in 1960s, was initially the first engineer who started working in the area of face recognition (Bledsoe, 1966). Bledsoe's work was for an intelligence agency and very few papers were published related to the area of his work. Chan and Bisson, beside Bledsoe, have worked by applying the computer for recognition of the human faces (Mian, 2011). Development of a semi-automatic system was used as a prototype for the facial recognition system. Computers were using information for face recognition from the semi-automatic system, where data of collected faces was determined by face coordinates input by humans.

Even now face recognition is an undeveloped area of video-based work; however, research has grown in recent years. It represents an innovative obstacle to explore and that is recognizing face images from video signals. In near future, modern laptops will be replaced by mobile phones. Consequently, the goal is to develop and design a constant security structure determined by application of facial recognition from video signal and to empower better security advancements. Determination is important, since almost all the main businesses are running on mobile phones these days. Hence, it is decisive to design a mobile phone with a developing biometric system for automated face recognition. It is very difficult to distinguish if it is easy for humans to extract facial expressions independently from the identity of the subject. How can a biological implementation of a computerized face recognition system identify faces? Sinha et al. (2006) have presented the key goal of computer vision for creating automated face recognition which is divided to nineteen parts, all based upon biometric facial security implemented on mobile devices (Kremić, 2011). Today we have come to an extent where we are presenting the face recognition from video still image for android mobile phones. In this chapter, we will present our work as well as the accomplished work of Kremić and Subasi (2016) vis a vis facial recognition solutions.

30.2 Background

In the recent years, smartphones play an important role for the adaptation of security mechanisms based on biometrics. Different types of modalities have been used to implement mobile based biometric recognition such as the use of face, gait and iris (Derawi, Nickel, Bours, & Busch, 2010; Kurkovsky, Carpenter, & MacDonald, 2010; Kwapisz, Weiss, & Moore, 2010; Tao & Veldhuis, 2010), electrocardiogram (ECG), (Biel, Pettersson, Philipson, & Wide, 2001; Choi, Lee, & Yoon, 2016; Islam, Alajlan, Bazi, & Hichri, 2012; Kang, Lee, Cho, & Park, 2016; Merone, Soda, Sansone, & Sansone, 2017; Odinaka et al., 2012; Odinaka, O'Sullivan, Sirevaag, & Rohrbaugh, 2015; Safie, Soraghan, & Petropoulakis, 2011; Sidek & Khalil, 2013; Sidek et al., 2014; Venugopalan, Savvides, Griofa, & Cohen, 2014) and electroencephalogram (EEG) (Campisi & La Rocca, 2014; Chen et al., 2016; Fraschini, Hillebrand, Demuru, Didaci, & Marcialis, 2015; Klonovs, Petersen, Olesen, & Hammershoj, 2013; Kumari & Vaish, 2015; Rodrigues, Silva, Papa, Marana, & Yang, 2016). Face, fingerprint, iris and DNA determine biological and/or behavioural characteristics of the individual used for biometric identification (Da Silva, Fred, Lourenço, & Jain, 2013). Therefore, principles of uniqueness, universality and acceptability are achieved by these personalities (Jain, Bolle, & Pankanti, 2006). Furthermore, research for the development of a biometric identification system based on an individual's characteristics with uniqueness, universality, and acceptability is needed for biometric applications to achieve biometric identification tasks through user-friendly systems.

The potential solutions by implementing a biometric security system for authentication can play a positive role, because necessity of security is needed to secure stored data with individual information or business information. This is very important because with mobile phones, when connected on corporate networks, the safety and protection of data could be at risk. Therefore, there exists a need to implement cutting-edge biometric techniques (Klonovs et al., 2013). Moreover, traditional mobile login methods like numerical or graphical passwords, and face recognition are vulnerable to passive attacks. Biometric characteristics are the fingerprints, iris scans, or voice recognition etc. Biometric authentication characteristics have one major drawback though—they cannot easily be changed and are impossible to replace if they are stolen. A biometric authentication system based on ECG and/or EEG can overcome this issue, but they need a more complicated EEG and ECG data acquisition device. Furthermore, it is common for intruders to gain access to personal information of their victims by watching them enter their passwords into their mobile screens from a close proximity (Arteaga-Falconi, Al Osman, & El Saddik, 2016). With this in mind, a mobile biometric authentication algorithm based on ECG and/or EEG is proposed. With this proposal, the user will safely login to the mobile device to gain access as well.

Mobility has become an increasingly important element of mobile biometric. The feasibility of subject identification techniques on mobile devices is imperative because of the demanding requirement for improved security to store personal information on mobile devices. Possible mobile biometric applications such as identifying customers in financial institutions, confirming voters in elections or even identifying automobile drivers are conceivable future applications. These circumstances need consistent, reliable and easy to use identification methods to protect personal information and individual identity against unauthorized access (Sidek et al., 2014).

Mian (2011) described an online learning approach to video based on a face recognition system. Video recognition in the past few years has increased. During the literature review we have not come across the research done yet related to mobile systems. The capacity of mobile phones and its processing power has increased (Choi, Toh, & Byun, 2011b). The work (Choi et al., 2011b) is dealing with research regarding the limited factors in low-quality image, limited computing power, limited memory and batch-based asymmetric trainings. Face recognition belongs to the non-linear problems. Biometric models of facial recognition are found to be very unstable because of emotional instability. Arandjelović & Cipolla (2009) argue that biometric security is different from classic methods and the advantages of biometric models of security over traditional methods are that biometric models cannot be stolen.

30.3 Material and Method

Recognition of face and video consists of three main approaches: face detection and face normalization, feature extraction, identification and verification. In previous research that was conducted—face recognition from video sequence—this method has originated from a still image. There are few systems that were implemented where video sequence was an input, and the output was trying to identify the faces in the video. Most of the research in literature is related to different classification methods for recognizing faces from video, and in most cases a single image. What they have been showing in their research studies is extraction of 2D and 3D faces from video. Mian (2011) has shown extensive work related to the face recognition model.

The early research was described in Kumar, Singh, and Kumar (2010) by introducing the example based learning for view based human face detection. In Jain and Li (2011) a probabilistic method and research of application has been introduced. A very common technique being used among studies and literature is the PCA (principle component analysis). In many research projects (Kremić, 2011; Kremić & Subasi, 2016; Kremić, Subasi, & Hajdarevic, 2012) the client server model for face recognition related to mobile phone authentication has been introduced.

Eigenface based: In a work by Sirovich and Kirby (1987) was an established approach for efficient application of facial expression with PCA techniques (Kremić, 2011; Kremić & Subasi, 2016; Kremić et al., 2012). Their goal of the approach is to represent a face as a coordinate system. The vectors that make up this coordinate system were referred to as Eigen pictures. Later, Turk and Pentland (Marques, 2010) used this approach to develop a eigenface-based algorithm for recognition. A known problem of visual pattern recognition is face recognition (Marques, 2010). The face is considered a 3D (three dimensional) object with its varying illumination, pose and expression. In order to be identified, it is transformed into two dimensional images. As shown in Figure 30.1, we can see that process of face recognition consists of four models. Those models are: (1) detection, (2) alignment, (3) feature extraction and (4) matching.

The face detection process segments the face areas from the background. Face alignment has the goal of achieving more accurate localization where face detection

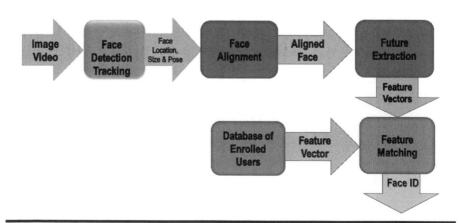

Figure 30.1 Process flow of recognition model.

provides estimates of the location and scale of each detected face. As explained by Arandjelović and Cipolla (2009), and Kumar, Singh, and Kumar (2010), facial components such as eyes, nose, mouth and facial outline are located on the location points. The feature extraction process is done after the face is normalized geometrically and photometrical. The approach of the face extraction is very important to perform because it provides information that is useful in distinguishing different faces among many in a database. In the process of face matching, extracted feature vectors of the input face are matched. There exist different pattern approaches, but here it is presented with PCA and has been implemented and integrated with mobile application for face recognition.

30.3.1 Overview

In the very early development of our history the modus of artificial recognition has been used. There a few handful examples as fingerprints and hand print pictures. The fingerprints were innovative and brought through Babylon merchants. The fingerprint was first time introduced around 500 B.C. Referring to hand print pictures in caves created approximately 3100 years ago shows this thinking belongs to prehistoric man. The very first phase of studying is image processing. The second part, or to say upgraded version, of continuation of this study is the model of face recognition. In 1970 (Kresimir, Grgic, & Marian, 2008) has described the proposal of face recognition within modern technology development. The method by name PCA is the first that has been proposed and is in use still today. The mote and purpose of researching such an application is in connection with security models; some examples are electronic passports, applications using login methods, biometric security and others. Besides research that has been developed in image processing and analysis, biometric research plays a role in every day of life (Kresimir et al., 2008). The reason is because face recognition presents the key security identification model that is in connection with a biometric system. As well, the face recognition model is under very active research in the fields of computer vision and pattern recognition (Kresimir et al., 2008).

30.3.2 Human Biometric System

The face recognition was developed under the area of image analysis. Such a model is very thought-provoking to work and develop. The focus is to be able, with an artificial computer, to differentiate the face's surface. The ordinary human–person is reasonably good in knowing and identifying faces (as well objects) that they previously have learned and memorized. Many questions arise in this research and some of those are:

1. *In terms of memory how are all of these objects over the years being stored into human brain?*
2. *What is the memory?*

3. *How are we able to memorize and to learn to distinguish all people among all that we have learned?*
4. *How many humans are capable to fast learn new faces and to be able to instantly know them, to identify them and to recognize them?*
5. *Are humans capable to recognize, let's say in one hour of glancing at a thousand faces, to recognize them instantly? What is the rate?*

Individuals are good in knowing, recognizing and identifying faces that are known to them. And working on this research and development is very strenuous, where the goal is to develop the system that will be able to recognize faces and objects. Woodrow W. Bledsoe (1966), back in the 1960s and Marques (2010) and Martin, Lu, Bui, Plataniotis, and Hatzinakos, (2009) were the very first engineers who worked to solve this problem. Their work has been related to several intelligence agencies and to the U.S. Department of Defense (Marques, 2010; Martin et al., 2009). Afterwards, upon completing research for the intelligence agencies, a very limited number of research reports related to subject of face recognition were published. In the research paper published in 1968 by Bledsoe, "Semiautomatic facial recognition" showed what has been conducted at Stanford Research Institute. Beside Bledsoe there are Chan and Bisson who have contributed in a process of computer automations for recognizing faces. A semi-automatic system was the very first in applying the automatic computer-oriented face recognition and identification model. The model was able to select coordinates and to use this information for recognition. Still, 50 years after this has been introduced we are still looking for answers to learn more and to develop a system with very high accuracy. The inconsistences where we are seeking answers are in:

- Illumination
- The facial expressions
- The human head rotation

Measurements of face feature, for example to measure ear size or to measure the distance between eyes, has conducted in Bell Laboratories under Goldstein, Harmon and Lesk (Goldstein et al., 1971). Measuring features automatically has begun under research of Fischler and Elshanger in 1973 (Fischler et al., 1973; Marques, 2010). The techniques of eigenface in image processing extensively known as Principle Component Analysis (PCA) was introduced by Sirovich and Kirby who have subjugated for all these years. Moreover, this research developed its child under new roads as the application and research related to recognizing objects and humans from video. Over the years and for years to come technology will change; for example, smart phones are replacing laptops and due to this transfer in technology the research will play a major role in security. This will be very significant since most of our business and personal plans are stored and we are running all of this information retrieved out of our mobile devices. In particular, a concept is to develop a computer-oriented system with an application of for various machine techniques that will be able to automatically detect human faces from different technological thresholds.

30.3.3 Connection of Brain

The difficulty of recognizing inverted faces in a class of stimuli was the research question of Diamond and Carey back in 1968 (Diamond et al., 1986). In the conclusion, they emphasized that faces were not unique, under the term when they are expected to represent in memory with special features. In (Kremić et al., 2012) was described that their concept was sustained with patients who have prognosis. These were a special neurological conditions and they were very challenging for identifying familiar images (Marques, 2010; Martin et al., 2009).

Development of information immediately begins with our thoughts in our brain, since the brain can be considered a human operating system and is the most complex system in our nature; for example, humans are capable of watching TV and typing on a computer while watching TV. Therefore, the process of these two activities is performing simultaneously in our brain.

We could say *Neural networks are nonlinear and highly complex system.* The future brings us to the edge where the imagination of science fiction is becoming reality and today we are working on machines that are able to share processes and to work simultaneously like a human brain. The impact of research in artificial neural networks is showing the blooming efforts in the performance of machine computing. The study is established and rooted in understanding brain activates. As we have said, the brain represents complex systems, nonlinear systems and parallel computing systems; moreover, the edifice of the brain is made out of neurons. Information in the brain is being constantly processed. For example, when we see someone who is familiar or known to us, our brain, through our system, is able to recognize and to tell who the person is. By recognizing a person, our brain in association with our memory system and visual system is performing the task of a facial recognition system. The aim is to develop a computational system to perform recognition based on human roots. By implementing such a system, it is evident that any computational facial recognition system will perform faster in recognizing humans than the human itself. One of the question that rises is: *How much time will a computer need to be able to execute the model?* The view is broader and must be comprehensive. In the first phase, the artificial system must be acquainted with the set of procedures. In the following step, a model needs to be trained. In one particular study, the model has been trained with one thousand images. Conducted image were stored in a database. In the humble judgment this represents a high level of computing. Neurophysiologist McCulloch and the logician Pits in 1943 produced AI neuron. The idea is to develop a model that will be able to participate in cognitive methods.

30.3.4 Module of Visual Protection

Protection of data has been the task for many decades. Entering the digital age, we have begun with the age of digital privacy. Based on that, we are focusing on improving the model of data protection via introducing the model of facial recognition. Very basic elements in relation with digital data protection are cryptography and computer image and vision system.

30.3.5 Method

Emphasize of this work is to describe and to prototype the model that will be able to significantly expand security on mobile phones. Birth of this research was delivered from digital image processing and artificial intelligence. Now we are witness to the application of artificial intelligence in biometric security, facial recognition, etc. An introduced model, under which we have conducted methodology, development, testing, etc., represents improvements in security aligned with recognition of faces from static and dynamic signals. It represents characteristics of security in communication between server and mobile phone. Therefore, the communication is handled via protocols Simple Object Access Protocol - SOAP. Images conducted from a mobile phone camera are frequently having issues; for example, low resolution determined on light, noise, facial expressions, etc. In the area of medicine, biometry and pattern, this research has great application. The focus of outcome in this research primarily should be in encompassing an application for protecting conducted face images for identification and authentication. In the first step this will be embedded to the model. The model is based on mobile to server architecture. The recognition method consists of a model whose task is to recognize a person from an image and retrieve information. Then, following, extend a model via involving the process of face detection and recognition. Images represent the input element in this model. Through the client, captured images were sent to the server. Upon sending images to the server, they are processed. In the MATLAB® method, recognition has been stored and it simulates performance for detection and recognition.

The face video recognition model is a proposed system for extending the security, where, at the moment, systems have a dilemma with forgery, theft, etc. It involves considerable development in biometric identification security system. Methods and techniques in pattern recognition were used sufficiently for identification of characteristics. The proposed system uses pattern recognition techniques in order to identify the characteristics. Such a similarity in this thesis and idea of mobile to server face recognition is found in the movie *The Quantum of Solace*. In this movie there was a scene where James Bond (Daniel Craig) captures images of suspected enemies by using his mobile phone which then sent images to the headquarters in London. Within a few seconds, he receives information on each of the images that were sent. This was just a movie, but the logic rationalization behind the system existed. Today, within advanced technologies that we have today, we cannot say that this is something impossible to develop. Detecting and recognizing faces is very challenging for the reason that faces have ample variability in poses, shapes, sizes and texture. The challenge in face detection and recognition is discussed in Kresimir et al. (2008), Martin et al. (2009), and Burnette (2015).

30.4 Operational Concept

In the work (Kremić, 2011; Kremić & Subasi, 2016), mobile phones were described as 'computer-in-medium'. Moreover, security issues arose. Regarding the applications that are running on those mobile phone 'computer-in-mediums', the request for security has increased (Jain & Li, 2011; Kumar et al., 2010). Previously introduced models must be restructured and made to assimilate with innovative methodology. Mobile infrastructure of 3G and 4G networks has improved considerably. The development of such applications has increased due to consumer requirement to secure information which exist on smart phone devices (Kremić, 2011; Kremić & Subasi, 2016). Methodology must be aligned with protecting user data e.g., PIN (personal identification number).

Method could potentially be used both on SIM—Subscriber Identity Module and PDA. Both, PDA and SIM are password oriented. Equally, PIN and passwords have been in conventional use for decades. However, this has been implemented through method–altered coding. In digital systems PINs and passwords remain to be violated. Hacking passwords or PIN is based on assumption. The study obtained in the work *"Beyond the PIN" is shown*: In a work (Jain & Li, 2011; Kumar et al., 2010), has initiated that 34% of 297 respondents did not use the PIN as a method for authentication on their mobile devices. In the study is research affiliated with security, where it was found that 70% surveyed were interested in security and 69% were willing to invest for the security of their devices. Since mobile evolution has happened and momentum gained, the ultimate request came for building a forward–thinking model for security. Observing new approaches of security, we will propose the face–recognition model of security for mobile authentication (Kremić, 2011; Kremić & Subasi, 2016) to diminish frauds. This will play a major role in authentication's security, and a new generation of mobile devices will have a crucial role in industries, government, business (Kremić, 2011; Kremić & Subasi, 2016):

- ▪ **Banks organization**: Financial sectors have introduced Federal Financial Institutions Examination Council FFIEC strategy. In FFIEC methods of authentication have been introduced. The primary function of strategies is to embargo banned transactions. Problems arise when it comes to development of the model that will be able to communicate between the bank and client. Implementation of face-recognition will reduce deception in the future (Kremić, 2011; Kremić & Subasi, 2016).

- **Mobile Network Operators**: This process is oriented towards the authentication solution. The mobile network operator's (MNO) idea is to emphasize significance of security, in particular, segments of reliable authentication methods. This will enable user benefits for safer data accessing (Kremić, 2011; Kremić & Subasi, 2016).

- **Technology providers**: The purpose of cutting-edge approaches are to be updated with requirements that are needed for business. Vendors are encouraged to apply new applications and to upgrade existing. This will enable them to meet the needs and condition requested by customers (Kremić, 2011; Kremić & Subasi, 2016).

In the work of (Kremić, 2011; Kremić & Subasi, 2016) was described that the role of the mobile phone's performance has increased. The PIN represents the most frequent technique used for verification. Perhaps PIN is not a sufficient method for protection regarding sensitivity of data. A diverse authentication approach is proposed to strengthen the structure within (Kremić, 2011). It empowers the system to redress potential weaknesses (Kremić, 2011). The face–recognition approach shows advanced authentication approaches for accessing authorized systems. Up-to-date applications for the authentication process is no longer an issue for granting authorization. Discussed possible solutions will boost confidence to the system. An advanced level of confidence permits users to access different aspect of services offered via mobile device system (Kremić, 2011).

30.4.1 Machine Learning Methods and Techniques

Inductive Learning: Mythology that applies inductive learning has been used to detect faces. Algorithms like Quinlan's C4.5 or Mitchells FIND-S have been used for this purpose (Kresimir et al., 2008).

Information: Markov random fields (MRF) can be applied to model contextual limitations of patterns in face images and their features. The Markov approach maximizes the discrimination among classes (to distinguish whether in an image exists a face or not) by applying the Kullback Leibler divergence (Kresimir et al., 2008).

Hidden Markov Model: The application of the *Hidden Markov Model* (HMM) has been used for face detection. The advantage of modeling reliable HMM is akin to setting up the output of probability, which can be trusted. Facial features represent states in the model. Usually they are denoted as pixel strips. Probability of evolution among states usually are the margins among selected pixel strips. In the example of Bayesian, HMMs mostly practice jointly with other methods; with main function to build detection algorithms (Kresimir et al., 2008).

Sparse Network of Winnows: SNoWs were first used for detection by Yang et al. (2000). They defined a sparse network of two linear units, or target nodes, one representing face patterns and the other for the non-face patterns. The SNoW had an incrementally learned feature space. Newly labeled cases served as a positive example for one target and as a negative example for the remaining target. The system proved to be effective at the time, and less time consuming (Kresimir et al., 2008).

Naive Bayes Classifier: Naive Bayes is a probabilistic approach that makes use of semantics in order to represent, use, and learn knowledge, and it has the capacity to reach good success levels. It has been found out that Naïve Bayes can compete with some other more sophisticated classifiers and outperform them. The basic principle of that approach is to always use the simple things. With some datasets though, Naive Bayes cannot perform well enough. Since attributes are regarded as if they were independent when the class is considered, the learning process is skewed by the redundant attributes. Naive Bayes' power to detect is undermined because of the dependencies between attributes. Many components basically are not normally dispersed. We may well use other distributions. If we know that a specific attribute will possibly come after some other distribution, the procedures for standard estimation can be utilized. If we are not sure about the real distribution, we can make use of kernel density estimation, which does not expect a specific distribution for the attribute values. Another thing we can do is just allocating different values to the data at first (Han, Pei, & Kamber, 2011). In Kremić (2011) Schneiderman and Kanade define an entity in algorithm for recognition whose development was estimated by Bayesian Classifier. Overall, their algorithm showed good results on frontal face detection. Bayes Classifiers have also been used as a complementary part of other detection algorithms (Kremić, 2011; Kresimir et al., 2008).

Artificial Neural Networks (ANN): A set of input and output units which are connected form artificial neural networks (ANN). A weight that is associated with each connected unit exists in that unit. The network acquires the information by adjusting the weights until it has the ability to anticipate the correct class label of the input tuples. Artificial neural network units can also be described as connectionist learning because it provides connections between units. Artificial neural networks have long training times and that's why it is proper for applications in which it is doable. They demand a number of parameters. Those parameters should generally be determined experimentally like the network topology or structure. One of the advantages of neural networks is that they have a high tolerance of noisy data. The other advantage is that they are able to categorize untrained patterns. We have several types of neural networks and neural network algorithms that are different from each other. The most famous algorithm is named as backpropagation. The backpropagation algorithm practices learning on a multilayer feed-forward neural network. It is learning from a set of weights used for prediction, if the class label of tuples occurs repetitively. A multilayer feed-forward neural network is comprised of an input layer, one or more hidden layers, and an output layer. A nonlinear function is practiced to the weighted input. Multilayer feed-forward neural networks have the ability to design the class prediction as a nonlinear combination of the inputs. According to viewpoint of statistics, they do nonlinear regression. If multilayer feed-forward networks possess enough hidden units and training samples, then they might finely approach any function (Han et al., 2011).

Distribution based: This was first proposed by Sung. The aim was for object and pattern detection. In general, the idea was to sufficiently collect large numbers of samples. Collection was used for pattern class detection by covering all possible sources in an image. The first step is to choose appropriate feature space. This must have been embodied in pattern class. The class is the distribution of all its permissible image appearances (Kremić, 2011; Kresimir et al., 2008). The next step uses a trained classifier. The purpose of a trained classifier is in identifying instances of targets in pattern class. This is based in background image patterns. These patterns represent distance calculations among input and distribution. This is enabled by applying class representation in certain spaces. For example, Fisher discriminant or PCA are used in artificial face recognition patterns in subspace (Kresimir et al., 2008).

Eigenface based: The approach for calculating efficient face representation by applying PCA (Principal Component Analysis) was developed by Sirovich and Kirbey. The idea is to represent a face in a design of a coordinate system. The vectors that make up this coordinate system were referred to as eigenpictures. Later, Turk and Pentland used this approach to develop an eigenface based algorithm for recognition (Kremić, 2011; Kresimir et al., 2008).

Support Vector Machine (SVM): A method used for the classification process of both linear and nonlinear data is named as support vector machines (SVMs). An SVM, which is an algorithm in a nutshell, make use of a nonlinear mapping in order to turn the original training data into an upper level dimension. It researches for the linear optimal separating hyperplane in this new dimension like a decision boundary by which the tuples of one class from another are being separated. A hyperplane can always separate data from two classes by using a proper nonlinear mapping to an adequately high dimension. This hyperplane is achieved by the SVM with support vectors that are important training vectors and margins which are identified by the support vectors. Other methods are not that apt for overfitting. A compact description of the learned model is also provided by the support vectors that are gained (Han et al., 2011). There is no straight line which separate the classes, and in the case of the data are not possible to separate linearly. SVMs are able to find nonlinear decision boundaries, like nonlinear hypersurfaces within input space. The explanation of how the linear approach is extended is that a nonlinear SVM is obtained with the extension of the approach for linear

SVMs in two main steps. When we use a nonlinear mapping, we turn the original input data into a higher dimensional space. After we transform the data into the new higher space, linear separating hyperplane in the new space is found in the second step. A quadratic optimization problem is obtained as a result and the usage of the linear SVM formulation is able to find an answer for this problem. The maximal marginal hyperplane that is present in the new space matches to a nonlinear separating hypersurface in the original space (Han et al., 2011). So, an optimal hyperplane should minimize the classification error of the unseen test patterns. This classifier was first applied to face detection by Martin et al. (2009).

K-Nearest Neighbour (k-NN): When we give large training sets to the k-nearest-neighbour method, it requires a lot of labour. We use this method broadly for pattern recognition. Nearest-neighbour classifiers with the help of analogy depend on learning. Analogy means the comparison of a given test tuple with training tuples which are similar to it. The n symbol shows the training tuples. A speck in an n dimensional space is symbolized by each tuple. This is how training tuples are kept in an n dimensional space. When there is an unknown tuple, the pattern space for k training tuples are searched for by a k-nearest-neighbour classifier. These tuples must be the closest ones to the unknown tuple. We describe "closeness" with a distance metric like Euclidean distance. That is to say the difference between the matching values of each numeric attribute is taken in tuple X1 and X2, is squared, and is added to each other. The total compiled distance count helps us to take the square root. The values of each attribute are generally normalized, and this provides prevention for attributes that have large ranges in the beginning, like income from beating attributes which have smaller ranges in the beginning like binary attributes. In order to classify k-nearest-neighbour, the tuple that are not known are selected as the most common class among its k-nearest-neighbours. As "k" is equal to 1, we select the unknown tuple in the class of the training tuple. This tuple must be the closest one to it in pattern space. How can a good value of k be determined? The answer can be that determination of k value can be done experimentally. As the beginning, we consider that k is 1 and we employ a test set to guess the error rate of the classifier. We redo the same process for each time by allowing k to increase one more neighbour. The *k* value which has the lowest error rate might be assigned. To sum up, if the number of training tuples is bigger, the value of k will be bigger too. So, it is possible to base numeric prediction decisions and classification on a bigger portion of the kept tuples. Distance based comparisons are used by nearest-neighbour classifiers. Those distance based comparisons inherently allocate equal weight to each attribute. So, in the case that irrelevant or noisy attributes are given, they may be harmed by poor accuracy. Yet, in order to integrate attribute weighting and the pruning of noisy data tuples, this method has been altered (Han et al., 2011).

CART: Classification and regression tree is a modern decision tree learner. It utilizes minimal cost-complexity pruning. Although it carries the same name as CART learner, it does not carry CART's features. The minimum number of instances on each leaf, the training data to build the tree, and the quantity of cross validation in the pruning can all be set (Han et al., 2011). The CART (Breiman, Friedman, Stone, & Olshen, 1984) includes a decision tree breeder for discrete classes that were similar to the classes of C4.5. It also included a design in order to induce regression trees. The CART contained methods like handling nominal attributes and replacement devices to attend to missing values. Nonetheless, model trees were only introduced by Quinlan (1992). In Han et al. (2011) they investigated how to use model trees to generate rule sets, but did not use partial trees. Wang and Witten (1996) gave an extensive description and application of model tree induction. Despite having a drawback in that the structures that they bring about are not blurred and not helpful in understanding the nature of the solution, we also use neural nets in order to predict numeric quantities.

REPTree: In a REPTree, a decision or regression tree is made with the help of gain–variance reduction and the built tree is pruned with reduced error pruning. As it is balanced for speed, just the values for numeric attributes are classified for one time. As in the case of C4.5, missing values are attended to through separating instances into pieces. The number of folds for pruning, maximum tree depth, minimum number of instances on each leaf, and minimum proportion of training set variance for a split (only for numeric classes) can all be determined (Han et al., 2011).

ADTree: An alternating decision tree is for two class problems by making use of boosting. The number of boosting iterations can be tuned to fit the dataset and the aimed complexity-accuracy tradeoff. The tree receives three nodes from each iteration, one being split node and other two being prediction nodes if nodes cannot be melded. The given search method is the extensive one while the other methods are faster. Saving instance data for visualization is an option. LADTree can deal with multiclass problems that rest on the LogitBoost algorithm (Hall, Holmes, & Frank, 1999) LADTree can also tune the number of boosting iterations to fit the data and it sets the size of the generated tree (Han et al., 2011).

C4.5 Decision Tree: Quinlan (1986) was the developer of C4.5 decision tree. In this algorithm, tests for which training examples have the same result are eliminated as they are not very important. Therefore, they are not contained in the decision tree if they do not have minimum two outcomes which have a minimum number of instances. The given value for the minimum is 2, yet we can control it and raise it for tasks with noisy data. Candidate splits are taken into consideration in the case that they cut a specific number of instances. There is MDL-based adjustment for splits on numeric attributes. In the case that a certain numeric attribute at the node which is for splitting has S candidate splits, we take out *log2(S)/N* from the information gain, in which case N stands for the number of instances at the node. Quinlan (1986) designed that heuristic in order to avoid over-fitting. After that subtraction, we might find out that the information gain is negative. If we do not have attributes that have positive information gain, which is a kind of pre-pruning, the tree will stop growing. This is indicated at this point since it could be unexpected to get a pruned tree although post pruning is not active (Hall et al., 1999).

Random Forests (RF): We can envision that the ensemble has classifiers, each of which is a decision tree classifier. In that case that group of classifiers is a forest. We produce individual decision trees by using an arbitrary array of attributes at each node in order to determine the split. Every tree relies on the values of random vector taken individually and have the same distribution allocated for all trees in the forest. Amid the classification, each tree decides and the most popular class is chosen. We can form random forests by making use of bagging together with random attribute selection. In order to raise the trees, the CART approach is used. We raise the trees to maximum size possible and they are not pruned. Random forests, which are created by random input selection, are named as Forest-RI. Forest-RC, on the other hand, makes use of random linear combinations from the input attributes. It does not randomly choose a subset of the attributes, but forms new features which are linear combinations of the current attributes. This means that we obtain an attribute by specifying L, which is the number of original attributes that are supposed to be combined. We arbitrarily select L attributes and add them together that are with coefficients which are uniform numbers on [−1,1]. We generate F linear combinations and make a search over those in order to get the best split. When we have a few available attributes, then this kind of random forest is beneficial because we can reduce the correlation between individual classifiers. The larger the number of trees in the forest, the closer the generalization error for a forest comes. That's the reason why over-fitting is not a problem. If the strength of the individual classifiers is high, a random forest is more accurate. It also relies on the measure of the dependence between the individual classifiers. The optimum thing to do would be to empower the individual classifiers but not raise their correlation. Random forests are indifferent to the number of attributes that are chosen for consideration at the splits. Since they consider much lower numbers of attributes for each split, they do well on bigger databases. Providing internal estimates of variable importance, random forests can act quicker than both bagging and boosting (Han et al., 2011).

Rotation Forest (RoF): Rotation forest (RoF) are classifier ensembles that rely on feature extraction. So as to form the training data for a base classifier, we split the feature set arbitrarily into K subsets, in which case K is a parameter of the algorithm, and we PCA to each subset. With the aim of preserving the variability information in the data, we retain all principal components. Hence, K-axis rotations emerge to make the new features for a base classifier. Individual accuracy and diversity in the ensemble both at the same time are supposed to be strengthened by the rotation approach. Preferred decision trees are named forest because of their sensitivity to rotation of the feature axis. We try to acquire accuracy by saving all principal components and using all of the data set in order to train each base classifier (Rodriguez, Kuncheva, & Alonso, 2006).

In the work of pattern recognition, there are problems which exists as: *object recognition, character recognition etc.* These were solved by applying the method of *neural network*. The application of this is in the example of face detection. Previous research shows the application of neural networks was used to learn certain objects, in this case human faces. This can be applied as well to detect faces in different patterns. The challenge was in finding and representing classes of the "*images that does not include faces image.*" There are other ways to apply neural network and to calculate a discriminant function. By measuring distance, discriminant functions will be able to do pattern calcification. In some examples, they have tried to find an optimal boundary among face images and non-face images (Kresimir et al., 2008).

30.5 Android Established Biometrics' Security System

With the expansion of mobile phone consumption, there are requests for greater levels, in particular for data security needs and its protection. Features in cutting-edge mobile technologies as: *touch screens, Wi-Fi, Bluetooth*, etc., are established for one user universal network. By connecting to any open Wi-Fi network is the reason security is rising. The ability of today's smart phones are the capability to establish connection on e-mails; to connect to one's bank account; to connect on video systems, etc. Moreover, this shows a great need in implementing the new level of security. Following all the above, we have come with a solution to propose a biometric level of security by using facial features for recognition (Kremić & Subasi, 2011, 2016).

The very high demand of new technologies is relying on these new approaches for increasing levels of security. Boosted usage of mobile phones or smart machines at *Carnegie Mellon Research Center* was introduced in early research work, connecting with solution to facial recognition and detection (Hull, Liu, Erol, Graham, & Moraleda, 2010). Architecture described in *client-server* was proposed in (Hull et al., 2010).

The advancement of the model is shown in Kremić and Subasi (2011), Kremić (2011), and Kremić and Subasi (2016). Face recognition has become field for itself for research (Mohamed & Yampolskiy, 2011; Choi, Ro, & Plataniotis, 2011a), mainly for innovative technologies. The main attention of face recognition is in its development. During the implementation, achieving success was shown in Kremić and Subasi (2011). It presents realization and implementation of facial expression recognition and detection on the smartphone *Samsung Galaxy S – Android based operating system.* During the implementation, simulation was done on emulator *DROID.* The MATLAB has been used as the server where facial images were stored. In work (Kremić, 2011), part of the facial recognition and detection was conducted on MATLAB. Yet, the main goal is to succeed in developing a functional face recognition segment; the main contribution and challenge in the end is to have a well–designed application. The general idea is to have a reliable level of data safety and to increase mobile security. Smart phones are integration parts of security, computation, digital communication, etc. Therefore, security for smart phones has become more important. The system itself is structured in a form of client-server architect design. On the server, information is being processed. Upon processing information, the following step is identification as described more in Kremić and Subasi (2011). If a person has been recognized and identified, access will be granted, otherwise the system will decline it.

30.5.1 What is Android and Why Use It?

Various smart phone architectures exist as: iPhone, Windows Mobile, Symbian, BlackBerry, Java Mobile Edition, Linux Mobile (LiMo), and others. Android is the first mobile platform proposes (Marques, 2010) because:

1. It is free, open and a Linux based open source platform (Marques, 2010);
2. A part-architecture created by stimulated Internet mashups (Marques, 2010);
3. Many different approaches—in package out of the box (Marques, 2010);
4. Life cycle of application is manageable (Marques, 2010);
5. Graphic and sound have high quality (Marques, 2010);
6. Portable over variety of hardware (Marques, 2010);

Android has moved ahead with its implementations for mobile application. During its time of increased development, it has set up new standards. With its new approaches, Android gives opportunities to developers to be able to implement reliable and function systems.

In the book (Marques, 2010) has described life cycle follows as:

■ onCreate(Bundle): This process is called when the activity first starts up. We can use it to perform one-time initialization such as creating the user interface (Marques, 2010).
■ onCreate(): This process takes one parameter and it is either **null** or is in same state information previously by the onSaveInstanceState()method (Marques, 2010).
■ onResume(): When activity starts interacting with the user, this method is called.
■ onPause(): This activity is called, when activity is almost to go into the background, and mostly since different activity has been started (Marques, 2010).

- onStop(): When activity is no longer active and visible to the user and perhaps will not be requested for a while, this process is called (Marques, 2010).
- onRestart(): This indicates activity as being displayed when activity that was stopped was requested by user (Marques, 2010).
- onSaveInstanceState(Bundle): When process of reinitialization happens from a state earlier saved by the onSaveInstanceState(), this process is called (Marques, 2010).

30.5.1.1 Android: Application Architecture

The Android's architecture allows developers to determine their own concepts of components. It enables them to reuse it and therefore, they are able to share the activities, intents, services, and data with other relevant applications. Several things are defined in the Android SDK. It is necessary that the programmer or developer is familiar with developing on Android OS. Crucial segments are: activities, intents, services and content providers.

Activities: An activity describes user interface screen. The application determines if there can be one or more activities defined in the program. Each activity is in charge for saving its own states; therefore, it can be restored later as part of the application life cycle (Marques, 2010).

Intents: This mechanism is used for calling a specific action. In Android's Intent, all activates go through. Intents gives authorization for replacing or reusing components (Mohamed & Yampolskiy, 2011).

Services: This runs in the background. User's interaction is not needed (Mohamed & Yampolskiy, 2011).

Content Providers: It is a set of data. Data are wrapped up in a custom API to read and write it. For sharing data among applications, using content provider is the best solution (Mohamed & Yampolskiy, 2011). In JAVA all programs are written. Dalvik virtual machine is used for execution of Android's program.

30.5.1.2 The Dalvik Virtual Machine

The Dalvik Virtual Machine represents important segments of Android. Usage of DVM is more requested than Java Virtual Machine (JVM). It runs on the Linux kernel. It is used for low-level functionality. The Android system includes both hardware and software. It is managed by using Dalvik as middle tier.

30.5.1.3 Biometric System and Application

After testing PCA on MATLAB for face recognition is done, (Clarke & Furnell, 2007), next phase is to develop the application on DROID emulator. A DROID emulator was set up for Android Samsung Galaxy S. The image of faces were captured. A function called *fakeProcessing* was created to simulate camera activity. The images of faces were saved on the computer's desktop. This simulates capturing image by user mobile phone camera.

30.5.1.4 Running and Testing Application

Firstly, a tomcat server is started. Upon initialization of the tomcat server, the MATLAB runs. On the emulator we have added on the image to simulate the process of capture face image from a mobile phone as shown on Figure 30.2. When image is stored on the SD card, the emulator is started as shown on Figure 30.3. Then, we have started our application called DroidAuth. When running, the application is shown Figure 30.2. The following process is process of authentication. When the process of authentication is started, the image is sent to the server. On the server side is MATLAB. The authentication process is working on PCA (Jain & Li, 2011; Kremić, 2011).

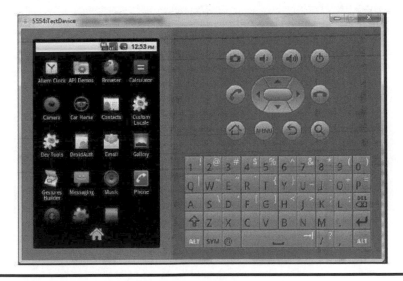

Figure 30.2   Emulator of Android OS.

Name	Size	Date	Time	Permissions	Info
▷ 📂 data		2011-06-12	14:16	drwxrwx--x	
◢ 📂 mnt		2011-07-14	13:17	drwxrwxr-x	
▷ 📂 asec		2011-07-14	13:17	drwxr-xr-x	
▷ 📂 sdcard		1970-01-01	00:00	d---rwxr-x	
▷ 📂 secure		2011-07-14	13:17	drwx------	
▷ 📂 system		2010-06-30	21:06	drwxr-xr-x	

Threads Allocation Tracker File Explorer

Figure 30.3   SD card file system.

30.5.1.5 Mobile Security

Mobile security highly depends on data storage and authentication. Therefore, in this paper we are as well introducing s model for authentication to secure it with the visual identity. The security of mobile devices also depends on s mobile operating system such as Android, iPhone, BlackBerry, Symbian, JME or WinMobile. There are different security levels and some of those are:

Normal: The consequences on applications from a normal threat are minor. Usually, it can grant some rights to the application.

Dangerous: The grants related to the settings and to SEND SMS are considered very dangerous. Android has the possibility to let the user knows when these permissions are installed.

Signature: The signature is granted only on the application level. And this can hide and keep public interface anonymous.

Signature or System: This varies with signature, except it allows images to grant the access. Nascent mobile application security brings with it new issues, which are different from the desktop security application. When speaking about Android, we can say that Android is a platform which is based on Linux kernel, which provides a security mode.

30.6 Architecture

The model consists of a mobile cellular phone side and server side. Comparing it to the initial research (Kremić, 2011; Kremić & Subasi, 2011; Kremić et al., 2012), changes were made toward the application improvements. In here on the cellular side the *DroidAuth* application, developed in JAVA, is running. In between is HTTP which enables communication between server and cellular side. On the server side MATLAB is running. The purpose of MATLAB is to simulate the authentication engine running. The server receives the video which is a capture via cellular-mobile side and is sent to the server. When it is sent to the server, faces from video were extracted. After the faces were extracted, there is a PCA running on server side. The PCA is used for recognition. After PCA, the application determines when authentication should happen and under which state of security.

There is a user database consisting of a biometric profile. Principle component analysis feature vectors which are being sent to biometric database, then go through the process of matching. If they are matched, the application accepts and user is being authorized ,and if not it is sent back to the beginning of the process. Both of these are visually described in Figure 30.4 shows the process flow.

Principle Component Analysis: The aim of the principle component analysis is to help in face recognition. In this application we have used the PCA method

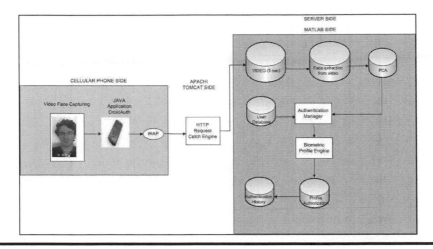

Figure 30.4   System architecture.

for recognition. The faces were captured via mobile camera. After capturing, the process of face extraction was done. The aim of PCA is to help automatize the process of face recognition and attempt to find the identity of a certain facial images according to those in the biometric database (Figure 30.5).

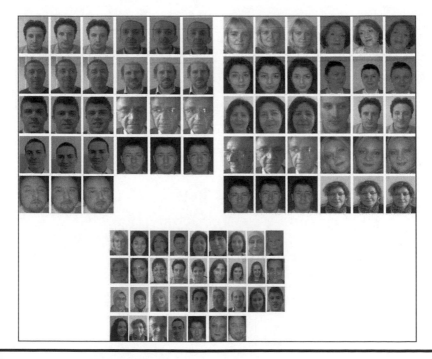

Figure 30.5   Database example.

30.7 Testing and Results

The results presented here are just the small data set of 40 persons from the IBU Biometric Data set. Each person has 20 different face images. For face recognition we have performed on the DroidAuth application PCA. The accuracy we have calculated is shown if Formula 1 described. For the mobile phone we have used the Samsung Galaxy S. The accuracy overall achieved in here is 92.64%. We have determined the Euclidian size between test images and training images. The threshold of the images is 10e+16. In Table 30.1 are shown results where males were recognized 100%. The problems come with females, especially those who are coloring their hair. We can see that females with darker hair are having higher accuracy achievements than females with light/blond hair.

$$\text{Accuracy} = \frac{\text{Matched Faces}}{\text{Total Number of Face Images in Database}} \times 100\% \quad (30.1)$$

In Figure 30.6 is shown the graphical representation of results plotted from Tables 30.2 through 30.4.

Table 30.1 Application of Biometric System

Areas	Application
Information Security	Access security (OS, database)
Access Management	Secure access authentication (restricted access)
Biometrics	Person identification (national ID)
Law Enforcement	Video surveillance
Personal Security	Home Video surveillance system
Entertainment – Leisure	Video Camera application

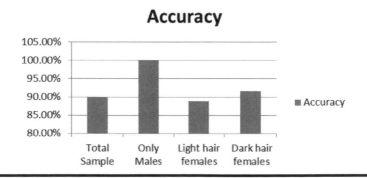

Figure 30.6 Graphical representation of results.

Table 30.2 Form of Authentication

From	Examples
What we know	Password, PIN, pass phrase
What we have	Token, CAC cards, RSA
What we are	Biometric: fingerprint, iris, speech pattern

Table 30.3 Results for Different Groups

Description	Matched	Sample	Accuracy
Total Sample	36	40	90.00%
Only Males	9	9	100%
Light hair females	8	9	88.88%
Dark hair females	11	12	91.66%

Table 30.4 Classification Performance of Different Classifiers

	Accuracy (%)	F-measure	ROC Area	Kappa
ANN (MLP)	92.6923	0.923	0.983	0.925
k-NN	95	0.95	0.974	0.9487
SVM	92.9487	0.929	0.995	0.9276
Random Forest	96.7949	0.968	0.999	0.9671
C4.5	84.2308	0.841	0.928	0.8382
Random Tree	86.2821	0.862	0.93	0.8592
REPTree	73.8462	0.738	0.932	0.7316
LAD Tree	73.8462	0.734	0.982	0.7316
NB	90.641	0.899	0.991	0.9039
Rotation Forest	94.8718	0.949	0.997	0.9474
CART	83.0769	0.831	0.93	0.8263

The result shown in this paper, are presenting that *Random Forest, SVM* have the highest recognition rate. This was achieved by extracting feature vectors. Testing of ANN, k-NN, SVM, Random Forest, C4.5, LAD Tree, etc., was done by using Weka. Using these we can see the different performance for each of them. The highest achieved result are presented by Random Forest. Random Forest performs 96.79%. While testing, 30 trees were constructed. Number of cross validation fold $k = 10$. F – measure of Random Forest is 96%, 0.968 respectively. ROC of Random Forest is 0.999 and is higher than SVM, ANN, CART. ANN performs 92.69%, 0.92 respectively. F – measure of ANN (MLP) is 0.923. ROC of ANN (MLP) is 0.983 and is higher than k-nn 0.974. k-NN has accuracy 95%, higher than SVM, C4.5, Random Tree, REPTree, NB, LAD Tree, and lower than Random Forest. F-measure of k-NN is 0.983. ROC of k-NN is 0.983.

The behaviour of histogram values of face images performed on SVM linear kernel delivers high accuracy. For training, the SVM and the appropriate classifier C were selected. The optimal values of C where results perform better is C = 100. We can see that Random Forest tree performs nearly well as an SVM linear kernel. Besides all the above mentioned, such models incorporated with real–time face recognition, an expert system may be improved with such higher accurate results via incising the versatile number of parameters.

30.8 Conclusion

The unsolved problems today with variations are: Illumination, head rotation and face expression. Research for measurement of facial features of ear size and between the eye distances has been done by Goldstein, Harmon and Lest in Bell Laboratories (Goldstein et al., 1971). In 1973, Fischer and Elschanger has started to calculate distance and to measure comparable features automatically (Fischler et al., 1973, Marques, 2010). Eigenface in image processing was introduced by Kirbey and Sirovich. Their technique is known as Principle Component Analysis (PCA). Principle component analysis has been dominated for many years. The problem of recognition attracts a level of new research, especially in the future to try to develop a recognition system which will involve. Yet, we still fully did not comprehend how the human brain is working and which kind of recognition performance is done; therefore, there is plenty ahead to do in developing fully with higher-level accurate systems.

30.9 Summary

This chapter addresses methods related to facial recognition and detection as methods for mobile security. In this chapter are addressed machine learning techniques. The work discusses information security, access management and personal security. Implementation of facial recognition authentication models on the mobile system has shown achievement of 96% accuracy. Significant research has been conducted. There is still sufficient space for continuing research work on this subject. With mobile phones consumption, the old-fashioned method of user authentication have changed forever. This change brings with it important security issues. Conventional PIN techniques will be gradually abandoned and ultimately replaced. Augmenting the required level of intelligent authentication will not be a question of pass or fail, but rather of confirming the identity of the user. An important question to future research stays in video and speech recognition in mobile phone security as part of the authentication. Artificial intelligence, both with machine learning and pattern recognition, will try to provide accurate results in self-learning the biometric system of human recognition system. The algorithms and their application will play a major role in digital security. The unsolved problems today with variations include illumination, head rotation and facial expression. The recognition problem attracts a high level of interest and research, especially as future students of the subject seek to develop a recognition system which will detect emotions. Yet, we still do not fully comprehend how the human brain operates or what kind of recognition technique is required to unlock its many mysteries. Therefore, much lies ahead in developing not only a system with greater accuracy but also one which can penetrate beneath the skin of its human subjects. No doubt many problems remain to be solved in the area of artificial recognition. But the future will bring us closer to discovering a computer which can have, show and detect emotion when recognizing humans. The gauntlet is thrown before future researchers. They must rise to the challenge and continue striving towards a model that will be able to construct a comprehensive image from feature vectors.

References

Alhussain, T., Drew, S., & Alfarraj, O. (2010). Biometric authentication for mobile government security. *Presented at the Intelligent Computing and Intelligent Systems (ICIS), 2010 IEEE International Conference on, IEEE* (Vol. 2, pp. 114–118).

Arandjelović, O., & Cipolla, R. (2009). A pose-wise linear illumination manifold model for face recognition using video. *Computer Vision and Image Understanding, 113*(1), 113–125.

Arteaga-Falconi, J. S., Al Osman, H., & El Saddik, A. (2016). ECG authentication for mobile devices. *IEEE Transactions on Instrumentation and Measurement, 65*(3), 591–600.

Biel, L., Pettersson, O., Philipson, L., & Wide, P. (2001). ECG analysis: A new approach in human identification. *IEEE Transactions on Instrumentation and Measurement, 50*(3), 808–812.

Bledsoe, W. W. (1966). The model method in facial recognition. *Panoramic Research Inc., Palo Alto, CA, Rep. PRI, 15*, 47.

Breiman, L., Friedman, J., Stone, C. J., & Olshen, R. A. (1984). *Classification and Regression Trees.* Boca Raton, FL: CRC Press.

Burnette, E. (2015). *Hello, Android: Introducing Google's Mobile Development Platform.* Dallas, TX: Pragmatic Bookshelf.

Campisi, P., & La Rocca, D. (2014). Brain waves for automatic biometric-based user recognition. *IEEE Transactions on Information Forensics and Security, 9*(5), 782–800.

Chen, Y., Atnafu, A. D., Schlattner, I., Weldtsadik, W. T., Roh, M.-C., Kim, H. J., ... Fazli, S. (2016). A high-security EEG-based login system with RSVP stimuli and dry electrodes. *IEEE Transactions on Information Forensics and Security, 11*(12), 2635–2647.

Choi, H.-S., Lee, B., & Yoon, S. (2016). Biometric authentication using noisy electrocardiograms acquired by mobile sensors. *IEEE Access, 4*, 1266–1273.

Choi, J. Y., Ro, Y. M., & Plataniotis, K. N. (2011a). A comparative study of preprocessing mismatch effects in color image based face recognition. *Pattern Recognition, 44*(2), 412–430.

Choi, K., Toh, K.-A., & Byun, H. (2011b). Realtime training on mobile devices for face recognition applications. *Pattern Recognition, 44*(2), 386–400.

Clarke, N. L., & Furnell, S. (2007). Advanced user authentication for mobile devices. *Computers & Security, 26*(2), 109–119.

Da Silva, H. P., Fred, A., Lourenço, A., & Jain, A. K. (2013). Finger ECG signal for user authentication: Usability and performance. *Presented at the Biometrics: Theory, Applications and Systems (BTAS), 2013 IEEE Sixth International Conference on, IEEE* (pp. 1–8).

De Carrera, P. F., & Marques, I. (2010). Face recognition algorithms. Master's thesis in Computer Science, Universidad Euskal Herriko.

Derawi, M. O., Nickel, C., Bours, P., & Busch, C. (2010). Unobtrusive user-authentication on mobile phones using biometric gait recognition. *Presented at the Intelligent Information Hiding and Multimedia Signal Processing (IIH-MSP), 2010 Sixth International Conference on, IEEE* (pp. 306–311).

Fischler, M. A., & Elschlager, R. A. (1973). The representation and matching of pictorial structures. *IEEE Transactions on Computers, 100*(1), 67–92.

Fraschini, M., Hillebrand, A., Demuru, M., Didaci, L., & Marcialis, G. L. (2015). An EEG-based biometric system using eigenvector centrality in resting state brain networks. *IEEE Signal Processing Letters, 22*(6), 666–670.

Goldstein, A. J., Harmon, L. D., & Lesk, A. B. (1971). Identification of human faces. *Proceedings of the IEEE, 59*(5), 748–760.

Hall, M., Holmes, G., & Frank, E. (1999). Generating rule sets from model trees. In *Proceedings of the Twelfth Australian Joint Conference on Artificial Intelligence* (pp. 1–12), Sydney, Australia. Berlin, Germany: Springer-Verlag.

Han, J., Pei, J., & Kamber, M. (2011). *Data Mining: Concepts and Techniques*. Burlington, MA: Elsevier.

Hull, J. J., Liu, X., Erol, B., Graham, J., & Moraleda, J. (2010). Mobile image recognition: architectures and tradeoffs. *Presented at the Proceedings of the Eleventh Workshop on Mobile Computing Systems & Applications, ACM* (pp. 84–88).

Islam, M. S., Alajlan, N., Bazi, Y., & Hichri, H. S. (2012). HBS: a novel biometric feature based on heartbeat morphology. *IEEE Transactions on Information Technology in Biomedicine, 16*(3), 445–453.

Jain, A., Bolle, R., & Pankanti, S. (2006). *Biometrics: Personal Identification in Networked Society* (Vol. 479). New York: Springer Science & Business Media.

Jain, A. K., & Li, S. Z. (2011). *Handbook of Face Recognition*. New York: Springer.

Jain, A. K., Nandakumar, K., & Ross, A. (2016). 50 years of biometric research: Accomplishments, challenges, and opportunities. *Pattern Recognition Letters, 79*, 80–105.

Jain, A., Ross, A. A., & Nandakumar, K. (2011). *Introduction to Biometrics*. New York: Springer Science & Business Media.

Kang, S. J., Lee, S. Y., Cho, H. I., & Park, H. (2016). ECG authentication system design based on signal analysis in mobile and wearable devices. *IEEE Signal Processing Letters, 23*(6), 805–808.

Klonovs, J., Petersen, C. K., Olesen, H., & Hammershoj, A. (2013). Id proof on the go: Development of a mobile EEG-based biometric authentication system. *IEEE Vehicular Technology Magazine, 8*(1), 81–89.

Kremić, E. (2011). Face recognition: Advanced security model for mobile phones. Master thesis dissertation, International Burch University, Sarajevo, Bosnia and Herzegovina.

Kremić, E., & Subasi, A. (2011). The implementation of face security for authentication implemented on mobile phone. *International Arab Journal of Information Technology*, 414–419.

Kremić, E., & Subasi, A. (2016). Performance of random forest and SVM in face recognition. *International Arab Journal of Information Technology, 13*(2), 287–293.

Kremić, E., Subasi, A., & Hajdarevic, K. (2012). Face recognition implementation for client server mobile application using PCA. *Presented at the Information Technology Interfaces (ITI), Proceedings of the ITI 2012 34th International Conference on, IEEE* (pp. 435–440).

Kresimir, D., Grgic, M., & Marian, S. B. (2008). *Recent Advances in Face Recognition.* Croatia: I-Tech.

Kumar, S., Singh, P., & Kumar, V. (2010). Architecture for mobile based face detection/recognition. *International Journal on Computer Sciences and Engineering, 2*(3), 889–894.

Kumari, P., & Vaish, A. (2015). Information-theoretic measures on intrinsic mode function for the individual identification using EEG sensors. *IEEE Sensors Journal, 15*(9), 4950–4960.

Kurkovsky, S., Carpenter, T., & MacDonald, C. (2010). Experiments with simple iris recognition for mobile phones. *Presented at the Information Technology: New Generations (ITNG), 2010 Seventh International Conference on, IEEE* (pp. 1293–1294).

Kwapisz, J. R., Weiss, G. M., & Moore, S. A. (2010). Cell phone-based biometric identification. *Presented at the Biometrics: Theory Applications and Systems (BTAS), 2010 Fourth IEEE International Conference on, IEEE* (pp. 1–7).

Marques, I. (2010). Face recognition algorithms.

Martin, K., Lu, H., Bui, F. M., Plataniotis, K. N., & Hatzinakos, D. (2009). A biometric encryption system for the self-exclusion scenario of face recognition. *IEEE Systems Journal, 3*(4), 440–450.

Merone, M., Soda, P., Sansone, M., & Sansone, C. (2017). ECG databases for biometric systems: A systematic review. *Expert Systems with Applications, 67*, 189–202.

Mian, A. (2011). Online learning from local features for video-based face recognition. *Pattern Recognition, 44*(5), 1068–1075.

Mohamed, A. A., & Yampolskiy, R. V. (2011). An improved LBP algorithm for avatar face recognition. *Presented at the Information, Communication and Automation Technologies (ICAT), 2011 XXIII International Symposium on, IEEE* (pp. 1–5).

Odinaka, I., Lai, P.-H., Kaplan, A. D., O'Sullivan, J. A., Sirevaag, E. J., & Rohrbaugh, J. W. (2012). ECG biometric recognition: A comparative analysis. *IEEE Transactions on Information Forensics and Security, 7*(6), 1812–1824.

Odinaka, I., O'Sullivan, J. A., Sirevaag, E. J., & Rohrbaugh, J. W. (2015). Cardiovascular biometrics: Combining mechanical and electrical signals. *IEEE Transactions on Information Forensics and Security, 10*(1), 16–27.

Quinlan, J. R. (1986). Induction of decision trees. *Machine Learning, 1*(1), 81–106.

Quinlan, J. R. (1992). Learning with continuous classes. *Presented at the 5th Australian Joint Conference on Artificial Intelligence*, Singapore (Vol. 92, pp. 343–348).

Rodrigues, D., Silva, G. F., Papa, J. P., Marana, A. N., & Yang, X.-S. (2016). EEG-based person identification through binary flower pollination algorithm. *Expert Systems with Applications, 62*, 81–90.

Rodriguez, J. J., Kuncheva, L. I., & Alonso, C. J. (2006). Rotation forest: A new classifier ensemble method. *IEEE Transactions on Pattern Analysis and Machine Intelligence, 28*(10), 1619–1630.

Safie, S. I., Soraghan, J. J., & Petropoulakis, L. (2011). Electrocardiogram (ECG) biometric authentication using pulse active ratio (PAR). *IEEE Transactions on Information Forensics and Security, 6*(4), 1315–1322.

Sidek, K. A., & Khalil, I. (2013). Enhancement of low sampling frequency recordings for ECG biometric matching using interpolation. *Computer Methods and Programs in Biomedicine, 109*(1), 13–25.

Sidek, K. A., Mai, V., & Khalil, I. (2014). Data mining in mobile ECG based biometric identification. *Journal of Network and Computer Applications, 44*, 83–91.

Sinha, P., Balas, B., Ostrovsky, Y., & Russell, R. (2006). Face recognition by humans: Nineteen results all computer vision researchers should know about. *Proceedings of the IEEE, 94*(11), 1948–1962.

Sirovich, L., & Kirby, M. (1987). Low-dimensional procedure for the characterization of human faces. *Josa A, 4*(3), 519–524.

Tao, Q., & Veldhuis, R. (2010). Biometric authentication system on mobile personal devices. *IEEE Transactions on Instrumentation and Measurement, 59*(4), 763–773.

Venugopalan, S., Savvides, M., Griofa, M. O., & Cohen, K. (2014). Analysis of low-dimensional radio-frequency impedance-based cardio-synchronous waveforms for biometric authentication. *IEEE Transactions on Biomedical Engineering, 61*(8), 2324–2335.

Wang, Y., & Witten, I. H. (1996). *Induction of Model Trees for Predicting Continuous Classes*. Hamilton, New Zealand: University of Waikato, Department of Computer Science.

Yang, M. H., Roth, D., & Ahuja, N. (2000). A SNoW-based face detector. *Advances in Neural Information Processing Systems* (pp. 862–868).

Zualkernan, I., Aloul, F., Shapsough, S., Hesham, A., & El-Khorzaty, Y. (2017). Emotion recognition using mobile phones. *Computers & Electrical Engineering, 60*, 1–13.

Chapter 31

Biometrics-Based Authentication Scheme for Cloud Environment

G. Jaspher Willsie Kathrine

Contents

DOI: 10.1201/9780429435461-36

31.1 Introduction

In cloud computing, dedicated systems, storage spaces and processors are maintained
to provide solutions to the users. Here the user pays for use rather than contribut-
ing for use as in grid computing. The definition for cloud computing (Klem et al.
2008) is given as, "The Cloud is a large-scale distributed computing paradigm that is
driven by economies of scale, in which a pool of abstracted, virtualized, dynamically
scalable, managed computing power, storage, platforms, and services are delivered
on demand to external customers over the Internet". Cloud computing and is gaining significance due to the widespread use of broadband Internet services. Cloud
computing has been developed by the basic framework of Infrastructure as a Service
(IAAS), Platform as a Service, Security as a Service and Software as a service.

According to the National Institute of Science and Technology (NIST) (Mell
and Grance 2011) the main characteristics of cloud computing are on-demand self
service, rapid elasticity and metered service. This metered service makes cloud similar to the grid form of utility computing. The types of cloud based on deployment
are termed as private cloud: limited to and organization or industry, public cloud:
accessible to public, community cloud: shared by several organizations and hybrid
cloud: a combination of any of the above types of cloud deployment. In some cases,
private cloud is not considered as a cloud service until all the internal features of the
organization are modified as per cloud requirements.

In the initial stages of cloud computing only a homogeneous Service Provider
(SP) was in existence and there was no need for a single sign on (SSO). But now, the
scenario includes a SP who provides more than one service and so, there is a need
for single sign on SSO to be provided by using the proxy credentials for each user.
The biometric based user authentication scheme is designed for a SP who provides
more than one service.

31.2 Related Work

In cloud computing the registration of a new user and the future login are dependent on the credit card details and the user's email address (Foster et al. 2008).
Hence, there is a need for a more secure authentication scheme to enhance the usage

of the cloud resource both for the resource provider and the user. An identity based cryptography method (Yan et al. 2009) was proposed to increase cloud security. In this scheme each user is provided a federated identity management in the cloud such that each user and each server has its own unique identity. In another identity-based cryptographic system (Schridde et al. 2010), each user and server is allocated a unique identity hierarchically by the system. An enhanced identity based authentication scheme for cloud computing was proposed with the usage of identity based encryption and signature schemes (Li et al. 2009). The identity based schemes were presented to reduce the complexity of certificate based security schemes.

A trusted cloud computing paradigm was proposed which included a trusted third party for user and server authentication (Zissis and Lekkas 2012; Shen et al. 2010). Since trusted computing depends more on a third-party compromise, in security it is very high if the third party becomes invalid. Smart card based authentication schemes with role based access control have been proposed (Choudhury et al. 2011; Urien et al. 2010). To make the protocol aware of internal as well as external denial of service (DoS) attacks, a solution using a multi-level adaptive technique to analyse a user's request before the authentication process was proposed (Darwish et al. 2015). An elliptic curve based anonymous authentication was proposed for securing a mobile cloud environment (Yang et al. 2016). A theoretic biometrics-based multi-cloud server based authentication scheme for authenticating a user to big data and Cloud of Things server (CoT) was proposed (Kumari et al. 2017). A security enhanced multi-factor biometric authentication scheme is proposed to overcome biometric recognition error, slow wrong password detection, off-line password attack, user impersonation attack, ID guessing attack, etc (Choi et al. 2017). The proposed scheme has been analysed by the Burrows-Abadi-Needham logic (BAN). The proposed scheme has an increased computational cost and can be utilized where the computational cost efficiency is not required.

31.3 Need for Belief Logics

Belief logic is utilized to discuss the absoluteness of a cryptographic protocol by formal means. The widely followed belief logic BAN (Burrows et al. 1990) is the foundation for all other belief logics. The limitations of BAN logic is the indistinguishable representation of certain variations in the protocols. These variations in protocols maybe significant in deciding the security effectiveness of the protocol (Nessett 1990, Boyd and Mao 1994). An extension to BAN logic is given as Gong, Needham, Yahalom (GNY) logic (1990) and Syverson Van and Oorschot (SVO) logic (Syverson and Van Oorschot 1994). Belief logic is based on the assumption that the analysis of the algorithms can be done on the basis of logical equations to check the security completeness of the given algorithms. Any breach in security can be identified by analysing each step in the algorithm through the belief logic based analysis. To analyse the biometrics-based user authentication scheme, on the basis of logical analysis against replay attacks, GNY logic is considered. The basic formulae and statements common to the formulation of the cryptographic schemes are given below.

A formula is equivalent to a variable which is in turn referred to as a bit string that is used in GNY logic. Each string has a particular value in an execution. X and Y are considered as a range in the formulae. Some formulas in GNY logic are (Gong et al. 1990),

(X, Y): indicates conjunction of two formulae X & Y.

$\{X\}_{+K}, \{X\}_{K^{-1}}$: indicates symmetrically encrypt and decrypt X with key K.

$\{X\}_{+K}, \{X\}_{-K}$: indicates asymmetrically encrypt/ decrypt X with a public key +K and private key –K.

$D_{N_U}(E_{N_U}\{SED, h(K_S), K_S\})$: indicates a one-way function with input X.

$^*X$: X is not originated here.

The formulae are depicted as statements in GNY logic. P and Q are considered as the principals in the GNY logic. In our security scheme user A can be related to P and the server B can be related to Q of GNY logic.

$P \triangleleft X$: P is told X

$P \ni X$: P possesses X

$P| \sim X$: P once conveyed X

$P| \equiv \neq (X)$: P considers that X is new

$P| \equiv \phi(X)$: P considers that X is identifiable

$P| \equiv P \overset{S}{\leftrightarrow} Q$: P considers that S is a suitable secret for P and Q

$P| \equiv \overset{+K}{\mapsto} Q$: P considers that +K is a suitable public key for Q

$P \triangleleft {}^*X$: P is told X that he did not communicate previously in the present run

31.4 Biometric Security Preliminaries

"Bio" is a word derived from the Greek word "bios" which means "life". Metric is derived from the Greek word "metron" which means "measure". Measuring data from a living organism for unique identification is biometric authentication. Biometric data for human beings include fingerprint, palm print, gait, facial features, iris and now it has extended to even heartbeat. Many biometric based matching techniques have been proposed by authors for unique user authentication. This part of the chapter analyses the well used biometric matching techniques.

An iris template, facial feature, fingerprint or multimedia, etc. represent the biometric data (Al Bouna et al. 2009). Fingerprint matching techniques for verification and identification is broadly classified as image-based, correlation-based and minutiae-based (Maio et al. 2003). The matching based on a fingerprint based verification scheme is shown in Figure 31.1.

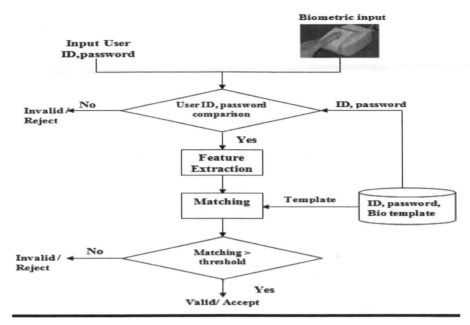

Figure 31.1 Basic biometrics-based verification system.

A verification algorithm based on proposed representation of the finger minutia was proposed, tested and found to be optimal (Tico and Kuosmanen 2003). But minutia collection devices need to be very accurate else even a valid user can be rejected. Image based fingerprint verification approaches were identified (Jain et al. 1999, Jain et al. 2000, Teoh et al. 2004) to perform the extraction of the fingerprint features directly from the unprocessed image such as a gray-level fingerprint image.

Image based techniques can be disturbed by non-linear distortions and noise in the image. In the correlation-based approaches (Bazen et al. 2000) the spatial association between equivalent pixels is calculated for approximating the degree of resemblance between the input fingerprint image and template for different alignments. A FingerCode scheme (Jain et al. 2000) was proposed that takes into account the local features and global features of the given fingerprint into a character vector of set length. The generic representation of oriented texture is dependent on the extraction of a core point in the fingerprint image. A variant of the Finger Code scheme was proposed (Ross et al. 2003) in which the fingerprint images and the overall minutiae information are aligned together. The proposed scheme was considered to be efficient and easy to use than utilizing the core point alone for the alignment of the image pair. A method for verification solely based on image-based fingerprint was proposed (Nanni and Lumini 2006a). In this image-based fingerprint scheme, a set of training fingerprints are used to determine the parameters solely dependent on the user. These parameters characterize the variance contained in the training fingerprints. While a set of test fingerprints are input to the system for verification, each of them are matched to each of the training fingerprints of the affirmed person. More biometric based authentication schemes which have used biometric templates have been discussed (Li et al. 2011, Li and Hwang 2010, Chang et al. 2004). The advantages of using an image based verification scheme have been justified as (Nanni and Lumini 2009), the high capability of image-based schemes to deal with low quality images in obtaining a reliable minutiae set gives an increase in the performance in verification. The fusion of a minutiae based scheme with an image based scheme (Ross et al. 2003) was proposed and the option of indicating a fingerprint as a point in a vector space by generating a character vector of preset length was also discussed (Nanni and Lumini 2006b). The generation of a fixed length value helps to combine the output with a random number such as a key to generate a Biohash code (Jin et al. 2004, Lumini and Nanni 2007). The BioHashing method proposed (Lumini and Nanni 2007) has been proven to be secured in the worst case scenario, which is that of an imposter stealing the hash key value. The texture descriptors taken from the fingerprints can also be used for BioHashing (Nanni and Lumini 2008). Robust hashing was proposed (Sutcu et al. 2005) where it is debated that it is computationally hard to get the pre-image of the template and it is computationally difficult to identify the original template from the deduced pre-image.

A BioPhasor technique was proposed (Teoh et al. 2007) where the rows of the orthogonal transformation matrix are used as an imaginary value and added to the biometric vector to obtain a set of complex vectors. The argument of the values from each vector is averaged and quantized to obtain the final binary template. A biometric based remote user authentication technique for multi-server environment has been proposed (Neha et al. 2017). It uses a key stroke based multi-server authentication model. A comparison has been done of the normal key stroke to biohashed key stroke authentication. An optimal Equal Error Rate (EER) rate of 0.15% is achieved in comparison to the plain key stroke value of 0.231% Equal Error Rate (EER). A fusion method is proposed (Manasa et al. 2104) that maximally correlates information captured from both features thereby removing the redundant information, which results in a more compact representation of the biometric feature. The biometric traits fused are fingerprint, palm print and iris modalities. Biometric feature extraction and recognition based on the ear was proposed (Pflug et al. 2012). The structure of the ear is not only distinctive, but also permanent, it does not change during the life of a human being. A novel biometric modality based on typing behaviour of the user was proposed (Roth et al. 2014). In this, through the usage of a webcam, the user's typing pattern is captured and a pattern is generated using real-time computer vision algorithms. This method has shown an improvement when compared with keystroke dynamics. A multifactor biometric authentication system for a cloud computing environment was proposed (Ziyad and Kannammal 2014). Palm vein and fingerprint biometrics are used together. The palm vein biometric data is stored in smart cards and the fingerprint data is stored in the central database of the cloud server. Fingerprint based user verification and identification is the most user-friendly and relatively easy technique for biometric data access.

Table 31.1   Comparison of Image-Based Biometric Schemes

Technique	Transformation	Final Representation	Security
FingerCode – Jain et al. (2000)	Random matrix convolution	Vector	Low
Gabor + Local Binary Pattern (LBP) – Nanni et al. (2008)	Fourier Transform and Tessellation by square overlapping grid	Vector	Medium
BioHashing – Jin et al. (2004)	Random Matrix Multiplication	Vector	High Medium if key stolen
Improved BioHashing – Lumini et al. (2007)	Multiple times random matrix multiplication and normalization	Vector	High

Table 31.1 gives an overall summary of the biometric template based comparison schemes. For the sake of a high security and less false rejection rate the Equal Error Rate (EER is the rate at which the false acceptance and false rejection is equal and very low) of each of the existing schemes is considered. The lower the EER rate, the higher the security of the biometric based comparison scheme. Database 2 in Fingerprint Verification Competition (FVC) DB 2002 (Fingerprint Verification Competition (FVC) 2002) has optimum conditions for usage and hence it is considered for use in the biometrics-based user authentication scheme. This database consists of 800 images of 100 fingers with 8 impressions per finger obtained using an optical sensor. The size of the images in this database is 296 × 560 pixels and the resolution of the sensor is 569 dpi. Six images of DB2 are of good quality while 2 images are out of focus in such a way that the core point is not clearly visible.

Table 31.2   Equal Error Rate Value for the Biometric Comparison Schemes

Technique	DB1	DB2	DB3	DB4
FingerCode – Jain et al. (2000)	10	9.8	25.5	14.8
Fingerprint recognition Scheme – Nanni et al. (2006)	5.5	**5.2**	18.3	8.4
Gabor + Local Binary Pattern (LBP) – Nanni et al. (2008)	3.7	**2.4**	5.5	3.7
BioHashing – Teoh Beng Jin et al. (2004)	8	8	16	9.6
Improved BioHashing – Lumini et al. (2007)	4	**3.75**	11	4.5

Table 31.2 gives the data obtained from the comparison of the various EER values of the already presented biometric schemes. The EER values have been considered for FVC 2002 database to select the optimal database for consideration as an input for the specific biometric comparison scheme. Since EER are ratios there is no unit.

Based on the EER value of the Table 31.2, the DB2 of FVC 2002 is considered efficient for carrying out image based template generation and comparison.

31.5 Biometrics-Based Authentication Scheme for Cloud Application

In order to enhance the security and to make it applicable to mobile devices in the future, a smart card based biometric user authentication scheme is proposed. To avoid problems occurring due to key management, smart cards can be used. It is assumed that the biometric data sensor/device is available in the system used by the user. The framework of the biometric based user authentication scheme is shown in Figure 31.2.

Similar to any smart card based scheme, in the biometric based user authentication scheme there exists a mandatory registration phase. In the registration phase, the user is requested to enter his/her biometric data into the SP database. Privacy as well as non-repudiated user authentication is a must for cloud computing. This is due to the fact that it involves data access, storage and metering/paying for the resource used. The smart card assumed to be used in the biometric based authentication scheme is a contactless type of a smart card. Though contactless smart cards have some security threats, it can be removed by the usage of strong cryptography (Kundarap et al. 2010). In many cases the user identifier (ID) refers to the username that is provided by the user. But in the biometric based authentication scheme, the identifier for every user is based on the username and the concatenation of the data related specifically to the server of the SP. Such a method can help identify the validity of the user identity specific to the SP. The notations used in this chapter are given in Table 31.3.

During the registration phase, the user's identifier, biometric data and hashed password is collected by the SP and stored in the smart card.

The data stored in the smart card can be denoted as, $h(PW_i), ID_i, y_i$ where $y_i = E_x\{B_i \oplus ID_i\}$. The value of 'x' indicates the secret key of the server. The data are all stored in hashed form and not in the open data form to add integrity. Every operation being performed by the user and server from login onwards is assumed to be monitored by a monitor. Since multiple services are being serviced by the SP, a proxy is issued at the end of every login.

The sensor in the reader will have an in-built liveness detector to ensure that the biometric data is the live data and not data collected from a previous scan.

The data which is transmitted is also encrypted so that it is unfeasible for an attacker to grab the value at that instant. Nonce values are used which ensures the

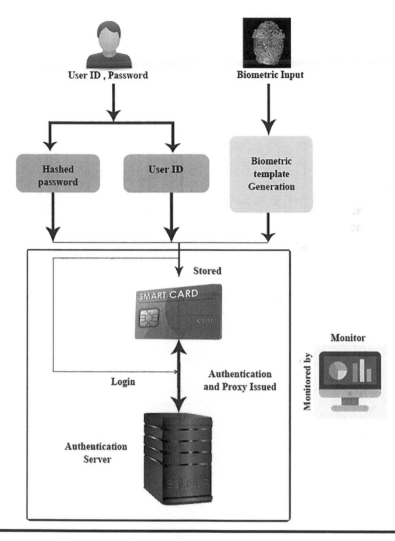

Figure 31.2   Biometric authentication scheme.

freshness of all the actions. This method of storage makes sure that the client's data is not tracked by others. During Login, the user transmits a set of data for valida-tion to the Authentication Server (AS). The message transfer during each round of the biometric based authentication scheme is shown in Figure 31.3.

When the client and the server both satisfy the validation criteria, then the data transfer will occur. If the client validation does not succeed it is rejected or the cli-ent is requested to start the authentication from the beginning of the login phase. As in every initial handshake message, the client sends its identifier, password and along with these the client's biometric data. In the biometric scheme, there is a biometric linking phase and a biometric verification phase.

Table 31.3   Notations Used

S_{ID}	Identity of Server
ID_i	Identity of client
B_i	BioHash data of client
(PW_i)	Password of client
$h(.)$	One-way hash function
P_k, S_k	Public-private key pair of server
x	Secret key of server
$\oplus$	The Exclusive-OR Operation
N_u, N_p	Nonce value generated by client
N_s	Nonce value generated by server
I	I=1,2,....n, where n denotes all users of the SP
ID_P	Proxy Identity of client
E_{P_k}, D_{P_k}	Encryption, decryption of asymmetric key
E_{Nx}, D_{Nx}	Encryption, decryption of symmetric nonce key
E_x, D_x	Encryption, decryption of symmetric key
K_S, K_P	Session Key and Proxy Key

A nonce value N_u is generated which is combined with the identifier of the client to generate the dynamic identifier for the client. This identifier is computed by concatenation of the original identifier and the nonce value generated for that session. During the handshake message, there is a nonce value generated which ensures the freshness of the whole scheme and avoids the origins of a replay attack. During login, the user enters the live bio-data for which a biohash is generated along with the issued ID and known password. The smart card compares the hashed password with the data stored in the smart card. The BioHash (Jin et al. 2004, Maio and Nanni 2006) is XORed with the hashed password to generate a much more secure biometric template. A nonce value N_u is generated which is also combined with the identifier of the client. These values along with the service requirement are sent to the AS. The AS matches the hashed password and the biometric data with the data stored in the database and confirms the identifier of the client. The nonce value is computed. The AS then sends its identifier along with a nonce value. The session key 'K$_s$', is generated by the AS. This

C   : Input PW_i & B_i where B_i is the biohash of the client.

$$SB_i = h(PW_i) \oplus B_i$$

$$y_i = E_x \{B_i \oplus ID_i\}$$

$$CID_i = ID_i \oplus N_u$$

$C \rightarrow S: E_{P_k} \{h(PW_i), SB_i, CID_i, S_{ID}, y_i\}$

S   : $D_{S_K} (E_{P_k} \{h(PW_i), SB_i, CID_i, S_{ID}, y_i\})$

$$N_U = CID_i \oplus ID_i$$

Check $h(PW_i)$ and SB_i

$$D_x(y_i) = (B_i \oplus ID_i)$$

Compare stored B_i with received B_i

$$SED = N_s \oplus S_{ID}$$

$S \rightarrow C: E_{NU} \{SED, h(K_s), K_s\}$

C   : $D_{NU} (E_{NU} \{SED, h(K_s), K_s\})$

$$N_s = SED \oplus S_{ID}$$

From K_s, $h(K_s)$ is calculated and compared.

Generate nonce value N_p

$C \rightarrow S: E_{N_s} \{sign(previous\ received\ messages), N_p\}$

S   : $D_{N_s} (E_{N_s} \{sign(previous\ received\ messages), N_p\})$

Check signed data

$$ID_P = ((ID_A \oplus ID_B) \| K_P)$$

$S \rightarrow C: E_{N_p} \{ID_P, CT_{init}\}$

Figure 31.3   Login and mutual authentication of the biometric based authentication scheme.

key is transmitted in encrypted form along with a hashed value of the key. The client decrypts the data sent by the server and confirms that the data has been sent by the server by computing the nonce value N_s.

The client proves its validity by sending a signed message of the hello message along with a nonce N_p. Once the signed message is validated, the AS sends the client proxy credentials for service access. In the biometric based authentication scheme, the dynamic identifier CID_i is used to generate a proxy for the service requested by the client. The monitor server keeps a check on the operations of the AS and the user.

31.6 Completeness of the Biometric Based Authentication Scheme

The biometric based authentication scheme is analysed for newness to avoid replay attacks and man-in-the-middle attacks through GNY logic.

31.6.1 Protocol Description

The proposed scheme is transformed into the form of $P \to Q : X$. The private key of the server is denoted as $-K$ and the public key related to the private key is shown as $+K$. The user is denoted as A and the server is denoted as B for the proposed protocol.

$$A \to B: \left\{ (ID_A \oplus N_U), (h(PW_A) \oplus B_A), ID_B, h(PW_A), \{B_A \oplus ID_A\}_x \right\}_{+K}$$

$$B \to A: \left\{ (N_S \oplus ID_B), h(K_S), K_S \right\} N_U$$

$$A \to B: \left\{ \left\{ h(K_S), K_S, h(PW_A), (N_S \oplus ID_B), CID_A, (h(PW_A) \oplus B_A), ID_B \right\}_{sign}, N_P \right\}_{N_S}$$

$$ID_B$$

The above equations are parsed through the parser. The parser produces $P| \sim X$ and $Q \triangleleft X$ for each description $P \to Q{:}X$. The parser scrutinizes all statements of the form $P| \sim X$ and $P \triangleleft X$ for each principal P. For every formula Y in $P \triangleleft X$, if Y does not appear in the line $P| \sim X$, the parser will add a star symbol before Y. The parser discards all lines of the form $P| \sim X$. Equation outputs after going through the parser are as follows:

$$B \triangleleft * \left\{ (ID_A \oplus {}^*N_U), {}^*SB_A, ID_B, {}^*h(PW_A), \{{}^*B_A \oplus ID_A\}_x \right\}_{+K} \sim\rangle A \Big| \equiv A \overset{N_U}{\leftrightarrow} B$$

$$A \triangleleft * \left\{ {}^*(N_S \oplus ID_B), {}^*h(K_S), K_S \right\} N_U \sim\rangle B \Big| \equiv A \overset{N_S}{\leftrightarrow} B$$

$$B \triangleleft \left\{ \left\{ h(K_S), K_S, h(PW_A), (N_S \oplus ID_B), CID_A, (h(PW_A) \oplus B_A), ID_B \right\} sign, {}^*N_P \right\}$$
$$N_S \sim A \Big| \equiv A \overset{N_P}{\leftrightarrow} B$$

$$\{ (((h(ID_A) \oplus n_u \oplus ID_B) \| K_P), CT_{init} \}_{n_p}$$

31.7 Goals

31.7.1 Message Content Authentication

1. B considers that the message in the first flow is identifiable

$$B \Big|\equiv \phi \big\{ (ID_A \oplus N_U), (h(PW_A) \oplus B_A), ID_B, h(PW_A), \{B_A \oplus ID_A\}_x \big\}_{+K}$$

2. A considers that the second flow message is identifiable

$$A \Big|\equiv \phi \big\{ (N_S \oplus ID_B), h(K_S), K_S \big\}_{N_U}$$

3. B considers that the third flow message is identifiable

$$B \Big|\equiv \phi \left\{ \begin{bmatrix} h(K_S), K_S, h(PW_A), (N_S \oplus ID_B), CID_A, \\ (h(PW_A) \oplus B_A), ID_B \end{bmatrix} sign, N_P \right\}_{N_S}$$

4. A considers that the message in the fourth flow is identifiable

$$A \Big|\equiv \phi \big\{ ((ID_A \oplus ID_B) \| K_P), CT_{init} \big\}_{N_P}$$

31.7.2 Message Origin Authentication

1. A considers that B told the message in the second flow

$$A \Big|\equiv B \big|\sim \big\{ (N_S \oplus ID_B), h(K_S), K_S \big\}_{N_U}$$

2. B considers that A told the message in the third flow

$$B \Big|\equiv A \big|\sim \left\{ \begin{bmatrix} h(K_S), K_S, h(PW_A), (N_S \oplus ID_B), CID_A, \\ (h(PW_A) \oplus B_A), ID_B \end{bmatrix} sign, N_P \right\}_{N_S}$$

3. A considers that B informed the message in the fourth flow

$$A \Big|\equiv B\Big|\sim \left\{\left(\left(ID_A \oplus ID_B\right)\|K_P\right),CT_{init}\right\}_{N_P}$$

31.7.3 General Identity Authentication

B considers that A holds the hashed password and the original biometric to generate the template

$$B\Big|\equiv A \ni \left(h\left(PW_A\right),SB_A\right)$$

31.7.4 Session Key Material Establishment

A considers that B considers that Nu is a secret shared between A & B

$$A\Big|\equiv B\Big|\equiv A \overset{N_U}{\leftrightarrow} B$$

A considers that Nu is a secret shared between A & B

$$A\Big|\equiv A \overset{N_U}{\leftrightarrow} B$$

B considers that A possesses Nu

$$B\Big|\equiv A \ni N_U$$

B considers that A considers that Nu is a secret shared between A & B

$$B\Big|\equiv A\Big|\equiv A \overset{N_U}{\leftrightarrow} B$$

31.8 Assumptions List

The assumptions made for the analysis of the proposed scheme are

■ The string N_U is generated by A in the scheme so that A possesses N_U and considers N_U is new.

$$A \ni N_U, A\Big|\equiv\# \left(N_U\right)$$

■ Since server's identity ID_B is public, A considers that ID_B is identifiable.

$$A \!\mid\!\equiv \phi(ID_B)$$

■ The string N_U generated by A is a session key generated in the present message. Therefore, it is assumed that A considers that N_U is an apt undisclosed data between A and B.

$$A \!\mid\!\equiv A \overset{N_U}{\leftrightarrow} B$$

■ A considers that the server B is the right authority on getting appropriate session key data N_S shared between A and B

$$A \!\mid\!\equiv B \!\mid\!\Rightarrow A \overset{N_S}{\leftrightarrow} B$$

■ B holds the private key $-K$, the public key $+K$ and secret key x
$B \ni -K, B \ni +K, B \ni x$
■ The string N_S is generated by A in the scheme so that A possesses N_S and considers N_U is new.

$$B \ni N_S, B \!\mid\!\equiv\!\neq (N_S)$$

■ The string N_P is generated by A in the scheme so that A possesses N_P and considers N_P is new.

$$A \ni N_P, A \!\mid\!\equiv\!\neq (N_P)$$

■ The string N_P generated by A is a session key generated in the present message transfer. Therefore, it is assumed that A considers that N_P is an apt secret between A and B.

$$A \!\mid\!\equiv A \overset{N_P}{\leftrightarrow} B$$

■ Since B keeps the ID table, B considers that ID_A is identifiable

$$B \!\mid\!\equiv \phi(ID_A)$$

31.9 Logical Analysis

The proposed scheme is analysed in accordance to the logical hypothesize in the GNY logic.

31.9.1 The First Flow

$$\frac{B \lhd \left\{ (ID_A \oplus {}^*N_U), SB_A, ID_B, h(PW_A), \{B_A \oplus ID_A\}_x \right\}_{+K}, B \ni -K}{B \lhd \left((ID_A \oplus {}^*N_U), SB_A, ID_B, h(PW_A), \{B_A \oplus ID_A\}_x \right)} \text{(T 4)}$$

If B is told $(ID_A \oplus {}^*N_U), SB_A, ID_B, h(PW_A), \{B_A \oplus ID_A\}_x$ with the public key $+K$ encrypted than the server holds the corresponding private key $-K$ then the server is considered to have also been told the decrypted contents of that encrypted formula

$$\frac{B \lhd \{B_A \oplus ID_A\}_x, B \ni x}{B \lhd (B_A \oplus ID_A)}$$

If B is told encrypted formula $(B_A \oplus ID_A)$ with key x the server B possesses, then the server is believed to have been informed the decrypted values of the encrypted equation.

$$\frac{B \models \phi(ID_A), B \ni x}{B \models \phi\{B_A \oplus ID_A\}_x} \text{(R 1, R 2)}$$

If B considers that the formula ID_A is identifiable and holds the key x then the server B is entitled to believe that the encrypted equation $B \lhd \{B_A \oplus ID_A\}_x$ of which $B \lhd \{B_A \oplus ID_A\}_x$ is a part which is identifiable. Therefore it is proved that the secret in the smart card is proved by the server.

$$\frac{B \models \phi\{B_A \oplus ID_A\}_x, B \ni +K}{B \models \phi\left\{ \{(ID_A \oplus {}^*N_U), SB_A, ID_B, h(PW_A), \{B_A \oplus ID_A\}_x \right\}_{+K}}$$

If B considers that the formula $\{B_A \oplus ID_A\}_x$ is identifiable and holds the public key $+K$, then B is entitled to believe that the encrypted equation, $\left\{ (ID_A \oplus {}^*N_U), SB_A, ID_B, h(PW_A), \{B_A \oplus ID_A\}_x \right\}_{+K}$, of which $\{B_A \oplus ID_A\}_x$ is a part which is identifiable. Therefore, it is proved that the server B can identify the communication in the first run of the proposed scheme.

31.9.2 The Second Flow

$$\frac{A \lhd \{(N_S \oplus ID_B), h(K_S), K_S\} N_U, A \ni N_U}{A \lhd \{(N_S \oplus ID_B), h(K_S), K_S\} N_U} (T3)$$

If A is told a formula $((N_S \oplus ID_B), h(K_s), K_s)$ encrypted with the key N_U is possessed by A then A is believed to have been informed the decrypted values of the encrypted equation.

$$\frac{A| \equiv \phi(ID_B), A \ni N_U}{A| \equiv \phi\{(N_S \oplus ID_B), h(K_S), K_S\}_{N_U}} (R1, R2)$$

If A considers that the formula ID_B is identifiable and A holds the key N_U, then A considers that formula $\{(N_S \oplus ID_B), h(K_S), K_S\}_{N_U}$, of which ID_B is a part that is identifiable. Therefore, it is proven that A can recognize the equation in the second run of the proposed scheme.

$$\frac{A| \equiv \phi(ID_B), A \ni N_U, A| \equiv \#(N_U)}{A| \equiv \#\{(N_S \oplus ID_B), h(K_S), K_S\}_{N_U}} (F1, F7)$$

If A considers that the formula ID_B is identifiable and A has the key N_U and considers that it is new, then A considers that the encrypted equation $\{(N_S \oplus ID_B), h(K_S), K_S\}_{N_U}$ of which ID_B is a part is new. Therefore, it is proved that A identifies that the message in the second flow of the proposed scheme is new.

$$A \lhd *\{(N_S \oplus ID_B), h(K_S), K_S\}_{N_U}, A \ni N_U,$$

$$\frac{A| \equiv A \leftrightarrow B, A| \equiv \phi(ID_B, N_S), A| \equiv \#(N_U)}{A| \equiv B|\sim\{(N_S \oplus ID_B), h(K_S), K_S\} N_U, A| \equiv B \ni N_U} (I1)$$

If all of the conditions hold: (1) A receives the formula $(N_S \oplus ID_B), h(K_S), K_S$ encrypted with the key N_U and marked with a non-originated mark; (2) A possesses N_U; (3) A considers that N_U is an apt secret between A and B; (4) A considers that the formula $(N_S \oplus ID_B), h(K_S), K_S$ is identifiable because ID_B is identifiable and (5) A considers that N_U is new, A considers that B once informed $\{(N_S \oplus ID_B), h(K_S), K_S\}_{N_U}$ and that B possesses N_U.

Therefore, it is proven that: (1) A considers that the second message is from the server in the proposed scheme B and (2) A considers that the server B has the temporal key N_U.

31.9.3 The Third Flow

$$
\cfrac{B \lhd \left\{ \left[\begin{matrix} h(K_s), K_s, h(PW_A), (N_S \oplus ID_B), CID_A, \\ (h(PW_A) \oplus B_A), ID_B \end{matrix} \right]_{\text{sign}}, N_P \right\}_{N_S}, B \ni N_s}{B \lhd \left(\left\{ \left[\begin{matrix} h(K_s), K_s, h(PW_A), (N_S \oplus ID_B), CID_A, \\ (h(PW_A) \oplus B_A), ID_B \end{matrix} \right]_{\text{sign}}, N_P \right\} \right)}
$$

If B is told the formula $\left(\{ h(K_s), K_s, h(PW_A), (N_S \oplus ID_B), CID_A, (h(PW_A) \oplus B_A), ID_B \}_{\text{sign}}, N_P \right)$ encrypted with the key N_S that B possesses, and then B is believed to have been informed the decrypted values of the encrypted equation.

$$
\cfrac{B \mid \equiv \phi \,(\text{signed message}), B \ni N_S}{B \mid \equiv \phi \left\{ \left[\begin{matrix} h(K_S), K_S, h(PW_A), (N_S \oplus ID_B), CID_A, \\ (h(PW_A) \oplus B_A), ID_B \end{matrix} \right]_{\text{sign}}, N_P \right\}_{N_S}} \quad (R\,1, R2)
$$

Signed message denotes $\{ h(K_S), K_S, h(PW_A), (N_S \oplus ID_B), CID_A, (h(PW_A) \oplus B_A), ID_B \}_{\text{sign}}$. If B considers that ID_B is identifiable then the formula of which ID_B is a part is identifiable. Therefore, it is proven that B can identify the third flow of the proposed scheme.

$$
\cfrac{B \left| \begin{matrix} \equiv \phi((h(K_S), K_S, h(PW_A), (N_S \oplus ID_B), CID_A, \\ (h(PW_A) \oplus B_A), ID_B)_{\text{sign}}, N_P), B \mid \equiv \#(N_S), B \ni N_S \end{matrix} \right.}{A \left| \begin{matrix} \equiv \#\{\{h(K_S), K_S, h(PW_A), (N_S \oplus ID_B), CID_A, \\ (h(PW_A) \oplus B_A), ID_B \}_{\text{sign}}, N_P \}_{N_S} \end{matrix} \right.} \quad (R\,1, R2)
$$

If B considers that the formula ID_B is identifiable and B has the key N_S and considers that it is new, then B considers that the encrypted equation $\{\{h(K_S), K_S, h(PW_A), (N_S \oplus ID_B), CID_A, (h(PW_A) \oplus B_A), ID_B \}_{\text{sign}}, N_P \}_{N_S}$, of which ID_B is a part is new. Therefore, B can recognize the third flow message of the proposed scheme as new.

$$B \triangleleft *\{\{h(K_S),K_S,h(PW_A),(N_S \oplus ID_B),CID_A(h(PW_A) \oplus B_A),$$

$$ID_B\}_{sign},N_P\}N_S,B \ni N_S,$$

$$\cfrac{B \underset{B \equiv A \leftrightarrow B,B}{\overset{N_U}{\left|\begin{array}{l} \equiv \phi(\text{signedmessage}, N_P,), \\ A| \equiv \#((\text{signedmessage},N_P)) \end{array}\right.}}}{B| \equiv A|\sim(\text{signedmessage},N_P),} \tag{13}$$

$$B|\equiv A \left|\begin{array}{l} \sim \{\{h(K_S),K_S,h(PW_A),(N_S \oplus ID_B),CID_A(h(PW_A) \oplus B_A), \\ ID_B\}_{sign},N_P\}N_S,B|\equiv A \ni N_S \end{array}\right.$$

If all of the conditions hold: (1) B receives the formula $\big(\{h(K_S),K_S,h(PW_A),$ $(N_S \oplus ID_B),CID_A(h(PW_A) \oplus B_A),ID_B\}_{sign},N_P\big)$ encrypted with the key N_S and marked with a non-originated mark; (2) B possesses N_S; (3) B considers that N_S is an apt secret between A and B; (4) B considers that the formula $\big(\{h(K_S),K_S,h(PW_A),(N_S \oplus ID_B),CID_A(h(PW_A) \oplus B_A),ID_B\}_{sign},N_P\big)$ is identifiable because ID_B is identifiable and (5) B considers that N_S is new, A considers that B once informed $\{\{h(K_S),K_S,h(PW_A),(N_S \oplus ID_B),CID_A(h(PW_A) \oplus B_A),ID_B\}_{sign},N_P\}N_S$ and that B possesses N_S.

Therefore, it is proven that: (1) B considers that the third flow message of the proposed scheme is from the A and (2) B considers that the A has the temporal key N_S.

31.9.4 The Fourth Flow

$$\cfrac{A \triangleleft \sim \{((ID_A \oplus ID_B)\|K_P),CT_{init}\}_{N_P},A \ni N_P}{A \triangleleft (((ID_A \oplus ID_B)\|K_P),CT_{init})} \tag{T 3}$$

If A is told the formula $((ID_A \oplus ID_B)\|K_P),CT_{init})$ encrypted with the key N_P that it possesses, then A is considered to have also been told the decrypted contents of the encrypted equation.

$$\cfrac{A|\equiv \phi((ID_A,ID_B)A \ni N_P)}{A|\equiv \phi\{((ID_A \oplus ID_B)\|K_P,CT_{init}\}_{N_P}} \tag{R 1,R 2}$$

If A considers that the formula ID_A and ID_B is identifiable and has the key N_P, then A is entitled to believe that the formula $\{((ID_A \oplus ID_B)\|K_P,CT_{init}\}_{N_P}$, of which ID_A and ID_B are parts which are identifiable. Therefore, it is proven that A can identify the message in the fourth flow of the proposed scheme.

$$\frac{A\vert\equiv\phi((ID_A\oplus ID_B)\Vert K_P,CT_{init}),A\vert\equiv(N_P),A\ni N_P}{B\vert\equiv\#\{(ID_A\oplus ID_B)\Vert K_P,CT_{init}\}_{N_P}}\text{(F7)}$$

If A considers that the formula ID_A and ID_B is identifiable and has the key N_P and considers that it is new, then A is entitled to believe that the encrypted equation $\{(ID_A\oplus ID_B)\Vert K_P,CT_{init}\}_{N_P}$, of which ID_A and ID_B are parts which are new. Therefore, it is proven that A can identify the message in the fourth flow of the proposed scheme is new.

$$A\vartriangleleft *\{(ID_A\oplus ID_B)\Vert K_P,CT_{init}\}_{N_P},A\ni N_P,$$

$$\cfrac{A\left\vert\equiv A\overset{N_P}{\leftrightarrow}B,,A\left\vert\begin{matrix}\equiv\phi((ID_A\oplus ID_B)\Vert K_P,CT_{init}),\\[4pt]B\vert\equiv\#((ID_A\oplus ID_B)\Vert K_P,CT_{init})\end{matrix}\right.\right.}{A\left\vert\begin{matrix}\equiv B\vert\sim((ID_A\oplus ID_B)\Vert K_P,CT_{init}),\\[4pt]A\vert\equiv B\vert\sim\{(ID_A\oplus ID_B)\Vert K_P,CT_{init}\}_{N_P},A\vert\equiv B\ni N_P\end{matrix}\right.}\text{(I1)}$$

If all of the conditions hold: (1) A receives the formula $((ID_A\oplus ID_B)\Vert K_P,CT_{init})$ encrypted with the key N_P and marked with a non-originated mark; (2) A possesses N_P; (3) A considers that N_P is an apt secret between A and B; (4) A considers that the formula $((ID_A\oplus ID_B)\Vert K_P,CT_{init})$ is identifiable because ID_B is identifiable and (5) A considers that N_P is new, A considers that B once informed $\{(ID_A\oplus ID_B)\Vert K_P,CT_{init}\}_{N_P}$ and that B possesses N_P.

Therefore, it is confirmed that: (1) A considers that the fourth flow message of the proposed scheme is from B and (2) A considers that the B has the temporal key N_P.

Therefore, it is proven that there exists a newness value included in all of the messages. Due to this newness of data, man-in-the-middle attack, snooping attack, which can lead to replay attack, and modification attack can be avoided.

31.10 Performance Analysis

31.10.1 Communication Cost Comparison

For comparison of communication cost between the authentication schemes, only the dominant communication costs in bytes are considered. Such costs include cost incurred due to the certificate generation, encryption and signing of messages. The comparison of the biometric based authentication scheme is with the Secure Socket Layer (SSL) (Freier et al. 1996) based authentication since the cloud computing authentication basis is the SSL protocol and ID based authentication scheme for

Table 31.4   Comparison of Communication Cost

SSL BASED AUTHENTICATION (Freier et al. 1996)		ID Based Scheme (Li et al. 2009)		The Biometric Based Authentication Scheme	
Certificate	RSA Signature	IBS Signature	IBE Ciphertext	ECC Based Ciphertext	ECDSA Signature
2	2	1	1	1	1

Cloud Computing (IBACC) (Li et al. 2009). Identity based Signing (IBS) and Identity based Encryption (IBE) are considered in the IBACC scheme.

The communication cost details are observed in Table 31.4 and it is evident that the biometric based authentication scheme has the major communication cost involving elliptic curve cryptography (ECC) based encryption and ECC based signature. The main advantage of an ECC based scheme is its low key size (160 bits when compared to 1024 of RSA). It also has the advantage of more effort required for breaking ECC based schemes. ECC has also been proven to be useful for handheld devices (Alghazzawi et al. 2011). This reduced communication cost indicates that the biometric based authentication scheme can also be extended to mobile handheld devices.

31.10.2   Computation Cost and Long-Term Storage Comparison

The computation cost of SSL based authentication, ID based authentication scheme for Cloud Computing (IBACC) and the biometric based authentication scheme includes only the operations which encompass encryption, decryption, signing and certificate generation/verification. The biometric based authentication scheme uses ECC based encryption and verification and the SSL based authentication uses RSA for encryption, decryption and signing. IBACC uses ID based encryption and signing. The cost of SSL based authentication is increased due to the certificate generation and maintenance.

Computation cost of the biometric based authentication scheme is compared with SSL based authentication and IBACC in Table 31.5. The operations done in the biometric based authentication scheme is much less when compared to SSL based authentication and IBACC schemes. The bit size used in the RSA scheme is higher (1024 bits) than the ECC (160 bits). In the ID based scheme there is a need for the maintenance of ID table, ID revocation list and the escrow problem.

The long-term storage values denote the need of the storage required for the respective schemes. Based on the long-term storage requirements, the capacity of the server/database required for the application is determined. In the biometric based authentication scheme there is only the need for storage of the BioHash of every user which is also stored in hashed form. The short-term storage requirements will be almost the same as storage of short term keys, nonces, proxy identities, etc., for all the three schemes.

Table 31.5 Comparison of Computation Cost and Storage

	SSL BASED AUTHENTICATION (Freier et al. 1996)	*ID Based Scheme (Li et al. 2009)*	*The Biometric Based Authentication Scheme*
Client	1 ENC$_{RSA}$, 1 SIG$_{RSA}$ and certificate verification	1 ENC$_{ID}$ and 1 DEC$_{ID}$	1 ENC$_{ECC}$ and 1 VER$_{ECC}$
Server	1 DEC$_{RSA}$, 1SIG$_{RSA}$ and Authenticating client	1 DEC$_{ID}$ and 1 V ER$_{ID}$	1 DEC$_{ECC}$
Long-Term Storage	Certificates	Identity based values and attributes	BioHash

31.11 Simulation

31.11.1 Simulation Platform

CloudSim (Calheiros et al. 2011) is a Java based simulation platform for creating a cloud environment. New modules of clients and resources can be integrated into CloudSim by rewriting the interfaces. P4 machines with 3.0 GHz CPU, 4 GB RAM, Windows XP Operating System and Java2 SDK 1.4 are used. Openss l0.9.7 is used to generate the SSL based authentication scheme. In the biometric based authentication scheme, ECC of 160 bits is used for the asymmetric encryption. For symmetric encryption a nonce based encryption scheme is used which further enhances the privacy of the scheme. The nonce key size is assumed to be 128 bits to enhance security. The public domain fingerprint database FVC2002-DB2 is taken as the input for our fingerprint. One hundred user fingerprints each with 6 impressions are considered as the biometric input. The threshold value for the BioHash computation is taken as $\tau = 0.06$, in 5 steps (value of p) with 5 permutations (value of q) for a key space of 5 values. For secure hash based operations SHA 256 is used.

31.11.2 Simulation Results and Analysis

Table 31.6 and Figure 31.4 shows the comparison of the communication cost of the biometric based authentication scheme in relation to the existing schemes. The biometric based authentication scheme has a communication cost of 8% of SSL based authentication scheme and 26% of IBACC.

From Table 31.6, it is clear that the biometric based authentication scheme has a much lesser communication time of an average of 463 bytes when compared to the 1810 of IBACC and 5852 bytes of SSL based authentication scheme.

Table 31.7 and Figure 31.5 shows the time taken for the purpose of user authentication for all three protocols. All the protocols have the required underlying

Table 31.6 Comparison of Communication Cost of the Biometric Based Authentication Scheme with Existing Scheme for Cloud Environment

No. of Users	The Biometric Based Authentication Scheme (Bytes)	Identity Based Scheme (IBACC) (Bytes)	SSL Based Scheme (Bytes)
10	462	1782	5858
20	925	3665	11702
30	1386	5450	17549
40	1849	7238	23382
50	2312	9127	29237
60	2774	10919	35082
70	3237	12698	40964
80	3701	14482	46813
90	4164	16292	52664
100	4627	18071	58519

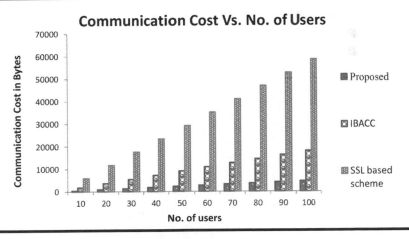

Figure 31.4 Comparison of communication cost.

feature of scalability, but the time taken is optimal for the biometric based authentication scheme user authentication.

The authentication time for the biometric based authentication scheme is reducing the time taken by the SSL based authentication scheme by 11% and the biometric based authentication scheme is 19% of that of IBACC. The time taken for authentication is also very low when compared with the IBACC and SSL based authentication scheme.

Table 31.7   Comparison of Authentication Time

No. of Users	The Biometric Based Authentication Scheme (ms)	Identity Based Scheme (IBACC) (ms)	SSL Based Scheme (ms)
10	106	560	980
20	209	1133	1953
30	311	1700	2941
40	415	2271	3934
50	517	2833	4902
60	625	3411	5885
70	743	3977	6869
80	849	4553	7844
90	955	5122	8825
100	1063	5684	9801

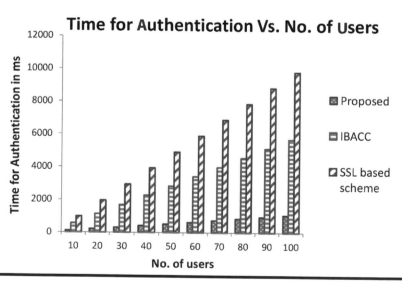

Figure 31.5   Comparison of authentication time.

The biometric based authentication scheme has a much lesser time when compared to the existing schemes. The biometric based authentication scheme has an average authentication time of 106 ms when compared to that of 569 ms for IBACC and 981 ms of SSL based authentication scheme.

The computation time in the server side is also proven to be optimal and much less time when compared with both IBACC and SSL based authentication. This is attained since the biometric based user authentication scheme does not time for storing certificates, IDs and retrieval of any such data. This reduction in process will enable the server to provide services to other valid registered users (Figure 31.6, Table 31.8).

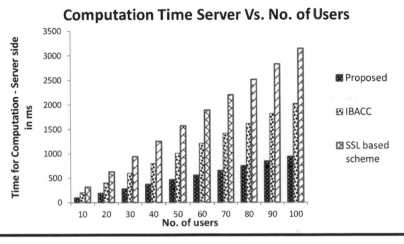

Figure 31.6   Comparison of computation time of server.

Table 31.8   Comparison of Computation Time – Server

No. of Users	The Biometric Based Authentication Scheme (ms)	Identity Based Scheme (IBACC) (ms)	SSL Based Scheme (ms)
10	94	202	315
20	186	403	629
30	278	602	940
40	371	800	1250
50	463	1005	1566
60	555	1209	1884
70	649	1412	2196
80	745	1613	2509
90	840	1817	2824
100	933	2020	3140

31.12 Summary

Image based identification of a user is the highest level of security that can be provided for any user level access. In recent years cloud and big data are gaining popularity due to their ubiquitous nature. Cloud is a ubiquitous computing technology dependent on geographically distributed computing entities like storage servers, dedicated systems and software. A cloud environment has dedicated systems, servers to provide the service promised by the service providers. As cloud computing is gaining more popularity, more importance is given to security issues such as, authentication, access control, storage, storage security and virtualization. Secure user authentication is one of the main necessities of cloud computing in order to avoid loss for a cloud service provider and to provide secure service to the valid user. A secure biometric based authentication scheme is proposed which provides secure user identification, mutual authentication, session key issue and proxy issue in cases where a single cloud SP provides more than one service. Cryptographic algorithm such as elliptic curve cryptography (ECC) is used for secure key generation and exchange. A new data is added in each round of the message communicated, to include freshness in the biometric based authentication scheme to resist against replay attack. The biometrics-based authentication scheme has optimal communication and computation cost and hence, it can also be utilized for mobile cloud users.

References

B. Al Bouna, R. Chbeir, and S. Marrara. 2009. Enforcing role based access control model with multimedia signatures. *Journal of Systems Architecture*. 55(4):264–274.

D. M. Alghazzawi, T. M. Salim, and S. H. Hasan. 2011. A secure proxy blind signature scheme using ECC. In: Fong S. (Ed) *Networked Digital Technologies*. Communications in Computer and Information Science. 136. Springer, Berlin, Germany.

A. M. Bazen, G. T. B. Verwaaijen, S. H. Gerez, L. P. J. Veelenturf, and B. Zwaag. 2000. Correlation-based fingerprint verification system. In *Proceedings of the Program for Research on Integrated Systems and Circuits*. pp. 205–213.

C. Boyd and W. Mao. 1994. On a limitation of BAN logic. In: Helleseth T. (Eds.) *Advances in Cryptology—EUROCRYPT'93*. Lecture Notes in Computer Science. 765.

M. Burrows, M. Abadi, and R. Needham. 1990. A logic of authentication. *ACM Transactions on Computer Systems*. 8(1):18–36.

R. N. Calheiros, R. Ranjan, A. Beloglazov, C. A. F. De Rose, and R. Buyya. 2011. Cloudsim: A toolkit for modeling and simulation of cloud computing environments and evaluation of resource provisioning algorithms. *Software-Practice and Experience*. 41:23–50.

C.-C. Chang and I.-C. Lin. 2004. Remarks on fingerprint-based remote user authentication scheme using smart cards. *ACM SIGOPS Operating Systems Review*. 38(4):91–96.

Y. Choi, Y. Lee, J. Moon, and D. Won. 2017. Security enhanced multi-factor biometric authentication scheme using bio-hash function. *PLoS One* 12(5): e0176250. doi:10.1371/journal.pone.0176250.

A. Choudhury, P. Kumar, M. Sain, H. Lim, and H. Jae-Lee. 2011. A strong user authentication framework for cloud computing. *IEEE Asia-Pacific Services Computing Conference.* pp. 110–115.

M. Darwish, A. Ouda, and L. F. Capretz. 2015. A cloud-based secure authentication (CSA) protocol suite for defense against Denial of Serice (DoS) attacks. *Journal of Information Security and Applications.* 20:90–98.

I. Foster, Y. Zhao, I. Raicu, and S. Lu. 2008. Cloud computing and grid computing 360-degree compared. *Grid Computing Environments Workshop.* 1–10.

A. O. Freier, P. Karlton, and Kocher P. C. 1996. The SSL Protocol, Version 3.0. INTERNET-DRAFT, draft-freier-ssl-version3-02.txt, (accessed on September 2017).

FVC2002, http://bias.csr.unibo.it/fvc2002 (accessed on July 2017).

L. Gong, R. Needham, and R. Yahalom. 1990. Reasoning about belief in cryptographic protocols. *IEEE Computer Society Symposium on Security and Privacy.* pp. 234–248.

A. K. Jain, R. Bolle, and S. Pankanti. 1999. *Biometrics: Personal Identification in Networked Society.* Kluwer Academic Publications, Boston, MA.

A. K. Jain, S. Prabhakar, L. Hong, and S. Pankanti. 2000. Filterbank-based fingerprint matching. *IEEE Transactions on Image Processing.* 5(9):846–859.

A. T. B. Jin, D. N. C. Ling, and A. Goh. 2004. Biohashing: Two factor authentication featuring fingerprint data and tokenised random number. *Pattern Recognition.* 37(11):2245–2255.

M. Klem, R. Cohen, J. Coplan, and D. Gourlay. 2008. Twenty experts define cloud computing. SYS-CON Media, http://cloudcomputing.sys-con.com/read/612375_p.htm (accessed September 2017).

S. Kumari, X. Li, F. Wu, A. K. Das, K. K. R. Choo, and J. Shen. 2017. Design of a provably secure biometrics-based multi-cloud-server authentication scheme. *Future Generation Computer Systems.* 68:320–330.

A. Kundarap, A. Chhajlani, R. Singla, M. Sawant, M. Dere, and P. Mahalle. 2010. Security for contactless smart cards using cryptography. Recent Trends in Network Security and Applications. CNSA 2010. *Communications in Computer and Information Science.* 89:558–566.

C.-T. Li and M. S. Hwang. 2010. An efficient biometrics-based remote user authentication scheme using smart cards. *Journal of Network and Computer Applications.* 33(1):1–5.

X. Li, J.-W. Niu, J. Ma, W.-D. Wang, C.-L. Liu. 2011. Cryptanalysis and improvement of a biometrics-based remote user authentication scheme using smart cards. *Journal of Network and Computer Applications.* 34(1):73–79.

H. Li, Y. Dai, L. Tian, and H. Yang. 2009. Identity-based authentication for cloud computing. *LNCS* 5931:157–166.

A. Lumini and L. Nanni. 2007. An improved biohashing for human authentication. *Pattern Recognition* 40:1057–1065.

D. Maio, D. Maltoni, A. K. Jain, and S. Prabhakar. 2003. *Handbook of Fingerprint Recognition.* Springer, Dordrecht, the Netherlands.

D. Maio and L. Nanni. 2006. MultiHashing, human authentication featuring biometrics data and tokenised random number: A case study FVC2004. *Neurocomputing.* 69:242–249.

N. Manasa, A. Govardhan, and C. Satyanarayana. 2014. Fusion of multiple biometric traits: Fingerprint palmprint and Iris. *Bio-inspiring Cyber Security and Cloud Services: Trends and Innovations.* pp. 287–320. Springer, Berlin, Germany.

P. Mell and T. Grance. 2011. The NIST definition of cloud computing. National Institute of Standards and Technology, Special Publication 800–145.

L. Nanni and A. Lumini. 2006b. A novel method for fingerprint verification that approaches the problem as a two-class pattern recognition problem. *Neurocomputing.* 69:846–849.

L. Nanni and A. Lumini. 2006a. Two-class fingerprint matcher. *Pattern Recognition.* 39(4):714–716.

L. Nanni and A. Lumini. 2008. Local binary patterns for a hybrid fingerprint matcher. *Pattern Recognition.* 41:3461–3466.

L. Nanni and A. Lumini. 2009. Descriptors for image-based fingerprint matchers. *Expert Systems with Applications.* 36:12414–12422.

D. M. Nessett. 1990. A critique of the burrows, abadi, and needham logic. *ACM SIGOPS Operating Systems Review.* 24(2):35–38.

A. Pflug and C. Busch. 2012. Ear biometrics: A survey of detection feature extraction and recognition methods. *Biometrics IET.* 1:114–129.

A. Ross, J. Jain, and Reisman. 2003. A hybrid fingerprint matcher. *Pattern Recognition.* 36(7):1661–1673.

J. Roth, X. Liu, and D. Metaxas. 2014. On continuous user authentication via typing behavior. *IEEE Transactions on Image Processing.* 23:4611–4624.

C. Schridde, T. Dornemann, E. Juhnke, B. Freisleben, and M. Smith. 2010. An identity-based security infrastructure for cloud environments. *IEEE International Conference on Wireless Communications, Networking and Information Security (WCNIS).* pp. 644–649.

Z. Shen, L. Li, F. Yan, and X. Wu. 2010. Cloud computing system based on trusted computing platform. *International Conference on Intelligent Computation Technology and Automation.* 1:942–945.

Y. Sutcu, H. T. Sencar, and N. Memon. 2005. A secure biometric authentication scheme based on robust hashing. *Proceedings of ACM Multimedia and Security Workshop.* pp. 111–116.

P. Syverson and P. C. Van Oorschot. 1994. On unifying some cryptographic protocol logics. *IEEE Computer Society Symposium on Research in Security and Privacy.* pp. 14–28.

A. B. J. Teoh, K.-A. Toh, and W. K. Yip. 2007. 2N discretisation of biophasor in cancellable biometrics. *Advances in Biometrics,* Lecture Notes in Computer Science. pp. 435–444. Springer, Berlin, Germany.

M. Tico and P. Kuosmanen. 2003. Fingerprint matching using an orientation-based minutia descriptor. *IEEE Transactions on Pattern Analysis and Machine Intelligence.* 25:1009–1014.

P. Urien, E. Marie, and C. Kiennert. 2010. An innovative solution for cloud computing authentication: Grids of EAP-TLS smart cards. *Fifth International Conference on Digital Telecommunications.* pp. 22–27. IEEE.

L. Yan, C. M. Rong, and G. S. Zhao. 2009. Strengthen cloud computing security with federal identity management using hierarchical identity-based cryptography. In the *First International Conference on Cloud Computing.* pp. 167–177. Springer, Berlin, Germany.

X. Yang, X. Huang, and J. K. Liu. 2016. Efficient handover authentication with user anonymity and un traceability for mobile cloud computing. *Future Generation Computer Systems.* 62:190–195.

D. Zissis and D. Lekkas. 2012. Addressing cloud computing security issues. *Future Generation Systems.* 28:583–592.

S. Ziyad and A. Kannammal. 2014. A multifactor biometric authentication for the cloud. *Computational Intelligence Cyber Security and Computational Models.* Springer, New Delhi, India. pp. 395–403.

Printed and bound by CPI Group (UK) Ltd, Croydon, CR0 4YY

17/10/2024

01775656-0019